f 21

BATH COLLEGE OF HIGHER EDUCATION

Author

Title

Stock

The Victoria History of the Counties of England

EDITED BY WILLIAM PAGE, F.S.A.

A HISTORY OF
SOMERSET

VOLUME I

THE
VICTORIA HISTORY
OF THE COUNTIES
OF ENGLAND
SOMERSET

PUBLISHED FOR

THE UNIVERSITY OF LONDON
INSTITUTE OF HISTORICAL RESEARCH

REPRINTED FROM THE ORIGINAL EDITION OF 1906

BY

DAWSONS OF PALL MALL

LONDON

1969

Issued by
Archibald Constable and Company Limited
in 1906

Reprinted for the University of London
Institute of Historical Research
by
Dawsons of Pall Mall
16 Pall Mall, London, S.W. 1
1969
SBN: 7129 0375 5

Reprinted by Stephen Austin and Sons Ltd., Caxton Hill, Hertford

INSCRIBED
TO THE MEMORY OF
HER LATE MAJESTY
QUEEN VICTORIA
WHO GRACIOUSLY GAVE
THE TITLE TO AND
ACCEPTED THE
DEDICATION OF
THIS HISTORY

THE ADVISORY COUNCIL
OF THE VICTORIA HISTORY

GENERAL ADVERTISEMENT

The Victoria History of the Counties of England is a National Historic Survey which, under the direction of a large staff comprising the foremost students in science, history, and archæology, is designed to record the history of every county of England in detail. This work was, by gracious permission, dedicated to Her late Majesty Queen Victoria, who gave it her own name. It is the endeavour of all who are associated with the undertaking to make it a worthy and permanent monument to her memory.

Rich as every county of England is in materials for local history, there has hitherto been no attempt made to bring all these materials together into a coherent form.

Although from the seventeenth century down to quite recent times numerous county histories have been issued, they are very unequal in merit ; the best of them are very rare and costly; most of them are imperfect, and many are now out of date. Moreover they were the work of one or two isolated scholars, who, however scholarly, could not possibly deal adequately with all the varied subjects which go to the making of a county history.

In the VICTORIA HISTORY each county is not the labour of one or two men, but of many, for the work is treated scientifically, and in order to embody in it all that modern scholarship can contribute, a system of co-operation between experts and local students is applied, whereby the history acquires a completeness and definite authority hitherto lacking in similar undertakings.

The names of the distinguished men who have joined the Advisory Council are a guarantee that the work represents the results of the latest discoveries in every department of research, for the trend of modern thought insists upon the intelligent study of the past and of the social, institutional and political developments of national life. As these histories are the first in which this object has been kept in view, and modern principles applied, it is hoped that they will form a work of reference no less indispensable to the student than welcome to the man of culture.

THE SCOPE OF THE WORK

The history of each county is complete in itself, and in each case its story is told from the earliest times, commencing with the natural features and the flora and fauna. Thereafter follow the antiquities, pre-Roman, Roman and post-Roman ; ancient earthworks ; a new translation and critical study of the Domesday Survey ; articles on political, ecclesiastical, social and economic history ; architecture, arts, industries, sport, etc. ; and topography. The greater part of each history is devoted to a detailed description and history of each parish, containing an account of the land and its owners from the Conquest to the present day. These manorial histories are compiled from original documents in the national collections and from private papers. A special feature is the wealth of illustrations afforded, for not only are buildings of interest pictured, but the coats of arms of past and present landowners are given.

HISTORICAL RESEARCH

It has always been, and still is, a reproach that England, with a collection of public records greatly exceeding in extent and interest those of any other country in Europe, is yet far behind her neighbours in the study of the genesis and growth of her national and local institutions. Few Englishmen are probably aware that the national and local archives contain for a period of 800 years in an almost unbroken chain of evidence, not only the political, ecclesiastical, and constitutional history of the kingdom, but every detail of its financial and social progress and the history of the land and its successive owners from generation to generation. The neglect of our public and local records is no doubt largely due to the fact that their interest and value is known to but a small number of people, and this again is directly attributable to the absence in this country of any endowment for historical research. The government of this country has too often left to private enterprise work which our continental neighbours entrust to a government department. It is not surprising, therefore, to find that although an immense amount of work has been done by individual effort, the entire absence of organization among the workers and the lack of intelligent direction has hitherto robbed the results of much of their value.

In the VICTORIA HISTORY, for the first time, a serious attempt is made to utilize our national and local muniments to the best advantage by carefully organizing and supervising the researches required. Under the direction of the Records Committee a large staff of experts has been engaged at the Public Record Office in calendaring those classes of records which are fruitful in material for local history, and by a system of interchange of communication among workers under the direct supervision of the general editor and sub-editors a mass of information is sorted and assigned to its correct place, which would otherwise be impossible.

THE RECORDS COMMITTEE

Sir Edward Maunde Thompson, K.C.B.   C. T. Martin, B.A., F.S.A.
Sir Henry Maxwell-Lyte, K.C.B.   J. Horace Round, M.A., LL.D.
W. J. Hardy, F.S.A.   S. R. Scargill-Bird, F.S.A.
F. Madan, M.A.   W. H. Stevenson, M.A.
F. Maitland, M.A., F.S.A.   G. F. Warner, M.A., F.S.A.

FAMILY HISTORY

Family History is, both in the Histories and in the supplementary genealogical volumes of chart Pedigrees, dealt with by genealogical experts and in the modern spirit. Every effort is made to secure accuracy of statement, and to avoid the insertion of those legendary pedigrees which have in the past brought discredit on the subject. It has been pointed out by the late Bishop of Oxford, a great master of historical research, that ' the expansion and extension of genealogical study is a very remarkable feature of our own times,' that ' it is an increasing pursuit both in America and in England,' and that it can render the historian most useful service.

CARTOGRAPHY

In addition to a general map in several sections, each History contains Geological, Orographical, Botanical, Archæological, and Domesday maps; also maps illustrating the articles on Ecclesiastical and Political Histories and the sections dealing with Topography. The Series contains many hundreds of maps in all.

ARCHITECTURE

A special feature in connexion with the Architecture is a series of ground plans, many of them coloured, showing the architectural history of castles, cathedrals, abbeys, and other monastic foundations.

In order to secure the greatest possible accuracy, the descriptions of the Architecture, ecclesiastical, military, and domestic are under the supervision of Mr. C. R. Peers, M.A., F.S.A., and a committee has been formed of the following students of architectural history who are referred to as may be required concerning this department of the work :—

ARCHITECTURAL COMMITTEE

J. Bilson, F.S.A., F.R.I.B.A.
R. Blomfield, M.A., F.S.A., A.R.A.
Harold Brakspear, F.S.A., A.R.I.B.A.
Prof. Baldwin Brown, M.A.
Arthur S. Flower, F.S.A., A.R.I.B.A.
George E. Fox, M.A., F.S.A.
J. A. Gotch, F.S.A., F.R.I.B.A.

W. H. St. John Hope, M.A.
W. H. Knowles, F.S.A., F.R.I.B.A.
J. T. Micklethwaite, F.S.A.
Roland Paul, F.S.A.
J. Horace Round, M.A., LL.D.
Percy G. Stone, F.S.A., F.R.I.B.A.
Thackeray Turner

GENEALOGICAL VOLUMES

The genealogical volumes contain the family history and detailed genealogies of such houses as had at the end of the nineteenth century seats and landed estates, having enjoyed the like in the male line since 1760, the first year of George III., together with an introductory section dealing with other principal families in each county.

The general plan of Contents and the names among others of those who are contributing articles and giving assistance are as follows :—

Natural History.

    Geology. CLEMENT REID, F.R.S., HORACE B. WOODWARD, F.R.S., and others

    Palæontology. R. L. LYDEKKER, F.R.S., etc.

    Flora   { Contributions by G. A. BOULENGER, F.R.S., H. N. DIXON, F.L.S., G. C. DRUCE, M.A.,

    Fauna   F.L.S., WALTER GARSTANG, M.A., F.L.S., HERBERT GOSS, F.L.S., F.E.S., R. I. POCOCK, REV. T. R. R. STEBBING, M.A., F.R.S., etc., B. B. WOODWARD, F.G.S., F.R.M.S., etc., and other Specialists

    Prehistoric Remains. SIR JOHN EVANS, K.C.B., D.C.L., LL.D., W. BOYD DAWKINS, D.Sc., LL.D., F.R.S., F.S.A., GEO. CLINCH, F.G.S., JOHN GARSTANG, M.A., B.LITT., and others

    Roman Remains. F. HAVERFIELD, M.A., LL.D., F.S.A.

    Anglo-Saxon Remains. C. HERCULES READ, F.S.A., REGINALD A. SMITH, B.A., F.S.A., and others

    Domesday Book and other kindred Records. J. HORACE ROUND, M.A., LL.D., and other Specialists

    Architecture. C. R. PEERS, M.A., F.S.A., W. H. ST. JOHN HOPE, M.A., and HAROLD BRAKSPEAR, F.S.A., A.R.I.B.A.

    Ecclesiastical History. R. L. POOLE, M.A., and others

    Political History. PROF. C. H. FIRTH, M.A., LL.D., W. H. STEVENSON, M.A., J. HORACE ROUND, M.A., LL.D., PROF. T. F. TOUT, M.A., PROF. JAMES TAIT, M.A., and A. F. POLLARD

    History of Schools. A. F. LEACH, M.A., F.S.A.

    Maritime History of Coast Counties. PROF. J. K. LAUGHTON, M.A., M. OPPENHEIM, and others

    Topographical Accounts of Parishes and Manors. By Various Authorities

    Agriculture. SIR ERNEST CLARKE, M.A., Sec. to the Royal Agricultural Society, and others

    Forestry. JOHN NISBET, D.Oec., and others

    Industries, Arts and Manufactures

    Social and Economic History   } By Various Authorities

    Ancient and Modern Sport. E. D. CUMING and others.

        Hunting

        Shooting   } By Various Authorities

        Fishing, etc.

        Cricket. HOME GORDON

        Football. C. W. ALCOCK

The Vale of the Parrett.

THE
VICTORIA HISTORY
OF THE COUNTY OF
SOMERSET

EDITED BY WILLIAM PAGE, F.S.A.

VOLUME ONE

PUBLISHED FOR
THE UNIVERSITY OF LONDON
INSTITUTE OF HISTORICAL RESEARCH
REPRINTED BY
DAWSONS OF PALL MALL
LONDON

County Committee for Somerset.

The Rt. Hon. The Earl Waldegrave, P.C.

The Rt. Rev. The Lord Bishop of Bath and Wells

The Rt. Hon. Sir Richard H. Paget, Bart., P.C.

The Rt. Hon. Sir Edward Fry, P.C.

The Rt. Hon. Henry Hobhouse, P.C., J.P.

Sir C. T. Dyke Acland, Bart.

Sir E. H. Elton, Bart.

Sir Edward Strachey, Bart, M.P.

Sir Cuthbert Slade, Bart.

Sir Henry Peto, Bart.

The Very Rev. The Dean of Wells, F.S.A.

H. Bailward, Esq.

The Rev. E. H. Bates, M.A.

H. H. P. Bouverie, Esq., J.P.

Col. James R. Bramble, J.P., F.S.A.

Edmund Buckle, Esq.

The Rev. Canon Church, M.A., F.S.A.

The Rev. Preb. W. E. Daniel, M.A.

R. E. Dickinson, Esq., J.P.

F. J. Fry, Esq., D.L.

A. J. Goodford, Esq., D.L., J.P.

Emanuel Green, Esq., F.S.A., F.R.S.L.

The Rev. W. H. P. Greswell, M.A.

The Rev. J. Hamlet

The Rev. Preb. Hancock, M.A., S.C.L., F.S.A.

The Rev. C. H. Heale.

C. E. H. Chadwyck Healey, Esq., K.C., F.S.A.

The Rev. Canon T. Scott Holmes, M.A.

Col. W. Long, J.P., C.M.G.

George F. Luttrell, Esq., D.L., J.P.

H. G. Montgomery, Esq., M.P.

W. R. Phelips, Esq., D.L., J.P.

The Worshipful Chancellor Rogers

T. B. Silcock, Esq., M.P.

A. F. Somerville, Esq., J.P.

William Speke, Esq., D.L., J.P.

E. J. Stanley, Esq., D.L., J.P.

The Rev. Charles S. Taylor, M.A., F.S.A.

E. B. Cely-Trevilian, Esq, J.P.

The Rev. F. W. Weaver, M.A., F.S.A.

Col. A. Welby

H. H. Wills, Esq.

The Rev. H. H. Winwood, M.A., F.G.S.

CONTENTS OF VOLUME ONE

CONTENTS OF VOLUME ONE

CORRIGENDUM.

Page 231, line 7, *for* fig. 9 *read* fig. 10.

LIST OF ILLUSTRATIONS

LIST OF ILLUSTRATIONS

LIST OF ILLUSTRATIONS

LIST OF MAPS

* *Not reproduced in this edition owing to technical difficulties.*
† *Reproduced in black and white in this edition.*

PREFACE

ALTHOUGH Somerset has many claims to a complete history, the *History and Antiquities of the County of Somerset*, by John Collinson, published in 1791, is the only work that can be said to treat the history of the county in any way fully. Collinson had little opportunity of referring to original sources, hence his work lacks the exactness and exhaustiveness which are now looked for in a work of this nature.

A more ambitious scheme for a county history was that of William Phelps, who published the first part of his *History and Antiquities of Somersetshire* in 1835, but only seven parts were issued and the work was left incomplete.

It may be mentioned that the Rev. R. W. Eyton, among his various works on the Domesday Book, published in 1880 a digest of the Great Survey under the title of the *Survey of Somerset*, although this of course cannot be reckoned as a county history.

The present volume has been unfortunately delayed on account of unforeseen difficulties, but it is hoped that the delay has enabled the work to be made more complete than could otherwise have been the case.

The Editor wishes to express his acknowledgements to Sir Henry C. Maxwell Lyte, K.C.B., and the Rev. E. H. Bates, M.A., for advice and help in the revision of articles, and to thank the Society of Antiquaries, the Royal Archæological Institute, the Somerset Archæological and Natural History Society, the Bath Natural History and Antiquarian Field Club, the Cambridge Antiquarian Society, the Glastonbury Antiquarian Society, the proprietors of the *Bath Herald* and Mr. G. C. Dymond for illustrations and the use of blocks.

The Editor wishes also to acknowledge the assistance of his late colleague, Mr. H. A. Doubleday, during whose editorship the earlier part of this volume was passed through the press.

The Index to the Domesday Introduction and Text will appear in Volume V.

TABLE OF ABBREVIATIONS

Abbrev. Plac. (Rec. Com.) . . . Abbreviatio Placitorum (Record Commission)
Acts of P.C. . . . Acts of Privy Council
Add. . . . . Additional
Add. Chart. . . Additional Charters
Admir. . . . . Admiralty
Agarde . . . . Agarde's Indices
Anct. Corresp. . . Ancient Correspondence
Anct. D. (P.R.O.) A 2420 . . Ancient Deeds(Public Record Office) A 2420
Ann. Mon. . . . Annales Monastici
Antiq. . . . . Antiquarian or Antiquaries
App. . . . . Appendix
Arch. . . . . Archæologia or Archæological
Arch. Cant. . . Archæologia Cantiana
Archd. Rec. . . Archdeacon's Records
Archit. . . . . Architectural
Assize R. . . . Assize Rolls
Aud. Off. . . . Audit Office
Aug. Off. . . . Augmentation Office
Ayloffe . . . . Ayloffe's Calendars

Bed. . . . . Bedford
Beds . . . . Bedfordshire
Berks . . . . Berkshire
Bdle. . . . . Bundle
B.M. . . . . British Museum
Bodl. Lib. . . . Bodley's Library
Boro. . . . . Borough
Brev. Reg. . . . Brevia Regia
Brit. . . . . Britain, British, Britannia, etc.
Buck. . . . . Buckingham
Bucks . . . . Buckinghamshire

Cal. . . . . Calendar
Camb. . . . . Cambridgeshire or Cambridge
Cambr. . . . . Cambria, Cambrian, Cambrensis, etc.
Campb. Ch. . . Campbell Charities
Cant. . . . . Canterbury
Cap. . . . . Chapter
Carl. . . . . Carlisle
Cart. Antiq. R. . Cartæ Antiquæ Rolls
C.C.C. Camb . . Corpus Christi College, Cambridge
Certiorari Bdles. (Rolls Chap.) . Certiorari Bundles (Rolls Chapel)
Chan. Enr. Decree R. . Chancery Enrolled Decree Rolls
Chan. Proc. . . Chancery Proceedings
Chant. Cert. . . Chantry Certificates (or Certificates of Colleges and Chantries)
Chap. Ho. . . . Chapter House

Charity Inq. . . Charity Inquisitions
Chart. R. 20 Hen. III. pt. i. No. 10 . Charter Roll, 20 Henry III. part i. Number 10
Chartul. . . . Chartulary
Chas. . . . . Charles
Ches. . . . . Cheshire
Chest. . . . . Chester
Ch. Gds. (Exch. K.R.) . Church Goods (Exchequer King's Remembrancer)
Chich. . . . . Chichester
Chron. . . . . Chronicle, Chronica, etc.
Close . . . . Close Roll
Co. . . . . County
Colch. . . . . Colchester
Coll. . . . . Collections
Com. . . . . Commission
Com. Pleas . . . Common Pleas
Conf. R. . . . Confirmation Rolls
Co. Plac. . . . County Placita
Cornw. . . . . Cornwall
Corp. . . . . Corporation
Cott. . . . . Cotton or Cottonian
Ct. R. . . . . Court Rolls
Ct. of Wards . . Court of Wards
Cumb. . . . . Cumberland
Cur. Reg. . . . Curia Regis

D. . . . . Deed or Deeds
D. and C. . . . Dean and Chapter
De Banc. R. . . De Banco Rolls
Dec. and Ord. . . Decrees and Orders
Dep. Keeper's Rep. Deputy Keeper's Reports
Derb. . . . . Derbyshire or Derby
Devon . . . . Devonshire
Dioc. . . . . Diocese
Doc. . . . . Documents
Dods. MSS. . . Dodsworth MSS.
Dom. Bk. . . . Domesday Book
Dors. . . . . Dorsetshire
Duchy of Lanc. . Duchy of Lancaster
Dur. . . . . Durham

East. . . . . Easter Term
Eccl. . . . . Ecclesiastical
Eccl. Com. . . . Ecclesiastical Commission
Edw. . . . . Edward
Eliz. . . . . Elizabeth
Engl. . . . . England or English
Engl. Hist. Rev. . English Historical Review
Enr. . . . . Enrolled or Enrolment
Epis. Reg. . . . Episcopal Registers
Esch. Enr. Accts. . Escheators Enrolled Accounts
Excerpta e Rot. Fin. (Rec. Com.) . Excerpta e Rotulis Finium (Record Commission)

Exch. Dep.	Exchequer Depositions
Exch. K.B.	Exchequer King's Bench
Exch. K.R.	Exchequer King's Remembrancer
Exch. L.T.R.	Exchequer Lord Treasurer's Remembrancer
Exch. of Pleas, Plea R.	Exchequer of Pleas, Plea Roll
Exch. of Receipt	Exchequer of Receipt
Exch. Spec. Com.	Exchequer Special Commissions
Feet of F.	Feet of Fines
Feod. Accts. (Ct. of Wards)	Feodaries Accounts (Court of Wards)
Feod. Surv. (Ct. of Wards)	Feodaries Surveys (Court of Wards)
Feud. Aids	Feudal Aids
fol.	Folio
Foreign R.	Foreign Rolls
Forest Proc.	Forest Proceedings
Gaz.	Gazette or Gazetteer
Gen.	Genealogical, Genealogica, etc.
Geo.	George
Glouc.	Gloucestershire or Gloucester
Guild Certif. (Chan.) Ric. II.	Guild Certificates (Chancery) Richard II.
Hants	Hampshire
Harl.	Harley or Harleian
Hen.	Henry
Heref.	Herefordshire or Hereford
Hertf.	Hertford
Herts.	Hertfordshire
Hil.	Hilary Term
Hist.	History, Historical, Historian, Historia, etc.
Hist. MSS. Com.	Historical MSS. Commission
Hosp.	Hospital
Hund. R.	Hundred Rolls
Hunt.	Huntingdon
Hunts	Huntingdonshire
Inq. a.q.d.	Inquisitions ad quod damnum
Inq. p.m.	Inquisitions post mortem
Inst.	Institute or Institution
Invent.	Inventory or Inventories
Ips.	Ipswich
Itin.	Itinerary
Jas.	James
Journ.	Journal
Lamb. Lib.	Lambeth Library
Lanc.	Lancashire or Lancaster
L. and P. Hen. VIII.	Letters and Papers, Hen. VIII.
Lansd.	Lansdowne
Ld. Rev. Rec.	Land Revenue Records
Leic.	Leicestershire or Leicester
Le Neve's Ind.	Le Neve's Indices
Lib.	Library
Lich.	Lichfield
Linc.	Lincolnshire or Lincoln
Lond.	London
m.	Membrane
Mem.	Memorials
Memo. R.	Memoranda Rolls
Mich.	Michaelmas Term
Midd.	Middlesex
Mins. Accts.	Ministers' Accounts
Misc. Bks. (Exch. K.R., Exch. T.R. or Aug. Off.)	Miscellaneous Books (Exchequer King's Remembrancer, Exchequer Treasury of Receipt or Augmentation Office)
Mon.	Monastery, Monasticon
Monm.	Monmouth
Mun.	Muniments or Munimenta
Mus.	Museum
N. and Q.	Notes and Queries
Norf.	Norfolk
Northampt.	Northampton
Northants	Northamptonshire
Northumb.	Northumberland
Norw.	Norwich
Nott.	Nottinghamshire or Nottingham
N.S.	New Style
Off.	Office
Orig. R.	Originalia Rolls
O.S.	Ordnance Survey
Oxf.	Oxfordshire or Oxford
p.	Page
Palmer's Ind.	Palmer's Indices
Pal. of Chest.	Palatinate of Chester
Pal. of Dur.	Palatinate of Durham
Pal. of Lanc.	Palatinate of Lancaster
Par.	Parish, Parochial, etc.
Parl.	Parliament or Parliamentary
Parl. R.	Parliament Rolls
Parl. Surv.	Parliamentary Surveys
Partic. for Gts.	Particulars for Grants
Pat.	Patent Roll or Letters Patent
P.C.C.	Prerogative Court of Canterbury
Pet.	Petition
Peterb.	Peterborough
Phil.	Philip
Pipe R.	Pipe Roll
Plea R.	Plea Rolls
Pop. Ret.	Population Returns
Pope Nich. Tax. (Rec. Com.)	Pope Nicholas' Taxation (Record Commission)
P.R.O.	Public Record Office
Proc.	Proceedings
Proc. Soc. Antiq.	Proceedings of the Society of Antiquaries
pt.	Part
Pub.	Publications
R.	Roll
Rec.	Records
Recov. R.	Recovery Rolls
Rentals and Surv.	Rentals and Surveys

TABLE OF ABBREVIATIONS

Rep. . . . . Report
Rev. . . . Review
Ric. . . . . Richard
Roff. . . . . Rochester diocese
Rot. Cur. Reg. . Rotuli Curiæ Regis
Rut. . . . . Rutland

Sarum . . . . Salisbury diocese
Ser. . . . . Series
Sess. R. . . . Sessions Rolls
Shrews. . . . Shrewsbury
Shrops. . . . Shropshire
Soc. . . . . Society
Soc. Antiq. . . Society of Antiquaries
Somers. . . Somerset
Somers. Ho. . . Somerset House
S.P. Dom. . . . State Papers Domestic
Staff. . . . . Staffordshire
Star Chamb. Proc. Star Chamber Proceedings
Stat. . . . . Statute
Steph. . . . . Stephen
Subs. R. . . . Subsidy Rolls
Suff. . . . . Suffolk
Surr. . . . . Surrey
Suss. . . . . Sussex
Surv. of Ch. Livings Surveys of Church Livings
　(Lamb.) or (Chan.)　　(Lambeth) or (Chancery)

Topog. . . . . Topography or Topographi-
　　　　　　　cal
Trans. . . . . Transactions
Transl. . . . . Translation
Treas. . . . . Treasury or Treasurer
Trin. . . . . Trinity Term

Univ. . . . . University

Valor Eccl. (Rec. Valor Ecclesiasticus (Record
　Com.)　　　Commission)
Vet. Mon. . . . Vetusta Monumenta
V.C.H. . . . . Victoria County History
Vic. . . . . . Victoria
vol. . . . . . Volume

Warw. . . . . Warwickshire or Warwick
Westm. . . . . Westminster
Westmld. . . . Westmorland
Will. . . . . William
Wilts . . . . Wiltshire
Winton. . . . Winchester diocese
Worc. . . . . Worcestershire or Worcester

Yorks . . . . Yorkshire

GEOLOGY

FEW counties in England present so great a diversity of scenery as Somerset, and none possesses a greater variety of geological formations. Although the land nowhere attains the dignity of a mountain, yet the older rocks which form the more solid framework of the county stand out boldly on Exmoor and in the Quantock Hills of west Somerset, in Crook Peak and other portions of the Mendip Hills, and rise to a lesser elevation on Broadfield Down in north Somerset. Along the borders of the county to the east and south-east there are ranges of secondary rocks, connected north of Bath with the Cotteswold Hills, and extending southwards in a series of escarpments to the neighbourhood of Wincanton and Yeovil, and thence along the Blackdown Hills to near Wellington. They form a kind of crescent, from the centre of which the older rocks of Mendip proceed westwards. Between these hilly grounds fertile vales and rich moorlands stretch irregularly inland from the shores of the Bristol Channel.

The stratified and igneous rocks met with are as follows :—

Period	Formation	Character of the Strata	Approximate thickness in feet
Recent and Pleistocene	Alluvium	Silt, clay, and peat . .	10 to 60
	Blown Sand	Fine sand	20
	Marine Sand (Burtle Beds)	Shelly sand and shingle with bands of sandy limestone	12
	Cave Deposits	Red earth and stalagmite with bones	10
	Valley Gravel	Gravel, sand, and loam .	10 to 30
	Plateau Drift	Angular and pebbly gravel	2
Cretaceous	Middle Chalk	Soft limestone with few flints	150
	Lower Chalk	Soft limestone and marl; phosphatic nodules at base	200
	Upper Greensand . . .	Calcareous grit, chert, sandstone, and sands .	100 to 180
	Gault	Bluish-grey clay . . .	70 to 90

Period	Formation	Character of the Strata	Approximate thickness in feet
Jurassic — Oolitic	Corallian	Oolitic limestone, calcareous sandstone and sand	120
	Oxford Clay	Stiff grey clay and shale, with septaria . . .	400
	Cornbrash	Rubbly limestone . . .	20
	Forest Marble and Bradford Clay	Flaggy oolitic limestone, sand and sandstone, and clay	100
	Great Oolite	Oolitic and shelly limestone	80 to 110
	Fullonian or Fullers' Earth	Grey marly clay, with fullers' earth and argillaceous limestone . .	150
	Inferior Oolite	Oolitic and shelly limestone	40 to 80
	Midford Sands (Passage Beds)	Buff sands with bands and nodules of calcareous sandstone.	20 to 150
Jurassic — Liassic	Upper Lias	Dark clay and pale argillaceous limestone . .	10 to 40
	Middle Lias	Hard brown ironshot limestone, sands and sandy shale	100
	Lower Lias	Dark blue clay and limestone	up to 350
New Red Sandstone Series or Permo-Triassic	Rhætic Beds	White limestone, black shale, and grey marl .	50
	Upper (Keuper) Marls passing locally into Dolomitic Conglomerate	Red and variegated marl and conglomerate . .	up to 750
	Upper Sandstone . . .	Red sandstone	200
	Conglomerate	Conglomerate with limestone and other fragments. . . , . .	75
	Lower Marls	Marl with sandstone . .	120
	Lower Sandstone and Breccia	Red sandstone and breccia	500
Carboniferous — Coal Measures	Upper Coal Measures. .	Shales and sandstones with seams of coal . . .	2,200
	Pennant Grit	Chiefly red and grey sandstones.	2,500 to 3,000
	Lower Coal Measures .	Shales and sandstones with seams of coal . . .	2,800
Carboniferous	Millstone Grit	Hard compact sandstone, with shales	500 to 900
Carboniferous — Carboniferous Limestone Series	Upper Limestone Shales .	Shales with bands of limestone and grit . . .	500 to 600
	Carboniferous Limestone .	Hard blue and grey limestone with nodules of chert	1,500 to 3,000
	Lower Limestone Shales .	Soft greenish-grey shales with bands of limestone	320 to 500

GEOLOGY

Period	Formation	Character of the Strata	Approximate thickness in feet
Old Red Sandstone and Devonian	Upper Old Red Sandstone Upper, Middle, and Lower Devonian	Hard red sandstone and quartzose conglomerate Hard sandstones and grits, slates and occasional limestones	over 2,000 thickness unknown
Igneous Rocks (*of various ages*)	Volcanic Ashes and Lava Andesite Felsite, etc.		

With such a list of formations the great diversity of soil and feature in Somerset will readily be understood. The soils indeed are but little modified by material drifted from a distance ; they are due so directly to the outcropping formations that geological boundary lines may be traced across ploughed fields from the evidence of weathered fragments of the underlying rocks. On the elevated moorlands of Exmoor and the Quantocks the heather, dwarf oak and whortleberry abound, and the red deer in places runs wild. On the tablelands of Mendip and Broadfield Down, amidst wild and cultivated tracts, we find excellent pasturage for sheep. The Oolitic and Liassic uplands are partly under plough cultivation, while the slopes of these stonebrash hills are studded with orchards. The clay vales of Lias and New Red Marl form rich pastures, and the levels in particular are noted grazing and dairy lands, one of the products being the famous Cheddar cheese. More than half the land is under permanent pasture, and the county is essentially an agricultural one ; but it is by no means wholly so—there are mines of coal and iron, famous building stones, fullers' earth, peat moors or turbary lands, lime and cement works, and formerly there were important mines of lead and zinc of which the refuse heaps are now worked.

As might be expected Somerset has had a considerable share in the development of geological knowledge. As early as 1719 the relations of its Coal Measures to the overlying 'Red earth' and 'Lyas' were pointed out by John Strachey, while towards the close of the eighteenth century William Smith, 'the father of English Geology,' was actively engaged in setting out and superintending the works for the Somerset coal canal, thereby gathering much of that knowledge of the succession of the strata and of their characteristic fossils which formed so important a part of the foundation of geological science.[1] Subsequently Buckland, W. D. Conybeare, Thomas Weaver and William Lonsdale determined the geological structure of various portions of the county in the masterly way characteristic of those old workers. The Geological Survey under the direction of De la Beche depicted on maps the superficial areas over which the many different strata are exposed, a task aided

[1] *Memoirs of William Smith*, by Professor John Phillips, 8vo (London, 1844). Many of Smith's early observations were published by the Rev. Joseph Townsend, rector of Pewsey, in his *Character of Moses Established for Veracity as an Historian*, 4to (Bath, 1813).

by William Sanders of Bristol, who afterwards personally surveyed a large part of Somerset between Bristol and the Mendip Hills, and published in 1862 a map on the scale of 4 inches to a mile.

The researches of numerous other observers during the latter half of the nineteenth century largely increased our knowledge, and among these we are indebted especially to Charles Moore of Bath. Since his death local interest in geology has ever been fostered by the Rev. H. H. Winwood, also of Bath.[1]

DEVONIAN

Geologists are far from unanimous with regard to the age and correlation of some of the grits and slates met with in that large and picturesque moorland region of west Somerset which extends from the Quantock Hills on the east to Exmoor on the west.[2]

The rocks classed as Devonian are there so folded and faulted that no reliable estimates can be made of their thickness, but the main lithological groups can be traced across country through Exmoor with generally an east and west strike to the Quantocks, where the general trend is north-west and south-east ; and these divisions, first marked out by Etheridge, have been surveyed in more detail by Mr. W. A. E. Ussher. Later researches have however thrown considerable doubt on the regularity of the succession which they depicted.[3]

On parts of Exmoor and the Brendon Hills (1,344 feet high) there is a group of much folded and highly cleaved slates, known as the MORTE SLATES, which for many years were regarded as an unfossiliferous set of beds overlying the Ilfracombe group in the Middle Devonian series.

In 1890, however, the late Dr. Henry Hicks discovered fossils in these Morte Slates at Woolacombe in north Devon, and elsewhere in the neighbourhood. Although the specimens were much distorted and in a bad state of preservation, he was able to recognize *Lingula*, *Orthis*, *Stricklandinia*, *Cardiola*, and some others of Silurian aspect, and he maintained that the rocks were the oldest in north Devon.[4] Continuing his researches into west Somerset, Dr. Hicks was successful in finding fossils in the Morte Slates of the Oakhampton slate quarry near Wiveliscombe, and in calcareous bands in the slates at Treborough on the Brendon Hills. Here he obtained the trilobites *Homalonotus* and *Dalmanites*, also *Strophomena*, *Chonetes*, and other forms suggestive of the Lower Devonian period.[5] These observations led Dr. Hicks to conclude that in the

---

[1] A bibliography of works on the Geology of Somerset to 1875 was compiled by W. Whitaker and H. B. Woodward, 'Geology of East Somerset and the Bristol Coalfields' (*Geol. Survey*), 1876 ; see also for Jurassic papers up to 1895, 'The Jurassic Rocks of Britain' (*Geol. Survey*), vol. v. (1895).

[2] See De la Beche, *Report on the Geology of Cornwall, Devon and West Somerset*, 8vo (London, 1839) ; and *Mem. Geol. Survey*, vol. i. p. 1 (1846) ; John Phillips, *Palæozoic Fossils of Cornwall, etc.* 8vo (London, 1841) ; and papers by Sedgwick and Murchison, Lonsdale, etc.

[3] Etheridge, *Quart. Journ. Geol. Soc.* vol. xxiii. p. 568 ; papers by Ussher, *Proc. Somerset Arch. and Nat. Hist. Soc.* vols. xxv., xxxv., xlvi. ; also A. Champernowne and Ussher, *Quart. Journ. Geol. Soc.* vol. xxxv. p. 532, and *Geol. Mag.* 1881, p. 441.

[4] Hicks, *Quart. Journ. Geol. Soc.* vol. lii. p. 354 ; *Proc. Geol. Assoc.* vol. xiv. pp. 357, 433.

[5] *Quart. Journ. Geol. Soc.* vol. liii. p. 438.

GEOLOGY

Morte Slates we have life-zones belonging to both Upper Silurian and Lower Devonian, and although his views have not as yet been fully accepted, his discovery of fossils in beds previously regarded as barren is of the utmost importance, while his contention that the beds in west Somerset are Lower, rather than Middle, Devonian has received the support of the Rev. G. F. Whidborne and Mr. J. E. Marr.

The famous iron ores of the Exmoor and Brendon Hills occur in these slaty rocks, and for the most part above certain calcareous bands which are impersistently seen in the slates. The late Sir Warington Smyth observed that these 'ores of iron occur both in regular strata and in veins; and it is evident that they were known and worked by our forefathers, although the common tradition of their having been opened by the Romans, and the term " Roman Vein " attached to one locality would seem, I think, of less weight than the probability of their having been wrought about the time when Queen Elizabeth invited German miners to England, supported as it is by the name *Eyesen* Hill by which one of the ancient workings is still known.'[1] Nodules of iron ore have been met with in the shales in the Exe valley north-east of Simonsbath, but the ore has been obtained mainly from lodes which have been extensively worked at Raleigh's Cross in the Brendon Hills, where one lode is from 2 to 20 feet wide. The lodes yield brown iron ore, with also goethite and much manganese ore, occasionally copper pyrites, and some hæmatite (red iron ore) at the surface, whilst at a depth the brown ore passes into sparry ore (carbonate of iron). According to Smyth a series of parallel fissures must originally have been opened in the slaty rocks, nearly concordant with the general planes of stratification. These, after being filled with carbonate of iron, some quartz and fragments of the containing rock, were dislocated, while much of the ore was changed from carbonate to peroxide of iron. The occurrence of pebbles of hæmatite in the New Red strata of west Somerset seems to indicate that the infilling of the fissures was of earlier date than those red rocks.

Elsewhere among the older Devonian Rocks the FORELAND GRITS, comprising the fine grained red, grey and purplish grits, extending from the Foreland in Devonshire to Porlock Hill, rise up in North Hill and Grabbist Hill to the west and south of Minehead, and again appear in Dunster Park. On the coast they form bold precipitous fronts to the stormy seas of the Bristol Channel. Resting apparently upon these grits, though in faulted relationship with them in west Somerset are the slaty grits and schists known as the LYNTON BEDS, which yield *Spirifer hystericus*, and appear at Oare and the north end of Luccot Hill. The connection between these rocks and the Morte Slates has yet to be determined.

The Lynton Beds are surmounted by a great series known as the HANGMAN GRITS, which include fine and coarse grained grits, speckled with red, and contain some slaty bands and occasional fossils such as *Natica* and *Myalina*. These rocks, which may possibly be equivalent to

[1] Smyth, *Quart. Journ. Geol. Soc.* vol. xv. p. 106; M. Morgans, ibid. vol. xxv. p. 255.

the Foreland Sandstones, form fine moorland ranges, including the prominent Dunkery Beacon (1,707 feet), Croydon Hill (1,251 feet), and the higher portions of the Quantocks with Wills Neck (1,261 feet).

Above the Hangman Grits is a series known as the ILFRACOMBE SLATES, comprising slates with occasional bands of limestone, which are sometimes conspicuous, but elsewhere occur in strings, and these in many places have been entirely dissolved away along the outcrop.

These rocks are described by Mr. Ussher as forming high long-backed ranges, with frequent conical hills of lesser elevation than the grits below and above them. They extend from Exmoor towards the Brendon Hills, and occur on the eastern borders of the Quantocks, where at Great Holwell, Asholt and Dodington the limestones are best developed. Here the Rev. H. H. Winwood found a number of fossils, including crinoids, brachiopods, and the coral *Favosites cervicornis*. Gritty beds locally occur in this division as noted by Mr. Ussher, and these appear in inliers among the New Red rocks east of the Quantocks.

Still higher in succession is a third series of grits, the PICKWELL DOWN SANDSTONES, variously coloured green, grey and purple grits with slates, which form barren moorlands intersected by the river Barle north-west of Dulverton, and extending eastwards by Winsford and Exton Hills and over Haddon Down.

To the south of Dulverton there is a tract of the higher Devonian slaty and gritty rocks grouped as BAGGY and PILTON BEDS, which pass upwards into the Lower Culm Measures near Brushford. These Lower Carboniferous rocks, so well known to the south at Bampton in Devonshire, do not enter conspicuously into the geology of west Somerset, although strata of equivalent age occur elsewhere in the county as noted further on.

In the great mass of Devonian rocks, which represent the hardened sands and muds of ancient sea bottoms, there are evidences of local volcanic activity in certain ashy beds which occur at the base of the Ilfracombe Series between Cockercombe and Adscombe on the Quantocks.

In the Morte Series there is a rock referred to by Mr. Ussher as the Bittadon felsite, which outcrops east of Exton Hill at Armoor and Withiel Florey 'apparently at or near the same horizon'[1]; while a syenitic rock was observed many years ago by Leonard Horner in the Ilfracombe Series at Hestercombe, north of Taunton, where the adjacent slates have been altered into a kind of hone stone.

The economic products of the Devonian rocks include the iron ores before mentioned, as well as slates and other materials employed for local building purposes and road metal.

If the Lower Devonian rocks merge into the Upper Silurian, so do the Upper Devonian into the Carboniferous, and there is every probability that the usually accepted Devonian group of Devonshire is in reality a more comprehensive system than the Old Red Sandstone which

---

[1] See also T. G. Bonney, *Geol. Mag.* p. 207 (1878).

it has been taken to represent. Mr. Ussher indeed has remarked 'that the Upper Devonian Beds may be in part at least equivalent to what is called the Lower Carboniferous Slate Series of the south of Ireland ; and if so, such correlations as the Pickwell Down Beds with the Upper Old Red Sandstone are natural.' The strata may be grouped as follows :—[1]

North Devon and West Somerset		East Somerset	
	Upper Culm Measures	Coal Measures Millstone Grit	Carboniferous
	Lower Culm Measures	Upper Limestone Shales Carboniferous Limestone	
Upper Devonian	Pilton and Baggy Beds	Lower Limestone Shales	
	Pickwell Down Sandstone	Upper Old Red Sandstone	
Middle Devonian	Ilfracombe Beds		
Lower Devonian and Silurian	Hangman Grits Lynton and Foreland Beds and Morte Slates		

UPPER OLD RED SANDSTONE

The Old Red Sandstone which forms a nucleus to the Mendip Hills, and rises at intervals from near Frome to Black Down north of Cheddar, consists for the most part of red and variegated sandstone, with sandy marls and towards the upper part beds of quartzose conglomerate. The conglomerates are conspicuous between Downhead and Beacon Hill to the north-west of Shepton Mallet, where in places they have been disintegrated into a loose gravel.

The Old Red Sandstone also occurs at Portishead and along the shores of the Avon near Abbots Leigh. Remains of the fish *Holoptychius* have been recorded from Portishead, otherwise but few traces of fossils have been found in this formation in Somerset.

On the Mendips the rock forms tracts of moorland together with pasture and arable ground, but the soil, a reddish stony loam, is not rich. Springs issue at the junction with the Lower Limestone Shales, which flank the Old Red Sandstone and hold up water in the joints and weathered portions of that formation. Economically the rock is not much used, except for building walls and for local road mending.

On the summit of the Mendips, extending westwards from Downhead to Beacon Hill, there are masses of igneous rock (andesite) sufficiently hard to be quarried for road metal at Moon's Hill south of Stoke

---

[1] See also Hull, *Quart. Journ. Geol. Soc.* vol. xxxvi. p. 255.

Lane. Attention was first called to these exposures by Charles Moore, and they have since been frequently examined. According to Sir A. Geikie and Mr. A. Strahan they appear to rise intrusively through the Old Red Sandstone, and may possibly belong to the Carboniferous volcanic series referred to later on.

CARBONIFEROUS LIMESTONE SERIES

The lowest Carboniferous strata in east Somerset are the LOWER LIMESTONE SHALES which occur between the Old Red Sandstone and the Carboniferous Limestone. They form passage-beds and are well shown above Burrington Combe on the Mendips and in the Avon gorge. In the ascending series we find that the higher beds of Old Red Sandstone alternate with shales and thence merge into the main mass of greenish grey and bluish-grey shales, above which the shales alternate with bands of limestone, which pass gradually into the Carboniferous Limestone.

Fossils are not uncommon in these beds ; they include the trilobite, *Phillipsia*, also many fish-remains, crinoids, bryozoa, and brachiopods such as *Spirifera*, *Chonetes* and *Strophomena*.

The shales which occur between the harder masses of Old Red Sandstone and Carboniferous Limestone have suffered erosion so that they occupy belts of lower ground often wet and boggy from the direct rainfall or from springs which issue from the bordering rocks. In by-gone days these shales, which are sometimes black, have led to fruitless trials for coal.

The CARBONIFEROUS or MOUNTAIN LIMESTONE forms some of the more picturesque parts of Somerset, and it well deserves the name of ' Scar Limestone,' which it received in the north of England on account of the numerous scarps of rock which characterize the land. In Somerset it forms the mass of the Mendip Hills, with its many charming rocky gorges, combes and caverns, as at Cheddar, Ebbor, Burrington and Frome on the Mendips, at Cleeve and Brockley on Broadfield Down. While however the rock frequently appears at the surface, there is elsewhere a rich red soil, a residue from the decomposition of the rock, and this supports an excellent herbage for sheep.

A fine section of the rocks is to be seen in the gorge of the Avon, where it cuts Leigh Down in Somerset, and Clifton and Durdham Downs in Gloucestershire. The upward succession from the Old Red Sandstone and Lower Limestone Shales may be traced from Cook's Folly towards Clifton, where the Upper Limestone Shales and Millstone Grit appear. The Carboniferous Limestone is there to a considerable extent repeated by the Great Clifton fault, which has thrown down the beds on the north to an extent estimated by Prof. C. Lloyd Morgan at 1,100 feet.[1] This great dislocation has produced much disturbance in the strata. The lower portion of the Carboniferous Limestone, seen in the

---

[1] *Proc. Bristol Nat. Soc.* ser. 2, vol. iv. (1885).

Black Rock quarry, comprises dark bituminous limestone crowded with crinoid remains, *Spirifera*, etc. ; higher up there occur bands with many fish remains, then a series of oolitic limestones, and some shaly beds ; while in the upper beds we find layers with *Terebratula hastata* and *Productus*, others with the trilobite *Phillipsia*, also *Orthoceras*, *Bellerophon*, *Murchisonia* and *Euomphalus*, and corals such as *Lithostrotion* and *Cyatho-phyllum*. The upper beds are worked in the Great quarry of Durdham Down, where fluor-spar occurs in crevices of the rock.

Near the Suspension Bridge at St. Vincent's Rocks the famous Hotwell Spring of Clifton issues from the higher beds of the Limestone ' at the rate of 60 gallons per minute, at a tolerably uniform temperature of 70° Fahr.' Its principal constituent is carbonate of lime; it contains also salts of soda and magnesia, but only to the extent of 44 grains to the gallon.[1]

The thermal waters of Bath which issue through the Keuper and Rhætic Beds probably arise also from the Carboniferous Limestone.[2] Judging by their temperature, 104 to 120° Fahr., Prestwich suggested that the depth from which they come is about 3,500 feet. Hence they may be regarded as natural artesian wells, fed perhaps to some extent from the sea, which in the Severn estuary is bordered in places by Carboniferous Limestone, and this rock also rises up in the Holmes islets. The chief ingredient in the waters is sulphate of lime, with also sulphate and chloride of sodium, and chloride of magnesium, etc. Altogether they contain from 144 to 168 grains per gallon, and the discharge is about 385,000 gallons daily. Traces of copper and other metals have been found in the Bath waters, and in connection with them it is interesting to bear in mind that almost every element is contained in sea water, while in the Carboniferous Limestone of Walton near Clevedon traces of gold as well as silver have been found. It should also be mentioned that at Bathampton Spa tepid saline waters were encountered in a boring, and saline waters were tapped in a coal-shaft at Twerton.

The Bath waters often bring up sand as well as nuts, insects and even fossils from the alluvial deposits and other strata through which they emerge ; moreover they leave a deep red ochreous deposit, and tinge with a red colour the bordering rocks.

The surface of the Carboniferous Limestone is so fissured and jointed that water readily finds its way downwards, and impurities also are readily washed in ; hence while considerable reservoirs of water occur in fissures and caverns below ground, there is no certainty of finding a copious and wholesome supply at any particular spot.

Since British and Roman times ores of lead and zinc (galena and calamine), as well as ochres, have been obtained from the Carboniferous Limestone and Dolomitic Conglomerate. In the time of Edward IV.

---

[1] Stoddart, *Proc. Bristol Nat. Soc.* ser. 2, vol. i. p. 313 (1876).
[2] See Lyell, *Address to Brit. Assoc.* (1864) ; Prestwich, *Geology, Chemical and Physical*, p. 166 ; and C. Moore, *Proc. Bath Nat. Hist. Club* (1870).

there were established certain 'Laws and Orders of the Mendip Miners,' which contain interesting clauses connected with the working of the ores.[1] The extent of the old workings is shown by the 'hills and hollows' that occur here and there on the Mendip plateau, from Green Ore, Egar (or Eaker) Hill and Priddy, northwestwards to Charterhouse Warren, Rowberrow and Shipham.

In old times shafts were sunk to depths of 6 or 12 fathoms, and rarely to 20 or 30 fathoms. The ores were sometimes found in regular courses or grooves, whence the old miners were known as 'groovers,' and the mineral veins were found especially in the Carboniferous Limestone, and occasionally in the Dolomitic Conglomerate. At other times the ores occurred in large masses or hulks lying horizontally; in these cases in the Dolomitic Conglomerate. Particular accounts of the methods of mining have been published by Giles Pooley and others.[2]

For many years no fresh material has been obtained from the rocks, lead being procured in sufficient quantities from the slags and slimes left by the old workers. Large accumulations of this kind have been found here and there at Stoke Hill, near Priddy, Charterhouse, East Harptree, and in the Tar valley near Chewton Mendip. In all cases the deposits are found on or near areas of Lower Limestone Shales, as in such situations water was held up and could be utilized for washing the material that had been brought from the mines. The fine silty material or slime, when calcined, yields about 5 per cent of lead, and the slags yield about 20 per cent, the average being about $12\frac{1}{2}$ per cent. The slags left by the Romans have proved to be the richest.

In 1890 manganese-ore and iron-ore (hæmatite) were worked at Dursdon at the head of Ebbor Gorge. Trenches excavated in the Dolomitic Conglomerate showed nests of manganese-ore, associated with a little copper-ore, cerussite (carbonate of lead) and mendipite (oxy-chloride of lead). The occurrence of mendipite was interesting, as it had hitherto only been recorded from Churchill. Quite recently Mr. L. J. Spencer has detected crystals of leadhillite (sulphate and carbonate of lead) in the ancient slags.

A small mass of Carboniferous Limestone, at one time thought to be Devonian, appears at Cannington Park, north-west of Bridgewater. It has yielded *Lithostrotion* and other Carboniferous fossils.[3] Its relations to the Devonian rocks near by are not clear owing to coverings of Trias, and although there is no evidence of unconformity Mr. Ussher is inclined to think that a pre-Triassic fault of great magnitude may occur there and stretch eastwards between Glastonbury and Shepton Mallet. This might affect the underground extent of Coal Measures, and there-

[1] John Billingsley, *General View of the Agriculture of Somerset*, p. 23 (1797).
[2] See H. B. Woodward, *Lead and Zinc Mines of the Mendips, Geol. of East Somerset*, etc. p. 167; *Proc. Geol. Assoc.* vol. xi. p. cxcix.; *Notes on the Lead Industry of the Mendip Hills*, by Thomas Morgans, *Trans. Fed. Inst. Mining Engineers* (1901).
[3] See E. B. Tawney, *Proc. Bristol Nat. Soc.* ser. 2, vol. i. p. 380.

GEOLOGY

fore he would commend trial-borings for coal at Highbridge, Burnham, Wedmore, or Mark, rather than in the area to the south of the supposed fault.[1]

There is evidence of volcanic activity in Carboniferous times in Somerset as in Derbyshire, and further particulars have recently been gathered by Sir A. Geikie and Mr. A. Strahan, who observe that successive outflows of vesicular lava and showers of volcanic detritus were here and there spread over the floor of the sea in which the Carboniferous Limestone was deposited.[2] No evidence of any central vent was observed, but it is probable there were orifices near Weston-super-mare, Uphill and Wrington Warren. Near Weston the volcanic rocks appear at Spring Cove and at Middle Hope.

The UPPER LIMESTONE SHALES, although not represented on the Geological Survey map, were long ago recognized by Buckland and Conybeare ; they comprise shales with bands of limestone and grit, and are exposed in the Avon gorge, where their thickness is estimated at 600 feet by Prof. Lloyd Morgan.

Representatives of these beds should be looked for between Mells Green and Ashwick, as well as near Emborrow and to the south-west of Ebbor Rocks, where doubt has been thrown on the occurrence of Lower Limestone Shales locally marked on the Geological Survey map. It would be interesting to find evidence of beds corresponding in character with the chert beds and culm limestones with *Posidonomya becheri*, which occur near Bampton and Burlescombe in Devon.

These Lower Carboniferous strata were all deposited in marine areas, with in places bands and reefs of coral.

MILLSTONE GRIT

This formation comprises beds of hard close-grained grit or quartzite with ferruginous specks, and with subordinate beds of shale and occasional seams of coal. It has received the name of ' Farewell Rock,' from the fact that when reached in mining there is no longer any chance of getting profitable coal.

Fossils mostly in the form of casts are met with, and they have been described in an essay by Fort-Major Thomas Austin.[3] Shallow-water conditions prevailed at this period, the formation being probably of estuarine origin.

The stone has in places been quarried for building material and road stone, and here and there it has yielded a good deal of hæmatite. It appears in the Avon gorge by the Hotwells, on the western side of Ashton Vale, at Leigh Down near Winford, and between Binegar and Mells on the northern side of the Mendip Hills. Traces occur near Ebbor and Dinder on the southern side of the range. The absence of

[1] Ussher, *Proc. Somerset Arch. Soc.* vol. xxxvi. p. 117 (1891) ; Champernowne and Ussher, *Quart. Journ. Geol. Soc.* vol. xxxv. p. 546.

[2] *Summary of Progress of Geol. Survey* for 1898 (1899), p. 104.

[3] *The Millstone Grit, its Fossils*, etc. 8vo (London, 1865).

any outcrop of Millstone Grit near Clevedon, Clapton-in-Gordano and Tickenham may be due to faulting.

COAL MEASURES

The Carboniferous Limestone and other strata, including the Coal Measures, have been bent into folds, in the hollows of which we find those portions of the conformable Coal Measures that have escaped denudation.

Three of these Coal basins are exposed or partially exposed at the surface : (1) That of Radstock, which is connected with the Bristol Coalfield ; (2) that of Nailsea ; and (3) that of Clapton-in-Gordano. To the south of the Mendips there is doubtless another tract of Coal Measures beneath the vale which extends from Brent Knoll to Glastonbury and Evercreech.

The limits of the basins to the north of the Mendips can be fairly well defined, but those of the probable basin on the south are wholly unknown (see p. 10). Nevertheless there is no unexplored tract in England from which coal might so confidently be expected as in this southern area beneath the Lias and New Red rocks, at a depth approximately of about 1,000 feet ; and it will be observed that to the north of the Mendips the Coal Measures occupy the lower grounds and are there largely concealed by Lias and New Red rocks which were deposited to some extent in a broad channel hollowed out of the softer Carboniferous strata.

The scenery of the coal districts in Somerset is far more agreeable than in some other coalfields in this country, because so much of the area is covered with the fertile Red Marls and other secondary strata. These indeed are locally so reduced in thickness that coal is worked near Radstock beneath the Inferior Oolite.

Some picturesque parts of the Coal tract are formed by the Pennant Grit which stands out boldly in wooded heights near Temple Cloud, Pensford, and along the Avon between Keynsham and Bristol. These sandstone rocks hold much water, but it is not as a rule serviceable for domestic supplies. The soil, a sandy loam, is not very fertile, nor is that on the shaly portions of the Coal Measures which give rise to a yellow clay. In places where there is much iron ore in the strata the soil is a bright red, often brighter in colour than that yielded by the New Red rocks.

For our knowledge of the Coal Measures we are indebted largely to the observations of the late G. C. Greenwell, J. Anstie, and J. Prestwich, but chiefly to Mr. J. McMurtrie of Radstock, who is still at work in the area.

The strata are generally divided as follows :—

Upper Division	Radstock and Farrington Series	Sandstones and shales with eight seams of coal	about 1,000 feet	Radstock, High Littleton, Pensford
		Red shales	about 150 feet	
		Sandstones and shales with six seams of coal usually worked, and others	about 1,000 feet	Farrington Gurney, Clutton
Pennant Grit		Chiefly grey, green and red sandstones, with occasional seams of coal	about 2,500 feet	North of Brislington, Pensford, Temple Cloud, Babington and Holcombe
Lower Division	New Rock and Vobster Series	Sandstones and shales with numerous seams of coal and some ironstones	about 2,800 feet	Long Ashton and Bedminster; Newton St. Loe and Twerton; Nailsea, Vobster

The district about Radstock is noted for the variety and excellent preservation of the fossil plants in the Coal Measures.

In the Upper Series the best seam of coal does not exceed 2 feet 4 inches in thickness; in the Lower Series there is a seam 8 feet thick. As remarked by Mr. McMurtrie it is mainly owing to its geographical position, being (at present) the most southerly coalfield of England, that the thin seams met with, especially in the Upper Series, have been worked with profit. He adds that 'one favourable feature connected with the Somerset and Bristol coalfield deserves to be mentioned, namely, the absence of fire-damp, which in practice has not been met with at all in the Upper Division, and in the Lower Division is chiefly confined to the deeper seams of the Vobster and the Nettlebridge valley, Ashton Vale and Bedminster, so that the district has to a large extent been spared from those disastrous explosions which unhappily occur in other parts of Great Britain.'[1] The deepest mine at Farrington is 1,794 feet, where some of the lower seams in the Farrington series are now being worked.

Many remarkable dislocations and disturbances have affected the Coal Measures, especially in the vicinity of the Mendip Hills, where the beds are so crushed and folded that the same seam has been passed through two or three times in a shaft. The softer Coal Measures have been much more contorted than the bordering hard rocks. The Radstock slide-fault or overlap-fault is a dislocation or overthrust whereby the strata are locally duplicated over a breadth of 350 yards in a fairly horizontal manner, the vertical displacement amounting to about 60 yards.

Connected with these disturbances and with the folds which occur in the Mendip Hills are the isolated masses of Carboniferous Limestone

---

[1] *Trans. Fed. Inst. Mining Eng.* (1901).

which occur at Luckington and Vobster. These masses have been attributed to overfolding from the Mendip Hills, to an independent inverted and faulted anticline, and to a thrust-plane.[1]

Although the general structure of the Mendip Hills is usually expressed in the term 'Mendip anticlinal,' the tableland is in reality formed of a series of denuded anticlines which trend in an easterly and westerly direction, and thus do not coincide with the north-westerly and south-easterly direction of the range. There is evidence of at least five folds, the summits of which in four instances, Beacon Hill, Pen Hill, North Hill and Black Down, have been laid bare sufficiently to expose the Old Red Sandstone. As in the case of other noteworthy folds in the secondary rocks of the south and south-east of England, the strata on the northern sides of these anticlines usually plunge downwards more steeply than on the southern side, and there are vertical strata and symptoms of overfolding at Churchill Batch, near East End, Leigh-upon-Mendip, and in the Steep Holme which is a continuation of the Black Down anticline.

In the Clapton-in-Gordano district there are also tracts of Carboniferous Limestone overlying Coal Measures, and the structure has in Professor Lloyd Morgan's opinion been produced by a double system of faulting.[2]

The disturbances in the Somerset coalfield are of a character similar to those well known to have affected the coalfields of Belgium and the north of France, where faults, contortions and overthrusts are the rule rather than the exception.

The highest strata in the coalfield, as remarked by Mr. McMurtrie, occur probably near Pensford, where there is a considerable thickness of unproductive strata above the Radstock series.[3]

The formation was laid down over an extensive estuarine and fluviatile area, with marshy tracts where luxuriant growths of giant club-mosses, horsetails (Equisetaceæ) and ferns furnished material for the seams of coal.

There is abundant evidence of great unconformity between the Carboniferous and other older rocks and the secondary strata. Excellent examples are to be seen in the vales near Frome and Wells, and in the Avon gorge near Bristol ; moreover remarkably even eroded surfaces of highly inclined strata are sometimes preserved beneath a mass of Dolomitic Conglomerate, Lias, or Inferior Oolite. These old platforms occur at various levels beneath the main plain of denudation of the Mendips, and for the most part represent different stages of erosion, although locally they may be displaced by faults.

The break between the Coal Measures and the New Red rocks was marked by considerable disturbance of the older rocks, the Mendip anticlines and coal basins were produced with their attendant dislocations,

---

[1] See *Proc. Geol. Assoc.* vol. xi. pp. clxxviii., ccxv. (references) and 485.
[2] *Proc. Bristol Nat. Soc.* ser. 2, vol. v. p. 42.
[3] *Proc. Bath Nat. Hist. Club*, vol. ii. p. 460.

and the whole area suffered vast denudation. Ramsay calculated that the loss from Mendip amounted in places to 6,000 feet.[1] In any case the present tableland is a plain of erosion, dating originally from Permo-Triassic times and being perhaps again and again buried up and revealed and further wasted away during later periods.

The secondary strata commencing with the New Red rocks were for the most part deposited in a subsiding area so that newer layers stretched over a wider tract and overlapped those previously laid down.

NEW RED SANDSTONE SERIES OR PERMO-TRIASSIC

Resting for the most part irregularly on the worn surfaces and upturned edges of the older rocks is the great series of New Red rocks, which in west Somerset probably include strata of Permian and Triassic ages. These were for the most part accumulated in a large inland sea area, an arid region with sand drifts and saline waters.

A traverse of the country from Wiveliscombe to Taunton shows the following succession :—

Keuper	Upper red and variegated Marls	Taunton
	Upper Sandstone	Wellington, Milverton, Fitzhead
Bunter	Conglomerate	Thorn St. Margaret
Permian	Lower Marls with occasional Sandstone. .	} Wiveliscombe
	Lower Sandstone and Breccia	

These divisions are again met with in the vale which extends to Stogumber, but in Mr. Ussher's opinion the higher strata overlap and entirely conceal the lower as we proceed from Williton westwards to Porlock.[2] Throughout this district the rocks are a good deal faulted, and although the main sequence is well established the subdivisions are themselves subject to so much local change that it is difficult to interpret some areas.

The *Breccias* are made up mainly of fragments of Devonian slate and grit, and are well seen near Stogumber. They are irregularly interstratified with sandstone. The *Lower Marls* are used for brick making near Wiveliscombe.

The *Conglomerates* are of a more mixed character than the Breccias and contain, in addition to fragments of grit and slate, large pebbles of Devonian and Carboniferous Limestone which are picked out in the quarries for lime burning ; while the rock itself is worked for building purposes, as at Tipnoller near Wiveliscombe and Vellow near Stogumber. In aspect it resembles the Dolomitic Conglomerate of the Mendips, but is in the main of older date.

[1] *Mem. Geol. Survey*, vol. i. p. 297 (1846).
[2] *Quart. Journ. Geol. Soc.* vol. xxxii. p. 367, and *Proc. Somerset Arch. Soc.* vol. xxxv. for 1889.

The *Upper Sandstone* forms a pleasant country with deep sandy lanes near Wellington, Milverton, Halse, Williton and Minehead, and also in places along the southern and eastern sides of the Quantocks. It may be seen again near Yatton, Chew Magna, Brislington and St. Anne's by Bristol. Both sandstones and conglomerate are usually good water-bearing strata.

The *Upper* (*Keuper*) *Marls* which extend over the vale of Taunton border the Devonian rocks along the western side of the Quantocks with a steep easterly dip. Here however we find no evidence of an ancient cliff-margin, and probably the older rocks of Quantock were not above water during the Triassic and Liassic periods. The Marls extend to Carhampton, Dunster, Minehead and Porlock, but they are best exhibited in the cliffs on either side of Watchet and also on the foreshore, where they occur in faulted relationship with the Rhætic Beds and Lower Lias. Here much gypsum or alabaster occurs in the cliffs: it appears in nodules, bands and also in veins which traverse the beds in all directions. It is found also near Somerton.

Over this intervening area the Marls fringe the marsh lands and form islands in it. At Compton Dundon a boring was carried to a depth of 519 feet in search of Coal Measures, but although the locality is a promising one the boring was not carried deep enough to reach the base of the Upper or Keuper Marls.

Approaching the Mendip Hills we find evidence of marginal accumulations in the *Dolomitic Conglomerate*—beds of breccia and conglomerate formed mainly of angular and rounded fragments of Carboniferous Limestone, cemented sometimes by a dolomitic (or magnesian limestone) matrix, more often by ferruginous matter and carbonate of lime. Much of the limestone material is evidently due to subaerial waste of the land, being talus or angular detritus cemented at or near the spots where it accumulated, while other portions have been more or less rolled. Remnants of this Dolomitic Conglomerate occur along the higher grounds of Mendip as well as along the borders of the range, where the marls and conglomerate dovetail one into the other; while in the Radstock coal field to the north of the Mendips the conglomerate is generally found at the base of the marls.

These facts indicate that while the conglomerate originated at the early stages of the Keuper period, its formation continued along the margin of the area of deposition until the close of the period.

At Draycot near Cheddar the stone has been quarried for building purposes, while near West Harptree some hard siliceous beds occur in association with the marls and conglomerates.

Fine sections of Conglomerate have been opened in the Avon gorge, where Dinosaurian remains were found. Here too, as near Wells and elsewhere, celestite (sulphate of strontian) and baryto-celestite have been found, as well as 'potato-stones,' geodes lined with calcite and quartz crystals (known locally as 'Bristol diamonds'). The Marls extend over the Vale of Wrington and Ashton Vale, and everywhere they yield a fertile soil, supporting good meadow and pasture land as well as orchards.

At Winford there are 'reddle pits,' or ochre and umber works, in ferruginous deposits which occur at the base of the New Red rocks and in joints and hollows of the subjacent Carboniferous rocks.

The RHÆTIC BEDS, the latest stage of the Trias, form a connecting link between that system and the Lias. In general they comprise the following subdivisions :—

	Feet
White Lias with hard compact limestone known as the Sun Bed at top, and Cotham or Landscape Marble at the base	10 to 25
Black shales with *Avicula contorta*, occasional bands of limestone, sandy layers, and one or more bone-beds	12 to 30
Green and grey marls which shade downwards into the red and variegated marls of the Keuper	10 to 30

These beds are well exhibited on the coast at Blue Anchor, Watchet, St. Audries and in many an inland section, notably at Queen Camel, Puriton, Shepton Mallet, Uphill, Saltford and Pylle Hill south of Bristol. They occur in the escarpment of the Polden Hills, where as elsewhere the junction of the green and grey marls with the underlying red marls is often conspicuously shown in the ploughed fields.

The green and grey marls are linked by some authorities with the Keuper marls into which they graduate, but they indicate the beginning of the change which ushered in the Rhætic fauna, they have yielded similar fish remains, while the black marly bands and the pale limestone bands seen in the green and grey marls at St. Audries foreshadow the black shales and White Lias.

The fossils indicate conditions of an inland salt lake subject to irruptions of the sea, a phase which occurred between the inland sea or lacustrine conditions of the Keuper and the open sea conditions of the Lias. Among the characteristic fossils are *Avicula contorta, Pecten valoniensis, Cardium rhæticum, Pleurophorus* and *Gervillia*, as well as fish remains and plant remains (*Naiadita*).[1]

In fissures of the Carboniferous Limestone near Frome many Rhætic fossils were obtained including the oldest known mammal *Microlestes*, and teeth of the fishes *Acrodus, Hybodus, Gyrolepis* and *Saurichthys*.

One of the most remarkable bands in the Rhætic series is the Landscape Marble so well known to visitors at Clifton near Bristol.[2] The stone, which is from an inch or two to about 8 inches in thickness, occurs at the base of the White Lias and is sometimes represented by a persistent layer of banded limestone of compact texture. Where this limestone occurs in isolated and more or less nodular masses with a

[1] See Moore, *Quart. Journ. Geol. Soc.* vol. xvii. p. 483, xxiii. p. 449; Wright, ibid. vol. xvi. p. 374; Dawkins, ibid. vol. xx. p. 396, *Geol. Mag.* (1864), p. 257; Etheridge, *Proc. Cardiff Nat. Soc.* 1873; and E. Wilson, *Quart. Journ. Geol. Soc.* vol. xlvii. p. 545.
[2] Described in 1745 by E. Owen, *Observations on the Earths, Rocks, Stones and Minerals for some miles about Bristol,* etc. See also H. B. Woodward, *Geol. Mag.* (1892), p. 110; 'Jurassic Rocks of Britain' (*Geol. Survey*), vol. iii. p. 30, and vol. v. p. 230; B. Thompson, *Quart. Journ. Geol. Soc.* vol. l. p. 393.

crinkly surface, there the aborescent markings which pervade the stone are met with. The darker patches which represent the landscape are tinted by carbonaceous matter, and the features have been attributed to the escape of bubbles of gas ; while the crinkly surfaces and some modifications of the landscape, which varies considerably, appear to be due to the changes produced amid the variously tinted calcareous mud during its solidification.

Sandy beds with *Pullastra arenicola* occur on Harptree Hill and near Wedmore, a locality where there is a hard shelly limestone used for building stone.

A sulphur spring at Queen Camel rises probably at the base of the White Lias from the decomposition of pyrites in the Rhætic shales. Limited supplies of good water are sometimes obtained from the White Lias.

LIAS

The Lias formation occupies a considerable portion of Somerset and is one which from its fossiliferous character offers many attractions to the collector. The beds were formed in marine areas and under somewhat varying conditions as regards depth, the sandy beds in the Middle Lias being shallow-water deposits. The argillaceous limestones were to some extent due to the mechanical waste of old cliffs formed of Carboniferous Limestone.

The LOWER LIAS almost everywhere rests conformably on the White Lias of the Rhætic Beds, but near Bristol and northwards it rests directly on the Cotham or Landscape Marble, and there probably the higher Rhætic Beds have been subject to contemporaneous erosion. The Lower Lias comprises two main divisions—the lower of limestones with alternating bands of clay or shale presenting a 'riband-like appearance'; the upper of clay and shale with occasional bands or nodules of limestone.

The fossils, which are many and varied, include large saurians, fishes, many ammonites, belemnites and other mollusca, corals, crinoids, etc.

So marked in vertical distribution are many of the ammonites that they have been taken to indicate life-zones, and these, although not rigidly separated one from another, are yet fairly constant, and the order of sequence is never inverted.[1] The following are the main zonal divisions :—

Ammonites capricornus	Mainly clays or shales with occasional bands
„ jamesoni	
„ armatus	and nodules of limestone and much pyrites.
„ oxynotus	
„ semicostatus	
„ bucklandi	Alternating limestones and clays or shales,
„ angulatus	the limestones sometimes preponderating.
„ planorbis	

In the southern part of the county the Lower Lias is exposed along

[1] References to various observers will be found in the *Memoir on Jurassic Rocks of Britain*, vol. iii., by H. B. Woodward (1893).

a scarp overlooking the vale of Taunton where the lower division is quarried here and there as at Thurlbeer and Curry Rivel.

The higher clayey beds extend over the area below Castle Neroche, at Ashill and Isle Abbots, to the west of Ilminster and near Chard. At the last-named locality the presence of dark bituminous shales led many years ago to a fruitless trial for coal. Similar trials were also made at Badgworth and near Glastonbury. Further on at Langport and Somerton the stone beds are exposed in many places, and at Keinton Mandeville they are largely quarried for paving and building stone.

At Queen Camel the limestone beds are well developed, being over 100 feet thick, but their thickness is less along the Polden Hills where the stone is extensively quarried, especially at Street. This locality is famous for its saurian remains, *Ichthyosaurus* and *Plesiosaurus*, some of them described in a rather fanciful work, *The Great Sea Dragons*, by Thomas Hawkins, who at one time resided at Sharpham Park, and collected many specimens which are now in the Natural History Museum at South Kensington.

At Dunball near Puriton Blue Lias lime and cement are manufactured. Here some of the lower beds are pale and resemble White Lias, but the mass of the limestones is little more than 20 feet thick, the higher beds with *Ammonites bucklandi*, elsewhere mainly limestone, being locally represented by clays and shales.

The clayey division is present over a large area from Ilchester to Castle Cary and Evercreech, and at Marston Magna the famous Ammonite Marble, consisting of nodular masses of limestone packed with small examples of *Ammonites obtusus* and *A. planicosta*, was at one time found.

At Pylle by Pennard Hill the limestones are seen at the lime and cement works, and the country northwards by Pilton to Shepton Mallet shows many a quarry in a region much broken by faults.

Approaching the Mendip Hills near Shepton Mallet we come upon curious pale granular and shelly limestones precisely like the Sutton Stone of Glamorganshire, yielding *Ammonites johnstoni*, *Pecten pollux*, *Lima*, *Ostrea multicostata*, etc. Like the beds in South Wales the Lias assumes different characters in proximity to the Carboniferous Limestone, which locally formed shore-lines. Here and there also we find conglomeratic beds with pebbles of the older rock.

On the summit of the Mendips south of East Harptree there are cherty beds yielding an assemblage of Lower Lias fossils similar to that above mentioned, with also *Ammonites planorbis*. Ochre has been worked from the ferruginous clay partings associated with the chert.

In west Somerset, along the coast from near Stolford by Kilve to Watchet and Blue Anchor, and inland near Selworthy west of Minehead, we find interesting exposures of the Lower Lias limestones. Again on the western extremity of the Mendips near Uphill we find a tract of Lower Lias, Rhætic Beds, and Red Marls faulted against the Carboniferous Limestone.

North of the Mendips near Radstock and Paulton the Lower Lias is much attenuated as pointed out by Moore, who considered that the hill range formed a barrier which prevented the accumulation of much sediment. The zones are crowded within small limits, there is evidence of reconstruction of layers and of pauses in deposition accompanied by phosphatic nodules and phosphatized fossils. In some cases, as E. B. Tawney observed, 'there really was not sufficient sediment to be the burial ground of distinct zones of life.' In this region *Spirifera walcotti* is a common fossil. There are also bands of ironshot limestone, the grains in which were found by Dr. G. J. Hinde to be mostly fragments of echinoderms. Further north there are modifications of the Lower Lias limestone at Downside on Broadfield Down, where there is a massive sparry rock with *Cardinia*, *Modiola* and *Ostrea*, approaching in character some of the beds seen near Shepton Mallet.

At Twerton and Weston near Bath, at Saltford and Keynsham, there are fine quarries in the Lower Lias limestone and many ammonites have been obtained. Hence arose the tradition that St. Keyna of Keynsham resided in a wood full of serpents, and her prayers converted them into stone.

The limestones as a rule form a brashy clayey soil whereon turnips are grown, while the clays form land suitable for pasture, wheat and beans.

The formation is not calculated to yield a large amount of water owing to the intercalation of shales, but wells at Street, Somerton and other places have afforded limited supplies. Saline waters have been met with at Horton near Ilminster and at Alford Well, Castle Cary ; chalybeate water at Capland Spa near Ashill ; and sulphuretted water at Shapwick and Burnham.

The MIDDLE LIAS occupies a lesser area than the Lower Lias, being usually exposed on the slopes of escarpments. It comprises the following sub-divisions :—

> Hard iron-shot limestone known as the Rock-bed or Marlstone.
> Micaceous sands with indurated masses of calcareous sandstone.
> Laminated sands and clays passing down into blue micaceous clays.

The lower beds are characterized by small examples of *Ammonites margaritatus*, but the more sandy or loamy beds yield as a rule few fossils, and when present they are often tender and difficult to preserve.

The Marlstone has yielded a large series of fossils for our knowledge of which we are especially indebted to C. Moore. The commoner fossils are *Ammonites spinatus*, *Pecten æquivalvis*, *Gryphæa cymbium*, *Rhynchonella tetrahedra* and *R. acuta*.

The beds are exposed in many a quarry opened for road metal near Ilminster, South Petherton, Yeovil, Pennard Hill and Glastonbury, and they occur also on Brent Knoll.

North of the Mendips in Somerset the Marlstone rock-bed is not often to be seen, and the beds in general appear to be mainly represented by clays in the neighbourhood of Bath ; but it is possible that here as near Yeovil the thin rock-bed has been dissolved away along the outcrop. At Ilminster the Marlstone was found by Moore to yield locally 15 or 16 per cent of metallic iron. Elsewhere in the midland counties the calcareous beds have been more wholly replaced by iron ore, and have been extensively worked.

Springs are thrown out from the sands, which usually yield a fair amount of water. The Holy Well and Chalice Well at Glastonbury are thus supplied, the water being chalybeate, while at Dillington near Ilminster there is a saline well.

The UPPER LIAS comprises at its base bands of pale earthy and nodular limestone and clay, and higher up clays and sandy shales which pass up into the Midford Sands. The formation has attained much fame as a fossiliferous division from the labours of Moore, who collected extensively from the basement beds. In the neighbourhood of Ilminster and onwards to that of Yeovil he discovered many saurians and remarkable fishes, as well as cephalopods, insects and crustaceans ; and among them were specimens of fossil cuttle-fishes with the ink-bag containing fossil sepia. These fossils he obtained from yellow limestone nodules, the shape of which roughly conformed to the enclosed organism, so that he could often predict before breaking the block the nature and even the genus of the fossil that was preserved. Many of the nodules however yield no fossils.

Ammonites annulatus, *A. communis*, *A. bifrons* and *A. serpentinus* (*falcifer*) are usually to be found in the basement beds of the Upper Lias. The limestone was formerly used for building purposes at Yeovil. The beds occur here and there on Pennard Hill, at Glastonbury Tor and Brent Knoll, where the stone and its fossils have been used for road mending.

North of the Mendips there are few clear sections of the Upper Lias.

MIDFORD SANDS

The Midford Sands, so named from the hamlet of Midford about 3 miles south of Bath, form a connecting link between the Lias and the Oolites. Where the sequence is complete there is a gradual passage from the Upper Lias clays through sandy clays into yellow micaceous sands. These sands contain bands and nodular masses of sandy and shelly limestone, which mark the incoming of those conditions which characterized the Inferior Oolite. The hard bands are conspicuous in the railway cuttings near Yeovil, while the more shelly bands occur at North Perrot, and coalesce at Ham Hill to form a mass of famous freestone, a brown stone of pleasing appearance, worked since Roman times, and seen to advantage in the old mansions of the district. Deep sandy lanes or hollow ways characterize the country near Yeovil and Crewkerne, and these trackways, which are often bounded by thick hedgerows, are deeply excavated beneath the bordering ground, the erosion being due mainly to the wear and tear of rain and streams along old bridle-paths.

The lower beds of the Midford Sands yield *Ammonites jurensis, A. striatulus,* and *A. variabilis* ; the higher beds are usually much more fossiliferous and yield *A. opalinus* and more abundantly *Rhynchonella cynocephala, Terebratula infra-oolitica* and other brachiopods. In many localities we may obtain no fossils. The sands occur along the borders of the oolitic hills from Crewkerne to near Doulting ; they cap the Tor at Glastonbury and Brent Knoll, and appear less persistently to the north of the Mendips. Springs are thrown out at the junction with the Lias clays beneath.

INFERIOR OOLITE

The Inferior Oolite, which consists of a variable series of limestones, shelly and oolitic, forms a conspicuous belt in the county.

The lower portion is characterized by *Ammonites murchisonæ* (named after Lady Murchison), and the higher portion by *A. humphriesianus* and *A. parkinsoni.*

As we proceed from the neighbourhood of Yeovil and Bruton northwards the lower beds disappear, and near the Mendips and further north by Radstock and onwards to Bath only the higher portion with *A. parkinsoni* is represented, except in the outlier of Dundry.

In the southern part of the county near Yeovil the series is but poorly developed as regards thickness, but it is remarkably fossiliferous, as is the Lias under similar conditions.

The beds are quarried near Crewkerne, Misterton and Haselbury in south Somerset, while along the eastern borders the higher beds are quarried in many places from Milborne Port to Castle Cary and onwards, and they yield in abundance *Rhynchonella spinosa.*

Near the Mendips the Doulting stone is extensively worked ; it consists of oolitic and sparry limestone—much of the latter being detrital and formed of fragments of crinoids cemented by calcite. Near Frome the Inferior Oolite becomes conglomeratic where it rests on the older rocks of Mendip. Northward it occurs through the Radstock district to Bath, but it presents no features of special interest. In some of the quarries near Bath the stone exhibits cavities due to the dissolution of shells.

At Dundry Hill (765 feet) we find a conspicuous outlier of Inferior Oolite where the main subdivisions are well represented and have yielded a rich harvest of fossils. The principal freestone, a hard pale brown and imperfectly oolitic stone, is in the highest strata (zone of *Ammonites parkinsoni*) with coral beds on top ; lower down there are richly fossiliferous iron-shot oolites with *A. sauzei, A. brocchii* and many other forms of mollusca; lower still are beds with *A. concavus, A. murchisonæ,* etc., and representatives of the Midford Sands with *A. opalinus, A. aalensis, A. striatulus,* etc.[1]

Mr. W. H. Hudleston has pointed out the close connection between the Dundry Inferior Oolite and that of the neighbourhood

[1] S. S. Buckman and E. Wilson, *Proc. Bristol Nat. Soc.* ser. 2, vol. viii. p. 188.

GEOLOGY

of Sherborne in Dorset, and this clearly indicates an open sea communication during the period around what is now the western end of the Mendip Hills.[1]

Springs are abundant at the base of the Inferior Oolite and Midford Sands. Chalybeate springs occur at Lyncombe Spa, Bath, and at Goathill, south of Milborne Port; while at East Chinnock between Yeovil and Crewkerne saline water has been met with.

GREAT OOLITE SERIES

Above the Inferior Oolite there is a great clay formation known as the FULLONIAN or FULLER's EARTH because at Midford and Wellow there occur in it beds of economic fuller's earth 4 to 7 feet thick. In mass the formation is 150 feet thick and more, and it includes bands of soft earthy limestone some 20 or 30 feet thick in places, known as the Fuller's Earth Rock. These bands of rock as well as the clays yield numerous fossils, amongst which are *Ammonites subcontractus*, many lamellibranchs such as *Ostrea acuminata, Isocardia* and *Pholadomya*, and brachiopods such as *Rhynchonella varians* and *Waldheimia ornithocephala*.

The formation is well developed near Crewkerne, where it is worked for brick-making, and it extends from near Milborne Port to near Bruton on the slopes beneath the fine escarpment formed of the Forest Marble, and thence onwards by Frome to the neighbourhood of Bath. The Fuller's Earth Rock is seen in railway cuttings near Milborne Port and south-east of Shepton Montague, also at Egford Bridges near Frome and Lansdown, Bath. The soil as a rule is cold and wet, but it yields good meadow land and well timbered hedgerows.

The peculiar detergent properties of the fuller's earth are due rather to the physical character than to the chemical composition of the earth; it is not plastic like ordinary clay, but falls to a powder under water.

The GREAT or BATH OOLITE forms an important and conspicuous part of north-east Somerset, in the high grounds of Lansdown, Little Salisbury Hill, Bonner Down, Bathampton Down (672 feet) and Odd Down. It consists of a mass of limestones, with some marly and clayey partings, and the stone beds are oolitic and shelly.

Broadly speaking there are two main divisions, the upper comprising false-bedded shelly oolites and marls, some freestone and very hard rag beds; and the lower comprising fine oolitic beds comparatively free from shells and furnishing most of the best freestone. The full thickness to the east of Bath is from 100 to 110 feet.

The mass of the freestones which have been worked are included in a thickness of about 50 feet, but the main freestone or ground bed is from 12 to 14 feet thick and is the lowest bed worked. The beds diminish in thickness towards Bradford-on-Avon and finally disappear to the south-west of that town, near Farleigh Hungerford and Norton St. Philip. The evidence leads to the conclusion that the Great Oolite has

---

[1] *Address to Geol. Section, Brit. Assoc.* (1898).

suffered erosion locally and to a certain extent contemporaneously during the succeeding period of the Bradford Clay and Forest Marble.[1]

Although the fauna and flora of the Great Oolite period are rich and varied when we take into account the Stonesfield Slate, yet that portion of it though feebly represented by certain beds on Lansdown is not locally very fossiliferous.

The shelly beds and rags are largely made up of comminuted shells, fragments of echini and crinoids, and there are many bryozoa and minute gasteropods in some layers. The principal fossils are *Ostrea sowerbyi*, *Pecten vagans*, *Lima cardiiformis* and *Terebratula maxillata*, while here and there, as on Farley Down above Bathford, and Combe Down, a coral bed yielding many species has been described by Mr. R. F. Tomes.[2]

Although Bath stone is quarried on Combe Down, Odd Down and other places, by far the larger quantity of stone is obtained at a depth by shafts and tunnels at Box, Corsham and Bradford-on-Avon in Wiltshire.[3]

Old terraces of cultivation known as lynchets occur on some of the oolitic scarps in the Avon valley, as well as on the Liassic slopes of Brent Knoll ; and Canon H. N. Ellacombe has drawn attention to the former presence of vineyards on the slopes of Claverton Down and other places near Bath.[4]

The FOREST MARBLE is remarkably false bedded and current bedded. No more variable formation is to be met with. In its changeful series we find clays and shales, sands and sandstones, shelly and oolitic limestones and much lignite. The curious track-marks and ripple-marks on the surfaces of many slabs show that it was deposited under shallow-water conditions. Ochreous clay-galls probably originated from rolled masses of clay, while the structure of the oolitic beds, the grains being irregularly mingled with comminuted shells and lignite, or scattered in a sandy as well as in a calcareous matrix, suggest the notion that they may have been derived from the local erosion of the Great Oolite.

At the base of the Forest Marble there is usually found in the south-west of England a bed known as the BRADFORD CLAY about 10 to 12 feet thick, with at its base a fossiliferous band yielding the pear encrinite (*Apiocrinus parkinsoni*), and many brachiopods such as *Waldheimia digona*, *Terebratula coarctata*, etc.[5] Although not well exposed in Somerset it has been observed at Farleigh Hungerford, Charterhouse Hinton, and in a boring for coal at Buckland Dinham.

The limestones which as a rule form a central mass in the Forest Marble, underlaid and overlaid by clays and shales with bands of limestone, stand out in a bold escarpment at Windmill and Charleton Hills near Charleton Horethorne, at Bratton and Scale Hill near Bruton, near

[1] H. B. Woodward, *Jurassic Rocks of Britain*, vol. iv. p. 254.
[2] *Quart. Journ. Geol. Soc.* vol. xli. pp. 174–9.
[3] An account of the working of the stone is given by the Rev. H. H. Winwood, *Proc. Geol. Assoc.* vol. xiv. p. 347.
[4] *Proc. Bath Nat. Hist. Club*, vol. vii. pp. 36, 42.
[5] Some of these fossils were figured by John Walcott in his *Descriptions and Figures of Petrifactions found in the Quarries, Gravel Pits, etc. near Bath* (1779).

Wanstrow, and thence by Cloford to Frome. Many a quarry may be observed and the stone is extensively used at Frome. In this neighbourhood the occurrence of sandy beds is noticeable, and they are to be seen at Buckland Dinham, and especially at Charterhouse Hinton, where large concretionary masses or 'doggers' of sandstone occur. The beds were noticed by William Smith under the name 'Hinton Sand and Sandstone.' On the Wiltshire borders some of the thin bands of limestone have been employed as stone tiles for roofing.

CORNBRASH

This formation was so named because it yields a brashy soil suitable for the growth of corn, and where exposed in quarries it is a rubbly yellow limestone which in most localities yields numerous fossils. *Ammonites macrocephalus* is characteristic, but more abundant though seldom well preserved are many lamellibranchs such as *Avicula echinata, Myacites, Gresslya, Pecten vagans* and *Pholadomya*; brachiopods, especially *Terebratula intermedia* and *Waldheimia obovata*; and the echinoderm *Echinobrissus clunicularis*. These may often be picked up on the ploughed fields. The formation was probably slowly deposited in tranquil waters and at a greater depth than other members of the Great Oolite series.

The Cornbrash is exposed at Closworth, Sutton Bingham, East Coker and again at Henstridge, Templecombe, Wincanton and Upton Noble, where hard limestone suitable for building purposes is obtained. Further on it is seen at Marston Bigot near Frome, at Road and Tellisford.

The Cornbrash yields water in shallow wells above the clays of the Forest Marble. It will be observed that a succession of villages on this account arose on the formation, but owing to unsatisfactory sanitary arrangements these supplies have nowadays often to be condemned. At Templecombe a boring carried to a depth of 172 feet encountered saline water.

OXFORD CLAY

This great clay formation, so well developed near Oxford, forms the extensive vale of pasture and meadow land below Penselwood, and thence by Witham Park to Berkley near Frome.

It is a marine formation divided for convenience into zones characterized by species of ammonites, which in upward succession are *Ammonites calloviensis, A. ornatus* and *A. cordatus*. Large examples of *Gryphæa dilatata* occur in the upper beds. The lowest zone includes locally some bands of calcareous sandstone known as the Kellaways Rock, from Kellaways in Wiltshire, where its numerous fossils early attracted attention. The rock bands are nowhere conspicuous in Somerset, but their occurrence at South Brewham has been recorded.

Septaria are found in the formation, and the dark shales, which are sometimes bituminous and contain a good deal of lignite, led to a fruitless trial for coal at Brewham.

CORALLIAN

These rocks, which are well exposed in north Dorset, extend into Somerset at Cucklington and Stoke Trister to the east, and in an outlier at Higher Hatherley, to the south-west of Wincanton. They are the highest Jurassic strata exposed in Somerset.

There is a gradual passage upwards from the Oxford Clay, and large oysters *Gryphæa dilatata* are found in the sandy clays which mark the incoming of the Corallian. These clays give place to sands with concretionary masses of calcareous sandstone, which yield *Ammonites perarmatus*, *A. cordatus*, etc.

The upper Corallian Beds include oolitic freestones, sandy and shelly limestones, clays and sometimes ferruginous beds, as near Sturminster Newton in Dorset and Westbury in Wiltshire. In these upper beds *Ammonites plicatilis*, *Chemnitzia heddingtonensis*, *Cidaris florigemma* and *Echinobrissus scutatus* are usually to be found.

The strata are water-bearing, but at Horwood Wells, south-east of Wincanton there are saline waters which probably issue from lower strata.

Prior to the overspread of the Upper Cretaceous rocks the Jurassic strata were tilted, faulted and folded, and to a great extent eroded. These phenomena took place after the deposition of the Wealden strata and during or prior to the accumulation of the Lower Greensand, while afterwards during the Upper Cretaceous period a more extensive plain of denudation was formed when Gault, Upper Greensand and Chalk were spread successively across the worn outcrops of the Jurassic and Triassic series.

Of all the present escarpments none of course were formed until after the Cretaceous strata were so far removed as to expose the Jurassic plain.

CRETACEOUS

The GAULT and UPPER GREENSAND, which have been grouped together under the name Selbornian by Mr. Jukes-Browne,[1] appear in Somerset along the northern borders of the Blackdown Hills south of Wellington; also near Chard and Crewkerne; again at Penselwood and Kilmington north-east of Wincanton, and thence they extend to near Frome.

The Gault itself, grey sandy micaceous clay with occasional phosphatic nodules, is the clayey lower portion of this group. It is from 70 to 90 feet in thickness in east Somerset near Penselwood, but it is hardly perceptible in the Blackdown Hills, where the sandy conditions of the Upper Greensand prevail and replace the clayey beds. These beds in east Somerset represent only the Lower Gault zones of *Ammonites interruptus* and *A. lautus*. They have also yielded *A. splendens*, *A. beudanti* and *A. denarius*, but although not well exposed they have been

---

[1] 'The Cretaceous Rocks of Britain,' by A. J. Jukes-Browne and W. Hill (*Geol. Survey*), vol. i. pp. 176, 234, etc. (1900).

recognized along the borders of the Greensand hills from near Penselwood to the east of Frome, in a band which at one time was regarded
as Kimeridge Clay. A brickyard at Flintford near Rodden has been
opened in the Gault.

The Upper Greensand is more important, and forms a bold scarp in
the Blackdown Hills overlooking the vale of Taunton, and extending
thence by Buckland St. Mary to Chard and Crewkerne.

As observed by Mr. Jukes-Browne the thickness increases from
about 100 feet near Crewkerne to 180 feet near Chard, and it is about
150 feet in east Somerset. It comprises in descending order calcareous
sandstone, chert beds, and green, grey and buff sands ; and among other
fossils it has yielded *Ammonites rostratus, Arca, Pleuromya, Exogyra conica,
Pecten (Neithea) quadricostata, P. quinquecostata* and *Cardiaster fossarius*.

The Upper Greensand is an important water-bearing formation,
springs being thrown out at its base where it rests on the Lias near
Chard or on the Gault north of Wincanton. Bruton is supplied from
springs near Kilmington. The region is naturally a healthy one, though
in some places pollution of water arises from defective sanitary arrangements.

Penselwood has long been famous for the old Pen pits whence
nodules of hard cherty sandstone were formerly dug for the manufacture of whetstones. The pits from which they were dug have been
regarded as early British pit-dwellings, and much has been written on
this subject.[1]

The soil on the Greensand is variable, that near Kilmington being
more fertile than it is near Crewkerne and Chard.

The CHALK occupies small areas in Somerset, including the western
extremity of Salisbury Plain and tracts between Chard and Crewkerne.

The Chloritic Marl, a fossiliferous glauconitic marl from 1 to 2 feet
thick, occurs at the base of the Chalk at Snowdown by Chard,[2] and
Kilmington. It yields *Ammonites rotomagensis, A. varians, Holaster sub-
globosus*, var. *altus*, also the sponge *Stauronema carteri*, and it contains phosphatic nodules.

The Lower Chalk, including the Chalk Marl, is about 200 feet
thick, and occurs near Chard, Crewkerne, and at Long Knoll, while
above it on White Sheet Down there are beds of Middle Chalk with
the Melbourne Rock at the base.[3]

PLEISTOCENE AND RECENT

A great break occurs between the Chalk and the next records
which have been preserved in Somerset. The Chalk as a deep sea
deposit no doubt overspread the entire county. Whether any Eocene
strata extended over the area it is impossible to say ; the nearest repre-

---

[1] See Rev. H. H. Winwood, *Proc. Somerset Arch. Soc.* vol. xxv. ; and H. B. Woodward, *Midland
Naturalist* (1883).

[2] H. B. Woodward, *Geology of England and Wales*, ed. 2, p. 392 (1887).

[3] A. J. Jukes-Browne and J. Scanes, *Quart. Journ. Geol. Soc.* vol. lvii. p. 96 ; Fitton, *Trans. Geol.
Soc.* ser. 2, vol. iv. p. 256.

sentatives occur within twenty miles of the eastern borders, while patches of flint shingle, probably of Eocene derivation, lie on the Chalk at Chitterne St. Mary near Heytesbury.[1] Eocene pebble beds indicate that locally the Chalk was upraised to form land areas, and this being the case agents of erosion partly marine and estuarine, largely subaerial, must have commenced the work of destruction which ever since, amid changing conditions and with greater or less potency, has been going on. The Miocene period, characterized by great earth movements which upraised Chalk and Eocene strata, was one during which subaerial erosion occurred on a large scale. The Severn drainage may have been defined; and there can be little doubt that the mass of the Chalk and other Cretaceous strata were removed from the greater part of Somerset before Pliocene times.

The removal of these formations unbared a plain of Jurassic and Triassic strata through which perhaps only in west Somerset the older rocks protruded, the inequalities elsewhere being filled up. Along this plain, and fed by springs from the Chalk and Greensand and ultimately from other sources, the Avon and its tributaries in the north, the Brue and Parret in the south, have carved out their courses. The Avon cut through hard and soft rocks, deeply trenching its course along what is now the Avon gorge before the bordering lowlands of Lias and New Red Rocks had been excavated[2]; and this lower part of its course was naturally deepened before the river had completed its picturesque channel through the Oolites above Bath. The long continued erosion has enabled the rivers to reach what is termed the base level of erosion over the greater length of their courses, and their channels are subject now to widening rather than to deepening processes.

Waste along the present hills and scarps is seen in the landslips which now and again occur along the oolitic hills near Bath. Thus at Hedgemead below Lansdown, and again at Beechen Cliff on the south side of Bath, the Inferior Oolite has slipped over the Lias clays; while at Bathampton and Claverton there have been slips of Great Oolite over the unstable foundation of Fuller's Earth Clay.

Knolls like Glastonbury Tor and Brent Knoll are striking monuments of denudation. Others near Ilminster, Montacute, South Cadbury and Castle Cary, not far removed from the main escarpment, indicate how the severance of such outliers may take place. Subterranean drainage and erosion in the first instance lead to the formation of underground channels in the impervious Lias clays beneath the porous Midford Sands and the limestones of the Inferior Oolite. The limestones themselves may be in part wasted by chemical dissolution, and if channels are formed in subjacent strata slight subsidences must take place here and there, and pave the way for the disconnection of portions of the main limestones to form outliers. The subsequent more complete

[1] See Prestwich, *Quart. Journ. Geol. Soc.* vol. xlvi. p. 144 ; and *Geol. Mag.* p. 412 (1898).
[2] See Jukes, *Geol. Mag.* p. 444 (1867) ; and C. Lloyd Morgan, *Proc. Bristol Nat. Soc.* ser. 2, vol. iv. (1885).

isolation of the severed masses is due to the superficial and subterranean erosion by rain and streams. In the case of Brent Knoll and Glastonbury Tor the influence of estuarine waters that once spread over the Somerset levels must have helped to complete the denudation. The slightly basin-shaped arrangement of the strata in both these outliers has helped in their preservation. The effects of subterranean erosion are also seen where valley gravel rests on furrowed surfaces of clays such as those of the Lias near Bath.

Elsewhere along the Mendip plateau and that of Broadfield Down the effects of chemical as well as mechanical erosion are evident in the deep ravines and caverns. A few of the ravines may have been initiated in the Triassic period, and have been re-excavated and deepened in later times, but Cheddar, Ebbor, Burrington, Brockley and Cleeve and most others probably belong in the main to the post-Pliocene period. Many of the great fissures on Mendip originating along joint planes or lines of fracture have been so enlarged as to form a series of caverns, and in some cases where erosion has proceeded further a deep ravine has resulted. The solvent action of carbonated water, aided by frost and streams, mainly contributed to produce the effect.

In the case of Cheddar the dip has exercised much influence on the shape of the cliffs, the one side with the inward dip standing up boldly and precipitously, while the other, the dip slope, affording abundant evidence of disintegration, showers of detritus now and then falling on to the road and in old times into a deep natural gully. The cliffs are perhaps the finest of their kind in England, and they rise at one point to a height of 420 feet above the level of the road.

Several of the streams which issue at the foot of the Mendip Hills take their rise from swallet holes in the Carboniferous Limestone of the plateau. Among these are St. Andrew's and other springs at Wells, the Axe (derived from Priddy) which issues at Wookey Hole, and the Cheddar water.

These waters flowing through limestone areas carry away much carbonate of lime in solution, but under certain conditions they redeposit it on the roofs and floors of caverns in the form of stalactites and stalagmites, or elsewhere in pipes; and in some instances, as near Coleford, Darshill near Shepton Mallet, and Chilton-upon-Polden, there are deposits of tufa left by petrifying springs.

While the Avon was cutting its rocky course the area of the Bristol Channel was evidently a great vale of Lias which spread from Watchet to the Glamorganshire coast, while the Inferior Oolite of Dundry and and the Midford Sands of Brent Knoll were connected with the main escarpments. This broad vale was trenched by the Severn drainage and afterwards widened by estuarine and marine action. The plain of marine erosion is now well seen in the wide rocky platform which is exposed at low tide at Watchet, but the sea must in Pleistocene times have cut its way up to some of the Limestone cliffs near Weston-super-Mare, as there we find traces of raised beaches.

In this brief sketch no reference has been made to the Glacial period, prior to which the main features throughout England were produced. Evidences of the Great Ice Age in Somerset are few and local. Unlike many other areas it was not buried beneath a mantle of ice, nor overspread with deposits of boulder clay or drift gravel. For this reason the soils of Somerset are for the most part local, bearing a direct relation to the sub-strata. No doubt the area has been affected by Pleistocene climatic changes and fluctuations in level, but from later Tertiary until comparatively recent times it has been subject chiefly to waste by rain, rivers and sea rather than to deposit.

The striated surfaces of Devonian sandstone observed near Porlock by W. C. Lucy, and the 'terminal curvature' of the slaty rocks near Wiveliscombe noted by D. Mackintosh,[1] are features which may have been produced by local agents.

Relics of early stages in denudation are met with in the shape of chalk flints, and pebbles of quartz and quartzite, which have been found here and there on the surface and in chinks of the Oolites on Farley, Bathampton and Claverton Downs. Small patches of gravel have also been observed on Clevedon Down.

Valley gravels here and there fringe the rivers and occur in scattered patches in the vales, but the only extensive superficial deposits are those which occupy the alluvial moorlands.

Along the Avon valley there are here and there small areas of river gravel, and these have yielded in places remains of Pleistocene mammalia such as we find in the older deposits of the Thames valley. These include mammoth or *Elephas primigenius*, also *E. antiquus*, rhinoceros, musk ox and reindeer.[2] Thus at Freshford, Bathampton, Bath and Keynsham there are deposits of gravel made up of local materials, the limestones of the Lias and Oolites, together with harder materials of the Carboniferous group and Old Red Sandstone derived from tributary streams which rise in the Mendips. At Larkhall, Bath, as much as 30 feet of gravel and loamy beds have been observed.

Valley gravel occurs at Wells and Wookey, along the Brue valley near Bruton and Castle Cary, and over the Lias vale bordering the rivers Yeo and Cary near Ilchester and Langport, at Babcary, Milton, Puddimore and other places. Patches of clayey gravel largely composed of chert detritus from the Greensand hills occur from near Chard to Broadway, at Ashill and other places.

At Taunton the valley gravel has yielded rhinoceros and Irish elk, as well as remains of alder, ash and oak timber ; and in this neighbourhood one Palæolithic implement was obtained by W. Bidgood. In the vale extending to Williton there are patches of gravel largely derived from the New Red conglomerates.

Possibly of the same age as some of the valley gravels into which they may have merged, are the remnants of raised beaches made up

[1] *Quart. Journ. Geol. Soc.* vol. xxiii. p. 323.
[2] Moore, *Proc. Bath Nat. Hist. Club* (1870).

mainly of Carboniferous Limestone pebbles with occasional flints, and preserved on platforms of the limestone at Anchor Head and Wood-spring Hill north of Weston-super-Mare.[1] They lie from 20 to 30 feet above high-water mark, and are covered by blown sand, by rubble or talus of ancient date, and by recent talus. The beaches yield *Mytilus edulis, Cardium edule, Tellina balthica, Ostrea edulis, Buccinum undatum* and *Littorina littorea*. All these species and others such as *Scrobicularia* are found in the so-called Burtle Beds. These comprise sands with occasional pebbles, sometimes cemented into hard bands, which occur in patches on the Lias or Red Marl in the moorlands at Burtle between Glastonbury and Highbridge, and at Middlezoy and Chedzoy near Bridgewater. Whether these Burtle Beds were contemporaneous with the raised beaches or were due to later incursions of the sea over the low lands is not certain.

The older rubble drift above the raised beaches has yielded remains of hyæna, bear, mammoth and rhinoceros. Hence these deposits may be compared with some of the valley gravels, with the older cave deposits, and with bone fissures such as occur on the Oolitic hills near Bath, where remains of rhinoceros, bison and lemming have been obtained. It must be remembered however that the Pleistocene period was a long one and attended by considerable physical changes, and that in South Wales Mr. R. H. Tiddeman has pointed out that subsequent to the raised beaches and the infilling of some of the caverns in Gower the local boulder drift was accumulated.[2]

Many caverns occur in Somerset, the more noteworthy being those of Cheddar, which contain fine stalactites, Wookey Hole, Burrington, Banwell and Uphill.[3] The Lamb Cavern near East Harptree is an extensive one, in which formerly there were lead workings.

The hyæna den of Wookey Hole, worked out by Professor W. Boyd Dawkins, is a fissure in the Dolomitic Conglomerate distinct from the large cavern in the Carboniferous Limestone. It has yielded remains of hyæna, cave lion, bear, badger, mammoth, rhinoceros, Irish elk, etc., together with implements of flint and chert of somewhat rude workmanship. Many of the bones bear evidence of having been gnawed by hyænas. Professor Dawkins expressed the opinion that at the time of the occupation of these caves a great plain extended over much of what is now the Bristol Channel. The land must indeed have stood higher previous to the accumulation of the more recent alluvial deposits, probably to the extent of 50 or 60 feet. Proof of this is to be gathered from the depth of these more recent deposits, and from the evidences of old forest growth at their base at Porlock [4] and elsewhere. The marsh-lands as near Bridgewater are made up of a succession of fluviatile and

---

[1] E. C. H. Day, *Geol. Mag.* p. 115 (1866) ; Prestwich, *Quart. Journ. Geol. Soc.* vol. xviii. pp. 286, 300.

[2] *Geol. Mag.* p. 441 (1900).

[3] See Buckland, *Reliquiæ Diluvianæ* ; Rutter, *Delineations of the County of Somerset* (1829) ; and Dawkins, *Quart. Journ. Geol. Soc.* vol. xviii. p. 115, vol. xix. p. 260 ; and *Cave Hunting.*

[4] See Godwin-Austen, *Quart. Journ. Geol. Soc.* vol. xxii. p. 1.

estuarine mud deposits, gravel and sand, and peat, with evidence of plant growth at more than one horizon. Remains of an old forest at Stolford were long ago recognized. Occasionally the peat is found in a compressed and indurated condition known locally as pill coal.

Peat is extensively dug to a depth of 14 or 15 feet on the moors between Glastonbury and Highbridge, especially near Ashcot, Shapwick and Edington. It is largely composed of the common sedge, bog moss, reeds and rushes.

The alluvial deposits have yielded remains of existing land and freshwater mollusca, and of such animals as *Bos taurus* var. *longifrons*, roe deer, goat, sheep, horse and dog.

The estuary of the Severn is noted for the extensive mud flats bordering it at low tide, and which are liable, as near the mouth of the Parret, to constant changes. The turmoil of the tidal waters agitates this silty material, and Weston-super-Mare has gained the name of 'Weston-super-Mud' from the fact that at low tide there is an extensive area of sandy silt and the waters are clouded with the suspended matter. This is borne down to a large extent by the rivers which drain into the Severn Sea, but is partly derived from the waste of the cliffs.[1]

At Bridgewater the material is utilized in the formation of the celebrated scouring bricks, named Bath bricks from the original manuturer, Mr. Bath. Tanks or slime-batches have been constructed on the borders of the Parret, into which the tidal waters are admitted and the slime is allowed to subside. This slime contains about 70 per cent of fine siliceous matter.

The marshlands over considerable areas lie beneath high water level, in some places as much as 8 or 10 feet, but they have since Roman times been more or less protected by artificial embankments, while the dunes of blown sand between Burnham and Woodspring, north of Weston-super-Mare, have likewise checked the inflow of the sea. The rivers too have been embanked and their courses have locally been modified, but in times of long continued heavy rain the dykes and sluggish rivers are unable to carry off the land drainage which is held up by the tidal waters ; and from these causes and the occasional bursting of a bank or overflow of a stream the marshes are sometimes inundated for many square miles.[2] The fine silty material then deposited helps to fertilize these large areas of dairy and grazing ground. In times of flood Athelney, a low hill which rises from the alluvial moors between Langport and Bridgewater, is liable to become an island ; but Glastonbury Tor, the Isle of Avalon, has probably never been surrounded by water in the historic period, though situated in the midst of marshes and bogs.

In ancient times the uplands were extensively wooded, and remains of the Mendip forest above Wells and Cheddar, of Selwood forest which

---

[1] W. J. Sollas, *Quart. Journ. Geol. Soc.* vol. xxxix. p. 611 ; see also *Geology of East Somerset*, etc. p. 159.

[2] See Rev. W. Phelps, *Prx. Somerset Arch. Soc.* vol. iv. p. 91.

stretched from Frome to Wincanton, and of the forests of North Petherton, Neroche and Exmoor which occupied much of southern and western Somerset were long unenclosed, some portions until the middle of the eighteenth century. The most prominent heights were early fortified, and the history of these earthworks and of the still older lake dwellings near Glastonbury link geology with human history. Indeed since Roman times some geological changes have taken place, and alluvium and peaty beds have been accumulated to a depth of 12 feet at Bath and on the levels of Burnham and Huntspill.

PALÆONTOLOGY

AMONG many other claims to the best attention of the student of vertebrate palæontology, Somerset has a special pre-eminence on account of having yielded the earliest known evidence in Britain of the existence of mammals. Indeed, there are no earlier representatives of the group known from any part of the world. In referring the remains in question to the Mammalia it must however be borne in mind that they may prove to belong to creatures intermediate between reptiles and the living duckbill (*Ornitho-rhynchus anatinus*) of Australia, which is one of the two lowest existing mammals. These presumed mammals are known only by teeth and are assigned to a genus (*Microlestes*) originally described from the Trias of the continent, but to species different from the continental. Certain of these teeth, now in the Bath Museum, were obtained from a fissure in the Rhætic strata of Frome, and named by Sir R. Owen *Microlestes moorei*, in honour of Mr. C. Moore, the well known collector of Somerset fossil vertebrates. Another tooth, preserved in the museum at Oxford, was collected by Professor W. B. Dawkins in the Rhætic of Watchet, and named by him *Hypsiprymnopsis rhæticus*, on the supposition that it indicated a creature allied to the modern rat-kangaroos of Aus-tralia. It appears however to be undoubtedly referable to the same genus as the Frome specimens, if indeed it be specifically distinct. If, as is stated to be the case, it was found in undisturbed Rhætic strata it is of the highest importance as definitely fixing the Triassic age of the former. For as the Frome teeth were obtained from a fissure in the Rhætic, it is obvious that they might perfectly well be of post-Triassic origin.

Leaving then these highly interesting teeth, we pass on to the consideration of the fossil fish of Somerset, among which several are peculiar to the county. The oldest of these occur in the Carboni-ferous strata of the county,[1] where they are represented by *Cladodus mirabilis*, a primitive shark of the group Ichthyotomi. Among the true sharks (Selachii) a tooth from Clevedon in the British Museum belongs to the well known *Psammodus rugosus*, whose large pavement-like crushing teeth are common in Carboniferous strata. Other teeth from Clevedon have curved and elevated crowns, and belong to *Delto-*

[1] See *Cat. Foss. Fish. Brit. Mus.* i. 17.

ptychius gibberulus, a member of the family *Cochliodontidæ*. The Carboniferous strata of the same locality have likewise yielded numerous teeth referable to *Orodus ramosus*, a pavement-toothed shark belonging to the family (*Cestraciontidæ*) typified by the existing Port Jackson shark.

The formations newer than the Carboniferous have yielded a large number of peculiar fishes, one of the most interesting being *Diplodus moorei*[1] from the Keuper, which is only known from Somerset, and indicates the survival in the early Secondary of the Palæozoic cladodont type (Ichthyotomi). Specimens from the Rhætic strata of the county indicate the occurrence of *Hybodus minor*, a fairly common cestraciont shark. Among species of uncertain affinity described on the evidence of fin-spines, the one known as *Nemacanthus monilifer* is indicated by a small spine from the Rhætic of the county. Other Rhætic fishes are the ganoid *Sargodon tomicus* and *Saurichthys acuminatus*, both of which have a wide distribution.

From the lower Lias three species are known, namely the pavement-toothed shark *Acrodus nobilis*, of which teeth (termed by quarry-men in some parts of the country fossil leeches) and fin-spines are met with at Weston and Keynsham near Bath ; the ganoid *Pholidophorus stricklandi*, of which remains occur at Glastonbury (the only other locality for the species being Leicestershire) ; and another ganoid, *Mesodon liassicus*, which is known from Langport.

Special interest attaches to the Upper Liassic fishes of Ilminster, a fine series of which, now in the Bath Royal Literary and Scientific Institution, were collected by the late Mr. C. Moore. These specimens have been described by Dr. A. Smith Woodward in a paper contributed to the *Proceedings* of the Bath Club.[2] They belong to a zone in the Lias represented elsewhere in Würtemberg, Bavaria, Calvados and Vassy in France, and Whitby in Yorkshire.

The first is a ganoid, *Lepidotus elvensis*, originally described from Würtemberg, and belonging to a well known genus in which the crushing teeth are button-shaped and the polished scales large and rhomboidal. Fragments too imperfect to admit of specific determination indicate the occurrence of a representative of another ganoid genus, *Dapedius* ; but of much more interest is a fine and apparently unique specimen of an unnamed species of the genus *Caturus*, which occurs typically in the lithographic limestones of Bavaria. The special interest of *Caturus*, as remarked by Dr. Woodward, consists in its being almost identical in regard to the structure of the head, skeleton and fins with the rhombic-scaled *Eugnathus*, although its whole body is invested with thin overlapping scales. The most numerous of the Ilminster fishes belong however to the Mesozoic ganoid genus *Pachycormus*, which represents a family whose members present a curious superficial resemblance to the modern sword-fishes ; the Cretaceous *Protosphyræna* being one of the *Pachycormidæ* in which a true sword was developed. The

[1] See A. S. Woodward, *Ann. Mag. Nat. Hist.* ser. 6, iii. 299 (1889), and *Cat. Foss. Fish. Brit. Mus.*
[2] Vol. viii. 233 (1896).

Ilminster species apparently include the typical *Pachycormus macropterus*, the smaller *P. curtus*, *P. esocinus*, and an unnamed small-scaled form. Other remains suggest a species which may belong either to *Pachycormus* or the allied genus *Saurostomus*, while a head in the British Museum belongs to a species of *Pholidophorus*, perhaps identical with *P. germanicus* of Würtemberg and Whitby. *Leptolepis bronni*, a more modern type of ganoid, is also met with at Ilminster.

From the Great Oolite of the county teeth of two common Mesozoic sharks, *Strophodus magnus* and *Hybodus grossiconus*, have been obtained, both belonging to the family *Cestraciontidæ*; and also the ganoid *Lepidotus tuberculatus*. In the Upper Greensand of Kilmerton we have a more modern type of shark represented by a tooth in the British Museum referable to the common Cretaceous *Oxyrhina mantelli*.[1]

Of the fossil reptiles of Somerset, one of the earliest appears to be the small carnivorous dinosaur *Thecodontosaurus platyodon*, of which there are two teeth in the British Museum from the upper Trias of the county. This species is typically from the Trias of Bristol, but other dinosaurian remains from the Rhætic of Wedmore near Glastonbury have been considered to represent two genera and species peculiar to the county. These have been named[2] *Avalonia sanfordi* and *Picrodon harveyi*, but further evidence seems desirable to show their distinctness from one another and also from the widely spread Triassic genus *Zanclodon*.

Remains of large marine saurians belonging to the genera *Ichthyosaurus*, *Plesiosaurus*, etc., are exceedingly abundant in the lower Liassic strata of Bath, Glastonbury, Street and Watchet, where many more or less nearly entire skeletons have been obtained. A fine series of such specimens are exhibited in the British Museum, several of which are the types of the species they represent. Ichthyosaurs, it may be mentioned, have very large heads, short necks, paddles composed of a number of polygonal bones articulated together to form a pavement, and the bodies of the vertebræ very short, deeply cupped, and quite separate from the arches protecting the spinal cord. Some of them reach thirty feet in length, and all have a ring of bones in the white of the eye. Most of the species from the county belong to the group with broad paddles, among them being *Ichthyosaurus communis* from Bath and Street, *I. conybeari* from Saltford near Bath, and *I. intermedius* from Street. The very distinct and gigantic *I. platyodon* is common in the county, and there are certain bones from Watchet in the Boulogne Museum which may indicate yet another species of the genus.

The Liassic plesiosaurs differ from the ichthyosaurs not only by their elongated necks and small heads, but likewise by the structure of their paddles, the bones of which are of normal form and do not make a pavement. The bodies of the vertebræ too are relatively longer, less deeply cupped, and more firmly articulated to the arches, while there are no ossifications in the ball of the eye. *Plesiosaurus compressus* has been

---

[1] See *Cat. Foss. Fish. Brit. Mus.* i. 379.   [2] See Seeley, *Geol. Mag.* decade 4, v. 1–9 (1898).

met with in the lower Lias of at least one locality in the county. *P. dolichodirus* occurs at Bath and Watchet, *P. hawkinsi* at Street, and *P. macrocephalus* at Street and at Weston near Bath. The species *Plesiosaurus eleutheraxon* was named from remains found at Street, and vertebræ from the same locality have been made the type of a nominal species under the name of *P. subconcavus*, while others from Weston have been described as a second nominal species with the title of *P. subtrigonus*. Of the allied genus *Thaumatosaurus*, distinguished by the proportionately larger head, two species occur in the lower Lias of the county, namely *T. arcuatus* and *T. megacephalus*. Part of a lower jaw in the British Museum, which is probably from Street, forms one of the types of the former species, of which remains also occur at Bath. The second species is typified by an entire skeleton in the British Museum from some locality in the county.

Reptilian remains from other Mesozoic deposits appear to be rare in Somerset. A peculiar species of long-nosed crocodile of the genus *Steneosaurus* is typified by a skull from the Great Oolite of Bath described by Sir R. Owen as *S. temporalis*. The common Cretaceous *Ichthyosaurus campylodon* is represented in the county by teeth and vertebræ from the Upper Greensand of Kilmerton ;[1] and a large-headed representative of the pliosaurs occurs in the lower Chalk of Frome in the form of the widely spread *Polyptychodon continuus*.

As regards Tertiary Mammalia, Somerset is celebrated on account of the large number of remains obtained from the limestone caves of the Mendips, of which a magnificent series are preserved in the Museum of the Somerset Archæological and Natural History Society at Taunton.[2] The earliest of these caves to be explored was that of Hutton near Weston-super-Mare, which was known to contain bones so long ago as the middle of the eighteenth century. This cave, together with the neighbouring ones of Banwell, Bleadon, Goat's Hole in Barrington Combe, Sandford Hill and Uphill were explored by Messrs. Beard and Williams between 1821 and 1860, while the so-called hyæna den of Wookey Hole, on the south side of the Mendips near Wells, was worked in 1859 and following years by Professor W. B. Dawkins and others. It was one of the first caverns in England where articles of human manufacture were found in association with the remains of extinct mammals. In addition to the abundance of hyænas at Wookey Hole, the Mendip mammalian fauna is especially characterized by the number of remains of lions, as it likewise is by a few indications of the presence of the wolverine, or glutton, an animal scarce in British Pleistocene deposits.

Among the Carnivora from the Mendip caverns may be mentioned the Pleistocene lion (*Felis leo spelæa*), which occurs at Banwell, Bleadon, Sandford and Wookey, the leopard (*F. pardus*) from Banwell and

---

[1] See *Cat. Foss. Rept. Brit. Mus.* ii. 18 ; misprinted Kilmenton.
[2] See W. B. Dawkins, *Cave Hunting*, p. 292 et seq. (1874), and W. A. Sanford, *Catalogue of Mammalia in Taunton Museum.*

PALÆONTOLOGY

Bleadon or Hutton, the wild cat (*F. catus*) at Bleadon, the Egyptian cat (*F. maniculata*), the Pleistocene variety of the spotted hyæna (*Hyæna crocuta spelæa*) from Banwell, Bleadon and Wookey, the wolf (*Canis lupus*) and fox (*C. vulpes*) from Banwell, Bleadon and Sandford, the otter (*Lutra lutra*) from Banwell and Bleadon, the badger (*Meles meles*) from Banwell and Wookey, the marten (*Mustela martes*) from Bleadon, the wolverine (*Gulo luscus*) from Banwell and Bleadon, the brown bear (*Ursus arctus*), including the so-called grizzly, and the great cave-bear (*U. spelæus*).

The Somerset cave rodents, according to Mr. W. A. Sanford,[1] include the common hare (*Lepus europæus*), mountain hare (*L. timidus*), Pleistocene hare (*L. diluvianus*), Siberian hamster (*Cricetus songarus*), water-vole (*Microtus amphibius*), field-vole (*M. agrestis*), bank-vole (*Evotomys glareolus*), Norwegian lemming (*Lemmus lemmus*), banded lemming (*Dicrostonyx torquatus*), an apparently extinct species of suslik (*Spermophilus erythrogenoides*), and the common pica (*Ochotona pusilla*).

Another vole, *Microtus ratticeps*, has also been recorded from the caves of Somerset ; this being apparently the only known instance of the occurrence of this continental species in Britain.

Among the hoofed mammals may be mentioned the Pleistocene bison (*Bos priscus*), the wild ox (*B. taurus primigenius*), the red deer (*Cervus elaphus*), giant fallow deer, commonly called ' Irish elk ' (*C. giganteus*), roe (*Capreolus capreolus*), reindeer (*Rangifer tarandus*), wild boar (*Sus scrofa*), woolly rhinoceros (*Rhinoceros antiquitatis*), leptorhine rhinoceros (*R. leptorhinus*), wild horse (*Equus caballus fossilis*), mammoth (*Elephas primigenius*), and straight-tusked elephant (*E. antiquus*).

Remains of bats are rare in British caves, but bones provisionally assigned to White's bat (*Pipistrellus noctula*) have been recorded from Banwell and Hutton caves.

There are also certain Pleistocene deposits other than those in caverns from which mammalian remains have been obtained in the county. Teeth or bones of the horse have, for instance, been found in a raised beach at Weston-super-Mare, as well as in superficial deposits at Bath and Larkhall. The mammoth also occurs at the two localities last-mentioned, while the straight-tusked elephant, woolly rhinoceros and reindeer are recorded from Larkhall, and the wild boar from both Larkhall and Ilminster.

[1] *Quart. Journ. Geol. Soc.* xxiv. 444 (1869).

BOTANY

SOMERSET has a mild climate, damper than that of counties situated further east, but drier and more bracing than that of Devon and Cornwall. The surface is for the most part hilly, but only Dunkery Beacon exceeds by a very little 1,700 feet, so that we look in vain for any trace of a distinctively mountain flora. Great levels, hardly above sea level, border the rivers Brue and Parrett, and stretch from the Bristol Channel to the base of Mendip. Of its area of 1,042,487 acres, about 65,000 acres are uncultivated, about 45,000 consist of mountain and heath land used for pasture, 45,000 of woods and plantations, while the remainder is under cultivation.

So far as present knowledge extends the phanerogamic flora of Somerset includes 1,042 species. Ferns and fern allies number 41, and 7 species of *Characeæ* have been recorded. It is believed that a very few out of this number have become extinct during the past half century or thereabouts. These are *Vicia lutea, V. hybrida, Parnassia palustris, Aster Linosyris, Cyperus longus, Cladium jamaicense, Carex dioica, C. Davalliana.* Some few others have been recorded on perhaps insufficient grounds, but it is hoped that most of them may yet be confirmed.

As is only natural, the flora of Somerset consists mainly of plants having a wide distribution in the British Isles, but no less than 43 species belong to Watson's 'Atlantic' group, which consists of plants having a markedly western range in Great Britain, while only 15 can be assigned to his Scottish or Highland groups, and 5 belong to his 'Germanic' group.

Among the more noticeable plants of the 'Atlantic' group which occur may be mentioned the following : *Meconopsis cambrica, Arabis stricta, Helianthemum polifolium, Dianthus cæsius, Vicia bithynica, Sedum rupestre, Trinia vulgaris, Aster Linosyris, Inula crithmoides, Wahlenbergia hederacea, Lithospermum purpureo-cæruleum, Sibthorpia europæa, Pinguicula lusitanica, Melittis Melissophyllum, Euphorbia Paralias, Cyperus longus* (extinct), *Scirpus numidianus, S. Holoschænus, Rhynchospora fusca* ; and among ferns *Hymenophyllum tunbridgense, Asplenium lanceolatum,* and *Lastræa æmula.*

'Scottish' and 'Highland' species may be recognized in *Alsine verna, Vicia Orobus, Rubus saxatilis, Drosera anglica, Saxifraga hypnoides, Hieracium Schmidtii, Andromeda polifolia, Empetrum nigrum, Listera cordata,* and a few others besides the following ferns : *Cryptogramme crispa,*

I   41   6

Asplenium septentrionale, Polypodium Phegopteris ; and a clubmoss, *Lycopodium alpinum.*

'Germanic' species are *Bupleurum rotundifolium, Chenopodium ficifolium, Polygonum mite* and *Carex depauperata.*

The following plants are (so far as the British Islands are concerned) found only in Somerset :—

Pæonia corallina on Steep Holm, but certainly originally introduced.

Dianthus cæsius, Cheddar gorge and in another small ravine between Cheddar and Wells.

Vicia hybrida, extinct and perhaps accidentally introduced.

Hieracium stenolepis, Cheddar gorge.

Verbascum Lychnitis var. *micranthum,* woods near Porlock.

Euphorbia pilosa, near Bath and supposed by some to have been introduced by the Romans.

Carex Davalliana, extinct.

Arabis stricta is confined to a very limited area in the immediate vicinity of Clifton, partly in Somerset and partly in Gloucestershire.

Helianthemum polifolium occurs only in Devon and Somerset.

Althæa hirsuta has been found in Herts, Kent and Gloucestershire.

Pyrus latifolia var. *decipiens* seems to be confined to Somerset and Denbighshire.

Sedum album, which is common in many places as an ' escape,' may be native in Somerset and on the Malvern Hills.

Hieracium lima has been recorded only (so far as the writer knows) from Somerset and west Yorkshire.

Cyperus fuscus, always rare, has been found only in Surrey, Hants, Dorset and Somerset.[1]

The following Somerset brambles have as yet been recorded from very few other counties, but it is probable that in time their range will prove to be much greater than at present known :—

Rubus cariensis, R. Questierii and *R. Lintoni,* the last of these being at present known only from Somerset, Monmouth and Norfolk.

---

[1] *Cyperus fuscus* was at one time found in Middlesex, but no longer exists there. I have always understood that it was known to have been intentionally introduced there.

BOTANY

SUMMARY OF ORDERS

	Genera	Species		Genera	Species
PHANEROGAMIA			48. Boragineæ	8	16
1. Ranunculaceæ	10	31	49. Convolvulaceæ	2	6
2. Berberideæ	1	1	50. Solanaceæ	3	4
3. Nymphæaceæ	2	2	51. Plantagineæ	2	6
4. Papaveraceæ	4	8	52. Scrophularineæ	15	34
5. Fumariaceæ	2	5	53. Orobancheæ	1	5
6. Cruciferæ	21	44	54. Lentibularineæ	2	4
7. Resedaceæ	1	2	55. Verbenaceæ	1	1
8. Cistineæ	1	2	56. Labiatæ	19	40
9. Violaceæ	1	7	57. Illecebraceæ	1	1
10. Polygaleæ	1	3	58. Chenopodiaceæ	6	17
11. Caryophylleæ	11	40	59. Polygonaceæ	2	23
12. Portulaceæ	1	1	60. Thymelæaceæ	1	2
13. Hypericineæ	1	9	61. Loranthaceæ	1	1
14. Malvaceæ	3	6	62. Santalaceæ	1	1
15. Tiliaceæ	1	1	63. Euphorbiaceæ	2	11
16. Lineæ	2	3	64. Urticaceæ	4	6
17. Geraniaceæ	3	14	65. Myricaceæ	1	1
18. Ilicineæ	1	1	66. Cupuliferæ	6	6
19. Empetraceæ	1	1	67. Salicineæ	2	11
20. Celastrineæ	1	1	68. Ceratophylleæ	1	1
21. Rhamneæ	1	2	69. Coniferæ	3	3
22. Sapindaceæ	1	1	70. Hydrocharideæ	2	2
23. Leguminosæ	16	56	71. Orchideæ	9	21
24. Rosaceæ	12	104	72. Irideæ	1	2
25. Saxifrageæ	4	8	73. Amaryllideæ	2	3
26. Crassulaceæ	1	9	74. Dioscoreæ	1	1
27. Droseraceæ	1	3	75. Liliaceæ	13	18
28. Halorageæ	3	8	76. Junceæ	2	19
29. Lythrarieæ	2	3	77. Typhaceæ	2	6
30. Onagrarieæ	3	13	78. Aroideæ	2	2
31. Cucurbitaceæ	1	1	79. Lemnaceæ	1	4
32. Umbelliferæ	28	44	80. Alismaceæ	3	4
33. Araliaceæ	1	1	81. Naiadaceæ	5	20
34. Cornaceæ	1	1	82. Cyperaceæ	8	64
35. Caprifoliaceæ	4	6	83. Gramineæ	35	81
36. Rubiaceæ	4	14			
37. Valerianeæ	3	8	Total genera and species	393	1,042
38. Dipsaceæ	2	5			
39. Compositæ	40	85	**SUMMARY OF VASCULAR CRYPTOGAMS**		
40. Campanulaceæ	4	8			
41. Ericaceæ	5	7	84. Filices	13	29
42. Monotropeæ	1	1	85. Equisetaceæ	1	7
43. Plumbagineæ	2	3	86. Lycopodiaceæ	1	4
44. Primulaceæ	7	11	87. Marsileaceæ	1	1
45. Oleaceæ	2	2			
46. Apocynaceæ	1	1	Total genera and species	16	41
47. Gentianeæ	4	6			

A HISTORY OF SOMERSET

The ten districts[1] into which the county is divided are founded on the river basins, and are consequently of very unequal size. They are (1) Dulverton; (2) Minehead; (3) Taunton; (4) Ilminster and Yeovil; (5) Somerton; (6) Axe; (7) Wincanton; (8) Glastonbury; (9) Mendip; (10) Bath and Bristol.

I.—DULVERTON

This district occupies the extreme south-west of the county, and is in length about twenty-one miles, while the breadth varies from three to eleven. It is extremely hilly, the northern boundary following the line of the watershed between the Bristol and English Channels, and attaining at Dunkery Beacon a height of 1,700 feet above the sea. It is drained by the rivers Exe and Barle, which unite a little to the south of Dulverton station close to the county boundary. The geological formation is Devonian, and the surface except for the narrow river valleys almost entirely moorland. Consequently the flora is comparatively poor in species, only a little over 400 having been as yet detected. Among these it is curious to find a foreign valerian (*Valeriana pyrenaica*), which the writer found in 1883 abundantly in a plantation near Higher Combe farm above Dulverton. In 1891 it formed a marked feature in the vegetation in the valley of the Barle for at least two or three miles.

The following interesting plants may also be noted as occurring in the district :—

Aquilegia vulgaris, L.
Meconopsis cambrica, Vig.
Sagina subulata, Presl.
Poterium officinale, Hook. f.
Sedum anglicum, Huds.

Valerianella carinata, Lois.
Carex pallescens, L.
— lævigata, Sm.
Avena pubescens, Huds.

II.—MINEHEAD

This comprises a narrow strip of country reaching from the Devon border on the west to Stert Point at the mouth of the Parrett on the east, and is bounded on the north by the shores of the Bristol Channel. The extreme length is about thirty-four miles, but the greatest breadth does not exceed six. It is watered by a number of small streams which descend from Exmoor and the Brendon Hills. Dunkery Beacon reaches 1,707 feet; Lucott Hill, 1,512; Elworthy Barrow, 1,290; and North Hill near Minehead, 1,011. Many of the valleys are well wooded and of great beauty. The coast line affords very little of interest from a botanical point of view, being for the most part shingly, backed by low cliffs. Westward of Minehead the cliffs rise to a much greater height, but very few rock plants are to be found upon them. Minehead Warren is an extensive sandy flat which affords shelter to some interesting plants ; among others the rare catchfly (*Silene conica*), which was discovered in 1894 by Miss May, and the fenugreek (*Trigonella ornithopodioides*). Towards Stert Point the coast becomes very low and sandy. The geological formations are the Devonian, which constitutes the uplands of Exmoor and the Brendon and Quantock Hills ; the Trias in the valleys stretching from Porlock between the Brendon and Quantock Hills ; and the Rhætic exposed on the coast at Watchet.

The following are among the more interesting plants of the district :—

Meconopsis cambrica, Vig.
Fumaria pallidiflora, Jord.
Silene conica, L.
Erodium maritimum, l'Herit.
Trigonella purpurascens, Lam.
Vicia lathyroides, L.
— silvatica, L.
Rosa pimpinellifolia, L.
Pyrus latifolia, Syme
     var. decipiens, N. E. Brown
Sedum rupestre, Huds.
— Forsterianum, Sm.
Hieracium Schmidtii, Tausch.
Pyrola minor, Sw.

Atropa Belladonna, L.
Limosella aquatica, L.
Sibthorpia europæa, L.
Verbascum Lychnitis, L.
Melittis Melissophyllum, L.
Empetrum nigrum, L.
Listera cordata, R. Br.
Epipactis palustris, Crantz.
Ophrys muscifera, Huds.
Scirpus numidianus, Vahl.
Carex divisa, Huds.
Agrostis setacea, Curt.
Gastridium australe, Beauv.

[1] These districts are the same as those used in the writer's *Flora of Somerset*.

BOTANY

III.—TAUNTON

This district comprises the country drained by the river Tone and by the small streams which, having their sources among the Blackdown Hills, empty themselves into the Parrett below Langport. The chief hills are the south-eastern Quantocks to the north-west, which attain a height of 1,262 feet at Will's Neck, and the Blackdowns on the south (Wellington Monument, 900 feet ; Staple Hill, 1,035 feet).

The Quantocks are of Devonian age, and limestone beds are worked at Asholt and Stowey. The Tone valley from west of Wiveliscombe to Taunton and the country from Stowey to Bridgwater and Langport consist of rocks of Triassic age. Rhætic beds are found along the south-eastern border of the district, and the Blackdown Hills belong to the Upper Greensand.

The greatest breadth of the district from east to west is twenty-four miles, and from north-east to south-west twenty miles.

The flora of the district is a fairly rich one. Among the more interesting plants we may mention :—

Aconitum Napellus, L.	Chrysosplenium alternifolium, L.
Silene anglica, L.	Sium latifolium, L.
Stellaria palustris, Retz	Sibthorpia europæa, L.
Alsine verna, Bartl.	Pinguicula lusitanica, L.
Radiola linoides, Roth.	Listera cordata, R. Br.
Genista anglica, L.	Polygonatum multiflorum, All.
Vicia bithynica, L.	Convallaria majalis, L.
Pyrus torminalis, Ehrh.	Potamogeton alpinus, Balb.

IV.—ILMINSTER AND YEOVIL

This district is drained by the upper waters of the Parrett and its tributary the river Isle. The northern boundary is formed by the river Yeo, another tributary of the Parrett, from Trent, where it enters the county from Dorset, to Langport. From east to west the extreme length is twenty-one miles, while the breadth averages about ten. Except along the southern border this is a low-lying district. Chard, on the watershed of the English and Bristol Channels, is about 300 feet above sea level. The geological formations of the district differ altogether from those of the three preceding districts, being practically confined to the liassic and oolitic series. Roughly speaking a line drawn from Staple Fitzpaine to Trent would have the lias to the north and the oolite to the south.

The flora is but poor as compared with that of the Minehead and Taunton districts, hardly 620 species having been as yet detected. This is probably owing in a great degree to the barren nature of much of the soil towards the south, especially to the west of Yeovil where the ' Midford Sands ' are largely developed. Three or four species however find their only Somerset stations in this district. These are the mousetail (*Myosurus minimus*), which has been twice found in the neighbourhood of Yeovil ; *Teesdalia nudicaulis* (I know no English name for it), which was detected by the Rev. J. Sowerby near East Chinnock ; a rare and very beautiful rose (*Rosa leucochroa*), which I found in a lane near Chard ; and the star thistle (*Centaurea Calcitrapa*) below Ham Hill.

Other interesting plants of the district are :—

Cerastium quaternellum, Fenzl.	Campanula patula, L.
Sagina ciliata, Fr.	Lamium hybridum, Vill.
Saxifraga granulata, L.	Ophrys muscifera, Huds.
Campanula Rapunculus, L.	

V.—SOMERTON

This district comprises all that part of the basin of the Parrett which lies to the north of the Parrett and the Yeo. In length it extends twenty-seven miles with an average width of about six miles. On the north the Polden Hills form for many miles a natural barrier separating this district from the valley of the Brue. Their southern slopes consist of beds of Rhætic age which also extend in a southerly direction by High Ham to Langport. Further to the east a broad band of ' blue lias ' crosses the district, while still further east we meet with the Midford Sands and fuller's earth. The western end of the district is formed by Sedgemoor, a level tract of post-Pliocene age, once (it is said) a storehouse of rare plants, but now completely drained. Eastwards the country becomes more hilly, but the hills do not reach any very considerable elevation.

The flora is by no means a rich one, only about 540 species having been recorded from the district. Of these by far the most interesting is a very rare mallow (*Althæa hirsuta*) which was detected by Mr. J. G. Baker in 1875 in Butleigh Woods, and considered by him to be certainly native. With this opinion I quite coincide. In some years the plant is extremely abundant.

Some other more or less interesting plants of the district are :—

Papaver hybridum, L.	Sambucus Ebulus, L.
Nasturtium amphibium, R. Br.	Onopordon Acanthium, L.
Astragalus glycyphyllos, L.	Utricularia vulgaris, L.
Vicia gracilis, Loisel.	— minor, L.
Poterium officinale, Hook. fil.	Chenopodium ficifolium, Sm.
Bupleurum rotundifolium, L.	Potamogeton coloratus, Hornem.
Caucalis daucoides, L.	— alpinus, Balb.

VI.—AXE

This consists partly of a narrow strip along the south-western border of the county which drains into the river Axe, and partly of a bit of country four or five miles long but only a few hundred yards wide, stretching along the ridge of the Blackdown Hills and draining into the Culm, a tributary of the Exe. A very small tract of land about Otterford drains into the river Otter. Staple Hill, where districts III., IV. and VI. meet is 1,035 feet high; at Chard the watershed between districts IV. and VI. falls to about 300 feet. The Blackdown Hills are of Upper Greensand age, and chalk occurs at Combe St. Nicholas, Chard, and Cricket S. Thomas.

Owing to its small area the flora is somewhat limited, but 417 species have already been detected. Chard Common is a particularly interesting piece of ground and is well worth visiting by the botanist. All the three British species of sundew (*Drosera*) grow there, besides several other plants of more or less rarity.

A few interesting plants of the district are :—

Draba muralis, L.	Drosera anglica, Huds.
Hypericum dubium, Leers.	Galium uliginosum, L.
Radiola linoides, Roth.	Lathræa Squamaria, L.
Genista anglica, L.	Myrica Gale, L.
Rosa glauca, Vill.	

VII.—WINCANTON

Like the last this is a very small district. It occupies the south-eastern corner of the county and is drained by the river Cale and the Bow brook (tributaries of the Stour) into the English Channel. The southern part consists of a level tract bounded on the west by a range of low hills belonging to the 'Cornbrash' (oolitic) series. In the valley of the Cale we meet the 'Oxford Clay' and a little to the north the 'Coral Rag.' In the north of the district the country becomes more picturesque and hilly, and the 'Upper Greensand' is again met with. The small detached portion to the north round Kilmington consists of chalk. Long Knoll rises to a height of 948 feet.

Though the area is so small the flora is of considerable interest, and close upon 600 species have been already detected within the limits. The chalk milkwort (*Polygala calcarea*) grows on Long Knoll, which is its only station in the county. A rare rose (*Rosa pseudorusticana*), which is however thought by Mr. Moyle Rogers to be a hybrid, occurs near Templecombe and rather plentifully in hedges below Henstridge; and the tiny bastard pimpernel (*Centunculus minimus*) may be found about Castle Orchard.

Other interesting plants of the district are :—

Corydalis claviculata, DC.	Polygonum minus, Huds.
Silene anglica, L.	Carex axillaris, Good.
— noctiflora, L.	— depauperata, Good.
Galium erectum, Huds.	— strigosa, Huds.
Gentiana campestris, L.	

VIII.—GLASTONBURY

This district consists of the valley of the Brue and extends across the middle of the county from Wiltshire to the Bristol Channel. For the most part it is of very moderate elevation, the western part from Glastonbury to the sea being almost a dead level. The

BOTANY

'peat moor' reaches from Glastonbury to Burtle. On the north the boundary is formed by the watershed of Mendip, reaching a height of 979 feet at Maesbury.

'Old Red' sandstone is found in the extreme north of the district, and the Rhætic beds are exposed at Croscombe, Wells and Wedmore. A belt of 'lias' crosses the district in a southerly direction from Shepton Mallet, and further east oolitic rocks appear. The flat lands below Glastonbury are of post-Pliocene age.

From east to west the length of the district is twenty-eight miles. In breadth it varies from six to twelve miles.

This is one of the most interesting parts of the county to the botanist, and undoubtedly the richest portion consists of the 'peat moor.' Unfortunately some of the rarest species have already disappeared and the list of 'extinctions' continues steadily to increase, owing to the destruction of the old surface and the removal of the peat for a depth of several feet. Still however much remains. The grass of Parnassus (*Parnassia palustris*) was found by Sole in 1782 in old pits of Burtle Moor. It has not been seen since. The cranberry (*Vaccinium Oxycoccos*) is another instance : it was last gathered many years ago (I believe by the Rev. J. G. Hickley), and I fear that yet another heathwort (*Andromeda polifolia*) is hardly likely to be seen again. I have not been able to find it since 1883.

The following list includes some of the more interesting plants of the district :—

Ranunculus Baudotii, Godr.
— Lingua, L.
Draba muralis, L.
Crambe maritima, L.
Dianthus deltoides, L.
Stellaria palustris, Retz
Althæa officinalis, L.
Genista anglica, L.
Lathyrus Aphaca, L.
— nissolia, L.
— palustris, L.
Lythrum hyssopifolia, L.
Bupleurum tenuissimum, L.
Cicuta virosa, L.
Peucedanum palustre, Mœnch.
Onopordon Acanthium, L.
Wahlenbergia hederacea, Reich.
Campanula patula, L.
Vaccinium Oxycoccos, L.

Andromeda polifolia, L.
Statice Limonium, L.
Hottonia palustris, L.
Lithospermum purpureo-cæruleum, L.
Rhinanthus major, Ehrh.
Pinguicula vulgaris, L.
— lusitanica, L.
Utricularia vulgaris, L.
— minor, L.
Chenopodium ficifolium, Sm.
Polygonum maritimum, L.
— mite, Schrank.
Rumex maritimus, L.
Myrica Gale, L.
Herminium monorchis, Br.
Rhynchospora fusca, R. et S.
Carex divisa, Huds.
— filiformis, L.

IX.—Mendip

This comprises the north-western portion of the county, and is drained by streams debouching into the Bristol Channel between the mouths of the Brue and the Avon. The chief rivers are the Axe and the Yeo (not to be confused with other streams similarly named which have been mentioned in connection with districts IV., V. and VI.). In outline the district is triangular, with the apex to the north. The length from north to south is about twenty-one miles, and from the extremity of Brean Down on the west to the point where districts VIII., IX. and X. meet is about nineteen.

'Old Red' sandstone occurs in many places on Mendip, as on the top of Blackdown, also in the north-west at Portishead Down. But the rock which gives so interesting a character to many places in the district is the mountain limestone. The south-west and west portions of Mendip belong to this formation, which extends also from Portishead to Clevedon and thence to Clifton. It forms also the promontories of Swallow Cliff, Worle Head and Brean Down, and the island of Steep Holm. The coal measures form two small basins in the north of the district. Triassic conglomerates are found locally along the flanks of Mendip. The marsh lands are of post-Pleistocene date.

The flora is exceedingly rich, nearly 850 species of phanerogams having been detected within the limits. This is due to the wonderful diversity of soil and situation : an extensive coast line, marshy lowlands, hills and promontories of limestone, boggy hollows on the sandstone, and heights ranging from sea level to 1,067 feet at the summit of Blackdown.

The Cheddar pink (*Dianthus cæsius*) finds here its only British station, and it is to be hoped that it will long continue to flourish in spite of the danger to which it is exposed at the hands of those who make a trade of selling the roots. Goldielocks (*Aster Linosyris*) used to grow on rocks near Weston-super-Mare, but has not been seen for many years. Two or three rare hawkweeds (*Hieracium lima, Schmidtii* and *stenolepis*) occur at Cheddar. Two rare umbellifers, honewort (*Trinia vulgaris*), which occurs in several places on the limestone, and an eryngo (*Eryngium campestre*), perhaps originally introduced at Worle Hill, merit notice. The snake's head (*Fritillaria Meleagris*) may be found in a meadow near Compton Martin. A small kind of galingale (*Cyperus fuscus*), till lately considered to be a very doubtful native of this country, was discovered in September, 1900, in considerable quantity below Weston-in-Gordano by Mr. Coley.

The following is a list of the more interesting species :—

Thalictrum collinum, Wallr.	Statice auriculæfolia, Vahl.
Helleborus fœtidus, L.	Lithospermum purpureo-cæruleum, L.
Meconopsis cambrica, Vig.	Atropa Belladonna, L.
Lepidium latifolium, L.	Orobanche elatior, Sutton
Thlaspi alpestre, L.	— Hederæ, Duby
Helianthemum polifolium, Pers.	Chenopodium urbicum, L,
Dianthus Armeria, L.	Rumex maritimus, L.
— cæsius, Sm.	Polygonum Raii, Bab.
Arenaria verna, L.	Daphne Mezereum, L.
Geranium sanguineum, L.	Cephalanthera pallens, Rich.
Erodium maritimum, l'Herit.	Orchis ustulata, L.
Vicia Orobus, DC.	Ophrys muscifera, Huds.
Spiræa Filipendula, L.	Polygonatum officinale, All.
Saxifraga hypnoides, L.	Fritillaria Meleagris, L.
Sedum rupestre, L.	Cyperus longus, L.
Eryngium campestre, L.	— fuscus, L.
Trinia vulgaris, Hoffm.	Schænus nigricans, L.
Galium silvestre, Poll.	Carex humilis, Leysser
Aster Linosyris, Bernh.	— montana, L.
Inula crithmoides, L.	— depauperata, Good.
Hieracium lima, F. J. Hanb.	— extensa, Good.
— Schmidtii, Tausch.	Festuca loliacea, Huds.
— stenolepis, Lindeb.	— uniglumis, Sol.

X.—BATH AND BRISTOL

This, which is the largest of the ten districts, occupies the north-eastern corner of the county and comprises all that part of the valley of the Avon which lies within the county of Somerset. The principal tributary streams are the Frome, the Midford brook and the Chew. The surface is hilly, but none of the hills reach any very great height. The extreme length is thirty miles, the greatest breadth about nineteen. 'Old Red' sandstone occurs at Maesbury and on Downhead Common; 'mountain limestone' and 'millstone grit' near Clifton; while the 'coal measures' occupy a considerable area in the centre of the district. Further east 'Rhætic' beds are exposed in several places, while ' lias' is found round Dundry Hill and between Bath and the Mendips. The remainder of the area is occupied by rocks belonging to the oolitic series.

The flora is a rich one, more than 800 phanerogams having been detected within the limits. Two sedges (*Carex dioica* and *C. Davalliana*) which were formerly found near Bath have since become extinct. A very rare rockcress (*Arabis stricta*) grows on the limestone on both sides of the Avon near Clifton, this being its only British station. Two willow herbs (*Epilobium lanceolatum* and *E. Lamyi*) find their only Somerset habitat in a few spots between Bath and Bristol. The bastard toadflax (*Thesium linophyllum*) occurs on Claverton Down; and the rare spurge (*Euphorbia pilosa*) is also found near Bath (its only British station). Here it has been known for more than three hundred years, but it is possible that it may have been originally introduced by human agency.

The species most worthy of notice are :—

Arabis stricta, Huds.	Cerastium pumilum, Curtis
Cardamina impatiens, L.	Arenaria tenuifolia, L.
Draba muralis, L.	Geranium sanguineum, L.
Cochlearia anglica, L.	— rotundifolium, L.
Hutchinsia petræa, R. Br.	Astragalus glycyphyllos, L.
Dianthus deltoides, L.	Potentilla verna, L.
Silene noctiflora, L.	Saxifraga granulata, L.

BOTANY

Sedum album, L.
Epilobium lanceolatum, Seb. et Maur.
— Lamyi, F. Schultz.
Wahlenbergia hederacea, Reichb.
Campanula patula, L.
Pyrola minor, L.
Cuscuta europæa, L.
Atropa Belladonna, L.
Pinguicula vulgaris, L.
Polygonum dumetorum, L.
Thesium linophyllum, L.
Euphorbia pilosa, L.
Juniperus communis, L.
Cephalanthera pallens, Rich.
Orchis ustulata, L.
Ophrys muscifera, Huds.
Herminium Monorchis, R. Br.

Polygonatum officinale, All.
Convallaria majalis, L.
Allium oleraceum, L.
Ornithogalum pyrenaicum, L.
Fritillaria Meleagris, L.
Gagea fascicularis, Salisb.
Juncus compressus, Jacq.
Acorus Calamus, L.
Potamogeton decipiens, Nolte.
— Friesii, Rupr.
Eleocharis acicularis, R. Br.
Scirpus Caricis, Retz
Carex axillaris, Good.
— digitata, L.
Gastridium australe, Beauv.
Bromus madritensis, L.

THE BRAMBLES (*Rubi*)

Somerset may fairly claim to possess one of the richest bramble floras in Britain, though I know of no forms which are entirely confined to the county. No less than sixty-five 'species' have been already detected within our limits, and some twenty-four subordinate forms may be added, so that very nearly ninety varieties of this protean genus find a home in the county. Most of the botanical districts are fairly rich with the exception of those which I have named (IV.) Ilminster and Yeovil and (V.) Somerton. Speaking generally it may be said that very little of interest will be found when 'blue lias' comes to the surface. Perhaps some of the best bramble ground may be found along the ridge of Blackdown and near Chard (district VI.) and near Pen Selwood (district VII.); but the combes near Dulverton (district I.) and about Minehead and Dunster (district II.) will amply repay a careful search.

Among our most noteworthy forms must be first mentioned the stone bramble (*R. saxatilis*, L.), which though abundant further north is hardly known south of the Severn, except in the extreme south-west —Cornwall, Devon and Somerset—and with us only in two places, both in the north of the county. Other species interesting from their general rarity or for some other reason are *R. suberectus*, Anders.; *R. opacus*, Focke; *R. Rogersii*, Linton; *R. cariensis*, Rip. et Genev.; *R. imbricatus*, Hort.; *R. dumnoniensis*, Bab.; *R. gratus*, Focke; *R. mollissimus*, Rogers; *R. micans*, Gr. et Godr.; *R. Questierii*, Lefv. et Muell.; *R. Borreri*, Bell Salt.; *R. criniger*, Linton; *R. Drejeri*, G. Jenson; *R. rudis*, Wh. et N.; *R. scaber*, Wh. et N.; *R. pallidus*, Wh. et N.; *R. Lintoni*, Focke; *R. longithyrsiger*, Bab.; *R. rosaceus*, Wh. et N., remarkable for its extraordinary abundance almost to the exclusion of other forms over several miles of country near Chard; *R. acutifrons*, Ley; not quite typical, but too near to be separated; *R. hirtus*, W. et K., var. *rotundifolius*, Bab.

CRYPTOGAMEÆ VASCULARES
LYCOPODIACEÆ

Four species of clubmoss occur in Somerset. Of these the stag's-horn moss (locally known as lady's knives and forks) (*Lycopodium clavatum*) is the least rare, having been found in five districts. The remaining three species are all exceedingly rare, though possibly the marsh clubmoss (*L. inundatum*) may have been overlooked in some places. The following is a list of the species :—

Lycopodium clavatum, L.	Lycopodium inundatum, L.
— alpinum, L.	— selago, L.

EQUISETACEÆ

Seven species of horsetail are found in Somerset. Four of these are very common. Another, the wood horsetail (*Equisetum silvaticum*), is rare and local, having been as yet detected in only four districts ; the remaining two, known as the Dutch rush (*E. hyemale*) and the variegated rough horsetail (*E. variegatum*), are known only from Weston-super-Mare, where they were discovered in the year 1900 by Mr. H. Corder. I append a list of the species :—

Equisetum arvense, L.	Equisetum limosum, Sm.
— maximum, Lam.	— hyemale, L.
— silvaticum, L.	— variegatum, Schleich.
— palustre, L.	

MARSILEACEÆ

Only one species of this order is known in Britain, and that is extremely rare, unless much overlooked, in Somerset, where it has only been noticed by Sole on Blackdown and by Dr. H. F. Parsons at Monckton Combe in district X.

Pilularia globulifera, L.

FILICES

As might be expected from its great diversity of surface and from the mildness and comparative dampness of the climate, Somerset gives a home to a considerable proportion of the British ferns, twenty-six out of thirty-eight species being found within our limits, and to this number may be added three 'sub-species.' The richest districts are (II.) Minehead and (IX.) Mendip ; but several others, especially (VIII.) Glastonbury and (X.) Bath and Bristol, are not far behind. The poorest district is (V.) Somerton, where only ten species have been as yet detected.

The species which, from their greater rarity or from some other cause, are the most interesting to the county botanist are the parsley fern (*Cryptogramme crispa*), a mountain species, which has been found in one place in the extreme west of the county ; two spleenworts (*Asplenium lanceolatum* and *A. septentrionale*) ; a filmy fern (*Hymenophyllum tunbridgense*)—all extremely rare and known only in the Minehead district ; the bladder fern (*Cystopteris fragilis*), common on limestone on Mendip, but very rare in the west, where I have only found it on a wall at Dulverton ; the marsh fern (*Nephrodium Thelypteris*), nearly or quite confined to the peatmoor below Glastonbury ; the hay-scented fern (*N. æmulum*), a western species ; the oak fern (*Polypodium Dryopteris*), one of our rarest species, occurring only on rocky ground by the river

BOTANY

Barle ; the beech fern (*P. Phegopteris*), also confined to one station on a hillside above Wells ; the limestone polypody (*P. calcareum*), chiefly on limestone rocks in the Mendip district ; the royal fern (*Osmunda regalis*), not uncommon on the peatmoor ; while the adder's tongue (*Ophioglossum vulgatum*) and the moonwort (*Botrychium Lunaria*), though by no means common, are fairly distributed through the county.   The following is a list of the species :—

Hymenophyllum tunbridgense, Sm.
Pteris aquilina, L.
Cryptogramme crispa, Br.
Lomaria Spicant, Desv.
Asplenium lanceolatum, Huds.
— Adiantum-nigrum, L.
— marinum, L.
— Trichomanes, L.
— Ruta-muraria, L.
— septentrionale, Hull.
— Filix-fœmina, Bernh.
— Ceterach, L.
Scolopendrium vulgare, Sm.
Cystopteris fragilis, Bernh.
Aspidium aculeatum, Sw.

Aspidium angulare, Willd.
Nephrodium Thelypteris, Desv.
— Oreopteris, Desv.
— Filix-mas, Rich.
— spinulosum, Desv.
— dilatatum, Desv.
— æmulum, Baker.
Polypodium vulgare, L.
— Dryopteris, L.
— calcareum, Sm.
— Phegopteris, L.
Osmunda regalis, L.
Ophioglossum vulgatum, L.
Botrychium Lunaria, Sw.

THE MOSSES (*Musci*)

The moss flora of Somerset is undoubtedly a rich one, and it is to be regretted that so little systematic work has been done amongst the mosses of the county.   Such local records as the writer has been able to discover are meagre in the extreme.   Parts of the county, including such interesting and promising districts as the Quantocks, the borders of Exmoor and the peat marshes near Glastonbury, would seem not to have been worked for mosses at all.   Under these circumstances it would be futile at present to attempt anything like a *list* of the mosses of Somerset.   It is proposed therefore merely to enumerate, with a few notes, the rarer and more interesting species which are known to occur in the county.   The writer's qualification for even this slight work is a poor one, as he has resided in the county during one year only at Wells.   The wealth of Somerset mosses may be judged by the fact that during his short residence at Wells he found, within an easy walk of the city, no less than 160 kinds of mosses ; and it will be noticed that the species enumerated below were mostly found there. Other records, with one or two exceptions, are taken from Dr. Braithwaite's work on the British mosses now nearing completion.   The nomenclature of the species here given is that adopted by Mr. Dixon in his *Handbook of British Mosses*, which is now in general use amongst students.

Seligeria pusilla, B. & S.   *Hampton Rocks, Bath.*   Hunt, 1867

Dicranella Schreberi, Schp.   Near *Wells,* 1886

Campylopus subulatus, Schp.   Near the Tumuli, *Chipstable, Wiveliscombe,* 1888

Dicranum Bonjeani, De Not. ; β. juniperifolium, Braithw.   *Dippy Down, Wookey,* 1887.   In grass

Fissidens tamarindifolius, Wils. Bare soil in hollows of grassy slope by path leading to *Datchetts* from *Bristol Road*, *Wells*, 1887. Several other species of the genus are found about *Wells* and in the county generally, but this is the only one that is at all rare, so far as the writer knows

Grimmia orbicularis, Bruch. Walls in several places about *Wells*, 1887. Very fine specimens were found, particularly on a wall near the asylum

Phascum curvicolle, Ehrh. Bare earth, *Wells*, 1887. Associated with Pottia recta, P. bryoides, P. cuspidatum

Pottia Heimii, Fürur.⎫
— crinita, Wils.⎬ *Failand*. Sir E. Fry
— Wilsoni, B. & S. *Minehead*. Miss Gifford, 1867

Tortula cuneifolia, Roth. *Minehead*. E. M. Holmes
— marginata, Spr. *Pope's Walk, Bath*. Mrs. Hopkins, 1861

Barbula rigidula, Mitt. *Rookham, Wells*, 1887
— cylindrica var. vinealis, Brid. Walls at *Wells*, fruit, 1887
— sinuosa, Braithw. Stones in damp places, *Wells*, 1887
— Hornschuchiana, Schultz. *Wells*. Not uncommon on stony ground, 1887

Weisia crispa, Mitt. *Failand*. Sir E. Fry
— microstoma, C. M. *Wells*, 1887
— crispata, B. & S. Crevices of limestone rock, 1887. Common in many parts of England, but only recently distinguished from Weisia tortilis and W. viridula, with which it had doubtless been often confounded

(Weisia) tenuis, C. M. *Bath*. E. M. Holmes

Trichostomum crispulum, Bruch.; β. elata. *Cheddar*. Boswell, 1873. The type is very common about limestone rocks and walls
— mutabile, Bruch. *Leigh Woods*, in abundant fructification, which is rare. E. M. Holmes
— nitidum, Schp. Common in the *Mendip* region on walls and rocks

Pleurochæte squarrosa, Ldb. *Wells*, 1887. Not uncommon on stony ground on *Tor Hill*

Cinclidotus Brebissoni, Husn. *Wells*. Sometimes on rocks, but more often on trees by streams

Zygdon Forsteri, Wils. *Minehead*. Miss Gifford. One of the rarest British mosses

Ulota crispa, Brid. *Chipstable*, near *Wiveliscombe*, 1888

Orthotrichum tenellum, Bruch. On an elm, *Wells*, 1887

Breutelia arcuata, Schp. This beautiful species occurs on *Dulcote Hill, Wells*, and on the *Mendips* near *Cheddar*, and probably also in other subalpine districts of the county. It is seen at its best by cascades in mountainous districts

Bryum Tozeri, Ldb. *Minehead*. E. M. Holmes

Bryum pendulum, Schp. 'Walls near *Bristol*,' Thwaites, 1844. There is nothing to indicate whether this moss was found in Somerset, but it is included here as having been possibly found in the county. It should not be confounded with the far more common B. inclinatum, Bland.
— torquescens. B. & S. *Wookey*, near *Wells*, 1887
— provinciale, Philib. A rare species found in 1887 at *Cheddar* and other places on the *Mendips* near *Wells*. Occasionally fertile on thin earth about limestone rocks. The sterile cushions of this moss are very large, and their dark colour makes it easy to know it from other species
— murale, Wils. On walls, *Worminster, Wells*, 1887
— roseum, Schreb. *Wells*, 1887

Mnium. The seven commoner species of the genus are found at *Wells* and doubtless in other humid parts of the county

Cryphæa heteromalla, Mohr. On trees by *Bristol road, Wells*, 1887. Like some other tree mosses this species has a decided preference for the elder

Neckera pumila, Hedw. On poplars at *Chipstable*, near *Wiveliscombe*, 1888. Sparingly on trees at *Wells*

Pterygophyllum lucens, Brid. *Failand*. Sir E. Fry

Habrodon Notarisii, Schp. A small but good specimen found on a tree at *Wells*, 1887. This is a rare and local moss found more often in the north of England and Scotland, where it evinces a preference for the sycamore

Antitrichia curtipendula, Brid. Sparingly at *Ebbor Gorge* near *Wells*, 1887

Porotrichum (Thamnium) alopecurum, Mitt. Plentiful about *Wells*, where it flourishes and even fruits in ordinary hedge-banks. It is usually found on shaded rocks near falling water

Anomodon longifolius, Hartm. On shaded rocks at *Ebbor Gorge* near *Wells*, associated with A. viticulosus and other mosses. One of the few stations where this species has been found in the British Islands. 1886

Cylindrothecium concinnum, Schp. Fine at *Cheddar*, 1887

BOTANY

Orthothecium intricatum, B. & S. Crevices of rocks near *Wells*, 1887 .

Brachythecium salebrosum, B. & S. *Failand*. Sir E. Fry. Rare

Eurhynchium curvisetum, Husn. Stones on margins of streams and under damp walls, *Wells*, 1886. Not common

— Teesdalei, Schp. *Wookey Hole* near *Wells*, 1886

— circinatum, B. & S. Rocks about the *Mendips*

— meridionale, De Not. On a wall at *Wells*, 1886. The only known occurrence of this moss in Britain. It is not uncommon in the Mediterranean region

— striatulum, B. & S. Common about *Wells* on shaded limestone rocks, where it fruits abundantly

Eurhynchium megapolitanum, Milde. Sandhills at *Burnham*, 1887

— rotundifolium, Milde. Between *Wells* and *Wookey Hole* on stones by the road under a hedge amongst nettles and rubbish, 1887. It has recently been found also in Gloucestershire. Very rare

Plagiothecium latebricola, B. & S. On a rotting log in a deep ditch surrounding a wood near *Wells*, 1887

Amblystegium confervoides, B. & S. On damp stones, *Ebbor Gorge, Wells*, 1887; *Leigh Woods*. E. M. Holmes. Usually regarded as a northern species

— Sommerfeltii, Myr. *Weston-super-Mare*. Sir E. Fry

Hylocomium. Five species occur at *Wells*, and are doubtless plentiful in other parts of the county

The above list is short, but it will be observed that it contains the records of some of the rarest British mosses, two of them at the time when they were found being new to Britain. It is much to be hoped in the interests of British bryology that careful attention will be paid to further research amongst the Somerset mosses.

SCALE MOSSES (*Hepaticæ*)

Comparatively few species of *Hepaticæ* have been recorded as occurring in the county. The following list, contributed by Dr. H. F. Parsons, includes chiefly common species collected in the north of the county and on the Upper Greensand in the east. The only exceptions are *Porella lævigata*, Carr. et Pears ; *Trichocolea tomentella*, Nees ; and *Reboulia hemisphærica*, Raddi, which are more characteristic of subalpine or hilly districts ; and *Gymnocolea affinis*, Dum., which is a local species found on chalk or limestone.

Frullania dilatata, Dum. *Beckington*
— tamarisci, Dum. *Wells*
Radula complanata, Dum. *Laverton*
Porella lævigata, Carr. et Pears. *Nettlebridge*
— platyphylla, Carr. et Pears. *Lullington*
Trichocolea tomentella, Nees. *Berkley Woods*
Kantia Trichomanis, Carr. et Pears. *Vallis, Frome*
Lepidozia reptans, Dum. *Gare Hill*
Diplophyllum albicans, Dum. „
Cephalozia bicuspidata, Dum. „
Lophocolea bidentata, Dum. *Beckington*

Lophocolea heterophylla, Dum. *Gare Hill*
Chiloscyphus polyanthus, Dum. *Gare Hill, Berkley*
Plagiochila asplenioides, Dum. *Beckington*
Gymnocolea affinis, Dum. *Norton St. Philip*
Fossombronia pusilla, Dum. *Gare Hill*
Pellia epiphylla, Corda. *Mendips*
Metzgeria furcata, Dum. *Vallis, Chilcompton*
Marchantia polymorpha, Nees. *Frome*
Reboulia hemisphærica, Raddi. *Wells*
Fegatella conica, Corda. *Beckington*

FRESHWATER ALGÆ

The freshwater algæ of Somerset appear to have been very little investigated by botanists, although the numerous streams and the boggy moorland between Glastonbury and the sea should furnish a large number of species. The few hitherto recorded are chiefly the result of the investigations of the late Mr. C. E. Broome and

Dr. G. H. K. Thwaites in the neighbourhood of Bath, and to those of Dr. H. Franklin Parsons in the neighbourhood of Frome in the east of the county.

CYANOPHYCEÆ
Nostoc commune, Vauch. *Beckington*
— verrucosum, Vauch. *Wells*
Phormidium inundatum, Kütz. *Bath thermal water*
— corium, Gomont. *Bath thermal water*
Oscillaria tenuis, C. Ag. *Bath thermal water*
— muscorum, Carm. *Laverton*
Symploca lucifuga, Harv. *Orchardleigh*
Tolypothrix coactilis, Kütz. *Orchardleigh*
Rivularia botryoides, Carm. Weirs in *River Frome*

CHLOROPHYCEÆ
Porphyridium cruentum, Näg. *Frome*
Tetraspora lubrica, Roth. *Berkley*
Hyalotheca dissiliens, Sm. *Stoke Hill* near *Wells*
Staurastrum margaritaceum, Ehr. *Stoke Hill* near *Wells*
Spirogyra nitida, Kütz. *Frome*
Vaucheria dichotoma, Lyngb. *Frome*

CHLOROPHYCEÆ (*continued*)
Enteromorpha intestinalis, Link. *Laverton*
Cladophora glomerata, Kütz. *River Frome*
Chroolepus aureus, Kütz. *Wells*
Cladophora insignis, Ktüz. *Bath thermal water*
Chætophora elegans, C. Ag. *Oldford* near *Frome*
— endiviæfolia, C. Ag. *Orchardleigh*

CHARACEÆ
Chara fragilis, Desv. 3, 5, 9, 10
— aspera, Willd. 9
— hispida, Linn. 9, 10
— vulgaris, Linn. 3–5, 7–10
    var. longibracteata, Kütz. 7, 10
    „ papillata, Walb. 9
Nitella flexilis, C. Ag. 10
— opaca, C. Ag. 2
Tolypella glomerata, Leonh. 8

RHODOPHYCEÆ
Batrachospermum moniliforme, Roth. *Oldford* near *Frome*
Lemanea fluviatilis, C. Ag. *River Frome*

In the above list the Characeæ follow the Chlorophyceæ, in which position they are placed by Engler in *Die Naturlichen Pflanzenfamilien*, although by some botanists they are considered to be more nearly allied to the mosses. The species given are taken from the Rev. R. P. Murray's *Flora of Somerset*, and the districts are those given in his work.

MARINE ALGÆ

The shore of Somerset, owing apparently to the immense quantity of mud brought down from the rivers Severn and Parrett, are extremely poor in marine algæ, and consequently few algologists have investigated its marine flora. Miss Isabella Gifford, who was for many years a resident at Minehead, published in 1853, in the *Proceedings* of the Somerset Archæological and Natural History Society, pp. 116–23, an account of the marine flora of Somerset, and also in the same year, under the title of the *Marine Botanist*, brought out an illustrated work on the British seaweeds, but in the latter only the rarer species found in Somerset are mentioned, with their localities. Her exploration of the Somerset shore does not appear to have extended further than Porlock on the west and Blue Anchor on the east. Dr. H. F. Parsons, who visited Clevedon, reports only two species of Fucus from that locality. A visit by the writer to Minehead, Porlock and Blue Anchor convinced him that the algal flora within tide marks is exceedingly scanty, the majority of the weeds found in this district being evidently thrown up from deep water after storms. Nevertheless the list includes a few species worthy of notice. *Ectocarpus Holmesii*, Batt., which was discovered by Miss Gifford on wooden piles near the quay at Minehead and distributed under the name of *E. crinitus*, Carm., subsequently proved, on comparison with well fruited specimens found at Torquay by the writer, to be a new species; it is described by Mr. Batters in the *Journ. Linn. Soc.* xxiv. 450. *Stenogramme interrupta*, Mont., one of the rarest of British seaweeds, which is recorded elsewhere only from Plymouth and Penzance, was found by Miss Gifford in tetrasporic fructification in 1848; but this kind of fructification appears to have been unknown to Harvey when the *Phycologica Britannica* was published. *Nitophyllum versicolor* is another species which is exceedingly rare in this country, being only recorded from Ilfracombe and Orkney in Great Britain. Until quite lately the fructification of this species was unknown. *Grateloupia filicina* as found at Minehead differs from the typical pinnate form of the plant, and has the more or less forked character of the variety *intermedia*, Holmes and Batt.

The collection of Somerset algæ, including about fifty species, made by the late Miss I. Gifford, is now in the possession of the Taunton Castle Museum, and the writer having been courteously permitted to see these specimens the following species were detected unnamed among them, viz. (1) *Ceramium transcurrens*, Kütz., belonging to the subgenus *Acanthoceras*, which was found by Miss Gifford parasitic on *Corallina* in Porlock Bay in July 1888, and does not appear to have been previously noticed in Great Britain; it differs from *C. echionotum* in having spines on one side only, and from *C. acanthonotum* in having tetraspores only on the outer side; (2) *Anabæna torulosa*, Lagerh., parasitic on (3) *Rhizoclonium riparium*, Harv.; (4) *Melobesia corticiformis*, Kütz.; (5) *M. farinosa*, Lamour; (6) *M. verrucata*, Lamour; (7) *Hapalidium roseolum*, Kütz.; 4 to 7 were parasitic on *Rhodymenia Palmetta*, Grev.; the last apparently not having been previously detected as a British plant.

The neighbouring shores of north Devon from Lynton to Saunton are particularly rich in marine algæ, and it is therefore probable that dredging off the Somerset coast might prove it to be richer than is indicated by the muddy shores within tide marks.

CYANOPHYCEÆ
  Anabaena torulosa, Lagerh.
CHLOROPHYCEÆ
  Enteromorpha compressa, Grev.
  — intestinalis, Link.
  Ulva latissima, J. Ag.
  Chætomorpha ærea, Kütz.
  Rhizoclonium riparium, Harv.
  Cladophora utriculosa, Kütz., var. lætevirens, Hauck.
  — rupestris, Kütz.
  Bryopsis plumosa, C. Ag.
PHÆOPHYCEÆ
  Punctaria latifolia, Grev.
  Ectocarpus confervoides, Le Jolis
  — Holmesii, Batt.

PHÆOPHYCEÆ (*continued*)
  Ectocarpus siliculosus, Kjellm.
  — tomentosus, Lyngb.
  Pylaiella litoralis, Kjellm.
  Arthrocladia villosa, Duby
  Cladostephus spongiosus, C. Ag.
  Halopteris filicina, Kütz.
  Laminaria digitata, Edmonst.
  Saccorhiza bulbosa, De la Pyl.
  Fucus vesiculosus, Linn. *Clevedon*
  — serratus, Linn. „
  Ascophyllum nodosum, Le Jolis.
  Pelvetia canaliculata, Decne et Thur.
  Dictyota dichotoma, Lamour.
  Taonia atomaria, J. Ag.
  Dictyopteris polypodioides, Lamour.

RHODOPHYCEÆ

Porphyra laciniata, C. Ag.
Gelidium corneum, Lamour., f. clavata, Grev.
Chondrus crispus, Stackh.
Gigartina mamillosa, J. Ag.
Stenogramme interrupta, Mont.
Gymnogongrus Norvegicus, J. Ag.
Callophyllis laciniata, Kütz.
Catenella Opuntia, Grev.
Gracilaria confervoides, Grev.
Calliblepharis ciliata, Kütz.
Rhodymenia palmetta, Grev.
Lomentaria articulata, Lyngb.
Plocamium coccineum, Lyngb.
Nitophyllum Gmelini, Harv.
— laceratum, Grev.
— Bonnemaisonii, Grev.
— versicolor, Harv.
Deleseria alata, Lamour.
Laurencia pinnatifida, Lamour.
Polysiphonia urceolata, Grev.
— fastigiata, Grev.
— nigrescens, Grev.

RHODOPHYCEÆ (continued)

Brongniartella byssoides, Bory.
Dasya coccinea, C. Ag.
Pleonosporium Borreri, Näg. Clevedon, Blue Anchor, Minehead
Rhodochorton Rothii, Näg.
Callithamnion tetricum, C. Ag.
Plumaria elegans, Schmitz.
Ceramium Deslongchampsii, Chauv. Blue Anchor, Bossington
— rubrum, C. Ag., f. corymbosum, J. Ag.
— echionotum, J. Ag.
— (Acanthoceras) transcurrens, Kütz. Porlock
— acanthonotum, Carm.
— flabelligerum, J. Ag. Blue Anchor
Grateloupia filicina, C. Ag., f. intermedia, Holmes et Batt.
Dumontia filiformis, Grev.
Polyides rotundus, Grev.
Melobesia corticiformis, Kütz.
— farinosa, Lamour.
— verrucata, Lamour.
Hapalidium roseolum, Kütz.

LICHENS (Lichenes)

The lichen flora of Somerset has only been investigated, more or less locally, by two residents in the county, viz. the late Mr. C. E. Broome of Batheaston and Dr. H. Franklin Parsons, formerly resident at Beckington. The late Mr. Joshua of Cirencester also collected many species in the Mendips.

It will be seen from the localities given in the following list that the oolite of Bath and its neighbourhood and the mountain limestone of the Mendips furnish by far the larger number of the species recorded. But there is no doubt that they by no means represent the large number that might be expected to occur on these strata. The rocks at the high elevation of Exmoor and the old red sandstone may be expected to yield many more species when they have been thoroughly explored. The genera *Calicium, Cladonia, Parmelia, Physcia, Pertusaria, Opegrapha, Graphis* and *Verrucaria* are as yet represented by very few species, although it is certain that many more should occur in the county. Hitherto a cryptogamic flora of the county does not appear to have been published, and the list of species is therefore given in detail from such records as are available, chiefly those in the British Museum, and a list of those in the herbarium of Dr. H. F. Parsons, which was kindly supplied by that gentleman.

The following species are of especial interest as having been recorded only for the county of Somerset, so far as Great Britain is concerned : *Pterygium centrifugum*, Nyl.; *Leptogium placodiellum*, Nyl.; *Lecanora granulosa*, Nyl.; *L. percænoides*, Nyl.; *Lecidea chondrodes*, Mass.; *Verrucaria linearis*, Leight.; *V. corniculata*, Leight. All these occur on calcareous

BOTANY

rocks. The rarer species in the list, but which are found also in other counties, are *Collema chalazanum*, Ach.; *Collemopsis Schæreri*, Nyl.; *Placodium cirrochroum*, Cromb.; *Lecanora epixantha*, Nyl.; *L. teichophila*, Nyl.; *L. Bischoffii*, Nyl.; *L. Prevostii*, Fr.; *L. decipiens*, Ehrh.; *L. spilota*, Fr., f. *ochracea*, Cromb.; *L. candida*, Web.; and *Verrucaria Borreri*, Leight. All these species are characteristic of the limestone districts. Of the other rare species, *Solorina saccata*, Ach., occurs on the carboniferous limestone; *Lecidea pachycarpa*, Nyl., occurs on very old trees; *L. Flotovii*, Nyl., usually on elms; and *Arthonia spadicea*, Leight., generally on hazel; *Opegrapha hapaleoides*, Nyl., is found near Clifton (on the Somerset side of the Avon), but elsewhere only at Doughruagh in Ireland.

COLLEMACEI

Pterygium centrifugum, Nyl. *Cheddar*
Collema chalazanum, Ach. „
— auriculatum, Hoffm., sub-sp. granosum, Nyl. *Cheddar, Leigh Woods*
— flaccidum, Ach. *Beckington*
— pulposum, Ach. *Lullington, Bathampton*
— tenax, Ach. *Mendips*
　　var. coronatum, Körb. *Claverton*
— crispum, Ach. *Standerwick*
　　sub-sp. ceranoides, Nyl. *Bathampton*
— cheileum, Ach. *Bathampton*
— granuliferum, Nyl. *Cheddar, Bathampton, Weston-super-Mare, Leigh Woods*
— cristatum, Hoffm. *Road*
— polycarpon, Körb. *Cleeve Hill*
— nigrescens, Ach. *Beckington*
— multipartitum, Sm. *Mendips, Yatton*
Collemodium plicatile, Nyl. *Mendips*
— turgidum, Nyl. *Chew Magna*
— Schraderi, Nyl. *Cheddar, Bathampton*
Leptogium pusillum, Nyl. *Freshford*
— subtile, Nyl. *Clevedon*
— microscopicum, Nyl. *Cheddar, Yatton, Porlock, Weston-super-Mare* (in fruit)
— placodiellum, Nyl. *Cleeve Hill*
— lacerum, Gray. *Cheddar*
　　f. fimbriatum. „
　　sub-sp. pulvinatum, Nyl. *Bathampton*
— scotinum, Fr. *Chew Magna*
　　var. sinuatum, Malbr. *Holwell*
Collemopsis Schaereri, Nyl. *Babington, Bathampton*

LICHENACEI

Calicium curtum, Turn. and Borr. *Brewham*
Cladonia pyxidata, Fr. *Bathampton, Standerwick*
　　var. pocillum, Fr. *Bathampton*
— cervicornis, Schaer. „
— furcata, Hoffm. *Brewham*
　　f. palamæa, Nyl. *Bathampton*
— pungens, Floerke, sub-sp. muricata, Cromb. *Bathampton*

LICHENACEI (*continued*)

Cladonia coccifera, Schær.
　　f. cornucopioides, Fr. *Beacon Hill, Mendips, Shapwick Moor*
Cladina rangiferina, Nyl. *Beacon Hill*
Ramalina farinacea, Ach. *Farleigh-Hungerford*
— fraxinea, Ach. *Road*
— fastigiata, Ach. *Standerwick*
— pollinaria, Ach. *Vallis*
Usnea dasypoga, Nyl. *Laverton*
Evernia prunastri, Ach. „
Parmelia perlata, Ach. *Berkley, Brewham*
— tiliacea, Ach. *Beckington*
　　sub-sp. carporhizans, Cromb. *Dunster Tower*
— saxatilis, Ach. *Lullington, Tellisford*
— caperata, Ach. *Great Elm*
— subaurifera, Nyl. *Lullington*
— physodes, Ach. *Standerwick*
Stictina fuliginosa, Nyl. *Wells*
— sylvatica, Nyl. *Asham Wood near Frome*
Lobaria pulmonaria, Hoffm. *Wells, Redlynch*
Solorina saccata, Ach. *Leigh Woods, Cheddar, Nettlebridge in Ashwick*
Peltigera canina, Hoffm. *Holwell*
— horizontalis, Hoffm. *Leigh Woods, Great Elm*
— polydactyla, Hoffm. *Chatley near Norton St. Philip*
Physcia flavicans, DC. *Wells, Redlynch*
— parietina, De Not. *Frome*
— ciliaris, DC. *Beckington, Lullington*
— pulverulenta, Nyl., sub-sp. pityrea, Nyl. *Road*
— stellaris, Nyl., sub-sp. tenella, Nyl. *Rudge*
— cæsia, Nyl. *Beckington*
— obscura, Nyl. „
Pannularia nigra, Nyl. *Bathampton, Beckington*
Squamaria crassa, Sm. *Cleeve Hill, Cheddar*
Placodium murorum, Leight. *Beckington*
— callopismum, Mudd. *Bathampton*

LICHENACEI (*continued*)

Placodium cirrochroum, Cromb. *Yatton, Weston-super-Mare*

Lecanora granulosa, Nyl. *Cheddar*
— xantholyta, Nyl. *Bathampton*
— vitellina, Ach. *Road*
— epixantha, Nyl. *Cheddar*
— cerina, Ach. *Standerwick*
— vitellinula, Ach. *Yatton, Weston-super-Mare*
— irrubata, Nyl. *Bathampton*
— candicans, Schaer. *Wells, Cleeve Hill, Bathampton, Walton-in-Gordano*
— chalybeia, Schaer. *Yatton*
— variabilis, Ach. *Bathampton*
  f. ecrustacea, Nyl. „
— sophodes, Ach. *Brewham*
— exigua, Nyl. *Beckington*
— teichophila, Nyl. *Bathampton*
— Bischoffii, Nyl., var. immersa, Cromb. *Yatton, Weston-super-Mare*
— galactina, Ach. *Cleeve Hill, Bathampton*
— subfusca, Nyl. *Beckington*
— rugosa, Nyl., var. geographica, Nyl. *Bathampton*
— albella, Ach. *Huxham Green*
— Hageni, Ach. *Wellow*
— argopholis, Ach. *Cleeve Hill*
— erysibe, Nyl., sub-sp. proteiformis, Nyl. *Bathampton*
— atra, Ach. *Beckington, Walton-in-Gordano*
— parella, Ach. *Vallis*
— calcarea, Somm. *Bathampton*
— Prevostii, Fr. „
  f. melanocarpa, Stiz. „
— percænoides, Nyl. *Yatton*
Pertusaria globulifera, Nyl. *Standerwick*
— amara, Nyl. *Great Elm*
— communis, DC. *Frome*
— pustulata, Nyl. *Hinton Abbey*
— Wulfenii, DC. *Standerwick, Batheaston*
Phlyctis agelæa, Kœrb. *Bathampton*
Urceolaria scruposa, Ach. „
— gypsacea, Ach. *Bathampton, Bathford Hill*
Lecidea decipiens, Ehrh. *Frome*
— lurida, Sw. *Bathford, Cheddar*
— chondrodes, Mass. *Yatton*
— lucida, Ach. *Porlock*
— flexuosa, Fr., f. æruginosa (Borr.). *Standerwick, Tellisford*
— vernalis, Ach. *Road, Bathford*
— parasema, Ach. *Beckington, Brewham*
— spilota, Fr., f. ochracea, Ach. *Batheaston*

LICHENACEI (*continued*)

Lecidea confluens, Web. *Batheaston*
— jurana, Schaer. *Bathampton*
— calcivora, Ehrh. *Cheddar*
— canescens, Dicks. *Road (ft.)*
— alocizoides, Leight. *Weston-super-Mare*
— candida, Web. *Cleeve Hill*
— cæruleo-nigricans, Leight. *Bathford*
  f. glebosa, *Yatton*
— Lightfootii, Leight. *Orchardleigh*
— lenticularis, Ach., f. nigricans, Arn. *Bathampton*
— subnigrata, Nyl. *Bathampton*
— fallax, Hepp. *Leigh Woods*
— alboatra, Hoffm. *Norton St. Philip, Laverton*
— aromatica, Leight. *Bathampton, Holwell*
— abietina, Ach. *Road*
— sphæroides, Nyl. *Bathampton, Holwell*
— pachycarpa, Nyl. *Great Elm*
— premnea, Ach. *Porlock*
— endoleuca, Nyl. *Bathampton*
— effusa, Leight. var. fuscella, Fr. *Bathampton*
— cupularis, Ach. *Bath*
— Flotovii, Nyl. *Leigh Woods*
— episema, Nyl. *Yatton*
Opegrapha atra, Pers. *Norton St. Philip*
— saxicola, Ach., var. Chevallieri, Leight. *Bathampton*
— varia, Pers. *Standerwick*
— hapaleoides, Nyl. *Clifton (Somerset)*
Arthonia spadicea, Leight. *Leigh Woods*
— Swartziana, Ach. *Vallis*
— cinnabarina, Nyl. *Berkley*
Graphis scripta, Ach. *Berkley, Brewham*
Endocarpon miniatum, Ach. *Cheddar, Wells*
— rufescens, Ach. *Great Elm*
  f. lachneum, Ach. *Cheddar*
Verrucaria nigrescens, Leight. *Vallis*
— plumbea, Ach. *Cheddar*
— viridula, Ach. *Batheaston*
— rupestris, Schrad. *Wells*
— Borreri, Leight. *Cheddar*
— conoidea, Fr. *Leigh Woods*
— gemmata, Ach. *Batheaston*
— epidermidis, Ach., f. fallax, Nyl. *Leigh Woods*
— chlorotica, Ach., f. trachona, Tayl. *Batheaston*
  f. codonoidea, Leight. *Weston-super-Mare*
— linearis, Leight. *Cheddar*
— nitida, Schrad. *Brockley Combe*
— olivacea, Borr. *Berkley*
— corniculata, Leight. *Weston-super-Mare*

BOTANY

FUNGI

Although a large part of Somerset is still practically unexplored as regards its fungus flora, it includes districts which have been searched as thoroughly as any in England, and may in fact be regarded as having been centres of mycological study for a considerable number of years. These districts have yielded a large number of species new to science, and a still larger number recorded for the first time as British, and amongst the workers who have contributed to this result the first place must be given to Christopher Edmund Broome, M.A., F.L.S. (1812–86), who came to reside at Wraxall near Bristol in 1844. The frequent occurrence of the name of this place as a locality for fungi shows that Mr. Broome was then working industriously at this group of plants. In a short time he moved to Clifton, and in 1848 to Batheaston, where he resided until his death in 1886. He was indefatigable in searching for specimens and enthusiastic and conscientious in their study, and enriched the British lists with a large number of species both of the larger forms and of those requiring the microscope for their determination. He was for nearly forty years associated with the Rev. Miles Joseph Berkeley, M.A., F.R.S. (1803–89), in a series of papers on Fungi,[1] and the initials 'B. & Br.' are known wherever these plants are studied throughout the world. The latter distinguished botanist, the 'prince of British mycologists,' was a frequent visitor at Batheaston, and as the plants described or recorded by Mr. Broome in the above-mentioned papers must have come under his notice, we may fairly claim him as a Somerset worker.

Mention must next be made of George Henry Kendrick Thwaites, F.R.S. (1811–82), who was intimate with Mr. Broome, and made excursions with him in search of fungi, especially of subterranean species. He was local secretary for Bristol of the Botanical Society of London, and in 1849 he was appointed superintendent of the Botanic Garden at Peradeniya, Ceylon, whence he sent 1,200 species of fungi to Messrs. Berkeley and Broome for description and publication. Dr. H. O. Stephens of Bristol and Mr. J. Aubrey Clark of Street were also workers in this branch of botany, and their names, as well as that of Dr. Thwaites, have been given to several species of fungi which they discovered in this county.

In the Bristol district, which comprises the parts of Gloucester and Somerset included in Sander's map of the Bristol coalfield, fourteen years' work has resulted in a list of 1,431 species,[2] more than half of which were found in Somerset, but many of the species recorded for Gloucester have also been noticed in the former county. For many rare species, principally from Clevedon and Yatton, the writer is indebted to Mr. Edmund Wheeler of Clifton, who has made a very large number of beautiful and accurate watercolour drawings of fungi, mostly from

---

[1] *Ann. Nat. Hist.* and *Ann. and Mag. of Nat. Hist.* 1844–83.
[2] 'The Fungi of the Bristol District,' by Cedric Bucknall, Mus. Bac., in *Proc. Bristol Nat. Soc.*, 1877–91.

Somerset specimens. These drawings have been presented to the national collection at South Kensington, where they are now exhibited.

THE BATH DISTRICT

Mr. Broome published a series of papers on the fungi of this district,[1] which includes Bath, Batheaston, Bathampton, Bathford, Farleigh, etc. ; and a supplementary list by Mr. G. Norman, F.R.S.A., has appeared of species found by Mr. R. Baker, principally at Claverton. Some of the most noteworthy are as follows : amongst the white-spored agarics the esculent fir-cone mushroom, *A. (Amanita) strobiliformis*, and the parasol mushroom, *A. (Lepiota) procerus*, 'one of the most delicate of fungusses' (Badham). A fine and rare purple-spored species, *A. (Psalliota) augustus*, allied to the common mushroom, has occurred at Claverton, and also a rare *Paxillus, P. panæolus*, first found by the writer at Blaize Castle Woods near Bristol (Glos.), and these are probably the only stations known in Britain. Other uncommon species from the same locality are *Lenzites sepiaria* ; the fine but poisonous *Boletus Satanas* ; *Trametes suaveolens*, smelling of aniseed ; and the rare vaulted earth-star, *Geaster fornicatus*. The edible morel, *Morchella esculenta*, as well as the less common *M. semilibera*, have been found at Batheaston, and numerous species of truffle and other subterranean fungi, one of which, *Melanogaster variegatus*, has been sold in the Bath market under the name of 'red truffle.' Another species, *Stephensia bombycina*, was dedicated by Tulasne to Dr. H. O. Stephens, of whom in his great work on Hypogæous Fungi he speaks in the highest terms.

At Street Mr. J. Aubrey Clark has found several agarics new to science or to Britain : *A. (Tricholoma) pessundatus*, *A. (Clitocybe) membranaceus*, several species of the genus *Hygrophorus*, and *Hydnum nigrum*.

THE BRISTOL DISTRICT

Crossing the Avon gorge, which here is the boundary between the two counties, by the Suspension Bridge, we arrive at the Leigh Woods, which have been the hunting ground for mycologists for sixty years, and which in a favourable season are prolific in gill-bearing and tube-bearing fungi (*Agaricini* and *Polyporei*), as well as in a large number of less conspicuous species which only careful search will reveal, and of hypogæous fungi, which can only be found by raking the soil. Here may be seen the handsome fly agaric, *A. (Amanita) muscarius*, with its vermilion white-warted pileus, of which the juice is used in some countries as an intoxicant, with several others of the same subgenus ; the beautiful but more sober coloured *A. strangulatus* ; *A. solitarius*, lately found here for the first time in Britain ; and the more common esculent *A. rubescens*. In one spot in 1882 quite a colony of small species of *Lepiota* appeared, including a new species, *A. Bucknalli*, with the odour of gas tar ; a new variety, *A. granulosus* var. *rufescens* ; *A. citrophyllus*, first found in Ceylon by

---

[1] *Proc. Bath Nat. Hist. and Antiq. Field Club,* 1869–86.

Dr. Thwaites ; and *A. seminudus*, the smallest member of the group. On dead twigs of gorse will be found a minute and delicate agaric, *A. electicus*, perhaps not yet known from any other station ; and on dead bracken the rare and beautiful rose-coloured *A. pterigenus* has been found by a lady mycologist, Miss Dickson. The genus *Hygrophorus* is represented by a species smelling like the goat-moth, *H. cossus* ; another like russian leather, *H. russocoriaceus* ; and the rather uncommon *H. arbustivus*.

The milk-bearing agarics (*Lactarius*) abound, the most conspicuous being *L. torminosus*, with very acrid milk and a woolly-margined pileus. Another fine species with yellow milk (*L. scrobiculatus*) was found here for the first time in Britain. Species of *Russula*, some of brilliant and others of sober colours, are abundant, some being acrid and poisonous, others mild and esculent. Some rare species with an arachnoid veil and brown spores (*Cortinarius*) are to be found, including the magnificent *C. triumphans*, *C. Riederi*, *C. largus*, and one with brilliant red rooting fibres (*mycelium*), *C. Bulliardi*. Of the less fleshy species of the *Agaricini*, the rare *Schizophyllum commune* has been found on dead branches, and *Boletus candicans* is a fine representative of the fleshy tube-bearing fungi. Of the club-bearing fungi *Clavaria Ardenia*, which occurred abundantly in 1868 (C. E. Broome) and has since been found by Miss Dickson, is the most noteworthy. The Leigh Woods may be considered classical hunting ground for the subterranean fungi (*Hypogæi* and *Tuberacei*), it being here that Mr. Broome, who was an adept at their discovery, found many of the species recorded in our lists. Perhaps the first mention of his name in connection with fungi is by the Rev. J. M. Berkeley, who writes : ' I am indebted for the greater part of the hypogæous fungi, which I have now the pleasure of recording as British, to the unwearied research of C. E. Broome, Esq.' On the occasions on which the writer has had the pleasure of accompanying Mr. Broome on fungus hunting expeditions, the rake was generally in use with successful results. On one well remembered expedition in these woods *Octaviana compacta*, *Hymenogaster vulgaris*, *H. tener*, *Hydnobolites cerebriformis* and *Elaphomyces granulatus* were found. *Hydnangeum carotæcolor*, conspicuous from its bright colour on the surface of the soil, and *Octaviana Stephensii*, dedicated to Dr. Stephens by Tulasne, also occur, the latter only here and in a plantation on the same range of hills.

Many of the dead oak branches lying on the ground are stained dark green by the mycelium of one of the *Pezizæ*, *Helotium æruginosum*, the mature cups of which may often be seen growing on them. The wood thus stained is used in the manufacture of Tunbridge ware. A few years ago some other species of the same order grew on patches of burnt ground, *Peziza melaloma*, *P. omphalodes* and *P. hinnulea*, together with some agarics which habitually occur in a similar situation, *A. atratus* and *A. carbonarius*, and also *A. maurus*, *A. hepaticus*, *A. cyathiformis* and *Polyporus perennis*, all in the greatest luxuriance and profusion.

Many species of the *Discomycetes* and the *Sphæriacei* will be mentioned in the accompanying lists. A common species of the latter order, *Hypoxylon concentricum*, is conspicuous on old ash trunks, forming rusty-black nodular masses several inches in diameter. In a field at Abbots Leigh some interesting species have been found, one of which, *A. (Amanita) ovoideus*, has only once been met with in this country ; the tall amanita, *A. excelsus* ; the poisonous stinking amanita, *A. phalloides* ; *Cortinarius laniger* ; and *Russula Du Portii*, smelling like fresh crabs. In the woods are *A. (Lepiota) clavipes* ; *A. (Inocybe) asterospora* ; *Cortinarius flexipes* ; *Russula Queletii* ; and amongst *Sphagnum*, in a small pond, *Mitrula paludosa*, a member of the *Elvellacei*, with a yellow head on a pale stem.

At Clevedon Mr. Wheeler found *Agaricus (Annularia) lævis*, almost simultaneously with its discovery at Kew by Mr. Massee, the only species of the sub-genus which has been recorded as British. It is characterized by its pink spores and ringed stem. Other interesting species from the same locality are *A. (Pluteus) roseo-albus, Hygrophorus calyptræformis* and a new species belonging to the *Pezizæ, Lachnella fragariastri*. The beautiful but fœtid latticed stinkhorn, *Clathrus cancellatus*, has occurred in a hothouse. At Brockley Coombe the writer has found *A. (Tricholoma) inodermius, Cortinarius brunneus, Russula cutefracta, Boletus pachypus, Tremella viscosa* and the esculent gigantic morel, *Morchella crassipes*. The large and brilliant orange peziza, *P. aurantia*, has occurred at Nailsea, and *Polyporus roseus* at Yatton (Mr. Wheeler).

The following is a list of the species which were first discovered in Somerset, either as new to science or to the British flora.[1] A few of the species were met with almost simultaneously in other parts of England :—

AGARICINI

Agaricus (Amanita) ovoideus, Bull. *Abbots Leigh*
— (Amanita) adnatus, Bull. *Quantocks*
— „ solitarius, Bull. *Leigh Woods*
— (Lepiota) granulosus var. rufescens, B. & Br. *Leigh Woods*
— (Lepiota) Bucknalli, B. & Br. *Leigh Woods*
— (Lepiota) citrophyllus, B. & Br. *Leigh Woods*
— (Tricholoma) pessundatus, Fr. *Street*
— „ colossus, Fr. „
— „ cælatus, Fr. *Bath*
— „ sordidus, Fr. *Great Elm*
— „ panæolus, Fr. *Street*
— (Clitocybe) membranaceus, Fl. Dan. *Street*
— (Collybia) ventricosus, Bull. *Bathford*
— „ floccipes, Fr. *Leigh Woods*
— „ eustygius, Cooke. „

AGARICINI (*continued*)

Agaricus (Collybia) coracinus, Fr. *Batheaston*
— „ inolens, Weinm. *Street*
— „ plexipes, Fr. *Leigh Woods*
— (Mycena) cohærens, A. & S. *Batheaston*
— (Mycena) sacchariferus, B. & Br. *Batheaston*
— (Mycena) electicus, Bucknall. *Leigh Woods*
— (Pluteus) spilopus, B. & Br. *Bath*
— „ salicinus, Pers. *Leigh Woods*
— (Entoloma) Bloxami, B. & Br. *Leigh Down*
— (Clitopilus) popinalis, Fr. Near *Bath*
— „ undatus, Fr. *Batheaston*
— „ vilis, Fr. *Leigh Woods*
— (Pholiota) squarrosus var. Mulleri, Fr. *Leigh Woods*

[1] This list is arranged according to Cooke's *Handbook of British Fungi*, except that in the *Discomycetes* Phillip's *British Discomycetes*, and in the *Pyrenomycetes (Sphæriacei)*, Massee's list of British Pyrenomycetes in *Grevillea*, vols. 15–19, are followed. This has been rendered necessary by the great increase in the number of species, and the changes in nomenclature since the handbook was published. The *Mycetozoa* will be treated separately.

BOTANY

AGARICINI (*continued*)

Agaricus (Inocybe) Clarkii, B. & Br. *Street*
—   „   descissus, Fr. *Somerset*
— (Psilocybe) sarcocephalus, Fr. *Leigh Woods*
— (Psilocybe) leucotephrus, B. & Br. *Batheaston*
— (Psathyrella) subatratus, Batsch. *Batheaston*
Cortinarius (Phlegmacium) fulgens, Fr. *Bathford*
— (Phlegmacium) largus, Fr. *Leigh Woods*
— (Myxacium) Riederi, Fr.   „
— (Inoloma) Bulliardi, Pers.   „
— (Dermocybe) cinnabarinus, Fr. *Street*
— (Telamonia) macropus, Fr. *Leigh Woods*
— (Telamonia) laniger, Fr. *Abbots Leigh*
—   „   pericelis, Fr. Near *Bath* (?)
—   „   flexipes, Fr. *Abbots Leigh*
— (Hygrocybe) Armeniacus, Fr. Near *Bristol*
— (Hygrocybe) decipiens, Fr. *Leigh Woods*
Paxillus lividus, Cooke.   „
Hygrophorus ceracinus, Berk. *Street*
— caprinus, Fr. *Bath*
— livido-albus, Fr. *Street*
— cinereus, Fr. *Great Elm*
— fornicatus, Fr. *Batheaston*
— Clarkii, B. & Br. *Street*
— metapodius, Fr.   „
Lactarius scrobiculatus, Scop. *Leigh Woods*
— turpis, Weinm.   „
— camphoratus, Fr.   „
Russula integra, Fr.   „
— aurata, Fr.   „
Marasmius urens, Fr. Near *Bristol* (H.O.S.)
— terginus, Fr. *Batheaston*
— archyropus, Fr. Near *Bristol* (H.O.S.)
— calopus, Pers.   „   „
— amadelphus, Fr. *Bath*
— spodoleucos, B. & Br. *Batheaston*

POLYPOREI

Boletus viscidus, L. *Bristol* (H.O.S.)
— parasiticus, Bull. *Clifton*
Polyporus brumalis, Fr. *Portbury*
— fulvus, Fr. *Batheaston*
— nitidus, Fr. *Bristol* (H.O.S.)
— bombycinus, Fr. *Portbury*
— micans, Ehb. *Leigh Woods*
— vitreus, Fr. Near *Bath* (?)
— obducens, Pers. *Failand*
— Stephensii, B. & Br. = Trametes serpens, Fr. *Leigh Woods*
Trametes Bulliardi, Fr. *Bathampton*
Merulius porinoides, Fr. *Leigh Woods*
— rufus, Pers. *Wraxall*
Porothelium Friesii, Mont. *Wraxall*
— confusum, B. & Br. *Leigh Woods*

HYDNEI

Hydnum nigrum, Fr. *Street*
— fuscoatrum, Fr. *Leigh Woods*
— Weinmanni, Fr. *Bristol*
— anomalum, B. & Br. *Langridge*
— bicolor, A. & S. *Batheaston*
— niveum, Pers. *Leigh Woods*
— stipatum, Fr.   „
Irpex fuscoviolaceus, Fr. „ *Leigh Woods*

AURICULARINI

Kneiffia setigera, Fr. *Wraxall*
Thelephora fastidiosa, Fr. *Bristol*
— cæsia, Fr. *Leigh Woods*
Cyphella ochroleuca, B. & Br. *Batheaston*
— fraxinicola, B. & Br.   „
— dochmiospora, B. & Br.   „
— faginea, Libert. *Abbots Leigh*

CLAVARIEI

Clavaria aurea, Schæff. *Leigh Woods*
— formosa, Pers. *Bathford Down*
— crocea, Pers. *Wraxall*
— argillacea, Fr. *Leigh Woods*
— fumosa, Pers. *Frome*
Calocera striata, Fr. *Batheaston*
— glossoides, Fr. *Leigh Woods*

TREMELLINI

Tremella epigæa, B. & Br. *Leigh Woods*
— versicolor, B. & Br. *Bathampton*
Dacrymyces macrosporus, B. & Br. *Batheaston*
— deliquescens, Bull. *Batheaston*
— sebaceus, B. & Br. *Bath*
— vermiformis, B. & Br. *Bathford*
— cæsius, Fr. *Leigh Woods*
Apyrenium armeniacum, B. & Br. *Batheaston*
Hymenula punctiformis, B. & Br. *Batheaston*

HYPOGÆI

Octaviana asterosperma, Vitt. *Leigh Woods*
— Stephensii, Tul. *Clifton*
Hydnangeum carotæcolor, Berk. *Leigh Woods* (H.O.S.)
Hysterangium nephriticum, Berk. *Leigh Woods*
— Thwaitesii, B. & Br. *Leigh Woods*
Rhizopogon rubescens, Tul. *Portbury*
Hymenogaster muticus, B. & Br. *Bristol*
— vulgaris, Tul. *Leigh Woods*
— olivaceus, Vitt. Near *Bath* (?)
— tener, Berk. *Leigh Woods*
— Thwaitesii, B. & Br. *Portbury*
— variegatus var. Broomeianus, B. *Bath*

TRICHOGASTRES

Lycoperdon atropurpureum, Vitt. *Leigh Down*

SPHÆRONEMEI

Phoma nothum, B. & Br. *Batheaston*
— radula, B. & Br.   „
— depressum, B. & Br.   „

SPHÆRONEMEI (*continued*)

Phoma samarorum, Desm. *Batheaston*
— sticticum, B. & Br.   „
— exiguum, Desm.   „
Sphæropsis mutica, B. & Br.   „
Diplodia paupercula, B. & Br.   „
Hendersonia arcus, B. & Br.   „
— mutabilis, B. & Br.   „
— polycystis, B. & Br.   „
— Stephensii, B. & Br. *Bristol*
— princeps, B. & Br. *Batheaston*
— Avellanæ, B. & Br. *Bathford*
Septoria primulæ, Buck. *Leigh Woods*
— medicaginis, Rob. & Desm. *Leigh Woods*
Cystotricha striola, B. & Br. *Batheaston*
Excipula chætostroma, B. & Br. *Leigh Woods*
— fusispora, B. & Br. *Batheaston*
Myxormia atroviridis, B. & Br. *Bathford*
Bloxamia truncata, B. & Br. *Batheaston*
Prosthemium stellare, Reiss. Near *Bath* (?)
Discella platyspora, B. & Br. *Batheaston*
— abnormis, B. & Br.   „

MELANCONIEI

Melanconium elevatum, Corda. *Batheaston*
Coryneum macrosporum, Berk.   „
— compactum, B. & Br. *Wraxall*
Glæosporium umbrinellum, B. & Br. *Batheaston*

TORULACEI

Torula abbreviata var. sphæriæformis, B. & Br. *Wraxall*
— hysterioides, Corda. *Batheaston*
Speira toruloides, Corda.   „
Bactridium Helvellæ, B. & Br. *Batheaston*
Septonema elongatispora, Preuss.   „
Sporidesmium polymorphum, Corda. *Wraxall*
— uniseptatum, B. & Br. *Batheaston*
— opacum, Corda. *Bath*
Dictyosporium elegans, Corda. *Brockley*
Gymnosporangium lateritium, B. & Br. *Bath*

CÆOMACEI

Synchytrium taraxaci, De Bary & Wor. *Batheaston*
— mercurialis, Fckl. *Batheaston*

STILBACEI

Stilbum melleum, B. & Br. *Congresbury*
— cunieferum, B. & Br. *Batheaston*
Graphium stilboideum, Corda.   „
Fusarium heteronema, B. & Br. „
Chætostroma stipitatum, Corda. „
Endodesmia glauca, B. & Br.   „

DEMATIEI

Arthrobotryum atrum, B. & Br. *Batheaston*
— stilboideum, Corda. *Langridge*
Dendryphium comosum, Wallr. *Batheaston*
Periconia brassicæcola, B. & Br.   „
Œdocephalum læticolor, B. & Br.   „

DEMATIEI (*continued*)

Stachybotrys atra, Corda. *Batheaston*
Haplographium delicatum, B. & Br. „
Monotospora sphærocephala, B. & Br. *Batheaston*
Helminthosporium sticticum, B. & Br. *Batheaston*
— dendroideum, B. & Br. *Batheaston*
Spondylocladium fumosum, Preuss. *Batheaston*
Acrothecium simplex, B. & Br. *Batheaston*
Trisporium elegans, Corda. *Brockley Coombe*
Cladosporium nodulosum, Corda. *Wraxall*
Gonotosporium puccinioides, Corda. *Somerset*

MUCEDINES

Rhinotrichum Thwaitesii, B. & Br. *Leigh Woods*
— repens, Preuss. *Leigh Woods*
Monosporium saccharinum, B. & Br. *Batheaston*
Coccotrichum brevius, B. & Br. *Leigh Woods*
Verticillium apicale, B. & Br. *Wraxall*
Oidium microspermum, B. & Br. *Batheaston*
Dactylium melleum, B. & Br. *Batheaston*
Cylindrium septatum, Bon.   „
Myxotrichum ochraceum, B. & Br. *Bath*
Gonytrichum fuscum, Corda. *Batheaston*

SEPEDONIEI

Psilonia discoidea var. lateritia, B. & Br. *Bath*

ANTENNARIEI

Antennaria semiovata, B. & Br. *Bath*

PERISPORIACEI

Perisporium vulgare, Corda. *Batheaston*

HELVELLACEI

Leptoglossum olivaceum, Pers. *Leigh Down*

PEZIZÆ

Peziza leucomelas, Pers. *Ashton*
— brunneoatra, Desm. *Leigh Woods*
— glumarum, Desm. *Batheaston*
— subhirsuta, Schum.   „
Hymenoscypha Candolleana, Lév. „
— nitidula, B. & Br.   „
— amenti, Batsch. *Langridge*
Belonidium minutissimum, Batsch. *Batheaston*
Helotium deparculum, Karst. *Ashton*
— phyllophilum, Desm. *Leigh Down*
Mollisia aquosa, B. & Br. *Batheaston*
— nervisequa, Desm.   „
— elaphines, B. & Br.   „
— Arctii, Phillips. *Leigh Woods*
— euphorbiæ, B. & Br. *Batheaston*
Lachnea coprinaria, Cooke.   „
— theleboloides, A. & S.   „

BOTANY

PEZIZÆ (continued)

Lachnella calyculæformis var. latebricola, Rehm. *Batheaston*
— brunneola var. fagicola, Phil. *Brockley Coombe*
— prasina, Quelet. *Cheddar*
— escharodes, B. & Br. *Bath*
— barbata var. pellita, Pers. *Brockley Coombe*
— fugiens, Phil. *Abbots Leigh*
— micacea, Pers. *Leigh Woods*
— araneocincta, Phil. *Leigh Down*
— siparia, B. & Br. *Batheaston*
— fragariastri, Phil. *Clevedon*
Tapesia rhabdosperma, B. & Br. *Leigh Down*

ASCOBOLEÆ

Ascobolus glaber, Pers. *Bathford*
— viridis, Curr. *Leigh Woods*
— immersus, Pers. *Batheaston*
Saccobolus Kerverni, Crouan. *Bathford*
— depauperatus, B. & Br. „
Rhyparobius Cookei, Boud. *Batheaston*
— dubius, Boud. *Bathford*
Ascophanus microsporus, B. & Br. *Batheaston*
— granuliformis, Crouan. *Batheaston*
— cinereus, Crouan. „
— consociatus, B. & Br. *Langridge*
Calloria lasia, B. & Br. „
— cornea, B. & Br. *Batheaston*
— inflatula, Karst. *Leigh Woods*

DERMATEÆ

Dermatea cinnamomea, DC. *Leigh Woods*

PATELLARIACEÆ

Patellaria lignyota, Fr. *Wraxall*
— olivacea, Batsch. *Batheaston*

STICTEÆ

Propolis chrysophæa, Pers. *Batheaston*
Stictis pteridina, Phil. & Buck. *Leigh Woods*
— graminum, Desm. *Batheaston*

PHACIDIACEI

Phacidium simulatum, B. & Br. *Langridge*

TUBERACEI

Tuber macrosporum, Vitt. Near *Bristol*
— excavatum, Vitt. *Batheaston*
— brumale, Mich. „
Pachyphlœus citrinus, B. & Br. *Portbury*
Stephensia bombycina, Tul. *Batheaston*
Hydnobolites cerebriformis, Tul. *Leigh Woods*
Balsamia vulgaris, Vitt. *Abbots Leigh*
— fragiformis, Tul. *Bathford*
Genea sphæria, Tul. *Leigh Woods*
Elaphomyces granulatus, Fr. *Portbury*

HYPOCREACEÆ

Cordyceps myrmecophila, Ces. *Leigh Woods*
— pistillariæformis, B. & Br. *Batheaston*

HYPOCREACEÆ (continued)

Hypocrea inclusa, B. & Br. *Leigh Woods*
— vitalba, B. & Br. „
Nectria inaurata, B. & Br. *Bath*
— citrinoaurantia, Desm. *Batheaston*
Hypomyces rosellus, A. & S. *Leigh Woods*
— Broomeianus, Tul. *Batheaston*
Dialonectria furfurella, B. & Br. *Batheaston*
— arenula, B. & Br. *Batheaston*
— graminicola, B. & Br. „
— helminthicola, B. & Br. „
Lasionectria rousselliana, Mont., var. viridis. *Batheaston*
— flavida, Fr. *Leigh Woods*
Gibberella Saubinetii, Mont. *Batheaston*

XYLARIÆ

Xylaria bulbosa, B. & Br. *Bath*

DOTHIDEACEÆ

Homostegia nigerrima, B. & Br. *Bath*
Hypospila viburni, Buck. *Abbots Leigh*

DIATRYPEÆ

Diatrype pyrrhocystis, B. & Br. *Batheaston*
Valsa tetraploa, B. & C. „
— bitorulosa, B. & Br. „
— hystrix, Sacc. *Leigh Down*
— syngenesia, Fr. *Batheaston*
— nidulans, Niessl. *Leigh Down*
— pustulata, Desm. *Leigh Woods*
Cryptovalsa Nitschii, Fckl. *Leigh Woods*
Pseudovalsa fusca, Buck. „
Fenestella hapalocystis, B. & Br. *Batheaston*
— tetratrupha, B. & Br. „

EUTYPEÆ

Eutypa ulicis, Berk. *Langridge*
— elevata, Berk. *Batheaston*
Diaporthe Tulasnei, Ntke. *Portbury*
— revellens, Ntke. *Leigh Woods*
— Quereus, Fckl. „

CUCURBITARIÆ

Cucurbitaria naucosa, Fr. *Batheaston*

SUPERFICIALES

Byssosphæria epochnii, B. & Br. *Bath*
Chætosphæria cupulifera, B. & Br. *Batheaston*
Lasiosphæria exilis, A. & S. *Wraxall*
— felina, Fckl. *Batheaston*
— membranacea, B. & Br. *Langridge*
— fulcita, Buck. *Leigh Woods*
— macrotricha, B. & Br. *Batheaston*
Venturia barbula, Cooke. *Wraxall*
— exosporioides, Desm. *Batheaston*
— Eres, B. & Br. „
Chætomium rufulum, B. & Br. „
Psilosphæria rhytioides, B. & Br. „
Rosellinia papaveracea, B. & Br. „
Melanomma pædida, B. & Br. *Langridge*
Sordaria sparganicola, Ph. & Pl. *Yatton*
var. velata, Buck. *The Avon, Somerset*
— polyspora, Ph. & Pl. *Leigh Down*

SUPERFICIALES (*continued*)
  Sordaria vesticola, B. & Br. *Batheaston*
PERTUSÆ
  Conosphæria rhodobapha, B. & Br. *Bath-easton*
  — brachythele, B. & Br. *Batheaston*
  — pertusa, Pers. *Bath*
  — melina, B. & Br. *Batheaston*
  Amphisphæria obliterans, B. & Br. *Bath-easton*
LOPHIOSTOMACEÆ
  Lophiostoma pulveracea, Sacc. *Pill*
  — caulium, Fr. *Batheaston*
CERATOSTOMEÆ
  Ceratostomella ligneola, B. & Br. *Portbury*
  — lampadophora, B. & Br. *Batheaston*
ENDOXYLEÆ
  Xylosphæria melanotes, B. & Br. „
  — hemitapha, B. & Br. *Bath*
  Physalospora farcta, B. & Br. *Bath-easton*
  Anthostoma gastrinoides, Ph. & Pl. *Leigh Woods*
  — appendiculosa, B. & Br. *Batheaston*
  Didymosphæria trivialis, B. & Br. „

ENDOXYLEÆ (*continued*)
  Didymosphæria celata, Curr. *Batheaston*
  — dochmia, B. & Br. „
  Leptosphæria vagabunda, Sacc. *Leigh Woods*
  — nectrioides, Speg. *Leigh Woods*
CAULICOLÆ
  Phomatospora endopteris, Ph. & Pl. *Leigh Down*
  Metasphæria Thwaitesii, B. & Br. *Bath-easton*
  — anarithma, B. & Br. *Batheaston*
  Rhaphidospora cariceti, B. & Br. *Batheaston*
  — eucrypta, B. & Br. „
  — helicospora, B. & Br. „
  Anthostomella tomicum, Lév. „
  Didymosphærella conoidea, Niessl. *Leigh Woods*
  — palustris, B. & Br. *Batheaston*
  Heptameria nigrans, Desm. „
  — dolioides, Auers. *Keynsham*
  — unicaudata, B. & Br. *Batheaston*
  Pleospora verecunda, Curr. „
FOLIICOLÆ
  Sphærella Tassiana, De Not. *Ham Green, Pill*
  — anarithma, B. & Br. *Batheaston*

MYCETOZOA

Although these curious organisms are fairly common, and may often be found on decaying wood, bark, dead leaves, etc., they are little known except to the mycologist, who claims them as coming within his range of study, or to the biologist, who sees in them a possible connecting link between the animal and vegetable kingdoms. The older mycologists, both British and continental, gave figures of the *Mycetozoa* then known to them in their illustrated works on fungi, among the British authors Sowerby and Greville giving coloured figures of a considerable number of species.

The Swedish botanist, E. Fries, placed them next to the puff-ball order (*Trichogastres*) under the name of *Myxogastres*, and later Wallroth substituted the name *Myxomycetes* (slime-fungi). When the mode of germination of the spores became known, it was found that the affinity with fungi was not so close as had been supposed, and De Bary gave them the name of *Mycetozoa*, thus indicating an affinity with the animal kingdom.

A brief outline of the life history of this group will enable the reader to form some idea of the difficulty which has been experienced in assigning to it its true position in the organic world.

The spores germinate in the presence of moisture and give rise to minute masses of protoplasm called *swarm-cells*. These acquiring *flagella* become motile, coalesce and form a jelly-like mass, the *plasmodium*, which creeps about on the surface or in the substance of dead wood, leaves, etc., enveloping and digesting bacteria and other food material, thus increasing in size, and in the case of some of the larger species sometimes forming a mass several inches in diameter. The plasmodium then becomes stationary, assumes various forms according to the species, dries up and produces receptacles or *sporangia* containing the spores, and generally a *capillitium* of flexible or rigid threads, which are either free or connected to the stem and sporangium-wall.

There are thus two distinct stages in the development of these organisms, in the first of which they bear a resemblance to some of the lower forms of animal life and in the second approach more nearly to the fungi. For further information the reader is referred to an excellent little work, *The Mycetozoa*, by the Right Hon. Sir Edward Fry and Miss Agnes Fry, in which the latest views on this interesting subject are clearly set forth; and for systematic description of the species to the works of Cooke, Massee and Lister.

THE BATH DISTRICT

As in the case of the fungi, C. E. Broome was one of the first workers in this county, and added many species to the British lists. Of the species which he met with in the neighbourhood of Bath may be mentioned *Badhamia utricularis*, whose greyish subglobose sporangia are borne on branched yellowish stalks, and contain dark spores and a capillitium of flat bands with granules of lime; *Physarum leucopus*, with sporangia on a white furrowed stalk, and capillitium consisting of delicate white threads connecting knots filled with lime; *Stemonitis fusca*, growing in fascicles of cylindrical sporangia whose walls are formed by a network of fibres springing from a central stem; several species of the genus *Trichia*, some of which are sessile and more or less globose like little yellow seeds, and others stalked and pear-shaped, and all containing spores and beautifully sculptured spiral threads of a brilliant golden yellow; *Margarita metallica*, with shining iridescent sporangia and an abundant capillitium of grey threads.

Amongst Mr. Broome's collection in the British Museum Mr. Lister has discovered a specimen of the rare *Dianema Harveyi*, probably collected at Batheaston, and which has only been recorded for one other locality in England and one in America. Another species of the same genus, *D. depressum*, has been found at Claverton by Mr. R. Baker, who also records *Brefeldia maxima*, one of the largest of the *Mycetozoa*, whose purplish-brown æthalia, filled with spores of the same colour, sometimes attain a breadth of 6 inches.

THE BRISTOL DISTRICT

In the Leigh Woods may be found *Badhamia hyalina*, with masses of balloon-shaped sporangia, which with the rigid capillitium are pure white when the dark spores have escaped; *Craterium pedunculatum*, like little yellow goblets with a chalky-white cover; *Spumaria alba*, forming confluent rugose masses of considerable size on leaves and living grasses; *Cribaria argillacea*, with lead-coloured plasmodium and net-like sporangia full of clay-coloured spores ; *Arcyria alba* and *A. incarnata*, belonging to a genus containing several beautiful species of different colours, with generally ovate or elongated sporangia and a conspicuous capillitium consisting of threads marked with half rings, nodules, spines, etc. ; *Lycogala miniatum*, with a pinkish plasmodium, and sporangia sometimes of the size and appearance of a small strawberry, afterwards becoming pinkisk-grey and shining, and full of spores of the same colour.

In the neighbourhood of Failand a large number of species has been collected by Miss Agnes Fry, to whom I am indebted for records of seventeen species and varieties as well as for additional localities. Amongst these may be mentioned : *Physarum viride*, belonging to a genus in which the sporangia, stems and limeknots are variously and brilliantly coloured—in the present species yellow, greenish or orange, the plasmodium being yellow ; *Fuligo septica*, 'flowers of tan,' sometimes found on tan in conservatories, with sporangia coiled and anastomosing, and forming æthalia ; *Chondrioderma spumarioides*, belonging to a genus in which the sporangium wall is double, the outer being calcareous and like an egg-shell, often separating from the inner membranous layer ; *Lamproderma irideum*, an abundant and beautiful species with a brilliantly iridescent globose sporangium on a slender stem and capillitium of delicate threads radiating from the stem to the circumference ; *Dictydium umbilicatum*, an elegant species in which the plasmodium is purple, and the sporangium wall is formed of ribs radiating from the top of the stem and connected by delicate transverse threads, the spores being pale red.

In the following list the species are arranged according to Lister's monograph :—

Ceratiomyxa mucida, Schrœt. *Leigh Woods, Failand*
Badhamia hyalina, Pers. *Leigh Woods, Claverton*
— utricularis, Bull. *Batheaston, Failand*
— panicea, Rost.   „   „
Physarum leucopus, Link. *Batheaston*
— citrinum, Schum. *Portishead*
— viride, Pers. *Tyntesfield, Failand*
— nutans, Pers. *Leigh Woods, Failand*
    var. aureum. *Batheaston*
— compressum, Alb. and Schw. *Failand*
— didermoides, Rost.   „
— bivalve, Pers. *Portbury*
— conglomeratum, Fr. *Yatton*
Fuligo septica, Gmel. *Freshford, Failand*
Craterium pedunculatum, Trent. *Batheaston, Failand, Leigh Woods*
— leucocephalum, Ditm. *Batheaston, Failand*
— mutabile, Fr. *Batheaston*
Leocarpus vernicosus, Link. *Leigh Woods, Failand*
Chondrioderma spumarioides, Rost. *Failand*
— Michelii, Rost. *Batheaston*

Chondrioderma floriforme, Rost. *Claverton*
Didymium difforme, Duby. *Batheaston, Failand, Leigh Down*
— Serpula, Fr. *Claverton*
— clavus, Alb. & Schw. *Batheaston, Failand, Yatton*
— nigripes, Fr. *Leigh Woods, Failand*
    var. xanthopus. *Batheaston, Failand*
— effusum, Link. *Batheaston, Failand*
Spumaria alba, Bull. *Leigh Woods, Failand*
Stemonitis fusca, Roth. *Leigh Woods, Failand*
— fusca var. rufescens. *Batheaston*
— splendens, Rost., var. flaccida. *Failand*
— ferruginea, Ehrenb. *Leigh Woods, Failand*
— Smithii, Macbride. *Charlton*
Comatricha obtusata, Preuss. *Batheaston, Leigh Woods, Failand*
— typhoides, Rost. *Failand*
Enerthenema elegans, Bowm. *Batheaston, Leigh Woods*
Lamproderma irideum, Mass. *Failand*
— violacea, Rost. *Batheaston, Failand*
Amaurochæte atra, Rost. *Halse House*

Brefeldia maxima, Rost. *Claverton*

Cribaria argillacea, Pers. *Abbots Leigh, Failand*

— aurantiaca, Schrad. *Failand*

— intricata, Schrad. *Leigh Woods, Clevedon*

Dictydium umbilicatum, Schrad. *Charlton*

Licea flexuosa, Pers. *Failand*

Tubulina fragiformis, Pers. *Failand, Brockley Coombe*

Dictydiæthalium plumbeum, Rost. *Batheaston, Leigh Woods*

Trichia favoginea, Pers. *Leigh Woods*

— affinis, De Bary. *Failand*

— persimilis, Karst. *Batheaston, Failand*

— scabra, Rost. *Bath, Failand*

— varia, Pers. *Batheaston, Failand*

— contorta, Rost. *Leigh Woods, Failand*

— fallax, Pers. *Batheaston, Leigh Woods, Failand*

— Botrytis, Pers. *Leigh, Failand*
     var. lateritia. *Failand*
     „ flavicoma. „

Oligonema nitens, Rost. *Abbots Leigh*

— furcatum, Bucknall. „

Hemitrichia rubiformis, Lister. *Batheaston, Failand*

— clavata, Rost. *Batheaston, Clevedon, Failand*

Arcyria ferruginea, Sauter. *Failand*

— albida, Pers. *Leigh Woods, Failand*
     var. pomiformis. *Leigh Woods, Failand*

— punicea, Pers. *Failand*

— incarnata, Pers. *Leigh Woods, Failand*

— flava, Pers. „ „

Œrstedtii, Rost. *Failand*

Lachnobolus circinans, Fr. *Halse House*

Perichæna chrysosperma, Lister. *Batheaston*

— depressa, Lib. *Clevedon, Failand*

— corticalis, Batsch. *Batheaston, Leigh Woods, Failand*

— variabilis, Lister. *Yatton, Failand*

Margarita metallica, Lister. *Batheaston, Leigh Woods*

Dianema Harveyi, Rex. *Batheaston*

— depressum, Lister. *Batheaston, Claverton*

Lycogala miniatum, Pers. *Batheaston, Leigh Woods, Failand*

ZOOLOGY
MOLLUSCS
NON-MARINE

Favoured in its situation and the quality of its soil, the county of Somerset yields a record of inland mollusca above the average, not only in the number of forms but in the abundance of individuals.

Out of the 139 species recorded for the British Islands no less than 112 have been found in the county, and possibly one or two more may yet be added, such for instance as *Vitrea lucida*.

The general facies of the assemblage is typically western, although the more peculiar forms are wanting.

Amongst records which cannot be accepted are those of *Vertigo substriata*, *V. alpestris*, *Succinea oblonga* and *Assiminea grayana*. The last named form is strictly confined to the Thames estuary, and its occurrence in a Somerset list must be due to a misidentification. *Succinea oblonga* has only been doubtfully recognized amongst *rejectamenta* of the Brue, and if correct the specimen probably came from a Pleistocene deposit. *Vertigo substriata* is a mistaken identification of Miller's record of *Turbo sexdentatus* which is *Vertigo antivertigo*, while *V. angustior* comes from a Gloucestershire locality.

The principal papers on the district are those by the Rev. Canon A. Merle Norman, D.C.L., F.R.S.,[1] and by Mr. E. W. Swanton.[2]

A. GASTROPODA

I. PULMONATA

a. STYLOMMATOPHORA

Testacella maugei, Fér. [Introduced] Long Ashton ; Castle Cary ; Taunton ; Bridgewater
— *haliotidea*, Drap. Bridgewater
— *scutulum*, Sby. Leigh Woods, Bristol
Limax maximus, Linn.
— *flavus*, Linn.
— *arborum*, Bouch.-Chant.
Agriolimax agrestis (Linn.)
— *lævis* (Müll.)
Amalia sowerbii (Fér.). Hatch Beauchamp ; Beer Crowcombe ; Clevedon
— *gagates* (Drap.)
Vitrina pellucida (Müll.)
Vitrea crystallina (Müll.)
— *alliaria* (Miller)

Vitrea glabra (Brit. Auct.). Creech Hill, near Bruton ; Hatch Beauchamp
— *cellaria* (Müll.)
— *nitidula* (Drap.)
— *pura* (Ald.)
— *radiatula* (Ald.). Elsdon Hill ; Clevedon Hill ; Leigh Woods, Bristol
— *nitida* (Müll.)
— *fulva* (Müll.)
Arion ater (Linn.)
— *elongatus*, Coll. Wainsgrove
— *hortensis*, Fér.
— *circumscriptus*, John.
— *intermedius*, Norm. Wincanton ; Glastonbury
— *subfuscus* (Drap.). Eastern part of the county
Punctum pygmæum (Drap.)
Pyramidula rupestris (Drap.)

---

[1] *Proc. Somerset Archæol. and Nat. Hist. Soc.* x. 131.　　　　[2] *Journ. of Conch.* ix. 187, 237.

Pyramidula rotundata (Müll.)
Helicella virgata (Da C.)
— *itala* (Linn.)
— *caperata* (Mont.)
— *barbara* (Linn.). Sandhills of the coast
— *cantiana* (Mont.). Bristol district
Hygromia fusca (Mont.)
— *granulata* (Ald.). Ashley Marsh, Bristol
— *hispida* (Linn.)
— *rufescens* (Penn.)
Acanthinula aculeata (Müll.)
Vallonia pulchella (Müll.)
Helicigona lapicida (Linn.)
— *arbustorum* (Linn.)
Helix aspersa, Müll.
— *nemoralis*, Linn.
— *hortensis*, Müll.
Buliminus montanus (Drap.). Mendips ; Bristol and Bath districts
— *obscurus* (Müll.)
Cochlicopa lubrica (Müll.)
Azeca tridens (Pult.). Brockley Coombe, Bristol
Cæcilianella acicula (Müll.) Bristol ; Taunton ; Yeovil, etc.
Pupa secale, Drap. Local, in the northern parts of the county
— *cylindracea* (Da C.)
— *muscorum* (Linn.)
Sphyradium edentulum (Drap.) Wincanton ; Yeovil ; *rejectamenta* of stream at Bratton St. Maur
Vertigo antivertigo (Drap.). Bath ; Bristol ; *rejectamenta* of Avon and stream at Shepton Montague
— *pygmæa* (Drap.)
— *pusilla*, Müll. ⎫ Near Bristol, in *rejecta-*
— *angustior*, Jeff. ⎭ *menta* of the Avon
Balea perversa (Linn.)
Clausilia laminata (Mont.)
— *bidentata* (Ström.)
— *biplicata* (Mont.). Leigh Woods, Bristol
— *rolphii*, Gray. Long Ashton, near Bristol
Succinea putris (Linn.)
— *elegans*, Risso.

b. Basommatophora

Carychium minimum, Müll.
Melampus denticulatus (Mont.) ⎫ Banks of the
Alexia myosotis (Drap.) ⎬ Avon near
Leuconia bidentata (Mont.) ⎭ Pill
Ancylus fluviatilis, Müll.
Velletia lacustris (Linn.)
Limnæa auricularia (Linn.)
— *pereger* (Müll.)
— *palustris* (Müll.)
— *truncatula* (Müll.)
— *stagnalis* (Linn.)
— *glabra* (Müll.). Bratton St. Maur
Planorbis corneus (Linn.)
— *albus*, Müll.
— *glaber*, Jeff. Clevedon, Bristol
— *nautileus* (Linn.)
— *carinatus*, Müll. Kenn Moor
— *marginatus*, Drap.
— *vortex* (Linn.)
— *spirorbis*, Müll.
— *contortus* (Linn.)
— *fontanus* (Lightf.)
Physa fontinalis (Linn.)
— *hypnorum* (Linn.)

II. PROSOBRANCHIATA

Paludestrina ventrosa (Mont.). Avonmouth ; Shirehampton ; The Pill, Clevedon
— *stagnalis* (Bast.). River mouths on the coast
Bithynia tentaculata (Linn.)
— *leachii* (Shepp.)
Vivipara vivipara (Linn.) Dunster ; Bath ; Avon Canal
— *contecta* (Millett). Weston-super-Mare
Valvata piscinalis (Müll.).
— *cristata*, Müll.
Pomatias elegans (Müll.)
Acicula lineata (Drap.). *Rejectamenta* of the Avon below Bristol ; of the Brue below Castle Cary ; of the stream at Bratton St. Maur ; Brockley Coombe
Neritina fluviatilis (Linn.).

B. PELECYPODA

Dreissensia polymorpha (Pall.)
Unio pictorum (Linn.) River Avon ; River Brue ; Bath Canal
— *tumidus*, Retz. River Avon ; River Brue, near Street
Anodonta cygnæa (Linn.)
Sphærium rivicola (Leach). Bath Canal ; Keynsham ; Harwood
— *corneum* (Linn.)
— *ovale* (Fér.). Kennet and Avon Canal ; River Avon

Sphærium lacustre (Müll.)
Pisidium amnicum (Müll.)
— *pusillum* (Gmel.). Avonmouth ; Bedminster
— *nitidum*, Jenyns. Pond, third railway bridge from Clevedon ; River Brue at Street
— *fontinale* (Drap.). Besides the type, the variety *henslowiana* is found in the Leigh Woods and in the Kennet and Avon Canal, Clevedon

INSECTS

With the exception of butterflies and moths, which are always favourites with collectors, the insects of Somerset have been very much neglected, and it does not appear that any local lists have ever been published. Among naturalists resident in the county collectors of the less known orders of insects are conspicuous by their absence, and while a very complete list of the Lepidoptera has been compiled by Mr. A. E. Hudd, the remainder are little more than sketches for others to enlarge upon, and are drawn up chiefly from my own collections, made for the most part in the immediate neighbourhood of my house at Batheaston and during occasional visits to the shore of the Bristol Channel. Their meagre appearance however must not be taken to indicate that the insect fauna of Somerset is less rich in species than that of most other counties; indeed it is probably more so. The majority of insects feed on plants, some confining themselves to special plants, which may be abundant, rare or altogether absent, according to the nature of the soil on which they grow.

Somerset is a large county of varied physical aspect, being both maritime and inland, while its geology includes the Devonian, Old Red Sandstone, Mountain Limestone, Coal Measures, New Red Sandstone (Trias), Lias, Oolite, Greensand and Chalk, with extensive alluvial deposits, from which it possesses a rich and varied flora, and justifies our expectation of finding an equally rich and varied insect fauna.

In the early part of last century a good deal of insect collecting was done in the western counties, Stephens in his *Illustrations of British Entomology* recording a very considerable number as having been taken at Bristol. Now although it is probable that more than half of these were found in the Leigh Woods and other places on the south side of the river Avon, still, on account of the uncertainty, I thought it best to omit them altogether from the following lists.

To each name is added a locality where the insect was found, even when it is considered as common everywhere ; and when not taken by myself, I have added the name of my authority, for my own experience quite confirms that of Canon Fowler, who, in his *British Coleoptera*, says : 'Very few beetles are really common in the sense of being generally distributed, and on the other hand very few are really rare; the majority of the so-called scarce species are locally abundant and may be found in numbers if their habits are discovered.'[1]

[1] My best thanks are due to the following gentlemen for the assistance they have kindly given me : Mr. E. Saunders, in naming some of the Hymenoptera ; Mr. H. J. Charbonnier, with notes on the Hymenoptera and Diptera ; Messrs. H. Donisthorpe, C. W. Dale, W. Macmillan, and C. Bartlett, with notes on the Coleoptera ; and Mr. A. E. Hudd for advice and general help.

A HISTORY OF SOMERSET

ORTHOPTERA

The order Orthoptera includes earwigs, cockroaches, grasshoppers and crickets, and is but poorly represented in Britain, the total number of species being about forty-two.

There are six species of earwig, only two of which are common; seven cockroaches, of which three species have been introduced from abroad; of grasshoppers twenty-four, and of crickets five species.

FORFICULIDÆ
  Labia minor, L.   *Batheaston*
  Forficula auricularia, L.   „
BLATTIDÆ
  Periplaneta orientalis, L.   *Batheaston*
ACRIDIIDÆ
  Stenobothrus viridulus, L.   *Batheaston*
  — rufipes, Zett.   „
  — bicolor, Charp.   „

ACRIDIIDÆ (*continued*)
  Stenobothrus parallelus, Zett. *Batheaston*
  Gomphocerus maculatus, Thunb. „
  Leptophyes punctatissima, Bosc. „
LOCUSTIDÆ
  Meconema varium, Fab.   *Batheaston*
  Locusta viridissima, L.   *Burnham*
  Thamnotrizon cinereus, L.   *Batheaston*
  Gryllus domesticus, L.   „

NEUROPTERA

The Neuroptera include bird-lice, stone-flies, dragonflies, May-flies, caddis-flies, scorpion-flies and lacewing-flies.

One of the Hemerobiidæ, *Psectra diptera* is a great rarity, having been found only in Somerset. Regarding it, Mr. C. W. Dale says: 'This, which was taken at Langport by my father on June 27, 1843, is the only specimen that has ever been taken in England, and there are only six others known in Europe' (*Dorset Nat. Hist. and Ant. Field Club*, (1900), xxi. 223).

Sympetrum sanguineum, Müll.   *Burnham*
Libellula depressa, L.   *Batheaston*
Cordulegaster annulatus, Latr.   „
Æschna cyanea, Müll.   „

Calopteryx virgo, L. *Oareford*
Ischnura elegans, Lind. *Batheaston*
HEMEROBIIDÆ
  Psectra diptera. *Langport* (Dale)

HYMENOPTERA

The order Hymenoptera includes ants, bees, wasps, sawflies and ichneumon-flies, and is by many considered the highest order of insects.

Of ants there are in Britain about twenty-five species, of which five have been introduced. Bees and wasps number about 350 species, and the sawflies are very numerous.

The great majority of this order however consists of parasitic hymenoptera, whose use to mankind is scarcely appreciated by the general public. Many of the most injurious insects are only kept within due bounds by their means.

Dr. Sharp says that the destructive Winter Moth (*Cheimatobia brumata*) is known to be subject to the attacks of sixty-three species of hymenopterous parasites, and that so abundant are these latter that late in the autumn it is not infrequently the case that the majority of caterpillars contain these destroyers.

INSECTS

This order is remarkable for the fact that in it parthenogenesis frequently occurs, and this is sometimes accompanied by alternation of generations.

ACULEATA

HETEROGYNA

FORMICIDÆ
Formica fusca, Latr. *Batheaston*
— rufa, L. *Minehead*
Lasius fuliginosus, Latr. *Batheaston*
— niger, L. „
— flavus, DeG. „

MYRMICIDÆ
Myrmecina latreilli, Curt. *Batheaston*
Tetramorium cæspitum, L. „
Myrmica rubra, L. „

FOSSORES

SCOLIIDÆ
Tiphia femorata, Fab. *Burnham*

POMPILIDÆ
Pompilus plumbeus, Fab. *Burnham*
— chalybeatus, Schiödte. „
Salius fuscus, L. *Freshford* (Charbonnier)

SPHEGIDÆ
Tachytes pectinipes, L. *Burnham*
Trypoxylon figulus, L. *Batheaston*
— attenuatum, Sm. *Taunton* (Charbonnier)
Ammophila hirsuta, Scop. *Burnham*
— sabulosa, L. *Minehead*
Pemphredon lugubris, F. *Freshford* (Charbonnier)
Passalœcus insignis, V. de Lind. *Batheaston*
Mimesa unicolor, V. de Lind. *Taunton* (Charbonnier)
Gorytes mystaceus, L. *Batheaston*
Nysson dimidiatus, Jur. *Minehead*
Mellinus arvensis, L. *Burnham*
— sabulosus, F. „
Oxybelus uniglumis, L. „
— mucronatus, F. „
Crabro clavipes, L. *Batheaston*
— capitosus, Shuck. *Freshford* (Charbonnier)
— palmipes, L. *Taunton* (Charbonnier)
— elongatulus, V. de Lind. *Freshford* (Charbonnier)
— cribrarius, L. *Batheaston*
— peltarius, Schreb. *Burnham*
— vagus, L. „
— cephalotes, Panz. *Batheaston*
— chrysostoma, Lep. • „
— interruptus, DeG. *Burnham*

DIPLOPTERA

VESPIDÆ
Vespa crabro, L. *Batheaston*
— vulgaris, L. „
— germanica, F. „
— sylvestris, Scop. „
— rufa, L. „
— norvegica, F. „

EUMENIDÆ
Odynerus spinipes, L. *Freshford* (Charbonnier)
— melanocephalus, Gmel. *Freshford* (Charbonnier)
— lævipes, Shuck. *Batheaston*
— callosus, Thoms. „
— parietum, L. *Burnham*
— pictus, Curt. *Freshford* (Charbonnier)
— trimarginatus, Zett. *Burnham*
— trifasciatus, Oliv. *Freshford* (Charbonnier)
— parietinus, L. *Batheaston*
— gracilis, Brullé. *Minehead*
— sinuatus, F. *Burnham*

ANTHOPHILA

COLLETIDÆ
Colletes fodiens, Kirb. *Burnham*
— marginata, Sm. *Minehead*
— daviesana, Sm. *Freshford* (Charbonnier)
Prosopis communis, Nyl. *Minehead*
— signata, Panz. *Freshford* (Charbonnier)
— brevicornis, Nyl. *Minehead*

ANDRENIDÆ
Sphecodes gibbus, L. *Freshford* (Charbonnier)
— subquadratus, Sm. *Batheaston*
— pilifrons, Thoms. *Burnham*
— puncticeps, Thoms. „
— similis, Wesm. *Batheaston*
Halictus rubicundus, Chr. *Freshford* (Charbonnier)
— leucozonius, Schr. *Batheaston*
— lævigatus, Kirb. „
— cylindricus, F. „
— albipes, Kirb. „
— longulus, Sm. „
— pauxillus, Schk. „
— tumulorum, L. „
— smeathmanellus, Kirb. „
— morio, F. *Minehead*

ANDRENIDÆ (*continued*)
Andrena cingulata, F.　*Batheaston*
— albicans, Kirb.　　　　　"
— trimmerana, Kirb.　*Freshford* (Charbonnier)
— rosæ, Panz.　*Freshford* (Charbonnier)
— cineraria, L.　*Batheaston*
— thoracica, F.　　　　"
— nitida, Fourc.　　　"
— fulva, Schr. (Francis)
— clarkella, Kirb. (Francis)
— nigro-ænea, Kirb.　*Minehead*
— gwynana, Kirb.　*Batheaston*
— varians, Rossi.　*Minehead*
— albicrus, Kirb.　*Batheaston*
— chrysosceles, Kirb.　　"
— labialis, Kirb.　　　　"
— minutula, Kirb.　　　"
— nana, Kirb.　*Freshford* (Charbonnier)
— afzeliella, Kirb.　　"　　　　"
— wilkella, Kirb.　　"　　　　"
Cilissa hæmorrhoidalis, F.　*Bath* (Saunders)
Nomada sexfasciata, Panz.　*Batheaston*
— succincta, Panz.　　　"
— lineola, Panz.　　　　"
— alternata, Kirb.　　　"
— ruficornis, L.　　　　　"
— ochrostoma, Kirb.　*Freshford* (Charbonnier)
— fabriciana, L.　*Leigh* (Charbonnier)
— flavoguttata, Kirb.　*Flax Bourton* (Charbonnier)

APIDÆ
Megachile willughbiella, Kirb.　*Freshford* (Charbonnier)
— centuncularis, L.　*Burnham*
— argentata, F.　*Burnham* (Saunders)
Osmia rufa, L.　*Batheaston*
— pilicornis, Sm.　*Leigh Woods* (Saunders)
— cœrulescens, L.　*Freshford* (Charbonnier)
— leucomelana, Kirb.　*Leigh Woods* (Saunders)
— spinulosa, Kirb.　*Cheddar* (Charbonnier)
Anthidium manicatum, L.　*Cheddar* (Charbonnier)
Melecta luctuosa, Scop.　*Freshford* (Charbonnier)

APIDÆ (*continued*)
Melecta armata, Panz.　*Batheaston*
Anthophora pilipes, F.　　　"
Psithyrus rupestris, F.　*Freshford* (Charbonnier)
— vestalis, Fourc.　*Batheaston*
— barbutellus, Kirb.　　　"
— campestris, Panz.　*Freshford* (Charbonnier)
Bombus venustus, Sm.　*Freshford* (Charbonnier)
— agrorum, F.　*Batheaston*
— hortorum, L.　*Ashton* (Charbonnier)
　　v. harrisellus, Kirb.　*Batheaston*
— pratorum, L.　　　　　"
— lapidarius, L.　　　　"
— terrestris, L.　　　　"
　　v. lucorum, Sm.　　　"
Apis mellifica, L.　　　　"
SIRICIDÆ
Sirex gigas, L.　*Batheaston* (Broome)
TENTHREDINIDÆ
Tenthredo lachlaniana, Cam.　*Batheaston*
— moniliata, Klug.　　　　"
— bicincta, L.　　　　　　"
— mesomela, L.　　　　　"
— olivacea, Klug.　　　　"
— lateralis, Fab.　　　　"
— viridis, L.　　　　　　"
Tenthredopsis cordata, Fourc.　"
— nigricollis, Cam.　　　"
— nassata, L.　　　　　"
— microcephala, Lep.　*Minehead*
Macrophya neglecta, Klug.　*Batheaston*
— punctum-album, L.　　　"
Allantus arcuatus, Forst.　　"
— scrophulariæ, L.　　　"
Dolerus fissus, Htg.　　　"
— fulviventris, Scop.　　"
— gonagra, Fab.　　　　"
— hæmatodis, Schr.　　　"
— oblongus, Cam.　　　　"
Strongylogaster angulatus, Thoms.　*Minehead*
Crœsus septentrionalis, L.　*Batheaston*
Trichiosoma lucorum, L.　　"
Hylotoma cyaneo-crocea, Forst.　"
Rhodites rosæ, L.　　　　"

COLEOPTERA

Beetles differ from other insects in having a hard external integument, and by the first pair of wings, which are of no use in flying, taking the form of tough chitinous wing covers, from which they get the name Coleoptera or sheath-wings. They exist in enormous numbers, Dr. Sharp considering them to form the predominant order of insects in the present epoch. He estimates the number of species now known at about 150,000, and about 3,500 of these have been found in Britain. They vary very greatly in their habits, and though many constantly conceal themselves, beetles, if searched for, are to be found everywhere, and some can live and thrive under the (apparently) most adverse circumstances. Nearly two years ago a stick of Spanish liquorice was brought me which contained a few small white maggots. I put this into a closed glass jar, and in a short time the maggots changed to beetles, *Anobium paniceum*, L., which have since passed through several generations, the liquorice gradually diminishing, while the number of beetles, living and dead, constantly increases, although they have had no moisture, except what they could get from the air in a very dry room, and I have little doubt that the race will survive until all the liquorice has been consumed.

Many beetles are very injurious to our crops and trees, while some are beneficial, in that they feed on and destroy noxious insects.

Among the former are wireworms, the most destructive of farm pests; they are the larval forms of various Click Beetles (*Agriotes lineatus*, L., *A. obscurus*, L., *A. sputator*, L.) and live for several years as grubs, eating the roots and underground shoots of plants, and thus destroy much more than they require as food. Among these are the Hop-flea (*Plectroscelis concinna*, Marsh.); the Turnip-fly (*Phyllotreta nemorum*, L.); the Turnip-gall Weevil (*Ceuthorrhynchus pleurostigma*, Marsh.); the Bean Beetle (*Bruchus rufimanus*, Boh.); the Pea Weevil (*Sitones lineatus*, L.); the Asparagus Beetle (*Crioceris asparagi*, L.); one of the Carrion Beetles, *Silpha opaca*, L., the grub of which attacks mangold-wurzel and beet. The following do much injury to forest trees: the Elm-bark Beetle (*Scolytus destructor*, Ol.), which makes galleries between the bark and the wood; the Pine Beetle (*Myelophilus piniperda*, L.); the Pine Weevil (*Hylobius abietis*, L.); while others are very injurious to fruit trees, the Apple-blossom Weevil (*Anthonomus pomorum*, L.); the Nut Weevil (*Balaninus nucum*, L.), responsible for maggoty nuts; the Nut-leaf Weevil (*Strophosomus coryli*, F.), which attacks the foliage of hazels and various other trees. The Leaf-Weevils, *Phyllobius oblongus*, L., and *P. maculicornis*, Germ., do occasionally much mischief in orchards. The Shot-borer (*Xyleborus dispar*, F.) injures many kinds of fruit trees by eating tunnels through the wood; the Raspberry Beetle (*Byturus tomentosus*, F.), which as a beetle attacks the blossom, and as a maggot destroys the fruit; *Otiorrhynchus tenebricosus*, Herbst, *O. picipes*, F., and *O. sulcatus*, F., do injury to fruit trees. The Rose Chafer (*Cetonia aurata*, L.) and the Garden Chafer (*Phyllopertha horticola*, L.) are both very destructive, while the Cockchafer (*Melolontha vulgaris*, F.) in its beetle state attacks the leaves of most of our common deciduous trees, doing at times considerable harm to apple, plum and cherry; while the grubs cause even greater damage by eating the grass-roots in pasture land, as well as those of mangold, potato and turnip.

It was formerly thought that the ground beetles, the *Geodephaga*, were exclusively carnivorous, but it is now known that several among them,

Harpalus ruficornis, F., *Pterostichus vulgaris*, L., *P. madidus*, F., and *Calathus cisteloides*, Panz., do injury to strawberries.

On the other hand the various species of *Coccinella*, the Ladybirds, are among our best friends, as both in the winged and in the larval state they destroy enormous quantities of aphides.

The following list is most imperfect; the only person, so far as I have been able to discover, who systematically collected beetles in Somerset was the late Mr. Gillo of Bath, but unfortunately he never published a complete list of his captures, and I do not know what became of his collection.

The entries against his name in the following list were found scattered in various periodicals, *Entomologist's Monthly Magazine*, *Entomological Record*, *Young Naturalist*, etc.

Of the two largest British beetles, one, the Stag Beetle (*Lucanus cervus*, L.) seems rare. I have never seen it in west Somerset, though its place is taken by its smaller relative, *Dorcus parallelopipedus*, L., which is abundant. Mr. Macmillan found it at Castle Cary. The Great Water Beetle (*Hydrophilus piceus*, L.) is plentiful near Glastonbury, and apparently was always so, as many of its wing cases (some now in the Glastonbury Museum) were found among the prehistoric remains of the British lake village.

A few rare beetles have been found. The late Mr. Gillo took near Bath, in 1885, *Amara nitida*, Sturm., a species then new to Britain (*E. M. M.* xxii. 240), and the late Mr. Blatch found at Porlock, in 1896, *Quedius reparius*, Kellner, the first recorded as taken in this country.

CICINDELIDÆ
  Cicindela campestris, L. *Batheaston*
  — hybrida, v. maritima, Dej. *Burnham*
CARABIDÆ
  Cychrus rostratus, L. *Batheaston*
  Carabus catenulatus, Scop. ”
  — nemoralis, Müll. *Bath* (Gillo)
  — violaceus, L. *Batheaston*
  — nitens, L. *Castle Cary* (Macmillan)
  — granulatus, L. *Batheaston*
  — monilis, F. ”
  Notiophilus biguttatus, F. ”
  — substriatus, Wat. *Cheddar*
  — aquaticus, L. *Batheaston*
  — palustris, Duft. *Bath* (Gillo)
  Leistus spinibarbis, F. *Batheaston*
  — fulvibarbis, Dej. ”
  — ferrugineus, L. ”
  Nebria complanata, L. *Burnham* (Gillo)
  — brevicollis, F. *Batheaston*
  Loricera pilicornis, F. ”
  Clivina fossor, L. ”
  — collaris, Herbst. *Bath* (Gillo)
  Dyschirius thoracicus, Rossi. *Minehead*
  — impunctipennis, Daws. *Burnham*

CARABIDÆ (*continued*)
  Dyschirius salinus, Schaum. *Weston-super-Mare* (Wollaston)
  — globosus, Herbst. *Burnham* (Gillo)
  Broscus cephalotes, L. *Castle Cary* (Macmillan)
  Badister bipustulatus, F. *Batheaston*
  — sodalis, Duft. *Bath* (Gillo)
  Chlænius vestitus, Payk. *Bath* (Gillo)
  — nigricornis, F. *Bath* (Gillo)
  Acupalpus meridianus, L. *Batheaston*
  Bradycellus distinctus, Dej. *Bath* (Gillo)
  — verbasci, Duft. *Batheaston*
  Harpalus punctatulus, Duft. *Bath* (Gillo)
  — azureus, F. *Bath* (Gillo)
  — rupicola, Sturm. *Batheaston*
  — puncticollis, Payk. ”
  — rufibarbis, F. *Bath* (Gillo)
  — ruficornis, F. *Batheaston*
  — æneus, F. ”
  — consentaneus, Dej. *Minehead*
  — rubripes, Duft. *Batheaston*
  — latus, L. ”
  — quadripunctatus, Dej. *Cheddar* (Blatch)
  — tardus, Panz. *Minehead*
  — anxius, Duft. *Burnham*

INSECTS

CARABIDÆ (*continued*)
Harpalus serripes, Schön. *Cheddar*
— ignavus, Duft. *Minehead*
Dichirotrichus pubescens, Payk. *Clevedon*
  (Gillo)
Anisodactylus binotatus, F. *Batheaston*
Stomis pumicatus, Panz. „
Platyderus ruficollis, Marsh. „
Pterostichus cupreus, L. „
— versicolor, Sturm „
— madidus, F. „
— oblongo-punctatus, F. *Porlock* (Blatch)
— niger, Schall. *Batheaston*
— vulgaris, L. „
— anthracinus, Ill. *Burnham*
— nigrita, F. *Batheaston*
— minor, Gyll. *Burnham* (Gillo)
— strenuus, Panz. *Batheaston*
— diligens, Sturm „
— picimanus, Duft. „
— inæqualis, Marsh. „
— vernalis, Gyll. „
— striola, F. „
Amara fulva, Dej. *Burnham* (Gillo)
— apricaria, Sturm. *Batheaston*
— consularis, Duft. *Bath* (Gillo)
— aulica, Panz. *Batheaston*
— rufocincta, Dej. *Bath* (Gillo)
— livida, F. *Bath* (Gillo)
— ovata, F. *Batheaston*
— similita, Gyll. *Batheaston*
— acuminata, Payk. „
— nitida, Sturm. *Bath* (Gillo)
— tibialis, Payk. *Burnham* (Gillo)
— lunicollis, Schiod. *Batheaston*
— familiaris, Duft. „
— lucida, Duft. *Burnham* (Gillo)
— trivialis, Gyll. *Batheaston*
— communis, Panz. *Minehead*
— plebeia, Gyll. *Bath* (Gillo)
Calathus cisteloides, Panz. *Batheaston*
— flavipes, Fourc. *Burnham* (Gillo)
— mollis, Marsh. „ „
— melanocephalus, L. *Batheaston*
— micropterus, Duft. *Minehead*
— piceus, Marsh. „
Taphria nivalis, Panz. „
Pristonychus terricola, Herbst. *Batheaston*
Anchomenus dorsalis, Müll. „
— albipes, F. *Minehead*
— oblongus, Sturm. *Bath* (Gillo)
— parumpunctatus, F. *Batheaston*
— viduus, Panz. *Bath* (Gillo)
  v. mæstus, Duft. *Clevedon*
— scitulus, Dej. *Bath* (Gillo)
— fuliginosus, Panz. *Batheaston*
— gracilis, Gyll. *Burnham*
Olisthopus rotundatus, Payk. *Bath*
  (Gillo)
Tachys bistriatus, Duft. *Batheaston*

CARABIDÆ (*continued*)
Bembidium rufescens, Guér. *Porlock* (Blatch)
— quinquestriatum, Gyll. *Batheaston*
— obtusum, Sturm „
— guttula, F. „
— mannerheimi, Sahl. *Clevedon*
— riparium, Ol. *Batheaston*
— doris, Panz. *Weston-super-Mare* (Wollaston)
— minimum, F. *Weston - super - Mare* (Wollaston)
— lampros, Herbst. *Batheaston*
— tibiale, Duft. *Porlock* (Blatch)
— decorum, Panz. „ „
— nitidulum, Marsh. *Bath* (Gillo)
— quadrimaculatum, Gyll. *Batheaston*
— littorale, Ol. *Batheaston*
— pallidipenne, Ill. *Burnham* (Gillo)
— varium, Ol. *Minehead*
Tachypus flavipes, L. *Batheaston*
Trechus micros, Herbst. *Bath* (Gillo)
— minutus, F. *Batheaston*
  v. obtusus, Er. *Bath* (Gillo)
Pogonus chalceus, Marsh. *Clevedon* (Gillo)
Lebia chlorocephala, Hoff. *Bath* (Gillo)
Demetrias atricapillus, L. *Batheaston*
Dromius linearis, Ol. „
— agilis, F. „
— quadrimaculatus, L. „
— quadrinotatus, Panz. „
Blechrus maurus, Sturm „
Metabletus foveola, Gyll. „
— truncatellus, L. *Burnham*
Brachinus crepitans, L. *Bath* (Gillo)

HALIPLIDÆ
Haliplus obliquus, F. *Burnham* (Gillo)
— confinis, Steph. *Weston-super-Mare*
  (Fowler, *Brit. Col.*)
— mucronatus, Steph. *Burnham* (Gillo)
— flavicollis, Sturm. *Bath* (Gillo)
— fulvus, F. „ „
— variegatus, Sturm. *Burnham* (Gillo)
— cinereus, Aubé. *Clevedon*
— ruficollis, DeG. *Glastonbury*
— fluviatilis, Aubé. *Burnham* (Gillo)
— lineatocollis, Marsh. *Clevedon*

PELOBIIDÆ
Pelobius tardus, Herbst. *Burnham*

DYTISCIDÆ
Noterus sparsus, Marsh. *Glastonbury*
Laccophilus interruptus, Panz. *Midford*
— obscurus, Panz. *Glastonbury*
Hyphydrus ovatus, L. *Midford*
Cælambus versicolor, Schall. *Midford*
— inæqualis, F. *Bath* (Gillo)
— confluens, F. *Burnham* (Gillo)
Deronectes depressus, F. *Bath* (Gillo)
Hydroporus pictus, F. „ „
— rivalis, Gyll. *Porlock* (Blatch)
— dorsalis, F. *Burnham*

79

DYTISCIDÆ (continued)

Hydroporus lineatus, F. *Glastonbury*
— palustris, L. *Bath* (Gillo)
— erythro-cephalus, L. *Burnham* (Gillo)
— pubescens, Gyll. *Bath* (Gillo)
— lituratus, F. *Batheaston*
Agabus guttatus, Payk. *Porlock* (Blatch)
— biguttatus, Ol. " "
— nebulosus, Forst. *Bath* (Gillo) " "
— chalconotus, Panz. *Glastonbury*
— bipustulatus, L. "
Ilybius fuliginosus, F. "
— fenestratus, F. "
— ater, DeG. "
— obscurus, Marsh. *Burnham*
— guttiger, Gyll. *Burnham* (Gillo)
Colymbetes fuscus, L. *Minehead*
Dytiscus punctulatus, F. *Burnham* (Gillo)
— marginalis, L. *Burnham*
— circumflexus, F. *Burnham* (Gillo)
— dimidiatus, Berg. *Glastonbury*
— Hydaticus transversalis, Berg. *Glastonbury*
— Acilius sulcatus, L. *Burnham*

GYRINIDÆ

Gyrinus urinator, Ill. *Bath* (Gillo)
— elongatus, Aubé. *Clevedon*
— natator, Scop. "
— marinus, Gyll. *Midford*

HYDROPHILIDÆ

Hydrophilus piceus, L. *Glastonbury*
Hydrobius fuscipes, L. "
— oblongus, Herbst "
Anacæna limbata, F. *Clevedon*
Philhydrus testaceus, F. *Burnham* (Gillo)
— maritimus, Thoms. *Glastonbury*
— minutus, F. *Bath* (Gillo)
Cymbiodyta ovalis, Thoms. *Burnham* (Gillo)
Enochrus bicolor, Gyll. *Midford*
Laccobius sinuatus, Mots. *Minehead*
— alutaceus, Thoms. *Burnham* (Gillo)
— minutus, L. " "
— bipunctatus, F. *Midford*
Berosus affinis, Brull. *Burnham*
Helophorus rugosus, Ol. *Bath* (Ste., *Illus.*)
— aquaticus, L. *Castle Cary* (Macmillan)
— æneipennis, Thoms. *Porlock* (Blatch)
— affinis, Marsh. *Dunster*
— brevipalpis, Bedel. *Clevedon*
Octhebius marinus, Payk. *Weston-super-Mare* (Wollaston)
— æratus, Steph. *Burnham* (Gillo)
Hydræna gracilis, Germ. *Porlock* (Blatch)
Cyclonotum orbiculare, F. *Clevedon*
Sphæridium scarabæoides, F. *Batheaston*
— bipustulatum, F. *Clevedon*
         v. marginatum, F. *Bath* (Gillo)
Cercyon hæmorrhoidalis, Herbst. *Batheaston*

HYDROPHILIDÆ (continued)

Cercyon melanocephalus, L. *Batheaston*
— pygmæus, Ill. *Porlock* (Blatch)

STAPHYLINIDÆ

Aleochara brevipennis v. fumata, Grav. *Batheaston*
— lanuginosa, Grav. *Batheaston*
Microglossa gentilis, Märk. *Weston-super-Mare* (Crotch)
Oxypoda hæmorrhoa, Mann. *Porlock* (Blatch)
— annularis, Sahl. *Nettlecomb* (Fowler, *Brit. Col.*)
Ocyusa maura, Er. *Batheaston*
Ocalea castanea, Er. *Porlock* (Blatch)
Dinarda dentata, Grav. *Weston-super-Mare* (Crotch)
Atemeles emarginatus, Payk. *Batheaston*
— paradoxus, Grav. *Weston-super-Mare* (Crotch)
Myrmedonia cognata, Märk. *Batheaston*
Astilbus canaliculatus, F. "
Callicerus obscurus, Grav. *Bath* (Gillo)
Notothecta anceps, Er. *Porlock* (Blatch)
Homalota currax, Kr. " "
— pavens, Er. " "
— cambrica, Woll. " "
— eximia, Sharp " "
— silvicola, Fuss. " "
— analis, Grav. *Batheaston*
— exilis, Er. *Porlock* (Blatch)
— xanthopus, Thoms. *Doniford* (Fowler, *Brit. Col.*)
— atramentaria, Gyll. *Batheaston*
— sordida, Marsh. *Porlock* (Blatch)
— testudinea, Er. " "
— subsinuata, Er. *Batheaston*
— fungi v. dubia, Sharp. *Porlock* (Blatch)
Leptusa fumida, Er. " "
Bolitochara lucida, Grav. *Nettlecomb* (Fowler, *Brit. Col.*)
— bella, Märk. *Somerset* (Fowler, *Brit. Col.*)
Myllæna elongata, Matth. *Porlock* (Blatch)
— gracilis, Matth. *Batheaston*
— brevicornis, Matth. *Porlock* (Blatch)
Hypocyptus longicornis, Payk. *Batheaston*
Tachyporus obtusus, L. "
— formosus, Matth. "
— solutus, Er. "
— pallidus, Sharp "
— chrysomelinus, L. "
— humerosus, Er. "
— hypnorum, F. "
— pusillus, Grav. "
— brunneus, F. "
Tachinus subterraneus, L. "
— rufipes, L. "
— laticollis, Grav. *Bath* (Gillo)
Megacronus analis, F. *Clevedon*

INSECTS

STAPHYLINIDÆ (continued)

Bolitobius lunulatus, L.   *Batheaston*
Quedius microps, Grav.   *Nettlecomb* (Fowler, *Brit. Col.*)
— fulgidus, F.   *Batheaston*
— xanthopus, Er.   „
— fuliginosus, Grav.   „
— tristis, Grav.   „
— picipes, Mann.   *Clevedon*
— molochinus, Grav.   *Batheaston*
— nigriceps, Kr.   *Bath* (Gillo)
— maurorufus, Grav.   *Batheaston*
— umbrinus, Er.   *Clevedon*
— scintillans, Grav.   *Bath* (Gillo)
— auricomus, Kies.   *Porlock* (Blatch)
— rufipes, Grav.   *Bath* (Gillo)
— riparius, Kellner.   *Porlock* (Blatch)
Creophilus maxillosus, L.   *Batheaston*
Leistotrophus nebulosus, F.   „
Staphylinus pubescens, DeG.   *Bath* (Gillo)
— stercorarius, Ol.   *Batheaston*
— cæsareus, Ceder   „
Ocypus olens, Müll.   „
— brunnipes, F.   *Minehead*
— fuscatus, Grav.   *Bath* (Gillo)
— cupreus, Rossi.   *Batheaston*
— ater, Grav.   „
— morio, Grav.   „
— compressus, Marsh.   „
Philonthus splendens, F.   „
— intermedius, Boisd.   „
— laminatus, Creutz.   *Clevedon*
— æneus, Rossi.   *Bath* (Gillo)
— atratus, Grav.   *Batheaston*
— politus, F.   „
— lucens, Er.   *Clevedon*
— varius, Gyll.   „
— marginatus, F.   *Batheaston*
— cephalotes, Grav.   „
— fimetarius, Grav.   *Bath* (Gillo)
— sordidus, Grav.   *Batheaston*
— ebeninus v. corruscus, Grav.   *Batheaston*
— sanguinolentus, Grav.   *Clevedon*
— cruentatus, Gmel.   *Batheaston*
— varians, Payk.   „
— ventralis, Grav.   *Porlock* (Blatch)
— micans, Grav.   *Batheaston*
Cafius fucicola, Curt.   *Clevedon* (Gillo)
— xantholoma, Grav.   *Burnham* (Gillo)
Xantholinus fulgidus, F.   *Batheaston*
— glabratus, Grav.   „
— punctulatus, Payk.   *Clevedon*
— ochraceus, Gyll.   *Batheaston*
— atratus, Heer.   *Porlock* (Blatch)
— tricolor, F.   *Bath* (Gillo)
— linearis, Ol.   *Batheaston*
— longiventris, Heer.   „
Baptolinus alternans, Grav.   *Clevedon*
Othius fulvipennis, F.   *Batheaston*

STAPHYLINIDÆ (continued)

Lathrobium boreale, Hoch.   *Batheaston*
— filiforme, Grav.   *Somerset* (Ste., *Illus.*)
— multipunctum, Grav.   *Batheaston*
Achenium depressum, Grav.   *Weston-super-Mare* (Wollaston)
— humile, Nic.   *Batheaston*
Stilicus orbiculatus, Er.   *Porlock* (Blatch)
— rufipes, Germ.   *Batheaston*
— similis, Er.   „
— geniculatus, Er.   *Bath* (Gillo)
Medon melanocephalus, F.   *Porlock* (Blatch)
Sunius filiformis, Latr.   *Burnham*
— angustatus, Payk.   *Batheaston*
Pæderus littoralis, Grav.   „
Dianous cærulescens, Gyll.   *Bath* (Gillo)
Stenus guttula, Müll.   *Porlock* (Blatch)
— juno, F.   *Batheaston*
— guynemeri, Duv.   *Porlock* (Blatch)
— speculator, Er.   *Clevedon*
— providus, Er.   *Batheaston*
— declaratus, Er.   „
— crassus, v. littoralis, Thoms.   *Weston-super-Mare* (Fowler, *Brit. Col.*)
— argus, Grav.   *Batheaston*
— nigritulus, Gyll.   „
— brunnipes, Steph.   „
— subæneus, Er.   „
— fuscicornis, Er.   „
— flavipes, Steph.   „
— pallitarsis, Steph.   „
— nitiduisculus, Steph.   *Porlock* (Blatch)
— similis, Herbst.   *Batheaston*
— tarsalis, Ljun.   „
— latifrons, Er.   „
— fornicatus, Steph.   *Weston-super-Mare* (Fowler *Brit. Col.*)
Platystethus arenarius, Fourc.   *Batheaston*
Oxytelus sculptus, Grav.   *Minehead*
— laqueatus, Marsh.   *Batheaston*
— inustus, Grav.   „
— sculpturatus, Grav.   „
— complanatus, Er.   *Dunster*
— tetracarinatus, Block.   *Batheaston*
Ancyrophorus aureus, Fauv.   *Porlock* (Blatch)
Lesteva pubescens, Mann.   *Porlock* (Blatch)
— sicula, Er.   „   „
Omalium rivulare, Payk.   *Batheaston*
— exiguum, Gyll.   „
— punctipenne, Thoms.   *Porlock* (Blatch)
— rufipes, Fourc.   *Batheaston*
— vile, Er.   *Somerset* (Ste., *Illus.*)
— iopterum, Steph.   *Batheaston*
— concinnum, Marsh.   *Somerset* (Ste., *Illus.*)
— striatum, Grav.   *Clevedon*
Hapalaræa pygmæa, Gyll.   *Batheaston*
Eusphalerum primulæ, Steph.   „
Anthobium ophthalmicum, Payk.   „
— torquatum, Marsh.   „

I   81   II

I   81   II

STAPHYLINIDÆ (continued)
Proteinus ovalis, Steph. *Batheaston*
— atomarius, Er. *Somerset* (Ste., *Illus.*)
Megarthrus denticollis, Beck. *Bath* (Fowler, *Brit. Col.*)
— affinis, Mill. *Bath* (Gillo)
— depressus, Lac. *Batheaston*
— hemipterus, Ill. *Somerset* (Ste., *Illus.*)
Prognatha quadricornis, Lac. *Batheaston*

PSELAPHIDÆ
Bythinus bulbifer, Reich. *Batheaston*
Euplectus punctatus, Muls. *Porlock* (Blatch)
— signatus, Reich. *Leigh Woods* (Gorham)

SCYDMÆNIDÆ
Scydmænus collaris, Müll. *Batheaston*
Euconnus denticornis, Müll. „

SILPHIDÆ
Agathidium nigripenne, Kug. *Batheaston*
Liodes glabra, Kug. *Bath* (Gillo)
Anisotoma calcarata, Er. *Batheaston*
— furva, Er. *Brent Knoll* (Rye)
Hydnobius punctatissimus, Steph. *Uphill* (Fowler, *Brit. Col.*)
Necrophorus humator, F. *Batheaston*
— mortuorum, F. *Bath* (Gillo)
— vestigator, Heer. *Batheaston*
— ruspator, Er. *Bath* (Gillo)
— interruptus, Steph. „ „
— vespillo, L. *Batheaston*
Necrodes littoralis, L. *Bath* (Gillo)
Silpha opaca, L. *Castle Cary* (Macmillan)
— thoracica, L. „ „
— rugosa, L. *Batheaston*
— lævigata, F. „
— atrata, L. „
Choleva angustata, F. „
— cisteloides, Fröhl. „
— nigricans, Spence. *Bath* (Gillo)
— nigrita, Er. *Batheaston*
— tristis, Panz. „
— chrysomeloides, Panz. „
— watsoni, Spence. *Bath* (Gillo)
Ptomaphagus sericeus, F. *Batheaston*
Colon brunneum, Latr. *Portishead* (Fowler, *Brit. Col.*)

HISTERIDÆ
Hister quadrimaculatus, L. *Castle Cary* (Macmillan)
— cadaverinus, Hoff. *Batheaston*
— bimaculatus, L. *Castle Cary* (Macmillan)
Carcinops minima, Aubé. *Burnham* (Gillo)
Abræus globosus, Hoff. *Porlock* (Blatch)
Onthophilus striatus, F. *Bath* (Gillo)

SCAPHIDIIDÆ
Scaphidium quadrimaculatum, Ol. *Batheaston*
Scaphisoma boleti, Panz. *Nettlecomb* (Fowler, *Brit. Col.*)

TRICHOPTERYGIDÆ
Trichopteryx chevrolati, All. *Batheaston*
Nossidium pilosellum, Marsh. „
Ptenidium evanescens, Marsh. „
Orthoperus atomus, Gyll. *Weston-super-Mare* (Fowler, *Brit. Col.*)
Sericoderus lateralis, Gyll. *Cheddar* (Fowler, *Brit. Col.*)

COCCINELLIDÆ
Subcoccinella 24-punctata, L. *Midford*
Anisosticta 19-punctata, L. *Minehead*
Adalia bipunctata, L. *Batheaston*
Anatis ocellata, L. *Minehead*
Coccinella 10-punctata, L. „
— 11-punctata, L. *Castle Cary* (Macmillan)
— 7-punctata, L. *Batheaston*
Halyzia 14-guttata, L. „
— conglobata, L. „
— 22-punctata, L. „
Scymus capitatus, F. *Leigh Woods* (E.M.M. xxxiv. 186)
Chilocorus similis, Rossi. *Minehead*
Exochomus quadripustulatus, L. „
Coccidula rufa, Herbst „

ENDOMYCHIDÆ
Endomychus coccineus, L. *Batheaston*

EROTYLIDÆ
Dacne rufifrons, F. *Batheaston*

PHALACRIDÆ
Phalacrus corruscus, Payk. *Minehead*
— championi, Guill. „
Olibrus bicolor, F. *Batheaston*

MICROPEPLIDÆ
Micropeplus porcatus, Payk. *Bath* (Gillo)

NITIDULIDÆ
Brachypterus pubescens, Er. *Batheaston*
Epuræa æstiva, L. „
— melina, Er. „
— longula, Er. *Nettlecomb* (E.M.M. xxi. 96)
— florea, Er. *Batheaston*
Nitidula bipustulata, L „
Omosita colon, L. „
— discoidea, F. „
Meligethes rufipes, Gyll. „
— fulvipes, Bris. *Clevedon*
— æneus, F. *Batheaston*
— ovatus, Sturm. *Nettlecomb* (E.M.M. xxi. 266)
— picipes, Sturm. *Batheaston*
— obscurus, Er. *Clevedon* (Fowler, *Brit. Col.*)
Ips quadriguttata, F. *Porlock* (Blatch)

COLYDIIDÆ
Orthocerus muticus, L. *Burnham*
Cerylon histeroides, F. *Batheaston*
— ferrugineum, Steph. *Porlock* (Blatch)

CUCUJIDÆ
Rhizophagus ferrugineus, Payk. *Batheaston*
— bipustulatus, F. *Batheaston*

INSECTS

MONOTOMIDÆ

Monotoma conicicollis, Aubé. *Porlock* (Blatch)

— formicetorum, Thoms. *Porlock* (Blatch)

— brevicollis, Aubé. *Cheddar* (Fowler, *Brit. Col.*)

— quadricollis, Aubé. *Cheddar* (Fowler, *Brit. Col.*)

— longicollis, Gyll. *Cheddar* (Fowler, *Brit. Col.*)

LATHRIDIIDÆ

Lathridius angulatus, Humm. *Batheaston*

Coninomus nodifer, Westw. „

Enicmus transversus, Ol. „

Cartodere elongata, Curt. *Porlock* (Blatch)

Melanophthalma gibbosa, Herbst. *Batheaston*

— fuscula, Humm. *Batheaston*

CRYPTOPHAGIDÆ

Diphyllus lunatus, F. *Batheaston*

Telmatophilus caricis, Ol. *Minehead*

— brevicollis, Aubé. *Weston-super-Mare* (Crotch)

Cryptophagus scanicus, L. *Batheaston*

— cellaris, Scop. „

— pubescens, Sturm „

Myrmecoxenus vaporariorum, Guér. *Weston-super-Mare* (Crotch)

Atomaria atricapilla, Steph. *Batheaston*

— analis, Er. *Batheaston*

— ruficornis, Marsh. *Weston-super-Mare* (Wollaston)

MYCETOPHAGIDÆ

Mycetophagus quadripustulatus, L. *Batheaston*

— atomarius, F. *Porlock* (Wood)

BYTURIDÆ

Byturus tomentosus, F. *Batheaston*

DERMESTIDÆ

Dermestes vulpinus, F. *Castle Cary* (Macmillan)

— murinus, L. *Bristol, Somerset* (Bartlett)

— lardarius, L. *Castle Cary* (Macmillan)

Attagenus pellio, L. *Batheaston*

Anthrenus varius, F. „

— claviger, Er. „

BYRRHIDÆ

Byrrhus pilula, L. *Batheaston*

— fasciatus, F. „

— dorsalis, F. „

Aspidiphorus orbiculatus, Gyll. *Langport* (Dale)

PARNIDÆ

Parnus prolifericornis, F. *Porlock* (Blatch)

— auriculatus, Panz. *Glastonbury*

HETEROCERIDÆ

Heterocerus sericans, Kies. *Weston-super-Mare* (Fowler, *Brit. Col.*)

LUCANIDÆ

Lucanus cervus, L. *Castle Cary* (Macmillan)

Dorcus parallelopipedus, L. *Batheaston*

Sinodendron cylindricum, L. „

SCARABÆIDÆ

Copris lunaris, L. *Bath* (Gillo)

Onthophagus nutans, F. „ „

— ovatus, L. „ „

— cænobita, Herbst „ „

— vacca, L. *Brent Knoll* (Fowler, *Brit. Col.*)

— fracticornis, Payk. *Bath* (Gillo)

— nuchicornis, L. *Burnham* (Fowler, *Brit. Col.*)

Aphodius erraticus, L. *Burnham* (Gillo)

— subterraneus, L. „ „

— fossor, L. *Batheaston*

— fœtens, F. „

— fimetarius, L. „

— scybalarius, F. *Burnham* (Gillo)

— ater, DeG. *Batheaston*

— constans, Duft. „

— granarius, L. *Bath* (Gillo)

— rufescens, F. „ „

— porcus, F. „ „

— tristis, Panz. *Minehead*

— pusillus, Herbst. *Bath* (Gillo)

— quadrimaculatus, L. *Castle Cary* (Macmillan)

— merdarius, F. *Batheaston*

— inquinatus, F. „

— sticticus, Panz. *Bath* (Gillo)

— punctato-sulcatus, Sturm. *Batheaston*

— prodromus, Brahm. „

— contaminatus, Herbst „

— obliteratus, Panz. *Minehead*

— luridus, F. *Batheaston*

— rufipes, L. „

— depressus, Kug. „

Heptaulacus sus, Herbst. *Burnham* (Fowler, *Brit. Col.*)

Oxyomus porcatus, F. *Bath* (Fowler, *Brit. Col.*)

Psammobius sulcicollis, Ill. *Burnham* (Fowler, *Brit. Col.*)

Ægialia arenaria, F. *Burnham*

Geotrupes typhœus, L. *Castle Cary* (Macmillan)

— spiniger, Marsh. *Batheaston*

— stercorarius, L. *Castle Cary* (Macmillan)

— mutator, Marsh. *Batheaston*

— sylvaticus, Panz. *Dunster*

— vernalis, L. *Minehead*

Trox scaber, L. *Castle Cary* (Macmillan)

Hoplia philanthus, Füss. *Dunster*

Serica brunnea, L. *Batheaston*

Rhizotrogus solstitialis, L. „

Melolontha vulgaris, F. „

83

SCARABÆIDÆ (continued)
Phyllopertha horticola, L.   Minehead
Anomala frischii, F.   Burnham
Cetonia aurata, L.   Batheaston

BUPRESTIDÆ
Aphanisticus pusillus, Ol.   Bath (Fowler, Brit. Col.)

ELATERIDÆ
Lacon murinus, L.   Batheaston
Cardiophorus thoracicus, Er.   Somerset (Ste., Illus.)
Cryptohypnus riparius, F.   Bath (Gillo)
Ischnodes sanguinicollis, Panz.   Porlock (Wood)
Melanotus rufipes, Herbst.   Batheaston
Athous niger, L.   „
— longicollis, Ol.   „
— hæmorrhoidalis, F.   „
— vittatus, F.   Somerset (Ste., Illus.)
Limonius cylindricus, Payk.   Batheaston
Adrastus limbatus, F.   Bath (Gillo)
Agriotes sputator, L.   Batheaston
— obscurus, L.   „
— sobrinus, Kies.   „
— pallidulus, Ill.   „
Corymbites cupreus, F.   Dunkery
— metallicus, Payk.   Somerset (Fowler, Brit. Col.)

DASCILLIDÆ
Dascillus cervinus, L.   Dunster
Helodes minuta, L.   Batheaston
— marginata, F.   „
Cyphon variabilis, Thunb.   Minehead
Prionocyphon serricornis, Müll.   Bath (Gillo)

MALACODERMIDÆ
Platycis minutus, F.   Leigh Woods (Fowler, Brit. Col.)
Lampyris noctiluca, L.   Batheaston
Podabrus alpinus, Payk.   Bath (Gillo)
Telephorus rusticus, Fall.   Batheaston
— pellucidus, F.   „
— nigricans, Müll.   Minehead
— lituratus, F.   Batheaston
— figuratus, Mann.   Weston-super-Mare (Crotch)
— bicolor, F.   Batheaston
— oralis, Germ.   Langport (Dale)
— flavilabris, Fall.   Batheaston
Rhagonycha unicolor, Curt.   Bath (Gillo)
— fulva, Scop.   Batheaston
— testacea, L.   „
— limbata, Thoms.   „
— pallida, F.   „
Malthinus punctatus, Fourc.   Batheaston
— fasciatus, Ol.   „
— frontalis, Marsh.   Somerset (Ste., Illus.)
Malthodes mysticus, Kies.   Minehead
— minimus, L.   Batheaston
Malachius bipustulatus, L.   Batheaston

CLERIDÆ
Tillus elongatus, L.   Batheaston
Thanasimus formicarius, L.   „
Necrobia ruficollis, F. ⎫
— violacea, L.   ⎬ Bristol, Somerset (Bartlett)
— rufipes, De G. ⎭
Corynetes cœruleus, DeG.   Batheaston

PTINIDÆ
Ptinus sexpunctatus, Panz.   Batheaston
— fur, L.   „
Niptus hololeucus, Fald.   „
Hedobia imperialis, L.   Bath (Fowler, Brit. Col.)
Priobium castaneum, F.   Bath (Gillo)
Anobium domesticum, Fourc.   Castle Cary (Macmillan)
— paniceum, L.   Batheaston
Xestobium tessellatum, F.   Batheaston
Ochina hederæ, Müll.   Bath (Gillo)

CISSIDÆ
Cis bidentatus, Ol.   Somerset (Fowler, Brit. Col.)
— nitidus, Herbst.   Nettlecomb (Fowler, Brit. Col.)

CERAMBYCIDÆ
Aromia moschata, L.   Burnham
Clytus arietis, L.   Batheaston
— mysticus, L.   „
Rhagium inquisitor, F.   Porlock
— bifasciatum, F.   Batheaston
Toxotus meridianus, Panz.   Batheaston
Strangalia armata, Herbst.   Minehead
— melanura, L.
Grammoptera tabacicolor, DeG.   Bath (Ste., Illus.)
— ruficornis, F.   Batheaston
Acanthocinus ædilis, L.   Bath (Fowler, Brit. Col.)
Pogonochærus dentatus, Fourc.   Batheaston
Lamia textor, L.   Bath (Fowler, Brit. Col.)
Monochammus sutor, L.   Taunton (Fowler, Brit. Col.)
Tetrops præusta, L.   Bath (Gillo)

BRUCHIDÆ
Bruchus cisti, F.   Langport (Dale)
— rufimanus, Boh.   Batheaston
— atomarius, L.   „
— loti, Payk.   „

CHRYSOMELIDÆ
Orsodacna cerasi, L.   Leigh (Bartlett)
Donacia sparganii, Ahr.   Batheaston
— limbata, Panz.   Minehead
— bicolora, Zsch.   Bath (Fowler, Brit. Col.)
— simplex, F.   Minehead
Lema cyanella, L.   Batheaston
— melanopa, L.   „
Crioceris duodecem-punctata, L.   Bath (Ste., Illus.)
— asparagi, L.   Batheaston

INSECTS

CHRYSOMELIDÆ (*continued*)

Cryptocephalus aureolus, Suffr. *Bath* (Ste., *Illus.*)
— hypochæridis, L. *Batheaston*
— moræi, L. *Bath* (Fowler, *Brit. Col.*)
— bilineatus, L. *Langport* (Dale)
— pusillus, F. *Batheaston*
— labiatus, L. *Bath* (Ste., *Illus.*)
Timarcha tenebricosa, F. *Batheaston*
— violaceonigra, DeG. *Minehead*
Chrysomela marginalis, Duft. *Batheaston*
— banksi, F. *Minehead*
— staphylea, L. *Batheaston*
— polita, L. „
— orichalcia, Müll. *Bath* (Ste., *Illus.*)
— hæmoptera, L. „ (Gillo)
— gœttingensis, L. *Batheaston*
— menthrasti, Suffr. *Bath* (Ste., *Illus.*)
Melasoma populi, L. *Burnham*
Gastroidea polygoni, L. *Batheaston*
Plagiodera versicolora, Laich. „
Phædon tumidulus, Germ. „
— armoraciæ, F. „
Phyllodecta cavifrons, Thoms. *Batheaston*
— vitellinæ, L. „
Hydrothassa aucta, F. „
— marginella, L. „
Prasocuris junci, Brahm. *Minehead*
— phellandrii, L. „
Phyllobrotica quadrimaculata, L. *Bath* (Ste., *Illus.*)
Lochmæa suturalis, Thoms. *Cheddar*
Galerucella viburni, Payk. *Leigh* (Bartlett)
Adimonia tanaceti, L. *Bath* (Fowler, *Brit. Col.*)
Sermyla halensis, L. *Batheaston*
Longitarsus anchusæ, Payk. *Batheaston*
— castaneus, Duft. *Midford*
— luridus, Scop. *Batheaston*
— suturellus, Duft. „
— atricillus, L. „
— suturalis, Marsh. „
— pusillus, Gyll. „
— gracilis, Kuts. „
Haltica lythri, Aubé „
— oleracea, L. „
— pusilla, Duft. „
Hermæophaga mercurialis, F. *Batheaston*
Phyllotreta atra, Payk. „
— cruciferæ, Goeze „
— undulata, Kuts. „
— nemorum, L. *Minehead*
Aphthona virescens, Foudr. *Leigh Woods* (Gorham)
Batophila ærata, Marsh. *Batheaston*
Sphæroderma testaceum, F. „
— cardui, Gyll. *Minehead*
Podagrica fuscipes, L. *Weston-super-Mare* (Fowler, *Brit. Col.*)
Crepidodera transversa, Marsh. *Batheaston*

CHRYSOMELIDÆ (*continued*)

Crepidodera ferruginea, Scop. *Minehead*
— rufipes, L. *Midford* (Gillo)
— nitidula, L. *Burnham*
— helxines, L. *Minehead*
— aurata, Marsh. *Batheaston*
— smaragdina, Fourd. *Minehead*
Hippuriphila modeeri, L. *Somerset* (Ste., *Illus.*)
Chætocnema hortensis, Fourc. *Batheaston*
Plectroscelis concinna, Marsh. *Minehead*
Psylliodes affinis, Payk. *Batheaston*
— chalcomera, Ill. *Bristol, Somerset* (Bartlett)
— hyoscyami, L. *Batheaston*
Cassida viridis, F. „
— equestris, F. *Bath* (Ste., *Illus.*)

TENEBRIONIDÆ

Blaps mucronata, Latr. *Batheaston*
— similis, Latr. *Weston-super-Mare* (Fowler, *Brit. Col.*)
Heliopathes gibbus, F. *Burnham*
Opatrum sabulosum, Gyll. *Uphill* (Gorham)
Microzoum tibiale, F. *Burnham*
Phaleria cadaverina, F. „ (Fowler, *Brit. Col.*)
Scaphidema metallicum, F. *Batheaston*
Tenebrio molitor, L. „
Alphitobius diaperinus, Panz. „
Helops pallidus, Curt. *Burnham*
— striatus, Fourc. *Minehead*
Cistela luperus, Herbst. *Leigh Woods* (*E.M.M.* xxxiv. 186)
— murina, L. *Burnham*
Cteniopus sulphureus, L. *Burnham*

LAGRIIDÆ

Lagria hirta, L. *Batheaston*

MELANDRYIDÆ

Hypulus quercinus, Quens. *Leigh Woods* (Gorham)

PYTHIDÆ

Rhinosimus ruficollis, L. *Somerset* (Ste., *Illus.*)
— viridipennis, Steph. *Batheaston*
— planirostris, F. „

ŒDEMERIDÆ

Œdemera nobilis, Scop. *Minehead*
— lurida, Marsh. *Batheaston*
Oncomera femorata, F. „
Ischnomera cœrulea, L. „

PYROCHROIDÆ

Pyrochroa serraticornis, Scop. *Batheaston*

MORDELLIDÆ

Mordellistena pumila, Gyll. *Langport* (Dale)
Anaspis frontalis, L. *Batheaston*
— pulicaria, Costa. *Minehead*
— rufilabris, Gyll. „
— geoffroyi, Müll. *Batheaston*
— ruficollis, F. „

MORDELLIDÆ (continued)

Anaspis flava, L.   *Batheaston*

— maculata, Fourc.   „

ANTHICIDÆ

Notoxus monoceros, L. *Burnham* (Fowler, *Brit. Col.*)

Anthicus floralis, L.   *Bath* (Gillo)

MELOÏDÆ

Meloe proscarabæus, L.   *Batheaston*

— violaceus, Marsh.   „

ANTHRIBIDÆ

Brachytarsus varius, F.   *Brent Knoll* (*E.M.M.* xxxiii. 106)

Platyrrhinus latirostris, F.   *Batheaston*

CURCULIONIDÆ

Rhynchites cœruleus, DeG. *Porlock* (Blatch)

— æquatus, L.   *Minehead*

— minutus, Herbst.   *Brockley* (Bartlett)

— pauxillus, Germ.   *Langport* (Dale)

Apion pomonæ, F.   *Bath* (Ste., *Illus.*)

— ulicis, Forst.   *Minehead*

— malvæ, F.   „

— miniatum, Germ.   *Batheaston*

— hæmatodes, Kirby.   *Bath* (Gillo)

— pallipes, Kirby.   *Bath* (Fowler, *Brit. Col.*)

— rufirostre, F.   *Minehead*

— difforme, Germ.   *Batheaston*

— apricans, Herbst   „

— trifolii, L.   „

— dichroum, Bedel   „

— nigritarse, Kirby   „

— stolidum, Germ.   „

— æneum, F.   „

— onopordi, Kirby   „

— carduorum, Kirby   „

— virens, Herbst   „

— æthiops, Herbst   „

— striatum, Kirby   „

— immune, Kirby   „

— ononis, Kirby   „

— ervi, Kirby   „

— gyllenhali, Kirby   „

— unicolor, Kirby   „

— meliloti, Kirby   „

— livescerum, Gyll.   *Burnham*

— seniculum, Kirby.   *Batheaston*

— tenue, Kirby   „

— simile, Kirby   „

— curtisi, Walt.   „

— sedi, Germ.   *Bath* (Fowler, *Brit. Col.*)

— violaceum, Kirby.   *Batheaston*

— humile, Germ.   „

Otiorrhynchus tenebricosus, Herbst.   *Batheaston*

— fuscipes, Walt.   *Brockley* (Bartlett)

— scabrosus, Marsh.   *Batheaston*

— ligneus, Ol.   „

— picipes, F.   „

— sulcatus, F.   „

CURCULIONIDÆ (continued)

Otiorrhynchus rugifrons, Gyll.   *Burnham*

Trachyphlœus scaber, L.   *Batheaston*

— laticollis, Boh.   *Porlock* (Blatch)

— spinimanus, Germ.   *Batheaston*

Cænopsis waltoni, Schön.   *Somerset* (Ste., *Illus.*)

Strophosomus faber, Herbst.   *Bath* (Fowler, *Brit. Col.*)

— coryli, F.   *Leigh* (Bartlett)

Exomias araneiformis, Schr.   *Batheaston*

Sciaphilus muricatus, F.   „

Liophlœus nubilus, F.   „

Polydrusus micans, F.   „

— tereticollis, De G.   *Leigh* (Bartlett)

— pterygomalis, Boh.   *Batheaston*

— chrysomela, Il.   *Burnham* (Fowler, *Brit. Col.*)

Phyllobius oblongus, L.   *Batheaston*

— calcaratus, F.   „

— urticæ, DeG.   *Bath* (Ste., *Illus.*)

— pyri, L.   *Batheaston*

— argentatus, L.   *Batheaston*

— maculicornis, Germ.   *Batheaston*

— pomonæ, Ol.   „

— viridiæris, Laich.   „

Philopedon geminatus, F.   *Burnham*

Barynotus obscurus, F.   *Batheaston*

— elevatus, Marsh.   *Bath* (Gillo)

Alophus triguttatus, F.   *Midford* (Gillo)

Sitones griseus, F.   *Burnham*

— regensteinensis, Herbst.   *Minehead*

— crinitus, Herbst.   *Batheaston*

— tibialis, Herbst   „

— hispidulus, F.   „

— flavescens, Marsh.   „

— puncticollis, Steph.   *Minehead*

— lineatus, L.   *Batheaston*

— sulcifrons, Thunb.   *Batheaston*

Hypera punctata, F.   „

— rumicis, L.   *Burnham*

— suspiciosa, Herbst.   *Somerset* (Fowler, *Brit. Col.*)

— variabilis, Herbst.   *Batheaston*

— murina, F.   *Burnham*

— plantaginis, DeG.   *Somerset* (Ste., *Illus.*)

— nigrirostris, F.   *Batheaston*

Cleonus sulcirostris, L.   *Weston-super-Mare* (Ste., *Illus.*)

Lixus bicolor, Ol.   *Minehead*

Larinus carlinæ, Ol.   *Weston-super-Mare* (Fowler, *Brit. Col.*)

Liosoma ovatulum, Clairv.   *Batheaston*

Liparus coronatus, Goeze   „

Hylobius abietis, L.   *Brockley* (Bartlett)

Orchestes quercus, L.   *Batheaston*

— alni, L.   „

  v. ferrugineus, Marsh.   *Somerset* (Ste., *Illus.*)

— ilicis, F.   *Somerset* (Ste., *Illus.*)

INSECTS

CURCULIONIDÆ (*continued*)

Orchestes stigma, Germ. *Somerset* (Fowler, *Brit. Col.*)
— saliceti, Payk. *Somerset* (Fowler, *Brit. Col.*)
Grypidius equiseti, F. *Bath* (Fowler, *Brit. Col.*)
Erirrhinus scirpi, F. *Minehead*
— acridulus, L. *Bath* (Ste., *Illus.*)
Thryogenes nereis, Payk. *Batheaston*
Dorytomus vorax, F. *Porlock* (Blatch)
— maculatus, Marsh. *Batheaston*
— pectoralis, Gyll. *Somerset* (Fowler, *Brit. Col.*)
Bagous alismatis, Marsh. *Bath* (Ste., *Illus.*)
Miccotrogus picirostris, F. *Batheaston*
Gymnetron beccabungæ, L. *Portishead* (Fowler, *Brit. Col.*)
Mecinus pyraster, Herbst. *Batheaston*
— circulatus, Marsh. *Somerset* (Ste., *Illus.*)
Anthonomus pedicularius, L. *Batheaston*
— rubi, Herbst. *Batheaston*
Nanophyes lythri, F. *Bath* (Fowler, *Brit. Col.*)
Cionus scrophulariæ, L. *Batheaston*
— blattariæ, F. „
— pulchellus, Herbst. *Bath* (Fowler, *Brit. Col.*)
Cryptorrhynchus lapathi, L. *Somerset* (Ste., *Illus.*)
Cœliodes quercus, F. *Somerset* (Ste., *Illus.*)
— ruber, Marsh. „ „
— cardui, Herbst „ „
— quadrimaculatus, L. *Batheaston*
Poophagus sisymbrii, F. *Somerset* (Ste., *Illus.*)
— nasturtii, Germ. *Weston-super-Mare* (Crotch)
Ceuthorrhynchus contractus, Marsh. *Batheaston*
— geographicus, Goeze. *Somerset* (Ste., *Illus.*)

CURCULIONIDÆ (*continued*)

Ceuthorryhnchus pollinarius, Forst. *Batheaston*
— trimaculatus, F. *Batheaston*
Ceuthorrhynchidius nigrinus, Marsh. *Somerset* (Ste., *Illus.*)
— terminatus, Herbst. *Batheaston*
— mixtus, Muls. *Porlock* (Bennet)
— troglodytes, F. *Minehead*
Rhinoncus gramineus, Herbst. *Weston-super-Mare* (Fowler, *Brit. Col.*)
— castor, F. } *Somerset*
— bruchoides, Herbst. } (Ste.,
Litodactylus leucogaster, Marsh. } *Illus.*)
Limnobaris T-album, L. *Burnham* (Fowler, *Brit. Col.*)
Baris picicornis, Marsh. *Batheaston*
Magdalis carbonaria, L. *Minehead*
— armigera, Fourc. *Leigh Woods* (*E.M.M.* xxxiv. 186)
— barbicornis, Latr. *Bath* (Gillo)
Calandra granaria, L. *Bristol, Somerset* (Bartlett)
Cossonus ferrugineus, Clairv. *Somerset* (Ste., *Illus.*)
Stereocorynes truncorum, Germ. *Bath* (Gillo)

SCOLYTIDÆ

Scolytus destructor, Ol. *Batheaston*
Hylastes ater, Payk. „
— opacus, Er. *Leigh Woods* (*E. M. M.* xxxiv. 186)
— palliatus, Gyll. *Bath* (Fowler, *Brit. Col.*)
Hylesinus fraxini, Panz. *Weston-super-Mare*
Xylocleptes bispinus, Duft. *Midford* (Gillo)
Dryocætes villosus, F. *Somerset* (Ste., *Illus.*)
Trypodendron domesticum, L. *Porlock* (Blatch)

STYLOPIDÆ

Stylops melittæ, Kirby. *Batheaston*
Elenchus tenuicornis, Kirby. *Bruton* (*E. M. M.* xxviii. 250)

LEPIDOPTERA

The butterflies and moths recorded from Somerset form a much greater percentage of the British species than is the case with any other order of insects, probably in consequence of their having been much more widely collected than any other order. Although there are few localities in the county where any but the most generally common species are now to be found in abundance, nevertheless a considerable number of rare and interesting insects have been recorded during the last century, some of which are still to be found in their favourite haunts, though others have not been seen for many years past.

The butterflies for instance make a fair show in the list, no less than sixty-one of the sixty-eight British species being recorded, or if we include the reputed species *Parnassius apollo* and *Polyommatus chryseis* (both of which are said to have been taken in the county) the Somerset butterflies number sixty-three. Of these about a dozen species have not been met with for many years, and some are doubtless extinct. The only British butterflies missing from the county list are *Melitæa cinxia* and *athalia*, *Erebia epiphron* and *blandina*, *Cænonympha typhon*, *Thecla pruni*, *Lycæna bætica* and *Hesperia actæon*. Some of these have also been reported from Somerset on somewhat doubtful authority, but rather than include in our list any species which have never been taken in the county, it has been decided to exclude, until further evidence is produced, four butterflies and dozens of moths which have been recorded as natives.

From the end of the eighteenth century to the present time there have been collectors of Lepidoptera resident in Somerset, but unfortunately very few of them have recorded their experiences. It will be seen however from our list that most of the printed records have been consulted, and that a few rare species, such as the original 'Bath-white' (*Pieris daplidice*) and the Large Blue (*Lycæna arion*), were found in the county so long ago as 1795, when Lewin published his book on British butterflies.

Somerset is the only English county in which all the six British 'Hook-tips' have been met with. The rare *Drepana sicula*, found only in the Leigh Woods amongst the small-leaved lime trees (*Tilia parvifolia*) which are there so abundant, is probably soon doomed to extinction as a native of our islands. It is found only at rest, never on the wing, and seems to be getting scarcer year by year. *D. lacertula*, Hub., has also become very scarce in the district, and has not been seen in its old haunts near Bristol for the last twenty years.

Thanks to a number of entomologists still, or till recently, resident in various parts of the county, we have been able to compile a fairly representative catalogue, but doubtless when some of the more remote districts of the Mendips, and the moors and marshes have been further explored, many additions will be made to the list.[1]

[1] It has not been thought necessary in all cases to give the names of the recorders for each locality after the names of the insects. In the case of species from Bristol district, Leigh Woods, etc., where no other authority is named I am myself responsible for the records. Species from the following localities, when not otherwise stated, are given on the authority of the entomologists named, who have either published lists or sent them to me :—

Ashbrittle near Wellington : Mr. F. Milton

Bath : Mr. Thomas Greer. Species not in Mr. Greer's list are from a catalogue by Dr. Terry in *The Historic Bath Guide* (1864) ; these are all marked ('Terry only')

Bathampton : The late Mr. J. G. Ross

Batheaston : Colonel Linley Blathwayt

Blackdown Hills : Mr. F. Milton

Brislington : The late Mr. Sircom

Bridgwater : Mr. Arthur Cottam, Mr. H. Corder, and the Rev. A. P. Waller

Castle Cary : Mr. W. Macmillan

Clevedon : Mr. J. Mason

Crowcombe (Quantocks) : Rev. J. Seymour St. John

Evercreech : Rev. E. Hallett Todd

Frome (Whatley, near) : Rev. J. S. St. John

Glastonbury (Baltonsborough, near) : Rev. J. S. St. John

Portishead : The late Mr. J. N. Duck

Sampford Arundel : Mr. F. Milton

Stoke-sub-Hamdon : Mr. W. Walter

Taunton : Mr. F. C. Woodforde (generally confirmed by the late Mr. Bidgood of Taunton Museum) ; a few species on the authority of Mr. A. S. Tetley (marked 'Tetley')

Wellington : Mr. F. Milton

Wells : The late Dr. H. W. Livett

Weston-super-Mare : The late Mr. G. R. Crotch

Yeovil : Mr. T. Parmiter

INSECTS

RHOPALOCERA

Papilio machaon, L. In the early part of the last century our only British Swallow-tail was recorded by Samouelle, in the *Entomologist's Useful Compendium*, to be found 'near *Bristol*. Between 1800 and 1815 specimens were taken in Somerset by the Rev. M. Newman at *West Camel* and the Rev. R. Burney at *Rympton* (Dale).[1] In 1856 one was taken by Mr. G. R. Crotch near *Weston-super-Mare*, and in the following year one was caught by Mr. Knight at *Portishead*. In 1862 a specimen was caught in the market place at *Taunton*, and was taken to Mr. Bidgood by the captor. In 1864 Dr. Terry records it as 'rare, near *Bath*.' One was captured in 1880 on *Durdham Down* near *Bristol*, and lastly a fine specimen was caught on June 17, 1900, on *Lodge Hill* near *Castle Cary* by Mr. Brake, as recorded by Mr. Macmillan in the *Castle Cary Visitor* for July, 1900. The occurrence of so many specimens of this fine butterfly so far west makes one wonder whether the species is quite so local in our country as it is generally supposed to be

[Parnassius apollo, L. In his *Lepidoptera of the British Islands*, i. 311, Mr. C. G. Barrett says one or two specimens of this doubtful British species were reported from near *Portishead*. I have been unable to ascertain any particulars as to the name of captor and date, but as Portishead is on the Bristol Channel, and ships from various foreign ports are constantly entering the docks, or passing close by on their way to Bristol, etc., it is quite possible these beautiful butterflies may have been brought from some French or Spanish port, and flown ashore at Portishead. This beautiful insect cannot therefore be claimed as a native of the county]

Aporia cratægi, L. As in other parts of England, the 'Black-veined White' has not been seen for many years. It was formerly common in many parts of the county, and has been recorded from near *Bath* (Terry), *Clevedon* (Hudd), *Langport* (Bidgood), *Portishead*, *Weston-super-Mare* and *Worle* (G. Harding)

Pieris brassicæ, rapæ and napi, L., are all abundant throughout the county
— daplidice, L. The original 'Bath White,' so named by Lewin, 'from a piece of needlework executed at Bath, by a young lady, from a specimen of this insect, said to be taken near that place' (Lewin's *Insects of Great Britain*, vol. i. 1795), has long disappeared. But there is still in the Bristol Museum collection a specimen which is probably the 'one captured by J. S. M. in a field near Keynsham, in 1818,' recorded by Dale as 'in the cabinet of Mr. Miller, of Bristol' (*Mag. Nat. Hist.* for 1831). Mr. Miller, who was curator of the Bristol Museum, was the father of the well-known artist William J. Müller

Anthocharis cardamines, L. Fairly common in lanes

Leucophasia sinapis, L. The pretty little 'Wood White' is fairly common in some woods in the *Taunton* district, but is very scarce in the northern part of the county. Near *Bath* (Terry); *Clevedon*, a single specimen by Mr. Braikenridge; *Cothelstone Woods* (Tetley); *Orchard Portman Woods* (Corder, Rawlinson, Tetley and Waller); *Sampford Arundel* (Milton); *Stoke-sub-Hamdon*; 'woods near *Taunton*, not uncommon in May and August, the earlier brood much the commoner' (Bidgood); 'woods near *Taunton* and on the *Quantocks*, local but sometimes abundant' (Woodforde); one at *Tickenham* (Braikenridge); *Weston-super-Mare* (Crotch)

Colias hyale, L. Rare near *Bath* (Terry), *Bedminster* (a few specimens in 1900, Hudd), *Bridgwater* in 1890 (Corder and Cottam), *Castle Cary*, *Clevedon*, *Orchard Wood*, *Taunton*, etc. Never common in the county and not found except in some years, generally when it is abundant further south
— edusa, Fab. Throughout the county, generally scarce, but some years abundant. *Bath, Bathampton, Bristol, Bridgwater, Burnham, Castle Cary, Clevedon, Frome, Staple-Fitzpaine, Stoke-sub-Hamdon, Taunton, Wells, Weston-super-Mare*. The var. helice has been recorded from *Bedminster, Bridgwater* (Cottam and Corder), *Burnham* (Col. Blathwayt and Smith), *Frome* (St. John), *Stoke-sub-Hamdon* (Walter), *Taunton, Wells* and *Weston-super-Mare*

[1] See 'Historic Notes on Papilio Machaon in England,' by Mr. C. W. Dale, in the *E. M. M.* for February, 1902, p. 37.

Gonepteryx rhamni, L. Generally distributed, but not very common

Argynnis selene, S., and euphrosyne, L., are both fairly common in some woods and on downs, especially in the *Taunton* district, but they have become very scarce in the northern part of the county, where they were once common

— lathonia, L. Only one specimen of 'the Queen of Spain,' has been recorded, taken near *Nailsea*, about 1858 (Naish)

— aglaia, L., adippe, L., and paphia, L., are all generally distributed throughout the county, and may be found most years in suitable localities. Like the other Fritillaries they are all more plentiful in the central and southern parts of the county than in the north. They are hardly ever found of late years in *Leigh Woods* or in other localities near *Bristol*. In fact only a single specimen of A. paphia has ever been recorded from *Leigh Woods*, so far as I am aware, a specimen caught by Mr. Prideaux in July, 1894

Melitæa artemis, Hub. Fairly common in marshy meadows near *Bath*, the *Blackdown Hills, Clevedon, Hallatrow, Langport, Portishead, Stoke-sub-Hamdon, Taunton, Winscombe, Wells, Weston-super-Mare*, etc. Very local, and much less common in most localities than formerly

Vanessa c-album, L., used to be fairly common in the northern parts of the county, and is still found near *Bath, Bathampton* (Ross), *Clevedon* (Hudd), *Crowcombe, Leigh Woods, Taunton, Weston-super-Mare*. It has been abundant this year (1901) in *Gloucestershire*, and several specimens have been seen in my garden at *Clifton*

— polychloros, L. Not common. *Bath, Bathampton, Bridgwater, Castle Cary, Clevedon, Crowcombe, Orchard Portman, Stoke-sub-Hamdon, Taunton, Wells, Weston*. Mr. Braikenridge tells me it used to be common at *Clevedon* fifty years ago. None have been seen there of late

— urticæ, L. Abundant among nettles everywhere

— io, L., atalanta, L., and cardui, L., are all generally distributed and fairly common

— antiopa, L., the 'Camberwell Beauty,' has several times been noticed since 1844, when James Francis Stephens saw one in *Goblin Coombe* near *Yatton*,

as recorded in the *Zoologist*, vol. iii. A specimen was taken near *Flax Bourton* in 1866, one near *Bridgwater* by Mr. Dale (*Mag. Nat. Hist.* vol. v.), two near *Bridgwater* in 1900 (Corder), one at *Chilton Polden* in 1870 now in the Clifton College collection, two in *Orchard Portman Woods* (Bidgood), one near *Chard* (Dale), one near *Taunton* (Crotch), and two on *Mendip* near *Wells* in 1872, one of which was captured by Dr. Livett. It is also recorded by Dr. Terry as 'rare near *Bath*'

Limenitis sibylla, L. Only a few specimens of the 'White Admiral' have been found in the county. One was taken in *Gribb Wood, Bratton Seymour*, in 1893, by Mr. Swanton (Macmillan). Mr. Bidgood recorded one from *Norton Fitzwarren*, and Mr. Crotch one from the neighbourhood of *Weston-super-Mare*. One was taken on the north bank of the Avon near *Clifton*, and several are said to have been taken and seen at *Brockley Coombe*

Apatura iris, L. A few recorded from *Brockley Woods* in 1870 (Last), *Brockley Coombe* (I. W. Clarke), *Clive Coombe* (F. D. Wheeler), and woods near *Winscombe* (T. H. Ormston Pease). No records from the southern portions of the county, where it ought to be found

Arge galatea, L. Scarce at *Bedminster, Brean Down* and *Clevedon*, where it was once common. Still plentiful on the *Polden Hills* and other places near *Bridgwater* (Corder), *Baltonsborough* near *Glastonbury*, and *Crowcombe* on the *Quantocks* (St. John); *Hatch* (Tetley), *Portishead, Taunton* and *Weston-super-Mare*

Satyrus egeria, L., and megæra, L., are fairly common in most parts of the county

— semele, L., swarms on limestone hills near *Bristol, Bridgwater*, the *Mendips, Quantocks*, etc.

— janira, L., and tithonus, L., are perhaps the two most abundant butterflies in the district, being found in thousands most years

— hyperanthus, L., is common in woods, but not nearly so plentiful as the last-named

Cænonympha pamphilus, L., is one of the most plentiful and most generally distributed of our butterflies, and is found sometimes even in gardens in *Bristol*

Thecla rubi, L., and quercus, L., are common in many parts of the county, the latter being plentiful in oak woods, where the curious larvæ are sometimes to be found in abundance on the leaves round the trunks of the trees

— w-album, Knock, is not very common except near *Bristol, Brockley Coombe* and *Weston-super-Mare*, where the larvæ are sometimes abundant on wych-elms

— betulæ, L. Recorded from 'near *Bath*' (Terry); *Neroche Forest*, 1885 and 1898 (Tetley); *Orchard Wood* near *Taunton*, where some specimens were taken by Mr. Spiller in 1864 and 1865, and by Mr. Corder more recently, and from *Brockley Coombe* near *Bristol*, where one was caught in 1861 by Mr. Harvey

Polyommatus phlœas, L. Common everywhere in the district on heaths and downs. Some good varieties have been met with

— dispar, Haw. There can be no doubt, I think, that the now extinct 'Large Copper' was formerly taken in *Somerset*. The late Mr. Bidgood of the Taunton Museum had no doubt on the subject, as is shown in the following notes which I received from him a few weeks before his death. The specimens, or rather some remains, are still in the Taunton museum : 'A specimen (was) in an old collection made in the early part of the century and presented to the Somerset Archæological and Natural History Society, about 1860, by Mr. Woodland, who told me that it was taken at Langport. There were two or three specimens in the Queckett Museum also, but so badly decayed from damp and moth that there was no chance of saving them ; only just enough to swear by ' (the late Wm. Bidgood, in his MS. *Catalogue of Lepidoptera occurring in the neighbourhood of Taunton*)

Later Mr. Bidgood wrote : ' About the year 1864 Mr. Woodland gave me a small collection of butterflies taken near *Langport* early in the century ; among them were two or three P. dispar, which he told me were taken by himself. In his early days he had taken care of them, but he got old and neglected them, so that when they came to me they were dilapidated. I preserved every bit I could. Among them were two or three specimens of the "Purple-edged Copper," P. chryseis, which he informed me were taken with the dispar.

' Early in the last century the late Professor Queckett and his brother (a banker at Langport) formed a museum in the " Hanging Chapel " there. This was transferred to our society about 1876–7. The collection had been much neglected, so that when I went to take possession I found everything covered with mildew, moth was playing havoc with the birds and mites with the insects. There were here also three or four dispar, which I was assured by the family were taken at *Langport*, and also two or three P. chryseis. This was confirmed by Mr. W. Bond Paul, who died in 1896, aged over eighty. He told me he remembered the insects well, but they were taken before his collecting days. This Mr. Paul had a long series of L. arion taken by himself at *Langport* ; he gave a pair to the (Taunton) museum collection ' (W. Bidgood *in. litt.*, Jan., 1901)

It was reported, but I could not ascertain particulars, that a specimen of the ' Large Copper ' was taken near *Clevedon* about 1869 or 1870. Not being able to find either the exact date or the name of the captor I did not record it in my *Catalogue of the Lepidoptera of the Bristol District*, but it is quite possible, I think, that it was found there. The late Mr. G. R. Crotch recorded a specimen from near *Weston-super-Mare* in 1856 : ' C. dispar fell ignobly, slain by the hat of a friend, who kindly made the spoil over to me in utter ignorance of its rarity ' (*Intelligencer*, ii. 165 ; iv. 21)

[Polyommatus hippothoe, L. (chryseis, Hub.), seems formerly to have been occasionally taken in England. Lewin in his *British Butterflies* (1795) says (p. 86) : 'I once met with two of these butterflies settled on a bank in the marshes in the month of August.' Mr. Bidgood informed me there were remains of two or three specimens in an old collection presented to the Taunton Museum, which he understood had been taken in the marshes near *Langport*, early in the nineteenth century, by Mr. Woodland. Specimens were also in the Queckett collection from the same locality]

Lycæna argiades, Pallas. Two specimens were taken by Dr. Marsh near *Frome* in 1874, the first captured British specimens of this pretty little ' tailed blue. Two were taken in Dorset by the Rev. O. Pickard-Cambridge in 1885. (See Barrett's *Lepidoptera of the British Islands*, i. 69)

Lycæna ægon, Schiff., is very local and uncommon in the county except near *Bridgwater*, where it has been taken freely by Mr. Cottam and Mr. Corder. It has been reported from near *Bath*, *Clevedon*, *Sidcot* (Corder), *Taunton* (Bidgood) and *Weston-super-Mare*

— agestis, Hub., seems to be generally distributed and common on limestone hills and downs

— icarus (alexis), Hub., is common everywhere. In hot summers a third brood occurs, very much smaller than the earlier form

— adonis, Fab. Very scarce in the county, the only records being from the neighbourhood of *Bath*, where it was found by Dr. Terry and by Mr. Greer ; one specimen from the *Polden Hills* near *Bridgwater* by Mr. Corder, *Pickeridge* near *Taunton* by Mr. Bidgood, *Radstock* by Dr. Livett, and *Stoke-sub-Hamdon* by Dr. Walter

— corydon, Fab. Common on hills near *Bath, Bridgwater, Frome, Taunton, Wells, Weston, Brean Down*, the *Mendips*, etc. Scarce near *Bristol, Clevedon*, etc.

— argiolus, L., is abundant throughout the county amongst holly bushes, and unlike most butterflies seems to be commoner near *Bristol* than it used to be

— acis, Fab. Recorded by Lewin : 'The last week in August, 1763, I took two or three, flying in a pasture field at the bottom of a hill near *Bath*' (*Insects of Great Britain*, p. 80). Near *Bath* (Crotch) ; a specimen from *Leigh Down* near *Bristol* was caught about 1867, and was in the collection of Mr. W. H. Grigg of Bristol

— alsus, Fab., is widely distributed, but very local, being found in some localities only in the corner of a field, or a space of a few dozen yards on a hillside. It is reported from *Brockley, Bath, Clevedon, Crowcombe, Portishead, Sidcot* (Corder), *Taunton, Wells, Weston, Wookey*, etc.

Lycæna arion, L. This fine butterfly was formerly taken in several places in the county, but has not been met with of late years. Lewin recorded it from 'hills near *Bath* on the wing the middle of July' (1795). In the early part of the last century Mr. W. Bond Paul used to take arion freely near *Langport*, and some specimens were presented by him to the Taunton Museum. Mr. Crotch met with some near *Weston-super-Mare*. So far as I know none have been taken in the county for the last forty years

Nemeobius lucina, L. Local, but common in a few localities : near *Bath* (Terry), *Bridgwater* (Cottam), *Neroche Hill* and *Orchard Portman* near *Taunton* (Tetley and others), *Stoke-sub-Hamdon* (Walter), *Warleigh Wood* near *Bath* (Braikenridge)

Syrichthus alveolus, Hub., Thanaos tages, L., and Hesperia sylvanus, Esp., are all fairly common on downs and clearings in woods throughout the county

Hesperia comma, L., is scarce and local. Near *Brockley* (Last), *Bath* (Terry), *Clevedon* and *Weston - super - Mare* (Rev. H. Tanner)

— linea, Fab. Common in some places, but local. *Bath, Bathampton, Crowcombe, Clevedon, Loxley Wood* near *Bridgwater, Leigh Woods* (Prideaux), *Taunton, Wells, Weston*

— lineola, Ochs. A specimen in the Taunton Museum collection was said to have been taken in the neighbourhood by the late Mr. Rawlinson of that town (Bidgood) (see Barrett, *Lepidoptera of the British Islands*, vol. i.)

Cyclopædes palæmon, Pall. (paniscus, Fab.). The late Mr. Bidgood, who included this very local butterfly in his MS. list of Lepidoptera taken near *Taunton*, wrote me a few weeks before he died : 'The paniscus record is all right,' but he did not give details. Dr. Terry reported it as 'rare near *Bath*,' but I feel some hesitation in accepting it as a Somerset species without further evidence. A single specimen has been recorded from Gloucestershire

HETEROCERA

NOCTURNI
SPHINGES

Smerinthus ocellatus, L., populi, L., and tiliæ, L., are all fairly common and generally distributed

Acherontia atropos, L., and Sphinx convolvuli, L., are found in most parts of the county, and are sometimes almost common. With the preceding species and other 'Hawk Moths' they have been taken at 'light,' especially at the electric lights in *Taunton* (Tetley)

Sphinx ligustri, L.   Common everywhere

— pinastri.   In 1863 a specimen was taken by Miss Bicknell at *Hinton St. George*, at rest on a tree-trunk, and is in the collection of the Institute at Crewkerne (Spiller, *Ent.* vi. 104 ; Barrett, *Insects of the British Islands*, ii. 29)

[Deilephila euphorbiæ, L. Reported from near *Taunton* by Mr. Rawlinson (*Zoologist*, xv.).   Probably a mistake]

— galii, Schiff.   *Bridgwater* (Dale, Newman and others), *Langport* (Macmillan and Newman), *Clevedon* (Braikenridge), *Stoke-sub-Hamdon* (Walter), *Taunton* (one 1868, Woodforde ; several at electric light, Tetley), *Weston-super-Mare* (Crotch, Clark and Rawlinson)

— lineata, Esp.   One taken at *Clevedon* is in the collection of Mr. Braikenridge ; a specimen was taken in 1888 at electric light at *Taunton* by Mr. Tetley ; and one was captured by Mr. Aldridge flying over flowers at *Weston-super-Mare* (*Ent.* v. 169)

Chærocampa celerio, L.   Two specimens were taken in October, 1886, by Mr. Mason, flying over flowers in the garden at *Clevedon Court*.   One was caught at 'light' at *Taunton* by Mr. Buckland, and two others from the same locality were seen by Mr. Bidgood.   A fine specimen was caught in September, 1869, by a lady in her drawing-room at *Weston-super-Mare* (Mathew), and two were recorded from the county in 1884 (St. John)

— porcellus, L.   Near *Bath, Brislington, Brent Knoll, Cheddar, Clevedon, Sidcot, Taunton, Weston-super-Mare*.   Not common

— elpenor, L.   *Bath, Bathampton, Brislington, Bridgwater, Clevedon* (sometimes common, Mason), near *Frome, Stoke-sub-Hamdon, Taunton, Wellington* (Milton), *Weston-super-Mare*

Macroglossa stellatarum, L.   Generally distributed and sometimes abundant

— fuciformis, L.   Scarce near *Bath* (Terry), *Leigh Woods, Portbury Woods*, over flowers of rhododendron

— bombyliformis, Esp.   Rare near *Bath* (Terry) ; one at *Bratton Seymour* (Macmillan), *Stoke-sub-Hamdon* (Walter)

Trochilium bembeciformis, Hub.   Taken by Mr. Jefferys and Mr. Mason at *Clevedon*, by the Rev. E. Hallett Todd at *Evercreech*, and by Mr. Macmillan at *Castle Cary*

Sesia myopæformis, Bork.   Scarce in old orchards near *Bristol, Bedminster* (Barton), *Brislington*(Grigg) and near *Bath* (Terry)

— culiciformis, L.   Recorded only from *Bedminster*, where a single specimen was taken by Mr. Ficklin, and from *Stoke-sub-Hamdon* by Dr. Walter

— formicæformis, Esp.   Near *Bath* (Dr. Terry), and a single specimen on the Somerset bank of the *New Cut, Bristol,* by Mr. S. Barton

— ichneumoniformis, W.V. Scarce near *Bath* (Terry), *Leigh Down, Bristol* (Vaughan) and *Weston-super-Mare* (Crotch)

— cynipiformis, Och.   A few specimens were caught in *Leigh Woods* by Dr. F. D. Wheeler many years ago.   No further records in the county

— tipuliformis, C. Common in some gardens amongst old and neglected currant bushes

Procris (Ino) statices, L., and geryon, Hub., are both reported from various parts of the county, the latter being sometimes plentiful on downs and hillsides, though it seems to have disappeared from some of its old localities.   Formerly it was common on slopes by the sea at *Clevedon*, but Mr. Mason says it is not now found there.   P. statices is recorded from near *Bath, Brockley* (Hudd), *Clevedon* (one locality only, Mason), near *Taunton* (Bidgood), *Stoke-sub-Hamdon, Weston-super-Mare*, etc.   There seems to be some confusion between these two species, and I expect several of those recorded as statices are really geryon

Zygæna trifolii, Esp., and loniceræ, Esp., the two 'Five-spotted Burnets,' are also frequently confused in collections, but both species are found in the county, the former near *Bath, Bathampton* (Ross), *Penselwood* (Macmillan), *Portishead, Stoke, Taunton* and *Weston* ; the latter, perhaps more scarce and local, near *Clevedon* (Mason), *Orchard Portman*, near *Taunton* (Tetley), *Portishead* (Harding), and *Weston-super-Mare*

— filipendulæ, L., is generally common, and some good varieties have been met with

BOMBYCES

Sarrothripa revayana, Tr. (undulana, Hub.), may be taken as a fair example of the divergence of opinion among entomologists on the subject of the classification of Lepidoptera.   In his *Manual* (1859), Stainton gave it a place at the commencement of the Tortrices ; South, in *The Entomologist List* (1884), gives it as the first of the Bombyces, immediately following the 'Burnets'; Meyrick (in 1896) places it between Nola and Halias, in the Arctiadæ; and Barrett, in his *Lepidoptera of the British Islands* (1900), among the Noctuæ, next to Gonoptera libatrix, L. When authorities differ so considerably, what is a poor student to do? The moth is not common, but has been reported from near *Bristol*, *Bridgwater*, *Clevedon*, *Leigh Woods*, *Portishead* and *Weston-super-Mare*

Earias chlorana, L. A local species, recorded only from *Ashcot*, near *Wells* by Mr. Harding, *Bridgwater* by Mr. Corder, *Walton Moor* near *Clevedon* by Mr. Mason, and *Bath* by Dr. Terry

Halias prasinana, L., is fairly common in oak woods

— quercana, Sch. (bicolorana, Fues.), has been taken near *Bath*, near *Bridgwater* by Mr. Corder, and bred from larvæ taken in *Leigh Woods* by Mr. George Harding

Nola cucullatella, L., is fairly common near *Bath*, *Bridgwater*, *Bristol*, *Burnham*, *Clevedon*, *Glastonbury*, *Minehead*, *Taunton*, *Weston*, etc.

— strigula, Schiff., is very local and scarce, but has been met with by Dr. Terry near *Bath*, by Mr. Mason at *Clevedon*, by Mr. Duck at *Portishead*, by Mr. Bidgood near *Taunton*, and by Mr. E. Wheeler at *Walton*

— confusalis, H.S., is recorded from *Castle Cary*, *Crowcombe* and the *Quantock Hills*, *Taunton* (Bidgood) and *Weston-super-Mare* (Crotch and W. H. Grigg)

Nudaria senex, Hub., was taken by Mr. Ross at *Bathampton* (one specimen only), on *Walton Moor* near *Clevedon* by Mr. Mason, and at *Stoke* by Dr. Walter

— mundana, L., is common on old walls on downs, etc., near *Bristol*, *Brislington*, *Bath*, *Brockley*, *Clevedon*, *Taunton*, etc.

Setina irrorella, Cl., is very local, and has only been recorded from near *Bath* by Dr. Terry and *Brockley Coombe* by Mr. Harding and Mr. Mason

Calligenia miniata, For., is generally distributed throughout the county, but not common. Near *Bath*, *Bridgwater*, *Clevedon*, *Leigh Woods*, *N. Petherton* (Corder), *Minehead* (Hudd), *Stoke*, *Taunton*, *Wells*, *Weston*. It sometimes comes to 'light'

Lithosia mesomella, L. Near *Bath*, *Bridgwater* (turf moor, Corder), *Stoke-sub-Hamdon*. Scarce

— griseola, Hub. Not scarce in damp meadows near *Bath*, *Bristol*, *Bridgwater*, *Castle Cary*, *Clevedon*, *Radstock* (Livett), *Portishead*, *Taunton*. The pale variety (stramineola, Dbd.) occurs with the type, but is rare

Lithosia lurideola, Z., is common and generally distributed

— complana, L., is found in marshy places near *Bristol*, *Clevedon*, *Bridgwater* (Sanders), *Taunton*, *Whatley* near *Frome* and *Weston-super-Mare*

— rubricollis, L., is local, but sometimes abundant in woods near *Taunton* (Tetley), and has been reported from near *Bristol*, *Brockley*, *Clevedon* and *Weston-super-Mare*. It flies high in the daytime, near the tree-tops

Gnophria quadra, L. Scarce at 'light.' Near *Bath* (Terry and Greer), *Wells* (two specimens by Dr. Livett) and *Yeovil* (one by Mr. Parmiter)

Emydia cribrum, L. Recorded only by Mr. Macmillan: 'Local, but not scarce near *Castle Cary*, 1900'

Deiopeia pulchella, L. The only Somerset specimen known of this beautiful insect is the one recorded by Stevens in 1847, in the *Transactions of the Entomological Society of London*, vol. i.

Euchelia jacobææ, L., is abundant everywhere amongst ragwort

Callimorpha dominula, L., has been reported only by Dr. Terry from near *Bath* and Dr. Walter at *Stoke-sub-Hamdon*. It is found occasionally in the *Bristol* district on the Gloucestershire side of the Avon and in several other localities in that county

Nemeophila russula, L. A local species, but sometimes common on heathy places round *Bath* (Terry), *Bridgwater* (Cottam), *Stoke* (Walter), on the *Quantocks* (Corder), *Crowcombe* (St. John), *Taunton* (Woodforde), *Milton Hill* near *Wells* (Westcott) and *Weston-super-Mare* (Crotch)

— plantaginis, L. Heaths and woods near *Bath*, *Bridgwater* (Cottam), *Holford* on the *Quantocks* (Corder), *Stoke* (Walter), *Taunton* (Bidgood) and *Weston*

Arctia caja, L., is common in many parts, but seems to have become scarce in the neighbourhood of *Bristol*. The 'Woolly-bear' is certainly not a garden pest in north Somerset

— villica, L., is occasionally met with in woods and lanes near *Bath*, *Bridgwater*, *Brislington*, *Clevedon*, *Crowcombe*, *Stoke*, *Taunton*, *Wellington*, *Weston* and *Yeovil*. Some have been taken at 'light'

Spilosoma fuliginosa, L., is scarce and local near *Bath, Bathampton, Burnham* (Corder), *Backwell* (Prideaux), *Clevedon, Crowcombe, Leigh Woods, Quantocks, Taunton, Weston*

— mendica, O., and lubricepeda, Esp., are both generally distributed, and the last-named is often too abundant in gardens in the larval state

— menthastri, Esp., is common, but S. urticæ is very rare, only three specimens being recorded, one near *Bath* by Mr. Greer, one on a gas lamp at *Taunton* railway station by Mr. Bidgood, and another near *Taunton* by Mr. Rawlinson

Hepialus humuli, L., is common over mowing grass throughout the district

— sylvinus, L., is local and not common, near *Bath, Bristol, Brislington, Bridgwater, Castle Cary, Clevedon, Leigh, Sampford Arundel, Taunton, Weston*

— velleda, Hub. Scarce near *Bath* (Terry), common on hills near *Minehead* (Hudd), *Frome* (St. John), *Danesborough Hill* and the *Quantocks* (Corder), near *Bridgwater* (Cottam)

— lupulinus, L. Generally distributed and common

— hectus, L. Widely distributed, but local. In woods near *Bath, Bristol, Castle Cary, Clevedon, Frome, Quantocks, Stoke, Taunton, Weston*, etc.

Cossus ligniperda, Fab. The well-known 'Goat Moth' and its destructive larvæ are sufficiently common throughout the county

Zeuzera æsculi, L., the 'Wood Leopard,' is sometimes met with, but is scarce and local. Near *Bath, Bathampton, Bridgwater, Bristol, Castle Cary, Stoke, Taunton* and *Wells*

Liparis chrysorrhœa, L. Scarce and local, near *Bath, Castle Cary*, and at 'light' at *Taunton* (Tetley) and *Weston-super-Mare*

— auriflua, Fab. (similis, Fues.). Abundant everywhere

Leucoma salicis, L. Rare at *Bath* (Terry), near *Bath* (Greer), *Bathampton* (Ross), *Leigh Woods* (1869, by the Rev. Joseph Greene), *Wells* (Dr. Livett)

Psilura monacha, L. Scarce near *Bath, Castle Cary, Frome, Stoke, Weston-super-Mare* (Grigg)

Dasychira pudibunda, L. Generally distributed and sometimes common

Orgyia antiqua, L. Abundant everywhere in gardens

Trichiura cratægi, L. Not common. *Ashbrittle* (Milton), *Bath, Bridgwater,*

Clevedon, Glastonbury, Leigh Woods, Orchard Portman, Taunton, Yeovil

Pœcilocampa populi, L. Generally distributed and common

Eriogaster lanestris, L. Sometimes very common in the larval state

Bombyx neustria, L., B. quercus, L., B. rubi, L., and Odonestis potatoria, L., are generally distributed and common

Lasiocampa quercifolia, L. Scarce and local near *Bath, Bridgwater*—larvæ on turf moor (Corder), *Bathampton* (Ross), *Castle Cary, Clevedon, Glastonbury, Shapwick, Radstock* (Livett), *Stoke, Taunton, Wellington* (Milton)

Endromis versicolor, L. Recorded only from near *Bath* by Dr. Terry and *Leigh Woods* near *Bristol* by Mr. P. H. Vaughan. It has not been seen for many years in either locality

Saturnia pavonia, L. Hills near *Bath, Bridgwater, Brockley, Frome, Quantock Hills, Stoke, Taunton, Wellington, Weston.* Larvæ sometimes common

DREPANULIDÆ

Drepana lacertula, H. Mr. Harding used to take this species among birch trees at *Leigh*, but it has not been noticed there of late. A few specimens have been caught by Mr. Corder on the turf moor near *Bridgwater*, and by the Rev. A. P. Waller at *Shapwick*

— sicula, W. V. The first British specimen of this still rare species was captured in *Leigh Woods* in May, 1837; a second was taken in June, 1856, by Mr. H. Bolt; and a third the same year by Mr. P. H. Vaughan. Five years then passed without any more captures, but in June, 1861, several specimens were taken by Messrs. G. Harding and C. Butler. Though every year the Leigh Woods were explored by several local collectors, no more D. sicula were seen till 1874, when Mr. W. H. Grigg captured three specimens and I met with one. Since 1874 a few specimens have rewarded the exertions of local entomologists most seasons. Mr. Grigg twice obtained eggs from captured moths, but Mr. Buckler, to whom they were sent, failed to rear the species, the larvæ dying while quite small. In September, 1875, Mr. Thomas beat a larva at *Leigh*, which was forwarded to and figured by Mr. Buckler, and produced an imago on June 12, 1876 (see 'Natural History of Drepana sicula,' *E. M. M.* xiv. 1–4, by W. Buckler). Many points in the life history of this interesting moth have still to be cleared up, among others the time of flight of the imago. Most of the specimens captured have been found at rest on low plants, the earliest and latest dates being May (end), 1837, and July 10, 1875. D. sicula does not appear to have been observed in England outside of Somerset. Some years ago I detected a slight difference between our form and those from the continent, which appears to be constant

Drepana falcula, Schiff. In woods near *Bath, Bathampton, Bridgwater, Clevedon, Leigh, Shapwick, Stoke-sub-Hamdon* and *Wells.* Not common

— hamula, Esp. Fairly common in oak woods throughout the county

— unguicula, Hub. Local and not often common, near *Bath, Brislington, Bridgwater, Brockley, Clevedon* and *Weston-super-Mare*

Cilix spinula, Sch. (glaucata, Scop.). Fairly common everywhere

PSEUDO-BOMBYCES

Dicranura furcula, L. Generally distributed but not common. *Ashton* and *Brislington* (Ficklin), *Bath, Bathampton, Bridgwater, Minehead* (Hudd), *Quantocks, Shapwick, Taunton, Weston-super-Mare*

— bifida, Hub. *Bath, Bathampton, Clevedon, Leigh Woods.* Mostly found in the larval state

— vinula, L. Fairly common everywhere

Stauropus fagi, L. Scarce and local. A fine specimen was found at rest in *Brockley Woods* by Mr. Jefferys in 1886. One was taken at *Taunton* in 1860 by Mr. Woodforde, and one of the curious 'lobster' larvæ was found by Mr. Ficklin in the *Leigh Woods* in August, 1877

Ptilophora plumigera, Esp. A single specimen is recorded from *Yeovil* by Mr. Parmiter

Pterostoma palpina, L. *Bath, Bathampton, Bedminster, Bridgwater, Clevedon, Minehead, Wells, Weston, Yeovil.* Not common

Lophopteryx camelina, L. Throughout the district, but not very common

— cucullina, Hub. One specimen was bred from a larva taken by Mr. Ficklin near *Bristol,* probably in the *Leigh Woods* in 1876

Notodonta dictæa, L. Not scarce near *Bath, Crowcombe, Clevedon, Leigh Woods, Taunton, Weston*

— dictæoides, Esp. *Clevedon, Leigh Woods, Weston-super-Mare.* Larvæ sometimes common at *Leigh,* but not easy to rear

— dromedarius, L. Scarce and local. The turf moor near *Bridgwater* (Corder), *Clevedon* (Mason), *Evercreech* (Todd), *Leigh Woods* (Vaughan), *Sampford Arundel* (Milton)

— ziczac, L. *Bath* (Greer), *Bridgwater, Brendon, Clevedon, Leigh Woods, Shapwick, Stoke, Taunton, Wells.* Several have been taken at light in the *Taunton* district, and the larvæ are sometimes common

— trepida, Esp. Recorded by the Rev. S. St. John from *Baltonsborough* near *Glastonbury*; from the *Leigh Woods, Bristol,* by Mr. Griffiths; and from near *Taunton* (pupæ taken by Mr. Crotch)

— chaonia, Hub. Scarce near *Bath* (Terry), *Brockley* (Sergeant, 1887), *Cleeve Coombe* (R. M. Prideaux, 1890), *Leigh Woods* (Vaughan and Bartlett), *Taunton* (Woodforde), *Weston* (Smallwood)

— dodonea, Hub. Recorded only by the Rev. E. Hallett Todd, who found some pupæ near *Evercreech*

Phalera bucephala, L. Abundant everywhere

Clostera curtula, L. Recorded only by Dr. Terry 'near *Bath,* rare, in May,' and Dr. Walter from *Stoke-sub-Hamdon*

— reclusa, Fab. (pigra, Hufn), is reported only by Dr. Walter from *Stoke.* Both these 'Chocolate Tips' used to be found near *Bristol,* but have not been met with of late years

Thyatira derasa, L., and T. batis, L. Both these beautiful species are found throughout the county, and are sometimes common at 'sugar' and flowers

Cymatophora ocularis, Gn. Scarce at 'light' and 'sugar.' Near *Taunton* (Tetley and others) and on the *Quantocks* (St. John)

— or, Fab. Scarce at 'sugar,' etc. Near *Bristol, Portishead, Stoke, Taunton* and *Orchard Portman*

— duplaris, L. Near *Bath, Bristol, Clevedon, Castle Cary, Leigh, Portishead, Stoke, Taunton, Wells, Weston,* etc. Not common

Asphalia diluta, Fab. Scarce in *Leigh Woods, Bristol* (Hudd), *Clevedon, Portishead, Stoke, Taunton* and *Weston-super-Mare*

Asphalia flavicornis, L. In birch woods. Not common near *Bristol*, *Clevedon*, *Leigh Woods*, *Stoke*, *Taunton*
— ridens, Fab. *Brislington* (Sircom), *Brockley* (Hudd), *Clevedon* (Mason), *Leigh Woods* (Grigg), *Stoke-sub-Hamdon*

NOCTUÆ

Byrophila glandifera, Hub. (muralis, Fors.). On old walls near *Bath*, *Bathampton*, *Bridgwater*, *Castle Cary*, *Clevedon*, *Stoke*, *Taunton*, *Wells*, *Weston-super-Mare*
— perla, F. Common everywhere
Demas coryli, L. *Ashbrittle* (Milton), *Bath*, *Brockley*, *Crowcombe*, *Bridgwater*, *Leigh Woods*, *Taunton*, *Portishead*. Not common
Acronycta tridens, Schiff. Near *Bath* (Greer), *Bristol*, *Bridgwater*, *Clevedon*, *Stoke*, *Wells*, *Weston-super-Mare* (Smallwood). Scarce
— psi, L. Common everywhere
— leporina, L. Near *Bath* (Greer), *Bathampton* (Ross), *Bedminster*, *Bridgwater*, *Castle Cary*, *Clevedon*, *Godney* near *Glastonbury* (Corder), *Leigh Woods* (Griffiths), *Stoke*, *Taunton*, *Wells*, *Witham Friary* (Todd). Not common
— aceris, L. Scarce and local. Near *Bath* (Greer), *Clevedon* (Jefferys), *Evercreech* (Todd), and *Weston-super-Mare*
— megacephala, F. Near *Bath* (Terry), *Bridgwater*, *Clevedon*, *Evercreech*, *Stoke*, *Taunton*, *Wells*, *Weston-super-Mare*, etc. Sometimes common at 'sugar'
— alni, L. Very scarce in the county. A few specimens only recorded from *Bathampton* (Ross), *Clevedon* (Mason and Sargeant), *Leigh Woods* (Greene), *Portishead* (Duck), *Taunton* (Buckland), *Wells* (Livett), and *Weston* (Smallwood). Larvæ on rose, alder, elm, hawthorn, etc.
— ligustri, F. Scarce and local. *Bathampton*, *Brislington* (Ficklin), *Bridgwater*, *Clevedon*, *Evercreech*, *Leigh*, *Orchard Portman*, *Portishead*, *Weston*
— rumicis, L. Common everywhere
Diloba cæruleocephala, L. Common everywhere
Leucania conigera, F. Generally distributed and not scarce ; at flowers, etc.
— lithargyrea, Esp. Common everywhere
— littoralis, Curt. Recorded only from the coast of the *Bristol Channel* by Mr. Crotch many years ago, and by Mr. George Harding in 1897
— comma, L., impura, Hub., and pallens, L., are all generally distributed and sometimes common

Leucania straminea, Tr., is found in marshy places near *Bridgwater*, *Clevedon*, *Glastonbury*, *Wells* and *Weston-super-Mare*, but is rare
Cœnobia rufa, Haw. (despecta, Tr.)., is very scarce in the county. A specimen was taken by Mr. Grigg at *Brislington*, and Mr. Mason has recorded a few from *Walton Moor* near *Clevedon*
Tapinostola fulva, Hub. Scarce near *Bath*, *Bridgwater*, *Bristol*, *Clevedon*, *Quantocks*, *Shapwick*, *Sedgemoor*, *Weston-super-Mare*
Nonagria typhæ, Esp. (arundinis, F.). Throughout the county where bulrushes grow ; especially common in the *Sedgemoor* district
— geminipuncta, Hatch. Marshy places near *Clevedon*, *Nailsea*, *Stoke-sub-Hamdon* and *Weston-super-Mare*. Larvæ sometimes common
Calamia lutosa, Hub. Near *Bridgwater*, *Bristol*, *Clevedon*, *Stoke-sub-Hamdon* and *Weston-super-Mare*. The moths may be found at rest on stems of reed, and are sometimes abundant
Gortyna ochracea, Hub. Near *Bath*, *Bicknoller*, *Bridgwater*, *Castle Cary*, *Clevedon*, *Evercreech* and *Weston*. Sometimes common
Hydræcia nictitans, B. Generally distributed and sometimes abundant at ragwort blossom and other flowers
— petasitis, D. Recorded only from *Taunton*, where a single specimen has been taken (Barrett, *Insects of British Islands*, v. 72)
— micacea, Esp. *Bath*, *Bridgwater*, *Brislington*, *Bristol*, *Castle Cary*, *Clevedon*, *Evercreech*, *Taunton*, *Weston*. Not common
Axylia putris, L., Xylophasia rurea, F., X. lithoxylea, F., and X. monoglypha, Huf. (polyodon, L.), are all generally common. X. sublustris, Esp., and X. hepatica, L., are rather more local, and X. scolopacina, Esp., is still more so, only having been taken near *Clevedon*, *Wells* and *Weston-super-Mare*
Dipterygia pinastri, L., used to be found by Mr. Crotch at *Weston*, and has been reported from *Stoke-sub-Hamdon*
Xylomiges conspicillaris, L., is occasionally found at light near *Taunton*, where several pupæ have been dug at roots of elms. Dr. Walter reports it from Stoke
Neuria reticulata, V., has been found near *Bath*, *Brislington*, *Castle Cary*, *Clevedon* and on the *Quantocks*

Neuronia popularis, Fab., is generally distributed and common

Heliophobus hispidus, Hub. Scarce and local, only reported from the *Quantocks* by Mr. St. John, and from *Stoke* by Dr. Walter. (The specimen taken by myself on *Clifton Down* in 1866 is the only Gloucestershire record)

Charæas graminis, L. Near *Bath, Bristol, Brockley, Clevedon, Quantocks, Stoke, Weston-super-Mare*

Pachetra leucophæa, V. The earliest recorded British specimens were said to have been taken near *Bristol* in the year 1816. One of these is now in the fine collection of Dr. P. B. Mason, of Burton-on-Trent. I have been unable to ascertain the exact locality of these captures, but in Rennie's *Conspectus*, p. 69, published in 1832, 'Somerset' is given as the only county for the species. None have been found in the west of England of late years

Cerigo matura, Huf. (cytherea, F.) Local and not common. Near *Bath, Bristol, Clevedon* and *Taunton*

Luperina testacea, Hub. Common everywhere
— cespitis, F. A single specimen was taken on *Leigh Down* near *Bristol* by Mr. Grigg in 1879, and Mr. Mason has met with a few at *Clevedon*

Mamestra abjecta, Hub., is found on the coast near *Weston-super-Mare* amongst Poa maritima, and M. albicolon, Hub., was taken in the same locality by Mr. Crotch and Mr. Knight ; M. anceps, Hub., is generally distributed, but not common ; M. furva, Hub., has been met with near *Bath, Clevedon, Glastonbury, Stoke* and *Weston* ; M. brassicæ, L., is too abundant everywhere, and M. persicariæ, L., is reported from *Bath, Clevedon*, the *Quantocks, Stoke, Taunton* and *Weston*, but not from the neighbourhood of *Bristol*

Apamea basilinea, Fab., A. gemina, Hub., and A. oculea, Gn., are common in most parts of the county ; A. unanimis, Tr., is reported from near *Bath, Bristol, Castle Cary, Clevedon, Stoke* and *Weston*, and is sometimes common at 'sugar' ; A. fibrosa, Hub., is reported from *Stoke* by Dr. Walter, and a single specimen was taken on the turf moor near *Bridgwater* by Mr. Corder

Miana strigilis, Cl., M. fasciuncula, Haw., M. furuncula, Vill., and M. arcuosa, Haw., are common nearly everywhere, and M. literosa, Haw., has been taken in many places in the county

Grammesia trilinea, B., and its variety bilinea, Caradrina morpheus, Huf., C. alsines, B., C. blanda, Tr., C. cubicularis, Bork., Rusina tenebrosa, Hub., and Agrotis puta, Hub., seem to be generally distributed, as also are A. suffusa, Hub., A. saucia, Hub., A. segetum, S., A. exclammationis, L., A. corticea, Hub., A. nigricans, L., and A. tritici, L. A. valligera, Hub., is reported only from near *Bath, Stoke* and *Weston-super-Mare*, a few specimens only ; A. cinerea, Hub., from *Bath, Clevedon* and *Weston* ; A. ripæ, Hub., formerly taken on the sands at *Weston* by Mr. Crotch, has recently been found there again by Mr. Harding ; A. aquilina, Hub., is scarce near *Clevedon* and *Weston* ; A. porphyrea, Hub., used to be common on heaths near *Bristol*, and is also found near *Bath, Bridgwater, Clevedon, Evercreech* and on the *Quantocks* ; A. agathina, Dup., is recorded only by Mr. Corder, 'larvæ taken on the *Quantocks*' near *Bridgwater*, and A. ravida, Hub., (obscura, Br.), by Mr. St. John from *Baltonsborough* near *Glastonbury*

Noctua glareosa, Esp., is reported only from near *Bristol, Clevedon, Castle Cary* and the *Quantocks* ; N. augur, F., from the same localities, and also *Bath, Bridgwater, Taunton* and *Wells* ; N. rhomboidea, Tr., from *Bristol* (Stainton), *Orchard Portman* (at 'sugar,' Woodforde), and *Taunton* (one specimen, Woodforde) ; N. plecta, L., N. c-nigrum, L., N. triangulum, H., N. brunnea, F., N. festiva, Hub., N. rubi, V., N. umbrosa, Hub., N. baja, Fab., and N. xanthographa, Fab., are generally distributed and often abundant ; N. dahlii, Hub., is recorded from near *Bristol* in Stainton's *Manual*, but I have been unable to find out his authority or the exact locality ; N. neglecta, Hub. (castanea, Esp.), has been taken at *Whatley* near *Frome* by Mr. St. John, and at *Weston* by Mr. Crotch

Triphæna janthina, Esp., T. fimbria, L., and T. interjecta, Hub., are generally distributed ; T. orbona, F., and T. pronuba, L., are abundant everywhere, and T. subsequa, Hub., is scarce and has been reported only by Mr. St. John from near *Frome*, and Mr. Macmillan from Castle Cary

Amphipyra pyramidea, L., A. tragopogonis, L., Mania typica, L., and M. maura, L., are common everywhere

Panolis piniperda, Panz., is plentiful in fir woods near *Bristol*, *Brockley*, *Clevedon*, *Portishead* and *Weston*

Tæniocampa gothica, L., T. instabilis, T. rubricosa, Fab., T. stabilis, V., T. gracilis, Fab., T. munda, Esp., and T. cruda, Tr., are all frequent visitors at sallow-bloom, and abundant as larvæ ; T. leucographa, Hub., is scarce at *Orchard Portman*, *Taunton* (Woodforde), and *Weston* (Crotch) ; T. opima, Hub. A few specimens from *Evercreech* (Todd), *Leigh Woods* near *Bristol*, *Orchard Portman* and *Taunton* ; T. populeti, Fab. *Bathampton* (Ross), *Taunton* (Woodforde), and *Weston* (Crotch)

Orthosia upsilon, Bork., is occasionally found near *Bath*, *Bristol*, *Bridgwater* and *Evercreech* ; O. lota, C., O. macilenta, Hub., Anchocelis rufina, L., A. pisticina, Fab., A. lunosa, Haw., A. litura, L., Cerastis vaccinii, L., C. spadicea, Hub., and S. satellitia, L., are all more or less common at ivy and 'sugar' throughout the county

Cerastis erythrocephala, F., has been taken at *Wells* by Dr. Livett, and at *Weston* by Mr. Crotch, and Dasycampa rubiginea, Fab., in the same places, and also near *Bristol*, *Bridgwater*, *Clevedon*, *Crowcombe*, *Glastonbury* and *Taunton*

Hoporina croceago, F., is very scarce, but a few have been met with near *Bristol*, *Crowcombe* and *Weston-super-Mare*

Xanthia citrago, L., is recorded only from *Bathampton* (Ross), *Bridgwater*, *Bristol*, *Castle Cary* and *Weston* ; X. cerago, F., X. silago, Hub., X. aurago, F., and X. ferruginea, Esp., are generally distributed and sometimes common. X. gilvago, Esp., is very rare, only two specimens having been recorded from *Clevedon* by Mr. Mason

Cirrhœdia xerampelina, Hub., has been found somewhat plentifully near *Bristol*, *Bath*, *Castle Cary*, *Clevedon*, etc., the pupæ being sometimes quite common at roots of ash trees

Tethea subtusa, F., has once been taken at *Clevedon* by Mr. Mason, and at *Weston* by Mr. Crotch, and T. retusa, L., is still more scarce, having been recorded only from *Brislington* by Mr. Vaughan

Euperia fulvago, Hub., is reported from *Keynsham* by Mr. Ficklin

Dicycla oo, L., from 'near *Bath*' (Dr. Terry only)

Calymnia trapezina, L., is abundant everywhere, and C. diffinis, L., and C. affinis, L., are generally distributed

Eremobia ochroleuca, Esp., is scarce at *Brislington* (Ficklin), *Taunton* (Woodforde), and *Weston* (Crotch)

Dianthœcia conspersa, Esp., has been taken in the *Leigh Woods* by the Rev. J. Greene, and near *Clevedon* by Mr. Mason ; D. capsincola, Hub., and D. carpophaga, B., are generally distributed and common ; D. cucubali, Fu., has been found near *Bath* (Greer), *Clevedon*, *Castle Cary* and *Weston* ; and a single specimen taken by Dr. Livett at *Wells* was identified by the late Mr. E. Newman as D. capsophila, Dup.

Hecatera dysodea, Hub., is recorded by Dr. Terry from *Bath*, and by Mr. Crotch from *Weston-super-Mare*

— serena, F., is more generally distributed. Near *Bath*, *Bristol*, *Castle Cary*, *Clevedon*, *Evercreech*, *Weston*, etc.

Polia chi, L., has been taken near *Bath*, *Clevedon* and *Yeovil*, and P. flavicincta, Hb., is common everywhere

Dasypolia templi, Th., is found at 'light' near *Bristol*, *Castle Cary*, *Clevedon*, *Taunton* and *Weston*

Epunda lichenea, Hb., has been reported from *Clevedon* (two specimens, Mason) and *Wells* ; E. lutulenta, Bk., from *Weston* by Mr. Crotch ; E. nigra, Haw., from near *Bath*, *Bristol*, *Clevedon*, *Nailsea* and *Weston* ; and E. viminalis, Fb., from most parts of the county

[Valeria oleagina, Fb. Specimens of this very rare insect are said by Stephens to have occurred near *Bristol* (*Illust. Br. Entom.* 1829), but probably in error]

Miselia bimaculosa, L. Dr. Leach's specimen, taken near *Bristol* in 1815, is still in the British Museum collection

— oxyacanthæ, L., is common everywhere

Agriopis aprilina, L., Euplexia lucipara, L., and Phlogophora meticulosa, L., are generally distributed and common

Aplecta herbida is local and not common, but has been taken near *Bath*, *Brockley*, *Bristol*, *Clevedon*, *Porlock* and *Weston* ; A. nebulosa, Huf., is reported from most of these places and also from *Castle Cary*, *Frome*, *Leigh* and *Taunton* ; A. tincta, B., has been found near *Bath* by Mr. Greer ; A. advena, Fb., near *Bath*, *Clevedon*, *Castle Cary*, *Glastonbury* and *Taunton*

Hadena adusta, Esp., *Bristol*, *Clevedon*, *Frome* and *Portishead* ; H. protea, B., H. dentina, Esp., H. oleracea, L., and H. thalassina, Rot., are generally common ; H. chenopodii, Fab., is very local near *Bath* (Terry), *Weston* (Crotch), and

Yeovil (Parmiter); H. suasa, Bork., is sometimes common at 'sugar' near *Bridgwater, Bristol, Clevedon, Portishead, Taunton, Weston*, etc.; H. pisi, L., on downs near *Bath, Bridgwater, Bristol* and *Weston*; H. contigua, V., is very rare near *Bathampton, Clevedon* and on the *Quantocks*; and H. genistæ, Bork., is not common but is found at *Bathampton, Brislington, Bridgwater, Castle Cary, Clevedon, Leigh, Portishead* and *Glastonbury*

Xylocampa lithoriza, B., is common in the northern part of the county, and Calocampa vetusta, Hb., C. exoleta, L., Xylina rhizolitha, Fb., X. semibrunnea, Haw., and X. petrificata, Fab., are not common but generally distributed

Asteroscopus cassinea, Hb., is found in all parts of the county, and is sometimes common at 'light'

Cucullia verbasci, L., and C. umbratica, L., are generally common [C. scrophulariæ, Esp., has once or twice been recorded, but requires confirmation]; C. absynthii, L., is found only on the coast near *Minehead*, where I have taken the larvæ; and C. chamomillæ, Sch., has once or twice been met with near *Bath* by Mr. Greer, and at *Clevedon* by Mr. Mason

Gonoptera libatrix, L., Habrostola urticæ, Hb., H. triplasia, L., Plusia chrysitis, L., P. iota, L., P. v-aureum, Gn., are fairly plentiful among flowers, and P. gamma, L., is, as elsewhere, probably the most abundant Noctua;[1] P. festucæ, L., is scarce and local, but has been taken near *Brislington* (Grigg), *Bridgwater* (Corder), *Clevedon, Sedgemoor* and *Weston-super-Mare*

Anarta myrtilli, L., is local on heaths and downs near *Bath, Bridgwater* and *Taunton*, and on the *Quantock* and *Blackdown Hills*

Heliodes arbuti, Fb., is local, but sometimes plentiful near *Bathampton* (Ross), *Castle Cary, Clevedon, Taunton* and *Weston*

Heliothis dipsacea, L., is scarce, but has been reported from *Bath, Clevedon* (one at 'light') and *Hinton St. George* (Hoskins); the very rare H. scutosa, Schiff., has once been found at *Weston* by Mr. Jones in 1877; H. peltigera, Schiff.,

has been taken at *Bath, Clevedon* and *Shapwick*, in *Wells* (Miles); and H. armigera, Hb., near *Bristol, Clevedon, Taunton* and *Weston*

Chariclea marginata, Fb., is found near *Bath, Bristol, Castle Cary, Clevedon, N. Curry* and *Weston*; Acontia luctuosa, Esp., has been recorded from near *Bath* and *Weston*; Erastria fuscula, Bork., from *Bath, Castle Cary* and *Weston*; Hydrelia uncula, C., from the moors near *Bridgwater* by Mr. Corder and Mr. Waller, and from near *Weston* by Mr. Crotch

Micra parva, Dup. One of the few British specimens of this pretty little species was captured on *Brean Down* in 1858 by Mr. Crotch

Phytometra ænea, Hub., Euclidia mi, Cl., and E. glyphica, L., are common on many heaths and downs

Catocala fraxini, L. A specimen was taken at 'sugar' in the *Leigh Woods*, close to the Clifton Suspension Bridge by Mr. Griffiths in 1880; C. nupta, L., used to be common near *Bristol*, and has been found at *Bath, Castle Cary, Clevedon, Evercreech, Leigh, Taunton, Wells* and *Weston*; C. sponsa, L., is reported only from near *Bath* and *Wells*

Aventia flexula, Sch., is scarce near *Bristol*, on the *Polden Hills* near *Street* (Corder), and *Sampford Arundel*

Toxocampa pastinum, Tr., has been taken by Mr. Woodforde at *Pickeridge Hill* near *Taunton*, by Mr. Mason at *Walton* near *Clevedon*, and by Mr. Crotch at *Weston*

Brephos parthenias, L., is sometimes plentiful among birch trees in *Leigh Woods*, and has also been recorded from near *Wells* (Westcott) and at *Bath* (Terry)[1]

GEOMETRÆ

Uropteryx sambucaria, Dup.; Rumia cratægata, L.; Metrocampa margaritata, L., and Epione apiciaria,[2] Schiff., are plentiful throughout the county. E. advenaria, Hb., is much more local, but is found near *Bath, Bristol, Portishead, Stoke, Taunton* and *Weston*. Venilia maculata, L., is found in many places, but seems to have become very scarce in some of its old haunts, such as the

[1] Both *Plusia illustris* and *P. orichalcea*, Hb., are given by Dr. Terry 'as rare near Bath in July,' but further evidence is required before we include them in our list, though the latter beautiful insect occurs in Gloucestershire.

[1] *B. notha*, Hub., and *Stilbia anomala*, L., are also recorded from near Bath by Dr. Terry, but require confirmation.

[2] Epione vespertaria, St., has been reported from near *Bath, Taunton, Stoke-sub-Hamdon* and *Wells*, but probably in error.

Leigh Woods and *Clevedon*. Angerona pruniaria, L., used to be common near *Bath* and *Bristol*, and is still found at *Clevedon*, *Portishead*, *Stoke*, *Taunton*, and *Weston*. Ellopia fasciaria, Schiff.; Eurymene dolobraria, L.; Pericallia syringaria, L.; Selenia illunaria, Hb.; S. lunaria, Schiff., and S. illustraria, Hb., are all found throughout the county where the respective food plants of their larvæ are plentiful. Odontopera bidentata, Cl.; Crocallis elinguaria, L., and Ennomos angularia, Bork., are common everywhere. E. tiliaria, Bork., and E. erosaria, Bork., are generally distributed, and sometimes common at 'light'; E. fuscantaria, Haw., seems to be more local, but is taken near *Bath*, *Bristol*, *Castle Cary*, *Clevedon* and *Taunton*. Himera pennaria, L., is common

Phigalia pilosaria, F.; Amphidasys prodromaria, W. V., and A. betularia, L., are generally distributed and not scarce. Nyssia hispidaria, W. V., used to be taken in some numbers at 'light' at *Taunton* by Mr. Spiller, but does not seem to be met with there now; it is also reported from *Bath* and *Stoke-sub-Hamdon*. Biston hirtaria is also recorded from the same places, but is never very common

Hemerophila abruptaria, Thn., and Cleora lichenaria, Huf., are generally distributed, and C. glabraria, Hb., has been once taken on the Quantocks near *Bridgwater* by Mr. Corder. Boarmia repandata, L., and B. rhomboidaria; Tephrosia crepuscularia, Hb., and T. buindularia, Bork., are fairly common. B. abietaria, Hb., is found among spruce firs in the *Leigh Woods* and at *Brockley*; T. extersaria, Hb., is occasionally taken in the same woods, and also T. punctulata, Hb., which is found also at *Weston-super-Mare* and near *Wellington*. Gnophos obscurata, Hb., is common in limestone districts

Pseudoterpna cytisaria, Schiff.; Geometra papilionaria, L., and G. vernaria, Hb.; Phorodesma bajularia, Schiff., and P. thymiaria, L., and Iodis lactearia, L., are reported from all parts of the county. Of the large emerald, G. papilionaria, Mr. Bartlett tells me the males may be caught flying round birch trees at night; he took a dozen in *Leigh Woods* on the night of August 3, 1892

Ephyra porata, F.; E. punctaria, L.; E. trilinearia, Bork.; E. omicronaria, Hb., and E. pendularia, L., are found in most woods, but the last is more local than the others, being reported only from *Bath*, *Clevedon*, *Leigh Woods* and *Weston*

Hyria auroraria, Bork., is very scarce and local, being recorded only from the turf moor near *Bridgwater* (Corder), *Taunton* (Spiller) and *Stoke* (Walter). Asthena luteata and candidata, Schiff., are generally distributed; A. sylvata, Hb., is reported from near *Bristol*, *Clevedon*, *Frome*, *Orchard Portman*, *Stoke* and *Taunton*; A. blomeri, Curt., among wych elms near *Bath*, *Bristol*, *Frome*, *Evercreech*, the *Quantocks*, *Weston*, etc. Eupisteria heparata, Haw., is very scarce near *Bristol*, *Castle Cary*, *Clevedon*, *Stoke* and *Taunton*, and Venusia cambrica, C., near *Bristol* and *Weston*. The genus Acidalia is well represented in the county, sixteen of the species being recorded. A. scutulata, Bork.; A. bisetata, Huf.; A. remutata, Hb.; A. imitaria, Hb.; A. aversata, L., and A. emarginata, L., are fairly common almost everywhere. The others are more local. A. trigeminata, Hw., is reported only from near *Bristol* (Stainton) and *Taunton* (Woodforde); A. dilutaria, Hb., from *Bath*, *Bridgwater*, *Minehead* and *Weston*; A. holosericata, Dup., from near *Bristol* and *Frome* (St. John); A. virgularia, Hb., is common in gardens amongst jasmine; A. ornata, Scop., has been taken at *Clevedon*, *Portishead* and *Stoke*; A. promutata, Gn., near *Bath*, *Bristol*, *Frome*, *Porlock*, *Wells* and *Weston*; A. subsericeata, Haw., near *Bristol*, *Clevedon* and *Weston*; A. immutata, L., at *Ashcott* near *Glastonbury* by Mr. Harding, *Shapwick Moor* by Mr. Waller, *Walton Moor* by Mr. Mason, and *Weston* by Mr. Crotch; A. fumata, St., on the *Quantocks* by Mr. St. John and near *Stoke* by Dr. Walter; and A. inornata, Haw., is not scarce on fir trees near *Bath* and at *Brockley Coombe*

Timandra amataria, L.; Cabera pusaria, L.; and exanthemaria, Scop., are common; and the variety of the latter, C. rotundaria, Haw., is occasionally found near *Bristol*. Corycia temerata, Hb., is reported from *Clevedon*, *Leigh Woods*, *Sidcot* and *Weston*; and C. taminata, Hb., from *Locksley Wood* near *Bridgwater* by Mr. Waller, and *Weston-super-Mare* by Mr. Crotch

Macaria alternata, Hb., has been reported from *Stoke* by Dr. Walter, from *Taunton* by Mr. Spiller, from two localities near *Taunton* by Mr. Stansell, from *Sampford Arundel* by Mr. Milton, and from *Yeovil* by Mr. Parmiter. M. notata, L., is much more local, having been found only near *Stoke*, *Wells* (Livett) and *Yeovil*; but M. liturata, Cl., and Halia wavaria, F., are widely distributed, and common

Strenia clathrata, L.; Panagra petraria, Hb.; Numeria pulveraria, L.; Fidonia atomaria, L., and F. piniaria, L., are generally distributed and common in suitable localities. Minoa euphorbiata, F., is scarce and local near *Bath*, *Brislington*, *Portishead* and *Weston*. Aspilates strigilaria, Hb., is reported from near *Bath*, *Sampford Arundel*, *Shapwick* and *Taunton*; A. citraria, Hb., near *Bath* (Terry) and *Wells* (Livett); and A. gilvaria, Fab., from *Nailsea* (Braund), *Stoke* (Walter), the *Mendips* near *Wells* (Livett), and *Weston-super-Mare* (Crotch)

Abraxas grossulariata, L., is abundant and variable. The Rev. Jos. Greene has bred some fine varieties from larvæ taken near *Bristol*. A. ulmata, Fab., is found in woods near *Bath*, *Bristol*, *Brockley*, *Clevedon*, *Stoke*, *Weston*, etc., but is not often common. [A. pantaria, L., 'said to have occurred in Oakhampton Park, Somerset' (Stainton's *Manual*, ii. 66), is not now included in the British list. No such place as 'Oakhampton Park' is known to me in the county.] Ligdia adustata, Schiff., and Lomaspilis marginata, L., are generally distributed

Pachycnemia hippocastanaria, Hub., has been taken by the Rev. St. John on the *Quantocks* near *Crowcombe*

Hybernia rupicapraria, Hb.,; H. leucophearia, Schiff.; H. aurantiaria, Hb.; H. progemmaria, Hb.; H. defoliaria, L., and Anisopteryx æscularia, Schiff., are generally distributed and sometimes abundant

Cheimatobia brumata, L., is common in most parts of the county, but C. boreata, Hb., is very local, being only reported from *Brislington* (Ficklin), *Leigh Woods* (Vaughan) and *Stoke* (Walter). Oporabia dilutata, Bork.; Larentia didymata, L., and L. pectinitaria, Fues., are common everywhere; L. multistrigaria, Haw.; L. olivata, Bork.; Emmelesia affinitata, St.; E. alchemillata,

L.; E. albulata, Schiff., and E. decolorata, Hb., are generally distributed; but E. unifasciata, Haw., is very scarce and local, having only been recorded from near *Weston* by Mr. Crotch and at *Bristol* by Mr. Harding

Eupithecia [1] venosata, Fb., is probably found everywhere amongst Silene inflata; E. consignata, Bork., has once been taken at *Portbury* (Clarke), and Mr. Woodforde caught two specimens at 'light' at *Taunton* in 1865. E. linariata, Fb., is not common, but is found at *Leigh*, *Portishead* and *Weston*; E. pulchellata, St., larvæ are sometimes common in foxglove flowers near *Clevedon*, *Minehead*, *Taunton* and *Weston*; E. centaureata, Fab., though absent from many of the lists, is probably generally distributed; E. succentaureata, L., is found near *Clevedon*, *Portishead*, *Walton* and *Weston*; E. subfulvata, Haw., is generally distributed but not very common; E. subumbrata, Gn., is scarce near *Bath* (Terry), and *Bathampton* (Ross); E. plumbeolata, Haw., near *Bath* (Terry), and *Weston-super-Mare* (Crotch); E. isogrammata, H.S., is common amongst Clematis in the northern part of the county. E. castigata, Hb.; E. lariceata; E. subnotata, Hb.; E. vulgata, Haw.; E. exiguata, Hb.; E. coronata, Hb., and E. rectangulata, L., seem to be found in suitable localities everywhere. E. satyrata, Hb., has been taken at *Yeovil* by Mr. Parmiter; E. virgaureata, Dbl., in *Leigh Woods* by Mr. Grigg and myself, and near *Glastonbury* by Mr. St. John; E. fraxinata, Crewe, was once taken at *Bathampton* by Mr. Ross; E. pimpinellata, Hb., used to be found on heaths and downs near *Bristol*; E. campanulata, H.S., larvæ not scarce in woods round Portbury; E. constrictata, Gn., I used to take on *Leigh Down* near *Bristol*; E. nanata, Hb., on heaths near *Bristol*, *Bridgwater*, *Evercreech*, *Taunton*, and on the *Quantocks*; E. albipunctata, Haw., in damp woods near *Bath*, *Clevedon*, *Portbury* (Greene), *Hutton* (Smallwood), etc.; E. expallidata, Gn., larvæ on golden-rod near *Bristol*, *Leigh*, etc., scarce; E. absyn-

---

[1] The genus Eupithecia does not seem to have been much studied or collected in the county, several of the lists received being marked with only two or three species from localities where many more are doubtless to be found. Nevertheless our catalogue contains no less than thirty-six species.

thiata, L., *Bath, Bristol, Castle Cary, Weston*, etc. ; E. minutata, Gn., scarce near *Bristol* ; E. assimilata, L., near *Bristol, Bridgwater, Frome* and *Weston* ; E. tenuiata, Hb., larvæ sometimes common in sallow catkins near *Bristol, Clevedon, Weston*, etc. ; E. subciliata, Gn., very rare near *Clevedon* (Mason) and *Weston* (Crotch) ; E. abbreviata, St., in oak woods ; E. dodoneata, Gn., scarce in *Leigh Woods* (Hudd) and near *Weston* (Smallwood) ; E. sobrinata, Hb., is found amongst juniper bushes near *Bath, Bridgwater, Clevedon* (Mason) and *Castle Cary* (Macmillan) ; E. pumilata, Hb., is not uncommon near *Bristol, Clevedon, Portishead* and *Taunton* ; and E. debiliata, Hb., has been captured at *Holford* near *Williton* by Mr. Corder

Lobophora sexalisata, Hb., has been found on *Walton Moor* near *Clevedon* by Mr. Mason, and at *Sampford Arundel* by Mr. Milton ; L. hexapterata, Schiff., is found on poplars near *Bristol* (Vaughan), *Clevedon, Stoke, Taunton, Weston* and *Yeovil* ; L. viretata, Hb., occurs in woods near *Bristol, Clevedon, Stoke* and *Weston* ; L. polycommata, Hb., near *Bristol* (Hudd), *Brislington* (Ficklin) and *Leigh* ; L. lobulata, Hb., near *Bath, Bristol, Clevedon, Taunton, Weston*, etc. [Thera simulata is marked on Mr. Crotch's list from *Weston*, but there are no other records from the county.] T. variata, Schiff., is common in fir woods, and T. firmata, Hb., is recorded from *Brockley Coombe* and *Weston* (Harding)

Hypsipetes ruberata, Fn., occurs near *Brislington* (Ficklin), *Clevedon, Stoke* and on the *Quantocks* ; H. impluviata, Hb., near *Bath, Bridgwater, Clevedon, Portishead, Stoke* and *Yeovil* ; H. elutata, Hb., is abundant everywhere. Melanthia rubiginata, Fb. ; M. ocellata, L. ; M. albicillata, L. ; Melanippe procellata, Fb. ; M. unangulata, Haw. ; M. rivata, Hb., and M. galiata, Hb., seem to be generally distributed, but not very common ; M. montanata, Bork., and M. fluctuata, L., are abundant everywhere ; M. hastata, L., has been taken near *Bath* (Greer) and *Clevedon* (Bird), and M. tristata, L., near *Brislington* (Vaughan), *Clevedon, Evercreech, Leigh* and *Stoke*. Anticlea sinuata, Hb., has only once been taken in Somerset, in *Orchard Wood* near *Taunton* by Mr. Spiller. A. rubidata, Fb. ; A. badiata, Hb. ; A. derivata, Bork. ;

Coremia propugnata, Fb. ; C. ferrugata, L., and C. unidentaria, Haw., are generally distributed. C. quadrifasciaria, L., is very scarce, and has only been recorded from near *Bath* (Terry), *Clevedon* and *Weston-super-Mare* (Crotch). Camptogramma bilineata, L., is abundant everywhere ; C. fluviata, Hb., is not scarce near *Bath, Bristol, Bridgwater, Clevedon, Sedgemoor, Taunton* and *Weston*. Phibalapteryx tersata, Hb. ; P. lignata, Hb., and P. vitalbata, Hb., are found in many localities. Scotosia dubitata, L. ; S. certata, Hb. ; S. vetulata, Schiff. and S. rhamnata, Schiff., are generall'y distributed and sometimes common . S. undulata, L., is very scarce, single specimens having been taken near *Bristol* by Mr. Bolt, near *Bridgwater* by Mr. Corder, and a few near *Clevedon* by Mr. Mason, and *Stoke* by Dr. Walter. Cidaria picata, Hb., is recorded from *Dodington* near *Williton* (Corder), *Taunton* (Woodforde), *Sampford Arundel* (Milton), *Stoke* (Walter) and the *Quantocks* (Waller). C. psittacata, Schiff. ; C. miata, L. ; C. corylata, Th. ; C. russata, Bork. ; C. immanata, Haw. ; C. suffumata, Hb. ; C. silaceata, Hb. ; C. prunata, L. ; C. testata, L. ; C. populata, L. ; C. fulvata, Fors. ; C. pyraliata, Fb., and C. dotata, Gn., are reported from all parts of the county. Pelurga comitata, L., is more local, being recorded only from near *Bath, Castle Cary, Stoke* and *Weston*

Eubolia cervinaria, Schiff., is local near *Bath, Bridgwater, Castle Cary, Clevedon* and *Weston*. E. mensuraria, Schiff. ; E. palumbaria, Bork., and E. bipunctaria, Schiff., are abundant in most places, especially on limestone. Mesotype lineolata, Hb., is abundant on the sandhills near *Burnham* and *Weston* ; Anaitis plagiata, L., is common everywhere. Chesias spartiata, Fuess., has been taken on the banks of the Avon near *Bristol* (Mann) and near *Stoke* (Walter). Mr. Crotch recorded the very local C. obliquaria, Bork., from near *Weston*, where it does not seem to have been seen of late years, but should be searched for. Tanagra chærophyllata, L., is widely distributed, and sometimes common in the central and southern parts of the county, but is scarce in the Bristol district

DELTOIDS

Rivula sericealis, Scop. Not scarce in damp woods near *Bristol, Castle Cary, Cleve-*

don, *Portishead*, *Leigh* and *Weston-super-Mare*. Herminia grisealis, Hb., is abundant everywhere ; H. tarsipennalis, Tr., is recorded from near *Bath*, *Bristol*, *Castle Cary*, *Clevedon*, *Leigh* and *Portishead*. H. cribralis, Hb.: Dr. Livett reported several specimens from the moors between *Glastonbury* and *Wells*, but none seem to have been observed there or elsewhere in the county of late. H. barbalis, Cl., is very scarce and local, recorded only from near *Bath* by Dr. Terry and from *Weston* by Mr. Crotch

Hypena crassalis, Fb., is very local amongst Vaccinium on downs near *Bridgwater* (Cottam) and *Porlock* (Corder) ; H. rostralis, L., is occasionally found in gardens near *Bath* (Terry), *Bridgwater* (Cottam), *Wells* and *Weston*. H. proboscidalis, L., is abundant everywhere. Hypenodes albistrigalis, Haw., and H. costæstrigalis, St., are found in woods near *Bristol*, *Clevedon*, *Portishead*, *Leigh*, etc., and sometimes come to 'sugar.' Schrankia turfosalis, Wk., is abundant in bogs and marshes near *Bridgwater*, flying at dusk (Barrett)

PYRALIDES

Cledeobia angustalis, Schiff., is fairly plentiful in August amongst stunted gorse bushes on the hills near *Dunster* and *Minehead*. Aglossa pinguinalis, L., and Pyralis farinalis, L., are generally distributed and common. P. glaucinalis, L., occurs near *Bath*, *Bristol*, *Brislington*, *Clevedon* and *Castle Cary*

Scoparia ambigualis, Tr. ; S. cembræ, Haw. ; S. dubitalis, Hb. ; S. mercurella, L., and S. angustea, St., seem to be generally distributed throughout the county. S. basistrigalis, Knaggs, is scarce, the only local specimens known to me being one caught in the *Leigh Woods* by myself and another from *Portbury* by Mr. George Harding. S. lineola, Curt., also occurs near *Bristol*. S. cratægella, Hb., is found near *Bristol*, *Brockley*, *Clevedon* and *Weston* ; S. resinalis, Gn., on trunks of trees near *Bristol* and *Clevedon* ; S. truncicolella, St., recorded in Stainton's *Manual* to have formerly been common near *Bristol*, is now rarely met with, but Mr. Mason has taken a few specimens at *Walton* near *Clevedon*. S. pallida, St., is common but local in marshy places on the banks of the *Avon* near *Bristol*, and near *Clevedon*

Stenopteryx hybridalis is common everywhere in grassy places. Pyrausta punicealis, Schiff. ; P. purpuralis, L. ; P. ostrinalis, Hb., and Herbula cespitalis, Schiff., seem to be generally distributed. Ennychia cingulalis, L., occurs near *Bristol*, *Bridgwater*, *Clevedon* and *Portishead* ; and E. anguinalis, Hb., near *Bristol*, *Bridgwater*, *Clevedon* and *Weston-super-Mare*. Agrotera nemoralis : a specimen of this rare insect was recorded from *Brislington* by Mr. Sircom, June 15, 1851. Endotricha flammealis, Schiff., has been found near *Bath*, *Bristol*, *Brislington*, *Bridgwater*, *Dunster* (Hudd), *Minehead* and *Weston-super-Mare*

Eurrhypara urticata, L., everywhere among nettles. Scopula lutealis, Hb., is reported from near *Bath*, *Bristol*, *Castle Cary*, *Clevedon* and *Weston* ; S. olivalis, Schiff., S. prunalis, Schiff., and S. ferrugalis, Hb., are generally distributed and common. Botys pandalis, Hb., is recorded only as a native of the county by the late Mr. Crotch, 'scarce near *Weston*' ; it occurs commonly in *Gloucestershire*. B. hyalinalis, Hb., and B. lancealis, Schiff., used to be found near *Bristol*, and the latter has been taken by Mr. Mason at *Clevedon*. B. verticalis, Schiff., is everywhere abundant ; B. fuscalis, Schiff., is found near *Bath* (Terry), *Brislington* (Sircom), *Portishead* (Duck) and *Weston-super-Mare* ; B. asinalis, Hb., common amongst Rubia peregrina throughout the county ; the presence of this species can always be detected from the white blotches made on the madder leaves by the larvæ. Mecyna polygonalis, Tr. : Mr. Mason met with a specimen of this rarity at *Clevedon* in 1895. Ebulea crocealis, Hb., is common among fleabane, and E. sambucalis, Schiff., among elders. Spilodes sticticalis, L., used to be common near *Bristol*, but seems to have disappeared from its old haunts of late ; it has also been reported from near *Bath* (Terry), and S. palealis, Schiff., has been taken on the *Quantocks* near *Bridgwater* by Mr. Corder. Pionea forficalis, L., is a garden pest everywhere in the larval state

Stenia punctalis, Schiff., a very rare species, was recorded from *Weston-super-Mare* by Mr. Crotch. Cataclysta lemnata, L. ; Paraponyx stratiotata, L. ; Hydrocampa nymphæata, L., and N. stagnata, Don., are all found in marshy places, on banks of rivers, etc., throughout the county

INSECTS

PTEROPHORI[1]

Platyptilia ochrodactyla, Hb., is occasionally found amongst tansy on the banks of the *Avon* near *Bristol* and at *Portishead*, but does not seem to have been recorded elsewhere in the county. P. bertrami, Rossl., is reported from *Portishead*, amongst yarrow, scarce. P. gonodactyla, Schiff., is common amongst colts-foot on railway banks, etc. Amblyptilia acanthodactyla, Hb., occurs near *Bristol* and *Weston-super-Mare*, and may sometimes be taken at ivy bloom ; A. cosmodactyla, Hb., is scarce near *Bath* and *Bristol*

Oxyptilus teucrii, Gr., is sometimes common on wood sage in *Leigh Woods, Brockley Coombe*, etc. ; O. parvidactylus, Haw., is taken occasionally at *Leigh, Portishead, Weston*, etc.

Mimæseoptilus bipunctidactylus, Haw., is not scarce on downs and hills near *Castle Cary, Clifton, Clevedon*, etc. ; M. zophodactylus, Dup., used to be taken on *Leigh Down* and other places near *Bristol* ; M. pterodactylus, L., is common in strawberry beds and amongst Veronica

Œdematophorus lithodactylus, Tr., is common amongst fleabane in August, on which plants the larvæ may be found in the previous month. Pterophorus monodactylus, L., is common everywhere. Leioptilus tephradactylus, Hb., is not scarce amongst golden-rod in the *Leigh Woods* and on the *Portishead* railway banks ; L. osteodactylus, Zell., is recorded from *Leigh Woods* and *Weston-super-Mare* ; L. microdactylus, Hb., occurs near *Bristol, Castle Cary, Leigh, Portishead*, etc., the larvæ being sometimes plentiful on hemp-agrimony

Aciptilia galactodactyla, Hb., is plentiful in the larval state on burdock, but the moths are seldom seen on the wing ; A. tetradactyla, L., is found at *Brislington* and near *Bristol* and *Weston* ; and A. pentadactyla, L., is generally distributed and common

Alucita polydactyla, Hb., is common in gardens amongst honeysuckle

CRAMBITES

Schœnobius forficellus, Thunb., is found occasionally near *Bristol, Brockley, Clevedon, Nailsea, Weston-super-Mare*, etc., but is

[1] The 'plumes' have not been much collected in Somerset, and with the exception of those recorded from the neighbourhood of *Bristol* we have little information as to the local species.

not common. Crambus falsellus, Schiff., has been recorded from *Minehead*, a single specimen caught by myself on the marsh near the sea in 1867, and from near *Bath* by Dr. Terry. C. pratellus, L. ; C. pascuellus, L. ; C. perlellus, Scop. ; C. tristellus, Fb. ; C. inquinatellus, Schiff. ; C. genicuellus, Haw. ; C. culmellus, L., and C. hortuellus, Hub., are generally distributed and often abundant. C. dumetellus, Hb., used to occur near *Bristol* and at *Portishead*, but I know of no recent captures ; C. pinetellus, L., is common in some places ; C. selasellus, Hb., has been taken by Mr. Macmillan near *Castle Cary*, and used to be found occasionally on the bank of the *Avon* near *Clifton*. C. chrysonuchellus, Scop., is common amongst Helianthemum vulgare

Anerastia lotella, Hb., has been taken by Mr. Macmillan on the coast near *Burnham*. Myelophila cribrum is common among thistles near *Bristol, Bridgwater, Cadbury Hill*, near *Yatton, Clevedon, Portishead* and *Weston*. Homœosoma sinuella, Fb., has been taken at *Clevedon* by Mr. Mason, and H. binævella, Hb., at *Weston* by the same collector. H. binævella and H. nebulella, Hb., are stated to be found near *Bristol* in Stainton's *Manual*, ii. 169–70. H. nimbella, Zell., and H. senecionis, Vaughan, *Leigh, Portishead*, etc.

Of the genus Ephestia there is some doubt as to old records, but E. elutella, Hb., is found probably all over the county, and other introduced species are quite sufficiently plentiful among dried figs, etc., in grocers' shops. Euzophera pinguis, Haw., occurs among old ash trees ; Cryptoblabes bistriga, Haw., is scarce, but has been found near *Bath, Bristol* (Stainton), *Leigh Woods* (Vaughan) and *Portbury* (Harding)

Phycis betulella, Goze, used to be found amongst birch trees in the *Leigh Woods*, and P. albietella, Z., among spruce firs at *Brockley Coombe*. P. carbonariella, F. (fusca, Haw.), and P. adornatella, Tr. (dilutella, Hub.), are reported from *Clevedon* by Mr. Mason ; and the last-named used to be taken on *Leigh Down*, not far from the Clifton Suspension Bridge, on ground now built over, where Pempelia palumbella, Fb., was also to be found in plenty. This latter insect is found on other heaths and downs in many parts of the county. Nephopteryx roborella, Zinck, is common in oak woods, and Rodophæa advenella, Zinck, amongst hawthorn hedges near *Bristol*, *Portishead*, *Clevedon*, etc. R. consociella, Hb., occurs near *Bristol*, *Clevedon*, *Leigh*, *Portishead* and *Weston*. R. tumidella, Zinck, is reported from *Leigh* and *Portishead Woods*. Oncocera ahenella, Zinck, is found near *Bristol*, *Bridgwater* and *Castle Cary*

Aphomia sociella, L., is generally distributed and common. Galleria melonella, L., is common near *Castle Cary* (Macmillan), and Meliphora grisella, Fb., is sometimes too abundant throughout the county where bees are kept

The *Tortrices* and *Tineina* have not had much attention paid to them by Somerset collectors either in the past century or at present. Mr. P. H. Vaughan and Mr. W. H. Grigg of Bristol have recorded their captures in the northern part of the county, and in the middle of the last century some rare species and a few additions to the British list were taken by Mr. Sircom of Brislington. With the exception of a list from Castle Cary and the neighbourhood, printed by Mr. Macmillan, we know little of the Micro-lepidoptera of the greater part of the county outside the Bristol district, and our list is therefore far from complete :—

TORTRICES

Tortrix podana, Scop. Generally common
— cratægana, Hb. Scarce ; in oak woods
— xylosteana, Linn. Abundant everywhere
— sorbiana, Hb. Common in oak woods near *Bath*, *Bristol*, *Brislington* and *Clevedon*
— rosana, Linn. Common everywhere
— diversana, Hb. *Bath*, *Castle Cary*, *Leigh Woods* ; scarce
— cinnamomeana, Tr. *Clevedon*, *Leigh Woods*, etc. The larvæ are sometimes common on larch
— heparana, Schiff. Common in woods
— ribeana, Hb. Common everywhere
— corylana, Fb. *Bath*, *Bristol*, *Castle Cary*, *Leigh*, etc. ; common
— unifasciana, Dup. Common amongst privet, etc.
— costana, Fb. *Clevedon*, *Keynsham*, *Leigh*, *Portbury* ; in marshy places
— viburnana, Fb.
— palleana, Hb. *Castle Cary* ; scarce
— viridana, Linn. Abundant everywhere
— ministrana, Linn. Common everywhere
— forsterana, Fb. Abundant in gardens among ivy
Dichelia grotiana, Fb. *Brislington*, *Clevedon* ; comes to 'sugar'
Leptogramma literana, Linn. *Bath*, *Bridgwater*, *Bristol*, *Castle Cary*, *Clevedon*, *Leigh Woods* ; not scarce in oak woods
— scabrana, Fb. *Bath*, *Bristol*, *Bridgwater*, *Clevedon* ; scarce
Peronea sponsana, Fb. *Bath*, *Bristol*, *Castle Cary*, *Clevedon*, etc. ; among beech trees

Peronea schalleriana, Linn. *Bath*, *Bristol*, *Bridgwater*, *Castle Cary*, *Clevedon*, *Leigh*, etc. ; among sallows
— comparana, Hb. *Brislington*, *Castle Cary*, *Clevedon*, etc. ; scarce
— variegana, Schiff. Common everywhere
— cristana, Fb. *Bath*, *Bristol*, *Clevedon*, *Portishead* ; scarce
— hastiana, Linn. *Bath*, *Bristol*, *Castle Cary* ; not common
— ferrugana, Tr. Common in woods and at ivy-bloom
— logiana, Schiff. (tristana, Hb.). *Bristol*, *Clevedon*, *Leigh* ; amongst Viburnum lantana
— aspersana, Hb. *Bath*, *Bristol*, *Clevedon* ; not common
Teras caudana, Fb. Widely distributed but not common
— contaminana, Hb. Common everywhere
Dictyopteryx lœflingiana, Linn. Common in oak woods
— holmiana, Linn. Amongst hawthorn ; common
— bergmanniana, Linn. Amongst roses ; the larvæ are sometimes destructive in rose gardens near *Bristol*
— forskaleana, Linn. *Bath*, *Bristol*, *Castle Cary*, *Clevedon*, etc. ; among maples
Argyrotoxa conwayana, Fb. Common among ash trees
Ptycholoma lecheana, Linn. Common in woods
Ditula semifasciana, Haw. *Bristol*, *Brislington*, *Clevedon*. Larvæ are sometimes found between leaves of sallow

Penthina corticana, Hb. (picana, Frol.). *Bristol, Castle Cary*; scarce in birch woods
— betulætana, Haw. *Bath, Clevedon, Leigh*; among birches
— sororculana, Zett. (prælongana, Gn.). A few specimens were taken in *Leigh Woods* by Mr. P. H. Vaughan
— pruniana, Hb. Abundant everywhere
— ochroleucana, Hb. *Bristol, Castle Cary*; among roses
— variegana, Hb. (cynosbatella, Wilk.). Common everywhere
— gentiana, Hb. Larvæ common in heads of teazles
— marginana, Haw. Taken by Mr. Vaughan on the bank of the *Avon* under *Leigh Woods*
Antithesia salicella, Gn. *Brislington, Castle Cary, Clevedon*. Scarce among willows; flies at dusk in June and July
Spilonota ocellana, Fb. Common everywhere. Mr. W. H. Grigg used to take the larvæ on Cratægus pyracantha in his garden
— lariciana, Zell. *Leigh*. Scarce amongst larch trees
— aceriana, Dup. *Bristol, Burnham*. On poplars; scarce
— dealbana, Frol. Generally common
— neglectana, Dup. *Leigh Woods*; scarce
— trimaculana, Haw. (suffusana, Zell). Common everywhere
— rosæcolana, Dbl. Abundant among roses
— roborana, Tr. A common garden pest
Pardia tripunctata, Fb. Common everywhere
Aspis udmanniana, Linn. *Bath, Bristol, Castle Cary, Clevedon*; plentiful among brambles
Sideria achatana, Fb. Formerly taken by Mr. Vaughan near *Bristol*, and reported by Dr. Terry from near *Bath*; not now found
Sericoris euphorbiana, Fr. Near *Bristol*. Mr. Grigg took a single specimen of this rare species on the Somerset bank of the *Avon*, near *Nightingale Valley, Leigh Woods*, in May 1880
— cespitana, Hb. Near *Bristol* and *Leigh Woods*; formerly plentiful but now scarce
— lacunana, Dup. Common everywhere
— urticana, Hb. Generally distributed and common
Euchromia mygindana, Schiff. Mr. Vaughan used to take this local species near *Pill*
Orthotænia antiquana, Hb. *Bristol, Castle Cary, Clevedon*; scarce
— striana, Schiff. *Bath, Bristol, Clevedon, Portishead*; common on tennis and croquet lawns

Eriopsela fractifasciana, Haw. *Leigh Down* near *Bristol*; they seldom fly, but may be found at rest on the grass
Phtheochroa rugosana, Hb. *Brislington, Clevedon*; scarce
Cnephasia musculana, Hb. Generally common
Sciaphila nubilana, Hb. *Bath, Bristol, Yeovil*; among hawthorn
— conspersana, Doug. *Castle Cary*; scarce
— subjectana, Gn. Generally common
— virgaureana, Tr. Generally common
— chrysantheana, Dup. *Bath, Bristol, Clevedon*; Mr. Grigg found larvæ on Inula conyza in July
— sinuana, St. Formerly near *Clevedon* (Stainton)
— hybridana, Hb. *Bath, Bristol, Castle Cary, Clevedon*
Sphaleroptera ictericana, Haw. *Bath, Bristol*, etc.; flies at night on railway banks; not common
Bactra lanceolana, Hb. Generally common in damp meadows
Phoxopteryx biarcuana, St. *Brislington, Castle Cary* and *Leigh Woods*
— lundana, Fb. Common in meadows
— derasana, Hb. *Brislington*; used to be taken by Mr. P. H. Vaughan
— mitterpacheriana, Schiff. Common in oak woods
— lactana, Fb. *Clevedon, Leigh, Portishead*; among poplars
Grapholitha ramella, Linn. *Clevedon, Leigh, Castle Cary*; among birches
— nisella, Cl. *Bristol, Brislington, Castle Cary, Clevedon, Leigh Woods*; larvæ common in sallow catkins
— cinerana, Haw. *Leigh Woods*; scarce among poplars
— campoliliana, Tr. (subocellana, Don.). *Bath, Castle Cary*; among sallows
— trimaculana, Don. Common among elms
— penkleriana, Fisch. *Leigh Woods*; sometimes common
— nævana, Hb. *Bristol, Castle Cary, Clevedon*; among holly
Phlœodes tetraquetrana, Haw. Generally common in woods
— immundana, Fisch. *Bristol, Castle Cary, Portishead*
Hypermecia cruciana, Linn. *Hanham, Saltford, Portishead*; among sallows
Batodes angustiorana, Haw. A common garden pest; the larvæ are partial to ripe grapes in my greenhouse
Pædisca bilunana, Haw. Sometimes plentiful among birch trees in *Leigh Woods*
— corticana, Hb. Abundant everywhere in woods

Pædisca profundana, Fb. Near *Bristol, Portishead, Yeovil*; among oaks

— ophthalmicana, Hb. *Bath, Bristol, Clevedon*; local and not common

— occultana, Dg. *Leigh Woods*; scarce among larch

— solandriana, Linn. Generally distributed

Ephippiphora similana, Hb. *Bath, Bristol, Castle Cary*; among birch

— cirsiana, Zell. Common in woods and fields

— pflugiana, Haw. Abundant among thistles

— brunnichiana, Frol. Abundant among coltsfoot

— turbidana, Tr. *Castle Cary*; among butter burr; scarce

— inopiana, Haw. Common on railway banks near *Bristol*, and on the banks of the *Avon* opposite *Clifton*

— fœnella, Linn. *Bath, Minehead*; not common

— nigricostana, Haw. *Leigh Woods*; scarce (Vaughan)

— signatana, Dg. *Leigh Down* (Vaughan)

— trigeminana, St. Common on railway banks, etc.

— tetragonana, St. *Brislington*; scarce

— populana, Fb. *Clevedon*; among sallows

— obscurana, St. *Leigh Woods*; bred from oak-galls

Olindia ulmana, Hb. *Castle Cary, Clevedon, Leigh*; scarce

Semasia spiniana, Fisch. *Leigh, Portishead*; not uncommon

— ianthinana, Dup. *Bristol, Clevedon*; among hawthorn

— wœberiana, Hb. Among fruit trees in gardens; common

Coccyx strobilella, Hb. *Leigh Woods*; among spruce

— argyrana, Hb. Common in oak woods

— tædella, Linn (hyrciniana, Usl.). Generally common among spruce

— nanana, Tr. *Clevedon, Leigh*; among spruce

Heusimene fimbriana, Haw. *Bristol, Clevedon, Leigh*; flies in the sunshine; scarce

Retinia buoliana, Schiff. Common in fir woods and plantations

— pinicolana, Db. *Brockley Coombe* and *Clevedon*; scarce

— turionana, Hb. *Clevedon* (Mason); among fir trees

— pinivorana, Zell. *Brockley Coombe* and *Clevedon*

Carpocapsa splendana, Hb. *Bristol, Leigh*; among oak

— pomonella, Linn. Abundant in orchards

Endopisa nigricana, St. (nebritana, Wilk.). *Bath, Brislington*; in pea-fields

Stigmonota perlepidana, Haw. *Belmont* near *Wraxall, Castle Cary, Clevedon*; among fir trees; common

— internana, Gn. *Castle Cary*; not common

— compositella, Fb. *Bristol, Brislington, Castle Cary, Portishead*; plentiful among clover in meadows

— nitidana, Fb. *Bath, Bristol, Portishead*; in woods

— regiana, Zell. *Bristol, Clevedon*; among sycamore

Dicrorampha politana, Hb. Banks of the *Avon* near *Bristol* and *Clevedon*; Mr. Grigg used to take larvæ in roots of tansy

— alpinana, Tr. *Bath, Bristol, Brislington, Keynsham, Leigh*; among tansy

— sequana, Hb. *Bath, Bristol, Clevedon, Keynsham*; local, but sometimes abundant on railway banks, etc., flying in the sunshine

— petiverella, Linn. Common everywhere among yarrow

— plumbana, Scop. *Castle Cary, Clevedon*; common on grassy banks

— plumbagana, Tr. *Castle Cary, Leigh*, etc.; larvæ in stems of yarrow

— acuminatana, Zell. *Brislington, Yeovil*; among ox-eye daisy

— simpliciana, Haw. *Brislington, Portishead*; among Artemisia, scarce

— tanaceti, St. *Keynsham* and near *Portishead*; among tansy in June and July

Pyrodes rhediella, Linn. *Bath, Bristol, Castle Cary, Clevedon, Portishead*; it flies over hawthorn in the daytime

Catoptria albersana, Hb. *Bristol, Brislington, Leigh Woods*; not common

— ulicetana, Haw. Abundant among furze

— juliana, Curtis. *Brislington* (Sircom)

— hypericana, Hb. Common among Hypericum

— cana, Haw. (scopoliana, Wk.). Plentiful among thistles

— scopoliana, Haw. *Leigh Woods*; among knapweed

— æmulana, Schil. *Portishead* railway bank; larvæ on golden-rod (Grigg)

— expallidana, Haw. *Leigh*; scarce (Vaughan)

— aspidiscana, Hb. *Leigh*, and on the *Portishead* railway bank; not scarce (Grigg)

Trycheris mediana, Fb. (aurana, Fb.). *Bristol, Brislington, Brockley Coombe, Castle Cary*; at rest on flowers, not common

Choreutes myllerana, Fab. (scintillulana, Hb.). *Brislington* and the banks of the *Avon* near *Clifton*; used to be common (Vaughan)

Symæthis pariana, Clk. *Bristol, Castle Cary*; scarce

— oxyacanthella, Linn. (fabriciana, St.). Abundant among nettles

Lobesia reliquana, St. (permixtana, Hub.). *Bristol* and *Leigh*; among oaks, flying in the daytime

Eupœcilia nana, Haw. *Leigh Woods*; among birch

— dubitana, Hb. *Bristol, Brislington, Leigh*; flies at dusk

— atricapitana, St. *Leigh Woods, Portishead* railway banks; among ragwort

— maculosana, Haw. Near *Bath, Castle Cary, Clevedon* and *Leigh Woods*; among wild hyacinth

— sodaliana, Haw. (amandana, H.S.). *Portishead*; among buckthorn

— hybridella, Hb. (carduana, St.). *Leigh Woods* and *Portishead* railway banks

— angustana, Hb. *Bath, Clevedon, Leigh*; not common

— curvistrigana, Wilk. *Leigh Woods*; larvæ common on golden-rod

— affinitana, Dg. *Avon* banks near *Clifton* (Grigg); among Aster tripolium

— udana, Gn. (griseana, St.). *Leigh Woods*; scarce

— notulana, Zell. *Brislington* (Sircom), *Clevedon*

— rupicola, Curt. *Brislington, Leigh Woods*; among hemp-agrimony

— roseana, Haw. *Clevedon* (Mason), *Portishead* railway banks; among teazels

— degreyana, Mch. *Portishead* railway bank under *Leigh Woods* (Grigg); scarce

— subroseana, Haw. Quarries on the *Avon* opposite *Durdham Down*

— ciliella, Hub. (ruficiliana, Haw.). *Bristol, Leigh, Castle Cary*; among cowslips

Xanthosetia zoegana, Linn. Generally distributed on dry hillsides and downs

— hamana, Linn. Plentiful among thistles

Chrosis tesserana, Tr. (aleella, Schz.). *Bristol, Castle Cary, Clevedon*; local

— bifasciana, Hb. *Leigh Woods*; a few specimens taken in May and June by Mr. Grigg and Mr. Harding; *Clevedon* (Mason)

Argyrolepia hartmanniana, Clk. (baumanniana, Schff.). Near *Bristol* and *Castle Cary*; scarce, in damp woods

— subbaumanniana, Wilk. *Leigh Woods*; scarce

— zephyrana, Tr. (dubrisana, St.). *Portishead* railway bank (Grigg); scarce

— cnicana, Dbl. *Castle Cary, Clevedon*; scarce, among thistles

— badiana, Hb. *Bristol, Clevedon*; among burdock; scarce

Conchylis dilucidana, St. Banks of the *Avon* near *Clifton*; larvæ common in stems of wild carrot

— straminea, Haw. *Bath* (Terry); in May, scarce

Tortricodes hyemana, Hb. Plentiful in oak woods

TINEINA

Lemnatophila phryganella, Hb. *Leigh Woods* near *Bristol*; scarce

Dasystoma salicella, Hb. Recorded from the *Quantocks* near *Crowcombe* by the Rev. Seymour St. John. It used to be common near *Bristol*, but has not been taken there of late years

Exapate gelatella, Linn. (congelatella, Clk). *Bristol, Brislington*; larvæ between united leaves of willow in July (Wilkinson)

Diurnea fagella, Schiff. Common everywhere

Epigraphia avellanella, Hb. *Bristol, Failand, Leigh Woods*; among young birch trees, not common

— steinkellneriella, Schff. *Bristol, Castle Cary, Leigh Woods*; among blackthorn, not common

Talæporia pseudo-bombycella, Och. *Bristol, Brislington*; larvæ on lichens

Fumea intermediella, Brd. *Bristol*; larvæ not uncommon

— radiella, Curt. *Bath*; in June, scarce (Terry)

Solenobia inconspicuella, Sta. *Bristol* district; larvæ on old walls

Psychoides verhuellella, Heyd. *Leigh Woods*; larvæ on Asplenium (Vaughan)

Xysmatodoma melanella, Haw. Near *Bristol*; larvæ on trunks of trees

— (Tinea) argentimaculella, Stn. The first specimen, taken by Mr. Sircom, is still, with the rest of his collection, in the possession of Mr. P. H. Vaughan of Redland, Bristol. Mr. Alan Hill also took some specimens near *Almondsbury, Glos.*, a few miles north of *Brislington*

Ochsenheimeria birdella, Curt. *Arno's Vale* near *Bristol*, and *Brislington*, by Mr. Sircom and Mr. Vaughan

Scardia corticella, Curt. (emortuella, Zell.). A specimen taken by Mr. Duck at *Portishead* is still in the collection of the Bristol Museum

— carpinetella, Hb. (parasitella, St.). *Leigh Woods*; scarce

— granella, Linn. Common in warehouses, etc.

— cloacella, Haw. *Bath, Bristol, Leigh, Portishead*; in woods

— ruricolella, Sta. *Leigh Woods, Taunton*, etc.

Scardia arcella, Fb. *Leigh Woods*, not rare (Vaughan) ; *Portishead*

Tinea ferruginella, Hb. *Leigh Woods*, scarce ; *Castle Cary*

— rusticella, Hb. Abundant everywhere

— tapetzella, Linn. Often too abundant in carpets and furniture

— albipunctella, Haw. *Brislington* and *Leigh Woods* (Vaughan)

— misella, Zell. *Castle Cary* ; scarce

— pellionella, Linn. Too abundant in houses

— fuscipunctella, Haw. Common everywhere

— pallescentella, Sta. Near *Bristol* (Grigg) and *Castle Cary* ; scarce

— lappella, Hb. *Brislington, Leigh, Portishead, Castle Cary* ; in woods

— nigripunctella, Haw. *Bath, Bristol* ; not common

— semifulvella, Haw. *Brislington, Leigh Woods, Castle Cary*

Phylloporia bistrigella, Haw. *Leigh Woods* ; among birches, scarce

Tineola biselliella, Sta. A household pest everywhere, in chairs, sofas, etc.

Lampronia quadripunctella, Fb. *Brislington, Leigh*, etc. ; among wild rose

— luzella, Hb. *Brislington, Leigh* ; scarce

— prælatella, Schiff. *Bristol, Leigh* ; among wild strawberry

— rubiella, Sta. Abundant sometimes among raspberry

Incurvaria muscalella, Fb. Abundant in hedges

— œhlmanniella, Hb. Common in the *Bristol* district

— capitella, Clk. *Brislington*, etc. ; among currant bushes

Micropteryx calthella, Linn. Common everywhere on flowers

— aruncella, Scop. *Bristol* (Stainton)

— seppella, Fb. *Bristol, Castle Cary, Clevedon* ; on flowers of veronica, etc.

— thunbergella, Fb. Abundant everywhere

— purpurella, Haw. *Bristol, Leigh Woods, Clevedon* ; common

— semipurpurella, St. *Leigh, Portishead* ; not common

— unimaculella, Zett. *Brislington, Leigh Woods*

— subpurpurella, Haw. Common everywhere

Nemophora swammerdammella, Linn. Generally plentiful

— schwarziella, Zell. *Bristol, Castle Cary, Leigh, Taunton* ; common

Adela fibulella, Fb. *Bristol, Brislington, Portishead* ; on flowers

— rufimitrella, Scop. *Brislington* (Sircom), *Castle Cary* (Macmillan), *Taunton* (Parfitt)

Adela sulzella, Schiff. (crœsella, Scop). *Bristol, Leigh, Portishead* ; in woods

— degeerella, Linn. *Bristol, Brislington, Portbury* ; scarce

— viridella, Linn. Abundant in oak woods

— cuprella, Th. *Brislington* (Sircom), *Portishead* (Duck)

Nematois cupriacellus, Hb. *Bristol, Leigh Woods* ; on teazels, scarce

Swammerdammia apicella, Don. ; combinella, Hb. *Bristol, Castle Cary, Clevedon, Portishead, Taunton* ; in gardens, not common

— lutarea, Haw. *Bristol, Castle Cary, Taunton* ; not common

— oxyacanthella, Dup. Common everywhere in hedges

— pyrella, Sta. *Bristol, Castle Cary, Taunton* ; common in gardens

— spiniella, Hb. ; cæsiella, St. *Castle Cary, Taunton*

Scythropia cratægella, Linn. *Bristol, Brockley Combe, Taunton*

Hyponomeuta plumbellus, Schiff. *Bristol, Leigh, Portishead* ; among spindle

— padella, Linn. Common in gardens

— cognatella, Tr. Common on spindle

— evonymellus, Linn. Near *Bristol* ; on Prunus padus

Prays curtisellus, Don. *Bristol, Castle Cary, Taunton*

Eidophasia messingiella, Fisch. *Brislington* ; flying over herbage before dusk, not uncommon (P. H. Vaughan)

Plutella cruciferarum, Zell. Abundant in gardens

— porrectella, Linn. *Bristol, Castle Cary, Leigh, Portishead*, etc. Common among rocket, Hesperis matronalis

Cerostoma sequella, Clerck. *Leigh, Brislington, Portishead* ; among sallows

— vittella, Linn. Generally common on tree trunks

— radiatella, Don. Abundant everywhere and very variable

— costella, Fb. Generally distributed in woods

— sylvella, Linn. *Bristol, Leigh, Portishead* ; in oak woods

— alpella, Schiff. *Portishead* ; among oak

— lucella, Fb. *Leigh Woods* ; scarce among oak

Harpipteryx scabrella, Linn. *Bristol, Leigh*, etc. ; not common

— nemorella, Linn. *Yeovil* ; scarce (Parmiter)

— harpella, Schiff. ; xylostella, Linn. Generally common among honeysuckle

Theristis caudella, Linn. ; mucronella, Scop. *Bristol, Brislington, Leigh Woods* ; commoner in the spring after hybernation

Phibalocera quercana, Fb. Abundant everywhere

Depressaria costosa, Haw. *Bristol, Brislington, Castle Cary, Clevedon, Portishead* ; among gorse

— flavella, Hb. ; liturella, Tr. *Bristol, Castle Cary, Keynsham* ; among knapweed

— umbellella, Sta. Abundant among furze

— assimilella, Tr. *Bristol* ; among broom, not common

— nanatella, Sta. *Bristol, Clevedon, Weston* ; among Carline thistle

— atomella, Hb. *Keynsham* (Sircom)

— arenella, Schiff. Common everywhere

— propinquella, Tr. *Castle Cary, Portishead* ; not common

— alstrœmeriana, Clk. Generally distributed among hemlock

— purpurea, Haw. *Brislington, Castle Cary, Portishead* ; not scarce

— hypericella, Hb. *Brislington, Leigh Woods,* etc. ; among Hypericum

— conterminella, Zell. *Brislington, Castle Cary* ; among sallow

— angelicella, Hb. *Leigh, Portishead* ; in damp woods

— ocellella, Fb. *Brislington, Portishead*

— yeatiana, Fb. *Bristol, Castle Cary, Portishead*

— applana, Fb. Common everywhere

— ciliella, Stn. Scarce near *Castle Cary*

— pimpinellæ, Zell. Taken by Mr. Sircom at *Brislington* in August, and by Mr. C. G. Barrett at *North Curry*

— discipunctella, H.S. ; pastinacella, Stn. Recorded from (*North Curry*) *Somerset* by Barrett (*E.M.M.* xiv. 160), *Portishead* (?)

— weirella, Stn. Scarce at *Castle Cary*

— chærophylli, Zell. *Yeovil* ; occasionally

— ultimella, Stn. Scarce near *Bristol,* and at *North Curry,* in thatch

— nervosa, Stn. Near *Bristol* ; larvæ common

— heracleana, Stn. *Bristol, Castle Cary, Leigh,* etc. ; larvæ common

Psoricoptera gibbosella, Zell. Not scarce on tree trunks in *Leigh Woods* (Vaughan)

Gelechia vilella, Zell. Recorded from *Somerset* by Barrett (*E.M.M.* xiv. 160)

— pinguinella, Tr. Near *Bristol, Keynsham,* etc. ; common on poplars

— populella, Hb. Among poplars and sallows

— lentiginosella, Zell. *Bristol, Brislington* ; among Genista, scarce

— ericetella, Hb. Common everywhere among heath

— mulinella, Zell. Common among furze

— sororculella, Hb. *Brislington* ; among sallow

Gelechia diffinis, Haw. *Bristol, Portishead* ; not common

— rhombella, Schiff. *Portishead* ; scarce, among apple

— distinctella, Zell. Taken near *Keynsham* by Mr. Sircom in 1851

Brachmia mouffetella, Schiff. *Brislington, Leigh* ; not common

Bryotropha terrella, Hb. Common everywhere

— senectella, Zell. *Leigh Woods* ; scarce

— affinis, Stn. *Bristol, Castle Cary, Portishead* ; on old walls

— umbrosella, Zell. *Burnham* (Macmillan)

— domestica, Haw. Common in gardens, etc.

Lita acuminatella, Sircom. First taken by Mr. Sircom at *Brislington,* and described by him in the *Zoologist* for 1850 ; larvæ on thistles

— maculea, Haw. *Bristol, Leigh, Portishead, Yeovil*

— maculiferella, Dg. *Bristol, Taunton* ; among Cerastium

— marmorella, Haw. *Portishead* ; scarce (Duck)

— obsoletella, Fisch. *Leigh, Portishead* ; larvæ on Atriplex

— atriplicella, Fb. *Leigh Woods* ; not common

Teleia proximella, Hb. *Leigh, Portishead* ; among birch

— notatella, Hb. *Leigh* ; among sallows

— vulgella, Hb. Common among hawthorn

— luculella, Hb. *Leigh* ; among oak (Grigg)

— scriptella, Hb. *Leigh, Taunton* ; among maple

— fugitivella, Zell. Scarce at *Castle Cary* (Macmillan)

— sequax, Haw. *Leigh* ; among rock-rose

Recurvaria leucatella, Clk. Common among hawthorn

Pœcilia nivea, Haw. ; gemmella, St. Scarce in *Leigh Woods* in July

Apodia bifractella, Mann. Common among fleabane

Ptocheusa inopella, Zell. *Leigh* ; among fleabane

Doryphora lucidella, Stn. Marshy places near *Portishead* in July (Duck)

Anacampsis tæniolella, Tr. Common on downs among Leguminosæ

— anthyllidella, Hb. Common among Anthyllis

Tachyptilia populella, Clk. *Bristol, Castle Cary* ; common

— temerella, Zell. *Brislington* (Vaughan)

Brachycrossata cinerella, Clk. *Bristol, Keynsham, Leigh, Portishead* ; amongst fern, common but local

Ceratophora rufescens, Haw. *Keynsham, Leigh*; flies at sunset

Cladodes gerronella, Zell. *Brislington, Hanham*; not scarce

Parasia carlinella, Dg. Common among Carline thistle

Cleodora cytisella, Curt. Abundant among fern on *Leigh Down* (Vaughan)

Chelaria hubnerella, Don. *Bristol, Castle Cary, Leigh*; common

Hypsilophus durdhamellus, Sta.; schmidiellus, Heyd. *Leigh*; among marjoram, on which the larvæ are sometimes plentiful in June

Harpella geoffrella, Linn. *Bristol, Castle Cary, Leigh, Portishead*

Dasycera sulphurella, Fb. Common in old woods and hedges

Œcophora minutella, Linn. *Brislington, Portishead*; common

— flavimaculella, Stn. (fulviguttella, Zell.). *Leigh, Brislington, Portbury*; among Angelica, not common

— angustella, Hb. *Brislington*; scarce

— lunaris, Haw. *Brislington*; scarce, on tree trunks (Vaughan)

— lambdella, Don. *Brislington, Hanham, Keynsham*, etc.; among broom

— fuscescens, Haw. *Bristol, Portishead*; not rare on heaths

— pseudospretella, Sta. Abundant everywhere

Œcogenia quadripunctella, Haw. *Bristol, Taunton*; at 'light'

Endrosis fenestrella, Scop. Abundant everywhere

Butalis grandipennis, Haw. Plentiful among furze on downs near *Bristol, Leigh*, etc.

— fusco-ænea, Haw. *Brislington*, by Mr. Sircom; *Portishead* (Duck)

— fuscocuprea, Haw. *Brislington, Leigh*; among Helianthemum

— variella, Stn. *Portishead*; scarce

Pancalia lewenhœkella, Linn. *Leigh Down* and *Portishead*; common

Acrolepia perlepidella, Stn. *Leigh Woods*. The larva was discovered there by Mr. Grigg mining in leaves of Inula conyza in the spring

— granitella, Tr. *Leigh, Portishead*; among fleabane

Röslerstammia erxlebenella, Fb. *Leigh Woods*. The larvæ were discovered by Mr. Grigg on leaves of the small lime, Tilia parvifolia

Glyphipteryx fuscoviridella, Haw. *Bristol, Pensford, Portishead*, etc.; plentiful

— thrasonella, Scop. *Avon* banks and *Portishead*; common

Glyphipteryx equitella, Scop. Common in gardens among stonecrop

— fischeriella, Zell. Common in grassy places

Perittia obscurepunctella, Stn. *Brislington* (Vaughan); among honeysuckle

Tinagma sericiella, Haw. *Keynsham* (Vaughan)

— stanneella, Fisch. *Brislington, Leigh Woods*; beaten from yews (Grigg)

— resplendella, Doug. *Brislington* (Sircom)

Argyresthia ephippella, Fb. *Leigh Woods* (Vaughan), *Portishead* (Duck)

— nitidella, Fb. Common among whitethorn

— spiniella, Zell. *Brislington* (Sircom)

— albistria, Stn. Common everywhere among sloe

— semifusca, Haw. *Portishead*; not common

— mendica, Haw. *Bristol, Castle Cary*; among sloe

— glaucinella, Zell. *Brislington, Leigh Woods, Portishead*

— retinella, Zell. *Castle Cary, Leigh, Portishead*; common among birch

— dilectella, Zell. *Bristol, Brislington*; among junipers

— curvella, Linn. *Castle Cary, Leigh*, etc.; in orchards

— sorbiella, Tr. *Leigh Woods*; scarce (Vaughan)

— pygmæella, Hb. *Bristol, Brislington, Hanham, Portishead*; among sallows

— gœdartella, Linn. *Bristol, Castle Cary, Leigh, Taunton*; among birch

— brockeella, Hb. Common in birch woods

— arceuthina, Zell. *Brislington*; among juniper (Sircom)

Cedestis farinatella, Dup. *Leigh Woods*; among fir, scarce (Grigg)

Ocnerostoma piniariella, Zell. *Leigh Woods*; among fir (Grigg)

Zelleria insignipennella, Stn. *Leigh Woods*; among yew, scarce (Grigg)

Gracilaria swederella, Th.; alchimiella, Scop. Common in oak woods

— stigmatella, Fb. *Castle Cary, Leigh Woods*; among sallows

— semifascia, Haw. *Castle Cary, Portishead*; not common

— elongella, Linn. Near *Bath, Bristol*, etc., in oak woods

— tringipennella, Zell. Common among plantain on railway banks

— syringella, Fb. Abundant among lilac in gardens

— auroguttella, Stn. *Leigh, Keynsham, Portishead*; among Hypericum

Coriscium brongniartellum, Fb. *Brislington, Keynsham*; among oaks

Coriscium cuculipennella, Hb. *Bristol, Portishead* ; among privet

Ornix avellanella, Stn. Common among nut bushes

— anglicella, Stn. *Bristol, Castle Cary, Leigh,* etc.; among hawthorn

— betulæ, Stn. Not scarce among birch in *Leigh Woods*

— fagivora, Frey. Bred from beech leaves by Mr. Vaughan

— guttea, Haw. *Bristol, Brislington, Castle Cary, Taunton* ; in orchards

Coleophora fabriciella, Vill. Banks of the *Avon* near *Keynsham* (Vaughan)

— alcyonipennella, Kol. *Brislington* (Sircom); among knapweed

— ochrea, Haw. *Leigh Down*; among Helianthemum

— lixella, Zell. *Leigh Woods* ; not scarce

— pyrrhulipennella, Tisch. *Leigh Down* ; among heath (Vaughan)

— albicostella, Haw. Abundant among furze

— anatipennella, Hb. *Bath, Bristol, Brislington* ; common

— ibipennella, Stn. *Leigh Woods* ; scarce among birch (Vaughan)

— conyzæ, Zell. One specimen was bred by Mr. Grigg from a larva found at *Leigh* feeding on Inula conyzæ

— therinella, Stn. *Leigh* ; among thistles

— troglodytella, Dup. Abundant among fleabane

— lineolea, Haw. *Bedminster* ; abundant in lanes

— murinipennella, Fisch. *Leigh Woods* ; three specimens (Grigg)

— cæspititiella, Zell. *Bristol, Clevedon, Leigh, Taunton, Yeovil* ; among rushes

— annulatella, Stn.; laripennella, Zett. ; abundant on the *Avon* banks near *Bristol*

— apicella, Stn. *Bristol* (Grigg), *Taunton* (Parfitt)

— virgaureæ, Stn. *Leigh Woods* ; among golden-rod

— juncicolella, Stn. *Leigh Down* ; among heath

— laricella, Hb. *Leigh* ; scarce, larvæ on larches

— albitarsella, *Leigh Woods* ; among ground ivy

— nigricella, Stn. Abundant among hawthorn

— fuscocuprella, Stn. ' *Bristol* ' is the only locality given for this species in Stainton's *Manual* (ii. 386). The larva is said to feed on hazel in the autumn 'in a nearly globular case.' I have taken such cases on nut leaves in *Leigh Woods,*

etc., but have not reared the moths (Hudd)

Coleophora gryphipennella, Stn. *Leigh Woods* ; among rose

— fuscedinella, Zell. Abundant among elms

— viminetella, Heyd. Banks of the *Avon* near *Bristol* and *Keynsham*

— olivaceella, Stn. *Bristol* ; one specimen by Mr. Grigg

— solitariella, Stn. *Taunton* (Parfitt)

— lutipennella, Zell. *Leigh Woods* ; common among birch

— limosipennella, Fisch. *Leigh Woods* ; larvæ on wych elms (Grigg)

Bedellia somnulentella, Zell. Scarce near *Taunton,* 1859 (Parfitt)

Batrachedra præangusta, Haw. *Keynsham, Leigh, Portishead* ; among sallows

Chauliodus chærophyllellus, Göze. *Castle Cary* ; scarce

Laverna propinquella, Stn. *Leigh Woods*

— lacteella, Stn. *Leigh Woods* (Grigg) ; among willow herb

— miscella, Schiff. *Leigh Woods, Brislington,* etc. ; among rock rose

— epilobiella, Sch. *Keynsham, Brislington, Leigh, Portishead*

— decorella, Stn. *Keynsham, Leigh,* etc. ; among willow herb

— atra, Haw. *Bristol, Castle Cary* ; larvæ in hawthorn berries

— vinolentella, H.S. Two specimens from *Leigh Woods* by Mr. Grigg

Chrysoclysta aurifrontella, Hb.; flavicaput, Haw. Common in hedges

Asychna modestella, Dup. *Taunton* ; among stitchwort (Parfitt)

— terminella, Dale. *Leigh Woods* ; among enchanter's nightshade

Antispila pfeifferella, Hb. *Leigh Woods* ; among dogwood

— treitschkiella, Fisch. *Leigh, Taunton* ; among dogwood

Stephensia brunnichella, Linn. *Leigh Down* ; not common

Elachista gleichenella, Fb. Among wild carrot on railway banks

— magnificella, Tgs. *Brislington, Leigh,* etc.; among Luzula in woods

— albifrontella. Plentiful on downs near *Bristol, Portishead,* etc.

— trapeziella, Stn. *Castle Cary,* scarce ; *Leigh Woods,* common

— cinereopunctella, Haw. Common in grassy places

— stabilella, Stn. *Portishead* railway bank under *Leigh Woods*

— bedellella, Sircom. *Keynsham, Leigh,* etc.; not common

— obscurella, Stn. *Leigh Down,* among grass

Elachista zonariella, Stn. Banks of the *Avon* near *Keynsham* (Vaughan)
— gangabella, Fisch. *Avon* banks under *Leigh Woods*
— tæniatella, Stn. Scarce at *Castle Cary*
— megerlella, Zell. *Leigh, Portishead, Taunton*; common in woods
— adscitella, Stn. *Brislington, Portishead* railway bank, etc.
— cerussella, Hb. Banks of streams among grasses
— biatomella, Stn. *Leigh Down* (Vaughan)
— collitella, Dup. *Failand, Leigh*; scarce (Vaughan)
— subocellea, Stn. *Taunton* (Parfitt)
— rufocinerea, Haw. Abundant everywhere
— cygnipennella, Hb. Abundant everywhere
Tischeria complanella, Hb. Common in oak woods
— marginea, Haw. Common among brambles
Lithocolletis roboris, Zell. Among oaks, not common
— hortella, Fb. *Brislington* (Sircom)
— amyotella, Dup. *Brislington*; scarce
— lantanella, Stn. Among guelder rose, larvæ common
— lautella, Zell. *Bristol, Brislington, Leigh*; among oak
— pomifoliella, Zell. Generally common
— coryli, Nic. Common among hazel
— spinicolella, Kol. *Brislington, Leigh*, etc.; in hedges
— faginella, Mann. Common among beech
— torminella, Frey. *Leigh Woods*; not common
— salicicolella, Sircom. *Brislington, Leigh*, etc.; among sallows
— carpinicolella, Stn. *Bristol*; scarce among hornbeam
— ulmifoliella, Hub. Common among birch
— spinolella, Dup. Common among sallow
— quercifoliella, Fisch. Plentiful among oak
— messaniella, Zell. Abundant among beech and evergreen oak
— corylifoliella, Haw. Plentiful among hawthorn bushes
— viminiella, Sircom. First taken by Mr. Sircom at *Brislington* and described by him in the *Zoologist* (vol. vi.). Mr. Vaughan says he never found them among sallows, but has taken larvæ in profusion on osiers near *Bristol, Hanham* and *Keynsham*, etc. It is also round at *Taunton*
— scopariella, Tisch. *Keynsham*, among broom (Vaughan)

Lithocolletis ulicicolella, Vaughan. First taken and described by Mr. Vaughan among furze near *Bristol*; also found at *Clevedon, Leigh*, etc.
— alnifoliella, Hb. Among alder near *Bristol, Brislington, Castle Cary*, etc.
— cramerella, Fb. Plentiful among oaks
— heegeriella, Zell. Generally common among oaks
— tenella, Zell. Scarce near *Bristol* among hornbeam
— sylvella, Haw. Common among maples near *Bristol*
— emberizæpennella, Bou. Scarce among woodbine at *Abbots Leigh, Brislington*, etc.
— nicelliella, Zell. Plentiful among hazel; *Bristol, Leigh, Portishead*
— schreberella, Fb. Among elms; *Bristol, Taunton*
— tristrigella, Haw. Abundant among elms
— trifasciella, Haw. Plentiful among honeysuckle
Lyonetia clerckella, Linn. Plentiful among apples
Phyllocnistis suffusella, Zell. Among poplar; scarce near *Bristol*
— saligna, Zell. *Taunton* (Parfitt)
Cemiostoma spartifoliella, Hb. *Brislington*; common (Vaughan)
— laburnella, Heyd. Abundant among laburnum
— scitella, Zell. Abundant in hedgerows
Opostega crepusculella, Fisch. *Brislington*; scarce (Sircom)
— spatulella, H.S. Taken at *North Curry* near *Taunton*, by Mr. C. G. Barrett, flying under elm trees
Bucculatrix aurimaculella, Stn. Common among ox-eye daisy
— ulmella, Mann. *Brislington* and *Leigh*; among oak
— cratægi, Zell. Plentiful among hawthorn near *Bristol*
— maritima, Stn. *Avon* banks near *Portbury* among sea aster
— boyerella, Dup. *Brislington*; among elm, not common
— thoracella, Thn.; hippocastanella, Zell. Larvæ abundant in leaves of small-leaved lime (Tilia parvifolia) at *Brislington* and *Leigh Woods*
— cristatella, Fisch. Common among yarrow
Nepticula atricapitella, Haw.; N. ruficapitella, Haw.; N. anomalella, Stn.; and N. pygmæella, Stn., are all generally plentiful in the larval state round *Bristol*, etc.
— oxyacanthella, Stn. Abundant among hawthorn

Nepticula viscerella, Doug. Scarce among elm
— catharticella, Stn. *Bedminster* ; not common
— septembrella, Stn. Plentiful at *Keynsham, Leigh Woods,* etc.
— intimella, Zell. *Brislington* (Sircom), *Keynsham* (Vaughan) ; among sallow
— subbimaculella, Haw. Abundant among oak
— argyropeza, Zell. Larvæ common at *Leigh* in fallen aspen leaves in October
— sericopeza, Zell.; louisella, Sircom. There are three specimens in Mr. Vaughan's collection taken at *Brislington,* two by himself and one by Mr. Sircom
— floslactella, Haw. Abundant among hazel
— salicis, Stn. Plentiful among sallow
— microtheriella, Stn. Abundant among hazel ; as many as thirty larvæ have been found in a single nut leaf
— turicella, H. Sch. (Tutt). *Clevedon* ; larvæ in beech leaves (Mason)
— ignobilella, Stn. *Bristol, Leigh* ; among hawthorn
— argentipedella, Zell. Among birch ; common

Nepticula tityrella, Doug. Plentiful among beech
— marginecolella, Stn. *Leigh Woods* ; plentiful among elm
— alnetella, Stn. *Bristol, Clevedon* ; among alder
— aurella, Fb. Larvæ plentiful in bramble leaves. Mr. Vaughan has found them also in leaves of Geum urbanum
— luteella, Stn. Plentiful among birch ; *Bristol, Leigh, Portishead*
— tiliæ, Stn. *Leigh Woods* ; among lime, Tilia parvifolia. Stainton says (*Nat. Hist. Tineina,* vii. 168), ' In this country this has only been noticed in the neighbourhood of Bristol '
Trifurcula squamatella, Stn. *Brislington* ; scarce
— immundella, Zell. *Brislington* ; among broom
— pulverosella, Stn. *Brislington* ; among wild apple (Vaughan)

NOTE.—At my request Mr. C. G. Barrett has kindly looked through the proof-sheets of this catalogue, and has made several additions and corrections to it.

DIPTERA

The Diptera, or two-winged flies, is an order of enormous extent, but these insects are not favourites either with collectors or with the general public. They are however of great use in the scavenger habits of their larvæ, though many are in this stage very injurious to plants, such as the Carrot-fly (*Psila rosæ,* Fab.) ; the Mangold-fly (*Pegomyia betæ,* Curt.), which mines the leaves of beet, mangold, etc. ; the Onion-fly (*Phorbia cepetorum,* Meade) ; the Crane-fly (*Tipula oleracea,* Linn.), which is sometimes the cause of enormous damage to corn and turnip crops, the grub gnawing the young plant just below the surface of the ground.

Quite lately one family, the *Culicidæ,* has attracted much notice from the discovery that one or two species of gnat of the genus *Anopheles* are the direct cause of malarial fever.[1]

CULICIDÆ
Culex ciliaris, L. *Freshford* (Charbonnier)
Anopheles bifurcatus, L. *Freshford* (Charbonnier)
CHIRONOMIDÆ
Chironomus plumosus, L. (Charbonnier)
TIPULIDÆ
Pedicia rivosa, L. *Wellington* (*E. R.* iii. 189)
Tipula oleracea, L. *Batheaston*
— gigantea, Schrk. ,,

TIPULIDÆ (*continued*)
Tipula nigra, L. *Shapwick* (*E. M. M.* xxviii. 268)
— scripta, Mg. *Wellington* (*E. R.* iii. 189)
— lutescens, F. ,, ,,
— ochracea, Mg. *Batheaston*
Pachyrrhina maculosa, Mg. *Batheaston*
BIBIONIDÆ
Dilophus febrilis, L. *Freshford* (Charbonnier)

[1] The families have been arranged in the order given by Dr. Sharp in the *Cambridge Natural History.*

BIBIONIDÆ (continued)
  Bibio marci, L.   Batheaston
  — leucopterus, Mg.   „
  — johannis, L.   „
  — clavipes, Mg.   Freshford (Charbonnier)
RHYPHIDÆ
  Rhyphus fenestralis, Scop.   Batheaston
STRATIOMYIDÆ
  Pachygaster ater, Pz.   Langport (Dale)
  Nemotelus uliginosus, L.   Minehead
  Oxycera formosa, Mg.   Batheaston
  — pulchella, Mg.   „
  — trilineata, F.   Puddimore Milton (Curt., B. E.)
  Stratiomys potamida, Mg.   Wellington (E. R. iii. 189)
  — riparia, Mg.   Wellington (E. R. iii. 189)
  — furcata, F.   Burnham
  Odontomyia viridula, F.   Minehead
  Chrysonotus bipunctatus, Scop.   Batheaston
  Sargus flavipes, Mg.   Batheaston
  — cuprarius, L.   „
  — infuscatus, Mg.   Freshford (Charbonnier)
  Microchrysa polita, L.   Batheaston
  Chloromyia formosa, Scop.   Freshford (Charbonnier)
  Beris vallata, Forst.   Freshford (Charbonnier)
  — chalybeata, Forst.   Freshford (Charbonnier)
  Actina tibialis, Mg.   Batheaston
LEPTIDÆ
  Leptis scolopacea, L.   Batheaston
  — tringaria, L.   „
  Chrysopilus auratus, F.   Freshford (Charbonnier)
  Atherix ibis, F.   Freshford (Charbonnier)
TABANIDÆ
  Hæmatopota pluvialis, L.   Batheaston
  Therioplectes micans, Mg.   Wellington (E. R. iii. 189)
  — tropicus, Mg.   Freshford (Charbonnier)
  Atylotus fulvus, Mg.   Wellington (E. R. iii. 189)
  Tabanus bovinus, L.   Wellington (E. R. iii. 189)
  — autumnalis, L.   Minehead
  Chrysops cæcutiens, L.   „
THEREVIDÆ
  Thereva nobilitata, F.   Freshford (Charbonnier)
  — plebeia, L.   Burnham
SCENOPINIDÆ
  Scenopinus fenestralis, L.   Freshford (Charbonnier)
BOMBYLIDÆ
  Bombylius discolor, Mik.   Batheaston
  — major, L.   „
  — minor, L.   Minehead

ASILIDÆ
  Leptogaster cylindrica, DeG.   Freshford (Charbonnier)
  Dioctria atricapilla, Mg.   Freshford (Charbonnier)
  — rufipes, DeG.   Batheaston
  — flavipes, Mg.   Minehead
  Antipalus varipes, Mg.   Batheaston
  Dysmachus forcipatus, L.   Burnham
  Asilus crabroniformis, L.   Batheaston
EMPIDÆ
  Empis tessellata, F.   Minehead
  — livida, L.   Freshford (Charbonnier)
  — nigritarsis, Mg.   „   „
  Rhamphomyia sulcata, Fln.   Batheaston
  Pachymeria femorata, F.   Freshford (Charbonnier)
DOLICHOPODIDÆ
  Dolichopus plumipes, Scop.   Batheaston
  — griseipennis, Stan.   Keynsham (Charbonnier)
  — æneus, DeG.   Batheaston
  Pœcilobothrus nobilitatus, L.   Keynsham (Charbonnier)
  Chrysotus læsus, W.   Freshford (Charbonnier)
  Argyra diaphana, F.   Freshford (Charbonnier)
PHORIDÆ
  Conicera atra, Mg.   Freshford (Charbonnier)
  Phora abdominalis, Fln.   Langport (Dale)
PLATYPEZIDÆ
  Callomyia leptiformis, Fln.   Leigh Woods (Dale)
CONOPIDÆ
  Conops quadrifasciatus, DeG.   Batheaston
  Sicus ferrugineus, L.   Minehead
  Myopa testacea, L.   Batheaston
SYRPHIDÆ
  Pipizella virens, F.   Freshford (Charbonnier)
  Pipiza noctiluca, L.   Freshford (Charbonnier)
  Chrysogaster hirtella, Lœw.   Minehead
  Chilosia maculata, Fln.   Batheaston
  — scutellata, Fln.   Freshford (Charbonnier)
  — pulchripes, Lw.   Batheaston
  — chloris, Mg.   „
  — mutabilis, Fln.   Freshford (Charbonnier)
  — albitarsis, Mg.   Batheaston
  — impressa, Lw.   Leigh (Charbonnier)
  — variabilis, Pz.   Batheaston
  — intonsa, Lw.   Freshford (Charbonnier)
  — œstracea, L.   Wellington (E. R. iii. 189)
  — cynocephala, Lw.   Batheaston

SYRPHIDÆ (*continued*)

Leucozona lucorum, L. *Batheaston*
Melanastoma quadrimaculatum, Ver. *Freshford* (Charbonnier)
— scalare, F. *Batheaston*
— mellinum, L. „
Platychirus albimanus, F. „
— peltatus, Mg. „
— scutatus, Mg. „
— clypeatus, Mg. „
— angustatus, Ztt. *Minehead*
Didea fasciata, Mcq. „
Syrphus lasiophthalmus, Ztt. *Leigh* (Charbonnier)
— umbellatarum, F. *Freshford* (Charbonnier)
— auricollis, Mg. *Minehead*
— cinctellus, Ztt. „
— balteatus, DeG. *Batheaston*
— bifasciatus, F. „
— luniger, Mg. „
— corollæ, F. *Minehead*
— annulatus, Ztt. „
— nitidicollis, Mg. *Freshford* (Charbonnier)
— vitripennis, Mg. *Leigh* (Charbonnier)
— ribesii, L. *Batheaston*
— grossulariæ, Mg. „
— lunulatus, Mg. *Minehead*
— albostriatus, Fln. *Batheaston*
— labiatarum, Ver. „
Catabomba pyrastri, L. „
Sphærophoria scripta, L. „
— menthrasti, L. *Minehead*
Xanthogramma ornatum, Mg. *Minehead*
Baccha elongata, F. *Minehead*
Ascia podagrica, F. *Batheaston*
Rhingia rostrata, L. „
Volucella bombylans, L. „
— pellucens, L. „
Arctophila mussitans, F. „
Sericomyia borealis, Fln. *Minehead*
Eristalis sepulchralis, L. *Midford*
— tenax, L. *Batheaston*
— arbustorum, L. „
— pertinax, Scop. „
— nemorum, L. „
— horticola, DeG. „
Myiatropa florea, L. „
Helophilus pendulus, L. *Ashton* (Charbonnier)
— lunulatus, Mg. *Shapwick* (*E. M. M.* xxviii. 268)
— trivittatus, F. *Cheddar* (Curt., *B. E.*)
Criorrhina oxyacanthæ, Mg. *Minehead*
— floccosa, Mg. *Batheaston*
— berberina, F. *Somerset* (Verrall)
Xylota segnis, L. *Minehead*
— lenta, Mg. „
— sylvarum, L. *Wellington* (*E. R.* iii. 189)

SYRPHIDÆ (*continued*)

Eumerus ornatus, Mg. *Freshford* (Charbonnier)
— lunulatus, Mg. *Freshford* (Charbonnier)
Syritta pipiens, L. *Batheaston*
Chrysochlamys cuprea, Scop. *Minehead*
Chrysotoxum arcuatum, L. *Wellington* (*E. R.* iii. 189)
— festivum, L. *Minehead*
— bicinctum, L. *Batheaston*
— cautum, Harr. *Minehead*
Microdon mutabilis, L. *Langport* (Dale)

MUSCIDÆ ACALYPTRATÆ

Blepharoptera serrata, L. *Freshford* (Charbonnier)
Dryomyza flaveola, F. *Freshford* (Charbonnier)
Tetanocera ferruginea, Fln. *Minehead*
— hieracii, Fabr. „
Limnia rufifrons, F. *Freshford* (Charbonnier)
— obliterata, F. *Freshford* (Charbonnier)
Elgiva albiseta, Scop. „ „
— cucularia, L. *Minehead*
Sepedon hæffneri, Fal. „
Psila fimetaria, L. „
Loxocera albiseta, Schrk. *Batheaston*
Platystoma seminationis, F. *Freshford* (Charbonnier)
Ceroxys pictus, Mg. *St. Vincent's Rocks* (Curt., *B. E.*)
Ptilonota guttata, Mg. *Freshford* (Charbonnier)
Seoptera vibrans, L. *Batheaston*
Acidia heraclei, L. „
Spilographa zoë, Mg. *Freshford* (Charbonnier)
Urophora solstitialis, L. *Minehead*
— aprica, Fln. *Minehead*
Tephritis vespertina, Lw. *Freshford* (Charbonnier)
Opomyza germinationis, L. *Freshford* (Charbonnier)
Sepsis cynipsea, L. *Batheaston*
Nemopoda cylindrica, F. *Shapwick* (Dale)
Saltella scutellaris, Fal. *Langport* „
Micropeza corrigiolata, L. *Batheaston*
Borborus geniculatus, Mcq. *Freshford* (Charbonnier)
Limnosina sylvatica, Mg. *Freshford* (Charbonnier)
Tichomyza fusca, Mcq. *Keynsham* (Charbonnier)
Sapromyza præusta, Fln. *Freshford* (Charbonnier)

ANTHOMYIDÆ

Polietes lardaria, F. *Minehead*
Hyetodesia erratica, Fln. *Freshford* (Charbonnier)

ANTHOMYIDÆ (*continued*)

Hyetodesia simplex, W. *Freshford* (Charbonnier)

— pallida, F. *Batheaston*

Spilogaster communis, Dsv. *Freshford* (Charbonnier)

Hydrotæa ciliata, F. *Batheaston*

— irritans, Fln. *Freshford* (Charbonnier)

Ophyra leucostoma, W. *Freshford* (Charbonnier)

Hydrophoria conica, W. *Batheaston*

Hylemyia strigosa, F. *Freshford* (Charbonnier)

Caricea tigrina, F. *Freshford* (Charbonnier)

Scatophaga lutaria, F. *Batheaston*

— stercoraria, L. „

Orygma luctuosum, Mg. *Minehead* (Charbonnier)

Cœlopa frigida, F. *Minehead* (Charbonnier)

TACHINIDÆ

Echinomyia ferox, Pz. *Wellington* (*E. R.* iii. 189)

— fera, L. *Minehead*

— ursina, Mg. *Leigh* (Charbonnier)

Micropalpus vulpinus, Fln. *Cheddar* (Charbonnier)

Olivieria lateralis, F. *Batheaston*

DEXIDÆ

Dexia vacua, Fln. *Cheddar* (Charbonnier)

Thelaira leucozona, Pz. *Cheddar* (Charbonnier)

SARCOPHAGIDÆ

Sarcophaga carnaria, L. *Minehead*

— atropos, Mg. *Keynsham* (Charbonnier)

— agricola, Mg. *Freshford* „

— nurus, Rnd. *Cheddar* „

MUSCIDÆ

Lucilia cæsar, L. *Batheaston*

— seratica, Mg. *Freshford* (Charbonnier)

Calliphora grœnlandica, Ztt. *Cheddar* (Charbonnier)

— erythrocephala, Mg. *Batheaston*

— vomitoria, L. *Burnham*

— sepulchralis, Mg. *Freshford* (Charbonnier)

Pollenia rudis, F. *Batheaston*

Musca domestica, L. „

— corvina, F. „

Pyrellia cadaverina, L. „

— lasiophthalma, Mcq. „

Mesembrina meridiana, L. „

Graphomyia maculata, Scop. *Cheddar* (Charbonnier)

Morellia hortorum, Fln. *Batheaston*

Cyrtoneura stabulans, Fln. „

Myiospila meditabunda, F. „

Stomoxys calcitrans. *Freshford* (Charbonnier)

ŒSTRIDÆ

Gastrophilus equi, F. *Wellington* (*E. R.* iii. 189)

— nasalis, L. *Wellington* (*E. R.* iii. 189)

Hypoderma bovis, DeG. *Batheaston*

HIPPOBOSCIDÆ

Ornithomyia avicularia, L. *Batheaston*

Stenopteryx hirundinis, L. „

Melophagus ovinus, L. „

BRAULIDÆ

Braula cæca, Nitz. *Batheaston*

HEMIPTERA

The Hemiptera include the bugs, plant-lice, etc., and are insects with mouth organs formed for piercing, and which gain their livelihood by sucking the sap of plants or the blood of insects. The number of species is very great, and although comparatively little attention has been paid to this order it is well worthy of special study. Dr. Sharp says, 'There is probably no order of insects that is so directly connected with the welfare of the human race as the Hemiptera; indeed if anything were to exterminate the enemies of the Hemiptera, we ourselves should probably be starved in the course of a few months.'

It is divided into two sub-orders, the Heteroptera and the Homoptera; the first of which, the bugs, contains about 430 British species; while the second is much more extensive, and includes the aphidæ or plant-lice, some of the most injurious of which are the Bean Aphis or 'Black Dolphin' (*Aphis rumicis*, Linn.); the Cabbage Aphis (*A. brassicæ*, Linn.); the Grain Aphis (*Siphonophora granaria*, Kirby), which attacks wheat, barley, oats and rye, sometimes doing much injury; the Hop

INSECTS

Aphis (*Phorodon humuli*, Schrank), which in some seasons has greatly ravaged the hop gardens of England; the Turnip Aphis (*Rhopalosiphum dianthi*, Schrank), which is most destructive to potatoes, turnips and swedes; it also attacks the tulip, crocus, fuchsia and numerous other plants, while in the autumn it infests the peach and nectarine; the 'American Blight' (*Schizoneura lanigera*, Hausm); and the Apple Aphis (*Aphis mali*, Fab.), both very destructive to apple trees.

The only rarity in the following list is *Aphelochorus æstivalis*, Fab., taken in the river Avon near Batheaston.

PENTATOMIDÆ
Corimelæna scarabæoides. *Burnham*
Podops inuncta, F. *Weston-super-Mare* (Blatch)
Sehirus bicolor, L. *Freshford* (Charbonnier)
Gnathoconus albomarginatus, Fab. *Minehead*
Sciocoris cursitans, F. *Burnham*
Ælia acuminata, L. *Minehead*
Neottiglossa inflexa, Wolff „
Peribalus vernalis, Wolff. *Weston-super-Mare* (Saunders)
Pentatoma baccarum, L. *Burnham*
— prasina, L. *Minehead*
Piezodorus lituratus, F. *Clevedon*
Tropicoris rufipes, L. *Batheaston*
Zicrona cœrulea, L. *Leigh Woods* (Charbonnier)
Acanthosoma hæmorrhoidale, L. *Batheaston*

COREIDÆ
Verlusia rhombea, L. *Burnham*
Coreus denticulatus, Scop. *Minehead*

BERYTIDÆ
Berytus minor, H.S. *Batheaston*

LYGÆIDÆ
Lygæus equestris, L. *Bath* (Saunders)
Nysius thymi, Wolff. *Minehead*
Plociomerus fracticollis, Schill. *Minehead*
Rhyparochromus chiragra, F. *Batheaston*
Stygnus rusticus, Fall. *Burnham*
Peritrechus geniculatus, Hahn. *Minehead*
Scolopostethus affinis, Schill. *Batheaston*
Drymus sylvaticus, F. „

TINGIDIDÆ
Orthostira parvula. *Batheaston*
Monanthia cardui, L. „
— costata, Fieb. *Langport* (Saunders, *Brit. Hem.*)
— quadrimaculata, Wolff. *Weston-super-Mare* (Saunders, *Brit. Hem.*)
— dumetorum, H. Schff. *Batheaston*

ARADIDÆ
Aneurus lævis. *Batheaston*
Velia currens, F. „
Microvelia pygmæa, Duf. *Batheaston*

HYDROMETRIDÆ
Gerris gibbifera, Schum. *Batheaston*
— najas, DeG. *Freshford* (Charbonnier)
— lacustris, L. *Midford*

REDUVIIDÆ
Reduvius personatus, L. *Batheaston*
Nabis lativentris, Boh. „
— major, Cost. „
— flavomarginatus, Scholtz „
— rugosus, L. „

SALDIDÆ
Salda saltatoria, L. *Minehead*
— orthochila, Fieb. „

CIMICIDÆ
Cimex lectularius, L. *Batheaston*
Lyctocoris campestris, Fab. „
Piezostethus galactinus, Fieb. „
Anthocoris nemoralis, Fab. „
— sylvestris, L. „
Triphleps niger, Wolff „
— minutus, L. „
Microphysa pselaphiformis, Curt. *Batheaston*
— elegantula, Baer. *Batheaston*

CAPSIDÆ
Acetropis gimmerthalii, Flor. *Batheaston*
Miris calcaratus, Fall. „
— lævigatus, L. *Freshford* (Charbonnier)
Megalocera erratica, L. *Batheaston*
— ruficornis, Fourc. „
Leptoterna ferrugata, Fall. „
— dolobrata, L. „
Lopus sulcatus, Fieb. *Weston-super-Mare* (Saunders, *Brit. Hem.*)
Phytocoris tiliæ, Fab. *Batheaston*
— longipennis, Flor. „
— varipes, Boh. „
— ulmi, L. *Batheaston*
Calocoris sexguttatus, Fab. *Batheaston*
— bipunctatus, Fab. „
— roseomaculatus, DeG. „
Oncognathus binotatus, Fab. „
Lygus pratensis, Fab. „
— lucorum, Mey. *Minehead*
— pabulinus, L. *Batheaston*
— contaminatus, Fall. *Freshford* (Charbonnier)

CAPSIDÆ (*continued*)
Camptobrochis lutescens, Schill. *Batheaston*
Liocoris tripustulatus, Fab. „
Capsus laniarius, L. „
Rhopalotomus ater, L. „
Dicyphus epilobii, Reut. „
— errans, Wolff „
Campyloneura virgula, H.S. „
Cyllocoris histrionicus, L. *Minehead*
— flavonotatus, Boh. *Batheaston*
Ætorhinus angulatus, Fab. „
Globiceps flavomaculatus, Fab. *Batheaston*
Orthotylus adenocarpi, Perr. *Midford*
Heterotoma merioptera, Scop. *Batheaston*
Malacocoris chlorizans, Fall. „
Harpocera thoracica, Fall. *Leigh Woods* (Charbonnier)
Atractotomus mali, Mey. *Batheaston*
Psallus ambiguus, Fall. „
— variabilis, Fall. „
— alnicola, D. and S. „
— sanguineus, Fab. „
— rotermundi, Schltz. „

CAPSIDÆ (*continued*)
Plagiognathus viridulus, Fall. *Batheaston*
— arbustorum, Fab. „
NAUCORIDÆ
Naucoris cimicoides, L. *Burnham*
Aphelochirus æstivalis, Fab. *Batheaston* (C. Broome)
NEPIDÆ
Nepa cinerea, L. *Burnham*
Ranatra linearis, L. *Midford*
NOTONECTIDÆ
Notonecta glauca, L. *Burnham*
v. maculata, Fab. *Glastonbury* (Dale)
Plea minutissima, Fab. *Clevedon*
CORIXIDÆ
Corixa geoffroyi, Leach. *Burnham*
— atomaria, Ill. *Clevedon*
— hieroglyphica, Duf. *Batheaston*
— sahlbergi, Fieb. *Clevedon*
— linnæi, Fieb. *Glastonbury*
— striata, L. *Midford*
— distincta, Fieb. *Clevedon*
— coleoptrata, Fab. *Midford*

HEMIPTERA HOMOPTERA

MEMBRACIDÆ
Centrotus cornutus, L. *Freshford* (Charbonnier)
ISSIDÆ
Issus coleoptratus, Geoff. *Batheaston*
CIXIIDÆ
Cixius pilosus, Ol. *Minehead*
— nervosus, L. *Batheaston*
CERCOPIDÆ
Triecphora vulnerata, Ill. *Minehead*
Aphrophra alni, Fall. *Batheaston*
— salicis, DeG. *Shapwick* (Dale)
Philænus spumarius, L. *Batheaston*
LEDRIDÆ
Ledra aurita, L. *Leigh Woods* (Charbonnier)
BYTHOSCOPIDÆ
Macropsis lanio, L. *Batheaston*

BYTHOSCOPIDÆ (*continued*)
Bythoscopus alni, Schr. *Batheaston*
— flavicollis, L. *Minehead*
TETTIGONIDÆ
Evacanthus interruptus, L. *Batheaston*
Tettigonia viridis, L. „
ACOCEPHALIDÆ
Strongylocephalus agrestis, Fall. *Batheaston*
Acocephalus nervosus, Schr. *Midford*
— albifrons, L. *Minehead*
— histrionicus, Fab. „
JASSIDÆ
Limotettix antennata, Boh. *Batheaston*
TYPHLOCYBIDÆ
Eupteryx auratus, L. *Batheaston*
PSYLLIDÆ
Psylla betulæ, L. *Minehead*
— alni, L. *Batheaston*

MYRIAPODA

Although it cannot be claimed that Somerset has been well worked so far as Myriapoda are concerned, since collections have been made at three localities only, it is not likely that further search will do much more than extend our knowledge of the distribution throughout the county of the species recorded in the subjoined list, and add a few species to it. Two or three species not yet obtained certainly await discovery, if their existence in Somerset may be inferred from what has been ascertained of their range in other counties in the south of England. Amongst the missing species which are common elsewhere may be mentioned *Lithobius melanops, Polyxenus lagurus, Glomeris marginata, Iulus sabulosus, I. pilosus* and *I. teutonicus*. Setting aside the last-named, about which there is room for doubt, it is safe to prophesy that the species here mentioned will be found as soon as collecting researches have been further extended.

Of the forms already discovered the rarest are unquestionably *Lamyctes fulvicornis, Polydesmus inconstans* and *Blaniulus fuscus*. Yet the scarcity or apparent absence of these species in other counties is probably attributable not so much to their rarity as to their having been overlooked or unsought for.

The specimens recorded below from Winsford were collected by Mr. F. C. Woodbridge. Winsford is a small village on the borders of Exmoor. Those from Blue Anchor and Leigh Woods were collected by Mr. R. I. Pocock. Blue Anchor is a small village lying between Watchet and Minehead on the coast of the Bristol Channel. Leigh Woods is situated in the extreme northern part of the county on the southern side of the river Avon, which here constitutes the boundary line between Somerset and Gloucestershire.

CHILOPODA

Centipedes

LITHOBIIDÆ

Short-bodied, swift-running centipedes, furnished with eyes and only fifteen pairs of legs.

1. *Lithobius forficatus*, Linn. *Syst. Nat.* ed. 10, p. 638 (1758).

Blue Anchor, Winsford, Leigh Woods.

The common large brown species met with everywhere under stones in gardens and backyards, as well as in fields and woods. Widely distributed in north and central Europe.

2. *Lithobius variegatus*, Leach. *Zool. Misc.* iii. 40 (1817).

Blue Anchor, Winsford, Leigh Woods.

This species is of peculiar interest on account of its being confined, so far as is at present known, to the British and Channel Islands. It is as large as the preceding, but may be at once distinguished by the different spinous armature of the legs and its variegated colouring.

3. *Lithobius melanops*, Newport. *Tr. Linn. Soc.* xix. 371 (1845).

Blue Anchor, Winsford.

Much resembling the preceding species in colour, but smaller and armed with 2 + 2 labial teeth.

4. *Lithobius calcaratus*, C. Koch. *Die Myr.-Gatt. Lithobius*, p. 86 (1862).

Blue Anchor, Winsford.

A smaller and blacker species than the last, with long antennæ and the legs of the last pair modified in the male. Widely distributed in central Europe.

5. *Lithobius crassipes*, C. Koch. *Die Myr.-Gatt. Lithobius*, p. 71 (1862).
Blue Anchor, Winsford.

Scarcely as large as *L. calcaratus*, paler and with shorter antennæ ; resembling a dwarfed *L. forficatus*, for the young of which it is frequently mistaken. Commonly distributed throughout central Europe.

6. *Lithobius microps*, Meinert. *Nat. Tidskr.* (3), v. 265 (1868).
Blue Anchor.

The smallest of the British species of *Lithobius* ; distinguishable by the small number of eyes on each side of the head.

7. *Lamyctes fulvicornis*, Meinert. *Nat. Tidskr.* v. 266 (1868).
Blue Anchor.

This species is no larger than *L. microps*. It is widely distributed on the continent, and, although infrequently met with, certainly ranges throughout the south of England. It is a small dark-coloured species, at once distinguishable from the species of *Lithobius* by the presence of a single eye on each side of the head, etc.

CRYPTOPIDÆ

Eyeless centipedes of medium length, with twenty-one pairs of short legs.

8. *Cryptops hortensis*, Leach. *Tr. Linn. Soc. Lond.* xi. 384 (1815).
Blue Anchor, Winsford.

Widely distributed throughout north and central Europe.

GEOPHILIDÆ

Long vermiform centipedes without eyes and furnished with a large but variable number of legs.

9. *Geophilus flavus*, De Geer. *Mèm. Ins.* vii. 561 (1778) (= *longicornis*, Leach).
Winsford, Blue Anchor, Leigh Woods.

Common throughout Great Britain and north and central Europe. This species is distinguishable by its long and cylindrical antennal segments.

10. *Geophilus carpophagus*, Leach. *Zool. Misc.* iii. 43 (1817).
Winsford, Blue Anchor.

Differing from the preceding and the rest of the British species by the 'ball and socket' method of articulation of its anterior sternal plates. Common in western Europe.

11. *Geophilus truncorum*, Meinert. *Nat. Tidskr.* iv. 94 (1866).
Blue Anchor.

This small and delicate species, which is widely distributed in the south of England and western Europe, is distinguished by the presence of three deep grooves on the anterior sternal plates.

12. *Linotænia crassipes*, C. Koch. *Deutschl. Crust.* etc., pt. 3, pl. 3 (1835).
Leigh Woods.

13. *Linotænia acuminata*, Leach. *Zool. Misc.* iii. 45 (1817).
Leigh Woods.

These two nearly allied species ot *Linotænia* are the two common British luminous centipedes which so frequently attract attention on damp evenings in the autumn by the emission of a phosphorescent secretion from their sternal glands. *L. crassipes* may be distinguished, amongst other characters, from *L. acuminata* by the deeper emargination of the anterior border of the coxal plate of the poison-jaws.

14. *Linotænia maritima*, Leach. *Zool. Misc.* iii. 44 (1817).
Portishead, near Avonmouth.

This species is nearly allied to *L. acuminata*, but is much larger. It is generally distributed in suitable localities round the shores of Great Britain and the continental coasts of the English Channel and North Sea. It occurs beneath stones between tide-marks or under cast-up seaweed. It was found by Mr. Pocock in vast numbers on a pebbly beach some two miles south of Portishead, under an accumulation of decaying seaweed marking the last high tide.

15. *Schendyla nemorensis*, C. Koch. *Deutschl. Crust.* ctc. pt. 3, pl. 4 (1837).
Blue Anchor, Winsford.

A small, delicate and widely distributed species, much resembling *G. truncorum* in size and general appearance.

16. *Stigmatogaster subterraneus*, Leach. *Tr. Linn. Soc. Lond.* xi. 385 (1815).
Blue Anchor, Winsford.

Widely distributed in Great Britain and the adjacent countries of Europe. Distinguished from the rest of the British species by its inflated porous anal pleuræ, and large number of segments.

MYRIAPODA

DIPLOPODA

Millipedes

POLYDESMIDÆ

Millipedes in which there are from nineteen to twenty body-segments, most of which are furnished, at least in the British species, with scent pores supported on larger or smaller lateral crests or keels.

17. *Polydesmus complanatus*, Linn. *Faun. Suecic.* ed. 2, p. 502 (1761).

Blue Anchor, Winsford.

The commonest and largest British species.

18. *Polydesmus inconstans*, Latzel. *Bull. Soc. Rouen* (2), xix. 269 (1883).

Blue Anchor.

A smaller and much scarcer species than the foregoing. Occurs also in the north of France and western Germany.

19. *Brachydesmus superus*, Latzel. *Die Myr. Öst. Ung. Mon.* ii. p. 130 (1884).

Blue Anchor.

Widely distributed in England and central Europe. The only species of the genus found in Great Britain. Distinguishable from the species of *Polydesmus* by possessing only nineteen body segments.

CHORDEUMIDÆ

Millipedes with thirty or thirty-two body segments furnished dorsally with six symmetrically disposed bristles, without pores and usually keeled like those of the *Polydesmus*.

20. *Atractosoma polydesmoides*, Leach. *Zool. Misc.* iii. 36 (1817).

Leigh Woods.

Widely distributed throughout the south of England and on the continent. With its large lateral keels, this species closely resembles an elongated *Polydesmus*.

IULIDÆ

Cylindrical millipedes with a large but variable number of segments, furnished with repugnatorial pores, but without large lateral plates.

21. *Iulus niger*, Leach. *Zool. Misc.* iii. p. 34 (1817).

Blue Anchor.

A large black species with a longish pointed tail and transverse grooves on the anterior portion of the segments. Common throughout England and the western countries of Europe.

22. *Iulus ligulifer*, Latzel. *Berl. Ent. Zeits.* xxxvi. 152 (1891).

Blue Anchor, Winsford.

Resembling the last in colour and the presence of a long pointed caudal process, but smaller and hairier and without transverse grooves on the anterior portion of the segments. Scarce in England, but widely distributed in central Europe.

23. *Iulus punctatus*, Leach. *Zool. Misc.* iii. 34 (1817).

Blue Anchor, Winsford, Leigh Woods.

A pale-coloured species with a lateral row of darker spots, and a bluntly clavate caudal process. Found in rotten wood. Distributed everywhere throughout central and northern Europe.

24. *Iulus britannicus*, Verhoeff. *Berl. Ent. Zeits.* xxxvi. 147 (1891.

Winsford.

A small brown species without caudal process. Fairly common in the south of England and western Europe.

25. *Iulus pusillus*, Leach. *Tr. Linn. Soc.* xi. 379 (1814).

Winsford.

A small black tailless species, with yellow dorsal band. Widely distributed, but not of common occurrence in England and the countries of western and central Europe.

26. *Blaniulus guttulatus*, Bosc. *Bull. Soc. Phil.* p. 12 (1792).

Blue Anchor.

A long, slender, eyeless species with the anterior extremity of the body pale and a line of blood-red spots on each side of the body. Widely distributed in Great Britain and central and northern Europe.

27. *Blaniulus fuscus*, Stein. *Jahr, Nat. Les. Graubündens*, p. 139 (1857).

Blue Anchor.

Not nearly so common in England as the preceding species, from which it may be at once distinguished by the presence of eyes. Widely distributed in central Europe.

ARACHNIDA

Two small collections only, including thirty-one species, have come to hand from the county of Somerset, one made at Clifton in the Leigh Woods, the other in the suburbs of Bristol, by Messrs. R. I. Pocock and F. P. Smith respectively.

ARANEÆ

ARACHNOMORPHÆ

DRASSIDÆ

Spiders with eight eyes, situated in two transverse rows. The tracheal openings lie immediately in front of the spinners. The tarsal claws are two in number, but the anterior pair of spinners are set wide apart at their base, and the maxillæ are deeply impressed across the middle.

1. *Drassodes lapidosus* (Walckenaer).
   Leigh Woods (R. I. P.).

2. *Prosthesima latreillii*, Simon.
   Leigh Woods (R. I. P.).

3. *Prosthesima pedestris* (C. L. Koch).
   Leigh Woods (R. I. P.).

PISAURIDÆ

Spiders with eight eyes in three rows, and three tarsal claws. The first row of eyes consists of four small eyes which are sometimes in a straight line, sometimes recurved and sometimes procurved. Those of the other two rows are situated in a rectangle of various proportions. *Pisaura* runs freely over the herbage, carrying its egg-sac beneath the body.

4. *Pisaura mirabilis* (Clerck).
   Bristol (F. P. S.).
   Very common; adult in June and July. Known also as *Dolomedes* or *Ocyale mirabilis*.

LYCOSIDÆ

The members of this family have also eight eyes, similarly situated to those of the *Pisauridæ*, the tarsal claws also being three in number. The spiders are to be found running freely and carrying their egg-sac attached to the spinners. Many of the larger species make a short burrow in the soil and there keep guard over the egg-sac.

5. *Lycosa ruricola* (De Geer).
   Leigh Woods (R. I. P.).

6. *Lycosa pulverulenta* (Clerck).
   Leigh Woods (R. I. P.).

7. *Pardosa amentata* (Clerck).
   Bristol (F. P. S.).

AGELENIDÆ

Spiders with eight eyes, situated in two transverse rows. Legs with three tarsal claws. The species of this family spin a large sheet-like web, and construct a tubular retreat at the back of it, which leads to some crevice amongst the rocks or the herbage or the chinks in the walls of outhouses, wherever the various species may happen to be found. The posterior pair of spinners is usually much longer than the other two pairs.

8. *Tegenaria silvestris*, L. Koch.
   Leigh Woods (R. I. P.).

9. *Tegenaria atrica*, C. L. Koch.
   Leigh Woods (R. I. P.).

10. *Cœlotes atropos* (Walckenaer).
    Leigh Woods (R. I. P.).

ARGIOPIDÆ

The spiders included in this family have eight eyes, situated in two rows, the lateral eyes of both rows being usually adjacent, if not in actual contact, while the central eyes form a quadrangle. The tarsal claws are three, often with other supernumerary claws. The web is

SPIDERS

either an orbicular (wheel-like) snare, or consists of a sheet of webbing beneath which the spiders hang and capture the prey as it falls upon the sheet.

11. *Araneus diadematus* (Clerck).
Leigh Woods (R. I. P.).

12. *Meta segmentata* (Clerck).
Leigh Woods (R. I. P.) ; Bristol (F. P. S.).

13. *Zilla* x *-notata* (Clerck).
Bristol (F. P. S.).

14. *Zilla atrica*, C. L. Koch.
Leigh Woods (R. I. P.).

15. *Lepthyphantes tenuis* (Blackwall).
Leigh Woods (R. I. P.).

16. *Bathyphantes concolor* (Wider).
Leigh Woods (R. I. P.).

17. *Linyphia triangularis* (Clerck).
Leigh Woods (R. I. P.).

18. *Macrargus abnormis* (Blackwall).
Leigh Woods (R. I. P.).

19. *Gonatium rubens* (Blackwall)
Bristol (F. P. S.).

THERIDIIDÆ

The members of this family have eight eyes situated very much like those of the *Argiopidæ*, but the mandibles are usually weak, the maxillæ are inclined over the labium, and the posterior legs have a comb of stiff curved spines beneath the tarsi. The web consists of a tangle of crossing lines, and the spider often constructs a tent-like retreat wherein the egg-sac is hung up.

20. *Theridion lineatum* (Clerck).
Bristol (F. P. S.).

21. *Theridion tepidariorum* (C. L. Koch).
Bristol (O. P. C.).

22. *Pedanostethus lividus* (Blackwall).
Leigh Woods (R. I. P.).

THOMISIDÆ

23. *Xysticus cristatus* (Clerck).
Leigh Woods (R. I. P.); Bristol (F. P. S.).

24. *Philodromus aureolus* (Clerck).
Leigh Woods (R. I. P.) ; Bristol (F. P. S.).

DICTYNIDÆ

The species possess the calamistrum and cribellum and three tarsal claws, but the eyes, eight in number, are situated in two transverse rows, the laterals being in contact. They construct a tubular retreat with an outer sheet of webbing, which is covered with flocculent silk made with the calamistrum with threads from the cribellum.

25. *Amaurobius ferox* (Walckenaer).
Leigh Woods (R. I. P.).
Known also under *Ciniflo*.

26. *Amaurobius similis* (Blackwall).
Leigh Woods (R. I. P.).
Known also under *Ciniflo*.

27. *Amaurobius fenestralis* (Strœm).
Leigh Woods (R. I. P.).
Known also as *Ciniflo atrox*.

OPILIONES

The harvestmen are spider-like creatures with eight long legs, the tarsi very long and flexible. Eyes simple, two in number, situated on each side of an eye eminence. Body not divided into two distinct regions by a narrow pedicle as in spiders ; abdomen segmentate.

28. *Phalangium opilio*, Linn.
Leigh Woods (R. I. P.).

29. *Oligolophus agrestis*, Meade.
Leigh Woods (R. I. P.).

30. *Nemastoma lugubre*, O. F. Müller.
Leigh Woods (R. I. P.).

31. *Liobunus rotundus*, Latreille.
Leigh Woods (R. I. P.).

CRUSTACEANS

The amicable rivalry which in some points exists between the neighbouring counties of Somerset and Devon has never extended to the catalogues of their crustacean fauna. The contest would have been too unequal, so far at least as marine species are concerned. So much fresh water mingles with the salt in that part of the Bristol Channel which forms the northern boundary of Somerset, that only by a kind of courtesy can the county be said to have a sea-coast. It seems therefore to have retired altogether with a proud reserve from a competition in which it could not hope to take a leading place. Its natural history societies and serials leave the subject of carcinology on one side, as if scarcely worthy of a passing regard. No doubt in geology and archæology, in botany and architecture, there have constantly been more obviously attractive objects of research. But there are some grounds for believing that even the modest branch of zoology here handled would well repay a patient student who could give time and trouble to its investigation. It would be unreasonable to expect a great harvest of rare crabs. Even the commoner Brachyura are not likely to be abundant. But, apart from these short-tailed decapods, the Malacostraca hitherto observed, few as they are, give assurance by their character and diversity that many companion species will eventually be found within the same territorial limits.

Among the Macrura, or long-tailed decapods, it is quite possible that the common lobster, *Astacus gammarus* (Linn.), may sometimes make its way up the Channel from Lundy Island, and it is highly probable that the river crayfish, *Potamobius pallipes* (Lereboullet), abundant in the Thames and Severn canal, may extend its range further westward. In regard to the latter species Mr. H. J. Charbonnier, of Bristol, in a letter dated August 21, 1901, says, 'I feel pretty sure that it occurs in Somerset.' He was unable however to make this statement more definite, so that it cannot be relied on for extending the distribution of the crayfish into this county. Leaving then the larger edible macrurans in the limbo of uncertainty, we must pass on to claim the occurrence of certain smaller but still useful and well esteemed forms, best known by the unscientific denomination of shrimps and prawns. Of these there are four species to be considered. They all belong to the same tribe, Caridea, which takes its name from *karis*, the Greek word for a shrimp. Little as they may at the first glance seem to resemble lobsters or crayfishes, they are essentially the same in structure. To impress this on the mind, nothing is needed but to take an opportunity of dismembering an example of a large species and another of a small one, so as carefully to compare the appendages of each in their orderly succession—eyes, antennæ, jaws and legs. The differences should be noted as well as the resemblances. When once such a comparison has been instituted with alert intelligence, a keener and kindlier regard is likely to be felt for every kind of crustacean, small or large, common or rare.

The massive front claws or chelipeds of the lobster and crayfish give them in our eyes an appearance very different from that of prawns and shrimps. But it should be borne in mind that in other regions there are shrimps as large as our crayfishes and prawns as large as our lobsters, and some of these great prawns have chelipeds longer than their bodies, so that in classification no exaggerated importance is attributed to size. A much more obscure feature separates all the Caridea with which we are here concerned from the larger British Macrura. In the latter the second and third pairs of legs are chelate, that is, the last two joints in these legs like the last two joints in the first pair form nippers, only they are nippers that are quite small instead of being massive. But in the Caridea the third pair of legs is always simple, its penultimate joint not being produced into a thumb to antagonize pincerwise with the finger-like terminal joint. By characters observed in the first two pairs of legs the Caridea are subdivided into four principal sections or legions. By what may for our purpose be described as a fortunate accident, the little flock of four species recorded in this county is distributed over three out of these four legions.

The first legion, Crangoninea, contains a single family, the Crangonidæ, which is here represented by the typical genus, *Crangon*, and the typical species of that genus, *Crangon vulgaris*, Fabricius, which may claim to be not only the common shrimp, but in most parts of England the commonest shrimp. By its extensive distribution, by its great abundance, by the facility with which it is captured on the shore and in shallow water, and by the appeal which it makes to the human palate this species holds a commanding position in popular notice and favour. Many, whom the logical definition of the class Crustacea would only bewilder, learn that the common shrimp is a crustacean with much satisfaction of mind. Its assignment to this county rests on rather slender but sufficient evidence. Adam White, in his *List of the specimens of British animals in the Collection of the British Museum* records it from 'Bridgwater : presented by W. Baker, Esq.'[1] This Mr. Baker of Bridgwater was a correspondent of Dr. Leach, and subsequently of Thomas Bell, both distinguished carcinologists, and one may be allowed to infer that the trusted correspondent of such men would neither have sent a lump of coal to Newcastle nor a common shrimp to the British Museum, unless such a specimen had been invested with the particular interest of coming from his own neighbourhood.

When crustaceans are being eaten little attention is paid to any-

[1] *Crustacea*, p. 37 (1850)

thing but the muscular part and the well flavoured liver-like glands. These, like every other constituent of the complex organism, have their scientific interest, but they are not much studied except by a few specialists. The ordinary student of natural history employs himself chiefly just upon those portions to which the consumer is most indifferent, except in so far as he is disposed to consider them a tiresome incumbrance. For distinguishing the Crangoninea from the other legions some of these parts must be taken into account. In the first legs of *Crangon* one of these distinctive features will be found. They do not end in a proper claw, after the pattern or with the action of a pair of tongs. They are subchelate, that is to say, chelate only in a partial or modified condition. The penultimate joint or 'hand,' as it is sometimes called, is not produced parallel to the finger, but has a widened end across which the finger closes like the jointed lid shutting down upon the body of a lady's card-case. In the second pair of legs the antepenultimate joint or 'wrist' is undivided. These legs in the common shrimp end in a true chela, though a very small one, but as such a chela is not found in all the genera it cannot be used as a character of the legion. It should not be thought that the whole interest of the subject is exhausted even when every cell and fibre, every limb and segment and gill of the adult animal has been examined. The evolution from the egg through several successive exuviations or moultings of the integument exhibits many surprising changes. The young one is far from having, to start with, the long array of appendages for which the fully grown find employment. Its eyes are for some time fixed instead of movable. The telson is triangular both first and last, but a curious thing is that the youthful telson broadens from a narrow base, then becomes quadrangular, and finishes up by being narrowest at the tip, where at first it was most broadly expanded.[1] Nature may be trusted not to make these changes out of mere caprice. In correlation with others, they express the endeavour to give the animal in the different stages of its existence the most favourable opportunities for feeding, migrating, and escaping dangers.

The second legion is called Polycarpinea or many-wristed, and the meaning of this peculiar name will help to explain one of the marks used as a characteristic of the preceding legion. It was there observed that the second legs had an undivided 'wrist.' The manner of speech that attributes a wrist to a leg is rather unconventional. The awkwardness of it is partly disguised if, instead of saying 'wrist,' we use the classical equivalent 'carpus' to designate the fifth or antepenultimate joint of the malacostracan trunk-limb. Normally these appendages are seven-jointed, but the simplicity of the counting is sometimes spoiled by coalescence, two joints running into one, and sometimes it is spoiled in the opposite direction by a joint being broken up into jointlets, as when

---

[1] See Sars, *Bidrag til Kundskaben om Decapodernes Forvandlinger*, pt. 3 (1890), and H. C. Williamson, 'On the larval stages of Decapod Crustacea—the Shrimp (*Crangon vulgaris*, Fabr.),' *Fishery Board for Scotland Report*, pt. 3 (1901).

a single bar of iron is converted into a chain of several links. This is what happens to the fifth joint in the second legs of the Polycarpinea. That legion comprises four families, the one with which we are here concerned being called the Pandalidæ from the premier genus *Pandalus*, Leach. The species *Pandalus montagui*, Leach, is a large, well known, and tolerably abundant English prawn, though not the commonest and most familiar kind to which that vernacular name is given. On parts of our east coast however it would seem to be the predominant form. But it occurs in several localities, and among these, according to Adam White, 'the Rev. Alfred Norman has found it at Clevedon in Somerset.'[1] It was till lately regarded as a character of the family that the front legs should be simple, but a French author, M. Maurice Caullery, found that this did not apply to a species which he examined from the Bay of Biscay. He suggested therefore that in regard to other forms observers might have overlooked the pincers owing to their extreme minuteness. On this point Mr. (now Dr.) W. T. Calman writes as follows : 'So far as concerns the British species, at any rate, I am able to confirm this suggestion of Mr. Caullery. A microscopic but perfectly formed chela is found on the first peræopods of all of them, including the familiar type of the genus, *P. montagui* . . . , which for more than three quarters of a century has been described as having the first legs "simple." Even under the microscope the chelate termination may easily escape notice, on account of the brush of setæ among which it is partly hidden. Closer examination however reveals the minute dactylus, separated from the propodus by a distinct articulation and, as it is easy to convince oneself by touching with a needle, freely movable. I am unable to say whether muscles for opening and shutting the chela are present. Both the fingers are slightly curved and a tuft of long curved setæ springs from the inner margin of each. The fingers are from one-twelfth to one-tenth of the whole length of the propodus in adult specimens of *P. montagui*, and proportionately a little longer in young individuals. No differences worthy of note are observable in the other British species.'[2] It may be further observed that in this genus the upper edge of the beak or rostrum is armed with teeth or spinules that are not rigid but movable, and that the second legs are not strictly a pair, one being considerably longer than the other. Among the British species, *Pandalus montagui* is distinguished by having the wrist in the shorter of these legs, which is on the right side, subdivided or annulated much more copiously than it is in the companion species.[3]

The third legion, the Monocarpinea, with undivided wrist in the second pair of trunk-limbs, could not by that feature alone be distinguished from the first legion. But whereas among the Crangoninea the second legs are feeble and generally short, in the numerous families of

---

[1] *Popular History of British Crustacea*, p. 126 (1857).
[2] *Annals and Magazine of Natural History*, ser. 7. iii. 28 (1899). The dotted space in the quotation marks only an omitted reference to an illustrative figure. The word 'propodus' is equivalent to 'hand' or penultimate joint.   [3] Loc. cit. p. 39.

the third legion they are as a rule long or strong, and if these marks happen to fail the first legs come to the rescue by being either simple or chelate, not subchelate as in the 'shrimps.' Two of the families are represented in this county, each so far as at present reported only by a single species. The Palæmonidæ, which are extensively distributed in the rivers as well as the seas of the globe, include *Leander serratus* (Pennant), the common prawn of British markets, together with other less common species of the same genus, and besides these a sort of amphibious species, *Palæmonetes varians* (Leach). The last is the only one as yet on record for Somerset. It is amphibious, not in the sense of being able to inhabit both land and water, but as being what is now called ' euryhaline,' latitudinarian as to salt, retentive of life in fresh water but not incapable of existence in brackish water or the sea. Accordingly Adam White, after mentioning various marine localities for this species, adds, ' the Rev. Alfred Norman finds it off the coast of Guernsey, and in a note he kindly informs me, " I have taken this species in great abundance at Clevedon, in a ditch far above ordinary high-water mark, of which the water was scarcely at all brackish ; it was in company with myriads of *Rissoa ventricosa*. I found some also further up in a stream of clear running water, along with *Aplexus hypnorum* and other freshwater shells." '[1] From this and other samples of careful observation it is easy to augur that, had Canon Norman, F.R.S., the distinguished naturalist referred to by White, spent much instead of little time in this county its crustacean records would have been wonderfully amplified.

The macruran species still remaining to be noticed belongs to the family Pasiphæidæ, of which the leading genus is *Pasiphæa*, Savigny. The species was first introduced as British by Adam White, Leach having left it unpublished, though with a manuscript name, *P. savigniana*, attached to specimens in the British Museum. Under the name *P. savignyi* Milne-Edwards in 1837 published a description of these specimens, but regarded their place of origin as ' Patrie inconnue.'[2] White, adopting the name *P. savignyi* given by Milne-Edwards, which he translates into ' Savigny's shrimp,' explains that the specimens came in part from Bridgwater, presented by W. Baker, Esq., and in part from Ireland, presented by the Rev. J. Bulwer.[3] Bell soon after identified the species with the earlier *Pasiphæa sivado*, Risso, and White in 1857 accepted this name, which he does into English as the ' sword shrimp.' Part of his account of it is well worth quoting. ' This shrimp,' he says, ' is very much compressed, and the body, when alive, is white and transparent, each joint being banded with red ; the eyes are black ; the antennæ and legs are red, and the tail-plates are dotted with red. I am indebted to the Rev. Alfred M. Norman for the following note : " This beautiful crustacean occurs in the British Channel at Clevedon, occasionally in

[1] *Popular History of British Crustacea*, p. 135 (1857).
[2] *Histoire Naturelle des Crustacés*, ii. 426.
[3] *List of the specimens of Crustacea in the British Museum*, p. 80 (1847) ; and *List British Animals in British Museum*, pt. iv. ; *Crustacea*, p. 43 (1850).

great abundance. It was called by the fishermen who procured them for me 'the White Shrimp.' It is taken in nets suspended from poles and placed near the mouth of the little stream that runs into the Channel at 'the Pill'; these nets are set to take shrimps, sprats and other fish which the tide as it goes out leaves in them. Although the fisherman is always on the spot to secure his fish as the tide recedes, he assures me he has never once seen a *Pasiphæa* alive. I conclude therefore that they cannot bear exposure to the air, and die instantly on leaving the water. Colour white, and the appearance jelly-like; the antennæ, articulations of the abdomen, pedipalps, hands and caudal laminæ are more or less coloured with rich crimson, as Risso has described Mediterranean examples. It is a most lovely and remarkable species."[1] This then may be regarded as the chief glory of the crustacean fauna belonging to this county. In appearance it has more the character of a prawn than a shrimp, though the insignificance of its rostrum at once discriminates it from the *Palæmonetes* before mentioned. The conspicuous long-fingered pincers of the first and second pairs of legs are also highly distinctive. In these limbs the slender thumb and finger are beautifully armed on the inner margin, each with a long comb of glass-like teeth, formed by articulated spines varying from forty to eighty in the several rows, the smallest number occurring on the thumb or immovable finger of the first pair and the highest on the movable finger of the second.

Of sessile-eyed Malacostraca the county records are still more scanty than those of the stalk-eyed division. This can be attributed with the utmost assurance not to dearth of species but to want of any long resident observers who thought it worth while to record them. Of the Isopoda the family Sphæromidæ yields a single species, *Sphæroma hookeri*, Leach, concerning which White remarks with a sort of customary formula that 'the Rev. Alfred Norman finds it at Clevedon and in Guernsey.'[2] The name of the family as of the genus refers to a particular habit and capacity in the animals comprised therein of assuming a spherical form. This is familiar to every one in a family of terrestrial isopods which will presently demand attention. In both families the adaptive structure is similar. That the Isopoda, including our common woodlice, are Malacostracan crustacea is by no means universally understood. The learned Savigny, whose name has been noticed above in connection with the genus *Pasiphæa*, demonstrated in 1816 the parity of organization between the stalk-eyed and sessile-eyed crustaceans. He made it clear that, though in general the former group have ten legs and the latter have fourteen, the difference depends only on the fact that the Decapoda have converted the first two pairs of legs into jaws or mouth-organs. The Tetradecapoda, retaining their seven pairs of appendages in more or less leg-like form, have also kept as a rule seven segments of the

---

[1] *Popular History of British Crustacea,* p. 137. It may be remarked that the 'pedipalps' are now more commonly spoken of as the third maxillipeds, the articulations of the abdomen as segments of the pleon, and that the caudal laminæ include the telson and the uropods, the latter being the appendages of the sixth pleon-segment. [2] Loc. cit. p. 245.

middle body freely movable one upon the other. This is managed by their having between one segment and another a transverse strip of integument not highly chitinized or solidified by carbonate of lime but thinly and flexibly membranaceous. Thus the segments can slide over one another to a certain degree when the body is extended, and on the other hand can usually be so far stretched apart as to enable the animal with the front of its forehead to touch the extremity of its tail. In some cases this only amounts to a process of doubling up, but in many of the Sphæromidæ, while the middle segments are dorsally distended, their lateral plates fold one over the other so that a compact little ball is produced, within which are sheltered the lashes of the antennæ, the mouth-organs, the more or less uniform legs and the delicate branchiæ of the pleon or tail. Whether *Sphæroma hookeri*, with two faintly marked longitudinal carinæ on the upper surface of its terminal segment, can thereby be effectively distinguished from the earlier *Sphæroma rugicauda*, Leach, is perhaps still open to question.

Of the land Isopoda or woodlice, in the family Armadillidiidæ, I can report *Armadillidium nasatum*, Budde-Lund, from Leigh Woods near Clifton. The members of this family are sometimes irreverently called ' pill-bugs,' in allusion no doubt as well to their shape when rolled up as to their actual use in ancient medicine. In these globe-forming animals the breadth is commonly about half the length. The species *A. nasatum*, meaning the Armadillidium with a nose, has evidently received its specific name in reference to the part called the epistome, by which it is pretty easily distinguished from *Armadillidium vulgare*. In the latter the epistome scarcely rises above the frontal line, but in *A. nasatum* it forms a subquadrangular plate much surpassing the frontal margin.[1] It is scarcely necessary to insist that at least several of the terrestrial isopods known to frequent the adjoining counties certainly also occupy the woods and gardens, the highways and byways, the underside of flat stones, the inside of ants' nests, and other their favourite retreats, as freely in Somerset as elsewhere.

In the companion group of the Amphipoda just one species may be said to save the situation. Of *Dexamine spinosa* (Montagu) the often quoted Adam White says once again that ' the Rev. A. Norman has found it at Clevedon, Somerset.'[2] When freshly captured this is among the brightest and most gaily coloured of its order. It may be regarded as in itself a guarantee that where it is found there also will occur many other species of Amphipoda of similar habits. Sand and sea-weed, various floating objects, muddy ooze and submerged timber supply them with food and shelter, so that within tide-marks, and in shallow water or in deep, all round our coasts many kinds are to be found, and some of them in great abundance. Without here entering into the minutiæ of their structure, it may suffice to say that the Amphipoda are completely distinguished from the other sessile-eyed group, the Isopoda, by the

[1] Budde-Lund, *Isopoda Terrestria*, p. 51 (1885).
[2] *Popular History of British Crustacea*, p. 178.

CRUSTACEANS

position of the breathing organs. The latter have their branchiæ, except in one aberrant section, situated in the caudal part or pleon. In the Amphipoda the respiratory sacs or vesicles, which are often simple, but sometimes pleated, twisted, or otherwise diversified, are always attached to limbs of the peræon or middle body.

That Entomostraca are well represented in this county is chiefly a matter of inference. It would be what logicians call a *petitio principii* to say that they are well represented in all counties, and therefore in this, but it would be a tolerably safe inductive conclusion. Of the Phyllopoda the shield-bearing *Apus cancriformis*, Schæffer, is recorded from Bristol and from Devonshire, and the elegant *Chirocephalus diaphanus*, Prevost, which unhampered by valves or carapace keeps up the rhythmical movement of its leaf-like limbs, is recorded in like manner both from Devonshire and the neighbourhood of Bristol. The old schoolmen are said to have propounded the subtle question whether angels in passing from place to place pass through the intermediate space. We may ask whether it is at all likely that the many-footed *Apus* or the translucent fairy shrimp could have possibly passed from Bristol into Devon without colonizing Somerset on their road. We know at any rate that in past ages the county was not destitute of phyllopods, since *Estheria minuta* var. *brodieana* is reported by Professor Rupert Jones from Somerset as occurring in the Rhætic formation, which consists of passage beds between the Lias and Trias.[1]

If the Phyllopods and the ubiquitous Cladocera have here to be taken on trust, for the third section of the Branchiopoda there is direct evidence. This section, the Branchiura, is a small one, and does not very clearly conform to the characters of the other branchiopods. It includes the single parasitic family of the Argulidæ, in which the species *Argulus foliaceus* (Linn.) has long been known in England and elsewhere as a parasite upon various freshwater fishes and tadpoles. Mr. H. J. Charbonnier, already mentioned, has informed me by letter that he once took it at Keynsham in one of the streams, and studied its behaviour in his aquarium with great delight. He attributed to it the death of some sticklebacks. From the scene of slaughter, in which the Argulus was observed swimming free, according to its wont after a satisfying meal, Mr. Charbonnier removed it to another aquarium where he had some other sticklebacks. Here, the letter continues, 'he was immediately seized and vigorously " chewed," but presently he slipped through the " gill " of his captor and creeping over his head proceeded to insert his rostrum just over the fish's brain.' In *Argulus* the second maxillæ are transformed into sucking discs by which the bloodthirsty little creature adheres to its involuntary host. A Japanese species has recently been made known in Europe, very far exceeding in size those found in European waters. The Japanese fishes would perhaps be content with the smaller pattern.

Of the Ostracoda species in Great Britain are very numerous.

[1] *Fossil Estheriæ, Palæontographical Society*, p. 67 (1862).

133

Some of these are rare, but several are so impartially distributed north and south, east and west, that they may reasonably be expected to occur in every county. They do not however tempt many observers to examine them. Not only are their bodies and limbs almost always very minute, but they are rather obstinately withdrawn from view by the owners whenever outside curiosity becomes in the least obtrusive. The desired privacy is secured by the pair of sheltering valves which make an ostracode look more like a tiny mollusc than a crustacean. Even after death the closure of the valves is very persistent, though not invincible in the hands of an expert. The only species actually recorded for Somerset seems to be *Cytheridea torosa* (Rupert Jones), which Dr. G. S. Brady reports from Weston-super-Mare on the authority of the Rev. A. M. Norman.[1] It belongs to the Podocopa, a tribe of the Ostracoda which manages to support existence without a heart. Within this tribe it is a member of the family Cytheridae, which generally have hard calcareous valves, uneven of surface, bare or sparingly hirsute, and united by a toothed hinge. The animals are incapable of swimming. The genus *Cytheridea*, Bosquet, was originally founded on forms from tertiary strata of France and Belgium. The species *C. torosa* is according to Dr. Brady rather exceptional in the genus, for while classing it as a true Cytheridea, he qualifies his opinion by adding that 'there remains one important character in which, so far as I know, this species stands alone among the Ostracoda, namely, the enormous number of ova borne at a single time by the female; how far this may prove to be of generic importance future investigations must show; it is at any rate an interesting fact, and one which fully accounts for the immense numbers in which the species is often found.'[2]

Of the Thyrostraca, that is, cirripedes or barnacles, apparently no definite record awards any to the Somerset coast. Yet many species must certainly reach its waters in attachment to the hulls of vessels and other floating objects. Of the sessile forms included in the family Balanidæ, at least the wide-ranging *Balanus improvisus*, Darwin, may be expected to rank as a resident on these shores. There can scarcely be anything in the conditions of the estuary to banish it from this part of the Bristol Channel, for this is 'a Balanus capable of living in freshwater and likewise in the saltest seas,' whereas 'even brackish water is a deadly poison to several, probably to most, species of the genus.'[3]

That even *B. improvisus* can live without an occasional savour of salt in its diet is not perhaps to be maintained, but since it can exist at Woolwich on the Thames, it may very well do the same at Weston on the Severn or on the Sea.

[1] *Transactions of the Linnæan Society*, vol. xxvi. pt. 2, p. 426 (1868). [2] Loc. cit.
[3] Darwin, *Monograph of Balanidæ*, Ray Society, p. 253 (1854).

FISHES

The fishes of Somerset have received a good deal of attention from the late Mr. W. Baker, who has contributed an excellent paper on the subject to the Somerset Archæological and Natural History Society in 1851 (*Proceed.* pp. 95–110). Very few additions have since been made to the list given by Mr. Baker, and which is the source whence the present account has been compiled. Day's great work on the British fishes contains but rare allusions to Somerset; although Baker's paper is quoted in the preface (p. iii.) it has evidently been overlooked in the preparation of the work.

As in other articles contributed to the *Victoria History of the Counties of England*, an asterisk prefixed to the name indicates a freshwater species and two asterisks denote occurrence in both fresh and salt water.

TELEOSTEANS

ACANTHOPTERYGII

*1. Perch. *Perca fluviatilis*, Linn.

**2. Sea Bass. *Morone labrax*, Linn. (*Labrax lupus*, Day).

3. Polyprion. *Polyprion americanus*, Bl. Schn. (*P. cernium*, Day).

This widely distributed sea perch, which occurs at great depths in the Atlantic Ocean, has occasionally been found on the south-west coast of England. Baker records it from the Somerset coast, nearly three feet long, and he mentions one in particular from the estuary of the Parret.

4. Common Sea Bream. *Pagellus centrodontus*, Delaroche.

This species appears under two names in Baker's list, viz. as the braize, *Pagrus vulgaris*, Cuv., and as the sea bream, *Pagellus centrodontus*, unless, following the error of Yarrell, the first name should be intended for the next species, which undoubtedly occurs in the Bristol Channel at certain seasons.

5. Pandora Sea Bream. *Pagellus erythrinus*, Linn.

6. Red Mullet. *Mullus barbatus*, Linn.

7. Common or Ballan Wrasse. *Labrus maculatus*, Bl.

Referred to by Baker under the names of *L. maculatus*, *L. lineatus* and *L. comber*.

8. Cuckoo Wrasse. *Labrus mixtus*, Linn.

L. variegatus and *L. carneus* of Baker.

9. Baillon's Wrasse. *Crenilabrus melops*, Linn.

C. tinca, *C. cornubicus* and *C. gibbus* of Baker.

*10. Miller's Thumb. *Cottus gobio*, Linn.

11. Father-lasher or Bull-head. *Cottus scorpius*, Linn.

12. Long-spined Bull-head. *Cottus bubalis*, Euphr.

13. Grey Gurnard. *Trigla gurnardus*, Linn.

14. Red Gurnard. *Trigla cuculus*, Linn.

15. Sapphirine Gurnard or Tubfish. *Trigla hirundo*, Linn.

16. Piper. *Trigla lyra*, Linn.

17. Lanthorn Gurnard. *Trigla obscura*, Linn.

18. Pogge or Armed Bull-head. *Agonus cataphractus*, Linn.

19. Lump-sucker. *Cyclopterus lumpus*, Linn.

20. Sea Snail. *Liparis vulgaris*, Flem.

21. Diminutive Sea Snail. *Liparis montagui*, Donov.

22. Spotted Goby. *Gobius minutus*, Gmel.

23. Two-spotted Goby. *Gobius ruthensparri*, Euphr.

24. Transparent Goby. *Aphia pellucida*, Nardo.

Recorded from the Bristol Channel by Day.

25. John Dory. *Zeus faber*, Linn.

26. Boar-fish. *Capros aper*, Linn.

Baker says this fish is very rare, but that he has met with specimens in Taunton market from the south coast, and in Bridgwater market from Stolford. The specimen figured in Yarrell's work is from the Taunton market.

27. Scad or Horse-mackerel. *Caranx trachurus*, Linn.

28. Mackerel. *Scomber scombrus*, Linn.

29. Swordfish. *Xiphias gladius*, Linn.

Baker mentions the capture of three specimens at the mouth of the Parret, and one, eight feet long, found by himself on the sands at Burnham in the summer of 1850.

30. Greater Weever. *Trachinus draco*, Linn.

31. Lesser Weever. *Trachinus vipera*, Cuv. & Val.

These poisonous fish are fortunately not abundant on the Somerset coast. The lesser weever is the rarer.

32. Dragonet. *Callionymus lyra*, Linn.

33. Angler. *Lophius piscatorius*, Linn.

Said to be not uncommon in Bridgwater Bay. Specimens of small size are often brought to market with other fish. Baker has seen a specimen from the estuary of the Parret, weighing eighty pounds.

34. Gattorugine Blenny. *Blennius gattorugine*, Bl.

35. Red Bandfish. *Cepola rubescens*, Linn.

Baker says this fish is rare on the Somerset coast, but a few have been taken in the estuary of the Parret in February, when they are believed to visit the coast for the purpose of spawning.

ANACANTHINI

36. Cod. *Gadus morrhua*, Linn.

37. Haddock. *Gadus æglefinus*, Linn.

38. Bib or Pont. *Gadus luscus*, Linn.

39. Power or Poor Cod. *Gadus minutus*, Linn.

40. Whiting. *Gadus merlangus*, Linn.

41. Pollack. *Gadus pollachius*, Linn.

42. Hake. *Merluccius vulgaris*, Cuv.

43. Fork-beard. *Phycis blennioides*, Bl. Schn.
Rare.

44. Lesser Fork-beard. *Raniceps raninus*, Linn.
Rare.

45. Ling. *Molva vulgaris*, Flem.

46. Five-bearded Rockling. *Motella mustela*, Linn.

47. Three-bearded Rockling. *Motella tricirrata*, Bl.

48. Holibut. *Hippoglossus vulgaris*, Flem.

Not uncommon, but generally small, a remark which applies also to the two following fishes.

49. Turbot. *Rhombus maximus*, Linn.

50. Brill. *Rhombus lævis*, Linn.

51. Common Topknot. *Zeugopterus punctatus*, Bl.

52. Megrim. *Lepidorhombus megastoma*, Donov.

53. Scald-fish. *Arnoglossus laterna*, Walb.

54. Plaice. *Pleuronectes platessa*, Linn.

55. Lemon Dab. *Pleuronectes microcephalus*, Donov.
Rare.

56. Smear Dab. *Pleuronectes cynoglossus*, Linn.

Two specimens are on record from Stolford, the types of Yarrell's *Platessa elongata*.

57. Dab. *Pleuronectes limanda*, Linn.

**58. Flounder. *Pleuronectes flesus*, Linn.

It is sometimes taken in clear streams far from tide rivers.

59. Sole. *Solea vulgaris*, Quens.

60. Lemon Sole or French Sole. *Solea lascaris*, Risso.
Rare.

61. Thickback. *Solea variegata*, Donov.
Rare.

62. Solonette. *Solea lutea*, Risso.
Rare.

PERCESOCES

**63. Grey Mullet. *Mugil capito*, Cuv.

**64. Lesser Grey Mullet. *Mugil chelo*, Cuv.

Grey mullet, says Baker, ascend the Parret beyond the reach of tide water, probably to spawn, as the fry of this species are found in the tributaries of the river in autumn. It is now well known that they spawn in the sea.

65. Atherine. *Atherina presbyter*, Jen.

66. Larger Launce or Sand-eel. *Ammodytes lanceolatus*, Lesauv.

FISHES

67. Lesser Launce. *Ammodytes tobianus*, Linn.

68. Garfish. *Belone vulgaris*, Flem.

Common in summer. Sometimes occurs in the Parret nearly up to Bridgwater.

69. Skipper. *Scombresox saurus*, Walb.

Baker records the capture of one specimen at Stolford.

70. Flying Fish. *Exocœtus volitans*, Linn.

An accidental visitor. The first record is of one from the Bristol Channel, ten miles from Bridgwater, in July, 1823; Baker mentions two or three from Burnham. A shoal was observed at the mouth of the Bristol Channel in July, 1876.

HEMIBRANCHII

**71. Three-spined Stickleback. *Gastrosteus aculeatus*, Linn.

The forms *trachurus, semiarmatus* and *liurus* are recorded by Baker.

*72. Ten-spined Stickleback. *Gastrosteus pungitius*, Linn.

73. Fifteen-spined Stickleback. *Gastrosteus spinachia*, Linn.

LOPHOBRANCHII

74. Broad-nosed Pipe-fish. *Siphonostoma typhle*, Linn.

75. Greater Pipe-fish. *Syngnathus acus*, Linn.

76. Snake Pipe-fish. *Nerophis æquoreus*, Linn.

HAPLOMI

*77. Pike. *Esox lucius*, Linn.

OSTARIOPHYSI

*78. Carp. *Cyprinus carpio*, Linn.

*79. Crucian Carp. *Cyprinus carassius*, Linn.
Baker records it from the Parret.

*80. Gudgeon. *Gobio fluviatilis*, Flem.

*81. Roach. *Leuciscus rutilus*, Linn.

*82. Dace. *Leuciscus dobula*, Linn. (*L. vulgaris*, Day).

*83. Minnow. *Leuciscus phoxinus*, Linn.

*84. Tench. *Tinca vulgaris*, Cuv.

*85. Bleak. *Alburnus lucidus*, Heck. & Kner.

In the western part of the county; not common.

*86. Loach. *Nemachilus barbatula*, Linn.

MALACOPTERYGII

**87. Salmon. *Salmo salar*, Linn.

In 1851 Baker complains of their becoming scarcer in the rivers.

**88. Trout. *Salmo trutta*, Linn.

'Salmon Trout, Bull Trout, Common Trout.'

'Very many books have been written on the genus Salmo, and of late years much has been done, through careful investigation, to lessen the confusion of supposed species and varieties of this genus; but there it still much more to be done to make the subject intelligible to inquisitive naturalists. The number of species in our books is reduced, and how many more will be found only varieties is yet to be learned.'—*W. Baker*, 1851. Most ichthyologists in 1901 regard the forms alluded to as mere varieties.

89. Anchovy. *Engraulis encrasicholus*, Linn.

Stated by Baker to be very fine at the mouth of the Parret.

90. Herring. *Clupea harengus*, Linn.

Does not visit the Somerset shores regularly in shoals.

91. Pilchard or Sardine. *Clupea pilchardus*, Linn.

Only a few stragglers are found on the Somerset coast.

92. Sprat. *Clupea sprattus*, Linn.

**93. Shad. *Clupea alosa*, Linn.

**94. Thwait. *Clupea finta*, Cuv.

This and the preceding species ascend rivers to spawn in fresh water.

APODES

**95. Eel. *Anguilla vulgaris*, Turt.

Breeds in the sea. Elvers ascend the rivers from March to May. The young, from Stolford, has been described by Yarrell as *Ophidium imberbe*. *Leptocephalus brevirostris*, Kaup, is the larval form.

96. Conger. *Conger vulgaris*, Cuv.

The larva has been described as *Leptocephalus morrisii*, Gron.

GANOIDS

**97. Sturgeon. *Acipenser sturio*, Linn.

Baker states very large sturgeons come up the Parret, sometimes almost to Bridgwater; one taken in 1850 was ten feet long and weighed 300 lb. These large fish are females full of roe, and generally taken in June and July. Small specimens from 6 to 20 lb. are not uncommon.

CHONDROPTERYGIANS

98. Rough Hound or Small-spotted Dog-fish. *Scyllium canicula*, Linn.
99. Tope. *Galeus vulgaris*, Flem.
100. Picked Dog-fish. *Acanthias vulgaris*, Risso.
101. Monk-fish or Angel. *Rhina squatina*, Linn.

102. True Skate. *Raia batis*, Linn.
103. Thornback. *Raia clavata*, Linn.
104. Flapper Skate. *Raia macrorhynchus*, Raf.

There is only one record of the occurrence of this skate on the Somerset coast, at Minehead, in April, 1838.

CYCLOSTOMES

**105. Sea Lamprey. *Petromyzon marinus*, Linn.

*106. Lampern. *Petromyzon fluviatilis*, Linn.

This and the preceding species are taken in the Parret.

*107. Mud Lamprey or Pride. *Petromyzon branchialis*, Linn.

Common in brooks.

REPTILES
AND BATRACHIANS

This section of the fauna formed the subject of an interesting paper by the late Mr. W. Baker in 1851 (*Proc. Somerset Arch. and N. H. Soc.* pp. 116–24), in which four reptiles and five batrachians are enumerated, in addition to an accidental visitor, *Chelone imbricata*, the hawk's-bill turtle, stated to have been caught in the river Parret. No species has since been added to the list. It is from this county that the palmated newt was first recorded as a British species, it having been discovered by Mr. Baker near Bridgwater in 1843. It is very remarkable that the presence of the natterjack toad, *Bufo calamita*, has not yet been ascertained in any part of Somerset.

REPTILES

LACERTILIA

1. Common Lizard. *Lacerta vivipara*, Jacq.
2. Slow-worm or Blind-worm. *Anguis fragilis*, Linn.

OPHIDIA

3. Common or Ringed Snake. *Tropidonotus natrix*, Linn.
4. Common Viper or Adder. *Vipera berus*, Linn.

BATRACHIANS

ECAUDATA

1. Common Frog. *Rana temporaria*, Linn.
2. Common Toad. *Bufo vulgaris*, Laur.

CAUDATA

3. Great Crested Newt. *Molge cristata*, Laur.
4. Common Newt. *Molge vulgaris*, Linn.
5. Palmated Newt. *Molge palmata*, Schneid.

BIRDS

The physical features of the county of Somerset are so diversified that an ornithologist might well expect to find a great variety of birds within its boundaries. In this hope he will not be disappointed, as although the list does not equal those for the counties of Devon and Cornwall, yet it cannot be said to compare unfavourably with those of many other counties. It must however be admitted that in a county possessing about seventy miles of seaboard and such a variety of hill and dale, moor and marsh, one would expect to find even a greater variety of birds than are at present known to occur.

Any one who examines the following list cannot fail to notice that quite a number of species have only been recorded once or twice as obtained within the county boundaries. It is natural to infer from this that these species are only waifs and strays which have drifted away from the lines of migration or have wandered from their usual haunts. In many cases this may be the true state of affairs, but I feel confident that closer observation and more readiness on the part of naturalists to record facts would prove that many of these so-called 'waifs and strays' may be far more often met with in the county than is generally supposed. To take one instance, the late Mr. Cecil Smith only mentioned one Somerset example of the common cormorant in his *Birds of Somersetshire* published in 1869, and even so keen a naturalist as the Rev. M. A. Mathew could not add to this record in his Revised List printed some twenty-four years later. I have however frequently noticed this bird in various places along the coast, and even suspect that it breeds in one locality. Without doubt there are several species mentioned in the following list which may truly be called accidental visitors. It is most improbable that the keenest field naturalist would ever again come across such species as the American hawk-owl, Egyptian vulture or black stork within the bounds of the county.

On comparing the list of birds of Somerset with those of Devon and Cornwall one is struck by the fact that some species rare in the first named county are comparatively common in the other two. For instance the great northern and red-throated divers, guillemots, razorbills and various species of terns are regularly to be met with on the Devon and Cornish coasts, but are rarely to be found in Somerset waters, and though not unknown in the latter county can only be regarded as occasional or passing visitors. But the reason why these birds avoid the coast of Somerset may easily be understood by any one who has a knowledge of their habits and the physical conditions which are most attractive to them. They all seek their prey in the water, and all but the terns pursue the fish beneath its surface, and the opaqueness of the water in the Bristol Channel, at any rate as far west as Minehead, cannot be said to offer them a tempting feeding-ground. Under the heading 'Red-Throated Diver' Mr. C. Smith remarked in his *Birds of Somersetshire*, 'probably they stop short at the muddy water; certainly it would occasionally rather puzzle them to see their prey in some parts of our channel, and diving in that thick muddy water must be something like walking in a London fog.'

We have mentioned above that a peculiarity in the county list of birds is that many species have only been noticed on one or two occasions. This feature, where not due to lack of observation, may perhaps be accounted for by the supposition that many migratory birds on their journey up and down the Bristol Channel do not as a rule stop either in Somerset or in the opposite counties of South Wales, but that occasionally a straggler drops away from the line of migration. The firecrest and red-breasted flycatcher, among others, have been thought to follow this route (D'Urban and Mathew, *The Birds of Devon*), and so possibly observation on the Steep Holm might add these two and other species to the county list. While on the subject of migration it may be mentioned that the absence of any important river which might serve as a flight-line to migrating birds is likely to modify the distribution of species in the county. It appears indeed that a stream of land birds enters the county by Bridgwater Bay and proceeds south-west after having diverged from the main stream which crosses England from the Wash to the Bristol Channel (vide *Birds of Devon*); but there is no large river running through the county, for the river Avon would only affect the northern district.

While considering the physical features of Somerset and their relation to the distribution of species, it seems advisable to arrange the county roughly into three main divisions, and then to treat of the whole coastline separately. The three main divisions comprise a central basin between two hilly districts, but it must be understood that these areas are not always very clearly defined, and that some parts of the county do not fall in very naturally with any of the three districts.

(1) One of the hilly districts occupies the north-east of the county and is separated from the central basin by the Mendip Hills. It consists of irregular heights sloping away towards the rivers Frome and Avon and is rich in parks and woodlands, particularly around Frome. This district, especially towards the eastern boundary of the county, is a favourite resort of the various species of warblers, the most remarkable of which is the marsh-warbler; three species of woodpeckers occur; the hawfinch and lesser redpoll breed somewhat freely, particularly in the neighbourhood of Bath, while the golden oriole, though only a rare visitor, seems to have been observed more often in this district than

elsewhere in the county. The Mendip Hills are also attractive to bird life, and in their rocky gorges the raven, peregrine falcon, and probably the chough used to breed in former years and may possibly do so still in one or two localities.

(2) The other hilly district comprises that part of the county to the west of Taunton. This includes the Quantock Hills with their thickly wooded slopes and combes, the Blackdown Hills on the borders of Devon, the Brendon Hills, the heather and whortleberry clad heights around Dunkery Beacon, and the wild moorland known as Exmoor Forest. A large portion of the land in the extreme west is over 1,000 feet above sea level, though there are no heights which attain to 2,000 feet. In this district the ring-ouzel, raven, common buzzard, black grouse, curlew, common snipe and wild duck still breed; the kite appears to have bred here formerly and the hen-harrier possibly does so still, though more information is wanted on the subject; trips of golden plover are seen in autumn and winter and some may breed on the moors, though the fact has yet to be established; the woodcock breeds sparingly in some of the coverts, and the grey wagtail, dipper and common sandpiper haunt the moorland streams, while the wood-warbler and nightjar are by no means uncommon in many of the hanging plantations.

(3) The central area, which is coextensive with the physical basin watered by the rivers Parret, Brue and Axe, contains no elevation except the low line of the Polden Hills and a few isolated knolls which rise out of the flat, alluvial deposits. This district includes the richest grazing grounds in the county; much of it is marsh or moorland and below sea level, and it is intersected in every direction by dikes or 'rhynes' as they are locally termed, which serve the double purpose of drains and hedges. To the north of the Polden Hills are extensive beds of peat known as the turf or peat moors. In the summer these moors are in parts covered with a luxuriant vegetation such as thick beds of alder and sallow and masses of plants of lower growth, among which the cotton grass, bog myrtle and the local *Osmunda regalis* may be found; the holes caused by cutting out the peat soon become filled with water and overgrown with flags, reeds and other vegetation, and the district presents just the features which might be expected to attract the more retiring species of birds. Far too little however is known of the birds which inhabit this district, and it would doubtless well repay careful investigation. To quote from the Rev. M. A. Mathew's Revised List mentioned above, ' we can still only sigh for knowledge respecting the birds of the peat-moor country, for almost absolutely nothing is known about its summer visitors, and the ornithologist can but picture to himself the rare aquatic warblers, the small rails, etc., which may visit it all undetected.' There are however many interesting species of birds which are known to breed on the levels of mid-Somerset. The lesser redpoll nests among the alders and sallows, and I came across several pairs this summer (1901) near Ashcott station and found a nest;

the wild duck and common snipe breed regularly, and the teal and shoveler do so occasionally ; the water-rail is well known in summer by the local name of 'skitty'; and the spotted crake, sometimes numerous in autumn, probably breeds more frequently than might be supposed ; careful search also would probably show that the marsh-warbler is a regular summer inhabitant of the levels of Somerset. During the winter months large areas of these low-lying lands are flooded, and in very wet seasons the country presents the appearance of a vast lake. Many species of ducks are then to be found on the floods, the wild duck, teal and wigeon appearing in the largest numbers ; but pintails, shovelers and many of the diving ducks put in an appearance and doubtless many rare species are shot by the local gunners and not recorded. Gulls and other sea birds are often driven inland to these districts, being usually met with after severe gales at sea; and among the other more interesting winter visitors may be mentioned the siskin, the marsh and hen-harriers, the short-eared owl and the common bittern. The latter bird is still far from rare, and sometimes quite a number are noticed during severe frosts. While treating of this central district of Somerset it is worth remarking that there is a duck decoy on Sedgemoor not far from the village of Walton, which appears to be the only one in the county which at the present time is regularly worked. Quantities of teal are sometimes taken and a good many wild duck, as well as other species in smaller numbers. It would be interesting to know what species of ducks were formerly taken here, but few records seem to have been kept.[1] Colonel Montagu in his *Dictionary of Birds* mentions having received specimens of the garganey teal from the Somerset decoys, and was informed that large numbers of wigeon were also taken.

(4) The coast line of Somerset, some seventy miles in length, presents a variety of features attractive to the shore-frequenting species. It is true there are no very lofty cliffs, but there are a few bold headlands such as Brean Down and Hurlstone Point, crumbling slopes wooded almost to the water's edge as in the extreme west, steep faces of low cliff as at Watchet and elsewhere, fine stretches of firm sand, ridges of shingle, lines of sand dunes, oozy estuaries of rivers and vast expanses of soft mud-flats, each of which have their attractions for various species of birds.

As far as I know the cliffs on the coast are nowhere tenanted by guillemots or any species of gulls, but on the Steep Holm, a rock in the Channel some 256 feet high and three miles off the end of Brean Down, both the herring and lesser black-backed gulls breed, and a pair of pere-

---

[1] Sir Ralph Payne-Gallwey, in his *Book of Duck Decoys*, published in 1886, mentions the following decoys in the county of Somerset : Sharpham Park, Shapwick, King's Sedgemoor (3) . . . in use ; Meare, Compton Dundon, Aller, Godney, Westbury, Stoke, Nyland, Cheddar Water and Kenn Moor, not in use. The only pool now in use (1901) is one of the three on King's Sedgemoor, on which I am informed the yearly take averages about 700 birds, chiefly teal. The combined average total for the three Sedgemoor pools for the years 1868–82 was 1,200 fowl, chiefly mallard and teal, but during the best season 3,000 birds were caught.

grine falcons still hold their own. A pair or two of this latter species probably breed also in the cliffs of the west in company with several ravens and at least two pairs of buzzards. Among the other species which find suitable breeding places on or near the coast may be mentioned the cirl-bunting, rock-pipit, wheatear, stonechat, common sheld-duck, stock-dove, kestrel, oyster-catcher, and ringed plover, while the white wagtail (*Motacilla alba*) appears regularly at the times of migration and a few probably stay to nest. Although we have touched on a similar subject before it will here be interesting to notice a few birds which nest on the opposite coast of Wales in the county of Glamorgan, but which do not at the present time appear to breed in Somerset. These species include the greater black-backed gull, common and lesser terns, chough, shag, guillemot, razorbill and puffin. It must be noted however that most of these species only breed, as far as Glamorgan is concerned, on the coast of Gower, where the water is clearer than it is higher up the channel, and so for the reason we have already noticed we hardly expect them to breed upon our coasts. It is however from autumn to spring that the greatest variety of birds may be seen on the coast. The bays with their shallow warm waters attract several species of diving ducks, the scaup in particular being abundant near Weston-super-Mare during the winter months. A variety of gulls spend the winter on the coast, and their numbers seem to vary with the numbers of the sprats which usually enter the Channel towards the end of the year. When these fish appear in large shoals they are followed by hundreds of gulls of which the commonest species is the black-headed gull. At low tide enormous mud-flats are left bare, and these are the favourite feeding-grounds of large flocks of dunlin, ringed plover and curlew ; while other wading birds such as knots and godwits are seen in smaller numbers ; the whimbrel also is common in May but rarer at the time of the return migration. Besides the mud-flats there are some fine stretches of sand and low rocks covered with seaweed which attract small parties of sanderlings and turn-stones and other species which appear to object to the mud. A few geese, in particular the white-fronted and brent geese, and even swans are met with in severe winters, and numbers of wild duck, wigeon and teal, which spend the night on the flooded marshes away from the coast, rest on the sea during the day. The most characteristic bird on the Somerset coast is undoubtedly the sheld-duck, or burrow-duck as it is locally called, and large parties may be seen at almost any season of the year feeding on the mud-flats at the edge of the tide.

We have drawn attention while treating of each species separately to those which are of rare occurrence or which appear to be increasing or decreasing within the county. In the present place it will only be necessary to make a few general remarks on the subject. Prominent among the disappearing species in Somerset as elsewhere are the larger birds of prey. The kite has vanished as a breeding species, and the common buzzard holds only a somewhat insecure tenure in the extreme west. The raven has forsaken some of its old haunts but clings to others with praiseworthy tenacity ; I know of a pair which nest yearly within a mile or two of one of the most populous towns in the county. The sparrow-hawk has in some districts been almost exterminated by the gamekeepers, and it is extremely doubtful whether any of the harriers or the chough can at the present time be claimed as breeding species, though the peregrine falcon is still to be met with in one or two localities. Reports also tend to prove that the land-rail is becoming very scarce in some districts.

It is more pleasant to deal with those species which appear to be on the increase in the county; here however we are on somewhat dangerous ground, for it is not always easy to decide whether increase of observation on the part of naturalists or real extension of range on the part of the species is the true cause of the apparent or real increase in numbers. There seems however to be little doubt that among the summer migrants the nightingale, reed-warbler and lesser whitethroat are all on the increase and spreading westward in the county. The hawfinch and lesser redpoll have certainly increased as breeding species, and the same remark is probably true of the stock-dove, especially as regards the coast. The common sheld-duck may also be included among the increasing species, thanks perhaps to an extension of the 'close time' which this bird enjoys within the limits of the county ; its headquarters are near Burnham, where it breeds in large numbers, and it is no uncommon sight to see a hundred or more together even in the middle of the breeding season. The black-headed gull is now a very abundant winter visitor to the coast, but this does not seem to have been always the case ; some thirty years ago Mr. C. Smith regarded it as only an occasional visitor, and added that he had never at any time of the year recognized the bird on the coast ; of late years a good many have been seen near Burnham throughout the summer months in the breeding plumage, which points to the possibility of some newly established nesting colony in the county.

The discovery of a British lake-village near Glastonbury in 1892 has afforded us an interesting peep at the ornithology of Somerset as it was some nineteen hundred years ago. Mr. Arthur Bulleid, the discoverer of the village, sent several bones of birds which he had found among other relics to Mr. C. W. Andrews. The latter gentleman examined these bones and made known the result of his researches in an article printed in the *Ibis*, 7th ser. vol. v. No. 19. The most interesting discovery was that of the bones of a species of pelican which after careful comparison were identified as belonging to *Pelecanus crispus*, Bruch. To quote from the article in the *Ibis* : 'In the present collection pelican bones are numerous . . . in several instances they must have belonged to young birds. This latter circumstance appears to indicate that these birds bred in the neighbourhood.' As might be expected many of the bones belonged to various species of the tribe of *Anseres*, but remains of the goshawk, white-tailed eagle, kite, barn-owl, cormorant, bittern, coot and crane were also identified. 'This assemblage of species,' continues Mr. Andrews, 'indicates the existence of a district of marsh and mere, haunted by flocks of pelicans and cranes, and in winter by swarms of wild fowl, which furnished the inhabitants of the pile-dwellings with food. Probably the birds were killed with a sling, for great quantities of pellets of clay well adapted for use with that instrument have been found. From time to time a stray sea-bird made its way to the spot, and the white-tailed sea-eagle no doubt found there a good hunting ground.'

A discovery like the above is exceedingly interesting, and one can only regret that so little appears to be known of the ornithology of Somerset even in comparatively modern times. The only two works I know of on the county birds which claim any attempt at completeness are those entitled *The Birds of Somersetshire*, by the late Mr. Cecil Smith, published in 1869; and 'A Revised List of the Birds of Somerset,' by the Rev. M. A. Mathew, printed in the *Proceedings of the Somersetshire Archæological and Natural History Society* for 1893. In drawing up the following list I have made much use of the above works, and my thanks are also due to a number of gentlemen who have furnished me with local lists and notes from various parts of the county, and so have helped me in my attempt, unsuccessful though it may be, to draw up a complete and up to date list of the birds of Somerset.

I have included in the following list 258 species, for which I consider there is sufficient evidence that they have all occurred in the county in a wild state, though it is possible that one or two, such as the little owl or black stork, may not have been truly wild birds. Seventy-five of these may be considered as residents and thirty-three as regular summer visitors, bringing the total of probable breeding birds to 108, while seven more, the chough, hen and Montagu's harriers, teal, shoveler, redshank and dunlin may all still breed occasionally in the county. It is hard to classify the remaining species as the groups often overlap, but there are some thirty-eight more which may be regarded as regular visitors either in winter or at the times of the spring and autumn migrations, while the remaining 105 species can only be regarded as occasional or accidental visitors. Twelve more have been included in brackets as of doubtful occurrence, and some others which have been clearly introduced or have escaped from captivity have been mentioned but not treated of separately. I shall perhaps be considered guilty of inconsistency for treating of the pheasant and red-legged partridge, which were originally introduced, as wild birds, and for omitting or dismissing with a few remarks other introduced species. It does not however seem to me reasonable to couple together birds which have settled down in a wild state with such species as, for example, the Canada goose, Egyptian goose or black swan. The line must be drawn somewhere, or we might find ourselves obliged to include in a local list escaped canaries or even parrots!

BIRDS

1. Missel-Thrush. *Turdus viscivorus*, Linn.
   Locally, Holm-Screech.
   A common resident.

2. Song-Thrush. *Turdus musicus*, Linn.
   A common resident.

3. Redwing. *Turdus iliacus*, Linn.
   Locally, Wind-Thrush.
   A winter visitor, usually common, but in some seasons is locally scarce.

4. Fieldfare. *Turdus pilaris*, Linn.
   A winter visitor, usually common.

5. White's Thrush. *Turdus varius*, Pallas.
   Two records : one secured at Hestercombe near Taunton, January 1870 (vide *Zool.* 1870, p. 2018) ; another shot at Langford, January, 1871 (*Zool.* 1871, p. 2607).

6. Blackbird. *Turdus merula*, Linn.
   Locally, Colley.
   A common resident, and has increased of late years.

7. Ring-Ouzel. *Turdus torquatus*, Linn.
   Locally, Mountain-Colley.
   Seen in various parts of the county, especially on the Mendips, during the spring and autumn migrations. Breeds in limited numbers in the Exmoor country.

8. Wheatear. *Saxicola œnanthe* (Linn.).[1]
   A fairly common summer visitor to such districts as are suited to its habits. Breeds freely among the sandhills near Burnham.

9. Whinchat. *Pratincola rubetra* (Linn.).
   A summer visitor, but local and not common.

10. Stonechat. *Pratincola rubicola* (Linn.).
    Resident. Local, but commoner than the whinchat. Frequents the coast line, the Mendips, the Quantocks and other suitable localities.

11. Redstart. *Ruticilla phœnicurus* (Linn.).
    A common summer visitor.

12. Black Redstart. *Ruticilla titys* (Scopoli).
    A winter visitor, somewhat irregular. There are many records from various parts of the county, and it probably occurs more frequently on the coast line than is generally supposed.

---

[1] Round brackets indicate that the original describer of the species did not employ the generic name which is now adopted.

[Red-spotted Bluethroat. *Cyanecula suecica* (Linn.).
There is a specimen in the Albert Memorial Museum at Exeter, which is stated to have been obtained in Somerset in 1856.]

13. Redbreast. *Erithacus rubecula* (Linn.).
    A common resident.

14. Nightingale. *Daulias luscinia* (Linn.).
    A summer visitor, and numerous in some localities. Seems to have increased of late years, and is spreading westward.

15. Whitethroat. *Sylvia cinerea* (Bechstein).
    A common summer visitor.

16. Lesser Whitethroat. *Sylvia curruca* (Linn.).
    A summer visitor, not very common. More frequently met with in the east of the county, but of late has spread westward. I have observed it as far west as Porlock.

17. Blackcap. *Sylvia atricapilla* (Linn.).
    A common summer visitor.

18. Garden-Warbler. *Sylvia hortensis* (Bechstein).
    A summer visitor, but far less common than the blackcap, and decidedly local. Perhaps least rare in the north east of the county.

[Dartford Warbler. *Sylvia undata* (Boddaert).
Mr. Stanley Lewis of Wells states that he discovered this species in 1900 in the Mendip Hills, and saw specimens at close quarters. As none were obtained the species is included in brackets.]

19. Goldcrest. *Regulus cristatus*, Koch.
    A common resident, and its numbers are considerably increased by migrants in winter.

[Firecrest. *Regulus ignicapillus* (Brehm).
Mr. H. St. B. Goldsmith, formerly of Bridgwater, writes that a friend of his accurately described to him a firecrest, which he saw in his garden near Bridgwater about twelve years ago. The occurrence however must be regarded as doubtful.]

20. Chiffchaff. *Phylloscopus rufus* (Bechstein).
    An abundant summer visitor.

21. Willow-Warbler. *Phylloscopus trochilus* (Linn.).
    A common summer visitor.

22. Wood-Warbler. *Phylloscopus sibilatrix* (Bechstein).

A summer visitor. Chiefly confined to the larger woods. Numerous in the wooded combes in the west of the county.

23. Reed-Warbler. *Acrocephalus streperus* (Vieillot).

A summer visitor. Local, but common in many localities. This species appears to have increased in the county of recent years, and nests commonly around Taunton, Bridgwater and Weston-super-Mare, and probably in suitable localities throughout the county.

24. Marsh-Warbler. *Acrocephalus palustris* (Bechstein).

Probably a regular summer visitor to the county. Nests have been found near Taunton, Bath, Bristol, Martock and elsewhere, and competent observers have noticed the species in other districts. Most of the nests have been discovered of recent years, but the species very possibly bred near Bath fifty years ago (*Zoologist*, 1901, p. 106). For accounts of the nesting of this species in the county see *Zoologist* for 1875, 1877, 1882, 1883, 1889, 1894, 1895, 1901.

25. Sedge-Warbler. *Acrocephalus phragmitis* (Bechstein).

A summer visitor. Common in suitable localities.

26. Grasshopper-Warbler. *Locustella nævia* (Boddaert).

A summer visitor. Local. It is reported as not uncommon around Bath, Bridgwater, Frome, Martock and Wellington. I have noticed it in the breeding season on the high ground behind Porlock Weir.

27. Hedge - Sparrow. *Accentor modularis* (Linn.).

Common resident.

28. Alpine Accentor. *Accentor collaris* (Scopoli).

Accidental. One shot in the Deanery garden at Wells in 1833 (vide Yarrell, i. 297, ed. 4).

29. Dipper. *Cinclus aquaticus*, Bechstein.
Locally, Water Colley.

Resident, but local. May be found by suitable streams throughout the county, particularly in the west.

30. Bearded Reedling. *Panurus biarmicus* (Linn.).

Accidental. Stated in Mr. Baker's notes to have occurred near Bridgwater. Mr. C. W.

Tucker of Bridgwater tells me that his father, who knew Mr. Baker, noticed a flock of these birds near Bridgwater about sixty years ago, so this was perhaps the occurrence to which Mr. Baker referred.

Mr. Stanley Lewis informs me that a male and female were shot near Wells in the spring of 1861, and were mounted by Mr. J. G. Hooper.

31. Long-tailed Tit. *Acredula rosea* (Blyth).

A common resident. An example of the white-headed continental form has been reported as obtained near Bridgwater in October 1871 (D'Urban and Mathew, *Birds of Devon*, p. 34, ed. 2).

32. Great Tit. *Parus major*, Linn.

A common resident.

33. Coal-Tit. *Parus britannicus*, Sharpe and Dresser.

A common resident.

34. Marsh-Tit. *Parus palustris*, Linn.

A common resident, but rather local.

35. Blue Tit. *Parus cœruleus*, Linn.

A common resident.

36. Nuthatch. *Sitta cæsia*, Wolf.

Resident. Fairly common, especially in orchards and the well timbered districts.

37. Wren. *Troglodytes parvulus*, Koch.
Locally, Kitty.

A common resident.

38. Tree-Creeper. *Certhia familiaris*, Linn.

A common resident.

39. Pied Wagtail. *Motacilla lugubris*, Temminck.
Locally, Dishwasher.

A common resident.

40. White Wagtail. *Motacilla alba*, Linn.

Not uncommon on the coast at the time of the spring migration. It has been seen, apparently nesting, in Leigh Woods near Bristol, and is probably a regular summer visitor to many parts of the coast, where it is doubtless often mistaken for the preceding species.

41. Grey Wagtail. *Motacilla melanope*, Pallas.

A fairly common resident. Numbers increased in the autumn. Nests sparingly throughout the county, and more commonly around Frome and in the extreme west.

42. Blue-headed Yellow Wagtail. *Motacilla flava*, Linn.

An occasional summer visitor. Has occurred at Taunton and elsewhere in the extreme west, and has perhaps nested at Wiveliscombe (Cecil Smith).

43. Yellow Wagtail. *Motacilla raii* (Bonaparte).
A summer visitor. Not uncommon.

44. Tree-Pipit. *Anthus trivialis* (Linn.).
A common summer visitor.

45. Meadow-Pipit. *Anthus pratensis* (Linn.).
A common resident.

[Richard's Pipit. *Anthus richardi*, Vieillot.
Accidental visitor. A pair seen near Clevedon, May 30, 1893 (*Zoologist*, 1893, p. 267).]

46. Rock-Pipit. *Anthus obscurus* (Latham).
A common resident on the coast.

47. Golden Oriole. *Oriolus galbula*, Linn.
A rare occasional summer visitor. Has been recorded about nine times from various parts of the county. The latest record appears to be that of a pair seen at South Stoke near Bath, June 1893.

48. Great Grey Shrike. *Lanius excubitor*, Linn.
A rare winter visitor. Has been obtained at least eight times.

49. Red-backed Shrike. *Lanius collurio*, Linn.
A summer visitor, and appears to be generally distributed throughout the county.

50. Woodchat Shrike. *Lanius pomeranus*, Sparrman.
An accidental summer visitor. One killed 'within a short distance of Bristol' (*Birds of Wilts*, p. 123). Mr. C. Prideaux possessed an adult specimen 'from Somersetshire' (*Zoologist*, 1852). The species has also been shot in Cheddar Wood (*A Mendip Valley*, p. 133, T. Compton).

51. Waxwing. *Ampelis garrulus*, Linn.
A rare occasional winter visitor. Has been recorded from the Bristol, Taunton and Winscombe districts and elsewhere in the county.

52. Pied Flycatcher. *Muscicapa atricapilla*, Linn.
A summer visitor, rare and usually only seen at the time of migration. A few pairs probably nest in the Exmoor district. A nest with five eggs was found near the Bristol city boundary, and within the county of Somerset in 1899 (Dr. J. A. Norton, Bristol).

53. Spotted Flycatcher. *Muscicapa grisola*, Linn.
A common summer visitor.

54. Swallow. *Hirundo rustica*, Linn.
An abundant summer visitor.

55. House-Martin. *Chelidon urbica* (Linn.).
An abundant summer visitor.

56. Sand-Martin. *Cotile riparia* (Linn.).
A common summer visitor. Rather local.

57. Greenfinch. *Ligurinus chloris* (Linn.).
A common resident.

58. Hawfinch. *Coccothraustes vulgaris*, Pallas.
Resident in some districts, only a winter visitor to others. Has increased as a resident during the last ten years, and now breeds frequently in the north-east of the county.

59. Goldfinch. *Carduelis elegans*, Stephens.
A resident. Generally distributed, but seems to be getting scarce in some localities.

60. Siskin. *Carduelis spinus* (Linn.).
A winter visitor. Somewhat local, but occasionally appears in fair numbers.

61. Serin Finch. *Serinus hortulanus*, Koch.
Accidental. One shot at Taunton, January or February 1866 (Cecil Smith, *The Birds of Somersetshire*, p. 180).

62. House-Sparrow. *Passer domesticus* (Linn.).
An abundant resident.

63. Tree-Sparrow. *Passer montanus* (Linn.).
Resident, but very local. Not uncommon round Bath, Bridgwater, Frome, Flax Bourton. This species is doubtless often overlooked.

64. Chaffinch. *Fringilla coelebs*, Linn.
Locally, Pink-twink, Whitefinch.
An abundant resident.

65. Brambling. *Fringilla montifringilla*, Linn.
A not uncommon winter visitor.

66. Linnet. *Linota cannabina* (Linn.).
An abundant resident. Numbers increased by arrivals in the autumn.

67. Lesser Redpoll. *Linota rufescens* (Vieillot).
A not uncommon winter visitor. Also a resident in some districts. Of late years it has been noticed breeding frequently in the Bath and Bristol districts. Nests have also been found in the peat-moor country, near Frome, Flax Bourton, Taunton, Bridgwater and Wellington, and it also breeds in all probability near Weston-super-Mare.

68. Twite. *Linota flavirostris* (Linn.).

An occasional winter visitor in small numbers, chiefly to the coast.

69. Bullfinch. *Pyrrhula europæa*, Vieillot.
Locally, Hoop.
A common resident.

[Pine-Grosbeak. *Pyrrhula enucleator* (Linn.).

A specimen is said to have been killed near Taunton about 1852, but little value can be attached to the record (vide *Zoologist*, 1852, 1877, 1890).]

70. Crossbill. *Loxia curvirostra*, Linn.

An irregular visitor, sometimes occurring in large numbers. It is reported to have nested near Bristol (Mathew, *Revised List*).

In the year 1791 a birdcatcher at Bath informed Colonel Montagu that he had taken a hundred pairs in the months of June and July (Montagu, *Ornith. Dict.*).

They seem to have been numerous in 1868; and in 1898, from September onwards, large flocks were observed in various parts of the county.

The larger form (*Loxia pityopsittacus*, Bechstein), is said to have occurred at Clevedon (*Zoologist*, 1888, p. 176).

71. Two-barred Crossbill. *Loxia bifasciata* (Brehm).

One shot out of a little flock at Keynsham near Bath by Mr. Maxwell, February 1895 (vide *Zoologist*, 1895, p. 110).

72. Corn-Bunting. *Emberiza miliaria*, Linn.

A local resident, common in some localities. It is numerous on the Bridgwater level.

73. Yellow Hammer. *Emberiza citrinella*, Linn.

An abundant resident.

74. Cirl Bunting. *Emberiza cirlus*, Linn.

A local resident. In the west of the county, especially around Bridgwater and Weston-super-Mare, it is common, and seems to prefer the vicinity of the coast. It is much rarer in the east, but seems to be not uncommon near Martock in the south.

75. Reed-Bunting. *Emberiza schœniclus*, Linn.

A resident. Not numerous, but well distributed in suitable localities.

76. Snow-Bunting. *Plectrophenax nivalis* (Linn.).

An occasional winter visitor, occurring fairly regularly in some districts.

77. Starling. *Sturnus vulgaris*, Linn.

An abundant resident. Enormous flocks may be seen in the autumn, due doubtless to immigration.

78. Rose-coloured Starling. *Pastor roseus* (Linn.).

A rare occasional visitor. Specimens have been taken at Taunton, Axbridge, Clevedon, 1895, and Laverton near Frome, 1869.

79. Chough. *Pyrrhocorax graculus* (Linn.).

At present only an occasional visitor. This species used formerly to breed on the cliffs near Minehead (C. Smith, *The Birds of Somersetshire*), and is reported to have done so at the Ebbor Rocks in the Mendips. It is improbable that it breeds within the county limits at the present time.

80. Nutcracker. *Nucifraga caryocatactes* (Linn.).

Accidental. The late Captain Tomlin of Rumwell House near Taunton possessed a specimen that had been shot near Bath. Colonel Montagu records one that was seen near Bridgwater in the autumn of 1805. Others are reported to have been seen at Cothelstone and North Petherton (Mathew, *Revised List*).

81. Jay. *Garrulus glandarius* (Linn.).

A resident. Common in some localities, where game is not strictly preserved.

82. Magpie. *Pica rustica* (Scopoli).

The same remarks apply to this species as to the preceding.

83. Jackdaw. *Corvus monedula*, Linn.

An abundant resident.

84. Raven. *Corvus corax*, Linn.

Resident. A pair nest annually on Brean Down, and the species may often be seen in the extreme west of the county, where a few pairs nest on the sea cliffs. Some old haunts, as for example the cliffs at Cheddar, have been deserted.

85. Carrion-Crow. *Corvus corone*, Linn.

Resident. Has been nearly exterminated in some localities, but is common in others, e.g. near Bridgwater and in the west country.

86. Hooded Crow. *Corvus cornix*, Linn.

A very rare winter visitor. Mr. C. Smith mentions three county specimens, and others have been procured at Rowberrow Warren, Tadwick and Puxton.

87. Rook. *Corvus frugilegus*, Linn.
An abundant resident.

88. Sky-Lark. *Alauda arvensis*, Linn.
An abundant resident.

89. Wood-Lark. *Alauda arborea*, Linn.
Resident. Scarce and local. I have noticed the species in summer near Porlock. In some districts it is getting scarcer than in former years, owing to the raids of bird-catchers.

90. Shore-Lark. *Otocorys alpestris* (Linn.).
A very rare winter visitor. Has been reported from Ashton, 1866, and Wraxall, 1874, both places being in the Bristol district.

91. Swift. *Cypselus apus* (Linn.).
An abundant summer visitor.

92. Alpine Swift. *Cypselus melba* (Linn.).
Accidental. A specimen obtained near Axbridge prior to 1851 (*Proc. of Somerset Arch. and Nat. Hist. Soc.* 1850).

93. Nightjar. *Caprimulgus europæus*, Linn.
A fairly common summer visitor. Appears to be well distributed.

94. Wryneck. *Iÿnx torquilla*, Linn.
Locally, Cuckoo's Mate, Barley Bird.
A summer visitor. Fairly common in the Bridgwater, Bath and Bristol districts, and occurs sparingly elsewhere in the county.

95. Green Woodpecker. *Gecinus viridis* (Linn.).
Locally, Woodwall, Rainpie.
A common resident.

96. Great Spotted Woodpecker. *Dendrocopus major* (Linn.).
Resident but nowhere common. This species is the rarest of the three woodpeckers in Somerset, but has been reported from many parts of the county. Not uncommon in the woods on the Quantock Hills.

97. Lesser Spotted Woodpecker. *Dendrocopus minor* (Linn.).
A local resident. Numerous in some localities.

98. Kingfisher. *Alcedo ispida*, Linn.
Resident. On some of the quieter streams, particularly in the west, it is not uncommon. Sometimes seen on the coast, and has nested at Brean Down.

99. Roller. *Coracias garrulus*, Linn.
Accidental. One at Orchard Portman near Taunton, many years prior to 1869 (Smith, *Birds of Somersetshire*, p. 272).

100. Bee-Eater. *Merops apiaster*, Linn.
Accidental. A specimen obtained at Bridgwater was in the collection of Mr. Stradling (*Zoologist*, 1881, p. 309). Mr. Mathew includes in his Somerset list three that were shot out of a small flock in May 1869 at Stapleton near Bristol. The locality however appears to be in Gloucestershire.

101. Hoopoe. *Upupa epops*, Linn.
A rare visitor. Specimens are reported from Priddy, spring 1859; Weston-super-Mare, 1858 and October 1860; Keynsham, May 1862; Monkton, spring 1866; Berrow, September 1892; Bleadon, summer 1895; Flax Bourton, April 1895; and Priston near Bath (*Zoologist*, 1892, p. 409).

102. Cuckoo. *Cuculus canorus*, Linn.
A common summer visitor.

103. Yellow-billed Cuckoo. *Coccyzus americanus* (Linn.).
Accidental. A female in perfect plumage was shot at Pylle on Oct. 6, 1901 (vide *Zoologist*, 1902, p. 26.)

104. White or Barn-Owl. *Strix flammea*, Linn.
Resident. Scarce in some districts owing to persecution, but common in others.

105. Long-eared Owl. *Asio otus* (Linn.).
An uncommon resident. Migrants probably arrive in the autumn.

106. Short-eared Owl. *Asio accipitrinus* (Pallas).
A winter visitor. Common in winter on the mid-Somerset levels. Colonel Montagu in the supplement to his Dictionary records that a great many of these owls occurred near Bridgwater during a plague of field mice.

107. Tawny Owl. *Syrnium aluco* (Linn.).
Resident. The commonest species, but much persecuted.

108. Tengmalm's Owl. *Nyctala tengmalmi* (Gmelin).
Accidental. A specimen was shot at Winscombe in 1859, and was in the collection of the late Mr. C. Edwards of Wrington (*Zoologist*, 1888, p. 176).

109. Little Owl. *Athene noctua* (Scopoli).
Accidental. One shot at Clevedon, in the year 1878, was in the collection of the late Rev. G. W. Braikenridge (*Zoologist*, 1879,

p. 32). This was possibly an escape from captivity, as many are imported from the continent.

110. Snowy Owl. *Nyctea scandiaca* (Linn.).

Accidental. One trapped on Exmoor end of March 1876 (vide *Zoologist*, 1876, p. 4900 ; 1893, p. 226).

111. American Hawk-Owl. *Surnia funerea* (Linn.).

Accidental. A specimen was shot near Yatton on August 25, 1847, while it was hawking for prey (vide Yarrell's *British Birds* i. 184, ed. 4).

[**Scops-Owl.** *Scops giu* (Scopoli).

A specimen is said to have been shot at Claverton in 1838 (vide the list of birds drawn up by Mr. Terry in the *Handbook to Bath*, 1888)].

112. Egyptian Vulture. *Neophron percnopterus* (Linn.).

Accidental. Two seen at Kilve near the Quantock Hills, October 1825, and one of them was shot (vide Yarrell's *British Birds*, i. 6, ed. 4).

113. Marsh - Harrier. *Circus æruginosus* (Linn.).

Extinct as a resident, and now only a rare visitor. One or two specimens are usually shot during the winter in the peat-moor country, where they are called buzzard-hawks.

114. Hen-Harrier. *Circus cyaneus* (Linn.).

Possibly still a resident, but if so only in very small numbers. A pair or two may still breed in Exmoor, but recent information is wanting. More than thirty years ago Mr. C. Smith considered that this species was almost extinct in the county.

115. Montagu's Harrier. *Circus cineraceus* (Montagu).

An occasional summer visitor. Mr. C. Smith considered this species to be more frequent in the county than the hen-harrier. It has been known to nest about forty years ago in Pixton Park near Dulverton, and young have been taken on the Blackdown Hills.

116. Buzzard. *Buteo vulgaris*, Leach.

Resident only in the extreme west of the county, but sometimes seen in other districts in autumn and winter. About two pairs still nest on the cliffs between Minehead and Glenthorne, where this summer (1901) I have seen the young in the nest. A pair nested at Hawkridge in 1890, and doubtless a few still maintain themselves inland in the Exmoor country. Mr. C. Smith considered that the species must at one time have been very plentiful in the west of the county.

117. Rough-legged Buzzard. *Buteo lagopus* (Gmelin).

An irregular winter visitor. Specimens have been obtained at Chargot Lodge and Burnham (Smith, *Birds of Somersetshire*). In the winter of 1875, when quite a flight of rough-legged buzzards visited Devonshire, two were obtained on the skirts of Exmoor (D'Urban and Mathew, *The Birds of Devon*, p. 148, ed. 2).

118. White-tailed Eagle. *Haliaëtus albicilla* (Linn.).

An occasional winter visitor. A good many specimens of this eagle have been either seen or obtained in the neighbourhood of Bridgwater and in the Quantock country. Colonel Montagu described one that was killed on the Mendips about the year 1811. An adult was shot at Stolford in November 1856, and an immature specimen was shot on the borders of Devon by Mr. Snow of Oare about the year 1870. Other specimens have been shot on the coast between Minehead and Bridgwater, and about the year 1890 a pair frequented the Quantocks and are said to have carried off some lambs (*Birds of Devon*, p. 150, ed. 2). The golden eagle (*Aquilla chrysaëtus*) has occasionally been reported from the west of Somerset, but the specimens seem always to have turned out to be immature examples of the white-tailed species. Bones of the goshawk (*Astur palumbarius*) have been identified from the remains of birds discovered near Glastonbury in the lake-dwelling (see Introduction), and in Mr. Terry's list in the *Handbook to Bath* it is stated that a specimen was shot at Claverton in 1833.

119. Sparrow-Hawk. *Accipiter nisus* (Linn.).

Resident. Common where game preserving is not too strictly indulged in.

120. Kite. *Milvus ictinus*, Savigny.

Once a resident, but now only a rare visitor. One shot near Yeovil in 1874 is in the Taunton Museum, and there are other local specimens in private collections. The latest records seem to refer to the year 1888, when a specimen was trapped at Chewton, and another shot in Cleeve Wood near Yatton (Dr. J. A. Norton, Bristol).

121. Honey-Buzzard. *Pernis apivorus* (Linn.).

A rare visitor in summer and autumn. The Rev. M. A. Mathew in his Revised List states that examples have occurred on the Quantock Hills, at Bagborough, Cothelstone, and the near neighbourhood of Taunton. A young male was shot at Cothelstone in the middle of June 1873, and a female was seen shortly afterwards in the neighbourhood, so it is likely that there was a nest close at hand. A specimen was shot near Wells in the spring of 1875 (Stanley Lewis, Wells).[1]

122. Peregrine Falcon. *Falco peregrinus*, Tunstall.

Resident in very small numbers. A pair breed annually on Steep Holm, and one or two eyries are perhaps left upon the coast. The species is reported to have bred formerly on Brean Down and on the Cheddar cliffs.

123. Hobby. *Falco subbuteo*, Linn.

A summer visitor. Occurs in the Taunton district, where it has nested in Stoke Wood. It has also been known to breed on the Blagdon Hills, and has been seen in the summer near Wells and Frome. The species may visit the county more often than is generally supposed.

124. Merlin. *Falco æsalon*, Tunstall.

A winter visitor. Not very uncommon in the west. A pair or two may possibly breed on Exmoor.

125. Red-footed Falcon. *Falco vespertinus*, Linn.

Accidental. A specimen was shot in Cheddar Wood by the late Arthur Tanner of Sidcot about the year 1860. It was for some time in Mr. Tanner's collection, where it was seen by Mr. F. A. Knight.

126. Kestrel. *Falco tinnunculus*, Linn.

A common resident. Breeds on the sea coast as well as inland.

127. Osprey. *Pandion haliaëtus* (Linn.).

A very rare visitor. None have been recorded in recent years. A specimen in the Taunton Museum was killed at Chargot Lodge in October 1859, and others have been obtained in the neighbourhood on ornamental sheets of water. In September 1887 a young female was taken alive on a boat in the Bristol Channel (*Zoologist*, 1887, p. 433). The upper waters of the Bristol Channel were probably, owing to their opaqueness, at no time attractive to this species. A pair

[1] Nests of the honey-buzzard, each containing four eggs, are said to have been discovered in the Mendips in the years 1897 and 1899 (*Ibis*, 8th ser. vol. i. No. 3. p. 515).

are said to have attempted to nest at Monksilver in 1847, but both were shot (vide *Ibis*, 1865, p. 9).

128. Cormorant. *Phalacrocorax carbo* (Linn.).

An uncommon visitor. Perhaps also a resident. There seem to be very few records of the occurrence of this species in the county, but it has been occasionally noticed on the coast, usually in the west where the water is clearer. I saw a pair on Steep Holm on April 20, 1900, and five together on June 25 of the present year (1901); some of these appeared to be young birds which may have been hatched out on the island.

129. Shag or Green Cormorant. *Phalacrocorax graculus* (Linn.).

A rare visitor. One was shot on the coast near Berrow, October 20, 1892 (*Zoologist*, 1894, p. 267). I have on several occasions seen either this or the preceding species on the coast in west Somerset, and other observers have had the same experience.

130. Gannet or Solan Goose. *Sula bassana* (Linn.).

Accidental. A young bird was washed ashore at Stolford in 1880, and others in immature plumage have been noticed on the coast. In 1890 an adult was taken near Martock, many miles inland (*Zoologist*, 1900, p. 557), and in September 1893 a party of four or five was seen at Denny Isle near the mouth of the Avon. The gannets which reach Somerset are probably stragglers from Lundy where a few pairs nest, or from Grassholm off the Pembroke coast, where there is a larger colony.

Bones of the crested pelican (*Pelecanus crispus*, Bruch.), belonging to both adult and immature birds, were discovered in the lake-dwelling near Glastonbury (see Introduction). A specimen of *Pelecanus onocrotalus* was shot on Exmoor in the year 1883, but was proved to have escaped from confinement (Yarrell, iv. 161, ed. 4).

131. Common Heron. *Ardea cinerea*, Linn. *Locally*, Crane.

Resident. There are heronries at Pixton Park near Dulverton, Knowle near Minehead, Halswell near Bridgwater, Brockley near Bristol, and Mells Park near Frome.

[Little Egret. *Ardea garzetta*, Linn.

Accidental. Mr. Edward Jesse in his *Country Life* (John Murray, 1844) mentions a little egret that was shot on Glastonbury Moor, and Mr. Terry records another in the *Handbook to Bath* as shot at Bathampton, 1841.]

132. Squacco Heron. *Ardea ralloides*, Scopoli.

An accidental visitor. One obtained near Bridgwater prior to 1850 (Yarrell, iv. 192, ed. 4).

133. Night-Heron. *Nycticorax griseus* (Linn.).

An accidental visitor. One obtained near Bridgwater was in the collection of Mr. Stradling. Another was shot near Glastonbury in 1881 (see *A Mendip Valley*, p. 173, T. Compton).

134. Little Bittern. *Ardetta minuta* (Linn.).

A rare occasional visitor. Mr. C. Smith knew of four Somerset specimens, and it has also occurred at Wells.

135. Bittern. *Botaurus stellaris* (Linn.).

A winter visitor. Specimens are still shot nearly every winter, and during severe frosts it is far from rare. The bittern, in all probability, used at one time to breed in the marshes of Somerset.

[American Bittern. *Botaurus lentiginosus* (Montagu).

Mr. Stanley Lewis of Wells informs me that he has examined two examples of the American bittern, which were shot near Glastonbury in November 1897.][1]

[White Stork. *Ciconia alba*, Bechstein.

Accidental. One obtained near Bridgwater (Baker, *Proc. of Somerset. Arch. and Nat. Hist. Soc.* 1850). A pair are said to have been shot on the church tower of Wick St. Lawrence in December 1897, but I have not been able to verify this statement.]

136. Black Stork. *Ciconia nigra* (Linn.).

Accidental. One shot on West Sedgemoor near Stoke St. Gregory, May 13, 1814. This bird recovered from its wounds, and was subsequently kept alive for some time by Colonel Montagu. Its skin is now in the British Museum, South Kensington.

137. Glossy Ibis. *Plegadis falcinellus* (Linn.).

A very rare visitor. The only record appears to be that of a specimen shot on the turf-moor near Shapwick in the autumn of 1859 (*Birds of Devon*, p. 199, ed. 2).

138. Spoonbill. *Platalea leucorodia*, Linn.

A very rare visitor. One was shot in November 1813 on West Sedgemoor, and another whose beak and skull are now in

[1] An American bittern is said to have been captured at Long Sutton during the winter of 1898. A photograph of this specimen appeared in *Cage Birds*, Feb. 15, 1902.

the Taunton Museum was shot on Curry Moor many years ago.

139. Grey Lag-Goose. *Anser cinereus*, Meyer.

A very rare winter visitor. It has been reported from the Severn coast.

140. White-fronted Goose. *Anser albifrons* (Scopoli).

A winter visitor. Not uncommon in severe winters, and probably the commonest species of goose which visits Somerset.

141. Bean-Goose. *Anser segetum* (Gmelin).

Not uncommon in severe winters.

[Pink-footed Goose. *Anser brachyrhynchus*, Baillon.

It is uncertain whether this species ever visits Somerset, but it may do so occasionally as it has occurred on the Welsh coast on the opposite side of the Channel. Mr. Sargent of Clevedon saw a goose which had been shot near that town in December 1887, which he thought was an example of this species.]

142. Barnacle-Goose. *Bernicla leucopsis* (Bechstein).

A specimen was sent to Colonel Montagu from Bridgwater in February 1809, and mention was made of it in his Dictionary. This appears to be the only county record.

143. Brent Goose. *Bernicla brenta* (Pallas).

A winter visitor to the coast in small numbers. Flocks of eight or ten have frequently been seen in the Bristol Channel.

The Canada Goose (*Bernicla canadensis*) and Egyptian goose (*Chenalopex ægyptiaca*) have been kept on various ornamental waters and escaped birds have occasionally been shot in the county.

144. Whooper Swan. *Cygnus musicus*, Bechstein.

A very rare winter visitor. A female was sent to Colonel Montagu from Bridgwater in 1805, and Mr. C. Smith records that he has seen specimens which had been shot on the marsh near Taunton.

145. Bewick's Swan. *Cygnus bewicki*, Yarrell.

An occasional winter visitor. In the winter of 1878 a large flock frequented the Somerset moors and others were seen near Glastonbury and Taunton. Wild swans are occasionally seen on the coast near Burnham. The mute swan (*Cygnus olor*) has been met with in an apparently wild state in the county, though doubtless in reality the species has only wandered from some ornamental water. The same may be said of the black swan (*Cygnus atratus*), of which five were shot near Bridgwater in 1858.

146. Common Sheld-Duck. *Tadorna cornuta* (S. G. Gmelin).

Locally, Burrow-Duck.

Resident. Common and increasing. Breeds on Steep Holm and all along the coast line, among sand hills and in crevices of the cliffs. The headquarters during the breeding season seem to be in the neighbourhood of Burnham, where 150 may sometimes be seen together. It is no uncommon sight to see a flock of 100 or more birds on the mudflats during the winter months, and sometimes 200 or even 300 may be seen together.

147. Mallard or Wild Duck. *Anas boscas*, Linn.

Locally, Brown Duck (female).

A winter visitor. Also a resident in limited numbers. Breeds sparingly on Exmoor, the turf moors and the levels near Bridgwater. In some seasons a good many are taken at the decoy near Walton.

148. Gadwall. *Anas strepera*, Linn.

A rare winter visitor. Mr. Cecil Smith recorded two specimens, one from the marsh near Taunton and one from near Dunster. One out of a pair was shot near Langport, January 10, 1889 (*Zoologist*, 1889, p. 149).

149. Shoveler. *Spatula clypeata* (Linn.).

Locally, Spoonbill.

A not uncommon winter visitor to the peat moors, where a few pairs have been known to breed.

150. Pintail. *Dafila acuta* (Linn.).

A somewhat rare winter visitor. Occurs both on the coast and inland. A few are usually taken each year at the Walton decoy.

151. Teal. *Nettion crecca* (Linn.).

A common winter visitor. A few have been known to nest in the peat moors in quite a wild state, and pinioned birds have of late years been turned down in this district and have hatched out broods. This is the commonest species which is at the present time taken in the Walton decoy.

152. Garganey. *Querquedula circia* (Linn.).

Not very rare as a summer visitor to the peat moors, but its nest has not been reported. Colonel Montagu received specimens from the Somerset decoys in the month of April, and was informed that it always appeared on the pools about that time.

153. Wigeon. *Mareca penelope* (Linn.).

A not uncommon winter visitor. At the present time they are rare on the decoy at Walton, but the case seems to have been different at the beginning of last century, when Colonel Montagu was informed by a decoy-man that more of this species were taken in the Somerset decoys than 'duck, teal and all other wildfowl collectively.'

154. Pochard. *Fuligula ferina* (Linn.).

Locally, Wigeon, Red-headed Curre.

A winter visitor to the coast and inland waters, but is not common.

155. Tufted Duck. *Fuligula cristata* (Leach).

Locally, Wigeon.

A fairly common winter visitor chiefly to the inland waters, where possibly a few occasionally nest.

156. Scaup-Duck. *Fuligula marila* (Linn.).

Locally, Black Duck, Diving Curre, Wigeon.

An abundant winter visitor to some parts of the coast. Small flocks begin to appear in the Channel about the middle of October, and a few birds remain until the end of April. During the winter flocks up to 300 in number may be seen in the bays near Weston-super-Mare.

157. Goldeneye. *Clangula glaucion* (Linn.).

A rare winter visitor. Occurs occasionally on the coast and on inland waters such as Barrow reservoir.

158. Long-tailed Duck. *Harelda glacialis* (Linn.).

A very rare winter visitor. The only record appears to be that of an immature bird shot near Weston-super-Mare, December 16, 1890 (*Zoologist*, 1891, p. 66).

159. Common Eider Duck. *Somateria mollissima* (Linn.).

A rare occasional winter visitor. A female was shot on Barrow reservoir in 1888 (*Zoologist*, 1889, p. 32), and a male was shot on the flooded moor near Glastonbury in 1896.

160. Common Scoter. *Œdemia nigra* (Linn.).

A not uncommon winter visitor to the coast. Occurs in flocks in the Channel and sometimes in company with scaup ducks and other wildfowl.

161. Velvet Scoter. *Œdemia fusca* (Linn.).

Has occurred occasionally on the Severn coast. A female in the Salisbury Museum is labelled Somerset. It is also 'observed in the Channel during winter, though in fewer numbers than the preceding,' i.e. the common scoter (*The Birds of Glamorgan*: Cardiff, 1900).

162. Goosander. *Mergus merganser*, Linn.

A not very rare visitor in severe winters. Several specimens have been obtained near Weston-super-Mare, Bridgwater and elsewhere.

163. Red-breasted Merganser. *Mergus serrator*, Linn.

A rare winter visitor. Immature birds have been seen and shot near Weston-super-Mare.

164. Smew. *Mergus albellus*, Linn.

A winter visitor and sometimes fairly numerous in severe seasons. Many have been obtained in the county.

165. Ring-Dove or Wood-Pigeon. *Columba palumbus*, Linn.

An abundant resident; great accessions in winter.

166. Stock-Dove. *Columba œnas*, Linn.

Resident, but not very numerous. Not uncommon in some inland districts and breeds also on the cliffs of west Somerset.

[Rock-Dove. *Columba livia*, Gmelin.

This species is reported to have been found breeding on Brean Down, Sand Point, Barton Rocks, Burrington Combe and the Cheddar Cliffs. It is impossible to say whether these records refer to the wild breed or only to escaped farmyard pigeons. I am strongly inclined to the opinion that the true wild rock-dove is not to be found anywhere in the county of Somerset.]

167. Turtle-Dove. *Turtur communis*, Selby.

A summer visitor. Somewhat local, but not uncommon in many parts of the county. It is reported to be increasing in numbers near Bristol. In 1900 a nest was found at Wraxall consisting almost entirely of pieces of old rusty wire (vide *Country Life*, August 11, 1900).

168. Pallas's Sand-Grouse. *Syrrhaptes paradoxus* (Pallas).

Accidental. In 1863 numbers of these birds visited the British Isles, but none seem to have been recorded for Somerset during that year. Several however were noticed during the visitation of 1888. Three were shot out of a flock of eleven on Steart Island on May 25, 1888, and on the same day two were seen at Charlinch near Bridgwater by the Rev. W. A. Bell. About the same time a small flock was seen at Nynehead, and others were reported from the neighbourhood of Weston-super-Mare, one specimen being procured near Portishead. The Rev. M. A. Mathew saw a flock of about twenty in a turnip field in the parish of Norton St. Philip at the end of June of the same year.

169. Black Grouse. *Tetrao tetrix*, Linn.

Resident in some localities. Numerous on Exmoor and around Dunkery Beacon, but rather scarce on the Quantocks. It is found also on the Blackdown, Brendon and Mendip Hills, though not in large numbers.

170. Red Grouse. *Lagopus scoticus* (Latham).

Accidental. One was shot on Blackdown in the Mendips by Mr. C. Edwards, September 24, 1884 (*Zoologist*, 1885, p. 147). Others are reported to have been taken near Weston-super-Mare, which were thought to have crossed the Channel from Wales (*A Mendip Valley*, p. 170).

171. Pheasant. *Phasianus colchicus*, Linn.
Introduced. Abundant in preserves.

172. Partridge. *Perdix cinerea*, Latham.
A common resident.

173. Red-legged Partridge. *Caccabis rufa* (Linn.).

Introduced. Some were turned out about eighty years ago on the Cheddar moors, but as they drove the English birds away efforts were made to get rid of them. Some were shot in this district in the years 1879, 1880 and 1884, while others are still occasionally met with in various parts of the county. A pair or two appear to be resident on Brean Down.

174. Quail. *Coturnix communis*, Bonnaterre.

A summer visitor. Numerous in some seasons. Several nests have been found recently near Bridgwater, and others have been reported from Cheddar and Sidcot, while the bird has been heard in the summer in the neighbourhood of Taunton.

175. Corn-Crake or Land-Rail. *Crex pratensis*, Bechstein.

A summer visitor. Occasionally seen in winter. This species is reported to be getting scarce in some districts.

176. Spotted Crake. *Porzana maruetta* (Leach).
Locally, Jackymo.

A migrant in spring and autumn. It is however sometimes numerous on the peat moors, where it is almost certainly resident throughout the year. Young broods have been met with in summer near Weston-super-Mare (D'Urban and Mathew, *Birds of Devon*, p. 277, ed. 2).

BIRDS

177. Little Crake. *Porzana parva* (Scopoli).

A very rare occasional visitor. An adult male, shot near Bridgwater, used to be in the collection of Mr. Stradling of Chilton Polden (*Zoologist*, 1881, p. 309).

178. Baillon's Crake. *Porzana bailloni* (Vieillot).

A rare visitor. An adult female was killed near Weston-super-Mare, September 1840. A bird of the year was obtained from near Taunton October 1870, and another, September 1874. A specimen was also shot at Stogursey in 1887.

179. Water-Rail. *Rallus aquaticus*, Linn.
Locally, Skitty.

A resident; not uncommon. Well known as a resident on the peat moor and in other suitable districts. Owing to its habits it is doubtless often overlooked.

180. Moor-Hen. *Gallinula chloropus* (Linn.).
A common resident.

181. Coot. *Fulica atra*, Linn.

A resident on suitable lakes and ponds, and also met with on the coast.

A specimen of the purple gallinule, *Porphyrio cœruleus* (Vandelli), was caught by a sheep dog in the parish of Badgworth on August 25, 1875. It was perhaps an escape from captivity (vide D'Urban and Mathew, *The Birds of Devon*, p. 282).

182. Crane. *Grus communis*, Bechstein.

A rare occasional visitor in spring and autumn. Specimens have been shot at Stolford near Bridgwater, October 17, 1865; South Brent May 1875; Wincanton, about 1880; and Stolford, December 1889. Remains of this species have been found in the lake dwelling near Glastonbury.

A specimen of the demoiselle crane, *Grus virgo* (Linn.), is said to have been picked up dead near Wincanton (vide *Science Gossip*, March 1876). The evidence however is very unsatisfactory (*Zoologist*, 1883, p. 333).

183. Great Bustard. *Otis tarda*, Linn.

Only one record. On September 27, 1870, Mr. J. E. Harting saw one alive on the Shapwick peat moor. He was at the time travelling on the Somerset and Dorset railway (vide *The Field*, January 14, 1871). Bustards were formerly found on the Wiltshire downs, and it is not unreasonable to suppose that a few from these localities used occasionally to visit the Mendips.

184. Little Bustard. *Otis tetrax*, Linn.

Accidental. An adult female in winter plumage was shot on the moor near Drayton, Oct. 19, 1894 (*Field*, Nov. 11, 1894).

185. Stone-Curlew. *Œdicnemus scolopax* (S. G. Gmelin).

A summer visitor. The species probably breeds in some parts of the county, though there is no record. It has frequently occurred on the Mendips and has been seen in summer near Radstock. In September 1898 a specimen was shot near Bridgwater. The species breeds on the Wiltshire downs.

186. Pratincole. *Glareola pratincola*, Linn.

A specimen was shot on the Mendips not far from Weston-super-Mare, some years ago (vide *Zoologist*, 1881, p. 309).

[Cream-coloured Courser. *Cursorius gallicus* (Gmelin).

In a list of the birds of Devon, published in *Trans. Plymouth Institution*, 1862–3, Mr. J. Brooking Rowe mentions that an example of this bird was obtained in Somerset, but no particulars are given.]

187. Dotterel. *Eudromias morinellus* (Linn.).

An occasional visitor on migration in spring and autumn. Seven were shot on the Mendips near Wells, May 1, 1869, and early in May of the same year a specimen was shot on the Steep Holm. In the middle of May, also in 1869, a small trip was seen at Weston-super-Mare, and on August 21, 1870, two specimens were obtained near Wells. Colonel Montagu was informed that eggs of this species had been taken on the Mendip Hills, but he suggested in his Dictionary that the eggs were those of the golden plover.

188. Ringed Plover. *Ægialitis hiaticula* (Linn.).
Locally, Bailie.

Resident. Very numerous on the coast in autumn and winter. Several pairs breed on Steart Island, Steart Point, on the sand dunes near Berrow church and elsewhere on the coast.

189. Kentish Plover. *Ægialitis cantiana* (Latham).

Accidental. The only record is that of an immature specimen shot some years ago on the coast near Burnham (Mathew, Revised List).

190. Golden Plover. *Charadrius pluvialis*, Linn.

An autumn and winter visitor. Found

both on the coast and inland districts and appearing sometimes in large numbers. Mr. Cecil Smith was informed that a few bred near Dunkery Beacon and on Exmoor, but there seems to be no direct evidence that it has ever nested in the county. I have seen small flights on Exmoor in August and September.

191. Grey Plover. *Squatarola helvetica* (Linn.).
Locally, Silver Plover.

A not uncommon winter visitor to the coast.

192. Lapwing. *Vanellus vulgaris*, Bechstein.

A numerous resident. Large flocks frequent the levels near the coast during the winter months.

193. Turnstone. *Strepsilas interpres* (Linn.).
An uncommon visitor to the coast. More frequent in autumn, but specimens in the nesting plumage have been obtained near Weston-super-Mare in early spring.

194. Oyster-Catcher. *Hæmatopus ostralegus*, Linn.
Locally, Sea-Pie.

A resident, but more numerous during the winter. About four pairs still nest on Steart Island and others on the shingle at Steart Point and elsewhere on the coast. I have seen sixty in a flock near Burnham in the middle of June, but conclude that many of these were not breeding birds. Small parties are common on the coast in winter, especially on the mud-flats near Burnham, where I have seen as many as 200 together.

195. Black-winged Stilt. *Himantopus candidus*, Bonnaterre.
Accidental. A specimen was shot near Bridgwater many years ago (*Zoologist*, 1881, p. 309), and another was shot on Sedgemoor near Wells, July 1896 (ibid. 1897, p. 511).

196. Grey Phalarope. *Phalaropus fulicarius* (Linn).

An irregular autumn visitor; sometimes numerous after stormy weather. Many were obtained in the county in 1866, and 1891 was another 'phalarope' year, when after a severe gale in October many were driven ashore on the south-west counties. It has sometimes occurred in Somerset, many miles from the coast.

197. Woodcock. *Scolopax rusticula*, Linn.
Resident in small numbers; great accessions in the autumn. A few breed on the wooded slopes of the Quantock Hills and elsewhere in the west, where it is at all times more numerous than in the east of the county.

198. Great Snipe. *Gallinago major* (Gmelin).
A rare irregular autumn visitor. It has been reported from near Glastonbury, Weston-super-Mare and the Exmoor country.

199. Common Snipe. *Gallinago cœlestis* (Frenzel).
Resident in limited numbers, but chiefly a winter visitor. Breeds on Exmoor and some of the levels of mid-Somerset, and has also been reported as nesting on the Quantocks, Brendon and Blackdown Hills. There are some very good 'snipe grounds' in the county, where sometimes a great many are shot in the winter.

200. Jack Snipe. *Gallinago gallinula* (Linn.).
A winter visitor. Common in some years.

201. Dunlin. *Tringa alpina*, Linn.
Locally, Purre.

Abundant on the coast from autumn to spring, and a few may be seen in the summer in the breeding plumage. Mr. Howard Saunders, in his *Manual of British Birds*, states that he has seen young dunlins on Exmoor hardly able to fly, so it is probable that a few nest in that district.

202. Little Stint. *Tringa minuta*, Leisler.
An occasional autumn visitor. It has been reported from Burnham and Weston-super-Mare.

203. Temminck's Stint. *Tringa temmincki*, Leisler.
A very rare winter visitor. Colonel Montagu received one shot out of a party of six near Bridgwater in September 1805. He referred to this bird under the heading 'Little Sandpiper,' but his description of the bird is now generally thought to apply to *T. temmincki*. Another specimen was shot on North Curry moor, November 14, 1874 (vide *Zoologist*, 1875, p. 4334).

204. Curlew-Sandpiper. *Tringa subarquata* (Güldenstädt).
A rare autumn visitor. Two were obtained at Weston-super-Mare, autumn 1893, and another in winter plumage was shot on a moor near Taunton. This species doubtless occurs more often than is supposed, as it might easily be overlooked among the thousands of dunlins which frequent the coast.

205. Purple Sandpiper. *Tringa striata*, Linn.

Occasionally seen on the coast in autumn. Specimens have been obtained from Bridgwater, Burnham, Weston-super-Mare and Minehead.

206. Knot. *Tringa canutus*, Linn.

An autumn visitor to the coast, not usually in large numbers.

207. Sanderling. *Calidris arenaria* (Linn.).

A not uncommon autumn visitor to the coast. The Rev. R. Chichester has informed me that he sees them every year in small numbers at Minehead, sometimes as early as the middle of August. Others have noticed them at Burnham and at Weston-super-Mare.

208. Ruff. *Machetes pugnax* (Linn.).

Now only a rare autumn visitor. This species used formerly to breed in the fens of Somerset (vide Yarrell's *British Birds*, ed. 4), and Colonel Montagu was informed that they were not uncommon in the fens about Bridgwater before these were drained and enclosed. In more recent times specimens in the breeding plumage have been secured near Taunton.

209. Bartram's Sandpiper. *Bartramia longicauda* (Bechstein).

Accidental. A specimen was shot more than forty years ago at Combwitch near the mouth of the river Parrett. This specimen was identified by the Rev. M. A. Mathew, and is now in the museum at Taunton Castle (*Zoologist*, 1877, p. 389).

210. Common Sandpiper. *Totanus hypoleucus* (Linn.).

A summer visitor. In some parts of the county it is only seen on migration in spring and autumn, but it nests commonly in the west by the Exmoor streams.

211. Wood-Sandpiper. *Totanus glareola* (Gmelin).

A rare passing visitor in spring and autumn. There are two records from the neighbourhood of Taunton. One, an adult shot on May 9, 1870, and the other a young bird shot in the autumn. These were formerly in Mr. Cecil Smith's collection.

212. Green Sandpiper. *Totanus ochropus* (Linn.).

A passing migrant in spring and autumn, not uncommon. Found on the coast as well as by inland streams and pools. Mr. C. Smith has received examples as early as August 8, and the Rev. M. A. Mathew has seen them in the summer near Weston-super-Mare in

so immature a state that he thought they had come from a nest in the neighbourhood.

213. Redshank. *Totanus calidris* (Linn.).

A not uncommon visitor in spring and autumn. I have evidence that a pair have nested quite recently on Steart Island, and it seems probable that the bird occasionally nests elsewhere in the county.

214. Spotted Redshank. *Totanus fuscus* (Linn.).

A rare irregular autumn visitor. Colonel Montagu received a specimen shot out of a small flock near Bridgwater. Two young birds were also procured in autumn several years ago, near Weston-super-Mare, and examined by the Rev. M. A. Mathew.

215. Greenshank. *Totanus canescens* (Gmelin).

A rare autumn visitor to the coast. A few specimens have been recorded from the neighbourhood of Burnham, and another was obtained at Huntspill, August 29, 1884.

216. Bar-tailed Godwit. *Limosa lapponica* (Linn.).

An occasional spring and autumn visitor to the coast.

217. Black-tailed Godwit. *Limosa belgica* (Gmelin.).

A very rare visitor. One out of a couple was shot near Bridgwater in February some year prior to 1869. Mr. Goldsmith has noticed specimens in the poulterers' shops in Bridgwater, shot in the neighbourhood ; but this species is evidently far rarer in the county than the bar-tailed godwit.

218. Common Curlew. *Numenius arquata* (Linn.).

Resident ; more numerous in winter. Breeds in the hilly country in the west and in some numbers on Exmoor. Very abundant on the mud-flats from autumn to spring, and many remain on the coast throughout the summer.

219. Whimbrel. *Numenius phæopus* (Linn.).
Locally, Checker, Cowslip Bird.

A visitor on migration. Common on the coast in spring but rarer in autumn. I have noticed them arrive as early as April 25, and seen them again on August 3.

220. Black Tern. *Hydrochelidon nigra* (Linn.).

Not uncommon both in spring and autumn. Mr. C. Smith heard of thirty being seen in one flock. Young birds have frequently been met with by the river Axe near Weston-super-Mare.

A specimen of the white-winged black tern was shot at Penarth, on the Welsh side of the Channel, in March 1891. It may therefore occasionally wander to the Somerset coast.

221. Sandwich Tern. *Sterna cantiaca*, Gmelin.

Accidental. A specimen was shot at Clevedon, April 22, 1890, and is now in the possession of Mr. E. Sargent of Clevedon.

222. Roseate Tern. *Sterna dougalli*, Montagu.

Accidental. Mr. Sargent has an adult, shot at Clevedon in the year 1898. I have examined the specimen, and the beautiful rose tint on the breast, though considerably faded, is still apparent.

223. Common Tern. *Sterna fluviatilis*, Naumann.

Sometimes seen in spring and autumn in the Channel and on the coast, but not common. It occasionally visits the flooded moors near Glastonbury.

224. Arctic Tern. *Sterna macrura*, Naumann.

Occurs rarely in spring and autumn. Large numbers of this and the preceding species were seen on the coast of the Bristol Channel in May 1842 (vide Yarrell, iii. 554, ed. 4).

225. Little Tern. *Sterna minuta*, Linn.

Occurs occasionally both on the coast and on the moors inland in spring and autumn.

226. Sooty Tern. *Sterna fuliginosa*, Gmelin.

Accidental. The Rev. M. A. Mathew saw an example of this tern which had been caught alive near Bath after stormy weather in October 1885 (*Birds of Devon*, p. 365, ed. 2).

227. Sabine's Gull. *Xema sabinii* (J. Sabine).

A rare winter visitor. Several young birds have occurred at Weston-super-Mare (vide *Zoologist*, 1863, 1865, 1867). Immature birds have also been obtained at Burnham, October 1893, and at Tickenham, September 1896.

228. Little Gull. *Larus minutus*, Pallas.

An irregular winter visitor. The Rev. M. A. Mathew had an immature specimen which had been shot on the sands at Weston-super-Mare about the year 1863. Another was shot at Clevedon, October 1888 (*Zoologist*, 1889, p. 32).

229. Black-headed Gull. *Larus ridibundus*, Linn.

An abundant winter visitor. From autumn to spring this is by far the commonest species of gull on the coast. Of late years several have been observed throughout the summer near Burnham in the breeding plumage, and so it is possible there may be a small nesting colony somewhere in the county, though I have not heard of one.

230. Common Gull. *Larus canus*, Linn.

A common winter visitor to the coast. Sometimes large flocks may be seen.

231. Herring-Gull. *Larus argentatus*, Gmelin.

Resident. May be seen on the coast at all seasons of the year, but not in large numbers. About twelve pairs nest on Steep Holm, but I do not think that there is any other nesting station in the county.

232. Lesser Black-backed Gull. *Larus fuscus*, Linn.

Resident. Not at any time common on the coast. Ten or twelve pairs nested this year (1901) with the herring-gulls on Steep Holm. I visited Steep Holm on June 25 of the present year, and consider that there were about twenty-three pairs of gulls breeding on the island, and perhaps rather more herring-gulls than black-backs.

233. Great Black-backed Gull. *Larus marinus*, Linn.

Seen occasionally on the coast. Colonel Montagu was informed that this species used to breed on Steep Holm, but that would be about 100 years ago. I do not know when they ceased to breed there, but there appear to be none at the present time. A few breed on the Gower coast, Glamorgan, on the opposite side of the Channel.

234. Glaucous Gull. *Larus glaucus*, Fabricius.

An irregular winter visitor. Several have been obtained at Weston-super-Mare from among the flock of gulls which enter the bay in pursuit of sprats. Yarrell's illustration was taken from a specimen shot on the river Severn near Bristol in 1840.

235. Iceland Gull. *Larus leucopterus*, Faber.

A rare winter visitor. Mr. Cecil Smith received an immature specimen from Weston-super-Mare which had been obtained on December 28, 1870. Another was taken inland at Somerton, December 12, 1881 (*Zoologist*, 1882, p. 71).

BIRDS

236. Kittiwake. *Rissa tridactyla* (Linn.).

A numerous winter visitor to the coast. Large flocks may often be seen, especially after stormy weather; but as a rule the species is not quite so numerous on the coast as the black-headed gull.

237. Ivory-Gull. *Pagophila eburnea* (Phipps).

An accidental visitor. Mr. C. Smith heard of one or two specimens which had been procured in the county.

An adult was caught in a trap at Weston-super-Mare in the winter of 1864 (vide *Zoologist*, 1865, p. 9470).

238. Great Skua. *Megalestris catarrhactes* (Linn.).

Accidental. One was shot at Berrow in December 1883 (vide *Zoologist*, 1896, p. 233). According to the report of the British Association Migration Committee, another specimen was seen off Minehead on October 16, 1886, and at the same time twelve Pomatorhine skuas and six Richardson's skuas were also noticed.

239. Pomatorhine Skua. *Stercorarius pomatorhinus* (Temminck).

Accidental. In October 1879 large numbers appeared off the south-west counties of England, and at that time examples were procured in Somerset at Minehead, Combwitch, North Curry, Weston-super-Mare and on Steart Island. Others occurred in the county in October 1880, and November 1893.

240. Arctic or Richardson's Skua. *Stercorarius crepidatus* (Gmelin).

Accidental. An adult was shot at Clevedon, December 1873, and an adult and two young at Stolford, autumn 1892.

241. Long-tailed or Buffon's Skua. *Stercorarius parasiticus* (Linn.).

Accidental. An adult was shot at Nynehead, October 1862, and an immature bird at Stolford, September 1873. In the autumn of 1891 numbers were blown by gales into the Bristol Channel, and a specimen was shot as high up as Clevedon.

242. Razorbill. *Alca torda*, Linn.

A straggler from Lundy and the South Wales breeding stations. Small parties may be seen in the Bristol Channel in autumn and winter.

243. Guillemot. *Uria troile* (Linn.).

An autumn and winter visitor to the Channel, when examples are sometimes taken on the Somerset coast. There seems to be no breeding station in the county.

244. Black Guillemot. *Uria grylle* (Linn.).

Accidental. An adult in winter plumage was taken near Quantoxhead prior to 1869 (C. Smith's *The Birds of Somersetshire*, p. 550).

245. Little Auk. *Mergulus alle* (Linn.).

Accidental, in winter. Several specimens have been at various times picked up dead or caught alive, doubtless having been driven in from the sea by storms. There are records for the years 1805, 1863 and 1884, both from the coast and inland. Mr. Stanley Lewis of Wells informs me that ten specimens have been taken during the last twelve years, principally from the flooded moors near Glastonbury.

246. Puffin. *Fratercula arctica* (Linn.).

Occasionally wanders up the Channel, and sometimes occurs on the coast. A young bird was caught alive at Cheddar, October 1888.

247. Great Northern Diver. *Colymbus glacialis*, Linn.

Accidental. Mr. Cecil Smith mentions an adult shot on the river at Nynehead, and states that one or two immature examples have occurred on the ponds at Chargot. A young bird was shot on the Barrow reservoir, January 20, 1881, and two were shot some years ago on the floating harbour at Bristol. Another was killed at Steart by a fisherman, November 1888.

248. Black-throated Diver. *Colymbus arcticus*, Linn.

Accidental. An adult was shot near Williton, December 1875, and an immature bird was killed near Burnham, December 9, 1895 (*Zoologist*, 1896, p. 233).

249. Red-throated Diver. *Colymbus septentrionalis*, Linn.

Accidental. A specimen was picked up near Taunton, March 28, 1867, and others were shot in the river near Bridgwater during the winters of 1890 and 1892. There are one or two other records, but this species as well as the two preceding can only be regarded as accidental visitors to Somerset.

250. Great-crested Grebe. *Podicipes cristatus* (Linn.).

A rare visitor. Mr. C. Smith recorded four county specimens. The species has also occurred on the Barrow reservoir, and doubtless on many other inland waters in the county. In January 1895 a specimen was picked up dead on the coast in the west of the county by Mr. A. Luttrell, and I possess an adult male shot at the mouth of the river Axe, November 2, 1901.

251. Red-necked Grebe. *Podicipes griseigena* (Boddaert).

Accidental. Taunton, February 1870; North Curry, February 1871 (*Zoologist*, 1871, p. 2563).

252. Slavonian Grebe. *Podicipes auritus* (Linn.).

Accidental. Mr. C. Smith knew of two examples from the neighbourhood of Taunton. It has also occurred on the Barrow reservoir in January 1885, and again in 1890.

253. Eared Grebe. *Podicipes nigricollis* (Brehm).

Accidental. A specimen was picked up dead near Bridgwater, July 1896 (*Zoologist*, 1896, p. 304).

254. Little Grebe or Dabchick. *Podicipes fluviatilis* (Tunstall).

A common resident in suitable localities. Found on the rhynes as well as the pools and larger pieces of water.

255. Storm-Petrel. *Procellaria pelagica*, Linn.

Occasionally picked up after gales, sometimes far inland. Colonel Montagu mentions a specimen from Bath, and a more recent example was obtained near Glastonbury, January 1897.

256. Leach's Fork-tailed Petrel. *Oceanodroma leucorrhoa* (Vieillot).

Accidental. Sometimes driven in by gales. Mr. C. Smith mentions two instances, one from Cothelstone, another from Weston-super-Mare. One was shot, October 1883, near the Clifton Suspension Bridge (*Zoologist*, 1884, p. 145), another was shot in December 1892, near Bridgwater (vide *Zoologist*, 1893, p. 22).

257. Manx Shearwater. *Puffinus anglorum* (Temminck).

Accidental. Has occurred after heavy gales. About seven examples have been procured both on the coast and inland, and others have been seen in the Channel.

258. Fulmar. *Fulmarus glacialis* (Linn.).

Accidental. Four specimens have been recorded: An adult from Weston-super-Mare, winter 1868 (*Zoologist*, 1869); an immature specimen from Stolford, October 1869; a third occurred near the mouth of the Avon, August 1878; and a fourth was obtained near Taunton, December 1883 (*Zoologist*, 1884).

A specimen of the 'gentoo' penguin (*Pygoscelis taeniata*) was picked up dead on the shore near Berrow, and is now in the possession of Mr. H. St. B. Goldsmith, late of Bridgwater. It was quite fresh when found, and had probably escaped from some ship.

MAMMALS

In the following account of the mammals of Somerset only those species have been included that are to be found in a wild state within its boundaries at the present time or have occurred within the last fifty years, either as residents or occasional visitors ; and those species have been omitted which have been extinct as residents for a longer period than half a century or are unlikely to occur even as accidental visitors.

In a county having such an extensive seaboard as Somerset has on the north, it might have been expected that seals and cetaceans would have occurred more frequently ; but besides being out of their usual track the waters of the Channel are so much discoloured by Severn mud, and also by the mud brought down by the Parrett into Bridgwater Bay, that the coast is exceedingly poor in marine life and offers but little attraction to these animals. Another cause that has tended to shorten the list has been the absence of evidence as to the *species* that have occurred from time to time, as specimens have been merely reported as a 'seal' or a 'whale.'

Several specimens of rorqual have at different times floated up the Bristol Channel or been stranded on the Severn coast, but such 'jetsam and flotsam' can hardly be considered as entitled to a place in the county fauna.

The roe deer has been omitted, although a specimen was found and hunted by the Seavington hounds in 1883 to the south of the Vale of Taunton ; yet this cannot be considered as having been anything but a stray from Dorset, where roe deer were introduced at the beginning of the nineteenth century.

There are two species of bats that further observations will undoubtedly add to the list, viz. the barbastelle and Natterer's bat. The former has been taken in Bristol just outside the county boundary and also in Wiltshire. The latter has occurred at Kingswood near Bath in the spring of 1874 (vide specimens in Bath Museum), and has also been found in Gloucestershire and in Dorset. There can be little doubt that these near neighbours hunted as often in Somerset as in the county where they were captured.

Mr. Richard Lydekker, F.R.S., in his handbook of British mammalia gives 43 land mammals (native and introduced) as at present inhabiting Great Britain, besides 4 species of seals and 19 species of whales. The present list enumerates 33 terrestrial forms besides 1 seal and 3 whales as forming the present mammalian fauna of Somerset.

The chief authorities on the mammals of the county are Baker, 'List of the Mammals of Somerset' in the *Proceedings of the Somerset Archæological and Natural History Society* for 1849–50 ; Fairbrother, *Mammals of Shepton Mallet* (1856) ; C. Terry, 'Fauna within a radius of 6 miles of Bath,' in Wright's *Historical Guide to Bath* (1864) ; T. Compton, *Winscombe Sketches* (1882) ; R. Lydekker, F.R.S., *Handbook of British Mammals* (1896) ; Prof. C. Lloyd Morgan, F.R.S., and H. J. Charbonnier in British Association *Handbook to Bristol and Neighbourhood* (1898), and various notes that have appeared at intervals in the *Zoologist*.

CHEIROPTERA

1. **Greater Horseshoe Bat.** *Rhinolophus ferrum-equinum*, Schreber.

Frequent in church towers and sometimes in caves. Abundant in Wells Cathedral and also at Hampton Rocks, Bath.

2. **Lesser Horseshoe Bat.** *Rhinolophus hipposiderus*, Bechstein.

Local and scarce. Generally found in caves or old quarries, in the old lead workings at Dundry and in other localities.

3. **Long-eared Bat.** *Plecotus auritus*, Linn.

Common and generally distributed. This species is the most easily tamed of our bats, and makes a most interesting pet.

4. **Great Bat or Noctule.** *Pipistrellus noctula*, Schreber.

Bell—*Scotophilus noctula*.

Common and generally distributed. Often found in numbers in old ash trees in June. Many of these colonies consist of females only. If disturbed they will often forsake the tree. This is a most useful species, as they destroy an immense quantity of 'chafers.' This bat produces one young one in May or early June.

5. **Pipistrelle.** *Pipistrellus pipistrellus*, Schreber.

Bell—*Scotophilus pipistrellus*.

Not uncommon in old houses and caves. In some localities rarer than the next species. It is not infrequently seen in early spring flying in bright sunshine.

6. **Whiskered Bat.** *Myotis mystacinus*, Leisler.

Bell—*Vespertilio mystacinus*.

Sometimes abundant in old roofs, also in caves and quarries. A colony containing more than 100 individuals was found in the roof of an old house at Keynsham on July 2, 1888. Some twenty specimens were captured and proved to be all females. Many of these gave birth to a young one within a day or two. These latter had pink bodies and nearly black heads and membranes ; they were quite naked and apparently blind, and measured $2\frac{1}{2}$ to 3 inches across the wings.

INSECTIVORA

7. **Hedgehog.** *Erinaceus europæus*, Linn.

Common in suitable localities. A female captured in June littered on the 24th. The young, three in number, appeared quite naked at first, but on the second day the spines, which were quite soft, began to show on the surface of the skin.

8. **Mole.** *Talpa europæa*, Linn.

Common. The cream coloured variety with rusty underparts occurs not infrequently. There is also a much rarer particoloured variety, black with large patches of white, in which the white fur is rather longer than the black.

9. **Common Shrew.** *Sorex araneus*, Linn.

Very common. This species is largely eaten by owls.

10. **Pigmy Shrew.** *Sorex minutus*, Pallas.

Bell—*Sorex pygmæus*.

Rather uncommon and local. It occurs in the Leigh Woods near Bristol.

11. **Water Shrew.** *Neomys fodiens*, Pallas.

Bell—*Crossopus fodiens*.

Local and sometimes scarce. Some specimens, such as those occurring in Leigh Woods, have the underparts dusky, approaching the form *remifer*.

MAMMALS

CARNIVORA

12. Wild Cat. *Felis catus*, Linn.

This is now extinct. The last occurrence was mentioned at a meeting of the Bristol Naturalists' Society in 1867 by the late president, William Sanders, F.R.S., who had 'seen a specimen, a few years before, that had been shot in the country south of Wells.'

13. Fox. *Vulpes vulpes*, Linn.
Bell—*Vulpes vulgaris*.

Common and preserved for purposes of sport. 'A pure white variety was killed in 1887 by the Taunton Vale Foxhounds' (Lydekker).

14. Pine Marten. *Mustela martes*, Linn.
Bell—*Martes abietum*.

Very rare, but probably still lingers on Exmoor, and through its roving habits may occur within the county at any time. A specimen in Taunton Museum was obtained at Dulverton.

15. Polecat. *Putorius putorius*, Linn.
Bell—*Mustela putorius*.

Formerly common, but now very rare. As the species still holds its own in several parts of Great Britain (in Wales in numbers) it will certainly be found occasionally, for during hard weather these animals migrate (sometimes in small packs) to great distances.

16. Stoat. *Putorius ermineus*, Linn.
Bell—*Mustela erminea*.

Common. Nearly white specimens have been shot near Taunton in January and also at the same time and place specimens in a brown coat as in summer. Nearly white specimens also occur during very mild winters.

17. Weasel. *Putorius nivalis*, Linn.
Bell—*Mustela vulgaris*.

Common. Often called by the country folk in west Somerset the *stoat*, while they term the former species the *weasel*.

18. Badger. *Meles meles*, Linn.
Bell—*Meles taxus*.

Fairly common and maintains its numbers in suitable places. A female caught near Shepton Mallet littered on February 16 (1899). The young were four in number, blind, and very slightly hairy.

19. Otter. *Lutra lutra*, Linn.
Bell—*Lutra vulgaris*.

Not uncommon in rivers and streams. As these animals often travel many miles during the night they may occur unexpectedly in any of the streams. Six years ago Messrs. George and Edward Parsons killed three females and one male in the river Tone at Bathpool near Taunton, three on one day and one on the next. The largest weighed about 19 lb. This species has also occurred at Bathford, Limpley Stoke, Congresbury, Creech St. Michael and elsewhere.

20. Common Seal. *Phoca vitulina*, Linn.

For reasons given in the introduction seals have rarely been recorded from the coast of Somerset. Mr. Sargeant of Clevedon reports that he saw one that had been shot in Lady Bay, Clevedon, on March 7, 1874.

RODENTIA

21. Squirrel. *Sciurus leucourus*, Kerr.
Bell—*Sciurus vulgaris*.

Common. Abundant in some localities.

22. Dormouse. *Muscardinus avellanarius*, Linn.
Bell—*Myoxus avellanarius*.

Local, but sometimes in plenty in Claverton Woods near Bath and at Portbury near Bristol.

23. Brown Rat. *Mus decumanus*, Pallas.

Very common in town and country; has been known to devour the grapes in a vinery. The melanic variety, *M. hibernicus*, has not been recorded, but may be found to occur.

24. Black Rat. *Mus rattus*, Linn.

Local. Occurs on the Somerset side of the Bristol Avon in warehouses and factories.

25. Ship Rat. *Mus alexandrinus*.

Often occurs on board ships and in Bristol warehouses. This species breeds freely with *Mus rattus*. Hybrid specimens are frequent, and often have white paws and a white patch on the breast.

26. House Mouse. *Mus musculus*, Linn.

Very common in buildings, though often found in the open country.

27. Long-tailed Field Mouse. *Mus sylvaticus*, Linn.

Very common in fields and woods, though sometimes found in houses in the suburbs of towns. This species lays up stores of corn or nuts for winter use.

28. Harvest Mouse. *Mus minutus*, Pallas.

Local and decidedly scarce in the more northern parts of the county, but fairly common a few miles from Yeovil. It consumes quantities of flies and insects, and makes a very pretty and interesting pet.

29. Water Vole. *Microtus amphibius*, Linn.
   Bell—*Arvicola amphibius*.

Very common. A black variety is said to occur. Water voles seem to have been excessively abundant in former times, as immense numbers of their bones and teeth are found in the loam filling the fissures in the limestone at Holwell near Frome, and in other localities.

30. Field Vole. *Microtus agrestis*, Linn.
   Bell—*Arvicola agrestis*.

Common and swarming in some seasons.

31. Bank Vole. *Evotomys glareolus*, Schreber.
   Bell—*Arvicola glareolus*.

Sometimes not uncommon in Leigh Woods near Bristol, where they have been seen in small scattered parties of eight or ten making their way down the valleys.

32. Common Hare. *Lepus europæus*, Pallas.
   Bell—*Lepus timidus*.

Fairly common in some parts of the county. Mr. Arthur Vassall of Harrow says that he has observed the lowland hares round Langport and Athelney move up to higher ground shortly before rain occurs in sufficient quantities to flood the district.

33. Rabbit. *Lepus cuniculus*, Linn.
   Very common.

UNGULATA

34. Red Deer. *Cervus elaphus*, Linn.

This grand member of the British fauna is still found in a wild state on Exmoor, where it has existed for many centuries. The question of whether the red deer at present found on the Quantocks is truly indigenous has been discussed at length in the *Proceedings of the Somerset Archæological and Natural History Society*, (xliv. i. 22), and the evidence adduced leads to the belief that the present red deer were introduced there about 1839, and that except as a straggler it did not occur on the Quantocks during the 150 or 200 years previous to that date.

CETACEA

35. Bottle-nosed Whale. *Hyperoodon rostratus*, Müller.

A whale of this species was found in Weston-super-Mare bay some twenty or twenty-five years ago, and was killed by some boatmen (Compton, *Winscombe Sketches*, p. 136).

36. Grampus or Killer. *Orca gladiator*, Lacépède.
   Bell—*Phocæna orca*.

Occurs occasionally. 'In March, 1864, ten of these whales entered the river Parrett, all of which were captured within a few miles of Bridgwater' (Lydekker). Mr. Sargeant of Clevedon saw two whales, probably of this species, killed in Little Harp Bay, Clevedon, on October 17, 1866.

37. Common Porpoise. *Phocæna communis*, F. Cuvier.

Not infrequently seen off the coast, and sometimes as far up the Channel as Portishead.

EARLY MAN

CHAPTER I. PLEISTOCENE SOMERSET

1. INTRODUCTORY

THE story of the arrival of man in Somerset, and of the gradual evolution of culture during untold ages, is an epitome of the history of mankind in Europe, north of the Alps and Pyrenees. Within the limits of this beautiful county all the principal events which stand out from the darkness of the past in the light of recent discovery find their place. The arrival of the first and oldest tribes of Palæolithic man, in the Pleistocene age, is recorded in the river gravels of the southern Axe, near Axminster. The animals which he hunted are represented by the discoveries at Freshford on the Avon, near Bath, and just above low-water mark at St. Audries, where the range of the Quantock hills descends to the shore of the Bristol Channel. The numerous caverns penetrating the range of carboniferous limestone hills, sweeping, from Weston-super-Mare and Uphill, through the Mendips eastward, reveal not merely the habitations of the cave-man, but also tell us the story of his surroundings.

If we turn from this glimpse of the arrival of primeval man in the Pleistocene age to the incoming of the peoples to whom we owe the beginnings of the culture of to-day, we find them amply represented by numerous discoveries, which fall within the usual classification applicable to the whole of the old world—the Neolithic age, the age of Bronze, and last, and more important than either, the Prehistoric Iron age.

In attempting to give an outline of the history of the population of the county, in the three divisions of the Prehistoric period, it must be confessed that the materials are so vast in quantity, and are increasing so rapidly, that it is impossible to give a finished and complete account within the limits of this work. This can only be done when the record is more complete than it is at present.

In all these four sections the record of man in Somerset is a mere fragment of the series of events which took place in the Pleistocene and Prehistoric periods not only in Britain but in the whole of France and Germany, and in a more remote degree in Spain and Italy.

A HISTORY OF SOMERSET

2. THE RIVER-DRIFT MAN AND HIS SURROUNDINGS IN SOMERSET

The numerous Palæolithic implements found during the last twenty years in the valley of the southern Axe, at Broom [1] near Axminster, prove the presence of the older section of the Palæolithic men, known all over middle and southern Europe as the men of the River-drift. There the numerous implements (figs. 1, 2, 3) in the deposits of sand and gravel, made for the most part of chert, recall to mind those of Amiens and St. Acheul, of Salisbury and of the region of the Solent.[2] They clearly belong to the same period as that during which the Isle of Wight was joined on the one hand to Hampshire, and on the other to the coast of France, when the River-drift men could follow in the hunt the herds of wild animals, as they passed northwards in their seasonal migrations, from France across the English Channel, then dry land, northwards along the line of the river Axe and of the Avon into Somerset. They represent nearly all the types found in England and the continent, some being perfectly fresh in shape, and others of them worn and rolled. They are obviously an accumulation formed in a favourite camping-place during a very long period of years, and mark unmistakably one of the lines of the migration of the River-drift man into Somerset. Broom is on the southern boundary of the county. They have also been found by Mrs. C. I. Elton in the district immediately to the north, near Whitestaunton Manor, Chard. The recent discovery [3] of twenty-three Palæolithic implements by Mr. G. T. Leslie to the south of Taunton, identical with one or other of the above types, and made of Upper Greensand Chert, indicates the route which was taken by the Palæolithic men as they ranged northwards. The implements have been obtained from the superficial deposits at Shoreditch, Staple Fitzpaine, on the north side of Staple Hill, and on Brook farm, Otterford. The makers therefore passed from the valleys of the Otter and the Yart, a tributary of the Axe, over the watershed into the vale of Taunton. No remains of the wild animals living in the district at the time have as yet been met with in this region. They have however been recorded from river gravels of the same age as those of Broom in the north of the county, in the valley of the Avon near Bath. At Loxbrook, Winwood has discovered the lion, Irish elk, reindeer, urus, bison, horse, woolly rhinoceros and mammoth. At Freshford, higher up the valley, the musk-sheep, bison, horse and mammoth have been found by the late Charles Moore and Winwood, while a fine tusk of mammoth, obtained in 1859 from the clayey subsoil overlying the reefs exposed at low water near St. Audries, by the late Sir Alexander Hood, extends the

---

[1] Evans, *Journ. Anthrop. Inst.* vii. 499 ; D'Urban, *Geol. Mag.* 1878, p. 37 ; *Trans. Dev. Assoc.* xvi. 501. They occur in vast numbers. Figs. 1 and 2 are in the Manchester Museum.

[2] See *V.C.H. Hants*, i. 253.

[3] I am indebted to Mr. J. E. Pritchard for this information and for allowing me to examine the specimens.

Fig. 1. Palæolithic Implement, Ballast Pit, Broom, Axminster.
Full size.

range, in the river deposits, of these animals as far to the north-west as
the Bristol Channel. It is obvious therefore that this remarkable group
of wild animals ranged over the whole of the county, and into the area
now occupied by the Bristol Channel. They extended further to the
north and to the east, up the valley of the Severn, beyond Gloucester
and Worcester, and their remains are met with in considerable abundance to the east and to the south in the river deposits near Salisbury,[1] in
which they lie intermingled with implements of the same type as those
of Broom. There can therefore be no doubt that the River-drift man
lived in this district at the same time as the above animals, or in other
words in the Pleistocene age.

River-drift man is proved by numerous discoveries in other places
to have been a hunter very poorly equipped for the chase. His only
cutting implements were splinters of flint and chert. Most of his implements and weapons were made of the same materials, rudely chipped
to an edge, sometimes fashioned into the shape of an axe-head, to be
used either in the hand, or fastened in a handle of withies (figs. 1, 2, 3),
or brought to a point, which may have been a spearhead, or carefully
chipped for scraping bones and skins, or made into borers ; but always
without trace of grinding. They were made of stones picked up by
the sides of the streams, either flint or chert. Their makers were
ignorant of all the arts, excepting those connected with the above rude
implements and weapons.

The use of implements and knowledge of fire are the two main
points which distinguished the River-drift man from the animals by
which he was surrounded. He was a hunter, but without the aid of
the dog, leading a wild nomad life, following the migratory wild
animals as they swung north and south from France to England, then
not an island, but a western portion of the continent ranging as far
to the north as Scandinavia, and as far to the west as the line now sunk
100 fathoms deep beneath the waters of the Atlantic.

3. THE RIVER-DRIFT MAN OLDER THAN THE CAVE MAN

The discoveries in Kent's Hole Cavern [2] near Torquay, and in the
caverns of Cresswell Crags,[3] prove that the River-drift hunter was the
first human inhabitant of Devon and of Derbyshire and Nottinghamshire
who has left any traces behind. In all these caverns the strata containing
his implements and weapons occur at the bottom, and are covered by
other and later accumulations containing implements and weapons of a
higher type, identical with those found under similar conditions in the
caves of Germany, Belgium, France and Switzerland. The men who
made them are known under the name of the Cave men, or Reindeer-

[1] Stevens, *Flint Chips*, p. 47 ; Evans, *Ancient Stone Implements*, p. 607 ; and *Quart. Journ. Geol. Soc. Lond.* xx. 168 ; Dawkins, *Early Man*, p. 161.
[2] Pengelly, *Brit. Assoc. Reports*, 1864–78.
[3] Dawkins and Mellow, *Quart. Journ. Geol. Soc. Lond.* xxxi. 67a ; xxxii. 240 ; xxxiii. 579 ; xxxv. June, 1879.

folk. In Britain therefore, as on the continent,[1] the River-drift men were the earliest human immigrants, and were followed in the course of long ages by the Cave men.

The length of the interval between the two must have been considerable when we take into account the fact that in Kent's Hole a sheet of crystalline stalagmite, in some places nearly 12 feet thick, separates the lower breccia, composed of fragments of limestone containing River-drift implements, from the upper cave earth with the implements of the Cave men. It was 'formed after the materials of the breccia were deposited, but before the introduction of the cave earth.'[2] The stalagmite in some parts of the cavern had been broken up and carried out of the cave before the first instalment of cave earth was deposited. We may therefore conclude that the interval was long enough not only to allow of the formation of the crystalline floor by the slow drip of water from the roof, but also of great physical changes in the district, by which it was subsequently broken up and partially carried away. It was long enough to allow of the evolution of the higher culture which characterizes the implements of the Cave men as compared with those of the River-drift men.

4. THE CAVERNS OF SOMERSET

In dealing with the Cave men we shall take the point of view offered by the study of the caverns of Somerset. The outliers of Carboniferous Limestone, on the southern side of the Bristol Channel, have long been known for their ossiferous caverns and fissures.[3] From a fissure in Durdham Down near Bristol, Miller obtained numerous bones, about the year 1820, among which Buckland identified the hind leg of a horse, the bones being kept in position by being imbedded in a mass of stalagmite. Subsequently the remains of bison, reindeer, lion, hippopotamus, mammoth, and the rare species of rhinoceros, *R. hemitœchus*, were discovered by Stutchbury. This cave is in Gloucestershire, close on to the northern border of Somerset, and is the only locality in the district which has furnished the remains of this rhinoceros and the hippopotamus. Both of these animals had been discovered in other caverns in Britain—in Kirkdale hyæna-den in Yorkshire and in the caves of Cresswell Crags on the borders of the counties of Nottingham and Derby. The latter is found in comparative abundance in the river deposits, and occurs in several of the caverns, ranging southwards from the vale of Pickering in Yorkshire, throughout the whole of middle and southern England.

The caves of the Mendip Hills were known to contain bones as early as the middle of the eighteenth century, when that of Hutton, near Weston-super-Mare, was discovered in mining ochre. The miners

[1] Dawkins, *Early Man*, p. 198.
[2] Pengelly, *Journ. Plymouth Inst.* Feb. 18, 1875, pp. 17, 18.
[3] For original authorities see Dawkins, *Cavehunting*, chap. viii.

FIG. 2.   PALÆOLITHIC IMPLEMENT, BALLAST PIT, BROOM, AXMINSTER.
Full size.

followed the ochre until they met with a chamber, the floor of which was formed of that material, with white bones on the surface, scattered through the mass, and projecting from the sides, roof, and floor of the excavation, in such quantities as to resemble the contents of a charnel house. Subsequently it was fully explored by Williams and Beard, the two gentlemen to whom we owe the exploration of the neighbouring caves of Uphill, Bleadon, Banwell, Sandford Hill and Burrington Coombe, during the period between 1821 and 1860.

All these caverns consist of chambers at various levels more or less connected with fissures, and from the perfect condition of the bones they are proved to have been inaccessible to the bone-destroying hyæna then inhabiting the district. Their contents were introduced, as is suggested by Buckland, from the surface, by streams, which have now ceased to flow, in consequence of the change in the physical geography of the district. These streams are now to be found in the limestone below the caverns at various levels, as for example at Burrington Coombe and Cheddar Pass. The red and grey mud, the sand and the pebbles in which the bones were imbedded, in many cases completely filling the chambers, are also materials left behind by the water. We may take the cave of Banwell as an example. It consists of two large chambers, the upper filled with thousands of bones of bison, horse and reindeer, collected out of the red silt, which filled it to the roof; the lower full of the undisturbed contents, silt, stones and bones mingled irregularly together. These chambers were connected with the surface by a vertical fissure, which apparently prevented the cave being used by the hyænas, who would have eaten up the perfect remains had they obtained access. They are however proved to have been living in the neighbourhood because their skulls, and antlers of reindeers scored by their teeth, have been found inside. These were probably swept in from the surface by the stream.

The strange assembly of animals, living and extinct, northern and southern, found in these caverns is recorded in the following table, where it is brought into comparison with that yielded by the caverns on the north side of the Bristol Channel, and by Kent's Hole near Torquay.[1]

[1] The references on which these tables are founded are given by the author in *Cavehunting*, pp. 359–62 ; *Quart. Journ. Geol. Soc. Lond.* 1872, p. 410 ; and *Early Man in Britain*, v.

TABLE OF MAMMALIA FROM PLEISTOCENE CAVES IN SOMERSET, DEVON AND SOUTH WALES

	Kent's Hole, Torquay	Uphill	Hutton	Bleadon	Banwell	Sandford Hill	Churchill	Burrington	Wookey Hole	Durdham Down	Pembroke Glamorgan Carmarthen Monmouth
Species living in temperate zone											
Pika	—	*	—	—	—	—	—	—	—	—	—
Water-vole	—	*	—	—	—	—	—	—	*	—	*
Wild cat	*	—	*	*	*	—	—	—	—	—	*
Wolf	*	*	*	*	—	*	—	—	*	—	*
Fox	*	—	*	*	—	*	—	—	*	*	*
Marten	—	—	—	*	—	—	—	—	—	—	*
Ermine	*	—	*	—	—	—	—	—	—	—	*
Otter	*	—	—	*	—	—	—	—	—	—	*
Brown bear	*	—	—	*	—	*	—	—	*	*	*
Grizzly bear	*	—	—	—	—	—	—	—	*	—	*
Badger	—	*	—	—	—	—	—	—	*	—	*
Horse	*	*	*	*	*	*	—	—	*	*	*
Bison	*	*	*	*	*	*	—	—	*	*	*
Urus	*	—	—	—	—	—	—	—	*	—	*
Stag	*	—	—	—	—	—	—	*	*	—	*
Roedeer	—	*	—	*	—	—	—	—	—	—	*
Wild boar	*	*	—	—	—	—	—	—	—	—	*
Species living in cold climates											
Cave man	*	—	—	—	—	—	—	—	*	—	—
Reindeer	*	—	—	*	*	*	—	—	*	*	*
Lemming	*	—	*	—	—	—	—	—	—	—	—
Norwegian lemming	—	—	*	—	—	—	—	—	—	—	—
Siberian ground squirrel	—	—	*	—	—	*	—	—	*	—	—
Hamster	—	—	*	—	—	—	—	—	—	—	—
Alpine hare	*	—	*	—	—	—	—	—	—	—	—
The glutton	—	—	—	*	*	—	—	—	—	—	—
The Arctic fox [1]	*	—	*	*	—	*	—	—	*	—	*
Species found in hot climates											
The River-drift man	*	—	—	—	—	—	—	—	—	—	—
Lion	*	*	*	*	—	*	—	—	*	*	*
Leopard	—	—	*	*	*	—	—	—	—	—	—
Caffir cat	—	—	—	*	—	—	—	—	—	—	—
Spotted hyæna	*	*	*	*	*	*	—	—	*	*	*
Hippopotamus	—	—	—	—	—	—	—	—	—	*	—

[1] The Arctic fox has been identified by Busk.

	Kent's Hole, Torquay	Uphill	Hutton	Bleadon	Banwell	Sandford Hill	Burrington	Wookey Hole	Durdham Down	Pembroke Caernarvon Glamorgan Monmouth
Extinct Species										
Straight-tusked elephant	—	—	—	—	—	—	—	—	*	*
Mammoth	*	—	*	*	—	—	*	*	*	*
Woolly rhinoceros . .	*	*	*	—	—	*	—	*	—	*
Small-nosed rhinoceros.	—	—	—	—	—	—	—	—	*	—
Irish elk	*	—	*	—	—	—	—	*	—	*
Cave bear.	*	—	*	*	*	*	—	*	—	*
Sabre-tooth lion . . .	*	—	—	—	—	—	—	—	—	—

We shall see later that this list of animals, now so widely scattered over remote parts of the earth, throws great light both on the climate and the geography of Somerset during the occupation of Britain by the River-drift men and the Cave men.

5. THE CAVE MEN OF WOOKEY HOLE

The presence of these two races of hunters in the south of England is proved by the discoveries in Kent's Hole near Torquay. The latter has been found only in one cave in Somerset, in Wookey Hole near Wells, explored in 1859–69, by Williamson, Willett, Parker, Sanford and the writer of this account. The cave, discovered in 1852 in making a water channel, is on the south side of a picturesque ravine, into which the river Axe rushes in full stream from a cavern at the bottom of an ivy-clad cliff about 200 feet high. It consists of a large entrance chamber running horizontally into the rock and passing into two narrow passages in the interior. Each of these passages terminates in a vertical fissure. The inner side of the entrance chamber also is in communication with the surface, since it contained the roots of trees growing on the ravine side above. We began our work by cutting our way into the chamber, which was packed to the roof with red cave-earth, stones and innumerable gnawed and splintered fragments of bone, teeth and antlers. The remains of the hyæna were very abundant and belonged to every age, from the youngest with its teeth uncut to the aged with teeth worn to a stump. There were also floors of hyæna dung at various levels above the rocky floor, proving that it was used as a den by those animals at various periods. Nearly all the remains in the cave bore the marks of the teeth of these animals, and obviously belonged to their victims. In the passages they were principally massed in two layers : one, 7 feet wide and 14 feet long and from 3 to 4 inches thick, with an area of 94 square feet ; the other, 6 feet wide, 14 feet long, and about the same thickness, with an area of 87 square feet. The total number of animals represented in the caves is very considerable. In 1862–3 we obtained from two to three thousand specimens, and the jaws and teeth were as follows :—

Cave hyæna	467	Woolly rhinoceros	233
Cave lion	15	Horse	401
Cave bear	27	Great urus	16
Grizzly bear	11	Bison	30
Brown bear	11	Irish elk	35
Wolf	7	Reindeer	30
Fox	8	Red deer	2
Mammoth	30	Lemming	1

The remains of these animals were so intermingled that they must have been living together at the same time. They lie large with small, and the light with the heavy. There is no evidence that the hyæna belonged to one geological period and the reindeer to another, as is suggested by James Geikie and Wallace;[1] or that the bears came in here to die, as in some of the German caves; or that the animals fell or were swept into open fissures and thence into caverns, as in the caves of Banwell and Hutton. The cave hyæna was the normal occupant, and the rest of the animals in the above list were his prey, dragged into and eaten in the cavern. It is probable that many of these animals, and more especially the larger and fiercer, lost their lives by falling from the top of the cliff at the head of the ravine; and it is likely that the hyænas hunted in packs, like the hyænas and wolves of to-day, and forced their prey over precipices. The ravine at Wookey is admirably situated for this method of hunting, and in all probability was used for this purpose, not only by the hyænas, but by the men whose implements and weapons were met with in the cave.

The implements (figs. 4, 5) discovered, for the most part on the floor of the chamber near the entrance, and in association with charcoal and burnt bones (one belonging to a rhinoceros) prove that the cave was used as a shelter by the second race of palæolithic hunters who occupied the caves of France, Switzerland and Belgium, while the wild animals of the caves of Somerset had unrestricted range from the British Isles southwards to the Pyrenees, the Mediterranean and the Alps.

The implements are about forty in number, and consist of flakes, scrapers, cutters and haches (fig. 4) made of flint and of chert from the Upper Greensand formation. The latter material was used, it must be remarked, by the River-drift men of Axminster, Chard and Taunton, and was probably brought to Wookey Hole by the Cave men who followed the same route as their predecessors northwards along the line of the Otter and the southern Axe. A trimmed flint (fig. 5) with the point broken off may have been the head of a spear, and a small triangular fragment of chert brought to a sharp point may have served for an arrowhead. Two rudely fashioned bone arrowheads were also found resembling in outline an equilateral triangle with the basal angles bevelled off. The whole group is identical with that of the Cave men of Cresswell Crags in Nottinghamshire and Derbyshire, and of Brixham and Kent's Hole in Devon, as well as with those of the

---

[1] Geikie, *The Great Ice Age*; Wallace, *Geographical Distribution of Animals*.

FIG. 3. PALÆOLITHIC IMPLEMENT, BALLAST PIT, BROOM, AXMINSTER.
Full size.

FIG. 4. PALÆOLITHIC IMPLEMENT, HYÆNA DEN, WOOKEY HOLE.
Full size.

FIG. 5. TRIMMED FLAKE OF FLINT, HYÆNA DEN, WOOKEY HOLE.
Full size.

caves of the continent.[1]   All indicate the same hunter stage of human culture—a stage immeasurably higher than that of the River-drift men who went before.   The Cave-men had better implements, and had the art of representing the animals on which they lived with an accuracy which is now only rivalled among hunting tribes by the Eskimos of the arctic regions.   The outlines of a horse scratched on the surface of a polished bone at Cresswell, the figure of a mammoth cut on a plate of mammoth ivory in Auvergne, and that of a reindeer grazing in happy ignorance of the hunter who left his sketch behind in a cave at Thayingen near the Falls of the Rhine, are true to nature, and show no mean artistic skill.

The daggers too found in the caves of Auvergne made of reindeer antler with handles carved into the shape of a kneeling reindeer, and of ivory with handles carved into the form of a standing mammoth, prove a mastery in the art of the sculptor unrivalled among the works of hunting races either of the past or of the present day—an art which after disappearing from the face of Europe for untold ages has been proved by recent discoveries to have flourished in Egypt some 5,000 years, and in the Ægean region 2,000 years B.C.[2]

The intimate association of the remains of the Cave men with those introduced into the cave by hyænas is explained by the fact that the latter cave-haunting animals were the normal occupants, driven out of their dens from time to time when the nomad hunters encamped there and kindled their fires for cooking.   Their visits were sufficiently long to allow of the making of implements in the cave and to allow of the accumulation of chips knocked off in the process. When the thin line of smoke disappeared, and the ashes of the fires were cold, the hyænas returned to the cave and ate up the remains of the animals left by the hunter.   These alternate occupations were continued until the cave was filled nearly to the roof with earth introduced by the rain, stones dropped from the roof and the fragments of the animals introduced by man and the hyænas.

6. THE GEOGRAPHY AND CLIMATE

The details given in the preceding pages enable us to ascertain the physical conditions under which the men of the River-drift and of the caves lived in the county.   If we examine the list of species given on page 172 we shall see that the mammalia of the Somerset caves ranged over the area of the Bristol Channel into Wales and Monmouthshire. They also ranged southwards as far as the caves of Devon and across the Channel into France, and westwards across the North Sea into Germany.   They are identical with those of the river deposits in

---

[1] Dawkins, *Early Man in Britain*, pp. 193, 198, 203, and generally chap. vii.

[2] In both these cases it was the outcome of a high civilization marked by the use of letters.   It was not, as Flinders Petrie supposed, in the case of the gold cups of Vapphio in Sparta, the work of an unlettered race, but of one proved by Arthur Evans' discoveries in Crete to have possessed at least two forms of writing.

Britain, France and Germany. It is therefore clear that the sea was no barrier to migration into the British Isles from the continent during the occupation of Somerset by the men of the River-drift and of the Caves.

The British Islands then stood at a height of at least 600 feet above their present level, and formed a portion of the continent with its shore line extending into the Atlantic as far as the hundred fathom line on the north and west.[1] The English Channel was then a broad valley traversed by a great river which received the drainage of the existing river systems, both French and English, and delivered it into the Atlantic to the north-west of the coast of Brittany. The Bristol Channel was land, and the Severn joined the streams draining the south of Ireland and formed a great river opening on the Atlantic to the south-west of Ireland. South-western England was the higher ground separating the valley of the Severn from the valley of the English Channel, and is proved by the soundings to have been continued westwards from Land's End, so as to form a water-parting between the two. Under these conditions the Pleistocene mammalia obtained free access to the British Isles in the migrations from France and Germany, and both the River-drift man and the Cave man could follow the migrating animals, on which they lived, as they wandered north and south, east and west, according to the food and the season. The River-drift man could advance northwards from the shores of the Mediterranean through France into the British Isles without meeting any physical barrier, and the Cave man could migrate freely northwards from the centre of France, and westwards from Germany and Belgium across the valleys of the English Channel and the North Sea, and along the upland, then 'the divide' between the two, now the Straits of Dover. It was under these conditions that both these races of Palæolithic man found their way into Somerset at successive times, the one from the south and the other from the south and east.

The groups too into which the mammalia of the caves naturally fall reveal the climate at the time. The first consists of those which are living in temperate climates and now amply represented in the fauna of the British Isles; the second of those now living in cold climates, such as the reindeer and arctic or alpine hare, and if we add the discovery in the gravel at Freshford, the musk-sheep, the most arctic of the mammalia. The presence of this group in Britain implies a severe climate. On the other hand, the third is now only living in warm regions—the lion, leopard, African lynx, Caffir cat, spotted hyæna and hippopotamus.

The same contradictory evidence is also presented by the examination of the extinct species found in the same stratum side by side. Some, such as the mammoth and woolly rhinoceros, which ranged over the whole of Northern Europe and Asia as far as the Arctic seaboard, are

---

[1] For evidence of this refer to Lyell, *Antiquity of Man*; Dawkins, *Early Man in Britain*.

northern, while others, such as the straight-tusked elephant, the small-nosed rhinoceros and the cave-bear, ranged over the south of Europe, and have not been found further to the north than the British Isles, and are therefore of southern habit.

This mingling of northern and southern forms in the same deposit is clearly explained by the fact that Britain then formed part of the continent, and enjoyed the extremes invariably presented by a continental climate—a severe winter and a hot summer, similar to that of Siberia. In the winter the reindeer and other arctic beasts would range to their most southern limit, the Pyrenees and the Alps, while in the summer the southern animals would migrate northwards from southern Europe to their northern limit in Yorkshire. Over this wide region devoid of physical barrier they would migrate according to the season to the north and to the south over the same feeding grounds, leaving their remains intermingled in the deposits of rivers and in caves.

7. THE RELATION OF THE RIVER-DRIFT AND CAVE MAN TO THE GLACIAL PERIOD

We must now consider the difficult and complicated question of the relation of these two races of Palæolithic man to the Glacial period.

The River-drift man is classified in the above list with the animals now living in warm or temperate climates, because he entered Europe from the south and ranged with the southern animals as far north as the British Isles, and as far to the south as Palestine, Arabia and the Indian Peninsula. His headquarters are to be looked for in the warm or the temperate zone. The Cave man is placed with the arctic animals, because he only occurs in northern and middle Europe in the regions in which they lived north of the Alps and Pyrenees. He is conspicuous by his absence from southern Europe, the Mediterranean and the warmer regions of the south. Were these races in Somerset pre-glacial, inter-glacial or post-glacial? From the discovery of the southern, the temperate and the arctic group of mammals in pre-glacial strata at Bielbecks[1] in Yorkshire and in post-glacial river gravels at Bedford[2] and at Hoxne in Suffolk,[3] it is clear that all three groups, leaving man out of account, inhabited the portion of the British Isles covered by the great mantle of glacial drift before the great changes in the geography and climate of Britain during the glacial period, as well as after the emergence of middle England from the waters of the glacial sea. In the two last-named localities River-drift implements have been met with, proving that there, at all events, the earlier race of man was present in post-glacial Britain. In the county of Somerset there is no

---

[1] Wolf, lion, stag, urus, bison, horse, small-nosed rhinoceros and straight-tusked elephant (*Phil. Mag.* vi. 225). The above species were identified by the writer in the York Museum.

[2] Lyell, *Antiquity of Man*, p. 215, fig. 50 ; Prestwich, *Quart. Journ. Geol. Soc. Lond.* xvii. 364.

[3] Lyell, *Antiquity of Man*, p. 219, fig. 31. The post-glacial age has been verified by the recent excavations carried out by a committee under the superintendence of Clement Reid (*Brit. Assoc. Rep.* 1896, p. 400).

evidence, because there are no boulder clays and no marks of glaciation in the county. The geographical change in the middle and northern parts of the British Isles, amounting, as Lyell has pointed out,[1] to a sinking of the land to a depth of 1,600 feet below its present level in the Snowdonian range, stopped short of an east and west line running through the Bristol Channel and the estuary of the Thames, and Somerset, Devon and Cornwall show no sign of the submergence. Nor are there any traces in this southern region of the presence of great masses of ice on the land such as are conspicuous in South Wales and the whole of the land to the north. Nor do we meet with any proof of the presence of local glaciers such as are abundantly met with in South Wales and further north on the higher ranges of hills. In this southern land then, as in the case of middle and southern Europe, it is impossible to correlate the River-drift and Cave men with the Glacial period. They were probably in Europe south of the above-mentioned line during the whole time that the glacial changes were taking place in the region to the north. It is very likely that the River-drift hunter, and possibly also the Cave man as he followed the wild animals in the hunt north-wards from the continent, may have seen from the Quantocks or the Mendips the hills of South Wales crowned with ice as he looked across the broad marshy valley of the Severn. He may too have noted how the great ice barrier to further migration north grew and developed at the beginning of the Glacial period. He may have wandered down to the shore of the Glacial sea in the area of the estuary of the Severn, and have hunted the reindeer, the bison, the horse and the mammoth over the area of the Bristol Channel as it again rose above the sea, and have noted from Uphill and Weston-super-Mare the glint of the smaller glaciers which descended from the higher hills in South Wales at the close of the glacial period. In Somerset Palæolithic man was probably pre-glacial, glacial, and post-glacial.

8. THE RELATION OF THE TWO RACES TO THE EXISTING PEOPLES

The River-drift man, as we have seen, preceded the Cave man, and was a hunter of a very low type. He cannot be identified with any known race, the few fragmentary remains of his skeleton only being sufficiently perfect to prove that he was a man, and not a 'missing link.' The Cave man, also a hunter, but better armed than his predecessor, led the same sort of life as the Eskimos, hunting the same animals, such as the reindeer and the musk sheep, as those which contribute to the food of the Eskimo of the arctic regions of America. In my opinion he was closely allied to, if not identical with, that northern race which stands isolated from all others. The discovery of his implements and weapons in the caves of Germany and in various refuse heaps in Siberia shows the line of his retreat when, at the close of the Pleistocene age, Palæolithic man and a large number of the beasts disappeared from

[1] Lyell, op. cit. pp. 322–9, figs. 42–4.

Europe—the northern animals, including the Cave man, retreating to the north, and the southern animals, and with them the River-drift man, retreating to the south, while owing to the geographical changes which took place, many animals, such as the woolly rhinoceros, mammoth and cave-bear, became extinct. Neither of the two races of Palæolithic man have left behind any marks in the existing population of Europe, or in the culture of the Neolithic peoples who succeeded them in the beginning of the Prehistoric age.

9. THE GEOGRAPHICAL AND CLIMATAL CHANGES AT THE CLOSE OF THE PLEISTOCENE AGE

Profound changes both in the geography and climate took place at the close of the Pleistocene age in the area of Britain.

A general depression of the land caused Britain to become an island, and the valleys of the North Sea and of the Irish Channel were covered by the waters of the sea. In consequence of this the climate became insular, and the extremes of continental temperature were no longer felt in summer and winter. To both these changes we may assign the extinction of some of the mammalia, and the retreat of others both to the north and to the south. Both these changes were probably very slow. They took place in the interval separating the Palæolithic man from his immediate successors in the Prehistoric period—an interval which marks off continental from insular Britain.

CHAPTER II. PREHISTORIC SOMERSET

1. DEFINITION OF PREHISTORIC PERIOD

Before we can adequately deal with Prehistoric Somerset it is necessary to define the meaning of the term.

The Prehistoric period covers all the events which took place between the Pleistocene age and the beginning of history, which in Somerset does not go further back than the conquest of the Romans. To it belong the great tracts of alluvia, the peat bogs, and the contents of some of the caverns, all being characterized by the presence of the remains of living wild mammals, together with those of the domestic animals introduced by man. Man appears in the Neolithic stage of culture, bringing with him the more important of the domestic animals, and the knowledge of many of the arts. Subsequently in the long course of ages bronze became known, and then iron, each material causing a profound change in the social condition of the people. Polished stone, bronze and iron are merely the symbols of three phases of culture almost world-wide, each higher and better than that which went before.

2. THE CAMPS AND FORTIFIED SETTLEMENTS

The prehistoric camps and fortified settlements, with few exceptions, have unfortunately not been sufficiently explored to allow of their being assigned to their proper archæological horizon. Some may be neolithic, but the majority belong to the bronze or iron ages. They are as follows :—

THE CAMPS AND FORTIFIED SETTLEMENTS OF SOMERSET, NOTICED IN THE 'PROCEEDINGS OF THE SOMERSETSHIRE ARCHÆOLOGICAL AND NATURAL HISTORY SOCIETY'

Banwell Hill, xv. i. 25

Ben Knoll, xii. i. 56

Brean Down, xii. i. 65

Brent Knoll, ix. ii. 145 ; xii. i. 64

Brimpton, iv. ii. 88

Burwell's Camp, xv. ii. 27, 30 ; xlvii. ii. 219

Cadbury (Wincanton), vii. i. 19 ; ii. 57, 60 ; viii. ii. 66 ; xxii. ii. 62 ; xxiv. ii. 84 ; xxvii. i. 53 ; xxix. ii. 110 ; xxxiii. ii. 79 ; xxxvi. ii. 8

Cadbury Camp, v. ii. 32, 45 ; (Twickenham), vi. ii. 113 ; x. i. 13 ; xxvii. i. 53

Cadbury (Yatton), i. ii. 59

Castle Neroche, i. ii. 45 ; v. ii. 30 ; xxiv. ii. 90

Cothelstone Hill, xxiv. ii. 196

Croydon Hill, vi. i. 6

Dolbury, v. ii. 32 ; xxxi. i. 16 ; xxix. ii. 104

Elworthy Barrows, i. i. 42 ; xxix. i. 45

Glastonbury Tor (Chalice Hill), ix. ii. 143, 144 (?)

Hamdon Hill, iv. ii. 78 ; v. ii. 35 ; xxiv. ii. 90 ; xxx. ii. 138 ; xxxii. i. 81

Hampton Down, vi. ii. 106

Kenny Wilkins Castle, v. ii. 35

Langport and neighbourhood, xi. i. 12 ; ii. 194

Lansdown, vi. ii. 122

Maesbury, xiii. i. 27

Maes Knoll, vi. ii. 111 ; xxii. ii. 64

Milborne Wick, vii. ii. 60 ; xvi. i. 34 ; xxii. ii. 63

Norton Fitzwarren, i. ii. 38 ; xviii. i. 43 ; xliv. ii. 198

Portbury, x. i. 22

Ponters Ball, ix. ii. 144

Small Down, xii. i. 5, 13

Solisbury, vi. ii. 107

Stanchester, iv. ii. 88 ; xxiv. ii. 47

Stantonbury, vi. ii. 100

Stokeleigh, vii. ii. 15 ; xlvii. ii. 224

Taunton Castle, xviii. ii. 61 (?)

Temple Combe, vii. ii. 62 ; xxii. ii. 63

Worle, Worlebury, ii. ii. 64 ; x. i. 14 ; iv. ii. 124 ; viii. ii. 68 ; xxxi. i. 13

Worle 'Belch,' xviii. ii. 70

CAMPS AND FORTIFIED SETTLEMENTS MARKED IN THE 6-INCH ORDNANCE MAPS OF SOMERSET

Aisholt on Quantocks

Banwell

Bath

Bathampton

Blackdown, Mendip

Bleadon, Mendip

Brewers Castle near Dulverton

Cannington Park

Dowesborough, Quantocks

Dinghurst, Mendip near Churchill

Dunball, north of Bridgwater

Dundon, south of Street

East Cranmore, Frome

Exford

Failand near Bristol

Kingdon near Mells

Kings Camp, Wiveliscombe

Monnsey Castle near Dulverton

Newbury, Frome

Newton, Bicknoller

Ruborough, Quantocks

Solisbury Hill, Bath

South Hay near Whitestaunton, Chard

Staddon Hill, Brendon

Stoberry, Dulverton

Stokeleigh, Bristol

Tedbury near Frome

Thorncombe Hill, Quantocks

Wadbury near Frome

3. THE DISTRIBUTION OF POPULATION IN PREHISTORIC TIMES

The county of Somerset is divided into three hilly regions, separated one from another by broad river valleys and marshes and low clay lands, which were for the most part covered with scrub and forest. The dry ranges of Dorset on the south-east, composed of chalk, are represented further to the west by the equally dry Upper Greensand hills, ending near Wellington in the Blackdown range. Northwards the hills of Dorset are continuous with the chalk downs of Wiltshire, past Shaftsbury and Warminster, to Yatesbury and Farringdon. Between them and the clay lands already alluded to are the irregular broken hills of the Greensands and Oolites, ranging from Crewkerne to Sherborne, Castle Cary, Bruton, Bradford and Chippenham. These broken hills link together the south-eastern portion of the county with the northern uplands represented by the Mendip range, composed of carboniferous limestone, and the irregular hilly district, composed of various rocks, as far as Bath and Bristol and the northern border.

The marshes of the Parrett and the Tone, and the low-lying district which they drain, formed of Triassic marls and Liassic clays, divide both these districts from the western division of Somerset, formed mainly of Devonian rocks, and extending from the border of Devon past Exmoor to the Bristol Channel, and eastwards to Wellington, Taunton and Bridgwater.

The distribution of the remains of prehistoric man in Somerset unfortunately at present mostly unclassified, follows the physical characters of the surface. They occur on the drier uplands. They are as a rule conspicuous by their absence in the lowlands now forming the 'Garden of England,' but then morass or forest. The settlements occur mainly in the hills, and were only extended to the bottom of the valleys towards the close of the prehistoric period, in the centuries which immediately preceded the Roman conquest of Britain. It will not be without interest to place on record the more important of these remains, in order that we may see the chief centres of population, and the roads by which they were linked together in prehistoric times, leaving the question of archæological age to be dealt with subsequently.

4. THE SOUTH-EASTERN UPLANDS

The prehistoric man, hunter, farmer and herdsman, found his way into Britain from the continent, and passed into Somerset, advancing westwards along the dry chalk downs of Dorset and of Wiltshire. The southern line of advance from the district where the chalk downs end to the west of Dorchester is marked by the ranges of Lower Greensand and Oolites and dry isolated outliers of Upper Greensand, ranging past Charmouth westward to Axminster and the Devon border. In this region the hut circles marking the sites of prehistoric villages, and the camps for the protection not only of the inhabitants, but of their flocks and herds during the time of attack, and the burial places, are so abundant as to show a long occupation by a people who were probably not small in numbers. These centres were joined together by roads mostly following the lines of the ridges, and therefore termed ridgeways on the maps, and bordered very generally by burial mounds. One of these roads passes from Sherborne northwards, past Sandford Orcas, to the great fortress of South Cadbury. A second road enters the county to the north of Mere, forming the county boundary as far as Jack's Castle ; from this point it sweeps to the south-west, to join the road from Sherborne close to the north of Cadbury. It is probably continued to Ilchester.

A third ridgeway passes from the south of Yeovil westwards to the great camp of Hamdon Hill, and thence, still westwards, between South Petherton and Seavington to Ilford and Castle Neroche, giving its name in later times to the village and forest of Broadway. From Castle Neroche it goes over Staple Hill and along the ridge of Blackdown, and onwards into Devon. From Castle Neroche a branch passes southwards by North Hay Barrow and Whitestaunton and the camp of South Hay. A second branch also passes southwards from the break between Staple Hill and Blackdown, by no less than six barrows, called Robin Hood's Butts, to the Devon border. Both these lateral branches are probably continued northwards along the existing roads to the ford over the Tone, the site of the modern Taunton. The vale of Bridgwater, ranging to Glastonbury and the marshes of the Axe, and consisting mainly of reclaimed morasses and low clayey hills, presents remarkably few traces of prehistoric inhabitants. We may however remark the isolated hill fort Dundon and the lake village at Glastonbury, which are linked together by the road passing northwards through Street to Wearyall Hill. We may also note the deep fosse to the east of Glastonbury at Ponter's Ball, which converted the peninsula into the ' Isle of Avalon ' and defended the approach from West Pennard. All three form one group, which belongs to the Prehistoric Iron age. The ridgeway, passing along the crest of the Polden Hills to a camp near Dunball, may probably be referred also to this date.

The isolated camp of Brent Knoll, to the north of Highbridge, and the barrow at Panborough near Theale, in the valley of the Axe, and that near Durston, are the only other traces of prehistoric settlement in the great flat district dividing the south-eastern division of the county from the range of the Mendip Hills. A few isolated implements, it is true, neolithic and bronze, have been met with in the marshlands ; but they do not imply the continuous occupation of the district by man, but merely the fact that he was an occasional visitant in the Neolithic and Bronze ages.

5. THE NORTHERN UPLANDS

The northern uplands are bounded on the south-west by the marshes of the Axe, and are united to the southern uplands by the broken Oolitic hills, ranging northwards past Frome to Bradford and Bath and westwards to Bristol. They are traversed by a network of roads. An ancient road passes westwards from Warminster, and the densely populated chalk downs of Wiltshire to Frome, and from thence under the name of the Ridgeway to East Cranmore, joins at this point the line of the Roman road to Maesbury Camp, and thence runs westwards on the top of the Mendips past Charterhouse, Shipham, to the south of Banwell and Hutton, ending at the harbour at the mouth of the Axe at Uphill. Along this part of its course it has been used by the Romans and is marked down in the maps as a Roman road. The pre-Roman camps however and pre-Roman barrows which abound in its neighbourhood prove that it is older than the Romans. At East Cranmore is a large irregular camp. Between Cranmore and Maesbury on the left are two barrows. Between the latter place and Shipham are more than twenty-one barrows, and one camp to the south of Blackdown. A branch road leading northwards in the direction of Churchill through a pass in the limestone has a barrow on the left, and is commanded by Dolbury and Dinghurst Camps. From Banwell a branch road passes over Woolvers Hill to end at the great fortress of Worle overlooking the Channel and Weston-super-Mare. There are two more camps near Banwell, a third near Bleadon, and a barrow near Uphill. On the ridge of Brean Down, on the other side of the estuary of the Axe opposite Uphill, are a camp and several hut circles. Another line of road from Frome westward passes two great hill fortresses, Tedbury and Wadbury, and at a short distance to the south is a third, Newbury. From this point the ridgeway sweeps to the south-west in the direction of Wells, joining the road from East Cranmore at Longcross. To the north-east of Frome, Barrow Hill marks the site of a burial mound near Buckland Dinham, and further to the north-west is Kingdon Camp on Mells Down, a little off the high road from Frome to Radstock. To the north of this latter place the road was probably continued close to a barrow on the left to Camerton. Between Camerton and Wellow many burial mounds have been destroyed in farming operations. One however at Stony Littleton, described later, has been preserved. It may be taken as a representative of the whole group.

The high road from Wells to Bath over the Mendip Hills probably follows the line of a prehistoric road. Before it reaches Emborrow it passes five burial mounds; between the latter place and Farrington Gurney is a sixth. From this point it sweeps past High Littleton and Farnborough. Between this place and Priston is a seventh, Priest Barrow. It joins the Fosse Way at the point where it intersects the Wansdyke as it approaches Bath. It is probably the ancient road to Bath superseded in later times by the junction with the Fosse in the direction of Portway Lane, Broadway and Norton Down.

The site of Bath was an important place in prehistoric times, and was undoubtedly the centre of a considerable population in the Prehistoric Iron age. Overlooking it are the two great fortified settlements of Bathampton Down and Solisbury Hill. From it a road passes northwards through Swanswick and Cold Ashton to join the ridgeway south of Dirham in Gloucestershire. This latter road runs by two camps and one burial mound as it ranges northwards from Bath over Lansdowne to the above junction.

The region north of the Mendip Hills, extending on the west to the Severn and on the east to the Avon, is traversed by three well-defined roads, proved to be prehistoric by the remains which cluster round them. Stratford Lane, running from the Mendips past Compton Martin, traverses at Staunton Drew the stone circles described in a later page. To the north of Norton Malreward it passes close to Maes Knoll

Camp, pointing towards Bristol. It probably joins the ridgeway passing from Maesbury Camp westwards over Dundry Hill, Barrow Hill, named after the barrow, and thence to Cadbury Camp near Yatton. The third runs westward from Stokeleigh Camp overlooking the gorge of the Avon at Clifton, past a prehistoric camp near Failand, and the great fortress of Cadbury on the ridge of Tickenham Hill to Clevedon. It was probably connected by a branch with the camp at Portbury. The prehistoric remains in the districts away from these roads are remarkably few. 'The Fairy Twt,' a burial mound near Batcombe, and Stantonbury Camp, on the line of the Wansdyke about two miles to the south-west of Corston, are the only two which I have been able to meet with. The last however may have been accessible by a branch road running southwards to join the Mendip road to Bath near Farmborough.

6. THE WESTERN UPLANDS

Prehistoric burying places and settlements cluster thickly along the ridgeway, traversing the Quantock Hills from St. Audries on the Bristol Channel, over Beacon Hill, Thornton, Lydiard, and Cothelstone in the direction of Taunton. Between Cothelstone and St. Audries there are sixteen barrows. On a westward branch from it, over Thorncombe Hill, are three more and an earthwork. On a north-eastern branch, between Crowcombe and Holford, is the fortress of Dowesborough and two barrows. On a second branch, passing eastward at the top of Aisholt Common, is another fortress, and on a third from Cothelstone is the great fortress of Ruborough. Among the few and isolated prehistoric remains to the east we must notice Tet Hill (Twt Hill) south of Stogursey, the camp at Cannington Park, overlooking the marshes of the Parret at Combwich, and the tumulus on North Moor, about two miles to the north of Stogursey.

The lower district, composed of Liassic and Triassic rocks, extending from Williton and Watchet to the south-east in the direction of Taunton, and dividing the Quantocks from the Brendon Hills and the uplands of Devon, yields few prehistoric remains. A barrow about a mile south of Watchet and a camp at Newton, about the same distance south of Bicknoller, are the only two recorded in the map. The latter, we must note, probably marks the site of the ford at which the western branch from the Quantock ridgeway crosses the stream at Newton in the direction of Stogumber and Elworthy.

The tumbled hills ranging from this tract of lowlands into Devon and northwards as far as the Channel present numerous traces of prehistoric man which are mainly grouped along the ridgeways. The camp of Norton Fitzwarren, about three miles from Taunton, and Kings Camp near Wiveliscombe mark a road, in one part of its course called Ridgeway Lane, ascending from the vale of Taunton into the hills in its passage westwards. To the north of Chipstable it passes two barrows and five more on Haddon Hill on its way to Dulverton. Here it passes

Stoberry Castle on the river Barle and becomes a true ridgeway, 'Ridge Road,' on the 6-inch maps, with the usual barrows as it goes over West Anstey Common into Devonshire. A second line of communication between the east and west is formed by the Brendon ridgeway sweeping westwards from the camp of Elworthy Barrows to Exmoor and the Devon border. Its course from Elworthy Barrows to Quarme Hill is marked by six barrows. Between the latter place and Exford it leaves the two camps of Staddon Hill and Exford on the left. The district between it and the southern or Haddon Hill ridgeway is penetrated by at least three roads with barrows: one southwards from Brendon Hill, the source of the Tone, to Lowtrow Cross, with one barrow; the second, thrown off at White Cross to the west of Exford, passes by the three barrows of Winsford Hill on its way to Dulverton; the third, starting about two miles further to the west, passes a barrow on its way to Withypool. Its further course is marked by a barrow on Withypool Hill, and by a second as it runs southwards to Hawkridge, and the two camps of Brewers Castle and Monnsey in the valley of the Barle. At Withypool Hill a branch sweeps westwards past Green Barrow over the common to Sandy Way, giving access to the hills between the Barle and the Dane.

The hills between the Brendon ridgeway and the Bristol Channel are traversed by three prehistoric ridgeways. One passes four barrows in its course from Old Cleeve over Croydon Hill to Timberscombe. The second, over Dunkery Hill, passes seven barrows (Robin How, Kit Barrow, Row Barrow, etc.) as it runs westward in the direction of Warren farm. From this point its further continuation to Saddle Gate along the watershed of Exmoor is marked by three barrows. On entering Devon its course is marked by eleven more on Challacombe Common. The third traverses North Hill, leaving four barrows on the left on Selworthy Hill. It is represented to the west of Porlock by the coach road which ascends Porlock Hill and passes three barrows before it reaches the border of Devon at County Gate on its way to Lynton.

The last of the ridgeways to be noted is that forming the boundary between Somerset and Devon, from Saddle Gate on the north to Sandy Way on the south, on the divide between the tributaries of the Taw and the Exe, passing ten barrows in its course and linking together all the ridgeways which radiate westwards from Taunton.

The ridgeways described above began as tracks connecting one settlement with another, which developed into roads fit for pack horses and in later times for wheeled vehicles. They form the earliest element in our complicated network of roads. They have survived because they occupy the lines of easiest access to the hills. They were probably tracks in the Neolithic, pack-horse roads in the Bronze, and were sometimes adapted, as in the case of that of the Mendip Hills, for the use of wheels in the Prehistoric Iron age. The general drift of the settled population was from the hills. The bottom of the valleys, and the lower grounds generally, were not occupied until the Prehistoric Iron age.

We must now deal with the county and its inhabitants in the Neolithic, Bronze, and Prehistoric Iron ages.

7. GEOGRAPHY OF BRITAIN IN THE NEOLITHIC AGE

We remarked at the close of the last chapter that the area of Britain was depressed beneath the sea level in the interval separating the Pleistocene from the Prehistoric period, and that an approximation was made to the existing shore line. It was however only an approximation. The submerged forests and peat bogs so amply represented on our shores prove that the downward movement had not ceased until a late period in the Neolithic age. It was probably continued into the succeeding Bronze age. The submerged forest, described by De la Beche and Godwin Austen,[1] on the coast of west Somerset occurs underneath the estuarine mud of the Severn at Porlock and Minehead, at a depth of 35 feet below high water, and the trees are seen rooted in the subsoil and ranging below low water. They have been met with at about the same level at St. Audries, and they are exposed in the deeply-cut channel of the river Parrett between Bridgwater and Boroughbridge. They extend underneath the peat bogs and alluvia drained by the Parrett, the Axe, the Yeo, and the low lying district generally near the estuary itself. They are equally well represented on the shores of South Wales. They have been met with in the excavations for the Barry Docks[2] at a depth of 55 feet below ordnance datum. They have been described by Hicks as extending between high- and low-water mark in Whitesand Bay in Pembrokeshire.[3] They are all mere fragments of one great forest of oak, ash and yew, which occupied the valley of the Bristol Channel at least as far as the 10 fathom line, if not further. This forest was inhabited by bears, stags, wild horses, as well as by the great wild oxen, and by small shorthorned cattle (*Bos longifrons* = *B. brachyceros*), which had been introduced into the country by man, and had reverted to feral conditions like the wild cattle in Australia.

In all four of the above-mentioned localities implements have been found, which prove that Neolithic man was an inhabitant of this forest. At Porlock, for example, Winwood and the writer of these pages not only found flakes and scrapers of the common Neolithic type in the old surface soil, after digging through the blue marine silt which covered it up, but we could mark the exact places where their makers sat, by the little heaps of splinters under the shade of a yew tree. We met with similar implements at Minehead under similar conditions. A Neolithic axe of polished flint has been discovered under similar conditions at Barry, and a well trimmed flint flake at Whitesand Bay.[4]

---

[1] *Quart. Journ. Geol. Soc. Lond.* xxii. 1.   [2] Ibid. lii. 479.   [3] Ibid. lii. 489.
[4] Ibid. lii. 479, 489.

EARLY MAN

8. NEOLITHIC MAN IN SOMERSET

The traces of Neolithic man in Somerset are remarkably few, when the large size of the county is taken into account. A few polished stone axes, a flint spearhead or two, and flint arrowheads and smaller implements, such as flakes and scrapers, have been met with, sometimes at the bottom of the peat, as for example at Burtle near Chilton-super-Polden, and generally in the surface soil and without association with either interments or habitations, as in the case of the Neolithic axe found at Whitfield near Wiveliscombe. They are however sufficient to prove that Neolithic man was present in the county, from Bath in the north-east to the border of Devon in the south-west. Two Neolithic axes have been discovered in the lake village of Glastonbury, which were without a doubt collected by the villagers in the Prehistoric Iron age (see p. 194). The polished stone axe found in Elworthy Barrows, a circular earthwork at the east end of the Brendon Hills, may have belonged to an inhabitant of that fortified village. The small sunken bases of huts known as 'hut-circles,' abundantly met with in higher places on dry ground, may in some cases mark the sites of Neolithic huts. Neither the one nor the other have however been sufficiently examined to allow of the Neolithic date being fixed beyond a doubt. It must be remembered that commanding positions have in all times been used for purposes of defence, and have been occupied by successive inhabitants of the county from the Neolithic age down to the time of the Roman Conquest. It is very strange that their burial places have not been discovered. Although many barrows have been explored, there is not one which can be assigned with certainty in Somerset to the Neolithic age.

If however the Neolithic implements and weapons are few in Somerset, the small dark descendants of the Iberian race who inhabited Britain and the whole of south-western Europe as far as the Straits of Gibraltar, in the Neolithic age, are still in evidence. Here and there in the present inhabitants of the county, as for example in the region of Pen Selwood and on the borders of Devon, the black eyes, the dark hair and the small stature, definitely Iberic, show that in Somerset, as elsewhere, the aboriginal element was Iberic. Tacitus describes the Silures, probably from information obtained from his father-in-law Agricola, as identical in complexion and hair with the inhabitants of the Iberian peninsula. The centre of their power at the time of the Roman Conquest was on the northern shore of the Bristol Channel, within sight of Somerset. Here they are of the greatest interest, because at the time of the Roman Conquest they were surrounded on every side by other races, constituting what Broca aptly calls 'an ethnological island,' isolated by invasion and by migration of newer peoples, from other islands of the same order, such as the Iberian island (Ireland) and the Iberian peninsula, both deriving their names from their aboriginal masters. It will be seen in our survey of the population in Somerset in the Prehistoric Iron age that this pre-Aryan southern race was abundantly represented in the county of Somerset.

We know from discoveries made in various parts of Britain and the continent that the Iberic race occupied the whole of Europe north of the Alps and the Straits of Gibraltar in the Neolithic age before the invasion of that region by the Goidelic (Gaelic) Celts. They probably occupied the whole of Germany, coming into prehistoric Europe with their flocks of sheep and goats and their small domestic cattle, their dogs, their hogs, and probably also their horses, from the south-east. They brought with them the knowledge of wheat and barley, and the arts of spinning and weaving, mining and pottery-making. They were the first people who used canoes made out of logs of wood hollowed with the aid of the stone axes and the use of fire. The arts which they introduced have had a continuous history in Somerset from that remote period down to the present day. Their domestic animals are represented by the existing breeds, and the people themselves are to be found in the existing population, sometimes in extraordinary purity, but generally more or less mingled with the successive conquerors of Somerset—the Goidel, the Brython and the West-Saxon.

9. SOMERSET IN THE BRONZE AGE

The inhabitants of Somerset in the Bronze age are amply represented by the implements and weapons which they left behind, as well as by their burial places, fortified villages and stone circles. A most remarkable group of implements and weapons has been obtained from the turbaries near Edington Burtle, some six miles to the west of Glastonbury. They include two palstaves, a flanged celt, a socketed celt, bronze dagger and four spearheads. In the same locality a wooden box was found, square outside, and with the inside scooped into an oval. It contained one sickle, unfinished as it came from the mould, and three others which had been used ; two armlets, three rings, a twisted torque and four palstaves. Another important group has been met with in Taunton, consisting of twelve palstaves, one socketed celt, a spearhead, razor, two sickles, a torque, armlet, five dress-fasteners or 'latchets,' two finger-rings and fragments of a bronze girdle composed of small rings. At Sherford also, close to Taunton, six palstaves and one spearhead were found in digging a drain. Among other finds a flat bronze celt from Staple Fitzpaine, and two sickles and a chisel from Sparkford may be quoted.[1]

10. THE BARROWS

The barrows of the Bronze age occur almost invariably on the higher ground, and consist either of earth or stones piled over a stone chamber or directly on the remains of the dead. In some the body had been interred in a sitting posture, in others it had been burnt and the

---

[1] For further information as to these finds see *Proc. Som. Archæol. and Nat. Hist. Soc.* Indexes. The specimens are in the Taunton Museum.

ashes placed in a sepulchral urn. In all the pottery is of the same rude type, made by hand, with little fragments of stone imbedded in the paste, and generally ornamented with patterns in chevrons and right lines. The tumulus at Broom Street, on the road from Porlock to Lynton, described by Elworthy,[1] may be taken as a type of barrows containing interments. It consisted of a chamber made of stone slabs 42 inches long by 22 wide and 18 inches high (fig. 6). The body had been folded into this small space. Along with the body a vase had been placed, $6\frac{1}{2}$ inches high and about 5 inches in diameter, with the usual ornamentation in right lines. The skull is identified by Beddoe and Garson with the round-headed type of man usually found in round barrows, in other words, to one of the Goidelic invaders who conquered the Neolithic aborigines in the west of England.

FIG. 6. NEOLITHIC STONE CIST, BROOM STREET.

The twinbarrow at Sigwell, explored by Rolleston and Pitt-Rivers, within about $1\frac{1}{2}$ miles of the great hill-fort near Wincanton, one of the three Cadburys, proves that there was a considerable variety in the mode of disposing of the dead. Two burials were met with, in neither of which an urn had been employed. The bodies had been burnt, and the bones had been picked out of the pyre and placed apart, one group in a bark coffin,[2] the other coffinless in the soil of the barrow. A few fragments of pottery proved that the burials belong to the Bronze age.

The chambered tomb of Stoney Littleton near Wellow described by Skinner in 1815,[3] and shortly after recorded by Hoare[4] and explored by Scarth, represents one of the most elaborate burial places of the Bronze age in the county. The form is oval (fig. 8), measuring 107 feet in length, 54 in breadth and 13 in height. The entrance (fig. 7) is to the

FIG. 7. ENTRANCE OF BARROW, STONEY LITTLETON (SCARTH).

south-west, and consists of a square aperture 4 feet high formed of two upright stone slabs set on edge and supporting a lintel 7 feet long and $3\frac{1}{2}$ wide. From this entrance two dry walls of stone sweep outwards

[1] Elworthy, *Proc. Som. Archæol. and Nat. Hist. Soc.* xlii. 57.
[2] *Som. Archæol. and Nat. Hist. Soc. Proceed.* xxiv. ii. 75.
[3] Ibid. viii. ii. 35.   [4] *Archæologia,* xix. 44.

and completely surround the burial place (fig. 8). Inside, a narrow passage 49 feet 6 inches long, with three recesses or transepts on each side,

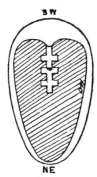

were formed of slabs of stone, also placed on end, and roofed with overlapping slabs, the whole forming a burial place of seven chambers (fig. 9). In the innermost recess (A) and in the two inner transepts (B C) human bones were found, while in the middle transept (D) there were burnt bones and rude pottery. A vertical stone slab (E) mapped off these inner chambers from the rest. The human skulls have been identified by Thurnam with the long skulls of the Iberic population. There is therefore evidence that in this burial place, as in the preceding, both cremation and inhumation were practised at the

FIG. 8.
GROUND PLAN OF BARROW, STONEY LITTLETON (SCARTH).

same time, and by the descendants of the Neolithic aborigines of Britain, who undoubtedly adopted the latter method of disposing of the dead from their Goidelic mas-

FIG. 9. PLAN OF CHAMBERS OF STONEY LITTLETON BARROW (SCARTH).

masters. This burial place forms one of a group of chambered long barrows ranging through Somerset into Gloucestershire on the one hand and into Wiltshire and Berkshire on the other.

11. THE RELATION OF THE BARROWS TO THE ROADS

The barrows on the Mendip Hills, which lie grouped along the road[1] passing from Maesbury Camp near Shepton Mallet on the east, westward as far as Uphill, have long excited curiosity. Those near Priddy on the top of the Mendips are mentioned by Stukeley and were examined by Skinner in 1815. In all cases the body had been cremated. In some the ashes were in urns, in others without urns, in stone cists or on slabs without cists. The urns are rude, handmade and adorned with a zig-zag ornament. Along with them were amber beads, an opaque glass bead, bronze spearheads, and arrowheads of bronze and of flint. These barrows are of various sizes, the largest being 12 feet high and 164 feet in circumference.[2] It is probable that some of the barrows may belong to the Neolithic as well as to the Bronze age. A second and a similar series of barrows marks the line of the ancient ridgeway on the Quantock Hills,[3] a third the line of the ridgeway on the top of the Brendon Hills, and a fourth that of Haddon Hill near Dulverton, while others crown the higher grounds on Exmoor. The great majority of these belong to the Bronze age, and from their association with existing tracks they give us a clue to the direction taken by the roads in use in the county in the Bronze age (see map of Prehistoric Somerset).

[1] See 1-inch contour map, sheets 280–279.   [2] Long, *Archæolog. Journ.* xv. 215.
[3] See 1 inch contour maps, sheets 294–5.

EARLY MAN

12. THE TEMPLES

The megalithic remains at Stanton Drew[1] in the valley of the Chew about 6 miles south of Bristol, although they are smaller, fall naturally into the same group with Avebury and Stonehenge. They consist of large stones found in the neighbourhood arranged in three circles, and others grouped in such a way that it is an open question as to their original purpose. The three circles are as follows : the smaller, or the north-east circle, has a diameter of 97 feet. At 145 feet to the south-west of this is the larger circle with a diameter of 368 feet ; while the third, 460 feet to the south-west, has a diameter of 145 feet. The two former circles have the remains of an avenue on the eastern side. A fourth group, 541 feet from the centre of the last circle, is called 'the cove,' and is close to the south-west of the church. Some of these stones are from 12 to 13 feet high. They have been obtained from various sources in the district, those composing the north-east circle being derived according to Lloyd Morgan from Harptree-under-Mendip, a distance of 5 miles, while some of those in the other two circles have been obtained at Leigh Down near Winford, a distance of 3 miles, the rest being derived from nearer localities. They were probably transported with the aid of ropes, rollers and levers, and erected on an inclined plane of earth which was afterwards removed. The entrances to the two circles were to the east as in many Neolithic burial places, such for example as Rodmarton and Littleton Drew, and in those of the Bronze age such as Bleasdale. The whole series undoubtedly marks the spot devoted to the same purposes as Avebury and Stonehenge, to the worship of the Great Unknown. They may at the same time have been ancient tombs, for there is no sharp line to be drawn between the tomb and the temple. There are innumerable instances in all religions of veneration for the dead and for the Great Unknown being represented by the same structure. In some cases, as at Arbor Low, Derbyshire, they enclose the burial mound, and at others, as in the case of Mule Hill near Port Erin in the Isle of Man, the burials have been carried on in cists in the circumference of the circle. In the case of Bleasdale[2] near Garstang in Lancashire, recently discovered, instead of stone, timber was used to form a circle 154 feet in diameter. Inside this on the eastern side was a smaller circle with a low mound outside, then a ditch, and inside this a small circle of large trunks of oak 30 inches in diameter, the entrance being on the eastern side, and splayed like that at Stoney Littleton. Inside was a low mound covering a group of urns containing the ashes of the dead and bearing the characteristic patterns of the Bronze age. In all these cases, with the exception perhaps of Mule Hill, the idea of temple and the idea of tomb are so closely united that they can hardly be separated.

[1] Stukeley, *Itinerarium Curiosum*, ii. 169 ; Long, *Archæol. Journ.* xv. 199 ; Scarth, *Som. Archæol. and Nat. Hist. Soc.* xiv. ii. 161 ; Dymond, ibid. xxiii. ii. 30 ; Lloyd-Morgan, ibid. xxxiii. ii. 37 ; (the last authority assigns a Neolithic age to the whole group of remains) ; Dymond, *Stanton Drew* (4to, 1896).
[2] Jackson, *Lancashire and Cheshire Antiquarian Soc.* xviii. (1902).

The circles probably represent the circular enclosure around the house of the living made of slabs of stone or of trunks of trees and are the veritable homes of the dead.

13. THE HUTS AND FORTIFIED TOWNS IN THE BRONZE AGE

The population was evidently centred in the higher grounds in the Bronze age, while the lower were covered by forest and morass, in which the burial places are conspicuous by their absence. The numerous hut-circles or bases of circular huts which occur in various parts of the county, and always in the higher grounds, unfortunately have not yet been explored with sufficient accuracy to be assigned to the Bronze age. We know, however, from discoveries made in Holyhead Island and elsewhere, that their habitations were round and formed of a wall of turf or rough stones some 3 feet high, and covered with a pointed roof either thatched or made with turfs. Inside they were subdivided by stone slabs into two or more imperfect rooms, each with its fireplace.

The evidence also is incomplete as to the fortified towns. Out of the many which exist in the county there is only one which can be proved to belong to the Bronze age by the discoveries which have been made in it—the great camp at Cadbury near Clevedon, consisting of a triple rampart and two fosses, which include an area of 4 acres. A bronze spear, now in the Taunton Museum, found in it, marks the age. Many others as yet unclassified probably may be referred to the Bronze age. Some, such as that at Dunster in the west, the great hill-fort of Hamdon about $1\frac{1}{2}$ miles to the south of Martock and that of Dundon about $4\frac{1}{2}$ miles south of Glastonbury, bear in their names the impress of the Goidels of the Bronze age. In all the *dun* means hill-fort in the Goidelic tongue, which was introduced into Britain at the beginning of the Bronze age. It therefore proves that they were used in that age, although they probably were used in later times for the same purposes, the new comer adopting the old name.

14. THE MEN OF THE BRONZE AGE IN SOMERSET

In dealing with the Neolithic inhabitants of Somerset it was pointed out that they are still represented in the existing population although their non-Aryan Iberic tongue, represented by the modern Basque, has been so completely lost that there is not a hill or a river in the county with a name traceable to an Iberic root. They were probably fewer in number and more scattered than their successors in the Bronze age. The Goidels invaded the adjacent parts of the continent in the Neolithic age, and after they had obtained from contact with the Mediterranean peoples the knowledge of bronze, and were armed with bronze daggers and spears, repeated their conquest of Gaul in the island of Britain, gradually mastering the Iberic aborigines and pushing their way to the remotest western and northern limits of the British Isles, including Ireland. Their conquest of Somerset was merely a part of this greater conquest. They did not drive away the existing population. They introduced the higher arts which are based upon the application of metal to the service of man. They introduced too the practice of cremation and a worship of the Unknown of which Stanton Drew is an illustration. They were a tall race, averaging about 5 feet 8 inches; they had round heads, broad faces, high cheek bones and aquiline noses. They belong to the blonde Goidelic section of the Celts, represented by the ancient Gaul, the existing Gael of the Highlands and the fair-haired Irish. Their language is still spoken by the Gael of the Highlands of Scotland and still lingers in the Isle of Man and in the west of Ireland. It has left its mark in almost every part of Britain in the names of rivers and hills. In Somerset the northern and the southern Axe (water) may be quoted among the rivers, and Dunkery Hill among the hills, as survivals of their language to the present day.[1]

15. THE CONQUEST OF SOMERSET IN THE PREHISTORIC IRON AGE

We have seen in the preceding pages that the county of Somerset was occupied during the Bronze age by the Goidelic invaders and the Iberic aborigines, and that they both lived side by side throughout the Bronze age. We have now to consider the occupation of Somerset by the Brythons in the Prehistoric Iron age. That younger branch of the Celtic race, after pushing through Gaul northwards and westwards, overran a very large part of Britain as far as the Highlands. They became the masters of the greater part of Wales. They did not however cross over into Ireland. When Britain became first known to the Greeks it was so completely identified with the Brythons that it bore their name. It may therefore be inferred that they passed over from the continent before, and probably very long before, the fourth century B.C., when the British Isles were first mentioned by Greek writers.[2] The Belgæ, a section of the same people, invaded Britain at a later time, and their northward progress was arrested by the Roman conquest before they had time to get beyond the southern counties. In dealing with the traces of the Brythonic occupation of Somerset I am unable to define the remains left by the Belgæ from those which belong to the earlier Brythonic tribes. With the arrival of the Brythons the connection of Britain with the continent grew stronger and the influence of the Mediterranean people caused a higher development of the arts in Britain than had been known before. There is no county in which the traces of this great change are more abundant than in Somerset—in the numerous hill-fortresses, and in the lake village near Glastonbury, recently explored by a committee, the work being under the direction of its discoverer Mr. Bulleid.

[1] The principal authorities for the facts used in dealing with the Bronze age are to be found in the *Proceedings of the Somerset Archæological and Natural History Society*, and the specimens are mostly to be found in the museums at Bristol and Taunton, to the curators of which, Messrs. Bolton and Gray, I am indebted for a list of specimens belonging to the Neolithic and Bronze ages.

[2] Aristotle, *De Mundo*, 3.

16. THE LAKE VILLAGE OF GLASTONBURY

The low-lying parts of Somerset, now mostly covered with peat, were great sheets of water fringed with morass in the Neolithic, Bronze and Prehistoric Iron ages. Consequently few prehistoric remains are to be found excepting at the ancient margins. One of these meres near Glastonbury was utilized for purposes of defence, and protected a lake village from attack—probably one out of many lake villages in the district as yet undiscovered.

The village (fig. 10) consists of a cluster of huts mostly round, built upon artificial platforms of clay and timber and surrounded by a stockade.[1] It was made on the edge of a mere now a tract of peat, and was thus protected from attack by the sheet of water and morass extending between it and Glastonbury, about 1 mile off. It was approached by two causeways on the north, the earlier of which was formed of blocks of lias and is 10 to 14 feet wide and 130 feet long, while the later was made of clay and rubble lias, and is 100 feet long. Both stopped short by 12 or 14 feet

FIG. 10. PLAN OF LAKE VILLAGE, GLASTONBURY.

of the entrance. This interval was occupied by water about 6 feet deep, and was probably bridged over by some kind of drawbridge. It was defended by a stockade consisting of piles 3 to 9 inches in diameter packed closely together, and irregular in outline, the irregularity being due to successive enlargements of the village. The stockade enclosed an area of about 400 × 300 feet, and between it and the huts a platform 8 to 10 feet wide, made of trunks of trees, and hewn timber with layers of brushwood and clay, rushes and bracken from 4 to 5 feet thick, rested on the peat, and gave access to the huts.

The huts are now marked by low circular mounds from 18 to 35 feet in diameter, formed of floors of clay thickening towards the centre to as much as 10 feet, each with a central hearth. Some of these mounds contained as many as ten floors, each representing a separate period of occupation. These clay mounds were based on a substructure of large

[1] 'The British Lake Village near Glastonbury,' *Glastonbury Antiquarian Society*; *British Assoc. Reports*, 1894–9. Figs. 10, 11, 12 are taken from Mr. Bulleid's drawings and photographs.

timbers placed side by side, brushwood, and logs 6 feet 6 inches thick, which rested on peat, and presented the following section :—

	ft.	in.
Soil, about	1	0
Large timbers	1	0
Brushwood	0	6 to 9
Timbers, olive brown peat and logs .	3	0
Decayed wood and dark peat . . .	1	6

The whole was kept in place by hundreds of piles.

On this substructure the sixty-five huts forming the settlement were placed, the whole floating so to speak on an accumulation of peat not less than 16 feet deep.

The remains discovered in and around this settlement, and preserved in the Glastonbury Museum, have unfortunately not yet been catalogued or described. The more important are as follows :—

Bronze Articles.—Curved bar (probably a key), rivet heads, studs, knob of scape of scabbard, mirrors, tweezers, bowl (see p. 199, fig. 11), needle, bands for wooden tubs.

Bronze Personal Ornaments.—Bracelets, rings, safety-pin brooches, penannular brooches, serpentine dress fastener like the eye of ' hook and eye,' pin.

Iron Implements.—Bill-hook, sickle, reaping hook, axe, adze, saw (small, tanged, with edge 1·5 inches long), gouge with handle 9 inches long, chisel, hammer, file, chain with round links, snaffle bit, rings, knife, handle of mirror.

Iron Weapons.—Spear-head or dagger, double-edged halbert, bar for making sword.

Leaden Articles.—Weight, line sinker for fishing, fishing net sinker, spindle-whorl.

Articles of Stone, Jet, Glass and Amber.—Querns of beehive type similar to those found at Northampton, grain rubbers, spindle-whorls (one is made out of *Ammonites bifrons*), pot boilers, whetstones, hammer stones, flint saws made out of flakes, flint flakes and cores, flint thumb-scraper, flint arrowhead, finger rings and armlets of Kimmeridge shale, two polished stone celts, probably preserved as charms, jet ring, amber beads.

Glass ring, small blue glass bead, ruby coloured glass bead with yellow streak, blue with white spirals, lump of glass for use in manufacture.

Articles made of Bone and Antler.—Pick made of antler of red deer, ferrules made of antler for wooden handles of tools, bone link for fastening dress, needles of bone and antler, knife handles of antler, weaving combs of antler, hammer-heads of stag's antler, antler stamps for making circles in ornamentation of the pottery, bone scoops, bone borers, bone shuttle, lathe-turned bone box with four oblong dice marked from one to six.

Pottery and Terra-cotta.—Large quantities of pottery were met with in the settlement, both handmade and turned on the wheel, fine and coarse, black and grey, and in one case red. The vessels have flat bottoms, and they are adorned with stamped circles, with flamboyant designs, and in some cases with incised lines in chevrons (see fig. 10). They are of the type usually found in settlements of the Prehistoric Iron age in Britain, and the ornamentation in flowing lines is obviously derived from southern Europe. The coarser hand-made vessels have been intended for common domestic use, and have the coarse paste with fragments of stone, found in pottery ranging in Britain from the Neo-

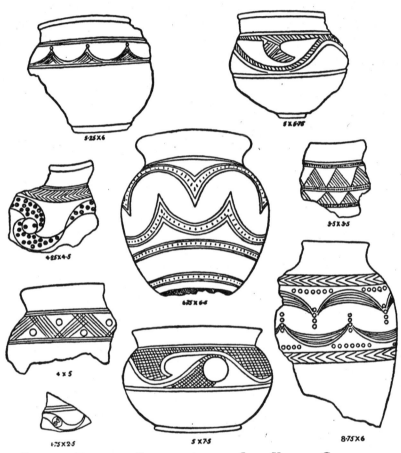

FIG. 12. DECORATED POTTERY FROM THE LAKE VILLAGE, GLASTONBURY.
Actual size is given in inches.

lithic age down to the close of the Roman occupation. Numerous fragments of this common archaic pottery have been met with in the recent excavations in Silchester. The ornamentation in chevron (fig. 12) is a survival from the Bronze age.

Numerous *terra-cotta* triangular loom weights have also been found of the type usually met with in settlements of the Prehistoric Iron age, such as Hunsbury near Northampton and Hod near Blandford in Dorset. Several thousand pellets for slinging—of the usual acorn shape, some burnt and others unburnt—were also discovered, along with pebbles of the same shape, selected from a beach. They are similar to the leaden *glandes* of the south of Europe.

196

Articles made of Wood.—The various articles made of wood have been preserved in the peat in almost their original perfection, and prove that carpentry in oak and ash was of a very high order in the settlement. Some have been lathe turned, others have been mortised, and in all the parts have been neatly fitted together. The following represents the more important and interesting finds :—

The mortised framework of two or more looms.

Tubs, buckets and bowls, mostly made of staves pegged together, while others have been cut out of the solid. They range from 6 inches to 2 feet 6 inches in height, and from a few inches to 2 feet in diameter. Some are ornamented with the same designs as those of the pottery.

Two wooden spoons.

Handles of awls, querns and other implements. Two reaping hooks, two axes, a saw and a gouge of iron have been found with perfect handles, some straight, others curved, and some with knobs.

Large mortised oaken beams. These were used in constructing the platforms on which the huts were built, and were fixed by piles. Others had small mortised holes on one side for the reception of the uprights of the hurdle which, covered with wattle and daub, formed the wall of the house, about 10 feet 3 inches long and 6 feet 3 inches high. The underside was cut for the reception of another similar timber, at right angles. It is therefore clear that some of the dwellings were rectangular and probably about 10 feet square, and with walls 6 feet high.

A door. This is 3 feet 6 inches high and 16 inches wide, made of one piece of oak with projections above and below, forming a pivot for movement in a socket. This shows the size and manner of hinging of the doors.

A ladder 7 feet long, with four steps made of split ash, each side having four mortised holes for the steps. The bottom step was secured by a wooden pin, and the top step originally made of wood had been replaced by plaited osiers. This ladder was probably used in thatching the roofs of the houses.

Wheels. An axle and several spokes, beautifully turned, prove that wheeled vehicles were in use on the adjacent land. The axle, 8 inches in diameter, was of ash, and had been worm-eaten before it was thrown away. The spokes were from 12 to 13·5 inches long. The diameter of the wheel therefore would be, allowing for the thickness of the felloes, about 3 feet. Another wheel cut out of the solid was 15 inches in diameter.

Two canoes, one 17 feet long, 2 feet broad and 1 foot deep, had been made out of an oak trunk, and was buried in the peat in the neighbourhood of the settlement.

The Animals found in the Refuse Heaps.—The following animals are represented in the refuse heaps : the British shorthorn (*Bos longifrons*), abundant ; the goat (*Capra hircus*), abundant ; the sheep (*Ovis aries*), abundant ; the hog (*Sus scrofa*), abundant ; the horse (*Equus caballus*), abundant ; the dog (*Canis familiaris*), rare ; the domestic fowl (*Gallus domesticus*), only one.   All these were the stock of the farms on the adjacent land.   The domestic fowl is represented by the spur of a cock.   It is probable that cockfighting was one of the sports in the settlement, and that the cocks were derived from Gaul, where cock-fighting was prevalent at the time of the Roman conquest.

The following wild animals have also been identified :—The wild cat (*Felis catus ferus*), rare ; the otter (*Lutra vulgaris*), rare ; the marten (*Mustela martes*), rare ; the stoat (*M. putorius*), rare ; the wolf (?) (*Canis lupus*), rare; wild boar (*Sus scrofa ferus*), many specimens ; the beaver (*Castor fiber*), rare ; the red deer (*Cervus elaphus*), many specimens ; the roe deer (*C. capreolus*), rare ; the water rat (*Arvicola amphibia*), abundant ; field mouse (*A. agrestis*), rare ; hedgehog (*Erinaceus europæus*).

The birds[1] identified by Dr. Andrews are as follows : Pelican, carrion crow, goshawk, kite, barn owl, common heron, common bittern, swan, wild goose, wild duck (including mallard), diver, puffin, crane, corncrake, grebe.   The identification of the pelican is of great interest, because it proves that that bird, now no longer found in north-western Europe, nested in the marshes of Glastonbury.[1]   Dr. Andrews sums up the evidence offered by the birds as to the conditions of life in the settlement as follows :—

> This assemblage of species indicates the existence of a district of marsh and mere haunted by flocks of pelicans and cranes, and in winter by swarms of wildfowl, which furnished the inhabitants of the pile-dwellings with food.   Probably the birds were killed with the sling, for great quantities of pellets of clay, well adapted for use with that instrument, have been found.   From time to time a stray sea bird made its way to the spot, and the white-tailed sea eagle, no doubt, found there a good hunting ground.

To this picture the study of the plants adds an appropriate setting. The forests bordering the marshes consisted of oak, ash, yew, alder and various willows.   There were hazel copses on the slopes and blackthorns on the clay lands, and vetches mingled with the grass in the glades ; while here and there were cultivated patches of ground golden in the autumn with barley.   This and the vetch and the sloe were among the stores found in the settlement.

From these discoveries we may infer that the inhabitants of this settlement were not only farmers and herdsmen but were advanced to an astonishing degree in the technical arts.   They used iron axes, adzes, gouges and saws in their wood-work ; they reaped their barley with iron sickles of various shapes.   They had iron chains : the *scoriæ* and the unfinished articles prove that the forges were in the village.   They smelted lead ore from the Mendip Hills and manufactured out of it spindle-whorls and weights for nets.   Some pieces of glass slag and fragments of crucibles make it probable that they carried on the manufacture of glass, ruby, blue and yellow, which they used for beads and rings and

[1] For a detailed account see Andrews 'On some Remains of Birds from the Lake-dwellings of Glastonbury, Somersetshire,' *Ibis*, July, 1899.

Fig. 11.   Bronze Bowl, Lake Village, Glastonbury.

other personal ornaments. They also were workers in bronze and tin, and were probably the makers of the beautiful bronze bowl (fig. 11) adorned with studs found in the village. They used bronze fibulæ, rings, pins and mirrors, and added to their personal charms by red ochre and powdered galena, the latter mixed with grease. They wore bracelets and armlets of Kimmeridge shale. They were also potters and used the lathe for the finer articles (fig. 12), although the coarser for common domestic use were made by hand. They were also spinners and employed the loom in weaving. They excelled in the arts of carpentry, as is shown by the well-squared holed and morticed beams, and the wooden buckets, dishes and bowls, many with flamboyant incised patterns, and by the well-fitted wheels, ladders, doors, as well as by the handles of their implements and weapons. Canoes of oak gave them access by water to the mainland. They cultivated barley on the adjacent land, and kept horses, the small prehistoric shorthorn (*Bos longifrons*), sheep, goats and pigs. They also hunted the red deer and roe in the forests and trapped the beaver and otter in the marshes. Among the birds on which they fed, wild geese, swans, ducks and pelicans may be noticed. In their herding and hunting they used big dogs. Their weapons were spears, arrows, slings, axes, bill-hooks, swords and daggers. They probably used the horse in warfare as well as for ordinary domestic purposes. Some of the bits are of iron and of the snaffle type still in common use. The discovery of a wooden wheel with beautifully turned spokes proves that horses were used for driving.

There is proof also of extended intercourse between the Lake villages and various parts of Britain and of southern Europe. The jet which they used probably came from Yorkshire, the Kimmeridge shale from Dorset, the amber from the eastern counties, or with more probability from the great centre of the amber trade to the south of the Baltic. The cocks were probably obtained from Gaul. The intercourse with the south is proved conclusively by the designs on the pottery (fig. 12) and by the bronze mirrors of Italo-Greek or Mykenæan origin. The bronze bowl too (fig. 11) is rivetted together in the same way, and by the same sort of rivets, as those used by the goldsmiths whose beautiful work, discovered in Mykenæ by Schliemann, is preserved in the museum at Athens.

Among the articles found in and around these huts it is interesting to note the spur of a cock, a set of dice, a 'potato-stone' and one perfect and another imperfect Neolithic flint celt of the Cissbury type—showing that the vices of cockfighting, gambling, and of collecting minerals and antiquities, were known in the settlement. These celts probably here, as elsewhere, had a superstitious value.

Nor are we without evidence as to the people living in the district at the time. The skulls found near the entrance of the stockade tell their own story. Some were cut and broken during lifetime, and some, including that of a woman, have been cut off the body and mounted on a spear, which has left its marks on its edges inside of the hole in the occiput for the admission of the spinal column into the brain-cavity. The heads had been cut off, carried on spears, and then placed on the stockade near the entrance as trophies. A few human bones found inside have been probably brought in by the dogs who gnawed them. Two entire skeletons of infants were found buried inside the stockade.

All the skulls belong to the small dark Iberic inhabitants, whose ancestors came into Somerset in the Neolithic age and were living also in the county in the succeeding age of Bronze. They probably do not belong to the community inhabiting this particular stockade, whose burial-place on the adjacent land has yet to be discovered. It must however be observed that from discoveries elsewhere in the county the Iberic race was very largely represented in Somerset in the Prehistoric Iron age.

The date of this 'Venice of the west' is fixed by the presence of brooches of a pattern common in the Mediterranean region at about 200 B.C. It is carried down to the period immediately before the Roman conquest, by the penannular brooches. Had it survived to a later time, it would undoubtedly have contained the coins, pottery and other remains invariably found in the Romano-British sites, which are amply represented in the county. It was destroyed before the Roman influence became all powerful in the district in the days of Claudius.

17. WORLEBURY AND THE OTHER FORTIFIED TOWNS.

Implements, weapons, ornaments and pottery, similar to those described above from Glastonbury, indicate the archæological age of several of the hill-fortresses of Somerset. Worlebury, explored by Warre, and more recently by Dymond and Tomkins,[1] may be taken as an example. Worlebury (fig. 13) crowns the precipitous headland, washed to the north and west by the Bristol Channel, and sloping southwards to the marshland, now covered in part by the villas and streets of Weston-super-Mare, but at the time of the occupation of the fortress probably a harbour. It was therefore in free touch with the sea. On the land side, to the south-east, it was connected, by a gentle rise above the marshes in the direction of Locking Head, with the ridgeway traversing the Mendips westward to Uphill, and used in later times by the Romans. It was also connected directly with Uphill by the line of dunes, giving free access southwards to the harbour at the mouth of the Axe, some three miles away, close under the hill fort of Brean Down, then probably an island. It occupied therefore a commanding position on the line of communication between Glastonbury and the other inland centres of the Prehistoric Iron age and the sea. We need not therefore wonder at the strength of its fortification. On the north side a limestone precipice renders fortification unnecessary. Where this ends to the east a wall formed of small blocks of limestone, built in sections faced with larger

[1] G. C. Dymond, *Worlebury*, 4to, new ed. 1902 ; G. C. E. Dymond and the Rev. H. G. Tomkins, *Worlebury*, 4to ; Warre, *Proc. Som. Archæol. and Nat. Hist. Soc.* ii. ii. 64 ; iv. ii. 124 ; v. ii. 32, 45.

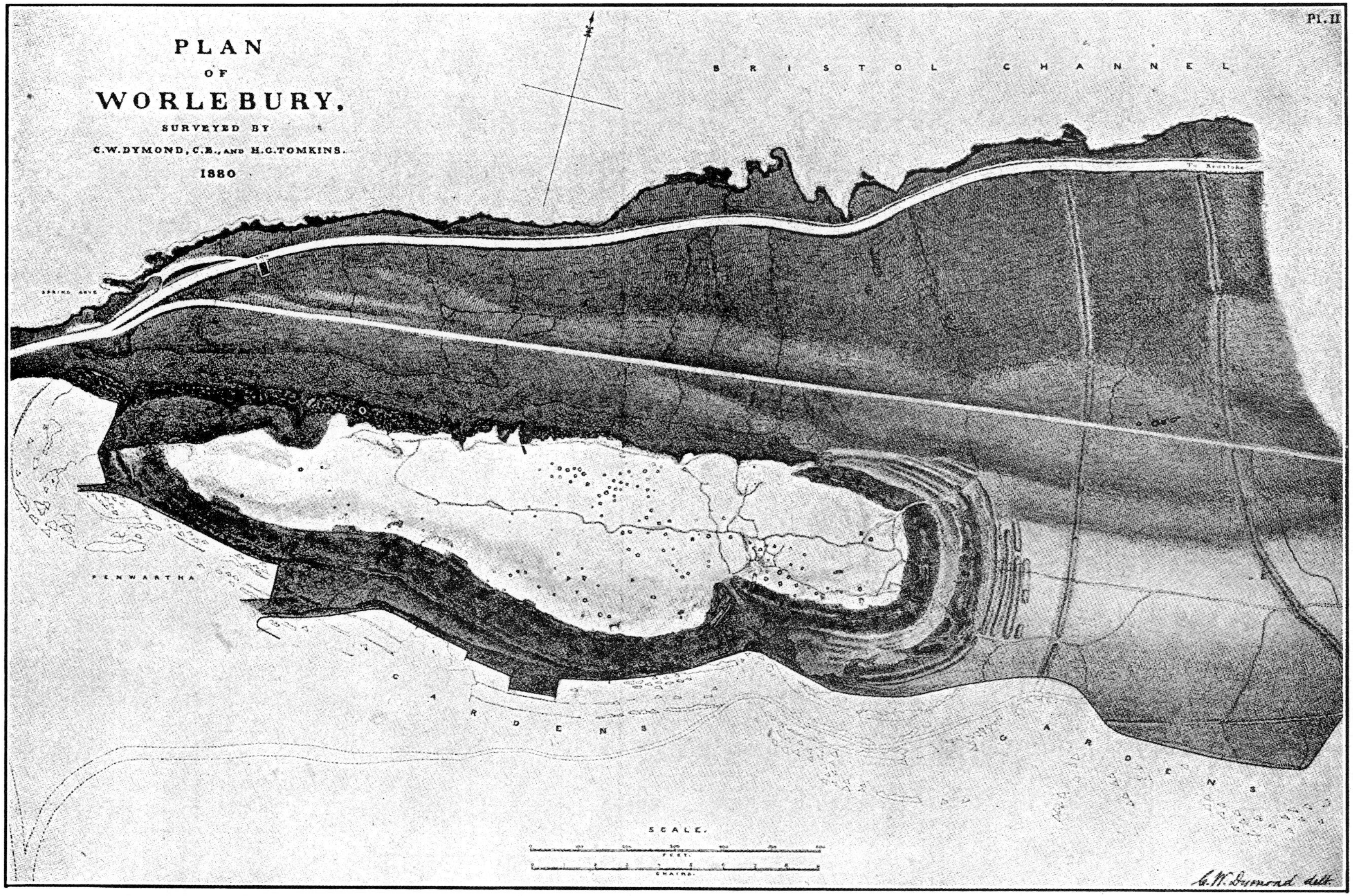
PLAN
OF
WORLEBURY,
SURVEYED BY
C.W.DYMOND, C.E., AND H.G.TOMKINS.
1880
Pl. II
BRISTOL CHANNEL
PENWARTHA
GARDENS
GARDENS
SCALE.
FEET.
CHAINS.
C.W. Dymond delt.

Fig. 13.

blocks, forms the inner line of defence 34 feet thick, sweeping round the promontory until it reaches the western end of the precipice. On the eastern side a second line of rampart sweeps round from the eastern to the western end of the precipice with an intervening fosse cut in the rock. The eastern side too being the weaker, the approach is rendered more difficult by four additional fosses cut in the rock and by breastworks. These probably extended also on the southern side until they met the precipice on the west, but their course has now been very nearly obliterated by the encroachment of gardens and villas. The area included within the inner rampart, $10\frac{1}{4}$ acres in extent, is further divided by a fosse, partly natural and partly artificial, into an eastern and western section, the former being the higher, and occupying the same relation that a Norman keep holds to its bailey.

The entrances are three in number. An ancient road, cut in the slope, winds up to the grand entrance on the south, and is about 13 feet wide, where it traverses the walls of the inner rampart. It is a flanking entrance. The second (fig. 14), also flanking, at the north-eastern angle, is 11 feet wide ; while the third, at the western end, approached by a flight of steps, is so ruined that its plan cannot be ascertained.

The structure of the walls is admirably shown by the excavations of Dymond and Tomkins. They are formed of blocks of limestone, taken out of the excavation for the fosses, and obtained also from the

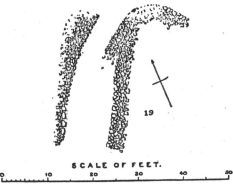

SCALE OF FEET.

FIG. 14. PLAN OF NORTH-EASTERN FLANKING ENTRANCE (DYMOND).

natural talus, faced with larger blocks. This process has been repeated until the whole thickness of the wall has been made. In some cases, as in the portion south of the grand entrance, it is composed of four sections, built one against the other (fig. 15), which probably, when perfect, were approached from the inside by a series of terraces. On the outside, in its present ruined state, it stands 16 feet from its base, and rises inside 8 feet above the ground. This method of construction is to be seen in prehistoric forts in other districts, where suitable stones are met with. In Wales, for example, the fortress of Tre Ceiri, and in the Arran Islands in Galway Bay those of Dun Angus and Dun Onacht may be quoted. The talus at the foot of the precipice on the north has been rearranged for purposes of defence and is approached by three passages or sally ports. There is also a fourth sally port leading directly to the spring on the shore at the west end of the fortress. The eastern approach was further defended by two lines of walling and fosse, extending from the line of cliff to the south. Here they are joined by a wall running east and west. They thus form two enclosures fitted both for defence and for herding the sheep, horses and cattle.

We must now review briefly the evidence as to the ancient possessors of this remarkable fortress, founded mainly on the discoveries of Warre, who was the first to explore scientifically the pit dwellings of Britain. No less than ninety-three pits have been recorded by Dymond within the area of the inner rampart, eighteen being in the

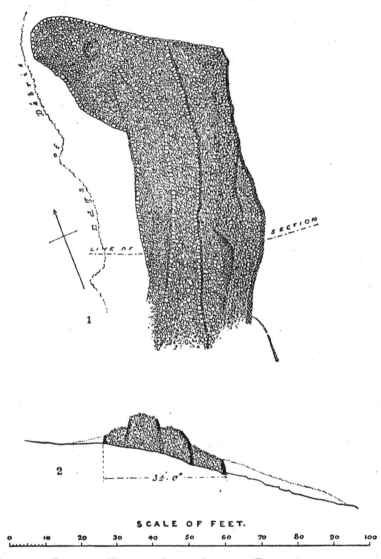

SCALE OF FEET.

FIG. 15. WALL OF GRAND GATEWAY (DYMOND).

eastern 'keep,' seventy-four in the western portion, and one in the fosse between the two. They vary in size from 3 feet × 2 feet 6 inches to 8 feet × 7 feet, and in depth from 3 to 6 feet. They are all excavated in the limestone rock, some having been the bases of dwellings while others have been used as granaries for the storage of wheat, barley and peas. They were circular excepting where the jointing of the rock made it necessary to take the stone out in rectangular blocks. In one group three pits lie so close together that Dymond suggests that they may have been under the shelter of one roof, while Warre writes of ring embankments surrounding the pits similar to those which have

WORLEBURY.

From a Drawing by C. W. Dymond.

recently been explored by the writer of this article in the fortress of Hod near Blandford, Dorset, a hill fort of the same Prehistoric Iron age as that of Worlebury. They contained the usual remains of food, comprising bones of hog, short-horned ox, horse, sheep or goat, stag and waterfowl. Small birds and limpets were also eaten. Iron spearheads, borers, chisels, sling stones, pot boilers, whorls for spinning and combs for weaving, a glass bead, and pottery identical with some of that at Glastonbury, were discovered, as well as quantities of wheat, barley and peas. The fortress obviously belonged to the farmers then occupying the district with their flocks and herds, and cultivating the slopes of the adjacent hills.

There is also ample proof that it was captured and burnt. The grain was converted into charcoal, and the carbonized remains of the wattlework of the huts, and the conversion of the limestone fragments into lime which had afterwards set, leave no room for doubt that it was destroyed by fire. The human skeletons in some of the pits, cut and hacked, prove that the inhabitants were massacred, and more or less covered by the débris thrown upon them. On one skull there is the unmistakable incision made by the sharp end of a bill-hook, similar to those found in the Lake village of Glastonbury ; on another are sword cuts ; and a third has been severed from the spinal column by a blow cutting clean through the atlas vertebra. Children were among the victims. The fortress had obviously been stormed and the inhabitants put to the sword.

The human skulls belong to the same oval-headed, Iberic type which has been already noted in those which adorned the entrance to the Lake village of Glastonbury, and presumably were the enemies of the villagers ; to a type which might be expected to be dominant in this district from its proximity to the Silures across the Bristol Channel, whose Iberic characteristics were noted by their conqueror Agricola, and recorded by his son-in-law Tacitus. In this district at this time they had probably been absorbed into the Brythons. It is not improbable that the destruction of Worlebury took place during the invasion of Brythonic Somerset by their kinsmen the Belgæ, the masters of this region at the time of the Roman conquest.

The fortress is represented in the plate as restored by Mr. Dymond. The view is taken from a point looking northward over the Bristol Channel and the Flat Holme to the coast of Wales and Monmouth.

Many of the other fortified towns, which occur on the line of the Mendip Hills eastward as far as Shepton, probably belong to the same age. Dolbury camp, for example, near Churchill, and Maesbury near Shepton Mallet, are composed of dry walling of the same kind as at Worlebury. The two latter stand in close relation to the ridgeway passing from Shepton westward along the Mendips to Uphill, and afterwards used as a Roman road.

The great camp at Cadbury near Wincanton has yielded ornaments and implements, pottery and sling stones, spindlewhorls and loom weights of the same type as those of Glastonbury, while that of Hamdon Hill near South Petherton has yielded iron swords roughly blocked out and in the same state of manufacture as those in the lake village. These are merely a few of the fortified towns which were occupied in the Prehistoric Iron age. In all probability the larger and better constructed hill forts throughout Somerset will be proved by future exploration to belong to this age. Nor must Bath itself be left out of consideration. The irregular area included by the Roman wall is so unlike the usual rectangular work of the Roman engineer that it is probably a pre-Roman site like that of Verulam (St. Albans) and Calleva Attrebatum (Silchester). The name Aquæ Sulis (the waters of the Celtic god Sul) implies that the hot springs were known in pre-Roman times.

18. THE SURVIVAL OF THE BRYTHONIC TONGUE

An examination of the names of places, rivers and mountains proves that the Brythonic, now represented by the Welsh, tongue prevailed over the whole of the county. This is proved by the numerous Pens and Combes, the 'Maes' (plain) in Maesbury, the 'Castel Rachich' (Rhag, Rhac spine) corrupted into Castel Neroche,[1] the 'Maen' (stone) in Mendip, and among the rivers, the Avon and the Parrett. The old name of the latter river Peryddon is to be found in Puriton, a village near its mouth. The Brythonic tongue survived in southern England until it became extinct in Cornwall at the end of the eighteenth century.

19. CONCLUSION

We have now come to the end of the story of the arrival of men in Somerset in remote times far beyond the reach of history. We have seen at its beginning the Palæolithic hunters, the River-drift men first and the Cave men afterwards, following the chase under conditions of life wholly continental and totally different to those of insular Britain. Then, after Britain had become severed from the continent, the Neolithic aborigines appear ; the small dark-complexioned Iberians were the first herdsmen and farmers. Next in the long course of the ages the blonde Goidelic Celts mastered the land and absorbed into their mass the conquered tribes, introducing the higher civilization of bronze ; and lastly, the iron-using Brythons in their turn conquered the Goidels and absorbed them into their own section of the Celts, bringing in with them a higher culture and a closer contact with the continental peoples and welding the smaller communities into larger centres of government.

The process was going on, and the Belgæ, the latest comers, were carving out for themselves a dominion in the county until the time when the Roman arms prevented any further intertribal warfare in Britain. At this point our story ends, to be taken up in due place by the historian of Roman Somerset.

---

[1] On the derivation of this and many other place names see Jones, *Som. Archæol. and Nat. Hist. Soc. Proc.* v. 73.

PREFATORY NOTE

FOR the following monograph I have searched the literature, printed and unprinted, as thoroughly as I could. I have also visited the chief sites—many of them familiar to me since my boyhood—and have examined the Museums at Bath, Bristol, Shepton, Taunton, and elsewhere. I owe sincere thanks to many helpers who are named in my pages, and above all to the Rev. H. H. Winwood, of Bath, without whose unfailing kindness and energy and knowledge I could not have achieved my task. For facilities and aid I am indebted at Bath to the Baths Committee and its Chairman, and to Mr. A. J. Taylor; at Bristol, to Mr. W. R. Barker; at Taunton, to Mr. Gray; and at Shepton, to the late Mr. John Phillis. It would be dishonest not to add that I have received other and no less valuable aid which I cannot here properly acknowledge. I desire also to express my gratitude to one now dead, who long ago encouraged a young student—the Rev. H. M. Scarth, Rector of Bathwick and of Wrington.

In citing published books I have used abbreviations which will, I think, be generally intelligible. But I may say that the two county histories by Collinson and Phelps, and the two histories of Bristol by Barrett and Seyer, are indicated simply by their authors' names.

I have also examined for this article much unpublished material, of which it may be convenient here to indicate the chief items: (1) The diaries and papers of the Rev. John Skinner, of Camerton, filling about 100 volumes in the British Museum, besides one in the Bath Institution; these relate principally to Camerton, but also to other parts of Somerset (*see* especially pp. 289 foll.). (2) Some important collections relating to Bath, commenced long ago by a Mr. Gulstone, bought by the late Colonel Long in 1866, and now the property of Colonel Long of Woodlands, Congresbury. (3) A large mass of drawings and notes, which concern all periods of Bath history, collected by the late Mr. J. T. Irvine while resident in Bath forty years ago, and bequeathed by him to the Edinburgh Museum of National Antiquities; they contain valuable details about Roman remains, among much that is less valuable and much that relates to medieval and modern Bath. (4) Lastly, I have found in the British Museum, the Bodleian, and the library of the Society of Antiquaries of London many scattered notes, some describing discoveries made in Bath during the eighteenth century, some referring to other places or dates, which deserve attention. In particular, the plan of the Roman baths at Bath gains from a use of these new sources.

The result of this re-examination of the existing remains, and the literature published and unpublished, is a survey of Roman Somerset that is, at any rate, much fuller than anything previously attempted. Aided as it is by the numerous illustrations allowed by the publishers, I hope that it may further the scientific study of the really important Roman antiquities in the county.

F. HAVERFIELD.

ROMANO-BRITISH SOMERSET

PART I.

1. SKETCH OF ROMAN BRITAIN

THE preceding chapter has shown that Somerset is unusually rich in striking Celtic antiquities. It is no less full of remarkable Roman remains. Though it lies far in the west country, and though much of it is marsh and much is moorland, it is certainly among the more noteworthy parts of southern Roman Britain.

Our account of this interesting region must needs be, like the preceding chapter, mainly archæological and not historical. It is true that when we pass from the Celtic to the Romano-British period, we begin to pass from the prehistoric to the historic. But we do not immediately reach the domain of full history. The allusions or narratives of ancient writers lend us their aid, but we cannot construct any continuous history of our subject, and we still depend chiefly on archæological evidence. In part this is due to the insufficiency of our knowledge, but to a still greater extent it is due to other causes. Even if we possessed a whole library of Roman literature about Roman Britain, we could not in this chapter attempt to write history. Two facts which are often overlooked limit us to a humbler though not an easier task.

The first of these facts is the character of the Roman Empire, of which Britain formed a province. Alike in its vast area and in its complex organization that Empire was constituted on a scale which dwarfs detail into insignificance. Its history—that is, its true history, apart from court scandals and imperial crimes—is the record of great developments slowly advancing among the peoples of three continents. It contains none of that continuity of individual life, that rapid succession of striking incidents, that quick growth of tendencies, which characterize the cities of ancient Greece or the little nations of modern Europe. Single men, local occurrences, are the least important items in its annals, and the fortunes of separate provinces are merged in the great movement of the whole mass. We may sketch the features of each or any province, its populousness, its degree of civilization, its mineral or agricultural or commercial wealth. We may string together in a rough narrative a few events connected with it. But we cannot write a real history of it, for it had no individual existence which the historian might trace.

A second fact imposes a still more serious limitation. When the Romans ruled our island it was not divided into its present counties or into any districts geographically identical with them. Neither the boundaries of the Celtic tribes nor those of the Roman administrative areas, so far as we know, agree with our existing county boundaries. When we study the Roman remains discovered in any one county, we deal with a division of land which for our purpose is accidental and arbitrary. The phrase 'Roman Somerset' is, strictly speaking, a contradiction in terms. We can discuss, as we shall presently do, the Roman remains found in our county, but we do so not because it is scientific, but because it is convenient. The topographical literature of our island is grouped so largely by counties that we can hardly treat the Roman antiquities on any other basis. But all the while we shall be dealing with an area which for our purpose has no meaning or unity. We can describe it; we cannot write its history.

These facts seem to justify a divergence from the plan followed by most county historians. Hitherto it has been customary to narrate the chief events recorded by ancient writers as occurring in Roman Britain, and to point out which of these events took place, or might be imagined to have taken place, within the county. The result is always to leave on the reader an impression that somehow or other the county possessed in Roman times a local individuality and a local history. In the following pages we shall adopt a different method. Utilizing the archæological evidence, which is now far better known and understood than a hundred years ago, we shall first sketch briefly the general character of Roman Britain and we shall then proceed to describe in detail the actual antiquities. We shall thus point out how far the district now called Somerset was an average bit of the Roman province.

The Roman occupation was commenced by the Emperor Claudius in A.D. 43. At first its progress was rapid. Kent and Essex were seized in a few weeks; then the army of invasion seems to have advanced into three divisions, the Second Legion moving south-west towards Somerset and Devon, the Fourteenth and Twentieth Legions north-west towards Shrewsbury and Chester, the Ninth Legion north towards Lincoln. Within three or four years the Romans held all the south and midlands as far as Exeter, Shrewsbury and Lincoln; part had been annexed, part left to 'protected' princes—for instance, the princes of the Iceni in what is now Norfolk and Suffolk. Then came a pause;

some thirty years were spent by Ostorius Scapula and his successors in reducing the hill tribes of Wales and Yorkshire, and during these years the protected principalities were absorbed. About A.D. 80 the advance into Scotland began ; about A.D. 124 the Emperor Hadrian built his wall from Tyne to Solway, and henceforward the Roman frontier was sometimes to the north, never to the south of this line.

The province thus acquired fell practically, though not officially, into two well-marked divisions, which coincide roughly with the lowlands conquered in the first years of the conquest and the hills which were conquered later (fig. 1). The former was the district of settled peaceful life, and in it we have to include the area now called Somerset. The troops appear to have been soon withdrawn from this district, and with a few definite exceptions there probably was not a fort or fortress throughout the south of our island after the end of the first century. It was the

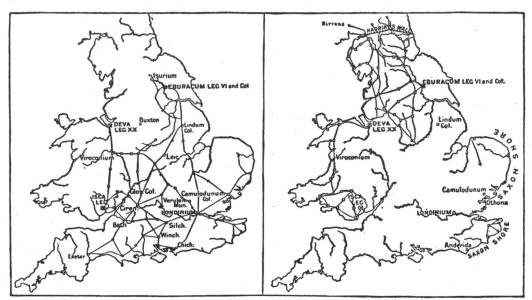

FIG. 1. THE CIVILIAN AND MILITARY DISTRICTS OF BRITAIN.

Roman practice, at least in the European provinces of the Empire, to mass the troops almost exclusively along the frontiers and to leave peaceful interior districts free from garrisons. Britain was no exception. The whole military force was stationed in Wales or in the north—that is, in the troublesome regions and on the Caledonian frontier. This military district was purely military ; it had its fortresses, roads and garrisons, but no towns or 'villas' or ordinary civilian life. The army which held it was perhaps forty thousand strong and ranked as one of the chief among the armies of the provinces. The most important element in Roman Britain was the military element.

With this military element however we are not here concerned. For our present purpose it is enough to note its existence in order to explain the rarity of Roman military remains in Somerset. But we may pause to examine the features of the non-military district, within which the area of our county lies. These features are not sensational. Britain was a small province, remote from Rome, and by no means wealthy. It did not reach the higher developments of city life, of culture and of commerce which we meet abundantly in more favoured lands, in Gaul or Spain or Africa. Nevertheless it had a character of its own.

In the first place, Britain, like all western Europe, became Romanized. Perhaps its Romanization was comparatively late in date and imperfect in extent, but in the end the Britons generally adopted the Roman speech and civilization, and in our island, as in Gaul and Spain and elsewhere, the difference between 'Roman' and 'provincial' practically vanished. When about A.D. 410 the Roman rule in Britain ended, the so-called 'departure of the Romans' did not mean an emigration of alien officials, soldiers and traders, such as we might see to-day if English rule ended abruptly in India or French rule in Algiers. It was administrative, not racial. Rome ceased to send to Britain high military and civil officials, and the imperial troops in the island were withdrawn or at least no longer reinforced from without. But the officials were not numerous; the troops had probably come long before to consist predominantly of local recruits, and we may believe that not many Romans actually 'departed.'

On the other hand, we know that the inhabitants of the island continued for years to think themselves 'Romani.' The gap between Briton and Roman, visible enough in the first century, had become almost obliterated by the fourth century. The townspeople and educated persons in Britain employed Latin, as casual words scratched on tiles or pottery assist to prove, while on the side of material civilization the Roman element reigned supreme. Before the Claudian conquest

FIG. 2. BRONZE TANKARD FROM ELVEDEN (SUFFOLK), ILLUSTRATING LATE CELTIC ART.

there had existed in the island a Late Celtic art of considerable merit, best known for its metal-work and earthenware, and distinguished by its fantastic use of plant and animal forms, its predilection for the 'returning spiral' ornament, and its enamelling. Somerset, as the preceding chapter has shown, provides us with many striking specimens of this art, and some illustrations are introduced here for further comparison (figs. 2, 3).

FIG. 3. LATE CELTIC POTSHERDS FROM THE GLASTONBURY LAKE VILLAGE
(Glastonbury Museum). $\frac{2}{3}$.

This art now vanished. In a few places, as for instance in some potteries of the New Forest and of the Nene Valley, its products survived as local manufactures, but even these were modified by Roman influences. Elsewhere, and not least in Somerset, we meet single specimens, usually of metal work, which are Late Celtic in style but occur with remains of the Roman period ; but these are sporadic, and their definite association with Roman objects is not always well attested. In general the Late Celtic art met the fate which overtakes every picturesque but semi-civilized art when confronted with an organized coherent culture. Almost every important feature in Romano-British life was Roman. The ground plans of the private houses form an exception ; they indicate in all probability that the Romans, coming to our shores from sunnier lands, accepted, as we might expect, some features of the native types of dwellings. But the furniture of these houses is Roman. The mosaic pavements and painted stucco and carved stone-work which adorned them, the hypocausts which warmed them, and the bathrooms which increased their comfort, were all equally borrowed from Italy. The better objects of domestic use tell the same

tale. The commonest good pottery is the red ware called Samian or Terra Sigillata (fig. 4). This was copied from an Italian original and manufactured in Gaul, and it completely superseded native manufactures as the fashionable and favourite ware. Nor were these foreign

FIG. 4. SAMIAN BOWL OF THE FIRST CENTURY A.D.

elements confined to the mansions of the wealthy. Samian bowls and rudely coloured plaster and makeshift hypocausts occur even in outlying hamlets.[1]

But though the Romanization was thus tolerably complete, it must be further qualified as a Romanization on a low scale. The more elaborate and splendid and wealthy features of the Italian civilization, whether material or intellectual or administrative, were rare or unknown in Britain. The finest objects of continental manufacture in glass and pottery and gold-work came seldom to the island, and the objects of local fabric rarely attained a high degree of merit. The choicer marbles and the finer statuary are still rarer—though there is one signal exception at Bath—and the mosaics are usually commonplace and lack distinction. Of Romano-British literature we have very little and that little owes its interest to other things than literary excellence. Of organized municipal

[1] R. Colt Hoare, *Ancient Wilts, Roman Æra*, p. 127 : 'On some of the highest of our [Wiltshire] downs I have found stuccoed and painted walls, as well as hypocausts, introduced into the rude settlements of the Britons.' The discoveries of the late General Pitt-Rivers fully confirm this.

or commercial or administrative life we have but scanty traces. The civilization of Roman Britain was Roman, but it contained few elements of splendour or magnificence.

We may distinguish in this civilization two local forms deserving special notice—the town and the villa. The towns of Roman Britain were not few. But as we might expect they were for the most part small. Many of them appear to have been originally Celtic tribal centres; then under Roman influence they developed into towns, like the tribal centres in northern Gaul. Scarcely any seems to have attained very great size or wealth, according to the standard of the Empire. The highest form of town life known to the Roman was certainly rare in Britain : the *coloniae* and *municipia*, the privileged municipalities with the Roman franchise and constitutions on the Italian model, were represented, so far as we know, by only five examples, the *coloniae* of Colchester, Lincoln, York and Gloucester and the *municipium* of Verulam, and none of these could vie with the greater municipalities of other provinces. But while lacking in size and magnificence, the towns of Roman Britain were in their way real towns ; if a modern term be allowed, we might best describe them as country towns. Most of them were walled, at least in the fourth century. Many of them had a *forum* built on the Roman plan, providing in Roman fashion accommodation for magistrates, traders and idlers. Not only the *coloniae* and *municipium*, which were ruled by prescribed magistrates and town councils, but many smaller places also must be regarded as having had some form of municipal life. They were, in their own way, Romanized.

Outside these towns the country seems to have been divided up into estates, known as 'villas,' and in this respect, as in its towns, Britain resembles northern Gaul. The villa was the property of a great land-owner, who inhabited the 'great house' if there was one, cultivated the ground close to it by slaves, and let the rest to half-serf *coloni*. The villa in fact was the predecessor of the mediæval manor. In Gaul some of the villas were estates of eight or ten thousand acres, and the land-owners' houses were splendid and sumptuous. In Britain we have no evidence to determine the size of the estates, and the houses—to which the term 'villa' is often especially applied—seem rarely to have been very large. A few can vie with continental residences ; many are small and narrow. The landowners, as in Gaul, were doubtless the Romanized nobles and upper classes of the native population, with but a slight infusion of Italian immigrants. The common assertion that they were Roman officers or officials may be set aside as rarely, if ever, correct. The wealth of these landowners must have been almost solely agrarian ; their lands were probably for the most part sheep runs and corn fields, and supplied the cloth and wheat which are mentioned by ancient writers as exported from Britain during the later Imperial period. The peasantry who worked on these estates or were otherwise occupied in the country lived in rude hamlets formed of huts or pit dwellings with few circumstances of luxury or even comfort. But even their material civilization

FIG. 3A.   LATE CELTIC COLLAR OF BRONZE, FOUND AT WRAXALL.
(From *Archæologia*, vol. liv.)

was Roman. Here, as among the upper classes, the Late Celtic art yielded largely to the strength of Italian influences.

In both town and country a remarkable feature is presented by the houses. Thoroughly Roman in their fittings, they are by no means

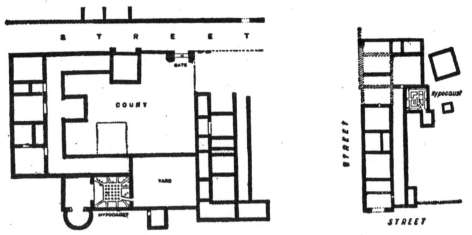

FIG. 5. PLANS OF COURTYARD AND CORRIDOR HOUSES AT SILCHESTER (scale 1 : 720). (The left-hand block shows a courtyard house with a corridor house adjacent ; the right-hand figure a small corridor house by itself.)

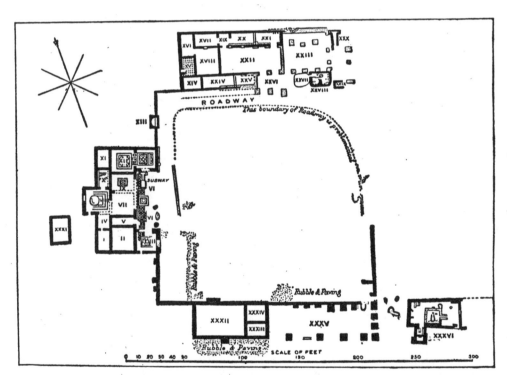

FIG. 6. VILLA, CONSISTING OF CORRIDOR HOUSE AND TWO BLOCKS OF FARM BUILDINGS ROUND A RECTANGULAR COURTYARD (BRADING, ISLE OF WIGHT). ROOM VI. IS THE CORRIDOR.

Roman in their ground plans.[1] In this respect they do not in the least resemble the houses of ancient Rome and Pompeii, nor are they very like

[1] The character of the Romano-British house was, I believe, first recognized by the Rev. H. M. Scarth.

the country houses which have been dug up in Italy. They belong instead to types which seem to occur only in Britain and northern Gaul, and they very possibly represent Celtic fashions, altered by Roman contact but substantially native. A common type is that sometimes called the Corridor type (fig. 5), which shows a straight row or range of rooms with a corridor running alongside of them and generally with some slight enlargement at one end or the other. Sometimes, as in the central building at Brading (fig. 6), both ends of the corridor terminate in rooms, and a rather different type of corridor house results. Another more elaborate type shows three rows of rooms and corridors set round an unroofed rectangular courtyard of considerable size. Very similar to this last is a type in which the buildings round the courtyard are not continuous, but stand isolated each in the middle of one of the three sides; in such cases the blocks may consist of corridor houses, of barns, outhouses and farm buildings of various plans (fig. 6). There appears to be no great difference between town and country in the distribution of these types, but the stateliest country villas seem to exhibit especially the courtyard types, and the second of the courtyard types occurs only in the country. In size the houses vary as widely as houses in all ages and countries. The corridor houses are as a rule the smallest, some of them measuring little more than 40 by 60 feet in length and breadth, while in the more imposing courtyard houses the yards alone are sometimes three times that area.

The local government of the country, so far as it is known to us, exhibits the same Romanization we have found in the general civilization of Britain. We can distinguish three units of administration. The five municipalities mentioned above had doubtless each its own territory, which it governed itself. The imperial domains, secondly, formed independent areas, under imperial officials. Their extent in Britain is uncertain, but we know that the mines were imperial property, and a villa on Combe Down (No. 19) perhaps supplies some slight indications of imperial estates of another kind. Thirdly, it seems that, as in northern Gaul, so in Britain, cantonal or tribal authorities ruled such parts of the country as were not municipal or imperial areas. These cantonal authorities represented the native chiefs and nobles of pre-Roman days. But they bore sway under Roman forms and titles ; they were called *duoviri*, like municipal magistrates, and their local meeting was styled *ordo* like the municipal senate. Of these, however, we have few traces in Britain and none in Somerset. The district does not even contain a town which can have served as a tribal capital, and its remains throw no light on the subject of the cantonal system in Britain.

One feature, not a prominent one, remains to be noticed—trade and industry. We should perhaps place first the agrarian industry, which produced wheat and wool. Both were exported in the fourth century, and the export of wheat to the mouth of the Rhine is mentioned by an ancient writer as considerable. Unfortunately the details of this industry are almost unknown : perhaps we shall be able to estimate it

better when the Romano-British 'villas' have been better explored.
Rather more traces have survived of the lead mining and iron mining
which, at least during the first two centuries of our era, was carried on
with some vigour in half a dozen districts—lead on Mendip in Somerset,
in Shropshire, in Flintshire and Derbyshire; iron in the Weald and the
Forest of Dean, and occasionally to a less extent elsewhere. Other
minerals were less important. The gold mentioned by Tacitus proved
very scanty. The far-famed Cornish tin seems (according to present
evidence) to have been worked comparatively little, and that late in the
Roman occupation. The chief commercial town was, from the earliest
times, Londinium (London). It was never, so far as we know, raised
to municipal rank, but was nevertheless a place of size and wealth and
perhaps the residence of the chief authorities who controlled taxes and
customs dues. The usual route to the continent for passengers and for
goods was from the Kentish harbours to Gessoriācum (Boulogne), but
the discovery of a pig of Mendip lead at the mouth of the Somme suggests that occasionally longer voyages were ventured.

Finally, let us sketch the roads. In doing so, we must dismiss
from our minds the Four Great Roads which are mentioned in some
early English documents and have frequently been called Roman. Three
of these four roads were Roman in origin, but the fourth was not, and
the idea of any such Four Great Roads is alien to the Roman road
system. Instead, we may distinguish four groups, all radiating from
one centre, London. One road ran south-east to Canterbury and the
Kentish ports. A second ran west and south-west, first due west from
London to Silchester, and thence by ramifications to Winchester and
Exeter, Bath, Gloucester and south Wales. A third, Watling Street,
ran north-west across the midlands to Wroxeter, and thence to the
military districts of the north-west; it also gave access to Leicester and
the north. A fourth ran to Colchester and the eastern counties, and
also to Lincoln and York and the military districts of the north-east.
To these must be added a long single road, the only important one which
had no connection with London and the only one with which in Somerset we shall be seriously concerned. This is the Fosse, which cuts
obliquely across from north-east to south-west, joining Lincoln, Leicester,
Bath and Exeter. These roads must be understood as being only the
main roads, divested, for the sake of clearness, of branches and intrica-
cies; and, understood as such, they may be taken to represent a reasonable supply of internal communications for the province. After the
Roman occupation had ceased, they were largely utilized by the English,
but they do not much resemble the roads of mediæval England in their
grouping or economic significance. One might better compare them
to the railways of to-day, which equally radiate from London.

Such, in the main, was that large part of Roman Britain on which
ordinary civilized non-military life prevailed—a land of small country
towns and large rural estates; permeated by the simpler forms of Roman
civilization, but lacking the higher developments; not devoid of natural

resources, but not rich ; a comfortable country perhaps, but an unimportant fraction of the Empire.

2. Sketch of Roman Somerset

From this brief sketch of southern Roman Britain we pass to the details of our own county. In general these details reproduce adequately the normal features which we have just described. But they are numerous and intricate, they include several items of peculiar interest, and it may be useful to summarize their principal characteristics before proceeding to discuss them one by one.

Somerset abounds with Roman remains. But the geographical distribution of these remains is very uneven. Some parts of the county were obviously well inhabited and well civilized ; other parts, whether inhabited or not, were certainly not inhabited thickly or in civilized fashion. Not only the wide marshes of the Brue and the Parret and the bogs and hills of Exmoor, but all the western portion of the county, even the pleasant vale of Taunton Deane, show but few vestiges of Romano-British life. The east and the north present a different picture. Here we meet ample traces of our period. Along the Fosse, which bisects the eastern half of Somerset, were towns and villages—a settlement at Bath, a tiny town or village at Ilchester, and perhaps a village at Camerton. Villas too and other marks of rural life are common on one side or the other of the same road ; they abound also in the north near Bristol and in the fertile vale of Wrington. Roughly and with certain obvious qualifications we may say that the districts east of Bridgwater were the districts of Romano-British life.

Besides these normal features, others less normal demand our attention. Bath, Aquae Sulis, the largest settlement and perhaps the only large one within the area of the county, was not an ordinary Romano-British town. It owed its existence to its hot mineral springs, and its most striking remains are those which are connected therewith—the ruins of its baths and the altars or tombstones of those who, successfully or unsuccessfully, sought the benefit of its waters. No doubt a population of others than invalids dwelt round the springs, as it does to-day. But, first and foremost, Bath was a bathing place. Let us add that its baths present one feature of signal interest which we might not expect. Among the carved stones of their ruins is a head, once the decoration of a pediment, which is the most remarkable piece of sculpture yet discovered in Britain. We know neither its sculptor nor his sources and inspiration, nor even his precise intention. But his work, in its astonishing vigour, is not only unique in Britain, it has hardly a rival in any province of the western empire.

Another noteworthy feature of Roman Somerset is furnished by the Mendip lead mines. Known, as it seems, to the pre-Roman Celts, they were worked by the Romans from the earliest period of their occupation ; they were amongst the few important industries of Roman Britain, and interesting (though, unfortunately, ill-recorded) relics of them have been at various times discovered. The sporadic finds of Roman remains in Somerset are also often noteworthy. Such are the numerous coin-moulds found along the northern slope of the Polden Hills, and the hoards of fourth-century silver coins which possess a special interest for numismatists. All these help to complete the picture of a remarkable area.

But this area, as our survey will show it to us, differs in some material respects from the Roman Somerset of many earlier writers. We have to forego much that they included. We can no longer call the great earthen camps Roman. The vast plateau of Hamdon Hill, Cadbury girt with its huge ditches, Castle Neroche dominating from its lofty summit the whole expanse of Taunton Deane, Dolebury looking out from its ramparts of piled stone over the vale of Wrington, Worlebury hanging heavy over Weston and the Channel—these and more are now recognized as dating from ages other and for the most part older than the Roman. We find Roman remains in some of them, but, except perhaps on Hamdon Hill, those remains are few and late and mostly coins; they prove no real habitation. Men sometimes say of such camps that, though not of Roman origin, they were occupied by the Romans. The phrase is unfortunate. The occupation must nearly always have been both slight and brief, and also Romano-British, that is, native, rather than really Roman. In the first four centuries of our era those camps, so far as they then existed, were what they are to-day, the stately ruins of a vanished world.

Again, we must exclude some British tribes which enthusiastic writers have assigned to Somerset. The Aedui, who are said to have migrated hither from Gaul, bringing with them the apple to Glastonbury, are a tolerably obvious fiction. The Cangi or Ceangi, whom some writers place on Mendip, are a real tribe, but their true home is in Flintshire.[1] We do not, indeed, know definitely the names of the Celtic tribes who in pre-Roman days inhabited the region which is now Somerset. Bath, as Ptolemy tells us, was in the territory of the Belgae, but the western limit of that territory is not recorded. Perhaps we might conclude that it lay east of Mendip, since no Mendip lead has ever been found with the stamp DE BELGIS or BELGICVM. But this is at the best a guess.

Once more, we must not seek in Somerset those defences which Ostorius is often stated to have erected near the Avon about the year A.D. 48. The Wansdyke has been called his Vallum, and his forts have been detected at neighbouring sites. But we now know that Wansdyke is, at least in large part, post-Roman (p. 371), while the alleged forts are either (like Worlebury) not Roman, or are sites of villages or villas.

[1] Camden put the Cangi in Somerset, quoting names like Cannington and Wincanton as proofs (i. 82, ed. Gough, 1806), but he hesitated about it, and elsewhere rightly put the Cangi in Flint (iii. 45). However, many have followed him without hesitation. Latterly Sir John Evans has resuscitated the idea (*Ancient British Coins*, p. 492), mainly on the ground that the Cangi were an important tribe and ought to have had a coinage, whereas the North Welsh tribes do not seem to have ever used coins. But the Cangi were not so very important, and the many pigs of Roman lead inscribed DECEANGI or the like, which have been found in or near Cheshire, fix the tribe to the Flintshire lead district. Whether its name was Cangi or Ceangi or Deceangi need not here concern us.

Moreover, the whole theory of the Ostorian forts has turned out an error. It rests on a bad text and a bad translation of Tacitus. The true text mentions neither a line of forts nor the river Avon. Probably it refers to a consolidation of the Roman dominion within the frontiers of the Severn and the Trent; in any case the Somerset archæologist can go his way untroubled by any heed of Ostorius.[1]

One more reflection, and that a rather different one, suggests itself concerning Roman Somerset. The county, as we have said, was in part well Romanized. It was also a part of Britain which the Saxons conquered comparatively late. Here, if anywhere, we should expect to see the form and fashion of the Roman epoch surviving into later days. We find nothing of the sort. Bath, it is true, stands on the site of Aquae Sulis, but we shall see below that Aquae Sulis lay waste for many years before English Bath was founded. Elsewhere in Somerset Roman and English sites coincide only in one case—Ilchester, and Ilchester was not an important Roman site. With this one exception the many towns of mediæval and modern Somerset—Taunton, Bridgwater, Wells, Shepton, Yeovil, Frome, Crewkerne, Ilminster, Chard, and others—are all of English origin. So, too, so far as we can judge, are the villages and even the roads except for portions of the Fosse Way. There is no continuity here between the English and their predecessors. The Somerset of Saxon and later days is a land from which Roman and Briton seem to have utterly vanished.

---

[1] Tacitus, *Annals*, xii. 31. The Ostorian forts have been detected in several parts of England with much misplaced ingenuity. Speculators would have done better, before theorizing, to have ascertained the true text of Tacitus and its probable sense. See further *Victoria History of Northamptonshire*, i. 213; H. Bradley, *Academy*, April–July, 1883, and the summary by Furneaux in his commentary on Tacitus.

ROMANO-BRITISH SOMERSET

PART II. BATH.

1. General sketch of Roman Bath. 2. Walls, gates, streets. 3. Internal buildings. 4. Temple of Sul and other remains found in 1790 and 1867. 5. Baths. 6. Private houses. 7. Cemeteries. 8. Inscriptions. 9. Uninscribed objects in stone. 10. Coins. 11. Other small objects.

1. GENERAL SKETCH OF ROMAN BATH

Bath lies in the deep valley of the Avon, between the lofty uplands of Lansdown on the north and Combe and Hampton downs on the south. The river, sweeping first against the slopes of Lansdown, then turning south to skirt the southern hills, and finally curving back towards the north, encloses between its northern bank and Lansdown a small expanse of low-lying and level land. That part of this expanse which is nearest the river is still liable to flood and must have been marsh in early times, but the rest of it is dry ground suitable for man to inhabit. Here stood the Romano-British settlement. Here too the medieval town, and hence in the last two hundred years the city has grown beyond the bottom of the valley and climbed the sides of the hills.

The reason for the occupation of the site is simple. In the level space within the fold of the river rise mineral springs, hot, medicinal, abundant ;[1] and their waters, suitable alike for drinking and for bathing, have power over gout and rheumatism and serious skin diseases. The ancient world suffered from these curses even more than the modern world, and sought eagerly for healing springs. Remote as the site of Bath is from the centres of population and activity during the Roman empire, its waters drew men to it, and its sheltered position, its mild climate and salubrious air added to its attractions. Other elements appear to have contributed comparatively little to its making. The site has no military strength. The river is not navigable. Even the deep valley in which Bath lies has less topographical importance than might be imagined. It divides, indeed, the hills of south Gloucestershire and of north Somerset, outliers respectively of Cotswold and Mendip. But it does not form a natural pass from any one important town or district to another ; and though it has been used between Bath and Bristol by Roman road and modern railway, the reason is because Roman and railway alike had reason to reach the hot springs. The natural route from London and the east to Bristol runs through Marlborough and Chippenham and Marshfield, north of Bath, as we find it running in the sixteenth century. Bath has not, like numerous towns, grown up beside a road. In the seasons of its prosperity, in the Roman period and in the last two hundred years, the roads have come to it.

The Romano-British settlement which thus rose beside the waters

---

[1] The supply at present averages half a million gallons a day ; the temperature varies from 104° to 120° Fahrenheit.

acknowledges its origin in its name. It is called Ὕδατα Θερμά, the hot springs, by the geographer Ptolemy, and Aquae Sulis in the Itinerary.[1] The identification of these names with Bath was first made in the early years of the sixteenth century and has since been universally accepted ; it is indeed beyond reasonable doubt. The contexts of Ptolemy and the Itinerary show that Ὕδατα Θερμά and Aquae Sulis must have been situated on a Roman road at or somewhere near modern Bath. At Bath we have hot springs and abundant Roman remains and a junction of Roman roads, and these features concur at no other place in southern Britain. The hot springs at Bath are indeed the only really hot springs in the whole of our island. At Bath moreover, and nowhere else, we have dedications to a goddess Sul or Sulis Minerva. We may safely accept the traditional view and place Aquae Sulis at Bath.[2]

The meaning of the second half of the name, Sulis, can hardly be doubted. As the inscriptions show, Sul or Sulis was the presiding deity of the springs. No reference to her occurs elsewhere,[3] and she is plainly a local goddess. We may compare her with Bormo, who presided over the Aquae Bormonis in central Gaul, and we may find in both an illustration of the elder Pliny's remark that 'healing springs increase the number of the gods under various names and encourage the growth of cities.' Presumably Sul or Sulis was a Celtic deity and Celtic philologists incline to connect her with the sun, who was female in early Celtic as in Teutonic languages.[4] The Romans equated her with Minerva, but that in itself proves little, except that she was a female and not a male deity.[5] Whether the nominative of her name was Sulis or Sul is uncertain : in the following pages I have used Sul as the shorter and most customary form.[6]

It is not its name only that the place owes to the waters. Aquae Sulis is one of the half-dozen sites in Roman Britain to which recognizable allusion is made in ancient literature. Londinium, Camulodūnum, Eburācum, Rutupiae are named ; the baths of Aquae Sulis are mentioned but not by name. In the third century of our era, one Caius Julius Solinus compiled an account of the curiosities of the world (*Collectanea rerum memorabilium*), and among them he includes the Bath waters.

[1] Itinerary, 486, 3. The MSS. there vary between Sulis and Solis, but the better MSS. (JLN) give Sulis. This is the more probable on the principle of *difficilior lectio potior*, for Sulis is more likely to have been corrupted into Solis than Solis into Sulis. Sulis is further supported by the numerous Bath inscriptions which mention Sul or Sulis Minerva, while Sol occurs only once (p. 241). among the Roman remains of the spot. Solis may therefore be regarded as out of the question.

[2] Other names are assigned by older writers to Bath—Βάδιζα, Caer Badon, Caer Palladur and the like—but they wholly lack authority. Aquae in Ravennas, 430, 5 is generally identified with Bath (for instance, by Holder, Hübner, Pauly and Wissowa), but it seems to be Buxton.

[3] The 'possible' references collected by M. Ihm (*Bonner Jahrbücher*, lxxxiii. 81) are all extremely improbable.

[4] So Rhys and Whitley Stokes. The latter writes to me that Sulis is the original Celtic word to which the Irish *suil* (eye) points, just as *sāvalis* is the strong form to which the Welsh *haul* (sun) points. Whether the Suleviae are connected is quite doubtful.

[5] The equation may, however, have been helped by the established Roman connexion of Minerva with medicinal art, seen in such details as Cicero's remark *Minerva sine medico medicinam dat* (*de divin.* ii. 123), the phrase Minerva Medica (C. vi.) and inscriptions such as C. xi. 1297 (Dessau 3134).

[6] It may be convenient to add that Samuel Lysons was the first who recognized Sul or Sulis as the true form. Previous writers corrupted it into Sublimis or Sulinis or the like.

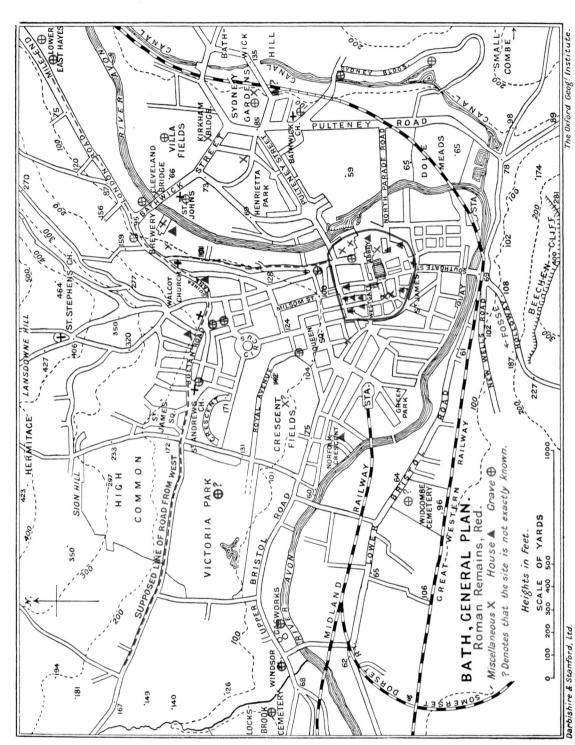

BATH, GENERAL PLAN.
Roman Remains, Red.
Miscellaneous X House ▲ Grave ⊕
? Denotes that the site is not exactly known.

Heights in Feet.

SCALE OF YARDS

0   100 200 300 400 500   1000

Fig. 7.

Darbishire & Stanford, Ltd.

The Oxford Geog.ˡ Institute.

ROMANO-BRITISH SOMERSET

He gives no name, but his words suit no other site in Britain and have been taken to denote Bath ever since the twelfth century.[1]

> Circuitus Brittaniae quadragies octies septuaginta quinque milia sunt. In quo spatio magna et multa flumina, fontes calidi opiparo exculti apparatu ad usus mortalium : quibus fontibus praesul est Minervae numen ; in cuius aede perpetui ignes nunquam canescunt in favillas, sed ubi ignis tabuit, vertit in globos saxeos (ed. Mommsen, 1895, p. 102).[2]

That is, in rough English :—

> In Britain are hot springs furnished luxuriously for human use : over these springs Minerva presides, and in her temple the perpetual fire never whitens into ash, but as the flame fades, turns into rocky balls.

Whence Solinus obtained these details is not known. He may have borrowed them with similar items from a lost second-century writer, but the point is not easy to settle. The details themselves seem to be correct enough. The luxurious equipment of the baths and the temple of Minerva will meet us below : the rocky balls are perhaps, as several writers have conjectured, cinders of the Somersetshire coal which crops out on the surface very close to Bath.

How early the hot springs drew men to the spot we have no means of ascertaining. Medieval writers assigned their discovery to a British prince Bladud, eight centuries before the Christian era. That is of course a pleasant romance. Yet it embodies the natural idea that the healing waters must have become known very early. The existence of the native deity, Sul or Sulis, further suggests that they were known before the coming of the Romans. Positive evidence however is wanting. The irregular outline of the area generally assigned to the Romano-British town has been cited by Sir R. C. Hoare, and by others following him, as a sign of Celtic origin ; while the paucity of Celtic objects recorded as found in Bath has struck other observers as a disproof of Celtic origin. But no force really attaches to either argument. The outline assigned to Aquae Sulis is much like the outline of many Roman towns in Italy and the provinces, and no reason exists for calling this outline Celtic or native. On the other hand, pre-Roman objects seem to occur rarely on sites which were seriously occupied during the Romano-British period, and yet some of these sites, such as Silchester, can hardly be conceived as having had no Celtic existence before the Roman Conquest.[3]

---

[1] *Geoffrey of Monmouth*, ii. 10 (in old editions, i. 13). Whence Geoffrey got the passage of Solinus, I do not know. It was well known : for instance, it is cited by Bede—though Geoffrey did not get it thence, nor did Bede connect it with Bath. But Geoffrey could easily have supplied the reference to Bath, for the baths of Bath were well known to him, and are often mentioned by writers more or less contemporary with him. See, for example, *Henry of Huntingdon*, i. 6 ; *Gesta Stephani*, pp. 37, 48 (Rolls Ser.) ; *Alex. Neckam*, pp. 401, 457 (Rolls Ser.).

[2] Hübner and others have proposed to read *praeest Sulis Minervae*. The proposal is not supported by MS. evidence nor is the change necessary. Still, it is an odd coincidence.

[3] One piece which may belong to pre-Roman Bath is a bronze jug which I exhibited to the Society of Antiquaries in 1905 (*Proc.* xx. 265, with plate). This must, however, be far anterior to the period immediately preceding the Roman occupation. Moreover, it may perhaps be, not a genuine relic of ancient Bath, but a modern collector's curiosity which got lost and re-found again. A British or Gaulish coin is said to have been found in Bath in 1827 with, or close to, a Roman burial.

Less doubt, fortunately, surrounds the Roman occupation. The evidence of coins, detailed below in section 10, suggests that the spot was inhabited at the very beginning of the Romano-British period, perhaps in the reign of Claudius, almost certainly in the reign of Nero (A.D. 54–68). Inscriptions, though not quite so early in date, tell much the same tale. One tombstone (No. 27) might well have been erected under Claudius or Nero ; another (No. 25) may be confidently referred to the years A.D. 71–85 ; two others (Nos. 28, 29) bear marks of the first century, and a fragment of a different kind (No. 10) seems to belong to A.D. 76. A piece of sculpture too, a large female head (fig. 52), is shown by the peculiar fashion of the hair to date from the last quarter of the first century. The general history of the Conquest points the same way. We should expect, *a priori*, that a site in the south of Britain and on the road to south Wales, would be occupied early, and inscriptions tell us that the lead mines of Mendip, 15 miles south-west from Bath, were worked under Roman control in A.D. 49, within six years of the first landing of the Claudian army (p. 338). Two pieces of literary evidence may also be here adduced. The elder Pliny, writing about A.D. 77, and briefly describing Britain, says nothing of Bath or its waters, while Tacitus, in his biography of Agricola (ch. 21) implies that the entrance of Roman civilization on a large scale into Britain began about A.D. 80. We may fairly conclude that the Roman or Romano-British life of Aquae Sulis began under Claudius or Nero and reached a considerable development towards the end of the first century.

The direction of that development can be stated with some confidence. Discoveries of inscribed and sculptured stones, foundations and buildings, potsherds and coins, however imperfectly recorded, are numerous and coherent enough to justify some negative and some positive conclusions. The place, to begin with, was not a military post. If any garrison was planted there, either in the early years of the Conquest or afterwards, it has left no trace of itself. No remains of military buildings have ever been discovered,[1] and the nine tombstones and altars of soldiers, which will be described below, indicate invalids visiting the waters rather than troops guarding them.[2] Nor was it a great municipality. We find in it neither any hint of town council or town officials, nor structural remains suggestive of forum or basilica such as occur at Silchester or Wroxeter or Cirencester.[3] Indeed the area occupied by buildings—at the

[1] The Praetorium alleged by Wood, the forts in Walcot alleged by Phelps and others, and the rectangular camp assumed by W. Esdaile (*Som. Proc.* xxxi. [1] 15) are absolute fictions. For the supposed third-century fort on Combe Down see Villa, No. 19.

[2] This is shown by the following facts. First, the soldiers named on the inscriptions belong to no one particular *corps* but to all the legions of the province. Secondly, the stones belong to very different dates—some to the first century and some to the second or third. These are features which do not occur at normal military posts. Moreover, the legion which is most likely to have been at Aquae Sulis, the Second Augusta, is mentioned only once and then on a late altar (No. 13). Nor indeed is a legionary garrison at the site like that of Bath at all probable. An auxiliary garrison would have been more probable, but we have only one auxiliary among the Bath soldiers (No. 29), and one swallow does not make a summer.

[3] The notion of Richard of Cirencester (that is, Bertram of Copenhagen) that Bath was one of nine *Coloniæ* in Britain, is a mere fiction.

most 23 acres—seems wholly inadequate to active and elaborate city life. If we examine the characteristics of the recorded remains, a different picture emerges (fig. 7). It is the picture of a small place, girt probably by a wall and ditch, and scantily provided with suburbs. Inside the walls, the chief feature is a suite of baths, lying south of the present Pump Room and Abbey Churchyard and stretching—so far as we know at present—100 yards from east to west and 60 yards from north to south. Near the west end was a temple of the presiding deity, Sul or Sulis, and perhaps other structures, and further west again more hot springs where the Cross Bath now stands. The remains of these buildings are abundant and striking ; they testify to substantial and splendid edifices and confirm the praise of Solinus. But they stand alone. They are the only large Roman edifices which we know in fact to have existed in Aquae Sulis. The rest of the area has yielded only walls and floors of dwelling houses, and these do not exceed in amount the accommodation which would be required by bathing visitors, by the officials of the baths and temple, and by some residents who might be attracted by the waters or the sunny sheltered valley. That there were such residents is suggested by one of the inscriptions, which seems to mention some sort of *collegium*, some club or guild, though it had apparently a rather intermittent life (No. 2). Aquae Sulis, in short, was primarily a watering-place and nothing more. It was a small example of the type to which Harrogate or Wiesbaden or Homburg belong ; we might, indeed, compare it with modern Bath itself, were it not that the developments of the last two centuries have increased the resident population beyond all semblance to the Romano-British settlement. Places of this sort were no less common in the ancient than in the modern world, though it is difficult to quote accurate parallels, since accurate statistics are rarely available.[1]

Who built the baths and owned the springs, whether the government or private speculators or some local authority, civil or religious, we do not know. But of the visitors we learn something from the inscriptions. Many were legionaries quartered in Britain. Three such came from the Sixth Legion at York, three from the Twentieth at Chester, one from the Second Adiutrix, also probably at Chester, and one from the Second Augusta at Caerleon. We have also one auxiliary from an *ala* in south Wales, and remains which indicate that other military tombstones have been lost. Other visitors are Romano-British civilians, such as a town-councillor (*decurio*) from the *colonia* at Glevum (Gloucester) and a stone-cutter or sculptor from Cirencester. Others again came from northern Gaul, from districts now represented by Trier, Metz

---

Scarth compares the baths of Sanxay at Herbord, some 20 miles west of Poitiers in France. But these are rather different. The remains there consist of a large temple and two shrines, a theatre, two suites of baths and some dwelling houses, one of which recalls the ' inn ' at Silchester. But the waters are not medicinal ; the baths differ from those of Bath in plan ; and the attraction to the place seems to have been the temple. That is, the baths were not the cause but the result of visitors, and Sanxay and Bath have only thus much in common, that in both the town-element is wholly subsidiary to something else. See Camille de la Croix, *mémoire sur les découvertes d'Herbord, dites de Sanxay* (Niort, 1883).

and Chartres. That these came to benefit by the waters is, of course, an assumption ; but it is an assumption which it would, in general, be unreasonable not to make, and it need not prevent our wondering whether in some cases the visitors came on other errands. For instance two stone-masons (Nos. 17, 21) may have been employed in building the baths or may have sought the excellent Bath stone.

Some of the visitors can be dated. A few of the soldiers certainly or probably came in the first century (Nos. 25, 27 foll.). Others, like the soldiers of the Sixth Legion and the Second Augusta and the decurion of Glevum, came in the second or later centuries. But, in general, we possess no chronological basis for a history of Romano-British Bath. We meet here the same paucity of datable evidence, or, it may be, the same absence of serious change, which we meet on most sites of Britain and indeed of the whole Roman empire. The place developed early. Baths and temple were doubtless erected in the first century, and altered and extended later.[1] Visitors were frequent in the later part of the first and in the second century and probably also later. One inscription may possibly refer to a growth of Christianity in the fourth century (No. 22). Coins suggest that the site was inhabited at least till A.D. 400. Into further detail our evidence does not permit us to go. We cannot, for instance, in the present condition of our knowledge, attempt to date the architectural fragments which have survived from baths or temple or other structures.

We know more, curiously enough, about the post-Roman period. Definite evidence exists to prove a great gap between Romano-British Aquae Sulis and English Bath. Possibly 'Aquae' survived in the old English name of the town, Acemannesceaster[2]; possibly 'Sulis' survives still in the name of Little Solsbury, the hill above Batheaston, though neither derivation appears to be at all certain. But the inhabitation of the site ceased. It was either abandoned, like Silchester, at the approach of the invading English, or it was overthrown by them. If we may accept the evidence of an English poem datable to the eighth century, we shall assign it the latter fate.[3] The town—says the unknown writer—was after stout resistance stormed, its buildings cast down, its inhabitants slain : 'death destroyed all.' In any case the English did not occupy it at once. Geological evidence proves that it lay waste for long years after the end of its Romano-British life.[4] In particular, the baths disappeared. Constructed below the natural surface in order to

[1] The pig of lead with Hadrian's name (No. 47 below) was perhaps brought to Bath in connexion with the leading of the large basins.

[2] So Freeman and Earle. Aquae, as I learn from Prof. Napier, might well become *Ake*—or *Ace*—since a medial *kw* was avoided in old English. But no satisfactory account has ever been given of the syllable *man* and some competent philologists prefer the medieval view that Akeman is a personal name. Recent controversies on the name (as in the *Athenæum*, August, 1890) have not been edifying.

[3] See 'The Ruin' preserved in the Exeter MS. and printed by Thorpe, *Codex Exoniensis*, p. 476, Earle, *Bath Field Club*, ii. 266 ; and most lately by Grein and Wülcker, *Bibliothek der angelsächsischen Poesie*, i. (1881), 296.

[4] C. Moore, *Bath Field Club*, ii. 42, iv. 155, confirmed by subsequent excavations. A coot's or teal's egg was found in August, 1882, among decayed vegetation on the edge of the large bath, and is preserved at the Pump Room.

enjoy a fuller inflow, they rapidly silted up. Their walls and roofs fell in. The hot springs, still forcing their way upwards, formed new pools at a higher level ; brushwood and water plants overgrew the débris, and marsh-fowl came to nest in the wilderness. The dates and details of the change are, of course, unknown. But the English conquered the vicinity of Bath about 577 and the desolation must have commenced then, if it had not begun before. At an uncertain date in the seventh or eighth century a small monastery was planted there, and perhaps the needs of its builders hastened the overthrow of the Roman buildings.[1] In the eighth century the ruins were visible but utterly desolate ; they have been described for us in phrases of singular beauty in the English poem mentioned above. Later, perhaps in the tenth century, the eastern part at least of the baths was hidden so deep in earth that men were buried above them.[2] Whatever masonry still rose above the surface was doubtless pillaged by Saxon and Norman builders, and though William of Malmesbury in the twelfth century was able to recognize the site as Roman, yet his language is vague, and in his day the visible ruins seem to have been few.[3] Aquae Sulis, in short, passed into oblivion. Even its baths were forgotten. No part of them remained in medieval use ; no part was employed as a definite foundation for a later edifice ; no medieval work has ever been detected in them.[4] The medieval Abbey House and the baths which grew into the King's and Queen's and Cross Baths do not correspond with Roman structures, and were apparently erected without any knowledge of them.[5] When Leland visited Bath about 1533 and Camden about 1600, and Horsley a century later, the only visible remains were inscriptions and sculptures, in part at least sepulchral, which had been inserted into the city walls.[6] But, all the while, buried deep in soft silt and mud, there remained intact the floors and foundations and lower walls of the baths and some portions also of the temple. The

[1] The traditional date for the foundation of Bath monastery is 676, but the earliest certain reference to it is in 781 (*Cart. Saxonicum*, i. 335, No. 241) [W. H. Stevenson].

[2] In 1755 Lucas records the discovery of a Saxon cemetery under the Abbey House and above the eastern part of the Baths. One coffin lay nearly level with the floor of a hypocaust room ; another was set on the broken shaft of a pilaster. The cemetery was dated by coins of Ethelred and Edmund (Lucas, *Essay on Waters*, iii. 224 ; *Soc. of Antiquaries' Minutes*, vii. 213, 19 June, 1755). Obviously the Roman ruins were covered with earth when these burials were made, and, as Lucas observed, Roman and Saxon were alike forgotten when the Abbey House was constructed. See also the account by W. Oliver, dated 24 June, 1755, in Add. MS. 6181, fol. 73.

[3] Irvine (*Brit. Arch. Assoc. Journ.* xxix. 380) argued that the Temple of Sul was still standing in the twelfth century. But his reasons are unsatisfactory, and we have no hint of such a thing in contemporary writers, like William of Malmesbury, who would naturally mention it. William of Malmesbury, *Gesta Pontificum*, ii. 90, practically mentions nothing but a theory of Roman origin. It has been suggested that the bath buildings mentioned in the *Gesta Stephani* (A.D. 1141-8) may be Roman (*Brit. Arch. Assoc. Journ.* xlii. 237). But I see no reason whatever for this suggestion.

[4] Davis (*Excavation of the Roman Baths*, p. 14) ascribed a medieval date to a lead cistern and channel connecting the two large baths (p. 257). But, so far as I know, there is no reason for this, and the cistern and channel are Roman.

[5] See, for example, the facts cited by Scarth, *Archæological Journal*, xl. 265.

[6] Davis (*Excavation*, p. 4) states that the Roman baths found in 1755 (p. 255) were partly open in Leland's time. But as a Saxon cemetery lay over them, this is clearly impossible. The old *Red Book of Bath*, under date 7 Dec. 1582, notes a medieval tombstone as existing *a dextra in ostio ruinosi templi quondam Minervae dedicati* (Burton, *Itin. Ant.* p. 262). But no one else mentions such a ruin, and it seems merely a bit of sixteenth-century antiquarianism.

re-discovery of these remains began in the eighteenth and continued through the nineteenth century. It is not yet complete.

2. WALLS, GATES, STREETS

In the preceding section I have tried to summarize what is known of Roman Bath. I pass on to describe in detail the remains which form the evidence for my summary—the walls, gates and streets; the

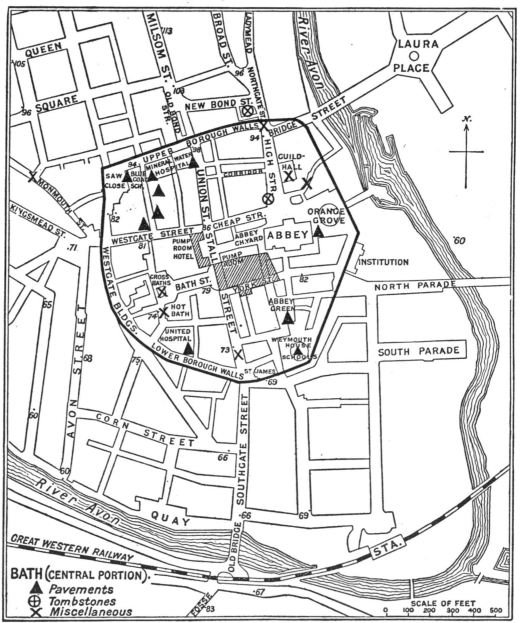

FIG. 8. ROMAN Bath.

buildings within the walls and in particular the temple, baths, and adjoining structures; the traces of dwelling houses; the cemeteries and other remains outside the walls; the inscriptions, architectural fragments, coins and other noteworthy objects. And first, the walls, gates and streets.

ROMANO-BRITISH SOMERSET

It has been generally assumed that Aquae Sulis was walled, and that the medieval walls, gates, and ditch reproduce roughly the lines of the Roman walls, gates and ditch—so that the Romano-British area would be a rough pentagon of about $22\frac{1}{2}$ acres and its circumference about 1,250 yards. The assumption is natural and may well be right. But it is proper to add that the direct evidence in favour of it is scanty. Along the north side, now called the Upper Borough Walls, the proofs seem to be adequate. Governor Pownall relates that in January 1795 the foundations of the Roman wall, 15 feet thick, were discovered underlying and wholly distinct from the medieval wall, at a point opposite the Mineral Water Hospital, where is now the end of Old Bond Street. He adds that the Roman north wall had previously been found at a point further west, near the Sawclose and the north-west corner of the medieval fortifications. Combining what he saw himself and what he was told, he judged the Roman wall to have consisted internally of rubble and hard cement, and to have been faced on each side with large blocks of a hard grit-stone. Some of these blocks, at a corner of the wall, weighed two tons each. There were no bonding-courses, but the unequal thickness of the facing-stones running into the interior acted as cramps. Similar finds were made soon after near the Northgate and a little west of it. In May 1803 the ancient wall was found here, composed of immense pieces of ashlar, and amongst them fragments of Roman columns, taken by the finders to be the relics of some noble edifice, demolished when the Roman wall was erected.[1] We may conclude, then, that the Roman north wall coincides in line with the medieval north wall, and that it was built, in a usual Roman fashion, with dressed stone on the faces and rubble and mortar inside. It seems also to have contained material taken from earlier Roman buildings, like many Roman town-walls, especially those erected in the third and fourth centuries. A notable feature is the large size assigned to the facing-stones. Possibly our accounts refer solely to blocks used at gates and towers, which are naturally more solid than the average ; possibly the facing of the north wall at Bath resembled that of the north wall of Roman Chester. In the latter case we shall assume the same cause at each place— the presence of sound and easily worked stone in great abundance.

No traces of Roman walls have been found elsewhere than along the medieval north wall. But what is true of one part of the medieval walls may well be true of all ; and since one part coincides with the Roman line, it is not improbable that the other parts may, in general, do the same. The distribution of Roman remains in Bath justifies this view. Within the compass of the medieval walls they abound ; where it ends, they end also, and though much has been found outside, it is

---

[1] For the finds of 1795 and earlier see Pownall, p. 27 ; for those of May 1803, see *Bath Herald*, 7 May 1803, *Gentleman's Magazine*, 1804 (ii.), 1006 and pp. 278-9 below. Duffield's *Bath Guide* (circa 1811), p. 35, mentions the discovery, 'about' 1806, at much the same spot, of fragments of a 'temple of Apollo, cornices, capitals and an inscribed fragment' (No. 40). These probably belong to the finds of 1803 : see also inscription No. 32 and fig. 53, p. 286. Governor Thomas Pownall, for whom see the *Dictionary of National Biography*, was a competent archaeologist.

obviously not continuous with the internal remains, and consists, indeed, for the most part of sepulchral relics. Serious doubt arises only in reference to the east wall. The north-east corner of the medieval town has yielded few Roman remains, and amongst those few are a tombstone dug up in High Street (No. 29) and some miscellaneous remains, generally called sepulchral (p. 263), dug up in Boatstall Lane behind the Police Station. The tombstone, which is an early one, might perhaps be older than the construction of the walls or might have been brought in from outside to be used as building material, and the record of the Boatstall Lane finds is imperfect. We must therefore leave unsettled the question whether the Roman and the medieval east walls coincided in position.

It would be fruitless to inquire the date of these Roman walls. In the western provinces of the empire, town walls seem to have been principally erected after A.D. 250, when the barbarian invasions grew formidable ; and if (as was thought in 1803) the Roman wall of Bath contained fragments from older Roman structures, we should naturally assign to it a comparatively late origin. Till further evidence emerges, it will be best to remain content with this probability.

For the position of the gates and streets we have even less evidence. No remains of the Roman gates have survived, and the descriptions which we possess of the medieval gates—now long demolished—do not suggest that Roman work survived in them, as it probably did in the medieval Eastgate of Chester, and as it still survives in the Newport at Lincoln. Nor can we derive a clue from the directions of the Roman roads which run to Bath, for they are not known with exactitude in the immediate vicinity of the town. We cannot trace the Fossway any nearer than Walcot church on the north or than Holloway on the south. We must acquiesce in a probability. If the medieval and Roman walls coincide, the gates in them may coincide also. When we pass on to the streets even probabilities fail us. No certain piece of Roman street has been found in Bath—neither pavement nor building frontage. No modern street has any real claim to represent a Roman street. The two which have been oftenest cited as Roman—Union Street and Stall Street—are certainly post-Roman, for Roman baths underlie Stall Street, and Union Street is of very recent origin.[1] Similarly, Bridewell Lane is proved to be post-Roman by the position of the pavement found under the front wall of the old " Sedan Chair " Inn, during the extension of the Mineral Water Hospital in 1884.[2] We must refrain at present from attempts to map the streets of Aquae Sulis. We may try rather to form some picture of the place from the remains of its buildings.

[1] Mr. J. T. Irvine claimed to have found a short piece of road (rough stones covered with fine gravel) under the Pump Room Hotel (*Bath Chronicle*, 6 Feb. 1868 : see fig. 9, p. 233) ; but, if a road at all, it stopped very shortly, and its age is unknown. The piece of road alleged by Mr. Scarth (*Brit. Arch. Assoc. Journ.* xxxv. 190) is not a road but pavement in the Baths. Mr. Scarth's views as to the gates and streets (*Brit. Arch. Assoc. Journ.* xiii. 259 = *Aquae*, p. 108) have been demolished by Mr. E. Green (*Archæological Journal*, xlviii. 178 ; *Bath Field Club*, vii. 116), but Mr. Green has not, I fear, established his own theory of a Roman street coinciding with Vicarage or Parsonage Lane. Major Davis (*Bathes of Bathe's Ayde*, p. 71) held a similar view, but it lacks real evidence.

[2] *Bath Field Club*, vi. 37. See p. 261, note 3.

3. INTERNAL BUILDINGS

Many buildings have been assigned to Aquae Sulis by previous writers—*praetorium, fabrica armorum, forum, basilica*, several temples, baths. Most of these are of course imaginary ; their existence is neither provable nor probable. The praetorium which the architect Wood in the eighteenth century thought to detect under the Mineral Water Hospital, and which the Ordnance Survey has since immortalized, is a mere fiction. When Wood suggested it he obviously had no idea of what a *praetorium* was, and the remains on which he based his idea bear no resemblance to a *praetorium*, but rather to a bath or a dwelling-house. The *fabrica armorum* which the same speculative writer placed in Spurriers' Lane (now Bridewell Lane) is a similar fiction. An inscription (No. 26) mentions a factory of arms as existing somewhere. Wood jumped to the conclusion that this was in Bath, and thought the street of the medieval spur-makers an excellent site for it ; and a more recent writer has called Bath 'the great Woolwich Arsenal of the Romans.' But the *fabrica armorum* was not in Bath, and the whole theory is baseless.[1] The forum and basilica are, in theory, more probable. But no inscriptions mention municipal life at Bath, and no structural remains indicative of forum or basilica have yet been found, either in the Abbey Churchyard, where the Forum is usually placed, or near the Guildhall, where Mr. E. Green puts it, or indeed anywhere in Bath. In this lack of evidence it is perhaps rash to assume *a priori* that Forum and Basilica were necessary in a watering-place hardly 23 acres in area. With the temples and the baths we reach firmer ground. We must indeed reject as baseless the notion of temples to Apollo and to Diana, and while we admit a temple to Minerva we shall find no evidence that it stood on the site either of the abbey or of the now vanished church of St. Mary Stall.[2] But when all these fictions have been rejected, there remains a goodly array of real edifices well worthy of attention. We may group them in three parts. First, the fragments of the temple of Sul, and other fragments found with them, which may or may not belong to the temple, but which cannot be discussed apart from it ; secondly, the baths ; thirdly, too often neglected, the remains which seem to belong to dwelling-houses.

4. THE TEMPLE OF SUL AND OTHER REMAINS FOUND IN 1790 AND 1867

There was certainly at Aquae Sulis a shrine or temple dedicated to Sul Minerva. The position of the goddess as presiding deity of the waters would require us to assume the existence of such a temple, even

---

[1] Wood, *Hist. of Bath*, pp. 170, 420 ; *Brit. Arch. Assoc. Journ.* xxix. 128. See p. 275.
[2] The reference to a temple of Minerva at this church, in the *Red Book of Bath* (A.D. 1582), is more probably due to antiquarian theory than to fact. Otherwise we should have heard of it from Leland or Camden. See p. 225 *note*.

if we possessed no direct evidence to the fact, and fortunately we are not reduced to assuming. Solinus tells us that the temple existed, and a tombstone, to be described below (No. 30), names a priest of the goddess. It is therefore quite justifiable to connect with this temple some remarkable remains. They seem to belong to a temple ; they are connected with Sul Minerva, and they occupy a spot where the temple may well have stood, adjoining the north-western corner of the baths and close to the springs whence the hot waters issued. These remains were found principally in the last decade of the eighteenth century ; a few additions were made in and after 1867. They were doubtless imperfect when found ; they have certainly been imperfectly recorded, and their interpretation is complicated by the fact that along with them were found other remains which may possibly have belonged to other temples or to structures of a different kind.

The first discoveries were made in September 1790. About that time extensive improvements were being effected by the Town Council in the centre of Bath, and among other changes the Pump Room was rebuilt and enlarged by the addition of what is now its western portion, the frontage to Stall Street. The remains with which we have to deal were found during the excavations required for this addition. No proper record was kept of the discoveries. The city architect, Baldwin, promised plans and details. But he speedily quarrelled with his town council ; he probably found the task of description beyond his archaeological powers ; certainly he published nothing. To some extent the gap was filled by two competent observers who chanced to visit the scene, Governor Pownall and Sir Henry Englefield ; some other contemporary notices have survived, and the architectural remains were carefully studied within a few years of their discovery by Carter and by Lysons. We remain however ignorant of many important details.[1]

The remains were found partly *in situ*, partly lying loose in the soil. The former comprised : (1) part of a wall with an attached pilaster ; (2) a pavement of large square freestone slabs, 12 feet below the surface— also described as ' a paved way with a channel to carry off the water ' ; and (3) some steps. Of the pavement only the east end seems to have been uncovered ; the rest of it was thought to extend under Stall Street westwards, but too little was laid open to show the kind of building to which it may have belonged. The steps were apparently at its east end, and are said by Englefield to have fronted east ; that is, they must have provided a descent from the pavement to a deeper level. Unfortunately

---

[1] Thos. Pownall, *Description of the Antiquities dug up in Bath in* 1790 (Bath, 1793) ; H. Englefield, *Archæologia*, x. 325 ; *Gentleman's Magazine*, 1791 (i.), 103 ; Cruttwell's and Duffield's *Bath Guides* ; Gough's *Add. to Camden*, i. 117 ; John Carter, *Ancient Architecture*, i. 8 (London, 1795) ; S. Lysons, *Reliquiæ Romano Britannicæ*, i. (London, 1802). Englefield's illustrations are very careless, Carter's rough but vigorous, those of Lysons admirably accurate and superbly reproduced. The objects found were the property of the town, and were placed by the civic authorities, first in a museum in Bath Street and afterwards in the Institution ; they are now mostly in the new Baths Museum and some few in the Institution. Some have disappeared in the lapse of time. I have noticed the chief detail, the head, in the *Revue Archéologique*, xli. 315, and in a paper read to the Society of Antiquaries on 30 April 1903.

none of these remains were measured nor were their positions planned, and it would be idle to make conjectures about them.[1]

Around these remains *in situ* the soil was full of architectural fragments heaped confusedly together, and most probably lying just where they had fallen when the building to which they originally belonged was ruined by man or time. Fifty or sixty pieces are said to have been taken out—half the carved tympanum of a temple (fig. 9); parts of rich cornice suitable to the tympanum (figs. 12, 13); a fine Corinthian capital, hollowed out behind (fig. 12); parts of a hollowed half column and base, which may belong to the capital; parts of a smaller tympanum (fig. 20); numerous pieces of attached pilasters and of bas-reliefs, representing the Four Seasons, which were connected with them (fig. 14); a bas-relief of a man in civilian dress, standing in a niche, two-thirds life size; a large corner-stone with figures in relief of Hercules and another deity (fig. 32); fragments of other less intelligible reliefs; two altars dedicated to Sul; parts of a long inscription recording (as it seems) the repair and repainting of a temple of Sul; several pieces of plainly moulded cornices and bases, and the like. Nor was the site then exhausted. In 1895 a sculptured stone was extracted from beneath the Pump Room, which fitted on to a piece found a hundred years earlier (fig. 16). More may well remain still undiscovered. Much too has doubtless perished unrecorded.

As soon as these architectural remains were found in 1790 it was perceived that they included part of one considerable temple, and possibly also of one or two smaller ones; and conjectural restorations were soon proposed by Pownall, Englefield and Lysons. The two former did not advance beyond combining the carved tympanum, cornice and Corinthian capital and column into the façade of a tetrastyle Corinthian temple. Lysons offered a complete restoration of this temple, and added to it the restoration of another smaller temple. His work is both able and attractive, and in respect to the larger temple is in many respects successful. His restoration of the supposed smaller temple is less probable, and in some important details of both buildings he is almost certainly wrong. He also treats the 'repairs' inscription unsatisfactorily, breaking it into two pieces in such a way that one part becomes untranslatable.

Further discoveries, which may be connected with those of 1790, were made in 1867–9, beneath and on the west side of Stall Street, opposite and north of the Pump Room. The occasion was the demolition of the White Hart Hotel and other houses, and the erection on their site of the Pump Room Hotel. Unfortunately these discoveries were no better recorded than those of 1790. The late Mr. J. T. Irvine,

---

[1] An extract, from (I believe) a local newspaper, in the *Soc. of Antiquaries' Minutes* (xxiii. 416), say that ' the pavement had three steps to the east downwards towards the King's Bath and four steps upwards to the west towards Stall Street.' (The same statement, distorted into unintelligibility, is given in Duffield's *Bath Guide* and Gough's *Add. to Camden.*) Here the pavement seems to be one at the bottom and not at the top of the steps mentioned in the text. It should be added that the water level here is hardly 15 feet below the surface.

then employed in Bath, collected numerous details ; but he left no proper plans, and his accounts of what he saw are both difficult to follow and intertwined with unverifiable and improbable theories and assumptions. According to him the chief discoveries were three. Under the north wing of the hotel was 'a bed of stone-dust and chippings,' which he took, quite arbitrarily, to be the stoneyard of Norman masons building St. Mary Stall. There was also here a small bit of 'Roman street.' Under the centre of the hotel were walls, from 2 to 3 feet thick, some running north and south, some east and west, much broken and interrupted, which he took to indicate low lean-to buildings round an open court, though, as far as recorded, they do not look like that (fig. 9). Under and east of the south wing was a ' platform ' of solid masonry, its top $8\frac{1}{2}$ feet below street level, with holes or tanks sunk into it, one of them 4 feet deep. Mr. Irvine identified the ' platform ' with the pavement found in 1790—though the two are at different levels—and explained the whole as the platform of a temple facing east with steps in front of it ; the holes or tanks he thought to be cesspools sunk in medieval or modern times. All these views are purely conjectural, and it would be idle now to criticize them, though for our present purpose we may regret that we possess no accurate details of the position, size and character of the ' platform.' Besides these supposed remains *in situ* a few pieces were found lying loose in the soil—a bit of cornice very like the cornice of 1790, found in 1867 lying on the alleged ' platform '; a bit of a different and very striking cornice, found in 1869 under the Westgate Street frontage of the new hotel (fig. 22) ; many very large building stones and some small objects :—the handle of a glass vessel adorned with a face ; Samian and other potsherds ; window (?) glass ; a small terra-cotta head of Egyptian type, and the like.[1]

A few further discoveries were made in 1895, as has been said, when Major Davis examined a part of the ground below the old Pump-room. An inscribed fragment was then found which fits on to a piece discovered in 1790 (fig. 16), and also some carved stones (p. 243). But no definite additions were made to our knowledge of the buildings.

No certain restoration of these remains has yet been offered and probably none is possible. Even the pleasing and scholarly designs of Lysons are open to grave objections in detail, and can only claim, at the most, to be partially correct. For the purpose of the present work it may be best to attempt no formal reconstruction, but to describe in due order the various architectural elements which can be traced in our remains. We shall find at the end that some probabilities emerge, and though we cannot restore the buildings, we shall gain a clearer idea of Aquae Sulis. We may group our remains under three heads : (1) those which seem to belong to the Temple of Sul, (2) those which form parts of

---

[1] Irvine, *Bath Chronicle*, 6 Feb. 1868, 8 April 1869, 28 April 1870 ; *Brit. Arch. Assoc. Journ.* xxix. 379 ; *Anastatic Drawing Society*, 1881, plate xxviii. ; 1882, plate xxxviii. Numerous rough plans and drawings, made or acquired by Mr. Irvine, are in the National Museum at Edinburgh, where I have been able to examine them with effective aid from Mr. J. H. Cunningham. The glass handle with a face on it resembles those figured by C. Roach Smith, *Roman London*, p. 121 ; a drawing is in Irvine's papers.

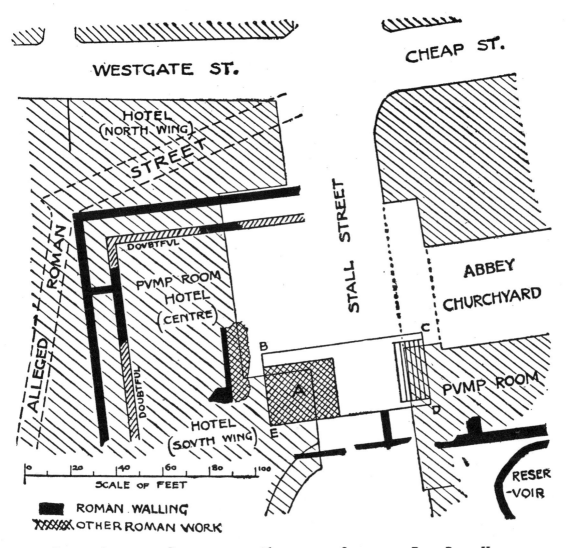

FIG. 9. STRUCTURAL REMAINS FOUND 1867-9 ON THE SITE OF THE PUMP ROOM HOTEL.

From plans by J. T. Irvine in the Edinburgh Museum (see p. 232).

A, Roman work taken by Irvine to be part of the Temple Platform.

B, C, D, E, Area of Temple Platform as conjectured by Irvine. It
will be obvious from the plan that A more probably belongs to the
remains immediately west of it, and the walls of the supposed
cloister must be connected with the same.

a Façade ornamented by figures of the Four Seasons, which may be connected either with the Temple or with the Baths, and (3) some detached pieces of considerable interest.

(1) The best preserved and most perfect of these architectural elements is a remarkable temple-pediment of which we possess many pieces and these singularly intact. When the temple was ruined by the hand of time or of man, these pieces must have fallen on to a soft and marshy surface, such as may well have existed round the baths in the period of their desolation. In consequence, we can reconstruct the pediment with some confidence and can thus recover for Roman Bath a rare and interesting feature. Hardly another site in the western provinces of the empire can show the remains of a sculptured pediment, and none perhaps can show so striking an example. At Bath six out of twelve slabs constituting the tympanum survive fresh and clean, and among these is the centre-piece. The tympanum, as we can reconstruct it, is not designed on strictly classical models : it combines details which follow good Roman precedent with unusual and indeed original features. In size it measured about 26 feet along its base and about 8 feet in height, and thus ended at the top in an angle which is less obtuse, and also less graceful, than ordinary Roman pediments.[1] Its decoration was elaborate, perhaps even excessive and somewhat awkwardly grouped (fig. 10). In the centre was a shield, upheld on either side by a winged figure like a Victory floating with her feet on a globe—a scheme to which Roman monuments supply abundant parallels. The ' Victories ' are only in small part preserved : of the left hand one the drapery and wings survive, of the right hand one the feet against the globe and the hands against the shield. Behind the ' Victories ' were presumably other figures, filling the lower angles of the tympanum, and we have one clue to these, an object on the right hand side which resembles the trunk of a human body terminating downwards in what looks like foliation—not impossibly an ornamented cuirass and apron. The space beneath the shield and ' Victories ' was filled, on the left, by a helmet with large cheek-pieces and a crest like an animal's head—an unusual Roman shape, though not devoid of approximate parallels. The corresponding figure on the right is lost, but there remains discernible a little owl, perched probably on some such object as a helmet or standard. A hand, holding a tiny stick (?), is visible between the body and the right wing of the owl, and it has been conjectured by Prof. Percy Gardner that, when the tympanum was perfect, the owl rested on a standard and the standard was ornamented by a hand holding a torch.

Above helmet and owl is the centre-piece of the tympanum (fig. 11), a circular shield decorated with two concentric wreaths of oak-leaves and acorns and, inside these, a round boss, 30 inches in diameter, carved in low relief. This carving is very remarkable. It shews a full face, framed in a broad border of hair, beard and moustache. The forehead

---

[1] Sharper angles appear, so far as I can learn, only on temple-shaped tombstones and in representations of temples on coins or elsewhere.

is sharply furrowed ; the eyebrows are emphasized and the eyeballs are indicated by deep round holes drilled in the middle of small circles in an unusual fashion, which recalls Roman metal rather than stone work. At the top and bottom the hair and beard are intertwined with snakes, while at the sides wings are inserted into the hair just above and behind the ears. The countenance, as a whole, has an intense and staring look, as of fear or pain, and was obviously intended to be regarded from a little distance. The details of the oak-wreaths, the balance of the hair and snakes, and the modelling of the singularly distinct features in 'Flach-relief,' are technically successful and have deservedly been praised. But the chief interest and importance of the work arises from its unconventional combination of attributes, which is not easy to explain, and its astonishing and almost barbaric vigour, which is probably without a parallel in the western Roman world.

The general design of the tympanum is plainly a group of arms and armour, such as occurs in varying forms on all kinds of Roman monuments, even on sarcophagi, and is constantly employed as mere decoration.[1] In the present case the design has been influenced by the cult of Minerva, the goddess identified with Sul as the patroness of the hot springs. The owl is the bird of Minerva and of no one else, and its appearance is, of itself, practically conclusive as to the artist's intention. The face on the shield, too, can be best interpreted as reproducing another attribute of Minerva, the face of the Gorgon Medusa, which frequently appears on her shield. The snakes and wings in its hair are peculiar to the Gorgon, and the strained and almost violent expression agrees well with that sensational type of Gorgon which Roman art affected. Moreover, the position of the face on a shield and a pediment is not inappropriate to the Gorgon. The Romans used the Gorgon's head as a common ornament for the centre of circular objects ; it is frequent on circular shields, whether of Minerva or of ordinary warriors, and, mounted on such a shield and upheld by allegorical figures, it forms the centrepiece of several temple-pediments represented in ancient art.[2] We can scarcely doubt that at Bath our artist intended to put a Gorgon's head on the shield of his pediment. Why, with that intention, he admitted a beard and moustaches and made his Gorgon male is less intelligible. Possibly he was following some original which had a bearded head instead of a Gorgon, and he thought to adapt this simply by adding the Gorgon's attributes. Possibly, through misunderstanding of some work of art, he added a beard to the normal Gorgon's face. The former

---

[1] Compare, for example, a Roman sarcophagus in the Ashmolean Museum at Oxford, often (though incorrectly) styled the Tomb of Germanicus (Michaelis, *Ancient Marbles in Great Britain*, p. 568). On the front of this two winged boys support a large round shield with a Gorgon's head on its centre, while on either side of them other winged boys play with a large helmet, a cuirass, lance and two greaves. Lysons may easily have known of this monument and borrowed from it the cupids which he introduces into his restoration of the Bath pediment. Compare also a tomb described by Benndorf, *Archäologisch-epigraphische Mittheilungen*, vi. 241, and W. Altmann, *Architectur und Ornamentik der antiken Sarcophage* (Berlin, 1902), p. 84 and illustration of tomb from the Via Salaria (fig. 30).

[2] Schreiber, *Hellenistische Reliefs*, xxxiv.-vii., xl. ; Clarac, plate 120 (Reinach's *Clarac de poche*, p. 20). The germ may perhaps be found at Olympia (Pausanias, v. 10, 4). On circular objects the hair is often arranged to form a border all round the head.

hypothesis may seem the simpler conjecture.[1] The latter has thus much in its favour, that in Hellenistic and Roman art, the Gorgon's head is occasionally corrupted into something not a pure Gorgon. For instance, among the dainty 'masks' used to decorate bronze and silver cups and *paterae*, we meet a type of Gorgon with attributes suggesting the sea, and some of these, though not bearded, are male in character.[2] Moreover in these 'masks' and in other Roman work—for instance, on marble cists and sarcophagi—the Gorgon's head is used promiscuously with, and indeed almost alternatively to, other heads, many of which are male and bearded. An artist who found the normal type of Gorgon already corrupted, as in the Sea-Medusa, might easily slip into a further corruption and combine the Gorgon's head from one 'mask' with the beard and moustache from another.[3]

Whatever its precise original, the head is among the most remarkable products of Roman provincial art in western Europe. Its marked individuality and astonishing vigour are hardly less extraordinary than its technical features. In the one respect, as in the other, it stands alone. The best sculptures found in the western provinces, in Gaul, Africa, Britain—the Venus of Arles or of Fréjus, the portraits of Martres Tolosanes, the tomb-reliefs of Neumagen, the sculpture-gallery of Cherchel and the rest—are in their various ways classical. This head is an exception. It has artistic merits. It is adapted from a classical original. But it is not itself classical. It reveals a spirit of wild freedom which is neither strictly Greek nor Roman, and students of the best Greek period would call it barbaric. Here for once we break through the conventionality of the Roman Empire, and trace a touch of genius. We cannot date the piece by its style or ornament, except in so far as the treatment of the eye-balls and the wreaths suggests the second or third century of our era. We do not know what else its artist wrought or whether he did one good work and no more. It will be only a guess if we ascribe to him the bold and unconventional fashion of some cornice fragments found with or near the tympanum (figs. 13, 22). At the end we leave this strange sculpture unexplained. But we shall not regret to have contemplated for a little the details of so virile and so unparalleled a work.

The rest of the temple of which this pediment formed part can

[1] In Wlgrim de Taillefer's *Antiquités de Vesone* (Périgueux, 1821), plate xx. (1), a shield is figured from a bas-relief, which has a bearded head in the centre.

[2] Brunn, *Griechische Götterideale*, pp. 37, 41 ; Schreiber, *Alexandrinische Toreutik*, pp. 345, 458 ; *Museo Borbonico*, v. plate 43. An example has been found as far north in Britain as Kirkcudbright : it is figured in the Anastatic Drawing Society's volume for 1879, plate xiv., and is now in Edinburgh Museum. It would be wrong to cite here the bearded Gorgons of early Greek art. The nearest parallel to the Bath head, and perhaps the only really close parallel, is supplied by a piece in the Grosvenor Museum at Chester, where a male bearded head with snakes appears on a small pediment. Unfortunately the piece is much damaged, and, if there were wings, they are no longer clear.

[3] That the head is a Gorgon has been affirmed by Lysons and others, but without any explanation of the beard. Various other interpretations have been offered—that it represents the Sun, or a watergod, or Sul—but none are satisfactory. Neither the Sun nor a watergod has a right to both wings and snakes, and the head of Sul would not have been put on a shield in this fashion. The symbolism suggested by Mr. Scharf in *Archæologia*, xxxvi. 187, is out of the question.

236

Fig. 11. Head of Gorgon from the Pediment of the Temple of Sul Minerva ($\frac{1}{7}$).

FIG. 12.   PART OF CORNICE (SEEN FROM BELOW: SCALE 1 : 5), CORINTHIAN CAPITAL, AND PART OF COLUMN,

FOUND IN 1790.

(From Photographs.)

only be recovered by conjecture. Some of the fragments found in 1790 have been usually and indeed reasonably considered to belong to it. These fragments are, first, a hollow [1] Corinthian half-capital, well designed and varying effectively from the general rule in that its foliation creeps on to the abacus (fig. 12) ; secondly, parts of a fine Corinthian half-column, 32 inches in diameter, also hollowed (and indeed so much so that the shell is barely 5 inches thick), fluted, and at top and bottom cabled ; thirdly, a hollow half-base, of less attractive workmanship, with a recess in front as for the end of a low balustrade ; and fourthly, some pieces of a striking cornice (fig. 13) richly adorned with fruit and flowers and noticeable for its small height, its very great projection and the absence of the usual modillions. These fragments are not unworthy of the pediment, and with their aid we can construct some conjecture of the temple. The capital and column show that it was Corinthian in style, like countless other Roman temples. The pedi-

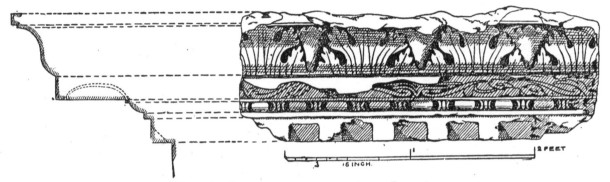

FIG. 13. CORNICE FOUND IN 1790 (FROM LYSONS).

ment (fig. 10) indicates a façade of four columns and a width of 26 feet. The diameter of the column indicates a height of, perhaps, 24 feet. The occurrence of a half-column and half-capital points to the use of engaged columns and a pseudo-peripteral ground-plan, such as occurs commonly in the Roman world. The groove in the base of the surviving column suggests that this stood at a corner of the *cella* next to the portico, and that a low balustrade ran out from it. But much of the temple has plainly perished or has not been discovered. We cannot tell its size, or its exact position, or whether it faced eastwards, with the steps found in 1790 in front of it, or westwards (as Gough incidentally alleges [2]), or otherwise. Here, as so often, we must wait for further evidence.

(2) A second structure, of which we possess remains, is a façade divided by engaged pilasters. These pilasters project 3 inches and are 18 inches wide ; each has five flutings, cabled at top and bottom ; the capitals are very plain, somewhat in Roman-Doric style (fig. 15). Between these

---

[1] The half-capital, half-column and base were, I supposed, hollowed to facilitate transport from the quarries : the block of stone on which the head is carved is also hollowed behind. It is curious (and not quite satisfactory) that the older writers do not mention in print that the pieces are hollow ; it is noted however by Lysons in a letter in the *Society of Antiquaries' Minutes*, xxviii. 353.

[2] Gough's *Add. to Camden*, i. 116. The assertion may be a mere error.

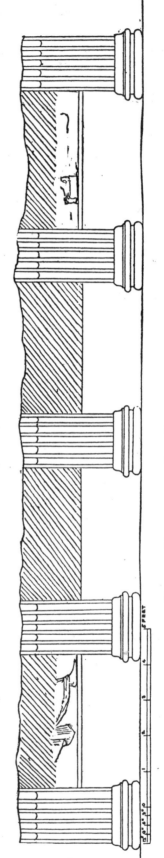

FIG. 14. FAÇADE OF THE FOUR SEASONS, PARTIALLY RESTORED.

238

pilasters, and also on the frieze above them, ran a long inscription or series of inscriptions, recording the repair and repainting of (probably) a temple of Sul Minerva (p. 267). Beneath the inscriptions, four of the

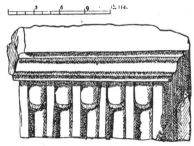
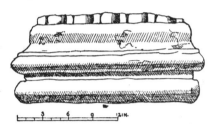

FIG. 15. CAPITAL AND BASE OF SQUARE PILASTER.

interpilasters, each 45 inches wide, contained panels carved in relief with figures of the Four Seasons, in a style that falls artistically far below the remains described in the preceding paragraphs. The seasons are

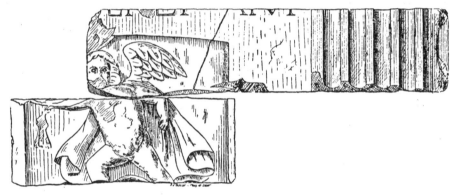

FIG. 16. ONE OF THE FOUR SEASONS.
The top piece was found in 1897–8, the bottom piece in 1790 ($\frac{1}{12}$). (From a drawing by Mr. A. J. Taylor.)

represented as winged boys, running, and holding appropriate emblems. Spring holds flowers, Summer corn, Autumn a bunch of grapes and Winter a billhook (figs. 16, 17). Spring and Summer run to the right,

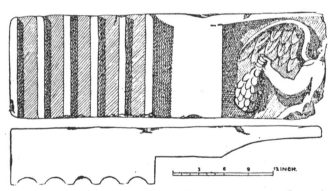

FIG. 17. ONE OF THE FOUR SEASONS ($\frac{1}{12}$) (FROM LYSONS).

Autumn and Winter to the left, and the pairs clearly matched each other. The billhook, suggestive of firewood rather than hedge-trimming, is an unusual feature [1]; in other respects the quartette is of a common type. It seems that the space beneath the Four Seasons was filled with other larger panels, with reliefs, but these are now almost wholly lost. One, or two, other interpilasters, 35 inches wide, contained a shell canopy with carving below and seemingly also above (fig. 18). Unfortunately we

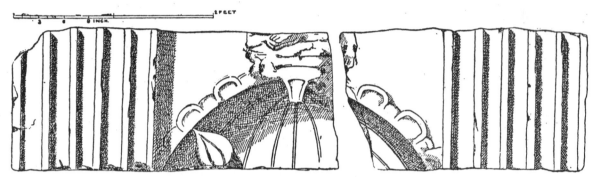

FIG. 18. TWO PIECES OF SHELL CANOPY (FROM LYSONS).

cannot venture into further detail. We do not know whether there were more than five (or six) interpilaster spaces ; the inscription, too, is very imperfect, and one piece of it, unless it was on the frieze, requires an interpilaster of 5 feet (No. 2).

However, we plainly have here a pilastered, sculptured and inscribed façade, which, as the inscription shows, was closely connected with the temple of Sul and later than it in date. Possibly it formed a decorated enclosure-wall or flanking façade. Possibly it was the north exterior wall of the Baths. A complete restoration is, however, impossible on our existing evidence. In my illustration (fig. 14), I have therefore ventured only to insert the Four Seasons, which seem certain. The reader must remember that the structure also included the shell canopies, and may have further included a door or doors, to which no definite place can be given. [2] But I may cite a proof that such grouping of temple and façade is quite natural. A well-known relief, now in the Palazzo dei Conservatori, shews the Emperor Marcus making a thankoffering in front of the Temple of Capitoline Jupiter at Rome. The Temple there appears as a tetrastyle building with Corinthian columns, and on the right of it is a façade of Roman Doric work with square pilasters, which is either an adjoining hall or part of the enclosure round the ' area ' of the Temple. [3]

(3) Other fragments indicate a pediment, measuring about 16 feet wide along the base of the tympanum and about $4\frac{1}{2}$ feet high (fig. 20).

[1] At Cirencester, Autumn has a bill-hook (Buckman and Newmarch, *Corinium*, Plate iv.).

[2] Lysons constructed from these remains, and from the pediment of the moon to be described in the next paragraph, a small temple front with four attached pilasters and no portico. But the absence of the portico is unusual, except in temple-shaped tombs, and the design admits only two of four Seasons and only a piece of the inscription, which, by itself, is unintelligible. Irvine (*Brit. Arch. Assoc. Journ.* xxix. 389) suggests a façade with five interpilaster spaces, each 45 inches wide. In the centre space he inserts a door, in each of the others a Season and a canopy ; the Season he puts in the centre of the space and the canopy below it on one side, thus by a lopsided arrangement equalizing the width required for the various elements. His scheme is ill-balanced, and his treatment of the inscription impossible.

[3] Jordan, *Topographie der Stadt Rom.* I. (2) 101.

In the centre, standing in relief in a round concave panel, was a bust of the moon goddess, with topknot in her hair, whip in her left hand and crescent beneath her face ; to the right of the panel are traces of a circular ornament, too fragmentary to be understood. The whole is artistically far inferior to the pediment described above (p. 234). It is comparable rather with the sculptures of the pilastered façade, and may perhaps have decorated some doorway or other part of it. Lysons and Carter record another fragment, now lost (fig. 19), which seems to have

been part of a similar panel contain-ing the rayed head of the sun, and it has been thought that perhaps two shrines of sun and moon flanked the temple of Sul. But the solar frag-ment is ill-shaped for a pediment, and it is not necessary that either piece should belong to a temple.

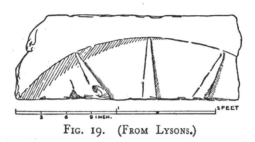

FIG. 19. (FROM LYSONS.)

(4) Three other pieces merit notice. They were found with or near the remains which we have described, but their relation to them is not clear. One, found in 1790, is a corner piece, 50 inches high on a pedestal 22 inches square, showing on each of its outer faces (the other two sides are plain) a figure in relief. On the left is a partly draped figure, not intelligible. On the right is Hercules, bearded, draped over the shoulder, holding in his right hand a large cup and in his left his club, which he rests on the ground. It is an example of Hercules Bibax, a common type in the Roman Empire, especially on bronze figurines (fig. 32).[1] A piece very similar in size and character now exists walled up in a buttress of Compton Dando church, 7 miles west of Bath : see the alphabetical index.

A second piece, also found about 1790, is a relief of a civilian about three-quarters life size, bearded, fully draped with cloak buckled on the left shoulder, standing erect in a plain niche, with dolphins sketched in the spandrils above it. The relief is broken across the middle, and knees and feet are altogether lost. In general appearance it is sepulchral, and may possibly be a tombstone brought into Bath at some period or other, Roman or later, as building material. Or it may represent some benefactor or prominent visitor to the baths.[2]

The third piece which claims notice was dug up in April 1869 from under the Westgate Street frontage of the north wing of the Pump Room Hotel. It is a fragment of cornice, 3 feet long and 18 inches high, of unusual character. It is decorated with foliation like a

---

[1] Now in the Institution. Warner's idea that these figures represent Maximian and Diocletian is most improbable ; nor is it easy to give the piece any special date. Pownall oddly took it to be ' Saxon or Gothic.'

[2] Pownall, p. 25, mentions the piece ; Carter (1794), and Warner (1797 and 1801) figure the upper half among the discoveries of 1790, and Lysons, plate ix. 1 (1802), figures the whole among the same. The lower part vaguely resembles a coarse sketch in the *Gentleman's Magazine* (1804, ii. 1006) of a piece found in Upper Borough Walls in 1803, and Scarth (*Aquae*, p. 81) states that this relief was found then and there. But as the whole of it was published before 1803 it cannot have been found in 1803. See further p. 227.

fleur de lys and a fantastic head (broken), which takes the place usually occupied by lions' heads along the top of classical cornices (fig. 22).[1] The fleur de lys occurs elsewhere at Bath and in other provincial work (fig. 34), but the free vigour of the head, and the size, depth and boldness of the carving are remarkable.   Possibly the fragment

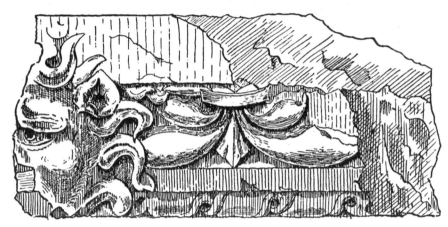

FIG. 22. ELEVATION AND SOFFIT OF CORNICE FOUND IN 1869.

comes from the same hand as the cornice and tympanum of the temple of Sul.   But it would be idle to speculate whether it belonged to that building.   We cannot, with our present knowledge, tell whether this and

---

[1] For accounts of the discovery see J. T. Irvine, *Bath Chronicle*, 8 April 1869; *Brit. Arch. Assoc. Journ.* xxix. 380; and *Anastatic Drawing Society*, 1881, plate xxviii.   The piece is now in the Bath Museum. I have to thank Mr. Alfred Taylor for excellent drawings of it, which I have reproduced (fig. 22).

FIG. 20. HEAD OF MOON GODDESS ($\frac{1}{1\frac{1}{2}}$).
(From a Photograph.)

FIG. 21. ONE OF THE FOUR SEASONS, SHEWING THE ROUGHNESS OF THE WORK ON THIS FAÇADE ($\frac{1}{5}$).
(From a Photograph.)

the two preceding pieces should be assigned to the temple and its precincts, or to the baths.

Some interest also attaches to the fragments (waists and thighs only) of two half-draped female figures which seem intended to form a pair, one moving to the right, the other to the left. They were found in 1895 to the north of the Baths under the Pump-room, along with the inscribed fragment No. 4 (fig. 16) and other less notable pieces, and are shewn in the upper part of fig. 37. The larger fragment measures 13 inches in height, 34 inches in length, and 22 in thickness.

5. THE BATHS

(i) History of the Excavation—(ii) General characteristics—(iii) Details—springs and reservoir; eastern wing; Great Bath; Circular Bath and western wing; sculptured and other remains.

(i) HISTORY OF THE EXCAVATION

Archaeologists have always agreed that Roman Bath must have had baths. Aquae Sulis would otherwise be a meaningless name. But the actual baths have only been revealed to us during the last century and a half, and in particular during the last twenty-five years. Throughout mediaeval and early modern times their position, extent and character remained wholly unknown. They were destroyed, or fell into decay, at the end of the Romano-British period. No part of them survived in use. No part is known to have been employed even as a foundation for a later bath. The earth and oblivion covered them. This oblivion lasted for twelve or thirteen centuries. When Camden and Guidott, Musgrave and Horsley, wrote of Aquae Sulis in the sixteenth, seventeenth and early eighteenth centuries, they wrote without a knowledge of its principal features.

The re-discovery of the forgotten structures began in the second quarter of the eighteenth century. The earliest recorded finds which can be connected with the baths were made in 1727, and probably belonged to the south-western part of them (p. 258). Unmistakable discoveries followed in the summer of 1755. At that time the mediaeval abbey (or priory) house, which adjoined the south-eastern corner of the abbey, was being demolished to make place for the Duke of Kingston's baths. Under the house were found, first, a tenth century cemetery, and beneath that, Roman masonry. This masonry proved to comprise a spacious swimming-basin with a small apsidal bath lying north of it, two large rooms fitted with hypocausts, some smaller rooms and a furnace—in short, nearly the whole eastern wing of the baths. A year or two later more was added. South of the swimming-basin, a second apsidal bath was uncovered, corresponding to the northern apsidal bath. West of the swimming-basin traces were detected of the east wall, pavement and steps of the Great Bath, and a conjectural but not wholly incorrect idea was gained of its size and character. These discoveries awoke wide interest among archaeologists. But they were not pursued, nor did chance add

243

greatly to them. A hundred and twenty years passed with little advance of knowledge. A part of the remains unearthed in 1790 may possibly belong to the baths building, as I have said above (p. 240). In or about 1800 and again in 1825 builders stumbled on structures which we can now recognize as connected with the Great Bath and the hypocausts south-west of it. In 1868–9 these hypocausts were again touched during the construction of an engine-room and chimney (now removed) over the north-west corner of the Great Bath. Other such isolated discoveries were made at other dates. But the real outline and extent of the baths remained as imperfectly known in 1878 as it had been a hundred years before. The plan given by Mr. Scarth in his *Aquae* in 1864 was in all important details the same as that which was published by Sutherland in 1760.

In 1878 a new epoch opened. The Corporation of Bath, already owners of the King's and Queen's Baths, now purchased the Kingston Baths and commenced engineering works for the better drainage of the site. In the course of these works notable Roman remains were discovered. Subscriptions were collected and definite excavations set on foot. Finally the enlargement of the Baths and Pump Room yielded further results. The whole inquiry was conducted by Major Davis, the city architect, and we have to thank his indomitable perseverance for the considerable area which was examined. His progress was naturally slow. The work was difficult and costly. The remains lay 15 or 20 feet below the present surface. Valuable modern houses had to be bought and removed. Interruptions from extraneous causes were unavoidable. But the work went forward. The general advance was from east to west. In 1878–80 the springs under the King's Bath and the Roman reservoir enclosing them were examined, and the culvert of the outfall drain on the north-east side of the baths was partly cleaned. In 1880–1 the north side and ends of the Great Bath were opened. In 1883–4 the hypocaust west of the Circular Bath and the passage north of it ; in 1885 the Circular Bath itself ; in 1885–6 the latrine and circular hypocaust ; and in 1887 the bath west of the Circular Bath were in succession explored. In 1893–5 the work was transferred to the north of the Great Bath, underneath the eastern extension of the Pump Room, and massive masonry of uncertain character was uncovered. Now too were revealed the 'dipping-place' (1894), the wooden duct (1895), and other details of the culvert already opened in 1878. At the same time a part of the ground below the old Pump Room was touched, and an inscribed fragment and other pieces extracted which belong to the same Roman structure as the remains found in 1790. Finally in 1896 a rectangular bath was excavated under Stall Street.

This long activity has provided the student of Roman Bath with abundant material. But that material is not always easy to interpret in detail. Difficulties arise from the nature of the remains. The Roman baths were used for three centuries or more. During that third of a millennium they must have undergone many changes. Rooms must have been added or removed, enlarged or divided up, passages made or unmade, drains dug or abandoned, and doors (as we chance to know) opened or closed. Further difficulties arise from the fortunes of the baths since their disuse. Saxon and Norman masons probably removed convenient stones. Later builders, erecting modern houses over the buried Roman ruins, sank their foundations down into the older work and produced, especially in the south-west corner, very serious confusion. Even in the better preserved parts important items like doors and drains often defy recognition. And, thirdly, difficulties arise from the inadequacy of our records. The accounts of the discoveries made in 1755–60 are creditable to their age. But they are not complete nor harmonious throughout. The accounts of the discoveries made in and after 1878 are equally open to criticism. The city architect, who conducted the work, had many merits. But he was not a trained archæologist, and he did not observe or register minutely his various discoveries. Thus he left to his successors too little information respecting the stratification of remains and the positions in which various objects were found. If I attempt to describe the baths in detail, and accompany the description with a plan on a larger scale than any yet issued, it is under obvious limitations.

AUTHORITIES

The discoveries of tiles made in 1727 in Stall Street are recorded in a sketch with brief text by Bernard Lens, a Belgian artist who worked much in Bath ; it is now in the Bodleian (Gough, Maps 28, p. 64), and a copy by Priscilla Combe is in the British Museum (King's Library, xxxvii. 26, O). See E. Green, *Bath Field Club*, vii. 118 (with reproduction of drawing), and *Arch. Journal*, xlviii. 177. A brief reference is in *Soc. of Ant. Minutes*, 12 March 1740.

The finds of 1755 are recorded minutely by Charles Lucas, *Essay on Waters* (London 1756), iii. 222–30. Lucas' plan was made for him, and he asserts that it is not quite exact, (p. 230) ; certainly plan and description do not tally. Nevertheless the plan was copied by Alex. Sutherland, *Attempts to Revive Ancient Medical Doctrine* (London, 1763), i. 16–22, who added some details found since Lucas wrote, and propounded the theory of the Great Bath, but otherwise followed Lucas closely. So too J. H. Spry, *Practical Treatise on the Bath Waters* (London, 1822), adding a few details found since 1763 ; hence Phelps (1836) and Scarth (1864). Other plans exist by William Hoare (Add. MS. 21577 B) and Jos. Stennett (A.D. 1755) (MS. 6211 fol. 132–137), which I have followed in some points in preference to Lucas. The Society of Antiquaries possesses a small plan by Hewitt in the Minutes, 10 May 1759 (viii. 159), and a plan and "perspective view" by G. Edwards (1760) showing the large bath and a part of the hypocausts. Other early accounts, too short to be very useful, are in the *Soc. of Ant. Minutes*, 26 June, 30 Oct. 1755, 10 May 1759, and 22 Jan. 1761, and *Gentleman's Mag.* 1755, p. 376. Stukeley's plan (Bodleian Library, Gough Maps 28), showing no southern apse, but a portico with six pillars, is obviously conjectural. Gough's illustration of the baths as found in 1755 (*Add. to Camden*, i. 114) is taken from a contemporary drawing, either that in B. M. King's Library, xxxvii. 26, C (undated and unsigned), or the original of that.

For the few finds made about 1800, when York Street was constructed, see Spry, pp. 16, 149. Some chance finds of 1825, made close to the corner of Stall Street and York Street are figured in Colonel Long's collection ; the houses then built were taken down in 1869 to make room for an engine and chimney, and this in turn was removed in 1886 ; see also Davis, *Excavations*, pp. 14 foll.

The discoveries of the last quarter of a century are described by the late Major Charles E. Davis, C.E., city architect, in his paper contributed to the *Transactions of the Bristol and Gloucestershire Archaeol. Soc.* viii. (1884), 89–113, reprinted with additions as *The Excavations of Roman Baths at Bath* (tenth ed. 1895), referred to below as *Excavations* ; in his pamphlet, *Guide to the Roman Baths* (42nd ed.1890), which contains much the same as the *Excavations* ; in a brief paper *Bath Field Club*, iv. (1881) 357, and also in his periodical reports to the city authorities (partly printed in the local newspapers). The Society of Antiquaries has a large plan by Mr. Mann. Other accounts are by Scarth, *Arch. Journal*, xl. (1883), 263, and *Bath Field Club*, vi. 75, mostly based on Davis; Irvine, *Brit. Arch. Assoc. Journ.* xxxviii. (1882), 92, etc. The record, as a whole, is inadequate.

My own plan of the baths is constructed from the plans in the British Museum and the Society of Antiquaries' Library, from new measurements taken for me by Mr. V. Saunders, and from much information supplied by Mr. A. J. Taylor. I have to thank the Baths Committee of the Bath Town Council for facilities very readily granted me, and Mr. Saunders for drawing this and other plans.

(ii) GENERAL CHARACTERISTICS OF THE BATHS

The Roman Baths, as at present known to us, agree in general position with the modern King's, Queen's and Kingston Baths. Described by modern boundaries, they may be said to lie between Stall Street, York Street, Church Street and the Abbey Churchyard, though, if we are to be exact, they do not extend quite so far north as the Churchyard, while they stretch beneath Stall Street and York Street. But they are not known to extend west of Stall Street so as to approach the Cross Bath, the Hot Bath and other adjacent baths. They cover, in all, about one acre, and measure roughly 110 yards from east to west and 40 yards from north to south.

Their original extent was somewhat greater. The remains as yet uncovered, it is plain, do not include the whole range of bath buildings. No façade, frontage or entrance has yet been traced, and both the eastern and western ends are imperfect. But the missing portions are probably not large. No discoveries have been made near either end which indicate any great extension eastwards or westwards beyond the area now opened. In particular the few Roman remains noted to the west of Stall Street resemble a well or fountain near the Cross Bath and some dwelling-houses, rather than any part of a bathing establishment. On the other hand the analogy of the plans of similar thermal baths surviving elsewhere (fig. 24) shows that the northern and southern sides of the baths, as known to us to-day, represent the original outer walls of the edifice at its central part. Probably, therefore, the whole area of the baths did not greatly exceed $1\frac{1}{2}$ acres. Certainly the common statement that it was 7 acres is a serious exaggeration.

The general disposition of the whole is evident. On the north side were the hot springs, rising directly into a reservoir which supplied the baths. The main building was long and somewhat narrow. In the middle of it was the principal bath, a large oblong basin suitable for swimming and immersion. East and west of this were several similar basins, smaller in size, various in shape. Beyond these again, at the eastern end and the south-west corner, were spacious rooms fitted with hypocausts and arrangements for hot air. A small dipping well, where drinkers could draw the waters, was provided on the east side of the springs. A latrine filled the centre of the south side. Behind the apses of the two largest baths were vacant spaces which may be yards. No entrances have yet been found. But the example of the other thermal baths (fig. 24) suggest that we should look for them at or near the eastern and western

FIG. 23. VIEW OF THE GREAT AND CIRCULAR BATHS, EXCAVATED 1880-5.

(From a model in the Baths Museum.)

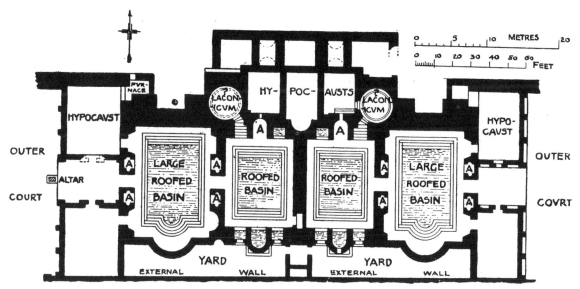

ROMAN BATHS AT BADENWEILER (GERMANY)

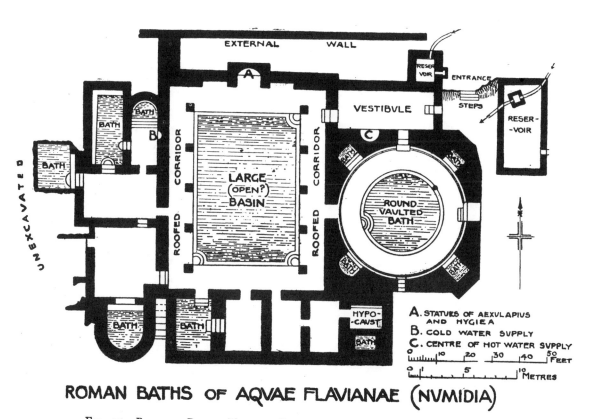

ROMAN BATHS OF AQVAE FLAVIANAE (NVMIDIA)

FIG. 24. PLANS OF ROMAN THERMAL BATHS, FOR COMPARISON WITH THOSE AT BATH.
(The rooms marked A at Badenweiler were perhaps used for charcoal stoves.)

247

ends. One point remains obscure—the division of the baths between the sexes. Some division doubtless existed. Mixed bathing was hardly thought respectable in Rome itself, and it ill suited the stricter manners of provincial life.[1] Possibly the western basins and hot rooms were separated from the eastern in some way that we cannot now detect, and the one was reserved for men, the other for women. Possibly the division was by hours, forenoon and afternoon.[2]

In workmanship and technical finish of building, the baths reach a high level. The masonry is solid and even. The piers and pilasters, though plain and severe, are also massive and dignified. The decorative pieces which survive show boldness and skill. Except that in two or three places corresponding piers or pilasters are not precisely opposite each other, the work is laid out well and truly. The general material is the local oolite, which is both abundant and easily worked, and is doubtless responsible in part for the size and stateliness of the structure. Brick was employed only for roofing and for hypocausts, and no traces occur of its use for bonding tiles. Indeed, the walling, as shown in fig. 29, consists of larger stones than is usual in Romano-British buildings where bonding tiles actually appear.

Throughout the whole range of bath buildings the general floor level, so far as we know it, is roughly the same, 13 or 14 feet below the present street level;[3] it is also lower than the ordinary Roman level, if we may judge by a gutter to be mentioned in a future paragraph. The baths, it seems, were sunk deep into the earth to ensure an easier inflow of water, and even the hypocausts were dug down to the same level.

We can now assign the Roman baths of Bath to their place among Roman baths in general. There were two distinct classes of these baths.[4] One class comprised the baths of ordinary life in town or country house. They were 'hot air' baths, and consisted principally of rooms heated to various temperatures, like modern Turkish baths. Such were the baths of Rome or Pompeii, of Italica or Silchester. The other class comprised the truly 'thermal' baths, that is, the hot-water baths supplied from natural hot springs possessed of healing virtues. Here the dominant feature was the use of basins suitable for immersion. These basins varied curiously in size and shape, but they were for the most part large enough for public bathing and deep enough for complete immersion and swimming. Hot rooms also occurred in these baths; and arrangements were doubtless made for drinking the waters, but these were subsidiary.[5] Such were the baths of Badenweiler in south-western Germany, of Royat in France, of Aquae Flavianae in Numidian

---

[1] Becker and Göll, *Gallus* (Berlin, 1882), iii. 152.   [2] *Lex Metalli Vipascensis*, i. 20.

[3] I have had measurements taken and find that the platform round the bath under Stall Street is 13 ft. 4 ins. below the street level, while the platform at the north-east corner of the Large Bath is 14 ft. 8 ins. below the level of the Abbey Churchyard just above it.

[4] The distinction between the two is obvious. But I have not found it definitely stated anywhere. As a rule the first class only is recognized.

[5] The ancients used thermal waters less than we do for drinking. But the notion that they never drank them is wrong. See for example Pliny, *N. H.* xxxi. 59, 60.

Africa, and many another.[1] To this second class the Roman baths of Bath obviously belong.   In it they claim a high place, partly because they are well preserved, partly because they are extensive and well built.   They deserve note also as being the only Roman thermal baths in which any provision for drinking the waters has been discovered.   But in general, they agree with the rest of their class in having, as their principal element, a series of basins suitable for swimming and immersion.   They agree also in affording us no hint of the various uses which may have corresponded to the various shapes and sizes of these basins.   In the detailed survey, therefore, to which we now pass, we shall have to leave unsolved the question why there was a plurality of basins.   We may guess that some of them were alternative baths, employed while the others underwent cleaning ; or that some were more select than others and their entrance charges higher ; or that some were of later date than others and were added as the baths grew popular and the original structure inadequate for the increasing crowds of bathers.   If we knew more of Roman thermal baths in general, and if the remains at Bath had been more minutely observed by their excavators, we might try to decide between these and similar guesses.   For the present, we must describe the remains left to us.

(iii) DETAILS OF THE BATHS

Our description of the baths naturally begins with the springs that feed them.   The baths proper, which we take next, may best be studied from east to west, almost (as it chances) in the order of their discovery, and may be divided into five parts.   These parts are, in succession, the eastern hypocaust rooms found in 1755, the large bath found at the same time, the Great Central Bath, the Circular Bath and other immersion baths adjacent to and west of it, and finally the hypocaust rooms in the south-west corner.   To these six sections we must append a seventh, embracing various remains found recently in the baths, but, from the inadequacy of our records, assignable to no definite part of them.

(1) SPRINGS AND RESERVOIRS

The springs of Aquae Sulis rose directly into a tank or reservoir set in an enclosure under the modern King's Bath.   The enclosure was roughly rectangular and measured about 45 by 65 feet.   Small doorways connected it with the baths south of it and with other structures north of it, the nature of which is unknown (see p. 252).   It has been called the main entrance to the bath buildings, but its doorways were too narrow for such a use, and its whole plan unsuitable.

The reservoir itself was an irregular octagon, about 50 feet in

---

[1] See H. Leibniz, *Die römischen Bäder von Badenweiler* (Leipzig, 1856) ; Alex. Petit, *Découverte à Royat des substructions d'un établissement thermal gallo-romain* (Clermont Ferrand, 1884) ; S. Gsell, *Monuments antiques de l'Algérie*, i. 237.   Compare the account of Amélie-les-Bains, near Perpignan in southern France, *Bulletin Monumental*, 1870, p. 620.

greatest diameter and 6 or 7 feet in depth. Its shape was doubtless determined by the positions of the springs. The bottom was open to admit the water, the sides were walled with good masonry, 3 ft. thick and 6 or 7 ft. high, and this was in turn coated with lead more than half an inch thick. Round the rim ran a low stone fence or parapet, plainly ornamented with sunk panels. Within it, near the sides, were six blocks, three round and three square, possibly pedestals or supports for some portico. The wall of the cistern was pierced with apertures, which were closed by wooden plugs a foot square. One aperture, on the south side, served the pipe which led south-east to the Great Central Bath. Another may have served the supply of the circular and adjacent baths which has not been traced in detail. A third, on the east side, opened into a large stone culvert which passed under an arch in the enclosure wall and ran along the north side of the eastern part of the baths, taking the overflow from the springs and the outfall from the baths. This culvert, at a point 15 ft. east from the edge of the reservoir, was utilized for the 'dipping-place,' which was approached from the north by a short flight of steps. Further east, it received the outfall from the large bath and from the basins found in 1755. Then it turned south-east and ultimately ran through the Institution Gardens to the river. For almost all its length from the dipping-place, so far as it was followed, it contained at its bottom a duct a foot wide and 8 in. deep, with oaken sides 4 in. thick, once perhaps cased in lead, which may have been the drain proper.[1] But this duct appears at one point to run for a little in another stone culvert, of which unfortunately we know practically nothing.

This group of remains was excavated partly in 1878–80 and partly about 1894–5. A portion of the culvert is still visible and restored to use. The reservoir itself has been covered in. It lies beneath the King's Bath, and in order not to interfere with that, it has been roofed in with concrete, and its roof now serves as a floor to the modern bath. But it has been cleaned out and an outlet provided by which the hot waters could rise up through the roof to the modern level, and thus it is restored to its Roman use as the great well of the baths. The lead which lined it was removed and sold for £70.[2] One of the purchasers gave a small piece to the British Museum.

Highly interesting remains were found in the excavation of the reservoir. In particular a small lead plate inscribed with a curse on some person or persons,[3] another lead plate, possibly inscribed but not now legible, and many coins of Vespasian, Domitian, Nerva, Trajan, Hadrian, Antoninus, Gallienus, Constantine, and others—that is, presumably, of all dates from the foundation of the baths to the end of the Roman period—were found close to the bottom. Both plates and coins

[1] Davis, *Excav.* p. 42.
[2] Davis, *Guide to the Baths*, pp. 11–12 ; J. T. Irvine, *Brit. Arch. Assoc. Journ.* xxxviii. 91 (from Mann, not quite accurate) ; Scarth, *Academy*, 16 April 1881. Scarth and Irvine state that the floor as well as the walls of the reservoir was leaded, but this seems wrong.
[3] Davis, *Athenaeum*, 15 May 1880, p. 641. For the details of the inscription, etc., see p. 282.

deserve notice. For here we touch on two pieces of ancient superstition. The reservoir was in effect the sacred spring of Sul, and the plate with its curse was dropped into it with the hope that the goddess would fulfil the imprecation on some enemy. The coins, on the other hand, belong to a gentler custom. They are offerings to the goddess of the waters, such as were thrown into sacred springs, whether thermal or other, throughout the ancient world. So the thermal spring of Bourbonne les Bains in France was found in 1876 to contain coins of almost every Roman emperor from Augustus to Honorius, the *stipes* or offerings of bather-worshippers.[1]

Other remains found in the reservoir must have come there at the time of its abandonment and ruin. Such were two square pedestals of stone, marked with Roman numerals and intended possibly to indicate the height of the water in the tank ; some shafts of columns and worked stones, including a Composite capital which perhaps measured originally 3 feet in diameter from volute to volute, many bones, nails and the like. These lay loose in the mud and débris which filled the reservoir, and their appearance suggested to the excavators that they came there by violence. If this conjecture be correct, the reservoir would appear to have been purposely wrecked at some date or other—presumably at the close of the Romano-British period.

Many small objects, again, were extracted from the culvert. The 'dipping-place' yielded two jugs and two cups or bowls of tin, a gold earring, two pewter charms or amulets, some fibulae, bracelets and the like. Some of these, and in particular the jugs and bowls, were doubtless lost by persons who came to draw water for drinking.[3] Some, on the other hand, may have been offerings thrown into the dipping place or perhaps washed out of the reservoir.

Further eastwards the culvert yielded in March 1878 a curious mask of nearly pure tin, measuring 13 inches long by 10 inches wide,

FIG. 25. TIN MASK, FOUND IN 1878.

and either originally flat or since flattened out (fig. 25). It has been called medieval, but it is almost certainly Roman. Its use, however, and its occurrence in the culvert are not easy to explain. One good

---

[1] *Bull. de l'Inst.* 1875, p. 133. Compare the coins found in the Well of Coventina on Hadrian's Wall, a non-thermal but sacred spring (Clayton, *Arch. Ael.* viii. [1880], pp. 23–33, who cites other parallels). A complete list of such cases would fill a large volume.
[2] Davis, *Guide*, p. 11. The numbered pedestals have not been preserved.
[3] Davis, *Excavations*, pp. 41–2. Most of the objects are now in the Pump Room.

judge has called it sepulchral, but the culvert is far from any known Roman burial.[1]

The oaken duct at the bottom of the culvert also yielded interesting relics which were scattered along it near the east end of the baths—the pins of two fibulae ; a bronze pin with a pearl ; a 'first brass' of Titus (A.D. 77–8 ; Cohen, 194) and two illegible 'small brass' coins; a barbed bronze fishhook, and some twenty-eight gems. These gems, intaglios on amethyst, sardonyx, chalcedony, onyx and the like, are engraved with ordinary subjects. Four represent gods, Jupiter seated and helmed, Mercury with caduceus and purse, Minerva (Roma) holding a little Victory, Fortune with rudder and horn of plenty. Five show a cupid, either climbing a tree, or riding a goat, or holding a butterfly and an inverted torch, or bending before a tree with an offering (?), or dancing with castanets. Four are horse scenes—a rider galloping and holding a large wreath, a nude charioteer in a *biga*, three four-horse chariots in an amphitheatre, two horses beside a column on which is a vase. Seven depict animals ; a lioness killing a deer, a large-horned goat, three cattle under a tree, a braying donkey, an eagle, a lion, and a mythological beast, beaked, horned, and winged. A young man who is purifying himself from a vase ; a chapletted female bust ; a cloaked shepherd milking a goat ; a figure on a couch (?) ; a group consisting of a *modius*, ears of corn, a pair of scales and a lamp ; and a few defaced designs complete the list. The gems have no special artistic merits. Some of them, indeed, are rudely executed. But they contribute an interesting item to the Roman remains of the baths. It has been ingeniously conjectured that they were lost by some lapidary selling gems and the like to visitors in the Baths.[2]

Finally, it is convenient to notice here the traces of buildings on the north side of reservoir and culvert. Here we might hope to find the connexion between the baths and the area opened in 1790, and partly with this hope some examination was made in 1890 of the ground directly north of the reservoir. But this underlies the Pump Room, and could be only explored in small part. The remains discovered were few and hard to explain, and threw little light on the buildings which had stood there. Two items deserve notice. A carved piece was found which fitted on to a fragment found in 1790, and bids us expect at this spot the building, whatever it was, which was adorned by the Façade of the Four Seasons. On the other hand two other pieces suggest a small independent monument. They were not discovered *in situ* ; one indeed had been used up as a step, and in consequence is much worn (fig. 37 bottom ; (fig. 38 right hand). But we can conjecturally reconstruct the monument to which they originally belonged (fig. 26). It was probably quadrangular, 6

---

[1] Davis, *Proc. Soc. Antiq.* vii. (1878), 403 ; compare *Arch. Journal,* xxxv. 100, *Brit. Arch. Assoc. Journ.* xxxiv. 248. The mask is now in the Baths Museum.

[2] Davis, *Reports to the Baths Committee,* printed *Bath Herald,* 3 May and 21 June 1895. The gems were submitted to Mr. Cecil Smith, who revised the subjects and assigned as their date the first or (at latest) the second century A.D. They are now in the Baths Museum. I have not had time myself to examine them minutely. Compare p. 337.

or $6\frac{1}{2}$ feet square, and of no great height. In each side it had a niche with bas-reliefs, one fragment of which is visible on one of the stones. Round the top ran a slight cornice, pleasantly decorated with foliation, and constructed in four quarter-pieces, of which the surviving stones are two. It may well have been an attractive monument, and as its stones were used up in later work, it may be ascribed to a comparatively early period in the history of the baths. Its use—possibly for a fountain, possibly for seats—and its position cannot now be determined.[1]

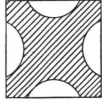

FIG. 26.

East of the reservoir the remains are less obscure. We can distinguish part of a colonnade running north and south with a gutter (indicating a court or other open space) on its east side, and at right angles to this a massive wall built east and west and incised with large masons' marks of Roman date.[2] The gutter occupies a higher level than the baths, being at its lowest point 5 feet above the pavement round the large bath, and the massive masonry may have belonged to a retaining wall which upheld the higher ground. Possibly the space between this and the wall of the Great Bath may have been a yard for the service of the baths, like similar spaces in other thermal baths (fig. 24).

(2) THE EASTERN HYPOCAUSTS

From the reservoir and adjacent structures, courts and yards, we pass to the baths themselves.

The hypocaust rooms at the east end of the bath buildings consisted of two large apartments, two small apses, a furnace and some imperfectly explored space. The two large rooms were ordinary hypocaust rooms, connected by a doorway, but differing slightly in level, the floor of the northern room being 18 inches the higher. Both floors were constructed of concrete, 4 inches thick, laid on tiles and supported by hypocaust pillars of square bricks, 4 feet high. Round the walls of both rooms stood rows of boxtiles, which, when found, were full of soot. The rooms, it is plain, were not heated through the floors but through the boxtiles. Some of these tiles served as chimneys for the smoke while the furnace was working : others were not opened until the smoke had cleared, and then let the hot air into the room.[3]

On the south of these two rooms were others provided also with hypocausts, but they have not been adequately examined. A detached column at the south extremity, if it has been correctly planned, suggests a portico and perhaps an entrance. On the north was a furnace, which showed visible marks of fire, burnt wood, charcoal and the like, at its outer mouth. On either side of this was a semi-

---

[1] Unpublished : information from Mr. A. J. Taylor and Mr. W. H. St. John Hope. The height is, of course, purely a matter of conjecture, and the length and breadth may have been greater. But the smallness of the cornice suits best the view taken in the text.

[2] Davis, *Bath Herald*, 2 August 1895 ; the remains are still open. For the masons' marks see p. 280.

[3] Jacobi, *Saalburg*, pp. 240, 245 ; O. Krell, *Altrömische Heizungen*, p. 48.

circular chamber with walls coated with six or seven coats of red plaster, and floors paved with mosaic[1] and sunk 30 inches below the level of the large northern room; the eastern chamber is said to have had an outlet on the floor.   These chambers were possibly hot water baths, but more probably perspiration rooms (*laconica*), and may have been heated by brasiers, while the outlet pipe would serve for the purpose of cleaning. North of these two chambers and the furnace were other rooms described as of 'ordinary work'—doubtless connected with the service of the furnace.   Hardly anything of this section of the baths is now visible.   For a bronze head perhaps found hereabouts see p. 288 note.

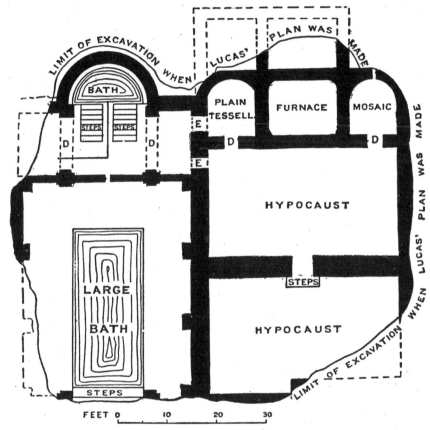

D.E. *Doors marked by Lucas'architect but judged wrong by Lucas.*
Those marked D are shewn also by Sutherland (1760) but not E

FIG. 27.   THE EASTERN BATHROOMS AS SHOWN BY LUCAS IN HIS PLAN.

Two points are doubtful in the account just given.   First, I have in my plan taken the northern wall of the northern hypocaust room to be in line with the general north wall of the baths—as is shown in contemporary plans by Hoare and Hewitt, and (almost) by Stennett, and as is implied in the measurements of Lucas.[2]   Secondly, I have given no doorway opening westwards at the north end of this section, while Lucas gives two (EE on fig. 27), both however—as he states—

[1] From a copy in the Bodleian Library (Gough, Maps 28, fo. 64b). Apparently the eastern chamber had mosaic, and the western one plain tessellation (figs. 27 and 30).

[2] Lucas' plan places this wall farther south (fig. 27), but he himself says it was not quite correct. Others however have copied him implicitly.

uncertain. For convenience I append a plan (fig. 27), on the same scale as my general plan, of the rooms and doors as generally shown.[1]

(3) THE LARGE BATH FOUND IN 1755

West of the hypocaust rooms, and connected with them by at least one door at the south end, is a long oblong hall, containing a large rectangular bath, with a small apsidal bath at each end. The large bath measured about 15 by 30 feet, and was 5 feet deep—the usual depth of the large baths at Bath. Steps gave access to it at the south end ; its sides were plastered, its floor flagged. A channel connected it with the Great Bath west of it, and at the end of this channel, 24 feet beyond the wall dividing the two bath-halls, was a leaden cistern. Apparently the eastern bath was supplied from the western, perhaps by some system of overflow. Round the bath was a flagged platform. The hall which contained it had plain square pilasters attached to the walls, and these doubtless supported a roof. We may, in any case, infer a roof from the fact that the bath was found full of broken tiles and mortar. The north end of this hall was closed by a wall with an unexplained opening in it, 10 inches wide. Beyond that was a pilastered gallery or chamber, with an apse on the north side of it and in the apse a bath 5 feet deep, entered by six steps and provided with a stone seat round the semicircle, 18 inches high. According to Lucas, the apsidal bath originally extended to the wall of the main hall and was subsequently reduced in size ; but this is hardly credible. The south end of the hall terminated in a similar apsidal bath, which was found three or four years after 1755.[2] This has not been fully explored, but doubtless formed the fellow to the northern apse. The means by which water was supplied to these apsidal baths is unknown. The northern apse may have received cold water from a pipe which also serves the large bath west of it, and which seems not to have been used for hot water, as it did not contain the deposit usually produced by the Bath hot waters. This apse has, in its floor, an outlet into the main outfall drain.

The doors of this section of the baths are uncertain, and are given differently by every writer. Traces exist, I think, of the two doors opening westwards which I have admitted to my plan. But the two doors placed by Major Davis in the wall between them are not in accordance with the older plans and drawings.[3] The doubtful door opening north on to the yard is attested by Hoare, Hewitt and Stennett. The two doors (DD, fig. 27) which flank the northern apse in Lucas' plan are, I think, consistent with existing remains. The plans of Hoare, Hewitt and Stennett agree in showing the easternmost of these doors as a wall and the other as a door.

---

[1] From examination of the spot subsequent to the printing of my plan I incline to think there may have been one door westwards, opposite the door leading further west to the Great Bath. The indications of it were pointed out to me by Mr. A. J. Taylor. The older plans, of Hewitt, Hoare, Stennett and Sutherland, all shew a wall here.

[2] Alex. Sutherland, *Attempts to revise Ancient Medical Doctrines* (London, 1763), i. 16–22.

[3] *Excavations*, plans 3, 4.

(4) The Great Bath found in 1880

Passing westwards from the large bath of 1755 we reach the largest of all the baths, which forms the centre of the whole suite. This is placed in a spacious hall measuring 68 by 110 feet. Round it runs a broad platform of freestone with patches of concrete, worn into holes by the feet of many bathers. Behind the platform on each of the north and south sides are three recesses, one rectangular and two semicircular, each about 18 feet wide, plastered red inside and used presumably as lounges for the bathers and their friends. The walls of these recesses, still standing on the north side 6 or 7 feet high, are constructed of coursed masonry 28 inches thick (fig. 29). They probably formed the outer walls of the baths at this point and looked on to yards and lumber spaces. On the north and south sides of the platform close to the water stand twelve rectangular piers, six each side, severe and massive. These doubtless supported whatever roof spanned the Great Bath. They correspond to twelve pilasters placed at the corners of the recess, and as these appear to be additions to the original plan, the detached piers may also (at least in their present form) be due to some alteration. The position of the mouldings supports this view. It suggests that the piers were originally square, but that afterwards need was felt for stronger supports, and they were enlarged by the addition of pilasters on both the water and the platform sides.

Unfortunately we can say little about the superstructure. There was a roof to the bath. Thus much is plain, since fragments of box-tiled roofage were found lying inside the bath. But its extent and character and height are uncertain. On general grounds we might be content with assuming something more like a shelter than a complete roof. Modern bathers have used the King's Bath for centuries without a roof. In Roman times the Great Bath may have served its purpose well, and yet have been incompletely roofed. Or it may have been roofed, and yet have had large apertures in the roofing. The surrounding platform, however, must in any case have been completely covered.

The bath itself is a great oblong, measuring 73 by 29 feet at the bottom and 83 by 40 at the top. It was floored with fine leaden sheets 5 by 10 feet in size, burnt together at the edges and not soldered, and laid on a thin layer of brick concrete backed by freestone. Six steps led down into it, and it has been noticed that the lowest steps are higher and narrower than the upper ones, and thus accommodate the buoyancy of the body in water. The inflow and outflow of the water was arranged principally on the north side. The hot water entered at the north-west corner through an oblong leaden channel 7 inches deep and 21 inches wide.[1] A bronze sluice at the north-east corner let out the overflow or used-up water. A small leaden pipe running along the north

---

[1] According to Major Davis there was here an arrangement for spraying the water. The traces of this are, however, not at all conclusive, and a hot spray is unlikely.

FIG. 28. THE GREAT BATH, EMPTY OF WATER.

FIG. 29. MASONRY OF WALL ROUND THE N.E. APSE OF THE GREAT BATH, EXTERIOR FACE.
The courses average 5 ins. each.
(From a Photograph).

FIG. 30. MOSAIC IN THE WESTERN SEMICIRCULAR CHAMBER, NORTH OF THE EASTERN HYPOCAUSTS.
(From Gough's papers in the Bodleian Lib.)

platform fed a small fountain in a carved pedestal at the middle of the north side and very possibly supplied it with cold water, either for douche or for drinking. Certainly it was not used for hot water since it was found to contain none of the characteristic deposit of the mineral springs. It also apparently supplied one of the baths further east.[1] In addition, the eastern end of the bath seems to have contained a leaden cistern, found in 1760, from which a channel led into the large bath of 1755.

Only four doors led into this great hall. Two, already mentioned, opened from the east. A third in the west wall gave passage to the Circular Bath, and a fourth—blocked up in Roman times and so shown on my plan—led from the north platform westwards into the corridor between the reservoir and the Circular Bath.

(5) THE CIRCULAR BATH AND ADJOINING APARTMENTS

The Circular Bath, excavated in 1885, lies immediately west of the large bath just described. It stands in a nearly square chamber measuring 33 by 39 feet, pilastered and once unquestionably roofed. Itself it is 29 feet in diameter and (when full) 5 feet deep. Its bottom is concrete faced with tiles and originally coated with lead. Its outfall drains run away southwards, as any one may see. One of them is a leaden pipe which connects the bottom of the east side with the stone drain of the latrine. The other is an overflow, which apparently leads to the same outlet. But the source whence the bath was supplied with water has not been discovered, despite excavations in search of it. Though it is within 25 feet of the reservoir, one good judge at any rate has considered it to be the cold plunge bath. Similar circular basins occur in most thermal baths, but nothing has been discovered anywhere to indicate their special use.

On the north of the Circular Bath was a passage or corridor separating it from the enclosure of the reservoir. This has undergone alterations in Roman times, and its object is now not clear. South of the Circular Bath and entered from it is a massively built room—perhaps adapted from an earlier structure—which served as a latrine, and beyond that a paved space about 25 by 40 feet in area, which may best be taken as having been an open court, perhaps with a stone bench or two in it.

Besides the Circular Bath we can trace in the western part of the buildings two other fairly large and deep immersion baths—one oval 26 feet long, and one rectangular and a trifle smaller. This latter has been called the cold bath,[2] but without any definite reason. It underlies Stall Street, and appears to belong to the western extremity of the suite of baths. Beyond it, so far as I can learn, nothing definite in the way of building or masonry has been traced. Unfortunately our knowledge of this western part is confused and faint. Modern builders have interfered

[1] Davis, *Excav.* p. 26, says it also supplied baths on the north and south of the Great Bath, but this is obviously wrong. The pipe or drain marks in the south-west corner of the platform do not seem connected with this, but are not very clear in themselves.

[2] Davis' *Guide*, p. 32. His measures are not quite the same as mine.

with it : the modern baths overlying it hindered complete uncovering, few details were recorded, and the drainage and communications are lost. A discovery made by Mr. A. J. Taylor since my plan was printed shows that a culvert ran along the north side of the oval and rectangular baths, but whether for supply or outfall is not clear.

(6) THE SOUTH-WESTERN HYPOCAUSTS

The hypocausts which lie south of the baths just noted are equally little known and for the same reasons. We can still see traces of some five hypocausts, fitted mostly with tubular bricks along the walls like the eastern hypocausts, and we can point out what seems to be a furnace which heated them. But a definite reconstruction of their character and interrelation is impossible.

We may however connect with them some discoveries made in 1727. At that time a sewer was being constructed along Stall Street, and at the bottom of a hole nearly 16 feet deep was found 'a row of bricks 20 in number made in the nature of stoves, all of one piece, hollow, $\frac{1}{2}$ inch thick within, 16 inches high. . . . Between each of them is put a strong and redish cimment of mortar and brickdust and a single tile. On the inside sticks a black-stuff very like soot : they are placed pretty regular one behind the other, so that you can thrust in a stick of 3 or 4 feet long towards the east side, going towards the King's Bath. They had all pieces of tile clapt before each hollow.' So runs the text to a picture now preserved in the Bodleian and (in copy) in the British Museum.[1] The locality in question seems to be just opposite the end of York Street,[2] and therefore close to the hypocausts which we have considered. Unfortunately neither plan nor notes make the character of the remains quite clear. But a drawing in Colonel Long's collection shows a very similar row of boxtiles—described as 'a floor composed of brick watercourses laid with a current northward'—found in 1825 under the south-west angle of the present baths, in the corner of Stall Street and York Street. Probably the two finds were made in the same locality, and we may therefore call the discoveries of 1727 the first discoveries of the Roman baths. In the drawings, the tiles found in 1727 and 1825 closely resemble the fragments of roof-tiling found in and near the Great Bath. But the mention of soot in them shows that part of them, at least, belonged to hypocausts, of which there were several close to the place of discovery, and were chimneys and passages for hot air from the hypocaust to the hot room above.[3]

With this we may connect another discovery, made a fortnight

[1] Original notes and sketch in Bodleian (Gough, *Maps* 28, p. 64) : see further p. 245; copy by Priscilla Combe in B. M. King's Library (xxxvii. 26, O). See E. Green, *Bath Field Club*, vii. 118 ; *Arch. Journ.* xlviii. 177. A reference to the finds of 1727 is in *Soc. Ant. Minutes*, iii. 283 (12 March 1740).

[2] The hole was dug on 25 July 1727, 'over against Alderman Ford's house in Stalls Street,' and the 'stoves' seem to have been found a few feet northwards. Mr. Ford's house (I am told) was at the junction of the south side of Bath Street and the west side of Stall Street, that is, almost opposite the end of York Street, but a trifle to the north.

[3] Confusion between the bath roof-tiling and hypocaust tubulation, odd as it may sound, is quite easy ; see Davis, *Bathes of Bathe's Ayde*, p. 82.

FIG. 31. BRONZE HEAD, PERHAPS OF MINERVA, FOUND IN 1727.
(From a Photograph. The original is about life size.)

Fig. 34. Minerva (p. 259).

Fig. 33. Goddesses and Worshippers (p. 259).

Fig. 32. Hercules Bibax (p. 241).

earlier than the preceding. On 12 July 1727 a remarkable head was dug up in the same sewerage works, at the same depth and about the same place (fig. 31). It is a bronze-gilt head of about life size. The gilding is still fresh, and so far as it survives it is singularly well preserved, but it has been broken round the neck, and something (perhaps a helmet) has been lost above the hair. Artistically it is a rather plain, classical head, of excellent workmanship, if not of the most refined conception, devoid of definite attributes, but obviously a goddess and not improbably Minerva. It may have ornamented some hall or entrance chamber in the south-west corner of the baths. Coins of Marcus and of the period of Diocletian and Constantine were found with it, but perhaps had no special connexion with it.[1] For another bronze head see p. 288 note.

(7) Sculptured and other Remains found in the Baths

It remains to notice some sculptured and architectural pieces found in the baths during the explorations of 1878–95, but under circumstances which have not been recorded.

Three of these represent deities—all rudely carved and inferior artistically to the average work in the baths.

(1) A relief of Minerva, in a gable-topped niche, 27 inches high, 18 inches wide (fig. 34). The goddess stands erect, draped and helmeted; her shield is on the ground to her left, with traces of Medusa's head on the boss and a fat owl perched on the rim; in her upraised right hand she holds her spear. It is a common type. Found in or near the Great Bath in April 1882.[2]

(2) A relief of Mercury, 14 inches high, 11 inches wide, nude, but with robe over left shoulder and under right arm; in his left hand his caduceus; near his right hand something now indistinguishable. A common type.

(3) A relief, 17 inches high by 13 inches broad, showing a woman seated, holding in her left hand a stick or wand over her shoulder: to her left an erect draped male figure with horns (?), and also holding club or stick over his left shoulder. Below, an animal and three little draped figures. Obviously a god and goddess, three worshippers and a victim. But precise identification is impossible. The pair of deities often found together in Germany, Mercury and Rosmerta, has occurred to me, but the attributes are not decisive (fig. 33).

Notice is also due to some various architectural fragments, some of which possess considerable excellence.

(4–7) In particular, four blocks arrest attention. They are slightly curved, and adorned on both sides, principally with bold and graceful

---

[1] It has attracted much notice and been frequently published—by John Wynter, *Of bathing at Bathe* (London, 1728), p. 11; *Vetusta Monumenta*, I. plate 34 (1730); Horsley, *Britannia Romana*, p. 327 (1732); Wood, *History of Bath*, p. 159; Warner, *Illustrations*, p. 69, and *History*, p. 335; J. Whitaker, *Antijacobin*, x. 344; Scarth, *Som. Proc.* iii. 89, and *Aquae*, frontispiece, but the only good illustrations are those in *Vetusta Monumenta* and in Horsley. The critics have called it sometimes Apollo and sometimes Minerva. It was kept for a long time in the Guildhall, and is now in the Pump Room.

[2] *Antiquary*, July 1882; Davis, *Guide*, p. 26.

foliation, but partly with figures, and above these a cornice seems to have slightly projected. Their general character will be clearest from the annexed illustrations (figs. 34A–6). What use they served is unknown. Possibly they crowned the columns of a circular structure in which the cornice could be seen from both sides; but we have no other vestige of such a structure.[1] They are generally supposed to have been found in the Great Bath, but no record exists of their discovery, and some dates given in Irvine's papers suggest rather that they, or some of them, were found in 1878–9 and therefore belong to the ornamentation of the reservoir. In any case the general similarity of their size and style seems to connect them together, while the excellence of their workmanship claims our notice.

(8) Another carved piece of far less merit is the head of a lion (or sphinx) with a mane—its face and legs broken—resembling an antefix. It was taken from the south-west corner of the Great Bath in the autumn of 1882 (*Antiquary*, Nov. 1882). A rather similar piece was unearthed in 1863 from under the markets (Scarth, *Aquae*, p. 137).

There remain purely architectural pieces. Drums and capitals or bases of columns, large and small, abound, but little can be suggested to fit them into any consistent whole. As proof of a large and stately building one may instance three drums and the base of a Doric column with a diameter of 28 or 29 inches and an original height of perhaps 17 feet, and two Doric capitals with shafts of 21 inches diameter; a drum of a fluted column with twenty-six flutes, nearly 28 inches in diameter; an ornate Corinthian capital found in the Great Bath; a fircone finial found in 1890 when the new laundry for the baths was built on the south side of York Street, but apparently inside the area of the baths; and finally two four-sided finials, one of them $17\frac{1}{2}$ inches high and measuring 8 by 11 inches at the base, found in the baths about June 1893, and the other $15\frac{1}{2}$ inches high, both broken. To these last, parallels have been found at Wellow (fig. 70), at North Wraxall, at Silchester, at Llantwit and elsewhere.[2] One is shown in the top of figure 38.

6. PRIVATE HOUSES

The temple of Sul and the baths were the dominant features of Aquae Sulis. But they obviously did not stand alone. Round them must have clustered the houses of officials and residents and the lodgings of visitors. Of these we have, as it seems, considerable traces. In particular, many mosaics have been found, which it is natural to attribute to private houses rather than to any extension of the baths.[3] These remains occur principally inside the circuit of the ancient walls and

[1] Davis, *Excavations*, p. 39, thinks them the backs of semicircular seats in the recesses round the Great Bath, but this is hardly likely. The circle implied by the curve of fig. 34, would probably have a diameter of 13 feet 4 inches.

[2] *Antiquary*, xxviii. (1893), pp. 44, 140; compare xxvi. 55 for Llantwit.

[3] The view of Mr. E. Green that mosaics would occur only in the principal or official houses (*Arch. Journ.* xlviii. 183) perhaps limits their use too much.

Fig. 34A. Carved Stone found probably in 1878–9 (⅐).

(The side shewn is slightly concave : the convex side has a smaller pattern.)

Fig. 35. Carved Stone found probably 1878–9 (⅐).

(The side shewn is slightly convex : the concave side is carved similarly. The section shews the projection of the cornice.)

Fig. 36. Carved Stone, found probably 1879 (⅐).

THREE OF THE CARVED BLOCKS FOUND IN THE PATHS (p. 260).

Fig. 38.

Fig. 37.

Groups of Miscellaneous Pieces found in the Baths since 1878.

(See pp. 243, 252, 260.)

indicate at least some comfortable houses. A few—some four or five—have been detected outside, but none, curiously enough, within 600 yards of the walls. They do not form real suburbs, but are isolated structures in the vicinity of Bath, except the remains found in Bathwick, which suggest something like a group of dwellings. None, either here or elsewhere without the walls, shew traces of wealth or comfort.

I. I take first those found within the walls. Most of these lie in the north-western corner of Aquae Sulis, on the site now occupied by the Mineral Water Hospital and the Bluecoat School immediately west of it.

(1) When the hospital was built in 1738, there was discovered at its south-east corner, 6 feet under the surface, a hypocaust with an ashpit (that is, a furnace) and two mosaics. One, 6 feet broad, was apparently a passage ; the other, 18 feet broad, and belonging to a room, showed a geometrical pattern of interlacing circles. A floor, flagged with common stone, and some walling were uncovered at the same time. Too little was detected or recorded to show the exact character of the building, but it would be most naturally explained as part of a private house.[1]

(2) More than a hundred years later, in 1859, when the hospital was enlarged by an extension westwards, a tessellated floors was found under the new building, 13 feet below the road level, along with concrete floors, ashpits (furnaces), walls, tiles, and miscellaneous coins (Trajan to Magnus Maximus), potsherds, bone pins and an incribed fragment (No. 15 below). The mosaic was a maeander fret of a common type in grey and white, somewhat poor in workmanship. It has been preserved *in situ*.[2]

Again in 1884 in a further extension, another and finer mosaic was found on the edge of Bridewell Lane, south of that detected in 1859, 3 feet below its level, and actually 8 feet underground. This displayed a geometrical pattern of conventional flowers in octagons, in white and blue-grey lias, red brick and purple sandstone, set in a border of herring-bone tiles. A plainer piece was also touched close by.[3]

A trifle west of these a still better mosaic, with a pattern of dolphins, seahorses and the like, was dug up from a depth of 15 feet beneath the Bluecoat School in 1859 and is still preserved there.[4] And finally a mosaic in red, white, and blue, never fully described and now lost, was discovered with coins and bricks in May 1814, near the corner of Westgate Street and Bridewell Lane.[5]

Further south, near Lower Borough Walls, extensive finds were made under the Royal United Hospital, when it was enlarged by the addition

[1] Wood, *Hist.* p. 270.
[2] *Bath and Cheltenham Gazette*, 11 May 1859; *Som. Proc.* xi. (2), 187; Scarth, *Aquae*, pp. 89, 94, plate xxxvi. D. The Institution has some of the objects found here.
[3] *Bath Field Club*, vi. 37, with photograph ; brief note in *Brit. Arch. Assoc. Journ.* xli. (1885) 98 ; *Building News*, 12 Sept. 1884 ; *Antiquary*, Nov. 1884. A small piece is preserved in the men's smoke room of the hospital. See p. 228.
[4] *Bath and Chelt. Gazette*, 9 June 1859; Scarth, *Aquae*, plate xxxvi.
[5] *Omnium Gatherum*, i. 25.

of the Albert wing in 1864–6. These comprised the foundations of a considerable building, hypocausts, an apsidal room, probably a bath, two other baths, a wall with a pilaster base attached, flue tiles, and especially a room of 12 by 15 feet containing a mosaic 10½ feet square, which showed a conventional rose inside a guilloche border (fig. 39). This latter was removed in 1898 and relaid in the Pump Room. In these remains we may perhaps have the private baths of a large residence.[1]

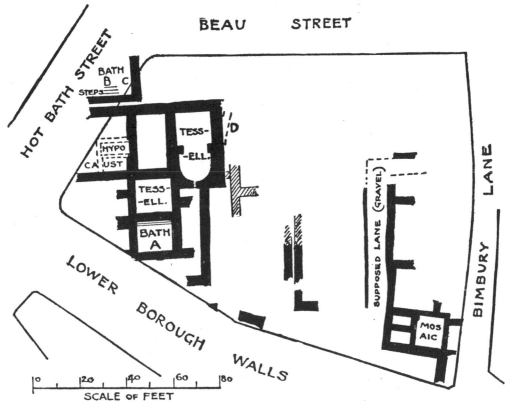

FIG. 39. REMAINS OF BUILDINGS, FOUND 1864–6, ON THE SITE OF THE UNITED HOSPITAL, ALBERT WING AND MEDICAL OFFICERS' QUARTERS.
From plans by J. T. Irvine and others.
A, Bath with stone floor and leaden discharge pipe; B, Bath floored with lead, 6 steps leading down to it; C, Pilaster; D, Stone culvert.

On the south-east side of the settlement a mosaic was found in June 1897, 10 feet deep under the Weymouth House Schools. It was decorated with a geometrical ornament, in red, white and blue, of guilloche, enclosing a central circle not preserved.[2] The further circumstances of the discovery have not been recorded. In the same quarter, but further north, a mosaic of red, white, and blue tesserae, apparently of a good pattern, was found in 1813 in Abbey Green, under the premises of a Mr. Crutwell 'on the south side of Swallow Street.' Of it also nothing further is recorded.[3] Some other items from this quarter are more dubious. Roman masonry is said to have been found under the east

[1] Bath and Chelt. Gazette, Aug. 1864; Scarth, Aquae, p. 136; Brit. Arch. Assoc. Journ. xxix. 379; Bath Field Club, ix. 56; Builder, 20 Aug. 1864; Intellectual Observer, vi. 217.
[2] Bath Chron. 17 and 25 June, 22 July 1897; Times, 18 June 1897; Antiquary, Aug. 1897.
[3] Omnium Gatherum, i. 25. Swallow Street, unfortunately, runs north and south.

end of the Abbey in 1833; and forty years later Mr. J. T. Irvine met with Roman wall stones and a bit of pillar, with window glass, Samian potsherds, etc., at the same spot, but it is not clear that these were *in situ*. Nor is it certain that the potsherds and blue and white tesserae found in 1843, in Orange Grove, east of the Abbey, were Roman, though it is natural to consider them so.[1] And, finally, doubt attaches to the true character of the remains found in 1824, in the alley called Boat Stall Lane or Fish Cross Lane, leading behind the Police Station to the East Gate. In one account they are said to have included masonry, the flue of a 'stove,' glass, bones, potsherds, and coins of about A.D. 250–325. But Scarth calls the bones human, and classes the whole find as sepulchral.[2]

II. Without the walls fewer remains of buildings have occurred, and still fewer tessellated floors. (1) The *Bath Chronicle* of 15 Oct. 1818 records a mosaic pavement as found in that year behind Norfolk Crescent, in Kingsmead, perhaps 180 yards from the present Midland Railway station. The situation is low and exposed to floods, and further details would have been desirable.

(2) In Walcot a coarse mosaic, with Samian and other potsherds, an inscribed fibula, a fragment of a military diploma, some glass, lead weights, and coins were found in May 1815 near the London Road, in making the Walcot Brewery, a little east of the present Cleveland Bridge. This seems to indicate a wayside house on the road from Aquae Sulis eastwards. Most of the finds passed into the collection of Mr. Cranch.[3]

(3) Remains of a columned structure were found in Dec. 1902, about a quarter of a mile from the site of Northgate, on the east side of Walcot Street and just north of the lane called Old Orchard. They consisted of five square pierbases, $5\frac{1}{2}$ feet apart, placed in a line running north and south and about 12 feet below the street level, and also flue tiles, potsherds, Samian and other, and a few coins of Constantine and Licinius. Close by was an old roadway taken to be Roman, but it was only $7\frac{1}{2}$ feet deep, and therefore considerably higher than the bases and presumably later in date. Some oak beams under the adjoining houses were probably modern work.[4]

(4) In Bathwick several remains have been found south of the Avon. Near the railway a piece of blue-grey and white tessellation, not fine work, was found long ago and given by Hunter to the Institution.[5] Near St. John's Church, a drain, a piece of wall, a broken column, and potsherds were found 7 feet deep in 1861. Quite recently,

[1] Irvine, *Brit. Arch. Assoc. Journ.* xlvi. 92, and *Bath Herald*, 2 Sept. 1893; *Gent. Mag.* 1833 (ii.) 269; 1843 (i.) 521. Earle, *Bath Field Club*, iv. (1881) 155, refers to a thirteenth century tessellated floor in Orange Grove. The remains found in 1894 when the White Lion Hotel was demolished, were not Roman.

[2] *Bath and Chelt. Gazette*, 21 Sept. 1824; Scarth, *Aquae*, 99; site on O. S. xiv. 5, 10. See p. 228.

[3] *Bath and Chelt. Gazette*, 20 Nov. 1816; Skinner in Add. MSS. 33661, p. 30, and 33665, pp. 16, 342; for the two inscribed objects see pp. 280, 283, and Lysons in *Soc. Ant. Minutes*, xxxiii. 160.

[4] Information from Mr. A. J. Taylor; note by J. P. E. Falconer, *Bath Field Club*, x. 316.

[5] *Bath Field Club*, ii. 479.

in 1900, fifty coins (Nero-Gratian), pottery, and an uninscribed altar, 18 inches high, with curious 'wings' (a parallel has since turned up at Silchester), have been unearthed close by the east side of Bathwick Street in Kirkham Buildings near the site of the now removed Old Bathwick Brewery. A pavement, finally, is said to have been found some time ago behind Daniel Street. But of this I have no details.[1]

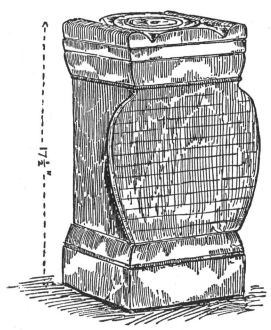

FIG. 39A. ALTAR, FOUND 1900.

(5) There remain to be recorded some few vestiges of building along the line of the Roman road which ran from Walcot Church by Julian Road towards the west. In sewering Guinea Lane in 1854–5, flue-tiles, coins of Commodus and others, Samian and other potsherds came to light,[2] and a little further west, near Christ Church and the Riding School, flue-tiles, sherds, coins.[3] In both cases we may argue from the flue-tiles to some sort of building. Further west, again, a gravelled Roman road was found in 1869–70, under the tower of St. Andrew's Church, and near it a wall, urn, and ashes, skeletons, and late Roman coins. This, however, might have been only a burial enclosure. A stone ' resembling a pineapple ' is said to have been discovered with the other remains, and a finial of this kind occurs frequently in Roman tombs.

It may be proper to add here a reference to the finds made in 1829–32 in forming Victoria Park. These included a considerable variety of pottery, mostly jugs, flasks and pitchers of common ware, and some fibulae, bronze rings and other small objects. They do not seem to be sepulchral, and may be connected with some vanished dwellings.[4]

7. CEMETERIES

Numerous Roman burials have been discovered round Bath. The principal cemetery lay along the Fosse Way, now the London Road, leading eastwards through the narrow level space between Lansdown and the Avon. Here were the most important graves and the most costly tombstones. Graves have also been found beside the continuation of the Roman road westwards through Julian Road and Victoria

[1] Information from Mr. Wallace Gill; *Bath Field Club*, x (i.), 1902, p. 16. See fig. 39A.
[2] *Bath and Chelt. Gazette*, 31 Jan. 1855; *Illustr. London News*, 10 Feb. 1855.
[3] *Bath and Chelt. Gazette*, 11 Dec. 1855.
[4] Bruce and Way, *Catalogue of Antiquities at Alnwick Castle* (Newcastle, 1880), Nos. 620–32; Archaeol. Instit. at Worcester, *Descriptive Catalogue*, 1862, p. 10.

Park, and between it and the Avon. Far fewer occur along the Fosse south of the Avon, and some seem to have no relation to any road.

The graves themselves are in general simple. A few stray pieces doubtfully indicate stately monuments.[1] A few tombstones bear reliefs; for instance, the familiar subject of a horseman riding over a fallen foe is here twice represented. But these do not attest much wealth or luxury, and most of the graves of which we know any details contain merely ashes in urns, or skeletons in coffins. It must be added that none of the discoveries has been recorded with sufficient minuteness to demand any detailed account in these pages.

Within the medieval walls only two very uncertain instances of Roman burials are known. The finds made in Boatstall Lane in 1824 (p. 263) may be sepulchral, but are of doubtful character. The tombstone of Vitellius Tancinus was found opposite the Town Hall in 1736, but it might have been brought in as building material in Roman or later times. It is curious however that both occur in the same part of Aquae Sulis, and the doubt might arise whether the Roman walls included this area (p. 228), if there were enough evidence to justify any decided view. In any case the coffins found in Orange Grove in 1815 and 1870 may quite as well be medieval as Roman.

Outside the walls to the north-east lay the chief cemetery, planted along the Fosse Way. Among its burials are those marked by the inscriptions of Murrius Modestus, Iulius Vitalis, Valerius Latinus, Antigonus of Nicopolis, and Vibia Iucunda, to which we may perhaps add the stones of the town councillor of Glevum, Rusonia Aventina, and Merc(atia ?) Magnii, found in or near the Northgate, and therefore not improbably taken as building material from their places beside the Roman road through Walcot. Here too we may mention the upper part of a rider relief, $2\frac{1}{2}$ feet wide, found long ago in Grosvenor Gardens, and doubtless, when perfect, provided with an inscription.[2] Humbler burials are also common—for example, coffins and skeletons, urns, coins, found in May 1815 near Cleveland Bridge and the Walcot Brewery; more found at the same spot in 1839, and more again found in 1867—a coffin and skeleton, two stone cists with burnt bones, potsherds (including first century Samian), and a Republican denarius (Cordius Rufus iiivir : B.C. 46).[3] Vaguer records indicate a stone coffin near to the tomb of Vitellius (Musgrave, *Brit. Belg.* p. 204), and a coffin with bones and ashes and coins of Faustina, found 'in Walcot' in 1818 (*Bath Chronicle*, 15 October 1818). Quite recently, in 1900, bones, potsherds and a rude coffin were found at the bottom of Guinea Lane, opposite Walcot church.[4] Further out of Bath on the same road, burials have been noted in Lam-

---

[1] The reliefs that once adorned the walls (p. 286), seen by Guidott, Dingley and others, may be to some extent sepulchral.

[2] Musgrave, *De Geta Britannico* (Iscae, 1714); Warner, *Illustration*, p. 9, and *Hist.* p. 32; *Som. Proc.* iii. (2), 102. It is often joined to the tombstone of Vitellius, but differs in size : see fig. 48, upper half. It has, of course, nothing to do with Geta.

[3] *Bath and Chelt. Gazette*, Nov. 1816; Scarth, *Aquae*, p. 98; *Som. Proc.* v. (2), 53; *Bath Field Club*, I. (iii.) 9, 18; Irvine's papers; *O. S.* xiv. (1), 20.

[4] *Bath Field Club*, x. 315; *Proc. Soc. Antiq.* xx. 248.

bridge. Here a sandstone coffin, two skeletons, two bronze rings and three pins were found in 1824.[1]

Burials also occur on the south side of the Avon, in Bathwick, where we have seemed to detect a small group of dwellings (p. 263). The tombstone of Calpurnius Receptus, priest of Sul, was discovered about 1795, in or near Sydney Gardens, and various stone coffins were dug up there in 1823, 1861 and 1866, one of them containing a horse's head.[2] Further, a wooden cist with a skeleton and three urns was found in 1857 in Villa Fields. Here also it may be mentioned that a stone coffin containing human remains and coins of the Lower Empire was found on "Hampton Down," that is, perhaps, on Bathwick Hill, in 1823–24.

On the north side of Bath burials are fewer. But skeletons, several coffins, potsherds, and coins of all four centuries (Vespasian, Pius, Constantine, Gratian), were found in Russell Street in 1818, 1836, and 1852, along the line of the Roman road. Higher up the hill, at the Hermitage, above Lansdown Crescent, two coffins with a skeleton, iron nails of various lengths (? nails of wooden coffins), potsherds, and part of an iron sword, were found in March 1808.[4] Whether we should call Roman the coffin said by Musgrave to have been found in Lansdowne Road, in 1716, and those unearthed in building St. Stephen's Church, may be doubtful.

On the west side of Bath burials occur fairly plentifully. The line of the Roman main road shows, it is true, few traces. Only at St. Andrew's Church do we meet with skeletons, urns, bones of a child, and late coins, found in 1869–70 (p. 264). Other reported discoveries seem doubtful, since the finds made in Victoria Park are probably not sepulchral, and the skeleton with sword-belt, mentioned by Scarth (*Aquae*, p. 110), may be post-Roman. South of this road, however, and nearer the Avon, we have more certain finds to catalogue. Such are sepulchral urns, etc., at the north-west corner of Queen's Square (Scarth, *Aquae*, p. 110); skeletons and black potsherds behind 11 Royal Crescent, found in 1888; coffins at Windsor Place, on the Upper Bristol Road, and the lodge of Locksbrook Cemetery; a skeleton and urn at the gasworks; and coffins (though of doubtful date) at Partis College.[5] A road probably led out of the west gate of Aquae Sulis, and some of these burials may have been placed along it.

Lastly, on the south side of the town, we must notice coffins, skeletons, and coins (Gallienus, Carausius, Constantine), found in 1843

---

[1] *Bath and Chelt. Gazette*, 22 June 1824; Scarth, *Aquæ*, p. 99: remains in the Institution.

[2] Scarth, *Aquae*, p. 101; *Brit. Arch. Assoc. Journ.* xvii. 232; *Proc. Som.* xxii. 28; *Arch. Journ.* xxiv. 60; *Bath Field Club*, III. (i.) 41; O. S. Whether the coffins found in Henrietta Park in 1882 were Roman seems open to doubt.

[3] *Gent. Mag.* 1824 (1), 508.

[4] *Bath Chronicle*, 16 Sept. 1852; Scarth, *Aquae*, pp. 99, 102, 133; *Som. Proc.* v. (2) 52; *Illustrated London News*, 30 Sept. 1854 and 10 Feb. 1856; *Gent. Mag.* 1852, ii. 407; O. S. xiv. (1) 13. The human and animal bones found in Julian Road opposite Morford Street in 1900 (*Bath Field Club*, x. 315) are of uncertain age.

[5] *Bath and Chelt. Gazette*, 7 Jan. 1863; Scarth, *Aquae*, p. 103; O.S.; the Rev. H. H. Winwood, *Bath Chronicle*, 11 May, 1888.

and 1859, in Lyncombe Cemetery, near the Foss, and a skeleton and coin of Crispus, found in 1860 in Smallcombe Bottom, far from any known road of Roman date.[1]

8. THE ROMAN INSCRIPTIONS OF BATH

The following section contains all the Roman inscriptions recorded as found in Bath. I have re-examined those which are extant and have revised the whole bibliography, and especially the earlier writers, and trust that in accuracy of text and fullness of detail I may have advanced on previous publications. The abbreviations are those used throughout this article, save that C = the seventh volume of the *Corpus Inscriptionum Latinarum* (Berlin, 1873), edited by the late Dr. Emil Hübner ; Eph = supplements to the same, edited in the *Ephemeris Epigraphica*, by Dr. Hübner and myself.

I. *Inscriptions found in or near the Baths and relating to the building or repair of the Baths or of the adjacent Temple of Sul Minerva.*

(1–4) Four fragments of similar stone, workmanship and lettering, connected with the façade of the Four Seasons mentioned above (p. 238). The lettering is in two lines, and in each case 3½ inches tall ; and, while good of its kind, suggests the second or third century rather than the first. All four pieces are now in the Bath Museum, except for two corners of Nos. 1 and 3. For the general character of the fragments see figs. 14, 16, 21 ; for the lettering, see the cut of No. 3, fig. 41.

(1) Fragment, now 33 inches long by 12½ inches high, found in or soon after 1790, when the Pump Room was rebuilt. From Lysons' drawing it seems that a part of the stone has been broken off since it was first discovered and that the original height was 20 inches and the piece belonged to a frieze.

> . . . C]laudius Ligur . . | . ae nimia vetus[tate conlapsum. . . .

The beginning of line 2 may be a vestige of *templum Sulis Minerv]ae : nimia vetus* is plainly the first part of a phrase common on Roman inscriptions. It would appear that one Claudius Ligur restored something, perhaps the temple of Sul, that had suffered through lapse of time.

Englefield, *Archaeologia*, x. 325, inaccurately ; Pownall, plate ; Carter, *Ancient Architecture*, i. plate vii. (1794) ; Warner, *Hist.* plate i. appendix ; Lysons, plate ii. ; Scarth, *Aquae*, p. 19 ; *C.* 39.

(2) Similar piece, 58 inches long by 12½ inches high, found about the same time and place, but apparently before No. 1. Its length shows that it did not belong to an interpilaster of the ordinary width, and we may put it on the frieze.

> . . . c]olegio longa seria . . | . sua pec]unia refici et repingi cur[avit. . . .

The first word can hardly be other than the dative or ablative of *collegium* : after *longa seria* (plainly a by-form for *serie*) we may supply *annorum*. The second line shows that a structure, presumably temple or baths, was repaired and repainted at the private expense of some one.

Pownall, plate ; Carter, pl. vii. ; Warner, *Hist.* plate i. ; Lysons, plate ii. ; Scarth, *Aquae*, p. 22 ; *C.* 39.

(3) Similar fragment. When first found, it measured 55 inches long by 10 inches high, and terminated to the left in the capital of a five-fluted pilaster similar to the pilasters of the Four Seasons façade. Now the left hand part is lost, and the block measures 23 by 9 inches. Found about the same time and place as Nos. 1 and 2. Fig. 41.

> C. Protaciu[s . .—. deae Su[l]is M[inervae. . . .

The *l* of *Sulis* was doubtless combined with the V to make V, and as the bottom of the letter is lost, it has disappeared. We may supply with *deae Sulis* either *sacerdos* or *templum*.

Pownall, p. 24, incorrectly; Carter, plate vii.; Lysons, plate vi.; Scarth, *Som. Proc.* iii. 90, and *Aquae*, p. 22; *C.* 39. Compare No. 5.

(4) Fragment 46 inches long by 11 inches high. At the right hand end are the lower extremities of some undecipherable letters, corresponding (so far as they survive) to the letters of Nos. 1–3; at the left is a five-fluted pilaster like that on No. 3, and below is part of a relief of a cupid which fits on to a piece of the Four Seasons façade. Found in the spring of 1895 under the Pump Room. Inedited: mentioned by Davis in a Report of the Baths Committee, *Bath Herald*, 2 April 1895. Fig. 16, from a drawing by Mr. A. J. Taylor.

The first three of these four pieces were supposed by the earlier writers who discussed them to belong to two different inscriptions and buildings. The first and second were attributed to the frieze of the temple of Sul, and the third was set by Lysons over the doorway into a smaller temple. Subsequently Hübner assigned all three to one inscription, which he supposed to have run along the front of some large structure, presumably the temple of Sul. But the more recent discovery of the fourth piece and a careful examination of the rest of the remains of the Four Seasons façade, show that both views are wrong. It is perhaps impossible to substitute for them any certain or even probable restoration. But some details seem clear. It is, in the first place, reasonable to ascribe all four pieces to one whole. But this whole is not the frontage of the Temple of Sul, but the façade of the Four Seasons. Secondly, in this façade two parts seem to have been inscribed. One inscription (or one part of it) ran along the frieze, and to this we may assign No. 1, which is plainly part of a frieze, and No. 2, which is too long to go elsewhere. On the other hand, Nos. 3 and 4 plainly belong to an inscription which ran along the façade below the cornice and between the interpilasters. That is, the frontage bore on its frieze an inscription in two lines, and on its interpilasters a second inscription, also in two lines. Possibly enough, the lower was a continuation of the upper row, but this we cannot now determine. All we can say is that Claudius Ligur, connected with some guild (*collegium*), restored and repainted a building ruined by lapse of time, and that C. Protacius did something else connected with Sul Minerva. It is obviously most likely that this double work was the restoration of the temple of Sul.[1] It is also possible that it concerned the baths.

---

(5) Fragment showing a five-fluted pilaster and capital (as in Nos. 3, 4), and immediately to the right of it the beginnings of two lines, the rest broken off. Said to have been dug up in 1790. Now not to be found.

D
V

Englefield, *Arch.* x. 319; *C.* vii. 38A. Englefield alone gives it, and as his copies of the inscriptions are bad, I suspect it is merely an error for the left hand part of No. 3. If not, it is an additional piece of the inscription between the pilasters of the Four Seasons façade.

---

(6) Fragment 13 inches square, bearing two letters $4\frac{1}{4}$ inches tall with a moulding immediately above: found in 1790, now at the Baths. The second letter is broken, but probably M, not N.

V̄M̄

Pownall, p. 25 (reading VN), Lysons, plate iv. Interpretation is plainly impossible, but it indicates a big inscription.

---

(7) Block 28 inches long by 19 inches high, with large $6\frac{1}{4}$ inch letters. Found in the Great Bath about 1880–5.

SSIL

Again interpretation is impossible, but a big inscription is indicated. Published by Davis, *Guide to Baths*, p. 13, and *Bristol and Glos. Archaeol. Soc.* viii. 107; hence Scarth, *Arch. Journ.* xlii. 14; Watkin, ibid. p. 156; myself, *Eph.* vii. 829. Davis thinks it was part of the frieze from the top of the colonnade round the large bath.

---

[1] For the painting of temples compare the examples of Champlieu and Sens in France (Caumont. *Abécédaire*, p. 222) and *Corpus Inscr. Lat.* ii. 4085 from Tarragona.

Fig. 40. Inscription of Vespasian (No. 10).

Fig. 41. Inscription of Protacius (No. 3).

Fig. 42. Lead Pig of Hadrian (No. 47).

Fig. 43. Military Diploma (No. 43).

ROMAN INSCRIPTIONS OF BATH.

(8) Fragment, 45 inches long by 11 inches high, found in May 1878 under Abbey Passage on the east side of the reservoir which received the springs, and north of the Circular Bath. It bears the beginnings of two lines of good letters 5 inches high.

T▲
ET

Interpretation is again impossible. Rubbing in Irvine's papers at Edinburgh: drawing (without scale) by R. Mann in the Library of the London Soc. of Antiquaries; Watkin, *Arch. Journ.* xxxv. 100, xxxvi. 163.

---

(9) Fragment of a column, 13 by 13 inches, found in the Baths after 1880. Just under the moulding of the capital are two letters, 2¾ inches tall, with a break in the stone after the second.

·ΛN

Unpublished. Probably a graffito scratched by a workman or other; compare the ABCD on a column at Caerwent (*Arch.* lvii. 303).

---

(10) Fragment of plain cornice of some small monument, with return at the right hand and traces of gable above, found in the Baths at an unknown date, detected among other débris in 1903 (fig. 40): unpublished. On the frieze, in 1½-inch letters—

≡VES·VII·Co≡

imp(eratore)] Ves(pasiano) septimum co[s, 'in the seventh consulship of Vespasian, A.D. 76.' This method of designating the date by only one consul, an emperor, is not uncommon, and many examples survive from the Flavian period.[1] The abbreviation **VES** for Vespasiano is very rare, but Rostowzew quotes a leaden tessera inscribed **IMP·AVG·VES**.

The stone appears to be the earliest datable inscription of Bath, and it is to be regretted especially that the circumstances of its discovery have not been recorded.

2. *Altars to Sul Minerva* (11–17) *and other deities* (18–24).

(11) Altar 50 inches high, 22 inches wide across the inscribed face, worn but legible, found in September 1790, 12 feet below the present surface, under some houses on the east side of Stall Street which were demolished when the Pump Room was rebuilt; the fragments Nos. 1–3 and many sculptured and worked stones were found close by. Now in the Institution.

Deae Suli pro salute et incolumitate Mar(ci) Aufid[i] Maximi, 7 leg. vi vic(tricis) : Aufidius Eutuches lib(ertus) v(otum) s(olvit) l(ibens) m(erito).

'To the goddess Sul, for the health and safety of M. Aufidius Maximus, centurion of the Legio VI Victrix, erected by his freedman Aufidius Eutyches.'

The sixth legion came to Britain about A.D. 120, and was posted at York. The altar is therefore later than that date. The centurion doubtless visited Bath for its waters.

Published, *Bath Chronicle*, 23 Sept. 1790; *Gent. Mag.* 1791 (I), 103; *Bath Guide*, pp. 8–10; Collinson, *Hist. and Antiq. Somers.* i. 9; Englefield, *Arch.* x. 326; afterwards by Warner, Gough (*Adds. to Camden*, confusing it with iv. 12); Lysons, plate x. 2, Colt Hoare, *Ancient Wilts*, p. 74; Scarth, *Aquae*, p. 50; *C.* 40. The text is certain, but the earlier copies are all in some details incorrect.

---

(12) Altar 11 inches high by 21 inches wide across the inscribed face, damaged at the beginning of several lines. A companion to No. 11, and found at the same spot but later, in 1792, so far as our meagre records let us judge. Now in the Institution.

Deae Suli pro salute et incolumitate Aufidi Maximi, > leg. vi. Vic(tricis), M(arcus) Aufidiu . . . mnus libertus v. s. l. m.

'To the goddess Sul for the health and safety of Aufidius Maximus, centurion of the Legis VI Victrix: erected by M. Aufidius . . . mnus, his freedman.'

First published by R. Warner, *Illustr. of the Roman Antiq. discovered at Bath* (Bath, 1797), p. 35, and *Hist.* appendix, p. 117; hence Gough (*Adds. to Camden*, but confusing with No. 11), Lysons, xi.; Colt Hoare, *Anct. Wilts*, p. 74; Scarth, *Aquae*, p. 49; *C.* 41. The text is certain except the *cognomen* of the freedman, generally given as 'Lemnus.'

---

[1] For example *Inscr. Helvet.* 78=Wilmanns, 1584; Wilmanns, 2771, **DOM CAES II COS**. *Domitiano Caesare iterum consule* (A.D. 73).

(13) Altar 44 inches high, 14 inches wide across the inscribed face, much worn. Found in the cistern of the Cross Bath, 13 feet below street level, in 1809. Now in the Institution.

Deae Suli Minervae et numin(ibus) Aug(ustorum) C. Curiatius Saturninus,) leg. ii. Aug-
(ustae) pro se suisque v. s. l. m.

'To the goddess Sul Minerva and the deities of the Emperors, Gaius Curiatius Saturninus, centurion of the Legio II Augusta (set this up) for himself and his household.'

The Legio II Augusta was posted at Caerleon (Isca Silurum) from an early date. Saturninus presumably came thence to bathe. As the stone has **AVGG·** at the end of line 3, it may belong to a period of joint rulers, either Marcus and Verus (A.D. 161–9) or any later pair.

First published by Lysons, plate xiii. 2 ; Warner, *Bath Guide* (1811), p. 13, very badly ; Scarth, *Brit. Arch. Assoc. Journ.* xvii. 13, and *Aquae*, p. 48 ; *C.* 42. The text seems certain.

---

(14) Small altar, 25 inches high, 8½ inches wide across the inscribed face, with a square hole on the top as if for a statuette. Found in 1774 in removing rubbish from the spring of the Hot Bath near S. John's Hospital (120 yards south-west of the King's Bath), see No. 18 Now in the Institution.

Deae Suli Minervae Sulinus Maturi fil(ius) v. s. l. m.
'Set up to Sul Minerva by Sulinus, son of Maturus.'

The local guide-books (1780, p. 18, etc.), and later writers state that numerous coins dating from Nero to Pius, mostly 'second brass,' were found with the altar. But as the altar was apparently not found *in situ* but among rubbish, we cannot deduce its age from the coins. For the name of the dedicator see No. 21.

Collinson, i. 13 ; R. Warner, *Illustration*, p. 15, and *Hist.* appendix, p. 116 ; Gough, *Adds. to Camden*, i. 118 ; Lysons, plate x. 4 ; Colt Hoare, *Anct. Wilts*, p. 74 ; Scarth, *Brit. Arch. Assoc. Journ.* xvii. 13, and *Aquae*, p. 47 ; *C.* 43 ; Dessau *inscr. select.* 4660. The text seems certain.

---

(15) Fragment of a thin slab of white foreign marble, 9 inches wide by 7 inches high. Found in 1861 during additions to the Mineral Water Hospital : a tessellated floor, coins and potsherds were found at the same time (see p. 261), but this fragment seems to be a stray piece, which may have no connexion with them. Now in the Institution.

Deae S[uli] Ti(berius) Cl(audius) T[i(berii) fil(ius)] Sollem[nis . . .
'Erected to Sul by Tiberius Claudius Sollemnis, son of Tiberius . . .'

The fragment contains the beginnings of three lines of a dedication to Sul ; traces of a fourth are visible but uncertain.

First published by Scarth, *Brit. Arch. Assoc. Journ.* xviii. (1862), 302 ; *Som. Proc.* xi. 188 (with a very bad illustration) ; *Archaeological Journal*, xix. 357 ; *Gentleman's Magazine*, 1862 (ii.) 209, and *Aquae* p. 77 ; *C.* 44.

---

(16) Part of a plain dedication, 12½ inches wide by 9½ inches high by 7 inches thick, broken at the bottom. Found in February 1879 built into a wall in York Street, on the south side of the Baths, during alterations connected with the modern baths. Now in the Baths Museum.

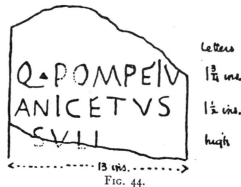

FIG. 44.

Q. Pompeiu[s] Anicetus Suli.
'Erected by Q. Pompeius Anicetus to Sul.'

A plain and humble offering, such as must have been not uncommon beside larger altars. Published *Bath Field Club*, iv. 261 ; Watkin, *Arch. Journ.* xxxvii. 136 ; Scarth, *Brit. Arch. Assoc. Journ.* xxxv. 191 ; *Eph.* vii. 828 ; myself, *Arch. Journ.* l. 283. The last line is wrongly given in all but the last-named passage.

---

(17) Plain dedication-stone, 21 inches high, 17 inches wide, and 8 inches thick, broken at the top and at the ends of the lower lines. Found near the Great Bath about 1880 : now in the Baths Museum. First published by myself, *Bulletin Archéologique*, January 1900 : hence Dessau 4661. The reading seems certain, and though something may possibly have been lost at the top, the inscription is probably almost complete.

> *Priscus Touti f(ilius), lapidariu[s], cives Ca[rnu]tenus Su[li ?] deae v. [s. l. m.*

'Priscus, son of Toutius, mason, member of the canton of Carnutes (in Gaul), to the goddess Sul (?).'

The inscription resembles that of Peregrinus (No. 20), and, like it, may belong to the first century A.D. Toutius is a Celtic name, derived from the Celtic *touta* (Irish *tuath*), 'a city' : the fact that the father has a Celtic name and the son a Latin name may point to the growing Romanization of the district in Gaul whence Priscus came (Chartres). Similar cases of a father with native name and a son with Roman name are common.[1] The contrary case, as in No. 14, Sulinus Maturi filius, is much rarer and probably denotes nothing important. Whether Priscus came to Bath in search of Bath stone or Bath waters, must remain doubtful, as in the case of Sulinus, No. 21.

Suli deae is a strange inversion of the usual order, but it is difficult to see how otherwise to complete the missing letters, unless, indeed, some local deity of the Carnutes was named here.

---

(18) Altar, 26 inches high, 10½ inches wide across the inscribed face. Found 19 July 1776, in the ruins of the Hot Bath (see No. 14). Now in the Institution. The text, which seems to me most probable, begins with six letters now lost :—

> *Dea(e) Diana(e) sacratissima(e) votum solvit Vettius Benignus l(ibens) m(erito).*
> 'To the most holy goddess Diana, Vettius Bolanus pays his vow.'

First published in the *Bath Chronicle* 25 July 1776 ; then in Collinson, i. 14 ; Warner, *Hist.* plate iii. 2 ; Whitaker, *Antijacobin*, x. (1801), 238 ; from Collinson, Gough, *Adds. to Camden*, i. 118 ; Lysons, plate xi. 4 ; Scarth, *Brit. Arch. Assoc. Journ.* xviii. 295, and *Aquae*, p. 66 ; C. 46, *Eph.* vii. 826. The earlier editors, the *Chronicle*, Collinson, Warner, Whitaker give **DEA·DIA** as the first lines of the inscription, and similarly the Rev. John Watson in 1776 read **DEA·D**. But these six letters are omitted by Lysons and all later writers, and, as we now see it, the stone begins **NA**. The six letters have been accordingly declared an interpolation of editors who could not understand **NA**. However, interpolation is unlikely in a brief contemporary note such as that of the *Chronicle*, and the top of the altar has obviously been smoothed flat at some recent time. It seems to me, therefore, fairly certain that the original commencement was **DEA·DIA**.[2] The letters which follow, **NA**, are fairly clear, though they have been read **PIA** (Lysons) and **RIA**. At the end the last letters are doubtful : **LM, LP, LPS** have all been read, and at present only **L** is discernible. But **L·M·** is the early reading, and I accept it accordingly.

The omission of the final *e* in the datives at the beginning recurs in No. 20, *Nemetona(e)*, and seems a mere barbarism.

---

(19) Top and bottom of an altar, originally perhaps about 3 feet high and 16 inches wide ; broken, weathered, hardly legible. Found in October 1871, in removing a portion of the building of the markets adjoining the Guildhall : now in the Institution, cemented together.

Published by C. E. Davis, *Proc. Soc. Ant.* v. 281 (hence *Som. Proc.* xxii. (2) 25 and C. 1351), not quite correctly. The reading of the first and last lines is certain : the rest is practically irrecoverable.

> **GENIO LOCI**
> **R.IAR...........**
> **V S L L M**

[1] See, for example, Boissier, *Afrique Romaine*, pp. 289 foll.

[2] If **DEA·DIA** be rejected, and **NA** accepted as the first letters, the only possible explanation seems *N(emesi) A(ugustae)*, as Hübner conjectures. But this abbreviation is intolerably harsh.

That is, the altar was dedicated to the genius of the place, and perhaps to other deities by some worshipper whose name is lost. The concluding formula, *v(otum) s(olvit) l(ibens) l(aetus) m(erito)*, is common enough.

---

(20) Altar, 32 inches high and 13 inches wide across the inscribed face. Found in or soon after June 1753, near the lower end of Stall Street and on its west side; afterwards in Dr. Oliver's garden, now in the Institution. No. 21 was found at the same time and place, and No. 22 at nearly the same (see fig. 48).

Peregrinus Secundi fil(ius) civis Trever, Loucetio Marti et Nemetona(e) v(otum) s(olvit) l(ibens) m(erito).

' Peregrinus, son of Secundus, member of the canton of Treveri (in Gaul) dedicates this to Mars Loucetius and to Nemetōna.'

Mars Loucetius (or Leucetius) and Nemetōna were Celtic deities, worshipped—sometimes together, as here—on the west bank of the Rhine. Peregrinus, coming from the district of the Treveri (now Trèves or Trier), was therefore paying a vow to his native gods when he set up this altar. As both he and his father bear Roman names, but not Gentile names, we may think that they lived in an age when the district of Trier was already in part Romanized but when the Roman franchise was still confined to a few. Such an age would be comparatively early in the history of the Empire, and perhaps the first century A.D. The lettering of the inscription also appears to be of an early type.[1]

J. Pettingal sent Stukeley a copy in Jan. 1754 (Stukeley's *Diaries*, iii. 182). Smart Lethieullier, Add. MS. 6181, p. 69. The text was first published by John Ward, *Philosophical Transactions*, xlix. (1755), p. 286, from a cast and readings of friends: afterwards by Collinson, Warner, Lysons (pl. xi. 2), Gough's *Add. to Camden*, and Scarth, *Brit. Arch. Assoc. Journ.* xvii. 9, *Aquae*, p. 42. The text is certain. The older writers read IOVCETIO in line 4, and explained it as *Iovi Cetio* or the like, but LOVCETIO was guessed by Grotefend (*Bonner Jahrbücher*, xviii. (1852), 243, Henzen Inscr. No. 5898, and McCaul, and is plain on the stone.

---

(21) Altar, 23 inches high, 17 inches wide and 11 inches thick, with its top hollowed as if for the pedestal of a statuette or something similar. Found with No. 20; now in the Institution.

Sulevis Sulinus scultor Bruceti f(ilius) sacrum f(ecit) l(ibens) m(erito).

' Sulinus, son of Brucetus, sculptor, erected this to the Suleviae.'

The Suleviae were a triad of probably Celtic goddesses, akin to the well-known Mother Goddesses : their monuments occur in several places in Britain and on the continent. Some writers have connected them with Sul Minerva, but Prof. Rhys declares that this view is philologically not very probable.[2]

Sulinus, son of Brucetus, is known also from an altar found at Cirencester in 1899— *Suleis Sulinus Bruceti, v. s. l. m.*, ' erected to the Suleviae by Sulinus son of Brucetus.' With this altar were found two reliefs of the Suleviae or the kindred Mother Goddesses, and ' so many other pieces of Roman stonework, some apparently new, in the sense of being unfinished or unused, as to suggest that the place in which they were found was the site of a workshop or stoneyard.' These pieces of stonework are of local Cirencester oolite, except one pedestal, which is of Bath stone.[3] It is probable, therefore, that Sulinus lived and worked at Cirencester, and visited Bath either to get Bath stone or to benefit by the waters. His name must apparently be connected with his patron saints, the Suleviae; on another Bath inscription (No. 14) it is the name of a votary of Sul.

As both he and his father bear Celtic names, we may think that, though Romanized enough to put up an altar with a Latin inscription, he had not the Roman franchise, and lived perhaps in the earlier Empire.

J. Pettingal sent Stukeley a copy in Jan. 1754 (Stukeley's *Diaries*, iii. 182). Smart Leth-

---

[1] For Leucetius and Nemetona see Holder's *Altkeltischer Sprachschatz* and Ihm in Roscher's *Lexicon*. For the phrase *civis Trever* see Mommsen in *Hermes*, xix. 28.

[2] Ihm, *Bonner Jahrbücher*, lxxxiii. 78–82 ; Siebourg, *de Sulevis* (Bonn, 1886) ; my article, *Arch. Æliana*, xv. 314–338.

[3] W. J. Cripps, *Proc. of the Soc. of Antiquaries*, xviii. 178. I have seen the inscription.

ieullier in Add. MS. 6181, p. 69. First published by John Ward, *Philosophical Transactions*, xlix. (1755), 286, from a cast and readings of friends; afterwards by Collinson, Warner, Gough's *Add. to Camden*, Lysons, pl. xi. 3; Scarth, *Aquae*, p. 52; C. 37. The text is certain.

---

(22) Altar, 35 inches high, 16 inches wide across the inscribed face. Found 29 June 1753, 5 feet underground among débris, in digging the foundation of a house in the lower part of Stall Street, outside the Baths area and not far from Nos. 20, 21. Now in the Institution (fig. 49).

Locum religiosum per insolentiam dirutum, virtuti et n(umini) Aug(usti) repurgatum reddidit
C. Severius Emeritus c(enturio) . . .(?)

'This holy spot, wrecked by insolent hands, has been cleansed and dedicated anew to the Excellence and Divinity of the Emperor, by Gaius Severius Emeritus, centurion.'

Locus religiosus means a shrine or temple, not, as Ward thought, a burial-place. The cause of its wrecking is naturally unascertainable. But the inscription may belong to the fourth century and commemorate a Pagan revival, such as that under Julian, when pagan shrines thrown down by Christians were re-erected. Two coins of Carausius (A.D. 287–293) were found under the stone, according to Stukeley, *Medallic Hist. of Carausius* (1787), i. 184, who cites the inscr. from Ward. But it does not seem to have been found *in situ*, and little stress, therefore, can be laid on their occurrence.

First published by John Ward, *Philosophical Trans.* xlviii. (1753), 332, from readings of friends; reprinted, *Universal Magazine*, xiv. (1754), 243; Cruttwell's *New Bath Guide* (ed. i. 1762), p. 9. Later, Collinson, i. 13; Warner, *Illustration*, p. 47, and *Hist.* appendix, p. 121; Gough, *Adds. to Camden*, i. 118; Lysons, plate xi. 1; Orelli, *Insc. Lat.* 2478; Scarth, *Brit. Arch. Assoc. Journ.* xviii. 296, and *Aquae*, p. 68. The text is certain, except in two details : *dirutum* might perhaps be *erutum*, and the last word, placed in small letters in a line by itself, may be read REC or PEC or the like, but is in any case unintelligible. The precise point of finding is also disputed. Ward says 'the lower end of Stall Street,' and adds that it lay among rubbish and the coins of Carausius were 4 or 5 feet lower. Others say the upper part of Stall Street, and Whitaker (*Antijacobin*, x. [1801] 239) asserts that 'as he understood from one who remembered the discovery,' it was found at the west end of the Pump Room and erect as standing in its original place. Ward's contemporary account seems however the safest guide.

---

(23) Block of stone 17 inches high, 19 inches wide, 28 inches thick, forming the lower part of a dedication and perhaps part of the base of a statuette or the like. Found in 1825 in digging the foundations of the United Hospital not far from the place where Nos. 20–22 were found in 1753; now in the Baths Museum.

. . Novanti fil(ius) pro se et suis ex visu possuit.

'. . . son of Novantius set up this . . . for himself and his family, directed by a vision.'
The name Novantius is formed like Gaudentius, Fulgentius, Amantius, Constantius, and the like, and occurs not uncommonly. *Possuit* is a variant for *posuit*, and also recurs elsewhere.

First published by Joseph Hunter, *Archaeologia*, xxii. 421 (with good illustration); then Scarth, *Brit. Arch. Assoc. Journ.* xviii. 300, *Aquae*, p. 73; C. 47. The text is certain.

---

(24) Bottom of an altar found in the Baths about 1880. Only the last letter of the last line remains.

M

This is obviously the conclusion of the regular formula *v(otum) s(olvit) l(ibens) m(erito)*. First edited by myself, *Eph.* vii. 830 and *Arch. Journ.* xlvii. 239.

3. *Tombstones of Soldiers* (25–29) *and Civilians* (30–36).

(25) Rectangular slab, 36 inches high, 26 inches wide, broken below. On the upper part is the ornament of a gable and rosette in low relief. Found before 1590 with No. 27 about a mile from the centre of Bath along the London Road. Transported with it in 1592 to a garden near Westgate, where both survived when Wood wrote in 1749. Both disappeared before Collinson wrote in 1791 (fig. 45 .

C. Murrius C. f(ilius) Arniensis Foro Iuli Modestus, mil(es) leg. ii Ad(iutricis) p(iae) f(idelis)
[c(enturia)] Iuli Secundi, ann(orum) xxv, stip(endiorum) . . . H(ic) s(itus) [e(st)].

'Gaius Murrius Modestus, son of Gaius of the tribe Arniensis born at Forum Iuli, soldier in the Legio II Adiutrix Pia Fidelis : he died aged 25, after . . . years of service (and) lies here.'

The Legio II Adiutrix was in Britain for a few years in the first century from about A.D. 70 till about A.D. 85. Tombstones of its soldiers have been found at Lincoln and in greater abundance at Chester, where it was probably quartered. Murrius was doubtless a temporary visitor to Bath, perhaps an invalid.

His birthplace and origin are involved in some obscurity. Forum Iulii was the name of at least five towns. The best known, now Fréjus in south-eastern France, was a Roman *colonia*, and provided many recruits for the legions. But the citizens of this town were normally classed in the tribe Aniensis, not in the tribe called Arnensis or Arniensis. Probably the stone-cutter has here blundered, and indeed confusions between the two names are not uncommon.[1] Even with this correction however it does not actually follow that Murrius was born at Forum Iulii. The legion to which he belonged was raised by enrolling

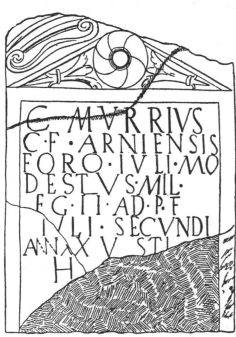

Fig. 45. Inscription 25.
(From Horsley.)

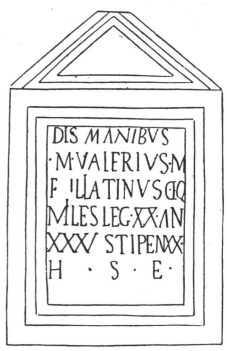

Fig. 46. Inscription 27.
(From Horsley.)

marines from the fleet in a crisis. The marines were not, as a rule, Roman citizens, and, when enlisted in the legion, had to receive the Roman franchise. With the franchise they received also a place in a tribe, and they were assigned to some Roman municipality as an official birthplace or domicile, irrespective of their natural birthplace. This presumably occurred in the case of Murrius.

First published by Camden (ed. 3, 1590) from a friend's copy and later seen by him (ed. 1600, p. 203) ; then by Thos. Johnson, *Thermae Bathonicae* (London, 1634) ; Guidott, *Appendix concerning Bathe* (London, 1669), p. 35, and *Discourse* (1676), p. 74 ; Dingley, *Hist. from Marble* (Camden Soc. 1867), i. p. xlv. ; Lister, *Philosophical Trans.* 1684, p. 457 (whence Musgrave, *Antiquitates Britanno-Belgicae*, i. 68) ; Gale, *Itin. Antonini*, p. 133 ; Horsley, p. 326 ; Stukeley, *Itin. Curiosum* (ed. 2), plate 41 ; John Wood, *Hist. of Bath* (Bath, 1749), ii. 420. Later writers depend on these, Collinson, i. 11 ; Gough, *Adds. to Camden*, i. 117 ; Scarth, *Aquae*, p. 61 ; *C.* 48, etc. The text is fairly certain. It seems from Johnson's and Dingley's accounts that there was a slight fracture before IVLI SECVNDI, and apparently also a centurial mark, and we may therefore supply the mark, as the sense requires.

[1] *Corp. Insc. Lat.* iii. 446, 14358 ; vi. 2381, 2608, 2664, 2926, 2942 ; *Notizie degli Scavi*, 1887, p. 67.

(26) Rectangular sepulchral slab with gable top, 75 inches high by 35 inches wide; in the gable is an ornament of flowers and an urn in low relief, much worn. Found in October 1708 near the London Road in Walcot, with (said Musgrave) a large and a small urn, containing ashes and bones.

Iulius Vitalis, fabricie(n)sis leg(ionis) xx V(aleriae) v(ictricis), stipendiorum ix a(n)nor(um) xxix, natione Belga, ex col(l)egio fabric(a)e elatus. Hic situs est.

'Here lies Iulius Vitalis, armourer of the Legio XX Valeria Victrix, of Belgic race, buried at the cost of the Guild of Armourers.'

Fabriciensis denotes a soldier employed in making or mending arms for the troops. Under the earlier Empire each legion had its *fabrica*: in the fourth and fifth centuries the government substituted *fabricae* in various cities chosen independently of the legions. As early as the end of the first century the armourers of the *fabricae* had begun to form guilds, and these guilds doubtless resembled the other *collegia* of the Empire, that is, they were primarily burial clubs. In the case before us, we may suppose that the *fabrica* was at Chester (Deva), the fortress of the XXth Legion; and that Vitalis, coming to Bath, perhaps for his health, died and was buried there at the cost of his guild. Various writers, English and foreign, have supposed that the *fabrica* was itself at Bath. But the *fabrica* of a legion must have been at or near its station; and Bath, having near it neither wood nor iron in abundance, was no proper place for such an institution—the alleged traces at Bromham (*Gent. Mag.* 1796, p. 472) are too far away and imaginary to boot.

Our inscription probably belongs to the second century. The evidence is not very decisive. The legionary *fabricae* seem only to have existed during the first three centuries; the *collegia* of *fabricienses* first appear about the termination of the first century; the lettering of the stone and the omission of the man's *praenomen* favour the second century, and the formula HSE at the end is commonest in the first century. The general trend of these facts favours the late first or early second century. The weighty opinion of Ritterling inclines to the later part of the second century. Jullian prefers the third century, and some English antiquaries have put it still later, but this seems to contradict definite facts which we know.[1]

The phrase *natione Belga* may denote either (as Mommsen supposes) a continental recruit from Gallia Belgica or a Briton of the tribe of Belgae. For the latter view we might cite as parallels a *civis Cantius* mentioned on a Colchester inscription and a soldier *natione Brigans* (from Yorkshire) named on a second century tombstone in Scotland. But such references to British tribes are scarce, and Britons rarely served even in the legions stationed in Britain.

First published by Thos. Hearne in his edition of Spelman's *Life of Alfred*, pp. 226–238 (Oxford, 1709) from a copy by Halley, and by Gale, *Itin. Antonini* (London, 1709), p. 134; then by Musgrave and Dodwell, *Iulii Vitalis Epitaphium* (Exeter, 1711), and *Brit. Belg. Antiq.* iv. (Exeter, 1720) (compare MS. Rawl. D 924, fol. 7, in Bodleian); Hearne, *Itin. of Leland*, viii. (ed. 1712), p. xxxii. from copies by Gale and Oddy; Horsley, *Britannia Romana*, p. 323; J. Wood, *History of Bath*, ii. 420; Stukeley, *Itinerarium Curiosum*, ed. 2, plate 41. Afterwards by Collinson, i. 7; Warner, *Illustration*, p. 1, and *History*, p. 121; Lysons, plate xii. 4; Gough, *Adds. to Camden*, i. 117; Scarth, *Aquae*, 59; Orelli, 4079; *C.* 49. The text is certain.

---

(27) Rectangular sepulchral slab, with a plain gable top, 38 inches high by 24 inches wide. Found, preserved, published and lost with the tombstone of Murrius Modestus (No. 25).

Dis Manibus M(arcus) Valerius M(arci) fil(ius) Latinus ŒQ miles leg(ionis) xx, an(norum) xxxv, stipen(diorum) xx. H(ic) s(itus) e(st).

'To the memory of Marcus Valerius Latinus, son of Marcus, CEQ, soldier in the Twentieth Legion, aged 35, soldier of 20 years' service: he lies here.'

The inscription probably belongs to the first century. That is indicated by the concurrence of such details as its shape, the formula *Dis Manibus* written out in full, the omission of the epithets *V(aleria) V(ictrix)* after *Leg. xx* and the letters H.S.E. The age of the man is probably given in round numbers, as often. It is not necessary to suppose that he enlisted at 15. The Roman military records seem to have shown the length of the man's service, but the length of his life must often have been imperfectly known.

---

[1] For the *fabricae* and their *collegia* see Jullian in Daremberg and Saglio's *Lexicon*, ii. 959; Waltzing, *Corporations Romaines*, i. 309, ii. 420, iii. 352, and the article in Pauly-Wissowa's new *Encyclopaedia*. The existence of such *collegia* in the first century is proved (as Dr. Ritterling points out) by a Carnuntum inscription, C. iii. 14358 (22). Generally, their origin is ascribed to Hadrian or even Severus.

Two points in the reading are doubtful. The letters FIL before Latinus were read variously by the early copyists: POL (Camden), ROL (Johnson), ΓΟL (Guidott), RF (Lister), RN (Dingley); Guidott (ed. 1676) and Horsley first read FIL: but, as Horsley doubted, the letters seem to have been slightly damaged. The letters after Latinus, ΟΕQ, have been so read by most copyists (CƎQ, Johnson; 6EQ, Guidott; ŒQ, Horsley CΛEQ Dingley). Probably, as Mommsen and Orelli have suggested, they may be expanded *C(olonia) Eq(uestri)* or *c(ivis Eq(uester)*, i.e. the man was born at Colonia Iulia Equestris, also called Noviodunum, now Nyon or Neuss in Switzerland. Horsley read ŒQ and interpreted it *d(ecurio) eq(uitum)*, but this is less probable (fig. 46).

---

(28) Lower part of a large sepulchral slab, 31 inches wide by 39 inches high. Found in digging the foundations for a house at East Hayes on the London Road, in Sept. 1792. Now in the Institution.

> . . . *Ser(gia tribu) A[nti]gonus Nic(opoli), emeritus ex legione xx, an(norum) xlv. H(ic) s(itus) e(st). G. Tiberinus heres f(aciundum) c(uravit).*

'(To the memory of . . .) Antigonus, of the Sergian tribe, of the town Nicopolis, time-expired soldier from Legio XX, aged 45. Erected by his heir Gaius (or Gavius) Tiberinus.'

The lettering, the formula HSE, and the omission of the usual 'Valeria Victrix' in the title of Legio XX, suggests that this may date from the first century.

Nicopolis is probably Actia Nicopolis in Epirus, founded by Augustus to celebrate his Actian victory. It was properly a Greek town. But it seems to have had a Roman municipal foundation attached—perhaps, like Lugudunum in Gaul—and it is mentioned once at any rate (*C.I.L.* iii. 7332) as a Roman *colonia*. It is not known to have belonged to the Sergian tribe. but some other municipalities established by Augustus did so belong, and there is no reason why this should not have done the same. Others have suggested Ulpia Nicopolis, founded by Trajan in Moesia not very far from the Danube. But that is not known ever to have acquired Roman municipal rights, nor can we in any way connect it with the Sergian tribe. It was also founded rather later than the end of the first century.[1]

First published *Bath Chronicle* 13 Sept. 1792; *Keene's Bath Journal*, 1 Oct. 1792; Warner, *History*, appendix, p. 122 and plate; Lysons, xii. (3); Scarth, *Brit. Arch. Assoc. Journ.* xviii. 290 and *Aquae*, p. 58, asserting incorrectly that the provenance is unknown. The text is certain, except the *cognomen* in the first line which seems to me . . . G°NVS and may have been *Antigonus*, though some faint traces of the first letter of the name looks like M as much as A.

---

(29) Lower part of a large sepulchral slab, 62 inches high by 36 inches wide: at the top are the remains of a bas-relief of a horseman riding over a fallen foe, and below is a sunk panel, 28 by 16 inches in size, bearing the inscription. Found 24 August 1736, in the old market-place, opposite the present Guildhall. Now in the Institution, joined to the upper part of a similar but rather smaller sepulchral bas-relief (27 inches high, 29 inches wide) found in Grosvenor Gardens (see fig. 48).

> *L. Vitellius Mantai f. Tancinus, cives Hisp(anus) Caurie(n)sis, eq(ues) alae Vettonum c(ivium) R(omanorum); ann(orum) xxxxvi, stip(endiorum) xxvi. H(ic) s(itus) e(st.*

'L. Vitellius Tancinus, son of Mantaius, by birth a Spaniard from Caurium, horseman in the Ala of Vettones, Roman citizens; aged 46, served 26 years. He lies here.'

Caurium was in the territory of the Vettones, in the east of the province of Lusitania. Tancinus is a common name in that district; names ending in -aius also seem not unfrequent, though Mantaius is as yet unknown. In this case the man was actually a Vettonian: in general the territorial recruiting of the *alae* and *cohortes* was imperfectly carried out.

The inscription, if we may judge by its shape and lettering, may well belong to the first century, when the *ala Vettonum* was perhaps in garrison at Y Gaer near Brecon.

Soc. Ant. Minutes, 14 Oct. and 23 Dec. 1736. First published in the *Gentleman's Magazine*, 1736, p. 622; communicated by W. Bowyer to Roger Gale in a letter dated 4 March 1738, see Bowyer's *Miscellaneous Tracts* (London, 1785), and Stukeley's *Letters*, iii. 182–191; Stukeley,

---

[1] *Corp. Insc. Lat.* iii. 6144, 7332; Mommsen, *Römische Geschichte*, v. 271, 281; Pick, *Antike Münzen Nordgriechenlands*, i. 184, 329.

Fig. 49. Altar (No. 22).

Fig. 48. Tombstone (No. 29, see also p. 265).

ROMAN INSCRIPTIONS OF BATH.

Fig. 47. Altar (No. 20).

Philosophical Transactions, 1748, p. 409 (text fairly correct, but wild emendations); Collinson, i. 12; Warner, *Illustrations*, p. 10, and *History*, appendix, p. 118; Lysons, plate xii. (1), good copy; Scarth, *Aquae*, p. 64. The text seems to be certain. Earlier editors vary principally as to the name *Mantai*, for which they give MANIAI (Stukeley), MANTANI, MANIALI, etc. The stone now has MANTΛI.

---

(30) Altar-shaped tombstone, 53 inches high, 22 inches wide across the inscribed face. Found in 1793 in or near Sydney Gardens, 4 feet underground; now in the Institution.

D(is) m(anibus) C. Calpurnius [R]eceptus, sacerdos deae Sulis: vix(it) an(nos) lxxv. Calpurnia Trifosa . . . coniunx f(aciundum) c(uravit).

'To the memory of Gaius Calpurnius Receptus, priest of Sul, aged 75. Set up by his wife . . . Calpurnia Trifosa.'

First published in the Bath Guides (1796, p. 11, etc.); then by Warner, *Illustrations*, p. 25, and *Hist.* p. 115 (incorrect); Lysons, plate xi. 3 (better); Gough, *Adds. to Camden*, i. 118 (inaccurate); Jos. Hunter, *Gent. Mag.* 1827, (i.) 392; Scarth, *Aquae*, p. 54, etc. The reading is certain except for some four or five letters between *Trifosa* and *coniunx*. Lysons read EPTE and conjectured the name Threpte; Hübner read IRᴱE and conjectured *lib(erta)et*; to me they seem LBᴣRT, *libert(a)*. The Greek female name Trifosa, that is Tryphōsa (Τρυφῶσα), was often borne, like other such Greek names, by persons of the freedman class in the Roman Empire, and therefore fits in well with *liberta*. The fact that the wife's Gentile name is the same as that of her husband also makes it not improbable that she was first his slave and subsequently his freedwoman and legal wife. It is not at all probable, on general grounds, that either a priest of Sul or his wife would be of high rank or good family.

---

(31) Fragment of a large stone, 40 inches long by 15 inches high, inscribed with two lines of 3-inch letters. As there is a blank space over the top, and the surviving words do not form the opening of the inscription, we may conclude that it was probably cut in two long lines, of which we have the middle, and ran round some funeral monument or structure more elaborate than an ordinary grave-slab. Recorded in the seventeenth century as then built into the city wall, a little west of the North Gate, with other Roman stones, but lost during the eighteenth century.

. . . dec(urio) coloniae Glev(ensis) . . . vixit an(nos) lxxx . . . ?

. . . town councillor in the municipality of Glevum . . . aged 80 . . . ?

Glevum (Gloucester) received its municipal charter as a *colonia* from Nerva (A.D. 96–8); compare *C.I.L.* vi. 336, *M. Ulpio Ner. Quinto Glevi mil(iti) fr(umentario) leg(ionis) vi victricis.* Its rank is also attested by the entry *Glebon colonia* in the Ravenna list, and by tiles stamped RPG (*respublica Glevensium*), which have been found in and near the place. The man, whose monument is partially preserved to us, was a town councillor of this *colonia* and came to Bath, probably for its waters, and died there.

Seen by Camden (ed. 5, 1600), p. 203; Guidott, *Appendix* (1669), p. 43, and *Discourse concerning Bath* (1676), p. 68; Dingley, *Hist. from Marble*, i. p. xlvi. (Camden Soc.); Lister, *Philosophical Trans. XIV.* (1684), p. 457, from friends, hence Musgrave, *Brit. Belg.* p. 68; Hearne in *Leland's Itinerary* (1712), ix. 154, from S. Gale and Thwaites, and *ibid.* (1768), ii. 68; R. Gale, *Itin. Antonini*, p. 129 (his own copy but misprinted: see MS. Rawl. D 924, fo. 7, 10 in the Bodleian); Horsley, p. 326; Stukeley (ed. 2), p. xli. Soon after Horsley saw it it disappeared, and later writers quote only from the preceding: Collinson, i. 10; Scarth, *Brit. Arch. Assoc. Journ.* xviii. 299, and *Aquae*, p. 63; *C.* 54. The numeral in the second line is doubtful. Camden read at first XXX (ed. 1600), and then LXXXVI (ed. 1607); Guidott read first LXXXVI, then LXXXVIII; Dingley, IXXXQVI; R. Gale and Horsley, LXXXQVI, and Hearne's correspondents LXXXoVI. Hübner suggests LXXX QV[INQVE, but the Q which appears in so many copies may be merely a leaf-stop ill represented in printed type. In that case VI may be the first letters of the name of the heir or other who set up the stone.

Leland (Hearne's edition, ii. 36) mentions a stone *vixit annos xxx*, which is generally taken to be this. But it is obvious from his description that it was quite a different kind of monument. See No. 36.

---

(32) Flat sepulchral slab, broken at the top, 37 inches long, 20 inches high, 4 inches thick. Found in the Borough Walls in May 1803; now in the Institution.

Rusoniae Aven[ti]nae, c(ivi) Mediomatr(icae) annor(um) lviii ; h(ic) s(ita) e(st). L. Ulpius
Sestius hvo(eres) f(aciendum) c(uravit).

'To Rusonia Aventina, by birth a Mediomatrican, aged 58. She lies here. Erected by her heir, Lusius Ulpius Sestius.'

The Mediomatrici were a Gaulish canton living round what is now Metz. The stone might well be a fairly early one, but the name Ulpius is commonest in the second century.

At the end of line 1 the stone now has AVƎNᚋ; originally it had no doubt AVƎNᛏ. The name Avenna, read by some antiquaries, is impossible.

First published *Gentleman's Magazine*, 1804 (ii.) 1006, very inaccurately; Lysons xxii, (1), fairly correctly; Scarth, *Aquae*, p. 56; *C*. 55. The text is certain, and the inscription may well be complete. For the finds of 1803 compare pp. 227, 279.

---

(33) Sepulchral slab with plain gable top, 24 inches high and broad. Found in 1809 in Upper Borough Walls near the north gate, under Cavanagh's Bank; now in the Institution.

D(is) M(anibus) Merc. Magnii alumna, vixit an(num) i, m(enses) vi, d(ies) xii.

'To the memory of Merc(atia) (?), fosterling of Magnius, aged one year, six months, twelve days.'

First published by Jos. Hunter, *Gentleman's Magazine*, 1829 (1), 31, and *Archaeologia* xxii. p. 420 (with illustration); Scarth, *Aquae*, p. 72; *C*. 57. The one doubtful point in the reading is the last letter of MERC or MERG; Hübner read G; to me it seems rather a C damaged.

---

(34) Oblong sepulchral slab, 36 inches long, 20 inches high, with a small figure in bas-relief at each end (see below). It was built up in the city wall between Northgate and Westgate in the sixteenth century, but was lost during the eighteenth century. The text is doubtful, but probably as follows :—

D(is) M(anibus) Succ(essae) Petroniae vix(it) ann(os) iii, m(enses) iv, d(ies) ix ? Vet(tius)
Romulus et Vict(oria) Sabina ? fil(iae) kar(issimae) fec(erunt).

'To Successa Petronia, aged 3 years, 4 months, 9 days; set up by Vettius Romulus and Victoria Sabina to their dearest daughter.' Successa Petronia is a mere variation on the usual order Petronia Successa, and parallels to it are not uncommon among women of what we might call the lower middle class.

First published by Camden (ed. 5, 1600), p. 204; Guidott, *Discourse* (1676), p. 70; Dingley, *Hist. from Marble*, p. 1 (Camden Soc.); Lister, *Philosophical Trans.* xiv. (1684), 457, whence Musgrave, *Brit. Belg.* p. 68; Hearne in *Leland's Itinerary* (1712), ix. 154, from S. Gale and Oddy, and (1768) ii. 63; R. and S. Gale in MS. Rawl. D. 924, fol. 7, 10 in the Bodleian; Stukeley, *Itin. Curiosum* (ed. 1, 1724), plate 49; Horsley, p. 327. Later writers depend wholly on the preceding: Scarth, *Aquae*, p. 70; *C*. 58, etc. The text is doubtful in respect of the parents' names, which are given differently in each different copy, and satisfactorily in none. How great the uncertainty is may be seen from the alternative guesses of Hübner, *Vet(tius) Romulus* or *Vepomulus* or *Pe(tronius) Omulus*. Dr. McCaul's suggestion, adopted above, seems as good as any. One would have expected the *nomen* Pet(ronius) rather than Vettius, but V seems to be supported by most copies. Certainty seems here quite unattainable.

Most copies of the inscription show two small figures in relief, one at each end of the inscribed slab, but the representations are too rude to enable us to explain them. Such supporters are of course not uncommon. But Dingley and Horsley combine to attest that these do not belong to the inscription. As the stone is lost, certainty is again not to be attained. It may be observed however that even if these figures do belong to the stone, they give no warrant for the theory of Dr. McCaul (*Britanno-Roman Inscriptions* [Toronto, 1863], p. 182) that the monument is Christian. The view is repeated by Haddan and Stubbs (*Councils and Ecclesiastical Documents*, i. 39), but there seems no reason whatever for it.

---

(35) Tombstone found in Walcot near the Bell Inn on the London Road, early in the seventeenth century; afterwards in possession of Alderman Parker, but soon lost.

First published by William Burton, *Commentary on Antoninus his Itinerary* (London, 1658), p. 262, from a MS. Latin account of Bath compiled (apparently) between 1640 and

1658; Thos. Philipot, *Villare Cantianum* (London, 1659), p. 250, imperfectly; Guidott, *Appendix* (1669), p. 40, and *Discourse* (1676), p. 72; hence later writers—from Burton, Stukeley, *Itinerarium* (ed. 2, plate 64); Collinson, i. 12; from Guidott, Musgrave, *Brit. Belg.* p. 72; Horsley, p. 328; C. 59.

There are two versions, the one of Burton, the other of Guidott.

VIBIA	VIBIA JUCUNDA
JUCUN	H·S·E·
DA	
AN XXX	
HIC SEPUL	
TAEST	

Burton's version may claim preference as the oldest; in either case we have the grave-stone of a female, Vibia Jucunda.

---

(36) Leland, in his *Itinerary* (vol. ii. [ed. Hearne], fo. 36), has the following passage :—

> I saw a Table [i.e. tablet or panel framed] having at eche ende an Image vivid and florishid above and beneth. In this Table was an Inscription of a Tumbe or Burial wher I saw playnly these words *vixit annos xxx*. The inscription was meately hole [? nearly whole] but very diffusely written, as letters for hole words and 2 or 3 Letters conveid in one.

This appears to be a fragment now lost. It differs wholly in shape and character from No. 31 above, with which it is often identified.

4. *Stone Fragments of Uncertain Significance.*

(37, 38, 39.) Three fragments, each (I think) with letters about 4 inches long, seen by Camden and others in the city walls, 37 between Northgate and Westgate and the other two between Westgate and Southgate. Like the other Roman stones in the walls, they were lost in the eighteenth century. The text of 39 is a little doubtful.

37	VRN	38	VLIA	39	LIIVSSA
	IOP		ILIA		ISVXSC

As Horsley remarks, nothing can be made of such imperfect fragments. We may think in the third to see part of the word *uxsor* for *uxor*, wife, but further conjecture seems useless. If one may judge by Dingley's drawings, it is not at all likely that the three belong together.

Camden (ed. 5, 1600), p. 204; Guidott, *Appendix*, pp. 39, 41, and *Discourse*, p. 70; Dingley, *Hist. from Marble* (Camden Soc.), i. pp. xl.–li.; Lister, *Philosoph. Trans.* xiv. (1684), 457; Stukeley, *Itin. Curiosum* (ed. 2, plate 41). Horsley, p. 328, has only 37 and 38, and cites 39 from Guidott, saying that none of the stones were legible in his time; a letter from Martin, Dec. 1730 (Gough Papers, Somerset 16 in Bodleian Library), has 38 and 39; Hearne, *Itin. of Leland* (1712), ix. 155=(1768), ii. 65 gives 39 only from Oddy and Thwaites. Later writers depend on the preceding. It seems needless to quote various readings of 39; that which I have given is supported by Lister and Martin, and the variations of other copies are slight.

---

(40) Oolite fragment, 26 inches long, 10 inches high, letters 3¼ inches tall. Found early in the nineteenth century, but the place and precise date are unknown; now in the Baths Museum. The stone breaks off in the middle of the initial S (?) and final V, and its lower edge is close to the lettering, but above there is a blank space, showing that the surviving letters had none above them.

SCORNƎIANV

This gives us the common *Cornelianu[s*, preceded probably by the final *s* of the man's *nomen*, but no more can be said as to the meaning. Published by Scarth, *Som. Proc.* iii. (1852), 108, and *Brit. Arch. Assoc. Journ.* xviii. 301 (inaccurate); and *Aquae*, p. 78; C. 60. Whether the letter before C is S or Ç has been doubted; it seems to me S.

I incline to identify with this another fragment, hitherto overlooked. This was found about 1806 (perhaps in 1803: see No. 32) in digging a foundation on the Borough Walls opposite the back gate of the Greyhound Inn, along with other Roman stones, cornices, capitals, etc. The fragment was placed in the Corporation Repository for Antiquities in Bath Street (a predecessor of the Baths Museum), and was said to be inscribed

CARNƎI V

Duffield's *Bath Guide*, n.d. (circa 1806), p. 35. The symbol ⊃ seems an attempt to reproduce the ⊒ of the stone which we actually have.

---

(41) Fragment, 15 inches high by 27 inches long, dug out at the time of the demolition of Westgate in 1776, from the foundation of Westgate House ; now lost.

Published in the *Bath Chronicle* 13 June 1776 (hence H. Lewis, *Bath Field Club*, iv. 145) ; Watkin, *Arch. Journ.* xxxvii. 145, xxxviii. 300, quoting from the papers of an eighteenth century antiquary, John Watson, who visited Bath in 1776 ; hence *Eph.* vii. 825.

AESVₒV
EₛCAN
I E N
D   M

No certain restoration is possible ; though it is natural to guess at *De]ae Su[li* in the first line. But the position of the find may suggest a tombstone.

---

(42) Masons' marks : (i.) on large blocks of stone in the wall outside the north wall of the Great Bath.

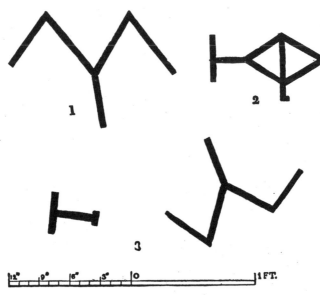

FIG. 50. MASONS' MARKS.
(Drawn by Mr. A. Taylor.)

These marks are deeply cut and large : for instance, in No. 5 the slanting strokes are 6–7 inches long, the vertical stroke 5 inches, and the extreme width of the whole 16½ inches In No. 2 the width of the whole is 16 inches, the head of the T is 4 inches long and its leg 4¾ inches long. These measurements greatly exceed those of ordinary mediaeval marks, and the stones on which they are cut may well be Roman and do not seem to have any signs of mediaeval date. They may therefore find a place here.

(ii.) A stone bearing a similar mason's mark, a large T, was found under the United Hospital (p. 262). A photograph is among Irvine's papers.

5. *Small Inscribed Objects, not being of Stone.*

(43) Fragment of a bronze plate, 1⅞ inches high and wide, inscribed with a military diploma (certificate of citizenship and other privileges) given to a discharged auxiliary soldier. Found in Walcot in 1815, probably about the same time and place as many other Roman remains, including an inscribed fibula (No. 49) ; first in the collection of Mr. Cranch, now in the museum at Huntingdon. I am indebted to the authorities of that museum for lately lending it me to examine carefully.

Noticed by Lysons, *Archaeologia*, xviii. 438 (hence Mommsen, c. iii. p. 901), but without the full text. Published, from a facsimile made by Lysons, by Watkin, *Arch. Journ.* xxxiii.

250, xxxiv. 318, xxxv. 72 ; from other tracings from the original, by J. C. Bruce, *Archaeologia Aeliana*, viii. 219, and Watkin, *Arch. Journ.* xxxvii. 141 ; from Bruce, Mowat, *Bulletin Épigraphique*, iii. 24, 309 ; from personal inspection by myself, *Eph.* vii. p. 341 and below. The text given below is, I think, fairly certain, as I was able to clean the bronze; it differs in one or two details from *Eph.* (fig. 43).

Inside Text.   *Outside Text.*

I N ET IITE
ITANNSVBP
RIBVSVESTIPE
EST·MISSIONE
ITIPSISLI

E STCIVITASII
VMFISQVASPOST
VLISINGVLAS
·VII· K· OCTOBR
TILARTIDIOCELE
RPROCVLEIANCVIP
PINQVOS
ALE

From the known formulae of these certificates we can restore the general tenor thus—[Imperator Caesar . . . equitibus et peditibus qui militaverunt in alis . . . et cohortibus . . . quae appellantur . . .] et iii e[t iv . . . et sunt in Br]itann(ia) sub P(?) . . . [quinis et vicenis plu]ribusve stipe[ndiis emeritis, dimissis hon]est(a) mission[e, quorum nomina subscripta sun]t, ipsis li[beris posterisque eorum civitatem dedit, et conubium c]um uxo[ribus quas tunc habuissent cum] est civitas ii[s data, aut si qui caelibes essent c]um iis quas post[ea duxissent, dumtaxat sing]uli singulas.

a.d.] vii K(alendas) Octobr(es . . . Ti. Lartidio Cele[re cos.
[alae i Aug. Gallo]r(um) Proculeian(ae) cui p[raeest . . .] Propinquos
. . . [ex grega]le . . .

That is, some Emperor, whose name is lost, granted in the usual fashion, to time-expired soldiers of auxiliary regiments in Britain, the franchise for them and their children and the right of legal marriage, provided they practised monogamy. This grant was made on the 25th of September in the consulship of Lartidius Celer (year unknown), and this particular certificate is in favour of a soldier serving in the ranks of the Ala I Gallorum Proculeiana under . . . Propinquos. Apparently the auxiliaries were discharged in large drafts, often with little heed to their having served too long. An imperial edict conferred the privileges above mentioned to all those discharged at any one time, and each soldier received a bronze copy of the edict, bearing in addition his name, rank, and so forth. The man now in question may have decided to settle at Bath after receiving his discharge, and hence it may be that his certificate is found there.

The date of the document can only be roughly ascertained. The lettering, if we compare it with other specimens, does not suit any earlier date than the latest part of the first century, and may well be later still. The phrasing *pluribusve stipendiis* first occurs about A.D. 80, and is common only in the second century ; on the other hand, the mention of *liberi posterique* ceases about A.D. 140. The Ala Proculeiana is known from another certificate found in 1879 at Chesters on Hadrian's Wall and dated A.D. 146, and we may well suppose that our Walcot diploma was issued in the first half of the second century.

M. Mowat argues from the spelling Propinquos, for Propinquus, that we should refer the diploma to a time near that of Claudius, who loved archaic spellings and made them fashionable. But -*uos* occurs not seldom on second century inscriptions, and is no proof of early date.[1] M. Mowat also attempts to identify the commandant of the Ala Proculeiana with a Pompeius Propinquus, procurator of Gaul, about A.D. 69, who had previously in all probability commanded an ala. This would be plausible, if only the dates fitted.

---

(44) Thin leaden plate, $2\frac{11}{16}$ inches square and $\frac{1}{20}$ inch thick, with eight lines of letters on it. Found 31 March 1880, in the great Roman reservoir under the King's Bath (p. 250), and near

---

[1] Ostia, Primitivos in A.D. 140 and 192 (*C.* xiv. 246, 251) ; Bovillae, Lascivos, A.D. 169 (*C.* xiv. 2408) ; Berytus, Ingenuos, about A.D. 200 (*C.* iii. 158) ; Aquincum, Genetivos, A.D. 189 (*C.* iii. 3494) ; Dacia, Primitivos, second century (*C.* iii. 1264).

the floor of the reservoir, 15 feet below the present water surface of the King's Bath. The inscription on it is written backwards; parts of the first four lines are uncertain (fig. 51).

Q(ui) mihi Vilbiam [?] involavit [?] sic liquat ⟨c⟩ com aqua ella [mu]ta ni q(ui) eam . . . l-vavit: Vinna vel(?) Exsupereus, [V]erianus, Severianus, Agustalis, Comitianus, Catusminianus, Germanill[a], Iovina.

'May he who carried off Vilbia (?), waste away like that dumb water, save only he who . . . her. (It may be) Vinna or Exsupereus or Verianus or Severianus or A(u)gustalis or Comitianus or Catusminianus or Germanilla or Iovina.'

The object is a curse on some one unknown, who offended the writer of the tablet. It was inscribed backwards, so that if discovered it should not be understood or counteracted, and was thrown into the fountain of Sul so that the goddess might learn of her votary's wrong and fulfil the curse. And, as the offender's name was unknown, various suspected persons are mentioned. Thus much is clear, and it is well in accordance with the practice of ancient life. Many instances are known in which wronged men or women in antiquity have inscribed their wrongs and prayers for revenge on tablets of some kind and laid them before a deity

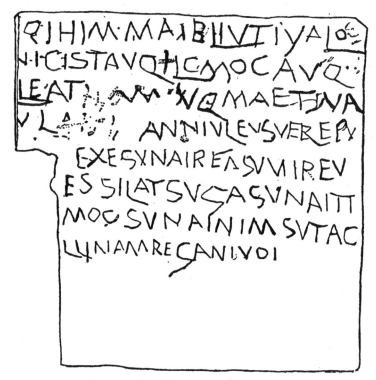

FIG. 51. THE BATH CURSE (No. 44), ¼
(Slightly altered from Zangemeister's Copy.)

deemed potent to punish. Thus, a hot spring near Arezzo has yielded a leaden tablet 3½ by 4¾ inches in size, thus inscribed :—

Q. Letinium Lupum, qui et vocatur Caucadio, qui est filius Sallusties Veneries sive Venerioses, hunc ego aput vostrum numen demando devoveo desacrifico, uti vos, Aquae ferventes, sive vos Nimfas sive quo alio nomine voltis adpellari, uti vos eum interematis interficiatis intra annum (C. xi. 1823).

Unfortunately several points remain obscure in the Bath tablet. Even the offence denounced is uncertain. Zangemeister, the decipherer of the bulk of the tablet, read not Vilbiam (**MAIBLIV**), as given above, but **MATELIV(M)**, that is *mantelium*, tablecloth. He supposed that the author of the curse had lost a tablecloth, and to make the fact plain to the goddess of the fountain, had written the one word which stated this, forwards instead of backwards. But the consensus of those who have seen the tablet favours the reading **MAIBLIV**, and after examining the object twice myself I can decipher nothing else. The name Vilbia, it is true, seems not to occur elsewhere. But it is no impossible name, and a woman unquestionably suits the situation better than a tablecloth.

Other obscurities beset the names of the suspected, whether *Vinna vel* or *Velvinna* should be read, whether *Exsupereus* or *exsuper e(i)us*, 'besides him,' and so forth. But for these it may be better to refer the reader to Prof. Zangemeister's elucidation. Anything like a full commentary would exceed even the tolerant limits of this work.

First published, Davis, *Bath Herald*, 24 April 1880; first adequately explained, Zangemeister, *Hermes*, xv. 588 (hence *Eph.* vii. 827), translated in a pamphlet, *Inscribed plate found beneath the Baths*, issued on behalf of the Bath Corporation. I may be excused from recalling to mind the strange errors of some who first attempted the decipherment. Audollent, *Defixionum Tabulae* (Paris, 1904), No. 104, adds nothing to the interpretation.

---

(45) Another tablet covered with scratches was found at the same time as the preceding. It has been recently examined by Mr. E. W. B. Nicholson, and a reading set forth in his paper, *Vinisius to Nigra* (London, 1904). I have carefully examined the tablet with this paper in my hand, and I regret to be altogether unable to accept the interpretation given in it. Whether the scratches on the tablet represent letters at all may be doubted, but so far as I can read them into letters, they do not correspond with Mr. Nicholson's decipherment. Compare *Revue Archéologique*, series iv. vol. 5 (1905), p. 448. The Baths have also yielded a leaden strap, now in the Baths Museum, bearing scratches which have not been deciphered, but may be letters.

---

(46) Medicine stamp of greenish stone, found in 1731 in a cellar in the Abbey yard, now lost. Inscribed on four sides with the labels of one T. Iunianus. Now lost. The Society of Antiquaries has casts, which seem to me to read as follows :—

1. T·IVÑANI·THALASSER
   AD CLARITATEM

   T. Iuniani, thalasser(os) ad claritatem.

2. T·IVNIANIPHOEBVMADQV
   ⁊ECVMQDELICTAAMEDICIS

   T. Iuniani phoebum ad qu[a]ecumque delicta a medicis.

3. T·IVNIANI·DIOXVM
   ADVETERESCICATRICES

   T. Iuniani dioxum ad veteres cicatrices.

4. T·IVNIANICRSOMAEL
   INMAD CLARITATEM

   T. Iuniani c(h)r(y)somaelin(u)m ad claritatem.

Minutes of the Soc. of Antiquaries, i. 289 (20 April 1732, stating that the stamp was found 'just outside the west gate'), iv. 210=13 Dec. 1744, and viii. 29=17 Nov. 1757; Gough, *Archaeol.* ix. (1789), 228: hence all later writers, including *C.* vii. 1318 and Espérandieu, *Signacula Medic. Oculariorum* (Paris, 1905), No. 175 (reprint from *C.* xiii. [3], 2). All the drugs occur on other stamps, except *Phoebum*, which, I suppose, must mean the 'bright' medicine or (it may be) the medicine of Phœbus Apollo.

---

(47) Pig of lead measuring 24 inches in length and 6 inches in width along the base, and weighing 195 lb. Found near Sydney Place, but above the canal, in 1809 (not in 1822); now at the Institution.

Jos. Hunter, *Archaeologia*, xxii. 421; Phelps, *Hist. and Antiq. of Somers.* i. 161 (inaccurate); Scarth, *Somers. Proc.* iii. (1852), 108; A. Way, *Archaeological Journal*, xvi. 34; Yates, *Somers. Proc.* viii. (1) 15; *Corp. Insc. Lat.* vii. 1209*d*. See fig. 42.

IMP·HADRIANI·AVG

Probably, as Scarth observed, from the Mendip mines, see p. 340. An iron key, found with the pig, is also preserved still at the Institution.

---

(48) Lead pipe, copied by Hübner (*Corp. Insc. Lat.* 1266) in the Institution about 1868. Found in 1825 at the south-west corner of Queen's Bath near junction of York Street and Stall Street—that is, *in* the Baths. Now in Baths Museum. It has raised letters in label, the letters 1⅞ inches high, the label 6⅜ by 2⅜ (including rim).

LDA

Probably the initials of maker or owner.

---

(49) Bronze fibula found, with many other remains in Walcot in the summer of 1815 (*Bath and Cheltenham Gazette*, 20 Nov. 1816); now lost. Said to read

TARRAS

Probably the name of maker or owner. We may compare a fibula found in Etruria (*C.* xi. 6719) marked ᴀRRIC.

(50) Fragment of glass, now in the Institution, apparently the bottom of a bottle, with an inscription in a circle on it. Unpublished.

.. RI ..

Possibly part of the stamp *Patrimonium* or *P. Atri Monimi ?*) , which occurs on glass found in Britain at York (*Eph.* vii. 1155), and at Densworth near Chichester (*C.* 1276), and abroad at various places for instance in the south of France (*C.* xii. 5696, 19).

---

(51) Samian stamps found in Bath.

No proper list has ever been made of the potters' marks on Samian ware found in Bath. The following is only a commencement of such a list, and is probably imperfect to a serious degree. It is, however, the best that I can compile at the moment.

ALBVCI—Mineral Water Hospital, 1859; Scarth, *Aquae*, p. 94; Institution.

AVENTINI · M—Institution.

CAITANI M.—Walcot; *Bath and Cheltenham Gazette*, 31 Jan. 1855.

OF CALVI—Near the north end of the Cleveland Bridge, Nov. 1867.

CAMVLINI—Baths (embossed second century ware).

CARANTINIM—Baths (ditto). Also Mineral Water Hospital, 1859; Scarth, *Aquae*, p. 94.

CARASIVS—Riding School near Christ Church; *Bath and Chelt. Gazette*, 11 Dec. 1856.

CASSI—Scarth, *Aquae*, p. 94.

CORNERTI M.—Ditto (read *Cobnerti*).

CVCAI · M—Institution. Broken at the beginning.

DECMIM—Institution.

DIOGIINIIƧ—That is, Diogenes; Institution, given 1857.

HABILIS · M—Found by J. T. Irvine under the Abbey in 1863–72.

MAMM—Institution.

MARITIVMIM—Ladymead, 1904; shown me by Mr. W. Gill.

MARTI—Russell Street, 1852; *Bath and Chelt. Gazette*, 31 Jan. 1855; *Illustr. London News*, 10 Feb. 1885.

MINIRIV—Scarth, *Aquae*, p. 94. Misread.

MVXIVLIIM—Found by Irvine under the Abbey (read *Muxtulli. m.*).

MF.OLIVI—Scarth, *Aquae*, p. 94. Misread.

OF NIG—Ditto.

OF MODE—Ditto.

PAVLLI · M—Institution.

PECVLIAR—Guinea Lane, 1854; *Bath and Chelt. Gazette*, 31 Jan. 1855; *Illustr. London News*, 10 Febr. 1855.

POTENTI...—Institution.

PRIWL—Institution.

PRITANI—Scarth, *Aquae*, p. 94.

QVINTIM—Russell Street (as MARTI).

SILVI OF—Scarth, *Aquae*, p. 94; Institution.

SOLE... *Ibid.*

OF · STVLP—Institution. The F is placed inside the O.

SVOBNEDOF—Guinea Lane, 1854 (as above).

SVOBNI · M—Institution.

TINT...—Found by Irvine under Abbey. Misread.

TITVR · OF—Scarth, *Aquae*, p. 94.

VERECVNNI—St. Andrew's Church, 1870 (read *Verecundi*).

VITAI—Institution.

Hübner attributes to Bath also REGINI · M. But the instance which he quotes was really found in Exeter (*Gent. Mag.* 1834 (ii.), 41).

APPENDIX

The following, often included among the inscriptions of Bath, have no proper place there.

(52) Bronze oval medallion, showing a female head with a jewelled frontlet on the forehead, facing to right, and in front of the face the inscription—

POMPEIA · I · C · V

Pompeia I(uli) C(aesaris) u(xor).

Picked up by a workman during the building of the Pump Room in 1790, and accepted by Warner, Whitaker, Scarth and others as Roman. But, as Hübner has pointed out, it is unquestionably modern, probably of the eighteenth century; the style of the head, the shape of the letters, and the character of the inscription, are all against it. First published by Warner, *History*, appendix, p. 123, with illustration; Whitaker, *Antijacobin*, x. (1801), 347; Scarth, *Aquae*, p. 84; *Som. Proc.* iii. (2), 110; *C.* vii. 2*.

(53) Tile, now in the Institution (No. 17), inscribed

Hübner (*C.* 1252), who gives a bad copy of this, ascribes its origin to Bath. Mr. Winwood has kindly looked up the Institution records for me, and tells me that it was found at Berkeley in Gloucestershire in 1865. I have seen a precisely similar tile at Berkeley, built into the south side of the choir screen (compare *Intellectual Observer*, vii. 312; *Brit. Arch. Assoc. Journ.* xxi. 234; *Eph.* iii. p. 142, No. 123). What exactly the letters mean, I do not know.

(54) Hübner, *Ephemeris*, iii. p. 114, mentions an inscription relating to the *ala Proculeiana*. This is the 'diploma' described above (No. 43).

9. UNINSCRIBED OBJECTS IN STONE

There remain to be described several objects in stone which have not found a place in the preceding lists because either their provenance or their character is obscure. These include a few pieces of carved stone which are still preserved, and others known to us only from earlier writers. They are necessary to complete the general picture of Aquae Sulis, though they cannot be definitely assigned to any one aspect or part of it.

(1) A colossal head of a woman, with her hair dressed in the style that obtained favour under the Flavian emperors, that is, in the last quarter of the first century. It is considerably over life size, and a statue on the same scale would stand at least 8 feet high. It was found in 1714 or 1715 'when ye way was mended were Walcot ajaunt to the City of Bath,' and was given to Dr. Musgrave of Exeter. After a long sojourn there, it has now returned to Bath. It may be a sepulchral bust of the first century.[1] Front view, fig. 52.

(2) A block of stone, 30 inches high by 18 inches wide and 10 inches deep was dug up in September, 1885, at the Cross Bath, nearly 20 feet underground (fig. 54). It is carved on three sides (the fourth is broken). On the shortest side is a snake coiled round a tree, and on one of the larger sides a dog standing beneath a tree. The other larger side has what seems to be the principal scene. On the left stands an undraped erect female figure; opposite her reclines a young man, draped across the knees, holding out a hand to draw her to him; above is an indistinguishable animal and a tripod. The precise reference of the scene is obscure. Professor Sayce, connecting the dog and snake with Aesculapius, conjectured that the two chief figures are meant for Apollo and Corōnis, mother of Aesculapius. In any case the piece seems to be of the same type as the well-known marriage of Zeus and Hera on a Selinus metope. Why it should have been found in the Cross Bath is not clear. Major Davis states that with it were found the walls of the Roman well and another altar, of which nothing else seems recorded. Mr. Scarth says that many coins were also dug up. It may be that the springs which now feed the Cross Bath, then merely bubbled up in a stone-girt fountain, that this monument decorated the well-head or its surroundings, and that the coins were thrown in by worshippers.[2]

---

[1] Gough, Maps 28, p. 56 (in Bodleian Library); Musgrave, *Brit. Belg* (Exeter, 1719), i. 212; Horsley, p. 329; Collinson, i. 14; Warner, *Illus.* p. xxvi. and *Hist.* p. 29; Scarth, *Aquae*, p. 27. The idea that the head represents Julia Domna is wrong. Now in the Baths Museum. The note in Gough's papers is the sole (and hitherto unpublished) record of its precise provenance.

[2] *Bath Herald*, 12 Sept. 1885; Winwood, *Bath Field Club*, vi. 79, with photographs; Scarth, *Proc. Soc. Ant.* xi. 104; Davis, *Guide*, p. 40. For another possible parallel to the main scene, see *Arch. Epigraphische Mitteilungen*, x. 222. The stone is now in the Baths Museum.

(3) A broken relief of a dog carrying a roe-deer over his back, found about 1860 under the foundations of a house on the London Road in Walcot, near the line of the Roman Fosse Way. The piece has some merit of vigour. It may possibly have adorned a tomb.[1]

(4) Headless and footless effigy of a man, possibly a military standard-bearer, 24 inches wide. Origin unknown; it resembles a piece figured in the *Gentleman's Magazine* (1804, ii. 1006), as found in May 1803 in the Upper Borough Walls with other Roman remains. See fig. 53.

(5) Some pieces seen by Leland, Camden, Guidott, Dingley, and Horsley in the city walls. Leland's own account of them is as follows :—

> There be divers notable Antiquitees engravid in Stone that yet be sene yn the Walles of Bathe betwixt the South Gate and the Weste Gate : and agayn betwixt the West Gate and the North Gate. (1) The first was the antique Hed of a man made al flat and having great Lokkes of Here as I have in a Coine of C. Antius. (2) The Secunde that I did se bytwene the South and North Gate was an Image, as I tooke it, of Hercules : for he held yn eche Hand a Serpent. (3) Then I saw the Image of a foote man *vibrato gladio et prætenso clypeo.* (4) Then I saw a Braunch with Leves foldid and wrethin into Circles. (5) Then I saw ij. nakid Imagis lying a long, the one imbracing the other. (6) Then I saw to antique Heddes with Heere as roselid yn Lokkes. (7) Then I saw a Grey-Hound as renning, and (8) at the Taile of hym was a Stone engravid with great *Romane* Letters, but I could pike no sentence out of it. (9) Then I saw another Inscription, but the Wether had except a few Lettres clere defacid. (10) Then I saw toward the West Gate an Image of a man enbracid with 2 Serpentes. I took it for Laocoon.

> Betwixt the Weste and the North Gate.

> (11) I saw 2 Inscriptions, of the wich sum wordes were evident to the Reader, the Residew clene defacid. (12) Then I saw the Image of a nakid Man. (13) Then I saw a stone having *cupidines et labruscas intercurrentes.* (14) Then I saw a Table having at eche Ende an Image vivid and florishid above and beneth. In this Table was an Inscription of a Tumbe or Burial wherin I saw playnly these wordes : *vixit annos xxx.* This Inscription was meately hole but very diffusely written, as Letters for hole Wordes, and 2 or 3 Letters conveid in one. (15) Then I saw 2 Images, wherof one was a nakid Manne grasping a Serpent in eche Hand, as I tooke it : and this Image was not far from the North Gate.

The relics gradually disappeared after Leland's time. Camden saw all of them except the inscriptions 11 and 14. Guidott saw many, which he figures on a plate not worth reproduction. But Dingley records only five; Gale in 1705 saw only seven or eight, Horsley and Wynter saw only two or three, and none survived the demolition of the walls in the middle of the eighteenth century. Detailed criticism of these remains seems unadvisable. The existing accounts of them are scanty, and the accompanying illustrations neither accurate nor drawn to scale. They must be taken as they have come down to us, as badly recorded examples of the Roman sculptures and carvings of Aquae Sulis.[2]

10. COINS

The Roman coins found in Bath have been of necessity recorded casually and imperfectly. A list of those known to me would, I think, serve no good purpose. But it may be well to point out that such a list would cover the whole four centuries of Roman Britain.

It would begin at an early date. Many coins of the first emperors and even a few of the Republic have been unearthed in Bath. The list of coins secured for the Corporation in 1879–98,[3] found principally in the baths, includes some 250 legible specimens, and of these 7 belong to Caesar and to the Republic, 3 to Augustus and Tiberius, 3 to Claudius, 7 to Nero, 10 to Vespasian. The Republican coins are perhaps in part survivals, for some of them may have been in circulation at any period in the first two centuries of the Empire.[4] But their number seems to indicate that Bath was inhabited, if not by Romans, at least by Britons, quite early in the first century. And equally the number of coins of Claudius, Nero and Vespasian indicates an early Roman occupation.

[1] Scarth, *Aquae*, p. 35 and plate ix. Now in the Institution.
[2] Leland (ed. Hearne, 1711), ii. fo. 35, Camden (ed. 1600), p. 203. Guidott, *Discourse of Bathe* (London, 1676), p. 72 and plate; Dingley, *Hist. in Marble* (Camden Soc.), i. p. xlvi.–li. with drawings; Horsley, p. 328; S. Gale, *Reliquiae Galianae*, ii. 1, p. 18; John Wynter, *Of Bathing in Bath* (London, 1728), pp. 10–11. Musgrave *Brit. Belg. Antiq.* (Iscae 1719), i. p. 70 repeats Guidott's plate.
[3] Report by E. C. Davey.
[4] Such is the denarius of Mark Antony (LEG. III). Compare *Archaeologia*, liv. 490.

FIG. 52. COLOSSAL HEAD OF FLAVIAN EPOCH (p. 285).
(From a Photograph. Scale about 1 : 5.)

FIG. 53. STANDARD-BEARER'S (?) EFFIGY (p. 286).
(From a Photograph. Scale about 1 : 13.)

Fig. 54. Monument found at the Cross Bath, 1885 (p. 285).
(From Photographs. Scale about 1 : 9.)

Similar evidence occurs elsewhere. The finds made in 1867–9 on the site of the White Hart (p. 231) included a bronze coin of Agrippa and another of Antonia Drusi. The finds at the Walcot Brewery in 1815 included 1 Augustus, 1 Claudius, 2 Nero, 1 Vespasian, all second bronze. A burial in the same neighbourhood contains a Republican issue B.C. 46. Guidott, writing to Aubrey as to coins found between 1665 and 1690, states that a triumviral coin of Antony occurred, and coins were common from Vespasian onwards.

In general, all periods of the Empire from Nero onwards seem to be fairly represented. But it has been noticed that the coins found in the baths fall into two chief groups. The earlier comprises coins of Nero, the Flavians, Trajan and Hadrian (A.D. 54–138). The latter comprises the fourth century. This may be due to accident, or to special incidents in the history of Bath that are not known to us. For, in general, second century coins are common in Britain, and the ' third brass ' of the middle of the third century overflow. Abundance of fourth century issues is, however, nothing strange.

The list of coins goes down to the end of the Empire. Magnus Maximus, Honorius, Arcadius are all represented, and it is plain that Bath was inhabited right up to the end of the Roman period.

Few hoards have been discovered—or at least recorded. In 1826 a metal pot holding half a peck of copper coins, Constantine and earlier, was found at the north end of Bathwick Street in the building of Cleveland Bridge.[1] In 1816 a packet of about 100 denarii is said to have been found near St. Swithin's Church on the west side of Trinity Court, Walcot, and to have contained 6 coins of Antony, 15 Republican, 1 Brutus, 1 Lepidus and Augustus, 5 Nero, 28 Vespasian, 2 Titus, 15 Domitian, 13 Nerva and 6 Trajan.[2] A third hoard is said to have been found near St. Swithin's Church in 1807, and to have comprised two rouleaux of 70 or 80 small silver coins, Roman, Numidian, and Carthaginian—'none later than the earlier Cæsars'. But this appears to have been a fraud of a Bath coin dealer.[3]

11. OTHER SMALL OBJECTS

In the preceding paragraphs we have described numerous and remarkable remains of sculpture and inscriptions. We might expect to meet in Bath an equal wealth of smaller uninscribed objects—pottery, fibulae, and the like. In reality, few have been recorded or preserved. The gems and pewter vessels discovered in the Baths and noticed above (p. 251) stand almost alone. Of other objects, whether found in the Baths or outside them, the list

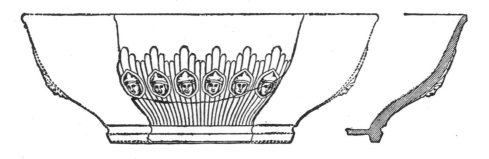

FRONT VIEW   SECTION

FIG. 55. SAMIAN BOWL, FOUND IN THE BATHS. (½)
(From a drawing by Mr. A. J. Taylor.)

is short and its details are somewhat insignificant. (1) The pottery includes much Samian, and among it embossed bowls of the first as well as of later centuries (Dragendorff, shapes 29, 30, 37). But Castor ware is scarce, and of the whole ceramic discoveries only two pieces demand individual comment. One is a Samian bowl from the Baths, adorned in a fashion to which I know no parallel (fig. 55). The other, found in the Sydney Gardens in 1828, is a cup of red paste, glazed black

1 *Gent. Mag.* 1826, ii. 160.
2 *Bath and Chelt. Gazette,* 20 Nov. 1816 ; *Aquae,* p. 98.
3 *Gent. Mag.* 1807, i. 269 ; Hunter, *Somers. Proc.* iii. (2) 109, whom I take to be referring to this plainly bogus hoard.

and decorated with a raised leaf pattern after a usual Samian fashion.[1] (2) Bronze objects are less common. Scarth, in his *Aquæ* (p. 85, pl. 35), can cite only one statuette of the class sometimes styled Penates, two keys, a spoon from Cheap Street, a couple of rings, a couple of armlets, and three or four fibulae, one of which shows the 'crossbow' pattern and belongs to the late third or the fourth century.[2] (3) Glass is even rarer, though a few good pieces have been found. This scarcity of smaller objects may be due in part to the continuous habitation of the site since Saxon times. In part, too, we may blame the carelessness of former antiquaries. Finds have been, doubtless, ill-recorded and collections made in Bath have been rapidly scattered. But this does not account for the whole of the scarcity. We can hardly resist the conclusion that, after all, Roman Bath was a small town. It contained little beyond its Baths and Temple. It owed its prosperity and its population largely to its visitors. The smaller finds thus confirm the verdict which our other evidence would lead us to pass. Roman Bath was before all things a spa.

[1] Scarth, *Aquæ*, plate xxxvii.; now in the British Museum.

[2] The British Museum has a charming silver fibula of crossbow pattern, decorated round the bow with an inlaid niello 'wave-pattern.' It was found long ago near St. James' churchyard, and is apparently the fibula mentioned by Scarth. The seated 'Lar' figured by Scarth was found in 1824–5 in Borough Walls. Another bronze 'Lar' of 'very beautiful design' was found in Monmouth Street and once belonged to Mr. Stradling of Chilton Polden (*Arch. Journ.* ix. 106). I may mention here a larger bronze object, a head of Diana (?), found according to Spry (p. 16) 'at the discovery of the Roman Baths,' that is, in 1755. It was in his time in the possession of Mr. Barker of Sion Hill, Bath: afterwards, apparently, it belonged to Mr. Smyth Pigott of Brockley Court (*Som. Proc.* ii. (1) 11), but I do not know its present home. It is described as being 'large and beautifully formed,' and does not deserve oblivion.

PART III.

1. CAMERTON

About six miles south of Bath the Fosse Way runs for more than two miles along a lofty plateau just 500 ft. above sea-level, which divides the Dunkerton and Radstock valleys. On the southern edge of this plateau, immediately above Radstock and close to the hamlet of Clan-

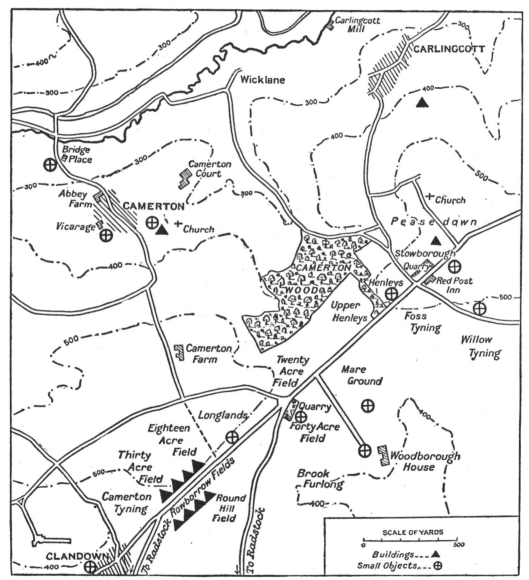

FIG. 56. THE NEIGHBOURHOOD OF CAMERTON.

down, in the parish of Camerton, is a spot beside the Roman road which has yielded remarkable remains (fig. 56). It is first mentioned, as it seems, by Collinson about 1790, who records briefly a tessellated pavement and coins[1] in this neighbourhood. It was explored in 1814 and succeeding

[1] Collinson, i. 102 (coins of Hadrian and Antoninus); iii. 329 (tessell).

years by the Rev. John Skinner, rector of Camerton from 1800 to 1839. It is still marked by Roman potsherds and tiles that lie about the fields, as I found when I visited the spot. But substantially all that we know of it is due to Skinner, and is contained in his papers and diaries. Skinner was an enthusiastic and industrious worker. But he seems to have been impulsive and unmethodical ; he had received no proper archaeological training, and his imagination not seldom ran away with his natural powers of observation. It is therefore difficult to extract from his materials any precise account of his finds, or to deduce any certain estimate of their significance. It would seem, however, that he discovered parts of a small village, and possibly also a local shrine which was regarded as holy both before and during the Roman period.[1]

The chief scene of his labours was in some fields beside the Fosse, north-east of Clandown, near the Round Hill tumulus. These fields were and still are called Thirty Acre Field, Eighteen Acre Field (these two now one field), and Longlands, on the north side of the Fosse, and Rowbarrow on the south side. The principal finds were made in Eighteen Acre Field. In total they consisted of a very uncertain number of small houses or other buildings, estimated by Skinner at eighteen, and many interesting lesser objects. The largest house, excavated in 1814–5, faced the Fosse, standing about 150 feet north of it, and contained five rooms and a semicircular open yard, of which the outline can best be gathered from fig. 57. It is not a normal outline, or one to which I can quote any precise

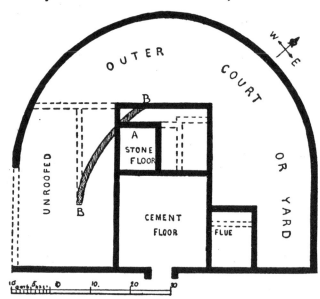

FIG. 57. LARGER HOUSE, EXCAVATED 1814–5.
(From Skinner.)

[1] Skinner himself published little. He communicated some details to *Gent. Mag.* 1827 (i.) 252, to *Omnium Gatherum*, i. (1814), 29 ; and to Phelps (pp. 151, 179). But most of his finds have to be collected from his papers. Of these, one volume, of no great importance for our present purpose, is in the Institution at Bath, and the bulk—100 volumes—in the British Museum ; see especially Add. MSS. 28794–5 and 33659–33665. Among the Museum volumes are more or less identical drafts for a comprehensive account and their illustrations, which want of health or of method prevented him from finishing. I have examined these volumes so far as time permitted, and hope to have selected the most important details. Some small part has been already published from Add. MS. 28974, or elsewhere, in *Som. Proc.* xi. (2) 174 and xxx. (1) 103. The objects found during the excavations are in part in Bristol Museum, but many seem to have disappeared. I may add that Skinner evolved a theory that his discoveries belonged to the ancient Camulodunum. This extraordinary view was combated at the time by Skinner's correspondent, Sir R. Colt Hoare, in a pamphlet issued 1827. In the following paragraphs I have taken no notice of it. A furthur account of Skinner may be found in the *Bath Field Club Proceedings*, ii. 282.

[2] Reduced from various plans by Skinner. These plans are not drawn to scale, and do not agree in details. I have harmonized them as I could. In fig. 57 the dotted lines represent uncertain walls, and the line B B a wall thought to be anterior to the rest.

parallel, though a building outside the Saalburg is somewhat similar. Nor can we now ascertain how far it is exact, for when the excavation was completed, the greater part of the walling was led away by Mr. Skinner or the farmer of the land as building material. More important are the smaller finds. The little 9 ft. room, marked A on the plan, yielded the lower part of a broken inscription; part of a freestone statuette 12 inches high; a pedestal with the feet of two adults and two children; a stone spear-head 5½ inches long; the capital of a freestone column 20 inches in diameter, and some painted stucco. The

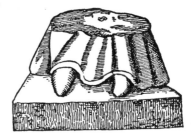

FIG. 58. BASE OF STATUETTE.

inscription is a bit of white lias, 7 inches long by 2½ inches high. It reads, so far as intelligible, in letters ⅝ inch high (fig. 73).

ΛIIVS
c|ONDEDIT
Severo |ETQVINTIANO COS

'Set up (by some one whose name is lost but perhaps ended in —*anus*) in the consulship of Severus and Quintianus,' A.D. 235.[1]

The statuette and stone spear-head suggested to Skinner the theory of a figure of Minerva with her spear. The pieces unfortunately do not fit in size, but the notion that we have here the vestiges of a local shrine is not impossible. Other discoveries, made in one part or other of the building, include Samian, some stamped **CLVPPIM** (or **GL—**) and **OF SECVN**, some embossed in second century style, a specimen of New Forest ware, a British coin and issues of Vespasian, Marcus, Tetricus, and Constantine, many fibulae, some glass, a leaden bracelet with a snake's head on it (an Italian device), a quern and many roof-slabs with nails.

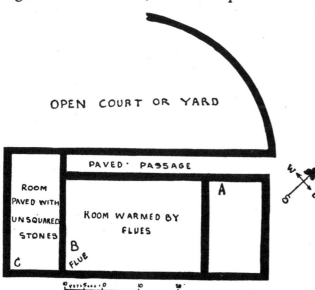

FIG. 59. SMALLER HOUSE, EXCAVATED 1817.
(From Skinner.)

A second and smaller house was found in 1817 about 50 feet west or north-west of the first, and about 200 feet from the line of the Fosse Way.

Here also we find rooms and a circular yard, but the yard now lies wholly behind and not around the building (fig. 59). The finds made in this house show that it was intended to be warmed and inhabited, and

---

[1] So Hübner completes it, *C.* vii. 63. Skinner (MS. 33661, p. 61), and after him Scarth (*Som. Proc.* xi. 181 ; *Brit. Arch. Assoc. Journ.* xviii. 304 ; *Aquae*, p. 79) prefer *Basso*, A.D. 289. But this is less likely. The stone is now in the Bristol Museum, where I have seen it.

its outline bears some relation to that of a corridor house. The principal objects found here were a bit of lead ore, 4 lb. in weight, much Samian and other pottery, including a thumb-vase, fibulae, bones, an iron lampstand (?), and three hoards of coins, all buried apparently just before the end of the third century. At the point A on the plan, 60 third brass were unearthed, dating from Gallienus, Valerian, Victorinus, Tetricus, Claudius Gothicus, Carausius and Allectus. At B, near or under the 'flue' which warmed the room, 114 third brass were found 'deposited in a small trench'; many were of Gallienus, Probus and Tacitus, a few of Claudius Gothicus, Quintillus, Aurelian, one of Carausius. At C a larger hoard of 334 coins was extracted from below two large stones, placed (as it seemed) purposely above it : the coins were of Gallienus, Probus, Tacitus and Claudius Gothicus.

Traces of other buildings were excavated to the south and west of the two just described, both in Eighteen Acre and in Thirty Acre Field, and others eastwards in Longlands, and Mr. Skinner estimated ten habitations in all on this side of the Fosse. But no definite remains could be made out. Broken walls, coarse pavements, flat-headed nails, roof-slates, coins and the like were found freely but no continuous walls or intelligible houses. Equally obscure were remains taken by Mr. Skinner to represent six small cottages, or the like, in Rowbarrow Field on the opposite side of the Fosse. Here he thought that he detected 'a connected line of habitations of artificers ; there being a number of flues and pieces of iron and lead ore found amongst the rubbish . also sepulchral urns let into the ground, within the walls of the houses. There were the remains of terras (cemented) floors to some of the houses, and fragments of painted stucco, red, yellow and green. Some of the foundation walls of these buildings were found under the road now called the Fosse.'[1] Samian was also found inscribed ALBVCIANI and SACIRO and a pelvis marked SBI on the lip, probably the same as a piece now in the Bristol Museum which seems to read ƆSBꟻ.

Of miscellaneous remains found in one part or another of this settlement, coins were the most abundant. They cover all periods. Two British ones occurred in Eighteen Acre Field ; other early issues are of Augustus, Agrippa, Drusus, Claudius, and Nero (1 each), Vespasian (6), Titus (4). Many belonged to the Constantinian family, and the series of those found up to 1818 ends with 2 Magnus Maximus, 7 Theodosius, 7 Arcadius and 8 Honorius.[2] Potsherds—Samian and coarser ware—abounded to the extent of 'bushels of every description,' and among the potters' stamps were VꟻALIS, OFLCVIRIL, OFCELI, DRVCVRSV, MARTIIO, CLAIIIIAE, CORNOI, ORPARRNT, IIIIXORI and ACVMR/S, these last perhaps misread. Much window and bottle glass, 40 fibulae, 7 spoons, 3 keys, 12 styles, many other iron and bronze pieces of various kinds, bone instruments, jet, two blue-stones, one with a dolphin and one

---

[1] Skinner, Add. MS. 33659, fo. 6.

[2] Phelps, p. 179, records also 26 silver coins of "Honorius, Arcadius and the later Emperors concealed, beneath two Roman tiles." This comes, I suppose, from Skinner, but I have not found any note of it in his papers.

with 'eastern characters' (possibly Abraxas), and so forth, are also recorded. In general the remains, as known to us by the copious sketches of Skinner, both attest by their number a fair-sized village and illustrate by their Roman character the general dominion of Roman culture in Britain. But especial interest attaches to a bronze object of Late Celtic design found in Eighteen Acre Field.[1] It may well be of earlier date, than the Roman conquest (fig. 61). A similar object, but of Roman style and date, has been found at Novaesium (Neuss).

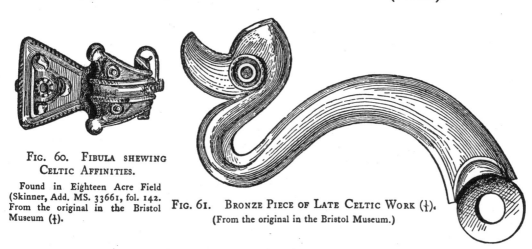

FIG. 60. FIBULA SHEWING CELTIC AFFINITIES.

Found in Eighteen Acre Field (Skinner, Add. MS. 33661, fol. 142. From the original in the Bristol Museum (⅓).

FIG. 61. BRONZE PIECE OF LATE CELTIC WORK (⅓). (From the original in the Bristol Museum.)

The Roman remains of Camerton lie thickest in the area which we have just been considering. But if Mr. Skinner is correct, they extend widely beyond its limits. Much was noted by him further north-east on the line of the Fosse, and in particular in Stowborough Field, opposite the Red Post Inn, better known in coaching days than now.[2] Here foundations, coins, pottery (including Samian stamped CAIVS . .), and graves dug in the rock were observed, and a silver coin of Vespasian was picked up close by. To the north, in Camerton village, coins (including a Tetricus, a Constantius, and a Constantine), potsherds, iron arrowheads, and a small bronze figurine of Vesta were noted. To the east, under Eckwick Hill on Oldbury, coins, potsherds and 'foundations of several houses' were recorded, and much the same was seen in Underdown Field on White Oxmead Farm. To the west near Clandown, in a field called Great Stanley's, 'foundations and roofing stones,' from local quarries were seen scattered over the surface, and ploughmen picked up coins and pottery, and further on two buildings, probably the residence and outhouses of a villa, were noted in the direction of Paulton (p. 315).

The general impression made by Mr. Skinner's list is that he saw Roman foundations everywhere. But this impression is perhaps a little unjust. A critical survey of his statements suggests rather that a loosely settled village did exist in Roman times on the Fosse Way near Clandown. The nucleus of this village was near Eighteen Acre Field, where (as we

---

[1] Fig 61, drawn from the original, now in Bristol Museum. See Skinner, Add. MS. 33661, fo. 86.
[2] Add. MS. 33662, fol. 96.

have said) there was possibly the shrine of some local god or goddess. But its houses may have been spread over a considerable area,[1] and some at least of Mr. Skinner's Roman masonry may be genuine vestiges of it. The period of this village is indicated fairly well by coins. It begins before or at the very opening of the Roman period. It ends only with the end of things Romano-British. During these four centuries the civilization of the site is predominantly Roman. A few objects suggest Celtic influences. In general we see that predominance of Roman fashions and Roman conventionality which marks the whole or almost the whole of Romano-British civilization.

2. ILCHESTER

Ilchester lies beside the river Yeo, in the centre of the broad, low expanse which intervenes between the higher lands near Somerton, Yeovil and Castle Cary. The marsh comes up to its western edge and the neighbourhood is liable to flood. But it occupies a central position and commands a crossing of the river, and hence at least in mediaeval times, it possessed some real importance. This importance has coloured the views generally held of its character in the Roman period. It was thought by early archaeologists, such as Camden, Gerard and Stukeley, to have been a large Roman town. But our survey will show that it more probably was what it is to-day, a poor and unimportant village, situated where the Fosse Way threw out a branch to Dorchester.

The remains actually recorded are few. Camden mentions coins, Gerard adds foundations, and emphasizes the preponderance of fourth century coins.[2] Stukeley visited the place himself and gives a much fuller account. He thought that he saw an enclosure with walls and ditches, measuring 200 by 300 paces. But these seem to be either mediaeval or imaginary. More solid finds which he records are brick and tessellated pavement, tiles, and coins, including one of Pius.[3] Later additions to this list are scanty. Another pavement was discovered in the grounds of Ivel House, Northover, in 1887,[4] and among smaller objects are a gold ring set with an *aureus* of Severus Alexander[5]; a bronze ornament of a face, inlaid with silver,[6] a fibula,[7] and two indications of burials, one, part of a skull with a coin from the Manor Farm, and the other, part of a leaden coffin from Northover House.[8] This is a

---

[1] Compare *Westdeutsche Zeitschrift*, xix. 1–67, or any similar case.

[2] Camden, *Britannia* (ed. 6, 1607), p. 162. Thos. Gerard, *Description of Somerset* (1633), printed in *Som. Record Soc.* xv. p. 204.

[3] Stukeley, *Itin. Curios.* (1724), p. 146; (ed. 1776), p. 155. Plate 72.

[4] *Somerset and Dorset N. and Q.* i. 26 (§ 35). Three *tesserae* are in Taunton Museum.

[5] *Brit. Arch. Assoc. Journ.* (1848), iv. 315, with illustration; *Somerset Arch. Proc.* (1853), iv. (2) 89. Now in Taunton Museum.

[6] *Somerset Arch. Proc.* xxxii. (1886) (1) 80. Now in Taunton Museum (Walter Collec.). The Walter Collec. also contains coins of Aurelian and Valentinian from Ilchester.

[7] Now in the British Museum; of unusual shape.

[8] *Somerset Arch. Proc.* (1871), xvii. 123; xxxii. (1886) (1) 80. Both in Taunton Museum; information from Dr. H. Norris of Petherton.

brief list, and it is all.[1] Of Phelps' prætorium, amphitheatre and equestrian camp there is no sign whatever. If the bridge over the Yeo is Roman, as it might possibly be in origin, there is no evidence to prove the fact.[2] No certain date can be assigned to the old causeway in the river, which is also said to be Roman, or to the earthworks mentioned by Buckler.[3] Even the enthusiastic Skinner, visiting the site in 1829, had to confess that hardly a vestige of the Roman occupation could be traced.[4] Here, we may be sure, stood no large Romano-British town.

Lastly, the name. Servetus in 1535 suggested Ischalis, or, as it should be spelt, Iscalis. He took this name from Ptolemy, and Camden and almost every one has since followed him.[5] Yet in reality little can be said for his view. In the first place Iscalis was only chosen because it began with the same letter as Ilchester. This similarity between the names is not great in itself, and etymologically it is delusive. For Ilchester was originally ' the Chester on the Ivel,' and that form of the river name appears in its ancient forms. For example, Florence of Worcester calls it Givelcaster, and others style it Ivelchester, which is a long way from Iscalis. And in the second place, Ptolemy is very likely here inaccurate. His name Iscalis may well be a confusion between Isca Silurum and Isca Dumnoniorum, as several scholars have conjectured. We must therefore be content to assign to Ilchester no Roman name.

3. HAM HILL

Ham or Hamdon Hill (fig. 62), forms the north-western extremity and almost the highest point in the irregular upland which rises three or four miles west of Yeovil. Jutting out from the main mass of this high ground, towering nearly 300 feet above the neighbouring plain of Martock, and fenced around three sides by a precipitous escarpment, its position is strong and stately beyond any in Somerset. Naturally it has been occupied from the earliest times. Round its summit runs a ring of huge entrenchments three miles in length, defending an area of 200 acres. Within this enclosure antiquities of many periods have come to light : Neolithic, Bronze Age, Celtic, and lastly Roman. Most of these have been discovered near the western face of the hill in the course of quarrying the Ham stone, with which innumerable Somerset churches and houses have been built. The Roman remains belong principally to a triangular peninsula which springs out at the north end of this western face. Unfortunately no record has been kept of the circumstances under which the different discoveries were made. Quarrymen have unearthed them in the course of their work, and local collectors, especially the late Mr. W. W. Walter, of Stoke-under-Ham,

[1] Collinson, indeed (iii. 298, 1791), talks of hypocausts, baths, mosaics, coins (Vespasian, Trajan, Pius) and ' almost every relic of Romanity.' But I think this is romance.
[2] Phelps, *Hist. of Somersets.* Introd. (1836), p. 166.
[3] *Ilchester Almshouse Deeds* (1866), pp. 173-4, 195-8.
[4] Add. MS. 33715, fol. 33.
[5] Horsley doubted, putting Iscalis at Wells, *Britannia Romana* (1734), p. 463. Iscalis, not Ischalis, appears to be the spelling of the best MSS. of Ptolemy.

have preserved them. But neither quarrymen nor collectors have adequately described the finds, and the detached and individual objects do not of themselves unfold the story of the hill.[1]

Plainly, however, the site was occupied in British and Roman times. Of Celtic remains assignable to a pre-Roman period we have such striking instances as pottery similar to that of the Glastonbury lake-village (figs. 3 and 63), a small bronze head of a bull (fig. 63, 12), an uninscribed British bronze coin, a comb, bits of a chariot wheel and weapons, and some of those iron bars resembling unfinished swords, which may perhaps be specimens of the iron coinage of the Britons mentioned by Caesar.[2]

Roman remains are more plentiful, and no less interesting. Among the bronze objects are some 38 scales, 1 inch in length, and $\frac{9}{16}$ inch in width, belonging to a breastplate. They are tinned alternately for decorative purposes, connected by tiny wire rings, and provided with holes by which they could be sewn on to a leather bodice. Similar pieces of scale armour have been found at many places in Britain—Hod Hill, Colchester, Catterick Bridge, Walltown and Great Chesters on Hadrian's Wall, Newstead near Melrose—and various sites abroad.[3] Other bronze objects are a dozen or more bow fibulae, including two uninscribed 'Aucissa' specimens, and one inscribed **AVCI22A** (see p. 343), a few penannular brooches, rings, buckles, a bell, a lamp found in 1848, and a bit of thin repoussé work of Late Celtic affinities and possibly of pre-Roman date (fig. 63, 4). Iron is also frequent in the shape of keys, knives, nails, chains, and the like ; the age of these, however, is not always certain. Various small objects in bone, including a die (fig. 63, 8), fragments of glass, a clay sling-bullet (fig. 63, 9), spindlewhorls, a few Samian potsherds including one stamped inside the base **ERTIVSF**, *Tertius fecit*, and many specimens of plainer grey ware, have also been preserved.

The recorded coins extend over all the first four centuries of our era from Augustus to Theodosius I, and are numerous. But in this point appearances may be deceitful. Unfortunately, those who have preserved them have not distinguished between coins discovered sporadically on the hill and coins found in two large hoards. Of these hoards, the most notable was discovered in 1882 at Bedmoor or

---

[1] The site is first noticed by Stukeley, *Itin. Cur.* (without mentioning remains). For remains see Collinson, iii. 310 ; R. C. Hoare, *Arch.* xxi. 39, with plan of camp (hence Phelps, *Introd.* p. 120) ; *Proc. Soc. Ant.* xi. 87 ; *Som. Proc.* iv. (1) 11, and (2) 87 ; xvii. (1) 59 ; xxx. (2) 138—only theories ; xxxii. (1) 48, 79, with plates of objects found ; C. Trask, *Norton sub Hamdon* (Taunton, 1898), pp. 18, 242. Brief references in *Brit. Arch. Assoc. Journ.* iv. 384 (bronze lamp found by a quarryman in 1848) ; *Arch. Journ.* x. 247. I am indebted to Mr. H. Norris for much information. The Walter and Norris collections are now in Taunton Museum : see H. St. G. Gray, *Guide to the Walter Collection* (Taunton, 1903) and the *Norris Collection* (1906). The 'amphitheatre' and 'Roman road' mentioned by some writers seem to me not to be Roman ; the stirrup (*Arch.* xxviii. 450) and bronze eagle are also, I think, later. My illustrations (fig. 63) are from photographs by Mr. Gray. For illustrations of other objects see *Som. Proc.* xxxii. 81 and Mr. Gray's *Guides*.

[2] *Classical Review*, 1905, p. 207 ; R. A. Smith, paper read to the Soc. of Antiq. on 26 January, 1905.

[3] C. R. Smith, *Coll. Antiq.* vi. 7, *Arch. Journ.* viii. 296, *Arch. Aeliana*, xvi. 441, xvii. p. xxxviii., Newstead excavations of Oct. 1905. See further, *Bericht des Vereins Carnuntum* 1899, p. 84 ; Bursian, *Aventicum*, plate xxi. 32, etc. The thing is not the rarity which it is sometimes stated to be. The Ham Hill scales were found on the south side of the Hill in Nov. 1885.

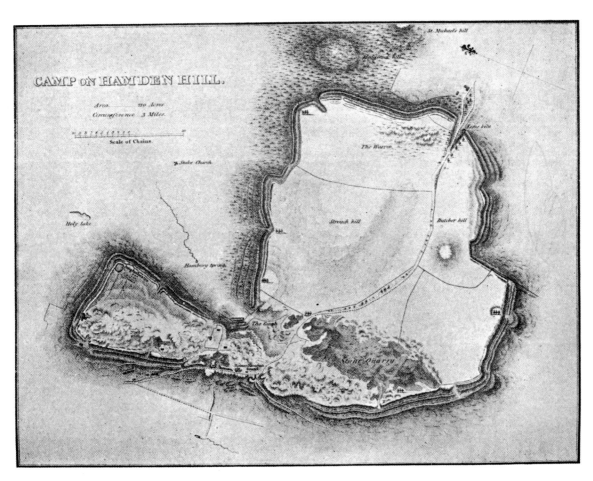

FIG. 62. PLAN OF HAM HILL.

(From *Archæologia*.)

FIG. 63.   REMAINS FROM HAM HILL, IN TAUNTON MUSEUM.
(From Photographs by Mr. Gray.)

1. Scale armour ($\frac{2}{3}$).   2, 3, 5, 6, 7, 10, 11.   Fibulae.   4.   Thin Repoussé Bronze of Late Celtic Style.
8. Roman Die.   9.   Clay Slingbullet.   12.   Bronze Head, Late Celtic.
13.   Potsherds (resembling those of Glastonbury, fig. 3).

Batemoor Barn, a site in Montacute parish just outside the south-east corner of the camp, at the point where a lane ascending from Montacute reaches the plateau. The hoard was contained in three good-sized amphorae. One of these, now at Taunton, is a large egg-shaped jar of coarse buff ware, about 11 inches high, with two very small handles. The coins are said to have numbered over 2,000, and to have consisted of Large Brass. No proper list was ever made, and most of them passed unregistered into collections in which they cannot now be distinguished. But Mr. C. R. Smith records 293, all much worn except the latest, a coin of Philip.

10 Domitian	1 Aelius	3 Lucius Verus
4 Nerva	35 Pius	2 Lucilla
40 Trajan	18 Faustina sen.	2 Commodus
133 Hadrian	25 Marcus	1 Crispina
2 Sabina	16 Faustina jun.	1 Philip

To these Mr. Franklin adds a First Brass of Severus Alexander, Mr. Norris had second century First Brass from Hadrian to Commodus, now at Taunton ; and Mr. Phelips of Montacute has coins of Augustus, Trajan and his successors to Albinus, Julia Mamaea, Severus Alexander and Postumus, which, or some of which, are said to come from this hoard. It would seem that the hoard was wholly of First Brass, and buried about the middle of the third century.[1] A second hoard was dug up about 1816 at some little distance south of Ham Hill. It was contained in a large earthen vase, and comprised coins of copper and white metal, many of them probably cast in moulds, from Volusian to Constantine (251–337), or according to another account from Aquilia Severa to Tetricus (220–272).[2]

It can hardly be doubted that, besides these two hoards, many coins have been discovered sporadically in the camp. But the indifference of finders, and perhaps even of collectors, has left us unable to distinguish such sporadic finds. We have a few statements that indicate their occurrence. But records of definite coins, found on Ham Hill and yet certainly different from the hoards just mentioned, are fewer than might be expected. We have therefore to rely on the general probability of such sporadic finds, and on the vague statements of our authorities, if we assert that coins have occurred not infrequently in the camp.[3]

After all, however, the character of the occupation remains obscure. Here, as at Hod Hill in Dorset and Borough Hill in Northampton-

---

[1] C. Roach Smith, *Num. Chron.* 1886, p. 96 ; *Proc. Soc. Antiq.* xi. 87 ; *Som. Proc.* xxxii. (2) 79 ; Norris, *South Petherton*, p. 15 ; lists in Mr. Gray's guide.

[2] R. Walter, *Som. Proc.* iv. (2) 88 ; H. Norris, ibid. xxxii. (1) 48. Some of the coins were acquired by these writers. Another hoard, of Third Brass of the Later Empire, seems to have been discovered long ago in an urn near Ham Hill, *Som. Proc.* iv. (1) 11. But its details have not yet been recorded.

[3] Collinson, iii. 310 (writing before either hoard was found) mentions 'many Roman coins.' H. Norris, *South Petherton*, p. 15, mentions three coins of Carausius, Allectus, and Constans, apparently unconnected with the hoards. So too *Som. Proc.* xvii. (1) 59, coins of Philip, Decius, Gallus, Volusian, etc. The Walter and Norris collections reach from Augustus to Theodosius, and must contain many coins unconnected with the hoards.

shire, men of the Roman period occupied an earlier site. But here their remains, however interesting, are comparatively few, and they lack indications of luxury. The scale armour may have been lost in the early years of the Roman conquest, when troops were pacifying southern Britain and constructing the Fosse to Exeter. The rest of the inhabitation may have been a survival from British days, or, in later times, a village of quarrymen working the excellent building stone, which was even then well known and used.

4. VILLAS AND RURAL DWELLINGS

From towns and villages we pass to the country outside them, and to the dwelling-houses of one sort or another which stood alone, or almost alone, scattered up and down the land.

Somerset is rich in such dwelling-houses. No less than 58 are known to us with more or less certainty and will be described below. Some of these are doubtful instances. But even when those are deducted, the total remains impressive. It is plain that Somerset was not a thinly inhabited or thinly civilized district in Roman days. But this conclusion is not true of the whole county. The Roman villas of Somerset occur almost wholly in its eastern half. Hardly a single example lies west of longitude 3°. Nor is this surprising. The marshes of West Somerset and its hills, Quantock and Exmoor, are ill adapted to a country population. Even the pleasant little vale of Taunton Deane lay too remote from roads, and too exposed, it may be, to the hill tribes and the Irish pirates to form a centre of rich and peaceful life. We find at Taunton some traces which suggest a village (p. 367). But, apart from this, the vale is almost as empty of remains as the very hills and marshes.

Within East Somerset we may group our 58 villas, at least for convenience, into five main divisions. These are (1) the villas near the Avon and the north-east edge of the county; (2) those in or near the Vale of Wrington and the basin of the northern Yeo; (3) those near and east of the Fosse between Bath and Ilchester; (4) a large series planted mostly on the irregular sweep of high land which runs round the marshes of the Parrett and the Carey, past Langport, Somerton, Street, and the Polden hills; and lastly (5) the villas in the extreme south, near South Petherton, Yeovil, and Chard.

Very few of these dwelling-houses have been excavated at all completely, and of many we know so little that we cannot feel sure of their exact character. Still it may be worth while to attempt—what has never been attempted as yet—to summarize and tabulate the chief recorded discoveries. Thus only can a reader gain some faint conception of this vanished rural civilization, with its country-houses and farms, its hamlets and its isolated cottages. Many of the houses, we shall find, were large and luxurious, though none of them rank in the very first class of Romano-British villas with Bignor and Chedworth and Woodchester. Others, again, were small and insignificant, and rather farmsteads than the residences of wealthy and highly civilized owners. In ground plan, so far as we know, they were normal. The two ordinary types, courtyard and corridor (p. 213), occur freely. Once only, at Yatton, does a distinct and different form of house seem to intrude (No. 11). The mosaics, again, appear to be normal. Their figures and their geometrical designs are often artistically good. But only one scene (No. 50) is really remarkable in subject, while of a local fashion, such as appears in Northamptonshire,[1] we meet hardly a trace (No. 19). One interesting piece of evidence is, however, supplied by these villas. Several have yielded Roman inscriptions, and one of these is a graffito on a potsherd (No. 23). This would seem to prove that even in the west of Britain the inhabitants of these houses used Latin, and the scratched potsherd suggests that this knowledge was not confined to the upper classes.

Some conclusions may also be drawn from the coins which have been recorded as discovered in these villas. Our lists of such coins are doubtless incomplete. Here, as elsewhere, we must allow for finds that have been forgotten and finds that have yet to be made. But in about two dozen cases we chance to possess fairly full accounts, such as may be used provisionally for historical purposes. They may form a basis for conjectures as to the periods when the Somersetshire villas were first built, were inhabited and were finally abandoned. It is, I fear, not easy to say when the settled life of the country districts began. Early coins are naturally rare in houses that have been continuously inhabited in after ages, and the absence of early coins is therefore not a conclusive proof that the house was built at a late period. Nor on the other hand is the occurrence of one or two early coins altogether decisive, since a few such issues lingered on in circulation long after their minting. The silver legionary coins of Mark Antony, for example, are known to have been current 100 or 200 years after his death. In the present case nine sites, Combe Down, Banwell, Chew Stoke, Paulton, Shepton, Chesterblade, Stanchester near Drayton, Coker and Wadeford have yielded coins of the first or second centuries, and these, or some of these, may have been occupied by A.D. 150 or earlier. On the other hand fourteen sites—Farley, Lansdown, Newton, Brislington, Long Ashton, Yatton, Wellow, Ditcheat, Street, Littleton, High Ham, Drayton and Chard contribute only third and fourth century issues, and those mostly later than A.D. 250. But after about 250 A.D., coins are commoner. Almost every villa yields specimens of the years A.D. 270–350. This is the period which must have seen the greatest extension and prosperity of Romano-British rural life and then, we may think, the villas were most definitely occupied. This conclusion is what we might expect on other grounds. The period in question was, as we chance to know from various evidence, a fragment of a happy age for Britain. It can be no accident that the farms and country houses of the province were then most numerous and, as it seems,

---

[1] *V.C.H. Northamptonshire*, i. 188.

most fully inhabited.   It is, however, less easy to decide how long the occupation lasted.   Ten sites were plainly inhabited till near the end of the fourth century—Lansdown, Newton, Combe Down, Shepton, Wellow, Chesterblade, Somerton, Coker, Chard and Wadeford.   Others show no evidence of life later than A.D. 350–360—such as Farley, Brislington, Yatton, Banwell, Wellow, Ditcheat and Drayton.   This may be due to the imperfection of our records.   But it can be otherwise explained.   The middle of the fourth century is the period when Saxon, Celt and Scot first became generally formidable to Britain.   Perhaps it is no accident that country houses, even in remote Somerset, began, as it seems, to be burnt or abandoned about that date.

I. THE VALLEY OF THE AVON AND THE NORTH-EAST OF SOMERSET (1–11).

(1) Farley Hungerford.   A Roman villa has been found in Temple Field half a mile north of Farley Hungerford near the farm road to Iford, 250 yards from the river Frome and close to the boundary of Hinton parish.   It was partly excavated by the Rev. John Skinner of Camerton in 1822, and was reopened between 1850 and 1860.   No plan of it seems to exist.   It is described as a structure measuring 33 feet by 114 feet in extent, containing a well constructed bath and tessellated pavements.   Coins of Tetricus, Magnentius and the Constantine family have been discovered here at one time or another.[1]   This villa is to be distinguished from another which stood half a mile east of Farley, across the Avon and perhaps across the Wiltshire border, above Stowford on a site which I have not been able precisely to identify.[2]

There is no reason to suppose that a villa occupied the site of Farley Castle.   A First Brass coin is said by Skinner to have been found there, but no other evidence exists of its inhabitation in Roman times.

(2, 3) Bathford.   Two houses or buildings have been noted in this parish, both situated at the foot of Bathford Hill on the east bank of the Avon, but about half a mile apart.

One of these was found in 1691 or 1692 in a field called Horselands, between the church and the river, or, more precisely, about 100 yards below the Low House farmstead, near an ancient ford.   The

[1] For the Templefield villa see J. E. Jackson, *Guide to Farley Hungerford* (London, 1879, ed. 3), and *Som. Proc.* iii. (2) 114; *Bath Herald*, 28 Sept. 1822; *Gent. Mag.* 1822 (i.) 113, and 1823 (ii.) 365; Skinner, Add. MS. 33656, p. 236; from Skinner, Phelps *Introd.* p. 179.   The site is marked in the O.S. six inch xxi. NE.   Phelps and Scarth (*Aquae*, p. 120) erroneously make two villas, one at Iford and one in Templefield.

[2] For the villa in Wiltshire see J. E. Jackson, as above, and Cox, *Magna Britannia*, p. 61.   This, I think, must be the villa in which Aubrey says that a mosaic was dug up in 1683.   It was, he says, 'in Sir E. Hungerford's park, in the Wiltshire part of it' (Bodl. Library, MS. Aubrey 15, fo. 103); hence Collinson, iii. 362, etc.   I am not quite sure, however, that I am right in putting the villa into Wiltshire. It was apparently in that county in 1683.   But the boundary seems to have changed since that time, and the Wiltshire Park Farm, with other land east of the Avon, is now in Somerset (O.S. xxi. NE.).   I am obliged to the Rev. R. W. Baker, vicar of Farley, for local information.

discovery is said to have consisted of a pavement 14 feet square, supported by a pillared hypocaust which, in its turn, seems to have stood on a mosaic floor. A spring of water was found beneath the building, and we may conjecture that the lower floor proved too damp and that another was, therefore, erected above it. Here perhaps, as in some other cases, the hypocaust may have served not for heating but for a dry basement. Two altars and an urn of coins are said to have come to light about the same time.[1]

The second building stood in Mumford's or Mompas Mead, between Bathford and Warleigh, near the point where Wansdyke reaches the Avon. This has yielded an elaborate square capital of the Composite order, discovered in the eighteenth century, as well as a stone coffin and various tiles or pipes, found more recently.[2]

Other Roman remains have been recorded from the parish which may be connected with one or other of the preceding. In particular, the seventeenth century antiquary John Aubrey tells us that a mosaic floor was laid open by drainers in May 1655. It was, he says, worked in the usual white (chalk), blue (lias) and red (brick) : in the centre was a rudely figured bird and in each of the four corners a " sort of knot." Below it was a hypocaust with stone pillars and also a spring of water. The mosaic was destroyed by visitors : another mosaic was noted near it but not excavated. Aubrey does not give the site of this discovery, but we may obviously connect it with Horselands and suppose that the floor left untouched in 1655 was that opened in 1691.[3] In addition, Collinson records a coin of Allectus as found in the vicarage garden in his own day.

(4) Langridge. Traces of a villa are stated to have been found near Langridge Rectory on the eastern declivity of Lansdown looking eastwards over the valley towards Swanswick. Singularly little, however, is recorded about it. In fact the only definite finds seem to be two or three stone coffins found near the rectory. These supply no evidence of their date and need not necessarily be Roman. As traces of a villa are said to have been found, it is difficult to imagine that there was not a villa. But until we can learn what these traces comprised, we cannot repress a lurking doubt as to its existence.[4]

(5) Lansdown. Traces of a Roman building were excavated by the Rev. H. H. Winwood and others in the late summer of 1905

---

[1] Letter of Mr. Vertue of Bath, in *Soc. Ant. Minutes*, iv. 19 (18 Sept. 1740); hence Collinson, i. 111, adding altars and coins; Gough, *Brit. Top.* ii. 226, and *Adds. to Camden*, i. 118; H. D. Skrine, *Bath Field Club*, v. (1885) 66.

[2] *Soc. Ant. Minutes*, xx. 48 (16 Dec. 1784); Collinson, i. 111; Scarth, *Aquae*, p. 119, with illustrations of capital; H. D. Skrine, *Bath Field Club*, v. (1865) 67; information from Col. H. M. Skrine of Warleigh. The capital is now in the Institution at Bath.

[3] Aubrey MS. 15, fol. 104, in the Bodleian; hence Scarth, *Aquae*, p. 119 (connecting it with Mumford's Mead, apparently by inadvertence), and H. D. Skrine, *Bathford and its Neighbourhood* (Bath, 1871), p. 23, and *Bath Field Club*, v. 65. This is the mosaic mentioned by Gibson in his ed. of Camden (1722, i. 87), and thence cited by Gough (*Adds. to Camden*, i. 111), but with a wrong date, 1644.

[4] Scarth, very briefly, *Aquae*, pp. 104, 125, and *Arch. Journ.* xi. 408; *Brit. Arch. Assoc. Journ.* xiii. 152 (stone coffin, with mediaeval interment supposed to be secondary); *Bath Field Club*, i. (ii.) 16 slight excavations in 1865), ii. 151 (stone coffin with female skeleton), v. 230 (coffin).

on the north side of Lansdown just within the Somerset boundary, near the Grenville monument, and immediately south of Battlefield House and grounds. The field in which the remains occur is steeply scarped on north and east and south, and the only easy approach is from the west. The remains include black soil, foundations of buildings, flagged floors, portions of columns and a female head in oolite, bricks and tiles, 59 coins ranging from Salonina to Valens (A.D. 253–378), many potsherds, but only a few pieces of Samian, fibulae—in particular, a circular disk-fibula enamelled in white and blue,—other bronze and iron fragments, some bits of glass, animals' bones, two rough-hewn stone coffins containing skeletons and iron nails, and some iron slag and iron-stone. One fragment of grey ware, apparently the hough of a cup, has stamped on it inside, in the manner of a very rude Samian stamp, the letters XIMV. This may be borrowed from the name Maximus. But, as used here, it has probably no other object than to give the general idea of a potter's stamp. The exact character of the building does not seem clear. But it is probable that we have to do with some late 'villa.' The excavations are to be continued.[1]

(6) North Stoke. Just below North Stoke Church, and between it and the village, there was found in 1888, under a mediaeval barn belonging to the Manor farm, a building measuring 11 feet by 102 feet, with an apse at one end. Other walling was noticed quite close and also bricks and tiles and three bases and one capital of oolite (indicating shafts of $6\frac{1}{2}$–$7\frac{1}{2}$ inches in diameter). The site was well chosen, for it is well watered and sheltered from the east and the north, and enjoys a good view over the west and south-west. A quarter of a mile east of the church on Little Down some interments were discovered in 1887: they included three skeletons, one in an oolite coffin with a few small nails. The Roman road—the so-called Via Julia—from Bath to Bitton and Sea Mills is supposed to have run close by, but a little lower down the hillside than the site of the villa.[2]

(7) Newton St. Loe. A Roman villa was brought to light here and partly uncovered about 1837, during the construction of the Great Western Railway from Bath to Bristol. It stood on ground that sloped gently towards the Avon, not far from the point where the Bath and Bristol road crosses the railway and on the south side of that road. Two distinct buildings were traced. One was lower down the slope than the other and was considered the more interesting. The portion of this which was excavated measured 55 feet by 102 feet, and consisted of a long corridor paved with mosaic, and rooms opening off it, some of which were provided with hypocausts. One of these rooms, in size 17 feet square,

---

[1] Information from the Rev. H. H. Winwood and Mr. Thos. Bush; notes in *Bath Herald*, 20 Sept. 1905; *Proc. Bath Branch of Som. Arch. Soc.* 1905, pp. 57–68; objects in the Institution at Bath. The black soil was analysed and found to owe its colour to particles of magnetic oxide of iron, many of which had the appearance of having been fused, as though iron had been smelted here in small quantities.

[2] Scarth, *Aquae*, p. 126; *Som. Proc.* xxxiii. (2) 146; *Bath Field Club*, ix. (1901), 50; *Bath Chron.* 8 Dec. 1887; information from Sir Henry Lawrence (owner of the site) and the Rev. F. Poynton; personal visit. Some of the objects are still preserved at the Manor farm. The coffin has been removed to the Sedbergh School Museum.

contained a figured mosaic in five colours—red (burnt brick), white and blue (local lias), brown (pennant grit), and green (lias marl from Bitton). Its subject was Orpheus seated within a central circle and surrounded by a circular series of beasts and trees. This was contained (as usual) in an oblong filled up with ordinary geometrical devices (lozenges, variations on the svastika pattern, etc.), noteworthy only for the patchwork fashion in which they are used (see No. 20, Wellow). Nichols states that the mosaics were found to be carefully covered up with slabs of stone to protect them, as if the last dwellers in the villa, when they abandoned it, still hoped one day to return and reoccupy it. Other mosaics were simpler. Smaller finds included painted wall plaster, window glass, tiles, potsherds, lead, nails and a few coins—1 silver Macrinus, bronze of Constans and Valentinian, 1 gold Honorius. Of the adjacent building nothing is recorded. It probably contained the servants' quarters and store rooms. Such second buildings are not rare in Roman villas (compare No. 22, Paulton).[1]

Burials have been detected in the neighbourhood of the villa. In 1869 quarrymen, working about a quarter of a mile away and nearer to Newton village, met with eight or nine interments, an urn with burnt bones, part of a wooden coffin with a 2-inch nail still in it, and also potsherds, coins of Probus and Constantine, and some bronze bits. More finds of the same character were made here during the next few years by Mr. Glover; the coins are said to have included 'Galba, Augustus, Pertinax, Constantine, Probus.' Finally in 1903, Mr. Falconer discovered more burnt bones, potsherds, a silver ring-key, a coin of Victorinus and some sandal nails. Some other burials have been found lately at Saltford, two miles to the north-west of Newton. But they can hardly be connected with this villa.[2]

(8) Burnett. At Burnett, in the parish of Corston and about halfway between that village and Marksbury, a Roman villa was discovered about 1830. A tessellated pavement and several small rooms, many potsherds and tiles, and, close by, two coins of Tetricus, have been recorded. An oolite coffin containing a woman's skeleton and iron nails (as of boots) near the feet, was found about 1890 in Lower Botmore Field in the same vicinity, and may possibly belong to one of the inhabitants of the house.[3]

(9) Brislington. A villa was discovered here in December 1899, during the construction of a new road close to the junction of Wick Lane and Bath Road. It was excavated at first by private efforts,

---

[1] W. L. Nichols, *Horae Romanae* (Bath, 1838, 4to), hence Scarth, *Aquae*, p. 114, with rough illustration of mosaic; brief notes in *Proc. Som.* xxii. (1) 64, *Arch. Journ.* xxxvi. 329, *Brit. Arch. Assoc. Journ.* ix. 74, and C. Bourne, *Great Western Railway* (1846), p. 24. A plan of the villa and drawings of several pavements is said to have been published in 1839 (London: Hearne, 31, Strand), but I have not seen it. Some bits of tessellation are in the Institute at Bath. The Orpheus mosaic was at first at Keynsham Railway Station, and then removed to Bristol, where it has since perished.

[2] *Bath Field Club*, ii. 143; *Bristol Mercury*, 8 Sept. 1903; *Antiquary*, xxxix. 293 (Oct. 1903); *Proc. Soc. Antiq.* xx. 248; J. P. E. Falconer, *Bath Field Club*, x. 312.

[3] For the villa see Scarth, *Aquae*, p. 126, writing from local information; for the coffin, *Journ. Brit. Arch. Assoc.* xlvii. (1891), 186.

and afterwards by the Bristol Museum Committee. The house was of the corridor type, facing south-west, and occupied an area of about 120 feet in length and 70 feet in depth (fig. 64). The walls were constructed of local stone : they were in parts much destroyed. Few, if any, traces of reconstruction or alteration were observed. Three apartments on the east side of the house, Nos. 1, 2, and the intervening passage, were floored with mosaics of conventional patterns—geometrical devices containing a cup or simple flowers—and probably the hypocaust and bath rooms (9, 10) at the other end of the building were similarly adorned. The central room, No. 5, had a flagged floor, a rubbish pit, and an open fireplace. It was thought by the excavators to have been an open court, and, indeed, parallels can be cited for unroofed spaces in such a position, though they do not appear to be common in

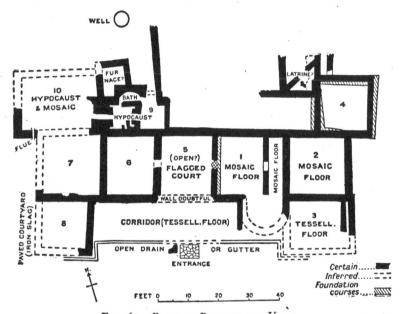

FIG. 64. PLAN OF BRISLINGTON VILLA.

Romano-British villas.[1] Among the smaller finds are painted wall-plaster ; pennant roofing slabs ; much pottery of the commoner sorts, though comparatively little Samian ; bottle and window glass and glass beads ; bronze pins and rings, and two bow fibulae ; many iron objects, such as nails, tools, horseshoes ; many broken bones of edible animals ; a lump of yellow ochre ; leaden weights, and a large tile eleven inches square, faintly scratched ⱶH///, or the like. Few coins were found, and those late and of copper (A.D. 267–361)—1 Victorinus, 1 Allectus, 1 Constantine the Great, 1 Constantinus II, 2 Constans, 3 Constantius II, and 1 illegible.

Notable objects were also taken out of the well, which was cleared to its full depth of 38 feet. Besides much indistinguishable rubbish, it yielded débris of building stone (at 24 and 36 feet), and tesserae (35 feet),

[1] Compare the villas at Cherington and Rodmarton (in Glouc.), and at Arlansart (*Annales de la Soc. archéol. de Namur*, xxiv. 11), and *Westdeutsche Zeitschrift*, xv. 14–17. The Littleton villa described below (No. 37) may also provide a parallel.

a coin of Constantius II (14 feet), 4 skulls and other human bones (32 feet). Beneath these were 7 pewter vessels, more or less fragmentary, (fig. 65) and, at the bottom, bits of wooden buckets. The pewter vessels were of shapes not uncommon in the fourth century : their metal, when analysed, proved to contain lead (62·5), tin (36·0), and a tiny trace of antimony (0·8). The largest pewter jug has scratched underneath it VIII∫, probably $8\frac{1}{2}$; a smaller jug has IIII, which may, however, be accidental. It is plain that the well at some time ceased to be used as a well, and was then filled with rubbish. The finding of building material in it suggests that this took place at the close of the history of the villa. Another interesting find was a considerable amount of iron slag and roasted ironstone, detected outside the west end of the house. This must not be taken to indicate any special industry in the modern sense of the phrase. We may think rather that those who dwelt here made iron objects for their own use, and perhaps also for their neighbours, though on a humble scale. I have failed to discover whence they obtained their ironstone ; no deposits of this substance occur near Bristol.

As a whole, the remains found at the villa point to a late date and a comparatively brief existence. It may have been built about the end of the third century, and it was apparently abandoned soon after the middle of the fourth. The occurrence of burnt roof tiles and the like suggests that it was burnt down.[1]

(10) Long Ashton. When the Bristol and Exeter Railway was constructed in 1838–9, traces of Roman buildings were found in the deep cutting between Long Ashton and Flax Bourton, just at the point where the Bristol and Weston road crosses the line, and apparently near what is now called Cambridge Batch, 300 yards east of Bourton station. Here foundations, worked stone, including capitals, a steined well, two oak coffins, coins, potsherds, and bronze spoons were found in the railway works. The coins appear to have been principally of the third and early fourth century, reaching from Severus to the Constantine dynasty. Some subsequent excavations promoted by the Rev. George S. Master, of Bourton Grange, yielded only Samian and other potsherds.[2]

(11) Failand Hill. Mr. Skinner states that in 1819 he noticed Roman remains near Failand on the high ground north-west of Long Ashton—vestiges of buildings, dark soil, potsherds and coins, mostly Third Brass. These may perhaps be connected with the coins of the

---

[1] W. R. Barker, *Account of remains of a Roman villa discovered at Brislington* (Bristol Museum), with plates of the mosaics, and to the same effect *Clifton Antiq. Club*, v. 78, 111, and *Bristol and Glouc. Archaeol. Soc.* xxiii. 289, xxiv. 283 ; brief references in *Antiquary*, April and November, 1900 ; remains in Bristol Museum. The alleged masons' marks mentioned in some accounts seem to me to be scratches.

[2] Felix Farley's *Bristol Journal*, 17 Nov. 1838, 9 Feb. 1839—the latter passage, which speaks of 'a village about a quarter of a mile in extent,' must be exaggeration ; G. S. Master, *Bristol Times and Mirror*, 17 Sept. 1897 ; coins of Tetricus (3) and Victorinus (1) from Cambridge Batch, in Bristol Museum ; information from Mr. C. Onslow Master. Collinson (ii. 304) briefly mentions foundations 'supposed to be Roman' at Yanley. That, however, is one and a half miles from Cambridge Batch (Ordnance Survey, v. NE.), and, whatever the foundations were, they cannot be connected with the buildings noticed in the text.

Lower Empire, massive foundations, and 'a military way leading towards Axbridge,' which Collinson records as found in Portbury parish. Col. Bramble has eight copper coins found long ago on Failand Hill— First Brass of Nero, Vespasian, Hadrian, Marcus, and Severus Alexander and Second Brass of Hadrian. The whole record is unsatisfactory, but it appears to point to some sort of house on Failand Hill.[1]

II. THE VALE OF WRINGTON AND ADJACENT DISTRICTS (12–18)

(12) Yatton. A Roman villa was detected here and excavated in 1884. It lies to the west of Yatton, among the low marshes near the Yeo, in a large meadow called Wemberham. So close is the site to the river that the eastern end of the foundations abuts on the embankment, and so low does it lie that, without a sea wall, it would be flooded at most high tides. The embankment of the Yeo must, therefore, have been commenced in Roman times. The house itself is small, covering an area of 65 by 150 feet (fig. 66), but it is not devoid of comfort and elegance. In arrangement it differs from the normal types of Romano-British houses. If the published plans of it are correct, an entrance on the north side seems to have led into an outer and an inner hall, and these in turn gave access to rooms lying

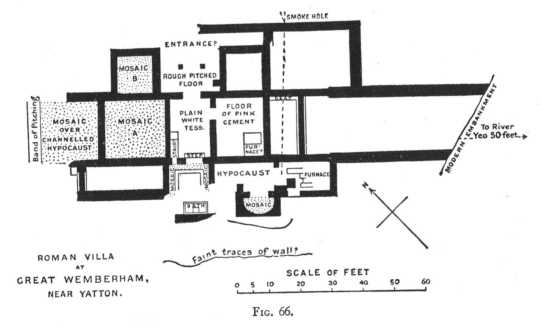

ROMAN VILLA
AT
GREAT WEMBERHAM,
NEAR YATTON.

SCALE OF FEET

FIG. 66.

right and left, and to bathing apartments at the back. There is also a possible trace of a staircase leading to lofts or an upper story. The best rooms lay to the right or west of the entrance. One (A in the plan) was floored with an elaborate mosaic of foliated geometrical pattern in red, white and blue (fig. 67). This has been called Christian, as the central panel of foliation somewhat resembles a cross. The same

[1] Skinner in Add. MS. 28794, p. 119; Collinson, iii. 141 (hence Gough and Phelps); *Clifton. Antiq. Club*, ii. 136, 173.

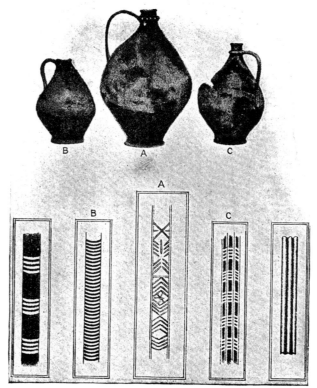

FIG. 65. PEWTER VESSELS FOUND IN THE WELL AT BRISLINGTON
AND ENLARGED SKETCHES OF THE PATTERNS ON THEM.
(See p. 305.)

feature however occurs elsewhere,[1] and appears to be merely ornamental. The room west of A had probably a similar floor, but it was too damaged to be reconstructed. A third mosaic adorned room B, a red, white and blue geometrical design, which when perfect may have had a central panel containing a two-handled cup or similar device. The rest of this wing of the house is known imperfectly, and is therefore not quite intelligible. At the back of the building were the baths, with some mosaic flooring. The left wing seems to have contained less well-furnished rooms. The two thick walls which run out from this wing towards the river are thought to have formed a boat-house and boat-channel, but no details of small objects or of silt and soil are recorded which either confirm or conflict with this idea. The smaller finds are of the ordinary kind—21 coins of A.D. 250–305 (or 360) ; potsherds, both Samian and other ; glass, iron and bone objects ; painted wall plaster, bricks, tiles and roofing slates ; and also some iron slag, less in amount, apparently, than that found at Brislington (No. 9).[2]

We may connect with this villa a discovery made in 1828 in the same field of Great Wemberham. This was a freestone coffin, shaped out of a solid block and very thick, with a stone lid, containing some fragments of a lead coffin and most of a human skeleton. We may also possibly connect a hoard found two miles away at Kingston Seymour.[3] For another possible house near Yatton, on Cadbury hill, see the Alphabetical Index under Yatton.

(13) Congresbury. About half a mile north-east of Congresbury village, at Woodlands, on the slope of Rhodyate Hill, traces of a small house or rural building have been noted. In 1867 Mr. White, then resident at Woodlands, uncovered two rooms, one with a hypocaust beneath it, and picked up abundant potsherds and other small objects, since lost. More recently Capt. Long, the present owner of Woodlands, has found pottery, including Samian and bronze implements, and has traced in the wood a boundary of loose stones enclosing several acres. One bit of Samian found here bears the mark RIIOGENI·M ; one coin, found in 1873, is a Third Brass of the middle of the third century. The mass of potsherds found by Mr. White has suggested the idea of a potter's kiln, to which the subsoil is fairly suitable.[4]

(14) Banwell. Traces of a Roman 'villa' have been noticed here in a field called Chapel Leases near the hamlet of Winthill, half a mile south of Banwell village, and on the south slope of Banwell Hill. The discoveries include foundations, bones and coins—1 large Brass

---

[1] As for example on a mosaic found under the Bank of England in 1805, figured by C. R. Smith, *Illustr. of Roman London*, plate xi., or on another found at Wiltingen in Germany, figured by F. Hettner, *Römische Mosaiken aus Trier*, plate ii.

[2] Scarth, *Proc. Soc. Antiq.* xi. 29 ; *Proc. Som.* xxxi. (2) 1–9 and 64–73, with plan of villa and figures of mosaics (here reproduced in part) ; *Brit. Arch. Assoc. Journ.* xl. 126, xliii. 353 ; *Num. Chron.* 1896, p. 239 ; remains in Weston Museum and at Brockley Court, which I have been permitted to examine.

[3] For the coffin see John Rutter, *North-west Somerset* (London, 1829), p. 70 ; for the hoard see the alphabetical index.

[4] Scarth, very briefly, *Som. Proc.* xxiii. (2) 9, and xxxiii. (2) 5 ; *Clifton Antiq. Club*, ii. (1891), 77 ; information from Capt. Long, and personal knowledge.

of Severus Alexander found in 1813, and 1 silver of Julian found in 1801. To these we may probably add 1 Julius Caesar, 1 Trajan and 8 late Third Brass, which are preserved in Glastonbury Museum and labelled 'found at Banwell,' and a British silver coin and some Roman coins of the fourth century found at Banwell before 1852. A burial at Wolvershill, a mile and a half north of Banwell village, lies too far away to be connected with any certainty with the Winthill remains. The cruciform earthwork on Banwell Hill has, I think, no claim to be considered Roman.[1]

(15) Shipham. In the parish of Shipham extensive foundations were discovered long ago in a field to the north of the Star Inn, about $\frac{1}{4}$ mile north-west of the point where a Roman road—the so-called Via ad Axium (p. 350)—is said to cross the turnpike from Bristol to Bridgwater. No excavation was made, but numerous bricks and potsherds were picked up on the surface, and also a few coins, and some parched wheat, which was thought to indicate the destruction of the villa by fire.[2]

(16) Havyatt Green, Wrington. Two different records seem to indicate a villa here.

(1) The *Gentleman's Magazine* states that tiles and part of a blue and red border of a mosaic were uncovered in 1856 at Lower Langford in digging up the foundations of an old wall. (2) A correspondent of Mr. Skinner writes that in 1817 foundations and Samian and other potsherds were found in making a new road from Bristol to Bridgwater, at Havyatt Green, about half-way between Dolebury and Broadfield Down, Redhill. That is practically in Lower Langford village. Hence we may assume that the two finds belong to one and the same villa. The Lyehole villa (No. 17) is about a mile and a half distant.[3]

(17) Lyehole, Wrington. At Lyehole, in the parish of Wrington, about two miles east of the village and two fields from the Lyehole farmhouse, in a pleasant and well-watered spot, traces of a villa were found and superficially examined in 1876. These traces were potsherds, bones, tiles, one or two tesserae from a pavement, wall plaster, a hypocaust in which the pilae were made in part with hexagonal roof-tiles, and foundations covering half an acre. No coins or metal implement of any description, except a flat-headed nail, came to light. Abundant traces of charred wood and burning showed that the villa had been destroyed by fire. The villa at Havyatt Green (No. 16) is a mile and a half distant. An old deep lane, now disused, once led

---

[1] George Bennet, MS. *Hist. of Banwell* (written about 1811–25), p. 5, and *Gent. Mag.* 1811, ii. 106; Skinner, Add. MS. 33726, p. 207; Williamson Collection in Glastonbury Museum; *Som. Proc.* iii. (1) 16; information from the Rev. C. Taylor and Mr. E. R. Bevan, and personal knowledge. For Wolvershill and for the cruciform earthwork on Banwell Hill, see the alphabetical index at the end of this chapter.

[2] Phelps, *Hist. of Somerset* (1836), Introduction, pp. 108, 135. Phelps' authority for the description of the Via ad Axium is Hoare, *Ancient Wilts*, ii. Roman aera (1819), but Hoare mentions no remains at Shipham. They must therefore have been noticed some time between 1819 and 1836.

[3] *Gent. Mag.* 1856 (ii.) 108; letter of J. Douglas to Skinner 18 June, 1817, preserved in Skinner's MS. in the Institution at Bath. Mr. Douglas was a most competent archaeologist.

Fig. 67. Restoration of Mosaic found at the Wemberham Villa near Yatton (p. 306).
(From *Somerset Arch. Proc.*)

from the site of Lyehole villa towards Havyatt Green, and might, I suppose, be a trace of a Roman communication-road.[1]

(18) Chew Stoke. Skinner records the occurrence of Roman remains on Pegnes Hill, apparently that now called Pagan's Hill, a quarter of a mile north of Chew Stoke Church. These remains, he says, comprised building stones, roof tiles, a freestone pinnacle like those found at Bath and Wellow (figs. 38, 70) and 40 or 50 coins of the second, third and fourth centuries. No other writer notices foundations here, but 29 silver coins from the place were added to Taunton Museum in 1882. These consist of 15 Republican issues and 14 Imperial coins from Tiberius onwards, ending with 1 Pius, 1 Severus Alexander and 1 Julia Maesa—a somewhat curious collection.[2]

III. VILLAS NEAR AND EAST OF THE FOSSE BETWEEN BATH AND ILCHESTER (19—31).

(19) Combe Down. Remains of a fair-sized house and of adjacent burials found in Monkton Combe parish, immediately south-east of Trinity Church, on the south slope of Combe Down overlooking the Midford valley. The villa was first noticed by Skinner and Warner about 1822 ; it was touched on again in 1854, and it was partly excavated in 1860 and the following years. It is described by Mr. Scarth as having been an example of the courtyard type, built round three sides of a rectangular yard. But no precise plan of it was taken, and only two sides were actually explored. One side, running north and south, contained three rooms and abundant roofing tiles, coins and bones. The other, running west and east, contained a hypocaust cut down into the rock and large rooms of which two measured 10 by 30 and 18 by 30 ft. An entrance gateway (of the yard?) is also said to have been found on the east side of the house. No tessellated pavements seem to have been noticed, but much wall plaster painted in stripes, flanged roof tiles and bricks. The smaller finds were numerous and interesting. There was pottery of every kind—Samian (CINI· M·F· and SACCINI· M) ; two characteristic cups of Castor ware, showing animals in the chase, 4 and 6 inches high, and other plainer wares. There were good pieces of delicate colourless glass from bottles ; ten bow-shaped fibulae in bronze, and bronze spoons, bracelets, styles, tweezers and a bell ; iron keys and the iron head of a javelin ; and much pumice stone, perhaps for dressing skins. The coins numbered about 230. Only a few were earlier than 290 A.D.—3 Second Brass (Antonia, the wife of Drusus ; Domitian, Faustina Senior) ; 2 denarii (Septimus Severus, Severus Alexander) ; and 8 Third Brass of Tetricus and Claudius II. About 197 out of the whole number of 230 belonged to the Constantinian period, and 16

[1] Scarth, *Proc. Soc. Antiq.* vii. 159, and very briefly *Som. Proc.* xxii. (2) 30 ; xxiii. (2) 10 ; xxxiii. (2) 4. For a few isolated coins found in Wrington village see the alphabetical index.

[2] Skinner's papers of the year 1830, in Add. MS. 33717, fol. 153 ; *Som. Proc.* xxviii. (i.) 78 ; information from Mr. Gray.

to Valens, Valentinian and Gratian. One small inscribed object was also discovered (fig. 67A)—a leaden seal about ¾ inch in diameter, inscribed with the figure of a stag couchant and the letters **PBR S**. The interpretation of the letters is unfortunately obscure. The analogy of tiles found in London stamped **P.P.BR. LON.** *publicani provinciae Britanniae Londinienses*, and **P.BRI.SAN.** *publicani Britanniae sanctae?* suggests that our Combe Down piece is a stamp of the *publicani* relating to taxes or dues in Britain. Perhaps, like the *piombi* used in the present day in Italy and elsewhere, it was affixed to some bale of merchandise which passed into or through the tax collectors' hands. In this case we might connect its occurrence here with an inscribed stone to be described two paragraphs below. This seems at any rate more probable than the only rival explanation, advanced by Mr. C. Roach Smith, that the seal was affixed to a pig of Mendip lead and that its letters mean *plumbum Britannicum signatum*. A lead seal affixed to a lead bar seems a superfluity. A somewhat similar lead seal, with a stag (?) standing and the letters **PB** is recorded from the fourth century site of Felixstowe on the Essex Coast.[1]

FIG. 67A. LEAD ROUNDEL FROM SKETCH BY IRVINE (⅓).

Close to the villa, but rather higher up the slope, we have traces of burials. Stone coffins were noted here in 1822, and more were excavated in 1854, partly in the spring and partly in the winter. In all two rows of burials were detected, 47 feet apart. The most northerly consisted of two stone coffins, with a skeleton and iron nails or studs, as if from boots, in each. One skeleton had an illegible brass coin in its mouth and three skulls at its feet, inside the coffin. Beside the coffins lay their displaced lids; one part of the lid covering the skeleton and coin bore a Roman inscription. The other row had three stone coffins, each with a skeleton and iron nails or studs inside, and beside the coffins the following: (a) an oblong stone box with a cover (14 by 20 inches) enclosing a horse's head and some other bones; (b) a stone cist (9 by 12 inches) with a lid and burnt human bones, and (c) two earthenware jars also containing burnt bones. A coin of Licinius was also picked up, but whether inside or near the second row of burials is not recorded, and other bones or skeletons were found lying outside the coffins. The burials appear to be principally if not wholly of late Roman date, though the horse's head is difficult to parallel.

Especial interest attaches to the inscribed slab, a block of stone 31 inches long by 18 inches high and 4 inches thick. It has of course nothing to do with the interments, but was used up again after its original purpose had expired, as part of a coffin lid. It reads (fig. 68):

---

[1] For accounts of the villa see Scarth and Cuming, *Brit. Arch. Assoc. Journ.* xix. 66 (with plate of Castor ware, glass, etc.), and *Aquae*, pp. 115 and 134 (list of coins) and similar plates (xlviii., xlix., 1); *Som. Proc.* v. 145. For the inscribed leaden ticket, see C. Roach Smith, *Trans. of the London and Middlesex Arch. Soc.* v. 433, and *Coll. Antiq.* ii. 68 (from J. T. Irvine); hence Watkin, *Arch. Journ.* xxxiv. 138, and Hübner, *Ephem.* iv. 707. A drawing of the seal is among Irvine's papers at Edinburgh. Where the object itself is, I do not know. A few remains from the villa (potsherds and stucco) are in the Institution at Bath.

*Pro salute Imp. Caes. M. Aur(elii) Antonini felicis invicti Aug(usti) n(ostri), Nae-
vius, Aug(usti) lib(ertus), adiut(or) proc(uratorum), principia ruina opressa (sic) a solo
restituit.*

'For the safety of our Emperor M. Aurelius Antoninus (probably Caracalla, A.D.
211–217), the Fortunate and Unconquerable, Naevius, freedman of the Emperor and
assistant to the Procurators, has restored from the ground-level the ruined Principia.' [1]

What exactly these *principia* were, is doubtful. The word usually
denotes the headquarters in a fort, and so it has been taken by most
writers to prove that a fort stood on Combe Down early in the third
century. However, no trace of such a fort has ever been detected.
Moreover, the existence of a fort on such a spot as the vicinity of
Bath about A.D. 215 is not especially likely, and an inferior civil official
—concerned with finance and a freedman by rank—is not in any case the
proper person to rebuild the most important structure in a military

Fig. 68.

establishment. It is possible that *principia* may here bear a civil
significance and denote a residence of some financial authority connected
with the procurators or an office of some Imperial estate. We do not
know the particular work performed by the procurators in question. It
is therefore useless to speculate on the minuter details of the problem.
But procurators in the provinces were frequently entrusted, among their
other duties, with the supervision of the *publicani* or middlemen who
farmed certain State taxes and revenues, and Naevius on Combe Down
may have stood in some such relation to the *publicani* whom we thought

---

[1] For the burials, see Scarth, *Som. Proc.* v. 60, 135, and *Aquae*, p. 116; brief notes in *Arch. Journ.*
xi. 289, 408; xii. 90, 178; xiv. 172, and *Brit. Arch. Assoc. Journ.* xii. 304. For the inscription, see
Brit. Arch. Assoc. Journ. xviii. 303, *Som. Proc.* v. 137, *Aquae*, p. 75, *Corpus Inscr. Lat.* vii. 62 and briefly
Proc. Soc. Antiq. First Series, iii. 149 (without text). The stone itself is now in the Institute at Bath,
where I have seen it. The reading seems certain, though the letters are somewhat worn. I can quote
no exact parallel for the civil sense which I propose to assign to *principia*. But an analogy may be found
in the uses of *praetorium* which, beside its military meanings, sometimes denoted the residential villa
occupied by the master of a private estate (Digest, xxxii. 91, 1; i. 16, 198, etc.). On an inscription
from Puteoli (*Corpus Inscr. Lat.* x. 1837) *principiola* plainly means a building which has nothing
to do with the headquarters of a fort, though the inscription is too fragmentary to tell us what it
actually is.

to detect on the leaden seal found in the villa. Our clues, however, are very scanty. It is rash to do more than suggest that we have here, not a fort, but some scattered vestiges of the Roman civil administration or the service of the Imperial domains.

On the whole, we seem to detect on this site two elements. One belongs to the Imperial administration at the opening of the third century A.D. The other is a residence, occupied possibly in the third century and more certainly in the fourth. It may be that the two are connected and that Naevius and his successors occupied the house of which we have traces. But as to this our evidence is silent. The house was, at any rate, inhabited till near the end of the fourth century. Then, as an abundant layer of ashes seems to indicate, it was burnt. It has been conjectured—as by Mr. Cuming—that some of the burials and some of the iron objects belong to a post-Roman and indeed an English date. That might imply that the site was afterwards occupied by the English. But the character of the objects hardly justifies the conjecture.

(20) Wellow. This parish contains the site of a large and sumptuous villa. It stood in what is now Upper Hayes, three-quarters of a mile west of Wellow church, halfway down a long hillside that slopes gently south-eastwards to Midford brook.[1] Portions of it have been explored on six different occasions. In 1685 a mosaic was found (A on plan). In 1737 this mosaic was reopened and two more were uncovered. In 1787 a visitor to the neighbourhood attempted a little piece of excavation. In 1807, a resident, Col. John Leigh of Combe Hay, reopened the three previously discovered mosaics and also broke fresh ground. In 1820–2 the Rev. John Skinner of Camerton (p. 290)

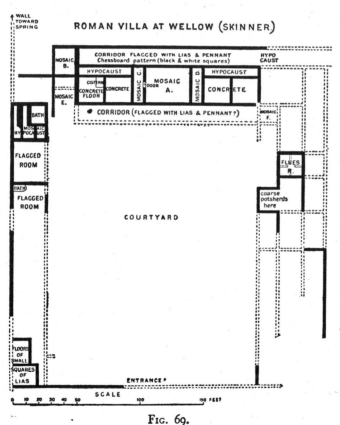

ROMAN VILLA AT WELLOW (SKINNER)

FIG. 69.

promoted a more or less systematic examination of the site. Finally in 1846 the Rev. C. Paul, vicar of Wellow, found a small building half a

[1] Part of the site, says Skinner (MS. 33657, p. 14), bore the name Blacklands, which often occurs on Roman sites.

MOSAIC PAVEMENT AT WELLOW

SCENE WITH FIGURES NOW UNINTELLIGIBLE

FEET

FIG. 71. WELLOW MOSAIC A.

mile from the villa, which may or may not belong to it and which may best be treated separately (No. 21).[1]

The villa itself was a normal instance of the courtyard house (fig. 69). With its yard, it occupied an area of about 248 by 262 feet. Its buildings ran continuously round the north, east and west sides of this area, while the south side was closed by a single wall, in which was doubtless the entrance. On the north side, looking down the yard, stood the principal dwelling, provided with a corridor or cloister on each side of it, and adorned with elaborate mosaics and warming apparatus. On its right hand, in the north part of the west wing, were the bathing apartments. The rest of the wings are imperfectly known to us, but seem to have contained servants' rooms and possibly stores, stables and the like. Some 'stoves for smelting iron and lead ore' noted by Skinner at R may be traces of a channelled hypocaust.

The small structural remains found in the villa comprise painted wall plaster, ridge and other tiles, hexagonal roofing slabs, a stone finial like that unearthed in the Baths at Bath (figs. 38, 70) and several striking mosaics. The principal pavement adorned the large room A (26 by 34 feet) It was unfortunately very fragmentary when first found in 1685 and has now, probably, entirely perished ; but enough has been recorded by successive observers to show its main character (fig. 71). Its general scheme is a central figured panel surrounded by interlacing squares and geometrical ornament. This is a common scheme in Roman mosaic work. But its application at Wellow is noteworthy, for the frame of geometrical ornament is

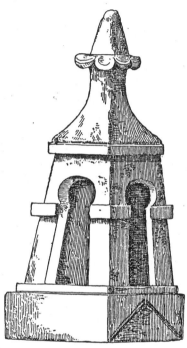

FIG. 70. FINIAL 18 INCHES HIGH.

[1] Our records of the excavation of this villa are very unsatisfactory. For the finds of 1685 see Aubrey's unpublished *Mon. Britann.* (Bodleian Library, MS. Aubrey 15, fo. 103), with illustration of the mosaic; Gale, *Antonini Iter* (London, 1709), p. 89, with roughly executed plate; brief note in Collinson, iii. 325. The excavations of 1737 are known only by a letter from the excavator, W. Prideaux, preserved in *Soc. Antiq. Minutes*, iii. 27 (23 June 1737), and three plates of mosaics in *Vetusta Monumenta*, i. 50–52. These are declared by Hoare (*Archaeologia*, xix. 45 note), Skinner and Lysons (*Soc. Antiq. Minutes*, xxxi. 379, 3 Dec. 1807) to be in part incorrect, and it is pretty clear that the largest (No. 50) is a most inaccurate restoration of the damaged mosaic found in 1685 (fig. 71). The others, however, which represent mosaics found in good preservation, seem to be fairly accurate. For the brief search made in 1787, see *Gent. Mag.* 1787, ii. 961, and *Gazetteer*, 10 Dec. 1787. Col. Leigh's operations in 1807 are noticed more or less briefly by S. Lysons, *Soc. Antiq. Minutes*, xxxi. 379; *Gent. Mag.* 1807, ii. 969; R. Warner, *Bath Guide* (1811), p. 133; Hoare, *Archaeologia*, xix. 45; and careful coloured drawings of mosaics opened by him are in the Bodleian (Gough, *Maps*, xxix. p. 26 f.). Skinner's excavations are recorded in his papers, Add. MS. 33657, etc. A plan and plates in folio were published by him and Weddell in 1823; from Skinner, Phelps *Introd.* p. 164. My plan of the villa is taken from Skinner and Weddell. My illustration of the principal mosaic is based on a comparison of the published plates in Gale's *Itinerary* and in Skinner and Weddell with the unpublished drawings in the Aubrey MSS. and Gough's papers in the Bodleian. It is, I believe, as correct as our materials permit. The Wollaston Collection at South Kensington contains drawings of the mosaics from *Vetusta Monumenta*. The notes on the 1737 finds in Lansd. MS. 827, p. 74, and Add. MS. 4452, p. 34 (miscatalogued as Wells) are of little value.

singularly rich and elaborate and contains a curiously large number of different patterns arranged somewhat unsymmetrically in small pieces, and, as it were, in patchwork. This appears to be due to design and not to mending.[1] Similar patchwork, though on a considerably smaller scale, occurs at Newton St. Loe (above, No. 7). But so far as I know, it is not common. Nor indeed is it so artistically successful that we should expect to meet it frequently. For despite its elaboration, or perhaps because of that, it is somewhat barbaric and perhaps a trifle oriental in conception. The narrow rooms or passages on either side of A (C and D in the plan) were floored with good geometrical mosaics suitable to corridors. That marked C, first found in 1737, contains five oblong partitions of common geometrical devices.[2] That marked D, opened in 1807, shows three oblong partitions, the centre made up of intersecting circles and the ends of diagonally bisected squares.[3] One other mosaic (B), first found in 1737, and reopened and partly destroyed in 1807, was an oblong floor in red, white, blue and dark brown or black (fig. 72). The centre was a square piece of singularly rich and elaborate key pattern : at each end were two conventional animals amongst still more conventional foliage, and the whole was bordered by a plain key pattern.[4] The other mosaics (rooms E, F and the bath) were so ill-preserved that reconstruction of their designs was judged by the excavators to be impossible. On the whole, the Wellow mosaics, though full of conventional elements and not devoid of barbaric extravagance, take a fairly high place among the tessellated pavements of Britain.

The smaller objects found in the villa are but scantily recorded. Skinner notes Samian and other potsherds, glass, a bronze spoon, two ring fibulae, an uninscribed fibula resembling the Aucissa type (p. 343), an iron ladle and handle, and late coins—of Severus Alexander, Gallienus, Allectus (noted by Warner), the Constantinian family and Valentinian.

The villa had round it outbuildings. From its north-west corner a wall ran northwards in the direction of an excellent spring, which was about 70 or 80 yards away. Near this wall were found many bones of edible animals—deer, pigs, sheep, oxen—and also the shells of oysters, cockles, limpets, periwinkles and the like. Here too was an outbuilding in which Mr. Skinner found upwards of a bushel of discarded pieces of blue and white lias and brick tesserae heaped together, as if (so he imagined) the outhouse were used for repairing the mosaic floors of the villa.

(21) Wellow. Besides the sumptuous house just described, other Roman buildings have been detected in the parish of Wellow. In

---

[1] Skinner and the artist of the coloured drawing in Gough's papers (see last note) record that the mosaic had been patched. But this was only in one small place—so small that I have omitted it from fig. 71.

[2] *Monumenta Vetusta*, plate 52 ; Skinner. The *Mon. Vet.* drawing seems correct, except that the partitions were perhaps oblong.

[3] Skinner ; Gough's papers in the Bodleian Library.   [4] *Mon. Vet.* plate 51 ; Skinner.

FIG. 72. WELLOW MOSAIC B.
(*Vetusta Monumenta.*)

1846 the vicar, the Rev. C. Paul, traced foundations, pavements and other signs of permanent Roman occupation about half a mile distant. Neither the position of this building nor the details of its plan and contents have been recorded. The principal discovery (fig. 74) seems to have been a sculptured stone 14 inches high and broad and $2\frac{3}{4}$ inches thick, bearing a bas-relief of two draped female figures, and an undraped male figure, all unfortunately headless. The female figures hold staves, or something similar, in each hand. The male figure has behind him a cloak dependent from his shoulders, and holds in his right hand a purse and in his left a staff. Possibly this is the end of a *caduceus* and the figure may be that of Mercury. But the identity of the two female figures is not clear. Other finds in this building were potsherds and much charred wood, the latter showing that the building had been burnt. Close by, a denarius of Augustus (Cohen, i. p. 70, No. 51) was picked up.[1]

Three other references to Roman buildings in Wellow parish occur in Mr. Skinner's papers.[2] He records foundations, coins and potsherds as noticed a mile west by south at Eckwick (or Eckweek) Farm and half a mile west by north at White Ox Mead. It is possible that the latter may be the site probed by Mr. Paul in 1846. He also mentions foundations, potsherds and a coin of Tetricus, as noticed in Shepherd's Mead, to the right of the road as one goes from Wellow towards Hinton.[3]

(22) Paulton. In January and the following months of 1818, Mr. Skinner, rector of Camerton (p. 290), excavated two adjacent houses in some fields on high ground between Paulton and Camerton. I have failed to discover the precise site. It is described as overlooking Clandown with a view into Wiltshire, and just south of the 'Ridgeway' road, to which Mr. Skinner attached an undue importance, and it appears to be rather

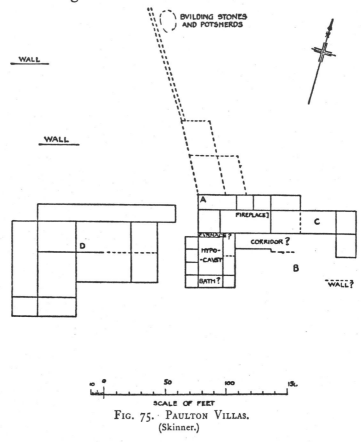

FIG. 75. PAULTON VILLAS.
(Skinner.)

[1] *Gent. Mag.* 1846 (ii.) 633; *Arch. Journ.* iv. 355, with cut of the sculpture. The piece was presented in 1851 to the Archaeological Institute (Bristol meeting, p. lxv.), and is now in the British Museum.
[2] Add. MSS. 33659, fol. 8; 33662, fol. 13; 33663, fol. 128.   [3] Add. MS. 33657 p. 67.

nearer to Paulton than to Camerton. The houses themselves, as planned by their excavator, appear to be a pair of ordinary rural dwelling-houses of the corridor type (fig. 75). Probably they belonged to the same estate; one may have sheltered the lord, and the other his servants or slaves. The eastern house was the better built. Like many corridor houses, it contained a special wing with a large

hypocaust. Room C was floored with cement, and its walls were plastered with stucco painted green, yellow, and brown. Two pits, 7 feet deep, containing coins of Pius and Faustina, a Samian cup, and a graceful urn of Castor ware (fig. 76), were found immediately north of the north-west angle of the house. Close by, at A on the plan, an interment was found in a corner of a room. Another interment—an urn with burnt bones and a silver coin of Pius—was in the front of the house at B. The second house was not so well built, but it is said to have contained some sort of tessellated floor. Among the ordinary objects recorded as found in these houses were pieces of Samian inscribed

FIG. 76. DARK BROWN URN, 5 INCHES HIGH, ORNAMENTED WITH LEAF PATTERN IN RELIEF, FOUND IN 1818: NOW IN BRISTOL MUSEUM.

SVORINEDO (misread for *Suobnedo*), ADVOOSIO (misread for *Advocisi officina*), and TIT.VRONIS.

Traces of other buildings or walls were noticed both on the north and on the south of these houses. But nothing definite can be made out of Mr. Skinner's plans, and it is likely enough that the remains belonged to outhouses, sheds, and enclosures.[1]

(23) Radstock. Two refuse pits were excavated in 1897 and 1898 in quarries on the south-east of Radstock. The first was found in Tyning quarry about 1,200 yards west of the Fosse. It yielded an iron nail, a quern, a spindle whorl, much black pottery, mostly British or earlier, but some perhaps Roman (?), much charcoal, burnt bones and teeth. The second was found near Radstock parish church, in Jubilee field, on the west of the road to Kilmersdon, and 1,320 yards south-west of the first. It was 6 feet deep, and measured 6 feet across at the top. It contained much black earth, charcoal, a large number of bones of animals, teeth, several bronze fibulae, tweezers, many iron nails, much common pottery, grey and black and red, embossed and other Samian, one piece with VIRIL scratched outside, flanged tiles, floor plaster and traces of wattle and dab.[2] These remains indicate the existence in the neighbourhood of either a villa, or (as has been also suggested) a Romano-British village, just off the Fosse.

[1] Skinner, Add. MS. 33659, p. 10, and 33661, pp. 168 foll.

[2] *Som. Arch. Proc.* xlv. (2) 108; *Bath Field Club,* ix. 202; information from the excavator, Mr. J. McMurtrie. Many of the remains are in the possession of Mr. McMurtrie, who allowed me to examine them.

FIG. 73. INSCRIPTION FROM CAMERTON (p. 291).

FIG. 74. RELIEF FROM WELLOW (p. 315).

(24) **Whatley.** Here was a good sized villa planted in open country close to a water brook, about two miles west of Frome, and immediately south of Whatley House, in a field called Chessil, just inside the north boundary of Nunney parish. It was discovered in August 1837, by men digging holes for posts, and was partly excavated in the following months, and again in 1848, and part of it is still open under the cover of a shed. Its ground plan has not been traced, but it seems to have consisted of at least one long row of rooms with hypocausts and apsidal chambers, as if of baths. The principal object found in it was a mosaic floor, worked in seven colours, and filling two large connected rooms, one rectangular and the other apsidal (fig. 77). The former showed a head of Cybele set amidst geometrical motives. In the other we have a procession of beasts, including an elephant, round a defaced central square which may have contained Orpheus. The smaller finds are painted wall plaster, tiles, window glass, Samian and other potsherds, spindlewhorls, a bronze figurine of a tiny deer (?), and

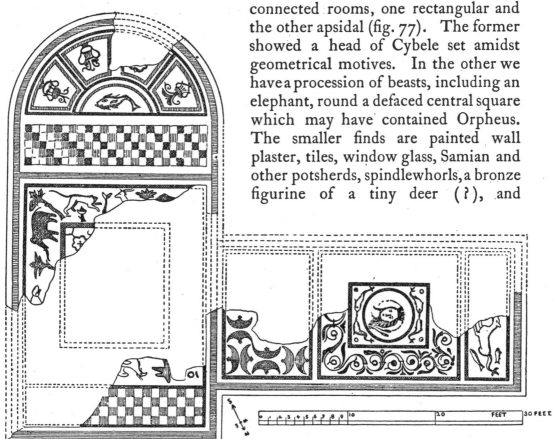

FIG. 77. ROMAN TESSELLATED PAVEMENT AT NUNNEY, SOMERSET.

numerous coins, almost all of which are copper of the late third and early fourth centuries. A lane called Whiteway runs from near the villa towards the village of Nunney.[1]

(25) **Shepton Mallet.** Interesting remains of inhabitation have come to light near Shepton, partly on the east and partly on the west

---

[1] *Gent. Mag.* 1838 (1), 435, 1839 (ii.), 77 ; *Som. Proc.* 1 (i.) 38, and more briefly xxi. (i.) 67, xxxv. (i.) 50, xxxix. (i.) 37. Mr. J. H. Shore, J.P., preserves many of the smaller objects at Whatley House, where he kindly let me examine them. Frome Museum has a model of the villa worked in stone by the late Jos. Chapman, but I am doubtful as to its correctness. The mosaic in fig. 77 is reproduced from a coloured drawing lent to me by Mr. Shore. A lithograph of it was published long ago by Bedford's Lithography (Redcliff Street, Bristol), but I have only once seen a copy. The drawings and reproductions of the mosaic which I have examined do not wholly agree in their measurements. It is still open to view, but less perfect than when originally found.

of the modern town. They have unfortunately not attracted the attention they deserve, and but for the wise exertions of the late Mr. John Phillis, we should know little about them.

(1) On the east of the town was a dwelling-house. It was planted close to the Fosse, and on the west side of it, about half way between Charlton and Cannard's Grave, just at the point where the Somerset and Dorset Railway crosses the Roman road. Its discovery was due to the doubling of that line in 1887, and, as too often happens in such cases, it was not followed up. But Mr. Phillis was able to note definite traces of walling about 40 feet in length, many roof slates of a thin shaley sandstone with the nails in them, and a well or rubbish pit 15 feet deep. The smaller finds, principally rescued by him, were interesting—not a little Samian, including a few embossed pieces of the first century (type, Dragendorff 29), and many of the second century (type 57), among it two stamps, **ERICI M** and **BVRRIO F** ; much common ware of many sorts, *pelves*, etc. ; over thirty fibulae, and among them an uninscribed Aucissa specimen and others of fairly early date ; bronze spoons, buckles, tweezers, and the like ; iron keys and nails and a knife blade, and some querns. The coins numbered over 120, and comprised 1 Republican, 22 of the first two centuries (1 Nero, 8 Claudius, 1 Vespasian, etc.), and many of the period 250–400. To these general finds of coins two hoards have probably to be added. One, consisting of perhaps 200 consular and imperial silver, buried in an earthen jar, seems to have been found at Charlton about 1880. The other is more dubious. Glastonbury Museum contains a large red urn found there in 1888, with 15 coins of the late third century and of Chlorus and Crispus. But it is not quite clear whether the 15 coins are or are not part of a hoard. Finally, in 1890 three skeletons with rings were found beside the Fosse near Charlton.[1]

(2) Besides these remains of houses and inhabitation, several potters' kilns have been found near Shepton. The fragments of one were noted by Mr. Phillis near the Charlton discoveries. Five others were found some years earlier on the west side of the town, when the Anglo-Bavarian Brewery (as it is now called) was built, in and after November 1864. One of the kilns first excavated is described as a circular structure excavated in the hill side, with a space in front, the floor 6 feet below the surface, the sides protected by stone jambs, the pottery shelf upheld by clay pillars, and perforated by nine holes of 3–9 inches in diameter, and the whole roofed by a dome (fig. 78). Several cups were found actually on the shelf or in the holes (fig. 79). The ware was of a red or buff colour, hard and somewhat resembling in texture the

---

[1] The late Mr. John Phillis described the remains to the Shepton Nat. Hist. Soc. on 22 Nov. 1887 (reprint from the *Shepton Mallet Journal*), but no further account has ever been published. I have to thank Mr. Phillis for much information ; I have also examined the interesting collection in Shepton Museum and some objects in private possession. The hoard of 200 silver coins passed, I understand, into the possession of the late Mr. Vonberg of Wells (compare *Som. Proc.* xxxiv. (1) 78) but was sold at his death. The fibulae and coins found in 1887 near Cannard's Grave (*Som. Proc.* xxxvi. (1) 61) may be another part of the finds described above. At Cannard's Grave itself (Mr. Phillis tells me) only a coin of Severus has been found.

modern flowerpot. Some black ware and a *pelvis* were also discovered, but no Samian occurred near the kilns. In an adjoining field a pit was soon after found, containing coins of the Constantine family, animal bones and other refuse.[1]

All these facts prove that the wayside of the Fosse south of Charlton was inhabited during all the Roman period, from the first to the fourth century. What was the precise character of the inhabitants must be left doubtful. It is not likely that the pottery kilns were employed during any great

FIG. 78.

number of years, or that the houses were inhabited principally by the potters. We may more probably have to deal with a wayside inn or a farm house or villa.

(26) West Cranmore. Skinner records a pavement found about 1800 at West Cranmore, and Sir R. C. Hoare notes coins and a fragment of a pavement. These are probably one and the same find.

FIG. 79.

It is surprising that nothing has since been heard of Roman remains at this place.[2]

(27) Chesterblade. At Chesterblade, two miles north-east of Evercreech, Mr. Joseph Allen found on his farm a few years ago some Roman remains indicating a villa or house. These were : foundations, potsherds, a lamp and coins (1 Domitian, 1 Hadrian, 2 Pius, 13 of *circa* A.D. 270–400). The site still awaits proper excavation. Its

[1] *Gent. Mag.* 1864, ii. 770 ; Scarth, *Som. Proc.* xiii. (2) 1–5 with plate here partly reproduced ; brief note in *Arch. Journ.* xxii. 163 ; letter and drawings from W. B. Caparn to C. R. Smith in the Fisher Collection in Exeter Museum ; remains in Taunton and Shepton Museums ; information from Mr. Phillis. It is unfortunate that in the Shepton Museum the objects found near Charlton and those connected with the kilns have not been wholly kept apart.

[2] R. C. Hoare, *Ancient Wilts*, Roman aera, p. 145 note ; Skinner, Add. MS. 33656, p. 100. One of the two probably learnt of the find from the other.

name may seem to suit Mr. Allen's discoveries, but it is unfortunately of obscure derivation. Mr. W. H. Stevenson tells me that the second half is doubtful in meaning, and the first may be from *caestel*, not from *ceaster*. It is, however, an old name occurring in the form 'Cestre-bald' in a Somerset Plea of A.D. 1225. The neighbouring camp on Smalldown, recently excavated, appears not to be Roman but of much greater antiquity.[1]

(28) Ditcheat. A villa was excavated in this parish by the late Colonel Woodforde about 1820. The site is a flat meadow called 'Laverns' on the north bank of the Brue and east of the road between Ansford Bridge and Brook House Inn, near to Castle Cary railway station. There were discovered, besides extensive foundations, a silver coin of Constantius II (Cohen 259), 6 or more bronze coins, including one or two of Tetricus, some 'coal money,' white and red tesserae of a mosaic, a curious circular armlet of what appears to be coal, potsherds and tiles. No proper record of the excavation exists, nor is anything now visible above ground.[2]

(29) Discove (about a mile south-east of Bruton). A tessellated pavement is said by Collinson to have been found here in 1711. But nothing more has been heard of it since, nor have I been able to learn anything by local inquiries.[3]

(30) Bratton. Insignificant foundations, tiles, coins, including two of Constantius II, pottery, etc., were found about 1832 on Castle Hill, a spur of Bratton Hill, and indicate a rural building of some sort. But we must wait for further evidence till we can decide its size and importance.[4]

(31) Bayford. Mr. George Sweetman of Wincanton tells me that a Roman villa is said to have been found in 1764 in building a new house at Bayford Lodge, a mile east of Wincanton, in the parish of Stoke Trister. No trace now remains of it. But its tradition has been consciously or unconsciously used by Mr. A. T. Quiller-Couch in his novel *The Westcotes*.

IV. VILLAS WEST OF THE FOSSE NEAR STREET, SOMERTON, LANGPORT AND THE POLDEN HILLS (32–50).

This group demands a preliminary observation. As the map shows, a very considerable number of villas is recorded from the neighbourhood of Somerton. For the most part they lie west or north

[1] For information as to the remains at Chesterblade I am indebted to Mr. Joseph Allen through the intermediation of the late Mr. John Phillis; Mr. Phillis also showed me the Roman lamp from the site. For 'Cestrebald' see *Somerset Record Society, Somerset Pleas*, No. 316. For Smalldown see Phelps, p. 111 and *Som. Proc.* xlix. 184, l. 35 foll.; in the recent excavations two bits of possibly Romano-British pottery were found, but they are very likely pre-Roman.

[2] Phelps, *Modern History of Somerset*, ii. 263; *Som. Proc.* xxxvi. (1) 61; *Arch. Journ.* xxxvi. 334; information from Rev. A. J. Woodforde, who possesses some of the objects mentioned above.

[3] Collinson, *Hist. of Somerset*, i. 215; hence Gough, *Adds. to Camden*, i. 99; *Gent. Mag.* 1823, i. 584.

[4] Phelps' *Hist. of Modern Somerset*, i. 221, hence *Murray's Handbook* (ed. 1899), p. 10; information from the late Bishop Hobhouse.

of it, on the high lands that fringe the eastern limits of the great marshes of the Parrett and Carey. Those nearest to Somerton were mainly excavated about 1820–30 by a local antiquarian, Mr. Samuel Hasell, and his results were very briefly published by Sir R. C. Hoare in a privately printed pamphlet. How far Mr. Hasell was competent for his task is not recorded. But I have a suspicion—which at least

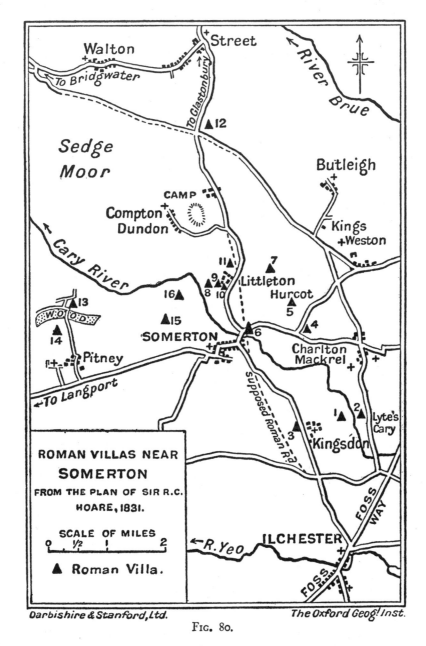

FIG. 80.

one good judge shares with me—that he was an enthusiast and saw foundations too easily. The case has been complicated by his successors. The Ordnance Survey marks on its six-inch sheets most of its villas and two new ones. The surveyors appear to have relied, partly on a map issued by Hoare (fig. 80) and partly on local information. The result is unsatisfactory. Hoare's map is quite rough, and the sites on it are necessarily also marked roughly. But the Ordnance map-makers seem to have transferred them mechanically to their own other-wise accurate map. The apparent precision which results from this process is of course illusory. The surveyors' local information is per-haps equally open to criticism. In consequence, several of the Ordnance sites are, as I believe, wrong. One certainly, near Hurcot, is physically impossible. Unfortunately, I have failed to secure any living witnesses to Roman remains on the sites in question, and the sites themselves, which I have visited, are now mostly under grass and afford little evidence to the visitor. Until, therefore, excavations be undertaken, or chance brings discoveries, it seems best to include the alleged villas with a full caution.

(32) Street (Butleigh Wootton). At Marshall's Elm, in the parish of Street, in a field and wood just north-east of the junction of the roads from Charlton Mackrell and Somerton, there was discovered about 1825 'the site of an extensive villa in Butleigh Bottom, in which, on a partial examination, were found coins of Claudius Gothicus and other Roman emperors.' Samian and other potsherds were picked up some time before 1850 near and east of the same spot. No traces are now visible, except that the ground has obviously been disturbed.[1]

(33) Kingweston. A villa is marked here by the Ordnance Sur-veyors about half a mile east of the village. This is not mentioned by Hoare, nor is anything recorded of it elsewhere. But perhaps we might connect it with some coins found at Barton St. David, half a mile away.[2]

(34) Copley (Kingweston). In Copley Wood, a little east of Littleton and in the parish of Kingweston, Sir R. C. Hoare records 'the sites of several small habitations irregularly interspersed over a con-siderable space of ground. They have been explored and produced coins of Constantine, Roman pottery, fibulae, angular tiles, etc., but no traces of mosaic pavements. The land around is high and barren.' No further record of the remains exists. The ruins of a stone building exist in Copley Wood at a spot called Magotty Pagotty. But so far as they are now visible on the surface, they might well be of fairly recent date. They are however marked as Roman by the Ordnance Surveyors.[3]

(35) Hurcot. A villa lay $1\frac{1}{4}$ miles north-east of Somerton, at Hur-cot Farm, only $\frac{1}{2}$ mile distant from the villas of Somerton and Charlton Mackrell (Nos. 36, 38). Hoare describes it as 'situated at the foot of a hill facing the south, and commanding a fine view of the neighbouring country ; it covers about half an acre of ground, and a clear spring of water rises at a short distance from the ruins. Traces of hypocausts, baths and

[1] R. C. Hoare, *Pitney pavement* (1832), No. 12; hence Phelps, *Hist. of Somerset*, Introduction p. 169; information from Mr. Clarke; personal visit. Site marked on O.S. lxiii. N.E.
[2] O.S. 6 inch No. lxiii. SE. on the authority of the late F. H. Dickenson and Col. F. W. Pinney ; for the coins see the alphabetical index.
[3] R. C. Hoare, *Pitney pavement* (privately printed 1832), No. 7 (see fig. 80 No. 7) ; hence Phelps, *Introd.* p. 168. Ordnance Survey, lxiii. SE. on the authority of Col. F. W. Pinney and F. H. Dicken-son. A High Street Furlong is marked on the map just to the NE. of Copley Wood. But it bears no outward signs to-day of Roman origin.

mosaic pavements were discovered.' The discovery was made in 1827 by Samuel Hasell, who, according to other records, found a good mosaic in a room measuring 12 by 14 feet, and another pavement, or it may be the same, of a purely geometrical pattern of guilloche and triangle, in the usual red, white and blue, measuring 4 feet square. But no further remains are recorded that might suggest the shape or size of the villa, or the approximate date of its occupation.[1]

(36) Charlton Mackrell. Sir R. C. Hoare states that a villa or other rural building was partially examined by Mr. S. Hasell about a mile east of Somerton, near the junction of the roads leading to that town from Charlton Mackrell and from Kingweston, just under Snap or Windmill Hill. The finds included ' herringbone walls, angular tiles, coins of Claudius Gothicus, with others of the Lower Empire, and instruments of iron,' but no mosaics, and the ruins seemed to have been previously disturbed. Nothing is now visible at or near the site marked by Hoare (fig. 80, No. 4), and the building appears to have been of humble character. About 1846, a parcel of forty coins dating from Constantius II to Theodosius was found somewhere near the building, and also three stone coffins of uncertain age.[2]

(37) Littleton. About a mile north of Somerton, and on the west of the road from Somerton to Street, two villas were excavated by Mr. S. Hasell, the first in 1822, and the second in 1827. Both were described by Sir R. C. Hoare.

(1) In the one case, close to Littleton itself, foundations were traced which at first appeared to belong to three distinct buildings, but which seemed on further excavation to form one large villa—possibly a courtyard house of the Brading type (fig. 6). Besides this, an adjoining area of about 30 acres was found to be ' entirely covered with buildings, and on digging deep into the soil, produced foundations of walls of herring-bone structure, bricks, tiles, coins, fragments of mosaics, etc.' This would indicate a village rather than a villa. But the ' area of 30 acres ' may be a serious exaggeration. It does not seem to be confirmed by any subsequent discoveries.

(2) About a third of a mile north of this a second villa was discovered. This was more carefully examined and described than most of the villas in this neighbourhood, and a plan was actually drawn (fig. 81). It lay ' in a pleasant meadow, with a fine stream running close to it,' and was a spacious structure, occupying, with outbuildings, an area of

---

[1] Skinner, in Add. MS. 33665, fol. 345 (letter from Hasell), and 33716, fol. 81 (drawing of geometrical mosaic) ; R. C. Hoare, *Pitney pavement* (1832), No. 6; hence Phelps, *Hist. of Somerset*, Introduction, p. 168 ; tesserae and potsherds in Taunton Museum. The O.S. 6 inch lxiii. SE. marks a villa to the NE. of Hurcot Farm. But the spot seems altogether unsuitable for a house ; the slope is much too steep and is scarred with little water-courses. More probably the villa lay to the west of the modern house and near to Dominie's well. This agrees better with Hoare's description of the site, and I noticed foundations here which may or may not be Roman. Pieces of Roman road and a ' camp ' are also marked on the Ordnance Survey lxiii. SE. near Hurcot. They seem, however, to lack evidence.

[2] R. C. Hoare, *Pitney pavement* (1832), No. 4 ; hence Phelps, *Introd.* p. 168. The site marked in the 6 inch O.S. seems simply borrowed from Hoare. For the coffins see *Arch. Journ.* ii. 209 ; for the hoard *Gent. Mag.* 1846 (i.) 76.

two and a half acres, arranged on the courtyard plan. Only the north side was excavated at all fully. There were found the principal apartments, consisting of a long corridor, measuring some 200 feet, and north of it a row of ten or eleven rooms, the largest measuring 16 by 20 feet, with four small rooms beyond them. The corridor seems to have been paved with mosaic originally, and mended with lias flags at a later date. Four rooms contained mosaics, which are said to have exhibited superior workmanship, but to have been much ruined. One had a representation of Bacchus (?) in the centre, and another an inscription, of which only the letters **FLA** remain. Three rooms were floored with lias flags or with terras. A hypocaust and furnace were found at the east and west ends, and flues in the centre room and in the small room to the west of it. South of the corridor and in the centre of it was a structure resembling a projecting porch, giving on to the courtyard. On the west side of this courtyard only one room was excavated, proving merely

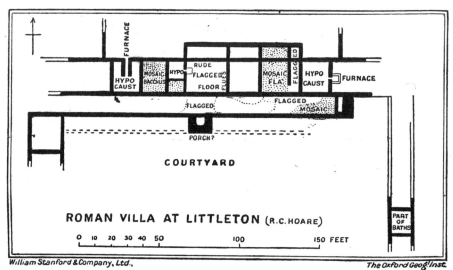

FIG. 81.

that there were buildings on this side. On the east side, 60 feet south of the main buildings, the baths were found, but were not entirely uncovered. This completes the list of ascertained rooms. Smaller remains included many potsherds, worked stone, and some coins dating from Vespasian onwards, but chiefly of the later Empire.[1]

In 1883 some coins of Postumus, Victorinus and Constantine were picked up at Littleton, and are now in the possession of Mr. Franklin of Taunton. From which of the two villas they came seems not to be recorded.[2]

(38) Somerton. Sir R. C. Hoare mentions a villa about ½ mile north-east of Somerton, on the line of the road to Charlton Mackrell and just north of the river Cary. It was excavated by Mr. Hasell,

---

[1] R. C. Hoare in *Gent. Mag.* 1827 (ii.) 113 and *Pitney pavement*, No. 11. W. Stradling, *Priory of Chilton Polden* (1839), p. 11, mentions 'a bason of Parian marble' from this villa, presented to him by the excavator, Mr. S. Hasell, but this is too good to be accurate. The two sites are marked on the Ordnance map (lxiii. SE.) apparently from Hoare.   [2] Hoare, *Pitney Pavement*, Nos. 15, 16.

'and Roman pottery, tiles, flues, and coins of Constantine, Antoninus, Victorinus, Postumus, etc., with foundations and tessellated floors,' were found. Other coins have since been picked up in the neighbourhood—two denarii of Hadrian, a 'First Brass' of Gordian, and some Third Brass from Constantine to Theodosius, indicating an occupation extending over the third and fourth centuries.[1]

(39) Two other villas in another part of this parish are marked by Sir R. C. Hoare on his map, but are not described in his text. They lie on the left bank of the river Cary, ¾ mile and a mile respectively north-west of Somerton. A villa, which might be the more northerly one, is marked by the Ordnance Surveyors near Etsome Farm, on the right bank of the river Cary. But if so, Hoare has put the house both on the wrong bank and on too high ground.

(40) King's Sedgemoor. Early in the nineteenth century Mr. S. Hasell found a Roman building below the peat on King's Sedgemoor near Somerton, and in it an iron ring or fibula 'cased in brass,' and a piece of bone (perhaps a handle) scored with the letters APRILIS, *Aprilis*,

FIG. 82. INSCRIPTION FROM KING'S SEDGEMOOR.
(*Archaeological Journal.*)

perhaps the name of the owner (fig. 82). No further details seem to be preserved of the building. It may however be that which the Ordnance Survey marks, low down on the marsh level, about 250 yards north-west of Etsome Farm in the parish of Somerton.[2]

(41, 42) Kingsdon. Hoare records two villas here.

(1) The first stood on the west of the village and of the road leading from Ilchester to Somerton, about halfway between these places. Here some small remains were found, but not examined in Hoare's time. Nothing has been since recorded, and the existence of a villa here remains to be proved.

(2) The second lies about half a mile east of Kingsdon, on the west bank of the river Cary, just opposite to the villa at Lyte's Cary. Hoare mentions 'the site of a large villa, which has not been opened, the fields in which it is situated being in tillage : but the plough has brought up to the surface Roman brick, tiles, etc.' This is better

---

[1] R. C. Hoare *Pitney pavement* (1832), No. 6, under the name Hurcot, hence Phelps, *Introd.* p. 168; *Som. Proc.* xxxi. (1) 45 (two denarii of Hadrian 'found at Somerton'); coins in the possession of Mr. Franklin. A Roman road is supposed to run close to it.

[2] W. Stradling, *Priory of Chilton Polden* (Taunton 1839), p. 16; *Arch. Institute*, Bristol meeting, p. lxv.; *Som. Proc.* xlviii. (1) 85; all referring primarily to the inscribed bone, which is, since 1902, in the Taunton Museum. For the site near Etsome Farm see Ordnance Survey 6 inch lxiii. SW. See the preceding entry (No. 39).

evidence that a villa existed than we have for the preceding item. But it is nevertheless unsatisfactorily meagre.[1]

(43) Lyte's Cary. A villa is noticed here by Sir R. C. Hoare,[2] to the east of the river Cary, and between it and the road leading north to Charlton Mackrell, just opposite to the villa in Kingsdon parish. It was examined by Mr. Hasell, and the recorded finds are said to have included 'a hypocaust and other Roman remains.'

(44) Pitney. Two villas have been discovered in this parish, both to the north of the village, about 500 yards apart. They occupy very different positions.

The best explored and possibly the largest of these villas was examined by Mr. Hasell in 1828-9. It occupies a ledge of nearly flat

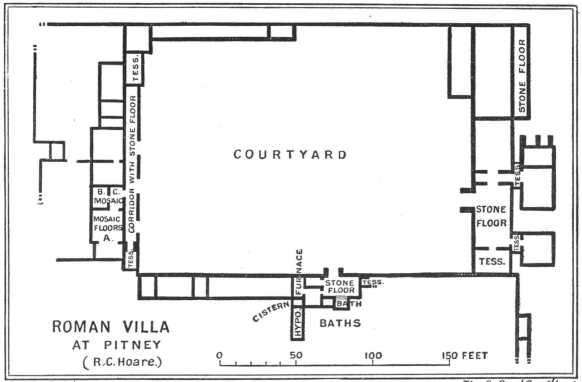

ROMAN VILLA
AT PITNEY
(R.C.Hoare.)

Darbishire & Stanford, Ltd.   The Oxford Geog! Inst.

FIG. 83.

ground, 45 feet above sea level, which intervenes between the marsh of King's Sedgemoor and the steep wooded side of Stowey or Stawell's Tree Hill (225 feet). The site, though cut off from a southern aspect, open only to the north, and somewhat secluded, is dry and well supplied with spring water. The villa itself formed a rectangular structure built round three sides of a large courtyard, the whole measuring 325 feet from east to west and 210 feet from north to south (fig. 83). At the west end of the courtyard was the house proper, a building of the corridor type, roofed with slates. Three rooms (A, B, C) were floored with mosaics

[1] R. C. Hoare, *Pitney pavement* (1832), Nos. 3 and 1. The second of these villas is marked on the Ordnance Maps (6-inch lxxiii. NE.) but the first is not.

[2] Hoare, *Pitney pavement* (1832), No. 2.

worked in four colours, which, to judge by drawings of them, were more ambitious than artistic. The principal room (A) was divided into two partitions (fig. 84). The larger half was paved with a square mosaic enclosing an octagonal scheme. In this, eight figures, alternately male and female, some draped, some undraped, each in its own triangular panel, are grouped round a central figure, and the four corners of the whole are filled with heads. The series was taken by Sir R. C. Hoare to represent the master of the house surrounded by his servants paying their dues to him, and he connected it with the Mendip lead industry. But this is highly improbable. These nude or half-draped figures do not represent the maidservants and menservants of a villa, or of an estate. Their costume sufficiently demonstrates that. Plainly they form some series of deities or mythological personages, chosen without regard to their coherence or congruity, unless, indeed, the artist had in mind some illustration of the loves of the gods. Certainly we can distinguish Mercury with his caduceus, Neptune with his trident, and a Mithraic figure with a Persian cap. The mosaic of the other and smaller part of the room A contained four figures (one defaced), which might be called the Four Seasons, set in a key pattern of guilloche bands. This mosaic was destroyed in 1836. The mosaic of room B (fig. 86) shows in a central circular panel an undraped man recoiling from a snake, striking at it and upsetting a pail which he carries. The scene has been explained as Hercules killing the Hydra, but it does not well suit that interpretation. The mosaic of room C is small and simple, a geometrical scheme of inter- lacing circles (fig. 85). Two other rooms in the building had tessellated floors; the rest, except the flagged corridor, were floored with earth or gravel. On the south side of the courtyard was a row of rooms ending in the baths. On the east was a block which may be assigned to the servants. The house appears to have been occupied for long years, since in some rooms three terras or plaster floors and a flagged one were found one above the other. The minor objects discovered in the excavation have been imperfectly recorded. Chief among them are two fragments, apparently sepulchral inscriptions, found in the courtyard. (*a*) PATER- PATRI-SANC

(*b*) **VIXISIN**
TRIGINTA
QVΛECAPI
NONOΛ

The second obviously contained some common sepulchral formula, such as *vixi sine ulla macula triginta annos*, 'I lived a spotless life for thirty years.' Among other recorded finds were painted wall-plaster, leaden water pipes and a clay plug, stone hypocaust-pillars and stone weights—once in Mr. Stradling's Museum at Chilton Polden. I have not been able to ascertain the present home either of the inscriptions or of the other objects.[1]

[1] R. C. Hoare, *The Pitney pavement* (8vo, privately printed, 1832), and *Gent. Mag.* 1828, ii. 361, and 1830, i. 17 (compare 1830, i. 546; 1833, i. 148; 1836, i. 194); from Hoare, Phelps *Introd.* p. 169. Coloured reproductions of the mosaics were issued by S. Hasell (copies in the Soc. of Antiq. Library and Taunton Museum). See also W. Stradling, *Priory of Chilton Polden* (Taunton 1839), p. 31; Skinner,

(45) The other Pitney villa was situated on the high ground south of the first villa, at an elevation of about 200 feet above the sea, with a good prospect south and west. It was first detected about 1828 and was partly explored in 1861 by Mr. Chambers. Foundations, a mosaic of circles and squares interlacing in common fashion, potsherds, roof-tiles, etc., were discovered. But no proper description was ever issued.[1]

(46) High Ham. A villa was excavated in 1861 about a mile south of High Ham church and half a mile west of Low Ham, on slightly rising ground near Sam's Cross. A plan is said to have been made, but no report was ever issued. Two mosaics were found, drawings of which, unfortunately ill-suited for reproduction, exist in Taunton Museum. One contained rectangular panels with conventional flowers and leaves inside a cable border. The other was a plain geometrical variation on a key pattern. The small objects found included a few coins of the later Empire (Allectus, Chlorus, Constantine), black ware and rims of mortaria, roof slates of shale, and bones.[2]

(47) Langport, Huish Episcopi. The position of Langport is significant. At this point the marshy levels beside the Parrett give way to higher land on both sides, and the river itself narrows, thus affording a convenient place for a bridge and one that was easily defensible. Earthworks, which may be of very early date, have been traced to the north-east of the town and the river, and Stukeley casually calls the site Roman, though without any apparent authority. Since Stukeley's time, Roman remains have actually been found. The 'Roman road' traced about 1863 along the lower road of Langport, may or may not be really Roman. But pottery and coins were picked up in 1867 close to the railway station on the west bank of the river, and in the parish of Huish Episcopi, and tiles appear to have been found earlier on the same site. Captain Long has three coins found somewhere in Langport—a Second Brass of Trajan, a Third Brass of the Thirty Tyrants and another of the fourth century. These remains, and especially the tiles, suggest the existence of a villa or building on the west bank of the river. But even this requires to be proved by excavations, and no more extensive occupation is even suggested by our present evidence.[3]

(48-49) Drayton, Curry Rivel. Two villas or houses have been detected about 900 yards apart, both close to the boundary which separates these parishes and near the eastern end of a low ridge of rising ground which juts out from the Blackdown range towards Langport and the river Parrett. Whether the two belonged to the same estate cannot be decided.

Brit. Mus. Add. MS. 33712, pp. 120–142, with sketches; *Corpus Inscr. Lat.* vii. 64 (from Hoare with a misreference to Phelps). I have given the inscription (b) as it is given in the original MS. of Hoare's pamphlet, now in my library. The site of the villa is marked on the Ordnance maps.

[1] J. Rutter, *Delineations of North West Somerset* (Lond. 1829), p. 170 note; *Som. Proc.* xi. (1) 22, drawing of mosaic in Taunton Museum. The site is marked on the Ordnance maps.

[2] *Som. Proc.* xi. (1) 33, 56; O.S. lxii. SE.; Taunton Museum.

[3] Stukeley, *Itinerarium*, ed. i. p. 147; ed. ii. p. 155; Gough's *Camden's Brit.* (1806), i. 98; *Som. Proc.* iv. (2) 46, xi. (1) 7, and (2) 196; O.S. lxxii. NE.; information from Capt. Long of Woodlands, Congresbury.

FIG. 84. PITNEY MOSAIC A.
(Scale 1 : 50.)

(*a*) In Drayton parish, and near its western edge, 560 yards west of the church, in a field called Broadwell (on the tithe map No. 337), walls, paving, plaster, potsherds, a bronze ring, four coins (Claudius Gothicus, Carausius, Magnentius, Third Brass ; Pertinax (?), (silver) ; skeletons and urns containing human bones, were found about 1861 and the principal objects were given to the Taunton Museum. Some 400 yards west of this, in Currey Rivel parish, part of a fibula, two bits of Samian and other potsherds came to light at the same time.

(*b*) At Stanchester in Curry Rivel parish, 700 yards east of the church, some tesserae from a floor, coins (First Brass of Pius and Trajan, and many later copper), Samian and other potsherds, bits of bronze, three whorls of Kimmeridge shale, and other small objects were found in 1865. Coins have also been found at Wiltown, another hamlet of Curry Rivel, lying on the south side of that village.[1]

(50) Bawdrip. A Roman villa seems to have stood in or very near this parish, possibly at Churchie Bushes, a field about half a mile east of Bawdrip village on the south slope of the Polden Hills. Paschal, writing in 1689 to Aubrey, mentions 'a pavement discovered in a ploughed field at Bawdrip some years ago.' Stradling, writing from Chedzoy in 1827 to Skinner, says that a villa had just been found in the next parish and on the south side of the Polden Hills, and had yielded black earth, flue tiles, potsherds, and a bluish-green bead. This bead appears to be the same as one found at Churchie Bushes, which was at first preserved in Mr. Stradling's museum and is now at Taunton. Churchie Bushes has also yielded a carved capital and some unglazed tiles, and might be accepted (subject to excavation) as the probable site of the villa. But it has also been identified as the site of a mediaeval chapel, and the matter is perhaps open to doubt.[2]

V. VILLAS NEAR THE FOSSE IN THE SOUTH OF THE COUNTY (51–58)

(51) East Coker. A villa was discovered in 1753 at a site which is described as about a mile and a half south of Yeovil, on the east side of the road leading to East Coker and near a good spring of water. Several rooms were distinguished and two mosaics, one figured and one of purely geometrical design. The figured mosaic (fig. 88) was laid over a hypocaust and measured 10 feet by 12 feet. Its colours were red, white

---

[1] Taunton Museum (Monckton Coll.) ; O.S. marking all three sites ; information from the Rev. R. Quick of Drayton, Mr. H. St. G. Gray and Dr. H. Norris. The Stanchester and Wiltown finds are mentioned in *Som. Proc.* xi. (1) 8, 56, and xviii. (1) 69. The name of the place appears in the Muchelney chartulary as ' Stankestlas ' (*Som. Record Soc.* xiv. 39) and its second half may come from *caestel*, not from *ceaster* (W. H. Stevenson).

[2] Andrew Paschal to Aubrey, 4 Nov. 1689, in MS. Aubrey, 13, fol. 83, and 15, fol. 110, in the Bodleian Library ; the pavement mentioned in MS. Aubrey 15, fol. 105, as found near to Knoll Hill in 1670, may well be the same (see p. 352). W. Stradling, letter to Skinner in Brit. Mus. MS. Add. 33665, fo. 337, and *Priory of Chilton Polden* (Bridgwater, 1839), p. 15 ; *Som. Proc.* xlvii. (1) 184. E. H. Brice, *Som. Proc.* xlix. (2) 187, mentions a statement by a Mr. Knott (whose father was vicar of Bawdrip till 1827) that a tessellated pavement had been found in the glebe land of the parish, and this may confirm Mr. Stradling's statement quoted in the text. But Mr. Brice himself takes Churchie Bushes to be the site of the mediaeval chapel called Ford Chantry. It is now grassland, and nothing ancient is discernible. The alleged villa at Slapeland in Chedzoy, noted by Mr. Stradling, must be different from the Bawdrip remains, whatever it be itself ; see the alphabetical index.

and blue, and its general scheme a circle enclosed in an oblong. Outside the circle in the corners of the oblong were Mercuries' heads, and at its two ends a dog chased a hare or stag. Inside the circle was a curious and unusual scene. In front a female figure, draped over the knees, reclined on a couch. Another female figure, fully dressed, stood by, and, according to some accounts, a third helped to affix a robe round the reclining figure. Behind stood a man fully clad, in the attitude of exposition. The whole has been explained as depicting a surgeon about to operate on a patient, and this view may serve in place of anything better. The other mosaic showed a purely geometrical design of lozenges, octagons, asiatic shields, and the like and measured

FIG. 88.   MOSAIC FOUND AT EAST COKER, 1753.

10 feet by 14 feet. The smaller finds made in the villa included bricks, tiles, iron objects and burnt bones, but have not been properly recorded.[1]

Further discoveries were made about 1818 or 1820 at the same spot, or very close to it, in a field called Chesil or Chessells. Foundations, hypocausts, two mosaics, one figured and one geometrical, painted wall plaster, tiles, potsherds and coins were discovered. The figured mosaic was a fragment of about $3\frac{1}{2}$ feet by 4 feet, representing two men returning from the chase carrying a spear each and a dead stag slung from a pole propped on their shoulders, with a small dog barking below the stag (fig. 87). The colours are blue-black, red and a yellowish drab, on a white ground. The coins were of Faustina (much defaced), Constantine, Crispus, Constantius (probably the second), Julian and Valens.[2]

[1] *Yeovil General Evening Post*, 23 June 1753; *Gent. Mag.* 1753, p. 293 (misplaced under Devon in the *Gent. Mag. Libr.* p. 40); Ducarel in Brit. Mus. Addit. MS. 6210, p. 72 (olim, p. 50); Collinson, ii. 340; Gough, *British Topogr.* ii. 226, and *Adds. to Camden*, i. 91. I here reproduce an unpublished drawing preserved in a copy of Collinson's *Somerset* in the Bodleian (Gough, *Som.* 10); it omits the third female figure—which indeed is said by those who mention it to have been much damaged. It seems from this drawing that the explanation of the mosaic given by C. R. Smith, *Coll. Ant.* ii. 53, cannot stand. The suggestion that it represents a Christian baptism is still less possible. The mosaic itself was destroyed soon after its discovery.

[2] Phelps, *Introd.* p. 167 (from Skinner, who visited the excavations and left a record in his diary, Brit. Mus. Addit. MS.); C. R. Smith, *Coll. Ant.* ii. 51, with a plate of the mosaic, from a sketch made at the time of its discovery; John Batten, *South Somerset* (Yeovil, 1894), p. 106; the mosaic itself is at Taunton. The site is marked on the O.S., half a mile north of North Coker hamlet, in the parish of East Coker, near the road to Yeovil and on the east side of it. Another drawing of the hunting scene is preserved in the Wollaston Collection of drawings of mosaics in the South Kensington Museum. It differs considerably in detail from the original: the deer is differently slung, the dog in the foreground is also different, and the colouring varies markedly. It is evidently restored and (like some other drawings in this collection) is not very trustworthy in detail. Mr. Smith's drawing is far more accurate, but in some points, and especially in colouring, is not quite satisfactory. My fig. 87 is taken from a photograph of the original, by Mr. H. St. G. Gray.

FIG. 85. PITNEY MOSAIC C (scale $\frac{1}{34}$).

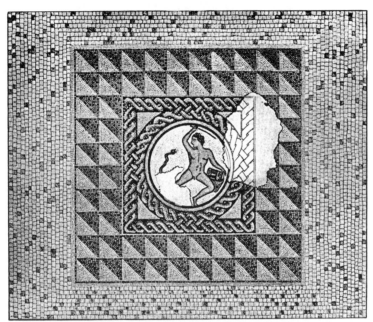

FIG. 86. PITNEY MOSAIC B (p. 327).
(From Hasell) $\frac{1}{34}$.

FIG. 87. COKER MOSAIC (p. 330).
(From a Photograph. Scale 1 : 15.)

ROMANO-BRITISH SOMERSET

It can hardly be doubted that the finds of 1753 and 1818–20 belong to the same villa, and that this formed a considerable and ambitiously ornamented structure, occupied, if not earlier, at any rate during the fourth century.

(52) West Coker. Here, in a field called Chessells, a villa was discovered and partially examined by Mr. John Moore in 1861. Few definite foundations were met with, but abundant evidences of a house, such as many blue and red tesserae from pavements, painted wall-plaster, tiles, roof slates and débris of building stone. The excavators thought that the villa had been burnt down, the spot rifled, and a subsequent building of rude character erected with burnt stones. Among the smaller finds were some pre-Roman items, suggesting that the site had been occupied at least by an interment of older date than the Roman period. The Roman items included Samian and other potsherds, many iron nails, some bits of bronze—including a rude statuette of Mars, 3 in. high, a bracelet and a pair of tweezers—bones of food animals and several coins—1 Lucilla, 1 Faustina, 1 Otacilia and Third Brass of Tetricus and other emperors to Valens, which show that the villa was occupied at least till near the end of the fourth century. Specially noteworthy is a bronze plaque, $1\frac{3}{4}$ inches high and $2\frac{3}{4}$ inches in length, on which an inscription has been punched—

DEO · MARTI
RIGISAMO
IVENTIVS
SABINVS
V · S · L · L · M

'To Mars Rigisamus, erected by Iuentius (that is Juventius) Sabinus.' Mars Rigisamus appears to be a Celtic deity Romanized; he occurs also on an inscription at Bourges in France. The whole of the West Coker remains suggest a house of some size and importance, and it is to be regretted that no proper plans or sketches have been published.[1]

(53) Norton sub Hamdon. At Norton sub Hamdon, near the Fosse, and underneath the south-west corner of Ham Hill, remains have been found in the village at Blackbarrowfield. These remains are : dark soil, potsherds, bones, an iron ring, a broken quern 6 feet deep, and also a well 39 feet deep, which, when excavated in 1897, yielded more potsherds, bones and querns, a small bronze fibula, tesserae, and a coin of Julia Mamaea (FECVN AVGVSTAE), this last found 6 feet deep. The tesserae indicate a pavement, and therefore a dwelling house of some sort.[2]

(54) South Petherton. In this parish three sites of Roman villas have been found or conjectured, but only one has adequate evidence.

---

[1] Moore, *Brit. Arch. Assoc. Journ.* xviii. 392, and xix. 322 ; the latter account is also given in *Gent. Mag.* 1864, i. 60 ; *Corp. Inscr. Lat.* vii. 61. In the *Assoc. Journ.* the dedicator's name is given as INVEN-TIVS, in the *Gent. Mag.* as IVENTIVS. The latter seems the more probable, since the name Inventius seems to occur nowhere else, while Iuventius and its byform Iventius are not uncommon ; see for example *Corp. Inscr. Lat.* vi. 20940–20958. For the Bourges inscription see *Corp. Inscr. Lat.* xiii. 1190.

[2] C. Trask, *Norton sub Hamdon* (Taunton, 1898), pp. 19, 240 ; information from Dr. Norris.

(1) A villa is said to have existed at Jailers' Mill, on the river Parrett, about a mile north-east of South Petherton, and about ¾ mile north-west of the Fosse. " Here," says Collinson, " remains of Roman buildings, coins, urns, paterae and terras were dug up."

(2) A pavement indicating another villa is reported to have been uncovered in 1673 at Watergore, half a mile south of South Petherton, and on the Fosse. But the earliest reference to it occurs in Collinson more than a century later, and is not to be received with any great confidence.

(3) Foundations are also said by Collinson to have been found at Wigborough, but these are more probably mediaeval, as Dr. Norris tells me.

Coins have been picked up one by one at various places all over this parish, and a hoard was dug up in 1720 at Petherton Bridge, near the first villa. Whether the two figures in relief built into the parapet of the bridge are Roman seems very doubtful.[1]

(55) Seavington. A villa was found and excavated here in 1861 and 1862, in a field called Crimmelford, or Curnelford Kapp, about ¾ mile south of St. Michael Seavington, and 300 yards west of the Fosse. It is situated on slightly elevated ground sloping gently to the south, with a good view of the open country all round. The entire building was not uncovered, the excavations were badly recorded, and the remains were immediately destroyed. Hence it is impossible to form any idea as to the character or the date of the villa. Several rooms were laid open, some with hypocausts under them, and two containing mosaics. One of these had a geometrical pattern in red, white, and blue ; the other was formed of squares of coarse red and white tesserae, while a third room was paved with red tiles about a foot square. Other remains included painted stucco from the walls, roof tiles, human skeletons, burnt bones, charcoal, potsherds, iron, bone pins and oyster shells, the débris of two ash pits.[2] A copper coin of Constantius II was found in 1889 in this parish, near Fowts, and coins are also ascribed to the neighbouring parish of Lopen (Alphabetical Index). These may be waifs from the villa.

(56) Chard. Two sites in this parish seem to have yielded significant remains. (1) Near St. Margaret's Chapel, on St. Margaret's Hill, in South Chard, quite close to the Fosse Way, remains were found in 1843, which may denote a villa of the third or fourth century. They consisted of tiles, tesserae, roof slates, opus signinum, potsherds,

---

[1] Collinson, *Hist. of Somerset* (1791), iii. 106, 7 ; he describes Jailer's Mill as in South Harp tithing, but he probably confused it with Petherton Mill. And as Wigborough and South Harp are quite close together, it is more probable that Wigborough was in the tithing of South Harp, and not Jailer's Mill. For the coins, see the alphabetical index. For the ' children ' on Petherton bridge, see a paper by H. Norris, *Somerset and Dorset N. and Q.*, June 1903, with illustrations.

[2] *Gent. Mag.* 1862 (1), 298 ; G. P. R. Pulman, *Book of the Axe* (1875), pp. 68, 69 ; H. Norris, *South Petherton*, p. 15, and *Som. Proc.* xxxvii. (1) 26. Tiles, tesserae, potsherds, fragment of mosaic, etc., in the Hull Collection at Chard, and in Taunton Museum. In the Walter Collection in the same Museum there is a rough drawing of one of the pavements. The site, still distinguishable by potsherds lying on the surface, is correctly marked on the Ordnance Map, lxxxviii. NE.

and coins dating from 250–380 A.D. (2) In a field near the Crew-kerne road, just east of the town, foundations of buildings and three Roman coins were turned up in 1856. The records of both these finds are vague and unsatisfactory. But they justify us in assuming the existence of one, or possibly of two, houses. For a few scattered smaller finds in the parish of Chard see the alphabetical index.[1]

(57) Wadeford. In a sheltered and well watered spot amidst the eastern Blackdown hills, at Wadeford, in the parish of Combe St. Nicholas, stood a Roman villa of considerable pretensions. It was first discovered in 1810, and some excavations were attempted about 1861. The plan of the edifice was not very clearly traced; possibly it belonged to the courtyard type (fig. 89). The contents are better known. In

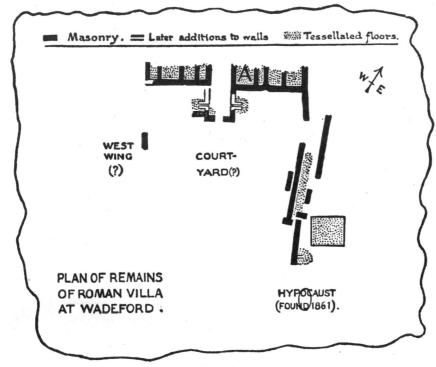

■ Masonry. = Later additions to walls ▨ Tessellated floors.

WEST WING (?)

COURT-YARD(?)

PLAN OF REMAINS OF ROMAN VILLA AT WADEFORD.

HYPOCAUST (FOUND 1861).

Fig. 89.

1810 two mosaics were unearthed. One, measuring 6 feet by 8 feet, showed a geometrical pattern of conventional flowers in circles and octagons in yellow, red, blue and grey on a white ground, the whole being set (as often) in a border of plain red brick tessellation (A on plan). The other pavement, 6 feet square, consisted of a central circular panel enclosed in two interlacing squares, which in their turn were contained by an octagon, while a square of maeander pattern bordered the whole. Both these mosaics perished soon after 1810 through frost. In 1861 five more pavements were found, all geometrical in pattern, mostly in very imperfect condition, and a hypocaust. The smaller

---

[1] Hull Collection in Chard Museum; G. P. R. Pulman, *Book of the Axe* (1875), p. 460. Sir R. C. Hoare (in Skinner's papers, Add. MS. 32839, pp. 125, 137) refers vaguely to a mosaic found at Chard, presumably about or before 1820. But this statement may quite well refer to the Wadeford villa (No. 57).

finds included tiles, painted wall plaster, roof slates ; a bronze hand, a ring fibula, and other small items in bronze ; many potsherds and some coins—five First Brass (one of Claudius I) and some Third Brass of Gallienus, Tetricus and others. Scattered remains have also been picked up elsewhere in the parish. Such are a gold coin of Valentinian (**RESTITVTOR REIPVBLICAE-SIRM**), 5 Constantinian coins found in 1858 in the churchyard, and a fibula found at Mill Court. But Davidson's idea of a Roman road leading from Castle Neroche to Streteford-on-the-Axe may safely be rejected.[1]

(58) Whitestaunton. In a sheltered nook high in the Blackdown hills, close to the church and manor house of Whitestaunton, is a spring known as St. Agnes Well, reputed in the vicinity to be tepid, and to possess slight medicinal qualities. Close by, the remains of a Roman villa were found about 1845 in altering the road, and were partially excavated in 1882–3 by the late Mr. Charles Elton, Q.C., M.P., owner of the spot. The discoveries included living and bath rooms, hypocausts, mosaic flooring of geometrical patterns (guilloche borders, svastika, etc.), painted wall-plaster, flue tiles, roofing slates, and many smaller objects ; Samian and other potsherds, window and other glass, metal and bone objects, lead piping and some balls of lead about the size of small oranges, iron slag, etc. Part of the villa is still open, but it does not reveal the general plan, which has still to be traced.[2]

5. THE LEAD MINES OF MENDIP

The high limestone plateau of Mendip, like the similar uplands of Derbyshire, was in old time rich with much store of lead, which was accessible on the surface and easily worked. This lead was known to the Britons before the Roman period ; it was fully worked by the Romans and by generations of medieval miners, and is even now the object of occasional enterprise. It is to this recent enterprise that we owe the most part of our knowledge of the Roman operations. Our earlier antiquaries were ignorant of them. Camden is silent about Roman mines on Mendip, and explains an inscribed pig of Roman lead as a triumphal record of a Roman victory. Even two centuries later his editor, Gough, though understanding well enough the pig of lead, has nothing to say about the mines. The first discoveries, as it seems, were due

---

[1] Phelps, *Introd.* p. 174 ; *Som. Proc.* i. (1) 28, xiii. (i.) 70 ; J. Davidson, *British and Roman Remains near Axminster* (London, 1833), p. 76, brief account ; Skinner, Addit. MS. 33665, fol. 338, ref. to mosaic found 1810 ; Pulman, *Book of the Axe*, p. 459 (based on some of the preceding references) ; remains in Taunton Museum and in the Hull Collection in Chard Town Hall. Drawings of the floral mosaics found in 1810 are reproduced by Lysons, *Rell. Britannico Romanae*, i. part iv., and in *Som. Proc.* xi. ; and others exist in the Walter Collection at Taunton and in the Wollaston Collection at South Kensington. A drawing, which I take to represent the other mosaic of 1810, is in the Walter Collection. Mr. John Brown has a few objects from the site at his house close by, which he allowed me to see. The position is correctly marked in the Ordnance Survey, 6 in. lxxxvii. SE.

[2] Elton, *Academy*, 1 Sept. 1883, reprinted in *Som. Proc.* xxix. (2) 98 ; *Antiquary*, viii. (1883) 226 ; remains at the Manor House, which Commander Elton kindly shewed me. In the absence of a plan, it is useless to discuss the arrangements of the rooms. But I do not think that those suggested by Mr. Elton are very probable.

to John Skinner, sometime rector of Camerton, and an enthusiastic explorer of Roman remains in his own parish and outside it (p. 290). He dug near Charterhouse on Mendip in 1819–20, and found traces of buildings and of lead-smelting of Roman date. Chance discoveries followed, and the existence of Roman mines in this region became generally recognized. But the principal part of our knowledge of these mines was not obtained till later. About 1867–76 attempts were made to resume the lead-mining, and in particular to resmelt the heaps of imperfectly treated ore left behind by Roman or medieval miners. To the archaeologist, though not perhaps to the financier, the result was most satisfactory. A vast quantity of Roman remains was obtained, and evidence revealed of an active mining industry and a large mining population in the Roman period. Unfortunately, the gains were not utilized. No proper watch was kept over the discoveries. No details were noted of the circumstances under which special objects were unearthed. No plans or drawings were prepared. Even the objects themselves were speedily scattered. Many were acquired by Mr. A. C. Pass of Clifton, by Sir Edward Hill and others. To-day, nearly thirty years after the time of discovery and dispersal, it is impossible to collect the scattered clues, or to give anything more than a general description.[1]

The Roman mining operations extended over a considerable area of Mendip between Blackdown on the north and the village of Priddy,[2] 4 miles away to the south, and finds have been made in various parts of this region. But the centre of activity lay just to the south of Blackdown (fig. 90). Here, close to the farm of Charterhouse and the meeting-point of the parishes of Blagdon, Charterhouse and Ubley, is the gentle well-watered valley of Blackmoor. The bottom of the valley is full of old mining refuse, and its northern slope, and in particular three fields called Town Field and Upper and Lower Rains Batch have yielded the largest part of the Roman remains found in the neighbourhood.

These remains unfortunately include very little that throws light on the arrangement and the buildings of the mining settlement. Skinner records bricks, tiles, mortar, and also lead *scoriae* as found by him in 1820 in Upper and Lower Rains Batch, and estimates the extent covered by remains at sixty acres. Sir R. Colt Hoare, who probably visited the spot with Skinner, mentions a large tract covered with square and circular foundations. Later writers speak of well-made drains three or four feet deep, foundations of huts, window glass, a layer of charcoal and *scoriae* two feet thick, and furnaces, some con-

[1] For Skinner's work see Addit. MS. 33656, etc., and MS. in the Bath Institution. For the finds of 1867–76 see *Intellectual Observer*, xii. (1867), 234; *Proc. Soc. Ant.* vi. 187; vii. 156; *Arch. Journ.* xxxiii. 196, 352; *Journ. Brit. Arch. Assoc.* xxxi. 129–142; xxxiii. 106, 251; *Proc. Som.* xxvii. (1), 76; *Bath Field Club*, iii. 335; *Cardiff Naturalists' Soc.* vii. (1875), 1–8. I have examined the collections in the Taunton and Bristol Museums, the latter of which now includes the cabinets of the late Mr. A. C. Pass, and have been allowed to reproduce some objects in these pages. Some sketches by the late J. T. Irvine are in the Library of the Soc. of Antiquaries.
[2] Skinner notes a coin of Trajan (A.D. 105) as found near Priddy (MS. 33716, p. 87), and potsherds have been and still are occasionally picked up round it. Some of these potsherds are in the Glastonbury and Bristol Museums: the former has a Samian bowl OF·LICIN. See also *Som. Proc.* xii. (1) 60.

taining traces of lead ore when found—all uncovered in the Town Field and very near it.[1] But they give no details, and nothing now survives to supply their omission. At the present day the one visible object of antiquity in the region is the so-called amphitheatre on the hillside a little north-west of the Town Field. It is a low, continuously circular bank of earth, enclosing a flat space some 75 feet in diameter. The bank rises 5–6 feet above the general level of the ground, and the interior is sunk about as much below the same level. We cannot decide its precise use, but it is ill-suited to form a pond or water reservoir, and the notion of a tiny amphitheatre is not wholly absurd.[2]

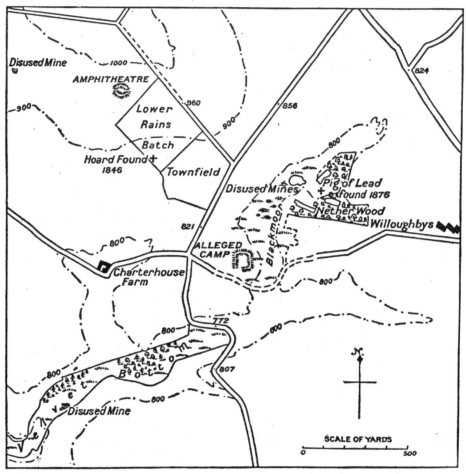

FIG. 90. CHARTERHOUSE MINING DISTRICT.

But if traces of buildings be few, movable objects abound. Lead may naturally take the precedence in our list. Not only do great quantities of *scoriae* and charcoal mark old mining sites, perhaps of various dates. Definitely Roman activity is attested by a dozen inscribed pigs of lead, to be enumerated below, and by others which,

[1] Skinner (see last note); R. C. Hoare, *Ancient Wilts* (Roman Aera), ii. 42; *Cardiff Nat. Soc.* vii.1–8; *Intell. Obs.* xii. 234; Rutter and Phelps merely repeat Hoare.

[2] O.S. marking two entrances which do not exist. I have examined it and have had it surveyed for this article. A second amphitheatre, said to have existed half a mile southwards (Scarth), needs more evidence to prove it. The Roman camp marked on the O.S. is to my eye fictitious.

FIG. 91. OBJECTS FROM CHARTERHOUSE, NOW IN TAUNTON MUSEUM.

1. Lead weights ($\frac{2}{3}$).   2. Clay Bullets ($\frac{2}{3}$).   3. Black incised ware ($\frac{2}{3}$).   4. Clay Crucibles ($\frac{2}{3}$).
5. Crucible with lead handle ($\frac{1}{2}$).   6. Brick imitating wicker work ($\frac{1}{2}$).   7. Parts of a lead pig ($\frac{3}{8}$).

(See p. 337.)

though uninscribed, have been found among Roman remains, such as four discovered by Skinner, which vary in weight from eighty to one hundred pounds. A mass of pure lead, weighing 78 lb., smelted (as it would seem) but never run into a mould, was found about 1875. Smaller lead objects are plentiful : weights, some of which form sets (p. 344), a lamp, sling bullets 3½ ounces in weight, a counter inscribed CATV, nails, a small pick which may have been a toy, clay crucibles with lead still adhering, and so forth.

Bronze and iron also occur freely. Bronze fibulae, in particular, are plentiful, and the Pass collection alone numbers some 230 bow fibulae, 20 disk fibulae, mostly enamelled, and various penannular specimens (fig. 92). One or two of the bow fibulae approach the La-Téne types, and may be pre-Roman. Two others, of the Aucissa style (fig. 97), belong to the first century of our era. None suggest so late a date as the fourth century. One of the disk fibulae is dragonesque, and another represents a rare ' shield ' type also found in the Derbyshire caves and elsewhere.[1] Besides these fibulae, we have to record a curious mask (fig. 94), a bell, keys, tweezers, pins, and the like—in all, a rich variety. Iron is also frequent, but naturally less well preserved. We find tools, chains (fig. 95), a chopper, a long knife, some rings, and five horseshoes, said by Mr. Scarth to be smaller than those now in use.[2]

The pottery includes the usual types. The Samian, preserved chiefly in the Taunton Museum, comprises embossed pieces of the first and second centuries (types 37, 38, 39 of Dragendorff and Dechelette). Interesting, though not at all uncommon, is a black ware with incised semicircles, for which see fig. 91. I may mention here also two bits of a small statuette in white clay, of a kind which is common especially in North Gaul and South Britain,[3] and some ten or twelve engraved signet gems, a few of which, such as the butting bull and the fishing cupid, shew good workmanship and may belong, as Mr. Lewis suggested, to the first century[4] (fig. 93). Sheet and bottle glass, bones and the usual débris also occur. To this list must be added three inscribed stones, all so fragmentary that they tell us little, and an oaken spade found 5 feet underground which may have a better claim than most of such finds to be called Romano-British. It was made of one solid block 21 inches long : its handle was square, and its blade, 11 inches long and 8 inches broad, was also squared at the sides. It is now in the Bristol Museum.

It remains to notice the coins. Of these it is impossible now to compile anything like a complete account. I can only give a list, drawn up by Mr. A. T. Martin, of some forty-five coins in the Pass collection, and supplement that by chance references in print and chance coins

---

[1] *V.C.H. Derby*, i. 234, fig. 34; *Archaeological Journal*, lxii. 265.
[2] *Proc. Bath Field Club*, iii. 339.
[3] C. R. Smith, *Coll. Ant.* vi. 48 ; *Cumb. and Westm. Arch. Trans.* xv. 504.
[4] S. S. Lewis, *Cambridge Antiq. Soc. Report*, 1877-8, and *Communications*, iv. 278, from which fig. 93 is taken. Compare p. 252 (gems found at Bath).

preserved elsewhere. The result is a long series, commencing with two British silver, two Republican and one Triumviral issue. The earliest Empire is represented by three coins of Tiberius, and thence onwards the list is continuous till the middle of the second century. The period A.D. 170–280 is less well represented. Constantinian issues are commoner, but the later part of the fourth century is a blank.[1] Only one hoard is known. This was discovered early in 1846 (not 1849) at Charterhouse, and the supposed spot is marked on the Ordnance Survey. It numbered some 900 coins, copper partly washed with silver, and covered the reigns of Claudius Gothicus, Aurelian, Tacitus, Probus, Carus, Diocletian, Maximian, etc., and was probably deposited, like many similar hoards, about the time of Carausius.[2]

Such are the Roman remains of Charterhouse, so far as I have been able to gather the details from scattered sources. They are few and fragmentary enough, but they enable us to attempt some general sketch of the history of Roman lead mining on Mendip. The lead, it would seem, was known to the Britons before the Roman conquest. Thus much we may infer from the early fibulae and British coins dug up at Charterhouse, and from the occurrence of lead objects in the pre-Roman village a few miles off, at Glastonbury. After the conquest, the Romans at once developed the mines. Within five or six years, as the inscribed pigs of lead demonstrate, they were busy smelting the lead. Probably its export had already begun. Some years ago there was found in a harbour of northern France a lead pig bearing Nero's name, which there is reason to connect with the Mendip mines,[3] and it would appear to have been lost in the disembarkation on the French coast. This activity continued for more than a century. Our series of inscribed pigs and our list of coins are almost continuous till the reign of Marcus and Verus (A.D. 161–9). But there we meet a pause. A similar pause at a similar date confronts us elsewhere in Britain and in other provinces where mines were worked.[4] It is often ascribed to the altered fortunes of the Roman Empire, which, at the close of the second century, suffered a heavy change from peace and good government to frontier wars and weak or cruel rulers. But in part it may be due to

[1] The details are :—2 silver British (1 Pass, 1 Sir E. Hill, see Evans, *Anc. British Coins*, p. 465); 3 Republican, of which one a legionary coin of Mark Antony (Pass); 1 plated silver and 2 bronze of Tiberius (Pass); 2 or 3 Claudius (Pass; *Brit. Arch. Assoc. Journ.* xxxi. 142); 2 Nero (Pass); 1 Vitellius (*Brit. Arch. Assoc. Journ.*); 1 silver and 2 bronze Vespasian (Pass; *Brit. Arch. Assoc. Journ.*); 1 Titus (Pass); 2 or 3 bronze Domitian (Pass); 1 silver Nerva (Pass); 3 silver and 3 bronze Trajan (Pass; *Proc. Soc. Ant.* vi. 187; *Brit. Arch. Assoc. Journ.*); 1 silver and 5 bronze Hadrian (Pass) 1 silver and 1 bronze Pius (Pass; Taunton Museum); 1 bronze Commodus (Pass); 1 base silver and 1 large bronze Severus Alexander (Pass); 2 bronze Tetricus (Pass, Skinner); 1 bronze Tacitus (*Proc. Soc. Ant.*; *Brit. Arch. Assoc. Journ.*); 2 bronze Probus (do.), 1 Third Brass Cl. Gothicus (Pass); 1 Maximian (Pass); 6 or 8 Constantinian (Pass; *Brit. Arch. Assoc. Journ.*) and 1 Licinius (*Proc. Soc. Ant.*). Waldron, in the *Cardiff Nat. Soc.* vii., mentions coins of Claudius, Trajan, Hadrian, Pius and Constantine. The seeming scantiness of coins dating from the late second and early third centuries has parallels at Bath (p. 287), and, indeed, elsewhere. At Bath, however, the scantiness extends to the middle of the third century, and may have a special cause. [2] *Dorset County Chronicle and Somersetshire Gazette*, March 19, 1846.

[3] Found at S. Valéry-sur-Somme : now in the St. Germain-en-Laye museum, where I have seen it (Cagnat, *Année Epigraphique*, 1888, No. 53). It bears the name also of the Second Legion.

[4] Hirschfeld, *Verwaltungsgeschichte* (ed. 2, 1905), pp. 156, 178.

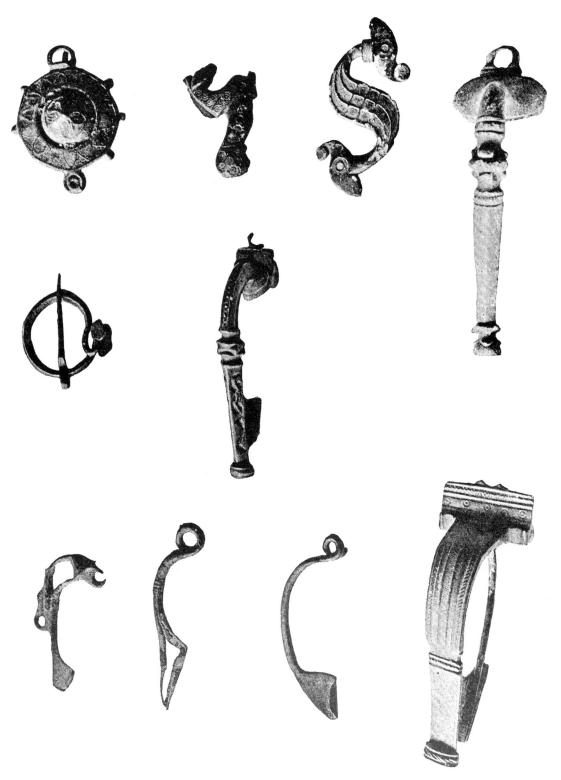

FIG. 92. FIBULAE FROM CHARTERHOUSE IN THE PASS COLLECTION.
(Bristol Museum). ¼.

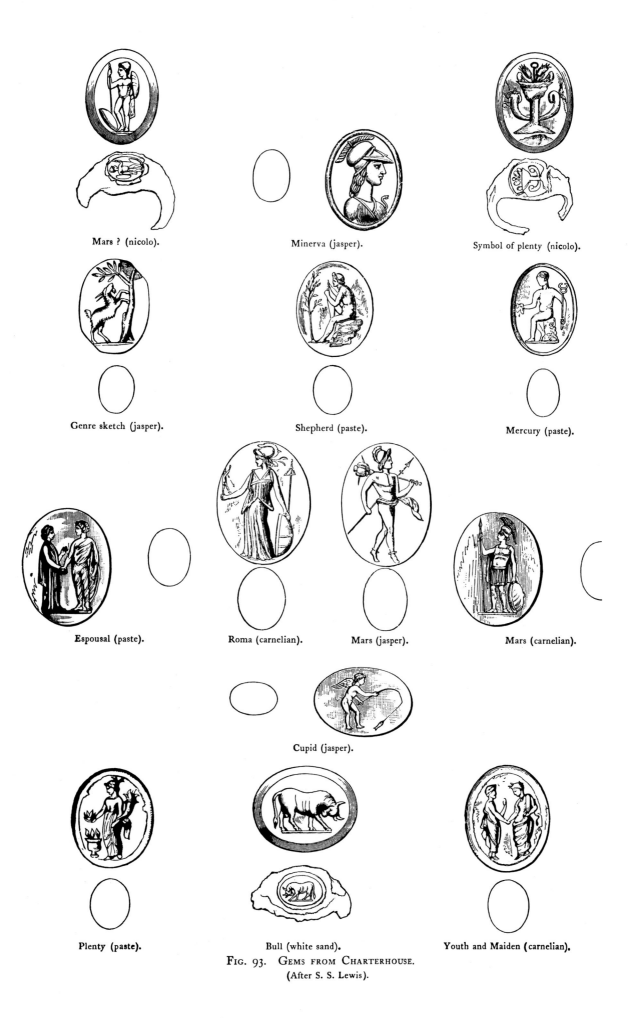

Mars ? (nicolo).

Minerva (jasper).

Symbol of plenty (nicolo).

Genre sketch (jasper).

Shepherd (paste).

Mercury (paste).

Espousal (paste).

Roma (carnelian).

Mars (jasper).

Mars (carnelian).

Cupid (jasper).

Plenty (paste).

Bull (white sand).

Youth and Maiden (carnelian).

FIG. 93.   GEMS FROM CHARTERHOUSE.
(After S. S. Lewis).

exhaustion of accessible ores, and in part perhaps to changes in system involving changes in the inscriptions relating to the system. It is at least unlikely that where easily workable ore remained, it should have been left unworked in the third century. The demand for lead cannot have then altogether ceased, however much it may have diminished, and one may wonder whether the production did not continue, though perhaps the system changed and the fashion (for example) of making up the metal into heavy pigs may have varied. At Charterhouse, at any rate, a stone fragment seems to date from the reign of Septimius Severus (A.D. 193–208), though it is too short for certain interpretation and might be otherwise explained (p. 340). The coins, too, may perhaps suggest a revival of activity after about A.D. 284 in the period of Carausius and the Constantines. But here the darkness which at no point leaves the history of the mines drops deeper down, and of the later fourth century we have no record.

Equally little is known of the administration. All the inscribed pigs of lead bear emperors' names, and it is plain the Mendip mines, like all or nearly all provincial mines, were Imperial property. But of the officials and miners we know nothing directly. In the early days, perhaps, the soldiers of the Legio II Augusta were employed, as soldiers not infrequently were, in connexion with the mines.[1] For the rest we can only say that the activity of the mines must have been considerable during the early empire. The abundance of small objects and in particular of fibulae indicates a very considerable population of miners gathered round the pools of Blackmoor and the smelting furnaces of Townfield. The character of some of these objects, for instance the fibulae and signet gems, points further to some amount of civilized life. The occurrence, lastly, of three stone inscriptions may supply cause for supposing that the Latin language was more or less understood by the miners.

But at the end it is clear that the picture is imperfect. One leaves it with the conviction that the long grassy slopes and woods around Blackmoor conceal more than has yet been found, and that further exploration might reveal the vestiges of definite buildings, the records of the local administration, the furnaces and moulds of the smelters, and the roads or communications by which the mining settlement on the upland plateau sent its goods to the outer world.[2]

INSCRIPTIONS OF THE MENDIP LEAD MINES

(1–3, stone ; 4–15, lead pigs ; 16–21, small inscribed objects)

(1) Stone about 10 inches wide by 17 inches high. Found in 1875 in pulling down a farm-building of Mr. Benjamin Panes at Charterhouse, north of the Town Field ; now lost.

The interpretation is uncertain. The opening suggests a dedication *I(ovi) o(ptimo) m(aximo)* [*et num(inibus)*] *Aug.* But the rest is obscure, except *domo Roma* in line 6, which suggests that some person named in the inscription was born in Rome. Professor Hübner pre-

---

[1] See p. 338, note 2. The Twentieth Legion similarly appears on a pig of lead.
[2] What little can as yet be said on this last point will be said on pp. 350–1.

ferred to regard the fragment as sepulchral. Unfortunately the reading is not certain. I have given the text according to three indifferent squeezes in the Library of the Society of

Antiquaries: **AVG** in line 2 seems to me certain, as it did to Scarth on the original stone: line 5 is doubtful, line 7 (except the **A**) fairly sure: I do not think there was an eighth line. Published by Scarth, *Bath Field Club*, iii. 336; Watkin, *Arch. Journ.* xxxiii. 354 from Scarth; Hübner, *Ephemeris*, iii. 121, from a poor squeeze.

(2) Fragment found at Charterhouse in 1873 or 1874; now lost. The letters *domin. Septimi* might indicate the Emperor Septimius Severus or one of his immediate successors, but the surviving piece is too small to yield any certain sense and other interpretations are possible.

I have given the text from a drawing by the late J. T. Irvine, in the Library of the Society of Antiquaries. Published by Scarth, *Brit. Arch. Assoc. Journ.* xxxi. 142 (badly); Hübner *Ephemeris*, iii. 121, reproducing Scarth's bad copy; Watkin, *Arch. Journ.* xxxiii. 354.

(3) Fragment found about the same time and place as the preceding, but said not to form

part of it; now lost. Its sense is, of course, irrecoverable. Published by the same writers as the preceding: I have copied a drawing by Irvine in the Society of Antiquaries' Library.

I have made considerable inquiries as to the fate of these stones and in particular of No. 1, but without result. No. 1 seems to have been last seen in the care of Mr. Scarth.

(4) Ploughed up in the reign of Henry VIII near Wookey Hole (Ochie Hole), the source of the Ochie or Axe, 5 miles south of Charterhouse: preserved for some time by the Duke of Norfolk in Lambeth, but soon lost. Size, weight and shape not recorded, except as *oblonga plumbi tabula*. Possibly it was merely the top surface of a pig, like Nos. 13–15, but Leland's Latin is not very explicit.

TI. CLAVD. CAESAR. AVG. P.M. TR. P. VIIII. IMP. XVI. DE BRITAN.

'Tiberius Claudius Caesar Augustus, pontifex Maximus, *tribunitia potestate* for the ninth year (A.D. 49), Imperator for the sixteenth time; from Britain.'

First published by Leland, *Assertio incomparabilis Arthuri*, London, 1544, fo. 23 a. (*Collectanea*, ed. Hearne, 5, p. 45). Hence, presumably, Camden (ed. 1, 1586), pp. 104–5, reading **CLAVDIVS** and dividing the text (wrongly, as is plain) into two lines after **P.M.**: from Camden, Lambarde (s.v. *Onky*) and many more, whom, as wholly third hand, it is needless to cite; Hübner, *C.* 1201, follows Camden also.

Leland and Camden took the object to be a trophy, but it is plainly a lead pig from the Mendip mines. Possibly enough the letters **DE BRITAN** may have been on the side and the rest on the face of the pig if it was a perfect specimen, but Leland gives the whole without division of lines.

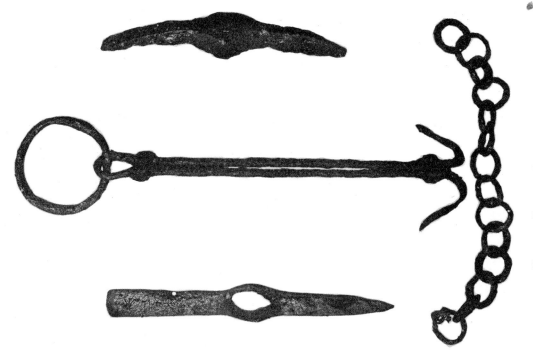

Fig. 95. Iron Implements (⅓).

Fig. 94. Bronze Mask (¼).

(Pass Collection.)

REMAINS FROM CHARTERHOUSE ON MENDIP.

(5) Pig of lead found in August 1853 near Blagdon, on the northern flank of Mendip; now in the British Museum. Weight 163 lb.; length at base, 24 inches ; width, 6¼ inches. Inscribed both on the top and on one side (fig. 96).

FIG. 96. (*Archaeologie.*)

On the top   **BRITANNIC⬛ · AVG · FI**

On the side, twice over   **V · ET · P**

'(The lead of) Britannicus son of Augustus, smelted in the consulship of Veranius and Pompeius (A.D. 49).' This explanation, first offered by Hübner, seems to be the best explanation of the inscription on the side. The top evidently refers to Britannicus son of Claudius, born in A.D. 42, heir to Claudius till superseded in favour of Nero in 48 or 49, murdered 55. It would seem unlikely that his name should be employed as it is here after 49.

First published by A. Way, *Arch. Journ.* xi. 278, xvi. 23 ; C. R. Smith, *Collectanea Antiqua*, iii. 258 ; brief mentions in *Proc. Soc. Ant.* ser. 2, iii. 198, 439 ; Hübner, *Corp. Insc. Lat.* vii. 1202. The text seems certain, though the last letter of the main inscription is blurred, and for the smaller one Way read **V · EIP · C** or **V · FTPC** and supposed this to denote the weight. I have not been able to examine the original (now in a cellar). But a squeeze sent me by Mr. R. A. Smith seems to shew **V · ET P⬛** and **V · ETP · C**, the last letter being, however, rather like an inverted **8 (8)** with a small top.

The parish of Blagdon extends right up to the Charterhouse mining centre, and this pig may quite possibly have been discovered there and not at the village of Blagdon.

(6) Pig of lead found at Charterhouse in June 1876; 172 lb. in weight, 23 inches long on its base and 19¾ inches on the chief inscribed face. Lettered on both top and side ; the letters on the top measure 1¼ inches high and those on the side $\frac{11}{16}$ inch. Formerly in the collection of Dr. Wood, of The Willoughbys, Charterhouse : now in the custody of his executors, to whom I am indebted for details and a rubbing.

IMP · VESPASIAN AVG

BRIT · EX ARG · VE

Imp(eratoris) Vespasian(i) Aug(usti) : *(plumbum) Brit(annicum) ex arg(entariis)* VE, ' belonging to the Emperor Vespasian : British lead from the silver works.' The sense of **VE** is unknown. The suggestion *ex argentaria ve(na)* seems unlikely, and no other has been advanced. Published by Scarth, *Proc. Soc. Ant.* vii. (1877) 158, with a poor illustration ; hence Watkin, *Arch. Journ.* xxxiv. 130 and Hübner, *Ephemeris*, iii. 141. The text seems certain : **VE** seems from the rubbing to be far more likely than **VF** or **VI**, which have been suggested.

(7) Pig of lead, 182 lb. in weight, found in July 1876 at Charterhouse, acquired by Dr. Wood of The Willoughbys and given by him in 1876 to the Bristol Museum, where it still is. The lettering is good, the stops triangular or foliated.

IMP · VESPASIANI · AVG

Copied by myself. Published by Scarth, *Proc. Soc. Ant.* vii. 159, and *Brit. Arch. Assoc. Journ.* xxxiii. 106; hence Hübner, *Ephemeris*, iii. p.141 (wrongly calling it a 'fragment') and Watkin, *Arch. Journ.* xxxiv. 131. I give the weight as it was given me in Bristol Museum : Scarth states it at 2 cwt. in one place and 296 lb. in another, but these figures are far too large and must be wrong.

(8) Part of a pig of lead, 15 inches long, 3½ inches wide, 2 inches thick, found at Charterhouse about 1874 : I do not know where it is now.

IMP·VESPASIA...

This is part of a pig resembling Nos. 6 and 7. It is, however, only a half of the top surface. This in the mould would be the bottom layer, and it seems that for some reason, this bottom layer became detached from the rest of the pig. The reason cannot of course now be determined. But the stratification so often observable in pigs of lead may help to explain it, since it would seem that the melted lead was poured into the mould in parcels, and therefore the cohesion between the layers might occasionally be imperfect. The bottom layer, which touched the lettering, would perhaps be the most likely to be detached, as it might cohere to the lettering instead of to its own pig.

Published by Scarth, *Brit. Arch. Assoc. Journ.* xxxi. 139 and *Proc. Soc. Ant.* vi. 188; hence Watkin, *Arch. Journ.* xxxiii. 353 and Hübner, *Ephemeris*, iii. p. 141.

(9) Found in 1822 near Sydney Buildings, Bath: weight, 195 lb.

IMP·HADRIANI·AVG

See the Bath inscriptions, No. 47. It can hardly be doubted that this pig came from the Mendip mines. It may have been intended for use in the Baths.

(10) Pig of lead found Sept. 1873 at Charterhouse: where now, I do not know. Weight, 223 lb.: the upper, inscribed, surface measures 19 by 2½ inches. The letters IIP seem to have been blurred in casting.

IMP·CAES·ANTONINI·AVG·PII P·P·

'(The lead of) the Emperor Caesar Antoninus Augustus Pius, father of his country.' This is the heaviest pig of Roman lead yet discovered in Britain. Published by Scarth, *Proc. Soc. Ant.* vi. 188, *Brit. Arch. Assoc. Journ.* xxxi. 138; hence Hübner, *Ephemeris*, iii. p. 141; and Watkin, *Arch. Journ.* xxxiii. 353.

(11–12) Two pigs of lead found in 1865 in Bristol, in making excavations on the old bank of the river Frome, in Wade Street. One (11) measuring on its inscribed face, 19 by 2¾ inches and weighing 76 lb., is in the British Museum. The other (12), weighing 89 lb., was at first in the collection of Mr. Edkins and is now in the Bristol Museum. Both pigs are imperfect in the first half of the name Antoninus, and probably came from the same mould (fig. 97).

Fig. 97. (*Archaeologia*).

IMP·CAES·A *nto* NINI·AVG·PII·P·P·

'(Lead of) the Emperor Caesar Antoninus Augustus Pius, father of his country' (A.D. 139–161).

Published by Scarth, *Proc. Soc. Ant.* ser. 2, iii. (1865), 198: hence *Gent. Mag.* (1866), i. 211; Way, *Arch. Journ.* xxiii. 278, from which I have taken my illustration; Hübner, *Corpus*, 1210. I have seen both pigs.

(13) Found early in the eighteenth century near Bruton, about sixteen miles south-east of Charterhouse: 21 inches long, 3½ inches wide, 2 inches thick, 50 lb. in weight. Preserved at first at Longleat: later in the collection of Matthew Duane (died 1785); now lost.

IMP·DVOR AVG ANTONINI
ET VERI ARMENIACORVM

'(The lead of) the two joint rulers, Antoninus (i.e. Marcus Aurelius) and Verus, called Armenian' (A.D. 164–9). The inscription is obviously the same as No. 14.

Published by Stukeley, *Itin. Curiosum* (ed. 1, 1724), p. 143 and *Medallic History of Carausius* (1757), i. 167; hence Horsley, p. 328; Ward, *Philosophical Trans.* xlix. 699, and others; Hübner, *Corpus*, vii. 1211; Soc. Ant. Minutes, 16 March 1758 = viii. 49.

(14) Fragment, 8 inches long, 3¾ inches wide and ¾ inch thick, found about 1874 at Charterhouse: now in the Taunton Museum. See fig. 91, bottom.

Imp. Duor(um) Augg. a⟩NTONINI
et Veri Armeniæ⟩CORVM

' (The lead of) the two Emperors, Antoninus (i.e. Marcus Aurelius) and Verus.' Marcus and Verus were conjoint rulers from A.D. 161–9 and bore the name *Armeniaci* from A.D. 163 or 164. The date of this pig is therefore about A.D. 164–9. Published by Scarth, *Brit. Arch. Assoc. Journ.* xxxi. 139 and *Proc. Soc. Ant.* vi. 189; hence Hübner, *Ephemeris*, iii. p. 141 and Watkin, *Arch. Journ.* xxxiii. 353; copied by myself.

(15) Similar fragment, 5½ inches long, 2¼ inches wide, and barely ¼ inch thick, found at Charterhouse about 1874: now in the Taunton Museum, where I have seen it. See fig. 91, bottom.

G
MENIA

It is obviously part of a pig like the preceding, but I am not sure that it comes from the same pig. Before **G** in the upper line over the **M** is a trace of what may have been **A** and the same occurs after **G**: this would give *A[ug]g. A*, as in the preceding inscription. Published by Scarth, *Proc. Soc. Ant.* vi. 189; Watkin, *Arch. Journ.* xxxiii. 353 from Scarth; Hübner, *Ephem.* iv. 206 from Watkin.

NOTE ON THE METAL OF THESE PIGS

Professor Gowland has analysed five of these pigs with the following results :—

Pig					Copper	Antimony	Arsenic	Dwt. of silver per ton
No. 5. Britannici	.	.	.	.	·043	·021	·014	166·6
„ 7. Vespasiani	.	.	.	.	·018	·017	nil	13·07
„ 9. Hadriani	.	.	.	.·	·025	·007	nil	13·37
„ 11. Antonini Pii	.	.	.	.	·024	·019	nil	22·0
„ 12. „ „	.	.	.	.	·029	·0083	nil	19·6

In addition each pig contains a minute trace of gold, but no trace of tin. It is plain, Mr. Gowland remarks, that all the lead of these pigs has been treated for the extraction of silver. It is plain, also, that in this process the original impurities of the ore, copper, antimony and the like, have been reduced to such small proportions that they do not help us in determining the character of the ore. Nor would they help us to refer a stray pig to its original mine by indicating the original character of the ore. Thus the pig found at Bath (No. 9, Hadriani) most closely resembles in analysis a pig found on Matlock Moor in Derbyshire, and one found at Charterhouse (Vespasiani, No. 7) most closely resembles another smelted near Matlock. But it is absurd to suppose that Somerset lead was taken to Derbyshire or Matlock lead to Mendip.

(16–17) Two bronze fibulae of the type known as Aucissa, and inscribed with that name: found at Charterhouse, in the collection of Mr. A. C. Pass. See fig. 98.

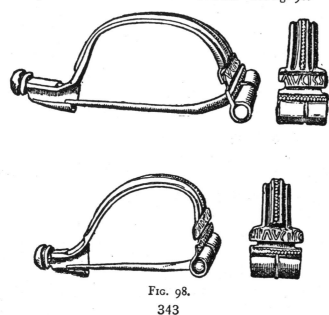

FIG. 98.

A HISTORY OF SOMERSET

(1) ΛVᴅSS *or* ΛVCISS (2) IIIΛVCISS

Copied by myself and published *Archaeological Journal*, lx. (1903), 240, lxii. 265. The readings seem fairly clear. In (1) the letters are so close that I am not sure if ᴅ or CI should be accepted, but CI is meant in either case. In (2) the first three strokes are ornament : there are also two slender strokes shown in the cut which seem accidental.

The Aucissa type of fibula is shown best by the accompanying cuts. Its features are a hinge instead of a spiral coil to work the pin, and a flat semicircular bow, widest above the hinge and decorated only by lines or beading running lengthwise. It occurs widely throughout the Roman Empire and even beyond it. Some thirty specimens are known which bear the name Aucissa : a few bear other names, and a vast number are uninscribed. They seem to belong chiefly to the Augustan period and the years immediately following : occasional specimens are found with remains assignable to the second half of the first century. See further my articles cited above.

(18) One of four small leaden roundels, barely an inch in diameter, bears the inscription

|CΛTV|

It is possible that the lettering may have been transferred from a bit of Samian. The Lydney Collection contains a small piece of lead inscribed DOCCIVSI—wrongly included by Hübner among the pigs of lead—which appears to have got its inscription similarly from an ordinary Samian stamp. The roundels were found at Charterhouse and are now at Bristol Museum in the Pass collection, where I have examined them.

(19) Four lead weights in the Pass Collection, marked respectively :—

::	107·17 grammes.	. .	53·64 grammes.
˙.	80·27 „	blank	25·85 „

Copied by myself : the standard is obvious. Drawings of these, by the late J. T. Irvine, are in the Library of the Society of Antiquaries.

(20) Four lead weights, in the Taunton Museum, stamped :—

II about 19½ oz. avoirdupois.
III 3 oz.
S 5¾ oz.
V₃ 11 oz.

Copied by myself and published *Arch. Journ.* xlix. 186.

(21) Some stamps on Samian pottery are preserved in Taunton Museum :—

OFLCVIRIL.. inside a fish-shaped label, broken at the end.
OF PATR
ROPVSᴵFE (*Corpus Inscr. Lat.* xiii. 10010, 1654).
A·POL·AVSTI
CRISPI
OF SILVINI
GENITORI₃
SILVANI
₃IIATICIOF (? *Asiatici officina*).
ΛISII·M (*Corpus Inscr. Lat.* xiii. 10010, 72).
OF·COTTO
CRISPINI·M
CRI₂PV₂ (?)
M·MON (?)
PATE...
PRIVAT..
REDITI·M
TITVRONIS

One *pelvis* has the mark Iᴵ II·V (*Bath Field Club*, iii. 341, not quite correctly given).

344

6. THE ROADS

The Roman roads in Somerset are few and easily described. Two roads led to Bath from the north-east and east, one from Cirencester and the Midlands, and the other from London, Silchester and Marlborough (Cunetio). Two roads equally led out of Bath to the west and the south-west. The former gave access to the neighbourhood of Bristol and the Severn ferry to South Wales. The latter ran through east Somerset and passed on by way of Chard, Axminster and Honiton to Exeter. Another road diverged from the Fosse at Ilchester and led to Dorchester (Durnovaria). And yet another, of which only a fragment can now be traced, served in some way the Mendip lead mines. This completes the list of certain roads. The doubtful ones are naturally more numerous. Two of these are not improbable, though they have not yet been proved. One—perhaps the best known and best supported—is supposed to have run from Salisbury (Sorbiodunum) along Mendip to Uphill and an alleged harbour on the channel. The other, which also has some claims to credence, is thought to have started at Glastonbury or Street, and, passing through the Somerton group of villas, to have joined the Fosse at Ilchester. Other roads have been conjectured which are far less probable than these. Roads indeed are the department in which Romano-British antiquaries have always exercised the greatest licence. It will be necessary to notice only two of these improbable roads.

(1) THE ROADS TO BATH FROM THE EAST AND NORTH-EAST

The two roads which approach Bath from the east and north-east demand few words. The course of each is well known. The north-eastern road, coming from Cirencester, enters the area of the county a couple of miles north of Batheaston. It runs along the top of Banner-down on the line of the modern high road and parish boundary, descends the hill by a steep straight drop down Morris lane—which is also followed by the parish boundary—and reaches the bottom of the valley near the third milestone from Bath. The eastern road descends Bathford (or Farley) Down—where its paving was noticed in 1882[1]— passes along the north of Bathford village and joins the other road at the same third milestone. Hence the combined roads run, first north-west and then south-west, into Walcot, along a line exactly represented by the modern London road. In Batheaston the Roman metalling is said to have been found underlying the modern roadway.

As is well known, the north-eastern road has been called, since Anglo-Saxon times, the Fosse. That is also the name of the Roman road from Bath to the south-west and Exeter. It is natural, indeed, to think of these two roads which run continuously in the same general direction, as one through route, on which Bath is only an intermediate

---

[1] *Bath Field Club,* iv. 135.

station. The Saxons obviously so regarded it.[1] It does not, however, follow that the Romans thought thus. They may have connected the road from Bath to Exeter with the road from Bath to London just as much as with the road from Bath to Cirencester. I have therefore preferred to treat the Fosse north-east of Bath separately from the Fosse south-west of it.

A piece of road which, if established, would supply an alternative to a portion of the eastern road, has been thought to run from Monkton Farley down Bathford Hill to the south of Bathford village, cross the Avon near Warleigh Ferry, climb Bathwick Hill, recross the Avon near the Pulteney bridge, and enter the Roman settlement by its east gate. It is admitted, however, by Mr. Scarth, that " this can only be discerned by the interments which have been found " in Bathwick, and the road has yet to be proved. A part of it, however, is probable enough. The group of remains, sepulchral and other, which occurs at the foot of Bathwick Hill near the Sydney Gardens (pp. 263, 266) indicates some village or suburb. This must have had communications with Aquae, and one of these communications may have led across the Avon to the east gate of the settlement. But apart from this, the suggested road has practically no evidence in its favour.[2]

(2) THE ROAD FROM BATH WESTWARDS TO THE SEVERN CROSSING AND SOUTH WALES

This road may, for convenience, be said to start from Bath. But it seems to have been regarded in Roman days rather as a continuation of the route from London, than as a road from Bath to the west. It does not, strictly speaking, start from Aquae. It diverges from the Fosse at Walcot church, half a mile east of the Roman settlement, and runs on westwards without entering the Roman area. Through modern Bath its course is roughly represented by Guinea Lane and Julian road. In Victoria Park it may have been joined by a road from the west gate of Aquae. But the evidence for such a road is scanty. It does not include any trace of an actual roadway and rests mainly on the probabilities of the case. Thence our road continues through Weston, mounts the neck of high land which joins Kelston Round Hill to Lansdown, runs close beneath North Stoke (p. 302) and drops sharply to the Avon valley and the 'station' or village at Bitton. West of Bitton, it coincides for some distance with the modern high road ; then, skirting

---

[1] The Fosse is mentioned by name in several pre-conquest charters relating to Gloucestershire and the Midlands. For Somerset we have only *Cod. Dipl.* 566 (A.D. 970, *Somerset Record Soc.* vii. (a) p. 32) : and *ibid.* 643 (about A.D. 1006, *Som. Rec.* vii. (a) p. 30) ; for some reason, which is not apparent, Kemble considered the latter charter to be spurious. Both refer to the road between Bath and Camerton. A curious Malmesbury charter (*Cart. Saxon.* 922) mentions *stratam publicam que ab antiquis* stret, *nunc* fos *nuncupatur.* This is dated A.D. 956. But it is plainly later than the Conquest (W. H. Stevenson), and smacks of the archæology of the early eleventh century. It cannot, therefore, be taken as proof that Fosse is only a late Saxon term.

[2] Scarth, *Aquae*, p. 110. The road is mentioned as probable by R. C. Hoare, *Ancient Wilts* (Roman aera), p. 73, and was, I believe, first suggested by Leman.

the north-east of Bristol, it crosses Durdham Down, where it has been excavated, sinks once more into the river valley and ends where the Trym flows into the Avon at Seamills.[1] Here was an important 'station.' It was first detected in 1712. Since that date, foundations of buildings, tiles, bricks, coins ranging from Republican times to Honorius, an inscribed tombstone (**SPES C SENTI**), and an immense number of small objects of all sorts, have been found in ever increasing abundance over an area stated (perhaps too enthusiastically) to extend to 50 acres.[2] Here, we may feel sure, began the *trajectus* or ferry to Caerwent and Caerleon and South Wales. We need not seek it at Aust Cliff or Portishead, or any other point on the Severn shore where neither abundant Roman remains nor Roman roads have been discovered.

This road is part of the Itinerary route from London to Caerleon. In the Itinerary it is described as follows:

Isca (Caerleon) to Venta Silurum (Caerwent) . . .	ix miles
Venta to Abone	xiv miles
Abone to Traiectus	ix miles
Traiectus to Aquae Sulis (Bath)	vi miles

It would at first sight seem natural to identify Traiectus with Bitton and Abone with Seamills. This solution, however, raises serious difficulties. Seamills is indeed not much more than nine miles from Bitton. But Bitton is ten or eleven, not six, Roman miles west of Bath, and no 'station' except Bitton exists on this part of the route. Again, no 'traiectus' worth the name occurs near Bitton nor indeed anywhere on the route except at the crossing of the Severn. The first difficulty can be solved by supposing a corruption in the text, and reading xi. for vi. The second has caused much perplexity. The remedy most often suggested is to transpose Abone and Traiectus, making Abone the name of the village at Bitton, which is within half a mile of the Avon, and identifying Traiectus with Seamills. Perhaps it would be better to suppose that Abone is Seamills and that Traiectus was put against it in the Itinerary : the double entry then was by error extended into two lines and Traiectus extruded the name corresponding to Bitton. In that case the original Latin text may have been :

(ab Isca) Venta Silurum	mpm viiii
Abone, Traiectus	mpm xiiii
,, (*Bitton*)	mpm viiii
Aquae Sulis	mpm xi

[1] The road has often been described, especially by the local historians, Barrett, Seyer, Coxe (*Hist. of Monmouthshire*, i. 13), Hoare; Ellacombe, *Hist. of Bitton*, p. 267; Martin, *Clifton Antiq. Club*, i. 58, and v. 75. It was excavated in 1901 on Durdham Down, and found to be 20–22 feet wide, and constructed in three layers—at the bottom a foot of sandy earth and limestone fragments; above that, six inches of reddish earth, and on top a layer of large rough stones bedded with occasional smaller stones. Excavations near Bath in 1903–4 showed only a *stratum* of ballast, and over that a layer of rounded stones 2–3 inches in diameter (*Proc. Soc. Antiq.* xx. 249).

[2] Abel Wantner, MS. *Hist. of Gloucestershire*, 1714 (in the Bodleian Library), fol. 231b ; Barrett, *Hist. of Bristol*, i. 10–12 ; G. W. Manby, *Sketches of Clifton Hotwells*, p. 15 ; Seyer, *Hist. of Bristol*, i. 142, 153 ; Skinner, Add. MS. 33719, fol. 43 ; A. Trice Martin, *Clifton Antiq. Club*, i. 61 ; Ellis, ibid. ii. 159, and iii. 168, 175 ; Pritchard, ibid. iv. 261, etc. The alleged remains near Blaise Castle, two miles to the north of Seamills (R. Atkyns, *Gloucestershire* (1712), p. 474, etc.), are certainly of less importance.

This view has the advantage of avoiding a transposition such as is not very common among the errors of the Itinerary MSS., while the mistake which it assumes, occurs often enough in lists of names of any sort.

The road is often called the Via Julia, and that name has been adopted in Julian Road at Bath and elsewhere along its course. It rests however on a mistake. Since Leland and Camden, antiquaries have been wont to support it by a couplet from the " De laudibus divinae sapientiae " of Alexander Neckam, abbot of Cirencester from 1213 to 1217.[1]

> Intrat et auget aquas Sabrini fluminis Oska
> praeceps : testis erit Iulia strata mihi.

And hence Richard of Cirencester, that is, Bertram of Copenhagen, in the eighteenth century invented the name Via Julia for the whole road from Bath to Caerleon. But it appears that the true reading of Neckam's line is not *Iulia* but *vilia*, and the whole theory therefore falls to the ground. It may be added that even if *Iulia* were the correct text, Neckam's words would still refer to Monmouthshire and not to Somerset or Gloucester.

(3) THE FOSSE, FROM BATH TO CHARD

This road is well attested and well known throughout all but the southernmost part of its course. For forty miles from Bath to Dinnington it usually coincides with existing roads and paths ; for just two-thirds of that distance it provides a boundary for thirty-two parishes ; it follows a significantly straight course and passes sites with significant names like Stratton, and it is mentioned under the title of ' Fos ' in very early charters. We need not here describe in detail what is shown on any good map and what has been fully recognized by several generations of antiquaries.[2] South of Dinnington, however, the trail is fainter. The Fosse here climbs the high range of Windwhistle Hill, towards which it has pointed since Ilchester, and its course is obscure. Probably it is represented by one of the deep lanes in Dinnington village ; then it may follow Nash Lane and Fisherway Lane, and descending from the hill to Street, enter and pass down the valley of the Axe by Titherleigh towards Axminster.[3] Its whole course seems to have been laid out by sighting on to certain elevated points, such as Beacon Hill on Mendip, Easton Hill near East Pennard and the summit behind Dinnington. This method was no doubt usually adopted by the Romans in constructing their roads. But it is more recognizable than usual on the line of the Fosse in Somerset.

[1] Neckam, *de naturis rerum*, ed. Wright (Rolls Series), p. 415, *de laud. div. sap.* iii. 886 ; Leland, *comment in cygn. cant.* (1545), *s.v.* Venta.

[2] Oddly enough, the 16th and 17th century writers knew little of it. Leland and Harrison say that it went to Bristol. They wrote probably without maps, and were influenced by Higden or some other mediaeval chronicler. Camden does not mention it at all by name. Speed (*Theatre*, 1611, p. 17) takes it through Dorchester. Even Hearne (*Essay on four roads*, in his edition of Leland, vi. 97) and Horsley regard the Somerset part of the Fosse as uncertain. Stukeley, however, traversed much of it, and added largely to the knowledge of its course (*Itin. Cur.* 1724, pp. 137, 146, 7), and Collinson in 1791 (i. 99) gives a detailed account.

[3] Collinson, i. 100 ; Davidson, *British and Roman Remains near Axminster* (London, 1833), p. 65.

ROMANO-BRITISH SOMERSET

The Fosse has been cut through several times. Early in the nineteenth century Skinner trenched it near Radstock, and found at the bottom 'a layer of large flat stones, then a foot and a half of earth and rubble, above that a course of small stones, with pavement or pitching stone on the surface.'[1] More recently it has been examined in the same neighbourhood by Mr. McMurtrie. It was found to measure at the top about 7 feet in width, at the bottom 11 feet, and to be about 3 feet thick. On either side were well-marked ditches. Six layers of metalling were discerned. They were as follows, in ascending order: (1) a bed of soil, (2) a layer of rubble stones thickest in the centre, being there 5 inches deep, (3) a bed of 'concrete,' 15 inches deep, consisting of broken stones of local oolite and lias mixed with lime, (4) a layer of finer material, $10\frac{1}{2}$ inches deep in the centre, made of local stone pounded fine and mixed with lime, (5) a course of paving stones of various sizes and shapes, put together as random work and cemented with lime. On this fifth layer the ruts of wheel tracks were discernible, 2 feet 9 inches apart.[2] With this description we may contrast what Stukeley said he saw, nearly two centuries earlier, on another part of the road. South of Ilchester he observed the road 'pav'd with the original work : 'tis composed of the flat quarry stones of the country, of a good breadth, lay'd edgwise, and so close that it look like the side of a wall fallen down.'[3] This paving may be later than the Romans.

(4) ILCHESTER TO DORCHESTER

This branch road needs no comment. It can be traced fairly continuously, leaving Ilchester on the line of the modern Yeovil road, passing west of Yeovil through lanes and fields, and then falling again into the modern high road to Dorchester.[4] It forms occasionally but not commonly a parish boundary, and few significant names occur along its course. But its straightness between two certain Roman sites seems to prove its Roman origin. Phelps states that its raised track was visible in many fields and that it was formed of flints brought from the neighbouring chalk downs.

(5) ROAD CONNECTED WITH THE MENDIP MINES

A fragment of Roman road—not, I think, hitherto noticed—can be traced on the north side of Mendip. It is only three or four miles long, and runs north-east and south-west, dividing the parishes of West Harptree and Compton Martin. It is attested by its straightness, its coincidence with parish boundaries, and the name Stratford Bridge. It was, I imagine, connected in some way with the Mendip lead mines. To judge by the parish boundaries, one might think that it climbed the steep scarp of Mendip and continued a mile or so along the plateau, till it met the line of the supposed Ad Axium road.[5]

[1] R. C. Hoare, *Ancient Wilts* (Roman aera, 1819), p. 77.
[2] *Som. Proc.* xxx. (2) 76, and l. (2) 108; *Bristol Mercury*, 25 March, 1904.   [3] *Itin.* p. 147.
[4] Phelps, *Introd.* p. 131.   [5] Ordnance Survey, xviii. SE.; xix. NW., SW.

(6) THE AD AXIUM ROAD

This road was first noticed by Sir R. C. Hoare, who made an elaborate survey of it on the surface. According to him, it ran from Salisbury westwards through Maiden Bradley, climbed Mendip near its eastern end, crossed the Fosse on Beacon Hill, skirted the pre-Roman camp at Maesbury, and passed on straight north-westwards to Charterhouse. From here its course lay along the south side of Black-down to near Shipham, then along the south side of Banwell Hill, and straight on over Bleadon Hill to Uphill and an alleged harbour at the mouth of the Axe. Its total length would be about 55 miles.[1]

I must confess to some scepticism concerning this road. Its actual traces are very scanty. Even Sir R. C. Hoare admits that large gaps impaired the continuity of the surface vestiges which he thought to detect. As laid down by him, it rarely coincides with any straight existing road, and still more rarely with any parish boundary. Between Salisbury and Charterhouse, a distance exceeding forty miles, it passes hardly any inhabited Roman site, and no village or town. Its supposed objective, the harbour at Uphill, rests on scanty finds of late coins (p. 368). I have carefully examined the supposed line of the road from Greenore on Mendip to Uphill, and have found no vestiges, even in ploughed fields and woods, that indicate a Roman road. The problem could be solved by excavation; without it the road seems to me to be unproven. The name 'Ad Axium' is in any case a modern invention.

(7) ILCHESTER TO STREET (OR MENDIP)

A road is often said to have branched off from the Fosse at Ilchester and run north-westwards through the Somerton villa district to Street, and perhaps to the Mendip mines. Its course has been laid down, principally, I believe, on the authority of Mr. S. Hasell, who excavated the Somerton villas.[2] But the available evidence, for it is scanty. The most definite remains that can be connected with it is an old corduroy road found in the moor north of Street, and close to Street church. The name of Street, if ancient, is significant, and Roman potsherds have been found in its churchyard.[3] But the road itself may be connected with Glastonbury Abbey quite as probably as with the Romans, and the rest of the supposed route shows even smaller traces of antiquity. In default of a critical examination, it must be called unproven.

(8) ALLEGED ROADS

(i) Bishop Clifford tried to trace a military road from Exeter to Caerleon.[4] He urged the evidence of the Antonine Itinerary, and the existence of suitable stations at Hembury Fort in Devonshire and at

[1] Hoare, *Ancient Wilts* (Roman aera), pp. 38 ; Skinner, Add. MS. 33726 ; information from Rev. C. Taylor.

[2] Add. MS. 33665, fol. 364 ; Hasell writes to Skinner that he thinks he has found traces near Kingsdon. See fig. 80.

[3] *Som. Proc.* xxvii. (2) 43 ; information from Mr. Jos. Clark of Street. See p. 367.

[4] *Som. Proc.* xxiv. (2) 22–31.

Taunton. But the passage of the Antonine Itinerary which he quotes is known to be interpolated ; Hembury Fort is certainly not Roman, and the remains at Taunton are not only too few to prove a Roman station, but include nothing that indicates a roadway.[1] Moreover, Bishop Clifford admitted that no traces of the road have ever been found. It must be added that his theory of a military, as distinct from a commercial road, is untenable ; and his idea that 'the twelfth Itinerary connects together all the great forts in the south and west of Britain' assumes forts at many places where we have no traces whatever of permanent Roman garrisons.

(ii) No better evidence exists for another road alleged by Phelps and other writers to have run from Ilchester through Sparkford, Galhampton, Redlinch Park and Kingston Deverill to Old Sarum. This appears to be a transmutation to Roman times of a British trackway supposed by Sir R. C. Hoare to have joined Ilchester and Old Sarum (*Anc. Wilts*, Roman Aera, p. 40). There does not appear to be any real reason for accepting either Roman or British road here.

7. MISCELLANEOUS FINDS

We have now surveyed all the well-attested remains in Somerset which indicate permanent inhabitation of definite places during the Roman period—the spa at Bath, the villages at Camerton, Ilchester and perhaps Ham Hill, the villas, the Mendip mines, the roads. There are left to be noticed a great number of discoveries, or alleged discoveries, which do not seem to suggest such permanent occupation. Some of these consist of objects, due probably to chance, such as isolated coins or potsherds accidentally lost or thrown away by some one passing. Others may belong to inhabited sites which our ignorance prevents us from recognizing as such. Others again are uncertain in age or in character, and demand notice rather because they have been styled, than because they actually are, Roman. All these can most conveniently be treated in a bibliographical list.

But it may be well to shorten this list by first noticing separately two special groups of finds. These cannot be classed under any of the preceding sections of this article. They demand fuller notice than suits an index. They have also—though this is an accident—a certain connexion in subject.

(a) REMAINS FOUND IN THE MARSHES ROUND THE POLDEN HILLS

The Polden Hills form a long thin ridge of upland, 200–300 feet above sea-level, which runs east and west between the neighbourhood of Glastonbury and that of Bridgwater, and divides the marshes of the Brue from King's Sedgemoor. Striking remains of both the British and the Roman periods have been found near their western end. We are here concerned only with the latter.

[1] See the alphabetical index (p. 361), under Taunton.

These remains do not include any very definite traces of dwellings. Perhaps there was a villa at Bawdrip, but it is not certain, and the villas ascribed to Chedzoy, Woolavington and Edington have, I think, no real evidence to prove them.[1] We have here to deal with a different kind, or rather two kinds, of remains. The first of these are coin-moulds made in clay, of which great numbers have come to light. In 1670, as Paschal writes to Aubrey, 'several hundreds of casting-moulds of fine clay' were found three or four feet deep, in low ground, on a site not easy to identify, but probably near Bawdrip, on the south side of the Polden Hills. The moulds bore the heads and names of Severus, Caracalla, Julia and Plautilla. Paschal sent a 'boxful' to the Royal Society, and Aubrey gave twenty to the Ashmolean Museum in Oxford, but both donations have disappeared.[2] A second discovery was made in 1801 on the north side of the Polden range, in digging a drain, a quarter of a mile north of the village of Chilton, in low ground on or near the Nidons. Here the Rev. J. Poole picked up some hundreds of moulds in a space of four feet square and at a depth of some nine inches. They bore the heads of Severus, Julia, Caracalla, Plautilla, Geta, Macrinus, Elagabalus, Severus Alexander, Julia Paula, and Mamaea.[3] More finds followed in 1835 in the same marsh, and probably about the same spot, between Chilton village and Edington Burtle—moulds bearing the heads of Commodus, Severus, Julia, Caracalla, Geta, Mamaea, and Severus Alexander, and two actual coins of base (apparently white) metal, one of Severus, and the other of Geta.[4] Yet a fourth discovery, of which fewer details are recorded, was made in Highbridge in 1804. Seven feet deep in the alluvial deposit, workmen who were excavating new drainage channels, found a layer of hard peat, and, lying upon it, Roman potsherds, bricks suggestive of kilns and several moulds for casting coins.[5] Lastly, an illegible mould preserved in Brighton Museum is said to have been found at 'Pointing Hill, near Bridgwater,' though its other history is lost.

Similar discoveries of clay moulds for casting coins have occurred elsewhere in Britain and in other parts of the western empire, Gaul, Germany, Noricum and Africa (Tunis), though apparently not in Italy or the east. They occur both in large towns and in remote and lonely places.

[1] For the Bawdrip villa, see p. 329; for Chedzoy and Woolavington, see the index. The Edington villa rests (ultimately) on information given by Andrew Paschal of Chedzoy to Aubrey (Bodleian Library, MS. Aubrey 15). Paschal states that a tessellated pavement came to light in 1670 'near the Knoll Hill, not far from Chedzoy,' where certain coin moulds were also found, and that the moulds were found 'in a village called Edington belonging to the parish of Murlinch' (fo. 105, 119–121). He also states that a mosaic was found, obviously about 1670, at Bawdrip (fo. 110 and MS. 13, fo. 83). His statements unfortunately are not clear or consistent in point of locality. There is a Knoll Hill at Moorlinch and a Knowle at Bawdrip—the latter being much the nearer to Chedzoy—while Edington is not in Moorlinch parish. On the whole, the evidence favours a villa at Bawdrip, and not at Edington or Moorlinch. But the matter is not clear.

[2] Bodl. Library, MS. Aubrey 15, fol. 105, 119–121: see last note. From Aubrey, Collinson, iii. 433, Gough, Phelps, etc.

[3] *Soc. Ant. Minutes*, xxviii. 433 (14 May, 1801); *Arch.* xiv. 99; hence Phelps, *Introd.* p. 175, etc.

[4] Phelps, p. 175, very briefly; W. Stradling, *Som. Proc.* i. (2) 58, and *Priory of Chilton Polden* (1839), p. 24; *Arch. Institute*, Bristol volume, p. lxvii.; specimens in Bristol Museum.

[5] *Som. Proc.* iv. (2) 103.

The period when they were principally made and used seems to have been that dark age of the Roman currency from about A.D. 210–280. The majority of the specimens bear the heads of Septimius Severus, his sons Caracalla and Geta, or their successor Elagabalus ; some show later emperors of the third century, while a few represent those of the second century or of the first half of the fourth century. Almost all appear intended for casting either denarii, and especially the debased denarii current in the third century, or bronze *folles* of the early fourth century.[1] Several theories have been advanced as to their use. They have been attributed to forgers, They have been attributed to the Government, attempting by travelling mints to supply local deficiencies in currency for the use of soldiers and traders. They have, thirdly, been ascribed to private coiners working to the same end with the sanction, or at least the acquiescence, of the State. Of these three origins the first is the most generally probable, and it alone is applicable to our present case. We can imagine forgers plying in the secret and lonely marshes of west Somerset. We cannot imagine the State sending thither a travelling mint, or private coiners, other than forgers, selecting the spot. Evidence, moreover, is wholly wanting which might prove that either travelling mints or authorised (or tolerated) private coiners really existed. Both are hypotheses, invented to suit the views of special writers. Both, so far as I can judge, are quite unnecessary.[2]

The coin moulds are not the only Roman remains in this district. On the north side of the Polden Hills the parishes of Edington, Chilton, Catcott, Cossington, Huntspill and Shapwick contain on their lower levels numerous small mounds, oval or round in shape, various in size, which rise up out of the marsh much like barrows on a flat plain. Many of these mounds were opened by Mr. W. Stradling in the early years of the nineteenth century. They proved to consist largely of fragments of Roman black ware, while near them were discovered platforms of clay and rude bricks lying thereon. These bricks resembled those used in kilns to keep earthenware in place during the process of firing. The finder accordingly took the platforms to be relics of kilns and the mounds to be refuse heaps of vessels damaged in the baking. Once or twice scoriae of iron or coal suggested ironworking, but the vast majority of the remains were pottery, and in some cases the pottery mounds and coin moulds were discovered side by side.[3]

A few other relics indicate Roman occupation here. In particular

---

[1] Some moulds for Second Brass coins are said to have been discovered in Somerset, at Whitchurch near Bristol ; compare the alphabetical index under Whitchurch. I have not seen these moulds, and it does not seem certain that they are for Second Brass at all.

[2] The latest and fullest account of these moulds is that of M. Babelon, *Traité des monnaies grecques et romaines* (Paris, 1901), i. 954. M. Babelon, however, inclines to believe some, at least, of the moulds to be authorised or official. See also J. G. Milne, *Num. Chron.* 1905, p. 353, and *V.C.H. Northants,* i. 198.

[3] Stradling, *Som. Proc.* i. (2) 57, and *Priory of Chilton Polden* (1839), p. 24. Sir H. de la Beche, *Geol. Report on Cornwall, Devon and Somerset,* p. 422, mentions 'potteries' at Bason Bridge (near Huntspill Level). Similar bricks were found in 1804 at Highbridge, seven feet deep, on the old peat surface, along with coin moulds and potsherds (*Som. Proc.* iv. (2) 103 ; see last note). The potsherds, etc., found at Burnham (*Som. Proc.* xv. (1), 43, Taunton Mus.), may also be noted here.

Mr. Stradling in 1838 found two small leather purses in a pottery mound. The one contained the smallest silver coins of the later Emperors and the other the smallest copper of the same era, and among the latter was a coin of Flaccilla, wife of Theodosius I. Constantinian coins have also come to light in the marsh at Shapwick and a fibula at Moorlinch.[1] In sum, we have proof that in Roman days man really dwelt on the edge of the marsh that skirts the Polden Hills. The occupation may have been confined to the third and fourth centuries. The occupants may have been few and shy and retiring. But they deserve a moment's consideration; for they belong to one of those secluded corners of former life which in every period of history are so hard to approach and comprehend.

(b) HOARDS OF LATE SILVER COINS

Numerous hoards of Roman coins have been discovered in Somerset. Most of these require no special notice and can be treated sufficiently in the index. But one remarkable feature is provided by an unusually large number of hoards of late silver coins, minted in the fourth century and buried or lost at dates near or even after its close. The reason for the occurrence of such hoards in the remote west is not clear. They are not in general common in England. Only one has been found in Worcestershire, one in Berkshire, none in the adjacent counties of Devon and Cornwall, and none in Warwickshire or Northamptonshire or Derbyshire, two in Hampshire (with three copper hoards of the same date) and two in Norfolk. Their distribution and metal, and, in some cases at least, their date forbid us to connect them with the march of Magnus Maximus on Rome in 387 or with the 'withdrawal of the legions' in 406. They seem to point rather to some special fortune or misfortune of Somerset about the beginning of the fifth century.[2] Such might be either attacks of Irish pirates or, at a later date, the retreat of the Romanized Britons from eastern Britain before the Saxons. But of the first we know so little that we can hardly use it safely, and the second appears to have come too late to explain coin hoards, in which many of the coins were certainly found in excellent preservation. It is, however, proper to add that while these hoards of late silver seem commoner in Somerset than in most parts of Britain, they are correspondingly commoner in Britain than elsewhere in the Empire. M. Blanchet, for instance, in his *Trésors de monnaies romaines en Gaule*, has no clear case to record of such a hoard in Gaul. Mommsen has observed[3] that, after about A.D. 360, silver was hardly used in the Empire for commerce,

---

[1] *Som. Proc.* xv. (1) 44, xxvi. (1) 79 ; coins in Taunton and Glastonbury museums. Mr. Stradling connected his two hoards with the forgers who (as he thought) would clip them for metal. But the dates do not suit.

[2] We cannot connect these coins with the silver of the lead mines, for they come to a great extent from external, and several indeed from eastern, mints.

[3] Mommsen—Blacas, iii. 133.

except in Britain. But he offers no explanation of the fact, and perhaps on our present imperfect statistics, it may be wise not to attempt one. The Coleraine hoard of 1506 silver coins (dating from A.D. 337–410 *circa*), silver ingots and other fragments may, of course, be connected with Irish pirates. But it is obviously due in the first instance to the use of silver coin in Britain, and must ultimately be explained by that fact.

(1) In making the Great Western Railway between Bath and Bristol, a hoard was found in 1839 at a spot which was intentionally concealed. It is said to have contained 250 silver coins; 150, which were examined, consisted of coins of Valens, Gratian and Magnus Maximus in about equal proportions. The mintmark was mostly Trier, and the reverses mostly 'Urbs Roma' and 'Virtus Romanorum.'[1]

(2) At Uphill, near Weston, a workman clearing rubbish in a cave in 1846 found potsherds and 129 silver and copper coins, mostly of Valentinian and Gratian. After the rubbish had been wheeled out of the cave, 'scores of these ancient coins' were further discovered lying mixed up with it. Over the place where the coins originally lay was a large fissure in the rock, and it was supposed at the time of discovery that the coins might have fallen through this. A coin of Julian and potsherds had been found in 1826 in this or a neighbouring cave.[2]

(3) A large hoard of silver coins was discovered about 1866 in the vicinity of Bristol or of Mendip at a spot which has not been revealed. The whole, or at least the bulk of it, to the number of 2,044 coins, is now in the cabinet of Sir John Evans, who has kindly given me the following analysis of it. The vast majority of the coins, 2,005, are ordinary *siliquae*; 32 are of the conventional medallion size, and 7 are small conventional *quinarii*. The emperors represented are :—

Emperor	Medallion	Middle size	Small size
Constans	1 medallion		
Constantius II.	8 ,,	186 middle size	
Gallus	1 ,,		
Julian	1 ,,	456 ,, ,,	
Jovian	1 ,,	15 ,, ,,	
Valentinian I.	5 ,,	57 ,, ,,	
Valens	4 ,,	295 ,, ,,	1 small size
Procopius		2 ,, ,,	
Gratian	4 ,,	233 ,, ,,	3 ,, ,,
Valentinian II.	4 ,,	254 ,, ,,	
Theodosius	2 ,,	175 ,, ,,	1 ,, ,,
Magnus Maximus		227 ,, ,,	1 ,, ,,
Victor		32 ,, ,,	
Eugenius	1 ,,	23 ,, ,,	
Honorius		12 ,, ,,	
Arcadius		36 ,, ,,	
Roma		2 ,, ,,	1 ,, ,,

Of these coins, two of Magnus Maximus, with mint marks of London under its fourth century title of Augusta (AVG and AVG PS), are noteworthy. The three coins of Roma are ascribed by Sir John Evans to the period of Valentinian and come from the Trier mint.[3]

(4) A far more striking and far better recorded find occurred in 1887 in the parish of East Harptree, near the summit of the north escarpment of Mendip, 800 feet above sea-level, close to the Frances Plantation and some three miles east of the Charterhouse mining settlement. The find was contained in a pewter vessel, 10¾ inches high, provided with a handle and exemplifying a shape not uncommon in the late Empire. The objects contained in this vessel were (1) a silver ring set with a cornelian intaglio of Mars; (2) five small ingots

[1] *Num. Chron.* ii. (1840), 144.
[2] *Gent. Mag.* 1846 (ii.) 633. For the find of 1826, see Rutter, p. 78.
[3] Information from Sir John Evans : brief notes by him, *Num. Chron.* 1867, pp. 62, 331, and 1888, p. 23.

of cast silver weighing respectively 818, 808, 644, 516, and 248 grains, and 1496 or more silver coins in excellent preservation. These coins were :—

Constantine I	1	Jovian	8
Constans	4	Valentinian I	165
Constantius II	340	Valens	199
Decentius	1	Gratian	60
Julian	718		

To these I may add 1 Constantius Gallus (66 grains), 1 Valentinian (68 grains) and 1 Valens (65 grains), medallions, shown me by Professor Oman and believed to be waifs from this hoard.

Of eleven mints represented, Arles sent 553 coins, Lyons 574, and Trèves 207, while the distant mints, Antioch, Constantinople, Nicomedia, contributed only 30. The coins were of three sizes. Most were small *siliquae* of 31–33 grains ; 8 averaged 49 grains, and 15 were medallions or double *siliquae* of 66 grains, coined largely in the distant mints.[1]

(5) Not long before 1859 an urn with a hoard of mixed silver and copper coins was found just outside or in the entrance to Wookey Hole. No proper account of it exists. But it seems certain that amongst the silver were issues of Constantius II, Julian, Valens and Gratian, and in particular a medallion or double *siliqua* of Gratian. The copper coins are said to have included small brass of the Constantine family, Valens, Valentinian, and Gratian and perhaps others.[2]

(6) In the marshes near Edington and Chilton Mr. W. Stradling discovered in a pottery mound (p. 353) two leather purses. One contained the smallest silver of the later Empire, and the other the smallest copper of the same age, including a coin of Aelia Flaccilla (died 388).

(7) At Holway, a south-eastern suburb of Taunton, a large hoard of late silver was found in 1821, and a few waifs from it (as it seems) were picked up in later years. No proper record was kept. It is said to have been stored in a Samian jar and to have ranged from Constans to Honorius and Arcadius. Like the Harptree hoard, it included many medallions or double *siliquae*—2 Constans, 2 Julian, 10 Valentinian, 4 Valens, 7 Gratian, 2 Valentinian II, 1 Magnus Maximus, 4 Theodosius and 1 Eugenius—mostly coined in eastern mints, and perhaps others not precisely recorded. Besides these, there was a much larger number of small silver *siliquae* of about the size of a sixpence or fourpenny bit.[3] See further p. 363.

(8) At North Curry, a village in the low country six miles east of Taunton, an urn with about 150 silver coins was ploughed up in July 1748. The coins were of Constantine, Constans, Julian, Valentinian, Valens, Gratian, Theodosius, Magnus Maximus, Honorius and Arcadius. One Gratian was of the size of a shilling—a medallion or double *siliqua* ; the rest were about the size of a sixpence or fourpenny piece.[4]

I may here add a tiny hoard noted on p. 292, and two hoards of the same date as the preceding, of which the metal is not recorded.

(*a*) At Milverton, six miles west of Taunton, a hoard was found in an urn about 1847. Only 45 coins are recorded, and apparently no more were discovered.

Julian	3	Theodosius	6
Valentinian I	3	Theodosius Maximus (*sic*)	16
Valens	7	Arcadius	1
Valentinian II	2	Faustina (*sic*)	7

Faustina must be an error for Fausta, and Th. Maximus may be an error for Magnus Maximus.[5]

(*b*) 40 coins ranging from Constantius II to Gratian and Theodosius, discovered about 1846 near a Roman villa found by Mr. S. Hasell near Charlton Mackrell (villa No. 36 above).

---

[1] J. Evans, *Num. Chron.* 1888, p. 23, full list with cuts of vessel and ring ; brief notices in *Proc. Soc. Antiq.* xii. 56 ; *Arch. Journ.* xlv. 94. The discovery reduced the market value of the medallions from about £3 to 15*s*. The Frances Plantation is marked O.S. xix. S.W

[2] *Num. Chron.* 1863 Proceedings, pp. 8, 11, *Som. Proc.* xi. 201 ('silver coins of Allectus and Commodus'—perhaps incorrect) ; xxvi. (1) 80 ; 15 Third Brass of 250–350 A.D. in Glastonbury Museum (Williamson Collection).

[3] *Num. Chron.* Proceedings, 23 Nov. 1843 ; *Som. Proc.* v. (1) 14 ; x. (1) 35 ; xxiv. (2) 105 ; xxvii. (2) 55 ; xlix. (1) 61 ; Pring, *Briton and Roman on the site of Taunton*, p. 105 ; some coins in Taunton Museum and in Mr. Franklin's Collection. By a misprint the hoard is sometimes assigned to Holwell.

[4] *Gent. Mag.* 1748, p. 405 ; hence Collinson, ii. 178, Gough, Phelps, etc. Pring, in *Som. Proc.* xxiv. (2) 109, says the find was made at a spot called Lillesdon.   [5] *Arch. Journ.* iv. 145.

ALPHABETICAL INDEX

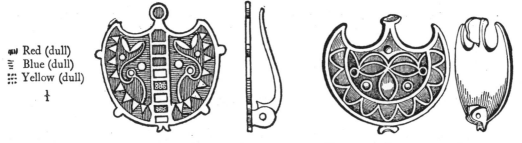

꙼ꙮ Red (dull)
≣ Blue (dull)
⁞⁞⁞ Yellow (dull)
¼

FIG. 99. BROOCH FROM WOLVERSHILL, ¼.   FIG. 100. BROOCH FROM IRCHESTER.

BLACKFORD.—See Wedmore.

BLAGDON.—Lead pig : see p. 341, No. 5.

BRATTON.—Building : see p. 320.

BREAN DOWN.—Scarth [*Som. Proc.* xxxi. (2) 13] says that ' all the surface of the down is marked with traces of Roman habitation.' This seems much exaggerated, but F. Warre mentions ' many Roman coins ' from here [*Som. Proc.* xii. (1) 66].

BRENT KNOLL.—Silver and copper coins in the earthwork on the knoll, and potsherds, including Samian, on it and at its base [Collinson, i. 196 ; Skinner in Add. MS. 33719, p. 99]. Barrett, *Hist. of Bristol*, p. 10, mentions coins of Trajan, Severus, and others in an urn on the knoll : hence Seyer i. 86. The alleged road found in the marsh, 6 feet below the surface, may be of any age [*Som. Proc.* iv. (2) 104].

BRIDGWATER.—Potteries on the Bridgwater levels, 300 yards from Basin Bridge [H. de la Beche, *Geological Report on Devon, Cornwall and Somerset*, p. 422]. Probably the same finds as some noted under Highbridge.

BRISLINGTON.—Villa : see p. 303. Hoard of 23 or more late copper coins, found in a ' metallic urn ' with potsherds, on Dr. Fox's Brislington estate about 1829 [W. R. Barker, *Acct. of Brislington Villa*, p. 6].

BRISTOL.—Leland (*Comment. in Cygneam Cantionem*, under Avona and Venta), H. Lhuyd, Andrew Hooke (*Bristollia*, 1748) and others, call Bristol Venta Belgarum. Seyer and others point to streets crossing at right angles in Roman fashion as evidence of a Roman town. But this is all fiction. The remains actually found are : coins at various spots (near the cathedral, the floating harbour, etc.), two lead pigs near the old course of the river Frome (p. 342), a lead coffin, etc., at Mina Road Brick Works, and a road and building outside the town on the Downs. These remains do not show that any part of the area of the modern city was inhabited in town-fashion in Roman times. See further, Seyer, i. 207 ; J. F. Nicholls, *Bristol Past and Present*, i. 24, 64 ; *Clifton Antiq. Club*, ii. 82, 160 ; iii. 125 ; v. 46 ; *Brit. Arch. Assoc. Journ.* xxxi. 63.

BRISTOL [near].—Hoard of 347 copper coins (in two sizes, but all smaller than *folles*) found about 1885 : the exact find-spot is not recorded. The coins were—1 Gallienus, 3 Probus, 1 Diocletian, 1 Carausius, 9 Maximin, 4 Licinius, 1 Licinius II, 279 Constantine I, 5 Crispus, 6 Constantine II. The hoard was deposited about A.D. 322. Quite half the coins bear the London mint-mark [John Evans, *Num. Chron.* 1885, p. 118].

—— [near].—Hoard found in 1839 in making the G. W. railway from Bath to Bristol : the exact site was concealed. It contained some 250 *denarii* : 150 examined belonged to Valens, Gratian, and Magnus equally : the mint-marks were mostly of Trier [*Num. Chron.* ii. (1840) 144.

—— [near].—For the hoard recorded by J. F. Nicholls, *Arch. Journ.* xxvii. 65, as found ' near Bristol,' see under Whitchurch (Philwood hoard).

BROCKLEY.—See Chelvey.

BROOMFIELD.—Scarth, *Som. Proc.* xxiv. (2) 10, says coins and querns have been found in Ruborough Camp in this parish. But he misquotes *Journ. Brit. Arch. Assoc.* xiii. 295, which really refers to Elm. See *Som. Proc.* xlix. (2) 173.

BRUTON.—Lead pig : see p. 342, No. 13.

Villa at Discove (since 1846 in this parish) : see p. 320.

BURNHAM.—Samian and other potsherds, bones, Kimmeridge clay objects found in clay pits [*Som. Proc.* xv. (1) 43 : Taunton and Exeter Museums]. Compare Highbridge.

BURNETT.—Building, p. 303, and compare Corston.

BURRINGTON.—Scarth [*Bath Field Club*, iv. 7 ; *Som. Proc.* xxiv. (2) 18 and xxxiii. (2) 5] says coins have been found in a cave in Burrington Combe. But the older writers mention no certainly Roman remains in these caves [Buckland, *Reliq. Antediluv.* ; Rutter, p. 117 ; Boyd Dawkins, *Som. Proc.* xii. (2) 169]. There is no reason to call Burrington Camp Roman.

BURTLES [near Edington].—See pp. 352-3, 356.

BUTLEIGH WOOTTON [near].—Villa : see Street, p. 322.

CADBURY.—This name occurs three times in Somerset, as noted below. It also occurs no less than three times on its borders, at Bitton [*Bath Field Club*, vii. 205], between Crediton and Tiverton, and near Chumleigh in Devon :—

    (1) Near Clevedon : see Tickenham and Clapton.

    (2) Near Yatton : see Yatton.

    (3) Near Sparkford. Here is a large earthen camp, 18 acres in extent, defended by

stupendous fosses. It was once popularly connected with King Arthur and called Camalet, perhaps because of the Camel close by. Roman remains appear to have been found in it, but our accounts are rather rhetorical and misty. Leland mentions ' foundations and rudera of walles ' (not necessarily Roman), and also ' much gold, sylver and coper of the Romaine coynes and many other Antique Thinges.' Selden repeats this. Stukeley mentions vast numbers of coins of Antoninus Pius and Faustina, worked stone, pavements, buildings, etc., and identifies the spot with the Colomeas (*sic*) of the Ravenna lists. But excavations made in the nineteenth century revealed, amid abundant pre-Roman matter, only one bit of Samian, one possibly Roman brick, and various coins, chiefly towards the east side of the hill [Leland, *Assertio Arturii*, p. 29, and *Itinerary* (ed. Hearne), ii. 47 ; Camden, i. 78 ; Selden, note to Drayton's *Polyolbion* (ed. 1612), p. 54 ; Stukeley, *Itin. Cur.* (ed. 2), p. 150. Hence Musgrave, *Antiq. Brit. Belg.* i. 172 ; Gough, *Adds. to Camden*, i. 192 ; Collinson, ii. 71 ; etc. For excavations and recent researches see *Som. Proc.* vii. 58, xvi. (1) 18, and especially xxix. 110 (plan by Dymond), xxxvi. (2) 12 ; *Bath Field Club*, i. (3) 100, vii. 83].

CAMERTON.—Village : see p. 289.

CARHAMPTON : see Dunster Park.

CASTLE CARY.—Coin of Pius found 1852 in South Cary Lane [*Som. Proc.* xxxvi. (1) 61]. For the Ditcheat villa, see p. 320.

CASTLE NEROCHE.—F. Warre [*Som. Proc.* v. (2) 29] argued for a late British fortification, slightly occupied in Roman times. But he could not cite any definitely Roman objects, and excavations made in 1903 revealed nothing Roman, but pointed mostly to a medieval occupation [Gray, *Som. Proc.* xlix. (ii.) 23–54]. The site, therefore, is not Roman.

CATCOTT.—See Edington, p, 352 foll.

CHARD.—Villas (1) at South Chard and (2) on the Crewkerne Road : see p. 332. Lesser finds in the neighbourhood are (1) a silver coin of Claudius picked up on Foxmore Hill about 1850, (2) a hoard of some 300 Third Brass Constantinian coins, found about 1836 at Court Pits field, Chard Farm, (3) Coins and a small vase at West Ford [G. P. R. Pulman, *Book of the Axe*, p. 460 : Hull Collection in Chard Town Hall].

Lewis (*Topogr. Dict.*) records an urn with many gold coins of Claudius, as found at Leigh House in May 1831. This is too good to be true. The metal may have been the bright brass (*orichalcum*) which is often mistaken by labourers for gold.

CHARLCOMBE (Bath).—At Cherry Wells, 2 bronze armlets and 2 ring-brooches [Scarth, *Aquæ*, p. 85].

CHARLTON.—(1) Near Shepton : see p. 318. (2) Mackrell, p. 323.

CHARTERHOUSE-ON-MENDIP.—Lead mines : see p. 334.

CHEDDAR.—Hoard of about 100 Third Brass Gallienus—Maximian and Diocletian (**PAX AVGGG** issued by Carausius), found in ploughing [*Journ. Brit. Arch. Assoc.* ii. 271].

A number of Roman coins, some Constantinian, were found about 1840, at Tanner's papermills, in the bed of the river [*Num. Chron.* ii. (1840) p. 206].

Potsherds, second brass coin of Domitian in churchyard, found 1886 ; Samain, coins of all dates found in churchyard and adjoining fields [*Axbridge Branch of Som. Arch. Soc.* i. (1898), p. 11]. The vicarage garden has yielded a denarius of Hadrian, 1 Victorinus, and about 10 fourth century coins, down to Valens, and Parsonage Pen 1 Pius and 5 fourth century coins to Valens [Preb. Coleman].

Near the cave mouth of the ' Roman Cave,' coins, fibulae, bones, potsherds found by Mr. Gough [information from E. A. Baker, 1903].

In the ' Long Hole ' cave Mr. Gough found in 1887–8 some bronze objects (armillae, tweezers, pins) and (if I understand aright) also some 10 or 12 coins—of Valens, Valentinian, Gratian and Constantius II—so far as legible. [Information from Preb. Coleman, kindly sent through Mr. H. E. Balch.] Possibly the same as the preceding.

CHEDZOY.—Coins found sporadically, amongst them a washed silver issue of Orbiana Augusta ; urns and fibulae found in 1701 near the church ; key (? Roman) in Taunton Museum [Collinson, iii. 94, hence Gough, *Adds. to Camden*, i. 98 ; *Som. Proc.* i. (2) 59 ; xlviii. (1) 84 ; Stradling, *Chilton Polden Mus.* (Bridgwater, 1839), pp. 13, 15, mentions 'a large Roman bead ' and ' an elegantly engraved key.' He also says (Preface, p. ii.) that he dug in Slapeland, a ' common field ' of Chedzoy, and found a nearly perfect hypocaust, of large Ham Hill stones, potsherds, scoriae of iron, and ashes. Close by, he found medieval masonry and architectural fragments probably belonging to a known chapel. Possibly the other remains may also be medieval. Stradling was somewhat enthusiastic. See p. 352 *note*.

CHELVEY (Brockley parish).—Hoard of 274 silver coins found Jan. 1808, 4 feet below the surface, in digging foundations for a new school. They were in a stone bottle and were said to be of 'Iulius Caesar': near was a large black urn full of human bones and ashes [*Gent. Mag.* 1808, i. 360; unfortunately an uncritical notice].

CHESTERBLADE.—Buildings: see p. 319. The neighbouring 'camp' on Smalldown is pre-Roman.

CHEW MAGNA.—Coins are vaguely alleged [*Clifton Antiq. Club*, ii. 163].

CHEW STOKE.—Villa, see p. 309. Twenty-nine silver coins [*Proc. Som.* xxviii. (1) 78].

CHEWTON.—Skinner alleges potsherds near the church and coins [Add. MSS. 33659 and 33663, p. 123].

CHIDLEY MOUNT.—Aubrey mentions coins and ruins of Roman age a mile and a half from Bridgwater, at 'Chiefe Chidley Mount.' This is identified in *Som. Proc.* xxiii. (1) 36, with a mound called by the Ordnance Survey (l. NE.) Downend, a quarter of a mile from Dunball railway station [Aubrey MS. 15, fol. 122, in the Bodleian Library: thence, briefly, Gibson, Gough, Reynolds]. Skinner mentions potsherds, including Samian, and late Imperial coins as found just at this point (Add. MS. 33716, fol. 105).

CHILCOMPTON.—Coin of Marcus [Collinson, ii. 127, hence Gough, *Adds. to Camden*, i. 105. But it is not clear that Collinson meant to assign the coin to this place].

CHILLINGTON.—Coins found in 1866; lead coffin found 1848–50. [Norris, *Som. Proc.* xxxvii. (1) 26; O.S.; the Hull collection at Chard contains a bit of the coffin.] A small bronze of Osiris, picked up here out of a lot of old metal in a blacksmith's forge, may be a waif from anywhere [*Proc. Soc. Antiq.* xi. 88; *Som. Proc.* xxxii. (1) 80].

CHILTON ON POLDEN.—Coin moulds: see p. 352 foll.

CHILTON TRINITY.—Silver coin of Empire [Jarman, *Hist. of Bridgwater*, p. 5].

CHINNOCK.—A large hoard was found in 1805 in Barrow Field, halfway between Middle and East Chinnock and on the north of the Yeovil and Crewkerne high road. It lay under human bones and rude potsherds, and was contained in two small pots of rude black ware. The coins, about 4,000, were apparently debased silver, Antoniniani and Third Brass of A.D. 253–282; only 300 were examined [*Gent. Mag.* 1805 (ii.) 1111].

CHISELBOROUGH.—Here Ward and Horsley inclined to put Iscalis. No Roman remains have been found here.

CHURCHILL.—See Dolebury (? coins) and Langford (villa).

CLAPTON-IN-GORDANO.—On Tickenham hill, near the border of Tickenham parish, 600 yards west of Cadbury Camp, 35 Third Brass of A.D. 253–305 (including Diocletian and Maximian **PAX AVGGG**, issued by Carausius), found about 1891. A few Third Brass (1 Valerian, 1 Tetricus, 1 Constans) and 1 silver Honorius had been found earlier, and also some querns and potsherds now in Taunton Museum [*Som. Proc.* xxvi. (1) 85; xxvii. (1) 76; *Clifton Antiq. Club*, iii. 117; Pritchard, *Numism. Chron.* 1896, p. 238]. For another and larger hoard found not far off, see Tickenham.

CLEVEDON.—(1) Potsherds and coins were found near Christ Church in 1876 [Ordnance Map].

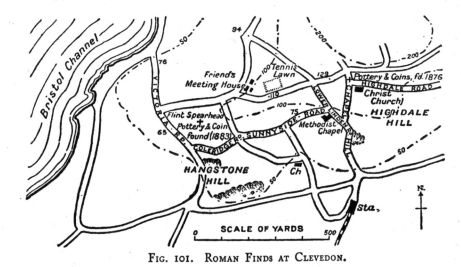

FIG. 101. ROMAN FINDS AT CLEVEDON.

(2) On the east side of Hangstone Hill (south of modern town) quarrymen found in 1879 some coins—1 Vespasian, 1 Hadrian, 2 Tetricus, etc.—fibulae, a sword with wooden

handle, rude potsherds, and human bones—perhaps burials, but date not clear [*Clevedon Mercury and Courier*, 13 Sept. 1879, hence *Arch. Journ.* xxxvi. 334, etc.]. The remains were taken to Cleveland Court and afterwards perished in a fire there.

(3) Samian and other potsherds, an illegible coin, animals' bones, were found in 1882 near the junction of Lower Linden Road and Sunnyside Road, when a new Wesleyan (Methodist) chapel was built [*Clevedon Mercury*, 19 Aug. 1882; hence *Antiquary*, 1882 (Oct.), p. 178].

(4) Potsherds, coins, and skeletons were found 180 feet north of Coleridge road and 300 feet east of Victoria Road in 1883 [*Clevedon Mercury*, 17 Feb. 1883; Ordnance Map].

(5) In Linden Road, 210 feet south of Constitutional Club, in making a tennis lawn, the workmen discovered 8 Constantinian coins, fragments of Upchurch ware and animals' bones [*Bristol Mercury*, 26 March, 1903; *Som. Proc.* xlix. (ii.) 185; Ordnance Survey].

The site of Clevedon was inhabited in Roman times, but probably not to any great extent. The inhabitation seems to have been confined to the ridge of high ground which runs west from Dial Hill, between the sea and the Land Yeo stream. Unfortunately, the finds have not been well recorded, and the very careful inquiries kindly made for me by Mr. J. E. Pritchard, F.S.A., show that the details are now locally forgotten. It is therefore rash to speculate on the character of Roman Clevedon—whether a little hamlet, or a villa, or farmhouse.

COCKMILL.—Large vessel containing a peck of coins of Aurelian, Probus, Tacitus, Gallienus, etc. [Phelps, p. 179, etc.].

COKER, EAST AND WEST.—Villas: see pp. 329, 331.

COMBE DOWN (BATH).—Villa and inscribed slab: see p. 309.

COMBE HAY.—Alleged villa on the hill above the village, very doubtful. Skinner, who alone mentions it, is not certain: Add. MS. 28795, fol. 7; 33663, fol. 127.

COMBE ST. NICHOLAS.—Villa at Wadeford, coins elsewhere in parish, p. 333.

COMPTON DANDO.—Sculptured stone walled into a buttress of the church. The stone is 48 inches high and about 16 inches square; the two sides not now visible are said to be plain; the two visible sides bear reliefs much damaged and weathered. One represents Apollo partly draped, standing facing sideways, his left leg raised, and above it his lyre held in his left hand while his right hand holds the plectrum close to it: face and shoulders lost. The other, a full-face relief, has been said to be Hercules, but is not identifiable in its present condition. The stone somewhat resembles a stone found at Bath in 1790 (p. 241) and carved on two sides with figures of two gods. Whence it came to Compton is unknown. It was first seen there in 1819 by John Skinner, who states that the other two sides were plain [Skinner, Addit. MS. 33663, p. 108; *Gent. Mag.* 1846 (i.) 78; *Arch. Journ.* ii. 272; Scarth, *Aquae*, p. 41, with fair illustration. I have examined the stone myself].

COMPTON DUNDON.—Mr. Franklin has 2 coins of Magnentius and 1 of (?) Augustus found here.

CONGRESBURY.—Supposed villa at Woodlands: p. 307.

Coins at Honey Hall, 1½ miles southwards, towards Churchill [Scarth, *Som. Proc.* xxiv. (1) 74; *Arch. Journ.* xxxvi. 335].

CONKWELL.—Potsherds and coins of Valens and Constantine [Skinner, Addit. MS. 33656, p. 150].

CONQUEST FARM.—See Lydeard St. Lawrence.

COPLEY.—See Kingweston.

CORSTON.—Villa (probably that at Burnett): see p. 303.

Oolite coffin with skeleton, nails (? of boots) near the feet, found in Lower Botmore field [*Journ. Brit. Arch. Assoc.* xlvii. 186].

CORTON DENHAM.—Urn containing 2 quarts of coins of Valerian, Gallienus, Tacitus, Probus, Florian, Aurelian, found Jan. 1722–3 [Stukeley, *Itin. Curiosum* (ed. 2), p. 149: hence Collinson, ii. 361; Gough, *Adds. to Camden*, i. 100; Reynolds, p. 435, etc.; Scarth, *Som. Proc.* xxiv. (2) 19; *Arch. Journ.* xxxvi. 334 records only urns. The date of the find is sometimes given as 1772, but Stukeley's MS. note in his copy of *Itin. Cur.* (ed. 1), p. 141 (now in the Bodleian) gives 1722, and so his printed text in the second edition. He took the information from the 'public papers'].

COSSINGTON.—See Huntspill, Highbridge.

COTHELSTON.—Vague references to coins in *Som. Proc.* i. (2) 43; xviii. (1) 45, etc.; *Arch. Journ.* xxxvi. (1) 74, all perhaps relating to the Lydeard St. Lawrence or other neighbouring hoard. W. H. Greswell, *Land of Quantock*, p. 26, mentions coins found in an old alder bed, but he has mixed up two sentences of *Som. Proc.* i. (2) 43. Probably nothing has really been found in this parish.

CRANMORE (WEST).—Villa : see p. 319.

CREWKERNE.—Coins of Trajan, etc., found at Crewkerne [Thos. Gerard, *Descr. of Somerset* (1633) in *Somerset Record Soc.*, xv. 65]. Coins of Pius, Gallienus, Constantine II, 1 each [Pulman, *Book of the Axe*, p. 235].

Hoard of about 130 Third Brass, Constantine I, Licinius, Crispus, found in 1872, just north of Combe Farm [Pulman, p. 72 ; *Proc. Som.* xvii. 124 ; *Archaeol. Cambrensis*, 1872, p. 272 ; Ordnance Survey].

CURRY (NORTH).—Hoard of late fourth century silver coins, p. 356.

CURRY RIVEL.—See Drayton, Stanchester.

DINNINGTON.—See Seavington.

DISCOVE.—Villa : p. 320.

DITCHEAT.—Villa : p. 320.

DOLEBURY (Churchill parish).—Large camp, not Roman. Roman coins are said to have been discovered in it, but there is no proper record of them [Collinson, iii. 579 ; hence Gough, *Adds. to Camden*, i. 122 ; Skinner in Addit. MS. 28974, p. 128, and 33663, p. 118 ; hence Phelps, p. 100 and (I think) Rutter, p. 115. See also *Som. Proc.* xxix. (2) 110 ; *Bath Field Club*, iii. 145].

DRAYTON.—Villa : p. 328.

DULVERTON.—Four Third Brass (3rd and 4th cent.), found in recent breccia [Bristol Mus.].

DUNKERTON.—' A few coins and mouldering urns,' [Collinson, iii. 337].

DUNSTER PARK (Carhampton parish).—Small copper coins of Maximian and Constantine, found about 1863, concealed under a stone in a gully in the Park, near the old Carhampton road : now in possession of Mr. Luttrell [*Som. Proc.* xxxv. (1) 47 ; J. Ll. W. Page, *Exploration of Exmoor*, p. 201 ; note from Sir Henry Maxwell Lyte].

There is no reason to consider either of the earthworks here to be Roman : Scarth has confused them [Savage, *Hist. of Carhampton*, p. 289].

EDINGTON.—Villa or building (doubtful), coin-moulds : see pp. 352–3, 356.

ELM.—Hoard of coins, chiefly of Constantine Junior, found in an urn in 1691 in Tedbury Camp or some adjacent earthwork [Stukeley, *Itin. Cur.* (ed. 2), p. 149, hence Collinson, ii. 206, Gough, *Adds. to Camden*, i. 112, etc].

A vague reference to querns and coins found at Tedbury occurs *Journ. Brit. Arch. Assoc.* xiii. 295.

EMBORROW.—Silver coins ploughed up near the church [Collinson, ii. 135].

ENGLISH COMBE.—Copper coin of Pius found in 1786 below English Combe Hill [Collinson, iii. 339].

Coins and potsherds in Farnham or Vernham Wood on Odd Down beside the Fosse [Skinner, Addit. MS. 28795, p. 261 ; hence, I think, Phelps, p. 146]. Two stone coffins found near Burnthouse Turnpike in 1822 [Scarth, *Som. Proc.* v. (2) 53].

EVERCREECH.—See Chesterblade.

EXMOOR.—Urns with coins found in 1831 near the sources of the Exe [Scarth, *Som. Proc.* xxiv. (2) 19 ; but perhaps a misquotation of Reynolds, p. 439].

FAILAND.—See Long Ashton.

FARLEY HUNGERFORD.—Villas : see p. 300. Skinner and a local guide (Bath, 1829) record a First Brass coin found in the Castle garden [Addit. MS. 33656, p. 239], but there is no reason to suppose that a villa stood on its site.

FARMBOROUGH.—At Hobbs Wall, large stone coffin containing a lead coffin, inside which was a skeleton : found 1886 [*Proc. Soc. Antiq.* xi. 313 ; *Clifton Antiq. Club*, i. 109]. Not necessarily but not improbably Roman.

FARNHAM WOOD.—See English Combe.

FILWOOD.—See Whitchurch.

FOSCOTE (NEAR RADSTOCK).—Skinner reports potsherds.

FRESHFORD.—Bronze key, once in possession of Martin Tupper, accepted as Roman by A. W. Franks [Letter from Tupper in Bath Institution Library. This may be the key reported in *Brit. Arch. Assoc. Journ.* x. 113 as from Fairford].

Rude potsherds in Bristol Museum.

GLASTONBURY.—The grey ware found on Wearyall Hill, now in Glastonbury Museum, does not seem to me Roman. The pile-dwellings in the moor near Glastonbury appear to be wholly of pre-Roman Celtic date. But Warner, *Hist. of Glastonbury* (1826), p. 153, *note*, states that 'many Roman coins had turned up either in the Abbey enclosure or at the foot of Tor Hill.' From the latter spot came a fine Vespasian, and Warner himself had a Hadrian from some part of Glastonbury. Still, he is doubtless right in thinking this was not a Roman site.

HADDON HILL (King's Brompton parish).—At the west end some coins dug up [Collinson, iii. 502 ; hence Lewis, *Topogr. Dict.* etc.].

HALLATROW.—Skinner notes stone coffins in Cheshills field [Add. MS. 33659].

HAM (HIGH).—Villa : see p. 328.

HAM HILL OR HAMDON HILL.—Many Late Celtic and Roman finds : see p. 295.

HARPTREE (EAST).—Hoard of late fourth century silver coins, p. 355.

HENSTRIDGE BOWDEN.—Bit of Samian and coarser potsherds found 1892 : shown me by Mr. G. Sweetman of Wincanton; now in Taunton Museum [*Som. Proc.* l. (1) 62].

HIGHBRIDGE.—Potsherds, tiles such as are used for pottery in kilns, coin moulds, etc. See pp. 352–3. Probably much the same as noted under Bridgwater, Burnham and Cossington.

HINTON CHARTERHOUSE.—Skinner alludes to foundations, coins and potsherds in Shepherd's Mead and coins at the Bulwarks [Add. MS. 28795, p. 261, and 33659 ; hence Phelps, p. 147]. The Roman *tesserae* mentioned as found in Hinton Abbey [*Gent. Mag.* 1830 (ii.) 578] must be medieval.

HOLFORD.—Coin of Constantine found above Alfoxton : another (illegible) coin found in Holford [W. H. Greswell, *Land of Quantock* (Taunton, 1903), p. 25].

HOLWAY.—Hoard of late fourth century silver found in 1821 near 2 skeletons. About 15 more coins of same period and metal found, with charred bones, etc., in another part of Holway, in 1870. A few copper coins (1 Domitian, 1 Trajan, 1 Pius, 1 Constantine and 8 more late silver coins, found sporadically since 1870 [*Proc. Som.* v. (1) 14 ; x. (1) 35 ; xxiv. (ii.) 105 ; xxvii. (2) 52 ; xlix. (i.) 61 ; *Proc. Numismatic Soc.* 23 Nov. 1843 ; Pring, *Briton and Roman on site of Taunton*, p. 105 ; coins in Taunton Museum and in collection of Mr. H. Franklin. The hoard is sometimes, by a miswriting, attributed to ' Holwell ']. See further under Taunton and p. 356.

HUISH CHAMPFLOWER.—Alleged *botontinus* : see my note under Banwell [*Som. and Dorset N. and Q.* Sept. 1903].

HUISH EPISCOPI.—See Langport.

HUNTSPILL.—Pottery mounds, etc., in the marshes : see pp. 352–3.

HURCOT (NEAR SOMERTON).—Villa : see p. 322.

IFORD.—See Farley Hungerford (villa) : p. 300.

ILCHESTER.—Village : see p. 294.

ILMINSTER.—Third Brass coin of Constantine I found in Ditton Street. Coin found at Dunpole [*Som. Proc.* xviii. (1) 71].

ISLE ABBOTS.—Potsherds at Walrond Park [*Proc. Som.* xxiii. (1) 83 ; Taunton Museum]

ISLE BREWERS.—Coins vaguely noted [*Som. Proc.* xxiv. (1), 74].

KELSTON.—Copper coins of Constantine I and Valentinian I in grounds of John Harington [Guidott (1676), p. 68]. Tiles under church [*Bristol and Glouc. Arch. Soc.* viii. 45].

KEN MOOR.—Coins : see Nailsea.

KEWSTOKE.—At St. Kew's Steps, fibula. Dymond, *Worlebury*, plate x. 17]. Cameos of Claudius, Nero and Vitellius are mentioned *Som. Proc.* ii (1) 13 as found here. But they may be modern.

KILMERSDON.—See Radstock.

KILTON, KILVE.—Collinson (i. 261) states that about the year 1700, many coins ' of Diocletian, Gallienus, Maximus, and some of the Thirty Tyrants ' were dug up at Putsham, a hamlet of Kilve. He also states (iii. 351) that about the year 1700 many coins of Antoninus, Alex. Severus, Gordian, Gallienus, Postumus, Faustina and Julia Mammaea were found near Kilton, and adds (iii. 532) that Roman coins have often been dug up at Putsham. Kilton and Kilve are adjacent parishes, and perhaps Collinson has given two different accounts of one and the same hoard. Scarth mentions coins at ' Putcombe ' (*Som. Proc.* xxiv. (2) 10) —apparently an error for Putsham.

KING'S SEDGEMOOR.—Building, bone inscribed ΛPRILIS : see p. 325.

KINGSDON.—Two villas : p. 325.

KINGSTON SEYMOUR.—Hoard found in 1884 of 800 Third Brass—Gallienus, Salonina, Postumus, Tetricus, Cl. Gothicus, Victorinus [*Proc. Soc. Antiq.* xi. 31 ; *Som. Proc.* xxxi.; (2) 7 ; the coins are now in the possession of Mr. Smyth Pigott of Brockley Court]. See Yatton.

KINGWESTON.—Villa and coins, p. 322. The villa is sometimes assigned to Charlton Mackrell.

KNOWLE (or KNOLL) HILL.—Alleged villa : pp. 329, 352 *note*.

LANGFORD (LOWER).—Villa : p. 308. In or near Churchill parish.

LANGPORT.—Supposed villa on west bank of river Parrett, in Huish Episcopi parish. See p. 328

LANGRIDGE.—Supposed building : p. 301.

LAVERTON.—For Peart Wood, see Woolverton.

LEIGH DOWN (Long Ashton parish).—Hoard of coins : see Long Ashton (2).

LITTLETON.—Villas : p. 323.

LOCKSBROOK.—See Bath, p. 266.

LONG ASHTON.—(1) Villas or buildings at Cambridge Batch (see p. 305) and Failand (p. 305).

(2) A noteworthy hoard was found in 1817 on Leigh Down in Long Ashton parish —500 or perhaps 1,000 denarii and (it is said) 1 copper coin. It was at once dispersed, but Seyer saw 242, all apparently silver, which had been purchased by various persons. Of these he gives a full list. Besides 3 dubious, they are (Seyer, i. 163–174) :—

9 Late Republic.	6 Marcus.	7 Geta.
1 Tiberius.	7 Faustina, jun.	5 Elagabalus.
2 Nero.	1 Verus.	1 Jul. Soaemias.
1 Otho.	2 Lucilla.	1 Severus Alexander.
13 Vespasian.	10 Commodus.	1 Jul. Mammaea.
3 Domitian.	1 Pertinax.	2 Maximin.
1 Nerva.	2 Albinus.	1 Pupienus.
8 Trajan.	80 Sept. Severus.	5 Gordian.
3 Hadrian.	23 Julia Domna.	2 Philip.
10 Pius.	18 Caracalla.	1 Salonina.
2 Faustina, sen.	5 Plautilla.	1 Constantius II.

The occurrence of the last coin, that of Constantius II (Cohen, 343), dating from A.D. 337–361, is puzzling. Not only is it 100 years later than the next latest coin, but it has also no proper place in a hoard of first, second, and early third century silver. Many hoards are known which contain a few Republican issues and Imperial silver extending down to the beginning or middle of the third century (*Archæologia*, liv. 492). But the addition of fourth century silver is unknown. Probably, therefore, the coin of Constantius may have been included erroneously by one of the purchasers of the coins actually found on Leigh Down.

(3) Hoard found in 1815 near Old Fort, in demolishing a 'tumulus': potsherds and over 150 (perhaps 300) copper coins of Lower Empire. A local farmer said there were also one or two gold coins, including a Crispus **VOTXX** (probably misread for **VOT XV FEL XX**) but these must have been merely bright copper. The *vota* coins of Crispus are all copper [Seyer, *Bristol*, i. 81, 160 ; Phelps, p. 177].

(4) Potsherds on the bank sloping down from Stokeleigh Camp to the Avon [*Som. Proc.* xlvii. 227 ; *Clifton Antiq. Club*, ii. 178].

LOPEN.—Coins vaguely mentioned *Gent. Mag.* 1862 (1) 298 ; Pulman, *Book of the Axe*, p. 70 ; Mr. Franklin at Taunton has a bronze Hadrian and a bronze Valerian from this parish. But the Seavington villa (p. 332) is close by, and the coins may all be waifs from it.

LUXBOROUGH.—Iron pickaxe, wooden spade, etc., found in shaft of old iron mine, supposed to be vestiges of Roman ironworkings : coins are also alleged to have been found here [*Som. Proc.* viii. 18 : *Bath Field Club*, iii. 420, vi. 144]. The tools are in Taunton Museum : I do not think it is possible to be certain of their age but see no reason to think them Roman. The district above Dunster contains much Brown Haematite ore. But there is no good evidence that it was mined in Romano-British times.

LYDEARD ST. LAWRENCE.—Large hoard of late third century coins, ill-recorded. A sixteenth century local antiquary, printed by Hearne, *Peter Langtoft*, states that in 1666 two large earthen pitchers were dug up, one in Lydeard St. Lawrence parish, and the other at Capton in Stogumber parish. Each, he says, weighed 80 lb. (? 10,000 Third Brass). He does not distinguish the hoards and entirely misunderstands them. But from his account it is clear that they consisted chiefly or wholly of Antoniniani and Third Brass of circa 250–275 A.D.—Gallienus, Postumus, Victorinus, Tetricus, Claudius Gothicus, Quintillus, Aurelian, and perhaps also Septimius Severus and Trajan Decius. It is a little odd that *two* very large hoards of the same size and character should have been dug up in the same neighbourhood at the same date. See further my article in *Arch. Journ.* lix. 342. The hoards are often put down, as one find, to Conquest Farm in Bishop's Lydeard, but this is an error.

LYTES CARY.—Villas : see p. 326.

MAESBURY.—Urn containing coins of Vespasian, Domitian, Trajan, Hadrian, Faustina, found on the line of Fosse [*Som. Proc.* xii. (1) 60].

MAESKNOLL.—I see no reason for calling Maesknoll ' tump ' a *botontinus*, as Nicholls does. For finds hereabouts, see Whitchurch.

MARSTON BIGOT.—The so-called ' Roman earthwork,' of which a plan is given in Add. MS. 6214, pp. 29–30, seems much later.

MELLS.—Coin of (?) Hadrian [*Gent. Mag.* 1794 (ii.) 703].

MENDIP.—Two hoards have been found on Mendip, about six miles from Frome, of which the exact locality has been concealed. One had 230 coins, dates not known. The other had 452 copper and was deposited about A.D. 335 (1 Tetricus, 16 Helena, 209 Constantine I, 11 Fausta, 4 Constantinian, 68 Crispus, 88 Constantine II, 15 Constantius II, 4 Licinius) [John Evans, *Num. Chron.* vi. (1866) 157].

MIDFORD.—Skinner mentions casual coins found opposite the castle, and on the hill above the village and in the village [Addit. MS. 28795, p. 261]. O.S. xiv. SW.

MIDSOMER NORTON.—Skinner mentions coins and potsherds near the church [Add. MS. 33659].

MILVERTON.—Hoard of late fourth century silver coins : p. 356.

MONTACUTE.—For Hamdon (or Ham) Hill, see p. 295.

MOORLINCH.—Large fibula, Stradling, *Priory of Chilton Polden* (1839), p. 12.

NAILSEA.—Three urns full of coins (some Constantinian), dug up near Nailsea Wall which divides Nailsea moor from Ken moor [Barrett, p. 19 ; Seyer, i. 163 ; from Barrett, Gough, *Adds. to Camden,* i. 123, etc.].

NEWTON ST. LOE.—Villa, p. 302.

NORTH STOKE.—Villa or building : p. 302.

NORTHOVER.—Suburb of Ilchester : p. 294.

NORTON FITZWARREN.—Potsherds, perhaps from a kiln, found in 1861–2 in making the Watchet railway [*Som. Proc.* xi. (1) 33, 56 ; xviii. (1) 44 ; xlvii. (1) 86 ; Taunton Museum ; Ordnance Survey lxx. NW]. Hearne, *Peter Langtoft,* p. 452, gives a curious tradition of burials, which apparently has no archaeological value.

NORTON MALREWARD.—See Whitchurch.

NUNNEY.—(1) Whatley villa, p. 317.

(2) Remarkable hoard found about 1860 on West Down Farm, between Holwell and Leighton, in an earthen jug. At least 250 coins were found, 10 British gold, 232 British silver, 4 Roman *denarii* of republican date (Aemilia, Julia, Junia, Servilia), and 1 imperial of Caligula, and 5 Second Brass, 1 Agrippa, 2 Antonia, 2 Claudius [J. Evans, *Numismatic Chronicle,* 1861, pp. 8, 133]. This hoard is plainly one of those which were buried during and on account of the Roman conquest (cf. *Num. Chron.* 1897, p. 293).

NYNEHEAD.—Hoard in urn, details not preserved [*Arch. Journ.* xxxvii. 107 ; *Som. Proc.* xi. (1) 52.

OCHIE HOLE.—See Wookey Hole.

ORCHARD WYNDHAM.—' Mother Shipton's Tomb ' in Blackdown Wood, close to Orchard Wyndham House, near Williton. This is a slab of stone 7 feet high by 3½ feet broad, with a Roman inscription and relief. It is not, however, ancient, but a modern copy of a genuine Roman tombstone found before A.D. 1600 at Maryport, in Cumberland, and now at Nether Hall, where I have seen it. The copy is declared a copy by the existence of the original and by the shapes of the letters and by two errors in the text. It was apparently made from an engraving in Alex. Gordon's *Itin. Septentrionale* (1726), plate xlv., with a wreath added from another plate. As it is not mentioned by Collinson, but is noticed by Phelps, it was probably put up between 1790 and 1836. The reason for its erection can be conjectured. The Earls of Egremont, from 1751 till 1837 owned both Orchard Wyndham and property near Maryport, and the third Earl, George (1763–1837), was a prominent antiquary and collector [Phelps, p. 174 ; Wm. George in the *West Somerset Free Press,* June and July, 1879, reprinted in a pamphlet *On an inscribed stone at Orchard Wyndham* (Bristol, 1879) ; Soc. Ant. Scrapbook ; *Proc. Soc. Antiq.* vi. 512. The history of the stone was first traced by Mr. George : the case against its genuineness is, however, even stronger than he states].

PAULTON.—Villa, between Paulton and Camerton, p. 315.

PENPITS, PENSELWOOD.—The remains here are in general neither Roman nor in any way connected with the Roman period. But earlier diggings for quernstones may have continued during that time. Querns of Penselwood stone are said to have been found in a Roman villa at Bradford Abbas, in Dorset, while the remains excavated at Penselwood in and about 1879, and now stored at Taunton Museum, contain one or two bits of tile and pottery which *may* be Roman. [For the excavations see *Som. Proc.* xxiv., xxv., xxx.; *Bath Field Club*, iv. 304; *Report* by Pitt-Rivers (London, 1884); *Arch. Journ.* xl. 288; *Somerset and Dorset N. and Q.* ii .82; *Report* of Wells Archaeol. Soc. 1896, p. 12]. In any case the theories of the late Mr. Kerslake are to be rejected.

PERROTT (NORTH).—Potsherds, including Samian (**ATILIAtO**), triangular bricks (? for kilns) 2 First Brass of Vespasian and Domitian [*Proc. Som.* xxvi. (1) 86; Taunton Museum].

PETHERTON (SOUTH).—Foundations at Wigborough, Watergore, Southharp : possibly villas : see p. 331.

Hoard, 6 pecks of coins in a pot, dug up about 1720 at Petherton Bridge, where the Fosse crosses the Parrett [Stukeley, *Itin. Cur.* (ed. 2), p. 156 : hence Collinson, iii. 106, Reynolds, p. 458, etc.].

Many coins, mostly of A.D. 250–350, found sporadically in the fields round South Petherton : some in collections of Mr. H. Norris and of Mr. Franklin. [Information from Mr. Norris.] A British uninscribed silver coin has also been found here [Taunton Museum].

PRESTON PLUCKNETT.—Four urns found 1901–3, near Roman road from Ilchester to Dorchester [Taunton Museum; *Som. Proc.* xlix. (1), 57].

PHILWOOD.—See Whitchurch.

PITNEY.—Two villas : p. 326.

PORTBURY.—Doubtful villa : p. 305.

PORTISHEAD.—The idea of a Trajectus hence to Caerwent (Isca Silurum) seems untenable.

PRIDDY.—Potsherds, traces of mining. See Charterhouse, p. 335 *note*.

PUTSHAM.—See Kilve.

PYLLE.—See Cockmill.

RADSTOCK.—Villa or building, 600 yards south of St. Nicholas Church, on west side of the road to Kilmersdon : see p. 316.

SALTFORD.—Coffin of Bath stone, child's bones, nails, found 1901 [*Proc. Soc. Ant.* xx. 247].

SEAVINGTON.—Villa : p. 332.

SELWORTHY.—A few coins at Brandish or Brandy Street [F. Hancock, *Hist. of Selworthy* (Taunton, 1897), p. 4]. A Roman road has been traced past Selworthy, but on inadequate evidence. The whole neighbourhood contains very few early remains of any date [C. Chadwyck-Healey, *West Somerset* (London, 1901), introd.]. The name Stratford in the parish (*Proc. Som.* xlvi. (1) 15) is, of itself, no proof.

SHAPWICK.—Coins found in the peat, p. 353.

SHEPTON MALLET.—Villa or building at Charlton, kiln on west side of town : p. 317.

SHIPHAM.—Building near the Star Inn : p. 308.

SHUTSHELVE.—Hearthstone and metal, ashes, lead, fibulae, bones, 2 skeletons, urns—found towards Winscombe [*Arch. Journ.* xxxvi. 335].

SOMERTON.—Villas : see p. 320.

SPARKFORD HILL.—Skeleton, fibula, coin, found 1845 [*Som. Proc.* li. (i) 73; Taunton Mus.].

STANCHESTER.—(1) In Curry Rivel parish, near Drayton, p. 328.

(2) In Stoke sub Hamdon, north of the village. Here stones burnt by fire have been noted, but no other remains of any age on the actual spot [H. Norris, *Som. Proc.* iv. (2) 88]. See p. 371.

STANTON PRIOR.—Coins, 1 Maximian, 1 Gallienus, and perhaps others [*Bath Field Club*, ii. 144; Skinner, Add. MS. 28795, p. 261]. Perhaps waifs from the Corston villa, p. 303.

STAPLE FITZPAINE.—The forge, horseshoes, scoriae of iron, etc., accepted by Scarth as Roman [see *Som. Proc.* v. (1) 17, (2) 47; xxiv. (2) 10], are probably not Roman. The notion that Staple is *Stabula* seems the only reason why they were ever called so. Some of the horseshoes are in Taunton Museum.

STERT POINT.—No reason exists for calling this Uxella, as Camden, Musgrave and others do.

STOGUMBER.—Hoard found at Capton in 1666 : see under Lydeard St. Lawrence.

STOGURSEY (STOKE COURCEY).—Copper coin of Constantine, found at Burton [*Som. Proc.* xxxviii. (1) 76].

STOKE LEIGH.—See Long Ashton.

STOKE, NORTH.—See North Stoke (villa, p. 302).

STOKE ST. MICHAEL (STOKE LANE).—A worn Second Brass of Faustina and 4 small copper coins of Constantine, found in 1865 [Hull Collection, Chard].

STOKE SUB HAMDON.—See Stanchester.

STOKE TRISTER.—See Bayford (alleged villa, p. 320).

STREET [near Glastonbury].—Roadway in the marsh near the churchyard : p. 350.
Potsherds (Samian and other) found in and near the churchyard [*Som. Proc.* xxvii. (2) 43 ; Glastonbury Museum ; information from Mr. Jos. Clark of Street]. For the villa near Marshall's Elm, see p. 322 : it is often put down to Butleigh Wootton.

STREET [near Chard].—See Winsham.

SUTTON (or SUDDON).—See Wincanton.

SUTTON (LONG).—Coins of about A.D. 250–300, Samian and other potsherds, burial urns and burnt bones, 2 skeletons, bevelled piece of ' Lydite,' pair of iron shears—all found in a field on the south side of the road from Sutton to Ilchester and Somerton [*Som. Proc.* xl. (2) 272].

SUTTON MALLET.—On north edge of King's Sedgemoor, silver coin of B.C. 69 (M. PLAETORIVS) ploughed up [*Gent. Mag.* 1810, ii. 609].

SWAINSWICK.—Stone coffin with 3 glass vessels, two double-handled and one *ampulla*—the latter now at Alnwick—found 1840 [Scarth, *Aquae*, p. 96 ; Bruce and Way, *Catal. of the Antiq. at Alnwick Castle* (Newcastle, 1880), No. 546, p. 96—both with illustrations].

TAUNTON.—The Roman remains found here seem to be (1) coins and ' divers other antiquities ' found near the castle about 1643 ; (2) denarius of Vespasian found about 1750 in St. James' parish ; (3) potsherds found in the Bishop's Hull cemetery in 1858 and now in the Museum, rude and perhaps not Roman ; (4) potsherds found in Fore Street in 1861 ; (5) coin of Magnentius found on the south side of the town, now in possession of Mr. Franklin ; (6) coins and burials at Holway, south-east of the town (see Holway, in this list) ; (7) potsherds at Norton Fitzwarren, farther away to the north-west (see Norton). (8) gold coin of Valens found in garden of J. Champante [*Gent. Mag.* 1825, ii. 261].
Other alleged remains are unauthentic. That Bathpool lane on the north-east of the town and Hoveland lane and Ramshorn bridge on the south-west [Ordnance Survey, lxx. SE.] are in any sense Roman is a baseless assertion, nor is there the least reason for calling Silver Street Roman [as is done, *Som. Proc.* xxiv. (2) 101]. The idea that Taunton had a Roman name, Thonodunum, is equally unfounded. That name is quite modern, appearing first in Collinson, and is simply a latinization of Camden's ' Thonton.'
On the whole, we conclude that Taunton was not a Romano-British site, though there may have been a village at Holway, connected with the burials. See Toulmin's *Hist. of Taunton* (ed. 1, 1791), p. 4 ; re-edited by C. G. Webb (Taunton, 1874), p. 7 ; Scarth, *Som. Proc.* viii. (1) 11 ; J. H. Pring, *Briton and Roman on the site of Taunton* (Taunton, 1880) and *Som. Proc.* xxiv. (2) 101 ; xxvii. (2) 52. Pring was an enthusiastic believer in a Roman Taunton, but his arguments are largely worthless.

TAUNTON [near].—Gold coin of Constantius II., **VOT XXX**, found near Taunton [*Soc. Ant. Minutes*, 7 Dec. 1780]. First Bronze of Maximian, found 1886 [Mr. Franklin].

TEMPLE CLOUD.—Alleged building on Cloud Hill, copper and silver coins, a potful of copper coins under the hedge bounding the earthwork on the west. So Skinner, as quoted by Phelps, p. 150. Skinner held Temple Cloud to be Templum Claudii, corresponding to his Camalodunum around Camerton (p. 289), and this impossible idea may have led his enthusiastic glance to exaggerate the finds at Temple Cloud.

THEALE.—See under Wedmore.

TICKENHAM.—Hoard, found in 1821, on the hill near Limebrock lane (? Lime Ridge) half a mile from Cadbury Camp. The coins were small copper, a few washed over with white metal ; Seyer saw 168, which included coins of Gallienus—Diocletian and Maximian A.D. 253–286. Coins seem to have also been found in the same spot 40 or 50 years earlier. Seyer adds that foundations of old buildings existed there, but nothing is recorded as to their age [Barrett, p. 19 ; hence Seyer, i. 162, Rutter, p. 234, Phelps, p. 177, etc.]. For another hoard found near Cadbury Camp, see above, under Clapton.
———Querns, coins, potsherds [*Som. Proc.* xxvii. (1) 76].

TINTINHULL.—Some bits of a leaden coffin, now in the Walter Collection at Taunton, are said to have been found in the north of this parish, at Beerly or Berely Farm, two miles west of Ilchester, between the Yeo and the Fosse Way. Mr. Walter (as I learn) thought there were remains of a Roman villa at this spot, and obtained *tesserae* thence. But these do not seem to have been preserved, and the spot is not otherwise known as Roman. (Gray, *Guide to Walter Collection*, p. 33, putting Berely at Stoke-under-Ham instead of at Tintin-hull ; information from Mr. Gray, in correction.)

TWERTON.—Stone coffin—containing earth and large-headed short iron nails: outside it, a skeleton and close by a bit of stone pillar and potsherds, found in 1872 near the Temperance Hall. Other stone coffins were found in 1865, but their age is less certain [*Bath Field Club*, iii. 477].

The Roman villa sometimes ascribed to Twerton belongs to Newton (p. 302).

UPHILL.—The supposed harbour and village Ad Axium near the mouth of the Axe seem to lack evidence. F. Warre [*Som. Proc.* xii. (1) 66] says that foundations were plainly visible and many Roman relics had been found, but he gives no details, and the only actual discoveries seem to have been made at the cavern. This yielded a coin of Julian and potsherds, found about 1826, either in it or just outside its mouth, and over 129 copper and silver coins, chiefly Valentinian and Gratian, and potsherds, found about 1846 when earth inside the cave was cleared out [Phelps, *Modern*, i. 25 ; Rutter, p. 78 ; *Gent. Mag.* 1846, ii. 633]. The names Cold Harbour and Borough Walls, which attracted Sir R. C. Hoare, and which are indeed his only evidences for Roman occupation, except one bit of Samian, [*Roman Aera*, p. 43] do not prove very much. The bronze signet, inscribed **OR**, said to have been found about 1820 in a tumulus ' near ' Uphill, with 4 bronze studs and 14 red glass beads [F. A. Knight, *Seaboard of Mendip* (1902), p. 25] seems to me certainly post-Roman. For the road supposed to come down to the coast at Uphill see the section on the Mendip road (p. 350).

The name Ad Axium was invented by Leman and accepted by Hoare as a convenient appellation. It has not any ancient authority and no one connected with it ever claimed that it had. Nor is there any reason to put Iscalis (see p. 295) at Uphill, as some do.

UPTON.—Coins (1 denarius of Trajan and 7 bronze, including 1 Trajan) found in 1847 on the boundary of Upton and Withiel parishes [*Somerset Co. Gazette*, 9 Sept. 1882, cited by J. Ll. W. Page, *Exploration of Dartmoor*, p. 215].

WADEFORD.—See Combe St. Nicholas (villa : p. 333).

WARLEY.—See Bathford.

WATERGORE.—See South Petherton (alleged villa : p. 331).

WEARE.—Coin, found 1870 [*Som. Proc.* xxiv. (2) 18]. This is probably the Second Brass of Pius from Weare, now in Captain Long's collection at Congresbury.

WEDMORE.—Large brass coin of Augustus, found at Blackford [*Som. Proc.* xxiv. (2) 18]. Glastonbury Museum has a similar coin from Northload, Theale, or the same, differently located.

Two or three coins (1 Probus) and perhaps potsherds, found at Heath House [*Wedmore Chronicle*, pp. 121, 138, 204, 363, 378]. Captain Long has a Third Brass of the fourth century from Wedmore.

The remains found at Mudgley are not Roman [*Proc. Soc. Antiq.* viii. 170 ; *Bath Field Club*, iv. 283 ; *Wedmore Chron.* p. 26 ; Glast. Museum].

WELLINGTON.—F. T. Elworthy [*Notes on Wellington*, 1892] cites the names Ford Street, Silver Street as proofs of Roman origin. But they prove nothing : no Roman remains seem ever to have been found in the town. Mr. Franklin has a First Brass of Trajan found somewhere ' near ' it.

WELLOW.—Villas : p. 312.

WELLS [near].—Coin of Postumus [*Proc. Soc. Antiq.* (ser. 1) iv. 303]. The pavements noted in Brit. Mus. Add. MS. 4452, p. 34, belong to Wello(w), not to Wells.

WEMBERHAM.—See Yatton (villa : p. 306).

WESTON [near Bath].—Alleged villa, imperfectly recorded [*Bath Field Club*, i. (1) 83]. Two bronze statuettes, found 1825 [Bath Institution]. The Late Celtic spoons found here (*Bath Field Club*, ii. 113, etc.) are presumably pre-Roman.

WHATLEY.—Villa : p. 317.

WHITCHURCH.—Two stone coffins, found in 1886, south of the village between Lion's Court Farm and Maes Knoll. Near them have been found sporadically some coins (2 Faustina, 2 Lucilla, 11 Commodus, 1 Crispina, 1 Sept. Severus, 1 Postumus, 1 Maximin, 1 Constantine II) and some ' Second Brass ' coin moulds—fragmentary, illegible and not certainly *Second* Brass—potsherds (including Samian) and bones [F. Ellis, *Clifton Antiq. Club*, i. 165 ; ii. 161 ; iii. 21]. Three skeletons found in 1869 in the railway cutting below Maes Knoll may be connected with these finds [*Bath Field Club*, i. (1) 6].

Hoard found in 1869 at Philwood or Filwood farm, 2 miles north of the village—urn containing (1) many First Brass of Claudius and his successors to Maximian (A.D. 43–300) ; Trajan, Hadrian, Pius, Faustina, Gallienus, are named as represented and Hadrian's coins are said to have been commonest, and (2) some thousands of 'minims,' ⅛ to ⅜ inch in diameter. Nicholls saw some 200 First Brass and 800 minims [J. F. Nicholls, *Arch. Journ.* xxvii. (1870) 69 and *Bristol Past and Present*, i. 25 ; Scarth, *Som. Proc.* xxxi. (2) 7, from Nicholls ; *Clifton Antiq. Club*, i. 165]. The combination of such early and late coins is rare and leads one to think that perhaps the earlier coins belonged to an early hoard discovered later and then reburied with the later coins. The 4 minims and late Third Brass deposited in the Baths Museum at Bath by J. P. E. Falconer, probably come from this hoard.

WHITESTAUNTON.—Villa : p. 334.

WIGBOROUGH.—Villa : p. 331.

WILTOWN.—Coins : see Curry Rivel, p. 329.

WINCANTON.—Urn full of coins, found 1720 [Stukeley, *Itin. Cur.* (ed. 2) p. 150 ; hence Collinson, ii. 33, etc.]. Another urn, with half a peck of coins (incl. Tetricus) found a little above Sutton or Suddon towards Beacon Ash, with potsherds, knife, etc. [ibid.].

Rude tessellated floor, stone column, slab with dog-tooth pattern, potsherds, found at Old Barn, a mile west of Wincanton [*Som. Proc.* xvi. (1) 5, 14, Plate ; Wincanton Field Club, *Report*, 1901, p. 15 ; information from Mr. George Sweetman]. I incline to think the column and slab certainly medieval, and the floor and potsherds probably of that date.

Alleged villa at Bayford Lodge (east of Wincanton), see p. 320.

WINSFORD HILL.—Inscribed pillar, locally called the 'Longstone,' on Winsford Hill, 2 miles west of the village. The letters are *Carataci nepus* (fig. 102), where *nepus* stands for *nepos*, and is apparently the Goidelic formula denoting membership of a family. As Rhys con-

FIG. 102. WINSFORD (EXMOOR).

jectures, the stone may have been set up by one of the Goidels who invaded South Wales and Devon about the fifth century and left Ogams there [Rhys, *Academy*, Aug. 1890 and *Archaeol. Cambrensis*, ser. 5, viii. (1891) 29 ; Page, *Expl. of Exmoor* (London, 1890), p. 91, and *Proc. Som.* xxxvi. (2) 82 ; *Somerset and Dorset N. and Q.* i. 263 ; ii. 164]. The *n* of *nepus* was found after the cut was made from which my fig. is reproduced.

WINSHAM.—Coins found between the village and Street hamlet, near the probable course of the Fosse, in 1684 and later [Collinson, ii. 479 ; Pulman, *Book of the Axe*, p. 363].

WIVELISCOMBE.—Coins, chiefly Trajan, Pius, Tacitus, Gallienus, found in 1711 in an earthwork called the Castle, a mile east of the town [Collinson, ii. 488].

Hoard of 1,600 large brass (' size of a half-penny ') found in an urn near Wiveliscombe. They belonged to Diocletian, Maximian, Constantius I, Maximin, Fl. Val. Severus, Constantine I, and are said all to have borne the figure of Mars and the legend Genio Populi Romani [Musgrave, *Antiq. Brit. Belg.* i. 20 ; Gibson's *Camden* (1772) i. 74, confusing the two hoards ; Collinson, ii. 488 ; Gough, *Adds. to Camden*, i. 95-6, following Gibson].

Leaden coffin found Aug. 1870, in making the Devon and Som. Railway, a mile from Wiveliscombe, 8 feet deep : the lead was much corroded and there were traces of a wooden coffin inside it : the head lay to the north [Gray, *Som. and Dorset N. and Q.* ix. (1904) lxv. ; Taunton Museum].

WOOKEY HOLE.—Lead pig : p. 340, No. 4.

Hoard of late silver and copper coins found about 1862 : see p. 356.

Rude Romano-British potsherds, Samian and late coins found recently.

WOOLAVINGTON.—The ruins of a Roman villa are said by Mr. Stradling to have been found at Coombe, three quarters of a mile south-east of Woolavington and almost in Cossington parish. A 'fibula or buckle' was picked up at the same time. Nothing, however, has since been noticed to confirm the statement; and here, as at Chedzoy, Mr. Stradling may have ' seen too much ' [W. Stradling, *Priory of Chilton Polden* (1839), p. 12].

WOOLVERTON.—Coins at Peart Wood [*Arch. Journ.* xxxvi. 335]. In Laverton parish.

WORLEBURY.—The camp is pre-Roman, as excavations in 1851 and since have abundantly shown. But in 1833 11 coins were found among the débris on the south-west side of Worlebury, Second Brass of Tiberius, Nero, Vespasian, Domitian, Hadrian and Marcus, First Brass of Marcus, Mammaea, Maximin, and two Large Brass of Constantius II, while a few rude potsherds of Roman date, some other trifles, and some 200 or 250 Third Brass of the third and fourth centuries were found in 1852 and show that part of the site was, at least temporarily, occupied in the later Roman times by peasants or others, till as late as Valens. [For the Roman remains see *Som. Proc.* iv. (2) 125 ; *Journ. Brit. Arch. Assoc.* xxxi. 266 ; Clifton, *Antiq. Club,* iii. 243 ; Dymond's *Worlebury* (ed. 2), pp. 81, 115 ; Taunton Museum.]

WRAXALL.—Coins found in 1815 on hill overlooking the rectory, lying in a patch of black earth 300 yards across. They were copper: Seyer saw 1 Pius, 4 Cl. Gothicus, 18 Constantinian. Whether a hoard, is not clear [Seyer, i. 161, hence Phelps, p. 177 ; Rutter, p. 226, etc.].

WRIGLETON.—Guidott (1676), p. 66, says : a silver coin of Trajan was found 5 miles from Bath at Wrigleton. This may be Writhlington, near Radstock.

WRINGTON.—Villas or buildings at Lye hole (p. 308) and Havyatt's Green (p. 308). Coin of Postumus found in the village ; also coin of Diocletian found 1881 [Scarth, *Som. Proc.* xxxiii. (2) 15]. The Diocletian, if genuine, seems to be a variety of Cohen (ed. 2), No. 458, 459 : it is said to have been inscribed IMP C DIOCLESIANVS PI FE AVG and SPES PVBLICA S P (letter from Mr. Scarth).

WRITHLINGTON.—Skinner here found potsherds and a coin of Vespasian [Add. MS. 33659]. See also Wrigleton above.

YANLEY.—Villa alleged in Long Ashton parish, p. 305 *note.*

YATTON.—Villa at Wemberham : p. 306.

Burials and buildings near Cadbury. Before 1849 a small cemetery, skeletons, a hoard of Second and Third Brass of later Empire, including one of Orbiana (circa A.D. 225), in a large urn were found at the foot of Cadbury Hill [*Som. Proc.* i. (2) 59]. In June, 1877, on the north side of the top of Cadbury Hill was found a rude stone cist, skeleton, bits of Samian, Caistor, etc., roof tiles, etc. [*Som. Proc.* xxiii. (2) 8].

YEOVIL.—The finds reported by Collinson, iii. 204 (villa) ; Gough, *British Topogr.* ii. 226 (mosaic) and *Proc. Soc. Antiq.* ser. 2, ii. 203 (fibula, etc.) belong to Coker (p. 329).

UNCERTAIN LOCALITY.—See under Bristol and Mendip.

APPENDIX I

THE NAME 'COLD HARBOUR'

As I have stated in other volumes of the *Victoria History,* the connection of the name ' Cold Harbour ' with Roman sites seems to me to be far less well established than is usually assumed. It may be, therefore, worth while to add here the Somersetshire evidence, for comparison with the preceding pages. The name occurs, so far as I can learn, ten times in the county : (1) about 1½ miles west of Glastonbury, towards Meare ; (2) at Milborne Port, as Mr. Bates informs me ; (3) at a hamlet near Dundry (Collinson, ii. 105) ; (4) Cold Harbour Hill and Lane at Hardington Mandeville ; (5) at Uphill, near the sea shore and the mouth of the Axe ; (6) at Paulton ; (7) in the parish of East Cranmore, south of Cranmore Park ; (8) on the side of Brendon Hills, ½ mile south of Treborough Church ; (9) in Wayford parish, on the edge of Dorset ; and (10) between Hindon and Fonthill (Hoare, *Arch.* xxxiii. 127). In addition, the parish of Horsington contains a Dark Harbour. Only two of these sites, Uphill and Paulton, can be in any way connected with Roman remains, and at neither is there evidence to connect the actual spot called Cold Harbour with the remains. Somerset, therefore, agrees with the other counties which I have examined in indicating no real relation between the name ' Cold Harbour ' and Roman antiquities. What the name means must, I fear, be left undetermined. It is very common. But Mr. W. H. Stevenson tells me that it never occurs in early documents, and even the date of its origin is unknown.

ROMANO-BRITISH SOMERSET

APPENDIX II

THE NAME 'CHESTER'

It is well known that ' chester ' and ' caistor,' and similar forms, when used as place-names or parts of place-names, denote sites occupied in the Romano-British period. Such sites are not necessarily the sites of Roman forts. They are quite as often, or oftener, the sites of villas or towns where no soldiery was stationed. However, besides this familiar use, the name also occurs occasionally in places where no Roman remains have been found, and sometimes where no such remains are at all likely to have ever existed. These places are commonest in the north of Northumberland and across the Cheviots. But they are not confined to that region, and in this connection it is desirable to examine the cases of ' chester ' in Somerset. Seven cases are known to me : (1) Ilchester, a Romano-British village ; (2) Stanchester in Curry Rivel parish, site of a villa or farm ; (3) Stanchester in Stoke sub Hamdon, where no remains definitely assignable to the Roman period have occurred ; (4) Chesterblade in Ever-creech, site of a farm, but perhaps not a true case of the name (see p. 320) ; (5) Newchester near Merriott, north of Crewkerne ; (6) Stilchester in Barwick parish, a little south of Yeovil ; and (7) Chestercroft, mentioned in the boundaries of North Petherton Forest A.D. 1298 (Collinson, iii. 60 *note*). No Roman remains have been found at any of the three last-named places. Thus, four out of seven Somersetshire ' chesters ' have yielded no traces of Roman occupation. It must be left for future research to decide whether in these cases the name has not its proper meaning or whether our knowledge is defective.

APPENDIX III

THE WANSDYKE

The Wansdyke—' Wodnesdic ' in tenth century charters (Kemble, *Cod. Dipl.* 502, 566)—is an ancient and extensive earthwork which traverses north Somerset and central Wiltshire. It can be traced almost continuously for over 45 miles, from a point near Maes Knoll, 4 miles south of Bristol, to a point near Chisbury, 5 miles south-east of Marlborough. Originally it may perhaps have stretched further east and west, but this is uncertain. It consists, generally, of a mound running east and west, with a capacious ditch to the north of it. But occasionally it is interrupted by short gaps in which mound and ditch are absent, and General Pitt-Rivers conjectures that the line was here marked by an abattis of felled trees. Very diverse dates have been assigned to the work. Many writers ascribe it to the Romans, and in particular to Ostorius Scapula. All our evidence, however, goes to show that it is post-Roman. General Pitt-Rivers' excavations, indeed, only demonstrated that it was not pre-Roman (*Excavations in Bokerly and Wansdyke*, 1892, pp. 29, 245). But the dyke itself is not of Roman shape or construction, and, as it runs for several miles along the top of the Roman road from Bath to Silchester and London, it cannot have been erected before that important highway had passed out of use. The student of Roman Somerset and Wilts has, therefore, no concern with this puzzling earthwork.

ANGLO-SAXON REMAINS

IF reliance can be placed on an entry in the Anglo-Saxon Chronicle under the year 577, and on the judgment of successive editors who agree in identifying a place there mentioned, archæology has a fixed starting-point for the treatment of post-Roman Somerset. The battle of Deorham, the event referred to, is the first recorded in the Anglo-Saxon history of the west, but though the site is generally acknowledged to be Dyrham, there is no clear indication of the route by which the invaders reached the fertile valley of the Severn. It is natural to imagine the advance on Bath to have been along the upper Thames valley, but it occurred to Professor Freeman,[1] and possibly to others, that the Saxons worked their way gradually west from the region of Southampton Water, by way of Salisbury, to Exeter. If this route were ever adopted for operations against the Britons of the west it was of a much later date than the advance against the Roman inhabitants of the Cotswolds ; and it is more probable that Ceawlin led his West Saxons from the upper valley of the Thames, where evidence of their early occupation is abundant, southwards into what is now the county of Somerset.

The year 577 saw not only the reduction of the three Romano-British townships and the death of their chieftains, Conmail, Condidan and Farinmail, but also the complete isolation of the West Britons, who could no longer act in concert with the North Welsh of our modern Wales, and were step by step compelled to retire into Cornwall. Through Somerset their retreat is marked by sundry entries in the Anglo-Saxon Chronicle, but for two generations after Deorham there seems to have been no decided activity on the part of the English in this region. It is probable that their energies were fully occupied elsewhere, for the soil of Somerset has yielded next to nothing characteristic of the pagan Saxon. The national collection contains only three objects of the kind from Somerset, and two of these (fig. 4) are brooches of a type best represented in the important series from Long Wittenham, Berks ; but specimens have been found in many parts of southern England, and they cannot be considered characteristic of any particular branch of the Anglo-Saxon stock. The third (fig. 3) is of more importance, and was evidently made in imitation of a type common

---

[1] Somersetshire Archæological and Natural History Society, *Proceedings* (1874), pt. ii p. 7.

in the Isle of Wight and apparently confined originally to the Jutish area. A specimen in the British Museum from Chessell Down, Isle of Wight, not only corresponds in size and outline, but explains the incised lines which have little meaning as they stand, but are survivals of the garnet settings that enriched the earlier examples. By itself this brooch can tell us little of the Sumorsætan, but it is interesting to note that Jutish forms are occasionally met with in the burials of Wiltshire and Berkshire; and its discovery with others at Ilchester, as well as the derived character of its ornamentation, justify its attribution to the second half of the seventh century, when the Saxon conquerors had reached the Parret.

Another discovery was made not far from this station on the Fosse Way. In the Castle Museum at Taunton there is an iron shield-boss of the usual pattern, that was found on Ham Hill (Hamdon) between Yeovil and South Petherton; and a Saxon dagger and spear-butt are said to have been found in one of the hut-circles on Worle Hill.[1] This site has been excavated with success, and proved to be a stronghold of an earlier population; so that the Saxon relic is here but slender evidence of occupation to any extent in the period preceding the conversion of Wessex. That was not accomplished till the middle of the seventh century, and till that date, perhaps for some time longer, it was customary to bury the warrior fully armed and the housewife with her ornaments and domestic utensils.

So far then there are some slight indications that the Saxons did not occupy in force the territory they had conquered, at any rate beyond the Bristol Avon, though the land immediately to the south of Bath no doubt passed into their hands with the Roman city; and archæological researches lend support to the theory that for three parts of a century the West Saxon territory was here bounded to the south by the earthwork known as Wansdyke.

There exist few earthworks to which a definite date can be assigned, and fewer still that can be ascribed with certainty to the Anglo-Saxon period; but what may prove a notable exception can be traced to this day in Somerset and Wilts. The Wansdyke has a course of about sixty miles, and runs from the marsh-land near the Severn at Portishead, passing by Bath to the north of Devizes, through Savernake Forest to Chisbury Camp, where it turns southward in the direction of Andover. As far as Marlborough its continuity is clear except in places where, to judge from the nature of the soil, dense woodland already formed a natural defence.

Throughout its length the dyke or rampart was strengthened by a ditch on the northern side, and was evidently intended to meet a hostile advance from that quarter. The scientific and elaborate excavations of the late General Pitt-Rivers on the line of this and the kindred work

---

[1] Somersetshire Archæological and Natural History Society, *Proceedings* (1856–7), vii. pt. ii. p. 51. The bone comb found on this site with an iron spearhead, and exhibited in 1864 to the British Archæological Association (*Journal*, xx. 329, see also xxiv. 61), may have been of early British date.

called Bokerly have for ever disposed of the theory that both were erected by the Belgæ before Cæsar's time, as step by step they forced a passage into the heart of the country from the southern coast. References to archæological literature on the subject are furnished by the General,[1] who was careful to distinguish between the tangible results of his excavations and the comments he thought fit to make upon them. It was in this judicious spirit that he pronounced the Wansdyke to be of Roman or post-Roman origin ; and though the evidence of date is more decisive in the case of Bokerly Dyke, he was disposed to regard them as almost contemporary. The more southern earthwork is proved by coins to have been thrown up at or after the time when the Roman forces and officials withdrew from Britain ; and a partial examination of the larger work afforded grounds for the belief that the Roman road from Marlborough to Bath was of earlier date and for some distance ran beneath the rampart.[2]

There is little choice then but to assign the Wansdyke to the period between the Roman and Saxon dominations. On what occasion this barrier was erected it is difficult to surmise, but it may well have served to arrest the southern advance of the Teutonic occupants who settled near the upper Thames and left but few traces of their presence during the pagan period in the counties further to the south.

It is true that Wiltshire is comparatively rich in Saxon grave relics ; but the cemetery at Harnham Hill near Salisbury has been assigned to the Christian period on independent evidence,[3] and it is possible that other Saxon graves in the county were not much earlier. In reliance therefore on data afforded by excavation, the suggestion may be hazarded that the Wansdyke marked the first, and Bokerly a subsequent, line of defence against West Saxon encroachment from the Thames.

So far as Somerset is concerned the written records point to the same conclusion, and the tale of the Anglo-Saxon Chronicle may now be resumed.[4] In 652 a forward step was taken by Cenwalh, third in descent from Ceawlin, and an English victory is recorded at Bradford-on-Avon. Six years later the Saxon king advanced his frontier to the Parret, thus including the fastnesses of the Polden Hills. From the Parret the next advance was to the coast, for in 682, after an interval of a quarter of a century, the Britons were driven to the sea by Centwine. In the meantime Wessex had been involved in domestic struggles, and at least the first ten years of the succeeding interval were occupied with the Kentish campaigns of Ceadwalla and Ine. The victory of the latter king in 710 comes immediately after the abdication of the Mercian king

[1] *Excavations in Bokerly Dyke and Wansdyke* (1892), iii. 25 ; see also pp. xiii. 246.

[2] Somersetshire Archæological and Natural History Society, *Proceedings*, vi. pt. ii. p. 101, and vii. pt. ii. pp. 9, 50. The view expressed in volume for 1876, pt. i. p. 63 must be erroneous.

[3] Davis and Thurnam, *Crania Britannica*, pt. ii.

[4] T. Kerslake, 'The first West Saxon Penetration into Somersetshire,' Somersetshire Archæological and Natural History Society, *Proceedings* (1876), pt. ii. p. 61.

Cœnred,[1] and Ine no doubt availed himself of such an opportunity of extending his dominion in the west, where the interests of Mercia and Wessex were beginning to clash.

The entry under 710 in the Anglo-Saxon Chronicle is of special interest as giving the name of the British king against whom this campaign of the West Saxons was directed ; and a contemporary letter of Aldhelm bears independent testimony to the historical character and political importance of King Geraint. It is open to conjecture that the defeat of the Britons compelled them to retire to the hills of Exmoor, and thus leave what is now the western portion of the county in English hands. The extent of this new accession to the West Saxon realm may indeed be marked by the county border as it exists to-day, in which case the Sumorsætan would have been in full possession early in the eighth century. The further doings of King Ine, the foundation of Taunton and the civil war that necessitated the razing of that fortress by his queen in 722 belong rather to the political history of the county, and are not essential to a treatment of the Anglo-Saxon remains recovered from the soil. For our present purpose the important points are the successive advances of the English, as recorded in their own chronicles (rather than in those of the conquered Britons), and the collateral evidence of British survivals under Anglo-Saxon rule. In this connection some ethnological evidence may be adduced. ' It is a fact that the people of the eastern half of the county have, on the whole, broader heads, lighter hair and darker eyes than those of the western half. In all these respects the eastern men approach more to the ordinary English, the western to the Irish standard. These are the clearest and most important differences between them, and are very much what we might have expected to discover.'[2] As to the line of separation, a local observer has stated his opinion that there is a notable difference in physique, as well as in dialect, between the people to the east of the Parret and those to the west of it—the eastern men being larger and having more of the Saxon type.[3] There are obvious reasons therefore why the actual relics of the conquerors are scanty in these parts ; for, to leave its mark on the speech and stature of the inhabitants, the frontier must have been maintained for a considerable period, and the conquering Saxon held at bay.

Though earlier traces of the Sumorsætan are for the most part wanting, the county has yet produced a relic of Anglo-Saxon times that for intrinsic value and historical interest far surpasses anything of the period. It was in 1693 that what has long been known as the 'Alfred jewel,' was discovered during some excavations about three miles from

[1] Professor Freeman on King Ine, Somersetshire Archæological and Natural History Society, *Proceedings* (1872), pt. ii. p. 41.
[2] Dr. Beddoe, ' Ethnology of Somerset,' Somersetshire Archæological and Natural History Society, *Proceedings* (1873), xix. pt. ii. p. 65 ; pt. i. p. 37.
[3] Mr. Prankard of Langport, quoted in same paper, p. 70. See also Mr. F. T. Elworthy's paper, ' On the Grammar and Dialect of West Somerset ' (1876), pt. i. p. 43, and pt. ii. p. 31.

a site that is intimately connected with the heroic figure whose millenary has recently been celebrated.

The Isle of Athelney lies very near the meeting-place of Tone and Parret, and the mound now known as King Alfred's Fort commands the junction of the streams. To the north-west, about half-way to Bridgwater, is an estate known either as Newton or Petherton Park, the villages of North Petherton and North Newton being little over a mile distant. The discovery took place in the park, which was then the property of Sir Thomas Wrothe, and five years later the jewel was in the hands of his uncle, Colonel Nathaniel Palmer of Fairfield. In 1717 it passed to the latter's son Thomas, who carried out his father's wishes by presenting it to the Bodleian Library. It has thus been the property of the University of Oxford for nearly two centuries, and is to-day perhaps the greatest treasure of the Ashmolean Museum.

The first description of the jewel was contributed to the *Philosophical Transactions* (No. 247, 1698) by Dr. William Musgrave of New College, and published by Dr. Hans Sloane, who had been elected secretary of the Royal Society in the very year of the discovery. It would be tedious to record the numerous notices that have since appeared, but special mention must be made of the elaborate account in the first volume of Hickes' *Thesaurus* (1705), pp. 142–4.

The full-size drawings (figs. A, B, C, D) will render a lengthy technical description unnecessary, and its general features can be presented in a few lines. An oval framework of gold encloses an enamelled plaque, which is protected by a thick slab of crystal. The figure is in cell-work, the coloured enamels being separated and the outlines traced by means of vertical partitions of gold attached to the plate, which serves as the base and is engraved with a floral design on the back. The open-work lettering passes all round the sloping edge of the crystal, except where a monster's head projects from the point of the oval and provides a socket for a thin rod that was originally fastened by a rivet still in position.

To account for the existence and character of such a product of the goldsmith's art is a task of greater difficulty, and what internal evidence there is must be reviewed. The Anglo-Saxon inscription is clear enough : + AELFRED MEC HEHT GEWYRCAN, or, in modern English, 'Alfred ordered me to be worked.' The Roman forms of the letters are here of little evidential value as they were in common use on the coinage of the time ; but the peculiar character of the language is unmistakable. HEHT is really a Mercian form, and Professor Earle said that both MEC and HEHT were archaic in the ninth century, the one being never, and the other rarely, found in the prose of the tenth century. MEC had been superseded by ME, while HEHT had given place to HÊT; but the older forms were still at the service of the poet, who sometimes retained them for metrical reasons. Both MEC and ME are Anglian forms, and the occurrence of the former in West Saxon poetry is due to its retention when the poems were altered into the dominant dialect; nor is it impossible that Alfred employed an Anglian goldsmith.[1] The old form of the personal pronoun occurs twice in similar phrases on a gold ring of about King Alfred's time, now in the national collection, and favours the common attribution of the Alfred jewel.

An ornament of such costliness and splendour must have been executed for a person of no mean station, and the occurrence of the name of Aelfred in such a context would alone justify a belief that the relic once belonged to the founder of England's greatness. Other pieces of jewellery connected with the royal family have, by a fortunate accident, come down to us from that time, and in the British Museum are the gold finger-rings of Alfred's father, Ethelwulf, and of his sister, Ethelswitha. The belief, thus further encouraged, is rendered almost a certainty by the fact that the Alfred jewel was dug up in the immediate neighbourhood of Athelney, the scene of the king's humiliation before his enemies the Danes. It was in 878 that the fortunes of England were at their lowest ebb, and Athelney the only English ground that was not given over to the heathen raiders. There we know that Alfred was, devising means for his country's deliverance; so that, accepting the connection of the jewel with the great Alfred as more than probable, the temptation becomes stronger to fix its date and place of origin with more precision.

The absence of the regal title from the inscription is an argument in favour of dating its manufacture before 871; but if the attractive theory, put forward a quarter of a century ago, is the correct one, it is more likely that the jewel was made some time after 878 and presented to the abbey which the king devoutly founded on the Isle of Athelney, when peace was at length secured at Wedmore.

With all deference to the lately deceased scholar from whose charming monograph on *The Alfred Jewel* many of the above details have been derived, it cannot be conceded that the latest theory as to its use is preferable to that of Bishop Clifford. At the Bridgwater meeting of the Somersetshire Archæological Society in 1877 the Bishop of Clifton put forward the view that the Alfred jewel was the head of an 'æstel of (the value of) 50 mancuses' such as the king sent with a copy of his translation of Pope Gregory's Pastoral to every bishop's see in the kingdom. Now in the preface to that translation, written some time after 890, Alfred mentions as one of his instructors in Latin the mass-priest John, whom he made Abbot of Athelney; and it is therefore by no means improbable that a copy with its æstel came in due course to the monastery. What the æstel was is uncertain,[2] but from its Latin equivalent, *indicatorium*, it was clearly a small rod or pointer to be used

---

[1] Additional notes on the grammar of the inscription have been kindly furnished by Mr. W. H. Stevenson.

[2] Æstel is described as a book-mark in Lye's *Dictionarium*, but in Toller's edition of Bosworth's *Anglo-Saxon Dictionary* it is said to be a tablet for memoranda, consisting of two waxed leaves joined together by a hinge and framed or covered with gold to the value of 50 mancuses. Mr. Sweet admits that his rendering ('clasp') is purely conjectural (*Gregory's Pastoral Care*, p. 473); and it is translated 'stylus' in Elfric's Glossary.

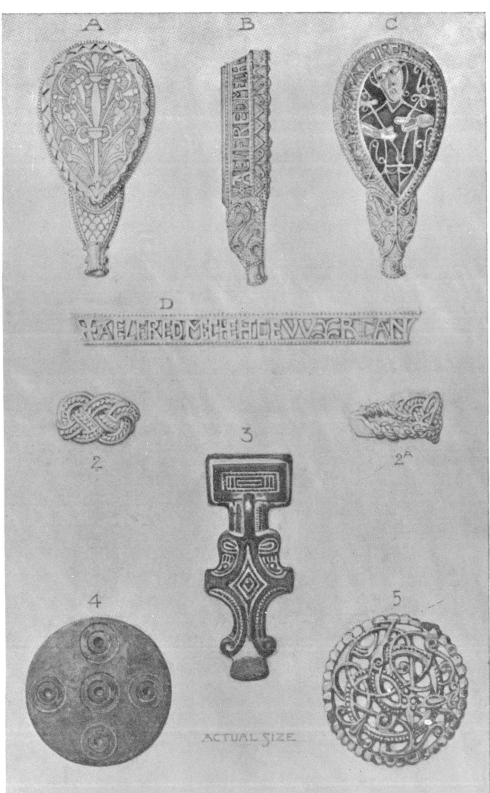

ANGLO·SAXON·REMAINS·FROM·SOMERSET

C.PRÆTORIUS.F.S.A

with the volume, and perhaps inserted in the binding. That the Alfred jewel had originally a rod of some stout but perishable material inserted in the socket is obvious; and it may be that, of the royal gift to Athelney, the æstel-head alone survived. It is true that none of the existing copies (those belonging to the sees of Worcester, Canterbury, and Sherborne) retains any pointer of this description; and the form of the jewel is not adapted, as Bishop Clifford himself supposed, to the hand. Much less is the remarkably similar jewel[1] from Minster Lovel, Oxon, likewise preserved in the Ashmolean Museum. This was to all appearance used for the same purpose, belonging to the same period; and, while it is easily conceivable that Oxford possesses two æstel-heads dating from the revival of letters under Alfred, it is surely improbable to a degree that either jewel was originally the central ornament of a crown or coronet. The suggestion that they severally graced the helmets of Anglo-Saxon war-lords is even less plausible, and other conjectures as to their use are as numerous as the interpretations of the central figure of the Alfred jewel.

The halo which can perhaps be detected on the front, would testify to the religious character of the subject, but opinions are divided as to the identity of the figure. Whether the representation is of the glorified Saviour or the Pope of Rome, even (as some have suggested) of St. Cuthbert or St. Neot, the two 'sceptres' are clearly the essential attribute, though not sufficiently distinctive for purposes of identification. They may be seen as attributes of Our Lord in the Gospels of St. Chad, of the late eighth century, and in the Book of Kells.[2]

A dissertation on the technique of the enamels would here be out of place, but comparison with a golden ouche or brooch formerly in the Roach Smith collection and found in London, shows that portraiture in the same style and material was not unknown on jewellery at that time both in England and abroad.[3] Whether all or any examples found in this country were of home manufacture or imported from the continent can only be decided by the production of more evidence than is at present available. Meanwhile the fact that the enamelling is the least satisfactory part of the Alfred jewel will weigh, even with the most sceptical, in favour of its insular origin. The Anglo-Saxon goldsmiths were famous, and a craft that could produce the wonderful jewellery of the Kentish graves in the seventh century would be quite equal to producing the Alfred jewel at the end of the ninth, when Christianity had brought civilization in its train. Moreover our museums show that enamelling, as well as other elaborate methods of decoration, were practised both in this country and in Ireland with eminent success before the year 900. The famous Ardagh chalice, which is enamelled by three distinct methods, belongs to that period.

---

[1] Figured in colours in Professor Earle's *The Alfred Jewel*, p. 47.   [2] Ibid. p. 77.
[3] A very similar piece of work, probably found in north Germany, is compared by Dr. Franz Bock with Hiberno-Scottish productions of the seventh and eighth centuries and figured in *Die byzantinischen Zellenschmelzen*, pl. xxiv. fig. 2; see p. 366.

The influence of an art best represented by discoveries on Irish soil may without difficulty be traced on the Alfred jewel itself. The so-called boar's head that holds the socket at the base of the jewel is nothing but an example in the round of what is more often seen in the illuminated manuscripts of the Irish school.[1] Parallels in metal are less frequently found in this country than in Scandinavia, but are even there attributed to Irish influence.

The artistic influence of the Irish school, spread through northern Europe by the zeal of missionaries, culminated about the year 900,[2] and is perhaps again exemplified in Somerset by a remarkable open-work brooch of gilt-bronze (fig. 5) discovered in Pitney churchyard some years ago. The front is slightly convex and is ornamented in a most pleasing manner with an animal form that can be distinguished among the interlacing curves. In style it differs altogether from the early Anglo-Saxon treatment of animal forms, and bears a very close resemblance to the design of a book-binding[3] preserved in the museum of the Royal Irish Academy and no doubt found in Ireland.[4] Its date is not determined, but the binding is if anything a little later than the Pitney brooch.

Another relic of more than local interest may perhaps be dated from a consideration of the site of its discovery. A gold finger-ring (fig. 2), now exhibited in the Pump Room at Bath, was found during excavations for the new Guildhall above some graves, and about three feet higher than the present basement floor level, at a spot near the back entrance and opposite the Central Police Station. It is formed of two sets of four wires, the bezel or front being composed of two figures of 8 interlaced, the strands consisting of two twisted wires with a single wire on either side of them. At the back the tapering wires are hammered together into a diamond-shaped joint that is itself a characteristic feature of gold and silver work in the Viking period (A.D. 700–1000). There is evidence that for a long time after the capture of Bath by the Saxons the Roman buildings were suffered to decay; but the city was no longer waste when Edgar was there crowned king in the year 973. Hence there is nothing improbable in the view that the ring was manufactured in the tenth century, and was subsequently lost on the Roman site by some important personage, perhaps at the very time of the coronation.

In the same collection is a leaden obituary cross that was fully described[5] by the late Major Davis, who was the hon. curator of the Corporation Museum. The accompanying illustrations[6] will sufficiently

---

[1] Westwood, *Facsimiles of Anglo-Saxon and Irish Miniatures*, plates 3, 18, 20 : all attributed to the eighth century.

[2] Sophus Müller, *Die Thier-ornamentik im Norden*, p. 92.

[3] Figured by Miss Margaret Stokes in *Early Christian Art in Ireland*, fig. 46, p. 110.

[4] Irish pilgrims are said to have settled at Glastonbury, and educated St. Dunstan in the first half of the tenth century. See Stubbs, *Life of St. Dunstan* (Rolls Series), pp. lxxviii. lxxxiii.

[5] *The Saxon Cross found in Bath, July*, 1898, by Chas. E. Davis, F.S.A.

[6] Photographs by W. G. Lewis, Bath : full size.

[Front]

[Back]

Leaden Coffin-plate found at Bath.

indicate its size and character, but the inscriptions on both sides, which were engraved on a wax model and transferred to the lead by casting, may here be set out at length, mainly in accordance with a reading by Mr. Blakiston included in the pamphlet already referred to. The front has the names of the four evangelists round the border, and four titles of the Deity, viz. **ELOE**, or **ELOI**, **ADONAI**, **SABAI** and **ΘEOI**, between the arms of the cross. These titles are of special interest as being of Gnostic origin and generally used in the middle ages as words of power.

Down the centre is a Latin invocation :—

Qui in virtute crucis mundum (*purgavit*)
Tartara disrupit claustra celestia a*peruit*
Et omnibus dedit p*acem* fidelibus Sa*lutem*

the words and letters in *italics* being supplied. This may be translated· ' He who by the power of the Cross redeemed the world, burst asunder the gates of Hell, opened those of Heaven, gave peace to all and salvation to the faithful.'

On the arms the inscription is apparently as follows, between the symbolic letters Alpha and Omega :—

Christe *omnium hominum* cunabula cuncta *disponens*
Pur*ifica me* squalore sorde voluta*tam*
Supplex ti*bi Domine* deposco miserere *mei*

which may be rendered : ' O Christ, who orderest the birth of all, purify me who am polluted by the stain of sin, I suppliantly beseech Thee, O Lord, have mercy on me.'

The inscription on the back is of a more personal character and professes to give the date :—

Anno ab incarnatione Domini nostri d*ie*
xv Kal. Octobris . . . Eadgyvu . . .
congregationis soror

This may mean that Eadgyvu, a sister of the community, died in the year . . . after the Incarnation of Our Lord, on the 17th September.

The cross was probably attached to the coffin of Sister Eadgyvu, belonging to some convent in or near Bath ; but her identification with the wife of King Edward the Martyr is anything but certain, and Mr. W. H. Stevenson points out that the use of *v* for *f* in Eadgyvu indicates the eleventh century. If the latter date is correct, comparison should rather be made with the inscribed leaden crosses[1] of that period found at Bury St. Edmunds and elsewhere, one of which may be seen in the national collection.

---

[1] Society of Antiquaries, *Proceedings*, iii. 47, 165 ; iv. 211.

DOMESDAY SURVEY

IF for our knowledge of the great Survey of 1086 we were dependent in Somerset on Domesday Book alone, we should find in it few points of general or special interest.   Manor follows manor in regular, monotonous succession ; the assessment, the number of ploughs required for working the land, the number actually possessed by the lord and by the peasants respectively, the number of these peasants arranged according to their classes, the water-mills, the amount, roughly reckoned, of meadow, pasture and woodland, and the value, past and present, of the manor, all these are duly recorded, together with the name of the Englishman who had held it before the Conquest and that of the baron or under-tenant to whom it had passed in what the record terms 'King William's time.'   But we look in vain for those glimpses of history, those little incidental touches which bring us, in some counties, face to face, as it were, with real men and women, and lift for a moment the veil that still hides from our eyes the meaning of the Norman Conquest.

Happily, however, we possess for the south-west of England, including the county of Somerset, two auxiliary sources of information which supplement, on certain points, the evidence of Domesday Book. The first of these is known as the 'Exon Domesday,' the other as the 'Geld Inquest' or *Inquisitio Geldi*.   The nature of these records requires to be briefly explained, for a good deal of confusion on the subject appears to exist.

As was explained by Sir Henry Ellis, under whose superintendence they were printed by the Record Commission,[1] the MS. sheets containing both of them were 'bound up in two volumes about the end of the fourteenth or beginning of the fifteenth century,' but so carelessly that they had to be separated again and 'arranged as they are now printed, in the most obvious order,' for the Record Commission's edition.   They were bound up in one volume, which is still in the custody of the dean

---

[1] *Domesday Book*, vol. iv. ('Additamenta'), 1816.

and chapter of Exeter, whence is derived the name 'Exon Domesday.' Ellis distinguished quite rightly between (1) 'its main body,' which 'is supposed, so far as it extends, to contain an exact transcript of the original rolls and returns made by the Conqueror's Commissioners at the time of forming the General Survey from which the Great Domesday itself was compiled,' and (2) the '*Inquisitio Geldi* or Taxation of the Hundreds,' which he discussed at some length. He also rightly connected the latter with the great levy of 'geld' (land tax) at the rate of six shillings on the hide 'at the end of the year 1083 or the beginning of 1084.'[1] He seems to have erred only in writing—

> Certain it is that the Record itself bears evidence that the tax was raised at the time of the Survey ; that it was connected with it ; and that, at least in the Western Counties, it was collected by the same Commissioners.

But, in Ellis' time, the actual date of the great Domesday Survey seems to have been deemed uncertain ; he himself knew from the colophon at the end of the eastern counties volume that 'it is evident that it was finished in 1086,'[2] and from the contents of both volumes that some parts of them could not be previous to '1085 or even later.' Yet the contradictions of chroniclers seem to have influenced his mind.

Mr. Eyton, who made such extensive use, in his monographs on Somerset and Dorset in Domesday, of the Exeter volume, wrote of that 'priceless document,' the geld-inquest, as follows—

> The true and authentic title of this Record is 'Inquisicio Gheldi.' Because the place of its custody has happened for centuries to have been the same with that of the Exon Domesday, and because the older Record Commission caused it to be printed and bound up with the Exon Domesday, this Inquest is usually spoken of and quoted as part of the Exon Domesday. Nothing can be more erroneous, nothing more suggestive of further error. The Inquest is two years older than any Domesday.
> A minute examination of this Inquest suggests that it was used, though not implicitly followed, by the Domesday Commission which afterwards visited the five Counties in question. Its date and nature, therefore, demand our immediate attention. . . .
> The date of the Inquisicio Gheldi was therefore the first three months of 1084.[3]

From what has been said above, it will doubtless be seen that this is scarcely fair to Ellis, who had so carefully distinguished the *Inquisitio* from the rest of the MS., or indeed to the Record Commission. For the *Inquisitio* was not merely preserved in the same custody ; it was actually part of the same MS., and a close comparison of the two portions, distinct though they are, suggests that their collocation had a definite meaning and purpose.[4]

On the other hand, if it was wrong to charge the Record Commission with having combined for the first time two distinct records, it

---

[1] These extracts are all taken from his Introduction to the volume.
[2] *General Introduction to Domesday*, i. 4.   [3] *Notes on Domesday* (1880), pp. 2–3.
[4] The subject is too wide a one to be fully investigated here, but one may point out that the arrangement of counties is peculiar, and is the same in both ; also that the assessment of the demesne of a manor in 'hides,' which is ignored in Domesday Book, plays a large part in the *Inquisitio Geldi*, and is duly recorded throughout in the other portion of the MS.

is perfectly true that their publication under the single title 'Exon Domesday' tends to cause confusion. In the MS., as at present arranged, they are so 'sandwiched' together that they could hardly be published separately[1]; but it would be better to speak of the whole as 'the Exeter Book,'[2] and to refer to its component portions, as will be done in this work, as the 'Exon Domesday' and '*Inquisicio Geldi*' respectively.

Of this 'Exeter Book' the importance can hardly be overrated so far as the Domesday Survey of the south-west is concerned. In Domesday Book, for instance, the usual hundredal headings are omitted in the case of Somerset, and we are therefore dependent for our knowledge of its Hundreds at the time, and for the identification of several doubtful manors, on the *Inquisicio Geldi*. Mr. Eyton, mentioning this, observes that 'the way in which the two Records, the Gheld-Inquest and Domesday, explain and supplement one another may be almost said to double the antiquarian value of the great Record.'[3] Of the other portion it is sufficient to say that a question arose, when deciding on the treatment of the Survey in Somerset, whether the text of the 'Exon Domesday should not be adopted in preference to that of Domesday Book, as approaching more closely to that of the original returns. It was only the desire to render the series of *Victoria Histories* as uniform as possible that led to the adoption here also of the great Exchequer volume as the standard text. As to the MS. itself, it was brought up to London for exhibition at the time of the Domesday Commemoration (1886), and Dr. De Gray Birch then described it as 'closely resembling Domesday Book in its general form and palæography,' and as ' of the eleventh century.'[4]

Enough, perhaps, has now been said of the tools with which we have to work in studying the Somerset Survey. It must, however, be borne in mind that the record of that Survey was made Hundred by Hundred, and that the original rolls in which that Survey was contained were lost at an early date. Even in the Exon Domesday their contents are entirely rearranged, while in Domesday Book they are rearranged on yet another system and also reduced by omitting certain details throughout.

[1] Professor Maitland states that the geld-inquests are placed ' at the beginning of the Exeter Domesday' (*Domesday Book and Beyond*, pp. 2, 478). But this is not so. Only those for Wilts and Dorset are there placed (pp. 1–11, 12–26). Those for Devon will be found on pp. 59–65, for Cornwall on pp. 65–7, and for Somerset on pp. 67–75, 489–90.

[2] In the same volume (' Additamenta ') of the Record Commission's Domesday the twelfth century Winchester Inquests are printed with the title ' *Liber Wintoniensis*,' though Ellis, in his Introduction to it, styles it ' The Winton Domesday ' (p. xv.). The confusion caused by the title ' Exon Domesday ' is illustrated by the statement of even so ardent a Domesday student as Mr. Freeman, who, after pointing out that Milo Crispin is found in Domesday Book as a successor of Wigod of Wallingford, added : ' It would seem however, from three entries in the Exeter Domesday (4, 9, 16), that the Western estates of Wigod did not pass to Miles without King William taking a large toll of them to his own use. The entry in all three cases is, " Rex habet xviii. hidas de terra Wigoti, Milo vi. hidas " ' (*Norman Conquest*, iv. 733). These three entries are but variants of one, and are taken from the *Inquisitio Geldi*. And, moreover, the king's ' 18 hides ' were in Corsham, which had been held by Earl Tostig, and had nothing to do with Wigod. The words ' de terra Wigoti ' should be read in connexion with ' Milo,' not with ' xviii. hidas.' In Jones' *Wiltshire Domesday* (1865) the survey and the geld inquest are similarly confused (pp. 153 et seq.).

[3] Preface to *Somerset Survey*, p. 3.

[4] *Domesday Studies*, pp. 490–1. Compare *Domesday Book* (S.P.C.K.), p. 53, and *Domesday Studies* p. 654.

A HISTORY OF SOMERSET

As the primary object of the Domesday Survey was the ascertainment of the county's right assessment for the (Dane)geld, that is, the original land-tax, the principle on which it was assessed is the first point to be considered. Down to a few years ago Mr. Eyton's views held the field. Set forth in his *Key to Domesday*,[1] and repeated in his studies on the Somerset Survey,[2] his conclusions were as follows. He rightly rejected the view, formerly prevalent, that the hide was an areal measure, and recognized that it was a unit of assessment unconnected with area. In his opinion 'hidage was intended to be an index of one or more of three things, viz., of liability in the first place ; of capacity or intrinsic value in the second ; of adventitious or extrinsic value in the third.'[3] The hidation of Dorset was regulated, he held, by 'royal favour, intrinsic wealth and extrinsic advantages.'[4] The only special feature distinguishing the Somerset hidation from that of Dorset was that 'the chief, we may almost say the only, intrinsic faculty which will have regulated the value of Somerset manors was fertility of soil ; that this faculty was the very first to be considered when the hidation of any Somerset manor was originally prescribed is evident on every page of Domesday.'[5]

In my *Feudal England* (1895) I advanced a new theory on the subject based on the extraordinary number of vills assessed at five hides or some multiple of five hides. From this fact I argued that assessment was not regulated by area or value, but was of an arbitrary character, being so arranged as to apportion among the vills of a Hundred its total assessment in blocks of five or ten hides. This arrangement is much clearer in some counties than others, and Somerset is not a county in which it is obvious to the eye. I was able to show, however, that even here sufficient traces are found to show that this system prevailed.[6] This theory, which is altogether opposed to that of Mr. Eyton, was emphatically adopted by Professor Maitland in his *Domesday Book and Beyond* (1897), and has since been elaborately applied to Somerset by the Rev. E. H. Bates.[7] Mr. Bates contends that the local assessments can, in practice, be explained by my theory, if the county be 'arranged in twelve districts, containing one or more Hundreds apiece,' and each district 'sub-divided into blocks containing assessments of twenty hides, with a few double and triple instances.' Whether his conclusions be accepted or not, the number of Somerset vills assessed in terms, as a mathematician would say, of the five-hide unit is far too large to be accounted for by any theory but that of an artificial arrangement based upon that unit. We find, on examining Mr. Bates' tables, that, putting aside his own combinations, Somerset had no fewer than sixty vills assessed at 5 hides each, thirty-eight at 10 hides, ten at 15 hides, fourteen at 20 hides, three at 30 hides and two at 40 hides and 50 hides respectively. These, it will be seen, account between them for 1,290 hides, that is, for more than

[1] *A Key to Domesday. . . Analysis and Digest of the Dorset Survey* (1878), pp. 3–16.
[2] *An Analysis and Digest of the Somerset Survey* (1880), pp. 20–8.
[3] *Key to Domesday*, p. 6.   [4] Ibid. p. 12.   [5] *Somerset Survey*, p. 25.
[6] *Feudal England*, pp. 61–2.
[7] 'The Five-hide unit in the Somerset Domesday' (*Somerset Arch. Soc. Proceedings* [1899], vol. xlv).

half the total assessment of the county.[1]   But when to these indisputable cases we add, from Mr. Bates' tables, those in which the assessments of two or more adjoining vills have clearly been combined in a multiple of the five-hide unit—as was certainly done in Cambridgeshire[2]—we discover that apparent exceptions can thus be reconciled with the rule in a goodly number of cases, and that the evidence for its application is very considerably strengthened.

One of the interesting facts emerging from Mr. Bates' analysis is the marked difference in character of the assessments in different parts of the county.   For instance, in the portion bordering on Gloucestershire (a county in which the prevalence of the 'five-hide unit' is marked) we find, to the west of Bristol, Wraxall assessed at 20 hides, Easton in Gordano and Portbury (adjoining it on the north) at 20 hides between them, Long Ashton (adjoining it on the east) at 20 hides, Blackwell and Barrow Gurney (adjoining them on the south) at 10 hides each, and Yatton (adjoining Wraxall) at 20 hides.   Or again, to the south-west of Bath we have the adjoining vills of Twerton, English Combe, Newton St. Loe and Corston assessed, all four, at 10 hides each, while close by, to their south-east, are Hinton Charterhouse, Norton St. Philip, Road and Laverton, all similarly adjoining, and all similarly assessed at 10 hides each. Or, again, if we pass to the south of the county, along the Dorset border, we find a group of adjoining manors—North Perrott,[3] Haselbury and Hardington—assessed at 10 hides each, while Coker, Pendomer and Sutton Bingham, immediately adjoining them on the east, were assessed repectively at 15, 5 and 5 hides.[4]   It is almost inconceivable that such figures as these, speaking so plainly as they do of an artificial system, should have failed to arouse in Mr. Eyton's mind grave doubts as to his own theory, or have done nothing to open his eyes to the true meaning of hidation.   But he belonged, as we shall see, to that class, all too numerous, of antiquaries who can only look at evidence in the light of the theories they hold, and who strive to fit facts to theory rather than theory to facts.

Keeping, however, to the point of the differences presented by districts, we find, at the other end of the county, the district stretching, in Mr. Bates' words, 'from the mouth of the Parret to Exmoor Forest,' vills assessed not only at much smaller amounts, but also in irregular figures.   Not merely the virgate or quarter of a hide, but even the 'fertine' or quarter of a virgate, occurs repeatedly in the record of assessment.   It may even be said that in the western half at least of this district we lose sight altogether of the 'five-hide unit.'   Arid though such investigation may seem, there can be no question that this contrast, well defined as it

---

[1] Mr. Eyton reckoned the Domesday total as 2,321 hides, 2 virgates and 11 acres (*Somerset Survey*, i. 144).   The figures I have given in the text are probably within the mark.

[2] See my *Feudal England*, pp. 47–8.

[3] South Perrott, across the border, was assessed in Dorset at 5 hides.

[4] It will be observed that, while not committing myself to Mr. Bates' application and development of my theory, I cannot agree with Mr. Whale's assertion 'that as regards Somerset the 5 hides unit is a myth' (*Principles of the Somerset Domesday*, 1902).

is, is very closely connected with the early history of the county. In the east we find a system of assessment resembling that which prevailed in the counties to its east and south-east; in the west we recognize a system approximating to that of Devon. Somerset, we are thus reminded, stands between Wessex and 'West Wales.'

From assessment we must now pass to measures of actual area. Having rightly abandoned the attempt of the older antiquaries to assign to the Domesday 'hide' a fixed area, Mr. Eyton devoted himself with ardour to the fascinating task of proving that its lineal and areal measures were so exact that they give us, when interpreted on his method, the actual acreage of the parish to which they refer. In the preface to the two volumes treating of the Somerset Survey he wrote as follows :—

> After many months' study of the Somerset Domesday the Author finds nothing to disturb, but very much to support, those principles of criticism and those methods of analysis which were adopted in his 'Key to Domesday' as 'illustrated by the Dorset Survey.' Domesday thus examined, county after county, becomes a Science more and more exact . . . The same principles, the same rules, of Domesday mensuration and values will derive added strength from the Somerset Survey.[1]

Now this is a matter which must be discussed, for it stands at the threshold of our inquiry. Either Mr. Eyton discovered the true 'key to Domesday,' or the whole of his elaborate calculations, based as they are upon that 'key,' crumble into dust.

Let us first grasp clearly what Mr. Eyton held as to the Domesday phrase 'land for x ploughs,' a formula which meets us on every page. Even the casual reader could hardly fail to be struck by the arbitrary character of the numbers entered in Domesday as those of the ploughlands on many manors at the very outset of the Survey. Taking Mr. Eyton's own tables we find that on the king's land ten manors or groups of manors of ancient demesne[2] have the number of their ploughlands recorded. One is credited with 100 ploughlands, four with 50, one with 30 and one with 20. In only three cases are the numbers odd.[3] Yet it did not strike Mr. Eyton as at all peculiar that in no fewer than four cases the arable land should, as he reckoned it, be exactly 6,000 acres. Of the fifteen manors in which the king had succeeded the family of Godwine, one is assigned 60 ploughlands, one 50, two 40, two 15, two 10 and one 5. For those which had come to him on the death of Queen Edith the figures are : One 100, two 40 and one 10.[4] In all this Mr. Eyton saw nothing peculiar, nor were his suspicions aroused by the fact that the vast and scattered manor of Taunton is assigned 100 ploughlands, or that on the Glastonbury manors we get such figures as 40, 30, 20, 15, 10, 5 in some twenty cases, including four of 30 and six of 20.[5]

Of the area of such ploughlands Mr. Eyton wrote as follows :—

> The normal capacity of the Plough-gang, or One-team-land, was 120 statute acres . . . the normal plough-land, the *Terra unius carrucæ* was 120 acres.[6]

[1] *Somerset Survey*, pp. 1, 14. [2] See p. 394 below. [3] *Somerset Survey*, i. pp. 1, 2.
[4] Ibid. ii. 3–6. [5] See pp. 460–467 below. [6] *Somerset Survey*, i. pp. 29, 30.

For proof we are referred to his Dorset book, where we read as follows :—

> The *Terra ad unam carucam*, or plough-gang . . . is, if not quite a definite ex-
> pression, intended in Domesday to denote an area of arable land, nearly if not always
> constant . . . we may reasonably seek to determine the average (*sic*) contents of a
> Dorset plough-gang . . .
>
> Let the *Terra ad unam carucam* or plough-gang stand then, for the present at
> least, as proximately (*sic*) implying 120 Domesday acres, and the same number of
> modern statute acres.[1]

Now I do not wish to press the point unduly—for it is not of great
consequence—but on the basis of this conclusion as to the 'normal' or
'average' plough-gang, Mr. Eyton assumed throughout that each individual plough-gang with which he had to deal contained 120 acres,
neither more nor less.[2]

Yet this inconsistency is of small or no account when compared with
his conclusions on 'the more precise system of mensuration . . . by which
the meadows, the pastures, the woodland and the wilds . . . were meted
in Domesday.'[3] It is a wonderful instance of the power of self-delusion,
and a further warning to those who subordinate facts to theory, that Mr.
Eyton was able to convince himself that he had proved his case in Dorset,
and that the Somerset evidence did but confirm its truth. For it is open
to fatal criticism from three different quarters. The first and most obvious
criticism is that when we find Domesday using as its unit of measure-
ment the 'league' (*leuga*)—which Mr. Eyton (rightly, I think) deemed
to be 12 furlongs or a mile and a half—it can only be making a vague
estimate. At Winscombe, for instance, there was, we read, 'una leuga
pasturæ in longitudine et latitudine, silva ii leugas long. et una leugam
lat.' (fo. 90). But Mr. Eyton treated such measures as these as accurate to
a yard, and worked them out as representing 120 acres of pasture and
2,880 acres of woodland. Adding 3,600 acres for thirty plough-gangs,
and 60 acres of meadow, he arrived at a total of 6,660 for the 'Domesday acreage' as against an actual 'parochial acreage' of 4,140.[4] But such
discrepancies appear not to have troubled him in the least. At Congresbury the woodland and pasture are reckoned by Domesday in the same
crude fashion : 'pasture 2 leagues long and half a league wide ; woodland $2\frac{1}{2}$ leagues long and half a league wide' (fo. 87). Again accepting
these measurements as absolutely exact, Mr. Eyton produced 'Wood-land
1830 acres' and 'Pasture 1440 acres,' which brought up the total Domesday acreage of Congresbury 'to 3,567 acres in excess of the aforesaid
parochial measurements.' 'From this,' he added, 'it follows' that the
manor 'had attached to it a quantity of arable land, wood-land, and

---

[1] *Key to Domesday*, pp. 23, 24. So too in *Somerset Survey* (i. 75) he 'converts these plough-lands
into statute acres, reckoning 120 statute acres as the average (*sic*) equivalent of the *Terra ad unam
carucam*.'

[2] Mr. Whale appears to agree wholly on this point with Eyton, for he writes defending him
against Mr. Bates : 'Eyton knew too much of his subject to doubt for an instant that "Terra ad
unam carucam" represented a *fixed* area, however difficult to decide what that fixed area is' (*Principles
of the Somerset Survey* [1902], p. 6). Yet Eyton himself, we have seen, spoke of an 'average' or 'normal' plough-gang, as if its area were *not* 'fixed.'

[3] *Key to Domesday*, p. 24.   [4] *Somerset Survey*, i. 206. Compare p. 391 below.

pasturage, which has never been brought within the parochial boundaries of Congresbury and Wick St. Lawrence.'[1] It was by such easy assumptions that he disposed of these discrepancies. In Hinton St. George, for example, he could find no room for the '720 acres' of woodland which the Domesday figures gave him, so dismissed them 'as being very probably in another parish,' and then claimed the remaining acreage as what he required.[2] Having stated his views on Domesday mensuration, he began his 'theories tested by examples' with the Dorset manor of Shillingstone. For this manor Domesday, he wrote :—

> gives (according to our principles and calculations of measurement) an area of (1,920 acres of ploughland + 183 acres of meadow + 3,360 acres of pasture + 2,070 acres of wood) 7,533 acres to this Manor, while the present Parish of Shillingstone is only 2,223 acres. The explanation . . . is that the bulk of the pasture-land and all the woodland (say 5,310 acres) were mere adjuncts, probably, nay demonstrably, lying at a distance ; in other Parishes, and, it may be, in other Hundreds.[3]

In his wonderful table of 'the exacter measures of the Dorset Domesday' he even went so far as to make his figures balance by assuming that '22,277$\frac{3}{4}$' acres were 'designedly omitted in Domesday because irrelevant to the Survey,'[4] and even further assumed an area of '5,531$\frac{1}{4}$ acres appurtenant to the Royal Forests.'[5] Misdirected ingenuity could scarcely go further than this.

The second criticism of Mr. Eyton's theories of Domesday mensuration admits of being briefly stated. Any student who investigates the matter will find that he could only arrive at the 'Domesday acreage' of his tables by assuming, however unconsciously, that the woodland, pasture, etc., was invariably composed of compact, strictly rectangular blocks like those of an American city. To imagine the county of Somerset or of Dorset laid out in such blocks as these is a conception that one can only describe as unthinkable. But the theorist has a way of shutting his eyes to the working of his theory in practice and of divorcing it from facts.

The third and perhaps the most fatal of these critical objections requires to be driven home. When Mr. Eyton accounted for discrepancies between his 'Domesday acreage' and the actual relative area by bold assumptions such as we have seen, he either had some evidence to support them, or he had not. In the latter case they were mere guesses, introduced only to account for his discrepancies. The test is found in those cases where he plausibly accounted for a difference that existed only in his own imagination. It is obvious that in these cases the explanation he offered must have been quite as imaginary as the difference it was invented to explain. I may venture to quote, from a paper of my own, an instance in point.

> It should be noted that on the title-page of his *Key to Domesday* Mr. Eyton places prominently 'its exactitude of mensuration.' It might almost be described as having been a passion with him to account for every acre in each county on which he wrote.

---

[1] *Somerset Survey*, i. 125.   [2] Ibid. p. 31.
[3] *Key to Domesday*, p. 57.   [4] Ibid. pp. 146, 148.   [5] Ibid. p. 148.

At first sight, no doubt, his results are wonderful. Every item is exactly accounted for. Yet, alas! this perfect system will not bear the strain of test. When Mr. Eyton was sure of the total for which he had to account, he was generally able to account for it. But sometimes the total turned out to be wrong after he had accounted for it quite satisfactorily under the impression that it was right. And this, I fear, is fatal. Take, for instance, the case of Drayton in his analysis of the Staffordshire Survey. Mr. Eyton considered that the area for which he had here to account was 3,315 acres. He reckoned up its two constituent manors, the king's and Thurstan's, which contained between them 9 ploughlands—that is, according to what he terms his 'oft-repeated theory,' 1,080 acres + '20 acres of meadow, and (as I,' he adds, 'compute the measurements,) 1,440 acres of wood' (p. 63). One can make nothing of this but 2,540 acres. Yet Mr. Eyton must have reckoned it, by an error of over 1,100 acres, at 3,653 acres, for he tells us that 'the Domesday measures' of these two manors 'imply 338 acres more' than the 3,315 that he had to account for. This supposed excess he at once disposes of by informing us that 'these 338 acres were in Cautwell' (p. 64). But, alas! in his *errata* he frankly confesses that the existence of two manors at Drayton was on his part 'a delusion,' as one of the two had been included in error, and that his calculations in Drayton were consequently 'mostly inept'![1]

Again, I have been able to show that in Staffordshire what was really the same estate was by him, in three separate places, reckoned at 616, 6,580 and 5,370 acres![2] In Somerset, owing to the same cause (his mis-reading of Domesday), we can apply the same criticism. He rather carelessly read Domesday as assigning to Milborne Port a liability to *half* a night's ferm[3] (instead of three-quarters), and then, finding it commuted for a sum equivalent to three-quarters, promptly produced an explanation to account for the supposed discrepancy.[4] Of this I observed in my *Feudal England* (p. 113) :—

> Great masses of Mr. Eyton's work consist of similar guesses and assumptions. Now, if these were kept scrupulously apart from the facts, they would not much matter ; but they are so inextricably confused with the real facts of Domesday that, virtually, one can never be sure if one is dealing with facts or fancies.

The climax, perhaps, is reached in his treatment of the Dorset boroughs, which have to be compared with these on the royal demesne in Somerset. His singular misconception of the Domesday entries concerning them led him to make assumptions as to area which rested only on his error.[5]

It has been absolutely necessary to show, once for all, that all these assumptions have no real foundation, for there is reason to believe that they even affected Mr. Eyton's identifications, several of which have been found to need correction. It is not so much, I must repeat, on the ploughlands as on the woodland and pasture that Mr. Eyton went astray. Yet even on the ploughlands Mr. Bates rejects his theory that their area was always 120 acres,[6] and cites Professor Maitland's cautious conclusion that when that theory threatens difficulty

---

[1] *Domesday Studies* (1888), pp. 223-4.   [2] Ibid. pp. 224-5.
[3] See p. 394 below for the meaning of this phrase.
[4] *Somerset Survey*, pp. 77-8. For a similar explanation of a supposed fall in value at Stafford see *Domesday Studies*, pp. 214-5, where I have shown that he had similarly misunderstood the Survey.
[5] See, for proof of this, *Feudal England*, pp. 113-4.
[6] *Somerset Archæological Society Proceedings*, xlv. 2, 54. Compare p. 389, note 2 above.

it can almost always be prevented by the intervention of some plausible hypothesis about shifted boundaries or neglected wastes. More than this has not been done. Always at the end of his toil the candid investigator admits that when he has added up all the figures that Domesday gives for arable, meadow, wood and pasture the land of the county is by no means exhausted. Then the residue must be set down as 'unsurveyed' or 'unregistered,' and guesses made as to its whereabouts. Then further this method involves theories about linear and superficial measurements which are, in our eyes, precarious.[1]

As against 'Eyton's theory' Professor Maitland asserts that 'the teamland' was 'no areal measure.'[1]

The student, in fact, must dismiss from his mind, as a wholly base-less delusion, the idea that those responsible for the Survey set themselves the herculean task of measuring out the land. As even Mr. Whale has justly admitted :—

> Domesday items of area are after all only roughly approximate ; the great purpose of the survey was fiscal, other items incidental. Not a tittle of evidence exists of a survey of area. The whole work was completed in less than a year. When the jury . . . answered in multiples of plough lands, very rarely taking notice of a half, we may safely conclude that fragments of a plough land were disregarded ; in other words, the question was answered without previous thought and with limited knowledge.[2]

A very little thought will show that certain information could easily be given and that other information could not. The assess-ment of a manor, or the amount of dues paid by custom to the Crown, were matters for exact statement ; it was also possible to state accur-ately the number of plough-oxen on the land, the figures of the live-stock and the classes of peasantry. But it was not possible to give exact measurements of the land, nor would such measurements directly affect taxation. They would to a large extent be little better than guess-work, and to base upon them an exact acreage is obviously out of the question.

Another of Mr. Eyton's delusions needs to be here exposed, for it is one on which he expressed himself in terms of great confidence. We read in the preface to his *Somerset Survey* (p. 11) :—

> In his translation of Domesday entries Collinson uniformly adopted the error which confused the *carucata terræ* with the *terra ad unam carucam*. It is difficult to see how any one with the Exon survey of any county before him could remain in such an error. Nevertheless there are Domesday scholars, of deserved repute, still living and still writing, who abide by this inveterate misconception. Would they but study the original text more critically, would they but accept the precise interpretation furnished by the correlative expressions of the Exon Survey, they might at length learn that the Domesday Commissioners and scribes did not crowd nearly every sen-tence of their works with a vain tautology, nor yet indite matter which, well and literally translated, could fail to be significant in every word.

Oddly enough it was the writer himself who swept aside the language of the Exon Survey and its scribes when he found it in con-

---

[1] *Domesday Book and Beyond*, pp. 431–2. It appears to be necessary to insist on this, for Mr. Whale, in his *Principles of the Somerset Domesday* (1902), holds that 'the investigations of Professor Maitland and others scarcely leave it longer doubtful that Eyton is right in accepting 120 statute acres as the extent of the *terra ad unam carucam*.'

[2] *Principles of the Somerset Survey* (1902), p. 8.

flict with his own theory on the subject. Observing that at Bedminster the *terra ad unam carucam* of Domesday Book was entered in the Exon Domesday in one place (p. 83) as *terra unius caruce* and in another (p. 489) as *I carrucata terræ*, he promptly disposed of the latter phrase by writing—

> Here the word *carucata* is improperly used. It was merely a clerical error, the clerk describing one thing in terms of another.[1]

The truth is that the scribe, on the contrary, knew what he was doing and simply employed a synonym after the manner of his kind.

The great lordship of Taunton affords us another illustration. Let us place the geld-roll for Taunton Hundred and the survey of Taunton in the Exon text side by side :—

GELD ROLL	EXON SURVEY
Habet adhuc episcopus W. in Tontona xx carrucatas terræ quæ nunquam reddiderunt Gildum.[2]	Exceptis his predictis hidis habet ibi episcopus terram ad xx carrucas quæ nunquam redd[id]it gildum.[3]

Here the synonymity of the phrases is placed beyond doubt. And yet Mr. Eyton had no difficulty in persuading himself that the *terram ad xx carrucas* of the second passage should be read in conjunction with a subsequent entry of woodland, pasture and meadow 'to make the 20 plough-lands into true carucates' by the addition of '4,360 acres of other land' ![4] But on turning to the Exon text we find that this woodland, etc., is not assigned, as he makes it, to these twenty ploughlands, but to the whole lordship of Taunton,[5] a very different matter.

Mr. Eyton's views on the 'carucates' of Somerset will be found on pp. 20, 28–9 of his *Somerset Survey*,[6] and were criticized by me on pp. 202–4 of *Domesday Studies* (1887), where I showed that the *terra I caruce*, or ploughland, of Domesday was equated in the *Inquisitio Eliensis* by *I carucata* or *I carucata ad arandum*. The geld carucate (*carucata ad geldum*) of northern England was quite another matter ; but with that we have nothing to do in Somerset.

From this preliminary but necessary discussion we may now at length turn to the distribution of the lands of the county at the time of the great Survey.

Somerset was a county in which the king's lands were of great extent and importance. For, as was duly explained by Mr. Eyton, he held in 1086, not only the ancient demesne of the Crown, which had been held by Edward the Confessor, but the forfeited possessions of Harold and his relatives, and the broad estates of Queen Edith, which had escheated to the Crown at her death in 1074. To these were added a few manors which had been held by Wulfward the White (*Albus*), a thegn apparently of that queen, so that one cannot wonder that, in all, the

---

[1] *Somerset Survey*, i. 28 *note*.   [2] *Exon Domesday*, p. 67.   [3] Ibid. p. 161.
[4] *Somerset Survey*, i. 191–2.   [5] *Exon Domesday*, p. 162.
[6] Compare his *Key to Domesday* (Dorset), pp. 16–23, for the Dorset ones.

manors in William's own hands occupy no less than five columns of Domesday Book.

Taking in succession these constituents of King William's holdings, we have first to deal with the 'ancient demesne,' which is not distinguished from the rest in Domesday Book itself, but which is defined in the Exon Domesday as 'D[omi] nicatus regis in Sumerseta' (p. 82).[1] This consisted, as is shown in Mr. Eyton's table,[2] of twelve manors : Carhampton, Williton, Cannington, North Petherton, South Petherton, Curry Rivel, Frome, Bruton, Somerton (with the 'borough' of Langport), Cheddar (with Axbridge), Bedminster, Milborne Port (with Ilchester). These manors possessed two distinctive features : in the first place they were not liable to pay 'geld' (or land tax), and were therefore not assessed in 'hides' (or units of taxation) ; in the second, they had formerly paid to the Crown, instead of a rent in money, the *firma unius noctis* (or supply in kind to the Court), and had been grouped, on an ancient system, for the purpose.[3] This grouping is so remarkable that I here give, from my *Feudal England* (pp. 111–2), the details of the money commutation for this ancient burden :—

	£	s.	d.	
North Petherton	42	8	4	One whole *firma* commuted
South Petherton	42	8	4	for £106 0s. 10d.
Curry Rivel	21	4	2	
Frome	53	0	5	One whole *firma* commuted
Bruton	53	0	5	for £106 0s. 10d.
Somerton (with Langport)	79	10	7	One whole *firma* commuted
Cheddar (with Axbridge)	21	0	2½	for £100 10s. 9½d.
Milborne Port (with Ilchester)	79	10	7	Commutation for three-quarters of a *firma*.
Bedminster	21	0	2½	

Williton
Carhampton } One whole *firma* commuted for £105 16s. 6¼d. (E.D.),
Cannington } or £105 17s. 4½d. (D.B.).

I have already spoken of Mr. Eyton's error in taking the Milborne payment as commutation for half instead of (as it was) for three-quarters of a *firma*.[4] With his suggestion that Milverton, if not Bath itself, had formerly belonged to this group of manors of ancient demesne I cannot agree,[5] while his assignation to the twelve manors of certain estates as appendages was avowedly tentative.[6]

[1] Mr. Eyton began his account of the 'ancient demesne' (*Somerset Survey*, i. 72 ; ii. 1–2) by speaking of 'the title given for this class of estate by the Exon Domesday, viz., "Dominicatus Regis ad regnum pertinens in Sumerseta,"' and explaining that the king held it '*jure regni* or *jure coronæ*.' It is of some importance, therefore, to correct his quotation. The practice of the Exon Domesday varied somewhat strangely. In Somerset it headed this class of estate as in the text above, while it entered in quite another place (p. 94) the 'Terre regis quas tenuit Godwinus comes et filii ejus in Sumerseta,' which in Domesday Book follow the others without any break. In Devon, on the other hand, the phrase 'dominicatus regis' is applied to those lands which had been held by the family of Godwine (p. 84), while 'd[omi]nicatus regis ad regnum pertinens' is applied to those which the king held as of ancient demesne (p. 75). In Dorset both classes are combined under the single heading 'dominicatus regis' (p. 26). [2] *Somerset Survey*, ii. 1–2.

[3] This same system can be traced on royal demesne manors in the neighbouring counties of Gloucestershire, Wilts, Hants and Dorset. [4] See p. 391, above.

[5] The almost nominal assessment of Milverton seems to have led him to this conclusion. But there is no trace of the distinctive *firma* system in connection with it. Both Milverton and Bath had escheated to the Crown, and, as was the practice with escheats, were granted out again not long afterwards. [6] *Somerset Survey*, i. 74–5.

There was yet another feature by which these manors were characterized, although it was not, like the two others, distinctive and peculiar to them. This feature was that each of them, as Mr. Eyton explained, was the head of an old Hundred, to which it gave its name.[1]

One finds it very difficult to say on what ground Mr. Eyton, while rightly urging that to each of these manors was attached the lordship of the Hundred named after it and that the Court of the Hundred was probably held within its limits, insisted that the manor itself was always extra-hundredal.[2]

As I had occasion to observe, many years ago, ' Mr. Eyton had, unluckily, a provoking habit of occasionally omitting his evidence, and thus rendering it impossible to judge of the correctness of his induction'.[3] The witness of Domesday as to those counties in which it gives hundredal headings is dead against his assertion. The best parallel, perhaps, is afforded by the case of Hampshire, in which the royal demesne manors had been similarly held by King Edward, were similarly free from assessment to geld, and had similarly contributed on an ancient system to the ' day's ferm,' or rent in kind. Yet Domesday distinctly enters them as *intra*-hundredal.[4]

The issues of the king's manors, the *Terra regis* of Domesday, formed the nucleus of that *firma comitatus* for which the sheriff answered at the Exchequer and which constituted so important an element in the revenue of our Norman kings. Here one is again compelled to differ from Mr. Eyton's views, for the interpretation of a notable passage in the Somerset Domesday is at stake. With the king's manors of ancient demesne the sheriff, Mr. Eyton held, had at that time nothing to do :—

> It is worth note that in no instance of the Twelve Royal Manors of Somerset is a manor said by Domesday to be in the ferm or custody of the Sheriff of the County.

[1] The only exception was Curry Rivel, of which the Hundred had the name of Abdick. Mr. Eyton's suggestion that it was so named to avoid confusion with North Curry and the Hundred named after it scarcely seems adequate.

[2] 'It may be proved of many, and it is probable of most of the 23 named estates of Royal Demesne that, though extra-hundredal and ingeldable themselves, they were the *Capita* of so many Hundreds, that is, that the king, in virtue of his holding such and such an estate of Ancient Demesne, was Lord of such and such an Hundred' (*Key to Domesday*, Dorset, p. 81). 'The twelve Royal Manors of Somerset, though themselves extra-hundredal, had each its appropriate hundred—that is, the king being lord of this or that manor, was thereby lord of a certain hundred ; and the *Curia* of the said hundred was probably held within the precincts of the relative manor' (*Somerset Survey*, i. 74).

[3] *Domesday Studies* (1887), i. 213.

[4] See for instance Domesday, i. 39 :—
' IN BASINGESTOCH H[UN]D[RET]
Rex tenet in dominio BASINGESTOCHES. Regale manerium fuit semper. Nunquam geldum dedit nec hida ibi distributa fuit. . . .
CLERE tenet rex in dominio. De firma regis E[dwardi] fuit et pertinet ad firmam diei de Basingestoches. Numerum hidarum nescierunt. . . .
ESSEBORNE tenet rex in dominio. De firma regis E[dwardi] fuit. Numerum hidarum non habent. . . .
Hec tria maneria, Basingestoc, Clere, Esseborne reddunt firmam unius diei.'
The whole passage is most instructive for comparison with the similar groups of royal demesne manors in Somerset. Of Bruton, for instance, we read :—' Nunquam geldavit, nec scitur quot hidæ sunt ibi.' On this Mr. Eyton comments : ' Bruton itself, though it gave name to the Hundred, . . . was a manor of the *Vetus Dominicum Coronæ*, non-hidated and consequently (*sic*) in no Hundred whatever' (i. 74). The case of Basingstoke shows that ' consequently ' is merely an assumption of Mr. Eyton's, and a wrong one.

Such manors were *extra comitatum* always. In William's time they were *extra vice-comitatum* also. . . . The Royal manors were fermed or managed by special Præpositi, not necessarily, nor always, resident, who were answerable to the Crown for fixed rents, whatever were the profits or losses of management.[1]

Evidence to the contrary could be produced from several other counties, but we need go no further than the immediately adjacent one of Gloucestershire to find in a single column of Domesday proof that the sheriff was responsible for the *firma* from manors of ancient demesne.[2] Next to Gloucestershire comes Worcestershire, where the language of Domesday on the subject is pre-eminently clear and decisive : ' de dominicis Maneriis regis reddit (vicecomes) cxxiii lib. et iiii sol. ad pensum ' (fo. 172).

The reason for insisting upon this fact is that a passage in the Somerset Survey is of absolutely unique value as proving that, before Domesday and even before the Conquest, the twelfth century exchequer system of crediting the sheriff, at his annual account, with a fixed sum in respect of such royal manors or portions thereof as had been granted out to subjects was already in full operation. The passage in question is found in the entry on Cheddar :—

' De hoc Manerio tenet Giso episcopus unum membrum WETMORE, quod ipse tenuit de rege E[dwardo]. Pro eo computat Willelmus vicecomes in firma regis xii lib. unoquoque anno ' (fo. 86)[3] ; ' sed episcopus tenuit de rege Edwardo longo tempore ante obitum regis E[dwardi] '[4]

I need not here repeat the argument in which I showed that *computare* was the technical word used at the exchequer for this system.[5] Ignorance of that fact, unfortunately, led Mr. Eyton, not only to miss the interest of the passage, but to give it an interpretation altogether erroneous :—

We have not noticed in this column an annual rent of £12 stated by Domesday to be paid by Bishop Giso for Wedmore as if it were a member of Cheddar. . . . Bishop Giso's payment of a rent for Wedmore was only a temporary incident. Elsewhere (p. 147, Exon) Domesday surveys the manor as the Bishop's in all integrity. . . .

Wedmore was not then, in any strict sense of the term, a *member* of Cheddar. It was not Royal Demesne ; it was *intra Vicecomitatum* and *intra Hundredum*, and geldable. All that we can suppose is that, owing to some claim of the Crown, Wedmore had been seized by the sheriff, William de Moione ; but Bishop Giso had been con-

---

[1] *Somerset Survey*, i. 73–4.
[2] See Domesday, i. 163, col. *a* :—
[Slaughter.] 'De hoc manerio reddebat quod volebat vicecomes T.R.E. . . . Modo vicecomes accrevit ibi. . . .' [Westbury.] 'Hoc manerium reddebat unam noctem de firma . . . de remanenti invenit vicecomes totam firmam. . . . In Cheftesihat Hundret tenuit E[dwardus] rex Langeberge . . . T.R.E. reddebat vicecomes de hoc manerio quod exibat ad firmam. . . . In Bliteslaw Hundret tenuit rex E[dwardus]. . . . 'Hoc manerium reddebat dimidiam firmam noctis T.R.E. . . . Vicecomes tamen reddit totam firmam. . . . Alwi vicecomes misit hæc [membra] extra firmam.' It will be observed that the cases of Longborough and Aure are further destructive of Mr. Eyton's theory that such manors were ' extra-hundredal.'
[3] This passage is found in the same form in the Exon Domesday (pp. 82, 479), but in the former place the scribe has, for ' unoquoque anno,' written in error ' 1 quoque anno,' while in the latter he has omitted ' anno.'
[4] This phrase is omitted in the Exchequer text, but occurs in both entries in the Exon Domesday.
[5] *Commune of London and other Studies*, pp. 73–4.

tinued in formal possession, at a stipulated rent. The rent was received from him by the said Sheriff, who was probably instructed to hand it over to the King's Provost at Cheddar. The affair was quite ephemeral. Doubtless Giso had recovered full seisin even while the Domesday Commissioners were in Somerset.[1]

The whole idea is illusion. Domesday does not state that the bishop paid a rent for Wedmore, and the sheriff neither received this imaginary rent, nor made it over to that ' Provost at Cheddar,' whose existence rests solely on another erroneous assumption which I have exposed above.[2] Wedmore had undoubtedly formed part, as Domesday states, of the ancient demesne till Edward the Confessor granted it out to Bishop Giso some quarter of a century before the date of the Survey. Oddly enough, Mr. Eyton was fully aware of this grant.[3]

Other features of this group of manors, such as the arbitrary reckoning of its ploughlands,[4] the royal boroughs that it included, and its richly-endowed churches, are discussed under other heads, but attention may be drawn here to the cases of estates which had been added to these manors or had been subtracted from them.[5] The latter, as was pointed out by Mr. Eyton, appear in Domesday assessed in terms of the hide, in spite of the fact that the manor from which they had been withdrawn had not been so assessed.

At the close of that group of manors with which we have been dealing Domesday begins a fresh column with that section of the king's lands which had come to him by the forfeiture of the whole house of Godwine. These, as explained above (p. 394), are entered in the Exon Domesday in a separate place with a distinct heading, and, as Mr. Eyton pointed out, there is found at the head of a folio towards the close (but in a smaller handwriting) the title ' mansiones de comitatu.' He therefore styled them ' the comital manors,' a name which we may adopt. It has also been adopted by Professor Maitland, on the strength of this Somerset heading confirmed by the phrase *comitales villæ*, which he cites from the ' Pseudoleges Canuti.'[6] He observes that the existence of such manors held *ex officio* may account for the vastness of those estates which appear in Domesday as having formerly been held by the house of Godwine, and that ' the wealth of the earls is a matter of great importance.'[7] But neither he nor Mr. Eyton, it would seem, noticed the great peculiarity by which these manors are, in Somerset, distinguished. This consists in the entry of their rentals on a quite peculiar system : (1) They are entered as renders (' reddit '), not as values (' valet ') ; (2) the sums rendered are ' de albo argento ' ; (3) in at least ten out of the fifteen cases they are multiples of the strange unit £1 3s.[8] Whatever may be the explanation of this singular system, it differentiates the comital manors very clearly from others. I have shown that there are visible traces, in the adjacent county of Devonshire, of the rents of the

---

[1] *Somerset Survey*, i. 76 ; so too (i. 107) ' he sometime paid a yearly rent to the Royal Manor of Cheddar. But the Bishop had held it (free) under King Edward.'

[2] See p. 396.   [3] Op. cit. i. 109, where he cites Edward's grant from the *Monasticon*.

[4] See p. 388.   [5] See p. 426 below.   [6] *Domesday Book and Beyond*, pp. 167–8.

[7] Ibid.   [8] See *Feudal England*, p. 115.

comital manors being based on a duodecimal system,[1] but it is not nearly so peculiar as that of their Somerset rentals.

The difficult question of the 'third penny' (*tercius denarius*) as appurtenant to comital manors will be discussed below in connection with finance, but this would seem to be the fitting place in which to speak of those by whom the manors were held. Although it would be naturally expected that all comital manors would remain in the hands of Harold himself, it will be found that his mother Gytha, his brother Earl Tostig, his sister Gunhild, and his own son Godwine, were among their holders. We cannot tell, however, whether they had received them from Harold or from his father Godwine, his predecessor in the earldom. But it is the tenure of Crewkerne that is the real puzzle. As was duly pointed out by Mr. Eyton, who discussed the matter at some length,[2] Crewkerne was 'by far the most valuable of the comital manors of Somerset,' and yet it had been held by 'Eddeva,' a lady whose identity is not disclosed. Now it is one of the problems of Domesday, as Mr. Eyton observed, whether its Edith 'the fair,' 'the beautiful,' 'the rich,' was identical with Edith 'Swan's neck' (*Swanneshals*), Harold's mistress, and probably the mother, in Mr. Freeman's opinion, of his son Godwine mentioned above. As to this problem Mr. Freeman held that 'there is absolutely no evidence either way.'[3] Mr. Eyton, discussing the question as to who was the tenant of Crewkerne, summed up strongly in favour of its being 'Edith the Fair,' who was, he suggested, 'of the race of Godwin'; but I do not think his reasoning sound. Even if the manor had previously belonged, as he held, to King Edward—which seems to me doubtful[4]—it does not follow that the king must have given it to 'Eddeva,' and that, therefore, 'Eddeva' cannot have been Harold's mistress. Harold might well have obtained it from the king and then bestowed it upon her. Moreover, 'Edith the Fair' was in no case a daughter of Godwine, nor have we any reason to suppose that she was even 'of kin to him.' It is difficult, therefore, to see how she obtained the manor unless it was given her by Harold.

I agree with Mr. Eyton in thinking that the manors of 'Estalweia,' Banwell and Lullington, which had also been held by Harold, were not 'comital manors'; but I differ from his view that Temple Combe ('Come'), which had been held by his brother Leofwine, was one of them, for which supposition there seems to be no ground.

The third division of King William's lands consisted of those which had come to him on the death of Queen Edith. These have a separate heading in Domesday Book, while in the Exeter Domesday they are, further, entered in a separate place (p. 104). It is worth observing that the form of her name is 'Eddid' in the former and 'Editda' in the

---

[1] *Commune of London and other studies*, pp. 70-1.
[2] *Somerset Survey*, ii. 82-3.
[3] *Norman Conquest* (2nd ed.), iii. 792.
[4] Alone among the 'comital manors,' no doubt, it was not assessed for geld; but Mr. Eyton admitted that, though a king's manor, it was not of the 'ancient demesne' group. Its render of £46 appears to me to stamp it as always a 'comital manor.'

latter, which is more akin to our modern form than the usual 'Edeva' of Domesday or Mr. Freeman's 'Eadgifu.' The queen's Somerset possessions were exceptionally valuable and extensive, including, as they did, the lordship of Bath. Of those in the king's hands at the time of the Great Survey we learn from Mr. Eyton's table that the assessment was about 140 hides and the value the then large sum of some £320. But, in addition to the manors that had passed to the king, she had also held others at Luccombe (now Luckham), Selworthy, Combe Hay and Twerton; but these were, comparatively, of little value.

The fourth and last section of the king's great holding was composed of the lands of Wulfward White (*Albus*) and receives, in both texts, a separate heading like the lands of the queen, of whom Wulfward, we shall see, had acted as officer. So shadowy are the names of the great English thegns who meet us as holding lands on the eve of the Conquest, and so slight our knowledge of the distribution of their lands that it is worth our while to ascertain the history, position and estates of Wulfward so far as possible, the more so as he clearly escaped, doubtless through the queen's influence, the general wreck at the Conquest. The first point to attract our attention, in his as in other cases, is the scattered character and great extent of the lands held by an English thegn. Mr. Eyton did something to trace his estates in Domesday,[1] but his search was not exhaustive. In Dorset he had held at least Pentridge and Silton ; in Hampshire (fo. 43*b*) he is entered as having held Hayling Island of Queen 'Eddid' as an 'alod,' Domesday adding that he had received half of it for life only from Queen Emma (Canute's widow) and had died in King William's time.[2] Far away in Kent he had held a manor with 'sac and soc' (fo. 1*b*, 9); while in Middlesex, as 'a thegn of King Edward,' he had owned three manors (fo. 129–30). Tracing him from Somerset in another direction, he had held land in Wilts under the Bishop of Salisbury (fo. 66); in Gloucestershire Hatherop had been his (fo. 169), and in Oxfordshire a part of Cold Norton (fo. 160), while in Buckinghamshire he and his wife Eadgifu ['Eddeva'] had held land, between them, at some ten different places, which were assessed in all at about sixty hides. Even in distant Lincolnshire 'Wlward Wite' was one of those notabilities who enjoyed 'sac and soc' (337), a fact which proves that he was the 'Wlward' who had held a valuable manor at Butterwick in that county. I have also no doubt, myself, that he was the 'Wlward' whom Ernulf de Hesdin had succeeded in a valuable Berkshire manor, which is now Newbury (fo. 62*b*). We thus connect him with ten counties.

In Somerset itself, besides the manors of Corton Denham, Mudford and Pitney, he had held estates at Stanton Drew and Burnett under Queen Edith's lordship of Keynsham, and the latter was still in possession of his widow in 1086, a pitiful fragment of his wide estate. Mr. Eyton showed that Wulfward was present, in 1068, at William's court and at that of

---

[1] *Somerset Survey*, pp. 86–7 ; *Key to Domesday* (Dorset), p. 112 *note*.
[2] This Hampshire entry is not mentioned by Mr. Eyton.

Queen Edith in 1072, witnessing in both cases Somerset grants. The geld roll implies that he was still living in 1084. From the Buckinghamshire entries we may gather that his daughter was given by Queen Edith to 'Alsi,' who was only allowed, however, to obtain land with her in that one county.[1]

From the king's land we may now at length pass to that of his subjects.

Awarding to the churchmen the precedence they invariably receive in Domesday, we have first to deal with the Bishop of Winchester. Pitminster and Rimpton he held as abbot of the Old Minster (St. Swithun's); Bleadon was apportioned to his monks; but these possessions become insignificant when compared with his lordship of Taunton. Three folios of the Exon Survey and about a column of Domesday Book are devoted to this lordship alone, and they supply material for a dissertation on many points of historical interest and institutional importance. While its local aspects have been discussed very fully by Mr. Eyton, it is Professor Maitland who has done most to illuminate its origin and character by his comments in *Domesday Book and Beyond*, in which work it is referred to in eight separate places. The first three points to be settled are: (1) How did the bishop come by Taunton? (2) What did 'Taunton' comprise? (3) Which were the places that owed suit and service to Taunton?

Walchelin, the Norman Bishop of Winchester, had obtained Taunton, Mr. Eyton tells us, by 'gift' or 'grant' of the Conqueror. It will be best to quote his own words :—

> The great Somerset Manor of Taunton had been before the Conquest a possession of Stigand, sometime bishop of Winchester, sometime Archbishop of Canterbury, sometime occupant of both sees together.
>
> After the Conquest, King William gave, or perhaps we should say confirmed, Taunton to Walchelin, the first Norman bishop of Winchester. The King conceded it, not as a personal and heritable feud, but as an endowment of the church of Winchester.
>
> There are many records of this gift (*sic*): but we hardly appreciate its munificence and its fulness till we turn to Domesday. . . .
>
> The elaborate care bestowed upon the Record and its unusual comprehensiveness are accounted for in a postscript which runs as follows :—'De his terris' (the adjuncts of Taunton) 'semper jacuerunt consuetudines et servitium in Tantone, et Rex Willelmus concessit istas terras sancto Petro' (the church of Winchester) 'et Walchelino episcopo, sicut ipse' (Rex) 'recognovit apud Sarisberiam audiente Episcopo Dunelmensi, cui præcepit ut hanc ipsam concessionem suam in Brevibus scriberet.'
>
> If we venture to translate somewhat freely, and to expatiate somewhat enthusiastically on this unwonted text, we trust at the same time to say no more than years of study and an ever growing tendency to prefer *facts* to *views* will warrant.[2]
>
> . . . On him (the bishop of Durham), then, did William, King of the English, being at Salisbury, enjoin that he should take present and diligent note of the King's declared intentions touching the quality and extent of his grant of Taunton (*sic*) to Bishop Walchelin ; and that when he (the bishop of Durham) should, in the course of

---

[1] Mr. Eyton suggested in a footnote (p. 87) that the Corton Denham entry in the Exon Domesday contains a confusion with this Alsi. But I think he misunderstood the alteration therein. The name of Wulfward as its holder T.R.E. was underlined for deletion and that of 'Alti' (*sic*) substituted, because Wulfward had received the manor since the coming of William, a fact of some interest.

[2] The italics are Mr. (Eyton's) own.

his circuit, be in Somerset, he should enter a memorandum of such, the king's 'concession,' on the Rolls of the Survey—'in brevibus,' as the King named the elements of that, the contemplated Record, which men afterwards called Domesday Book.[1]

It will be seen at once that Mr. Eyton here speaks of the grant in one place as that of 'the adjuncts of Taunton,' and in another as that of 'Taunton'; and that his evidence for both statements is the 'postcript' cited above. Now I do not hesitate to say that this postscript referred neither to Taunton nor to its adjuncts, but to two estates in Lydeard (St. Lawrence) and (Angers)leigh, of which Domesday expressly tells us that they had been 'added' to Taunton,[2] and were held of Bishop Walchelin by grant (*concessionem*) of King William.[3] And this conclusion is in harmony with the evidence of the whole entry, which shows that Walchelin had but stepped at Taunton, as elsewhere, into his predecessor's shoes.

As against these additions the bishop's great lordship had suffered three encroachments,[4] though these were not serious. The Count of Mortain, John the Usher, and Alvred 'de Hispania' had thus secured between them $4\frac{1}{8}$ 'hides.' Mr. Eyton wrote of this as a 'grant made by King William . . . in qualification, or perhaps in non-anticipation of the King's more general grant of Taunton and its appurtenances to the Bishop of Winchester'[5]; but this latter 'grant' was, we have seen, an error, and as these encroachments are also found among the 'terræ occupatæ,'[6] there can be no reason for doubting that they were merely such aggressions as were frequent on church lands in the early days of Norman rule. In such cases the lands were rarely recovered by the church.

It is partly by comparing the Taunton lordship with those in other counties held by the Bishops of Winchester, and partly by invoking the evidence of Anglo-Saxon charters, that Professor Maitland has been able to bring the lordship of Taunton into relation with its fellows and to direct us on the right path for tracing its earlier history. In the first place he has drawn our attention, in Hampshire, to 'the great Chilcombe estate of the church of Winchester, which stretched for many a mile from the gates of the royal city,' and which was granted as 100 hides; in Wiltshire to its great Downton estate, entered in Domesday as 100 hides; and in Somerset to 'Taunton' as the name of a territory comprising several parishes. From these instances he draws the inference that 'whenever the West-Saxons conquer new lands they cede a wide territory to their bishop.'[7] In other words the bishops, he held, had acquired these territories 'in very early days.'[8]

When from the character of these great lordships, with the special privileges attached to them, we pass to what we can learn of their history, we find evidence which throws, I think, a curious reflex light on the

[1] *Somerset Survey*, i. 12–13. On p. 11 the passage cited is described as 'an abnormalism of great interest . . . a piece of Domesday history such as is not to be foundon any other page of the great Record.'
[2] *Exon Domesday*, pp. 163, 481. Compare p. 444 below.
[3] *Domesday*, i. 87*b*. [4] Compare p. 427 below.
[5] *Somerset Survey*, p. 194. [6] *Exon Domesday*, p. 480.
[7] *Domesday Book and Beyond*, pp. 496–500. [8] Ibid.

Domesday Survey of Somerset. Although primarily interested in matters of justice and jurisdiction, Professor Maitland incidentally brings before us privileges of another kind. For the former he refers to a document of special interest as follows—

> in a book [1] of fairly good repute we may read of the grand liberties with which in 904 King Edward endowed the Bishop of Winchester's large estate at Taunton— that estate which in subsequent centuries was to become the classical example of colossal manors.[2]

The critical study of such documents is not yet sufficiently advanced for us to say with certainty which of these ancient texts are wholly or partly spurious ; but it is always a sound principle to accept admission of liabilities even if we look with suspicion on assertion of privileges and rights. I am, therefore, disposed to accept as genuine the important passage which follows, the more so as it is in harmony, we shall find, with known facts. Professor Maitland's rendering is this—

> Taunton, which belonged to the Bishop of Winchester, had been bound to provide one night's entertainment for the King and nine nights' entertainment for his falconers, and to support eight dogs and a dog-ward, to carry with horses and carts to Curry and to Williton whatever the King might need, and to conduct wayfarers to the neighbouring royal vills. To obtain immunity from these burdens the bishop had to give the King sixty hides of land.[3]

We have here, in this grant of a thousand years ago, that *firma unius noctis* with which we have already met as the due payable from royal manors or groups of manors in Somerset,[4] and it is at least suggestive that the ' 100 ploughlands ' of Taunton are parallel in Domesday Book with the ' 100 ploughlands ' of the Williton group or of the Bruton and Frome group, each of which was liable to provide the *firma unius noctis*. But it is the further burden of providing for hawk and hound and for carriage of the king's stuff from one of his manors to another that gives to this evidence, I think, a genuine look. As Professor Maitland has said of such charters—

> Apparently the king, the under-king, even the ealdorman, has a certain right of living at the expense of his subjects, of making a progress through the villages and quartering himself, his courtiers, his huntsmen, his dogs and horses upon the folk of the townships, of exacting a ' one night's farm ' from this village, a ' two nights' farm ' from that.[5]

In Somerset, indeed, Domesday mentions nothing beyond the ' night's farm,' but other counties supply us with examples, evidently archaic, of payments for hawk and hound, for sumpter horse or for

---

[1] This term is here used in the specialized sense of a ' land-book ' or Anglo-Saxon charter.

[2] *Domesday Book and Beyond*, p. 276.

[3] Ibid. p. 272. The Latin runs : ' Erat namque antea in illo supradicto monasterio pastus unius noctis regi et viii canum et unius canicularii pastus et pastus novem noctium accipitrariis regis et quicquid rex vellet ducere usque ad Curig vel Willettun cum plaustris et equis et si advene de aliis regionibus advenirent debebant ducatum habere ad aliam regalem villam quæ proxima fuisset in illorum via' (Birch, *Cartularium Saxonicum*, ii. 273). Curry (Rivel) lay some ten miles to the east of Taunton, and Williton some thirteen to its north-west.

[4] See p. 394 above.   [5] *Domesday Book and Beyond*, p. 236.

carriage (*avera*).[1] A careful examination of the record reveals payments for hounds of £23 from Oxfordshire and from Warwickshire respectively (ff. 154*b*, 238), and of £42 from Northants (fo. 219), while in Gloucestershire three royal manors had to supply them with 3,000 loaves (*panes*) apiece, and in Beds two of them paid respectively £6 10*s.* 0*d.* and £3 5*s.* 0*d.* for the same purpose.[2] In six counties also we have identical payments for a hawk and for a sumpter horse. Looking at the whole evidence, I am disposed to think that the Somerset 'night's farm,' of which we read in Domesday, included certain 'customary' payments such as are mentioned in other counties, and indeed in the above Taunton charter, as additional. This might explain certain differences and oddly uneven sums in the totals of the money equivalents.

Another indication of the early date at which Taunton must have passed into the bishop's hands is found in the extraordinary privileges with which its lordship was endowed. In this respect it is instructive to compare it with the Bishop of Worcester's Hundred of Oswaldslow, in which that prelate enjoyed similarly exceptional privileges.[3] The 'customary dues' enjoyed at Taunton by the bishop, its lord, included the profits of certain 'pleas of the highest class,' as Professor Maitland terms them, together with the local 'hundred-pence, Peter's pence and churchscot.' It was at Taunton that the pleas were held, and to Taunton that men were compelled to go when they had to make oath or to undergo the ordeal.[4]

As to the second portion of our inquiry, 'the vills implied in the Domesday survey of Taunton,' as Mr. Eyton has expressed it,[5] he made them to be Kingstone (13½ miles distant), Combe Florey, Nynehead Flory, Withiel Florey (16 miles distant),[6] Corfe, Orchard Portman, Ruishton, Staplegrove, Trull, Cothelstone, Bishop's Hull, Otterford and Bishop's Wood, and part of Bishop's Lydeard.[7] I have already discussed and rejected Mr. Eyton's system of obtaining from the Domesday figures exact measures of area, but one may point out that, applying them to the 'Taunton' of Domesday, he arrived at 16,659 acres as the total area implied.[8] But this was on the assumption that its ploughlands, containing 'about 120 statute acres,'[9] were '20 + 80 = 100.' But Professor

[1] The burgesses of Wallingford were bound to service by road or river to four neighbouring royal vills.

[2] The Record Commission's *Index rerum* to Domesday is very deficient on this point.

[3] See the *V.C.H. Worc.* i. 245.

[4] The very first of the customary dues appurtenant to Taunton is recorded as 'burgerist,' a mysterious word which occurs again in the survey of the comital manor of Cleeve. We there read that 'to this manor there belonged the third penny of "bu(r)gherist" from Williton and Carhampton and Cannington and North Perrott' (*Exon. Domesday*, p. 96), all of which were manors of royal demesne. Sir Henry Maxwell Lyte has been able to trace this word, in varying forms, as the name of a payment found in Somerset through the middle ages; but though it was clearly a local due from certain tithings and tenements, the origin of its name (which appears to represent 'borough-right') has not been ascertained. It is mentioned in the Taunton Charter of 904.

[5] *Somerset Survey*, i. 193.

[6] These places derived their suffixes from a family of Flury which held by knight service of the Bishops of Winchester. Hugh de 'Flury' held three knights' fees of the bishop, and Robert de 'Flury' three in 1166.

[7] *Somerset Survey*, i. 193, ii. 34.   [8] Ibid. i. 192, 195.

[9] In practice, however, he reckoned them, as usual, at exactly that amount and thus obtained his total.

Maitland read the text as 20 + 100[1]; which seems to me to be clearly right, especially if we examine Mr. Eyton's own table (ii. 33) ; and this gravely affects the total. He preferred the Hundred to the single vill as a test of his theories, and claimed that the Domesday Hundreds of Taunton and Pitminster, of which he reckoned the areas by 'the exacter measures of Domesday' at 33,814 statute acres, showed a discrepancy of only 8,672 acres 'between the two measurements, that of the 11th and that of the 19th centuries.' He therefore 'opined' that 'in this district or province the Domesday surveyors found some 8,672 acres of moor or waste of which they took no notice.' As already explained, it was by such assumptions that he endeavoured to explain away the failure of his so-called 'key.'

Our third point, the suit and service due to the bishop as lord of Taunton from the vills beyond its limits, is one of great importance. Professor Maitland on this subject, which is one of special interest to him, observes that—

> Within his immense manor of Taunton the bishop of Winchester has pleas of the highest class, and three times a year without any summons his men must meet to hold them.[2]

This is a somewhat serious slip, due to misapprehension. The Domesday Book text, which he cites as his authority in a note, is particularly clear upon the point. After closing its survey of the great manor of Taunton it begins a new paragraph thus :—

> Istæ consuetudines pertinent ad Tantone, burgheristh, latrones, pacis infractio, hainfare, denarii de Hundret et denarii Sancti Petri, Circieti,[3] ter in anno tenere placita episcopi sine ammonitione, profectio in exercitum *cum hominibus episcopi*. Has denominatas consuetudines reddunt in Tantone hæ terræ :—

Then follows a list of the places (*terræ*) which rendered the above dues and services, places which were not 'within,' but without the manor of Taunton, and from which the men of other lords assembled for pleas, host, and so forth '*with* the men of the bishop' (*cum hominibus episcopi*). In addition to the dues described above, the lords of all these places, we read lower down, had to be buried at Taunton—which brought, if one may speak colloquially, more grist to the bishop's mill[4]—and finally all who dwelt within them were bound, as already mentioned, to swear their oaths and undergo their ordeals at Taunton. In short the whole paragraph deals with *consuetudines*—the normal term in such cases —due to the great manor of Taunton from lands outside it and forming an addition to its value.

But some of these places enjoyed exemption from one or more of these duties, and of such exemption both the Surveys contain careful

---

[1] *Domesday Book and Beyond*, p. 113. Both in Domesday Book and in the Exon Survey the text distinctly supports this view.

[2] Ibid. pp. 87–8. So too on p. 102 : 'The tenants of the bishop of Winchester "hold the bishop's pleas" at Taunton.'

[3] This word is omitted by Prof. Maitland.

[4] Compare the writer's remarks on Burton Abbey's right to *sepultura*, in *Eng. Hist. Rev.* xx. 279.

record. The variants here in their texts are of some interest and importance ; both for instance agree in stating that Stoke (St. Mary) and 'Scobinalre' (or 'Scobindare') were exempted from the duty as to the host, while Bagborough was free from this and from the burial provision (*sepultura*) as well ; but while Norton Fitzwarren, Bradford, Halse and Heathfield are entered together in Domesday Book among the places owing all the duties, the Exon Survey enters them apart as owing (only) attendance at the pleas, Peter's pence, and (apparently) Hundred pence.[1] Again, the Exon Survey includes 'Lediart et Lega' among the places liable to all the dues, while Domesday Book does not ; but the latter duly asserts that they had been so liable when dealing with them lower down as having been 'added' to Taunton.[2] The Exon Survey here indulges in needless repetition.

There was no other lordship belonging to the church in Somerset comparable, even distantly, to Taunton in importance. But the great fief of the Bishop of Coutances fills some five and a half columns of Domesday Book. This fief, however, like that of the Bishop of Bayeux —which was represented in Somerset by one manor only—was akin, in reality, to the lay baronies and was so dealt with on the bishop's death. The fact that it did not descend, in later days, as a whole makes it difficult to trace the devolution and, therefore, the identity of its manors as recorded in 1086. Of the true church lands in the county the most important were those of the Bishop of Wells, and of the abbeys of Bath, Glastonbury, Muchelney and Athelney. In the early days of the Conqueror's reign the see of Wells had recovered the manor of Banwell, which had been wrested from it by Harold, but there are signs in Domesday that the imposition of knight-service on lands of the Church[3] was already making itself felt in the frequent mention of knights (*milites*) as quartered on the bishop's manors. But the famous abbey of Glastonbury was the chief sufferer in Somerset, and its chroniclers' complaints of the loss of its lands by their distribution among the Norman knights are confirmed by the Domesday Survey. Portions of its thegnland were annexed to the fief of the Bishop of Coutances, but its chief loss was caused by the imposition on the abbey of a *quota* of forty knights.[4] To supply this large contingent knights had to be enfeoffed, which involved the practical alienation of many a manor. Domesday shows a number of these in the hands of Roger de Courcelles, whose successors were responsible for ten knights, that is for a fourth part of the abbey's large *quota*. Muchelney was only called upon to provide one knight and Athelney escaped free.

Somerset was the only county in which St. Peter's of Rome re-

---

[1] 'Debent ire ter in anno ad placita episcopi et redd[er]e denarii (*sic*) Sancti Petri in Tantona et den' in hundreto.' The first of these provisions is important as confirming my contention that not merely the bishop's 'men,' but those of other lords had to attend his pleas.

[2] 'De his terriss emper jacuerunt consuetudines et servitium in Tantone.' This confirms my contention that these words in the Exon Survey (where they also appear) refer to those two manors alone (see p. 401 above).

[3] See *Feudal England*, p. 278. The bishop's *quota* in the twelfth century was 20 knights.

[4] Ibid.

ceived an English manor as the reward of the Pope's encouragement of William's conquest. On it he bestowed the Puriton estate, and on his own abbey of St. Stephen of Caen the richly endowed church of his royal manor of 'Cruche' (Crewkerne). To the lot of the abbey of Jumièges there fell the much less richly endowed church of his manor of Chewton Mendip. Foreign churchmen shared the spoils; Maurice, who had just been appointed to the see of London, was holding in 1086 the churches of Ilchester (St. Andrew's), Congresbury, and North Curry, the first of which, with its valuable glebe, had been detached from the possessions of Glastonbury; Richer d'Andely, who had secured the church and glebe of Stogumber, was a Norman who held three churches in the neighbourhood of Southampton, and four houses in that town together with certain manors in the county. The wealthy church of Frome, as well as that of Milborne Port, was in the hands of Reinbald, a remarkable man of uncertain origin, who enjoyed the favour of William as of Edward, and whom I have elsewhere styled 'the first great pluralist.'[1]

In this county Domesday displays a singular lack of system in dealing with the churches in the king's gift. Some are dealt with in their normal place, under 'Terra regis,' but to others is assigned a special section, 'Clerici tenentes de rege,' which is oddly sandwiched in between the church tenants and the lay. From this special section we learn that Peter, bishop of Chester, who had died shortly before the survey, had held the royal churches of North Petherton, Carhampton, and Kilmersdon. Peter, who had been a chaplain of William's, and possibly of Edward's before him,[2] had also obtained a small estate at Buckland St. Mary. In Dorset he had secured a hide, probably glebe land,[3] while in Berkshire he was provided for out of a glebe estate at Wantage, his 'son' Reinbald also obtaining a manor.[4] Another chaplain was Stephen, who held Milverton church, while Erchenger, who had secured that of Cannington, must also have been a foreigner. An English priest, Alviet, is entered in this section, but not in connection with any church, while three other Englishmen included in it were apparently not priests, but holders of small estates in almoin,[5] as were certainly three nuns who are comprised in it. Indeed the Exeter Domesday arranges (pp. 178–181) these lands very differently, throwing together sections xi, xii, xiii, xv, and xvi of the Exchequer text into a confused group, to which it gives the heading: 'Terra (sic) que date sunt Sanctis in elemosina in Sumerseta.' In the Somerset returns at the great inquest of 1212 we find a small holding at Holnecote (in Selworthy) still held by the true almoin tenure (free from all service but prayer) and seem to be told that Edith the nun was really the widow of a man slain in the king's service.[6]

---

[1] *Feudal England*, p. 427.   [2] Ibid. p. 320.
[3] Eyton, *Dorset Domesday*, p. 122 *n.*   [4] Domesday, 57, 58.
[5] These are usually entered in Domesday as the King's *elemosinarii*.
[6] 'Abel de Hunecot tenet dim. virg. terræ in Hunecot de domino Rege per oracionem, quam Willelmus Rex Angl. dedit Edithe in puram et perpetuam elemosinam quia vir suus occisus fuit in servicio domini Regis' (*Testa de Nevill*, 162).

Nigel the physician, who, in this as in five other counties, had succeeded Spirtes the priest, had bestowed a manor in Somerset as in Wilts on the Norman abbey of Montebourg ; and that of Grestain had obtained from its patron, the Count of Mortain, the manor of Norton-sub-Hamdon. The Earl of Chester had given Henstridge to his own abbey of St. Sever, but, on the whole, the alien churchmen had not obtained much. It was at a later date than this that Cluniac monks made their home in the priory of Montacute below the castle of its founder, the Count of Mortain.

On one result of the Norman Conquest on church lands in Somerset we obtain light from the survey, not of Somerset, but of Bedfordshire and of Bucks. The 'Old Minster' of St. Swithun, Winchester, had suffered heavily from the change ;[1] but in Somerset its actual loss was confined to the manor of Crowcombe and to Heal, a dependency of Taunton which William's grasping brother, the Count of Mortain, had seized. Crowcombe had been given to the minster by Harold's mother— apparently after her husband's death (1053)—who gave Bleadon at the same time.[2] Bleadon duly appears in Domesday as apportioned to the support of the monks of Winchester after as before the Conquest ; but in another part of the great survey we find estates in Bedfordshire and in Bucks held by Geoffrey, Bishop of Coutances, 'in exchange for Bleadon.'[3] This would seem to imply that the bishop had laid hands on Bleadon, and had only disgorged it on receiving compensation in another part of the kingdom. Possibly the excuse in both cases was that the manors had belonged to the house of the dead 'usurper.'

Everywhere the English houses were liable to Norman spoliation ; Athelney had lost to Ralf de Limesi its manor of Bossington in Porlock, although its issues were specially assigned to the monks' support ; and Cerne Abbey had failed to regain an estate in South Cheriton which Alwold had leased from it for life, because, as in similar instances, it was confused with his own land. Another example of this fruitful source of loss to religious houses occurs at Wheathill, which Elmer had held of Glastonbury Abbey, 'nec poterat ab ea separari.' At the survey it is found in the hands of Serlo de Burci, evidently because he had obtained the lands of this Elmer or Almar. The nuns of Shaftesbury, however, had added to their solitary manor of Combe Abbas that of Kilmington, which was given them by this same Serlo, when his daughter took the veil among them.

With the church lands, as with those of the king,[4] Domesday betrays a lack of system. Under the fief of Roger 'de Corcelle' we read that his three hides at Puckington had formerly been held 'of St. Peter's church,' which Mr. Bates holds to be Muchelney Abbey. Yet under Muchelney's fief we cannot trace Puckington or find the abbey making any claim to this estate. In the entry which follows those on Puckington, we read that the $1\frac{1}{8}$ hide to which it relates was held of

---

[1] See *V.C.H. Hampshire*, i. 416.   [2] *Annales Monastici*, ii. 26.
[3] Fols. 145*b*, 210.   [4] See p. 406 above and p. 426 below.

Muchelney Abbey, 'nec poterat ab ea separari.' In this case we have the further information that the land is ' de xx hidis de Draitune et est Tainlande.' We turn to Drayton, a Muchelney manor, but the only encroachment recorded under it is one of 'two hides, which the details prove to be distinct. But, with the help of the Exon Survey, we discover that Domesday only accounts for $11\frac{5}{8}$ hides of desmesne, 5 hides in the hands of the villeins, and 2 hides of encroachment. There remains, therefore, to be accounted for $1\frac{3}{8}$ hide, which would more than cover this holding of Roger. The fact that such encroachments are sometimes recorded under the religious houses affected, and sometimes not, makes it extremely difficult to trace them out.

A curious feature, in this county, of the Exchequer Domesday is the appearance, in the margin of the text, against the entries of certain manors, of a Maltese cross. We find it against the Count of Mortain's manors of Crowcombe and Heal, of which he had robbed St. Swithun, as of Tintinhull and Kingstone, of which he had deprived Glastonbury. It calls our attention to the fact that Roger ' de Corcelle' was holding at Long Sutton land which two thegns had held of Athelney Abbey, ' et non poterant ab ea separari ' ; it stamps Roger Arundel as the wrongful holder of Ash Priors, stolen from the bishop of Wells ; and it stands against the record of Glastonbury's right to Brompton' Ralph and Clatworthy, two manors which William de Moion had contrived to annex to his fief.[1] But it does not distinguish all the losses which had been inflicted on the Church. In its place, however, an accusing finger points to Stratton-on-the-Fosse and Middlecote, of which Glastonbury had been robbed by the grasping bishop of Coutances. Glastonbury and Athelney, which had suffered most at the hands of the newcomers, group together, at the end of their fiefs, some of their chief losses, from which we learn that Roger ' de Corcelle' had been preceded by his father, who had obtained Limington by giving in exchange five hides which he held of Glastonbury with no power to separate them therefrom. To Athelney's loss of Long Sutton we are indebted for one of those double entries, which sometimes prove so instructive :—

De eadem terra hujus Manerii tenet Rogerius de Corcel ii hidas invito abbate. Duo taini tenebant de æcclesia T.R.E. nec inde poterant separari. Terra est ii (*sic*) car. quæ ibi sunt in dominio, et vi (*sic*) acræ prati. Valet l sol. Duo homines tenent de Rogerio (91).

Dodeman et Warmund tenent de Rogerio Sutone. Duo taini tenuerunt T.R.E. de æcclesia Adelingi et non poterant ab ea separari et geldabant pro ii hidis. Terra iii (*sic*) car. In dominio sunt iii (*sic*) car. . . . Ibi viii (*sic*) acræ prati, Valet l sol. (94 b).

The ' thegnland' so often spoken of in Somerset was held of the church by thegns, one of whom, at the time of the survey, was still holding two hides at Chard of the bishop of Wells.

Of the lay tenants the Count of Mortain, half-brother to the Conqueror, was by far the most important, Mr. Eyton reckoning the assessment of his manors at over 342 hides and their annual value at £346 6s. 4d.

---

[1] 'Hæc terra fuit de æcclesia G. nec poterat inde separari T.R.E.' 'Hæc terra non poterat separari ab æcclesia G. sed erat ibi tainlande T.R.E.'

The figures for the fief of the Bishop of Coutances are slightly in excess of both these, but the count could claim, like the bishop, that he held nearly a tenth of the county, whether from the standpoint of assessment or from that of annual value.

A tenant-in-chief in twenty counties, the count can hardly be said to be associated specially with one, unless it was that of Cornwall, in which he practically reigned supreme ; for whether he was actually its earl or not, he was virtually the only lay tenant-in-chief within its borders. With Somerset, however, he also had a connection of a special kind, for it was there that he raised his castle of ' Montacute,'[1] which became, on the breaking up of his fief, the head of a great ' honour ' comprising his broad estates in the counties of Somerset and Dorset. Of him Professor Freeman wrote, speaking of the conquest of the West (1068) :—

> And there was one beyond all these, whose share of the spoils of England was greater than that of any other one man, and whose chiefest and richest rewards lay in the newly conquered lands. Robert, the son of Herlwin and Herleva . . . . now gathered in the richest spoil of all in the forfeiture of countless Englishmen within the Western shires . . . . The lord of the waterfalls[2] heaped together manor upon manor among the dashing streams of Devonshire and among the hills and islands of Somerset. And one spot came to him by an exchange with an ecclesiastical body, the possession of which, like the possession of Pevensey, seemed to mark him out as the very embodiment of the overthrow of England. The hill of Lutgaresbury, whence came the holy relic which had given England her war-cry, and which had been the object of the life's devotion of her king, now passed into the hands of one who was to wipe out its name and memory. The height, one of the peaked hills which form so marked a feature in the scenery of Somerset, was now crowned by a castle of the new Earl, which, under the French name of Montacute, became at once a badge of the presence of the stranger and an object of the bitterest hatred to the men of the Western lands.[3]

The ' exchange ' by which the count obtained from its owner, the abbot of Athelney, that manor of ' Bishopston ' on which he fixed as the site for his strong castle, was the manor of Purse Caundle, Dorset, which was only about half its size and one-third of its value. In the adjoining county of Devon the count, by a similar transaction, had given the Bishop of Exeter two manors 'in exchange for the site of his castle in Cornwall.'[4] Even the king himself, however, had only obtained a site for his important castle of Corfe (in Dorset) by giving to the abbess of Shaftesbury the advowson of Gillingham in exchange.[5] The count further improved his home estate by obtaining Tintinhull, close to Montacute, from Glastonbury Abbey, to which he gave ' in exchange ' Camerton, south-west of Bath, a manor of not half its value.

But the churches which suffered at the count's hand were by no means always fortunate enough to obtain even an ' exchange.' In addition to the lands of which, as we have seen, he had despoiled St. Swithun of Winchester,[6] he had laid his hands in addition on Kingstone, not far from his castle, a manor which Glastonbury Abbey had held

---

[1] ' Ibi est castellum ejus quod vocatur Montagud ' (see p. 483 below). Its ' porters ' are entered in Domesday as holding, under the Count, Stert in Babcary.

[2] The allusion is to the falls of the Canche in the picturesque district of Mortain.

[3] *Norman Conquest* (1871), iv. 168–70. Cf. *English Towns and Districts*, 128–9.

[4] 'Pro excambio castelli de Cornualia' (fo. 101*b*).

[5] Domesday, fo. 78, and *Testa de Neville*, p. 164.   [6] See p. 407 above.

before the Conquest. Yet these aggressions were as nothing when compared with his 'wide and reckless spoliation of ecclesiastical bodies,' as Mr. Freeman describes it, in Cornwall. Nor was the church his only victim ; the very manors of the king himself in Somerset had been encroached on or defrauded of dues by the count or by his vassals.[1] These vassals, as entered in Domesday, are of more than fleeting importance ; for, on the count's fief escheating to the Crown, they became tenants-in-chief, and their tenures were converted, as in the case of the vassals of the count's brother, Odo of Bayeux, into separate baronies.

So ardent a student of feudal genealogy as Mr. Eyton has left one little that is fresh to record about these vassals.[2] Two of the most interesting are the count's butler, whose name, 'Alvredus,' suggests Breton extraction, and Dru (*Drogo*) 'de Montagud,' as Domesday styles him, each of whom occurs about a dozen times as a tenant of the count in Somerset. The holdings of the former were of great extent, for the count enfeoffed him not merely in the south-western counties, but in others so far afield as Sussex and Northamptonshire ; his holdings were represented, in 1166, by a barony of ten fees which, although mainly in Somerset, was returned under Dorset, and which was held by his direct descendant, 'Richard the son of William.' The holdings of the Domesday 'Drogo' were represented similarly, in 1166, by a barony of ten fees held by his descendant 'Drogo de Monte Acuto.'[3]

It may, perhaps, be well here to caution the reader against the confusion surrounding the name of Montacute. The baronies held by members of the house which bore it were quite distinct from 'the fee of Montacute,' which was a phrase used alternatively with 'the fee of Mortain' for those baronies formed from the local portion of the great fief held by the Count of Mortain in Domesday. On the Pipe Roll of 1168 we find, under Somerset, such baronies described as 'of the fee of Montacute,' while on that of 1194 we actually find William de Montacute holding his barony 'of the fee of Montacute,'[4] the double use of 'Montacute' being here well illustrated. In 1166 we find, under Somerset, Richard del Estre making a return of the knights of his 'barony,' at the end of which he explains that 'three of them are of the barony of Montacute in Somerset, and the fourth of the Honour of Berkhampstead in Northamptonshire.'[5] Here 'the barony of Montacute' is used in its wider sense ; it is not merely that which was held by the family of the name, but the whole of that extensive honour of which the castle of Montacute was the head, just as 'the Honour of Berkhampstead' was that portion of the count's fief which had the castle of that name for its *caput*. It is in this sense that Bernard Pullus returns himself, under Dorset, in the same year as holding one fee 'of the

---

[1] See pp. 426, 428 below.   [2] See his *Somerset Domesday*, i. 59.
[3] There were, however, already two lines of this family under Henry II, and the pedigree, consequently, presents difficulties.   [4] *Red Book of the Exchequer*, p. 80.
[5] 'Tres etiam istorum sunt de baronia de Monte Acuto in Sumersete, et quartus de honore de Berkamestede in Norhantescire.' Berkhampstead itself, of course, was in Herts, but the fee spoken of was in Northants.

Honour of Montacute,' and the lord of Harptree as holding there a knight's fee ' of the Honour of Montacute of the fee of the Count of Mortain.'¹ In this latter return we have both phrases used, but in that of Richard son of William, the representative of Alvred the Count of Mortain's butler, his barony is described only as ten fees ' of the fee of Mortain.'²

Four centuries at least after the date of Domesday we still read of a knight's fee (or a small knight's fee) ' of Mortain,' in spite of the early dissolution of the count's immense fief. The reason for this persistence of the name is that the knight's fees that belonged to it enjoyed the peculiar privilege of paying only two-thirds as much scutage as others. This reckoning, however, was not absolutely exact ; investigation shows that when the ordinary fee paid one pound (240 pence) or one marc (160 pence) the fee ' of Mortain ' paid respectively 150 pence and 100 pence.

Before leaving the name of Montacute we must glance at the question of its origin, which presents some difficulty. In Domesday the castle itself is styled ' Montagud,' a form preserved in its later name. Dru (' Drogo ') was one of the count's four tenants who held a hide apiece there in 1086. But although he is styled in the survey ' Drogo de Montagud,'⁴ and Ansger (another of the count's great tenants) Ansger ' de Montagud,'⁵ the latter at least is in no way associated by it with the castle, and it is scarcely conceivable that Dru can have taken his name from his lord's castle, with which moreover he is not shown as more closely connected than his three fellow-tenants on the count's manor of ' Bishopston.'⁶ The family name appearing normally in its Latinized form alone, there is a doubt as to what it was ; but on the Pipe Roll of 1167 we find under Somerset the ' Monte Acuto ' of the chancellor's roll represented by ' Muntagu.' In the present department of La Manche, in which Mortain is situate, we have a Montaigu and a Montaigu-les-bois, from one or the other of which the name may well be derived.⁷

The castle itself presents a further difficulty, for although its name is undoubtedly French, like those of Richmond, Rougemont, or Belvoir, the 'peaked hill' from which it rose had its parallel at Mortain itself.⁸ Its name, however, is due, doubtless, to its own situation. Of it Mr. Freeman has finely said :—

> From the Peak which had now taken the name of Montacute, the fortress of the stranger Earl looked down like a vulture's nest on the surrounding hills and on the rich valleys at its foot. Of the castle itself not a stone is left.⁹ . . . But the

¹ *Red Book of the Exchequer*, pp. 218, 219.   ² Ibid. p. 220, and compare p. 410 above.

³ ' quorum tres milites non faciunt Regi servitium nisi quantum duo debent facere de cæteris baronibus Angliæ ' (see Dru de Montacute's return, in 1166, under Somerset, *Red Book*, p. 228).

⁴ See p. 526a below.   ⁵ See p. 526b below.   ⁶ See p. 483 below.

⁷ Sir Henry Maxwell Lyte, however, tells me that he considers the surname was derived from the Somerset castle.

⁸ We there still see, on the left bank of the Canche, 'le rocher taillé à pic et revêtu de plantes grimpantes qui portait autrefois un château fort, dont les restes sont insignificantes.'

⁹ It is by no means certain that, at the time of Domesday, there was a castle of stone on the hill, and it may safely be asserted that there could not have been one so early as 1069.

wooded height still covers the fosses which marked the spot which the men of Somerset and Dorset in those days looked on as, above all others, the house of bondage. . . . We read how the West-Saxons of Somerset, Dorset, and the neighbouring districts besieged the castle of Montacute.[1]

Whether the Count of Mortain obtained his widespread estates in the district in 1067 or 1068 the fact that it was already a stronghold in 1069 shows that he had lost no time in erecting it. And the fact that 'the two porters of Montacute' appear as holding Stert in Babcary tells us that its lord had made the same permanent provision for their support as he had been careful to do at his Sussex castle of Pevensey. The Montacute entry is of further interest as an illustration of the practice of assigning to leading tenants small estates in the immediate vicinity of the lord's castle. Thus we have here Alvred (the butler), Dru (de Montacute), Bretel (de St. Clair) and Donecan, all holding a hide apiece in the manor of Bishopston, in which stood the castle. Bretel (or Britel)—from whom Ashbrittle derives (as Mr. Eyton observes) its name—must have been called from St. Clair,[2] as was Hubert the count's tenant at Kingstone. His other principal tenants in the county were Mauger de Carteret, Ansger le Breton, who seems to have been also styled Ansger de 'Muntagud,' and who occurs in eight entries; and Robert Fitz Ivo, otherwise the constable, predecessor, we learn from Mr. Eyton, of the Beauchamps of Hatch Beauchamp. Among the count's tenants of less importance one may name William 'de Lestra,' who held of him at Bickenhall and Pointington in Somerset, and Catherston, Durweston, and Corscombe in Dorset, because his descendant Richard del Estre appears as a Somerset baron in 1166.[3] There is some confusion about his name, which appears in various forms; but it is clearly derived from Lestre near Valognes.[4]

Next in importance to the fief of the Count of Mortain were those of Roger 'de Corcelle,' Roger Arundel, Walter 'de Dowai,' and William de 'Moion.' The first of these, whose holdings cover more than five columns of Domesday, held so largely as a tenant-in-chief or under-tenant in the county, that 'there were not,' in Mr. Eyton's words, 'six Hundreds in Somerset of any capacity, in which this ubiquitous and omnivorous Feudalist had not some interest.' The persistent endeavour to make him the founder of the house of Churchill was very properly rejected by Collinson and, after him, by Eyton,[5] but I am prepared to go further. Although the name appears in Domesday as 'Corcelle' or 'Curcelle' normally, and only once (fo. 72b) as 'Corcelles,' it is found regularly enough in the next century as 'Corcelles' or 'Curcelles,' and I have elsewhere[6] derived it from Courseulles in the present 'Calvados,' north-north-west of Caen, on the coast. Roger is remarkable not only for the number of his Somerset tenures *in capite*, but also for that of the

1 *History of the Norman Conquest* (1871), iv. 272-3.   2 Department of La Manche.
3 See p. 410 above.   4 Department of La Manche.   5 *Somerset Domesday*, i. 60.
6 *Calendar of Documents preserved in France*, i. 575. Among the documents in that volume is found (p. 170) a grant by Roger de 'Curcella' of lands at Bernières-sur-mer (*Bernerie*), which actually adjoins Courseulles.

manors he held as an under-tenant, especially if, as Eyton asserts, he was the Roger 'Witen' who held of the Bishop of Coutances. The devolution of is wide estates remains, unfortunately, as subject to doubt as when Eyton investigated the problem.[1] Here one can say no more than that the baronial Malets succeeded him at Curry (Mallet) and in the bulk of his barony and his tenancies, but apparently under a fresh grant after a forfeiture of his fief, rather than by inheritance and descent.

The extensive barony of Walter (or Walscin) de Douai presents similar difficulty as to its devolution. Broadly speaking, however, it is found in the next century divided between the 'Honour of Castle Cary' (Somerset), of which his castle there was the head, and the 'Honour of Bampton,' which Devonshire manor was the head of this portion.[2] The former came into the hands of the Lovels, the latter into those of the Paynels.

Roger Arundel's fief, of thirty knights' fees, had passed to Gerbert de Percy in 1166[3] and was subsequently divided equally between the families of Newburgh and Fitz-Payn.[4] Alone among these great Domesday barons William de 'Moion' was destined to transmit his extensive fief, of which Dunster was the head,[5] to descendants of his own name until the line ended in heiresses about three centuries after the great survey.[6] Sheriff of the shire at the time of that survey, William derived the name, which became anglicized as Mohun, from Moyon (now in the 'Manche'), which lay some seven miles south of St. Lo.[7]

Neither of the two earls who were tenants-in-chief in Somerset had extensive estates in the county. Earl Hugh of Chester, as Mr. Eyton explained, had for his only vassal one of his Cheshire barons, William Malbanc; Count Eustace of Boulogne's chief tenant was Alvred of 'Merleberg,' lord of Ewias (Harold). This Alvred had for his predecessor, in Somerset as elsewhere, a certain Carle, whom he had succeeded at Chelwood, the only estate in the county that he held in chief; in accordance with a common Domesday practice he held the rest of Chelwood as a tenant of Count Eustace. Kingweston, held by the Countess of Boulogne, was subsequently bestowed by her on the Cluniac priory of Bermondsey.[8]

Next in importance to the lay tenants dealt with above were William de Eu, Turstin Fitz Rou and Serlo de Burci, who held between 50 and 60 hides apiece. William's predecessor in all but one of his Somerset manors was that great Wiltshire thegn, Alestan of Boscombe, whose estates, scattered over England, he obtained, as Mr. Eyton has shown, after their intermediate tenure by Ralf de Limesi. They were forfeited, however, on his fall, not long afterwards. Turstin is alleged

---

[1] *Somerset Domesday*, i. 60.   [2] See my *Studies in Peerage and Family History*, p. 60.

[3] In right of his wife Maud Arundel, as Sir Henry Maxwell Lyte observes.

[4] *Red Book of the Exchequer*, pp. 166, 169; Dugdale's *Baronage* (citing records), i. 572.

[5] 'Ipse tenet Torre, et ibi est castellum ejus' (see p. 501 below).

[6] The lords of Dunster have formed the subject of a monograph by Sir Henry Maxwell Lyte, which deals exhaustively with their history and their lands.

[7] *Dunster and its lords*, p. 1.   [8] *Studies in Peerage and Family History*, p. 153.

to have been identical with the bearer of the Norman 'gonfanon' at the battle of Hastings.[1] The devolution of his fief eluded even the researches of such a master of feudal history as Mr. Eyton proved himself to be; but it is now known that it must have been forfeited and then regranted to Winebaud de Ballon, a baron from Maine, who took his place as a lord of the March, and the heiress of whose house brought his estates in Somerset, as in other parts, to a branch of the line of Newmarch.[2] Serlo, who derived his name from Burcy near Vire (in the 'Calvados'), was father-in-law of William de Falaise, another Somerset baron. His barony, as Mr. Eyton has explained, is afterwards found in possession of the Martin family, and was usually known, from its chief manor, as the barony of Blagdon[3]; but considerable obscurity surrounds its devolution, as well as that of the fees which, like Roger de Courseulles, he held under Glastonbury Abbey.

The only other lay barons deserving of special notice are William de Falaise, whose chief holdings were in Devon, and whose daughter Geva brought Stoke to the Courcys; Alvred 'de Hispania,'[4] whose barony was shown by Mr. Eyton to be identical with that which was returned, under Somerset, in 1166 as held by Philip de Columbers; Edward de Salisbury (sheriff of Wilts), ancestor of the first Earls of Salisbury; Baldwin of Exeter, lord of Oakhampton and sheriff of Devon; Robert Fitz Gerold, whose estates passed to his nephew; Matthew de Mortagne, whose estates ranged through six counties from Somerset to Essex; and Ralf Paynel, a Yorkshire baron, who owed his Somerset manors to his obtaining the lands of Merlesweyn, a great thegn, the chief seat of whose power was in Lincolnshire, but who was a holder of land also in Gloucestershire, Devon and Somerset.

The last two pages of the survey of the county (fols. 98b, 99) present peculiar difficulties, difficulties duly recognized, but scarcely explained by Mr. Eyton. The normal practice in Domesday Book is to class together, where they exist, at the end of each county (1) the king's serjeants, who held their land by serjeanty; (2) the king's thegns, that is the few Englishmen who had either been allowed to hold some pitiful estate in the place of their former possessions, or found favour in Norman eyes and received a manor or more from the spoils. These 'thegns' are a class of peculiar interest as Englishmen, and are fairly numerous in the counties of Devon, Somerset, Dorset, Wiltshire and Hants. There was, however, in addition to these recognized classes, a third and limited class for which the Exchequer clerks had no definite name. These are they who appear at the end of the Somerset Survey as 'certain others.' Mr. Eyton's statement of the difficulty is as follows :—

> The Exchequer Domesday is by no means free from the blemish of misarrangement of Fiefs. It commences a survey of Humphrey Chamberlain's estates with a proper title, viz. 'Terra Hunfridi,' therewith treating his fief as the last of Somerset

[1] Eyton, *Dorset Domesday*, p. 76; *Somerset Domesday*, i. 65.
[2] *Studies in Peerage and Family History*, pp. 189–98.   [3] *Somerset Domesday*, i. 65–6.
[4] He is more likely to have derived his name from the village of Épaignes than (as Mr. Eyton and others have assumed) from Spain (see his *Dorset Domesday*, p. 77; and *Somerset Domesday*, i. 65).

baronies, yet still as a barony. It enters two manors proper to this category, and then, without giving any fresh title or note of interruption, lapses into a list of the estates of King's Serjeants. Then it gives a chapter entitled *Terra Tainorum Regis*, which proves, on examination, to be of the lands of the *Angli Taini* only, who are thus placed in an unusual precedency.[1]

Lastly, and out of all sequence and propriety, it gives a chapter entitled 'Item Hunfridi Terra et Quorundam aliorum.' Here it resumes its interrupted survey of Humphrey Chamberlain's estates, and registers the particulars of three manors. Then again, without any fresh title or note of interruption, it lapses into the estates of the Franci Taini, as they are called in the Domesday of other Counties.

The true arrangement of the Exchequer text would have been to have inserted this last chapter immediately after the two manors entitled *Terra Humfridi*, and then, when Humphrey's manors had all five been registered, to have inserted a new title, such as *Terræ Francorum Tainorum*.[2]

FRANCI TEGNI.—The perverse arrangement of both editions of the Somerset Domesday has led to the suppression of this Title in both Records. Nevertheless, collating the two, we are enabled to make out a Somerset list of those who in other counties would have come under this category . . . the 'French Thanes.'[3]

In no county is found a category of 'French Thanes'; indeed such a phrase might be described as a contradiction in terms.[4] One can only suppose that the writer must have had a vague recollection of the phrase 'Hugo de Luri et alii Franci' in the heading to the survey of Dorset, which is contrasted with 'Gudmund et alii taini' in the same heading (fo. 75). On comparing the arrangement under other counties, it seems tolerably clear that Domesday had in this matter no fixed practice, and that when it grouped, after tenants-in-chief, several 'Frenchmen' who held a manor or two apiece, it did not thereby imply that either in status or in tenure they differed from those who were entered, under separate headings, before them. In Somerset, for instance, the survey closes with the two-hide holding of Ansger 'de Montagud' at Preston Plucknett, Ansger being here grouped with 'certain others.' But under Devon this same Ansger is entered among the great tenants-in-chief (fo. 116), merely, it would seem, because he there held seven different estates. So too Ralf 'de Berchelai,' who figures in the same group, under Somerset, where he held half a hide, is placed, with a separate heading, as a tenant-in-chief, in Gloucestershire (fo. 168), where his two estates were assessed at $5\frac{1}{2}$ hides. Keeping still to neighbouring counties, we have seen that in Dorset Hugh de Luri heads a group similar to that at the end of the survey of Somerset. Yet in Northamptonshire, where his solitary holding was a very much smaller one, we find him entered separately among the great barons (fo. 224*b*).

We have here then a further instance of Domesday's capricious practice.[5] I cannot agree with Mr. Eyton in treating the group of Normans found both in Somerset and in Dorset as differing in status or

---

[1] But the thegns actually precede the serjeants in the survey of Wiltshire (J.H.R.).

[2] *Somerset Domesday*, i. 54–5. [3] Ibid. i. 68.

[4] There is mention in an Essex entry of a 'francus teignus,' but 'francus' there clearly means not 'French,' but free. See also p. 432 below.

[5] It is even possible that the real reason of this grouping arrangement in Somerset and Dorset was that the space available at the heading of each county was not large enough at its close to admit of numbering each tenant-in-chief separately.

tenure from their fellows, though I entirely concur with his view that ' the true arrangement of the Exchequer text would have been to have inserted the Somerset group in continuation of Humphrey the chamberlain's land.' But I cannot admit that the ' confusion probably arose in the indeterminate and complex position of Humphrey Chamberlain himself . . . as his very name suggests, he was or had been a king's sergeant, and in that quality the clerks gave him a third post at the head of the Servientes Regis.'[1] It was not Humphrey, but Robert ' de Odburvile,' who headed the king's serjeants[2]; and Humphrey (whose brother, Aiulf the chamberlain, was sheriff of the adjoining county of Dorset) was a tenant-in-chief in no fewer than nine counties. Three out of five of his Somerset estates had been added, we read, to Brictric's lands, which gives us a clue as to how he came by them. For the bulk of the lands held by that great western thegn, Brihtric the son of Ælfgar, had been given to Queen Matilda, with whom legend has associated his name, and various entries in Domesday show that Humphrey had been her chamberlain and had received estates from her.[3] Among the small tenures *in capite* which follow those of Humphrey is Tadwick, held by William ' Hosed ' and by Ralf brother of Roger de Berkeley.[4] The former is identified by the Exon Domesday as the tenant of Serlo de Burci at Ridge Hill, of the Bishop of Coutances at Pitcombe, and of Bath Abbey at Charlcombe. Next in order is ' Hugolin ' the interpreter, who held three estates, and who is probably identical with the Hugh ' latinarius,' who had held an estate in the New Forest (fo. 50b). He was an under-tenant of Bath Abbey at Bathampton, and had secured for himself a valuable house in Bath. In the geld-roll he appears under the noteworthy alias of ' Hugolinus legatus,' an alias which suggests that the ' Richard ' who appears with him in this group as holding a hide in Road (where he was also an under-tenant of the Bishop of Coutances), and who appears in the Exon Domesday as Richard ' Interpres,' was the Richard ' legatus ' who held, as a tenant-in-chief, the valuable manor of Tormarton in Gloucestershire (fo. 168b). The question as to his title at Road is obscurely stated in Domesday, and I have elsewhere suggested that the ' tenuit ' of the Exchequer record is a slip of the scribe for ' emit,' the word in the Exon Domesday, which makes sense of the passage.[5] With Ansger and Dru ' de Montagud ' I have already dealt. There remain only in the group ' Schelin,' who gave his name to Shillingstone, his Dorset manor ; Hugh (de Valletort) who held at Fodington of the Count of Mortain as well as of the king, and who probably derived his name from Vautort (Mayenne) some 25 miles south of Mortain, Odo the Fleming, and ' Eldred ' (the Aldret' of the geld-roll) who, at Brockley and Crandon, still held the lands which had been his before the Conquest. Even Mr. Eyton, who studied so long and to such good purpose both the Norman and the English holders of lands, did not attempt to identify

---

[1] *Somerset Domesday*, i. 54.
[2] ' Robertus de Odburville et alii servientes regis ' (fo. 86).
[3] This is expressly stated of two manors in Gloucestershire, one of which had been Brihtric's.
[4] Compare p. 417 below.   [5] See *Feudal England*, pp. 425–6.

Eldred ; but I believe him to have been identical with a man whose case was as interesting as it was exceptional. If so, he was the Eldred or Edred who appears in Devon to the west as holding three estates, two at least of which had been his before the Conquest (fo. 118), and the 'Aldred' who, in Wiltshire to the east, held five, two of which had been similarly held by himself before (fo. 73*b*), and finally the Eldred 'brother of Odo of Winchester,' who held land in Hampshire which he had similarly contrived to retain.[1] In all three of these counties he appears among the native thegns, as is shown by his name to be his right place ; and I conclude that only an obvious error has placed him in Somerset, among Normans.

Next in order are the king's serjeants. Robert de 'Odburvile,' who heads the list, was, says Mr. Eyton, 'a king's forester, and to foresters of King Edward he succeeded in some estates.'[2] I have not found the evidence for his office, and in only one of his five estates is he recorded to have been preceded by foresters. He is followed by John the usher, who had six estates in this county and two in Wiltshire. Next to him are Ansger 'Fower' (the hearth-keeper[3]) with four small estates and Ansger the cook, who, in addition to his own holding at Lilstock, had obtained possession of land belonging to the royal manor of Martock. This cook appears in Wiltshire also among the king's tenants by serjeanty, and is doubtless identical with the man of the name who had a small estate at Aveley far away in Essex. The name of Anschitil the parker speaks for itself. The appearance of one who must have been an Englishman among these foreign serjeants is noteworthy ; Edmund the son of 'Pagen,' who held three estates, is entered in Hampshire as an English thegn holding land in the New Forest district, with which he and his father seem to have been associated ; but the strange thing is that he is also found in Suffolk, where he had succeeded to a substantial manor held by his father 'Pagan' before the Conquest. The last tenure by serjeanty is that of the wife or widow of Manasses the cook, who himself appears as an under-tenant at Stalbridge in Dorset.

Of the 'king's thegns,' that is the Englishmen who, in 1086, were still allowed to hold land,[4] Harding son of 'Elnod,' or 'Alnod,' was 'clearly the greatest.'[5] He has been the subject of much discussion, rather because he was the probable ancestor of the historic race of Berkeley than because he was certainly the founder of the Somerset house of Meriet.[6] In the geld-roll of Crewkerne Hundred (1084) he is styled 'Hardinus de Meriet,' taking his name from his chief manor as did his descendants. Mr. Freeman, who was much interested in the subject, established the identity of this Harding, son of 'Elnod' or 'Alnod,'

---

[1] For his other Hampshire holdings see the *Victoria History* (i. 427–8) of that county, where I have worked them out.
[2] *Somerset Domesday*, i. 68.   [3] He is the Ansger 'focarius' of the Exeter book.
[4] Mr. Eyton, in accordance with the 'Exon' book, styles them 'the Anglo-thanes.'
[5] Eyton, *Somerset Domesday*, i. 69.
[6] See Freeman's *Norman Conquest* (1871), iv. 45, 165, 226, 757–60 ; Eyton, *Somerset Domesday*, i. 58–9, 69–70 ; Greenfield, *Genealogy of . . Meriet*, pp. 4–6 ; Ellis, *Domesday Tenants of Gloucestershire*, pp. 111–2.

with the ' Heardinc ' or ' Hierdinge ' son of ' Eadnoth,' who is found in Anglo-Saxon documents, and with the ' Herdingus ' son of ' Ednod,' who was alive when William of Malmesbury wrote,[1] and whose father, that historian tells us, fell in repelling the descent on Somerset by Harold's sons in 1068. This identifies the latter with the ' Eadnoth Stallere ' of the Chronicle, the ' Eadnothus Haroldi Regis stallarius ' of Florence, who commanded, they tell us, William's troops on that occasion. The Domesday holder of Meriet is also, clearly, the Harding ' filius Elnodi ' who acted as a justice itinerant for Devon and Cornwall in 1096.[2]

The great estates of Eadnoth did not pass to his son ; they are found in Somerset, as in other counties, in the hands of Hugh, Earl of Chester. A Berkshire entry (58b) enables us to prove the identity by styling the earl's predecessor ' Ednod stalre.' The succession of the Count of Mortain to a manor which had been Ordulf's, and to three[3] which Edmeratorius had held, is of interest because he had obtained the whole estates of both in Devonshire, as Mr. Eyton points out. The second of these great thegns, who is only styled ' Edmer ' in the Exchequer Domesday, is, in the Exeter Book, ' Edmeratorius,' which enables us to identify him with the Count's predecessor in his great lordship of Berkhampstead and other Hertfordshire lands. The Exeter book applies the term *Honor* to the vast holdings of these two thegns.

Restrictions of space and the usual difficulties attending their identification preclude any detailed description of those English thegns whom the Normans had dispossessed ; but some mention should be made of Mærleswegen the sheriff. Although Harold, it is said, had left him, after the battle of Stamford Bridge, in charge of the North, he is found witnessing as sheriff (i.e. of Lincolnshire) an early charter of William's.[4] But he must soon have gone into exile, for we find him among those who landed in the Humber in 1069 to join in the siege and storm of York. Although the seat of his power was in Lincolnshire and Yorkshire, another portion of his great possessions lay in Somerset, Devon and Cornwall. Apart from his distinctive name we have clear proof of identity in the fact that the whole of the estates of Ralf Paynel in Somerset and Devon had previously belonged to Mærleswegen, and that Ralf was also Mærleswegen's successor in his *mansio* at Lincoln itself and in his Lincolnshire lands. Of this great noble's Somerset estates four manors, which are not found in the hands of Ralf Paynel, were secured by Walter de Douai, while the only other had been annexed to the king's manor of South Petherton.

In the absence of a distinctive name or of a definite succession the identification of English thegns is apt to be rash work. On the one hand, the Domesday scribes were loose in the spelling of their names ;

---

[1] ' Vocabatur is Ednodus, domi belloque Anglorum temporibus juste insignis, pater Herdingi qui adhuc superest.' *Gesta Regum* (Rolls series) 313.

[2] See *Feudal England*, p. 330.

[3] Mr. Eyton says ' three,' but in the Camerton estate, which he had given in exchange to Glastonbury, Edmer had also been his predecessor.

[4] The *Commune of London*, pp. 29-30.

on the other, the student may confuse names which are wholly distinct. There can, virtually, for instance be no question that the Alverd, Aelvert, or Ailvert, who was Roger Arundel's predecessor in four Somerset manors was also the Alvert, Ailvert, or Aielvert who preceded him in three Dorset ones. Nor need we hesitate to see in him the 'Æilferth Minister' who was a witness, as Mr. Eyton points out, to Edward the Confessor's grant of Ashwick to Wulfwold, abbot of Bath in 1061.[1] But when that writer treats the 'Alward,' 'Elward,' and 'Olward' of Domesday as variants of his name, nay, when he further identifies him with Ælfred (*Aluredus*) sheriff of Dorset and lord of Lulworth before the Conquest,[2] it is time to call a halt. Again, when he suggests that 'Aluredus', a 'dapifer' of Queen Edith, who had held of her at Tiverton (Twerton), may have been the 'Alvered or Alverd' who held Bathwick, as a king's thegn in 1086 (and, similarly, before the Conquest), and also with 'Alured,' who held of Count Eustace,[3] it becomes necessary to point out that this last was no other than the well known Alvred (*Aluredus*) of Marlborough, a tenant-in-chief in six counties.

But with Tofig the sheriff at least we stand on sure ground. Not only before the Conquest, but even after, he acted as sheriff of Somerset. Mr. Freeman made him sheriff 'between 1061 and 1066,'[4] but he also, as Mr. Eyton points out, was the 'Tong (i.e. Tovig) Minister' who appears among the witnesses to the charter by which King William, in the summer of 1068, restored Banwell to the church of Wells.[5] And, one may add, he is actually the sheriff to whom King William addresses the charter by which he restored Winsham to Giso and the church of Wells.[6] His lands in Somerset were at Keynsham,[7] Buckland St. Mary, Bradon, Capland, Freshford, Discove in Bruton, Berkley and Lopen. Most of them are found at the time of the Survey in the hands of Harding of Merriott, the son of Eadnoth the Staller.

Tofig's Norman successor, at the time of the Domesday Survey, was that William de Moion whose seat and successors are the subject of a learned monograph.[8] We are here chiefly concerned with him as sheriff. Although the Survey gives us but indirect information on the county's administration and finance, I have here shown that William— in direct contradiction of Mr. Eyton's conclusion—was farming the royal demesne of Somerset in 1086.[9] He was also receiving and paying to the Crown—no earl having been appointed—the rent of the 'comital manors.'[10]

---

[1] *Somerset Domesday*, i. 155–6. [2] Ibid. [3] Ibid. 70, 85, 152.
[4] *Norm. Conq.* i. 769 (citing *Cod. Dipl.* iv. 171, 197, 199).
[5] *Somerset Domesday*, i. 80. [6] 10th Report *Hist. MSS.* iii. 29.
[7] Where he held under Queen Edith.
[8] *Dunster and its Lords*, by Sir H. C. Maxwell Lyte, K.C.B. [9] See p. 396 above.
[10] This we only learn from their entries in the Exeter Domesday. Mr. Eyton observes (i. 79) that ' with the exception of Bruneton (the exception probably being only an omitted statement) all the Comital Manors and Comital Dues were under the custody and responsibility of William.' But this remark should apply to Dulverton, the next manor on the list. Under Brompton (' Brunetone ') we read ' quando comes accepit,' which is not ' an omitted statement,' but (apparently) an error for ' quando vicecomes accepit.'

Dealing as we are here with administration and finance, one ought to say something of a difficult and obscure question, that of 'the third penny' (*tertius denarius*). In the adjoining county of Dorset we read under Puddletown, a comital manor which Harold had held: 'Huic etiam manerio Piretone adjacet tercius denarius de tota scira Dorsete.' Here we seem to recognize what is afterwards familiar as 'the earl's third penny,' that is the third part of the profit from the pleas (*placita*) of the shire.[1] But in Somerset the entries are perplexing. Under (King's) Brompton—which had been held by Harold's mother Ghida, and which heads the Comital Manors—we read that it no longer receives, as it used to do, the third penny of Milverton, a manor which had reverted to the king on Queen Edith's death. A little lower down, under Old Cleeve, which had been held by Harold, we have the puzzling entry: 'Huic Manerio adjacuit tercius denarius de Burgherist ${et \atop de}$ Caretone et Willetone et Cantetone et Nortpereth.' We distinguish the names of two units of royal demesne (1) Carhampton, Williton, and Cannington; (2) North Petherton; but what are we to make of 'Burgherist'? We have seen, under Taunton, that this term, as 'burgeristh,' remains as yet obscure to us; nor are scholars likely to accept Mr. Eyton's ingenuous view that it was 'burglary,' and connoted the *Placita Coronæ*.[2]

We must, I think, distinguish carefully the 'third penny' spoken of above and associated with rural manors[3] from that which Domesday, as I read it, associates only with the local boroughs. Nor do they differ only in the character of the places from which the payments are due; they differ also in that the latter is not due to a comital manor. Mr. Eyton, it is true, reckons as appurtenant to Henstridge the third penny of six towns,[4] a due which the record enters by itself; but in spite of this he, quite justly, pointed out reasons for doubting whether it was so appurtenant. The fact that, as we shall now see, it was distinctively burghal is further ground for rejecting that view.

In boroughs, or—to speak with more precision—in towns of a burghal character, Somerset appears in Domesday exceptionally rich. But the line of division between the manor and the nucleus of a rising town is here so difficult to draw that students of the Survey may well differ in the classifications they adopt. Mr. Eyton, Professor Maitland,[5] and Mr. Ballard[6] have each their own.

We may well start from that simple list which Domesday itself suggests. Standing by itself is the 'borough' of Bath, which was in the king's hands in 1086, and of which Edward the sheriff (of Wilts) was paying him 'the third penny.' Next to it would come the group

[1] *Geoffrey de Mandeville*, p. 287.   [2] Op. cit. i. 80.

[3] This is a carefully guarded phrase, because the Domesday entries do not actually tell us the source of the due.

[4] Op. cit. i. 52, 84; ii. 4.   [5] *Domesday Book and Beyond.*   [6] *The Domesday Boroughs.*

DOMESDAY SURVEY

of six places of which Domesday shows us William the sheriff (of Somerset) paying 'the third penny' to the king; these are Ilchester, Milborne Port, Bruton, Langport, Axbridge and Frome. All the six have 'burgesses' in Domesday [1] except Frome, which, however, has a market. Lastly we have Taunton, where all the burgesses belonged to its sole lord, the bishop of Winchester.

Mr. Eyton practically adopted this classification, but more recent students appear to have rejected it. Professor Maitland, after mentioning Ilchester and Bath, proceeds :—

Axbridge, Langport, and Milborne seem to be boroughs. Axbridge and Langport occur in that list of ancient fortresses which we have called the Burghal Hidage. Wells was an episcopal, Somerton a royal manor; we have no reason for calling either of them a borough.[2]

Mr. Ballard constructs a definite list, consisting of six 'composite' boroughs—Axbridge, Bath, Bruton, Ilchester, Milborne, Langport, and one simple borough Taunton.[3] To the mint as a test of burghal rank he has given special attention, and he points out that while Domesday speaks of mints at Bath and Taunton,[4] there are coins from pre-Conquest mints at Bath, Bruton, Ilchester and Langport.[5] But neither at Axbridge nor at Milborne is there any trace of a mint, while at Somerton, which was not a borough, there is.[6] On the whole his own evidence would seem to 'prove,' not 'that a mint was a necessary factor in the making of a borough,' but that it was not; for Milborne Port was a market town, as its name implies, and ranked, in the number of its burgesses, easily third among the towns of Somerset. Frome was probably on the border line between manor and market town.

A feature which has struck all students is that, while in Dorset to the south Domesday places four towns all by themselves at the head of the Survey, it does not accord this distinction to any town in Somerset. Mr. Eyton, in his chapter dealing with 'the royal burghs of Somerset,' wrote :—

The Burghs of Dorset were, doubtless, Royal Burghs; but they were distinct, and they were kept distinct in Domesday from the estates of Ancient Crown-Demesne. . . . But in Somerset, where every Burgh, except Bath, was but a mere appendage of some estate of Ancient Demesne, no such distinction could be made, and certainly none was attempted by the Domesday Commissioners.[7]

Again, Professor Maitland writes :—

If we compare the first page of the survey of Somerset with the first pages that are devoted to its two neighbours, Dorset and Devon, we shall probably come to the conclusion that the compilers of the book scrupled to put any Somerset vill on a par with Exeter, Dorchester, Bridport, Wareham and Shaftesbury.[8]

Mr. Ballard similarly notes that at the head of the Somerset survey there is only 'a blank space,'[9] which contrasts with Dorset. It is no

Bruton is credited with only five burgesses under *Terra Regis*, but Turstin son of Rolf had also eleven burgesses there appurtenant to his manor of Pitcombe adjoining it.

[2] Op. cit. p. 215. [3] Op. cit. p. 9. [4] Ibid. p. 77. [5] Ibid. p. 119. [6] Ibid. p. 120,
[7] *Somerset Domesday*, i. 49. [8] Op. cit. p. 177. [9] Ibid. p. 5.

doubt the case that the infant towns of Somerset were smaller than those of Dorset. With the exception of Bath, Ilchester was much the largest, having 108 burgesses; and these were fewer than those of Bridport, the smallest of the Dorset towns. Yet Malmesbury in the neighbouring county of Wiltshire is assigned the distinctive position at the head, although its burgesses were considerably fewer than those of Ilchester. We can also, I think, detect in Domesday the beginning of a Somerset town of which I have not yet spoken. This is Yeovil, of which we read that to William d'Eu's manor of Yeovil there had been 'added' twenty-two messuages (*masuræ*[1]), formerly held *pariter* by the men who dwelt in them. Obscure as is the previous status, we have clearly here the nucleus of a town which is unmentioned by the writers I have named, but of which the twenty-two householders compare not unworthily with the thirty-four burgesses of Langport, the thirty-two of Axbridge, or the seventeen of Bruton. It was not size alone that gave a town its importance. Nor indeed is size the test that Professor Maitland himself selects. That test he finds in 'tenurial heterogeneity,' that is to say in the fact that the burgesses do not all hold of one lord.[2] But when we apply this test to the Somerset and Dorset boroughs we find that this 'heterogeneity' is wholly absent at Bridport, a borough which Domesday emphatically places 'above the line,' while Bath, which stands below it, is 'a good example,' as Mr. Ballard observes,[3] of 'tenurial heterogeneity.' Other Somerset towns, as he says, display this feature, although obscurely entered as part of the *Terra Regis*.

This is perhaps the most important point about the Somerset boroughs, for it suggests that the compilers of Domesday Book—with that lack of system and love of variety which seems to us so strange—may after all have had no definite practice as to the placing of boroughs 'above' or 'below' the line.[4] Mr. Eyton found the distinction in the fact that the Somerset boroughs were 'interned' in groups of royal demesne, while the Dorset ones occupied a wholly different and independent position. But I have maintained that this view was wholly mistaken, and that Dorchester and Bridport, for instance, formed part, much as did Ilchester and Milborne Port, of a royal demesne group.[5]

The most important element, the centre of life, in these little towns was the market. Its value is not always recorded, but that of Ilchester, 'with its appurtenances,' was worth £11 a year, that of Frome £2 6s. 8d., and that of Taunton £2 10s. Crewkerne, although apparently only a rural manor, had a market worth £4 a year, while that of Milverton was worth ten shillings. Ilminster market brought in twenty shillings. The mention of eight smiths at Glastonbury hints at a small iron industry, of which plough-shares, probably, would be the

1 The Exeter Domesday calls them *masuræ terræ*.
2 Op. cit. pp. 178–182. 3 Op. cit. p. 7.
4 This conclusion would be parallel with my rejection of Mr. Maitland's view that Domesday employs *manerium* in a highly specialized sense, and my demonstration that *manerium* and *terra* were used interchangeably. Cf. p. 430 below.
5 *Feudal England*, pp. 113–4.

chief product. But ironstone would not be found in the lias of the Polden hills.[1] Nor can we connect with ironstone districts the curious dues in unwrought iron entered in the county. In the south, near Crewkerne, we have mention at Seaborough, Cricket St. Thomas, and Bickenhall, of a due from each free man of a 'bloom' of iron[2]; at Alford, near Castle Cary, eight such 'blooms' are receivable from 'the villeins'; and at (White) Staunton, on the Devonshire border, four 'blooms' are due in respect of 50 acres of pasture. Lexworthy (in Enmore) appears to be the only place where Domesday speaks of *plumbæ ferri*; its three mills rendered between them four of these *plumbæ*.

In Somerset, as in other counties at this early period, agriculture was the dominant occupation; the field and the meadow, the woodland and the stream, were the paramount sources of wealth.

Like that volume of Domesday Book which deals with the three Eastern counties, the Exeter book records the number of the live stock on the manors, which, although comprised, it is believed, in the original returns throughout the country, are omitted in the digest thereof in the larger volume of Domesday. The abstracts in this larger volume are concerned only with the plough-oxen, the teams of which were accounted the most important element in the agricultural system. Mr. Eyton, in his short, but very useful section on 'farming stock,'[3] tells us that the plough-teams in the county were notably fewer than the plough-lands :—

> The numerical inadequacy of the teams-in-stock to the plough-lands, specified to be available, was more constant in Somerset than in Dorset.

But the subject of this relation and of its actual meaning is still for Domesday students one of notorious difficulty.[4]

In a table constructed to show the proportion of plough-teams to other live stock for those counties in which we have material for such comparison, Professor Maitland selects these figures for Somerset :

Teams.	Beasts not of the plough.	Horses.	Goats.	Pigs.	Sheep.
202	82	16	49	198	1,506

But partial figures such as these prove nothing. Even the figures for a whole county may be in practice misleading, for the proportion would naturally vary in different districts. Swine we should expect in the woodlands; sheep are associated with marshlands; and cows we look for in the meadows down in the river valleys.

Very interesting in the records of the Survey are the wild (*silvaticæ*) or unbroken (*indomitæ*) brood-mares, a class of stock not mentioned above, though met with frequently enough in Somerset.

[1] It is to be observed, however, that Glastonbury Abbey obtained much iron from its manor of Pucklechurch on the other side of Bristol.

[2] Said to have been a four-square mass of iron about two feet long.

[3] Op. cit. i. 44.

[4] See Professor Maitland's *Domesday Book and Beyond*, pp. 410 et. sq., especially p. 424, where he observes that 'as we pass through the southern counties from east to west, the ratio borne by the team-lands to the teams steadily increases.'

The valuable tables of the Hundreds so laboriously constructed by Mr. Eyton tempt us to see whether it is possible to localize, through their mention, the industry of horse-breeding in the county. Certainly in and about the Hundred of Bempstone—that is between the Mendips and the mouth of the Parret—these mares are often mentioned ; we read of them at Wedmore (6), Tarnock in Badgworth (8), Burnham and Highbridge (12), Huntspill (6 + 14), and we also find them at Stoke Rodney (20). On the other hand, it seems to me that Mr. Eyton is right in holding that horse-breeding depended on the barons who held the fief. 'The bishop of Coutances,' he writes, ' the Comte of Moretain, and William of Moione were the chiefs who seem most to have encouraged this class of stock.' Analysis shows that the bishop is credited with about 130 mares, of which he kept 60 at Long Ashton alone. The Count's chief stud was at Cloford, near Frome, where he had 38, besides 34 elsewhere. That of William de Moiun was at Cutcombe, south-west of Dunster, where his mares were 39 in addition to 7 in Luccombe and 22 at Brewham. The bishop of Wells and the abbot of Glastonbury also did a little horse-breeding.

Milch-cows, as Mr. Eyton says, are not so often mentioned ' as to indicate that the county was to become famous for its dairy farms.' At Cheddar, it is true, we read of one cow only, but at Winscombe, north of the hills, there seem to have been sixteen. It is not, however, at all certain, in my opinion, that cows were not sometimes among the 'animalia,' which we can only translate as cattle. The entries of one cow are, I think, significant, as suggesting that it was kept for the use of the lord of the manor. Of cheese there is hardly any mention, nor were cows needed for it then, as ewes' milk was largely employed.[1]

Horses—as distinct from brood mares—are divided, Mr. Eyton writes, into two classes, *caballi* and *roncini*. Of the former, the riding horses, from whose name is derived the Spanish *caballero* (cavalier), 'Alured of Spain,'[2] he asserts, 'had a stock.' The reference is, I find, to the abbot of Glastonbury's fief, on which, at Woolavington, Alured had 'xiii caballos' *inter alia*. But the phrase is interlined, and over it is written the word 'roncinos,'[3] so that even this occurrence is open to question. The *roncini*—Chaucer's 'rounceys'—were most probably pack-horses, specially useful where the roads were few or bad.

The ewe-sheep, says Mr. Eyton, were 'common to nearly all Somerset estates,' and the she-goats ' more frequent in, but not peculiar to, the hill districts.' The large number of she-goats recorded at the Survey may come as a surprise to those who forget the important part they still play in lands where cows' milk is scarce or unprocurable.[4] The kid would be valued for its skin and its flesh, but milk would be the product of the goat.

The swine were fattened in the woodlands on the mast. In Somerset, as in Devon, the swineherds are a feature, the great majority

---

[1] *V.C.H. Essex*, i. 371.   [2] I have never accepted this rendering of ' de Ispania.'
[3] Exon Domesday, p. 149.   [4] *V.C.H. Essex*, i. 368-9.

of those entered in Domesday Book being found in these counties. To the king's manor of North Petherton no fewer than twenty swineherds contributed between them five pounds ; at King's Brompton fifteen of them paid thirty-five shillings ; and at East Coker ten swine were payable by the swineherd. Again, 'in William de Moione's forestal manor of Cutcombe six *Porcarii* paid an annual rent of thirty-one hogs.'[1] It was ingeniously suggested by Mr. Eyton that, comparing the payment at North Petherton with the render in kind of five swine, to the King, by the Bruton swineherd, the commuted value of a fat hog was one shilling. But this was only a 'surmise,' and cannot be taken for more.

The moorlands, which have always formed so prominent a feature of Somerset, and of which so many traces are preserved in its local nomenclature were, of course, far more extensive at the time of the great survey. But as they were of little or no value, Domesday was not much concerned with these *moræ*, as it terms them. Mr. Eyton points out, for instance, that at Wedmore the Exeter book speaks of moors which are worth nothing, and which Domesday Book ignores. In the north-east, 'moors' are mentioned in districts liable to inundation, at Yatton and Weston-in-Gordano. We read of them also to the south of Bridgwater, at Newton Huntworth and Edgeborough, to its west at Spaxton, and again, north of this, at Fiddington. A considerable moor which is entered at Wells would probably, as at Wedmore, be undrained land ; but that which is spoken of at Milborne Port in the south-east of the county may have been of a different character.

Meadow-land (*pratum*) that was mown for hay was a possession of some value, but pasture (*pastura*) occupied an indeterminate position between profitable and worthless land. The water-mills and (weir) 'fisheries' in the streams need not detain us, save for the solitary mention of ten fishermen (*piscatores*) at Glastonbury. The three vineyards, in the heart of the county at Glastonbury, Pamborough, and Meare, were doubtless introduced by Thurstan, the innovating abbot, together with his Norman archers. But there were also seven acres of vineyard at North Curry and a small one at Muchelney on the demesne. At Langport there is mention of a garden (*ortus*) from which the singular due was 50 eels, a render more suggestive of a 'fishery.'

Of the agricultural classes the most noteworthy are ' the small but interesting class of *coliberti*,'[2] otherwise styled in Domesday *buri* or burs. Professor Maitland deemed them 'distinctly superior to the *servi*, but distinctly inferior to the villeins, bordiers and cottiers.'[3] They are found in a group of counties extending from Buckinghamshire and from Shropshire to Cornwall, and in Somerset are fairly numerous, 218 being entered, as against 32 in Devon and 33 in Dorset, though in Wiltshire there are 260, and in Gloucestershire 103.[4] No fewer

---

[1] Eyton, op. cit. i. 43.   [2] *Domesday Book and Beyond*, p. 36.   [3] Ibid. 28, 36.
[4] These figures are taken from Ellis' *Introduction to Domesday*.

than 150 of those in Somerset are found on the King's manors, and here, it should be observed, they are systematically entered after the serfs and, like them, as belonging to the lord's demesne.[1] Indeed, at Frome, where there were no serfs, while there were six coliberts to the three demesne teams, I suspect that they took the place of the serfs in their normal proportion of two to each demesne team. Another interesting class are the holders by a money rent, the seven *gabulatores* who pay between them, at Cheddar, seventeen shillings. For this would seem to be their only mention by that name in Domesday.

We may now turn to the remaining point deserving of comment in this county.

The Domesday Survey brought to light in various parts of the country wholesale encroachments on the king's manors by the great barons and their vassals. His own reeves, at times, proved but unfaithful stewards, though they sometimes added to the king's demesno the small estates of private men, probably hoping to 'farm,' thereby, a larger area without having to pay a larger sum to the Crown.

Thus from Somerton, which stands at the head of the *Terra Regis*, half a hide had been filched by Alvred 'de Hispania,' while the estates (*terræ*) of three thegns had added five and a half hides to the manor. It is one more illustration of the lack of system in Domesday that, although Alvred's encroachment on Somerton is recorded under that royal manor, his similar diminution of (North) Petherton by the lands he had obtained at Wolmersdon and West Bower is recorded not under that royal manor, but under his own fief. In each case the land had been secured by 'Alwi,' his predecessor in title ; and in that of Wolmersdon, at least, Domesday records that the (king's) reeve had lent (*prestitit*) the land to Alwi in King Edward's time, reminding us that the king's interests might thus suffer loss even before the Conquest.

The king was even robbed of lands and dues by his own greedy brother, the Count of Mortain. From King's Brompton he had annexed a hide at Torrels Preston, 'quæ fuit de dominica firma.' Here we have a good instance of these double entries in Domesday, which are often so instructive.[2]

Rex tenet BRUNETONE. Ghida tenuit T.R.E. . . . De hoc manerio tenet Comes Morit' i. hidam in PRESTETUNE, quæ fuit de dominica firma T.R.E. Terra est iiii. car. Ibi sunt ii. car. Valet xl. sol. et valuit (86b).

Robertus tenet de Comite in PRESTITONE i. hidam. Hanc tenuit Heraldus Comes. Terra est iiii. car. In dominio est dim. car. cum i. servo et vi. vill. et ii. bord. cum ii. car. . . . Valet et valuit xxx. sol. Hæc terra jacuit in BURNETONE M[anerio] regis cum firma (92).

Now what are we to say of such a case as this ? Here are two entries describing the same estate, differing not only in their whole

---

[1] Professor Maitland shows that this was not so everywhere, and indeed, under Taunton the arrangement is somewhat different.

[2] Compare p. 408 above.

arrangement, but in the valuation past and present, in the number of ploughs upon the land, and in the name of the previous holder.[1]

It is clear surely that these entries cannot be taken from a common original; and yet how can there have been more originals than one? The answer, I take it, is that the entry found under the Count's fief is derived from the general return, while the entry under *Terra Regis* is derived from a special and separate return—*breve regis?*—made for the king's land. This conclusion is strongly supported by the fact that in the only transcripts of original returns which have come down to us, the entries for the king's manors are wanting.[2]

Let us see if the Exeter Domesday helps us. Under the Count of Mortain's fief we have, as usual, a slightly fuller entry, which expands the name of Robert into Robert son of Ivo, who was the Count's constable.[3] But in the entry of King's Brompton we have a far more important addition; for we there read that the hide at Preston was held of the Count by Hugh de Valletort![4] Here we have a really flagrant contradiction in addition to those already discovered in the text of the Exchequer Domesday.[5] If I am right in suggesting two independent returns, all the contradictions become explicable. And this suggestion is remarkably supported by the fact that King's Brompton appears in the Exchequer Domesday as 'Brunetone' under the King's land, and 'Burnetone' under the Count's, while it is similarly in the Exeter Domesday 'Brunetona' under the King's land (pp. 94, 474), and 'Burnetona' under the Count's (pp. 252, 478). This would appear to prove that the name was spelt differently in two independent returns.

The entries relating to the annexation of Eastham by the Count from the king's manor of Crewkerne, formerly Edith's, and its tenure under him by Turstin present no contradiction, but this is not inconsistent with the theory of two returns; and other entries of aggression under 'Terra Regis' are difficult, if not impossible, to discover on the fiefs of the alleged aggressors.

The alteration of the king's manors by the processes of accretion and diminution[6] find their parallels on the manors in private hands. Thus, for instance, William de Moiun had secured the valuable manor of Brewham, which had been held by Robert Fitz Wimarc the Staller, one of the Confessor's favourites;[7] but it had suffered diminution by

---

[1] For the record distinguishes carefully under 'Terra Regis' between Harold and his mother 'Ghida,' as previous holders; and as she survived the Conquest, they were both living on the day of King Edward's death, when they are both, we see, alleged to have held it. Possibly Ghida held it for life only, as dower, the land being Harold's eventually.

[2] See, for instance, *Inquisitio comitatus Cantabrigiensis* (Ed. Hamilton), p. 6.

[3] Mr. Eyton suggests that he was constable of Montacute Castle, and observes that he was ancestor of the house of Beauchamp of Hatch Beauchamp (i. 97, 140).

[4] 'Modo tenet eam hugo de valle torta de moritonensi comite' (p. 95).

[5] Mr. Eyton had duly noted this and the other contradictions, but could only make the awkward suggestion that the two entries may have related to two different hides, of which one was overlooked under King's Brompton. This, of course, would not explain the difference in the names of the previous holder of Brompton, on which he rightly insists.

[6] Compare the gains and losses of the Bishop of Winchester's lordship of Taunton (p. 401 above).

[7] He was succeeded as sheriff of Essex by his son Swegen, a great Domesday baron. His other and less valuable Somerset manor had passed to the Count of Mortain.

the subtraction of Witham, which Domesday, it should be noted, reckons in one place as two, and in another as three hides, and which, though inalienable from Brewham, had been grabbed by Roger 'de Corcelle.'[1] On the other hand the Brewham estate had been increased by the addition of three virgates which Almar, an Englishman, had held. All these cases speak of the confusion that accompanied the Conquest and of the need for such a check as must have been supplied by the compilation of the Survey.

The curious customary dues withheld from the king's manors are by no means consistently entered. Under South Petherton, a manor of ancient Crown demesne, we read that Cricket St. Thomas (a six-hide manor), held by Turstin of the Count of Mortain, had failed to pay its annual due of six ewes and lambs and a 'bloom' of iron from each free man since the count obtained that estate. It heads the account of his own fief, but there is nothing there of this liability. So too, Dulverton, one of Harold's manors, which was held by the king, was entitled, we read, to 24 sheep a year from Brushford, which was held from the count by Mauger, who withheld that due 'per comitem.' Under Brushford itself there is no mention of this due. Yet conversely, on the count's fief, the very next manor (also held by Mauger) is entered as owing a customary due to the king's manor of Curry. The same is recorded of six other estates on the same page, the due being always a ewe and lamb for a hide,[2] save in one instance, where a money payment suggests that the commuted value of the ewe and lamb was sixpence. Here the point is that there is no mention of this due under Curry itself. The same remark applies to the bishop of Salisbury's manor of Seaborough, in the account of which we read that it had been appurtenant to Edith's manor of Crewkerne, now the king's, from which its holder could not separate it, and to which he owed the customary due of twelve sheep with as many lambs, and from each free man a 'bloom' of iron.[3] But under Crewkerne itself there is no mention of this.

So, again, Ralf de Limesi is charged, under his own fief, with withholding 12 sheep a year due from his own manor of Allerford (in Selworthy) to the King's manor of Carhampton, though under the latter manor we hear nothing of that due. Exactly the same remark applies to Ralf de Pomerei's manor of Oare, lying near it in the wild north-western corner of the county. It had similarly been held by Edric, and owed the same due, which was similarly withheld.

As against these withdrawals of dues we find, under *Terra Regis*, the statement that there has been added to Williton an annual due

---

[1] Under William's fief the assessment is given as 3 hides, and under Roger's as 2 hides, the unjust transference being noted in both entries. I have found similar suggestive instances of Domesday's carelessness, but in this case we can correct its figures by the Exeter Domesday, which gives 2 hides in all its three entries (pp. 342, 407, 484).

[2] In one instance the due of a bloom of iron from each free man is mentioned in addition.

[3] 'jacuerunt in Cruche, M[anerio] regis, et qui tenebant inde non poterant separari, et reddebant in Cruche xii oves cum agnis et unam bloma ferri de unoquoque libero homine,'

from a manor of Alvred (de Hispania), which was not due in King Edward's day. One would expect to find complaint of this under that manor itself, but we find there nothing.

Apart from the record of the Taunton franchise there is singularly little in Somerset to illustrate legal antiquities ; but the phrase ' lord of the manor' (*dominus manerii*) occurs under Congresbury and Henstridge among Harold's lands. There are also two notable entries—one of them marginal—of estates, held by Robert de ' Odburvile.' The first of these relates to Withypoole, of which we read that Robert used to contribute in respect of it twenty shillings towards the revenue derived from the king's manor of Winsford, but that now it has been proved to be ' thegnland' (*diratiocinata est in tainland*) which had been held by Harold's brother (Tostig). Under Winsford itself we find another entry of this estate, which is there admitted to have been an addition (*addita*), but of which the retrocession and Robert's tenure are alike ignored ! Moreover, its three former holders are described as ' thegns,' not as ' foresters.' It is, further, explained that they used to render customary service to the reeve of Winsford, but gave him no rent (*absque omni firma donante*). Again, there is the marginal entry of Robert's nameless land, which it will be well to collate with the text of the Exeter book.

EXCHEQUER.	EXETER.
Hic Robertus habuit unam virgatam terræ quam tenebat Dodo libere T.R.E. Hec addita fuit Dolvertone manerio Regis. Modo dijudicata est esse tainland. Valet x. sol.	Rodbertus de Odburvilla habuit i. virgam terre quam tenuit Dodo pariter . . . . Hec addita fuit mansioni Regis que vocatur Dolvertona. Modo iterum dijudicata est esse Teglanda et valet per annum x. sol.

Here we have the *libere pariter* equation, both terms, evidently, excluding subjection to the manor of Dulverton. And, as in the preceding case, we find the law strong enough, or King William just enough, to secure the restoration of the land to its former free status, when that status had been proved. I do not, however, follow Mr. Eyton's observation that ' there are many similar appearances in Domesday of recent question and settlement of De Auberville's estates and position,'[1] for I cannot find Robert as a holder of land elsewhere than in Somerset.

The marriage portion may be said to occur in connexion with Serlo de Burci, for he, who had given with one of his daughters a manor when she became a nun, gave to another, on her marrying William de Falaise, the manor from which Woodspring Priory, in after days, derived its name.[2]

Cases of equally divided vills are always deserving of notice ; of such vills Puckington is an instance. It is the subject of two consecutive entries, of which each records an assessment of $1\frac{1}{2}$ hides, which in each was apportioned alike, viz. $1\frac{1}{8}$ hide on the demesne, and $\frac{3}{8}$ hide on the rest. Each portion had 6 acres of pasture and 66 of woodland and one

---

[1] Op. cit. i. 202.

[2] Burcy lay some thirty miles west of Falaise. For the Somerset manors and descendants of William de Falaise see the Eton College muniments calendared in 9th Report *Historical MSS. Com.* App. i. 353-5.

and a half ploughlands, while the only difference was in the acreage of meadow and in the number of peasants and their ploughs. All this points to Puckington having been one, and subsequently divided into two moieties, probably by two brothers. At the Conquest it was once more thrown into one manor by Roger 'de Corcelle', to whom both moieties had been granted.

The language in which Domesday describes this operation has an important bearing on its use of the term 'manor.' Prof. Maitland held that Domesday employs it as 'a technical term' . . . 'an accurate term charged with legal meaning.' If the words 'pro manerio' were added to 'tenuit,' this, he urged, distinguished the tenure and imparted a special meaning. As against this view I have been able to show that the terms *manerium* and *terra* were used indifferently, and that the addition of 'pro manerio' made no difference to the meaning.[1]

Now of the two Puckington entries in the Exchequer text the first has simply 'Leving tenuit' and does not speak of 'manor,' yet the second refers to it as 'huic manerio.' In the second we read 'Alward tenuit pro manerio,' and yet Domesday proceeds at once to speak of these two 'manors' as 'has ii *terras*.' In the Exeter text, on the other hand, the word 'mansio' (i.e. manor) is found not only in both the entries, but also in the rider, which runs 'has ii *mansiones*.' The perfect indifference with which Domesday employed or omitted the word is thus made manifest.

To the genealogist the Exeter text is a record of the greatest value; for it enables us at times to identify those of whom the Exchequer text gives us but the Christian names. From it, for instance, we obtain the surnames of such men as William d'Aumary (*de Almereio*), Richer d'Andeli, Bernard Pauncevolt, Britel de St. Clair, and Walter and William Hussey (*Hosatus*). From it also we learn the distinctive names of some Englishmen, such as Ælfwine 'Banneson,' whom we could not otherwise trace. Again, the Beatrice, who holds of Ralf de 'Pomerei' at Nether Stowey is entered in the Exeter book as Ralf's sister. Mr. Eyton pointed out that she also held of him a Devon manor, while she further held in that county two of William 'Capra,' who is similarly entered as her brother. On the strength of this he asserted that Ralph and William were brothers,[2] and although this may seem not absolutely clear, it is interesting to note that Roger 'Capra' and William his son were benefactors, in the next generation, to the Pommeraye abbey of St. Mary Du Val.[3]

Ralf, though of small account in Somerset, was a great man across its western border. Coming, as his name reminds us, from among the apple orchards of Normandy to make his home amidst those of Devon, he left his castle of La Pommeraye to gain a mightier lordship, and to found that rock fortress, in the heart of English woodlands, which still preserves his name in that of Berry Pomeroy.

[1] *Eng. Hist. Review*, xv. 293–302. Cf. p. 422, note 4 above. [2] *Somerset Domesday*, i. 64.
[3] *Cal. of Docs. France*, 536.

More famous, if less enduring, is the name of Ranulf Flambard, who held at Woodwick in Freshford under the abbot of Bath.

It is always a matter of considerable interest when we can identify in Domesday serjeanties which meet us in the records of the 13th century. Wigborough, for instance, in South Petherton is one of the six estates held in Domesday by John the Usher (*Hostiarius*) among the king's serjeants. And in 1212[1] Helen, holder of the ushership, is returned as holding Wigborough with her other lands in Somerset by usher-service.[2]

Long as this introduction may seem, it would be far longer if space permitted of discussing in detail the returns for the Hundreds to 'the geld-inquest,' as Mr. Eyton styles it. With infinite labour and patience he brought together in his work the entries in these returns and those in the Domesday Survey. To that work, therefore, the reader is referred should he desire to study this aspect of the Survey. Space also does not allow of discussing the relative merits of the Exeter and Exchequer texts or of the genesis of the former and the object with which it was compiled.

We may sometimes be called upon to make our choice between the readings of the Exeter and of the Exchequer Domesday. A notable case in point is discussed in my *Feudal England* (pp. 425–6), where I have urged that Richard the interpreter claimed to have bought (*emit*), not held (*tenuit*) Road from Reinbald the priest and chancellor. This involves our rejecting the Exchequer text's *tenuit*, but one may point out that, if it were not for the 't,' 'emit' and 'enuit' might very easily be confused by the scribe. It is held by some that the Exeter text is the more exact as well as the fuller, and although the errors of its rival cannot be of much consequence, it is possible that their view is right.

It has already been observed that lack of system in dealing with encroachments on the King's lands, as also on those of others, is a weak point in the Exchequer text.[3] Mr. Eyton claimed for the Exon text superiority in this respect, because it groups together such aggressions as 'Terræ occupatæ in Sumerseta' (pp. 471–489). But although it is convenient to have them thus brought together, there is no attempt at arranging them in any order, the lands of the King and of his subjects being mixed up in hopeless confusion.

Without entering on the many problems raised by the Exeter book[4] attention should be drawn to one of its features by which students, I think, have been misled. Its normal system of grouping estates is to deal in

[1] *The Commune of London*, p. 276.

[2] 'Elena Hostiaria tenet Wigeberga et alias terras suas in Sumerset per hostiaritatem de domino Rege' (*Testa de Nevill*, 162, cf. pp. 170, 173, and p. 171, where the serjeanty is defined as 'per quam debuit esse hostiarius Magne Aule per totum annum').

[3] p. 426 above.

[4] For the construction of its text the student may consult the Rev. T. W. Whale's paper on 'the history of the Exon Domesday' in the *Transactions of the Devonshire Association* (xxxvii. 246–283), which was only published after this Introduction was in type. Mr. Whale, who has enjoyed special facilities for examining the original MS., has there given useful tables of its contents, with notes on their original and later order.

turn with those of each tenant or class (1) under Devon (2) under Somerset. Thus we find grouped together :—

> Terræ Francorum militum (*sic*) in Devenesira.
> Terræ Francorum tegnorum (*sic*) in Sumersete Syra (pp. 421–433).
> Terræ servientium regis in Devenesira.
> Terræ servientium regis in Summerseta (pp. 439–445).
> Terræ Anglorum tegnorum in Devenesira.
> Terræ Anglorum tegnorum in Sumersetæ syra (pp. 445–457).

Here we have the origin of the misconception dealt with above.[1] The 'Anglo-thegns,' as writers on Devon and Somerset portions of Domesday call them, are the only true thegns, and are rightly recognized as such in the Exchequer text. The Exeter text is here not even consistent; for its French 'thegns' of Somerset are French 'knights' in Devon. The one term is, if one may say so, no less absurd than the other. For among the so-called ' knights ' in Devon is no less a man than ' Richard, the son of Count Gilbert,' one of the mightiest of Domesday nobles and the founder of the house of Clare. Two other Domesday barons, Ralf Paynel and Ralf de Limesi, both of them lords of vast fiefs, are no less strangely here classed among the 'knights' of Devon and the 'thegns' of Somerset. Why they should have been selected from among their fellows for this treatment, and why their respective manors should be entered, not by themselves, but hotch-potch among those of smaller men, is one of the unsolved mysteries, as yet, of the ' Exon ' Book. All that can be said is that, here at least, the Exchequer volume appears to advantage, classing, as it does, these magnates among their fellows, and entering their manors under their names instead of making them masquerade as French 'knights' or French 'thegns.' It is greatly to be hoped that the 'Exon' Book will some day receive at the hands of a trained scholar the full and critical treatment of which it stands in need and which may yet reveal its character, its origin, and its object.

[1] p. 415.

NOTE

THE reader should bear in mind throughout that the date of the Domesday Survey is 1086; that King Edward, to whose time it refers as 'T. R. E.' i.e. ' *tempore Regis Edwardi*,' died January 5, 1066; that the 'hide' was the unit of assessment on which the (Dane) geld was paid; that its subdivisions were: the 'virgate,' one-quarter of the hide; the 'ferling' (farthing), one-quarter of the virgate; and the acre, of which 120 went to one hide. The 'demesne' was the lord's portion of the manor, the peasantry holding the rest under him.

The Rev. J. Collinson prefixed to his History of the County, published in 1791, a copy of the Exchequer Domesday, with an index giving the modern names of places. On the whole the index quite deserves the praise bestowed upon it by the Rev. R. W. Eyton in his *Analysis and Digest of the Somerset Survey (according to the Exon codex) and of the Geld Inquest of* 1084, 2 vols., 1880. In this latter work the manors are arranged under the Hundreds mainly by means of clues afforded by a close study of the Geld Inquest. The identifications include nearly every manor mentioned, and correct not a few of Collinson's suggestions. In 1899 the present writer printed (*Som. Arch. Proc.* XLV. ii. 51) an analysis of the Survey arranged to show the prevalence of manors, single or grouped, containing a unit or multiple of five hides. In working it out he availed himself of the immense mass of additional information contained in the Somerset Record Society's volumes, of articles in the *Som. and Dors. Notes and Queries*, as well as of the six-inch maps of the Ordnance Survey. In 1902, the Rev. T. W. Whale issued an analysis of the Exeter codex and the Geld Inquest. A number of the identifications in the following pages are based upon corrections made therein. But even now finality has not yet been reached. The sites of manors long since obsolete are brought to light quite unexpectedly, and references in early records, by enabling the descent of manors bearing the same name to be accurately distinguished, give clues which eventually carry back their history to Domesday.

HERE ARE ENTERED
THE HOLDERS OF LANDS
IN SUMMERSETE

N.B.—[ ] enclose modern names and identifications; ( ) enclose translator's additions; ' ' enclose matter found only in the Exeter Domesday, including variant spellings.

I	KING WILLIAM	XXV	William de Moion
II	The Bishop of Winchester	XXVI	William de Ow
III	The Bishop of Salisbury	XXVII	William de Faleise
IV	The Bishop of Bayeux	XXVIII	William son of Guy
V	The Bishop of Coutances	XXIX	Ralph de Mortemer
VI	The Bishop of Wells	XXX	Ralph de Pomerei
VII	The church of Bath	XXXI	Ralph Pagenel
VIII	The church of Glastonbury	XXXII	Ralph de Limesi
IX	The church of Muchelney	XXXIII	Robert son of Girold
X	The church of Athelney	XXXIV	Alvred de Marlborough
XI	The church of St. Peter at Rome	XXXV	Alvred de Ispania
		XXXVI	Turstin son of Rolf
XII	The church of Caen	XXXVII	Serlo de Burci
XIII	The church of Monteburg	XXXVIII	Odo son of Gamelin
XIV	The church of Shaftesbury	XXXIX	Osbern Gifard
XV	Bishop Maurice	XL	Edward de Salisbury
XVI	Clerks holding of the king	XLI	Ernulf de Hesding
XVII	Count Eustace	XLII	Gislebert son of Turold
XVIII	Earl Hugh	XLIII	Godebold
XIX	The Count of Mortain	XLIV	Matthew de Mortain
XX	Baldwin de Execestre	XLV	Humphrey the Chamberlain
XXI	Roger de Corcelle		
XXII	Roger Arundel	XLVI	Robert de Odburvile and other serjeants of the king
XXIII	Walter Gifard		
XXIV	Walter or Walscin de Dowai	XLVII	The king's thegns

THE KING'S LAND.

The king holds SUMMERTONE [Somerton]. King Edward held it. It never paid geld, nor is it known how many hides are there. There is land for 50 ploughs. In demesne there are 5 ploughs and 4 serfs, and (there are) 80 villeins and 28 bordars with 40 ploughs. 'There are 2 riding-horses, 9 swine and 500 sheep.' There are 100 acres of meadow, and pasture 1 league in length and half a league in breadth. Wood(land) 1 league long and 1 furlong broad.

There (is a borough) which is called LANPORTH, 'LANPORDA' [Langport], in which dwell 34[1] burgesses paying 15 shillings, and there are 2 fisheries paying 10 shillings.

It (Somerton) pays yearly 79 pounds 10 shillings 7 pence at 20 pence to the ounce.

[1] Exet. Dom. reads: '24.'

THE HOLDERS OF LANDS

To this manor are added 3 estates (*terræ*)[1] which 3 thegns, Brisnod, Alvric and Sawin, held 'in parage (*pariter*)' T.R.E.; and they paid geld for 5½ hides. There are 7 villeins and 5 bordars with 4 ploughs. They pay 7 pounds 15 shillings. 'Brisnod held one of these, and paid geld for 4 hides, which 4 ploughs could plough. It is worth yearly 100 shillings. Alvric held one estate which paid geld for 1 hide; now Ogisius holds it and pays yearly 25 shillings. Sawin held half a hide T.R.E. and still holds it, and has there 1 plough and pays yearly 30 shillings in the king's ferm.'

From this manor (Somerton) has been taken away half a hide at DENESMODESWELLE [²], which was (part) of the demesne ferm of King Edward. Alvred de Hispania holds it, and it is worth 10 shillings.

The king holds CEDRE [Cheddar]. King Edward held it. It never paid geld, nor is it known how many hides are there. There is land for 20 ploughs. In demesne there are 3 ploughs and 2 serfs and 1 colibert, and (there are) 17 villeins and 20 bordars with 17 ploughs. And 7 rent-payers (*gabulatores*) pay 17 shillings.

In ALSEBRUGE [Axbridge] 32 burgesses pay 20 shillings. There are 2 mills paying 12 shillings and 6 pence, and 3 fisheries paying 10 shillings. 'There are 6 beasts, 15 swine and 100 sheep.' There are 15 acres of meadow and pasture 1 league in length and as much in width. Wood(land) 2 leagues in length and half a league in width. It (Cheddar) pays yearly 21 pounds and 2½ pence at 20 pence to the ounce.

Of this manor Giso the bishop holds a member (called) WETMORE [Wedmore], which he held of King Edward. For it William the sheriff reckons in the king's ferm 12 pounds every year. 'The bishop held it of King Edward long before his death.'

From this same manor has been taken away half a virgate of land which was of the demesne ferm of King Edward. Robert de Otburgvile holds it, and it is worth 15 pence.

These 2 manors, Somerton and Cheddar, with their attached members (*appenditiis*) paid the ferm of one night T.R.E.

fo. '88b'

The king holds NORT PERET [North Petherton]. King Edward held it. It never paid geld, nor is it known how many hides are there. There is land for 30 ploughs. In

demesne are 3 ploughs and (there are) 20 villeins, 19 bordars, 6 serfs, and 20 swineherds 'who pay 100 shillings' with 23 ploughs. 'And there are 2 beasts and 100 sheep.' And there is a mill which pays yearly 15 pence, and 100 acres of meadow, and 2 leagues of pasture paying 20 shillings. This manor pays 42 pounds 8 shillings 4 pence at 20 pence to the ounce.

The king holds SUDPERET, 'SUTPETRET' [South Petherton]. King Edward held it. It never paid geld, nor is it known how many hides are there. There is land for 28 ploughs. In demesne are 2 ploughs and 5 serfs and 22 coliberts, and (there are) 63 villeins and 15 bordars with 26 ploughs. 'There are 2 riding-horses, 1 cow, 12 swine and 63 sheep.' There is a mill paying yearly 20 shillings. There are 50 acres of meadow, and wood(land) 11 furlongs in length and 10 in width. It pays 42 pounds 8 shillings 4 pence at 20 pence to the ounce.

Of this manor Merlesuain held 2 hides in STRATONE [Stratton] T.R.E.; it was thegnland. It now pays 60 shillings in the king's ferm 'and 24 sheep.' From the same manor has been taken half a hide. Norman holds it of Roger de Curcelle, and it is worth 16 shillings.

To this manor T.R.E. there was yearly paid from Cruche, 'Cruca' [Cricket St. Thomas] a customary due (*consuetudo*). This was 6 sheep with their lambs, and from each free man 1 bloom (*bloma*) of iron. Turstin holds (Cricket) of the Count of Mortain, but he has not paid the due since the count has had the land.

The king holds CHURI [Curry Rivel]. King Edward held it. It never paid geld, nor is it known how many hides are there. There is land for 13 ploughs. In demesne are 3 ploughs and 5 serfs, and (there are) 20 villeins and 2 bordars with 10 ploughs. 'There are 1 riding-horse, 8 beasts, 11 swine and 64 sheep.' There are 40 acres of meadow, and wood(land) 2 leagues in length and 1 league in breadth. It pays 21 pounds 50 pence at 20 pence to the ounce.

From this manor has been taken away 1 virgate of land. Bretel holds it of the Count of Mortain. It is worth 10 shillings 8 pence.

These 3 manors, Nordperet and Sudperet and Churi, T.R.E. paid the ferm of one night with their customary dues.

fo. 86b

The king holds WILLETONE [Williton] and CANDETONE [Cannington] and CARENTONE

---

1 'mansiones' in Exeter Domesday.
2 This estate has not been identified.

435

[Carhampton]. King Edward held them. They never paid geld, 'and were never hidated,' nor is it known how many hides are there. There is land for 100 ploughs. In demesne there are 11½ ploughs and 11 serfs and 30 coliberts, and (there are) 38 villeins and 50 bordars with 37½ ploughs. 'There are 2 riding-horses and 11 swine and 350 sheep.' There are 2 mills paying 5 shillings and 104 acres of meadow. The pasture is 5 leagues in length and 3 leagues in breadth. Wood(land) 4 leagues in length and 2½ leagues in breadth. It (the group of 3 manors) pays 105 pounds 16 shillings 6½ pence at 20 pence to the ounce. T.R.E. (it)[1] paid the ferm of one night.

To this manor of Welletone is added half a hide.[2] Saric held it T.R.E. for 2 manors and paid geld for half a hide. There is land for 5 ploughs. There 6 villeins and 4 bordars have 3 ploughs. There are 4 acres of meadow. The wood(land) is 4 furlongs in length and 1 furlong in breadth. It pays 31 shillings 8 pence.

To the same manor is added another half hide at WAISTOU [Westowe in Lydeard St. Lawrence] which Alwin held 'in parage (*pariter*)' T.R.E. and paid geld for half a hide. There is land for 1 plough. It pays 40 pence. To the said manor[3] has been added half a hide, and it pays 7 shillings to the king's ferm.

From Alvred's manor of SELVERE [Monksilver][4] has been added to this manor a customary due of 18 sheep every year. T.R.E. this did not belong to Welletone.

'fo. '90b'

The king holds BEIMINSTRE, 'BETMINISTRA' [Bedminster]. King Edward held it. It never paid geld, nor is it known how many hides are there. There is land for 26 ploughs. In demesne there are 3 ploughs and 3 serfs, and (there are) 25 villeins and 22 bordars with 10 ploughs. 'There are 1 riding-horse and 9 beasts and 22 swine and 115 sheep.' There is a mill paying 5 shillings, and 34 acres of meadow. Wood(land) 2 leagues in length and

---

1 league in breadth. It pays 21 pounds and 2½ pence at 20 pence to the ounce.

The priest (*presbiter*) of this manor holds land for 1 plough, and it is worth 20 shillings. Of this manor 'Geoffrey' the Bishop of Coutances holds 112 acres of meadow and wood(land).

The king holds FROME [Frome]. King Edward held it. It never paid geld, nor is it known how many hides are there. There is land for 50 ploughs. In demesne there are 3 ploughs and 6 coliberts, and (there are) 31 villeins and 36 bordars with 40 ploughs. 'There are 24 swine and 93 sheep.' There are 3 mills paying 25 shillings, and a market (*mercatum*) paying 46 shillings and 8 pence. There are 30 acres of meadow and 50 acres of pasture. Wood(land) 1 league in length and the same in breadth. It pays 53 pounds and 5 pence at 20 pence to the ounce.

Of this manor the church of St. John of Frome holds 'in almoin' 8 ploughlands (*car. terræ*) as it did T.R.E. Reinbald is priest there.[5]

THE king holds BRUMETONE,[6] 'BRIUUETONA' [Bruton]. King Edward held it. It never paid geld, nor is it known how many hides are there. There is land for 50 ploughs. In demesne there are 3 ploughs and 5 serfs and 4 coliberts, and (there are) 28 villeins and 26 bordars with 18 ploughs. There are 5 burgesses and 1 swineherd 'who pays 5 swine every year. There are 80 sheep and 13 goats.' There are 6 mills paying 20 shillings, and 38 acres of meadow and 150 acres of pasture. Wood(land) 5 leagues in length and 1 league in breadth. It pays 53 pounds and 5 pence of 20 pence to the ounce.

This manor with the above (named) FROME T.R.E. paid the ferm of one night.

From this manor have been taken away 9 acres 'which were in the above named manor T.R.E.' which Bretel holds of the Count of Mortain 'in Retlis' [Redlynch], and they are worth 18 pence.

From this manor has been taken away half a hide in CILEMETONE [Kilmington]. Serlo de Burci holds it, and it is worth 10 shillings. They were part of the demesne ferm 'of the king in Briuueton [Bruton] T.R.E.'

From the same manor has been taken away 1 hide, 'which was (*jacebat*) there T.R.E.' Gozelin 'de Rivaria' holds it of Robert Fitz Girold. There is land for 3 ploughs.

---

1 The Exeter Domesday reads : 'these 3 manors (*mansiones*).'

2 The half hide may have included 'Imela' and 'Oda' mentioned in the Geld Inquest along with 'Waistou' as exempt. The manor of 'Imele' held by Roger de Corcelle comes in his schedule after places in Stogumber and Nettlecombe. 'Oda' might be Woodavent. This place was held by Robert Avenant in 1284 of the Barony of Donden, Corcelle's representative. Woodavent farm is in Nettlecombe. Imele is now lost.

3 Exet. Dom. has, 'huic predicte Cantoctonet.'

4 See p. 512.

5 Exet. Dom. adds : 'Modo tenet hanc Rainbald' et tenuit tempore Edwardi.'

6 The scribe evidently misread the five minims as 'Brumetona' instead of 'Briuuetona.'—J.H.R.

It was worth 'when Robert received it' 40 shillings, now 20 shillings.

The king holds MILEBURNE [Milborne Port]. King Edward held it. It never paid geld, nor is it known how many hides are there. There is land for 50 ploughs. In demesne are 4 ploughs and 5 serfs, and (there are) 70 villeins and 18 bordars with 65[1] ploughs. 'There are 2 riding-horses and 22 swine and 153 sheep.' There are 6 mills paying 77 shillings and 6 pence, and 170 acres of meadow. Wood(land) 2 leagues in length and 9 furlongs broad. Pasture 4 furlongs long and 2 furlongs broad, and 1 league of moor (mora).

In this manor are 56 burgesses with a market paying 60 shillings 'in the king's ferm.'

In GIVELCESTRE, 'GUILECESTRE' [Ilchester] are 107 burgesses paying 20 shillings. A market with its attached members (appenditiis) pays 11 pounds.

The whole of MELEBURNE with the aforesaid attached members pays 80 pounds of white silver less 9 shillings and 5 pence. T.R.E. it paid one half and one quarter of the ferm of one night.

Reinbald[2] holds the church of S. John with 1 hide. There he has 1 plough. It is worth 30 shillings.

fo. '103'

THE KING'S LAND, WHICH EARL GODWIN and his sons HELD IN SUMERSETA'[3]

The king holds BRUNETONE [King's Brompton]. Ghida held it T.R.E., and paid geld for 10 hides. There is land for 60 ploughs. Four[4] hides of it are in demesne, and there (are) 3 ploughs and 7 serfs; and (there are) 50 villeins and 17 bordars with 20 ploughs 'and 5 hides.' 'There are 15 swineherds who pay yearly 32 shillings.' There are 2 mills paying 3 shillings, and 60 acres of meadow. Pasture 3 leagues long and 1 league broad, and as much wood(land) in length and breadth. It pays 27 pounds 12 shillings 1 penny of white silver.

Of these 10 hides a priest holds 1 in almoin (elemosina) of the king. 'There is land for 2 ploughs.' There he has '3 virgates and' 1 plough and (there are) 4 villeins with 1 plough 'and one virgate.' 'There are 4 beasts, 9 swine, 30 sheep and 7 she-goats,'

and 3 acres of meadow. It is worth 20 shillings.

Of this manor[5] the Count of Mortain holds 1 hide in PRESTETUNE [Torrel's Preston in Milverton], which was part of the demesne ferm T.R.E. There is land for 4 ploughs; 2 ploughs are there. 'Hugh de Valletort holds it of the count, and has 1 plough and 3 virgates of land, and the villeins have 1 virgate and 1 plough.' It was and is worth 40 shillings.

From this manor has been taken away the third penny from Milverton which used to be paid T.R.E. there.

The king holds DOLVERTUNE [Dulverton]. Earl Harold held it T.R.E. and paid geld for 2½ hides. There is land for 11 ploughs. Of this there is in demesne 1 hide and there are 2 ploughs and 6 serfs, an there are 17 villeins and 6 bordars with 3½ ploughs 'and one hide and one half.' 'There are 6 beasts and 30 sheep.' There (are) 3 acres of meadow. Pasture 1 league long and half a league broad, and as much wood(land). It pays 11 pounds 10 shillings of white silver.

To this manor have been added 2 hides of land less half a ferling. 13[6] thegns held them 'in parage' (pariter) T.R.E. There is land for 10 ploughs. There are 8 villeins with 4 ploughs, and 3 acres of meadow, and pasture half a league long and 4 furlongs broad, wood(land) one league long and half a league broad. It is worth 64 shillings and 2 pence.

From this manor has been taken away a customary due (paid) from BRIGEFORD [Brushford], a manor of the Count of Mortain. It was 24 sheep yearly which were delivered there T.R.E. Mauger keeps it back by direction of (per) the count.

The king holds CLIVE [Old Cleeve]. Earl Harold held it T.R.E. and paid geld for 4 hides and 1 virgate of land. There is land for 33 ploughs. Of this there is in demesne 1 hide and there (are) 3 ploughs and 4 serfs and (there are) 19 villeins and 9 bordars with 18 ploughs 'and the rest of the land.' 'There are 1 riding-horse and 14 swine and 300 wether sheep (berbices) and 50 she-goats.' There are 2 mills paying 54 pence, and 24 acres of meadow. Wood(land) 1 league long and half a league broad. It pays 23 pounds of white silver; 'and when William de Moione received it it paid as much.'

---

[1] Exet. Dom. reads: '55½ ploughs.'
[2] Exeter Domesday reads: 'Reinbald the priest who serves the church.'
[3] This heading is in the Exeter Domesday only.
[4] In Exeter Domesday 3.

[5] Exeter Domesday reads: 'From this manor of the king's has been taken away 1 hide of land called Prestetona.'
[6] The Exchequer text reads 12, and is corrected in an interlineation.

To this manor belonged, 'T.R.E.,' the third penny of the Burgherist of Carentone and Willetone and Cantetone and Nordpereth [Carhampton, Williton, Cannington, North Petherton].

The king holds NETELCUMBE [Nettlecombe]. Godwin son of Harold[1] held it T.R.E. and paid geld for 2 hides and 3 virgates of land. There is land for 12 ploughs. Of this there is in demesne 1½ virgates where (are) 2 ploughs and 3 serfs, and (there are) 15 villeins and 4 bordars with 7 ploughs, 'and 1½ hides and half a virgate.' 'There is 1 riding-horse.' There are 6 acres of meadow and 100 acres of pasture and 50 acres of wood(land). It pays [2] pounds 12 shillings of white silver; 'and as much when W. received it.'

The king holds CAPINTONE [Capton in Stogumber]. Earl[3] Harold held (it)[4] and paid geld for 1 hide. There is land for 5 ploughs. Of this half a hide is in demesne where (is) 1 plough and (there are) 5 villeins with 1 plough 'and half a hide.' 'There are 4 beasts and 50 sheep.' There (are) 8 acres of meadow and 20 acres of pasture and 10 acres of wood(land). It pays 46 shillings of white silver, 'and as much when W. received it.'

The king holds LANGEFORD [Langford in Burrington]. Godwin son of 'Earl' Harold[5] held it T.R.E. and paid geld for 5 hides. There is land for 10 ploughs. Of this there are in demesne 1½ hides where (are) 1 plough and 4 serfs and (there are) 21 villeins and 4 bordars with 8 ploughs 'and 3½ hides.' 'There is 1 riding-horse and 3 beasts and 10 swine and 30 sheep and 18 she-goats.' There is a mill paying 7 shillings and 6 pence, and 8 acres of meadow and 100 acres of pasture and 30 acres of wood(land). It pays 4 pounds and 12 shillings 'and as much when W. (de Moione) received it.'

The king holds WINESFORD [Winsford]. Earl Tosti held (it) T.R.E. and paid geld for 3½ hides. There is land for 60 ploughs. Of this there is in demesne half a hide where (are) 2 ploughs and 9 serfs, and (there are) 38 villeins and 11 bordars[6] with 13 ploughs 'and the rest of the land.' 'There are 52 sheep.' There is a mill paying 6 pence, and 8 acres of meadow and 40 acres of wood(land). Pasture 4 leagues long and 2 leagues broad. It pays 10 pounds and 10 shillings of white silver.

To this manor has been added half a hide. 3 thegns held (it) in parage (pariter) T.R.E. and did customary service to the reeve (serviebant præposito per consuetudinem)[7] of the manor without paying any ferm (absque omni firma donante).[8] There is land for 4 ploughs. There (are) 3 villeins and 23 bordars. It pays 20 shillings 'and when W. de Moione received it, as much.'

The king holds CRICE [Creech S. Michael]. Gunnild held it T.R.E. and paid geld for 10½ hides. There is land for 8 ploughs. Of this there are in demesne 6 hides where (are) 2 ploughs and 6 serfs, and (there are) 20 villeins and 10 bordars with 6 ploughs 'and 4½ hides.' 'There are 1 riding-horse and 10 beasts and 10 swine and 48 sheep.' There is 1 mill paying 8 pence, and 8 acres of meadow. Pasture 1 league long and as much broad. Wood(land) 1 furlong long and as much broad. It pays 9 pounds 4 shillings of white silver 'and when W. (de Moione) received it as much.' A fishery is there, but it does not belong to the ferm.[9]

The king holds NORTCURI [North Curry]. Earl Harold held it, and paid geld for 20 hides. There is land for 40 ploughs. Of this there are in demesne 5 hides, where (are) 5 ploughs and 18 serfs and 23 coliberts, and (there are) 100 villeins less 5 and 15 bordars with 30 ploughs 'and 11 hides.' 'There are 1 riding-horse and 20 beasts and 20 swine and 100 sheep.' There are 60 acres of meadow and 50 acres of wood(land). Pasture 2 leagues long and 1 league broad. To this manor belong 5 burgesses in Langporth, 'Lantporta' [Lang-port], paying 38 pence, and 18 serfs and 4 swine-herds and 2 cottars. The whole (manor) pays 23 pounds of white silver 'and when W. (de Moione) received it as much.' There is a fishery which does not belong to the ferm;[10] and 7 acres of vineyard.

Bishop Maurice holds the church of this manor with 3 hides of the same land. He has there 7 villeins and 11 bordars and 2 serfs with 4 ploughs and 18 acres of meadow and

---

[1] 'f. Herold' is interlined.
[2] The number is omitted in both Domesdays. The Exchequer scribe has made a mark in the margin.
[3] 'Comes' is interlined.
[4] T.R.E. is omitted in the Exchequer text.
[5] 'f. Herold' is underlined.
[6] 'and 11 bordars' is interlined.
[7] Exon.:—'Debebant ire in servitium prepositi hujus manerii.'
[8] No rent was paid from that land.
[9] The fishermen contributed nothing to the rent due from the manor.
[10] See note under Creech St. Michael.

5 acres of pasture and 12 acres of wood(land). It pays 60 shillings.

Of the same land of this manor Ansger 'Brito' holds 1 hide of the Count of Mortain. It is worth 20 shillings.

The king holds CRUCHE [Crewkerne]. Eddeva held it T.R.E. It did not pay geld, nor is it known how many hides are there (*habentur*). There is land for 40 ploughs. In demesne are 5 ploughs and 12 serfs and 26 coliberts, and (there are) 42 villeins and 45 bordars with 20 ploughs. 'There are 2 riding-horses and 8 unbroken (*indomitæ*) mares and 9 beasts and 40 swine and 400 sheep and 64 she-goats.' There are 4 mills paying 40 shillings, and a market paying 4 pounds. There

fo. 87

(are) 60 acres of meadow. Pasture half a league long and 4 furlongs broad. Wood-(land) 4 furlongs long and 2 furlongs broad. It pays 46 pounds of white silver.

From this manor has been taken away ESTHAM [Eastham]. T.R.E. it belonged to the ferm of the manor and could not be separated from it. Turstin holds (it) of the Count of Mortain. It is worth 50 shillings 'and when the Count received it as much. Godwin the king's reeve (*prepositus*) held it in the ferm of Cruche, and paid geld for 2 hides. 2 ploughs could plough these (hides). Turstin has in demesne 2 ploughs and 10 bordars and 1 serf and 6 beasts and 11 swine and 45 sheep and 1 mill which pays yearly 12 shillings and 20 acres of wood(land) and 12 acres of meadow.'

The king holds CUNGRESBERIE [Congresbury]. Earl Harold held it T.R.E. and paid geld for 20 hides. There is land for 50 ploughs. Of this there are in demesne 5 hides where (are) 6 ploughs and 12 serfs, and (there are) 34 villeins and 34 bordars with 34 ploughs 'and 9½ hides.' 'There are 2 riding-horses and 20 beasts and 40 swine and 200 sheep and 40 she-goats.' There are 2 mills paying 17 shillings and 6 pence, and 250 acres of meadow. Pasture 2 leagues long and half a league broad. Wood(land) 2½ leagues long, half a league broad. It pays 28 pounds 15 shillings of white silver. 'And as much when W. the sheriff received it.'

Of the land of this manor 3 thegns, Alward, Ordric and Ordulf, hold 3 hides and 3 virgates of land 'as thegn-land.'[1] They held (it) T.R.E., nor could they be separated

from the lord of the manor. There are in demesne 3 ploughs and 4 serfs, and (there are) 6 villeins and 17 bordars with 3½ ploughs. 'There are 12 beasts and 10 swine.' There (are) 20 acres of meadow and 30 acres of wood(land). Total value 60 shillings.

Bishop Maurice holds the church of this manor with half a hide. It is worth 20 shillings.

Of the same land of this manor have been taken away 2 hides which belonged (*jacuerunt*) there T.R.E. Giso the bishop holds one, and it is worth 4 pounds 'and as much when he received it.' Serlo de Burci and Gislebert son of Turold hold another hide, and it is worth 40 shillings, 'and as much when they received it.'

The king holds CAMEL [East or Queen's Camel]. Ghida 'the countess' held (it) T.R.E. and paid geld for 8½ hides. But there are 15 hides there. There is land for 15 ploughs. Of this there are in demesne 5 hides where (are) 4 ploughs and 6 serfs, and (there are) 28 villeins and 10 bordars with 11 ploughs 'and 10 hides.' 'There are 1 riding-horse and 12 beasts and 20 swine and 300 sheep.' There are 2 mills paying 20 shillings and 100 acres of meadow and 100 acres of pasture and 100 acres of wood(land). It pays 23 pounds of white silver. 'And as much when W. the sheriff received it.'

'Manors belonging to the earldom.'[2]

The king holds COCRE [East and West Coker]. Ghida 'the countess' held (it) T.R.E. There are 15 hides there, and it paid geld for 7 hides. There is land for 15 ploughs. Of this are in demesne 5½ hides, where (are) 3 ploughs and 7 serfs and 4 coliberts, and (there are) 35 villeins and 42 bordars with 12 ploughs 'and the rest of the land.' 'There is 1 swineherd who pays 10 swine, and 1 riding-horse and 3 beasts and 20 swine and 150 sheep and 48 she-goats.' There (is) 1 mill paying 5 shillings and 100 acres of meadow. Pasture 1 league long and half a league broad. Wood(land) 8 furlongs long and 6 furlongs broad. It pays 19 pounds and 12 pence of white silver. 'And as much when W. the sheriff received it.'

The king holds HARDINTONE [Hardington Mandeville]. Gunnild 'daughter of Earl Godwin' held it T.R.E., and there are 10 hides there, and it paid geld for 5 hides. There is land for 10 ploughs. Of this there are in demesne 5½ hides where (are) 2 ploughs

[1] Exeter Domesday gives '3 hides,' and adds the figures of the 3 distinct holdings, making that total.

[2] 'Mansiones de comitatu.'

and 7 serfs and (there are) 16 villeins and 16 bordars with 8 ploughs 'and the rest of the land.' 'There are 1 riding-horse and 5 beasts and 100 sheep.' There (are) 40 acres of meadow. Wood(land) 5 furlongs long and 4 furlongs broad. It pays 12 pounds 14 shillings of white silver. 'And as much when the sheriff received it.'

The king holds HESTERIGE [Henstridge]. Earl Harold held (it), and paid geld for 10 hides. There is land for 16 ploughs. Besides these 10 hides there is land for 8 ploughs, which never paid geld. There are in demesne 5 ploughs and 8 serfs, and (there are) 37 villeins and 15 bordars with 16 ploughs 'and 10 hides.' 'There are 3 riding-horses and 1 cow and 22 swine and 438 wether sheep.' There is a mill paying 30 pence, and 160 acres of meadow. Pasture 1 league long and half a league broad, and as much wood(land). It pays 23 pounds of white silver. 'And as much when W. the sheriff received it.'

In this manor 1 free man held 9 acres of land and 2 acres of wood(land). They are worth 30 pence. He could not separate himself from the lord of the manor.

fo. '113'
EDITH (*EDDID*) THE QUEEN HELD THESE LANDS ENTERED BELOW

The king holds MILVERTONE [Milverton]. T.R.E. it paid geld for half a virgate of land. There is land for 16 ploughs. In demesne there are 1 plough and 3 serfs and 3 cottars, and (there are) 16 villeins and 7 bordars with 9 ploughs 'and the rest of the land.' 'There are 1 riding-horse and 40 sheep and 11 she-goats.' There (is) a mill paying 7 shillings and 6 pence, and 6 acres of meadow and 100 acres of pasture and 100 acres of underwood (*silva modica*).[1] There (is) a market paying 10 shillings. The whole manor pays 25 pounds by tale (*ad numerum*). In Queen Edith's time it used to pay 12 pounds.

The king holds MERTOCH [Martock]. There are 38 hides there. T.R.E. it paid geld for 13 hides. There is land for 40 ploughs. Of this (land) there are in demesne 8 hides, where are 3 ploughs and 6 serfs and 14 coliberts, and (there are) 65 villeins and 24 bordars with 28 ploughs 'and 30 hides.' 'There are 2 riding-horses and 23 beasts and 36 swine and 300 sheep less 16.' There (are) 2 mills paying 35 shillings, and 50 acres of meadow. Pasture 1 league long

[1] Exet. Dom. 'nemusculi.'

and as much broad. Wood(land) 1 league long and 2 furlongs broad. A fishery pays 5 shillings. It pays 70 pounds by tale, and 100 shillings more if Bishop Walchelin would have borne witness (*fuerit testatus*).

To this manor have been added 3 hides.[2] T.R.E. 3 thegns held them. They pay 4 pounds and 10 shillings in Mertoch.

From this manor have been taken away 1 hide and 1 virgate of land in CONTONE [Compton Durville in South Petherton], 'which used to belong to (*jacebat in*) Martocha.' Ansger the cook holds (it). There is land for 2 ploughs. There 4 men have 1 plough. It was worth 50 shillings; now 30 shillings.

From this manor have been taken away 1½ hides[3] [Westcombland in Buckland St. Mary]. Alric *Parvus* 'de Hantesyra' holds (it), and it is worth 40 shillings. 'And the same when Alric received it.'

The king holds CAINESHAM [Keynsham]. T.R.E. it paid geld for 50 hides. There is land for 100 ploughs. Of this (land) there are in demesne 15½ hides, where are 10 ploughs and 20 serfs and 25 coliberts and (there are) 70 villeins and 40 bordars with 63 ploughs 'and 17 hides.' 'There are 4 riding-horses and 10 beasts and 44 swine and 700 sheep and 70 she-goats.' There are 6 mills paying 60 shillings, and 100 acres of meadow and 100 acres of pasture. Wood(land) 1 league long and as much broad. It pays 108 pounds by tale. It used to pay 80 pounds 'when William Hosatus received it in ferm.'

To this manor belong 8[4] burgesses in Bath paying 5 shillings yearly.

Of these 50 hides Count Eustace holds in BELETONE, 'BELGETONA' [Belluton in Stanton Drew] 4 hides, and Alvred (holds) of him. '4 ploughs could till this.' Tovi held it for 1 manor T.R.E. There (are) in demesne '2½ hides and half a virgate and' 1½ ploughs with 1 serf, and (there are) 5 villeins and 2 bordars with 2 ploughs 'and 1 hide and 1½ virgates.' 'There are 10 beasts and 13 swine and 47 sheep

[2] Exet. Dom. reads 4 hides, and enters them thus: 'To this manor have been added 4 hides, 2 of which Alwin Banesone held T.R.E. It is called Accheleia [Oakley in Chilthorne Domer], and pays yearly 50 shillings in the king's manor of Mertocha. The other 2 hides 2 thegns held *pariter* T.R.E., nevertheless they paid by custom 40 pence in Martocha, and now (this) pays 40 shillings in Martocha the king's manor.'
[3] Exet. Dom. 'vi virge.'
[4] Exet. Dom. reads '7.'

and 10 she-goats.' There (is) a mill paying 15 shillings and 22 acres of meadow and 20 acres of pasture. Wood(land) 3 furlongs long and 2 furlongs wide. It was worth 3 pounds, now 4 pounds.

Of the same land of that manor Roger holds 10 hides in STANTONE [Stanton Drew]. 'Ulward Wyte,[1] held it freely, T.R.E.' '10 ploughs could till this.' He has there in demesne '5½ hides and' 1 plough and (there are) 15 villeins and 13 bordars owning 7 ploughs and 4½ hides. 'There are 87 sheep.' There (is) a mill paying 13 shillings and 15 acres of meadow. Pasture 4 furlongs long and 1½ furlongs broad, and as much wood(land). It is worth 100 shillings. 'And when Roger received it it was worth 4 pounds.'

Of the said land the Bishop of Coutances holds half a hide, and has there half a plough. It is worth 5 shillings. Ulward held (it), nor could (he) be separated from the manor.

The wife[2] of the said Ulward holds 1 hide of the above-mentioned 50 hides 'in BERNET [Burnett], which Ulward held freely T.R.E.' and has there 'half a hide and' 4 ploughs[3] with 3 serfs, and (there are) 3 villeins and 4 bordars 'with half a hide.' 'There are 6 swine and 100 sheep.' There (are) 12 acres of meadow and 4 acres of underwood (silva minuta). It was and is worth 4 pounds.

Alvric holds of that land 1 hide 'of thegnland' which Ulmar held T.R.E., nor could (he) be separated from the manor. 'This land can be tilled with 1 plough.' One plough is there. 'There are 100 sheep.' There are 17 acres of meadow and 2 acres of pasture. It is worth 20 shillings.

The king holds CIWETUNE [Chewton Mendip]. There are 29 hides there. T.R.E. it paid geld for 14 hides. There is land for 40 ploughs. Of this there are in demesne 18 hides, where (are) 9 ploughs and 20 serfs and 2 coliberts, and (there are) 18 villeins and 25 bordars with 19 ploughs 'and 11 hides.' 'There are 1 riding-horse and 35 swine and 800 sheep and 50 she-goats.' There are 5 mills paying 30 shillings less 5 pence, and 100 acres of meadow. Pasture 2 leagues long and 1 league broad. Wood(land) 1 league in length and breadth. In Bath 'are appurtenant' 4 burgesses 'who' pay 40 pence. It pays 50 pounds by tale. In the time of Queen Edith it used to pay 30 pounds.

The Abbot of Jumièges (de Gemetico) holds the church of this manor with half a hide of land. 'Three ploughs can till this.' There are 2½ ploughs there, and 2 serfs, and (there are) 2 villeins and 8 bordars and 8 cottars. It was and is worth 40 shillings. 'The abbot has half a virgate and half a plough in demesne, and the villeins have half a plough and the rest of the land.'

The king holds ESTONE [Batheaston]. There are 2 hides there, and it paid geld for 1 hide. There is land for 10 ploughs. In demesne there is '1 hide and' 1 plough, and 2 serfs and 7 coliberts, and (there are) 13 villeins and 3 bordars and 3 cottars with 5 ploughs 'and 1 hide.' 'There are 150 sheep and 24 she-goats.' There are 2 mills paying 100 pence, and 50 acres of meadow and of underwood (silva minuta) 2 leagues in length and breadth. These 2 hides were and are of the demesne ferm of the burgh of Bath (de dominica firma burgi Bade).

The king holds BADE [Bath]. T.R.E. it paid geld for 20 hides when the shire (scira 'vicecomitatus') paid geld. There the king has 64 burgesses paying 4 pounds, and 90 burgesses of other men (hominum)[4] pay there 60 shillings. There the king has 6 destroyed (vastas) houses.

That burgh with the foresaid Estone pay 60 pounds by tale and 1 mark of gold. Besides this the mint (moneta) pays 100 shillings. Edward 'the sheriff' pays 11 pounds for (de) the third penny of this burgh.

From this burgh 1 house has been taken away. Hugh the interpreter holds it, and it is worth 2 shillings.

William Moion pays of (de) the third penny of GIVELCESTRE [Ilchester] 6 pounds of 20 pence to the ounce. From MELEBURNE [Milborne Port] 20 shillings. From BRAUETONE, 'BRIUETONA' [Bruton] 20 shillings. From LANPORT [Langport] 10 shillings. From AISSEBRIGE [Axbridge] 10 shillings. From FROME 5 shillings.

ULWARD WHITE (ALBUS) HELD THESE LANDS ENTERED BELOW

The king holds CORFETONE [Corton Dinham]. T.R.E. it paid geld for 7 hides. There is land for 7 ploughs. Of this (land) there are in demesne 3½ hides and 1 ferling, where are 1 plough and 3 serfs, and

---

[1] This is the 'Ulwardus Albus' whose manors are grouped below (see Introduction).

[2] Probably his widow.

[3] Exet. Dom. assigns 2 ploughs to the desmesne and 2 to the villeins.

[4] Exet. Dom. reads: 'of the king's barons' (Barones regis).

(there are) 10 villeins and 8 bordars with 3 ploughs 'and the rest of the land.' 'There are 1 riding-horse and 4 swine and 100 sheep.' There are 6 acres of meadow. Wood(land) 2 furlongs long and 1 furlong broad. It was and is worth 7 pounds.

The king holds WITECUMBE [Whitcombe in Corton Dinham]. T.R.E. it paid geld for 5 hides. There is land for 4 ploughs. Of this (land) there are in demesne 3 hides and 3 virgates of land, where are 1 plough and 2 serfs, and (there are) 3 villeins and 3 bordars having 2 ploughs 'and the rest of the land.' There (are) 6 acres of meadow. Wood(land) 4 furlongs long and 1 furlong broad. It pays 4 pounds.

The king holds PETENIE[1] [Pitney Lorty]. T.R.E. it paid geld for 1 hide. There is land for 1½ ploughs. Humfrey holds there ½ hide, and he has there 1 plough. 'There are 1 riding-horse and 12 beasts and 6 swine and 45 sheep.' (He has) 6 acres of meadow and 4 acres of wood(land). It was and is worth 20 shillings. What the king has there is worth 10 shillings.

Warmund holds MUNDIFORD[2] [Mudford][3] in mortgage (vadimonium) of Ulward on the evidence of the king's writ (testimonio brevis Regis).[4] T.R.E. it paid geld for 5 hides. There is land for 5 ploughs. Of this there are in demesne 2 hides where are 2 ploughs, 'and the villeins have 3 hides and 3 ploughs.' 'There Garmund[5] has 4 villeins and 8 bordars and 2 serfs and 1 riding-horse.' There (are) 12 acres of meadow and as much of pasture. It was and is worth 3 pounds.

fo. 87b '173b'

THE LAND OF THE BISHOP OF WINCHESTER

The Bishop of Winchester holds TANTONE [Taunton]. Archbishop Stigand held (it)

T.R.E. and paid geld for 54 hides and 2½ virgates of land. There is land for 100 ploughs. Besides this (land) the bishop has in demesne land for 20 ploughs which never paid geld and there he has 13 ploughs. There (are) 80 villeins and 82 bordars and 70 serfs and 16 coliberts and 17 swineherds paying 7 pounds and 10 shillings. Between them all they have 60 ploughs 'and 37 hides.' There (are) 64 burgesses paying 32 shillings. 'There the bishop has 8 riding-horses and 30 beasts and 24 swine and 100 sheep.' There are 3 mills paying 100 shillings less 60 pence. The market pays 50 shillings, and from the mint (moneta) 50 shillings. There (are) 40 acres of meadow. Pasture 2 leagues long and 1 league wide. Wood(land) 1 league long and as much wide. When Walchelin the bishop received (it), it paid 50 pounds. Now it pays 154 pounds and 13 pence with all its appendages (appenditiis) and customary dues.

These customary dues belong to TANTONE. Burgheristh. Thieves (Latrones). Breach of the peace. Hainfare. Hundred pence and S. Peter's pence. Church-scot (Circieti). Thrice in the year the bishop's pleas to be held without summons (ammonitione). Setting out on military service (profectio in exercitum) with the bishop's men.

[6]The said customary dues are paid at (in) TANTONE by these lands: Talanda [Tolland], Acha [Oak], Holeforde [Holford in Lydeard St. Lawrence or Combe Flory][7] and

[1] Exeter Domesday reads :—'Ulward Wite had 1 manor which is called Peteneia which he himself held T.R.E. and paid geld for half a hide. Half a plough could till this. This the king has in his hand, and it is worth 10 shillings a year. Humfrey holds a manor which he held of Ulward Wite, and there is half a hide of land. One plough could till this.'

[2] Exet. Dom. rectius : 'Modiforda.'

[3] Identified by Mr. J. Batten (Som. Arch. Proc. xlv. ii. 186) with Up-Mudford manor near Yeovil.

[4] This does not imply that Ulward was living in 1086, but only that he had mortgaged the land to Warmund.

[5] This is the same name as Warmund.

[6] This paragraph is given with certain variations and greater definiteness in Exet. Dom. 'And from Talanda and from Acca and from Holeforda and Ubcedena and Succedena and from Maidenobroca and from Lafort and Lediart and Lega and Billa and Bela and Denichebede (so printed by Rec. Com.), and all these are bound to go on military service (ire in expeditionem) with the bishop's men, and when the lords of the above-mentioned lands die they are bound to be buried in Tantona. Bagueberga owes to Taunton (Tantone) the same customary service (consuetudinem) except (as regards) the army and burial, and from Scobinalre and from Stoca is due the same customary service except (as regards) the army, and Nortona and from Bradeforda and Halsa and Hafella are bound to go thrice in the year to the bishop's pleas, and to pay St. Peter's pence in Tantona, and (their) contribution (denarios) in the hundred, and the land of Hela and of Hilla was not able to be separated from Tantona, and all who dwell in the aforesaid lands, if they are going to be sworn or to undergo the ordeal, shall do (so) in Tantona.'

[7] There are three places of this name in Domesday. Moione's Holeford is the parish of Holford St. Mary, afterwards placed in Whitley Hundred, as in Kirby's Quest (1284) it was held by Alice de Furneis of John de Moun. Roger de Corcelle held the other two places of this name. Tenements in

Ubcedene and Succedene [Upper and Lower Cheddon Fitzpaine], Maidenobroche [Maidenbrooke in Cheddon], Laford [Ford in Norton Fitzwarren], Hilla and Hela [Hillfarrence, and Hele in Bradford], Nichehede [Nynehead Flory], Nortone [Norton Fitzwarren], Bradeford [Bradford], Halsa and Hafella [Halse and Heathfield], Scobindare[1] and Stocha [Stoke St. Mary]. These 2 estates (*terræ*)[2] do not owe military service (*exercitum*). They of Baweberga [Bagborough] owe these same services except military service and burial (*sepulturam*).[3] From all these lands those who have to make oath (*facturi sacramentum*) or undergo the ordeal (*judicium portaturi*) come to TANTONE. When the lords of these estates (*terris*) die, they are buried at Tantone.

Hilla and Hele T.R.E. could not be separated from Tantone. Of the aforesaid 54½ hides and ½ virgate of land, Geoffrey now holds of the bishop 4 hides and 1 virgate of land; Robert (holds) 4½ hides; Hugh 'de Villana' (holds) 2½ hides. 'Geoffrey has 3 hides and 4 ploughs in demesne; and the villeins have 1 hide 1 virgate and 3 ploughs; he has there 8 villeins and 13 bordars and 2 riding-horses and 38 beasts and 30 swine and 220 sheep and 22 acres of wood(land) and 16 acres of meadow, and it is worth 10 pounds. Robert has 3 hides and 4 ploughs in demesne; and the villeins have 1½ hides and 4 ploughs; he has there 8 villeins and 18 bordars and 8 serfs and 4 riding-horses and 28 beasts and 30 swine and 200 sheep and 16 acres of wood(land) and 16 acres of meadow and 1 mill (paying) 3 shillings, and it is worth 12 pounds. Hugh de Villana has 1½ hides and 2 ploughs in demesne; and the villeins have 1 hide and 3 ploughs; he has there 4 villeins and 6 bordars and 4 serfs and 2 riding-horses and 12 beasts and 16 swine and 60 sheep and 5 acres of wood(land) and 5 acres of meadow, and it is worth 100 shillings.'[4]

Holford St. Mary were held by John le Walshe of Roger de Newburgh (representative of Corcelle) in 1333 (*Inq. p. m.* 7 Edw. III. No. 26). It is likely that these holdings of Corcelle became the manors of Holford in Combe Florey and Lydeard St. Lawrence, which afterwards became Trebble's Holford and Riche's Holford respectively.

[1] Exet. Dom. 'Scobinalre'; doubtful. Perhaps, as placed with, near Stoke S. Mary.

[2] I.e. 'Scobindare' and 'Stocha.'

[3] The last service, mentioned below.

[4] In Domesday Book this passage is thus compressed: '10 ploughs are there in demesne, and 12 serfs, and (there are) 20 villeins and 27 bordars with 10 ploughs. There (are) 37 acres of meadow, and 43 acres of wood(land), and a mill worth (*de*) 3 shillings—this is Hugh's. In all (this) is worth 27 pounds.'

Also of the aforesaid hides Goduin holds of the bishop 2 hides less half a virgate of land; Leueva (holds) 2 hides; Alward (holds) 1 hide, 1½ virgates; Alvric and Edmer (hold) 3 hides; Lewi holds half a virgate of land. 'Goduin holds 1½ hides and 2 ploughs in demesne'; and the villeins have 1½ virgates and 1 plough; he has there 4 villeins and 5 bordars and 2 serfs and 1 riding-horse and 8 beasts and 10 swine and 100 sheep and 1 mill (paying) 40 pence, and 5 acres of wood(land) and 6 acres of meadow and 4 acres of pasture, and it is worth 40 shillings; when the bishop received (it) 20 shillings. Leueva has 1½ hides and 2 ploughs in demesne; and the villeins have half a hide and 1 plough; she has there 4 villeins and 5 bordars and 3 serfs and 1 riding-horse and 2 beasts and 50 sheep and 1 mill which pays 40 pence, and 3 acres of wood(land) and 6 acres of meadow and 8 of pasture, and it is worth 40 shillings; when the bishop received (it) 20 shillings. Alwald[5] has 1 hide and 1 virgate and 1 plough in demesne; and the villeins have half a virgate and half a plough; he has there 1 villein and 5 bordars and 2 serfs and 32 acres of wood(land) and 13 acres of meadow, and it is worth 20 shillings; and when the bishop received (it) 5 shillings. Alvric and Edmer his brother have 2½ hides and 2 ploughs in demesne; and the villeins have half a hide and 1 plough; they have there 4 villeins and 5 bordars and 6 serfs and 2 riding-horses and 16 non-working beasts (*animalia otiosa*) and 20 swine and 40 sheep and 20 acres of wood(land) and 20 acres of meadow, and it is worth 3 pounds; and when the bishop received (it) 20 shillings. Lewi has there half a plough in demesne and 1 acre of underwood (*nemusculi*), and it is worth 3 shillings, when the bishop received it 2 shillings.' 'The 8 thegns who held these lands T.R.E. could not be separated from the church.[6]

Also of the aforesaid hides the Count of Mortain holds 1 hide; Alvred (holds) 1 hide; John (holds) 2 hides and half a virgate of land; 'John the usher (*hostiarius*) has 1 hide and 1 virgate and half a virgate and 1 plough in demesne; and the villeins have 3 virgates and 1½ ploughs; he has there 6 villeins and 10 bordars and 2 serfs and 1 riding-horse and 1 mill, which pays 50 pence, and

[5] 'Alward' above.

[6] In Domesday Book this passage is thus compressed: '7 ploughs are there in demesne and 13 serfs, and (there are) 13 villeins and 20 bordars with 3½ ploughs. There (are) 2 mills, which pay 6 shillings and eightpence, and 45 acres of meadow, and 61 acres of wood(land). In all (this) is worth 8 pounds and 3 shillings.'

7 acres of meadow and 100 acres of pasture, and it is worth 30 shillings; when the bishop received (it) 20 shillings. Alvred de Hispania has there 4 villeins who have 1 plough and 2 acres of meadow; this pays 20 shillings; when the bishop received (it) 10 shillings. Alvred holds the 1 hide of the count, and has 3 virgates and 1 plough in demesne; and the villeins have 1 virgate and 1 plough; he has there 2 villeins and 7 bordars and 4 serfs and 1 riding-horse and 1 mill, which pays 10 shillings, and 5 swine and 15 acres of wood(land) and 10 acres of meadow, and it is worth 4 pounds, and when the bishop received (it) 40 shillings. These three estates (*terræ*) belonged to TANTONE T.R.E., and could not be separated from the church (of Winchester).'[1]

To this manor of Tantone have been added 2½ hides in Lidiard and Lega[2] [Lydeard St. Lawrence and Angersleigh] which one thegn held in parage (*pariter*) T.R.E., and could choose his own lord (*potuit ire ad quemlibet dominum*). Now Wlward and Alward hold (them) of the bishop by grant (*concessionem*) of King William. 'Wlward holds Lidiard and pays geld for 2 hides; 4 ploughs could cultivate these (hides); he has there 6 villeins and 2 bordars and 3 serfs and 15 acres of wood(land) and 9 arces of meadow and 100 acres of pasture, and it is worth 40 shillings; and when he received (it) as much. Alward holds Lega [Angersleigh], and pays geld for half a hide; one plough can cultivate this; he has there 1 bordar and 4 serfs and 33 acres of wood(land) and 2 acres of wood(land) and 2 acres of meadow, and it is worth 5 shillings; and when he received it, as much.'[3] The customary dues

[1] In Domesday Book this passage is thus compressed: '2 ploughs are there in demense and 6 serfs, and (there are) 12 villeins and 17 bordars with 3½ ploughs. There are 2 mills, which pay 14 shillings and 2 pence, and 19 acres of meadow, and 100 acres of pasture, and 20 acres of woodland. . . . and (these estates) were worth 70 shillings; they now pay 6 pounds and 10 shillings.' In this version the other ploughs are again recorded, and the 70 shillings valuation is referred to the time of King Edward, not to that of the Bishop's succession.

[2] This 'Lega' is perhaps Pyleigh, or West Leigh, in Lydeard St. Lawrence. As Leghe Episcopi it has a separate schedule in the Exchequer Lay Subsidy of 1327 (*Som. Record Soc.* iii. 148). In the same Hundred of Taunton are the schedules of Leghe Militis (Angersleigh) and 'Chappeleghe.'

[3] In Domesday Book this passage is thus compressed: 'There is land for 5 ploughs. There are 6 villeins and 3 bordars and 4 serfs and 11 acres of meadow and 100 acres of pasture and 49

and service from these estates (*terris*) always belonged to (*jacuerunt in*) TANTONE; and King William granted these lands to be held of S. Peter[4] and Bishop Walchelin as he himself recognised at Salisbury in the hearing of the Bishop of Durham,[5] whom he commanded to write this his grant on the returns (*hanc ipsam concessionem suam in brevibus*).

The same bishop holds PIPEMINSTRE, 'PINPEMINISTRA' [Pitminster]. Archbishop Stigand held (it) and paid geld for 15 hides. There is land for 20 ploughs. Of this (land) there are in demesne 5 hides, where are 2 ploughs, and there are 17 villeins and 8 bordars with 14 ploughs 'and 10 hides, and 4 serfs and 1 swineherd and 1 riding-horse and 20 swine and 36 she-goats, and 1 mill which pays 16 pence.' There (are) 6 acres of meadow and 400 acres of pasture and as many acres of wood(land). It was worth 13 pounds. Now 16 pounds.

The same bishop holds BLEDONE [Bleadon]. It was and is (appropriated) for the monks' table (*de victu monachorum*). T.R.E. it paid geld for 15 hides. There is land for 17 ploughs. Of this land there are in demesne 10 hides where are 3 ploughs and 8[6] serfs and (there are) 16 villeins and 10 bordars with 11 ploughs 'and 4 hides. There are 18 beasts and 10 swine and 250 sheep.' There (are) 50 acres of meadow, and pasture 1 league long and half a league broad. It was and is worth 15 pounds. Of these 10 hides Saulf holds of the bishop 1 hide 'which Sawald held T.R.E. and which could not be separated from the church,' and there he has 1 plough[7] with 1 serf and 1 bordar 'and 7 beasts and 6 swine and 100 sheep' and 16 acres of meadow and 1 acre of underwood. It is worth 20 shillings 'and when the bishop received (it) 10 shillings.'

The same bishop holds RINTONE [Rimpton]. Stigand held it T.R.E. and paid geld for 5 hides. There is land for 5 ploughs. Of this (land) there are in demesne 2 hides and 1 virgate of land and a half, where there are 3 ploughs and 2 serfs and (there are) 8 villeins and 7 bordars with 3 ploughs 'and the

acres of wood(land). It was and is worth 45 shillings.

[4] The Old Minster (now Winchester Cathedral).

[5] William de St. Calais, Bp. Dur. 1081–96, 'a valued counsellor of the King William I. of whom all men stood in awe,' *Dict. Nat. Biog.* ix. 82.

[6] Exet. Dom. '7.'

[7] Exet. Dom. '1½ ploughs.'

rest of the land. There are 1 riding-horse and 24 swine and 23 sheep.' There (are) 10 acres of meadow. Wood(land) 4 furlongs long and 1 furlong broad. It was and is worth 7 pounds.

THE LAND OF THE BISHOP OF SALISBURY

The Bishop of Salisbury, 'Osmund,' holds SEVEBERGE [Seaborough]. Alward held (it) T.R.E. and paid geld for 1½ hides. There is land for 1½ ploughs. Nevertheless there are 2 ploughs and 2 villeins and 4 bordars and 2 serfs [1] 'and 7 beasts and 5 swine and 59 sheep. In demesne are 3 virgates and 1 plough, and the villeins have 3 virgates and 1 plough.' There is a moiety of a mill paying 10 pence, and 9 acres of meadow and 10 acres of wood-(land). Pasture half a league long and half a furlong broad.

To this manor has been added another SEVEBERGE [Seaborough]. Aluer held (it) T.R.E. and paid geld for 1½ hides. There are 2 ploughs with 1 villein and 5 bordars. 'In demesne are 3 virgates and 1 plough, and the villeins have 3 virgates and 1 plough. There are 4 swine and 58 sheep,' and a moiety of a mill paying 10 pence, and 9 acres of meadow and 10 acres of wood(land). Pasture half a league long and half a furlong broad.

These 2 estates (terræ) do not belong to the bishopric of Salisbury (non sunt de episcopatu). Bishop Osmund holds them for one manor and Walter 'Tirell' of him. It was and is worth 60 shillings. T.R.E. they belonged (jacuerunt in) to CRUCHE [2] [Crewkerne], a royal manor, and their tenants could not be separated from it, and they paid by custom in CRUCHE [2] 12 sheep with their lambs, and a 'bloom' (bloma) of iron from every free man.

The same bishop holds CONTONE [Chil-compton] and Walter 'Tirell holds it' of him.[3] Alward held (it) T.R.E. and paid geld for 5 hides. There is land for 3 ploughs. In demesne are '3 hides and 3½ virgates and' 2 ploughs and 2 serfs and (there are) 5 villeins and 4 bordars and 7 cottars with 2 ploughs 'and the rest of the land. There are 2 riding-horses and 3 beasts and 8 swine and 100 sheep and 20 she-goats.' There is a mill paying 30 pence, and 14 acres of meadow and 80 acres of wood(land) and 1 league of pasture. It was and is worth 60 shillings.

THE LAND OF THE BISHOP OF BAYEUX

The Bishop of Bayeux holds COME [Temple-Combe] and Sanson (holds it) of him. Earl Lewin [4] held (it) T.R.E., and paid geld for 8 hides. There is land for 8 ploughs. Of this there are in demesne 5 hides, where are 3 ploughs and 7 serfs, and (there are) 10 villeins and 6 bordars with 2 ploughs. There (are) 40 acres of meadow and 40 acres of pasture and 60 acres of under-wood (silva minuta). It was and is worth 10 pounds. To this manor have been added 3 virgates of land in TORNIE.[5] Alward held (it) T.R.E. for one manor and paid geld for as much. There is land for half a plough. It was and is worth 13 [6] shillings.

THE LAND OF THE BISHOP OF COUTANCES

The Bishop of Coutances holds DOULES, 'DOUELIS' [Dowlish Wake and West Dow-lish]. Alward held (it) T.R.E. and paid geld for 2 hides and 1 virgate of land. 'William de Moncels holds it of the Bishop.' There is land for 1½ ploughs, which are there with 3 villeins and 3 bordars and 1 serf. 'There are 4 beasts and 7 swine and 32 sheep.' It was and is worth 24 [7] shillings. 'In demesne is 1 plough, and the villeins have half a plough.'

To this manor have been added 7 hides, which 3 thegns held in parage (pariter) T.R.E.[8] There are in demesne 2 ploughs and 2 serfs, and (there are) 11 villeins and 11 bordars with 5 ploughs. 'There are 1 riding-horse and 6 beasts and 19 swine and 21 sheep.' There (are) 44 acres of meadow and 4 fur-longs of pasture in length and as much in breadth, and 20 acres more. Wood(land) 8 furlongs long and 3 furlongs broad and 20 acres in addition (insuper). It is worth 6 pounds 10 shillings. William 'de Moncels' holds this land of the bishop.

---

[1] Exet. Dom. '1 serf.'

[2] Exet. Dom. 'Crucca' and 'Crucche.'

[3] In 1284 (Kirby's Quest, S.R.S. iii. 40) Roger Tyrel held half the vill of 'Childe Cumtone' of the Bishop of Salisbury.

[4] Leofwine.

[5] Exact equivalent not now known. In Exeter Dom.: 'Turnie' and 'Turnietta.' It is the 'Tour-negate' of a Final Concord concerning land in Wyke and Kingsbury in Milborne Port (Ped. Fin. 42 Ed. III. 33; S.R.S. xvii. 68); or the 'Tour-negate' of another Final Concord concerning lands in Toomer and Endeston in Henstridge, to the south of Templecombe; Ped. Fin. 14 Rich. II. 21, (S.R.S. xvii. 144).

[6] Exet. Dom. reads: '14.'

[7] Exet. Dom. '23.'

[8] Exet. Dom. adds: '2 thegns held 4 hides, and 1 thegn held 3 hides.'

The same bishop holds CAFFECOME [Chaff-combe], and Ralph, 'rufus,' (holds it) of him. Two thegns held it in parage (*pariter*) T.R.E., and paid geld for 3½ hides. There is land for 3 ploughs. In demesne 'are 3 hides and half a virgate and' one plough, and (there are) 2 villeins and 6 bordars having 1 plough and 1½ virgates. 'There are 8 beasts and 24 swine and 65 sheep.' There (is) wood(land) 8 furlongs long and as much broad. It is worth 40 shillings. To this manor has been added 1 hide and 3 virgates of land. Two thegns held it 'in parage' (*pariter*) T.R.E. for 2 manors. There is land for 2 ploughs. Three villeins there have these (ploughs). It is worth 20 shillings 'and as much when the bishop received it.' 'Ralph holds these 4 manors of the bishop for 1 manor.'

The same bishop holds HASECUMBE [Hescombe in Odcombe],[1] and William 'de Moncellis' (holds it) of him. 4 thegns 'Saric 1½ h., Alwin ½ h., Alwin ½ h., Godric 1 virg.' held it in parage (*pariter*) T.R.E., and paid geld for 2 hides and 3 virgates of land. There is land for 3 ploughs. In demesne are '1½ hides and' 2 ploughs with 1 serf, and (there are) 4 villeins and 8 bordars with 2 ploughs 'and 1 hide and 1 virgate. There are 10 beasts and 20 swine and 143 sheep.' There (are) 31 acres of meadow and 10 acres of underwood (*silvæ minutæ*). It was worth 40 shillings; now 50 shillings.

The same bishop holds STOCHES, 'STOCCA' [Rodney Stoke]. Alvied 'Pottoch' held it T.R.E. There are 5 hides and 1 virgate of land, and it paid geld for 4 hides. There is land for 5 ploughs. 'Roger Witen holds this manor of the bishop.' Of this (land) there are in demesne 2½ hides, where are (*et ibi*) 2 ploughs and 3 serfs, and (there are) 9 villeins and 3 bordars with 4½ ploughs 'and 1½ hides. There are 20 mares and 5 cows and 20 swine and 65 sheep and 68 she-goats.' There (is) a mill paying 3 shillings, and 15 acres of meadow. Pasture 2 leagues long and 1 league broad, and 2 shillings'(worth) more in addition (*desuper plus*).[2] Wood(land) 1 league long

---

[1] 'Hasecumbe.' Although hitherto identified with part of Ashcombe in Weston-super-Mare, the other part coming later in this schedule, its position in the sequence is in favour of its identification with Hescombe, an obsolete part of the parish of Odcombe, on the borders of Montacute and Tintinhull. In *Kirby's Quest* 'Etecumb' (Hececombe) in the Hundred of Tintinhull is held by Bret of Lacy as of the Barony of Trowbridge.

[2] Exet. Dom., 'tantum pascue quod reddit ii

and 1 furlong broad. It was worth 6 pounds. Now 4 pounds.

The same bishop holds ESSETUNE [Exton] and Drogo (holds it) of him. Edwin held (it) T.R.E. and paid geld for 3 hides and 1 ferling. There is land for 12 ploughs. In demesne are 'one ferling and' 2 ploughs and 6 serfs, and (there are) 20 villeins and 13 bordars with 7 ploughs 'and 3 hides. There are 6 swine and 60 sheep.' There (are) 8 acres of meadow and 60 acres of wood(land). Pasture 1 league long and as much broad. It is worth 6 pounds; 'and when the bishop received it 40 shillings.' Of this same land T.R.E. 3 virgates of land always belonged to (*jacuerunt in*) NETECUMBE [Nettlecombe], a manor of the king.

fo. 88

The same bishop holds WINEMERESHAM [Wilmersham in Stoke Pero], and Drogo (holds it) of him. T.R.E. it paid geld for 1 hide and 1 virgate of land. There is land for 5 ploughs. Of this (land) there are in demesne 3 virgates, where are (*et ibi*) 1 plough and 3 serfs, and (there are) 5 villeins and 3 bordars with 1 plough 'and 2 virgates. There are 5 beasts and 40 sheep and 30 she-goats.' There (are) 200 acres of pasture and as much of wood(land). It is worth 30 shillings.

The same Drogo holds of the bishop CHETENORE [Kitnor, now Culbone]. T.R.E. it paid geld for 1 hide and 1 virgate. There is land for 2 ploughs. 'In demesne are 1 hide and 1 plough, and the villeins have 1 virgate.' There are 2 villeins and 1 bordar and 1 serf with 1 plough, and 50 acres of pasture and 100 acres of wood(land). It is worth 15 shillings, 'and when the bishop received it, 5 shillings.' These 2 manors Osmund 'Estramin' held T.R.E.

Edmer holds of the bishop WIDICUMBE [Withycombe]. Alnod held (it) and paid geld for 3 hides T.R.E. There is land for 10 ploughs. In demesne are '1 hide and' 2 ploughs and 6 serfs and (there are) 14 villeins and 7 bordars with 8 ploughs 'and 2 hides. There are 1 riding-horse and 3 beasts and 10 swine and 40 sheep and 30 she-goats.' There are 10 acres of meadow and 550 acres of pasture and 100 acres of wood(land) less 4 acres. It was worth 4 pounds; now 6 pounds.

Azelin holds of the bishop HARPETREU

solidos per annum.' The value of the pasture is to be added to the value of the manor, 4 pounds.

[West Harptree]. Alric and Ulwi held it 'in parage (*pariter*)' T.R.E. for 2 manors and paid geld for 5 hides. There is land for 5 ploughs. Of this (land) there are in demesne 3 hides, where are (*et ibi*) 2 ploughs and 2 serfs, and (there are) 9 villeins and 1 bordar and 4 cottars with 3 ploughs 'and 2 hides. There are 1 riding-horse and 3 beasts and 12 swine and 46 sheep and 20 she-goats.' There (is) a mill paying (*de*) 5 shillings, and there are 40 acres of meadow. Pasture 8 furlongs long and 5 furlongs broad. Wood(land) 4 furlongs long and 2½ furlongs broad. It was and is worth 40 shillings. 'These 2 estates (*terræ*) the bishop holds for 1 manor.'

Azelin holds of the bishop HOTUNE [Hutton]. Two thegns held (it) T.R.E. for 2 manors and paid geld for 5 hides. There is land for 5 ploughs. There 'are 3½ hides and' 1 plough in demesne, and (there are) 5 villiens and 6 bordars having 2 ploughs 'and 1½ hides.' There (are) 30 acres of meadow and 200 acres of pasture and 15 acres of underwood (*silvæ minutæ*). It was worth 4 pounds; now 60 shillings.

Azelin holds of the bishop LILEBERE [1] [Elborough in Hutton]. Alward held (it) T.R.E. and paid geld for 3 hides. There is land for 4 ploughs. In demesne there are '2½ hides and' 2 ploughs with 1 serf, and (there are) 1 villein (*villano*) and 5 bordars with 1 plough 'and half a hide. There are 10 beasts and 12 swine and 200 sheep.' There (are) 20 acres of meadow and 40 acres of pasture. It was worth 60 shillings; now 40 shillings.

Herluin holds of the bishop WINTRETH [Winterhead in Winscombe]. Brictric held (it) 'of the abbot of Glastingesberie and could not separate (it) from the church' T.R.E. and paid geld for 1 hide. There is land for 2 ploughs. There they are with 2 villeins and 2 bordars and 2 serfs. 'In demesne are 3 virgates and 1 plough, and the villeins have 1 virgate and 1 plough.' 'There are 8 cows and 40 sheep.' There (are) 8 acres of meadow and 3 acres of underwood (*silva modica*). It was and is worth 20 shillings. These 3 manors belonged to (*erant de*) the church of Glastingberie T.R.E. Those who held them could not be separated from the church.

Herluin holds of the bishop AISECOME [Ashcombe in Weston-super-Mare]. Brictric

held it T.R.E. and paid geld for 3½ hides. There is land for 5 ploughs. In demesne there are '2 hides and 1 virgate and' 2 ploughs and 7 serfs, and (there are) 6 villeins and 5 bordars with 3 ploughs 'and 1 hide and 1 virgate. There are 30 beasts and 18 swine and 136 sheep and 60 she-goats.' There (are) 40 acres of meadow and 3 acres of underwood (*silva minuta*) and 100 acres of pasture. It was and is worth 100 shillings.

William holds of the bishop CLUTONE [Clutton]. Turchil held (it) T.R.E., and paid geld for 10 hides. There is land for 8 ploughs. In demesne there are '5½ hides and' 3 ploughs with 1 serf, and (there are) 10 villeins and 12 bordars with 6 ploughs 'and 4½ hides. There are 1 riding-horse and 12 beasts and 26 swine and 176 sheep.' There is a mill paying 30 pence, and 107 acres of meadow. Pasture 10 furlongs long and 4 furlongs broad. Wood(land) half a league long and as much broad. It was worth 3 pounds. Now 6 pounds.

William holds of the bishop TEMESBARE [Timsbury]. Ape held (it) T.R.E., and paid geld for 3 hides. There is land for 3 ploughs. In demesne there are '1½ hides and' 1 plough and 2 serfs, and (there are) 2 villeins and 1 bordar with 1 plough 'and 1½ hides. There are 1 riding-horse and 9 beasts and 14 swine and 60 sheep.' There (are) two-thirds (*duæ partes*) of a mill paying 3 shillings, and 26 acres of meadow, and as much of pasture. It was worth 26 shillings; now 50 shillings.

To this manor have been added 2 hides which Sibe held for 1 manor T.R.E., and paid geld for as much (*pro tanto*).[2] There is land for 2 ploughs, which are there with 1 serf and (there are) 1 villein and 3 bordars. 'In demesne are 1½ hides and 1 plough, and the villeins have half a hide and 1 plough. There are 5 beasts and 6 swine and 40 sheep.' There (is) the third part of a mill paying 2 shillings, and 16 acres of meadow and as much of pasture. It was worth 14 shillings. Now 30 shillings.

Ulveva holds of the bishop NORTONE [Norton Hautville and Malreward]. Alwold held it T.R.E. and paid geld for 5 hides. There is land for 8 ploughs. In demesne there 'are 4 hides and' 1 plough and 3 serfs, and (there are) 5 villeins and 11 bordars with 3 ploughs 'and 1 hide. There

---

Exet. Dom. *rectius* : ' Illebera.'

[2] Exet. Dom. : 'Temesbera which Sibe held *pariter.*'

are 1 riding-horse and 9 beasts and 18 swine and 147 sheep.' There is a mill paying 40 pence, and 34 acres of meadow and 6 acres of underwood (*silva minuta*) and 1 league of wood(land) in length and as much in breadth. It was worth 100 shillings; now 60 shillings.

Folcheran holds of the bishop CLAVEHAM [Claverham in Yatton]. Gonnil held (it) T.R.E. and paid geld for 2 hides. There is land for 3 ploughs. In demesne there are 'one hide and' 1 plough with 1 serf, and (there are) 3 villeins and 12 bordars with 2 ploughs 'and 1 hide. There are 1 riding-horse and 4 beasts.' There (are) 7 acres of meadow. Wood(land) 1 furlong long and as much broad. Underwood (*silva modica*) half a league long and as much broad. It was worth 20 shillings; now 30 shillings.

William holds of the bishop FERENBERGE [Farmborough]. Edric held (it) T.R.E. and paid geld for 5 hides. There is land for 5 ploughs.[1] In demesne there are '2½ hides and' 2 ploughs and 5 serfs, and (there are) 4 villeins and 3 bordars with 2 ploughs 'and 2½ hides. There are 1 riding-horse and 14 beasts and 215 sheep.' There (are) 77 acres of meadow and 74 acres of pasture. It was and is worth 4 pounds.

To this manor have been added 5 hides. Alvric held (them) T.R.E. for 1 manor, and paid geld for 5 hides. There is land for 5 ploughs. Nigel holds (them) of the Bishop. In demesne are '4 hides and' 2 ploughs with 1 serf and (there are) 1 villein and 5 bordars 'with 1 hide. There are 21 beasts and 14 swine and 68 sheep.' There (are) 77 acres of meadow and 74 acres of pasture. It was and is worth 4 pounds.

Fulcran and Nigell hold of the bishop CLIVEWARE [Clewer in Wedmore]. Turchil held it T.R.E. and paid geld for 3 virgates of land less 1 ferling. 'In desmesne is 1 virgate and half a plough, and the villeins have 1 virgate[2] less 1 ferling and 1½ ploughs.' There is land for 2 ploughs, which are there with 6[3] 'villeins and 10 acres of meadow. It is worth 15 shillings; and the same when received.'

[1] In the Exchequer text the number of the hides and ploughlands have been altered from '2' to '5'; the Exeter Domesday reads '2' in each case.

[2] A 'ii' interlined before '*vill. i. virg.*' is probably intended as a correction of the number of virgates, which should be 2.

[3] Exet. Dom. '4.'

Herluin holds of the bishop BICHEURDE 'BISCHEURDA' [Bishopsworth]. Alger held it T.R.E. and paid geld for 2 hides. There is land for 2 ploughs. In demesne is 1 plough and 3 serfs, and (there are) 2 bordars. There (are) 12 acres of meadow. Wood(land) 6 furlongs long and 1 furlong broad. In BRISTOU [Bristol] (are) 10 houses appurtenant. In BADE [Bath] (are) 2 houses paying (to it) 10 pence. It was worth 20 shillings; now 40 shillings.

Azelin holds of the bishop BISCOPEWRDE [Bishopsworth]. Edric held (it) T.R.E. and paid geld for 1½ hides. 'In demesne are 2½ virgates.' There is land for 2 ploughs which are there with 4 villeins and 4 bordars and 4 cottars. There (are) 10 acres of meadow and 45 acres of pasture. It was worth 20 shillings; now 30 shillings.

Azelin holds of the bishop WESTONE [Weston in Gordano]. Britnod held (it) T.R.E. and paid geld for 7 hides. There is land for 6 ploughs. In demesne there are '5½ hides and' 3 ploughs and 2 serfs and (there are) 6 villeins and 7 bordars with 3 ploughs 'and 1½ hides. There are 1 riding-horse and 8 beasts and 7 swine and 67 sheep and 24 she-goats.' There (are) 33 acres of meadow. Pasture 12 furlongs long and 8 furlongs broad. Wood(land) 7 furlongs long and 3 furlongs broad. It was and is worth 4 pounds and 10 shillings.

Roger 'Witen' holds of the bishop SANFORD [Saltford]. Four thegns held (it) 'in parage' (*pariter*) T.R.E. and paid geld for 4 hides. There is land for 6 ploughs. In demesne there are '1½ hides and' 3 ploughs and 6 serfs, and (there are) 7 villeins and 10 bordars with 4 ploughs 'and 2½ hides. There are 1 riding-horse and 13 swine and 120 sheep.' There (is) a mill paying 12 shillings and 6 pence, and 32 acres of meadow. It was and is worth 6 pounds.[4]

Roger 'son of Ralph' holds of the bishop ESTONE [Easton in Gordano]. Ailric held (it) T.R.E. and paid geld for 12 hides. There is land for 9 ploughs. In demesne are '5 hides and 3 virgates and' 2 ploughs and 3 serfs, and (there are) 14 villeins and 7 bordars with 7 ploughs 'and 6 hides and 1 virgate. There are 2 riding-horses and 3 unbroken (*indomitæ*) mares and 12 beasts and 20 swine and 200 sheep.' There (is) a mill

[4] Against this paragraph Exet. Dom. has in the margin a ✠.

paying 50 pence, and 36 acres of meadow and 30 acres of wood(land) and 100 acres of pasture. It was worth 10 pounds. Now 7 pounds.

William 'de Moncels' holds of the bishop PORTESHEV[1] [Portishead]. Alvric 'cild' held (it) T.R.E. and paid geld for 8 hides. There is land for 8 ploughs. In demesne are '6 hides and' 2 ploughs with 1 serf, and (there are) 9 villeins and 4 bordars with 5 ploughs 'and 2 hides. There are 8 beasts and 10 swine and 60 she-goats.' There is a mill paying 8 shillings, and 20 acres of meadow and 100 acres of pasture. Underwood (*silva minuta*) 12 furlongs long and 3 furlongs broad. It was and is worth 70 shillings.

William holds of the bishop WESTONE [Weston in Gordano]. Algar held (it) T.R.E. and paid geld for 3 hides and 1 virgate of land. There is land for 3 ploughs. In demesne are '2 hides and 3½ virgates and' 2 ploughs and 2 serfs and (there are) 4 villeins and 4 bordars with 2 ploughs 'and half a hide and half a virgate. There are 100 sheep.' There (are) 17 acres of meadow and 12 acres of underwood (*silvæ minutæ*). Pasture 12 furlongs long and 2 furlongs broad and 6 furlongs of moor (*moræ*).[2] It was and is worth 60 shillings.

Herluin holds of the bishop CLOTUNE[3] [Clapton in Gordano]. Algar held (it) T.R.E. 'in parage (*pariter*)' and paid geld for 5½ hides. There is land for 5 ploughs. In demesne are '3½ hides and' 2 ploughs and 2 serfs, and (there are) 10 villeins, and 10 bordars with 3 ploughs 'and 2 hides less 1 virgate.' 'There are 1 riding-horse and 16 beasts and 40 swine and 50 she-goats.' There (are) 50 acres of meadow. Pasture 18 furlongs long and 3 furlongs broad. Wood 7 furlongs long and 1 furlong broad. It was worth 40 shillings. Now 70 shillings.

Brungar, 'an Englishman,' holds of the bishop ATIGETE, 'ATTIGETTA' [Havyat in Wrington]. Tidulf held (it) T.R.E. 'in

1 The final 'v' of this name is interlined and faint, but Exet. Dom. reads : 'Portesheve.'
2 Exet. Dom. '*morarũ*.'
3 In the Supplement to *Kirby's Quest* (S.R.S. iii. 44), 1303, Clapton-in-Gordano is held by Rich. Artur of the Earl of Gloucester. This entry of 'Clotune' comes among other manors in Portbury Hundred, and may be considered as a clerical error for 'Cloptone.'

parage (*pariter*)' and paid geld for 1½ hides. There is land for 1 plough which is there in demesne with 3 bordars. 'There are 4 cows and 5 swine and 100 sheep and 50 she-goats.' There (are) 10 acres of meadow and 20 acres of wood(land). It was and is worth 20 shillings; 'and when the bishop received it, it was worth as much.'

The bishop himself holds one estate (*terram*) which is called CHEN, 'CHENT' [Kenn]. There is half a hide, where he has 1 serf. It is worth 5 shillings 'a year.'

Fulcran and Nigel hold of the bishop BACOILE [Backwell]. Turchil held (it) T.R.E. and paid geld for 10 hides. There is land for 14 ploughs. 32 villeins[4] and 21 bordars and 2 serfs there have these (ploughs). 'There is 1 burgess (*borgisũ*) who lives (*manet*) at Bath and pays yearly 32 pence. There are 23 swine.' There (is) a mill paying 4 shillings, and 24 acres of meadow. Pasture 1 league long and half a league broad. Underwood (*silva minuta*) 1 league long and 2 furlongs broad. It was and is worth 8 pounds; 'and when received, it was worth as much.'

Fulcran holds of the bishop BUDICOME [Butcombe]. Elward held (it) T.R.E. and paid geld for 3 hides. There is land for 3 ploughs. In demesne there is '1 virgate and' 1 plough and 2 serfs, and (there are) 11 villeins and 4 bordars with 5 ploughs 'and 3 hides less 1 virgate. There are 1 riding-horse and 6 beasts and 2 swine and 124 sheep.' There (is) a mill paying 20 pence, and 10 acres of meadow and 30 acres of wood(land). It was and is worth 4 pounds.

Nigel 'de Gurnai' holds of the bishop BERUE [Barrow Gurney]. Edric held it T.R.E. and paid geld for 10 hides. There is land for 14 ploughs. In demesne[5] are '5 hides and' 2 ploughs and 3 serfs and (there are) 15 villeins and 7 bordars 'with 5 hides and 12 ploughs. There are 2 riding-horses and 27 beasts and 14 swine and 152 sheep and 50 she-goats.' There is a mill paying 5 shillings, and 35 acres of meadow and 30 acres of pasture. Wood(land) 1 league long and 1 furlong broad. It was and is worth 10 pounds.

4 Exet. Dom. : '(Fulcran and Nigel) have there 2 hides (in demesne) and 32 villeins, who have 14 ploughs.'
5 Exet. Dom. : '(Nigel) has there 5 hides and 2 ploughs in demesne, and his villeins 5 hides and 12 ploughs.'

fo. 88b

The bishop himself holds PORBERIE [Portbury]. Goduin held (it) T.R.E. and paid geld for 8 hides. There is land for 18 ploughs. In demesne are ' 1 hide and 1 virgate and ' 2 ploughs and 13 serfs and (there are) 20 villeins and 17 bordars with 16 ploughs, 'and 6½ hides and 1 virgate. There are 2 riding-horses and 14 unbroken mares (*equas indomitas*) and 15 beasts and 18 swine and 216 sheep.' There are 2 mills paying 6 shillings, and 150 acres of meadow. Pasture 17 furlongs long and 2 furlongs broad. Wood (land) 1 league long and 5 furlongs broad. It was and is worth 15 pounds.

The bishop himself holds ESTUNE [Long Ashton]. Three thegns held (it) ' in parage (*pariter*)' T.R.E. and paid geld for 20 hides. There is land for 30 ploughs. In demesne are ' 6 hides less 1 virgate and ' 2 ploughs and 5 serfs, and (there are) 12 villeins ' 4 hides and 1 virgate,' and 6 bordars with 7 ploughs 'and 4 hides and 1 virgate. There is 1 riding-horse and 14 beasts and 12 swine and 27 sheep and 20 she-goats.' There is a mill paying 40 pence, and 25 acres of meadow. Pasture 1 league long and half a league broad, and 100 acres of wood(land). It was worth 12 pounds. Now 10 pounds.

Of the land of this manor Roger 'dispensator' holds 7 hides, and has there in demesne ' 4 hides less 1 virgate and ' 2 ploughs and 4 serfs and (there are) 8 villeins and 10 bordars with 5 ploughs 'and 3 hides. There are 2 riding-horses and 14 beasts and 22 swine and 36 sheep and 14 she-goats.' There (are) 18 acres of meadow and 30 acres of wood(land). It is worth 7 pounds, 'and when Roger received it 100 shillings.' Of the same land of this manor Guy the priest holds 3 hides and there he has 2 ploughs and 2 serfs, and (there are) 3 villeins and 2 bordars with 2 ploughs. 'There are 2 riding-horses and 13 beasts and 60 unbroken mares (*equas indomitas*) and 22 swine and 80 sheep and 30 she-goats.' It is worth 100 shillings, 'and when he received it 20 shillings.' To the church of this manor belongs 1 virgate of the same land.[1]

Roger 'Witen' holds of the bishop FIRFORD [Freshford].[2] Toui held (it) T.R.E.

and paid geld for 2½ hides. There is land for 3 ploughs. In demesne there are ' 1 hide and a half and half a virgate and ' 2 ploughs and (there are) 8 bordars 'who hold 1 hide less half a virgate' with 1 plough. 'There are 2 riding-horses and 8 beasts and 15 swine and 44 sheep.' (There is) half a mill paying 5 shillings, and 12 acres of meadow and 30 acres of pasture and 12 acres of underwood (*silvæ minutæ*). It was worth 40 shillings. Now 60 shillings.

Azelin holds of the bishop LANCHERIS [Langridge]. Ælsi held (it) T.R.E. and paid geld for 2½ hides. There is land for 5 ploughs. In demesne are ' 1 hide and ' 3 ploughs and 3 serfs and (there are) 5 villeins and 7 bordars with 2 ploughs 'and 1½ hides. There are 17 beasts and 4 swine and 194 sheep.' There is a mill paying 40 pence, and 4½ acres of meadow and 130 acres of pasture. It was worth 40 shillings. Now 60 shillings.

The bishop himself holds WICHE [Bathwick]. Alvric held (it) T.R.E. and paid geld for 4 hides. There is land for 4 ploughs. In demesne are ' 3 hides and 11 acres and ' 3 ploughs and 4 serfs and (there are) 1 villein and 10 bordars 'who hold 1 hide less 11 acres. There are 2 riding-horses and 14 swine and 250 sheep.' There is a mill paying 35 shillings, and 50 acres of meadow and 120 acres of pasture. It is worth 7 pounds.

To this manor has been added 1 hide in WILEGE, 'WLLEGA' [Woolley], which Alvric held T.R.E. for 1 manor and paid geld for 1 hide. 'Geoffrey holds it of the bishop.' There are 'in demesne 1 hide less 3 acres and ' 2 ploughs and 6 serfs and (there are) 9 bordars 'who have 3 virgates' with 1 plough. 'There are 1 riding-horse and 14 swine and 106 sheep and 33 she-goats.' There (are) 2 mills paying 2[3] shillings, and 20 acres of underwood (*silvæ minutæ*). It was and is worth 60 shillings.

Nigel 'de Gurnai' holds of the bishop WICHE [Bathwick]. Alvred held (it) T.R.E. and paid geld for 1 hide. There is land for 1 plough. It was and is worth 20 shillings.

The bishop himself holds CONTONE [Compton Dando]. Edric 'cild' held (it) T.R.E. and paid geld for 10 hides. There is land for 14 ploughs. In demesne 'are 3 hides and 3 virgates and ' 1 plough and 4 serfs and

---

[1] Exet. Dom.: 'Of the aforesaid hides a priest holds 1 virgate which belongs to the church.'

[2] A list of knights' fees held of the Earl of Gloucester in 1315 includes Freshford (*Inq. p. m.* 8 Ed. II. 68–69). Freshford occurs in Bishop Drokensford, *Register* in 1313 (*S.R.S.* i. 157).

[3] Exet. Dom. ' 10.'

(there are) 16 villeins and 6 bordars with 6 ploughs 'and 6 hides and 1 virgate. There are 1 riding-horse and 16 beasts and 14 swine and 120 sheep.' There are 2 mills paying 25 shillings, and 15 acres of meadow and 100 acres of pasture and 15 acres of wood(land). It was and is worth 10 pounds.

The bishop himself holds WEROCOSALE [Wraxall]. Alvric held (it) T.R.E. and paid geld for 20 hides. There is land for 26 ploughs. In demesne 'are 7½ hides and' 1 plough and 2 serfs and (there are) 34 villeins and 30 bordars with 25 ploughs 'and 8½ hides. There are 2 riding-horses and 2 unbroken mares (equæ indomitæ) and 24 beasts and 19 swine and 96 sheep.' There are 2 mills paying 12 shillings and 6 pence, and 150 acres of meadow and as much of wood(land). Pasture 2 leagues long and 7 furlongs broad. It was and is worth 15 pounds. Of the same land of this manor 1 knight (miles) holds 4½ hides of the bishop, and there he has [1] 2 ploughs with 3 villeins and 4 bordars. 'There are 70 sheep.' It was and is worth 50 shillings. To this manor has been added 1 hide which 1 thegn held 'in parage (pariter)' T.R.E. There is land for 1 plough. It is worth 10 shillings.

The bishop holds WENFRE [Winford].[2] Alwold held (it) T.R.E. and paid geld for 10 hides. There is land for 22 ploughs. Of this (land) Roger 'Witen' holds 4 hides, Folcran (holds) 5 hides, Colsuain (holds) 1 hide. In demesne they have 5 ploughs and there (are) 7 serfs and 19 villeins and 12 bordars with 14 ploughs. 'There are 2 riding-horses and 3 unbroken mares (equæ indomitæ) and 20 beasts and 21 swine and 320 sheep.'[3] There (is) a mill paying 40 pence, and 20 acres of meadow. Pasture 2 furlongs long and 1 furlong broad. Wood(land) 1 league long and 2 furlongs broad. The whole (manor) was worth 9 pounds 5 shillings. Now (it is worth) 20 shillings more.
To this manor has been added 1 hide which Alvric held T.R.E. Now Colsuain holds (it) of the bishop and has there 2 ploughs and 2 bordars. It was and is worth 25 shillings.

William 'de Moncellis' holds FUSCOTE [Forscote or Foxcote]. Aldida held (it)

T.R.E. and paid geld for 5 hides. There is land for 4 ploughs. In demesne are '3 hides and 3 virgates and' 2 ploughs and 3 serfs and (there are) 2 cottars and 3 villeins and 6 bordars with 2 ploughs 'and 1 hide and 1 virgate. There are 20 beasts and 29 swine and 177 sheep.' There is a mill paying 10 shillings, and 19 acres of meadow and 6 acres of pasture and 20 acres of underwood (silvæ minutæ). It was and is worth 4 pounds.

+ The same William 'de Moncellis' holds of the bishop STRATONE[4] [Stratton-on-the-Fosse]. T.R.E. Alwold[5] held (it) of the church of Glastingberie [Glastonbury], nor could he be separated from it, and he paid geld for 3 hides. There is land for 3 ploughs. In demesne are '2½ hides and' 2 ploughs and 3 serfs and (there are) 5 villeins and 6 bordars with 1½ ploughs 'and half a hide.' 'There is 1 riding-horse and 10 beasts and 27 unbroken mares (equæ indomitæ) and 21 swine and 317 sheep and 43 she-goats.' There is a mill paying 5 shillings, and 20 acres of meadow. Pasture 4 furlongs reckoning length and breadth (inter long. et lat.). Wood(land) 3 furlongs long and 2 furlongs broad. It was worth 50 shillings. Now 4 pounds, 'and 10 shillings.'
To this manor have been added 1½ hides in PICOTE [Pitcott in Stratton]. Wlmar held (it) T.R.E. 'in parage (pariter)' and could betake himself where he would (poterat ire quo volebat).[6] There is land for 1 plough. 'In demesne are 1 hide and 1 virgate, and the villeins have 1 virgate and half a plough.' There are 2 villeins and 2 bordars with 1 serf. There is a mill paying 40 pence, and 7 acres of meadow and 2 furlongs of pasture and 1 furlong of wood(land). It was and is worth 20 shillings. William 'de Moncellis' holds (it) of the bishop.

Nigel 'de Gurnay' holds of the bishop ENGLISCOME, 'INGELISCUMA' [Englishcombe]. One thegn held (it) T.R.E. 'in parage (pariter)' and paid geld for 10 hides. There is land for 10 ploughs. In demesne are '6½ hides and 1 virgate and' 3 ploughs and 6 serfs and (there are) 3 villeins and 17 bordars with 6 ploughs 'and 4 hides and 1 virgate. There are 2 riding-horses and 9 beasts and 24 swine and 137 sheep.' There are 2 mills

[1] Exet. Dom. adds: 'inter se et suos.'
[2] In Kirby's Quest, 'Wynfred'; Nom. Villar. of 1317, 'Wynfird.'
[3] These figures include the live-stock on the hide 'addita.'
[4] Against this entry + in Excheq. Dom., and also at Millescota, evidently to mark Glastonbury property alienated.
[5] Exet. Dom.: 'Wlwold the priest.'
[6] Exet. Dom.: 'cum terra sua poterat ire ad quemlibet dominum.'

paying 11 shillings and 7 pence. There (are) 12 acres of pasture and 100 acres of underwood (*silvæ minutæ*). It was and is worth 10 pounds.

The same Nigel 'de Gurnay' holds of the bishop TWERTON [Twerton]. Three thegns held (it) 'in parage (*pariter*)' T.R.E. and paid geld for 7½ hides. There is land for 10 ploughs. In demesne are '3½ hides and' 3 ploughs and 6 serfs and (there are) 7 villeins and 13 bordars with 6 ploughs 'and 3 hides. There are 2 riding-horses and 11 beasts and 17 swine and 200 sheep.' There are 2 mills paying 30 shillings, and 15 acres of meadow. It was and is worth 10 pounds.

Geoffrey 'Malrward' holds of the bishop TWERTONE [Twerton]. One thegn held (it) T.R.E. 'in parage (*pariter*)' and paid geld for 2½ hides. There is land for 2½ ploughs which are there in demesne with 4 bordars and 2 serfs. 'There are 2 riding-horses and 6 beasts and 18 swine and 200 sheep.' There are 2 mills paying 30 shillings, and 7 acres of meadow and 4 acres of underwood (*silvæ minutæ*). It was and is worth 60 shillings. Alvred 'the steward (*dapifer*)' held this estate (*terram*) of Queen Edith. Now the bishop holds it of the king, as he says.

Roger[1] holds of the bishop STOCHE, 'Estoca' [Radstock]. Alvied, Alwin, and Ælgar held (it) 'in parage (*pariter*)' T.R.E. and paid geld for 7 hides and 3 virgates. There is land for 9 ploughs. In demesne are '3½ hides and' 3 ploughs and 2 serfs and (there are) 9 villeins and 12 bordars and 3[2] cottars with 4 ploughs 'and 4 hides and 1 virgate.' 'There are 1 riding-horse and 5 beasts and 22 swine and 210 sheep.' There is a mill paying 13[3] shillings, and 12 acres of meadow. It was and is worth 7 pounds.

Ralf, 'rufus,' holds of the bishop HARDINTONE [Hardington]. Three thegns held (it) 'in parage (*pariter*)' T.R.E. and paid geld for 4 hides. There is land for 4 ploughs. In demesne are '3 hides and 1 virgate and' 2 ploughs and 4 serfs and (there are) 1 villein and 7 bordars with 3 ploughs 'and 3 virgates.

[1] The tenant Roger is apparently Roger Wythent, who gave the church of Stok to the church of Bath (*v.* the Martyrology in *Chartularies of Bath Priory, S.R.S.* vii. 159). In 1221 Roger de Clifton recovered the advowson of the church of 'Radestok' from the Prior of Bath (*Ped. Fin.* 5 Hen. III. 48 ; *S.R.S.* vi. 43).
[2] Exet. Dom. : '4.'
[3] Exet. Dom. : '12.'

There is 1 riding-horse and 6 beasts and 28 swine and 126 sheep and 2 asses.' There are 36 acres of meadow and 12 acres of underwood (*silvæ minutæ*). It was and is worth 4 pounds. In this manor is 1 hide belonging (*pertinens*) to HAMINTONE [Hemington]. Baldwin holds (it) and has common of pasture in this manor (*communem pasturam huic M.*).

Azelin holds of the bishop BABINGTONE [Babington]. Two thegns held (it) 'in parage (*pariter*)' T.R.E. and paid geld for 5 hides. There is land for 4 ploughs. In demesne are '4 hides and 1 virgate and' 2 ploughs and 7 serfs and (there are) 2 villeins and 2 bordars with 3 ploughs 'and 3 virgates. There are 3 cottars. There are 2 riding-horses and 1 beast and 13 swine and 200 sheep.' There (is) a mill paying 40 pence, and 12 acres of meadow and 15 acres of pasture. Wood(land) 6 furlongs long and 2 furlongs broad. It was worth 40 shillings. Now 60 shillings.

+ Azelin holds of the bishop MILLESCOTE [Middlecote in Babington]. Two thegns held (it) of the church of Glastingberie, nor could they be separated from it, 'and it was thegnland of the church T.R.E.,' and they paid geld for 5½ hides. There is land for 5 ploughs. In demesne are '2½ hides and' 1½ ploughs and 3 serfs, and (there are) 9 villeins and 6 bordars and 5 cottars with 5 ploughs 'and 3 hides. There are 2 beasts and 9 swine and 30 sheep.' There is a mill paying 6 shillings and 6 pence, and 3 acres of meadow. Pasture 4 furlongs long and 2 furlongs broad, and as much wood(land). It was worth 40 shillings. Now 4 pounds.

The bishop himself holds LOLIGTONE [Lullington]. Earl Herald held (it) T.R.E. and paid geld for 7 hides. There is land for 5 ploughs. In demesne are '4 hides and' 2 ploughs and 2 serfs and (there are) 7 villeins and 10 bordars with 4 ploughs 'and 3 hides. There are 2 riding-horses and 4 beasts and 16 swine and 220 sheep.' There (is) a mill paying 20 shillings, and 20 acres of meadow. Wood(land) 6 furlongs long and 2 furlongs broad. It was worth 4 pounds. Now 100 shillings.

The bishop himself holds HORCERLEI [Orchardleigh]. Three thegns held (it) 'in parage (*pariter*)' T.R.E. and paid geld for 5 hides. There is land for 4 ploughs. In demesne are '3 hides and' 3 ploughs and 2 serfs and (there are) 3 villeins and 9 bordars with 2 ploughs 'and 2 hides. There are 3 riding-horses and 14 she-goats.' There (is) a mill paying 12 shillings and 6 pence, and 24 acres of meadow. Wood(land) 6 furlongs long and 2 furlongs broad. It was and is worth 4 pounds.

Moyses holds of the bishop TABLESFORD[1] [Tellisford]. Edward held (it) T.R.E. and paid geld for 2 hides. There is land for 3 ploughs. In demesne are '1½ hides and' 2 ploughs and (there are) 5 cottars and 4 bordars with 1½ ploughs 'and half a hide.' 'There are 7 beasts and 13 swine and 95 sheep and 29 she-goats.' There (is) half a mill paying 7 shillings and 6 pence, and 7 acres of meadow and 10 acres of pasture and 1½ acres of wood(land). It is worth 30 shillings, 'and when the bishop received it 20 shillings.'

To this manor have been added 3 hides. Alviet held (them) 'in parage (pariter)' T.R.E. and paid geld for so much (pro tanto). 'Roger holds this of the bishop.' There is land for 4 ploughs. In demesne 'are 1 hide and 3 virgates and' 1 plough and 3 serfs and (there are) 3 villeins and 8 bordars with 2 ploughs 'and the rest of the land. There are 12 swine and 65 sheep and 24 she-goats.' There (is) half a mill paying 9 shillings, and 11½ acres of meadow and 30 acres of pasture and 4½ acres of wood(land). It was worth 60 shillings. Now 40 shillings.

The bishop holds '1 vill which is called' RODE [Road] for 3 manors. Seven thegns held (it) 'in parage (pariter)' T.R.E. and paid geld for 9 hides. There is land for 9 ploughs. Of this estate (terra) Robert holds of the bishop 1 hide. Moyses (holds) ½ hide. Robert (holds) 1½ hides. Roger (holds) 2½ hides. Sirewold (holds) 2½ hides. Richard 'the interpreter' (holds) 1 hide. In demesne are '8½ hides and' 7 ploughs and 6 serfs and (there are) 3 villeins and 29 bordars with 4½ ploughs 'and 2 virgates.' 'There are 2 riding-horses and 17 beasts and 45 swine and 375 sheep and 21 she-goats.' From the mills come (exeunt) 27 shillings, and (there are) 33 acres of meadow and 33 acres of wood(land) and 25 acres of pasture. The total value was 7 pounds 10 shillings. Now between them all it is worth 8 pounds 5 shillings.[2]

Nigel holds of the bishop CAIVEL [Keyford in Frome]. Levedai held (it) T.R.E. and paid geld for 1 hide and 1 virgate of land. There is land for 1 plough which is there in demesne with 12 cottars. 'There are 2 beasts and 13 swine and 26 sheep and 18 she-goats.' There (is) a mill paying 30 pence, and 6 acres of meadow and 5 acres of pasture. It was worth 10 shillings. Now 15 shillings.

fo. 89

Osmund holds of the bishop LITELTONE [Stony Littleton in Wellow]. Goduin held (it) T.R.E. and paid geld for 2 hides. There is land for 2 ploughs which are there in demesne with 1 bordar and 6 serfs. 'There are 1 riding-horse and 5 beasts and 15 swine and 200 sheep.' There (is) a mill paying 10 shillings, and 2 acres of meadow and 6 acres of pasture. It is worth 40 shillings, 'and when received 30 shillings.'

The bishop himself holds NIWETONE, 'NEWETONA' [Newton St. Lo]. Alric held (it) T.R.E. and paid geld for 3 hides. There is land for 4 ploughs. In demesne are '2½ hides and' 2 ploughs and 4 serfs and (there are) 4 villeins and 3 bordars with 2 ploughs 'and half a hide. There are 2 riding-horses and 12 beasts and 40 swine and 93 sheep.' There (is) a mill paying 7 shillings and 6 pence, and 9 acres of meadow and 40 acres of underwood (silvæ minutæ). It was worth 60 shillings. Now 100 shillings.

To this manor have been added 7 hides which 2[3] thegns held 'in parage (pariter)' T.R.E. There is land for 8 ploughs. 'In demesne are 3½ hides and half a virgate, and the villeins have 3 hides and 1½ virgates.' There are 14 villeins and 8 bordars and 7 serfs with 6 ploughs and 23 acres of meadow. It was worth 100 shillings. Now 10 pounds.

Azelin holds of the bishop FERENTONE [Farrington Gurnay]. Brismar held (it) T.R.E. and paid geld for 5 hides. There is land for 7 ploughs. In demesne are '3 hides and' 3 ploughs and 4 serfs and (there are) 7 villeins and 7 bordars with 4 ploughs 'and 2 hides. There are 2 riding-horses and 7 beasts and 7 swine and 100 sheep.' There are 100 acres of meadow. It was worth 50 shillings. Now 4 pounds.

Azelin holds of the bishop ESTONE [Stone Easton]. Three thegns, 'Saiulf, Alvric, Vlsi,' held (it) 'in parage (pariter)' T.R.E.

---

[1] In *Kirby's Quest*, 1284, 'Telesford' is held of the Earl of Gloucester.

[2] See Exet. Dom. for the different shares of the several tenants.

[3] Exet. Dom. reads '9.'

and paid geld for 4½ hides. There is land for 6 ploughs. In demesne are '3 hides and' 3 ploughs and 4 serfs and (there are) 5 villeins and 4 bordars and 2 cottars with 4 ploughs 'and 1½ hides. There are 1 riding-horse and 1 cow and 6 swine.' There is a mill paying 30 pence, and 40 acres of meadow and 40 acres of pasture. It was and is worth 70 shillings.

Azelin holds of the bishop HERPETREU [West Harptree]. Edric held (it) T.R.E. and paid geld for 5 hides. There is land for 4 ploughs. In demesne 'are 3 hides and' half a plough and (there are) 7 villeins and 4 bordars and 5 cottars with 3 ploughs 'and 2 hides. There are 5 beasts and 4 swine and 24 she-goats.' There is a mill paying 5 shillings, and 58 acres of meadow and 42 acres of wood(land). Pasture 1 league long and half a league broad. It was and is worth 40 shillings.

Robert holds of the bishop AMELBERGE[1] [Emborough]. Two thegns, 'Alnod and Ulfric,' held (it) 'in parage (*pariter*)' T.R.E. and paid geld for 3 hides. There is land for 4 ploughs. In demesne there are '1 hide and 3 virgates and' 2 ploughs and 2 serfs and (there are) 6 villeins and 4 bordars with 5 ploughs 'and 1 hide and 1 virgate, and 3 cottars. There are 1 riding-horse and 23 beasts and 25 swine and 158 wether sheep (*berbices*).' There (are) 29 acres of meadow. It was worth 20 shillings. Now 70 shillings.

The bishop himself holds CAMELEI [Cameley]. Two thegns, 'Sirewold and Orduald,' held (it) 'in parage (*pariter*)' T.R.E. and paid geld for 9 hides and half a virgate of land. There is land for 9 ploughs. In demesne are '4 hides and 3 virgates and' 3 ploughs and 13 serfs and (there are) 9 villeins and 1 bordar and 7 cottars with 4 ploughs 'and 3 hides and 1½ virgates. There are 2 riding-horses and 12 beasts and 21 swine and 150 sheep.' There is a mill paying 5 shillings, and 120 acres of meadow and 30 acres of pasture and 50 acres of underwood (*silvæ minutæ*). It was worth 7 pounds. Now 10 pounds.

Of this land of this manor Humfrey holds 1 hide and there he has 1 plough, and (there are) 3 villeins and 1 cottar with 1 plough. 'There are 12 beasts and 14 swine and 70 sheep.' There are 40 acres of meadow. It is worth 20 shillings.

William 'de Moncellis' holds of the bishop CHINGESTONE [Kingston Seymour]. Eldred held (it) T.R.E. and paid geld for 1 hide. There is land for 17 ploughs. In demesne are '1 virgate and' 3 ploughs with 1 serf and (there are) 18 villeins and 4 bordars with 11 ploughs 'and 3 virgates. There are 20 beasts and 31 swine and 120 sheep.' There are 40 acres of pasture. It was and is worth 6 pounds.

Of the land of this manor Fulcran holds of the bishop land for 1 plough and there he has 2 bordars. It is worth 3 shillings.

The same William 'de Moncellis' holds CHINGESTONE [Kingston Seymour] of the bishop. Four thegns, 'Alvric the priest, Siward, Saric, and Saiolf,' held (it) 'in parage (*pariter*)' T.R.E. and paid geld for 4½ hides. There is land for 7 ploughs. 'In demesne are 2 hides, and the villeins have the rest of the land.' There are 9 villeins and 8 bordars with 1 serf having 6½ ploughs. It was and is worth 60 shillings. T.R.E. this manor[2] paid geld for 1 hide only.

Roger holds of the bishop HELGETREU [Hallatrow in High Littleton]. Four thegns, 'a certain woman, Sirewold, Alward and Fordret,' held (it) 'in parage (*pariter*)' T.R.E. and paid geld for 5 hides less half a virgate of land. There is land for 6 ploughs. In demesne there are '3½ hides and' 1½ ploughs and (there are) 4 villeins and 3 bordars and 3 cottars with 2 ploughs 'and the rest of the land. There are 1 riding-horse and 17 sheep.' There are 27 acres of meadow and 33 acres of pasture. It was and is worth 60 shillings.

Ralf 'rufus' holds of the bishop LITELTONE [High Littleton]. Alwold[3] held (it) T.R.E. and paid geld for 5 hides. There is land for 5 ploughs. In demesne are '4 hides and 1½ virgates and' 2 ploughs with 1 serf, and (there are) 4 villeins and 6 bordars with 3 ploughs 'and the rest of the land. There are 6 beasts and 2 swine and 83 sheep.' There is a mill paying 50 pence, and 32 acres of meadow and 66 acres of pasture. In Bath (there is appurtenant) 1 burgess paying 15 pence. It was and is worth 60 shillings.

The same Ralf 'rufus' holds of the

---

[1] Mediæval variations are Emelebergh (*Kirby's Quest*), Emnebergh (*Nom. Villar.*), Empneberghe (*Excheq. Lay Subsidy*, 1327), Enbarowgh (*Inq. p.m.* John Butler, 17 Hen. VIII. Chanc. 43).

[2] Exet. Dom. reads, 'the aforesaid 5½ hides.'
[3] Exet. Dom.: 'Alnod.'

bishop OPETONE [Upton Noble].[1] Lesmer
held (it) T.R.E. and paid geld for 3 hides.
There is land for 3 ploughs. In demesne
are '2 hides and 1 virgate and' 1 plough
and 2 serfs and (there are) 5 villeins and
4 bordars and 2 cottars with 3 ploughs 'and 3
virgates. There are 4 beasts and 21 swine
and 30 sheep and 11 she-goats.' There are
5 acres of meadow. Wood(land) half a
league long and 4 furlongs broad. It was
and is worth 60 shillings.

Lewin holds of the bishop MEGELE
[Midghill in Chelvey]. Almar held (it)
T.R.E. and paid geld for 1 hide. There
is land for 2 ploughs which are there with
2 villeins and 3 bordars and 1 serf. 'In
demesne are 2 virgates and the villeins have
2 virgates and 2 ploughs. There are 4
beasts and 1 pig.' There are 6 acres of
meadow. It was worth 4 shillings. Now
20 shillings.

Ralf holds of the bishop WEREGRAVE[2]
[Weathergrove in Sandford Orcas]. Three
thegns held (it) 'in parage (pariter)' T.R.E.
and paid geld for 2 hides. There is land
for 1 plough which is there in demesne with
'1½ hides and' 2 serfs and (there are) 1 villein and 5 bordars and 2 cottars with half
a plough 'and half a hide. There are 2
swine and 56 sheep.' There is a mill paying 3 shillings, and 3 acres of meadow and
5 acres of wood(land). It was worth 20
shillings. Now 30 shillings.

Azelin holds of the bishop STANWELLE[3]
[Stowell]. Turmund held (it) T.R.E. and
paid geld for 3 hides. There is land for 4
ploughs. In demesne are '1½ hides and'
2 ploughs and 2 serfs and (there are) 5 villeins and 7 bordars and 2 cottars with 2
ploughs 'and the rest of the land. There are
2 riding-horses and 6 beasts and 20 swine and

140 sheep.' There (are) 16 acres of meadow
and 5 acres of pasture and 6 acres of underwood (silvæ minutæ). It was worth 40 shillings. Now 60 shillings.

'fo. 156'
VI. THE LAND OF THE BISHOP 'GISO' OF WELLS

The Bishop of Wells holds WELLE
[Wells]. He held (it) T.R.E. and paid geld
for 50 hides. There is land for 60 ploughs.
Of this (land) are in demesne 8 hides where
are 6 ploughs and 6 serfs and (there are) 20
villeins and 14 bordars with 15 ploughs 'and 6
hides. There are 2 riding-horses and 22 beasts
and 30 swine and 150 sheep and 24 she-
goats.' There are 4 mills paying 30 shillings,
and 300 acres of meadow. Pasture 3 leagues
long and 1 league broad. Wood(land) 2
leagues long and 2 furlongs broad and 3
leagues of moor. It is worth 30 pounds for
the use (ad opus) of the bishop.

Of that land of the same manor the canons
'of S. ANDREW' hold 14 hides. They have
there in demesne '6 hides and' 6 ploughs
and 8 serfs and (there are) 16 villeins and 12
bordars with 8 ploughs 'and 8 hides.' 'There
are 2 riding-horses and 12 beasts and 10 swine
and 100 sheep.' There are 2 mills paying
50 pence. It is worth 12 pounds.

Of that land of the same manor Fastrad
holds of the bishop 6 hides, 'which two thegns
held who could not be separated from the
church.' Richard (holds) 5 hides. Erneis
(holds) 5 hides, 'which a thegn held who
could not be separated from the church.'
There are in demesne '11 hides and' 6
ploughs and 10 serfs and (there are) 17
villeins and 16 bordars with 11 ploughs
'and 5 hides.' 'There are 2 riding-
horses and 40 beasts and 62 swine and 500
sheep.' There are 2 mills paying 10 shillings. Between them all it is worth 13
pounds.[4]

Of that land of the same manor Fastrad
holds of the bishop 2 hides. Ralf (holds) 2
hides. These 4 hides are part of the bishop's
demesne. There (are) in demesne 3 hides
and 2 ploughs and 3 serfs and (there are) 5
villeins and 5 bordars with 1 plough 'and 1
hide. There are 10 beasts and 6 swine and
50 sheep and 30 she-goats.' There is a mill
paying 7 shillings and 6 pence. Total value
70 shillings.

Of the same 50 hides the wife of Manasseh
holds 2 hides, but not of the bishop. It is
worth 20 shillings.

Besides these 50 hides the bishop has 2

---

[1] Opetone. Augustine de Plessy held 'Hupptone'
in Bruton Hundred of the Honour of Gloucester
in 1284, Kirby's Quest (Upetone in Nom. Villar.).

[2] There are two places of this name in the
county, both held of the Earl of Gloucester.
One is 'Wydergrave' in Hardington, near Frome;
the other is Wergrave in Sandford Orcas; both are
obsolete. Its position in the schedule between
Midgehill in Chelvey and Stowell in the Hundred
of Horethorne is dubious, but the balance is in
favour of the identification adopted.

[3] 'Estanwella.' This spelling appears in Kirby's
Quest in the Hundred of Horethorne, which
contains the modern Stowell. In the Nom.
Villar., 1317, and in the Exchequer Lay Subsidy of
1327 it is 'Stawelle.'

[4] Exet. Dom. gives the details of each holding.

hides which never paid geld T.R.E. Alward 'Crocco' and Edric hold (them) of the bishop. They are worth 30 shillings.

The same bishop holds CUMBE [Combe St. Nicholas]. Azor 'son of Torold' held (it) T.R.E. and paid geld for 20 hides. There is land for 16 ploughs. Of this (land) there are in demesne 8 hides where are 3 ploughs and 12 serfs and (there are) 15 villeins and 13 bordars with 12 ploughs 'and 12 hides. There are 12 beasts and 18 swine and 315 sheep and 1 riding-horse.' There (are) 12 acres of meadow and half a league of pasture reckoning (inter) length and breadth, and 1 league of wood(land) reckoning length and breadth. It was worth 10 pounds. Now 18 pounds.

The same bishop holds CHINGESBERIE [Kingsbury Episcopi]. He held (it) T.R.E. and paid geld for 20 hides. There is land for 24 ploughs. Of this (land) there is in demesne 6 hides where are 2 ploughs and 4 serfs and (there are) 16 villeins and 4 bordars with 11 ploughs 'and 6 hides. There are 1 riding-horse and 2 beasts and 4 swine and 30 sheep.' There are 2 mills paying 30 shillings, and 100 acres of meadow. Pasture 1 league long and 3 furlongs broad. Of the same land of this manor 3 knights (milites) and 1 cleric (clericus) hold 8 hides. It is worth for the use (ad opus) of the bishop 12 pounds. For the use of the knights 8 pounds.

The same bishop holds CERDRE [Chard]. He held (it) T.R.E. and paid geld for 8 hides. There is land for 20 ploughs. Of this (land) there are in demesne 2 hides where are 2 ploughs and 11 serfs and (there are) 20 villeins with 14 ploughs 'and 6 hides.' 'There are 1 riding-horse and 13 beasts and 20 swine and 300 sheep and 24 she-goats.' There is a mill paying 30 pence, and 20[1] acres of meadow. Wood(land) 2 leagues long and 4 furlongs broad, and as much pasture. Of the same land 1 thegn holds 2 hides who cannot be separated from the church. Total value 16 pounds.

The same bishop holds LITELANDE, 'LIT-TELANEIA' [probably in Huish Episcopi].[2] He held (it) T.R.E. and paid geld for 2 hides. There is land for 8 ploughs. Of this (land)

there is 1 hide in demesne where are 2 ploughs and 2 serfs and (there are) 3 villeins and 6 bordars with 2 ploughs 'and 1 hide. There is 1 riding-horse.' There are 12 acres of meadow and 100 acres of pasture and 20 acres of wood(land). It was and is worth 40 shillings.

The same bishop holds WIVELESCOME [Wiveliscombe]. He held it T.R.E. and paid geld for 15 hides. There is land for 36 ploughs. Of this (land) there are in demesne 3 hides, where are 4 ploughs and 8 serfs and (there are) 16 villeins and 3 bordars with 7 ploughs 'and 3 hides.' 'There are 1 riding-horse and 15 beasts and 12 swine and 70 sheep and 36 she-goats.' There is a mill paying 50 pence, 'and 34 acres of meadow and 200 acres of pasture and 80 acres of wood(land).

Of the land of this manor 3 knights (milites) hold of the bishop 9 hides, and there they have 16 ploughs. This land belongs to the demesne of the bishopric (episcopatus), nor can it be separated from the bishop. It is worth 10 pounds to the bishop. To the knights (it is worth) 15 pounds.

The same bishop holds WALINTONE [Wellington]. He held it T.R.E. and paid geld for 14 hides. There is land for 30 ploughs. Of this (land) there is in demesne 3 hides, where are 4 ploughs and 31 serfs and (there are) 53 villeins and 61 bordars with 25 ploughs 'and 9 hides.' 'There are 1 riding-horse and 17 beasts and 3 swine and 110 sheep.' There are 2 mills paying 15 shillings, and 105 acres of meadow. Pasture 1 league long and half a league broad. Wood(land) 3 furlongs long and as much broad.

Of the land of this manor John 'Hosti-arius' holds 2 hides of the villeins' land. Total value 25 pounds.

To this manor has been added 1 hide which Alveva held 'in parage (pariter)' T.R.E. for a manor. There is land for 3 ploughs which are there with 8 villeins and 4 bordars and 1 serf. There are 5 acres of meadow. Wood(land) 3 furlongs long and as much broad. It is worth 30 shillings.

The same bishop holds LIDEGAR [Bishops Lydeard]. He held it T.R.E. and paid geld for 10 hides less 1 virgate. There is land for 16 ploughs. Of this (land) there are in demesne 3 hides, where are 2 ploughs and 5 serfs and (there are) 20 villeins and 12 bordars with 6 ploughs 'and 4 hides.' 'There are 1 riding-horse and 10 beasts and 20 swine and 150 sheep.' There is a mill paying

---

[1] Exet. Dom. : '15.'

[2] A charter of Edward the Confessor to Bishop Giso mentions 'Lytleinge and Hywise.' As Huish Episcopi is not mentioned in Domesday, it is likely that at this date the parish was known by the first name, which has now disappeared.

31 pence, and 30 acres of meadow. Pasture 1 league long and 3 furlongs broad, and as much wood(land).[1]

Of the land of this manor 2 knights (*milites*) hold 3 hides of the villeins' land, and have 3 ploughs there. Total value 13 pounds; 'to the use of the bishop 10 pounds, to the use of the knights 3 pounds.'

fo. 89b

The same bishop holds BANWELLE [Banwell]. Earl Harold held (it) T.R.E. and paid geld for 30 hides. There is land for 40 ploughs. Of this (land) there are in demesne 6 hides where are 3 ploughs and 5 serfs, and (there are) 24 [2] villeins and 12 bordars with 18 ploughs 'and 7 hides.' 'There are 15 beasts and 15 swine and 30 sheep and 20 she-goats.' There (are) 100 acres of meadow. Pasture 1 league long and broad. Wood(land) 2½ leagues long and broad.

Of the land of this manor Serlo 'de Burci' holds of the bishop 3 hides. Ralf 'Tortesmains' (holds) 5½ hides. Rohard (holds) 5½ hides. Fastrad (holds) 1 hide. Bono (holds) 1 hide. Elwi 'Haussonna' (holds) 1 hide.[3] There are in demesne 9 ploughs and 5 serfs and (there are) 25 villeins and 15 bordars owning 13½ ploughs. 'Rohard has 6 unbroken (*indomitas*) mares and 1 riding-horse and 20 beasts and 30 swine and 100 sheep.' There (are) 2 mills belonging to Rohard paying 10 shillings. Ordulf has 1 mill paying 40 pence. The whole manor is worth 15 pounds for the use (*ad opus*) of the bishop. For the use of the men 15 pounds as well.

The same bishop holds EVRECRIZ [Evercreech]. He held it T.R.E. and paid geld for 20 hides. There is land for 20 ploughs. Of this (land) there are in demesne 3 hides, where are 3 ploughs and 6 serfs and there (are) 3 villeins and 10 bordars with 2 ploughs. 'and 2 hides.' 'There are 1 riding-horse and 25 beasts and 30 swine and 200 sheep.' There is a mill paying 7 shillings and 6 pence, and 60 acres of meadow and 200 acres of pasture. Wood(land) 1 league long and 1 furlong broad. It is worth 10 pounds. Of this land of the same manor Erneis holds of the bishop 7 hides. Macharius (holds) 1½ hides. Ildebert (holds) 1 hide. In demesne are 4 ploughs and 4 serfs and (there are) 5 villeins and 4 bordars with 2 ploughs. 'Erneis

and Macharius have 1 riding-horse and 14 beasts and 22 swine and 180 sheep.' Between them all it is worth 110 shillings.[4] Of the same land a priest and 2 other Englishmen hold 5 hides and 1 virgate of land. It is worth 4 pounds.

The same bishop holds WESTBERIE [Westbury]. He held it T.R.E. and paid geld for 6 hides. There is land for 8 ploughs. Of this (land) there are in demesne 3 hides where are 2 ploughs and 2 serfs and (there are) 6 villeins and 10 bordars with 5 ploughs ' and 3 hides.' 'There are 1 riding-horse and 10 beasts and 18 swine and 200 sheep.' There (are) 30 acres of meadow, and wood(land) 1 league long and 2 furlongs broad. It is worth 8 pounds.

Osmund holds of the bishop WINESHAM [Winsham]. Elsi held (it) T.R.E. and paid geld for 10 hides. There is land for 16 ploughs. Of this (land) there are in demesne 4 hides where are 3 ploughs and 12 serfs and (there are) 50 villeins with 9 ploughs 'and 6 hides.' 'There are 2 riding-horses and 13 beasts and 13 swine and 270 sheep, and 1 swineherd who pays 12 swine (yearly).' There (are) 2 mills paying 20 shillings, and 6 acres of meadow. Wood(land) half a league long and 1½ furlongs broad. It was worth 6 pounds; now 10 pounds.

The same bishop holds CHIWE [Chew Magna]. He held it T.R.E. and paid geld for 30 hides. There is land for 50 ploughs. Of this (land) there are in demesne 4 hides where are 6 ploughs and 14 serfs and (there are) 30 villeins and 9 bordars with 24 ploughs 'and 6 hides.' 'There are 2 swineherds who pay 24 swine (yearly) and 1 riding-horse and 9 beasts and 36 swine and 148 sheep and 46 she-goats.' There are 3 mills paying 20 shillings, and 100 acres of meadow and 50 acres of pasture. Wood(land) 2 leagues long and half a league broad. It is worth 30 pounds to the bishop.

Of the land of this manor Richard holds of the bishop 5 hides. Rohard (holds) 6 hides. Stephen (holds) 5 hides. Alvric 'de Stauue' (holds) 7 virgates. Ulvric (holds) 2 hides. There are in demesne '15 hides and' 7 ploughs and 8 serfs and (there are) 18 villeins and 27 bordars with 10 ploughs 'and 4½ hides.' 'They [5] have 2 riding-horses and 20 beasts and 24 swine and 300 sheep, and 80 she-goats and 1 cow.' There are 2 mills paying

---

[1] Exet. Dom. gives the breadth of the woodland as '2 furlongs.'

[2] Exet. Dom. : ' 23.'

[3] Exet. Dom. gives the details of each holding.

[4] Exet. Dom. gives the details of each holding.

[5] Stephen has no stock.

10 shillings. Between them all it is worth 13 pounds.[1]

The same bishop holds JATUNE [Yatton]. John the Dane (*Danus*) held (it) T.R.E. and paid geld for 20 hides. There is land for 22 ploughs. Of this (land) there are in demesne 6 hides where are 2 ploughs and 3 serfs and (there are) 10 villeins and 14 bordars with 6 ploughs 'and 2 hides.' 'There are 11 beasts and 15 swine.' There (are) 32 acres of meadow. Wood(land) 1 league long and 2 furlongs broad. Moors 1 league in length and breadth. It is worth 6 pounds to the bishop.

Of the land of this manor Fastrad holds of the bishop 5 hides. Ildebert (holds) 4 hides.[2] In demesne there are '5 hides and' 3 ploughs and 4 serfs and (there are) 18 villeins and 23 bordars with 11 ploughs 'and 5 hides.' 'There are 16 beasts and 30 swine.' Between them it is worth 9 pounds.[3]

A pasture called WAIMORA [Wemberham] is there which T.R.E. belonged to Congresb'ie [Congresbury], the king's manor.

Benthelin 'the archdeacon' holds of the bishop the church of this manor with 1 hide. It is worth 20 shillings.

The same bishop holds WEDMORE [Wedmore]. He held it T.R.E. and paid geld for 10 hides. Nevertheless there (are) 11 hides. There is land for 36 ploughs. Of this (land) there are in demesne 5 hides less 1 virgate where are 4 ploughs and 4 serfs and (there are) 13 villeins and 14 bordars with 9 ploughs 'and 5 hides and 1 virgate' and 18 cottars. 'There are 6 unbroken mares (*equæ indomitæ*) and 17 beasts and 3 swine.' There (are) 70 acres of meadow and 2 fisheries paying 10 shillings, and 50 acres of wood(land) and 1 league of pasture reckoning (*inter*) length and breadth. It was worth 20 pounds; now 17 pounds. 'Beside this there are moors which pay nothing.'

The canons of S. Andrew (of Wells) hold of the bishop WANDESTREU [Wanstrow]. They held it T.R.E. and paid geld for 4 hides. There is land for 4 ploughs. Of this (land) there are in demesne 2 hides where are 2 ploughs and 4 serfs and (there are) 5 villeins and 2 bordars with 3 ploughs

'and 2 hides.' 'There are 12 swine.' There (are) 12 acres of meadow. Wood-(land) 3 furlongs long and 2 furlongs broad. It is worth 3 pounds, 'and when the bishop received it it was worth 4 pounds.'

They[4] hold LITUNE [Litton]. They held (it) T.R.E. and paid geld for 8½ hides. There is land for 7 ploughs. Of this (land) there are in demesne 6½ hides where are 2 ploughs and 6 serfs and (there are) 8 villeins and 7 bordars with 4 ploughs 'and 2 hides.' 'There are 13 beasts and 40 she-goats.' There (are) 3 mills paying 10 shillings 'and 10 pence,' and 60 acres of meadow and 1,000 acres of pasture and 3 furlongs of wood(land) in length and breadth. It is worth 100 shillings.

The king holds the manor of MILVERTUNE [Milverton]. Giso the bishop held it T.R.E. and paid geld for 1 virgate of land.

Roger Arundel holds the manor of AISSE [Ash Priors] which T.R.E. belonged to (*jacebat in*) LEDIART [Bishops Lydeard] the bishop's manor. Bishop Giso held it and paid geld for 3 hides and 1 virgate. Roger holds (it) of the king unjustly. It is worth 3 pounds.

'fo. 185'

VII. THE LAND OF THE CHURCH OF BATH

The Church of St. Peter of Bath 'has a manor which is called BADE [Bath], which is the seat of that abbey (*caput ipsius abbatie*), which Sewold the abbot held T.R.E.'; has in the same borough 24 burgesses paying 20 shillings. There (is) a mill paying 20 shillings, and 12 acres of meadow. Total value 40 shillings.

The church itself holds PRISCTONE [Priston]. T.R.E. it paid geld for 6 hides. There is land for 8 ploughs. Of that (land) there are in demesne 2 hides where are 1 plough and 3 serfs and (there are) 7 villeins and 8 bordars with 6 ploughs 'and 4 hides. There is 1 riding-horse.' There is a mill paying 7 shillings and 6 pence, and 20 acres of meadow and 80 acres of pasture. It was and is worth 6 pounds.

The church itself holds STANTONE [Stanton Prior]. T.R.E. it paid geld for 3 hides. There is land for 3 ploughs. Of that (land) there is in demesne half a hide where are 1 plough and 5 serfs and (there are) 4 villeins and 3

---

[1] Exet. Dom. gives the details of each holding.

[2] Exet. Dom. : 'Of these 4 hides a certain woman Ailruna held 1 hide in parage (*pariter*) T.R.E. With this hide belongs (*jacet*) 1 pasture called Weimorham.'

[3] Exet. Dom. gives details of each holding.

[4] i.e. the canons of St. Andrew, the cathedral church of Wells.

bordars with 2 ploughs 'and 2 hides.' 'There are 1 riding-horse and 50 sheep.' There (are) 12 acres of meadow and 30 acres of pasture and 30 acres of underwood (*silvæ minutæ*). It was and is worth 3 pounds.

Walter 'Hosatus' holds of the church WIMEDONE, 'WIMMADONA' [Wilmington[1] in Priston]. One thegn held it of the church T.R.E. 'who could not be separated from it' and paid geld for 3 hides. There is land for 4 ploughs. In demesne there are '2 hides and 1 virgate and' 2 ploughs and 2 serfs and 7 bordars with 1 plough 'and 3 virgates.' 'There are 1 riding-horse and 300 sheep.' There (is) a mill paying 5 shillings, and 10 acres of meadow and 10 acres of pasture. It was and is worth 60 shillings.

The church itself holds WESTONE [near Bath]. 'Selwold the abbot held it' T.R.E. and paid geld for 15 hides. There is land for 10 ploughs. Of that (land) there are in demesne 8½ hides where are 2 ploughs and 7 serfs and (there are) 7 villeins and 10 bordars with 6 ploughs 'and 6½ hides.' 'There are 1 riding-horse and 200 sheep.' There (is) a mill paying 10 shillings, and 20 acres of meadow. Of underwood (*silvæ minutæ*) there is 1 league reckoning (*inter*) length and breadth. It was worth 8 pounds. Now 10 pounds.

The church itself holds FORDE [Bathford]. 'Selwold the abbot held it' T.R.E. and paid geld for 10 hides. There is land for 9 ploughs. Of that (land) there are in demesne 5 hides where are 2 ploughs and 6 serfs and (there are) 5 villeins and 7 bordars with 6 ploughs 'and 5 hides.' 'There are 1 riding-horse and 12 beasts and 8 swine and 112 sheep.' There is a mill paying 10 shillings, and 12 acres of meadow and 1 league of underwood (*silvæ minutæ*) reckoning length and breath. It was and is worth 10 pounds.

The same church holds CUME [Monkton Combe]. 'Sewold the abbot held it T.R.E.' and paid geld for 9 hides. There is land for 8 ploughs. Of that (land) there are in demesne 6 hides, 'less 1 virgate,' where are 3 ploughs and 6 serfs and (there are) 6 villeins and 8 bordars with 5 ploughs, 'and 3 hides and 1 virgate. There are 1 riding-horse and 12 swine and 72 sheep.' There are 2 mills paying 13 shillings and 6 pence, and 32 acres of meadow and 1 league of underwood

(*silvæ minutæ*) in length and breadth. It was worth 7 pounds. Now 8 pounds.

William 'Hosatus' holds of the church CERLECUME [Charlcombe]. One thegn held (it) of the church T.R.E. 'who could not be separated from it,' and paid geld for 4 hides. There is land for 4 ploughs. In demesne there are '2 hides and 3 virgates and' 2 ploughs and 3 serfs and (there are) 5 villeins and 4 bordars with 2 ploughs '1 hide and 1 virgate.' 'There are 1 riding-horse and 200 sheep.' There are 5 acres of meadow and 10 acres of underwood (*silvæ minutæ*). It was worth 50 shillings. Now 6 pounds.

The church itself holds LINCUME [Lyncombe]. 'Sewold the abbot held it T.R.E.' and paid geld for 10 hides. There is land for 8 ploughs. Of this (land) there are in demesne 7 hides where are 3 ploughs and 8 serfs and (there are) 4 villeins and 10 bordars with 3 ploughs 'and 2 hides. There are 1 riding-horse and 8 swine and 180 sheep.' There are 2 mills paying 10 shillings, and 30 acres of meadow and 200 acres of pasture. It was worth 6 pounds. Now 8 pounds.

Walter 'Hosatus' holds of the same church ESTONE [Batheaston]. Ulward the abbot held (it) T.R.E. and paid geld for 1½ hides. There is land for 2 ploughs. In demesne there are '1 hide and 1 virgate and' 1 plough with 1 villein and (there are) 8 bordars with 1 plough 'and 1 virgate. There are 250 sheep.' There are 2 mills paying 6 shillings and 8 pence. There (are) 2 acres of meadow. It was worth 30 shillings. Now 40 shillings. 'This estate (*terra*) cannot be separated from the abbey.'

Hugh 'the interpreter (*interpres*),' 3 hides,[2] and Colgrim 'an Englishman (*anglicus*),' 2 hides,[3] hold of the same church HANTONE [Bathampton]. Two thegns held (it) T.R.E. nor could they be separated from the church, and they paid geld for 5 hides. There is land for 6 ploughs. In demesne are 3 ploughs and 3 serfs and (there are) 3 villeins and 6 bordars with 3 ploughs. 'There are 1 riding-horse and 14 beasts and 180 sheep and 20 swine.' There (are) 28 acres of meadow and 6 furlongs of pasture reckoning length and breadth, and 10 furlongs of underwood (*silvæ minutæ*) in length and breadth. It is worth 110 shillings.[4]

---

[1] In *Kirby's Quest* 'Wuhumdone.' Wilmedon and Wylmyngdon in early Final Concords.

[2] Interlined.   [3] Ibid.
[4] Exet. Dom. gives the figures of the two holdings separately.

Ranulf Flambard[1] holds of the same church UNDEWICHE[2] [Woodwick in Freshford]. One monk of that monastery held (it) T.R.E. 'when it could not be separated,' and paid geld for 2½ hides. There is land for 3 ploughs. There are 5 bordars, and half a mill paying 5 shillings, and 12 acres of meadow, and 30 acres of pasture. It was and is worth 20 shillings.

The church itself holds CORSTUNE [Corston] 'which Sewold the abbot held T.R.E. and' paid geld for 10 hides. There is land for 9 ploughs. Of this (land) there are in demesne 5 hides where are 2 ploughs and 4 serfs and (there are) 5 villeins and 8 bordars with 3 ploughs 'and 5 hides.' 'There is 1 riding-horse and 6 swine and 62 sheep.' There is a mill paying 30 pence, and 6 acres of meadow. It is worth 8 pounds, 'and when the abbot received it it was worth 7 pounds.'

The church itself holds EVESTIE[3] 'which Wlnold the abbot held T.R.E. and' paid geld for 1 hide. There is land for 1 plough which is there in demesne and (there are) 3 serfs and 4 acres of meadow. It is worth 20 shillings.

The church itself holds ESCEWICHE [Ashwick] 'which Wlnold the abbot held T.R.E. and' paid geld for half a hide. There is land for half a plough. There is 1 serf and 2 villeins paying 42 pence, and 12 acres of meadow and 3 acres of underwood (silvæ minutæ). It is and was worth 42 pence.

All this land belonged to (jacuit in) the same church T.R.E., and could not be separated from it.[4]

1 'Flambard' interlined.
2 Exet. Dom. : 'Wdewica.'
3 No doubt the 'Geofanstiga' of King Edgar's charter to Bath Abbey (Bath Cartularies, i. 25 ; S.R.S. vii. 25. It is marked spurious by Kemble). Two of the bounds are the Camelon, the older form of the Cam brook, and the Bath 'herpath,' perhaps the Fosse way. In a later charter (S.R.S. vii. p. 112, Nos. 581, 582) the Prior of Bath acknowledges the tithes coming from the demesne of Robert de Boys in 'Evesty' within the limits of the parish church of Wellow to belong to the Abbey of Cirencester. A Final Concord of 29 Ed. I., No. 76 (S.R.S. vi. 314) mentions 'Eversy-juxta-Combe Hawey.' So the position of the place can be settled, but the name is quite obsolete.
4 This appears to refer to all the preceding manors.

VIII. THE LAND OF ST. MARY OF GLASTONBURY

'fo. 172.'

The church of Glastonbury has in the same town (villa) 12 hides which never paid geld. There is land for 30 ploughs. Of this (land) there are in demesne 10 hides less half a virgate, where are 5 ploughs and 17 serfs and (there are) 21 villeins and 33 bordars with 5 ploughs 'and the rest of the land.' There (are) 8 smiths (fabri). 'There are 5 riding-horses and 58 beasts and 20 swine and 20 sheep and 50 she-goats.' There are 3 arpents (arpenz) of vineyard, and 60 acres of meadow and 200 acres of pasture and 20 acres of wood(land) and 300 acres of underwood (silvæ minutæ). It is worth 20 pounds, 'when Abbot Turstin received it it was worth 10 pounds.'

To this manor belongs (adjacet) an island which is called MERE [Meare]. There are 60 acres of land. (There is) land for 1 plough which is there, and (there are) 10 fishermen and 3 fisheries paying 20 pence. 'There are 1 riding-horse and 13 beasts and 4 swine.' There are 6 acres of meadow and 6 acres of wood(land) and 2 arpents (arpenz) of vineyard. It is worth 20 shillings, 'and as much when the abbot received it.'

Another island belongs there which is called WADENEBERIE[5] [Pamborough in Wedmore]. There are 6 acres of land and 3 arpents (arpenz) of vineyard and 1 bordar. It is worth 4 shillings, 'and as much when the abbot received it.'

A third island belongs there, and it is called EDERISIGE [Edgarley in Glastonbury], in which are 2 hides which never paid geld. 'T.R.E. 1 thegn held these and could not be separated from the church.' There is 1 plough with 1 bordar, and 2 acres of meadow and 1 acre of underwood (silvæ minutæ). It is worth 15 shillings, 'and as much when the ab ot received it.' Goduin holds (it) of the abbot.

'fo. 161.'

The church itself holds WINESCOME [Winscombe]. T.R.E. it paid geld for 15 hides. There is land for 30 ploughs. Of this (land) there are in demesne 5 hides less 1 virgate where are 2 ploughs and 3 serfs, and (there are) 28 villeins and 6 bordars with 9 ploughs and 5 hides less 1 virgate. There are 8 cows and 16 swine and 30 sheep and 31

5 In Exet. Dom. 'Padenaberia.'

she-goats.' There is a mill paying 5 shillings, and 60 acres of meadow and 1 league of pasture (reckoning) in length and breadth. Wood(land) 2 leagues long and 1 league broad.

Of the land of this manor Roger 'de Curcella' holds of the abbot 2½ hides. Ralf 'Tortesmains' (holds) 1 hide and 1 virgate. Pipe (holds) ½ hide. There are 5 ploughs.[1]

This manor is worth 8 pounds to the abbot. To his men (it is worth) 55 shillings.

Of the land of this manor the Bishop of Coutances holds of the king 1 hide, 'and Herluin holds of him,' and it is worth 20 shillings. Brictric held (it) freely (*libere*) T.R.E., but he could not be separated from the church.

The church itself holds MIDELTONE [Milton Puddimore, now Podymore]. T.R.E. it paid geld for 6 hides. There is land for 6 ploughs. Of this (land) there are in demesne 4 hides and 7 acres, where are 2 ploughs, and (there are) 8 villeins and 6 bordars with 4 ploughs 'and 2 hides less 7 acres. There are 1 riding-horse and 3 sheep.' There (are) 50 acres of meadow and 100 acres of pasture. It was and is worth 6 pounds.

Roger 'de Corcelle' holds of the church LIDEFORD [East Lydford]. 'A thegn called' Alward (held it) T.R.E., nor could he be separated from the church, and it paid geld for 4 hides. There is land for 5 ploughs. Of this (land) there are in demesne 3 hides and half a virgate of land where are 2 ploughs and 6 serfs, and (there are) 6 villeins and 3 bordars with 1½ ploughs 'and one hide less half a virgate.' 'There is 1 riding-horse and 6 beasts and 13 swine and 160 sheep.' There is a mill paying 10 shillings, and 40 acres of meadow. It was and is worth 4 pounds.

The church itself holds SAPESWICH [Shapwick]. 'Alnod the abbot held it T.R.E. and' paid geld for 30 hides. There is land for 40 ploughs. Besides this (land) the abbot has land for 20 ploughs which never paid geld. There are 12 ploughs belonging to the villeins 'on that land,'[2] and elsewhere there are 4 ploughs in demesne where are 6 serfs, and (there are) 5 coliberts and 15 villeins and 16 bordars. 'There are 2 riding-horses and 23 beasts and 11 swine and 100 sheep.' (There are) 60 acres of meadow and 60 acres of pasture and 57 acres of underwood (*silvæ minutæ*).

Of these 30 hides Roger 'de Corcella' holds of the abbot 5 hides in SUTONE [Sutton Mallet], and 5 hides in EDWINETONE [Edington], and 5 hides in CEPTONE[3] [Chilton upon Polden], and 5 hides in CALDECOTE, 'CADICOTE' [Catcott]. Fourteen thegns held these (hides) T.R.E., and they could not be separated from the church. There are in demesne (altogether) '16 hides and 1¼ virgates and' 9 ploughs and 11 serfs, and (there are) 19 villeins and 23 bordars with 8½ ploughs 'and the rest of the land.' 'There are 5 riding-horses and 100 swine and 18 beasts and 185 sheep.' There are 100 acres of meadow less 1 and 31 acres of underwood (*silvæ minutæ*).[4]

Of the same 30 hides Alvred 'de Hispania' holds 5 hides in HUNLAVINTONE [Woolavington], 'which Alwi Banneson held T.R.E.' and has 2 ploughs there 'and 3 hides in demesne.' There (are) 5 serfs and 12 villeins and 8 bordars with 6 ploughs 'and 2 hides.' 'There are 13 horses[5] and 11 beasts and 33 swine and 151 sheep.'

Of the same land Warmund[6] holds half one hide 'of thegnland' of the abbot, and has there 1 plough and 4 bordars. It is worth 10 shillings.

This manor is worth to the abbot 12 pounds, 'and when Turstin the abbot received it 7 pounds,' to Roger 19 pounds, to Alvred 7 pounds.

The church itself holds SOWI [Weston Zoyland, Middlezoy and Othery]. 'Alnod the abbot held it T.R.E. and' paid geld for 12 hides. There is land for 20 ploughs. Of this (land) there are in demesne 5 hides where are 2 ploughs and 2 serfs and (there are) 12 coliberts and 27 villeins and 13 bordars with 14 ploughs 'and 7 hides.' 'There are 17 beasts and 18 swine and 50 sheep.' There are 30 acres of meadow and 12 acres of underwood (*silvæ minutæ*). It was worth 10 pounds. Now 24 pounds.

Walter 'de Duaco' holds of the abbot COSINTONE [Cossington]. Alwin Pic held (it) of the abbot T.R.E. and paid geld for 3 hides. There is land for 6 ploughs. Of

---

[1] Exet. Dom. gives details of each holding.

[2] Exet. Dom.: 'super illam terram quæ non reddidit gildum.'

[3] As there is no place of this name in or near Shapwick, and Chilton (on Polden) does not appear, it is probable that 'Ceptone' really refers to Chilton. In *Kirby's Quest* Robert de Cheltone holds Cheltone of Cecilia de Beauchamp (representative of Corcelle), who holds of the Abbot.

[4] Exet. Dom. gives separate details of each of these four holdings.

[5] *Caballi* with *roncini* written above.

[6] Exet. Dom. has 'Garmund.'

this land there is in demesne 1 hide where are 1 plough and 4 serfs and (there are) 9 villeins and 9 bordars with 5 ploughs 'and 2 hides.' 'There are 1 riding-horse and 6 beasts and 26 swine and 26 sheep.' There (are) 10 acres of meadow and 2 acres of underwood (*silvæ minutæ*). It was and is worth 6 pounds.

Roger 'de Corcella' holds of the abbot DEREBERGE [Durborough in Stoke Courcy, now Stogursey]. Oswold held (it) of the abbot T.R.E. and paid geld for 2 hides. There is land for 3 ploughs. There are 3 villeins and 3 bordars with 2 ploughs 'and 1 hide,' and in demesne (there is) half a plough 'with 1 hide. There are 6 swine.' There are 11 acres of meadow and 20 acres of pasture and 10 acres of wood(land). It is worth 30 shillings. When he received (it) it was worth 40 shillings.

Ailwacre holds of the abbot BLACHEFORD [Blackford, near Wincanton]. Alnod held it of the abbot T.R.E. and paid geld for 4 hides. There is land for 6 ploughs. In demesne are '2½ hides and' 3 ploughs and 5 serfs and (there are) 7 villeins and 10 bordars with 4 ploughs 'and 1½ hides. There are 1 riding-horse and 9 unbroken mares (*equæ indomitæ*) and 30 beasts and 24 swine and 84 sheep.' There (are) 115 acres of meadow and 43 acres of pasture and 47 acres of wood-(land). It is worth 100 shillings. When he received (it) 4 pounds.

Godescal holds of the abbot STAWELLE [Stawell]. Alward held (it) T.R.E. and paid geld for 2½ hides. There is land for 2½ ploughs. In demesne there 'are 2 hides and 1 virgate and' 1 plough, and 3 serfs, and (there are) 3 bordars with 1 plough 'and 1 virgate' and 20 acres of meadow. 'There are 5 riding-horses and 8 beasts and 200 sheep.' It is worth 40 shillings. When he received (it) 5 shillings.

The church itself holds WALTONE [Walton]. 'Alnod the abbot held it T.R.E. and' paid geld for 30 hides. There is land for 40 ploughs. Of this (land) 10 hides are in demesne, where are 4 ploughs and 4 serfs and (there are) 27 villeins and 12 bordars with 18 ploughs 'and 4½ hides.' 'There are 2 riding-horses and 10 beasts and 18 swine and 100 sheep and 30 she-goats.' There are 50 acres of meadow. Pasture 7 furlongs long and 1 furlong broad. Wood(land) 7 furlongs long and 3[1] furlongs broad. It is worth 15 pounds

[1] Exet. Dom.: '4.'

to the abbot, 'and when Torstin the abbot received it 100 shillings.'

Of these 30 hides Roger 'de Corcella' holds of the abbot 5 hides in CONTONE [Compton Dunden]. Walter 'de Duaco' (holds) 3 hides in AISSECOTE [Ashcott], and 3 hides in PEDEWELLE [Pedwell in Ashcott]. They[2] who held (them) T.R.E. could not be separated from the church. In demesne there are '6¾ hides and' 3 ploughs and 6 serfs and (there are) 15 villeins and 12 bordars with 8 ploughs 'and the rest of the land.' Roger has '1 riding-horse and 2 beasts and 46 sheep and 49 she-goats and' 20 acres of meadow and 6 furlongs of wood(land) in length and 1 furlong in breadth. Walter 'has 4 beasts and 23 swine and 55 sheep and' 12 acres of meadow and 40 acres of underwood (*silvæ minutæ*). Between them it is worth 8 pounds.[3]

Roger 'de Corcella' holds of the abbot BODESLEGE.[4] Winegod 'the priest' held it T.R.E. and paid geld for 3 virgates[5] of land. There is land for 1½ ploughs which are there with 7 bordars. 'In demesne are 1½ virgates and 1 plough, and the villeins have the rest of the land and half a plough.' 'There are 4 beasts and 2 swine.' There (are) 6 acres of meadow and 2 acres of wood(land). It is worth 10 shillings, 'and when received 6 shillings.'

The same Roger holds of the abbot DON-DEME [Dunden in Compton Dunden]. Algar held (it) T.R.E. and paid geld for 5 hides. There is land for 4 ploughs. Of this (land) there are in demesne 3 hides and half a virgate of land where are 2 ploughs and 4 serfs and (there are) 5 villeins and 10 bordars with 3 ploughs 'and the rest of the land. There are 5 unbroken mares (*equæ indomitæ*) and 2 riding-horses and 9 swine.' There (are) 40 acres of meadow and 10 acres of wood(land). It is worth 100 shillings. 'And when he received it 6 pounds.'

The same Roger holds of the abbot AISSE-COTE [Ashcott], and it belongs to Walton a

[2] Exet. Dom.: '2 monks at Contona; 2 thegns at Aissecota; Algar at Pedewilla.'
[3] Exet. Dom. 10 pounds.
[4] This is superfluous to the 20 hides of Butleigh. Its position in the schedule among portions of the great manor of Walton would lead to the belief that it is an obsolete ville, but again it is super-fluous. At present it must be left doubtful.
[5] Exet. Dom. reads iiii virg., the last stroke interlined.

manor of the abbot. 'Almer held it T.R.E. and' paid geld for 2 hides. There is land for 3 ploughs. 'In demesne are 1½ hides and 2 oxen (*boves*) in a plough, and the villeins have the rest of the land and 1 plough.' There are 2 villeins and 3 bordars and 2 serfs with 1 plough, and 4 acres of meadow. 'There are 1 riding-horse and 2 cows and 7 swine and 42 sheep and 8 she-goats.' It was and is worth 40 shillings.

Girard 'Fossarius' holds of the abbot GRAINTONE [Greinton]. Ulmer held (it) T.R.E. and paid geld for 2½ hides. There is land for 2½ ploughs. In demesne there 'are 2 hides and' 1 plough, and 5 serfs, and (there are) 2 bordars and 2 coliberts with 1 plough 'and half a hide. There are 4 beasts and 6 swine.' There (are) 20 acres of meadow and 3 acres of wood(land). It is and was worth 50 shillings.

The church itself holds LEGA [Leigh in Street]. 'Alnod the abbot held it T.R.E. and' paid geld for 4 hides. There is land for 10 ploughs. Of this (land) there are in demesne 2 hides. One of these was thegn-land, yet it could not be separated from the church. In demesne are 4 ploughs with 1 serf and (there are) 7 villeins and 10 bordars with 5 ploughs 'and 2 hides. There are 2 riding-horses and 8 beasts and 20 swine and 55 sheep.' There (are) 35 acres of meadow and 30 acres of pasture and 6 acres of wood(land). It is worth 8 pounds. 'And when T(urstin) the abbot received (it) 60 shillings.'

The church itself holds HAME [High and Low Ham]. 'Alnod the abbot held it T.R.E. and' paid geld for 17 hides. There is land for 20 ploughs. Of this (land) there are in demesne 5 hides and 2½ virgates where are 3 ploughs and 5 serfs and (there are) 22 villeins and 21 bordars with 8 ploughs 'and 3 hides and 1½ virgates.' 'There are 2 riding-horses and 17 beasts and 10 swine and 150 sheep.' There are 30 acres of meadow and 16 acres of wood(land). It is worth 10 pounds. 'And when Turstin the abbot received it, 4 pounds.'

Of the land of this manor Robert 'de Otborvilla' holds of the abbot 1 hide and 1 virgate, and Serlo 'de Burceio' (holds) 5 hides. Girard 'Fossarius' (holds) 3 virgates of land. Leuric and Alwold and Almar held (the lands) T.R.E., nor could they be separated from the church. In demesne are '4¼ hides and half a virgate and' 2 ploughs and 4 serfs and (there are) 2 villeins and 14 bordars with 2 ploughs 'and the rest of the land.' 'Between them they have 2 riding-horses and 3 mares and 14 beasts and 13 swine and 103 sheep.' There (are) 30 acres of meadow and 20 acres of pasture. Altogether it is worth 110 shillings. 'When they received the land, 115 shillings.'[1]

The church itself holds BODUCHELEI [Butleigh]. 'Alnod the abbot held it T.R.E. and' paid geld for 20 hides. There is land for 20 ploughs. Of this (land) there are in demesne 5 hides where are 5 ploughs and 7 serfs and (there are) 11 villeins and 7 bordars with 6 ploughs 'and 2½ hides.' 'There are 2 riding-horses and 12 beasts and 25 swine and 120 sheep.' There (are) 50 acres of meadow and 100 acres of wood(land). It is worth to the abbot 10 pounds, 'and when T(urstin the abbot) received it 60 shillings.'

Of the land of this manor Turstin son of Rolf holds 8 hides, Roger 'de Corcella' (holds) 2 hides. Two thegns[2] held (them) of the church T.R.E., and they could not be separated thence. In demesne are there '7 hides and' 4 ploughs and 6 serfs and (there are) 11 villeins and 6 bordars with 3 ploughs 'and the rest of the land.' 'There are 2 riding-horses and 3 beasts and 22 swine and 330 sheep and 32 she-goats.' There are 14 acres of meadow and 12 acres of underwood. Between them it was and is worth 7 pounds.[3]

Of the same land Alestan[4] holds of the abbot half a hide and there he has 1 plough. 'And 1 riding-horse and 60 sheep.' It is worth 10 shillings. 'And when he received it, 5 shillings.'

Humfrey 'the chamberlain' holds of the king 2 hides in LODREFORD [perhaps Butleigh Moor in Walton[5]], and it belongs to this manor. Alvric held (it) T.R.E., nor could it be separated from the church. There is land for 2 ploughs. It is worth 20 shillings.

[1] Exet. Dom. gives details of each holding.
[2] Exet. Dom. mentions '3 thegns' and 'Sirewold.'
[3] Exet. Dom. gives details of each holding.
[4] Exet. Dom. reads : 'Alward holds half a hide which Alestan held T.R.E.'
[5] Lodreford. Bowen's map of Somerset (1750) marks Loderford south-east of Walton, evidently close to Butleigh moor, now in the civil parish of Walton, but formerly a detached part of Butleigh. There is another 'Loderford,' hodie Lattiford, a detached part of the parish of Holton, situate in North Cheriton. Blackford, Holton and 'Loterforde' are in the Hundred of Whitley (*Excheq. Lay Subsidy*, 1327). In Domesday Humphrey the chamberlain is tenant both of Halton and Loderford, which rather points to Lattiford as being the modern representative of 'Lodreford.'

The same church holds PILTONE [Pilton]. 'Alnod the abbot held it T.R.E. and' paid geld for 20 hides. There is land for 30 ploughs. Besides this (land) the abbot has there land for 20 ploughs which never paid geld. In demesne are 10 ploughs and 15 serfs, and (there are) 21 villeins and 42 bordars with 10 ploughs upon the land which does not pay geld. 'There are 4 riding-horses and 35 beasts and 56 swine and 500 sheep and 42 she-goats.' There are 2 mills paying 10 shillings, and 46 acres of meadow and 40 acres of pasture. Wood(land) 1[1] league long and half a league wide. Of the land which does not pay geld Alnod the monk holds 1 hide of the abbot freely (*liberaliter*) by the king's grant (*concessu Regis*). This was thegnland, nor can it be separated from the church. The whole is worth 24 pounds. It was worth 16 pounds.

Of the land of this manor Roger 'de Corcella' holds 6½ hides in SEPETONE [Shepton Mallet], and 3 hides in CORISTONE [2] [Croscombe]. Uluert and Elmer held (them) T.R.E., and they could not be separated

fo. 90b

from the church. In demesne are '6 hides and 2½ virgates' 3 ploughs and 8 serfs and 13 villeins and 19 bordars with 6 ploughs 'and the rest of the land.' 'There are 1 riding-horse and 15 beasts and 37 swine and 600 sheep and 45 she-goats.' There are 2 mills paying 6 shillings and 3 pence, and 50 acres of meadow and 42 acres of underwood (*silvæ minutæ*). Pasture 3 furlongs long and 1 furlong broad. The whole is worth 9 pounds.

Of the land of the same manor Adret holds of the abbot 5 hides in UTONE [North Wootton], and Serlo 'de Burceio' (holds) 5 hides in PILLE [Pylle], and Ralph 'Tortesmains' (holds) 2 hides in the same PILTONE [Pilton]. Those who held them [3] T.R.E. could not be separated from the church. There are in demesne '7¼ hides and' 4½ ploughs and 8 serfs and (there are) 8 villeins and 18 bordars with 3 ploughs 'and the rest of the land.' 'There are 2 riding-horses and 19 beasts and 21 swine and 48 sheep and 16 she-goats.' There (are) 2 mills paying 4 shillings and 6 pence, and 36½ acres of meadow and 20 acres of pasture and 4 acres of wood(land). Between them it is worth altogether 7 pounds and 10 shillings.[4]

The church itself holds PENNARMINSTRE [East Pennard]. 'Alnod the abbot held it T.R.E. and' paid geld for 10 hides. Nevertheless there are 20 hides there. There is land for 12 ploughs. Of this (land) there are in demesne 12 hides where are 5 ploughs and 4 serfs and (there are) 17 villeins and 9 bordars and 10 cottars with 6 ploughs 'and 7 ploughs.' 'There are 2 riding-horses and 42 beasts and 25 swine and 55 sheep.' There (are) 30 acres of meadow and 40 acres of pasture. Wood(land) 1½ leagues long and 4 furlongs wide. It is worth 12 pounds to the abbot. 'When T(urstin) the abbot received it, 4 pounds.'

Of the land of this manor Serlo 'de Burceio' holds of the abbot 1 hide 'of thegnland which' Ailmar held T.R.E. There are 4 villeins who 'hold that hide and' have 2 ploughs, and 8 acres of meadow and 30 acres of wood(land). It was and is worth 30 shillings.

The church itself holds BALTUNESBERGE [Baltonsborough]. T.R.E. 'Alnod held it and' it paid geld for 5 hides. There is land for 6 ploughs. Of this (land) are in demesne 4 hides and 1 virgate where are 2 ploughs and 4 serfs and (there are) 5 villeins and 9 bordars and 3 cottars with 2 ploughs 'and 3 virgates.' 'There are 2 riding-horses and 16 beasts and 14 swine and 33 she-goats.' There is a mill paying 5 shillings, and 30 acres of meadow. Wood(land) 1½ leagues long and half a league wide. 'It was and is worth 6 pounds.'

The church itself holds DOLTIN [Doulting]. T.R.E. 'Alnod the abbot held it and' it paid geld for 20 hides. There is land for 20 ploughs. Of this (land) 12 hides are in demesne where are 2 ploughs and 5 serfs and (there are) 10 villeins and 6 bordars and 4 cottars with 6 ploughs 'and 2 hides.' 'There are 1 riding-horse and 4 beasts and 15 swine and 340 sheep.' There (are) 30 acres of meadow and 60 acres of pasture and 60 acres of underwood (*silvæ minutæ*). It is worth 14 pounds to the abbot, 'and when Turstin received it 6 pounds.'

Of this land Roger 'de Corcella' holds 3 hides and 1 virgate of land in CERLETONE [Charlton in Shepton Mallet], and elsewhere 2 hides and 3 virgates of land. 'Ulmar and Alward held them T.R.E. and could not be separated from the church.' In demesne 'are 4 hides and 2½ virgates and' 1 plough with 1 serf and (there are) 8 villeins and 6 bordars with 2 ploughs 'and 1 hide and 1½ virgates.' 'There are 1 riding-horse and 24 beasts and 4 swine and 320

---

[1] Exet. Dom.: '1½.'

[2] Exet. Dom. reads 'Coriscoma.'

[3] Exet. Dom. : Almer at Wootton ; Almar at Pylle ; Sirewold in Pilton.

[4] Exet. Dom. gives details of each holding.

sheep.' There (is) a mill paying 9 pence, and 23 acres of meadow and 10 acres of pasture and 30 acres of underwood (*silvæ minutæ*). It is worth 100 shillings. 'And when he received it 50 shillings.'[1]

The same church holds BATECUMBE [Batcombe]. 'Alnod the abbot held it and' T.R.E. it paid geld for 20 hides. There is land for 16 ploughs. Of this (land) there are in demesne 9 hides and 3 virgates of land where are 2 ploughs and 6 serfs and (there are) 4 villeins and 14 bordars with 3 ploughs 'and half a hide.' 'There are 2 riding-horses and 8 beasts and 9 swine and 150 sheep and 17 she-goats.' There is a mill paying 5 shillings, and 20 acres of meadow and 6 acres of pasture and 40 acres of wood(land). It is worth 7 pounds to the abbot. 'And when he received it 40 shillings.'

Of the land of this manor Roger 'de Corcella' holds 2 hides. Ulwi held (them) T.R.E. and could not be separated from the church. He has there 1 plough with 1 serf and 3 bordars. 'There are 1 riding-horse and 2 swine.' There (are) 12 acres of meadow and 10 acres of pasture. It is worth 20 shillings. 'And when he received it 40 shillings.'

Of the land of the same manor Azelin holds in WESTCUMBE [Westcombe in Batcombe] 7 hides and 3 virgates of land. Alfhilla 'the mother of the abbot' held (it) T.R.E. and could not be separated from the church. In demesne are '5 hides and 1 virgate and' 2 ploughs and 6 villeins and 7 bordars and 6 cottars with 1 serf owning (*habentes*) 2½ ploughs 'and the rest of the land.' 'There are 1 riding-horse and 11 beasts and 10 swine and 100 sheep.' There (are) 2 mills paying 5 shillings, and 12 acres of meadow and 12 acres of pasture and 10 acres of wood(land). It is worth 4 pounds and 10 shillings. 'And when he received it 20 shillings.' Two hides of this land were the villeins' land and the other virgates were thegnland.

The church itself holds MULLE [Mells]. 'Alnod the abbot held it and' T.R.E. it paid geld for 20 hides. There is land for 20 ploughs. Of this (land) there are in demesne 10 hides where are 2 ploughs and 2 serfs and (there are) 8 villeins and 7 bordars and 5 cottars with 3 ploughs 'and 3½ hides.' 'There are 1 riding-horse and 7 beasts and 15 swine and 100 sheep less 9.' There is a mill paying 5 shillings, and 15 acres of meadow and 12 acres of pasture. Wood(land) 1 league long and 2 furlongs broad. It is worth 10 pounds to the abbot. 'And when Turstin received it, 100 shillings.'

Of the land of this manor Godeve holds of the abbot 1 hide. Her husband (*vir ejus*) held (it) T.R.E., nor could it be separated from the church. It is worth 78 pence.

The Bishop of Coutances holds of the king 5½ hides belonging to this manor. Two thegns held (them) T.R.E., but they could not be separated from the church. Azelin holds (them) of the bishop.[2]

Walter 'Hosatus' holds of the abbot in WATELEI [Whatley] 4 hides. Ulgar a monk held (it) T.R.E. 'and paid geld for 5 hides'[3] and could not be separated from the church. There is land for 4 ploughs. Of this (land) there are in demesne 2½ hides where are 2 ploughs and 4 serfs, and (there are) 8 villeins and 5 bordars with 2 ploughs 'and 1½ hides.' 'There are 8 beasts and 100 sheep.' There is a mill paying 5 shillings, and 6 acres of meadow and 50 acres of pasture and 14 acres of wood(land). It is worth 70 shillings. 'And when he received it, 30 shillings.'

In the same manor John 'the usher,' (*ostiarius*), holds of the abbot 1 hide of the villeins' land. There is land for 1 plough which is there with 2 villeins. It is worth 15 shillings. 'And when he received it, as much.'

The church itself holds WERITONE [Wrington]. T.R.E. it paid geld for 20 hides. There is land for 32 ploughs. Of this land there are in demesne 11 hides where are 6 ploughs and 7 serfs, and (there are) 41 villeins and 12 bordars with 20 ploughs 'and 6 hides.' 'There are 46 beasts and 30 swine and 278 sheep and 47 she-goats.' There (are) 3 mills paying 14 shillings and 2 pence, and 44 acres of meadow and 200 acres of pasture. Wood(land) 2 leagues long and as much broad. It is worth to the abbot 30 pounds.

Of the land of this manor Roger 'de Corcella' holds 1½ hides of the abbot. A thegn held (it) T.R.E., and it could not be separated from the church. There are 3 ploughs and 2 villeins and 6 bordars. It is worth 30 shillings.

Of the same estate (*terra*) Saulf holds 1½ hides. He held (it) T.R.E. 'and could not be separated from the abbot.' There he has 1½ ploughs, and 1 villein with 4 cottars have 1 plough. It is worth 30 shillings.

---

[1] Exet. Dom. gives details of each holding.

[2] Millescote, now Middlecote, in Babington (see p. 452).

[3] This includes the hide held by John the usher.

The church itself holds MONECHETONE, 'MORCHETONA' [West Monkton]. T.R.E. 'Alnod the abbot held it and' paid geld for 15 hides. There is land for 20 ploughs. Of this (land) Walchel Bishop (of Winchester) holds of the abbot 5 hides and 1 virgate of land in demesne where are 3 ploughs and 7 serfs and (there are) 20 villeins and 7 bordars with 7 ploughs 'and 2½ hides.' 'There are 1 riding-horse and 22 beasts and 12 swine and 50 sheep.' There are 20 acres of meadow and 100 acres of pasture and 24 acres of wood(land). It is worth 7 pounds.

In the same place (villa) Roger 'de Corcella' holds of the abbot 4 hides and 3 virgates of land 'which 3 thegns held T.R.E.,' and Serlo 'de Burceio' (holds) 2½ hides. Those who held (them) T.R.E. could not be separated from the church. There are 4 ploughs in demesne and 3 serfs and (there are) 8 villeins and 11 bordars with 2½ ploughs. 'There are 6 swine and 20 sheep.' There are 19 acres of meadow and 40 acres of pasture. Between them it is worth 4 pounds and 10 shillings.

The church itself holds MERCESBERIE [Marksbury]. T.R.E. 'Alnod the abbot held it and' it paid geld for 10 hides. There is land for 8 ploughs. Of this (land) 4½ hides are in demesne where are 2 ploughs and 5 serfs and (there are) 6 villeins and 5 bordars with 3 ploughs 'and 3 hides.' 'There are 1 riding-horse and 29 swine and 85 sheep.' There (are) 19 acres of meadow and 40 acres of wood(land). It is worth 10 pounds.

A thegn holds 2½ hides of this estate (terra). It is worth 20 shillings. Oswald held (it) T.R.E., and it could not be separated from the church.

The same church holds DICESGET [Ditcheat]. T.R.E. 'Alnod the abbot held it and' it paid geld for 30 hides. There is land for 30 ploughs. Of this (land) 3 hides are in demesne where are 3½ ploughs and 2 serfs and (there are) 13 villeins and 18 bordars and 3 cottars (coscez) with 7 ploughs 'and 2 hides.' 'There are 2 riding-horses and 12 beasts and 20 swine and 123 sheep and 23 she-goats. There is a mill paying 7 shillings and 5 pence, and 40 acres of meadow, and pasture 6 furlongs long and 2 furlongs broad. Wood(land) 1½ leagues long and 2 furlongs broad. To the abbot it is worth 12 pounds.

Of the land of this manor Serlo 'de Burceio' holds 5½ hides in HORBLAWETONE [Hornblotton]. Ralph 'Tortesmains'(holds)6½ hides in ALENTONE [Alhampton in Ditcheat]. Nigel the physician (medicus) (holds) 5½ hides

in LAMIETA [Lamyat]. They[1] who held (these lands) T.R.E. could not be separated from the church. In demesne are 4 ploughs and 4 serfs and (there are) 29 villeins and 12 bordars and 3 cottars (coscez) with 15 ploughs. 'There are 1 riding-horse and 4 unbroken mares (equæ indomitæ) and 13 beasts and 37 swine and 138 sheep and 1 cow.' There are 3 mills paying 13 shillings and 4 pence, and 55 acres of meadow and 20 acres of pasture. Wood(land) 9 furlongs long and 1½ furlongs wide. Between them it is worth altogether 14 pounds and 10 shillings. It was worth 11 pounds.[2]

Of the same 30 hides Alfric and Evrard hold of the king 1 hide. A thegn held it T.R.E. nor could he be separated from the church. It is worth 20 shillings.

Of the same 30 hides, the Count of Mortain holds of the king 7 hides. A thegn held them T.R.E., nor could he be separated from the church. It is worth 100 shillings. 'And when he received it 7 pounds.'

The same church holds CAMERLERTONE [Camerton]. Edmer[3] held (it) T.R.E. and paid geld for 10 hides. There is land for 10 ploughs. Of this (land) 7 hides are in demesne where are 2 ploughs and 8 serfs and (there are) 6 villeins and 6 bordars with 2 ploughs 'and 2 hides.' 'There are 1 riding-horse and 13 swine and 154 sheep.' There are 2 mills paying 5 shillings, and 80 acres of meadow and 20 acres of pasture and 40 acres of wood(land). It is worth 7 pounds. 'And when Turstin the abbot received it, 6 pounds.'

Of the land of this manor Roger holds of the abbot 1 hide 'of thegn-land which Ailuin held T.R.E. and could not be separated from the manor (mansione),' and there he has 1 plough with 1 serf and 1 bordar. There are 10 acres of meadow and 6 acres of wood(land). It is worth 10 shillings. The Count of Mortain gave this manor to the abbot in exchange for TUTENELLE,' 'TITTENELLE' [Tintinhull].

Harding holds of the abbot CRENEMELLE [Cranmore]. He likewise (similiter) held (it) T.R.E., and paid geld for 12 hides. There is land for 10 ploughs. Of this land 6 hides are in demesne where are 1 plough and 6

---

[1] Exet. Dom.: 2 thegns at Hornblotton; 2 thegns 'pariter' at Alhampton; Spirtes (Sps) the priest at Lamyat.
[2] Exet. Dom. gives details of each holding.
[3] A blank space after Edmer. Exet. Dom.: 'Edmeratorius.'

serfs and (there are) 8 villeins and 2 bordars and 7 cottars with 3 ploughs 'and 6 hides.' 'There are 1 riding-horse and 15 she-goats.' There is a mill paying 30 pence, and 50 acres of meadow and 60 acres of pasture and 100 acres of wood(land). It is worth 4 pounds. This land cannot be separated from the church.

The church itself holds BRENTMERSE [Brent]. T.R.E. 'Alnod the abbot held it and' it paid geld for 20 hides. There is land for 30 ploughs. Of this (land) 4 hides are in demesne where are 8 ploughs and 5 serfs and (there are) 50 villeins and 47 bordars with 16 ploughs 'and 11 hides' and 20 acres of meadow. 'There are 1 riding-horse and 73 beasts and 60 swine and 82 sheep.' To the abbot it is worth 50 pounds. 'And when he received it 15 pounds.'

Of these 20 hides Roger 'de Curcella' holds of the abbot 1 hide. Ralph 'de Cuntevill' (holds) 5 virgates. Alfric 'son of Euerwacre' (holds) 5 virgates. Godvin 'the priest' (holds) 1½ hides. They[1] who held them of the abbot T.R.E. could not be separated from the church. In demesne there are 4 ploughs with 1 serf and (there are) 3 villeins and 5 bordars and 10 cottars with 3 ploughs. 'There are 1 riding-horse and 9 beasts and 10 swine and 86 sheep. There are 5 acres of meadow and 6 acres of underwood.' The value between them is 4 pounds and 10 shillings.[2]

Walcin '(de) Duaco' holds of the abbot LODENWRDE[3] [Edingworth in East Brent]. A thegn held (it) T.R.E., nor could he be separated from the church, and he paid geld for 2 hides. There is land for 5 ploughs. In demesne are '1 hide and' 2 ploughs and 4 serfs and (there are) 4 villeins and 5 bordars and 5 cottars with 4 ploughs 'and 1 hide.'

'There are 1 riding-horse and 15 beasts and 5 swine and 5 sheep.' It is worth 40 shillings, 'and as much when he received it.'

Erneis holds or the abbot DUNEHEFDE [Downhead]. Ulgar the monk held (it) T.R.E.,[4] and paid geld for 3 hides. There is land for 5 ploughs. Of this (land) 2 hides are in demesne, and there (are) 3 ploughs with 5 villeins and 4 bordars 'who have 1 hide.' There (are) 5 acres of meadow. Pasture 5 furlongs long and 2 furlongs broad. Wood(land) half a league long and as much broad. It was and is worth 40 shillings.

Siward holds 3 virgates of land of the church of Glastingberie in a manor which is called DINNITONE [Dinnington]. It is worth 13 shillings and 2 pence.

fo. 91

Maurice the Bishop 'of London' holds the church of St. Andrew in Givelcestre [Ilchester] with 3 hides of land of the king. Brictric held this (estate) T.R.E. of the church of Glastingberie, nor could he be separated from it. 'It is worth 100 shillings, and the same when Maurice received it.'

The Bishop of Coutances holds of the king Hutone, Eleberie, Hetsecome and Stretton [Hutton, Elborough in Hutton, Ashcombe in Weston-super-Mare, and Stratton-on-the-Fosse]. These estates (terræ) were thegnland T.R.E., nor could they be separated from the church. They are worth 100 shillings, and more. From them the church has no dues (servitium).

The Count of Mortain holds these manors of the king, Stane, Stoca and Stoca, Dreicote [perhaps Stone in East Pennard, Stoke-under-Ham, and Draycote in Limington.[5]] These estates (terræ) were thegnland in Glastingberie T.R.E., nor could they be separated from it. They are worth 14 pounds. 'Stane is worth 9 pounds, Stoca and Stoca 40 shillings, and Dregcota 40 shillings.'

The same count holds in the manor of BODECHELIE [Butleigh] 2 furlongs of wood(land) in length and 1 furlong in breadth, which T.R.E. was in Glastingberie.

Roger de Corcelle has one manor (called) LIMINGTONE [Limington] for which his father

[1] Exet. Dom. : 'two thegns and Alfric the reeve (prepositus).'
[2] Exet. Dom. gives details of each holding.
[3] Exet. Dom. reads: 'Iodena Wirda.' Being held temp. Domesday by Walter of Dowai, it may be identified with the manor of Edenworthy in Brent Mareys, a moiety of which was held by George de Cantilupe, son of William de C., as a member of the Barony of Worleston or Worle, this being also a holding of W. de Dowai (Inq. p.m. George de C., 1 Edw. I. 16). In the Rentalia of Glastonbury, temp. Abbot Michael de Ambresbury (1235-1252), Will. de Cantilupe and Helyas de Bello Campo held '1 fee at Edenewrth and Kington (in Wilts)' (S.R.S. v. 3). In the Nom. Villarum of 1317, John son of Thomas Beauchamp held 'Yadenworth' in the Hundred of Bempstone.

[4] Exet. Dom.: 'nor could he be separated from the church.'
[5] Som. Arch. and Nat. Hist. Proc. xlv. ii. 74-5.

gave in exchange 5 hides which he held of the church of Glastingberie, nor could they be separated from it (*inde*). From these (hides) the church loses its due (*servitium*).

'The abbot of Glastonbury has 20 manors in demesne in Somerset containing (*de*) 194 hides and 3 virgates and 40 carucates exempt (from geld) and 23 hides (which have been) always exempt. And he has in them in demesne 75½ ploughs, and 347 villeins and 325 bordars and 108 serfs and 19 coliberts and 10 fishermen, who have 160 ploughs. These (manors) are worth 288 pounds 4 shillings. The knights of the church have in the same county 50 manors containing 159 hides, 64 ploughs in demesne, 219 villeins, 249 bordars, 101 serfs and 2 coliberts, who have 99½ ploughs and (these manors) are worth 146 pounds. In the same county English thegns hold 11 manors containing 31½ hides and 2 carucates of land which never paid geld; they have 12½ ploughs in demesne; and 21 villeins, 48 bordars and 16 serfs, who have 11 ploughs; and (these manors) are worth 20 pounds and 15 shillings. This land is sufficient for 554½ ploughs. This land was (*emendata*) in the hands of Turstin the abbot at (*de*) 128 pounds.'[1]

fo. '188'

IX. THE LAND OF THE CHURCH OF MUCHELNEY

The CHURCH of ST. PETER of MICELENYE has 4 carucates of land which never paid geld in these islands, MICHELENIE, MIDELENIE and TORELIE [Muchelney, Middleney in Drayton, and Thorney in Muchelney]. There in demesne are 2 ploughs and 1 arpent of vineyard. There (are) 4 serfs and 3 villeins and 18 bordars with 2 ploughs. 'There are 1 riding-horse and 21 beasts and 6 swine and 30 she-goats.' There (are) 2 fisheries paying 6,000 eels, and 25 acres of meadow and 12 acres of wood(land) and 100 acres of pasture. It was and is worth 3 pounds.

The church itself holds CIPESTAPLE [Chipstable]. Celric held (it) T.R.E. and paid geld for 2½ hides. There is land for 6 ploughs. Of this (land) half a hide is in demesne where are 1 plough and 2 serfs and (there are) 16 villeins and 2 bordars with 5 ploughs 'and the rest of the land.' There are half an acre of meadow and 100 acres of pasture. Wood(land) half a league long and 2 furlongs broad. It is worth 50 shillings.

The church itself holds ILEMINSTRE [Il-

minster]. Liward the abbot held (it) T.R.E. and paid geld for 20 hides. There is land for 20 ploughs. Of this (land) 9 hides and 1½ virgates are in demesne where are 3 ploughs and 10 serfs and (there are) 25 villeins and 22 bordars with 20 ploughs 'and 10½ hides and half a virgate.' 'There are 2 riding-horses and 27 beasts and 33 swine and 40 sheep.' There are 3 mills paying 22 shillings and 6 pence and 80 acres of meadow. Wood(land) 3 leagues long and 1½ leagues broad. There (is) a market paying 20 shillings.

Of this estate (*terra*) 2 thegns, 'Livric the priest and Wlward and now his son Edward holds half a hide,' held 1½ hides who could not be separated from the church.

It is worth in all 20 pounds. When the abbot died it was worth 26 pounds.

The church itself holds ILE [Ile Abbots]. Godric held (it)[2] T.R.E. and paid geld for 5 hides. There is land for 5 ploughs. Of this (land) 3 hides are in demesne where are 2 ploughs and 6 serfs and (there are) 5 bordars with 2 ploughs 'and 2 hides.' 'There are 1 riding-horse and 25 beasts and 15 swine and 59 sheep.' There (is) a mill paying 15 shillings, and 40 acres of meadow and 7 acres of pasture. Wood(land) 3 leagues long and 1½ leagues broad. It was and is worth 4 pounds.

The same church holds ILE [another part of Ile Abbots]. Eduin held[2] (it) and paid geld for 1½ hides. There is land for 1½ ploughs. 'St. Peter has 1½ hides less 15 acres.' There are 3 bordars holding 15 acres. The rest (*alia*) is in demesne, and there are 10 acres of meadow and 7 acres of pasture. Wood(land) 3 furlongs long and 1 furlong broad. It is worth 16 shillings.

The church itself holds DRAITUNE [Drayton]. T.R.E. it paid geld for 20 hides. There is land for 15 ploughs. Of this (land) 11 hides and 2½ virgates of land are in demesne where are 6 ploughs and 10 serfs and (there are) 16 villeins and 14 bordars with 9 ploughs 'and 5 hides.' 'There are 3 riding-horses and 22 swine and 107 sheep.' There are 50 acres of meadow, and pasture 2 leagues long and 1 league broad. Wood(land) 2 leagues long and 1½ leagues broad.

Of these 20 hides Celric and Ulward hold 2 hides. Brictuin and Leving held them of the abbey T.R.E. nor could they be separated from it (*inde*). 'In demesne are 2 hides less 20 acres which 4 bordars hold.' There are 4 bordars and 3 acres of meadow and 35 acres

---

[1] This abstract is given only in the Exeter Domesday.

[2] Exet. Dom. adds '*pariter.*'

of pasture and 7 acres of wood(land). The whole is worth 10 pounds : ' 9 pounds for the benefit (*ad opus*) of the church and 20 shillings for the benefit of the thegns.' [1]

The church itself holds CAMELLE [West Camel]. T.R.E. it paid geld for 10 hides. There is land for 16 ploughs. Of this (land) 4½ hides are in demesne where are 4 ploughs and 5 serfs, and (there are) 7 villeins and 8 bordars with 6 ploughs 'and 4½ hides.' 'There are 2 riding-horses and 7 cows and 1 swine and 91 sheep.' There is a mill pay-'ng 10 shillings, and 60 acres of meadow and 60 acres of pasture.

Of these 10 hides Dodeman holds of the abbot 1 hide, and there he has ' 1 virgate and ' 1 plough and 3 villeins with 1 plough [2] 'and 3 virgates' and 2 acres of meadow. 'There are 4 beasts and 100 sheep.' The whole is worth 10 pounds and 10 shillings.[3]

The church itself holds CATHANGRE [Cathanger in Fivehead]. Wadel held (it) 'in parage (*pariter*)' T.R.E. and paid geld for 1½ hides. There is land for 1½ ploughs. 'In demesne is half a hide less 15 acres.' There is 1 villein with 1 bordar holding 15 acres. Of this estate (*terra*) Ingulf holds 1 hide and there he has 1 plough with 3 bordars. 'There are 5 beasts and 9 swine and 25 sheep.' There are 6 acres of meadow and 15 acres of wood-(land). 'Ingulf's share' is worth 20 shillings. The monks' share (*pars*) (is) 7 shillings. 'These 3 thegns' Godric (of Ile Abbots) and Eduin (of Ile Abbots) and Wadel (of Cathangre) did not belong to the abbey T.R.E.

'fo. 191'

X. THE LAND OF THE CHURCH OF ATHELNEY [ADELINGI]

The church of St. Peter of Adelingye holds ATILTONE [Ilton]. T.R.E. it paid geld for 8 hides. There is land for 12 ploughs. Four hides are in demesne where are 3 ploughs and 4 serfs and (there are) 10 villeins and 6 bordars with 4 ploughs 'and 2 hides.' 'There are 2 riding-horses and 6 beasts and 10 swine and 40 sheep.' There is a mill paying 7 shillings and 6 pence and 40 acres of meadow and 30 acres of pasture. Wood(land) 1 league long and another in breadth. It is worth 100 shillings.

[1] Exet. Dom. as usual gives the separate items for each holding.
[2] Exet. Dom. reads: ' 1½ ploughs.'
[3] Exet. Dom. values the abbot's portion at 9 pounds, and Dodeman's at 20 shillings ; 'and when he received it, 10 shillings.'

Of the land of this manor the Count of Mortain holds 2 hides which belonged to (*erant in*) that church T.R.E. There is land for 4 ploughs, and it is worth 30 shillings. ' Malger de Cartrai holds them of the count.'

The church itself holds SUTUNE [Long Sutton]. T.R.E. it paid geld for 10 hides. There is land for 16 ploughs. Of this (land) 4 hides are in demesne where are 2 ploughs and 4 serfs, and (there are) 8 villeins and 6 bordars with 6 ploughs 'and 3½ hides.' 'There are 6 beasts and 15 swine and 102 sheep.' There (are) 40 acres of meadow and 100 acres of pasture. To the abbot it is worth 8 pounds.

Of the same land Roger Brito holds half a hide and has 1 plough.

Of the land of this manor Roger de Corcelle holds 2 hides against the will of the abbot (*invito Abbate*). Two thegns held (them) of the church T.R.E., nor could they be separated from it (*inde*). There is land for 2 ploughs which are there in demesne and 6 acres of meadow. It is worth 50 shillings. Two men 'Garmund and Dudemann' hold it of Roger. 'There Dudemann has 8 beasts and 2 swine and 80 sheep ; and it is worth to the use of Dudemann 20 shillings, and to the use of Garmund 30 shillings.'

The church itself holds SEOVENAMENTONE [Seavington Abbots in Seavington St. Mary]. T.R.E. it paid geld for 2 hides. 'In demesne is 1 hide, and the villeins have 1 hide.' There (is) land for 2 ploughs which are there with 7 villeins and 3 bordars and 2 serfs. 'There are 1 riding-horse and 9 swine and 40 sheep.' There (are) 6 acres of meadow. It is worth 30 shillings.

The church itself holds HAME 'HAUMET' [Ham in Bridgwater]. T.R.E. it paid geld for 1 hide. There is land for 4 ploughs. In demesne are 'half a hide and' 1 plough and 4 serfs, and (there are) 1 villein and 7 bordars with 1 plough 'and half a hide.' 'There are 2 beasts.' There are 15 acres of meadow and 3 acres of underwood (*silvæ minutæ*). It is worth 30 shillings.

The church itself holds LEGE [Lyng]. One hide is there but it did not pay geld T.R.E. In demesne there are 'half a hide and' 2 ploughs and 6 serfs and (there are) 3 villeins and 4 bordars with 2 ploughs 'and half a hide.' 'There are 1 riding-horse and 2 beasts and 10 swine and 30 sheep.' There are 12 acres of meadow and 50 acres of wood(land). It is worth 40 shillings.

The Count of Mortain holds 2 hides in AISSELLE [Ashill], and Roger de Corcelle holds 2 hides of the manor of SUTONE [Long Sutton], and Ralph de Limesi holds 1 hide of the manor of BOSINTONE [Bossington in Selworthy]. These estates (*terræ*) belonged to (*jacebant in*) Adelingi T.R.E. and could not be separated from it.

XI. THE LAND OF THE CHURCH OF ROME [1]

The church of the blessed Apostle Peter at Rome holds of the king PERITONE [Puriton]. Eddid the queen held it T.R.E. Six hides are there, but it did not pay geld except for 5 hides. There is land for 12 ploughs. Of this (land) 3 hides are in demesne where are 2 ploughs and 4 serfs and there are 11 villeins and 4 bordars with 6 ploughs and '3 hides.' 'There are 2 cows and 60 sheep.' There (are) 150 acres of meadow and 150 acres of pasture. It is worth yearly 12 pounds.

XII. THE LAND OF ST. STEPHEN OF CAEN

The church of St. Stephen of Caen holds of the king the church of CRUCHE [Crewkerne]. There are 10 hides. There is land for 13 ploughs. Of this (land) 2 hides are in demesne where are 1 plough with 1 serf and (there are) 11 villeins and 2 coliberts and 17 bordars with 6 ploughs 'and 4½ hides.' 'There are 1 riding-horse and 25 sheep.' There (are) 10 acres of meadow, and of pasture half a league in length and in breadth.

Of these 10 hides a knight (*miles*) holds of the abbot 3 hides, and there he has '1½ hides and' 2 ploughs with 1 serf and 6 villeins and 2 bordars with 4 ploughs 'and 1½ hides.' 'There are 1 riding-horse and 5 beasts and 14 swine and 150 sheep.' He has a mill paying 5 shillings, and 10 acres of meadow and of pasture half a league in length and breadth.

To the abbot it is worth 7 pounds. To the knight 4 pounds.

XIII. THE LAND OF ST. MARY OF MONTEBURG

The church of St. Mary of Monteburg holds of the king a manor by the gift of Nigel the physician. Spirtes the priest held it T.R.E. and paid geld for 5 hides. There is land for 3 ploughs. Of this (land) 2½ hides are in de-

mesne where are 2 ploughs and 2 serfs, and (there are) 5 villeins and 12 bordars with 2 ploughs 'and the rest of the land.' 'There are 10 swine and 60 sheep and 18 she-goats.' There is a mill paying 30 pence and 20 acres of pasture. Wood(land) half a league long and as much broad. Now as formerly (*olim et modo*) it is worth 4 pounds.[2]

fo. 193b'

XIV. THE LAND OF ST. EDWARD

The church of St. Edward[3] holds CUMBE [Abbas-Combe in Templecombe]. T.R.E. 'Leveva the abbess held it and' it paid geld for 5 hides. There is land for 5 ploughs. Of this (land) 2½ hides are in demesne where are 2 ploughs and there are 4 villeins and 7 bordars with 2 ploughs 'and 2½ hides.' 'There are 1 riding-horse and 7 cows and 40 sheep.' In Meleburne [Milborne Port] are 6 burgesses paying 50 pence. (There is) a meadow 4 furlongs long and 2 furlongs broad. Wood(land) 3 furlongs long and 1 furlong broad. It was and is worth 6 pounds.

XV. WHAT MAURICE (BISHOP OF LONDON) HOLDS

Bishop Maurice holds of the king the church of ST. ANDREW.[4] Brictric held (it) T.R.E. and paid geld for 3 hides. There is land for 3 ploughs. In demesne are '1 hide and 3 virgates and' 2 ploughs and 3 serfs, and (there are) 1 villein and 6 bordars with 1 plough 'and 1 hide and 1 virgate.' 'There are 2 riding-horses and 9 beasts and 50 sheep.' There is a mill paying 20 shillings and 30 acres of meadow. It was and is worth 100 shillings.

XVI. WHAT THE KING'S CLERKS (*clerici*) (HOLD) [5]

Reinbald holds the church 'of St. John' of FROME with 8 ploughlands (*car. terræ*).[6] In demesne are 2½ ploughs and 4 serfs and (there are) 8 villeins and 12 bordars with 6 ploughs. 'There are 1 riding-horse and 3 beasts and

[1] Exet. Dom. arranges this and succeeding entries under 'Lands given in almoin' (fo. 196), that of Shaftesbury excepted.

[2] Eyton identifies this anonymous manor as one moiety of Nunney (*Dom. Stud. Som.* i. 158–60).
[3] i.e. the nunnery of Shaftesbury.
[4] Of Ilchester, v. ante p. 467.
[5] Exet. Dom. : 'Land which has been given to the saints in almoin.' The order of the entries runs : North Petherton, Edith the Nun, Bera, Cannington, South Petherton, Carhampton, Honicote, Waverdinestoc, Milverton, Crewkerne, Curry (Rivel), Ilchester, Puriton, Lege, Ragiol, Frome, (Nunney,) Kilmersdon.
[6] Exet. Dom. has '*carrucatas*.'

30 swine and 228 sheep.' There is a mill paying 5 shillings, and 35 acres of meadow. Wood(land) 6 furlongs long and 2 furlongs broad. It is worth 6 pounds.

Richer 'de Andeleio' holds the church 'of St. Mary' of WARVERDINESTOCH [Stogumber][1] of the king. 'Alvric held it' T.R.E. and paid geld for 2 hides. There is land for 4 ploughs. 'In demesne are 1½ hides and 3 ferlings, and the villeins have 1 virgate and 1 ferling.' There are 5 villeins and 4 bordars and 2 serfs with 2 ploughs. There are 3 acres of meadow and 20 acres of pasture and 4 acres of wood(land). It is worth 3 pounds and 4 cows. 'And when R(icher) received it, 30 shillings.'

fo. 91b

Erchenger 'the priest' holds of the king in the church of CANTETONE [Cannington] 2½ virgates of land, 'which Alvric the priest held T.R.E.' There is land for 2 ploughs. In demesne are 'half a hide and' half a plough with 1 villein and 6 bordars 'with half a virgate.' 'There are 3 cows and 9 swine and 10 wether sheep (*berbices*).' There are 7 acres of pasture and 30 acres of meadow and 4 acres of underwood (*silvæ minutæ*). It is worth 30 shillings.

Stephen the 'king's' chaplain holds the church of MILVERTONE [Milverton] with 1 virgate of land and 1 ferling. There is land for 1 plough. There (are) 10 acres of wood(land). It is worth 40 shillings.

Alviet the priest holds of the king 1 hide in SUDPERETONE [South Petherton]. 'He held it in almoin of King Edward.' There is land for 1 plough which is there with 1 bordar and 1 serf. 'There are 8 beasts and 11 swine and 50 sheep.' There (are) 8 acres of meadow. It is worth 20 shillings.

To the church of CARENTONE [Carhampton] belong (*jacent*) 1½ hides. 'Peter the bishop held it in almoin T.R.E., and now it is in the king's

[1] This place can be identified with the later Stokegomer, hodie Stogumber, by references to its ancient lords; Richer de Andeleio of the Exet. Domesday being replaced by John de Andeli, who held a tenement in demesne in 'Stoke Gunner' in 1226 (*Som. Plea Rolls* 9–10 Hen. III. 299; *S.R.S.* xi. p. 64). Walter de Andelys gave the advowson of 'Stokgummer' to the Bishop of Bath and Wells in 1256 (*Wells Cath. MSS., Hist. MSS. Report*, 1885). In *Kirby's Quest*, 1285, Robert de Andely holds 'Stokegommer' of Henry de Lacy, Earl of Lincoln. I have not found any example of the earlier form of the word outside Domesday.

hand.' There are in demesne 'half a hide and' 1½ ploughs, with a priest and 1 villein and 8 bordars 'with 1 hide and 1½ ploughs.' 'There is 1 riding-horse.' There are 40 acres of pasture and 15 acres of wood(land). It is worth 30 shillings. 'When the bishop died it was worth 40 shillings.'

To the church of 'St. Mary of' PERETUNE [North Petherton] belong (*jacent*) 3 virgates of land. There is land for 1 plough which is there. 'Rannulf the nephew of Peter after the bishop's death had the proceeds thence which the bishop had before. It is worth 20 shillings.'
Peter the bishop (of Chester) held these 2 churches. Now they are in the king's hand.

Liof holds 'BERA'[2] [Beere in Cannington] which he also held of King Edward and paid geld for 1 virgate of land. 'In demesne are 3 ferlings and half a plough, and the villeins have 1 ferling and half a plough.' There is land for 1 plough which is there with 1 serf and 2 bordars. 'There are 4 beasts and 5 swine and 5 sheep.' There is a mill paying 6 pence and 6 acres of meadow. It is worth 10 shillings.

Turstin holds LEGE [Abbot's Leigh]. His father held (it) T.R.E. and paid geld for 1 hide. There is land for 1 plough. There are 2 bordars. 'There are 2 beasts and 6 swine.' It is worth 10 shillings.

Godwin holds half a hide in a manor which is called Ragiol [Ridgehill in Winford] of the king in almoin. 'T.R.E. he held the whole manor.' It is worth 3 shillings.

In the church of CURI [Curry Rivel] is half a hide. There a priest has 1 plough. It is worth 12 shillings.

Edith (*Eddida*) the nun (*monialis*) has in almoin of the king 12 acres of land. There she has 80 acres of wood(land) and pasture. 'There she has 4 beasts and 4 swine and 11 sheep.' It is worth 5 shillings.

Two nuns (*nonnæ*) hold of the king in almoin 2½ virgates of land in HONECOTE [Huntscott in Wootton Courtney], 'which 2 thegns held in parage (*pariter*)' T.R.E. There is land for 2 ploughs. There is 1 plough and 5 acres of meadow. It is worth 5 shillings. 'When they received it, 10 shillings.'

[2] In the Exchequer Domesday (facsimile) this is written Ebra.

In 'the church of' CHENEMERESDONE, 'CHIVEMERESDONE' [Kilmersdon] there is half a hide of land. It is worth 10 shillings. Peter the bishop held (it). Now it is in the king's hand.

'fo. 282'

XVII. THE LAND OF COUNT EUSTACE

Count Eustace holds of the king NEWENTONE [Newton in North Petherton]. Lewin held (it) T.R.E., and paid geld for 1 hide and 1 virgate of land. There is land for 4 ploughs. Of this (land) 2½ virgates of land are in demesne where are 1 plough and 2 serfs and (there are) 7 villeins and 6 bordars with 3 ploughs 'and the rest of the land.' 'There are 2 swine and 35 sheep.' There is a mill paying 15 pence, and 7 acres of meadow and 33 acres of pasture and 17 acres of wood(land). It was and is worth 4 pounds. Alvred of Merleberg holds (it) of the count.

The same Alvred holds of the count COMMIZ 'COMMIT' [Combwich in Otterhampton]. Lewin held (it) T.R.E., and paid geld for 1½ hides. There is land for 6 ploughs. In demesne 'are 3 virgates' and 1 plough and 2 serfs and (there are) 2 villeins and 1 bordar with 2 ploughs 'and the rest of the land.' There (are) 26 acres of meadow and 10 acres of pasture and 2 acres of wood(land). It was worth 50 shillings. Now 40 shillings.

Evrard holds of the count LECHESWRDE [Laxworthy in Enmore]. Alward held (it) T.R.E., and paid geld for 1 virgate of land. There is land for 2 ploughs. In demesne 'are half a virgate' and half a plough and 4 serfs and (there are) 4 villeins[1] and 3 bordars[1] with 1½ ploughs 'and half a virgate.' 'There are 6 beasts and 5 swine.' There are 2 mills paying 2 blooms (plumbas)[2] of iron, and 3 acres of meadow and 20 acres of wood(land). It was and is worth 30 shillings.

The same count holds LOCHESTONE [Loxton]. Ulveva held (it) T.R.E., and paid geld for 5 hides. There is land for 7 ploughs. Of this (land) 4 hides are in demesne where are 2 ploughs and 2 serfs and (there are) 5 villeins and 6 bordars with 3 ploughs 'and 1 hide.' 'There are 3 beasts and 3 swine.' There is a mill paying 6 pence, and 50 acres

[1] Exet. Dom. reads : '3 villeins and 4 bordars.'
[2] Plumba = a dish used as a measure for ore, afterwards the due payable on the measure (Eyton, Som. Dom. i. 41).

of meadow and 60 acres of pasture and 6 acres of underwood (silvæ minutæ). It was and is worth 100 shillings.

Alvred holds of the count CELEWORDE [Chelwood]. Thuri held (it) T.R.E., and paid geld for 3 hides. There is land for 3 ploughs. Of this (land) 2½ hides are in demesne, and (there are) 3 villeins and 2 bordars with 1 plough 'and half a hide,' and the other (plough) is in demesne. 'There are 15 swine and 80 sheep.' There (are) 5 acres of meadow. Wood(land) 5 furlongs long and 1 furlong broad. It is worth 60 shillings. 'And when the count received it, 40 shillings.'

Alvred holds of the count BELGETONE [Belluton in Stanton Drew]. Tovi held it freely (libere) T.R.E., and paid geld for 4 hides. There is land for 4 ploughs. In demesne are '2 hides and 2½ virgates and' 1½ ploughs with 1 serf and (there are) 5 villeins and 2 bordars with 2 ploughs 'and 1 hide and 1½ virgates.' 'There are 10 beasts and 13 swine and 47 sheep and 10 she-goats.' There is a mill paying 15 shillings, and 22 acres of meadow and 20 acres of pasture. Wood(land) 4[3] furlongs long and 2 furlongs broad. It was worth 3 pounds. Now 4 pounds.

The Countess Ida of Boulogne[4] holds of the king CHINWARDESTUNE [Kingweston]. Ulveva held (it) T.R.E., and paid geld for 5 hides. There is land for 8 ploughs. Of this (land) 2 hides and 3 virgates are in demesne where are 2 ploughs and 6 serfs and (there are) 8 villeins and 8 bordars with 5 ploughs 'and 2 hides and 1 virgate and 5 acres.' 'There are 12 beasts and 12 swine.' There (are) 25 acres of meadow and 22 acres of pasture. Wood(land) 3 furlongs long and 1 acre broad. It was and is worth 6 pounds.

Maud holds of the count CONTITONE [Compton Bishop].[5] Ulnod held (it) T.R.E.

[3] Exet. Dom. reads : '3.'
[4] Boloniensis interlined in red.
[5] Contitone, held of Count Eustace by Maud. This was one of three places of the same name left unidentified by Eyton. The other two, with a total of 5 hides, belonging to Walter of Dowai, can be identified with part of Chilcompton. The only other parish of Compton on the modern map not provided with a Domesday prototype is Compton Bishop. This has generally been taken as a detached part of the great episcopal manor of Banwell; and it was certainly in the Bishop's hands in 1159 (Wells Cath. MSS. 15). Compton

and paid geld for 5 hides. There is land for 5 ploughs. Of this (land) there are in demesne 3 hides where are 2 ploughs and 4 serfs and (there are) 5 villeins and 10 bordars with 3 ploughs 'and the rest of the land.' 'There are 2 cows and 140 sheep.' There (is) a mill paying 64 pence, and 5 acres of meadow. Pasture 4 furlongs long and 2 furlongs broad. It is worth 100 shillings. 'When the count received it, 4 pounds.'

' fo. 286b '

XVIII. THE LAND OF EARL HUGH

Earl Hugh holds of the king TEDINTONE [Tetton in Kingston], and William of him. Ednod held (it) T.R.E., and paid geld for 1 hide. There is land for 4 ploughs. In demesne there is 'half a hide and' 1 plough, and 4 serfs, and (there are) 5 villeins and 8 bordars with 2 ploughs 'and the rest of the land.' 'There are 8 beasts and 6 swine and 60 sheep.' There (are) 5 acres of meadow and 100 acres of pasture and 40 acres of wood(land). It was and is worth 40 shillings.

William holds of the Earl SANFORD [Sampford Bret].[1] 'Alnod held it and' T.R.E. paid geld for 2 hides. There is land for 5 ploughs. In demesne are '1 hide and 3 ferlings and' 1 plough with 1 serf and (there are) 8 villeins with 1[2] plough 'and the rest of the land.' 'There are 3 beasts and 4 swine and 100 sheep.' There are 9 acres of meadow and 50 acres of wood(land) and a mill. It was and is worth 3 pounds.

William holds of the Earl ALRE.[3] Ednod held (it) T.R.E., and paid geld for ½ hide. There is land for 2 ploughs. 'In demesne are 1 virgate and 3 ferlings and 1 plough' with 1 serf and 1 bordar and 1 villein 'who has 1 ferling' and 1 acre of meadow

Bishop adjoins Loxton, another manor of Count Eustace. While it is not possible to decide the question, it is quite likely that one of the early bishops of the diocese may have obtained Compton for the see. Failing this, 'Contitone' must remain unidentified.

[1] It was held in 1284 (*Kirby's Quest*) by William le Bret of the Barony of Chester (which was Hugh's earldom). As in the case of Tetton and Alre, the family of Brett had succeeded William, whose surname Eyton considers to have been Malbanc (Eyton, *Som. Dom.* i. 58).

[2] Exet. Dom. reads : ' 2.'

[3] Possibly part of Bicknoller, anciently ' Bykenalra.'

and 36 acres of pasture and 6 acres of wood-(land). It was worth 20 shillings. Now 15 shillings.

The church[4] of St. Sever holds of the earl HENGESTRICH [Henstridge]. Ednod held (it) T.R.E. and paid geld for 4 hides. There is land for 3 ploughs. Of this (land) 3½ hides are in demesne where are 2 ploughs and 4 serfs and (there are) 6 bordars with 1 plough ' and half a hide.' 'There are 8 beasts and 5 swine.' There (are) 30 acres of meadow and 30 acres of pasture and wood(land) 4[5] furlongs long and 1 furlong broad. It is worth 4 pounds and 10 shillings. 'When the count received it, 5 pounds.'

'fo. 265 '

XIX. THE LAND OF THE COUNT OF MORTAIN

The Count of Mortain holds of the king CRUCHE [Cricket St. Thomas] and Turstin of him. Sirewold held (it) T.R.E. and paid geld for 6 hides. There is land for 5 ploughs. Of this (land) 4 hides are in demesne where are 3 ploughs and 2 serfs and (there are) 6 villeins and 5 bordars with 3 ploughs 'and 2 hides.' 'There are 14 beasts and 14 swine and 124 sheep and 24 she-goats.' There is a mill paying 12 shillings, and 1½ acres of meadow. Wood(land) 7 furlongs long and 2 furlongs broad. It was worth 4 pounds. Now 100 shillings.[6]

Malger holds of the count SEVENEHANTUNE [Seavington St. Mary].[7] Alward held (it) T.R.E. and paid geld for 7 hides. There is land for 7 ploughs. Of this (land) 5½ hides are in demesne where are 3 ploughs and 6 serfs, and (there are) 8 villeins and 7 bordars with 3 ploughs 'and 1½ hides.' 'There are 4 cows and 9 swine and 116 sheep.' There is a mill paying 5 shillings and 40 acres of meadow. It was worth 8 pounds. Now 100 shillings.

From this manor have been taken away 10 acres of wood(land) and 25 acres of moor (*moræ*) and meadow, and they are in Sudperet [South Petherton] the king's manor.

[4] Exet. Dom. reads : ' abbot.'

[5] Exet. Dom. reads : ' 3.'

[6] Exet. Dom. adds here the statement of the custom due to South Petherton, which will be found under the ' Terra Regis.'

[7] As nearly all Malger de Cartrai's holdings in this district came to the family of Vaux, this particular manor may be identified with Seavington Vaux or St. Mary.

Malger holds of the count CONTUNE [Compton Durvill in South Petherton].[1] Godric held (it) T.R.E. and paid geld for 3 hides. There is land for 3 ploughs. In demesne there are ' 2 hides and' 1 plough, and 6 villeins with 6 bordars have 1 plough ' and 1 hide.' ' There are 14 beasts and 42 sheep.' It is worth 60 shillings. ' When the count received it, 40 shillings.'

Ansger ' Breto' holds STANTUNE [White-staunton] of the count. Alward held (it) T.R.E. and paid geld for 3 hides. There is land for 8 ploughs. In demesne there are ' 1 hide and 1 virgate and' 1½ ploughs and 6 serfs and (there are) 18 villeins and 4 bordars with 3½ ploughs ' and 1 hide and 3 virgates.' ' There is 1 riding-horse and 7 beasts and 16 swine and 59 sheep and 13 she-goats.' There is a mill which pays nothing (*sine censu*),[2] and 260 acres of wood-(land) and 50 acres of pasture paying 4 blooms (*blomas*) of iron. It is worth 60 shillings. ' When the count received it, 30 shillings.'

The count himself holds SCEPTONE [Shepton Beauchamp]. Algar held (it) T.R.E. and paid geld for 6 hides. There is land for 4 ploughs. Of this (land) 4 hides less half a virgate are in demesne where are 1½ ploughs and 3 serfs, and (there are) 9 villeins and 3 bordars ' with 2 hides and half a virgate.' ' There are 1 riding-horse and 4 beasts and 7 swine and 64 sheep.' There are 15 acres of meadow. It was worth 100 shillings. Now 4 pounds.

Gerard holds of the count LOPENE [Lopen]. Alward held (it) T.R.E. and paid geld for 1 hide. There is land for 1 plough. There is 1 bordar with 1 serf and 10 acres of meadow. ' There are 3 beasts and 3 swine and 61 sheep.' It is worth 20 shillings, ' and when the count received it, 10 shillings.'

[3] + Robert ' the constable' holds of the count CRAWECUMBE [Crowcombe]. The church of St. Swithun of Winchester held (it) T.R.E. There are 10 hides but it paid geld for 4 hides only (*non geldavit nisi*). There is land for 12 ploughs. Of this land 1 hide is in

demesne where are 3 ploughs and 6 serfs and (there are) 31 villeins and 10 bordars with 10 ploughs ' and 9 hides.' ' There are 26 beasts and 26 swine and 70 sheep and 28 she-goats.' There (are) 11 acres of meadow and 20 acres of wood(land). Pasture 1 league long and half a league broad. It was and is worth 8 pounds.

Ansger ' Brito' holds of the count ISLE [Isle Brewers]. Ulnod held it T.R.E. and paid geld for 6 hides. There is land for 6 ploughs. In demesne are ' 4½ hides and' 2 ploughs and 5 serfs and (there are) 5 villeins and 4 bordars with 2 ploughs ' and 1½ hides.' ' There are 6 riding-horses and 27 beasts and 15 swine and 90 sheep and 60 she-goats.' There is a mill paying 14 shillings, and 17 acres of meadow. Wood(land) 3½ furlongs long and 2 furlongs broad. It is worth 100 shillings. ' When the count received it, 60 shillings.'

+ The count himself holds TINTEHALLE [Tintinhull]. The church [4] of Glastingberie held (it) T.R.E. There are 7 hides and 1 virgate of land, but it paid geld for 5 hides. There is land for 10 ploughs. Of this (land) 4 hides are in demesne where are 2 ploughs and 5 serfs and (there are) 19 villeins and 9 bordars with 8 ploughs ' and the rest of the land.' ' There are 2 riding-horses and 5 cows and 30 swine and 94 sheep.' There (is) a mill paying 30 pence and 60 acres of meadow and 200 acres of pasture and 57 acres of wood(land). It is worth 16 pounds. ' And when the count received it, 10 pounds.'

Drogo holds of the count 1 virgate of this land, ' a thegn held it in parage (*pariter*) T.R.E.,' and it is worth 1 marc of silver.

fo. 92

+ Hubert ' de St. Clare' holds of the count CHINGESTONE [Kingstone]. The church of Glastingberie held (it) T.R.E. and paid geld for 8 hides. There is land for 8 ploughs. Of this (land) 4 hides are in demesne where are 2 ploughs and 3 serfs and (there are) 11 villeins and 13 bordars with 5 ploughs ' and 3 hides and 1 virgate.' ' There are 38 swine and 61 sheep.' There (are) 41 acres of meadow. Wood(land) 6 furlongs long and 3 furlongs broad. It was and is worth 9 pounds. The church receives no due (*non habet servitium*) ' from this (estate).'

Malger holds of the count STOCHET [Stoke under Ham]. Alwin held (it) T.R.E. and

---

[1] Compton Durvile in 1284 (*Kirby's Quest*) was held by the heirs of Whytele of the heirs of Essehulle, i.e. Ashill, owned by Vaux.

[2] Exet. Dom. has : ' molendinum quod molit annonam suam' ; having no business outside the manor work (Eyton, *Som. Dom.* i. 41).

[3] This entry and those of Tintinhull and Kingstone below are marked with a cross, to show land alienated from the church. See also p. 451.

[4] Exet. Dom. reads : ' Alnod abbot of.'

paid geld for 2 hides and 1½ virgates of land. There is land for 3 ploughs. In demesne are ' 1 hide and 3 virgates ' and 2 ploughs and 7 serfs with 1 villein and 1 bordar ' who have the rest of the land.' ' There are 2 beasts and 20 sheep.' There is a mill paying 40 pence, and 10 acres of meadow. It is worth 40 shillings. ' When the count received it, 60 shillings.'

William ' de Corcella ' holds of the count DRAICOTE [Draycott in Limington]. Ulwi held (it) T.R.E. and paid geld for 2 hides. There is land for 3 ploughs. In demesne are ' 1 hide and 3 virgates and ' 1½ ploughs and (there are) 9 bordars with 1½ ploughs ' and 1 virgate.' ' There are 11 swine and 83 sheep.' There is a mill paying 15 shillings, and 26½ acres of meadow and 31 acres of pasture and as much of underwood (*silvæ minutæ*). It is worth 40 shillings. ' When William received it, 20 shillings.'

Robert holds of the count STOCHE [Stoke under Ham]. Five thegns[1] held (it) ' in parage (*pariter*) ' T.R.E. and paid geld for 5½ hides. There is also (*superest ibi*) 1 virgate of land which did not pay geld T.R.E. There is land for 8 ploughs. In demesne are ' 3 hides and ' 2 ploughs and 5 serfs and (there are) 2[2] villeins and 14 bordars with 3 ploughs ' and 2½ hides and 1 virgate.' ' There are 2 riding-horses and 12 beasts and 10 swine and 40 sheep.' There (are) 2 mills paying 9 shillings, and 25 acres of meadow and 2 furlongs of pasture and 3 acres of wood(land). It was and is worth 7 pounds.

Robert holds of the count STOCHET [Stoke under Ham]. Three thegns[3] held (it) ' in parage (*pariter*) ' T.R.E. and paid geld for 2 hides less half a virgate of land. There is land for 2 ploughs. There are ' 1½ hides in demesne and ' 4 bordars ' who have the rest of the land ' and 10 acres of meadow and 15 acres of pasture and 4 acres of wood(land). ' There are 6 cows.' It was and is worth 40 shillings.

Bretel holds of the count SEWELLE [Swell]. Alwald held (it) T.R.E. and paid geld for 3 hides. There is land for 4 ploughs. In demesne ' are 1½ hides and ' 1 plough with 1 serf, and (there are) 6 villeins and 12 bordars with 2 ploughs ' and 1½ hides.' ' There are 1 riding-horse and 7 beasts and 8 swine and

75 sheep.' There are 34 acres of meadow. Wood(land) 5 furlongs and 10 perches long and 2 furlongs broad. It is worth 60 shillings. ' When he received it, 40 shillings.'[4]

Malger holds of the count BRUCHEFORD [Brushford]. Ordulf held (it) T.R.E. and paid geld for 2 hides. There is land for 12 ploughs. In demesne ' are 1 hide and 1 virgate and 1 ferling ' and 1 plough and 12 serfs and (there are) 10 villeins and 5 bordars with 2 ploughs ' and half a hide and 3 ferlings.' ' There are 10 beasts and 2 swine and 60 sheep and 20 she-goats.' There is a mill paying 12 shillings and 6 pence, and 6 acres of meadow and 17 acres of wood(land). Pasture half a league long and 3 furlongs broad. It is worth 4 pounds. ' And when the count received it, 8 pounds.'

Malger holds of the count BREDE, ' BRETDA ' [North Bradon].[5] Alvric held (it) T.R.E. and paid geld for 1 hide. There is land for 1 plough. There is 1 bordar. It is worth 10 shillings. ' When the count received it, 20 shillings.'

This manor owes as a customary rent (*per consuetudinem*) one ewe with a lamb to CURI [Curry Rivel] the king's manor. ' Since Mauger received the land this customary rent has not been rendered.'

Malger holds of the count AISELLE [Ashill]. Two thegns held it ' in parage (*pariter*) ' T.R.E. and paid geld for 5 hides. There is land for 5 ploughs. In demesne are ' 3 hides and 3½ virgates and ' 2 ploughs and (there are) 4 villeins and 17 bordars with 2

---

[4] Exet. Dom. adds here the statement concerning 1 virgate detached from Curry Rivel ; see under ' Terra Regis.'

[5] There are four entries under this name (with variations), with a total of 5 hides. The Bradon of Harding son of Elnod is Goosebradon, whose superior lords were the family of De Meryet (*Inq. p.m.* John de Meriet, 1 Edw. II., no. 62). Bradon held of the Count by Drogo, rated at 2 hides, is South Bradon, in which Nicholas Reade held 2 hides of Will. de Montacute Earl of Salisbury in 1397 (*Inq. p.m.* 20 Ric. II. 35). Another Bradon also held of the Count by Drogo (de Montacute), rated at 1 hide, is the single hide held by Will. de Staunton of Will. de Montacute in 1397 as above. The fourth Bradon held of the Count by Malger de Cartrai, rated at 1 hide, should be the single hide in ' Bradene ' given by Gervase Ivas to Hugh de Montisorell c. 1220, and by him given to Muchelney Abbey (*Much. Cart.*, Nos. 14, 15, 16, *S.R.S.* xiv. p. 52). In *Nom. Villar.*, 1317, the Abbot of Muchelney and Cristina de Staunton are entered as owners in North Bradon.

---

[1] Exet. Dom. has : ' Edwi and his four brothers.'
[2] Exet. Dom.: ' 9.'
[3] Exet. Dom. : ' Aluiet, Suet and Alvert.'

ploughs 'and 1 hide and half a virgate.' 'There are 2 beasts and 70 swine and 20 she-goats.' There (are) 40 acres of meadow. Wood(land) 40 furlongs long and 20 furlongs broad. It is worth 60 shillings. 'When the count received it, 4 pounds.'

This manor ought to pay 30 pence to CURI, 'CHORI' [Curry Rivel] the king's manor. 'Since Mauger received the land this customary rent has not been rendered.'

Malger holds of the count BRADEWEI [Broadway]. Alnod held (it) T.R.E. and paid geld for 1 hide. There is land for 1 plough. There are 2 virgates in demesne and there are 3 villeins and 3 bordars 'who have 2 virgates and half a plough' with 1 serf. There (are) 12 acres of meadow and 4 acres of wood(land). It was and is worth 10 shillings.

Bretel holds of the count AISSE [Ashbrittle]. Wado held (it) T.R.E. and paid geld for 4 hides. There has been added 1 hide[1] which 2 thegns held. Altogether (in totum) there is land for 10 ploughs. In demesne are 2½ hides and 2 ploughs and 8 serfs and (there are) 16 villeins and 22 bordars with 4 ploughs 'and 3 hides.' 'There are 7 beasts and 10 swine and 80 sheep and 60 she-goats.' There are 2 mills paying 15 shillings, and 4 acres of meadow and 40 acres of pasture and 38 acres of wood(land). It was and is worth 100 shillings.

Bretel holds of the count GRINDEHAM [Greenham in Stawley]. Alric held (it) T.R.E. and paid geld for 1 hide. There is land for 2 ploughs. In demesne 'are 3 virgates and' 1 plough and 2 serfs and (there are) 3 villeins and 2 bordars with half a plough 'and 1 virgate.' 'There are 12 beasts and 7 swine and 40 sheep.' There is a mill paying 5 shillings, and 3 acres of meadow and 3 acres of pasture and 10 acres of wood(land). It is worth 15 shillings. 'When the count received it, 10 shillings.'

Bretel holds of the count APPELIE [Appley in Stawley]. Brismar held (it) T.R.E. and paid geld for 1 hide. There is land for 2 ploughs. 'There are in demesne 2½ virgates.' There are 2 villeins with 1 plough 'and 1½ virgates' and 2 acres of meadow and 3 acres of pasture and 3 acres of wood(land). It is worth 10 shillings.

Drogo holds of the count BREDDE, 'BRETDA' [North Bradon]. Celred held (it) T.R.E. and

paid geld for 1 hide. There is land for 1 plough which is there with 1 serf. There (are) 7 acres of meadow and 3 acres of underwood (silvæ minutæ). It is worth 15 shillings. 'When the count received it, 20 shillings.' This manor ought to pay as a customary rent (per consuetudinem) 1 ewe with its lamb to CURI, 'CHORI' [Curry Rivel] the king's manor. 'Since Drogo received the land, it has not been paid.'

Drogo holds of the count DONIET [Donyat]. Adulf, Sawin and Dunstan held (it) for 3 manors[2] T.R.E. and paid geld for 5 hides. There is land for 5 ploughs. In demesne 'are 4 hides and' 1 plough and 3 serfs and (there are) 6 villeins and 9 bordars with 2 ploughs 'and 1 hide.' 'There are 1 riding-horse and 12 unbroken mares and 9 beasts and 70 sheep and 30 she-goats.' There is a mill which pays no rent (sine censu),[3] and 20 acres of meadow, and 50 acres of pasture, and a park. It was and is worth 100 shillings.

This manor owes for a customary rent (per consuetudinem) to CURI, 'CHORI' [Curry Rivel] 5 ewes with their lambs. 'Since Drogo received the manor, it has not been paid.'

The count himself holds STAPLE [Staple Fitzpaine]. Two thegns held (it) 'in parage (pariter)' T.R.E. and paid geld for 10 hides. There is land for 9 ploughs. Of this (land) 7 hides are in demesne where are 3 ploughs and 6 serfs and (there are) 20 villeins with 6 ploughs 'and 3 hides.' 'There are 1 riding-horse and 10 unbroken mares and 10 beasts and 50 sheep and 100 she-goats.' There is a mill paying 30 pence, and 24 acres of meadow. Pasture half a league long and 1 furlong broad. Wood(land) 1 league long and 2 furlongs broad. It was worth 10 pounds. Now 12 pounds.

To this manor belongs an orchard (ortus) in Langeport, 'Lanporda' [Langport] paying (a rent of) 50 eels.

William 'de Lestra' holds of the count BICHEHALLE [Bickenhall]. Alvric held (it) T.R.E. and paid geld for 5 hides. There is land for 5 ploughs. In demesne are '1 hide and' 2 ploughs and 3 serfs and (there are) 9 villeins and 7 bordars with 3 ploughs 'and the rest of the land.' 'There are 1 riding-

[1] Exet. Dom. reads : ' 1½ hides.'

[2] Exet. Dom. reads : 'Hatulf held Doniet T.R.E. and paid geld for 2 hides ; to this manor has been added the land of 2 thegns who held in parage (pariter). Sawin held 1½ hides and Dunstan 1½ hides.'

[3] Exet. Dom. states : 'qui molit annonam suam': having no business beyond the work of the manor,

horse and 14 beasts and 3 swine and 7 she-goats.' There are 14 acres of meadow. Wood(land) 1 league long and 1 furlong broad. It was worth 20 shillings. Now 70 shillings.

This manor ought to pay as a customary rent (*debet per consuetudinem*) to Curi, 'Chori' [Curry Rivel], the king's manor, 5 sheep with as many lambs, and from each free man 1 bloom (*bloma*) of iron. 'Since William received the land from the count this rent has not been paid.'

Rainald 'de Valle torta' holds of the count Bere [Beer Crocombe]. Algar held it T.R.E. and paid geld for 5 hides. There is land for 4 ploughs. In demesne are ' 4 hides and' 3 ploughs and 4 serfs and (there are) 6 villeins and 7[1] bordars 'with 1 hide.'[2] 'There are 8 beasts and 4 swine and 21 sheep and 20 she-goats.' There (are) 20 acres of meadow and 12 acres of pasture and 5 acres of wood(land). It was worth 100 shillings. Now 60 shillings.

Robert 'the constable' holds of the count Hache [Hatch Beauchamp]. Godric and Goduin and Bollo held (it) T.R.E. as 3 manors, and paid geld for 5 hides.[3] There is land for 6 ploughs. In demesne are ' 4 hides and 3 virgates and' 2 ploughs and 3 serfs and (there are) 11 villeins and 4 bordars with 3 ploughs 'and 1 hide and 1 virgate.' 'There are 2 riding-horses and 16 beasts and 112 sheep and 58 she-goats.' There (are) 8 acres of meadow and 60 acres of wood(land). It was worth 8 pounds. Now 4 pounds.

From one of these hides which Bollo held there is due as a customary rent (*per consuetudinem*) to Curi, 'Chori' [Curry Rivel], 'the king's' manor, 1 sheep with a lamb. 'Since Robert received the land this rent has not been paid.'

Drogo holds of the count Torlaberie [Thurlbeare]. Ulviet held (it) T.R.E. and paid geld for 3 hides. There is land for 9 ploughs. In demesne are ' 1½ hides and' 2 ploughs and 5 serfs and (there are) 21 villeins with 7 ploughs 'and the rest of the land.' 'There are 1 riding-horse and 3 beasts and 12 swine and 60 sheep.' There (are) 15 acres of meadow and 20 acres of wood(land). It was and is worth 6 pounds.

---

[1] Exet. Dom.: ' 8.'

[2] Exet. Dom. allots the 3 ploughs to the villeins.

[3] Exet. Dom. reads : ' Godric held Hachia T.R.E. and paid geld for 2 hides ; to this have been added 2 other manors which 2 thegns held in parage (*pariter*). Godwin had 2 hides and Bollo 1 hide.'

Ansger holds of the count Torne [Thorn Falcon]. Algar held (it) T.R.E. and paid geld for 6 hides. There is land for 6 ploughs. In demesne are ' 3½ hides and' 2 ploughs and 3 serfs and (there are) 5 villeins and 4 bordars with 2 ploughs 'and the rest of the land.' 'There are 8 beasts and 7 swine and 130 sheep.' There (are) 8 acres of meadow and 2 acres of underwood (*silvæ minutæ*). It was and is worth 3 pounds.

Dodeman holds of the count Meriet [Merriott]. Lewin and Bristward held (it) 'in parage (*pariter*)' T.R.E. and paid geld for 7 hides. There is land for 7 ploughs. In demesne are ' 3½ hides and' 2 ploughs and 6 serfs and (there are) 10 villeins and 6 bordars with 4 ploughs 'and the rest of the land.' 'There are 1 riding-horse and 10 beasts and 15 swine and 35 sheep.' There are 3 mills paying 30 shillings, and 25 acres of meadow and of pasture half a league in length and breadth (*in long. et lat.*). It was worth 4 pounds. Now 7 pounds.

Turstin holds of the count Estham [Eastham in Crewkerne]. Godwin the king's reeve (*prepositus*) held (it) with Cruche [Crewkerne], the king's manor, and T.R.E. it could not be separated from the 'ferm' (*firma*),[4] and he paid geld for 2 hides. There is land for 2 ploughs which are there in demesne with 10 bordars and 1 serf. 'There are 6 beasts and 11 swine and 45 sheep.' There is a mill paying 12 shillings, and 12 acres of meadow and 20 acres of wood(land). It was and is worth 50 shillings.

Drogo holds of the count Cruchet [Cricket Malerbie].[5] Two thegns held (it) T.R.E. 'in parage (*pariter*),' and paid geld for 3 hides. There is land for 4 ploughs. In demesne there are ' 2½ hides and' 1 plough with 1 serf and (there are) 5 villeins and 4 bordars with half a plough 'and half a hide.' 'There are 5 beasts and 11 swine and 22 sheep.' There (are) 8 acres of meadow and 80 acres of wood(land). It was worth 10 shillings. Now 30 shillings.

Robert 'son of Ivo' holds of the count 1 hide in Prestitone [Torell's Preston in Milverton]. Earl Harold held it. There is land for 4 ploughs. In demesne are ' 2½ virgates and' half a plough with 1 serf and

---

[4] i.e. he could not alienate the land.

[5] In *Kirby's Quest*, 1284, Hugh de Courtney held Cricket Malerbe of Simon de Montacute as of his manor of Shepton Montacute.

(there are) 6 villeins and 2 bordars with 2 ploughs 'and the rest of the land.' 'There are 6 beasts and 7 swine and 27 sheep.' There is a mill paying 12 pence, and 5 acres of meadow and 3 acres of pasture and 11 acres of wood(land). It was and is worth 30 shillings.

This estate (*terra*) used to belong to (*jacuit in*) BURNETONE [Brompton Regis], the king's manor, with the ferm (*firma*).[1]

Ansger holds of the count in AISSE [Ashbrittle] 1 hide. Bristuin held (it) T.R.E. There is land for 1 plough which 2 villeins there hold. 'In demesne are 3¾ virgates, and the villeins have the rest of the land.' There are 1 acre of pasture and 2 acres of underwood (*silvæ minutæ*). It was and is worth 10 shillings.

Robert 'son of Walter' holds of the count HARPETREU [East Harptree]. Alduin held (it) T.R.E. and paid geld for 5 hides. There is land for 5 ploughs. In demesne are '3½ hides and' 2 ploughs, and (there are) 6 villeins and 6 bordars with 2 ploughs 'and 1½ hides.' 'There are 4 beasts and 1 pig and 10 she-goats.' There is a mill paying 5 shillings, and 40 acres of meadow and 60 acres of wood(land). Pasture 8 furlongs long and 5 furlongs broad. It was and is worth 40 shillings.

Two porters[2] of Montagud [Montacute] hold of the count ESTURT [Stert in Babcary]. Brisnod held (it) T.R.E. and paid geld for 2 hides. There is land for 3 ploughs. In demesne are '5 virgates and' 3[3] ploughs and 4 serfs with 1 bordar and 1 villein owning 1 plough 'and 3 virgates.' 'There are 1 riding-horse and 3 beasts and 15 swine and 30 sheep.' There (are) 16 acres of meadow. It was worth 30 shillings. Now 50 shillings.

[4]Drogo holds of the count BREDENE [Bradon]. Orde held (it) T.R.E. and paid geld for 2 hides. There is land for 2 ploughs which are there in demesne with '1 hide and 3 virgates and' 1 serf and 3 bordars 'who have 1 virgate.' 'There are 2 riding-horses and 16 beasts and 10 swine.' There is a mill paying 12 shillings and 6 pence, and 18

---

1 Exet. Dom.: 'in firma mansionis Regis.'
2 Exch.: *portarii.* Exet. Dom.: '*portitores.*'
3 Exet. Dom.: ' 2.'
4 This entry is written across the whole width of the page at the foot (pl. xiii. in Photozincographed Copy of Domesday), showing that it had been omitted at the proper place, which on the evidence of the Exeter codex is between Appley and Bradon.

---

acres of meadow and 20 acres of pasture and 20 acres of wood(land). It is and was[5] worth 40 shillings. This manor ought to pay as a customary rent (*per consuetudinem*) 2 ewes with their lambs to CURI, 'CHORI' [Curry Rivel] the king's manor. 'Since Drogo received the land this customary rent has not been paid.'

Alvred, 'the butler (*Pincerna*),' holds of the count BRADEFORD [Bradford]. Eduin[6] held
fo. 92b
(it) T.R.E. and paid geld for 5 hides. There is land for 8 ploughs. In demesne are '2 hides and' 2 ploughs and 5 serfs and (there are) 19 villeins and 7 bordars with 6 ploughs 'and 3 hides.' 'There are 2 riding-horses and 8 beasts and 14 swine and 40 sheep.' There is a mill paying 10 shillings, and 30 acres of meadow and 10 acres of pasture and 72 acres of wood(land). It was worth 8 pounds. Now 11 pounds.

Alvred holds of the count HELE [Hele in Bradford]. Eldred held (it) and paid geld for 1 hide. There is land for 3 ploughs. In demesne are '3 virgates and' 1 plough and 4 serfs and (there are) 2 villeins and 7 bordars with 1 plough 'and 1 virgate.' 'There are 1 riding-horse and 5 swine.' There (is) a mill paying 10 shillings, and 10 acres of meadow and 15 acres of wood(land). It was worth 40 shillings. Now 4 pounds.

+ This land T.R.E. could not be separated from Tantone the manor of Walchelin Bishop of Winchester.

Alvred holds of the count NORTONE [Norton Fitzwarren]. Osmund held (it) 'in parage (*pariter*)' T.R.E. and paid geld for 5 hides. There is land for 10 ploughs. In demesne are '1 hide and' 3 ploughs and 6 serfs and (there are) 13 villeins and 8 bordars with 8 ploughs 'and 4 hides.' 'There are 2 riding-horses and 7 swine and 50 sheep.' There are 2 mills paying 11 shillings and 3 pence, and 25 acres of meadow and 40 acres of wood(land). It was worth 8 pounds. Now 15 pounds.

Alvred holds of the count EFORD 'ÆFORD' [Ford in Norton Fitzwarren]. Teodric held (it) 'in parage (*pariter*)' T.R.E. and paid geld for half a hide. There is land for 1 plough which is there with 2 bordars, and there (are) 2 acres of meadow. It was worth 20 shillings. Now 30 shillings.

Rainald 'de Valle torta' holds of the count CERLETONE, 'CEORLATONA' [Charlton Adam,[1] alias East Charlton]. Three thegns with 1 cleric held (it) 'in parage (*pariter*)' T.R.E. and paid geld for 5 hides.[2] There is land for 6 ploughs. In demesne are '2 hides and' 3 ploughs and 6 serfs and (there are) 5 villeins and 6 bordars 'and 2 cottars' with $1\frac{1}{2}$ ploughs. 'There are 1 riding-horse and 5 beasts and 30 swine and 60 sheep.' There (are) 50 acres of meadow and 40 acres of pasture and 20 acres of underwood (*silvæ minutæ*). 'The manor is worth 6 pounds and as much when the count received it.'

The count himself holds CINIOCH [East Chinnock].[3] Edmer[4] held (it) and paid geld for 7 hides. There is land for 7 ploughs. In demesne are '$4\frac{1}{2}$ hides and' 3 ploughs and 4 serfs and (there are) 10 villeins and 12 bordars with 4 ploughs 'and $2\frac{1}{2}$ hides.' 'There are 1 riding-horse and 14 beasts and 122 sheep.' There is a mill paying 15 pence, and 60 acres of meadow and 20 acres of pasture. It was worth 100 shillings. Now 12 pounds.

Bretel holds of the count PERET [North Perrott]. Algar held (it) T.R.E. and paid geld for 10 hides. There is land for 8 ploughs. In demesne are '6 hides and' 1 plough and 2 serfs and (there are) 8 villeins and 12 bordars with 3 ploughs 'and 4 hides.' 'There are 2 beasts and 10 swine and 120 sheep.' There are 2 mills paying 14 shillings, and 18 acres of meadow. Wood(land) 6 furlongs long and 3 furlongs broad. It was and is worth 7 pounds.

Ansger 'Brito' holds of the count UDE-

COME, 'ODECOMA' [Odcombe]. Edmer held (it) T.R.E. and paid geld for 5 hides. There is land for 5 ploughs. In demesne are '2 hides and' 2 ploughs and 4 serfs and (there are) 10 villeins and 16 [5] bordars with 3 ploughs 'and 3 hides.' 'There are 36 swine and 126 sheep.' There is a mill paying 7 shillings and 6 pence. There (are) 20 acres of meadow and 12 acres of pasture and 1 furlong of underwood (*silvæ minutæ*). It was and is worth 100 shillings.

Alvred holds CEOLSEBERGE, 'CEOSELBERGON' [Chiselborough]. Two thegns held (it) 'in parage (*pariter*)' T.R.E. and paid geld for 5 hides. There is land for 5 ploughs. In demesne are '$1\frac{1}{2}$ hides and' 1 plough and 2 serfs and (there are) 10 villeins and 12 bordars with 4 ploughs 'and $3\frac{1}{2}$ hides.' 'There are 2 riding-horses and 10 beasts and 4 swine and 29 sheep.' There is a mill paying 15 shillings, and 38 acres of meadow and 3 acres of underwood (*silvæ minutæ*). It was worth 60 shillings. Now 100 shillings.

Malger holds of the count CINIOCH [Chinnock, Middle]. One thegn held (it) 'in parage (*pariter*)' and paid geld for 3 hides. There is land for 3 ploughs. In demesne are '2 hides and' 1 plough and 3 serfs and (there are) 2 villeins and 9 bordars with 1 plough 'and 1 hide.' 'There are 6 swine.' There (are) 36 acres of meadow. It was worth 4 pounds. Now 3 pounds.

Alvred holds of the count CINIOCH [Chinnock, West]. One thegn held (it) 'in parage (*pariter*)' T.R.E. and paid geld for 4 hides. There is land for 4 ploughs. In demesne are '2 hides and' 2 ploughs and 5 serfs and (there are) 5 villeins and 10 bordars with 2 ploughs 'and 2 hides.' 'There are 2 riding-horses and 4 beasts and 20 swine and 67 sheep.' There (is) a mill paying 10 shillings, and 40 acres of meadow and 2 acres of pasture. It is worth 4 pounds. 'When the count received it 3 pounds.'

The church of St. Mary of Greistan holds of the count NORTONE [Norton-sub-Hamdon]. One thegn held (it) 'in parage (*pariter*)' T.R.E. and paid geld for 5 hides. There is land for 5 ploughs. Of this (land) 2 hides are in demesne where are 1 plough and 5 serfs and (there are) 8 villeins and 6 bordars with 3 ploughs 'and 2 hides.' 'There are 1 riding-horse and 10 beasts and 17 swine and 40 sheep.' There (are) 2 mills paying 20

---

[1] John Fitzhamon son of Haimo, a tenant of the Count at Buckhorn Weston in Dorset, gave the church of Charlton Adam to Bruton Priory during the episcopate of Bishop Robert, 1142–1166 (*Bruton Cart.* 180 *seq.*; *S.R.S.* viii. 41; *Historic Notes on South Somerset*, by J. Batten, pp. 142–5).

[2] Exet. Dom. states: 'Reginald holds $4\frac{1}{2}$ hides of the count; in demesne 2, and $2\frac{1}{4}$ held by the villeins.' The $\frac{1}{2}$ hide wanting is not mentioned again.

[3] The three manors of this name, all being held of the Count, can be differentiated. The largest, held by the Count himself, is East Chinnock, as his son gave it to the monks of Montacute. The Chinnock held by Malger de Cartrai came, like so much of his property, to Vaux of Ashill. Will. de Albemarle held Middle Chinnock of the fee of Ashill in 1289 (*Inq. p.m.* W. de A., 17 Edw. I. 22). The third Chinnock held by Alred is therefore West Chinnock. Alred also held Chiselborough, and the two villages have always been closely connected.

[4] Exet. Dom.: 'Edmaratorus.'

[5] Exet. Dom.: '6.'

shillings, and 25 acres of meadow. Wood-(land) 2 furlongs long and 1 furlong broad. It was and is worth 100 shillings.

Alvred holds of the count PENNE [Pendomer]. Alward 'the hunter (*venator*),' held (it) 'of the king' T.R.E. and paid geld for 5 hides. There is land for 5 ploughs. In demesne are '3 hides and' 3 ploughs and 2 serfs and (there are) 5 villeins and 10 bordars with 4 ploughs 'and 2 hides.' 'There are 2 riding-horses and 4 unbroken mares and 12 beasts and 35 swine and 250 sheep.' There (are) 10 acres of meadow and 4 furlongs of pasture (reckoning) in length and breadth. Wood(land) 7 furlongs long and 3 furlongs broad. It was worth 40 shillings. Now 60 shillings.

The count himself holds CLOVEWRDE, 'CLOVESWRDA' [Closworth]. One thegn held (it) 'in parage (*pariter*)' T.R.E. and paid geld for 7 hides. There is land for 6 ploughs. In demesne are '4 hides and' 3 ploughs and 3 serfs and (there are) 10 villeins and 7 bordars with 3 ploughs 'and 3 hides.' 'There is 1 riding-horse and 9 beasts and 23 swine and 100 sheep and 100 she-goats.' There (is) a mill paying 15 shillings, and 12 acres of meadow. Wood(land) 4 furlongs long and 2 furlongs broad. It was and is worth 7 pounds.

Alvred holds of the count CLAFORD [Cloford]. Five thegns held (it) 'in parage (*pariter*)' T.R.E. and paid geld for 10 hides. There is land for 9 ploughs. In demesne are '5½ hides and' 3 ploughs and 2 serfs and 3 cottars and (there are) 12 villeins and 17 bordars with 7 ploughs 'and 4½ hides.' 'There are 2 riding-horses and 38 unbroken mares and 10 beasts and 50 swine and 150 sheep and 30 she-goats.' There is a mill paying 3 shillings, and 20 acres of meadow and 300 acres of pasture and 160 acres of wood(land). It was worth 7 pounds. Now 10 pounds.

The count himself holds GERLINTUNE, 'GERLINCGETUNA' [Yarlington]. Alnod held it T.R.E. and paid geld for 7 hides. There is land for 7 ploughs. In demesne are '4 hides and' 1 plough and 6 serfs and (there are) 8 villeins and 6 bordars with 2 ploughs 'and 3 hides.' 'There are 6 beasts and 3 swine and 60 sheep.' There is a mill paying 7 shillings. Wood(land) 6 furlongs long and 3 furlongs broad. It was worth 7 pounds. Now 100 shillings.

Drogo holds of the count UFETONE [Wool-

ston in North Cadbury]. Three thegns held (it) 'in parage (*pariter*)' T.R.E. and paid geld for 3 hides and 1½ virgates of land. There is land for 2½ ploughs. In demesne are '2½ hides and 1½ virgates and' 1 plough and 8 cottars with 1 villein and 5 bordars with 1 plough 'and half a hide.' 'There are 66 sheep.' There is a mill paying 30 pence, and 10 acres of meadow. It was worth 50 shillings. Now 40 shillings.

Drogo holds of the count SUTONE [Sutton Montis]. Bundi held (it) T.R.E. and paid geld for 5 hides. There is land for 5 ploughs. In demesne are '3 hides and 1 virgate and' 2 ploughs and 2 serfs and (there are) 3 villeins and 9 bordars with 2 ploughs 'and 2 hides less 1 virgate.' 'There are 11 swine and 106 sheep.' There is a mill from which no rent is paid (*sine censu*), and 16 acres of meadow and 8 acres of wood(land). It was and is worth 100 shillings.

Drogo holds of the count SCEPTONE, 'SHEPTUNA' [Shepton Montague]. Toli held (it) T.R.E. and paid geld for 5 hides. There is land for 5 ploughs. In demesne are '3 hides and' 2 ploughs and 8 serfs and (there are) 8 villeins and 5 bordars with 3 ploughs 'and 2 hides.' 'There are 2 riding-horses and 4 cows and 23 swine and 210 sheep.' There (are) 2 mills, from one of which no rent is paid (*sine censu*), the other pays 7 shillings and 6 pence. There (are) 30 acres of meadow. Wood(land) 10 furlongs long and 4 furlongs broad. It was worth 7 pounds. Now 100 shillings.

To this manor has been added STOCHE [Stoney Stoke in Shepton Montague]. Drogo holds (it) of the count. Robert son of Wimarc held (it) 'in parage (*pariter*)' T.R.E. and paid geld for 3 hides. There is land for 4 ploughs. In demesne are '1 hide and' 1 plough and 2 serfs and (there are) 5 villeins and 8 bordars with 2 ploughs 'and 2 hides.' 'There are 7 beasts and 11 swine and 50 sheep.' There (are) 5 acres of meadow and 2 acres of wood(land). It is worth 3 pounds. 'When the count received it, 4 pounds.'

Bretel holds of the count ROLIZ, 'RELIZ' [Redlynch]. Alvric held (it) and paid geld for 4 hides. There is land for 6 ploughs. In demesne are '3 hides and' 1 plough and (there are) 4 villeins and 3 bordars and 7 cottars with 1 plough 'and 1 hide.' 'There are 1 riding-horse and 20 swine and 20 sheep.' There (are) 15 acres of meadow. Wood(land) 2 furlongs long and half a furlong broad. It is worth 40 shillings. 'When the count received it, 4 pounds.'

Malger holds of the count CHINTUNE [Keinton Mandeville]. Two[1] thegns held (it) 'in parage (*pariter*)' T.R.E. and paid geld for 5 hides. There is land for 5 ploughs. In demesne are '4 hides and 1 virgate less 5 acres and' 3 ploughs and 5 serfs and (there are) 2 villeins and 4 bordars with 1 cottar owning 1½ ploughs 'and 3 virgates and 5 acres.' 'There are 5 swine and 85 sheep.' There are 30 acres of meadow. It is worth 4 pounds. 'When the count received it, 5 pounds.'

Richard holds of the count CREDELINCOTE [Carlingcott in Dunkerton.[2]]. Godeman[3] held (it) T.R.E. and paid geld for 3½ hides. There is land for 3 ploughs. In demesne are '3 hides and 1 virgate and' 2 ploughs with 1 serf and with 1 villein and 3 bordars 'who have 1 virgate.' 'There are 3 cows and 12 swine and 162 sheep.' There is a mill paying 5 shillings, and 10 acres of meadow. It is worth 50 shillings. 'When the count received it, 60 shillings.'

Alvred holds of the count ECEWICHE, 'EC-CHEWICA' [Wick in Camerton]. Alestan 'de Boscoina' held (it) T.R.E. and paid geld for 1 virgate of land. 'One plough can till this land.' There (are) 1 villein and 1 serf. It was and is worth 10 shillings.

Bretel holds of the count BERROWENE [South Barrow]. Almær held (it) T.R.E. and paid geld for 5 hides. There is land for 5 ploughs. In demesne are '3 hides and half a virgate and' 1 plough and 2 serfs and (there are) 10 villeins and 1 bordar and 4 cottars with 4 ploughs 'and 1 hide and 3½ virgates.' 'There are 1 riding-horse and 11 beasts and 15 swine and 65 sheep.' There are 8 acres of meadow and 20 acres of pasture and 40 acres of wood(land). It was and is worth 4 pounds.

Bretel holds of the count STOCHE [Stoke Trister]. Two thegns held (it) 'in parage (*pariter*)' T.R.E. and paid geld for 3 hides. There is land for 5 ploughs. In demesne are '1½ hides and' 1 plough and 7 serfs and (there are) 3 villeins and 8 bordars and 5 cottars (*coscez*) with 2 ploughs 'and the rest of the land.' 'There are 1 riding-horse and 11 beasts and 20 swine and 70 she-goats and 8

unbroken mares.' There is a mill paying 10 pence, and 15[4] acres of meadow. Wood-(land) 1 league long and 1 furlong broad. It was and is worth 60 shillings.

Bretel holds of the count COCINTONE [Cuck-lington]. Leving and Swain held (it) 'in parage (*pariter*)' T.R.E. and paid geld for 7 hides. There is land for 6 ploughs. In demesne are '3½ hides and' 1 plough with 1 serf and (there are) 12 villeins and 8 bor-dars with 2 ploughs 'and 3½ hides.' 'There are 4 cottars. There are 12 beasts and 13 swine and 129 sheep and 25 she-goats.' There (are) 22 acres of meadow. Wood(land) 18 fur-longs long and 4 furlongs broad. It was worth 7 pounds. Now 100 shillings.

Ansger holds of the count ALDEDEFORD [Alford]. Godric held (it) T.R.E. and paid geld for 5 hides. There is land for 5 ploughs. In demesne are '2½ hides and 1 virgate and' 1 plough and 3 serfs and (there are) 7 villeins and 4 bordars and 4 cottars with 2 ploughs 'and 2 hides and 1 virgate.' 'There are 20 swine.' There is a mill paying 7 shillings, and 50 acres of meadow, and from the vil-leins (are due) 8 blooms (*blomas*) of iron. It was worth 100 shillings. Now 4 pounds.

Robert 'son of Ivo' holds of the count BABA-CHAN[5] [Babcary]. Godric held (it) T.R.E. and paid geld for 2½ hides. There is land for 3 ploughs. In demesne are '1 hide and 1 virgate and' 2 ploughs and 3 serfs and (there are) 6 villeins and 4 bordars with 1 plough 'and the rest of the land.' 'There are 1 riding-horse and 10 beasts and 15 swine.' There are 14 acres of meadow and 8 acres of pasture. It was worth 50 shillings. Now 60 shillings.

Hugh 'de Valletorta' holds of the count FEDINTONE[6] [Foddington in Babcary). Celred held (it) T.R.E. and paid geld for 1 hide and 1½ virgates of land. There is land for 2 ploughs. In demesne are '1 hide and' 1 plough with 1 villein and 1 bordar with 1 plough 'and the rest of the land' and 4 acres of meadow. It was worth 30 shillings. Now 20.

Malger 'de Cartrai' holds of the count CLOPETONE [Clapton in Maperton]. Two thegns 'Wlua and Alvric his brother' held (it) 'in parage (*pariter*)' T.R.E. and paid

---

[1] Exet. Dom. has as an alternative reading : 'three.'

[2] Part is in Camerton.

[3] Exet. Dom. reads : 'Goderona.'

[4] Exet. Dom.: '16.'

[5] Exet. Dom. reads *rectius* : 'Babakari.'

[6] Exet. Dom. reads *rectius* : 'Fodintona.'

geld for 3 hides. There is land for 3 ploughs. In demesne are ' 2 hides and ' 1 plough and 2 serfs and (there are) 2 villeins and 3 bordars 'with 1 hide.' 'There are 2 beasts and 10 swine and 4 unbroken mares and 100 sheep and 22 she-goats. There are 2 furlongs of wood(land) in length and 1 in breadth.' It is worth 30 shillings. ' When the count received it, 3 pounds.'

Alvred holds of the count WESTONE [Weston Bamfield]. Brictuid held (it) T.R.E. and paid geld for 1 hide and 2½ virgates. There is land for 1 plough which is there with 5 bordars. ' There are 2 serfs. There are 2 riding-horses and 8 beasts and 10 swine.' There is half a mill paying 30 pence. ' There are 4 acres of wood(land) and 8 acres of meadow.' It was worth 20 shillings. Now 30 shillings.

Humphrey holds of the count 1 hide in GATELME [Goathill].[1] Godric held (it) T.R.E. There is land for 2 ploughs which are there with 2 villeins and 3 bordars. ' In demesne are 3 virgates and 1½ ploughs and the villeins have 1 virgate and half a plough. There are 2 closes (*masurae*) in Meleborna [Milborne Port]. There are 1 riding-horse and 2 cows and 15 swine and 50 sheep.' There is a mill paying 10 shillings, and 15 acres of meadow and 15[2] acres of wood(land). It is worth 30 shillings. ' When he received it, 20 shillings.'

[This entry is written across foot of fol. 92d.]

fo. 93

Warmund holds of the count in MELEBURNE [Milborne Port] 1 hide. ' Goduin held it T.R.E.' There is land for 1 plough which is there in demesne with 2 bordars and 2 serfs. ' There are 1 riding-horse and 1 cow and 20 swine.' There (are) 11 acres of meadow and a mill paying 16 pence, and 5 burgesses paying 3 shillings ' and 9 pence.' The whole is worth 20 shillings. ' When he received it, 15 shillings.'

The count himself holds MERSTONE [Marston Magna]. Four thegns held (it) ' in parage (*pariter*)' T.R.E. and paid geld for 5 hides. ' Leuerona held 3 hides, Edret held 1 hide, and Saward and his mother held 1 hide.' There is land for 5 ploughs. In demesne are ' 2 hides and 3 virgates and ' 1 plough with 1 serf and (there are) 5 villeins and 10 bordars with 3 ploughs ' and 2 hides and 1 virgate.' ' There are 1 riding-horse

and 16 swine. There (are) 40 acres of meadow and 30 acres of wood(land). It was and is worth 10 pounds.

Robert holds of the count MERSTONE [Marston Magna]. Five thegns held (it) ' in parage (*pariter*)' T.R.E. and paid geld for 2 hides. There is land for 2 ploughs. Five villeins there have these (ploughs) ' and the land ' and (there are) 2 bordars and 24 acres of meadow. It was worth 40 shillings. Now 60 shillings.

Drogo holds of the count in ETESBERIE [Adber in Trent] 3 virgates of land. Alwi held (it) T.R.E. There is land for half a plough which is there ' in demesne with 2½ virgates ' and 3 bordars ' who have half a virgate.' There (are) 6 acres of meadow and 10 acres of wood(land). It was and is worth 10 shillings.

Ansger holds of the count TRENTE [Trent]. Brisnod held (it) T.R.E. and paid geld for 7 hides. There is land for 5 ploughs. In demesne are ' 4 hides and ' 1 plough and 6 serfs and (there are) 7 villeins and 10 bordars with 4 ploughs ' and 3 hides.' ' There are 20 swine and 115 sheep.' There (are) 30 acres of meadow and 60 acres of pasture and 30 acres of wood(land). It was and is worth 8 pounds.

William holds of the count PONDITONE [Poyntington]. Adulf held (it) T.R.E. and paid geld for 2½ hides. There is land for 3 ploughs. In demesne are ' 1 hide and 5 acres and ' 1 plough and there are 4 villeins and 6 bordars with 2 ploughs ' and the rest of the land.' ' There are 1 riding-horse and 1 pig and 30 sheep.' There is a mill paying 32 pence, and half an acre of meadow and 20 acres of pasture. It is worth 40 shillings. ' When he received it, 30 shillings.'

Drogo holds of the count TORNE [Thorn Coffin]. Cheneve held (it) T.R.E. and paid geld for 1 hide and 1 virgate. There is land for 2 ploughs. In demesne are ' 1 hide and ' 1 plough and 3 serfs and (there are) 3 bordars.[3] ' There are 30 sheep.' There are 10 acres of meadow. It was worth 10 shillings. Now 20 shillings.

Ralph the priest holds of the count TORNE [Thorn Coffin]. Two thegns held (it) ' in parage (*pariter*)' T.R.E. and paid geld for 2 hides. There is land for 3 ploughs. In

---

[1] May be identified by its position in the schedule with Goathill, near Milborne Port.
[2] Exet. Dom.: ' 25.'

[3] Exet. Dom. reads : ' The villeins have a virgate ' but does not give their numbers.

demesne are '1½ hides and' 1 plough and (there are) 5 villeins and 2 bordars with 1 plough 'and the rest of the land.' 'There are 4 swine.' There are 14 acres of meadow. It was worth 40 shillings. Now 32 shillings.

Alvred holds of the count CILTERNE [Chilthorne Domer, or Vagg]. Brictuin held (it) T.R.E. and paid geld for 3 hides. There is land for 3 ploughs. In demesne are '2 hides and' 2 ploughs and 2 serfs and (there are) 3 villeins and 5 bordars with 2 ploughs 'and 1 hide.' 'There are 1 riding-horse and 7 beasts and 24 swine and 64 sheep.' There (are) 15 acres of meadow and 20 acres of wood(land). It was and is worth 60 shillings.

Alvred 'the butler (*pincerna*)' holds of the count CILTERNE [Chilthorne Domer, or Vagg]. Alwi held (it) T.R.E. and paid geld for 2 hides. There is land for 3 ploughs. In demesne are '1 hide and' 2 ploughs and 5 serfs and (there are) 2 villeins and 4 bordars with 2 ploughs, 'and 1 hide.' 'There are 1 riding-horse and 11 beasts and 24 swine and 115 sheep.' There are 30 acres of meadow. It was worth 30 shillings. Now 40 shillings.

Ansger holds of the count HUNDESTONE [Houndston in Brympton]. Three thegns held (it) 'in parage (*pariter*)' T.R.E. and paid geld for 1 hide. There is land for 1 plough which is there in demesne 'with half a hide and half a virgate and' with 2 serfs and (there are) 2 villeins and 3 bordars 'who have half a plough and the rest of the land.' 'There are 3 beasts and 50 sheep.' There are 3½ acres of meadow. It was worth 10 shillings. Now 20 shillings.

Ansger holds of the count in LOCHETONE, 'Locutona' [Lufton] 1 hide. Alwin held (it) T.R.E. There is land for 1 plough which is there in demesne and 2 serfs and (there are) 3 bordars. 'There are 1 riding-horse and 1 cow and 60 sheep.' There are 10 acres of meadow. It is worth 20 shillings. 'When he received it, 12 shillings.'

The count himself holds in GIVELE [Yeovil] 1 hide 'which is in demesne.' There is land for 2 ploughs. There are 2 bordars. It is worth 3 shillings.
In the same vill (*villa*) Amund holds of the count 1 hide. There is land for 1 plough which is there with 2 bordars. 'There are 5 beasts and 5 swine and 95 sheep.' There (is) a mill paying 5 shillings. The whole is worth 20 shillings. 'When received 10 shillings.'

Four thegns held these 2 hides T.R.E. and paid geld for so much.

Robert 'son of Ivo' holds of the count SOCHE [Sock Dennis]. Seven thegns held (it) 'in parage (*pariter*)' T.R.E. and paid geld for 3½ hides. There is land for 5 ploughs. In demesne are '2½ hides and' 2 ploughs with 1 serf and (there are) 8 villeins and 2 bordars with 2 ploughs 'and the rest of the land.' 'There are 5 beasts and 35 swine and 25 sheep.' There are 70 acres of meadow. It was and is worth 65 shillings.

The count himself has in demesne BISCOPESTONE, 'BISOBESTONA' [Bishopston[1]] and there is his castle which is called MONTAGUD [Montacute]. T.R.E. this manor paid geld for 9 hides ; and it belonged to the abbey of Athelney (*Adelingi*) and for it the count gave to that church a manor which is called CANDEL [Purse Caundle in Dorset]. In this manor there is land for 7 ploughs. Of this land 2½ hides are in demesne where are 2 ploughs and 4 serfs, and (there are) 4 villeins and 3 bordars with 2 ploughs 'and 1 hide.' 'There are 1 riding-horse and 100 sheep.' There is a mill paying 50 pence, and 15 acres of meadow.
Of these 9 hides Alvred 'the butler (*pincerna*)' holds of the count 1½ hides. 'He has 1½ ploughs and 6 bordars and 1 serf and 80 sheep. It is worth 28 shillings.' Drogo (holds) 1 hide 'and has 1½ ploughs and 5 bordars. It is worth 10 shillings.' Bretel (holds) 1 hide 'and has 1 plough and 2 bordars, and it is worth 10 shillings.' Donecan (holds) 1 hide 'and has there in demesne 1 plough and 6 bordars and it is worth 15 shillings.' This manor is worth to the count 6 pounds. To the knights it is worth 3 pounds and 3 shillings.

Dodeman holds of the count MUNDIFORD [Up-Mudford]. W(i)nulf held (it) T.R.E. and paid geld for 4½ hides. There is land for 4 ploughs. In demesne are '3 hides and 3 virgates and' 2 ploughs and 7 serfs and (there is) 1 villein and 7 bordars with 1 plough 'and the rest of the land.' 'There are 1 riding-horse and 6 beasts and 15 swine.' There (is) a mill paying 20 shillings, and 15 acres of meadow and 40 acres of pasture. It was and is worth 4 pounds.[2]

[1] The name of Bishopston disappeared, and was supplanted by Montacute.
[2] This entry in the Exchequer Domesday is entered at the bottom of fol. 93*a*. after the lands of Baldwin of Exeter. Its right place, as in the Exet. Dom., is between Chilthorne Domer and Montacute.

'fo. 315.'

XX. THE LAND OF BALDWIN DE EXECESTRE

Baldwin the sheriff (*Vicecomes*) holds HAMITONE, 'HAMINTONA' [Hemington] of the king. Siward held (it) T.R.E. and paid geld for 21 hides. There is land for 20 ploughs. Of this (land) 8 hides are in demesne where are 4 ploughs and 11 serfs and (there are) 26 villeins and 8 bordars with 12 ploughs 'and 12 hides.' 'There are 2 riding-horses and 19 beasts and 23 swine and 245 sheep and 58 she-goats.' There are 12 acres of meadow and 50 acres of underwood. Pasture half a league long and half a league broad. It was and is worth 19 pounds. Of this land 1 hide is in the open pasture (*in communi pastura*) in Hardintone [Hardington], a manor of the Bishop of Coutances (see ante, p. 452).

Drogo[1] holds of Baldwin APELIE [Appley in Stawley]. Norman held (it) T.R.E. and paid geld for 3 virgates of land. There is land for 2 ploughs. 'In demesne are 2 virgates and half a plough.' There are 4 villeins and 3 bordars 'who have 1 virgate and 1½ ploughs' and 5 acres of meadow and 10 acres of pasture. It is worth 15 shillings. 'When Baldwin received it, 5 shillings.'

The same (Drogo[1]) holds of Baldwin PORTLOC [Porlock]. Algar held (it) T.R.E. and paid geld for 3 hides. There is land for 12 ploughs. 'In demesne are 1½ hides.' There are 6 villeins and 3 bordars 'who have the rest of the land,' and 6 serfs and 300 acres of wood(land) and 500 acres of pasture. It was worth 4 pounds when he received it. Now 25 shillings.

'fo. 422.'

XXI. THE LAND OF ROGER DE CORCELLE

Roger de Corcelle holds of the king CURI [Curry Mallet]. Brictric held (it) T.R.E. and paid geld for 3½ hides. There is land for 4 ploughs. Of this (land) 1 hide is in demesne where are 2[2] ploughs and 2 serfs and (there are) 11 villeins and 7 bordars with 3½ ploughs 'and 2½ hides.' 'There are 1 riding-horse and 9 swine and 23 sheep.' There (are) 12 acres of meadow and 5 acres of pasture and half a league of wood(land) (reckoning) in length and breadth. It was worth 4 pounds. Now 100 shillings.

Roger himself holds CURI [Curry Mallet]. Celric held it T.R.E. and paid geld for 3½ hides. There is land for 4 ploughs. Of this (land) 1 hide is in demesne where is 1 plough with 1 serf and (there are) 10 villeins and 7 bordars with 3½ ploughs 'and 2½ hides.' 'There are 8 swine and 22 sheep.' There (are) 10 acres of meadow and 5 acres of pasture and half a league of wood(land) (reckoning) in length and breadth. It was worth 4 pounds. Now 100 shillings.

These 2 estates (*terras*) Roger holds as (*pro*) one manor.

Robert holds of Roger NIWETONE [North Newton in North Petherton]. Eilaf held (it) T.R.E. and paid geld for 3 virgates of land. There is land for 1 plough which is there with 1 villein and 5 bordars and 2 serfs. 'There are 21 beasts and 20 swine and 50 sheep.' There (are) 6 acres of wood(land). It is worth 20 shillings. 'When Roger received it, 10 shillings.'

Robert holds of Roger HATEWARE [Hadworthy in North Petherton]. Algar held (it) T.R.E. and paid geld for 1 hide. There is land for 1½ ploughs. 'In demesne are 2 virgates and 1 plough and' 2 serfs and (there are) 1 villein and 9 bordars 'who have the rest of the land and half a plough.' 'There are 1 riding-horse and 15 beasts.' There are 4 acres of meadow and 7 acres of wood(land) and 36 acres of pasture. It was worth 15 shillings. Now 20 shillings.

Of this hide W. de Douai has 1 virgate of land.

Geoffrey (*Gosfridus*) 'de Valle' holds of Roger PERI [Pury Furneaux, now Perry, in Wembdon]. Four thegns held (it) in parage (*pariter*) T.R.E. and paid geld for 1 hide and 1 ferling. There is land for 2 ploughs. In demesne are '3 virgates and' 1 plough and (there are) 2 villeins and 5 bordars with 1 'plough and 1 virgate and 1 ferling.' 'There are 1 cow and 2 swine and 12 sheep.' There are 33[3] acres of meadow and 43 acres of pasture and 37 acres of wood(land). It is worth 30 shillings.

William holds of Roger ULVERONETONE [in N. Petherton Hundred]. Alwi held (it) T.R.E. and paid geld for 1 hide and 1 ferling. There is land for 2 ploughs. In demesne are 'half a hide and' 1 plough with 1 serf and (there are) 3 villeins and 3 bordars with 1 plough 'and half a hide and

---

[1] Exet. Dom. reads : ' Rogo son of Nigel.'
[2] Exet. Dom. reads : ' one.'

[3] Exet. Dom. : ' 23.'

1 ferling.' 'There are 26 sheep and 3 swine.' There (are) 11 acres of meadow and 7 acres of pasture and 13 acres of wood(land). It was and is worth 22 shillings.

To this manor has been added 1 hide in PERI [Pury Furneaux, now Perry, in Wembdon]. Alward held (it) T.R.E. and paid geld for 1 hide. There is land for 2 ploughs. In demesne are 'half a hide and' 1 plough and there are 2 villeins and 3 bordars with 1 plough 'and half a hide.' 'There are 3 swine and 26 sheep.' There (are) 10 acres of meadow and 7 acres of pasture and 13 acres of wood(land). It was and is worth 20 shillings.

Anschitil holds of Roger CLAIHELLE [Clayhill in Cannington]. Ordgar held (it) T.R.E. and paid geld for 1 hide. There is land for 3 ploughs. In demesne are 'half a hide and' 1 plough and (there are) 2 villeins and 7 bordars with 2 ploughs 'and half a hide.' 'There are 4 beasts and 7 swine and 12 sheep.' There (are) 3 acres of meadow and 8 acres of pasture and 12 acres of wood(land). It was and is worth 20 shillings.

Robert 'Herecom' holds of Roger SIREDESTONE [Shearston in North Petherton]. Sired held (it) T.R.E. and paid geld for half a hide. There is land for 1 plough which is there in demesne with 'one virgate and' 1 serf and (there are) 2 villeins and 5 bordars with 1 plough 'and 1 virgate.' 'There are 6 beasts and 7 swine and 30 sheep.' It was worth 10 shillings. Now 15 shillings.

Anschitil holds of Roger RIME [doubtful, in N. Petherton Hundred]. Alwi held (it) T.R.E. and paid geld for half a virgate of land. There is land for 2 oxen. There is 1 bordar and 2 acres of meadow. It is worth 30 pence.

Anschitil holds of Roger CILLETONE [Chilton Trinity]. Godric held (it) T.R.E. and paid geld for 1 virgate of land. There is land for 1 plough. 'In demesne are 1 virgate and 3 ferlings.' There is 1 bordar. It was and is worth 20 shillings.[1]

Robert holds of Roger RACHEWORDE [Rexworthy in Durleigh]. Godric held (it) T.R.E. and paid geld for 1 virgate of land. There is land for half a plough. There are 2 bordars and 6 acres of wood(land). It was and is worth 4 shillings.

[1] Exet. Dom. adds 1 ferling for the bordar, making a total of 2 virgates.

Roger himself holds CERDESLING [Charlinch]. Alwi held (it) T.R.E. and paid geld for 1½ hides. There is land for 3 ploughs. In demesne are '1 hide and' 2 ploughs and 4 serfs and (there are) 3 villeins and 3 bordars with 2 ploughs 'and half a hide.' 'There are 1 riding-horse and 1 cow and 11 swine and 80 sheep and 30 she-goats.' There is a mill paying 6 pence, and 3 acres of meadow and 14 acres of pasture and 2 acres of wood(land). It was and is worth 40 shillings.

Roger himself holds CURIEPOL [Currypool in Charlinch]. Alwi held (it) T.R.E. and paid geld for 1 hide. There is land for 4 ploughs. In demesne are 'half a hide and' half a plough and (there are) 6 villeins and 5 bordars possessing (habent) 3 ploughs 'and half a hide.' There are 7 acres of meadow and 100 acres of pasture and 6 acres of wood(land). It was and is worth 40 shillings.

Geoffrey (Goisfria) 'de Valle' holds of Roger PUCHELEGE [Pileigh in Spaxton]. Almar held (it) T.R.E. and paid geld for 1 hide. There is land for 4 ploughs. In demesne are '1 virgate and' 2 ploughs and 5 serfs and (there are) 2 villeins and 4 bordars with 2 ploughs 'and 3 virgates.' 'There are 4 beasts and 39 sheep and 20 she-goats.' There (are) 6 acres of meadow and 6 acres of pasture. It was and is worth 40 shillings.

Geoffrey holds of Roger GODELEGE [Gothelney in Charlinch]. Alward held (it) T.R.E. and paid geld for half a hide. There is land for 2 ploughs. In demesne are '1 virgate and' 1 plough and (there are) 5 villeins and 5 cottars (coscez) with 1 plough 'and 1 virgate,' and 1 serf. 'There are 3 swine.' There (is) half a mill paying 10 pence, and 20 acres of pasture. It is worth 20 shillings. It was worth 30 shillings.

Geoffrey holds of Roger COLGRIN'S LAND, [in Cannington Hundred]. Colgrin held (it) T.R.E. and paid geld for half a virgate of land. There is land for 2 oxen. There are 3 bordars. It is worth 4 shillings. 'When Roger received it, 7 shillings.'

Robert holds of Roger OTRAMESTONE [Otterhampton]. Eduin held (it) T.R.E. and paid geld for half a hide. There is land for 1½ ploughs. 'In demesne are half a virgate and 1 plough.' There are 4 villeins and 1 bordar and 1 serf 'who have half a plough and the rest of the land.' 'There is 1 beast.' There are 2½ acres of meadow and 12 acres of pasture and 7 acres of underwood. It was and is worth 18 shillings.

fo. 93b.

Robert holds of Roger ULARDESTONE 'WL-WARDESTONA' [Woolstone in Stogursey]. Ulf held (it) T.R.E. and paid geld for half a hide. There is land for half a plough. There is 1 villein and 17 acres of meadow and 42 acres of pasture. It was worth 10 shillings. Now 15 shillings.

Alward holds of Roger HOLECUMBE [Holcombe in Aisholt]. He (*ipse*) held (it) T.R.E. and paid geld for 1 virgate of land. There is land for 2 ploughs. In demesne are 'half a virgate and' 1 plough and 2 serfs and (there are) 1 villein and 5 bordars with half a plough 'and half a virgate.' 'There are 12 beasts and 3 swine and 4 sheep and 12 she-goats.' There is a mill paying 6 pence and 75 acres of pasture and 15 acres of wood-(land). It was and is worth 10 shillings.

Anschitil holds of Roger DUDESHAM [Dodisham in Cannington].[1] Three thegns held (it) 'in parage (*pariter*)' T.R.E. and paid geld for 3½ virgates and 5 acres of land. There is land for 2 ploughs which are there with 6 bordars 'who have half the land.' There are 5 acres of meadow and 12 acres of pasture. It was and is worth 20 shillings.

Anschitil holds of Roger PERREDEHAM [Petherham in Cannington]. Godwin held (it) T.R.E. and paid geld for half a virgate of land. There is land for 1 plough. Four bordars there have this (plough) 'and all the land.' There (is) 1 acre of meadow. It was and is worth 10 shillings.

Anschitil holds of Roger CILDETONE [Chilton Trinity]. Leuegar held (it) T.R.E. and paid geld for half a hide. There is land for 2 ploughs. In demesne are 'half a virgate and' 1 plough with 1 serf and (there are) 2 villeins and 5 bordars with 2 ploughs 'and 1½ virgates.' 'There are 6 unbroken mares and 8 beasts and 12 swine.' There (are) 6 acres of meadow and 8 acres of pasture and 16 acres of wood(land). It was worth 20 shillings. Now 40 shillings.

Anschitil holds of Roger ALWIN's LAND [in Cannington Hundred]. Alwin held (it) T.R.E. and paid geld for 1 virgate and 1 ferling of land.

There is land for 1 plough which is there in demesne 'with all the land except 5 acres, and' with 1 bordar 'who holds the said 5 acres.' 'There are 10 beasts and 9 swine and 10 sheep.' There is a mill paying 12 pence, and 2 acres of meadow and 2 acres of pasture. It was and is worth 10 shillings.

Anschitil holds of Roger CILDETONE [Chilton Trinity]. Mereswet held (it) T.R.E. and paid geld for half a hide. There is land for 2 ploughs. Four villeins and 6 bordars have these (ploughs) there 'and the rest of the land,' and in demesne are 'half a virgate and' half a plough. 'There are 8 beasts and 12 swine.' There is half a mill paying 20 shillings. There (are) 6 acres of meadow and 8 acres of pasture and 16 acres of wood(land). It was and is worth 40 shillings.

Anschitil holds of Roger PILLOCH [in Cannington Hundred]. Godric held (it) T.R.E. and paid geld for half a ferling. There is land for half a plough. Nevertheless (*tamen*) in demesne is 1 plough 'and all the land except 10 acres.' There are 2 bordars 'who hold the said 10 acres. There are 2 beasts and 7 swine and 16 sheep,' and 3 acres of meadow and 7 acres of pasture. It was and is worth 6 shillings.

Anschitil holds of Roger STOCHELAND [Stockland Bristol]. Two thegns held (it) 'in parage (*pariter*)' T.R.E. and paid geld for 1½ hides. There is land for 2 ploughs which are there in demesne, 'with 3½ virgates and' 2 serfs and (there are) 3 villeins and 2 bordars with 1 plough 'and the rest of the land.' There (are) 24 acres of meadow and 12 acres of wood(land). It was worth 30 shillings when he received it. Now 65 shillings.

Anschitil holds of Roger EDEVESTONE [Idson in Stogursey]. Alwin held (it) T.R.E. and paid geld for 2½ hides. There is land for 4 ploughs. In demesne are '1 hide and 3 virgates and' 2 ploughs and 7 serfs and there are 7 villeins with 1 bordar owning 3 ploughs 'and 3 virgates.' 'There are 1 riding-horse and 10 beasts and 80 sheep.' There (are) 40 acres of meadow and 5 acres of wood(land). It was and is worth 100 shillings.

Robert holds of Roger RADEFLOTE [Radlet in Spaxton]. Godric held (it) T.R.E. and paid geld for half a hide. There is land for 2 ploughs. 'In demesne are 1½ virgates.' There (are) 1 villein and 2 bordars 'who

---

[1] Dodisham. in Cannington is mentioned in the will of Richard Michell, proved 1563-4 (F. Brown, *Som. Wills*, vi. 3). It is now obsolete.

have half a virgate,' and a mill paying 6 pence, and 5 acres of meadow and 24 acres of pasture and 1 acre of wood(land). It was worth 20 shillings. Now 15 shillings.

Ranulf holds of Roger SUINDUNE [in Cannington Hundred].[1] Alward held (it) T.R.E. and paid geld for 1 virgate of land. There is land for 1 plough which is there in demesne 'with all the land except 15 acres, and' 2 serfs and 5 bordars. 'There are 10 beasts and 8 swine, 50 sheep and 24 she-goats.' There is a mill paying 3 pence, and 1 acre of meadow and 3 acres of pasture and 7 acres of wood(land). It was worth 15 shillings. Now 20 shillings.

Herbert holds of Roger Teodric's Land [in Cannington Hundred]. Tedric held (it) T.R.E. and paid geld for 1 virgate of land. There is land for 1 plough. There are '2 oxen and' 1½ acres of meadow. It is worth 10 shillings. 'When he received it, 20 shillings.'

Robert holds of Roger Terram Olta [doubtful, perhaps Aisholt]. Alward held (it) T.R.E. and paid geld for 1 virgate of land. There is land for 1 plough. 'All except 10 acres is in demesne.' There are 2 bordars and 1½ acres of meadow. It was and is worth 10 shillings.

John holds of Roger ICHETOCHE [Edstock in Cannington]. Ulf held (it) T.R.E. and paid geld for 1 virgate of land. There is land for half a plough which is there in demesne 'with half a virgate and' with 7 bordars 'who have half a virgate.' 'There are 3 beasts and 20 sheep.' There (are) 20 acres of meadow and 7 acres of underwood. It is worth 12 shillings. 'When he received it, 10 shillings.'

William holds of Roger WIDIETE [in Cannington Hundred]. Edric held (it) T.R.E. and paid geld for 3 virgates of land. There is land for 1½ ploughs. 'In demesne are 1½ virgates and half a plough.' There are 2 villeins and 5 bordars with a plough 'and 1½ virgates.' 'There are 3 beasts and 3 swine and 3 she-goats.' There is a mill paying 6 pence. It was and is worth 15 shillings.

William holds of Roger STRENGESTUNE [Stringston]. Siward held (it) T.R.E. and paid geld for 1½ virgates of land. There is land for half a plough which is there in demesne with 1 bordar and 1 acre of meadow and 6 acres of pasture. It was and is worth 8 shillings.

Anschitil holds of Roger BLACHEMORE [Blackmore in Cannington]. Alvric held (it) T.R.E. and paid geld for 1 virgate of land. There is land for half a plough. To this manor has been added 1 acre of land which T.R.E. 1 thegn held 'in parage (*pariter*).' There are 2 bordars. The whole was and is worth 8 shillings.

William 'de Almereio' holds of Roger WORDE[2] [part of Knowle St. Giles]. Two thegns held (it) 'in parage (*pariter*)' T.R.E. and paid geld for 1½ hides. There is land for 3 ploughs. There are 10 villeins with 2½ ploughs, and 4 acres of meadow and 4 furlongs of wood(land) in length and 2 furlongs in breadth. It was and is worth 60 shillings.

The same 'William de Almereio' holds of Roger CHENOLLE [Knowle St. Giles]. Godric and Alvric held (it) 'in parage (*pariter*)' T.R.E. and paid geld for 1 hide and 1 virgate of land. There is land for 2 ploughs. In demesne are '3 virgates and' 1 plough, and (there are) 5 villeins and 4 bordars with half a plough 'and half a hide.' 'There are 6 beasts and 48 sheep.' There (are) 4 furlongs of wood(land) in length and 2 furlongs in breadth. It is worth 25 shillings. 'When Roger received it, 10 shillings.'

To this manor has been added ILLEGE [Ely in Knowle St. Giles [3]]. Bruning held (it) T.R.E. for a manor and paid geld for 3 virgates of land. There is land for 2 ploughs. There is 1 plough with 1 villein and 1 bordar and 1 serf. It was and is worth 15 shillings.

Girard 'Fossor' holds of Roger LOPTONE [4] [Lopen]. Lewin held (it) T.R.E. and paid

---

[1] Suindune. William de Horsya d d homage for his land of 'Swindon' to William Avenell, c. 1220 (*Som. Arch. Proc.* xliii. ii. 85). It might be Swang farm in Charlinch parish, but close to Cannington.

[2] Now obsolete. In *Kirby's Quest*, 1284, Alan de Furrell holds in South Petherton Hundred Knolle, Worth and Sregham (*sic*) for 1 fee of Hugh de Poinz, representative through Mallet of Roger de Corcello. In the *Inq. p.m.* of Nicholas Poyntz, 5 Edw. II. 62, Matthew Esse holds of him in Knoll, Worth, and 'Hillegh.' This last is the 'Illege' of Domesday, now Ely on the borders of Knowle and Chard.

[3] 'Chaffcombe and Illey.' Subsidy Roll for Som. 13 Henry IV. (*Bath Field Club Report*, 1900).

[4] Exet. Dom. reads *recte* : 'Lopena.'

geld for 1 hide. There is land for 1 plough, which is there in demesne with 'the hide and' 1 bordar. 'There are 66 sheep.' There (are) 10 acres of meadow. It is worth 20 shillings. 'When Roger received it, 10 shillings.'

Eldred holds of Roger SELVE [Monksilver]. He (*ipse*) held (it) T.R.E. and paid geld for half a hide. There is land for 1½ ploughs. 'In demesne is 1 virgate and' there (are) 1 villein and 2 bordars with 1 serf who have 1 plough 'and 1 virgate.' There (are) 3 acres of meadow and 62 acres of pasture. It was and is worth 20 shillings.

Alric holds of Roger SELVE [Monksilver]. Brismar held (it) T.R.E. and paid geld for half a hide. There is land for 1½ ploughs. 'In demesne are 1 ferling and 2 oxen.' There (are) 4 villeins with 1 bordar owning 1 plough, '1 virgate and 3 ferlings.' There (are) 6 acres of meadow and 16 acres of pasture and 16 acres of underwood (*silvæ minutæ*). It was and is worth 20 shillings.

Alric holds of Roger HALSWEIE [Halsway in Bicknoller, formerly in Stogumber]. He (*ipse*) held (it) T.R.E. and paid geld for 3 virgates of land. There is land for 3 ploughs. In demesne are '1½ virgates and' 1½ ploughs and 3 serfs, and (there are) 4 villeins with 1 bordar owning 1½ ploughs 'and 1½ virgates.' 'There are 50 sheep.' There (are) 3 acres of meadow and 400 acres of pasture. It is worth 20 shillings.

Alric holds of Roger COLFORDE [Coleford in Stogumber]. He (*ipse*) held it T.R.E. and paid geld for 3 ferlings of land. There is land for half a plough. Nevertheless in demesne there is 1 plough. 'There are 40 sheep.' It is worth 4 shillings.

Bertram holds of Roger HEWIS [Ludhewish in Nettlecombe]. Ulgar held (it) T.R.E. and paid geld for 3 virgates of land. There is land for 2 ploughs. In demesne are '2 virgates and' 1 plough with 1 serf and (there are) 3 villeins and 2 bordars owning 1 plough 'and 1 virgate.' There (are) 3 acres of meadow and 30 acres of pasture. It is worth 20 shillings.

Alric holds of Roger FESCHEFORDE [Vexford in Stogumber]. Domne held (it) T.R.E. and paid geld for half a hide. There is land for 1 plough. This (plough) 'and half a virgate' 2 villeins own there with 1 bordar, and in demesne are half a plough 'and 1½ virgates.' 'There are 2 beasts and 3 swine and 10 sheep and 8 she-goats.' There (are) 4 acres of meadow and 3 acres of pasture and 11 acres of wood(land). It is worth 10 shillings.

Robert holds of Roger FESCHEFORDE [Vexford in Stogumber]. Brismar held (it) T.R.E. and paid geld for half a hide. There is land for 2 ploughs. In demesne are '1 virgate and 1 ferling and' 1 plough, and (there is) 1 villein and 3 bordars owning 1 plough 'and the rest of the land.' 'There are 2 swine and 15 sheep.' There (are) 2 acres of meadow and 20 acres of pasture and 40 acres of wood(land). It was and is worth 17 shillings.

Alric holds of Roger IMELE, 'IMELA' [doubtful, but in Williton hundred]. Ulgar held (it) T.R.E. and paid geld for half a hide. There is land for 2 ploughs. In demesne is half a plough and 1½ acres of meadow and 4 acres of pasture. It is worth 5 shillings.

Roger himself holds CLIVE [Kilve]. Brictric held (it) T.R.E. and paid geld for 2½ hides. There is land for 4 ploughs. In demesne are '2 hides and 3 ferlings and' 2 ploughs with 1 serf and (there are) 5 villeins and 5 bordars with 2 ploughs 'and 1 virgate and 1 ferling.' 'There are 2 riding-horses and 9 beasts and 7 swine and 40 sheep and 50 she-goats.' There is a mill paying 6 shillings and 13 acres of meadow and 12 acres of wood(land). Pasture 1½ leagues long and half a league broad. It was and is worth 4 pounds.

To this manor has been added HILLE [Hill in Kilve]. Edwald held (it) (*pariter*) as a (*pro*) manor T.R.E. and paid geld for 2 hides. There is land for 2 ploughs. There (is) 1 villein and 5 bordars and 2 serfs owning half a plough. There is a mill paying 12 pence and 7 acres of meadow and 20 acres of wood(land). It was and is worth 30 shillings.

To this same manor has been added PERLESTONE [Pardlestone in Kilve]. Parlo held (it) 'in parage (*pariter*)' T.R.E. and paid geld for half a hide. There is land for 1 plough which is there in demesne 'with 1½ virgates' and (there are) 2 villeins and 4 bordars with half a plough. 'There are 13 sheep and 24 she-goats.' There (are) 3 acres of meadow and 12 acres of pasture and 6 acres of wood(land). It was and is worth 10 shillings. Norman holds (it).

THE HOLDERS OF LANDS

Geoffrey (*Goisfrid*) and William hold of Roger WAICOME [Weacombe in West Quantockshead]. Three thegns held (it) 'in parage (*pariter*)' T.R.E. and paid geld for 1 hide. There is land for 1½ ploughs. There is 1 bordar. The whole is worth 32 shillings.[1]

William holds of Roger WESTOU [Westowe in Lydeard St. Lawrence]. Edelwald held (it) T.R.E. and paid geld for 1 hide. There is land for 2 ploughs. In demesne are '3½ virgates and' 1 plough and 3 serfs and (there are) 2 villeins and 3 bordars with half a plough 'and half a virgate.' 'There are 26 sheep.' There (are) 4 acres of meadow and 8 acres of pasture and 15 acres of wood(land). It was and is worth 40 shillings.

Hugh holds of Roger ASCWEI [Ashway in Dulverton]. Alvric held (it) T.R.E. and paid geld for half a hide and one ferling. There is land for 6 ploughs. In demesne are '1 virgate and' 1 plough and 2 serfs and (there are) 11 villeins and 3 bordars with 2 ploughs 'and 1 virgate and 1 ferling.' 'There are 3 beasts and 12 swine and 26 sheep and she-goats.' There (are) 1 acre of meadow and 60 acres of wood(land). Pasture 1 league long and half a league broad. It is worth 25 shillings. 'When Roger received it, 20 shillings.'

William holds of Roger BROFORD, 'BROFORT' [Broford in Dulverton]. Ulwin held (it) T.R.E. and paid geld for 1 virgate of land. There is land for 2 ploughs. In demesne are 'half a virgate and 1 ferling and' 1 (plough) and (there are) 4 villeins owning the other (plough) 'and 1 ferling.' There (are) 5 acres of wood(land). It is worth 7 shillings. 'When Roger received it, 5 shillings.'

William holds of Roger BROFORD, 'BROFORT' [Broford in Dulverton]. Almar held (it) T.R.E. and paid geld for 1 ferling. There is land for half a plough. There are 2 bordars and 4 acres of wood(land). It is worth 26[2] pence.

Roger himself holds POTESDONE [Pixton in Dulverton]. Brictric held (it) T.R.E. and paid geld for 1 virgate of land. There is land for 2 ploughs. There (are) 20 acres of pasture and 3 acres of wood(land). It was and is worth 30 pence.

William holds of Roger POCHINTUNE [Puckington]. Leving held (it) T.R.E. and paid geld for 1½ hides. There is land for 1½ ploughs. 'In demesne are 1 hide and half a virgate and half a plough.' There are 3 villeins and 3 bordars and 2 serfs with 1 plough[3] 'and 1½ virgates.' 'There are 3 swine and 2 she-goats.' There are 11½ acres of meadow and 6 acres of pasture and 66 acres of wood(land).

To this manor has been added POCHINTUNE [Puckington]. Alward held (it) T.R.E. as (*pro*) a manor and paid geld for 1½ hides. There is land for 1½ ploughs. 'In demesne are 1 hide and half a virgate and half a plough.' There are 4 bordars with 1 villein and 1 serf 'and 1½ virgates and 2 oxen. There are 3 swine.' (There are) 2 acres of meadow and 6 acres of pasture and 66 acres of wood(land).

fo. 94

+ These 2 estates (*terras*) Leving and Alward held of the church of St. Peter [4] nor could they be separated from it T.R.E. It was worth 50 shillings. Now 60 shillings.

+ Ogis holds of Roger LAMORE [part of Drayton]. Suetth held (it) T.R.E. of the church of Mucelenie [Muchelney] nor could be separated from it and he paid geld for 1 hide and half a virgate of land, and it is part of the 20 hides of DRAITUNE [Drayton] and is thegnland. There is land for 1 plough which is there in demesne 'with 3½ virgates' and 6 serfs 'who hold 1 virgate.' 'There are 1 riding-horse and 7 swine.' There (are) 10 acres of meadow and 7 acres of wood(land). It was and is worth 20 shillings.

Roger himself holds EDMUNDESWORDE [Almsworthy in Exford]. Edric held (it) T.R.E. and paid geld for 1 virgate of land. 'There is land for 6 ploughs.' In demesne is 'half a virgate' and 1 plough and 2 serfs and (there are) 6 villeins and 9 bordars with 3 ploughs 'and half a virgate.' 'There are 1 riding-horse and 6 beasts and 47 sheep and 27 she-goats.' There (are) 8 acres of meadow and 30 acres of underwood (*silvæ minutæ*). Pasture 2 leagues long and 2 wide. It is worth 25 shillings. 'When he received it, it was altogether wasted (*penitus vastata*).'

[1] Exet. Dom. has : 'Geoffrey has 1 virg. and 1 bordar, who pays to him 7 shillings and 6 pence. The 3 virgates which William holds pay him 25 shillings.
[2] Exet. Dom. reads : '2 shillings and 6 pence.'
[3] Exet. Dom. gives the villeins ½ plough only.
[4] The next entry shows that the church of S. Peter is that of Muchelney Abbey.

I 489 62

Eileva holds of Roger DONESCUMBE [Downscombe in Exford]. Lesmer held (it) T.R.E. and paid geld for 1 ferling. There is land for 1 plough. There is 1 bordar with half a plough and (there are) 6 acres of meadow and 3 acres of wood(land) and 6 acres of pasture. It is worth 2 shillings. 'When he received it, it was wasted (*vastata*).'

Roger himself holds AISSEFORD [Exford]. Aiulf held (it) T.R.E. and paid geld for half a virgate. There is land for 2 ploughs. 'Roger has 1 ferling and half a plough between himself and his men, and the villeins have half a ferling.' There are 1 bordar and 1 serf with half a plough. 'There are 5 sheep.' There are 10 acres of meadow and 10 acres of pasture and 12 acres of underwood (*silvæ minutæ*). It is worth 3 shillings. 'When he received it, it was altogether wasted (*penitus vastata*).'

Ednod holds of Roger AISSEFORDE [Exford]. Edric held (it) T.R.E. and paid geld for 1 ferling. There is land for 1 plough. There is 1 bordar with half a plough. 'There are 4 beasts and 3 swine and 40 sheep and 10 she-goats.' There are 2 acres of wood(land) and 3 acres of meadow and 10 acres of pasture. It is worth 30 pence. 'When he received it, 2 shillings.'

Roger himself holds STOCHE, 'ESTHOCA' [Stoke Pero]. Ailhalle held (it) T.R.E. and paid geld for half a virgate of land. There is land for 2 ploughs. There is 1 plough[1] with 1 serf and 2 bordars. 'There are ( ) beasts and 7 swine and 20 sheep and 20 she-goats.' There are 50 acres of pasture and 60 acres of wood(land). It was and is worth 5 shillings.

Caflo holds of Roger BAGELIE [Bagley in Stoke Pero]. He (*ipse*) held (it) T.R.E. and paid geld for half a virgate of land. In demesne are '1 ferling and' 1 plough[2] and (there are) 2 bordars owning half a plough 'and 1 ferling.' There (are) 50 acres of pasture and 12 acres of wood(land). It was worth 12 pence. Now 40 pence.

Roger himself holds CUMBE [in Carhampton hundred]. Alric held (it) T.R.E. and paid geld for 1 virgate of land. There is land for 1 plough. There 'in demesne are

half a virgate and' half a plough with 1 bordar 'and half a virgate.' 'There are 1 swine and 8 sheep and 4 she-goats.' There (are) 16 acres of pasture and 18 acres of wood(land). It is worth 5 shillings.

Ogis holds of Roger ALRE [perhaps Aller in Carhampton]. Brismar and Edmar held (it) 'in parage (*pariter*)' T.R.E. and paid geld for half a hide. There is land for 1½ ploughs. In demesne are '1½ virgates and' 1 plough with 1 serf and 1 villein and 1 bordar who own half a plough 'and the rest of the land.' 'There is 1 riding-horse.' There (are) 60 acres of pasture. It is worth 8 shillings.[3] 'When Roger received it, 5 shillings.'

Alric holds of Roger GILDENECOTE [Gilcot in Carhampton]. Edwin held (it) T.R.E. and paid geld for half a hide. There is land for 1½ ploughs. 'In demesne are 1½ virgates and' there is 1 plough[4] with 3 bordars 'and half a virgate.' 'There are 2 beasts and 1 pig and 11 sheep and 11 she-goats.' There are 6 acres of meadow and 50 acres of pasture and 15 acres of wood(land). It is worth 10 shillings. 'When he received it, 3 shillings.'

William holds of Roger HUNECOTE [Huntscott in Wootton Courtney]. Alvric and Brictuin held (it) 'in parage (*pariter*)' T.R.E. and paid geld for half a hide and half a virgate of land. There is land for 2½ ploughs. There are 4 villeins with 1 bordar and they own 2 ploughs 'and hold the land of William.' There (are) 16 acres of pasture. It is worth 22 shillings.

Alric holds of Roger DOVRI, 'DOVERI' [Doverhay in Luccombe]. Eddeve held (it) T.R.E. and paid geld for 1 virgate of land. There is land for 1 plough. There (are) 2 villeins with 1 bordar. It is worth 8 shillings.[5] 'When Roger received it, 10 shillings.'

William holds of Roger HOLME [Hollam in Dulverton]. Godric held (it) T.R.E. and paid geld for 1 virgate of land. There is land for 2½ ploughs. 'In demesne is half a virgate.' There (are) 3 villeins and 4 bordars with 1½ ploughs, and half an acre of meadow and 30 acres of pasture and 14 acres of underwood (*silvæ minutæ*). It is worth 6 shillings. 'When Roger received it, 30 pence.'

---

[1] Exet. Dom. has : 'In demesne 1 ferling and half a plough, and the villeins have half a plough and 1 ferling.'
[2] Exet. Dom. reads : 'half a plough.'

[3] Exet. Dom. reads : '7 shillings and 6 pence.'
[4] Exet. Dom. divides the plough between the demesne and the villeins.
[5] Exet. Dom. reads : '7 shillings and 6 pence.'

William holds of Roger AISSEFORD [Exford]. Ulwin held (it) T.R.E. and paid geld for 1 ferling. There is land for 1 plough. There (are) 2 bordars with half a plough, 'and in demesne is 1 plough.' There (are) 3 acres of meadow and 10 acres of pasture. It was and is worth 30 pence.

Roger himself holds ESTONE [Stone in Exford]. Brictric held (it) T.R.E. There is half a virgate of land. There is land for 2 ploughs, but it 'has always been' waste (*vasta*) 'since Roger received it.'

Bertran holds of Roger FIFHIDE [Fivehead]. Aldred held (it) T.R.E. and paid geld for 1½ hides. There is land for 2 ploughs. In demesne are '1 hide and 1 virgate and' 1 plough and 2 serfs and 4 bordars 'who have 1 virgate.' 'There are 2 beasts and 15 swine and 40 sheep and 30 she-goats.' There (are) 15 acres of meadow and 20 acres of wood(land). It was worth 30 shillings. Now 40 shillings.

Ulward holds of Roger ERNESHELE [Earnshill]. Living held (it) T.R.E. and paid geld for half a hide. There is land for 1½ ploughs. In demesne are '1½ virgates and' 1 plough with 1 serf and 3 bordars 'who hold half a virgate.' 'There are 5 cows and 3 swine and 10 sheep.' There (are) 8 acres of meadow and 8 acres of pasture. It is worth 12 shillings. 'When Roger received it, 20 shillings.'

Ogis holds of Roger SANFORD [Sampford Arundel]. Alwin held (it) T.R.E. and paid geld for 2 hides. There is land for 7 ploughs. In demesne are '1 hide and' 2 ploughs and 5 serfs, and (there are) 11 villeins and 6 bordars with 3 ploughs 'and 1 hide.' 'There are 2 riding-horses and 11 beasts and 9 swine and 120 sheep.' There (is) a mill paying 8 pence, and 5 acres of meadow and 200 acres of pasture and 47 acres of wood(land). It was worth 20 shillings. Now 50 shillings.

Alric holds of Roger TORNE [Thorne St. Margaret]. Three thegns, 'Almer and his 2 brothers,' held (it) 'in parage (*pariter*)' T.R.E. and paid geld for 1 hide and 3 virgates of land. There is land for 5 ploughs. In demesne are '3 virgates and' 1 plough and 3 serfs and (there are) 9 villeins and 5 bordars with 3 ploughs 'and 1 hide.' 'There is 1 riding-horse and 5 beasts and 7 swine.' There is a mill paying 10 shillings and 4 acres of meadow and 30 acres of pasture and 8 acres of wood-

(land). It was worth 20 shillings. Now 40 shillings.

Geoffrey holds of Roger ANIMERE [Enmore]. Algar held (it) T.R.E. and paid geld for 1 hide. There is land for 4 ploughs. In demesne are '1 virgate and' 1 plough, and 2 serfs and (there are) 3 villeins and 3 bordars with 3 ploughs 'and 3 virgates.' There (are) 68 acres of wood(land). It was and is worth 40 shillings.

Geoffrey holds of Roger LECHESWRDE [Laxworthy in Enmore]. Orgar held (it) T.R.E. and paid geld for 1 virgate of land. There is land for 1 plough. 'In demesne is half a virgate.' This (plough) 2 villeins and 2 bordars there own 'with half a virgate.' There is a mill paying 2 blooms (*plumbas*) of iron, and 4 acres of wood(land) there. It was and is worth 15 shillings.

Geoffrey holds of Roger LECHESWRDE [Laxworthy in Enmore]. Adestan held (it) T.R.E. and paid geld for 1 virgate of land. There is land for 3 ploughs. 'In demesne is half a virgate.' There (are) 4 villeins and 4 bordars and 2 serfs owning 2 ploughs 'and half a virgate.' There is a mill paying 2 blooms (*plumbas*) of iron, and 5 acres of meadow and 20 acres of wood(land). It was and is worth 40 shillings.

Geoffrey holds of Roger BLACHESALE [Blaxhold in Enmore]. Leuric held (it) T.R.E. and paid geld for 1 virgate of land. There is land for 3 ploughs. 'In demesne is half a virgate.' There (are) 3 villeins and 3 bordars with one serf owning 2 ploughs 'and half a virgate.' There are 60 acres of wood(land). It was worth 20 shillings. Now 30 shillings.

Robert holds of Roger CEDER [Cheddar]. Adulf held (it) T.R.E. and paid geld for 2 hides and 1 virgate of land. There is land for 4 ploughs. In desmesne are 2 ploughs with 5 villeins and 5 bordars. 'There are 1 cow and 16 swine and 20 sheep.' There (are) 15 acres of meadow. It was worth 40 shillings. Now 30 shillings.

Robert holds of Roger SIPEHAM [Shipham]. Aldwin held (it) T.R.E. and paid geld for 4 hides. There is land for 6 ploughs. In demesne are '3 hides and 3 virgates and' 2 ploughs and (there are) 2 villeins and 7 bordars with 1 plough 'and 1 virgate.' 'There are 1 cow and 26 sheep.' There are 3 acres of meadow and 200 acres of pasture and 10 acres of underwood (*silvæ minutæ*). It was worth 40 shillings. Now 30 shillings.

Roger himself holds half a hide in PANTE-SHEDE[1] [in Banwell] and there he has half a plough with 1 serf. 'Godric held it T.R.E.' There is half an acre of meadow. It was and is worth 10 shillings.

Geoffrey 'de Valle' holds of Roger ACHE [Oake]. Domno held (it) T.R.E. and paid geld for $3\frac{1}{2}$ hides. There is land for 6 ploughs. In demesne are '1 hide and' 2 ploughs and 4 serfs and (there are) 14 villeins and 14 bordars owning $3\frac{1}{2}$ ploughs 'and $2\frac{1}{2}$ hides.' 'There are 14 swine and 62 sheep.' There (is) a mill paying 4 shillings, and 17 acres of meadow and 15 acres of pasture and 10 acres of wood(land). In Milvertone [Milverton] (is) 1 house paying 11 pence. It is worth in all 4 pounds. When he received it, it was worth 50 shillings.

William 'son of Robert' holds of Roger TALHAM, 'TALAM' [Tolland]. Ulwin held (it) T.R.E. and paid geld for 2 hides. There is land for 6 ploughs. In demesne are 'half a hide and 1 ferling and' 2 ploughs with 1 serf and (there are) 11 villeins and 4 bordars owning 4 ploughs 'and $1\frac{1}{2}$ hides less 1 ferling.' 'There are 2 cows and 14 swine and 50 sheep.' There (are) 10 acres of meadow and 15 acres of wood(land) and 60 acres of pasture. It was and is worth 50 shillings.

William holds of Roger HOLEFORD [Riches Holford in Lydeard St. Lawrence]. Adelwald held (it) T.R.E. and paid geld for half a hide. There is land for 1 plough. There (are) 2 bordars and 2 serfs and 1 acre of meadow and 10 acres of pasture and 1 acre of wood(land). It is worth 18 shillings.[2]

Alric holds of Roger HOLEFORDE [Trebles Holford in Combe Florey]. Alward held (it) T.R.E. and paid geld for half a virgate of land. There is land for half a plough which is there with 1 villein, and he pays 3 shillings.

[1] This place-name, though quite obsolete now, is mentioned in a charter of William I., by which Banwell was confirmed to Bishop Giso (*Som. Arch. Proc.* xxiii. ii. 56). It appears to have been upon the extreme west or north-west side of the parish (Rev. C. S. Taylor). As 'Ponteside juxta Banne-welle' it occurs in a Final Concord of 1318 (*Ped. Fin.* 2 Edw. II., 28).

[2] Exet. Dom. reads : '17 shillings and 6 pence. When Roger received it, 10 shillings.'

Norman holds of Roger LITELTONE [Littleton in Compton Dundon]. Almar and Osborn and Godric held it as (*pro*) 3 manors T.R.E. and paid geld for 3 hides. There is land for 4 ploughs. In demesne are '3 hides and' 2 ploughs and 3 serfs and (there are) 4 villeins and 3 bordars with 1 plough 'and the rest of the land.' 'There are 120 sheep.' There are 40 acres of meadow and as many acres of underwood (*silvæ minutæ*). It was and is worth 40 shillings.[3]

Robert holds of Roger : STALREWICHE, 'ESTALREWICCA' [Standerwick in Beckington]. Smewin held (it) T.R.E. and paid geld for $1\frac{1}{2}$ hides. There is land for 3 ploughs. In demesne are '1 hide and' 1 plough and (there are) 2 villeins and 7 bordars 'with half a hide.' There (are) 6 acres of meadow and 4 acres of wood(land). It was worth 50 shillings. Now 20 shillings.

Almar holds of Roger ECFERDINTONE [Egford in Frome]. Alvric held (it) T.R.E. and paid geld for 1 hide. There is land for 4 ploughs. 'In demesne is 1 virgate and' there (are) 6 villeins and 3 bordars with 3 ploughs 'and 3 virgates,' and 13 cottars. There (are) 6 acres of meadow and 60 acres of wood(land). It was worth 60 shillings. Now 40 shillings.

Almar holds of Roger FERLEGE [Farleigh Hungerford]. Smewin held (it) T.R.E. and paid geld for half a hide. 'In demesne are $1\frac{1}{2}$ virgates and' there (are) 1 villein and 3 bordars and 2 cottars owning 1 plough 'and half a virgate.' 'There are 3 swine.' There (are) 3 acres of meadow and 6 acres of wood(land). It was worth 20 shillings. Now 10 shillings.

Robert 'Greno' holds of Roger WITOCHES-MEDE [White Oxmead in Wellow]. Two thegns held (it) 'in parage (*pariter*)' T.R.E. and paid geld for 1 hide. There is land for 2 ploughs which are there in demesne with 'half a hide and half a virgate and' 1 serf and 6 bordars 'who have $1\frac{1}{2}$ virgates.' 'There are 1 riding horse and 1 ass and 12 swine and 120 sheep.' There (are) 3 acres of meadow and 30 acres of wood(land). It was and is worth 3 pounds.

William holds of Roger WITEHAM [Witham]. Erlebald held (it) T.R.E. and paid

[3] Exet. Dom. gives the figures for 2 manors separately. In that formerly Almar's the villeins have 2 ploughing oxen (*boves in carr'*).

geld for 2 hides. There is land for 3 ploughs. In demesne are '6 virgates and' 1 plough and 2 serfs and (there are) 4 villeins and 3 bordars and 4 coscez with 2 ploughs 'and half a hide.' 'There are 5 beasts.' There (are) 20 acres of meadow and 30 acres of pasture. Wood(land) 1 furlong long and half a furlong broad. It was worth 20 shillings. Now 30 shillings.

This estate (*terra*) T.R.E. used to belong to (*jacebat in*) Briweham [Brewham], a manor of William de Moion, nor could it be separated thence.

Erneis holds of Roger Briwetone [Bruton]. Godwin held (it) T.R.E. and paid geld for 1 hide and 1 virgate of land. There is land for 2 ploughs. There is 1 plough with 3 bordars and a mill paying 30 pence. It was and is worth 30 shillings.

Norman holds of Roger Bertone [Barton St. David]. Alestan held (it) T.R.E. and paid geld for 1½ hides. There is land for 2 ploughs. In demesne are '1 hide and' 1 plough and (there are) 2 villeins and 4 bordars with 1 plough 'and half a hide.' 'There are 18 swine.' There is a mill paying 5 shillings, and 24 acres of meadow and the same quantity of pasture. It was worth 40 shillings. Now 30 shillings.

To this manor belonged (*jacuit*) Chintone [Keinton Mandeville] T.R.E. There is 1 plough. The Count of Mortain holds (it). 'Almar held it, now Mauger of the count.'

Roger himself holds Limintone [Limington]. Saulf held (it) T.R.E. and paid geld for 7 hides. There is land for 8 ploughs. In demesne are '4 hides and 1 virgate and' 3 ploughs and 3 serfs and (there are) 1 villein and 13 bordars with 1 plough 'and 3 hides less 1 virgate.' 'There are 1 riding-horse and 3 cows and 20 swine and 80 sheep.' There is a mill paying 20 shillings and 60 acres of meadow. Pasture 12 furlongs long and 2 furlongs broad. It was and is worth 7 pounds.

Vital holds of Roger Essentone [Ashington]. Godwin held (it) T.R.E. and paid geld for 3 hides. There is land for 3 ploughs. In demesne is 1 plough with 1 serf and (there are) 2 villeins and 4 bordars with 1 plough. 'There are 5 swine and 20 sheep.' There (are) 43 acres of meadow and 20 acres of pasture. It was and is worth 40 shillings.

Vital holds of Roger Soche [Sock Dennis].

Tochi[1] held (it) T.R.E. and paid geld for 1½ hides. There is land for 2 ploughs. In demesne are 'one hide and' 1 plough and (there are) 3 bordars 'holding the rest of the land.' 'There are 15 sheep and 4 swine.' (There are) 10 acres of meadow and 15 acres of pasture. It was and is worth 15 shillings.'

Herbert holds of Roger Brunetone [Brympton Devercy]. Seulf held (it) T.R.E. and paid geld for 3 hides. There is land for 4 ploughs. In demesne are '1½ hides and' 2 ploughs and 2 serfs and (there are) 2 villeins and 8 bordars with 2 ploughs 'and 1½ hides.' 'There is 1 riding-horse and 6 swine and 60 sheep.' There (are) 13 acres of meadow and 4 acres of underwood (*silvæ minutæ*). It was worth 40 shillings. Now 60 shillings.

Roger himself holds half a hide which is worth 10 shillings. T.R.E. this (land) belonged to Barintone [Barrington] the king's manor.

+ Dodeman and Warmund hold of Roger Sutone [Long Sutton]. Two thegns held (it) T.R.E. of the church of Adelingi [Athelney] and could not be separated from it, and they paid geld for 2 hides. There is land for 3 ploughs. In demesne are 3 ploughs with 1 serf and (there are) 4 villeins and 3 bordars owning 1 plough. 'There are 9 swine and 1 cow and 214 sheep.' There (are) 8 acres of meadow. It is worth 50 shillings.[2]

XXII. THE LAND OF ROGER ARUNDEL

Roger Arundel holds of the king Halse [Halse]. Ailmar held (it) T.R.E. and paid geld for 4 hides. There is land for 7 ploughs. In demesne are '1 hide and' 2 ploughs and 3 serfs and (there are) 16 villeins and 7 bordars with 3½ ploughs 'and 3 hides.' 'There are 1 cow and 7 swine and 40 sheep.' There is a mill paying 10 shillings, and 8 acres of meadow and 12 acres of wood(land) and 20 acres of pasture. When he received (it), it was worth 100 shillings. Now 6 pounds. 'This estate is in (*de*) Taunton Hundred.'[3]

Roger himself holds Hiwis [Hewish Champflower]. Ailric held (it) T.R.E. and paid geld for 2 hides and 3 virgates of land. There is land for 12 ploughs. In demesne are 'half a hide and 1 ferling and' 2 ploughs and 5

---

[1] Exet. Dom. : 'Stochi.'
[2] Exet. Dom. gives the 2 holdings separately.
[3] This entry is in the margin of the Exeter Domesday.

serfs and (there are) 20 villeins and 6 bordars with 6 ploughs 'and 2 hides and 1 ferling.' 'There are 3 beasts and 100 sheep.' There is a mill paying 12 pence, and 20 acres of meadow and 60 acres of wood(land). Pasture 1 league long and half a league broad. It was worth when he received (it) 6 pounds. Now 7 pounds.

Roger himself holds WISLAGETONE, 'WYS-LAGENTONA' [Whitelackington]. Almar held (it) T.R.E. and paid geld for 10 hides. There is land for 10 ploughs. In demesne are '5 hides and 1 virgate and' 1 plough and 7 serfs and (there are) 9 villeins and 30[1] bordars with 7 ploughs 'and 4 hides and 3 virgates' and 7 swineherds paying 40 swine. 'There are 4 beasts and 9 swine and 44 sheep.' There is a mill paying 15 shillings and 50 acres of meadow and 61 acres of pasture and 240 acres of wood(land). It was worth when he received (it) 12 pounds. Now 9 pounds.

Richard holds of Roger DESTONE[2] [Durston]. Alwi held (it) T.R.E. and paid geld for 2 hides and 3 virgates of land. There is land for 4 ploughs. In demesne are '1 hide and $1\frac{1}{2}$ virgates and' 1 plough and 4 serfs and (there are) 4 villeins and 5 bordars and 4 cottars with 3 ploughs 'and the rest of the land.' 'There are 7 beasts.' There (are) 15 acres of meadow and 20 acres of pasture and 20 acres of wood(land). It was and is worth 40 shillings.

Ralph holds of Roger SANFORD, 'SANTFORT' [Sandford in Wembdon].[3] Ailward held (it) T.R.E. and paid geld for 1 hide and half a virgate of land and 1 ferling. There is land for 3 ploughs. In demesne are '3 virgates and' 1 plough and 3 serfs and there (are) 2 villeins and 4 bordars with 1 plough 'and the rest of the land.' 'There are 11 beasts and 23 swine.' (There are) 12 acres of meadow. It was and is worth 30 shillings. 'Of this manor 2 thegns held half a virgate, and they could not be separated from the manor.'

Ralph holds of Roger PERI [Perry Furneaux in Wembdon]. Ulvric held (it) T.R.E. and paid geld for half a hide. There is land for 1 plough which is there in demesne and 8 acres of meadow. 'There are 20 sheep.' It was and is worth 10 shillings.

Ralph holds of Roger 1 virgate of land in NEWETONE [Newton in North Petherton]. Bristwold held (it) T.R.E. There is land for half a plough. There (are) 1 acre of meadow and 2 acres of wood(land). It is worth 5 shillings.

Hugh holds of Roger FITINTONE [Fidding-ton]. Ailward held (it) T.R.E. and paid geld for 4 hides. There is land for 6 ploughs. In demesne are '3 hides and' 2 ploughs and 2 serfs and (there are) 6 villeins and 5 bordars with 3 ploughs 'and 1 hide.' 'There are 12 beasts and 11 swine and 60 sheep and 14 she-goats.' There (are) 2 mills paying 2 shillings, and 21 acres of meadow and 80 acres of pasture and 43 acres of moor and 42 acres of wood(land). It was and is worth 4 pounds.

Hugh holds of Roger TOCHESWELLE [Tux-well in Spaxton]. Estan held (it) T.R.E. and paid geld for 1 virgate of land. There is land for half a plough. 'In demesne is 1 ferling.' There (are) 2 villeins and 3 bordars owning 1 plough 'and the rest of the land.' There (are) 140 acres of wood(land) and 41 acres of moor and 40 acres of pasture. It was worth when he received (it) 20 shillings. Now 12 shillings and 6 pence.

Odo holds of Roger CUDWORDE [Cudworth]. Three thegns held (it) 'in parage (*pariter*)' T.R.E. and paid geld for $3\frac{1}{2}$ hides. There is land for 4 ploughs. In demesne are '$2\frac{1}{2}$ hides and' 1 plough and 2 serfs and (there are) 4 villeins and 2 bordars with half a plough 'and 1 hide.' 'There are 2 beasts and 12 swine and 60 sheep.' There (are) 4 acres of meadow. Pasture 8 furlongs long and 2 furlongs broad. It was worth 40 shillings. Now 30 shillings.

Robert 'de Gatemore' holds of Roger SCHELIGATE [Skilgate]. Goda held (it) T.R.E. and paid geld for 1 hide and 1 virgate of land. There is land for 4 ploughs. In demesne are '3 virgates and' 2 ploughs and 5 serfs and (there are) 5 villeins and 2 bordars with half a plough[4] 'and half a hide.' 'There are 10 beasts and 150 sheep.' There is a mill paying 10 pence, and 2 acres of meadow and 60 acres of wood(land). Pasture 4 furlongs long and 1 furlong broad. It is worth 30 shillings. 'When Roger received it, 40 shillings.'

The same (Robert de Gatemore) holds of Roger MILDETUNE [Milton in Skilgate]. Dunno held (it) T.R.E. and paid geld for 1

---

[1] Exet. Dom. : '25.'
[2] Exet. Dom. reads : 'Derstona.'
[3] Sanford. This place, though owned by Arundel, is not Sampford Arundel in Milverton Hundred, but Sandford in Wembdon. In 1284 it was held by Robert Fitzpayn, who succeeded to much of Arundel's property.

[4] Exet. Dom. gives the villeins 1 plough.

hide less 1 ferling. There is land for 3 ploughs. In demesne are '3 virgates less 1 ferling and' 1 plough and 2 serfs and (there are) 3 villeins and 1 bordar with 1 plough 'and 1 virgate.' 'There are 3 beasts and 3 swine and 30 sheep and 20 she-goats.' There (are) 2 acres of meadow and 5 acres of wood(land). Pasture 3 furlongs long and 1 furlong broad. It was worth 30 shillings. Now 20 shillings.

Robert holds of Roger RADINGETUNE [Raddington]. Two thegns held (it) 'in parage (pariter)' T.R.E. and paid geld for 2 hides. There is land for 8 ploughs. In demesne are '1½ hides and half a virgate and' 2 ploughs and 3 serfs and (there are) 5 villeins and 5 bordars with 4 ploughs 'and half a hide and half a virgate.' 'There are 4 beasts and 9 swine and 48 sheep and 5 she-goats.' There (is) a mill grinding for the hall (ad aulam molen.[1]) and 3 acres of meadow and 6 acres of wood(land). Pasture 4 furlongs long and 3 furlongs broad. It was and is worth 30 shillings.

Drogo holds of Roger TIMBRECUMBE [Timberscombe]. Alverd held (it) T.R.E. and paid geld for 1½ hides. There is land for 8 ploughs. In demesne are '3 virgates and' 1 plough and 2 serfs and (there are) 3 villeins and 8 bordars with 1 plough 'and 3 virgates.' 'There are 30 sheep and 10 she-goats.' There are 11 acres of meadow and 150 acres of pasture and 61 acres of wood(land). It was worth when he received (it) 100 shillings. Now 40 shillings.

To this manor has been added 1 ferling. Algar held (it) T.R.E. There is land for 1 plough. There is half a plough with 2 bordars and 8 acres of pasture and 4 acres of wood(land). It is worth 5 shillings. 'When he received it, 6 shillings.'

William holds of Roger CHEDESFORD [Kittisford]. Osmund Stramun held (it) T.R.E. and paid geld for 2 hides. There is land for 7 ploughs. In demesne are '1 hide and' 2 ploughs and 3 serfs and (there are) 5 villeins and 6 bordars with 3½ ploughs 'and 1 hide.' 'There is 1 riding-horse and 16 swine and 50 sheep.' There is a mill paying 7 shillings, and 3 acres of meadow and 10 acres of pasture and 12 acres of wood(land). It was worth 40 shillings. Now 60 shillings.

William holds of Roger 1 virgate of land in SIDEHAM [Sydenham in Bridgwater].

[1] Exet. Dom. has : 'molinus qui molit annonam suam.' A mill which yielded nothing beyond doing the work of the manor-house.

Cheping held (it) T.R.E. There is land for 1 plough. There (are) 15 acres of pasture. It is worth 15 pence. 'When he received it, 5 pence.'

Wido holds of Roger HASEWELLE [Halswell in Goathurst]. Alward held (it) T.R.E. and paid geld for 1 hide. There is land for 2 ploughs. In demesne are 'half a hide and half a virgate and' 1 plough and 2 serfs and (there are) 2 villeins and 3 bordars with 1 plough 'and the rest of the land.' 'There are 2 beasts and 10 sheep.' There are 14 acres of wood(land). It is worth 25 shillings. 'When he received it, 17 shillings and 6 pence.'

Robert holds of Roger CARI [Cary Fitzpaine in Charlton Mackrell]. Two thegns 'Alinc and Lovinc' held (it) 'in parage (pariter)' T.R.E. and paid geld for 1 hide less 1 ferling. There is land for 1 plough which is there in demesne with 4 cottars. 'There are 10 beasts and 9 swine.' There (are) 20 acres of meadow. It was and is worth 20 shillings.

Roger himself holds CERLETUNE [Charlton Mackrell alias West Charlton]. Alverd held (it) T.R.E. and paid geld for 3 hides. There is land for 6 ploughs. In demesne are 'half a hide and' 1 plough and 4 serfs and (there are) 3 villeins and 9 bordars with 3 ploughs 'and 2½ hides.' 'There are 1 riding-horse and 14 swine and 15 sheep.' There (are) 30 acres of meadow and 2 acres of wood(land). It was worth 6 pounds. Now 100 shillings.

Roger himself holds AIXE, 'AISXA' [Ash Priors]. Ailric held (it) T.R.E. and paid geld for 2 hides. There is land for 4 ploughs. In demesne are '1 hide and one half less 1 ferling' and 1 plough and 3 serfs and (there are) 5 villeins and 5 bordars with 2 ploughs 'and half a hide and 1 ferling.' There (are) 8 acres of meadow and 10 acres of wood(land), pasture 2 furlongs long and 1 furlong broad. It is worth 20 shillings.

+ To this manor has been added AIXA [Ash Priors]. Sawin held (it) of the Bishop of Wells and could not be separated from it T.R.E., and paid geld for 1 hide and 1 virgate of land. There is land for 3 ploughs. In demesne is 1 plough and the villeins owned 2¼ ploughs. It was and is worth 30 shillings. Roger holds (it) of the king and Givold (holds it) of him.

Roger himself holds OPECEDRE [Cheddon Fitzpaine]. Domno held (it) T.R.E. and paid geld for 3½ hides. There is land for 5 ploughs. In demesne are ' 1 hide and half a virgate and ' 1 plough and 2 serfs and (there are) 6 villeins and 6 bordars owning 3 ploughs ' and 1 hide and 1½ virgates.' There (are) 23 acres of meadow and 15 acres of pasture and 2 acres of wood(land). It was worth 50 shillings. Now 60 shillings.

Of the land of this manor Robert holds 1 hide and there he has ' in demesne half a hide and ' 1 plough with 1 serf and 5 bordars ' who have half a hide and 1 plough ' and a mill paying 3 shillings. ' There are 2 cows and 15 sheep and 5 she-goats.' There are 3 acres of meadow and 5 acres of pasture and 4 acres of wood(land). It was worth 15 shillings. Now 20 shillings.[1]

Roger himself holds CEDRE [Cheddon Fitzpaine]. Ulwin held (it) T.R.E. and paid geld for 2½ hides. There is land for 4 ploughs. In demesne are ' 1 hide and half a virgate and ' 1 plough and 3 serfs and (there are) 6 villeins and 6 bordars with 3 ploughs ' and the rest of the land.' There (are) 24 acres of meadow and 15 acres of pasture. It is worth 60 shillings. ' When Roger received it, 50 shillings.'

Roger Buissel[2] holds of Roger SUTONE [Sutton Bingham]. Ulward held (it) T.R.E. and paid geld for 5 hides. There is land for 5 ploughs. ' In demesne are 4½ hides and 1 ferling.' There are 6 bordars ' who have the rest of the land ' and 4 cottars and a mill paying 16 shillings. There (are) 12 acres of meadow. Pasture 3 furlongs long and 2 furlongs broad. It was worth 100 shillings. Now 30 shillings.

Roger himself holds BECHINTONE [Beckington]. Ailvert held (it) T.R.E. and paid geld for 10 hides. There is land for 10 ploughs. In demesne are ' 5 hides and 3 virgates and ' 2 ploughs and (there are) 9 villeins and 7 bordars owning 6 ploughs ' and 4 hides and 1 virgate.' ' There are 24 swine and 100 sheep and 50 she-goats.' There is a mill paying 20 shillings, and 12 acres of meadow and 8 acres of pasture and 100 acres of wood(land). It was worth when he received (it) 10 pounds. Now 6 pounds.

Robert holds of Roger BERCHELEI [Berkley]. Tovi held it T.R.E. and paid geld for 2½ hides. There is land for 3 ploughs. In

demesne are ' 2 hides and ' 2 ploughs with 1 serf, and (there are) 3 villeins and 4 bordars with 1 plough ' and 3 virgates.' ' There are 15 beasts and 9 swine.' There (is) a mill paying 12 shillings and 6 pence, and 6 acres of meadow and 70 acres of wood(land). It was and is worth 40 shillings.

Roger himself holds MERSITONE [Marston Bigot]. Aelvert held (it) T.R.E. and paid geld for 3½ hides. There is land for 5 ploughs. In demesne are ' 1½ hide and ' 1 plough and 2 serfs and (there are) 5 villeins and 14 bordars owning 5 ploughs ' and 2 hides. There are 9 beasts and 14 swine and 9 sheep.' There (is) a mill paying 6 shillings, and 16 acres of meadow and 100 acres of pasture. Wood(land) 1 league long and as much broad. It is worth 7 pounds. ' When Roger received it, 6 pounds.'

William ' Geral ' holds of Roger PENNE [Penselwood]. Britnod held (it) T.R.E. and paid geld for 3 hides. There is land for 3 ploughs. In demesne are ' 2 hides and ' 1 plough and (there are) 4 villeins and 8 bordars and 4 cottars with 1½ ploughs ' and 1 hide.' ' There are 3 beasts and 13 swine and 100 sheep.' There is a mill paying 40 pence, and 12 acres of meadow and 20 acres of pasture. Wood(land) 12 furlongs long and 4 furlongs and 12 perches broad. It was worth when he received it 7 pounds. Now 3 pounds.

Azelin holds of Roger ESLIDE [Lyde in Yeovil]. Godwin and Seric held (it) ' in parage (pariter) ' T.R.E. and paid geld for 2 hides. There is land for 2 ploughs which are there in demesne with ' 1 hide and 3½ virgates and ' 4 serfs with 1 bordar ' who has half a virgate.' ' There are 4 swine and 53 sheep.' There (are) 4 acres of meadow and 2 acres of wood(land). It was and is worth 40 shillings.

fo. 95. ' fo. 447 '

XXIII. THE LAND OF WALTER GIFARD

Walter Gifard holds of the king GERNEFELLE [Yarnfield in Kilmington] and William (holds it) of him. Ernebald held (it) T.R.E. and paid geld for 2 hides. There is land for 3 ploughs. In demesne are ' 1 hide and 2½ virgates and ' 2 ploughs with 1 serf and (there are) 5 bordars with 1 plough ' and 1½ virgates.' ' There are 2 cows and 25 swine and 124 sheep.' There (are) 20 acres of pasture and 60 acres of wood(land). It was worth 40 shillings. Now 30 shillings.

---

[1] Exet. Dom. adds : ' T.R.E. this was held by a widow who could not be separated from the manor. In demesne are half a hide and 1 plough.'

[2] Interlined ; Exet. Dom. reads : ' Boiscellus.'

THE HOLDERS OF LANDS

XXIV. THE LAND OF WALTER DE DOWAI[1]

Walter de Dowai holds of the king WORLE [Worle]. Esgar held (it) T.R.E. and paid geld for 6½ hides. There is land for 15 ploughs. In demesne are '3 hides and 1½ virgates and' 4 ploughs and 5 serfs and (there are) 22 villeins and 3 bordars with 9 ploughs 'with 3 hides and half a virgate.' 'There are 1 riding-horse and 24 beasts and 18 swine and 60 sheep.' There (are) 50 acres of meadow. Pasture 13 furlongs long and 2 furlongs broad. It was worth 10 pounds. Now 7 pounds.

Walscin holds STRAGELLE, 'ESTRAGELLA' [Stretcholt in Pawlett], and Renewald (holds it) of him. Levegar held (it) T.R.E. and paid geld for half a hide. There is land for 2 ploughs. In demesne are '1 virgate and' 1 plough with 1 serf and there are 3 bordars 'who have 1 virgate and half a plough' and 10 acres of meadow. 'There are 8 beasts and 14 swine and 32 sheep.' It was and is worth 50 shillings.

Renewald holds of W[alter] STRAGELLE, 'ESTRAGELLA' [Stretcholt in Pawlett]. Eddwold held (it) T.R.E. and paid geld for half a hide. There is land for 1 plough. In demesne are '1 virgate and' 2 ploughs and 2 serfs and (there are) 1 villein and 2 bordars with 1½ ploughs 'and 1 virgate.' 'There are 8 beasts and 43 swine and 31 sheep.' There (are) 10 acres of meadow. It is worth 50 shillings. 'When Walter received it, 40 shillings.'

Rademer holds of W[alter] WALLEPILLE [Walpole in Pawlett]. Edward 'Brit' held (it) T.R.E. and paid geld for 3 virgates of land. There is land for 1 plough which is there in demesne 'with 1½ virgates' and (there are) 1 villein and 3 bordars with half a plough 'and 1½ virgates.' It was and is worth 20 shillings.

Walter holds 1 virgate of land which is called DONEHAM [probably Downend or Dunball in Puriton]. Algar held (it) T.R.E. This is part of that land which the king gave to him between (the) two waters (inter duas aquas).[2] It is worth 12 pence.

[1] In Exet. Dom. : 'Walscin de Duaco.'
[2] Refers probably to the mouths of the Parret and Brue, in which case this is Downend, at one time a borough with provosts and a chapel (Som. Pleas, No. 229 and note ; S.R.S. xi. 52 ; Cal. Anc. Deeds, C. 2779).

Rademer holds of W[alter] CRUCE [doubtful].[3] Edward held (it) T.R.E. and paid geld for 1 virgate. There is land for 1 plough which is there in demesne with 'half a virgate and' 4 bordars 'who have half a virgate.' 'There are 3 beasts and 3 swine.' It is worth 10 shillings.

Rademer holds of W[alter] BURE [West Bower in Durleigh]. Saric held (it) T.R.E. and paid geld for half a hide. There is land for 3 ploughs. In demesne are '1 virgate and' 1 plough with 1 serf and (there are) 3 villeins and 2 bordars owning 2 ploughs 'and 1 virgate.' 'There are 15 beasts and 21 swine.' It was and is worth 40 shillings.

This land belonged T.R.E. to Melecome [Melcombe Paulet] which now Robert de Odborvile holds.

Walscin holds WERRE [Weare]. Alwacre held (it) T.R.E. and paid geld for 5 hides. Nevertheless there are 6 hides there. There is land for 8 ploughs. Of this (land) 3½ hides are in demesne where are 2 ploughs and 2 serfs and (there are) 5 villeins and 8 bordars with 2 ploughs 'and 2½ hides.' 'There are 18 beasts and 5 swine.' There are 2 mills paying 42 shillings, and 32 acres of meadow. When he received (it) it was worth 10 pounds. Now 100 shillings.

Fulcuin holds of W[alter] BAGEWERRE [Badgworth]. Two thegns, 'Sahulf and Alvric,' held (it) 'in parage (pariter)' for 2 manors T.R.E. and paid geld for 2 hides. There is land for 2 ploughs. In demesne are '1 hide and 3 virgates and' 1 plough and (there are) 2 villeins and 8 bordars with 1 plough 'and 1 virgate.' 'There are 10 beasts and 18 swine and 34 sheep.' There (are) 9 acres of meadow. It was worth 15 shillings. Now 20 shillings.

Ralph 'de Contiville' holds of W[alter] ALWARDITONE [Chapel Allerton].[4] Ulnod held (it) T.R.E. and paid geld for 5 hides. There have been added 6 hides which 2 thegns held 'in parage (pariter)' T.R.E. for 2 manors. Between them all (int. tot.) there is land for 8 ploughs. Of this (land) 9 hides less half a virgate are in demesne where are 3

[3] Perhaps the vill of 'Crosse juxta Bokelond' in Durston; Ped. Fin. 15 R. II. 23; S.R.S. xvii. 23.
[4] Alwarditone. In 1284 (Kirby's Quest) as 'Alewartun,' held of Hugh Lovel by Richard de Cunteville; and can thence be traced down to the modern Chapel-Allerton. Stone Allerton may be the 'addita' (Proc. Som. Arch. Soc. xlv. ii. 25).

ploughs and 4 serfs and (there are) 9 villeins and 9 bordars with 4 ploughs 'and 2 hides and half a virgate.' 'There are 4 beasts and 13 swine.' There (are) 40 acres of meadow and 300 acres of pasture. It was worth 8 pounds when he received it. Now 100[1] shillings.

Ludo holds of W[alter] TERNOC [Tarnock in Badgworth]. Alward held (it) T.R.E. and paid geld for 1 hide. There is land for 2½ ploughs which are there in demesne and 2 serfs and 4 bordars. 'There are 8 unbroken mares and 13 beasts.' There are 20 acres of meadow and of pasture 5 furlongs in length and as much in breadth. It is worth 20 shillings. 'When Walter received it, 15 shillings.'

Richard holds of W[alter] TERNOC [Tarnock in Badgworth]. Lewin held (it) T.R.E. and paid geld for 1 hide. There is land for 2½ ploughs. Nevertheless there are 3 ploughs in demesne 'with 3½ virgates and' 2 serfs and (there are) 1 villein and 2 bordars 'with 1 plough and half a virgate.' 'There are 1 riding-horse and 9 unbroken mares and 16 beasts and 14 swine and 45 sheep.' There (are) 30 acres of meadow and of pasture 6 furlongs in length and as much in breadth. It was worth 15 shillings. Now 25 shillings.

Hubert holds of W[alter] ALNODESTONE [Alston Sutton in Weare]. Two thegns held (it) 'in parage (pariter)' T.R.E. and paid geld for 4½ hides. There is land for 6 ploughs. In demesne are '4 hides less 1 virgate and' 3 ploughs with 1 serf and (there are) 6 villeins and 3 bordars with 2 ploughs 'and 3 virgates.' 'There are 23 beasts and 7 swine.' There (are) 15 acres of meadow and 20 acres of wood(land). It was and is worth 60 shillings.

Gerard holds of W[alter] BROCTUNE [Bratton St. Maur]. Elsi held (it) T.R.E. and paid geld for 4 hides. There is land for 8 ploughs. In demesne are '2 hides and 1 virgate and' 2 ploughs and 6 serfs and (there are) 7 villeins[2] with 4 ploughs 'and 2 hides less 1 virgate.' 'There are 10 beasts and 11 swine and 37 sheep and 23 she-goats.' There are) 4 acres of meadow and 6 furlongs of wood(land) in length and breadth. It was worth 7 pounds when he received (it). Now 4 pounds.

Richard holds of W[alter] MIDDELTONE, 'MILDELTUNA' [Milton in Worle]. Elwacre

[1] Exet. Dom. : '105.'
[2] Exet. Dom. adds : 'and 8 bordars.'

held (it) T.R.E. and paid geld for 1½ hides. There is land for 2 ploughs. There (are) 3 villeins owning 1 plough. It is and was worth 25 shillings.[3]

Renewar holds of W[alter] WINCALETONE [Wincanton]. Elsi held (it) T.R.E. and paid geld for 3½ hides. There is land for 7 ploughs. In demesne are '1 virgate and' 1 plough and 2 serfs and (there are) 16 villeins and 6 bordars and 5 cottars with 7 ploughs 'and 3 hides and 1 virgate.' 'There are 1 riding-horse and 14 beasts and 15 swine and 32 sheep.' There (are) 50 acres of meadow and as many of wood(land). It was and is worth 70 shillings.

To this manor has been added half a hide which Brismar 'the priest' held 'in parage (pariter)' for a manor T.R.E. and paid geld for half a hide. There is land for 5 ploughs. There Renew[ar] has 'in demesne 1 virgate and' 1 plough and 2 serfs and (there are) 7 villeins and 9 bordars and 2 cottars with 3 ploughs 'and 1 virgate.' There (is) a mill paying 30 pence and 60 acres of meadow and 30 acres of pasture and 100 acres of wood(land). It was and is worth 40 shillings. 'These 4 hides paid geld T.R.E. for 3 hides.'

Walter holds CARI [Castle Cary]. Elsi held (it) T.R.E. and paid geld for 15 hides. There is land for 20 ploughs. Of this (land) 8 hides are in demesne where are 6 ploughs and 6 serfs and (there are) 23 villeins and 20 bordars with 17 ploughs 'and 7 hides.' 'There are 2 riding-horses and 16 beasts and 20 swine, and 8 swineherds who yearly pay 50 swine, and 117 sheep.' There (are) 3 mills paying 34 shillings and 100 acres of meadow. Wood(land) 1 league long and half a league broad, and (there is) one burgess in Givelcestre [Ilchester] and another in Briwueton [Bruton] paying 16 pence and one halfpenny. When he received (it), it was worth 16 pounds. Now 15 pounds.

Fulk (Fulcuin) holds of W[alter] SPERCHEFORDE, 'SPARKEFORDA' [Sparkford]. Elwacre held (it) T.R.E. and paid geld for 5 hides and 1 virgate of land. There is land for 5 ploughs. In demesne are '2½ hides and a virgate and' 2½ ploughs and 6 serfs and (there are) 9 villeins and 7 bordars with 4 ploughs 'and 2½

[3] This entry occurs on the bottom of plate xix. col. a. of the photozincograph copy of Exchequer Domesday, and is evidently an addition. In the Exeter Domesday it comes immediately after Worle. After the entry of Worle in the Exchequer codex there is a small space which seems to have been intended for the 'Middeltone' entry.

hides.' 'There are 16 beasts and 19 swine and 72 sheep.' There is a mill paying 7½ shillings and 40 acres of meadow and 100 acres of pasture and 1 furlong of wood(land) (reckoning) in length and breadth. It was worth 4 pounds. Now 100 shillings.

Ulvric holds of W[alter] ALMUNDESFORD [Ansford]. Chetel held (it) T.R.E. and paid geld for 5 hides. There is land for 6 ploughs. In demesne are '3 hides and' 2 ploughs and 3 serfs and (there are) 5 villeins and 4 bordars with 5 ploughs 'and 2 hides.' 'There is 1 riding-horse and 9 beasts and 11 swine and 60 sheep.' There (is) a mill paying 7½ shillings and 20 acres of meadow and 20 acres of pasture. Wood(land) 4 furlongs long and 1½ (furlongs) broad. When he received (it), it was worth 4 pounds. Now 3 pounds.

Ralph holds of W[alter] BERUE [North Barrow]. Elsi held (it) T.R.E. and paid geld for 5 hides. There is land for 5 ploughs. In demesne are '3½ hides and half a virgate and' 2 ploughs and 3 serfs and (there are) 7 villeins and 5 bordars with 3 ploughs 'and 1½ hides less half a virgate.' 'There are 10 beasts and 24 swine and 73 sheep.' There (are) 25 acres of meadow, and of wood(land) 3 furlongs in length and 1 furlong in breadth. When he received (it), it was worth 100 shillings. Now 60 shillings.

Walscin holds BRUGIE [Bridgwater]. Merlesuain held (it) T.R.E. and paid geld for 5 hides. There is land for 10 ploughs. In demesne are '2 hides and' 3 ploughs and 5 serfs and (there are) 13 villeins and 9 bordars and 5 cottars with 8 ploughs 'and 3 hides.' 'There are 13 beasts and 7 swine and 61 sheep.' There is a mill paying 5 shillings and 10 acres of meadow and 100 acres of underwood (*silvæ minutæ*) and 30 acres of pasture. When he received it, it was worth 100 shillings. Now 7 pounds.

Ludo holds of W[alter] WADMENDUNE [Wembdon]. Merlesuain held (it) T.R.E. and paid geld for 2 hides. There is land for 8 ploughs. In demesne are '1 hide and' 2 ploughs with 1 serf and (there are) 5 villeins and 6 bordars[1] with 4 ploughs 'and 1 hide.' 'There are 1 riding-horse and 18 beasts and 20 swine and 30 sheep and 17 she-goats.' There (are) 10 acres of meadow and 13 acres of pasture and 5 acres of wood(land). When he received (it), it was worth 3 pounds. Now 4 pounds.

Renewald holds of W[alter] BAGETREPE [Bawdrip]. Merlesuain held (it) T.R.E. and paid geld for 2 hides. There is land for 8 ploughs. In demesne are '1 hide and' 1 plough and 6 serfs and (there are) 11 villeins and 7 bordars and 3 cottars with 5 ploughs 'and 1 virgate.' 'There are 1 riding-horse and 7 beasts and 20 swine.' There is a mill paying 4 shillings and 100 acres of meadow and 40 acres of pasture. It was worth 50 shillings. Now 60 shillings.

Renewald holds of W[alter] BREDENIE [Bradney in Bawdrip]. Alnod the reeve (*prepositus*) held (it) T.R.E. and paid geld for 1 hide. There is land for 1½ ploughs. 'In demesne are 4 virgates and 1 plough.' There is 1 villein and 5 bordars and 1 cottar and 1 serf with 1½ ploughs 'and 1 virgate.' There (are) 25 acres of meadow. It is worth 20 shillings. 'When he received it 15 shillings.'

Rademer[2] holds of W[alter] HURSI [Horsey in Bridgwater]. Elward 'Glebard' held (it) T.R.E. and paid geld for 2 hides. There is land for 7 ploughs. In demesne are '3 virgates and' 2 ploughs and 2 serfs and (there are) 8 villeins and 6 bordars and 3 cottars with 5 ploughs 'and 1 hide and 1 virgate,' and 24 acres of pasture. 'There are 1 riding-horse and 10 beasts and 20 swine and 50 sheep.' It is worth 4 pounds. 'When he received it, 60 shillings.'

Rademer[3] holds of W[alter] PAUELET [Pawlett]. Semar held (it) T.R.E. and paid geld for 1 virgate of land. There is land for 1 plough which is there in demesne with 1 serf and 2 bordars and 3 cottars and 5 acres of meadow. 'There are 8 beasts and 10 swine and 20 sheep.' It was and is worth 10 shillings.

W[alter] himself holds BURNEHAM [Burnham]. Brixi held (it) T.R.E. and paid geld for 4 hides. There is land for 12 ploughs. In demesne are 'half a hide and' 1 plough and 3 serfs and (there are) 7 villeins and 8 bordars[4] with 5 ploughs 'and 1½ hides.' 'There are 1 riding-horse and 6 mares and 6 beasts and 7 swine and 50 sheep.' There are 150 acres of meadow and 20 acres of pasture. It is worth 4 pounds. Of this land Rademer[5] holds of Walter 2 hides and there he has 1 plough 'and half a

---

[1] Exet. Dom. adds: '6 cottars.'

[2] Exet. Dom.: 'Raimar.'
[3] Exet. Dom.: 'Ramar.'
[4] Exet. Dom. adds: '3 cottars.'
[5] Exet. Dom.: 'Reinewal.'

hide' and 3 serfs and (there are) 7 villeins and 8 bordars and 3 cottars with 5 ploughs 'and 1½ hides.' 'There are 6 mares and 5 beasts and 6 swine and 50 sheep.' (There are) 150 acres of meadow and 20 acres of pasture. It is worth 4 pounds. 'When Walter received it, 6 pounds.'

W[alter] himself holds HONSPIL [Hunt-spill]. Elwacre held (it) T.R.E. and paid geld for 1 hide. There is land for 13 ploughs. In demesne are 'half a hide and' 2 ploughs and 5 serfs and (there are) 21 villeins and 5 bordars and 7 cottars with 11 ploughs 'and half a hide.' 'There are 14 mares and 8 beasts and 20 swine and 28 sheep.' There (are) 100 acres of meadow and 200 acres of pasture. It was and is worth 8 pounds.

W[alter] himself holds BRIEN [Breane]. Merlesuain held (it) T.R.E. and paid geld for 2 hides. There is land for 8 ploughs. In demesne are '1 hide and' 3 ploughs with 1

fo. 95

serf and (there are) 9 villeins and 7 bordars and 8 cottars with 3½ ploughs 'and 1 hide.' 'There are 10 beasts and 4 swine and 53 sheep.' There are 30 acres of pasture. It is worth 100 shillings. 'When Walter received it, 8 pounds.'

Ralph holds of W[alter] CONTUNE, 'COM-TUNA' [Chilcompton].[1] Elwacre held (it) T.R.E. and paid geld for 4 hides. There is land for 3 ploughs. In demesne are '3½ hides and half a virgate and' 2 ploughs and (there are) 4 bordars and 7 cottars and 1 villein with half a plough and 1½ vir-gates.' 'There are 2 beasts and 2 swine and 120 sheep and 70 she-goats.' There is a mill paying 6 pence and 12 acres of meadow and 10 furlongs of pasture in length and 2 furlongs broad, and 3 furlongs of wood(land) in length and 2 furlongs in breadth. It was and is worth 50 shillings.

To this manor has been added 1 hide called CONTUNE [Chilcompton]. Alric held (it) 'in parage (*pariter*)' for a manor T.R.E. and for so much he paid geld. There is land for 1 plough. There is half a plough 'and 3 vir-gates less 1 ferling' with 1 villein 'who has 1 virgate and 1 ferling,' and 2 bordars and 2 acres of meadow and 4 acres of pasture and 4 acres of under(wood). It was and is worth 10 shillings.

Ralph holds of W[alter] HARPETREU [West Harptree]. Elwacre held (it) T.R.E. and paid geld for 5 hides. There is land for 4 ploughs. In demesne are '4 hides and' 1 plough and 2 serfs and (there are) 5 villeins and 2 bordars with 2 ploughs 'and 1 hide.' 'There are 2 beasts.' There is a mill paying 5 shillings and 58 acres of meadow and 62 acres of wood(land). Pasture 1 league (reckoning) in length and breadth. It was and is worth 40 shillings.

Ralph holds of W[alter] ECEWICHE, 'HECUI-WICCA' [perhaps Wick in Brent Knoll].[2] Elwacre held (it) T.R.E. and paid geld for 1½ virgates of land and 8 acres. There is land for 1 plough. 'It is all in demesne.' There is 1 bordar. It is worth 10 shillings.

Rademer[3] holds of W[alter] ALSISTUNE [Alston Maris in Huntspill]. Alwold held (it) T.R.E. and paid geld for 1 hide. There is land for 3 ploughs. In demesne are '3 virgates and' 1 plough with 4 serfs and 1 villein and 4 bordars and 3 cottars, owning 1 plough 'and 1 virgate,' and 40 acres of pas-ture. 'There are 10 beasts and 19 swine and 45 sheep.' It was and is worth 20 shillings.

W[alter] himself holds HUNESPIL [Hunt-spill]. Alwin 'Godesunn' held (it) T.R.E. and paid geld for 3 virgates of land. There is land for 2 ploughs. In demesne there 'is a hide and' 1 plough and 4 serfs and (there are) 2 villeins and 5 bordars and 4 cottars with 1 plough 'and 1 virgate.' 'There are 6 wild (*silvaticæ*) mares and 12 beasts and 18 swine and 80 sheep.' There are 20 acres of meadow. It was and is worth 20 shillings.

Raimar the clerk (*clericus*) holds of W[alter] 'his brother' HIWIS [Huish in Burnham]. Chinesi held (it) T.R.E. and paid geld for 1 virgate of land. There is land for 1 plough which is there with 1 serf and 1 cottar and 3 bordars. 'There are 5 beasts and 10 swine.' It was and is worth 10 shillings.

Ralph 'de Contevilla' holds of W[alter] HIWIS [Huish in Burnham]. Ailwi held (it) T.R.E. and paid geld for 1 virgate of land. There is land for 1 plough which is there with 5 bordars. It was and is worth 10 shillings.

---

[1] In 1284 (*Kirby's Quest*) one moiety of this vill was held of the Bishop of Salisbury, and the other of the Barony of Hugh Lovel of Cary.

[2] Ecewiche. There are also places called Wick in Mark. Putting aside Chilcompton and Harptree, this notice comes in the schedule between Breane and Alston Maris in Huntspil.

[3] Exet. Dom.: 'Ramar.'

The same Ralph 'de Contevilla' holds of W[alter] ATEBERIE [Adber in Trent]. Elsi held (it) T.R.E. and paid geld for 1 hide and 1 virgate of land. There is land for 1 plough which is there 'in demesne with 1 hide and' 1 villein 'who has 1 virgate' and 1 bordar. There are 10 acres of meadow and 20 acres of wood(land). It was and is worth 15 shillings.

'fo. 356'

XXV. THE LAND OF WILLIAM DE MOION

William de Moion holds of the king STOCHELANDE [Stockland Bristol]. Algar held (it) T.R.E. and paid geld for 4 hides and 1 virgate of land. There is land for 5 ploughs. In demesne are '3½ hides and 1 virgate and' 3 ploughs and 6 serfs and (there are) 5 villeins and 4 bordars with half a plough 'and half a hide.' 'There are 3 riding-horses and 5 beasts and 15 swine and 74 sheep.' There is a mill paying 10 pence, and 48 acres of meadow and 12 acres of wood(land). When he received (it), it was worth 60 shillings. Now 4 pounds and 10 shillings.

To this manor has been added SEDTAMME-TONE [   ]. Alvric held (it) 'in parage (*pariter*)' T.R.E. for 1 manor and paid geld for 3 virgates of land. There is land for 1 plough. 'William has this in demesne.' There are 13 acres of meadow and 6 acres of wood-(land). It was and is worth 10 shillings.

He himself [William de Moion] holds TORRE [Dunster], and there is his castle. Alvric held (it) T.R.E. and paid geld for half a hide. There is land for 1 plough. There are 2 mills paying 10 shillings and 15 bordars and 5 acres of meadow and 30 acres of pasture. It was formerly worth 5 shillings. Now 15 shillings.

Hugh holds of W[illiam] TETESBERGE [per-haps Adsborough or Edgeborough in Creech St. Michael]. Six thegns held (it) 'in parage (*pariter*)' [1] T.R.E. and paid geld for 2 hides. There is land for 4 ploughs. In demesne are '3 virgates and' 1 plough and 3 serfs and (there are) 6 villeins and 12 bordars with 3½ ploughs 'and 1 hide and 1 virgate.' 'There are 3 beasts and 1 pig.' There (are) 6 acres of meadow and 100 acres of pasture and 10 acres of moor and 2 acres of wood-(land). It was and is worth 40 shillings.

Garmund holds of W[illiam] AILGI, 'AILI' [Eley in Over Stowey]. Algar held (it) T.R.E. and paid geld for half a hide. There is land for 2 ploughs. In demesne are '1 virgate less half a ferling' and 1 plough with 1 serf and (there are) 6 bordars with 1 plough 'with the rest of the land.' 'There is 1 riding-horse.' There are 10 acres of wood-(land). It was and is worth 20 shillings.

Robert holds of W[illiam] LEGE [Leigh in Winsham]. Sirewald held (it) T.R.E. and paid geld for 3 hides. There is land for 4 ploughs. In demesne are '2 hides and 2½ virgates and' 1 plough with 1 serf and (there are) 5 villeins and 2 bordars. 'There is 1 riding-horse and 6 beasts and 24 sheep.' There are 8 acres of meadow. Wood(land) 2 furlongs long and 1 furlong broad. It was formerly worth 30 shillings. Now 20 shillings.

Roger holds of W[illiam] STRATE, 'ESTRAT' [Street in Winsham]. Huscarl and Almar held (it) 'in parage (*pariter*)' T.R.E. and paid geld for 1½ hides. There is land for 2 ploughs. There are 3 villeins and 1 bordar with 1 plough and 1½ acres of meadow. Pasture 5 furlongs long and 2 furlongs broad. It was and is worth 15 shillings.[2]

Turgis holds of W[illiam] BURNETONE [Brompton Ralph]. Brictric held (it) T.R.E. and paid geld for 3½ hides. There is land for 12 ploughs. In demesne are '1 virgate and' 2 ploughs and 7 serfs and (there are) 16 villeins and 2 bordars with 8 ploughs 'and 3 hides and 1 virgate.' 'There are 1 riding-horse and 8 beasts and 5 swine and 107 sheep and 12 she-goats.' There is a mill paying 30 pence, and 6 acres of meadow and 20 acres of wood(land) and 1 league of pasture. When he received (it), it was worth 40 shillings. Now 4 pounds.
+ This land belonged to the church of Glastingberie nor could it be separated from it T.R.E., '(but) was thegnland there.'

Ogis holds of W[illiam] CLATEURDE [Clat-worthy]. 'A certain woman' Alviet held (it) T.R.E. and paid geld for 1½ hides. There is land for 7 ploughs. In demesne are '3 virgates and' 2 ploughs and 2 serfs and (there are) 16 villeins and 5 bordars with 5 ploughs 'and 3 virgates.' 'There are 1 riding-horse and 8 beasts and 20 swine and 100 sheep and 30 she-goats.' There is a mill paying 6 pence

---

[1] Exet. Dom. adds : ' potuerunt ire ad quemli-bet dominum.'

[2] Exet. Dom. inserts: 'Roger has 1 h. and 1 virg. in demesne and 4 oxen, and the villeins have 1 virg. and 4 oxen.'

and 5 acres of meadow and 25 acres of wood(land). Pasture half a league long and 4 furlongs broad. It was formerly worth 20 shillings. Now 40 shillings.

+ This land could not be separated from the church of Glastingberie, but was thegn-land there T.R.E.

W[illiam] himself holds UDECOME [Cutcombe].[1] Ælmar held (it) T.R.E. and paid geld for 3 hides. There is land for 15 ploughs. In demesne are '3 virgates and' 4 ploughs and 6 serfs and (there are) 18 villeins and 5 bordars with 5 ploughs 'and 1 hide and half a virgate.' There (are) 6 swineherds paying 31 swine. 'There are 36 unbroken mares and 2 riding-horses and 5 beasts and 3 swine and 250 sheep and 47 she-goats.' (There is) a mill paying 5 shillings, and 6 acres of meadow. Pasture 2 leagues long and 1 league broad. Wood(land) 1 league long and half a league broad. It was formerly worth 3 pounds. Now 6 pounds.[2]

Of the land of this manor 3 knights (milites) hold of W[illiam] 1 hide and half a virgate of land and there they have 2 ploughs 'and 3 virgates in demesne' and (there are) 4 villeins and 6 bordars with 1 plough 'and 1½ virgates.' 'There are 3 wild (silvestres) mares and 50 sheep.' There (are) 2 acres of meadow and 14 acres of wood(land). Pasture half a league long and 5 furlongs broad. It was and is worth 35 shillings and 6 pence. 'Three thegns held this land who could not separate (themselves) from the lord of the manor.'

W[illiam] himself holds MANHEVE [Minehead]. Algar held (it) T.R.E. and paid geld for 5 hides. There is land for 12 ploughs. In demesne are '2½ hides and' 3 ploughs and 12 serfs and (there are) 27 villeins and 22 bordars with 10 ploughs 'and 2½ hides.' 'There are 1 riding-horse and 16 beasts and 10 swine and 300 sheep.' There is a mill paying 3 shillings and 12 acres of meadow and 24 acres of wood(land). Pasture 4 leagues long and 2 leagues broad. When he received it, it was worth 100 shillings. Now 6 pounds.

W[illiam] himself holds AUCOME [Alcombe in Dunster]. Algar held (it) T.R.E. and paid geld for 1 hide. There is land for 3 ploughs. In demesne are '3 virgates and' 1 plough and 4 serfs and (there are) 3 villeins and 4 bordars

1 In *Kirby's Quest*, 'Codecombe.' In the *Geld Inquest* of 1084 'Codecoma' appears as the name of a Hundred. 'Udicome' is apparently a misreading for 'Codecome,' which is not found in Domesday.
2 Exet. Dom. : 'and 10 shillings.'

with 2 ploughs 'and 1 virgate.' 'There are 1 riding-horse and 5 beasts and 200 sheep.' There (are) 8 acres of meadow and 3 furlongs of pasture. It was and is worth 20 shillings.

Durand holds of W[illiam] BRUNE [Brown in Treborough]. Edwold held (it) T.R.E. and paid geld for 1 hide. There is land for 6 ploughs. In demesne are 'half a hide and' 2½ ploughs and 2 serfs and (there are) 13 villeins and 3 bordars with 4 ploughs 'and half a hide.' 'There are 2 riding-horses and 15 beasts and 23 swine and 190 sheep and 44 she-goats.' There (are) 1 acre of meadow and 80 acres of pasture and 12 acres of wood(land). It was formerly worth 20 shillings. Now 40 shillings.

Three knights (milites) hold of W[illiam] LANGEHAM [Langeham in Luxborough]. Three thegns held (it) 'in parage (pariter)' and paid geld for 1 hide. There is land for 6 ploughs. In demesne are 'half a hide and 1 ferling and' 3 ploughs with 1 serf and (there are) 5 villeins and 8 bordars with 3½ ploughs 'and the rest of the land.' 'There are 8 beasts and 3 swine and 75 sheep and 34 she-goats.' There is a mill paying 3 shillings and 4 acres of meadow and 60 acres of pasture and 36 acres of wood(land). It was and is worth 30 shillings.

Mainfrid holds of W[illiam] COARME [Quarme in Exton]. Ailward held (it) T.R.E. and paid geld for half a hide. There is land for 4 ploughs. In demesne is '1 virgate and' 1 plough with 1 serf and (there are) 5 villeins and 4 bordars with 1 plough 'and 1 virgate.' 'There are 2 unbroken (indomitæ) mares and 15 beasts and 42 wether-sheep and 20 she-goats.' There are 1 acre of meadow and 10 acres of wood(land). Pasture 5 furlongs long and 5 broad. It was formerly worth 7 shillings 'and 6 pence.' Now 15 shillings.

Richard holds of W[illiam] BICHECOME [Bickham in Timberscombe]. Two thegns held (it) 'in parage (pariter)' T.R.E. and paid geld for 1 virgate of land. There is land for 2 ploughs. In demesne is 'half a virgate and' 1 plough and (there are) 3 villeins and 6 bordars with half a plough 'and half a virgate.' There (are) 3 acres of meadow and 40 acres of pasture. It was formerly worth 6 shillings. Now 15 shillings.

W[illiam] himself holds BRADEWRDE, 'BRADEUDA' [Broadwood in Carhampton]. Alric held (it) T.R.E. and paid geld for half a hide. There is land for 1[1] plough which is there in demesne 'with 1½ virgates' and 2 serfs and (there are) 3 villeins and 2 bordars with 1 plough 'and half a virgate.' 'There are 2 riding-horses and 4 beasts and 60 sheep.' There (are) 5 acres of meadow. Pasture 1 league long and half a league broad. Wood(land) 1 league long and 4 furlongs broad. It was formerly worth 10 shillings. Now 15 shillings.

Ralph holds of W[illiam] AVENA [Avill in Dunster]. Alvric held (it) T.R.E. and paid geld for half a hide. There is land for 2 ploughs. In demesne is 'the whole except 12 acres and' 1 plough and (there is) 1 villein and 5 bordars with half a plough. 'There is one beast.' There (is) a mill paying 20 pence and 4 acres of meadow and 2 acres of wood-(land) and 50 acres of pasture. It was and is worth 10 shillings.

William [himself] holds STANTUNE, 'ESTANTONA' [Stanton in Dunster]. Walle held (it) T.R.E. and paid geld for 3 virgates of land. There is land for 2 ploughs. There 'are in demesne 2½ virgates and' (there are) 2 villeins and 2 serfs and 2 bordars with 1 plough, 'and half a virgate' and 5 acres of meadow and 40 acres of pasture. It is worth 15 shillings. 'When he received it, 7 shillings and 6 pence.'

To this manor has been added 1 virgate of land which 1 thegn held T.R.E. 'in parage (*pariter*)' for 1 manor 'and could betake himself to any lord' (*potuit ire ad quemlibet dominum*). There is land for 1 plough. There is 1 bordar and 3 acres of meadow and 50 acres of pasture. It is worth 3 shillings.

W[illiam] himself holds AISSEFORDE [Exford]. Domno held (it) T.R.E. and paid geld for 1 ferling. There is land for two oxen. There is 1 villein and 15 acres of pasture. It was and is worth 15 pence.

W[illiam] himself holds AISSEFORDE [Exford]. Sarpo held (it) T.R.E. and paid geld for 1½ ferlings. There is land for half a plough. But it has been laid down to grass (*jacet in pastura*), and it pays 12 pence.

fo. 96

Durand holds of W[illiam] STAWEIT [Stowey in Cutcombe]. Leving held (it) T.R.E. and paid geld for 1 virgate of land. There is land for 1 plough which is there in demesne 'with 3½ ferlings' and 1 villein and 1 bordar 'with half a ferling.' 'There are 4 beasts and 20 sheep.' There (are) 14 acres

of wood(land). It was worth 3 shillings. Now 10 shillings.

Durand holds of W[illiam] WOCHETREU [Oaktrow in Cutcombe]. Manno held (it) T.R.E. and paid geld for half a virgate of land. There is land for 1 plough. 'In demesne is 1 ferling and half a plough and' there are 2 villeins with half a plough 'and 1 ferling' and 4 acres of wood(land). 'There are 6 beasts and 50 sheep and 20 she-goats and 8 swine.' It was worth 4 shillings. Now 6 shillings.

·Durand holds of W[illiam] ALVRENCOTE [Allercott now in Timberscombe]. Lewin held (it) T.R.E. and paid geld for half a virgate. There is land for 2 ploughs. 'In demesne is 1 ferling and half a plough.' There is 1 plough with 2 villeins and 2 bordars 'and 1 ferling and 4 beasts' and 8 acres of pasture and 2 acres of wood(land). It was and is worth 6 shillings.

Geoffrey holds of W[illiam] MENE [East Myne in Minehead]. Lewin held (it) T.R.E. and paid geld for half a hide. There is land for 2 ploughs which are there in demesne and 4 serfs with 1 bordar. 'There are 107 sheep and 50 she-goats.' There (are) 1 acre of meadow and 4 acres of wood(land) and 50 acres of pasture. It is worth 15 shillings. 'When he received it, 10 shillings.'

Roger holds of W[illiam] BRATONE [Bratton in Minehead]. Alvric held (it) T.R.E. and paid geld for 3 virgates of land. There is land for 4 ploughs. In demesne are '2 virgates and' 2 ploughs with 1 serf and (there are) 2 villeins and 4 bordars with 2 ploughs 'and 1 virgate.' 'There are 12 beasts and 60 she-goats.' There are 2 acres of meadow and 100 acres of pasture. It was formerly worth 5 shillings. Now 30 shillings.

Roger holds of W[illiam] ERNOLE, 'HERNOLA' [Owl Knowle now in Timberscombe]. Paulinus held (it) T.R.E. and paid geld for 1 hide. There is land for 3 ploughs. In demesne are 3 virgates and' 1½ ploughs and 1 serf and 1 bordar and (there are) 4 villeins with 1 plough 'and 1 virgate.' 'There are 5 wild (*silvestres*) mares and 20 beasts and 16 swine and 120 sheep.' There is of underwood (*silvæ minutæ*) 1 league in length and half a league in breadth. It was formerly worth 5 shillings. Now 25 shillings.

Ranulf holds LOLOCHESBERIE [Luxborough]. Two thegns held (it) 'in parage (*pariter*)'

T.R.E. and paid geld for 1 hide ; 'one held 3 virgates the other 1 virgate.' There is land for 4 ploughs. In demesne is ' 1 virgate and ' 1 plough and 3 serfs and (there are) 6 villeins and 3 bordars with 3 ploughs 'and 3 virgates.' 'There are 6 beasts and 12 swine and 100 sheep.' There (are) 100 acres of pasture and 30 acres of wood(land). It is worth 20 shillings. 'When he received it, 15 shillings.'

Nigel holds of W[illiam] LOLOCHESBERIE [Luxborough]. Brismar held (it) T.R.E. and paid geld for 1 hide. There is land for 3 ploughs. 'In demesne is 1 virgate and 1 plough and there are 6 villeins and 3 bordars with 1 plough 'and 3 virgates.' There (are) 2 acres of meadow and 100 acres of pasture and 30 acres of wood(land). It was and is worth 15 shillings.

W[illiam] himself holds CANTOCHEVE [West Quantockshead]. Elnod 'the reeve (*prepositus*)' held (it) T.R.E. and paid geld for 3½ hides. There is land for 8 ploughs. In demesne are ' 2 hides and 1 virgate and ' 3 ploughs and 7 serfs and (there are) 10 villeins and 4 bordars with 6 ploughs 'and 1 hide and 1 virgate.' 'There are 2 riding-horses and 6 beasts and 8 swine and 200 sheep.' There (are) 16 acres of meadow and 50 acres of wood(land). Pasture 1 league long and 1 league broad. It was worth 3 pounds. Now 4 pounds.

W[illiam] himself holds CHILVETUNE [Kilton]. Alward and Leuric held (it) 'in parage (*pariter*)' for 2 manors T.R.E. and paid geld for 10½ hides. There is land for 10 ploughs. In demesne are ' 7½ hides and half a virgate and ' 4 ploughs and 7 serfs and (there are) 16 villeins and 6 bordars with 5 ploughs 'and 2 hides less half a virgate.' 'There are 4 riding-horses and 4 beasts and 10 swine and 130 sheep.' There (are) 60 acres of meadow and 60 acres of pasture and 100 acres of wood-(land). It was formerly worth 100 shillings. Now 7 pounds.

Of this land Ralph 'a knight (*miles*)' holds of W[illiam] 1 hide and has there 1 plough 'and 3 virgates and 1 ferling' and 2 villeins with 1 plough 'and 3 ferlings.' 'There are 4 beasts and 2 swine and 22 sheep and 5 she-goats.' There (are) 5 acres of meadow and 1 virgate of pasture. It is worth 20 shillings.

W[illiam] himself holds NIWETUNE [Newton in Bicknoller]. Alviet held (it) T.R.E. and paid geld for 4½ hides. There is land for 7 ploughs. In demesne are ' 3 hides less

1 virgate and 1 ferling and ' 2 ploughs and 4 serfs and (there are) 13 villeins and 4 bordars with 5 ploughs 'and 1 hide and 3 virgates and 1 ferling.' 'There are 2 riding-horses and 4 beasts and 6 swine and 80 sheep.' There is a mill paying 40 pence and 18 acres of meadow and 50 acres of wood(land) and of pasture 1 league (reckoning) in length and breadth. It was worth 60 shillings. Now 100 shillings.

W[illiam] himself holds ULVRETUNE, 'UL-TERTUNA' [perhaps Woolston in Bicknoller].[1] Britmar held (it) T.R.E. and paid geld for half a hide. There is land for 1 plough. There 'are 5 acres in demesne and ' 2 villeins and 2 bordars owning 2 ploughs. There (are) 7 acres of meadow and 10 acres of pasture and 7 acres of wood(land). It was formerly worth 10 shillings. Now 20 shillings.

Dudeman holds ELWRDE [Elworthy[2]] of W[illiam]. Dunne held (it) T.R.E. and paid geld for 4 hides.[3] There is land for 5 ploughs. In demesne are ' 1 virgate and ' 2 ploughs and 2 serfs and (there are) 9 villeins and 8 bordars with 3 ploughs 'and 2 virgates.' 'There is 1 riding-horse and 12 swine and 72 sheep.' There is a mill paying 4 shillings and 1½ acres of meadow and 120 acres of pasture and 50 acres of wood(land). It was formerly worth 20 shillings. Now 40 shillings.

Of this hide the king holds 1 virgate of land (as belonging) to the manor of Welletune [Williton].

Dudeman holds of W[illiam] WILLET [in Elworthy]. Dunne held (it) T.R.E. and paid geld for half a hide. There is land for 4 ploughs. In demesne is 'half a virgate and ' 1 plough with 1 serf and (there are) 9 villeins and 6 bordars with 3 ploughs 'and 1½

---

[1] Ulvretune. As 'Ulftuna', 'addita' of South Cadbury, called Wolferton in the *Inq. p.m.* Will. Montagu 13 Edw. II. 31, is Woolston ; and 'Ulmer-stone' becomes Woolmersdon; so 'Ulvretune' may be Woolston in Bicknoller. Agnes of Windsor, relict of the lord of Bicknoller, seems to have held land at 'Wulureston' under the lord of Dunster in 1236 (*Ped. Fin.* 20 H. III. S.R.S. vi. 85).

[2] The single virgate belonging to the King as of the manor of Williton must be the one virgate in 'Pirtochesworda,' noted in the *Geld Inquest* of Williton Hundred as rendering no geld, held by Dodeman and Richard (the verb being in the singular). The name is obsolete

[3] Exet. Dom. reads '4 virgates.' The Exchequer text has '*iij*' altered to '*iiij*', and '*virg*' has been changed to '*hid*' but without changing the numeral from 4 to 1.

virgates.' 'There are 1 riding-horse and 4 beasts and 3 swine and 100 sheep.' There is a mill which pays no rent (*sine censu*)[1] and 3 acres of meadow and 50 acres of pasture and 40 acres of wood(land). It was formerly worth 10 shillings. Now 20 shillings.

The same person [Dudeman] holds of W[illiam] 'the sheriff (*vicecomes*)' COLEFORD [in Stogumber]. Brictuin held (it) T.R.E. and paid geld for half a hide less 1 ferling. There is land for 2 ploughs. 'In demesne are 1½ virgates and' there 2 villeins have 1 plough 'and 2 ferlings.' It is worth 6 shillings. 'When he received it, 3 shillings.'

The same D[udeman] holds of W[illiam] 'the sheriff (*vicecomes*)' WACET [Watchet]. Alwold held (it) T.R.E. and paid geld for 1 virgate of land. There is land for half a plough. Nevertheless there is 1 plough with 1 serf and 1 bordar 'and 1 riding-horse.' There (is) a mill paying 10 shillings. It is worth 15 shillings. 'When William received it, 5 shillings.'

Hugh holds of W[illiam] TURVESTONE [Torweston in Sampford Brett]. Lefsin held (it) T.R.E. and paid geld for 1½ hides. There is land for 3 ploughs. In demesne are '1 hide less half a virgate and' 2 ploughs and (there are) 5 villeins and 6 bordars with 2 ploughs 'and half a hide and half a virgate.' 'There are 14 beasts and 2 swine and 88 sheep.' There is a mill which pays no rent (*sine censu*),[1] and 15½ acres of meadow and 11 acres and 46 acres of wood(land). It was formerly worth 30 shillings. Now 50 shillings.

Hugh holds of W[illiam] HOLEFORD, 'HULO-FORT' [Holford St. Mary[2]]. Alwold held (it) T.R.E. and paid geld for 1 hide. There is land for 2 ploughs, which are there in demesne with '3 virgates and' 1 serf and 1 villein and 5 bordars with 1 plough 'and 1 virgate.' 'There are 9 swine and 4 sheep and 64 she-goats.' There (is) a mill paying 10 pence and 3 acres of meadow and 60 acres of pasture and 4[3] acres of wood(land). It was formerly worth 10 shillings. Now 20 shillings.

Roger holds of W[illiam] 'the sheriff (*vicecomes*)' HARETREU [Hartrow in Stogumber]. Ulwold held (it) T.R.E. and paid geld for 1

hide. There is land for 4 ploughs. In demesne is '1 hide less 1 ferling and' 1 plough with 1 serf and (there are) 2 villeins and 6 bordars with 1 plough 'and 1 ferling.' 'There are 5 beasts and 3 swine and 20 sheep and 20 she-goats.' There is a mill paying 6 pence and 5 acres of meadow and 100 acres of pasture and 6 acres of wood(land). It was formerly worth 10 shillings. Now 20 shillings.

Meinfrid and Robert hold of W[illiam] CIBEWRDE [Chubworthy in Raddington]. Two thegns, 'Seric and Uthret,' held (it) 'in parage (*pariter*)' T.R.E. and paid geld for 1 hide. There is land for 3 ploughs. In demesne is '1 hide and' 1 plough and (there is) 1 villein and 4 bordars with half a plough. 'There are 9 beasts and 80 sheep and 32 she-goats.' There (are) 4 acres of meadow and 50 acres of pasture and 5 acres of wood(land). It was formerly worth 10 shillings. Now 12 shillings.

Turgis holds of W[illiam] COME [possibly Combe Sydenham in Stogumber]. Ailmer held (it) T.R.E. and paid geld for 1 hide. There is land for 3 ploughs. In demesne is 'half a hide and' 1 plough with 1 serf and (there are) 6 bordars with half a plough[4] 'and 1 ferling.' 'There are 3 swine and 300 sheep.' There is a mill which pays no rent (*sine censu*)[5] and 4 acres of meadow and 50 acres of pasture and of wood(land) 4 furlongs in length and 2 furlongs in breadth. It was formerly worth 15 shillings. Now 20 shillings.

Brictric holds of W[illiam] SORDEMANE-FORD [doubtful].[6] The same Brictric held (it) T.R.E. and paid geld for 1 virgate of land. There is land for half a plough. One bordar there has this (½ plough)[7] and 7 acres of wood(land). It was and is worth 6 shillings.

Nigel holds of W[illiam] BADEHELTONE [Bathealton]. Two thegns, 'Alvric and Algar,'

---

[1] Exet. Dom. reads : 'qui molit annonam suam.'
[2] Holeford. Now Holford St. Mary, which in 1284 (*Kirby's Quest*) was in the Hundred of Whitley, and was held of Mohun by Furneaux.
[3] Exet. Dom.: '104.'

[4] Exet. Dom. reads : 'iiii animalia in carr.'
[5] Exet. Dom. reads : 'molinus qui molit annonam suam.'
[6] Although occasionally mentioned, this place has hitherto defied identification. William de Mohun gave it to Cleeve Abbey. Schortmanesford and Durborough (in Stogursey) are mentioned in a Final Concord of 1256 (*Ped. Fin.* 40 Hen. III. 168). Shortmannesford appears in a list of knights' fees on the north side of Quantock held by John de Nevill of Essex (*Ped. Fin.* 32 Edw. III. 570, divers counties. *S.R.S.* xvii. 185).
[7] Exet. Dom. states the virgate with the half plough to be in demesne.

held (it) ' in parage (*pariter*) ' T.R.E. and paid geld for 2 hides. There is land for 5 ploughs. In demesne is ' 1 hide and ' 1 plough and 3 serfs and (there are) 12 villeins and 1 bordar and 5 cottars with 4 ploughs ' and 1 hide.' 'There are 3 beasts and 3 swine and 50 sheep and 50 she-goats.' There is a mill paying 7 shillings and 6 pence and 6 acres of meadow and 40 acres of pasture and 12 acres of wood(land). It was formerly worth 20 shillings. Now 50 shillings.

Ranulf holds of W[illiam] MANEWORDE [Manworthy in Milverton]. Ulf held (it) T.R.E. for 1 hide. There is land for 3 ploughs. In demesne are ' 3 virgates and 1 ferling and ' 1 plough with 1 serf and (there are) 3 villeins and 2 bordars with half a plough ' and 3 ferlings.' 'There are 1 riding-horse and 2 beasts.' There are 7 acres of meadow and 12 acres of wood(land) and 12 acres of pasture. It was formerly worth 10 shillings. Now 20 shillings.

Dodeman holds of W[illiam] RUNETONE [Runnington]. Two thegns held (it) ' in parage (*pariter*) ' T.R.E. and paid geld for 2 hides. There is land for 2 ploughs. In demesne are ' 1 hide and 3 virgates and ' 1 plough and 4 serfs and (there are) 1 villein and 8 bordars with 1 plough ' and 1 virgate.' 'There are 1 riding-horse and 4 beasts and 23 swine.' There is a mill paying 5 shillings and 8 acres of meadow and 10 acres of wood(land). It was formerly worth 20 shillings. Now 50 shillings.

Dodeman holds of W[illiam] POUSELLE [Poleshill in Milverton]. Ulvric held (it) T.R.E. and paid geld for half a hide. There is land for 2 ploughs. There is 1 serf there ' and 1 cow ' and 3 acres of meadow and 20 acres of wood(land). It is worth 10 shillings.

To this manor has been added 1 hide which 1 thegn held freely (*libere*)[1] T.R.E. There is land for 1 plough. It was and is worth 30 pence.

Mainfrid holds of W[illiam] LEGE [Leigh in Milverton]. Cheping held (it) T.R.E. and paid geld for half a hide. Nevertheless there is 1 hide. (There is) land for 2 ploughs. In demesne are ' 3 virgates and 1 ferling and ' 1 plough and 2 serfs and (there are) 2 villeins and 3 bordars with half a plough ' and 3 ferlings.' There is 1 acre of meadow and 12 acres of pasture and 20 acres of wood-

[1] Exet. Dom. reads : ' *pariter*.'

(land). It was formerly worth 5 shillings. Now 12 shillings.

Roger holds of W[illiam] STOCHE, 'ESTOCHET' [Stocklinch Magdalen].[2] Eddida held (it) T.R.E. and paid geld for 2 hides. There is land for 2 ploughs which are there in demesne with ' 1½ hides and 3 ferlings and ' 8 bordars ' who have 1 virgate and 1 ferling.' 'There are 14 sheep.' There are 8 acres of meadow and 4 acres of underwood (*silva minuta*). It was and is worth 30 shillings.

W[illiam] himself holds BRUNFELLE [Broomfield]. Alnod held (it) T.R.E. and paid geld for 3 hides. There is land for 10 ploughs. In demesne are ' 1 hide and 3 virgates and ' 1 plough and 8 serfs and (there are) 12 villeins and 2 bordars with 4 ploughs 'and 1 hide and 1 virgate.' 'There are 1 riding-horse and 13 beasts and 17 swine and 155 sheep and 16 she-goats.' There are 10 acres of meadow and 1 league of pasture and 1 league of wood(land reckoning) in length and breadth. When he received it, it was worth 40 shillings. Now 60 shillings.

W[illiam] himself holds LIDIARD [Lydeard Punchardon in Bishop's Lydeard].[3] Alric held (it) T.R.E. and paid geld for 2 hides. There is land for 6 ploughs. In demesne are ' 1½ virgates and ' 1 plough and 4 serfs and (there are) 10 villeins and 6 bordars with 1 plough ' and 6½ virgates.' 'There are 1 riding-horse and 5 beasts and 115 sheep.' There is a mill paying 8 shillings and 15 acres of meadow and 10 acres of pasture and 20 acres of wood(land). It was and is worth 7 pounds.

W[illiam] himself holds BAGEBERGE [West Bagborough]. Leuric held (it) T.R.E. and paid geld for 3 hides. There is land for 10 ploughs. In demesne are ' 3 virgates and ' 3 ploughs and 7 serfs and (there are) 21 villeins and 2 bordars with 4 ploughs 'and 2 hides and 1 virgate.' 'There are 2 riding-horses and 4 beasts and 6 swine and 150 sheep and 45 she-goats.' There (are) 11 acres of meadow and 200 acres of pasture

[2] In 1278 Adam and Joan Lysewys held a life interest in Stokelinch of John de Beauchamp (*Ped. Fin.* 6 Edw. I. 30). John de Beauchamp held property in ' Stockelinche ' of John de Mohun, lord of Dunster (*Inq. p.m.* John de B., 17 Edw. III. 58).
[3] Held in 1284 (*Kirby's Quest*) by Malet and Pyn of John de Mohun. Although in the parish of Bishop's Lydeard in the Hundred of Kingsbury West, it was reckoned as part of Taunton Dean Hundred.

and 10 acres of wood(land). It was and is worth 100 shillings.

W[illiam] himself holds Stoche [Stoke St. Mary]. Alward held (it) T.R.E. and paid geld for 2 hides. There is land for 6 ploughs. 'In demesne are 1 hide and 1 virgate and' there (are) 6 villeins and 2 bordars with 1 serf owning 2 ploughs 'and 3 virgates.' There (are) 1 acre of meadow and 200 acres of pasture and 6 acres of wood(land). It was and is worth 30 shillings.

Ralph holds of W[illiam] Herfeld [Heathfield]. Elwin held (it) T.R.E. and paid geld for 3½ hides. There is land for 6 ploughs. In demesne are '2½ hides and' 1 plough and 5 serfs and (there are) 7 villeins and 5 bordars with 1 plough 'and 1 hide.' 'There are 5 beasts and 71 sheep.' There is a mill paying 30 pence and 18 acres of meadow and 50 acres of pasture and 30 acres of wood(land). It was worth 30 shillings. Now 4 pounds.

fo. 96b

Turgis holds of W[illiam] Novin[1] [Nunney]. Colo held (it) T.R.E. and paid geld for 5 hides. There is land for 3 ploughs. In demesne are '4 hides and 1 virgate and' 1 plough and 4 serfs and (there are) 3 villeins and 8 bordars with 1 plough 'and 3 virgates.' 'There are 1 riding-horse and 8 beasts and 20 swine and 100 sheep.' There is half a mill paying 30 pence and 20 acres of meadow and as many of pasture and 100 acres of wood(land). It was formerly worth 40 shillings. Now 60 shillings.

W[illiam] himself holds Briweham [Brewham]. Robert son of Wimarc held (it) T.R.E. and paid geld for 12 hides. There is land for 15 ploughs. In demesne are '6 hides and' 4 ploughs and 2 serfs and (there are) 22 villeins and 28 bordars 'and 25 cottars' with 13 ploughs 'and 6 hides.' 'There are 3 riding-horses and 22 wild mares (*equæ silvestres*) and 17 beasts and 60 swine and 300 sheep.' There are 2 mills paying 9 shillings and 2 pence and 60 acres of meadow and 200 acres of wood(land). When he received (it), it was worth 12 pounds. Now 14 pounds and 12 shillings.

To this manor have been added 3 virgates of land. Almar held (them) 'in parage (*pariter*)' T.R.E. There is land for half a plough. There are 3 cottars. It was and is worth 5 shillings.

From this manor have been taken away 3[2]

hides which Erlebold held T.R.E. of Robert, nor could he be separated from the manor. Roger de Corcelle now holds them.

Warmund holds of W[illiam] Eiretone[3] [Cheriton North]. Ernui held (it) T.R.E. and paid geld for 3 hides. There is land for 3 ploughs. In demesne are '2 hides and 1 virgate and' 1½ ploughs and (there are) 1 villein and 4 bordars with half a plough[4] 'and 3 virgates.' 'There is 1 cow and 50 sheep and 15 swine.' There are 10 acres of meadow and as many of pasture and 12 acres of wood(land). It was and is worth 40 shillings.

'fo. 438'

XXII.[5] THE LAND OF WILLIAM DE OW

William de Ow holds of the king Watelege [Whatley in Winsham]. T.R.E. 'Alestan held it and' it paid geld for 1 hide. There is land for 1 plough. There are 2 villeins and 6 furlongs of wood(land) in length and 4 in breadth. It is worth 10 shillings.

W[illiam] himself holds Hantone [Hinton St. George]. T.R.E. 'Alestan held it and' it paid geld for 13 hides. There is land for 12 ploughs. Of this (land) there are in demesne 5 hides where are 4 ploughs and 5 serfs and (there are) 16 villeins and 24 bordars with 10 ploughs 'and 8 hides.' 'There are 36 beasts and 44 swine and 190 sheep.' There (are) 2 mills paying 7 shillings and 6 pence and 60 acres of meadow. Wood(land) 1 league in length and half a league broad. When he received (it), it was worth 12 pounds. Now 15 pounds.

Ralph 'Blowet' holds of W[illiam] Geveltone [Yeovilton]. T.R.E. 'Alestan de Boscome held it and' it paid geld for 8 hides. There is land for 8 ploughs. In demesne are '4 hides and' 3 ploughs and 4 serfs and (there are) 6 villeins and 4 bordars with 5 ploughs 'and 4 hides.' 'There are 2 riding-horses and 2 unbroken mares and 12 beasts and 16 swine and 100 sheep.' There are 2 mills paying 30 shillings and 90 acres of meadow and 40 acres of pasture. When he received (it), it was worth 9 pounds. Now as much.

the figure is set down as '2', and so in the Exet. Dom. in both schedules.

[3] Exet. Dom. *rectius*: 'Ciretona.'

[4] Exet. Dom. reads: '3 oxen.'

[5] The transcriber has mistaken the v in Moion's number xxv for i, and in consequence numbers wrongly to the end.

[1] Exet. Dom. *rectius*: 'Nonin.'

[2] In the entry in Roger de Corcelle's schedule

To this manor have been added 2 hides which 5 thegns held 'in parage (in paragio, pariter)' T.R.E. There is land for 2 ploughs. It is worth 30 shillings.

Herbert holds of W[illiam] LAVRETONE [Laverton]. T.R.E. 'Alestan held it and' it paid geld for 10 hides. There is land for 10 ploughs. In demesne are '6 hides and 3 virgates and' 3 ploughs and 2 serfs and (there are) 6 villeins and 8 bordars with 4 ploughs 'and 3 hides and 1 virgate.' 'There are 1 riding-horse and 3 beasts and 7 swine and 68 sheep and 15 she-goats.' There are 12 acres of meadow and 60 acres of pasture and 60 acres of wood(land). When he received it, it was worth 7 pounds. Now 8 pounds.[1]

Ralph 'Bloet' holds of W[illiam] HANTONE [Hinton Blewitt]. T.R.E. 'Alestan held it and' it paid geld for 8 hides. There is land for 6½ ploughs. In demesne are '5 hides and' 2½ ploughs and 4 serfs and (there are) 7 villeins and 3 bordars and 4 cottars with 3 ploughs 'and 1½ hides.' 'There are 1 riding-horse and 5 beasts and 17 swine and 25 she-goats.' There is a mill paying 4 shillings and 60 acres of meadow. Wood(land) 1 league long and 1 furlong broad. It was worth 6 pounds. Now 100 shillings.

Of this land Hugh 'Maltravers' holds of W[illiam] half a hide. It has always been worth 3 shillings.

Hugh holds of W[illiam] IVLE, 'IVLA' [Yeovil]. T.R.E. 'Alestan held it and' it paid geld for 6 hides. There is land for 6 ploughs. In demesne are '1½ hides and' 1 plough and 3 serfs and (there are) 11 villeins and 14 bordars with 6 ploughs 'and 4½ hides.'[2] 'There are 3 beasts and 5 swine and 32 sheep.' There is 1 mill paying 10 shillings and 33 acres of meadow and 30 acres of pasture. It was and is worth 8 pounds.

To this manor have been added 22 messuages (masuræ)[3] which T.R.E. 22 men held in parage (in paragio, 'pariter'). They pay 12 shillings.

Warner holds of W[illiam] CITERNE [Chilthorne Domer]. T.R.E. 'Alestan held it and' it paid geld for 1 hide. There is land for 1 plough. It is worth 10 shillings.

All these lands above mentioned Alestan Boscome held T.R.E.

W[illiam] himself holds TICHEHAM [Tick-

enham]. Saulf and Teolf, '2 thegns,' held (it) T.R.E. 'in parage (pariter)' and paid geld for 8½ hides. There is land for 9 ploughs. In demesne are '5 hides less 1 ferling and' 3 ploughs and 4 serfs and (there are) 12 villeins and 5 bordars with 6 ploughs 'and 3½ hides and 1 ferling.' 'There are 1 riding-horse and 7 beasts and 7 swine and 47 sheep.' There (are) 30 acres of meadow and 60 acres of pasture and 110 acres of wood(land). It was worth 100 shillings when he received (it). Now 6 pounds.

' fo. 369

XXIII. THE LAND OF WILLIAM DE FALEISE

William de Faleise holds of the king STOCHE [Stoke-Courcy, now Stogursey]. Brixi held it T.R.E. and paid geld for 4½ hides. There is land for 14 ploughs. In demesne are '2 hides and' 4 ploughs and 5 serfs and (there are) 38 villeins and 3 bordars and 3 coliberts with 10 ploughs 'and the rest of the land.' 'There are 3 riding-horses and 29 beasts and 10 swine and 250 sheep.' There is 1 mill paying 16 pence, and 150 acres of meadow and 19 acres of pasture and 100 acres of wood(land). When he received (it), it was worth 25 pounds. Now 20 pounds.

To this manor has been added half a hide which T.R.E. 1 thegn held in parage (in paragio, 'pariter') and was able to go where he would (poterat ire quo volebat).[4] There is land for 1 plough which is there with 1 bordar and 2 serfs. It has always been worth 10 shillings.

W[illiam] himself holds OTONE 'OTTONA' [Wootton Courtney]. Algar held (it) T.R.E. and paid geld for 3 hides. There is land for 10 ploughs. In demesne are '1 hide and 1 virgate and' 3 ploughs and 6 serfs and (there are) 10 villeins and 8 bordars with 3 ploughs 'and 2 hides.' 'There are 1 riding-horse and 13 beasts and 7 swine and 150 sheep and 18 she-goats.' There is 1 mill paying 10 pence and 4 acres of meadow. Pasture 1 league long and a half broad and as much wood(land). It was and is worth 100 shillings.

W[illiam] himself holds WORSPRING [Woodspring] by permission (concessu) of King William. Serlo 'de' Borci gave (it) to him with his daughter. Evroac held (it) T.R.E. and paid geld for 6 hides and 1 virgate of land. There is land for 12 ploughs.

---

[1] Exet. Dom. reverses the values.
[2] Exet. Dom. misreads carr' for hides.
[3] Exet. Dom: 'mansuræ terræ.'
[4] Exet. Dom.: 'potuit ire ad quemlibet dominum.'

In demesne [1] 'are 4 hides and 3 virgates and' there (are) 13 villeins and 6 bordars owning 6 ploughs 'and 1½ hides.' 'There are 16 beasts and 92 sheep.' There (are) 10 acres of pasture and 10 acres of underwood. It has always been worth 100 shillings.

To this manor have been added 3 hides which T.R.E. Alward and Colo held 'in parage (*pariter*)' for 2 manors and paid geld for 3 hides. There is land for 8 ploughs. In demesne are '2½ hides and' 3 ploughs and 4 serfs and (there are) 7 villeins and 4 bordars with 3 ploughs 'and half a hide' and 8 acres of pasture. 'There are 2 swine.' It has always been worth 4 pounds.

'fo. 386'
THE LAND OF WILLIAM SON OF WIDO

William son of Wido holds of the king HORSTENETONE [Horsington]. Savard and Eldeva held (it) 'in parage (*pariter*)' for 2 manors and they could go where they would (*quo volebant ire poterant*),[2] and they paid geld for 11 hides. There is land for 10 ploughs. In demesne are '4½ hides less 5 acres and' 1 plough and 4 serfs and (there are) 12 villeins and 10 bordars and 12 cottars with 7½ ploughs 'and 5 hides and 5 acres.' 'There are 1 beast and 16 swine and 5 sheep.' There is a mill paying 42 pence, and 100 acres of meadow. Pasture 6 furlongs long and 5 furlongs broad. Wood(land) 7 furlongs long and 6 furlongs broad. When he received (it), it was worth 8 pounds and 15 shillings. Now as much.

Of this land Ralph holds of William 1½ hides and there he has 1½ ploughs. 'There are 2 riding-horses and 6 beasts and 12 swine and 60 sheep.' It has always been worth 25 shillings.

Bernard holds of W[illiam] CHERINTONE [South Cheriton in Horsington]. Alwold held (it) T.R.E. and paid geld for 6 hides. There is land for 6 ploughs. In demesne are '4 hides less half a virgate and' 2 ploughs and 6 serfs and (there are) 5 villeins and 4 bordars and 2 cottars with 3 ploughs 'and 2 hides and half a virgate.' 'There are 1 riding-horse and 22 beasts and 28 swine and 3 sheep.' There (are) 125 acres of meadow. Pasture 5 furlongs long and 3 furlongs broad. Wood(land) 7 furlongs long and as much broad. When he received

[1] In Exchequer Dom. there is a gap here.
[2] Exet. Dom. : 'potuerunt ire ad quemlibet dominum.'

(it), it was worth 100 shillings. Now 6 pounds.

Of this same land Alwold purchased 5 hides of the Abbey of Cernel [Cerne in Dorset] for the term of his life (*in vita sua tantum modo*) and after his death the land ought to be restored to the Church.

'fo. 447b'
XXV. THE LAND OF RALPH DE MORTEMER

Ralph de Mortemer holds of the king WALTONE [Walton in Gordano], and Richard 'de Barra' (holds it) of him. Gunni 'the Dane (*Dacus*)' held (it) T.R.E. and paid geld for 3½ hides. There is land for 4 ploughs. In demesne are '2 hides and 1 virgate and' 1 plough and (there are) 7 villeins and 5 bordars with 3 ploughs 'and 1 hide and 1 virgate.' 'There are 1 beast and 5 swine and 43 sheep and 25 she-goats.' There (are) 20 acres of meadow and 100 acres of pasture and 50 acres of wood(land). When he received (it), it was worth 50 shillings. Now 20 shillings more, that is 70 (shillings).

'fo. 344'
XXVI. THE LAND OF RALPH DE POMEREI

Ralph de Pomerei holds STAWEI [Nether Stowey] and Beatrice 'his sister' (holds it) of him. Almer held (it) T.R.E. and paid geld for 1 virgate of land. There is land for 3 ploughs. In demesne are '3½ ferlings and' 2 ploughs and 3 serfs and (there are) 1 villein and 4 bordars 'with half a ferling.' 'There are 6 beasts and 60 sheep and 30 she-goats.' There are 2 acres of meadow and 6 acres of wood(land), and pasture half a league long and 4 furlongs broad. It was and is worth 20 shillings.

Ralph himself holds ARE [Oare]. Edric held (it) T.R.E. and paid geld for 1 hide. There is land for 6 ploughs. In demesne are 'half a hide and' 2 ploughs and 4 serfs and (there are) 7 villeins and 5 bordars with 4 ploughs 'and half a hide.' 'There are 20 beasts and 100 sheep.' There are 2 acres of meadow and 15 acres of wood(land). Pasture 2 leagues long and 1 (league) broad. It is worth 30 shillings. 'When he received it, 20 shillings.' This manor used to pay yearly to the king's manor of Carentone [Carhampton] for a customary due 12 sheep. Ralph keeps back this customary due.

XXVII. THE LAND OF RALPH PAGENEL

Ralph Pagenel holds of the king STOCHE-LAND [Stockland Bristol] and Ralph 'de Roileio' (holds it) of him. T.R.E. 'Merlesuain held it and' it paid geld for 3 hides. There is land for 5 ploughs. In demesne are '2½ hides and' 2 ploughs and 4 serfs and (there are) 7 villeins and 4 bordars with 3 ploughs 'and half a hide.' 'There are 6 beasts and 20 swine and 40 sheep.' There (are) 50 acres of meadow and 80 acres of pasture. It has always been worth 100 shillings.

The same Ralph holds of Ralph CANTOCHE-HEVE [East Quantockshead]. T.R.E. 'Merlesuain held it and' it paid geld for 7 hides. There is land for 20 ploughs. In demesne are '5 hides and 1 ferling and' 2 ploughs and 5 serfs and (there are) 13 villeins and 7 bordars with 7 ploughs 'and 2 hides less 1 ferling.' 'There are 4 swine.' There is a mill paying 7 shillings and 6 pence, and 20 acres of meadow and 50 acres of wood(land). Pasture 2 leagues long and 1 league broad. It was worth 11 pounds when he received (it). Now 8 pounds.

The same Ralph holds of Ralph HEWIS [Beggearn-Huish in Nettlecombe]. T.R.E. 'Merlesuain held it and' it paid geld for 1½ hides. There is land for 6 ploughs. In demesne are '3 virgates and' 2 ploughs and 5 serfs and (there are) 9 villeins and 6 bordars with 3 ploughs 'and 3 virgates.' 'There are 2 beasts and 1 riding-horse and 1 pig and 30 sheep.' There is a mill paying 3 shillings and 12 acres of meadow and 100 acres of pasture. It has always been worth 3 pounds.

The same Ralph holds of Ralph BAGEBERGE [Bagborough East]. T.R.E. 'Merlesuain held it and' it paid geld for 1 hide. There is land for 4 ploughs. In demesne are 'half a hide and' half a plough and 3 serfs and (there are) 5 villeins and 5 bordars with 2½ ploughs 'and half a hide.' There (are) 3 acres of meadow and 60 acres of pasture. It has always been worth 50 shillings.

Robert 'son of Roscelin' holds of Ralph NEUHALLE [Newhall in Holford]. T.R.E. 'Merlesuain held it and' it paid geld for 1 virgate of land. There is land for 2 ploughs. There are 2 bordars and half a league of wood(land). It has always been worth 10 shillings.

These lands above mentioned Merlesuain held T.R.E.

XXVIII. THE LAND OF RALPH DE LIMESI

Ralph de Limesi holds of the king COMICH [Combwich in Otterhampton] and Walter 'Arbalistarius' (holds it) of him. Liward held (it) T.R.E. and paid geld for 1½ hides. There is land for 6 ploughs. In demesne are '1 hide and' 1 plough with 1 serf and (there are) 4 villeins and 5 bordars with 2 ploughs 'and half a hide.' 'There are 5 beasts and 50 sheep.' There are 28 acres of meadow and 5 acres of pasture and 2 acres of wood(land). It has always been worth 40 shillings.

Walter himself holds LOCUMBE [Luccombe]. Queen Edith held (it) T.R.E. and paid geld for 2 hides. There is land for 8 ploughs. In demesne are '1 hide and' 3 ploughs and 2 serfs and (there are) 18 villeins and 6 bordars with 4 ploughs 'and 1 hide.' 'There are 1 riding-horse and 6 beasts and 6 swine and 100 sheep and 50 she-goats.' There are 5 acres of meadow and 50 acres of wood(land). Pasture 1 league long and half a league broad. It was worth 3 pounds. Now 4 pounds.

Ralph himself holds SELEURDE [Selworthy]. Queen Edith held (it) T.R.E. and paid geld for 1 hide. There is land for 5 ploughs. In demesne are 'half a hide and 2 ploughs and' 2 serfs and (there are) 7 villeins and 5 bordars with 3 ploughs 'and half a hide.' 'There are 1 riding-horse and 2 beasts and 4 swine and 60 sheep.' There is a mill paying 20 pence, and 5 acres of meadow and 60 acres of pasture and 40 acres of wood(land). It was worth 20 shillings. Now 25 shillings.

Ralph himself holds ALRESFORD [Allerford in Selworthy]. Edric held (it) T.R.E. and paid geld for 1 hide. There is land for 5 ploughs. In demesne are 'half a hide and' 2 ploughs and 2 serfs and (there are) 6 villeins and 2 bordars with 1 plough 'and half a hide.' 'There are 1 riding-horse and 1 swine and 60 sheep.' There is 1 mill paying 15 pence, and 6 acres of meadow and 20 acres of pasture and 1 acre of wood(land). It was worth 15 shillings. Now 20 shillings.

This manor used to pay yearly for a customary due 12 sheep to Carentone [Carhampton] the king's manor. Ralph has kept back this customary due to the present time.

+ Ralph himself holds BOSINTUNE [Bossington in Selworthy]. The Church of Adelingi [Athelney] held it T.R.E., and it was set apart for the monks' food (*de victu monachorum*), and paid geld for 1 hide. There is land for 5 ploughs. In demesne are 'half a hide and' 1 plough with 1 serf and (there are) 5 villeins and 2 bordars with 1 plough 'and half a hide.' Pasture 1 league in length and half a league in breadth. It was and is worth 20 shillings. The Church was seised of this manor when the king gave his land to Ralph.

Ralph himself holds TRABERGE [Treborough]. Edric held (it) T.R.E. and paid geld for half a hide. There is land for 5 ploughs. In demesne is 'all the land except 10 acres and' 1 plough. There is 1 villein, 'who has 10 acres,' and 30 acres of wood(land). Pasture 1 league long and as much broad. It is worth 7 shillings for it has been laid waste (*vastata est*).

Ralph himself holds EPSE [perhaps Rapps[1] in Ashill]. Ulward held (it) 'in parage (*pariter*)' T.R.E. and paid geld for half a hide. There is land for 1 plough. There is 1 villein and 16 acres of meadow. It is worth 3 shillings.

Ralph himself holds ALRE [Aller]. Ulward held (it) T.R.E. and paid geld for 2 hides. There is land for 4 ploughs. In demesne are '3 virgates and' 2 ploughs and 2 serfs and (there are) 5 villeins and 12 bordars with 2 ploughs 'and 1 hide and 1 virgate.' 'There are 12 beasts and 6 swine and 16 sheep.' There (are) 15 acres of meadow and 200 acres of pasture and 10 acres of wood(land). When he received it, it was worth 100 shillings. Now 6 pounds.

'fo. 436b'

XXIX. THE LAND OF ROBERT SON OF GEROLD

Robert son of Gerold holds of the king CERLETONE [Charlton Musgrove], and Godzelin (holds it) of him. Godman held (it) T.R.E. and paid geld for 5 hides. There is land for 12 ploughs. In demesne are '2 hides and' 3 ploughs and 7 serfs and (there are) 4 villeins and 15 bordars and 3 cottars (*coscez*) with 8 ploughs. There (is) a mill paying 5

shillings and 50 acres of meadow. Pasture 4 furlongs long and 3 furlongs broad. Wood(land) half a league long and as much broad. It was worth 10 pounds. Now 6 pounds.

Robert himself holds [2][? Charlton Horethorne].[3] Vitel held (it) T.R.E. and paid geld for 10 hides. There is land for 10 ploughs. In demesne are '4 hides and' 3 ploughs and 8 serfs and 4 coliberts and (there are) 11 villeins and 17 bordars with 5 ploughs. There (are) 30 acres of meadow and 100 acres of pasture. Wood(land) 3 furlongs long and 2 furlongs broad. When he received it, it was worth 18 pounds. Now he pays 100 cheeses and 10 bacons.

'fo. 447b'

XXX. THE LAND OF ALVRED DE MERLEBERGE

Alvred de Merleberge holds of the king CELLEWERT [Chelwood] and Nicholas (holds it) of him. Carle held (it) T.R.E. and paid geld for 5 hides. There is land for 5 ploughs. In demesne are '3 hides and' 1 plough and 4 serfs and (there are) 3 villeins and 4 cottars (*coscez*) with 1 plough 'and 2 hides.' 'There are 2 riding-horses and 12 swine and 100 sheep and 30 she-goats.' There (are) 7 acres of meadow and 30 acres of wood(land). It was and is worth 100 shillings.

'fo. 371b'

XXXI. THE LAND OF ALVRED DE ISPANIA

Alvred de Ispania holds of the king ULMERSTONE [Woolmersdon in North Petherton] and Walter (holds it) of him. Alwi held (it) T.R.E. and paid geld for half a hide. There is land for 3 ploughs. In demesne is '1 virgate and' 1 plough with 1 serf and (there are) 4 villeins and 13 bordars with 1 plough 'and 1 virgate.' 'There are 4 swine.' There are 10 acres of meadow and 20 acres of wood(land). It was and is worth 30 shillings.

To this manor has been added 1½ virgates of land. 'One virgate of' this land belonged to (*fuit de*) Peret [North Petherton] the king's manor. Alwi the reeve (*prepositus*) had possession (*præstitit*) T.R.E. It was and is worth 10 shillings. 'A thegn held the half virgate in parage (*pariter*).'[4]

---

[1] This has been identified with Rapps, a hamlet on the borders of Ilton, Ashill and Broadway. It appears as 'Apse' in the Assize Rolls of 1242-3 (*Som. Pleas*, No. 1184, *S.R.S.* xi.), and 'Lapse,' or 'Les Apses.' In *Nom. Villar.* it is the hamlet of 'Apse' in Broadway.

[2] Word omitted in both Domesday books.

[3] The statistics of the Hundred of Milborne, now Horethorne, in the *Geld Inquest* cannot be made complete without the inclusion of a large manor.

[4] See Eyton, *Som. Dom.* i. 185.

Alvred himself holds BUR [East Bower in North Petherton]. Alwi held (it) T.R.E. and paid geld for half a hide. There is land for 5 ploughs. 'There is 1 virgate in demesne.' There are 8 villeins and 6 bordars and 3 serfs 'with the rest of the land.' 'There are 1 cow and 2 swine.' It has always been worth 100 shillings.

To this manor has been added 1 virgate of land which belonged to (*fuit de*) the king's ferm (*firma*) in Peret [North Petherton]. There is land for 1 plough. It is worth 10 shillings. 'Samar held it T.R.E.'

Richard 'Demeri' holds of Alvred HUNTE-WORDE [Huntworth in North Petherton]. Alwi held (it) T.R.E. and paid geld for 1 hide. There is land for 2 ploughs which are there with 2 serfs and 7 bordars. 'There are 8 beasts and 60 sheep.' There are 4 acres of meadow and 10 acres of moor. When he received (it), it was worth 5 shillings. Now 20 shillings.

Ranulf holds of Alvred STRENGESTONE [Stringston]. Alwi held (it) T.R.E. and paid geld for 1 hide. There is land for 3 ploughs. In demesne are '3 virgates and' 2 ploughs and 4 serfs and (there are) 3 villeins with 1 plough 'and 1 virgate.' 'There are 8 beasts and 15 swine and 193 sheep.' There (are) 4 acres of meadow and 50 acres of pasture. It is worth 50 shillings. 'When he received it, 40 shillings.'

To this manor has been added half a virgate of land which Bristive held freely[1] T.R.E. There is land for half a plough. One villein there owns this (half plough). It has always been worth 5 shillings.

Alvred himself holds SPACHESTONE [Spaxton]. Alwi held (it) T.R.E. and paid geld for 2½ hides. There is land for 8 ploughs. In demesne is 'half a hide and' 1 plough and 2 serfs and (there are) 3 villeins and 2 bordars with 1 plough 'and half a hide.' 'There are 17 sheep.' There (are) 26 acres of meadow and 9 acres of wood(land). When he received (it), it was worth 50 shillings. Now the same (*similiter*).

Of the same land 1 knight (*miles*) holds of Alvred 1½ hides, and there he has '1 hide in demesne and' 2 ploughs and 3 serfs and 3 cottars and 6 villeins and 5 bordars 'with 2 ploughs and half a hide.' 'There are 16 swine and 37 sheep and 14 she-goats.' There (are) 4 acres of meadow and 120 acres of wood(land). It was worth 3 pounds. Now as much.

1 *Libere*; Exet. Dom. reads '*pariter*.'

Herbert holds of Alvred OTREMETONE, 'OTTRAMMETONA' [Otterhampton]. Estan held (it) T.R.E. and paid geld for 1 hide and 2½ virgates of land. There is land for 3 ploughs. In demesne are '1 hide and half a virgate and' 2 ploughs with 1 serf and (there are) 5 villeins and 3 bordars and 3 cottars with 2½ ploughs 'and half a hide.' 'There are 4 beasts and 11 swine and 45 sheep.' There (are) 5 acres of meadow and 3 acres of pasture and 3 acres of wood(land). It has always been worth 40 shillings.

Herbert holds of Alvred RADEFLOT [Radlet in Spaxton]. Estan held (it) T.R.E. and paid geld for half a hide less 1 ferling. There is land for 1½ ploughs. There are '3 ferlings in demesne and' 2 villeins with 1 bordar 'and 1 plough and 1 virgate,' and 5 acres of meadow and 21 acres of pasture and 3 acres of wood(land). It was and is worth 15 shillings.

Hugh holds of Alvred PLANESFELLE [Plainsfield in Over Stowey]. Edred held (it) T.R.E. and paid geld for 1 hide. There is land for 2 ploughs. There are 3 bordars and 1 serf and 2 acres of meadow and 15 acres of wood(land). When he received it, it was worth 20 shillings. Now 10 shillings.

Hugh holds of Alvred MULSELLE [Marsh Mills in Over Stowey]. Alwin held (it) T.R.E. and paid geld for 1 hide. There is land for 1 plough. There is 1 bordar with 1 serf and 15 acres of meadow. It has always been worth 15 shillings.

Richard holds of Alvred SELVRE [Monksilver]. Alwi held (it) T.R.E. and paid geld for 1½ hides. There is land for 9 ploughs. In demesne are 'half a hide and 3 ferlings and' 2 ploughs and 4 serfs and (there are) 11 villeins and 5 bordars with 7 ploughs 'and the rest of the land.' 'There are 1 riding-horse and 1 cow and 12 swine and 30 sheep.' There is a mill paying 3 shillings, and 2 acres of meadow and 160 acres of pasture. Wood(land) 3 furlongs long and 2 furlongs broad. It was worth 3 pounds. Now 4 pounds.

Alvred himself holds STALWEI [Nether Stowey]. Earl Herald held (it) T.R.E. and paid geld for 3 hides. There is land for 5 ploughs. In demesne are '2 hides and' 1 plough and 5 serfs and (there are) 8 villeins and 4 bordars with 2 ploughs. 'There are 9 beasts and 7 swine and 90 sheep.' There is a mill paying 4 pence, and 7 acres of meadow and 100 acres of pasture. Wood(land) 1½ leagues (reckoning) in length and breadth. 'It was worth when he received it, 8 pounds. Now 10 pounds.'

Osward and Ailward, '2 thegns,' hold of Alvred STALWEI [Nether Stowey]. They held it 'in parage (*pariter*)' T.R.E. and paid geld for 2 hides. There is land for 4 ploughs. In demesne are 1½ ploughs 'and all the land'[1] with 1 serf and (there are) 4 villeins and 3 bordars with 1 plough. 'There are 8 swine and 20 sheep.' There are 3 acres of meadow, 'and 1 league of wood(land).' It has always been worth 20 shillings. This land has been added to the lands of Alwi which Alvred holds.

Ranulf holds of Alvred ALFAGESTONE and LEDING[2] [Alfoxton in Holford, and Dyche in Stringston]. Alwi 'Baneson' held (them) T.R.E. and paid geld for 2 hides. There is land for 3 ploughs. In demesne are '1½ hides and' 1 plough with 1 serf and (there are) 4 villeins and 2 bordars with 2 ploughs 'and half a hide.' There (are) 8 acres of meadow and 30 acres of pasture and 35 acres of wood(land). It was and is worth 20 shillings.

Hugh holds of Alvred LEGE [Leigh in Old Cleeve]. Domno held (it) T.R.E. and paid geld for half a hide. There is land for 1½ ploughs. There are 2 bordars, and 2 acres of meadow. Wood(land) 3 furlongs long and half a furlong broad. It was and is worth 17 shillings. This land has been added to the lands of Alwi 'Banesone' which Alvred holds.

Hugh holds of Alvred RADEHEWIS [Rodhuish in Withycombe]. Alwi held (it) T.R.E. and paid geld for 1 virgate of land. There is land for 1 plough which is there in demesne with 1 bordar and 1 acre of meadow and 12 acres of pasture. When he received (it), it was worth 2 shillings. Now 6 shillings.

Robert and Herbert hold of Alvred STAWEI [Stawley]. Alwi 'Bannesonn' held it T.R.E. and paid geld for 3 hides. There is land . In demesne are '2 hides and 3 virgates and' 2 ploughs with 1 serf and (there are) 2 villeins and 4 bordars 'with 1 virgate.' 'There are 8 swine and 24 sheep.' There (are) 4 acres of meadow and 20 acres of wood(land). When he received (it), it was worth 100 shillings. Now 60 shillings.

Richard 'Demeri' holds of Alvred ILE [Ile

Brewers]. Alwi held it T.R.E. and paid geld for 2 hides. There is land for 2 ploughs. In demesne are '1 hide and' 1 plough with 1 serf and (there are) 8 villeins and 2 bordars with 1 plough 'and 1 hide.' 'There are 1 riding-horse and 1 cow and 60 sheep.' There (is) a mill paying 20 pence and 10 acres of meadow and 10 acres of pasture and 30 acres of wood(land). When he received (it), it was worth 20 shillings. Now 40 shillings.

Hugh holds of Alvred PRESTETONE [Preston Bowyer in Milverton]. Alwi held (it) T.R.E. and paid geld for 3 hides less 1 virgate. There is land for 5 ploughs. In demesne are '1½ hides and half a virgate and' 1 plough and 2 serfs and (there are) 14 villeins with 1 plough 'and the rest of the land.' 'There are 7 beasts and 5 swine and 48 sheep.' There is a mill paying 20 pence, and 8 acres of meadow and 15 acres of wood(land). When he received it, it was worth 30 shillings. Now 60 shillings.

fo. 97b

Walter, 'his brother,' 5 virgates, and Ansger 'Focarius,' 2 virgates of land, hold of Alvred GAHERS [Goathurst]. Alwi held it T.R.E. and paid geld for 1 hide and 3 virgates of land. There is land for 6 ploughs. In demesne are 'half a virgate and' 2 ploughs and 4 serfs and (there are) 13 villeins and 5 bordars with 4 ploughs 'and 1 hide and half a virgate.' 'There are 9 beasts and 10 swine and 60 sheep and 16 she-goats.' There are 62 acres of wood(land).[3] When he received (it), it was worth 70 shillings. Now the same (*similiter*).

Ranulf holds of Alvred MALRIGE [Merridge in Spaxton]. Alwi held (it) T.R.E. and paid geld for half a hide. There is land for 2½ ploughs. In demesne are '1 virgate and' 1 plough and 2 serfs and (there are) 4 villeins and 1 bordar with 1½ ploughs 'and 1 virgate.' 'There are 4 beasts and 31 sheep and 12 she-goats.' There is a mill paying 6 pence, and 30 acres of pasture and 20 acres of wood(land). It was and is worth 20 shillings.

Robert holds of Alvred CANTOCHE [Quantock, exact position doubtful]. Alwi held (it) T.R.E. and paid geld for 1 virgate of land. There is land for 1½ ploughs. Three villeins there have these (ploughs) and 8 acres of under-

---

[1] Exet. Dom. gives the villeins half a virgate.
[2] Exet. Dom. *rectius :* 'Ledich.'

[3] The Exet. Dom. divides the 2 holdings, and assigns all the stock and the woodland to Walter, as Ansger had no part in demesne. The figures after the tenants' names are interlineations.

wood (*silvæ minutæ*). When he received it, it was worth 20 shillings. Now 25 shillings.

Walter holds of Alvred HILLE [Hill Farrance]. Alwi held (it) T.R.E. and paid geld for 3 hides. There is land for 6 ploughs. In demesne are 'half a hide and' 1 plough and 4 serfs and (there are) 11 villeins and 4 bordars and 1 cottar with 1 plough 'and 2½ hides.' 'There are 6 beasts and 14 swine.' There is a mill paying 30 pence, and 17 acres of meadow and 10 acres of pasture and 17 acres of wood(land). It was worth 3 pounds. Now 4 pounds.

Alvred himself holds LOCHINTONE, 'LODUNTONA' [Luckington in Kilmersdon]. Alwi held (it) T.R.E. and paid geld for 5 hides. There is land for 5 ploughs. In demesne are '4 hides and 3 virgates and' 2 ploughs and 3 serfs and (there are) 8 bordars with 1 plough 'and 1 virgate.' 'There are 1 riding-horse and 8 beasts and 108 sheep and 31 she-goats.' There (is) a mill paying 10 shillings, and 12 acres of meadow. Wood(land) half a league long and 3 furlongs broad. When he received it, it was worth 6 pounds. Now 3 pounds.

Alvred himself held (*habuit*) ACHELAI [Oakley in Chilthorne Domer]. Alwi 'Baneson' held it 'in parage (*pariter*)' T.R.E. This manor has been added to Mertoch [Martock] the king's manor, and it is worth yearly 50 shillings.

'fo. 382b'

XXXII. THE LAND OF TURSTIN SON OF ROLF

Turstin son of Rolf holds of the king PIDECOMBE [Pitcombe]. Alwold held (it) T.R.E. and paid geld for 5 hides. There is land for 5 ploughs. In demesne are '4 hides and' 2 ploughs and (there are) 5 villeins and 19 bordars with 3 ploughs 'and 1 hide.' 'There are 1 riding-horse and 6 unbroken mares (*equæ indomitæ*) and 12 beasts and 60 swine and 104 sheep.' There are 2 mills paying 15 shillings and 22 acres of meadow and 5 acres of wood(land). In Briwetone [Bruton] (are) 11 burgesses paying 23 shillings. It is worth altogether 7 pounds. When he received it, it was worth 8 pounds.

Butolf holds of Turstin WITEHAM [Witham]. Chetel held (it) T.R.E. and paid geld for 1 hide. There is land for 2 ploughs. In demesne are '2½ virgates and' 1 plough and 'there are 3 villeins and' 6 cottars with 1 plough 'and 1½ virgates.' 'There are 12

beasts and 10 swine and 35 sheep.' When he received (it), it was worth 15 shillings. Now 20 shillings.

To this manor has been added 1 hide in WLTUNE, 'WLFTUNA,' [   ] which Chetel held (*pariter*) for 1 manor T.R.E. There is land for 1 plough which is there with 1 serf and 6 cottars. There are 2 acres of meadow. It is worth 10 shillings. When he received (it), it was worth 30 shillings.

This land has been added to the lands [1] of Adwold which Turstin holds.

Rippe holds of T[urstin] STORPE [2] [Eastrip in Brewham]. Alwin held (it) T.R.E. and paid geld for 1 hide. There is land for 1 plough which is there with 3 cottars. 'There are 3 cows and 12 swine and 30 sheep.' Wood(land) 1 furlong long and broad. It has always been worth 20 shillings.

Hugh holds of T[urstin] SINDERCOME [Syndercombe in Clatworthy]. Cerric held (it) T.R.E. and paid geld for 1 hide. There is land for 5 ploughs. In demesne are '1 virgate and' 1 plough and (there are) 7 villeins and 7 bordars with 3 ploughs 'and 3 virgates.' There (are) 17 acres of meadow and 1 league of pasture (reckoning) in length and breadth and 50 acres of wood(land). It was and is worth 20 shillings.

Turstin himself holds CADEBERIE [North Cadbury]. Alwold held (it) T.R.E. and paid geld for 12 hides. There is land for 12 ploughs. In demesne are '4 hides and' 3 ploughs and 6 serfs and (there are) 16 villeins and 20 bordars with 8 ploughs 'and 8 hides,' and there is 1 swineherd paying yearly 12 swine. 'There are 1 riding-horse and 31 beasts and 60 swine and 42 sheep.' There are 2 mills paying 22 shillings and 50 acres of meadow and 70 acres of pasture. Wood(land) 4 furlongs long and 1 furlong broad. It was worth 20 pounds. Now 12 pounds.

To this manor has been added WESTONE [Weston Bampfylde]. Alwi held (it) T.R.E. for a manor, and could go where he liked,[3] and paid geld for 2 hides and 2½ virgates of land. In demesne are '1½ hides and' 1½ ploughs and 2 serfs and (there are) 6 bordars with 1 plough 'and the rest of the land.' 'There are 1 riding-horse and 9 swine.'

---

[1] Exet. Dom. has 'ad honorem.'
[2] Exet. Dom. *rectius*: 'Estropa.'
[3] Exet. Dom. reads: 'poterat sibi eligere dominum secundum voluntatem suam cum terra sua.'

There is half a mill paying 45 pence, and 24 acres of meadow. Wood(land) 2 furlongs long and 1 furlong broad. It was and is worth 40 shillings. Richard holds (it) of Turstin.

Alwin holds of T[urstin] WESTONE [Weston Bampfylde]. He held (it) T.R.E. and paid geld for half a hide. There is land for half a plough. Nevertheless 1 plough is there with 1 villein. It is worth 10 shillings.

Bernard 'Pancewold' holds of T[urstin] SUDCADEBERIE [South Cadbury]. Alwold 'Calvus' held (it) T.R.E. and paid geld for 3 virgates of land. There have been added 2 hides and 1 virgate of land which 4 thegns held freely (libere)[1] T.R.E.. Altogether there is land for 3 ploughs. Bernard has 2 hides. A priest (clericus) (has) half a hide. One Englishman (has) half a hide. All these lands have been added to the lands of Alwold which Turstin holds.

'Besides these lands added which I have noted above,'[2] to this has been added 1 hide in ULTONE, 'ULFTONA' [Woolston in North Cadbury] which Alnod held freely (libere)[1] T.R.E. There is land for 1 plough. Leviet holds (it) of Turstin and has there 1 serf and 3 cottars (coscez) 'and 50 sheep' and 4 acres of meadow and 3 acres of underwood (silvæ minutæ). It is worth 10 shillings. 'When Turstin received it, 15 shillings.'

To this has been added CLOPTONE [Clapton in Maperton]. Alnod held (it) freely (libere)[1] T.R.E. and paid geld for 2 hides. There is land for 3 ploughs. Ralph 'Trencart' holds (it) of Turstin, and has there 1 plough with 1 villein and 4 bordars and 2 serfs. There (are) 10 acres of meadow and 4 furlongs of wood(land) in length and 2 furlongs broad. When he received it, it was worth 40 shillings. Now 20 shillings.

Alward holds of T[urstin] BLACHEFORD [Blackford]. He held (it) T.R.E. and paid geld for 1 hide. There is land for 1 plough, which is there with 3 bordars. 'There are 3 beasts and 8 swine and 40 sheep.' It is worth 15 shillings. 'When Turstin received it, 20 shillings.'

Geoffrey holds of T[urstin] CUNTONE [Compton Pauncefoot]. Alward held (it) T.R.E. and paid geld for 6 hides. There is land for 6 ploughs. In demesne are '3 hides

and' half a plough[3] and 4 serfs and (there are) 9 villeins and 11 bordars with 5 ploughs 'and 3 hides.' 'There are 4 beasts and 20 swine and 80 sheep.' There (is) a mill paying 8 shillings, and 15 acres of meadow. Wood(land) 4 furlongs long and 1 furlong broad. It is worth 100 shillings. Now 6 pounds.

Geoffrey holds of T[urstin] MALPERTONE, 'MALPERETTONA' [Maperton]. Alwold held it T.R.E. and paid geld for 5 hides. There is land for 6 ploughs. In demesne are '2 hides and' 2 ploughs and 10 serfs and (there are) 3 villeins and 9 cottars with 3 ploughs 'and the rest of the land.' 'There are 17 beasts and 20 swine and 80 sheep.' There are 2 mills paying 5 shillings and 5 pence and 5 acres of meadow and 10 acres of pasture. Wood(land) 5 furlongs long and 3 furlongs broad. It was formerly worth 8 pounds. Now 6 pounds.

Norman holds of T[urstin] WANDESTREU [Wanstrow]. Alwold held (it) T.R.E. and paid geld for 5 hides. There is land for 5 ploughs. In demesne are '4 hides and' 2 ploughs and 4 serfs and (there are) 4 villeins and 4 bordars with 1 plough 'and the rest of the land.' 'There are 5 riding-horses and 6 beasts and 27 swine and 86 sheep.' There (are) 36 acres of meadow and 30 acres of pasture. Wood(land) 1 league long and half a league broad. It is worth 3 pounds. Formerly 6 pounds.

Norman holds of T[urstin] CHAIVERT [Keyford in Frome]. Levedai held (it) T.R.E. and paid geld for half a hide. There is land for half a plough which is there in demesne with 4 cottars. 'There are 7 beasts and 8 swine and 14 sheep.' There (are) 4 acres of meadow and 4 acres of pasture. It is worth 7 shillings. 'When the count received it, 5 shillings.'

Bernard 'Pancewolt' holds of T[urstin] DUNCRETONE [Dunkerton]. Alwold held (it) T.R.E. and paid geld for 3 hides. There is land for 8 ploughs. In demesne are '1½ hides and' 4 ploughs and 8 serfs and (there are) 10 villeins and 6 bordars with 4 ploughs 'and 1½ hides.' 'There are 1 riding-horse and 11 beasts and 36 swine and 212 sheep.' There is a mill paying 7 shillings and 6 pence, and 6 acres of meadow. Pasture 4 furlongs long and 2 furlongs broad. It is worth 6 pounds. It was formerly worth 100 shillings.

---

[1] Exet. Dom. : 'pariter.'
[2] 'Preter has terras additas quas superius commemoravi.'

[3] Exet. Dom. reads : '4 oxen.'

To this manor has been added 1 virgate of land, and it is worth 5 shillings. Edwi held (it) freely (*libere*)[1] T.R.E.

Robert holds of T[urstin] CIRETUNE [South (?) Cheriton]. Alwold held (it) T.R.E. and paid geld for 2 hides. There is land for 2 ploughs. In demesne are '1½ hides and' 1 plough with 1 villein and 4 bordars 'and half a hide.' There (are) 6 acres of meadow, and 1 furlong of wood(land) (reckoning) in length and breadth. It is worth 30 shillings. Formerly it was worth 40 shillings.

‹ fo. 452 ›

XXXIII. THE LAND OF SERLO DE BURCI

Serlo de Burci holds of the king BLACHE-DONE [Blagdon]. Almar held (it) T.R.E. and paid geld for 10 hides. There is land for 10 ploughs. In demesne are '7½ hides and' 2 ploughs with 1 serf and (there are) 5 villeins and 8 bordars with 5 ploughs 'and 1½ hides.' 'There are 3 beasts and 13 swine and 50 sheep and 60 she-goats.' There (are) 2 mills paying 5 shillings, and 10 acres of meadow and 200 acres of wood-(land). Pasture 1 league (reckoning) in length and breadth. When he received (it), it was worth 10 pounds. Now 7 pounds.

Of this land Lambert holds 1 hide of Serlo and there he has 2 ploughs with 2 villeins. It is worth 20 shillings. 'In demesne are 3 virgates and 1 plough, and the villeins have 1 virgate and 1 plough.'

Four knights (*milites*) hold of S[erlo] OPO-PILLE [Uphill]. Ewacre held (it) T.R.E. and paid geld for 6½ hides. There is land for 10 ploughs. In demesne are '5 hides and 3 virgates and' 4 ploughs with 1 serf and (there are) 7 villeins and 4 bordars with 3 ploughs 'and 3 virgates.' 'There are 8 beasts and 25 swine and 100 sheep.' There (are) 70 acres of meadow and 100 acres of pasture. It was and is worth 6 pounds.

S[erlo] himself holds STOCHE, 'Stocca' [Chewstoke].[2] Ewacre held (it) T.R.E. and paid geld for half a hide. There is land for 1 plough, and with 1 serf it is there in demesne, and (there are) 1½ acres of meadow. 'There are 13 beasts and 12 swine and 27 sheep and 20 she-goats.' Wood(land) 4 furlongs long and 1 furlong broad. It is worth 10 shillings.

1 Exet. Dom. reads : '*pariter.*'
2 'Stocca' may be a part of Beechenstoke, now obsolete, as in 1326 fees in Morton and 'Bytthgne-stoke' were held of Will. Fitzwilliam Martin, who succeeded to much of Serlo de Burci's holding (*Inq. p.m.* 19 Edw. II. 100).

S[erlo] himself holds CILELE [Chillyhill Farm in Chewstoke]. Ewacre held (it) T.R.E. and paid geld for 3 virgates of land. There is land for 2 ploughs which are there with 1 villein and 1 bordar and 1 serf. There are 1½ acres of meadow. It is worth 15 shillings.

To this (land) has been added STOCHE [Chewstoke]. Alvric held (it) 'in parage (*pariter*)' T.R.E. for 1 manor and paid geld for half a hide. There is land for 1 plough which is there with 2 bordars and half an acre of meadow. It is worth 10 shillings. 'When Serlo received it, 20 shillings.'

Walter holds of S[erlo] ALDUIC [Aldwick in Butcombe]. Almar 'Atter' held (it) T.R.E. and paid geld for 2 hides. There is land for 5 ploughs. In demesne are '3 virgates and' 1 plough and 2 serfs and (there are) 4 villeins and 1 bordar 'with 1 hide and 1 virgate.' 'There are 1 riding-horse and 14 beasts and 11 swine and 14 sheep.' There is a mill paying 3 shillings, and 15 acres of meadow and 49 acres of wood(land). It was formerly and is now worth 40 shillings.

fo. 98

Guntard holds of S[erlo] RAGIOL [Ridghill in Winford]. Four thegns held (it) 'in parage (*pariter*)' T.R.E. and paid geld for 2 hides. There is land for 2 ploughs. In demesne is 1 plough with 1 serf and 1 villein. 'There are 15 beasts and 6 swine and 55 sheep.' There (are) 5 acres of meadow and 5 acres of under-wood (*silvæ minutæ*). It is worth 30 shillings. 'When Serlo received it, 20 shillings.'

To this (manor) has been added 1 hide and 1 virgate of land. One thegn held (it) freely (*libere*)[3] T.R.E. There is land for 3 ploughs. Walter 'Hosed' holds (it) of Serlo and has there 1 plough and 4 serfs with 1 villein and 1 bordar. 'There are 1 riding-horse and 4 beasts and 10 swine.' There (are) 3 acres of meadow and 3 furlongs of wood(land) (reckoning) in length and breadth. Formerly (it was worth) 10 shillings. Now 30 shillings. This land did not belong to Ewacre.

The Church of St. Edward [Abbey of Shaftesbury] holds of S[erlo] CHELMETONE, 'CHILMATONA' [Kilmington] for his daughter who is there. Alsi held (it) T.R.E. There are 5 hides but he paid geld for 1 (hide). There is land for 5 ploughs. In demesne are '4 hides and 1 virgate and' 1 plough and (there are) 4 villeins and 3 bordars with 4 ploughs 'and 3 virgates.' 'There are 14 beasts and 15 swine and 137

3 Exet. Dom. reads : '*pariter.*'

sheep.' There (is) 1 league of wood(land) in length and 3 furlongs broad. Formerly (it was worth) 30 shillings. Now 40 shillings.

S[erlo] himself holds LOVINTUNE [Lovington]. Three thegns 'Aelmar, and Siric, and a woman Alsille' held (it) 'in parage (*pariter*)' T.R.E. for 3 manors and paid geld for 6 hides. There is land for 8 ploughs. In demesne are '3 hides less 5 acres and' 2 ploughs and 2 serfs and (there are) 8 villeins and 9 bordars with 6 ploughs 'and 2 hides and 5 acres.' 'There are 16 beasts and 1 riding-horse and 11 swine and 80 sheep.' There is a mill paying 10 shillings and 40 acres of meadow. Wood(land) 4 furlongs long and 2 furlongs broad. Formerly (it was worth) 6 pounds. Now 100 shillings.

Of this land Lambert holds 1 hide and has there 1 plough with 3 villeins.[1] 'There are 2 swine.' There (are) 12 acres of meadow. It is worth 20 shillings.

+ Serlo himself holds WATEHELLE [Wheathill]. Elmer held (it) T.R.E. of the Church of Glastingberie, nor could he be separated from it, and he paid geld for 3 hides. There is land for 4 ploughs. In demesne are '2 hides and' 1 plough with 1 serf and 1 bordar. Formerly (it was worth) 40 shillings. Now 40[2] shillings.

Of this land Geoffrey holds 1 hide and it is worth 10 shillings.

S[erlo] himself holds CONTONE [Compton Martin]. Ewacre held (it) T.R.E. and paid geld for 5 hides. There is land for 5 ploughs. In demesne are '2 hides and 3 virgates and' 2 ploughs and 2 serfs and (there are) 5 villeins and 6 cottars and 5 bordars with 4 ploughs 'and 1 hide and 3 virgates.' 'There are 6 beasts and 7 swine and 17 sheep and 9 she-goats.' There are 15 acres of meadow and 1 league of pasture in length and 2 furlongs broad. Wood(land) 11 furlongs long and 9 furlongs broad. Formerly (it was worth) 100 shillings. Now 4 pounds.

Of this land Richard holds of S[erlo] 1 virgate and 1 ferling of land,[3] and has there 1 plough with 2 bordars and 5 acres of meadow. 'There are 12 beasts and 10 swine and 30 she-goats.' Formerly (it was worth) 5 shillings. Now 15 shillings.

S[erlo] himself holds MORTONE, 'MOR-

THONA' [Morton in Compton Martin]. Three thegns, 'Alvric, Aelric and Alwic,' held (it) 'in parage (*pariter*)' for 3 manors T.R.E. and paid geld for 5 hides. There (is) land for 5 ploughs. Godric holds 2 hides of this land and Elric (holds) 2 hides. In demesne are '3 hides and' 2 ploughs and (there are) 9 villeins and 11 bordars with 2 ploughs 'and 1 hide and 2 cottars. There are 19 beasts and 40 sheep.' There is a mill paying 5 shillings, and 40 acres of meadow and 15 acres of wood(land). Its value formerly and now is 3 pounds.

Of this land Richard holds 3 virgates of land and Humphrey (holds) 1 virgate of land. There is 1 plough 'and 2½ virgates in demesne' and (there are) 2 villeins and 3 bordars 'with 1½ virgates' and 18 acres of meadow and 4 acres of wood(land) and 2 acres of pasture. It was formerly and is now worth 15 shillings.[4]

Reynold holds of S[erlo] MUDIFORD [Mudford]. Elmar 'Atter' held (it) T.R.E. and paid geld for 3 hides. There is land for 3 ploughs. In demesne 'are 1½ hides and' 1½ ploughs and (there are) 3 villeins and 4 bordars with 2 ploughs 'and 1½ hides.' 'There are 3 beasts and 8 swine and 26 sheep.' Its value formerly and now is 3 pounds.

To this manor has been added STANE [Stone in Mudford]. Sared held it freely (*libere*) for a manor T.R.E. and paid geld for 2 hides. There is land for 1½ ploughs. 'There are 10 sheep.' It was formerly and is now worth 10 shillings.

'fo. 380'

XXXIIII. THE LAND OF ODO SON OF GAMELIN

Odo son of Gamelin holds of the king LOCUMBE [Luccombe] and Vital (holds it) of him. Fitel held (it) T.R.E. and paid geld for 1 hide. There is land for 6 ploughs. In demesne are 'half a hide and' 1 plough and 2 serfs and (there are) 8 villeins and 1 bordar with 2½ ploughs 'and half a hide.' 'There are 2 acres of meadow and 12 acres of wood(land) and 50 acres of pasture.' Its value formerly and now is 40 shillings.

'fo. 447'

XXXV. THE LAND OF OSBERN GIFARD

Osbern Gifard holds of the king CANOLE [Knowle in Bedminster]. Alnod 'Staller'

---

[1] Exet. Dom. adds : 'in demesne half a hide and half a plough, and the villeins have half a hide and half a plough.'

[2] Exet. Dom. reads : '30.'

[3] Exet. Dom. adds : 'the bordars have 1 ferling.'

[4] Exet. Dom. gives details of each holding.

held (it) T.R.E. and paid geld for 2 hides. There is land for 3 ploughs. In demesne are ' 1 hide and ' 1 plough and (there are) 5 villeins and 6 bordars with 2 ploughs 'and 1 hide.' 'There are 1 riding-horse and 8 beasts and 25 swine.' There (are) 16 acres of meadow and 20 acres of pasture. Wood(land) 2½ furlongs long and 1½ furlongs broad. Formerly (it was worth) 30 shillings. Now it is worth 40 shillings.

O[sbern] himself holds TELVVE [1] [Elm]. Donno held (it) T.R.E. and paid geld for 5 hides. There is land for 4 ploughs. In demesne are ' 4 hides and 1 virgate and ' 1 plough and 2 serfs and (there are) 3 villeins and 4 bordars with 3 ploughs 'and 3 virgates.' 'There are 1 riding-horse and 15 beasts and 16 swine and 250 sheep and 30 she-goats.' There are 2 mills paying 100 pence, and 14 acres of meadow and 16 acres of underwood (*silvæ minutæ*) and 14 acres of pasture. Formerly (it was worth) 3 pounds. Now 4 pounds.

O[sbern] himself holds UDEBERGE [Woodborough in Wellow]. Donno held (it) T.R.E. and paid geld for 1 hide. There is land for 2 ploughs. In demesne is 1 plough and 6 bordars with 1 serf 'who have half a virgate,' and 8 acres of meadow. 'There are 1 cow and 150 sheep.' Formerly (it was worth) 30 shillings. Now 40 shillings.

' fo. 437 '

XXXVI. THE LAND OF EDWARD OF SALISBURY.[2]

Edward of Salisbury holds of the king HANTONE [Hinton Charterhouse]. Ulwen held (it) T.R.E. and paid geld for 10 hides. There is land for 10 ploughs. In demesne are ' 5 hides and ' 3 ploughs and 9 serfs and (there are) 12 villeins and 15 bordars with 6 ploughs 'and 5 hides.' 'There are 3 riding-horses and 40 beasts and 250 sheep and 40 swine and 60 she-goats.' There are 2 mills paying 34 shillings, and 12 acres of meadow. Wood(land) 1 league long and half a league broad.

In BADE [Bath] are 2 houses, one paying 7 pennies and 1 halfpenny.[3] Formerly (it was worth) 10 pounds. Now it is worth 12 pounds.

[1] Exet. Dom. *rectius* : 'TELMA.'
[2] Exet. Dom. designates him throughout : ' *Vicecomes.*'
[3] Exet. Dom. reads : ' 1 domus in Bada quæ reddit per annum vii denarios et 1 obolum et alia mansura in eodem burdo vacua.'

E[dward] himself holds NORTUNE [Norton St. Philip]. Iving held (it) T.R.E. and paid geld for 10 hides. There is land for 10 ploughs. In demesne are ' 5 hides and half a virgate and ' 3 ploughs and 3 serfs and (there are) 3 villeins and 13 bordars with 3 ploughs 'and 5 hides less half a virgate.' 'There are 2 riding-horses and 20 beasts and 28 swine and 240 sheep.' There is a mill paying 5 shillings, and 20 acres of meadow and as much pasture. Wood(land) 1 league long and as much broad. Formerly (it was worth) 6 pounds. Now 7 pounds. Of these 10 hides King E[dward] gave to the aforesaid Iving 2 carucates of land.

' fo. 448b '

XXXVII. THE LAND OF ERNULF DE HESDING

Ernulf de Hesding holds of the king WESTONE [Weston near Bath]. Edric held (it) T.R.E. and paid geld for 5 hides. There is land for 7 ploughs. In demesne are ' 4 hides less half a virgate and 3 acres, and ' 2 ploughs and 10 serfs and (there are) 6 villeins and 1 bordar with 3 ploughs 'and 1 hide and half a virgate and 3 acres.' 'There are 6 riding-horses and 8 beasts and 16 swine and 250 sheep.' There is a mill paying 20 shillings, and 13 acres of meadow and 60 acres of pasture and 30 acres of wood(land). In BADE [Bath] (are) 3 houses paying 27 pence. Altogether formerly and now it is worth 8 pounds.

Engeler holds of Ern[ulf] TICHEHAM [Tickenham]. Edric held (it) T.R.E. and paid geld for 1 hide and 3 virgates of land. There is land for 3 ploughs. 'There are 5 virgates in demesne and ' there are 3 villeins and 1 bordar 'who have half a hide' and 1 serf and 6 acres of meadow. 'There are 2 beasts and 1 swine and 3 sheep.' Wood(land) 3 furlongs long and 1 furlong broad. It is worth 40 shillings. 'When he received it, 60 shillings.'

Engelram holds of Er[nulf] REDDENE [Rodden]. Edric held (it) T.R.E. and paid geld for 1 hide. There is land for 3 ploughs, which are there in demesne 'with half a hide' and 3 serfs and 28 bordars 'with half a hide.' 'There are 1 riding-horse and 20 beasts and 50 swine and 300 sheep.' There are 2 mills paying 15 shillings, and 20 acres of meadow and 30 acres of pasture. Wood(land) 1 league long and as much broad. Formerly and now it is worth 4 pounds.

'fo. 446'

XXXVIII. THE LAND OF GILBERT SON OF TUROLD

Gilbert son of Turold holds of the king CHIWESTOCH [Chewstoke] and Osbern (holds it) of him. Edric held (it) T.R.E. and paid geld for 1½ hides. There is land for 2 ploughs, which are there in demesne and 2 serfs and (there are) 2 bordars and 20 acres of meadow and 10 acres of underwood (*silvæ minutæ*). 'There are 5 unbroken mares and 18 beasts and 30 swine and 18 sheep and 15 she-goats.' Formerly (it was worth) 20 shillings. Now it is worth 30 shillings.

Walter holds of G[ilbert] TUMBELI[1] [Ubley]. Edric held (it) T.R.E. and paid geld for 5 hides. There is land for 5 ploughs. In demesne are '3 hides and 1 virgate and' 1 plough and 2 serfs and (there are) 5 villeins and 4 bordars and 4 cottars (*coscez*) with 3 ploughs 'and the rest of the land.' 'There are 5 beasts and 14 swine.' There is a mill paying 30 pence, and 35 acres of meadow. Pasture 1 league long and half a league broad, and as much wood(land). When he received (it), it was worth 100 shillings. Now as much.

The same [Walter] holds ESTONE [Stone Easton]. Edric held (it) T.R.E. and paid geld for 1 hide.[2] There is land for 1 plough which is there with 3 bordars. It pays 30 shillings.

'fo. 473b'

XXXIX. THE LAND OF GODE-BOLD

Godebold holds of the king CARME [Quarme in Winsford]. Albricht held it T.R.E. and paid geld for 3 virgates of land. There is land for 3 ploughs. In demesne are '2 virgates and' 1 plough with 1 serf and (there are) 3 villeins with 1 bordar 'and 1 virgate.' There (are) 3 acres of meadow and 50 acres of pasture. Formerly (it was worth) 20 shillings. Now it is worth 10 shillings.

'fo. 450'

XL. THE LAND OF MATTHEW DE MORETANIA

Matthew holds of the king CLIVEDONE [Clevedon] and Ildebert (holds it) of him. John 'the Dane' held (it) T.R.E. and paid

geld for 5½ hides and 2 ferlings. There is land for 6 ploughs. In demesne are '2 hides and' 2 ploughs with 1 serf and (there are) 8 villeins and 10 bordars with 4 ploughs 'and 3½ hides.' 'There are 7 unbroken mares (*equæ indomitæ*) and 1 riding-horse and 22 beasts and 25 swine and 115 sheep.' There (are) 46 acres of meadow. Pasture 1½ leagues long and as much broad. Wood(land) 2 furlongs long and half a furlong broad. Formerly (it was worth) 40 shillings. Now it is worth 4 pounds.

Rumald holds of M[atthew] CALVICHE [Chelvey]. Torchil held (it) T.R.E. and paid geld for 1 hide. There is land for 3 ploughs. In demesne are '1 virgate and' 1 plough and 2 serfs and (there are) 3 villeins and 4 bordars with 2 ploughs 'and 3 virgates.' 'There are 6 swine.' There (are) 6 acres of underwood (*silvæ minutæ*). Formerly and now (it is worth) 40 shillings.

From this manor has been taken away 1 virgate of land which Turchil held with the aforesaid land. The Bishop of Coutances holds (it).

Ildebert holds of M[atthew] MIDELTUNE [Milton Clevedon]. Ulward, 'Tumbi,' held (it) T.R.E. and paid geld for 10 hides. There is land for 6 ploughs. In demesne are '5 hides and' 2 ploughs and 4 serfs and (there are) 9 villeins and 9 bordars with 3 ploughs 'and 5 hides.' 'There is 1 riding-horse and 10 beasts and 18 swine and 160 sheep and 40 she-goats.' There is a mill paying 5 shillings, and 24 acres of meadow. Wood(land) 10 furlongs (reckoning) length and breadth. When he received (it), it was worth 100 shillings. Now 6 pounds.

fo. 98b. 'fo. 479b'

XLV. THE LAND OF HUMFREY[3]

Humphrey the chamberlain holds of the king CURI, 'CARI' [Lytes Cary in Charlton Mackrell]. 'Two brothers,' Ordric and Living, held (it) 'in parage (*pariter*)' T.R.E. and paid geld for 1 hide and 1 ferling. There is land for 1 plough which is there in demesne with 1 bordar and 2 cottars 'who have 7 acres

---

[1] Tumbeli. The first letter is a phonetic affix as in 'Telme' for Elm, and 'Tetesberge' for Adsborough. 'Ubbeli' appears in 1212 (*Ped. Fin.* 14 John III. *S.R.S.* vi. 28).

[2] Exet. Dom. reads : ' 1½ hides.'

[3] The number of the heading is corrected at this point.

This heading is misleading, as only the first two entries refer to him. In the margin of the Exchequer Domesday at this point is a *, with a similar mark on the next leaf at the heading ' Land of Humphrey and others.' In the Exeter Domesday the heading of XLV. is ' Lands of the King's serjeants in Somerset.'

of land.' 'There are 12 beasts and 100 sheep.' There (are) 20 acres of meadow. Formerly (it was worth) 20 shillings. Now it is worth 40 shillings. This land has been added to the lands of Brictric but the two (thegns) who held (it) T.R.E. could go where they liked.[1]

The same H[umphrey] holds CURI[2] [perhaps Tuckerscary in Charlton Mackrell]. Leving held (it) 'in parage (*pariter*)' T.R.E. and paid geld for 2 hides. There is land for 3 ploughs. In demesne are '1 hide and 1 virgate and' 2 ploughs and (there are) 3 villeins and 3 bordars with 1 plough 'and the rest of the land.' There (are) 24 acres of meadow. Formerly (it was worth) 30 shillings. Now it is worth 40 shillings; and this (land) has been joined to the lands of Brictric, but they who held them T.R.E. could go where they liked.

XLVI. Robert de Odburville holds of the king in WARNE [Wearne in Huish Episcopi] 2½ virgates of land which never paid geld. There is land for half a plough. There is 1 bordar with 1 serf. 'There are 4 beasts and 15 sheep.' It is worth 15 shillings. It was waste when he received it (*vastam accepit*).

'fo. 478b'
This Robert had 1 virgate of land which Dodo held freely 'in parage (*pariter*)' T.R.E. This has been added to DOLVERTONE [Dulverton] the king's manor. Now it has 'again' been decided to be (*dijudicata est*) thegn-land. It is worth 10 shillings.[3]

The same Robert holds half a hide in WIDEPOLLE [Withypool]. Three foresters 'Dodo, Almar and Godric' held (it) 'in parage (*pariter*)' T.R.E. There is land for 4 ploughs. From this (land) Robert used to pay 20 shillings to the king's ferm at WINESFORD [Winsford]. Now it has been declared (*diratiocinata est*) to be thegn-land.

The same Robert holds WILESFORDE, 'WELESFORDA' [Wellisford in Langford Budville]. Two thegns, 'Edric and Bruninc,' held (it) 'in parage (*pariter*)' T.R.E. and paid geld for 1 hide. There is land for 2 ploughs. In demesne are 'half a hide and' 1 plough and 2 serfs and (there are) 8 bordars owning 1 plough 'and 1 virgate.' 'There are 1

riding-horse and 18 beasts and 3 swine and 17 sheep.' There (are) 4 acres of meadow and 10 acres of pasture and 3 acres of underwood (*silvæ minutæ*). Formerly (it was worth) 10 shillings. Now it is worth 15 shillings. Of this hide the Count of Mortain holds 1 virgate and Bretel (holds it) of him.

'fo. 477b'
The same Robert holds MELECOME [Melcombe in North Petherton]. Saric held (it) T.R.E. and paid geld for 1½ virgates of land. There is land for 1½ ploughs, and they are there with 10 bordars. 'There are 3 cows and 40 sheep.' There (is) a mill paying 12 pence, and 10 acres of underwood (*silvæ minutæ*). Formerly and now it is worth 15 shillings.

From this manor has been taken away half a hide which T.R.E. belonged there. Walter (*Walscin*) de Dowai holds (it) with his manor of BUR [West Bower].

John the Usher (*Hostiarius*) holds of the king PEGENS, 'PEGHENES' [Horsey Pignes in Bridgwater]. Brictric held (it) T.R.E. and paid geld for 1 hide and 1 virgate of land. There is land for 2 ploughs. In demesne are 'half a hide and' 1 plough and (there are) 2 villeins with 1 bordar 'and half a virgate.' 'There are 8 beasts and 10 swine.' There is a priest[4] with 1 plough and 2 bordars 'and half a hide and 6 beasts and 6 swine and 33 sheep and it is worth 15 shillings.' There are 5 acres of meadow. Formerly (it was worth) 40 shillings. Now it is worth 30 shillings.[5]

The same John holds PERI [Perry Furneaux in Wembdon] 'and Robert holds it of him.' Orgar held (it) T.R.E. and paid geld for half a hide and half a virgate of land and half a ferling. There is land for 1 plough which is there; 'in demesne are 1 virgate and 1 ferling and half a plough,' and 2 villeins and 2 bordars 'have half a plough and the rest of the land.' There (are) 5 acres of meadow. Formerly (it was worth) 10 shillings. Now it is worth 15 shillings.

Stable holds of John NEWETUNE [North Newton]. Samar held (it) T.R.E. and paid geld for half a hide. There is land for 1 plough which is there with 1 virgate 'in demesne' and with 2 villeins and 2 bordars 'who have 1 virgate' and 3 serfs. 'There are 10 sheep and 10 she-goats.' There (are)

---

[1] This last par. in Exet. Dom. runs: 'potuerunt ire adquemlibet dominum.'

[2] Exet. Dom. *rectius*: 'Cari.'

[3] This paragraph is entered in the margin.

[4] Exet. Dom. reads: 'sacerdos de ecclesia istius villæ.'

[5] Including the priest's share.

5 acres of meadow and 5 acres of wood(land). Formerly (it was worth) 10 shillings. Now it is worth 15 shillings.

'fo. 478'
Robert holds of John CANDETONE [Cannington]. Semar held (it) T.R.E. and paid geld for half a hide. There is land for 1 plough which is there in demesne 'with 1½ virgates and' with 1 villein and 4 bordars[1] 'with half a virgate.' 'There are 4 beasts and 1 swine and 40 sheep and 24 she-goats.' There is a mill paying 5 shillings, and 23 acres of meadow and 6 acres of pasture. Formerly it was worth 15 shillings. Now it is worth 20 shillings.

John himself holds WINCHEBERIE, 'WINCHINBERIA' [Wigborough in South Petherton]. Alward held (it) T.R.E. and paid geld for 2 hides. There is land for 1½ ploughs and they are there with 2 villeins and 3 bordars 'who have 1½ virgates and 1 ferling and half a plough.' 'In demesne are 1 plough and 1½ hides and 1 ferling. There are 2 cows.' There (are) 8 acres of meadow. Formerly (it was worth) 20 shillings. Now 30 shillings.

'fo. 479'
John himself holds HUSTILLE [Huntstile, now in Goathurst]. Alward held (it) T.R.E. and paid geld for 1 virgate of land. There is land for 2 ploughs which are there with 'half a virgate in demesne and' 3 villeins and 4 bordars 'who have half a virgate and 1 plough.' 'There are 4 swine.' There (are) 10 acres of pasture. Formerly it was worth 10 shillings. Now it is worth 20 shillings.
Of this land half a virgate and 1 ferling T.R.E. belonged to 'the king's manor of' SVMERTONE [Somerton]. It is worth 5 shillings.

'fo. 477b'
Ansger Fower[2] holds of the king CILDETONE [Chilton Trinity]. Alwin held (it) T.R.E. and paid geld for 1 virgate of land. There is land for 1 plough which is there with '3 ferlings in demesne and' 1 villein 'who has 1 ferling and half the plough' and 1 serf. 'There are 3 cows.' There are 14 acres of meadow and 5 acres of pasture. Formerly (it was worth) 5 shillings. Now it is worth 15 shillings.

The same A[nsger] holds MICHAELISCERCE

[1] Exet. Dom. adds : 'who have 2 ploughing oxen.'
[2] Exet. Dom. : 'focarius.'

[St. Michaelchurch]. Alwi held (it) T.R.E. and paid geld for half a hide. There is land for 1 plough. Formerly and now it is worth 5 shillings.

The same A[nsger] holds SIWOLDESTONE [Sheerston in North Petherton]. Two thegns held (it) freely 'in parage (pariter)' T.R.E. and paid geld for 1 virgate of land. There is land for half a plough. Formerly and now it is worth 4 shillings.

'fo. 479'
The same [Ansger] holds DERLEGE [Durleigh]. Alsi held (it) T.R.E. and paid geld for 2½ virgates of land and 1 ferling. There is land for 3 ploughs which are there ; 'half a hide less 1 ferling and 1 plough are in demesne,' 4 villeins and 2 bordars and 3 serfs 'have 2 ploughs and the rest of the land.' There (are) 20 acres of wood(land). Formerly and now it is worth 20 shillings.

'fo. 478b'
Ansger the cook (coquus) holds of the king LULESTOCH [Lilstock]. Bricsic held it T.R.E. and paid geld for 5 hides. There is land [   ]. In demesne are '2½ hides and' 3 ploughs and 2 serfs and (there are) 11 villeins and 7 bordars 'with 1 hide and 3 ferlings,' and 20 acres of wood(land) in one place and in another wood(land) 1 league long and half a league broad. 'There is 1 cow and 25 swine and 10 sheep.' Formerly and now it is worth 100 shillings.

'fo. 477b'
Anschitil Parcher ('parcarius') holds of the king NEWETUNE [North Newton]. Osward held (it) T.R.E. and paid geld for 1 hide and 1 virgate of land. There is land for 3 ploughs which are there with '1 hide in demesne and' 8 bordars 'who have 1 virgate and 2 ploughs.' There (are) 15 acres of meadow and 20 acres of moor and 10 acres of wood(land). Formerly (it was worth) 40 shillings. Now it is worth 30 (shillings).

The same A[nschitil] holds HERDENEBERIE, 'HEDERNEBERIA' [perhaps Honibere in Lilstock]. Alvric held (it) T.R.E. and paid geld for 1 hide. There is land for 2 ploughs. There are 3 bordars with 1 serf, and 60 acres of pasture. Formerly (it was worth) 20 shillings. Now it is worth 5 shillings.

'fo. 479'
The same A[nschitil] holds MIDELTONE [perhaps part of Milton in Kewstoke]. Osward held (it) T.R.E. and paid geld for 1 hide. There is land for 1 plough which is

there with ' 3½ virgates in demesne and ' 1 villein and 2 serfs ' who have half the plough and half a virgate.' There (are) 6 acres of meadow and 2 acres of under(wood) and 20 acres of pasture. Formerly and now it is worth 15 shillings. ' Alward holds it of Anschitil.'

' fo. 478b '

Girard holds ERNESEL [Earnshill]. Leving held (it) T.R.E. and paid geld for 1 hide of land. There is land for 1 plough. There are 1 bordar and 2 serfs and 6 acres of meadow and 10 acres of wood(land). Formerly and now it is worth 30 shillings.

' fo. 480

Edmund son of Payn holds BERTUNE [Barton St. David] of the king. Jadulf held (it) T.R.E. and paid geld for 3½ hides. There is land for 6 ploughs. In demesne are ' 3 hides and 1 virgate and ' 1 plough with 1 serf and (there are) 2 villeins and 4 bordars and 6 cottars ' with 1 virgate.' ' There are 5 beasts and 4 swine.' There is a mill paying 10 shillings, and 50 acres of meadow and 60 acres of pasture. Formerly (it was worth) 6 pounds. Now 3 pounds.

From this manor has been taken away 1 hide which Mauger de Cartrai holds.

The same E[dmund] holds PICOTE [Pitcot in Stratton-on-the-Fosse]. Jadulf held (it) T.R.E. and paid geld for 3½ hides. There is land for 4 ploughs. In demesne are ' 2½ hides and ' 2 ploughs and 2 serfs and (there are) 3 villeins and 8 bordars with 2 ploughs. ' There are 1 riding-horse and 9 beasts and 45 sheep.' There is a mill paying 50 pence. There (are) 8 acres of meadow and 12 acres of pasture and 50 acres of wood(land). Formerly and now it is worth 4 pounds.

The same E[dmund] holds WALTUNE [Walton in Kilmersdon]. Elmar held (it) T.R.E. and paid geld for 3 hides. There is land for 4 ploughs. In demesne is ' all the land except 1 virgate and ' 1 plough and (there are) 1 villein and 6 bordars with 1½ ploughs ' and one virgate.' ' There are 15 sheep.' There are 6 acres of meadow and 40 acres of pasture. Underwood 1 furlong (reckoning) in length and breadth. Formerly (it was worth) 4 pounds. Now 40 shillings.

The wife of Manasses the cook (coquus) holds HAIA [Hay Street in Stone Easton]. Edric held (it) T.R.E. and paid geld for 2 hides. There is land for 2 ploughs. There are 2 bordars with 1 cottar and 6 acres of meadow and 12 acres of pasture. Formerly (it was worth) 20 shillings. Now it is worth 15 shillings.

The same [i.e. Manasses' wife] holds ESTONE [Stone Easton]. Aldwin held (it) T.R.E. and paid geld for 1 hide and 1 virgate of land. There is land for 2 ploughs which are there in demesne ' with 1 hide and ' with 1 villein and 3 bordars and 1 cottar ' who have 1 virgate.' There are 8 acres of meadow and 6 acres of pasture. Formerly and now it is worth 20 shillings.

' fo. 490 '

XLVII. THE LAND OF THE KING'S THEGNS.[1]

Brictric and Ulward hold of the king BOCHELANDE [Buckland St. Mary]. They also (idem ipsi) held (it) T.R.E. ' in parage (pariter) ' and paid geld for 1½ hides. There is land for 3 ploughs. In demesne are 2 ploughs and (there are) 2 villeins and 4 bordars. It is worth 20 shillings.

They held this land of Bishop Peter while he lived, and paid him 10 shillings. Now they hold (it) of the king, but since the bishop's death the king has had nothing from it.

Of this land the wife of Bolle held 3[2] virgates T.R.E.

Siward holds SEVENEMETONE [Seavington St. Michael]. T.R.E. it paid geld for 3 hides. There is land for 3 ploughs. In demesne are ' 2 hides and 3 virgates and ' 1 plough and 2 villeins and 3 bordars ' who have the rest of the land ' and 2 serfs and 8 acres of meadow. ' There are 1 riding-horse and 2 beasts and 10 swine and 120 sheep.' It is worth 3 pounds.

Harding son of Alnod holds LOPEN [Lopen] Tovi ' the sheriff ' held (it) T.R.E. and paid geld for 2 hides. There is land for 2 ploughs. In demesne are ' 1½ hides and 3 ferlings and ' 1 plough and 2 serfs and (there are) 2 villein. and 5 bordars ' with 1 virgate and 1 ferling ' and 20 acres of meadow. ' There are 1 riding-horse and 7 beasts and 10 swine and 150 sheep.' Formerly (it was worth) 20 shillings. Now it is worth 40 shillings.

' fo. 491b '

Harding holds BRADE [Goose Bradon]. Tovi held (it) T.R.E. and paid geld for 1 hide. There is land for 2 ploughs. ' Celric holds it of Harding and has 3 virgates and ' 1 plough

---

[1] Exet. Dom.: ' ANGLORUM TEGNORUM.'
[2] Exet. Dom. reads vi. for iii.

in demesne with 1 villein 'who has 1 virgate.' 'There are 50 sheep.' Formerly (it was worth) 20 shillings. Now 10 shillings.

The same [Harding] holds CAPILANDE [Capland in Hatch Beauchamp]. Tovi held (it) T.R.E. and paid geld for 1 hide. There is land for 2 ploughs. In demesne is 1 plough with 1 bordar and 1 serf· and 6 acres of meadow and 30 acres of wood(land). 'There are 3 beasts and 1 pig.' Formerly (it was worth) 5 shillings. Now it is worth 20 shillings.

To this manor has been added half a hide which belonged to (*fuit de*) CURI [Curry Rivel] the king's manor. It is worth 5 [1] shillings. 'When he received it, it was waste.'

The same [Harding] holds MERIET [Merriott]. Godwin held (it) T.R.E. and paid geld for 5 hides. There is land for 6 ploughs. In demesne are '2½ hides and' 2 ploughs and 2 serfs and (there are) 9 villeins and 6 bordars with 2 ploughs 'and the rest of the land.' 'There is 1 riding-horse.' There (is) a mill paying 5 shillings, and 10 acres of meadow and 3 furlongs of pasture. Formerly (it was worth) 100 shillings. Now it is worth 4 pounds.

Harding holds BOCHELAND [Buckland St. Mary]. Tovi held (it) T.R.E. and paid geld for 1 hide. There is land for 4 ploughs. 'Godwin holds it of Harding and has half a hide in demesne; and his villeins have half a hide. There are 6 beasts and 10 sheep and 20 she-goats.' There are 3 acres of meadow and 10 furlongs of pasture in

fo. 99

length and 4 in breadth. Wood(land) 2 furlongs long and 1 broad. Formerly (it was worth) 40 shillings. Now it is worth 10 shillings.

'fo. 493'
Harding holds DINESCOVE, 'DIGENESCOVA' [Discove in Bruton]. Tovi held (it) T.R.E. and paid geld for 1 hide. There is land for 3 ploughs. In demesne are '1½ virgates and' 2 ploughs with 3 villeins 'who have 2½ virgates and half a plough.' 'There is 1 riding-horse and 28 swine and 71 sheep.' There (are) 8 acres of meadow and 3 furlongs of pasture (reckoning) in length and breadth. Formerly and now it is worth 40 shillings.

'fo. 490b'
Brictric holds TOCHESWELLE [Tuxwell in Spaxton]. Godwin held (it) T.R.E. There

<hr/>

is half a virgate of land and it did not pay geld T.R.E. There is land for 1 plough. 'In demesne is half a plough and' there are 4 bordars with 1 serf. 'There are 4 acres of wood(land) and 7 acres of pasture.' Formerly and now it is worth 12 shillings and 6 pence.

Siward 'the falconer (*accipitrarius*)' holds DUNINTONE [Dinnington]. Edmar held (it) T.R.E. and paid geld for 3 hides. There is land for 3 ploughs, which are there with 6 villeins and 3 bordars. 'In demesne are 2 hides and 1 plough and the villeins have 1 hide and 2 ploughs.' There (is) a mill paying 8 pence, and 8 acres of meadow. Pasture 3 furlongs long and 2 furlongs broad. Wood(land) 3 furlongs long and 2 furlongs broad. Formerly (it was worth) 20 shillings. Now it is worth 40 (shillings).

'fo. 493b'
Siward 'the Hundred-man (*Hundrannus*)' holds ETTEBERE, 'EATTEBERA' [Adber in Trent]. He also (*idem ipse*) held (it) T.R.E. and paid geld for 1 hide. There is land for 1½ ploughs and they are there with 2 villeins and 3 bordars. 'In demesne are half a hide and 1 plough, and the villeins have half a hide and half a plough.' 'There are 7 beasts and 13 swine and 62 sheep.' There (are) 6 acres of meadow and 1 furlong of wood(land), (reckoning) in length and breadth. Formerly and now it is worth 20 shillings.

'fo. 491'
Dodo holds 'a manor in the hundred of Wellintuna [2] called' STAWE [Nether Stowey]. Siwold held (it) T.R.E. and paid geld for 3 virgates of land. There is land for 3 ploughs. In demesne is '1 virgate and' 1 plough and 3 serfs and 6 villeins and 2 bordars, and a mill which pays no rent (*sine censu*) [3] and 5 acres of meadow and 30 acres of pasture and 3 acres of wood(land). Formerly and now it is worth 20 shillings.

Ulf holds HAUECHEWELLE [Hawkwell in Dulverton]. He also (*idem ipse*) held (it) T.R.E. and paid geld for 1 virgate of land and 1 ferling and the fourth part of 1 ferling. There is land for 3 ploughs. 'Of this land Ulmar an Englishman holds 1¼ ferlings

<hr/>

[2] Although Wellington does seem to have given name to a Hundred (Eyton, *Som. Dom.* ii. 10), at this period it belonged to Bishop Giso's land, and afterwards to Kingsbury West, so it is probably a slip for Williton.

[3] Exet. Dom. reads : ' qui molit annonam suam.'

[1] Exet. Dom. reads : ' 6.'

' in parage (*pariter*).' Ulf has 1 ferling and 1 plough, the villeins have 1 plough, and Ulmar has 1 plough.' There are 3 ploughs with 1 serf and (there are) 3 villeins and 4 bordars. 'There are 4 beasts and 30 sheep and 40 she-goats.' It is worth 25 shillings.

Alward and his brothers hold STOCHE [Chewstoke]. Their father held (it) T.R.E. and paid geld for 3 hides. There is land for 2 ploughs which are there in demesne 'with 2½ hides and half a virgate and' with 1 villein and 1 serf and 13 bordars 'who have the rest of the land and half a plough. 'There is 1 riding-horse and 6 beasts and 5 swine and 17 sheep.' There (are) 15 acres of meadow and 8 acres of pasture. Formerly (it was worth) 60 shillings. Now it is worth 50 shillings.

'fo. 492'

GODWIN 'an Englishman' holds DRAICOTE [Draycott near Cheddar]. He and his mother held (it) T.R.E. and they were assessed (*defendebant se*)[1] for 1 virgate of land. There is land for half a plough. 'There he has 2 oxen.' It pays 2 shillings yearly.

Aldvi holds STOCHE [Chewstoke]. He also held (it) T.R.E. and paid geld for 1 hide and 3 virgates of land. There is land for 2 ploughs. There are 3 bordars and 2 serfs with 1 plough. There is a mill paying 6 shillings and 8 pence, and 6 acres of meadow. Pasture 5 furlongs long and 2 furlongs broad. Wood(land) 3 furlongs long and 2 furlongs broad. 'In demesne are 1 hide and 1 virgate, and there are 3 villeins who have 3 virgates and 1 plough, and 2 beasts and 2 swine and 8 sheep. It is worth 25 shillings.

Brismar 'an Englishman' holds HALBERGE [Haselbury Plucknett]. He also (*idem ipse*) held (it) T.R.E. and paid geld for 10 hides. There is land for 8 ploughs. In demesne are '5 hides and' 1 plough and 2 serfs and (there are) 8 villeins and 16 bordars with 5 ploughs 'and 5 hides.' 'There is 1 riding-horse and 8 beasts and 7 swine.' There is a mill paying 5 shillings, and 13½ acres of meadow and half a league of pasture (reckoning) in length and breadth, and as much wood(land). It is worth 8 pounds.

Alverd holds WICHE [Bathwick]. He also (*idem ipse*) held (it) T.R.E. and paid geld for 2 hides. There is land for 3 ploughs which are there with 2 villeins and 6 bordars and 3 serfs. 'In demesne are 1 hide and 2

[1] The sole instance of this formula in the county.

ploughs, and the villeins have 1 hide and 1 plough. There are 1 riding-horse and 8 swine and 60 sheep.' There is a mill paying 5 shillings, and 5 acres of meadow and 10 acres of thicket (*spinetum*). It is worth 40 shillings.

Donno holds BOCHELANDE [Buckland Dinham]. He also (*idem ipse*) held (it) T.R.E. and paid geld for 12 hides. There is land for 7 ploughs. 'In demesne are 8½ hides and 1 plough and the villeins have 3½ hides and 4 ploughs.' There are 5 ploughs and 11 villeins and 5 bordars and 7 serfs and 40 acres of meadow and 30 acres of underwood and half a league of pasture in length and 1½ furlongs in breadth, and a mill paying 7 shillings. 'In demesne are 8½ hides and 1 plough, and there are 2 beasts and 8 swine and 12 sheep.' Formerly (it was worth) 8 pounds. Now it is worth 100 shillings.

Agelric holds CVME [Combe Hawey]. Queen Edith (*Eddid*) held it T.R.E. and paid geld for 2 hides. There is land for 5 ploughs, which are there and 6 villeins and 5 bordars and 3 serfs. 'In demesne are 1 hide and 1 plough and the villeins have 1 hide and 4 ploughs, and there are 1 riding-horse and 3 beasts and 7 swine and 126 sheep.' There is a mill paying 50 pence, and 8 acres of meadow and 20 acres of wood(land). Formerly (it was worth) 20 shillings. Now 4 pounds.

Alvric holds LIDEFORD [West Lydford]. Brictric 'his father' held (it) T.R.E. and paid geld for 9 hides. There is land for 8 ploughs. There are 7 ploughs and 6 villeins and 9 bordars and 2 cottars and 8 serfs. 'In demesne are 5½ hides less half a virgate and 3 ploughs and the villeins have 3 hides and 1½ virgates and 4 ploughs, and there are 2 riding-horses and 20 beasts and 25 swine and 60 sheep and 25 she-goats.' There (is) a mill paying 15 shillings, and 60 acres of meadow and 30 acres of pasture and 1 league of wood(land) (reckoning) in length and breadth, and a swineherd paying 10 swine (yearly). Formerly and now it is worth 8 pounds.

Alvric holds SCEPEWORDE, 'SHEPBWURDA' [   ]. Brictric held (it) T.R.E. and paid geld for half a hide. There is land for half a plough. 'Rahir holds this of Alvric and has there 10 sheep.' It is worth 5 shillings.

Brictoward holds WRITELINCTONE [Writhlington]. Brictwold held (it) T.R.E. and paid geld for 6 hides. There is land for 5 ploughs and there they all are with 8 villeins [1] and 3 cottars. 'In demesne are 5 hides and 2 ploughs and the villeins have 1 hide and 3 ploughs, and there are 24 sheep.' There are 12 acres of meadow and 24 acres of pasture and 12 acres of underwood. Formerly it was worth 100 shillings. Now it is worth 4 pounds.

Huscarle holds 1 virgate of land which he also (*ipsemet*) held T.R.E. in ESTROPE [Eastrip in Brewham]. There he has half a plough,[2] 'and 4 beasts and 7 swine and 20 sheep.' It is worth 40 pence.

Osmer holds half a virgate of land in OTREMETONE [Otterhampton]. His father held (it) T.R.E. Of this (land) 2 parts have been taken away and placed in Candetone [Cannington] the king's manor.

*ITEM. THE LAND OF HUMPHREY AND OF CERTAIN OTHERS

'fo. 466'

Humphrey 'the chamberlain' holds BABE-CARI [Babcary]. Bruno held (it) freely[3] T.R.E. and paid geld for 2½ hides. There is land for 3 ploughs. Nevertheless in demesne are '1 hide and' 2 ploughs and 2 serfs, and (there are) 6 villeins and 3 bordars with 3 ploughs 'and 1½ hides.' 'There are 2 riding-horses.' There (are) 14 acres of meadow and 8 acres of pasture. Formerly (it was worth) 40 shillings. Now it is worth 50 shillings. This has been added to the lands of Brictric.

Humphrey holds ALTONE[4] [Holton], 'and Albric holds it of him.' Alnod held (it) T.R.E. and paid geld for 2 hides. There is land for 2 ploughs. In demesne are '1½ hides and' 1 plough and (there are) 1 villein and 4 bordars with half a plough 'and half a hide' and 1 serf. 'There is 1 riding-horse and 2 cows and 12 swine and 12 sheep.' There are 6 acres of meadow and 6 acres of wood(land). Formerly (it was worth) 20 shillings. Now it is worth 30 shillings.

Humphrey holds SANFORD [Sandford Orcas]. Three thegns held (it) freely[5] T.R.E. and paid geld for 6 hides. There is land for 6 ploughs and there they all are and 4 villeins and 15 bordars and 4 serfs and 8 acres of meadow. 'In demesne are 3½ hides less 1

ferling and 3 ploughs, and the villeins have 3 ploughs and the rest of the land. There are 2 riding-horses and 2 cows and 13 swine and 150 sheep.' Pasture 2 furlongs long and 1 furlong broad. Wood(land) 4 furlongs long and 1 furlong broad. Formerly (it was worth) 8 pounds. Now it is worth 9 pounds.[6]

'fo. 464b'

Odo of Flanders holds TIMESBERIE [Timsbury]. Gonuerd held (it) T.R.E. and paid geld for 5 hides. There is land for 4 ploughs. There are 2 ploughs and 5 villeins and 3 bordars and a mill paying 40 pence and 40 acres of meadow less 1, and 39 acres of pasture. 'In demesne are 3¾ hides and 1 plough and the villeins have 5 virgates and 1 plough. There are 56 sheep and 4 swine.' It is worth 3 pounds.

William Hosed holds TATEWICHE [Tadwick in Swainswick]. Three thegns, 'Siric, Codulf, and Waldin' held (it) 'in parage (*pariter*)' T.R.E. and paid geld for 1½ hides. There is land for 1 plough which is there in demesne 'with 1¼ hides' and 3 serfs and 2 bordars who have half a virgate, and half an acre of meadow and 10 acres of underwood. 'There is 1 riding-horse and 100 sheep.' Formerly (it was worth) 10[7] shillings. Now it is worth 30 shillings.

Ralph, 'brother of Roger' de Berchelai, holds TATEWICHE [Tadwick in Swainswick]. Godric held (it) T.R.E. and paid geld for half a hide. There is land for 1 plough which is there with 3 serfs. 'There are 89 sheep.' There (is) 1 acre of wood(land). Formerly (it was worth) 10 shillings. Now it is worth 15 shillings.

Hugolin the interpreter holds of the king HERLEI, 'HEORLEIA' [Warley in Bathford].[8] Azor held (it) T.R.E. and paid geld for 1 hide. There is land for 3 ploughs and so many are there with 1 villein and 5 bordars and 2 serfs. 'In demesne are half a hide and 2 ploughs and the villeins have half a hide and 1 plough. There are 100 sheep.' There is half an acre of meadow, and of underwood 3 furlongs reckon-

---

[1] Exet. Dom.: '3 villeins and 8 bordars.'
[2] Exet. Dom.: '4 oxen.'
[3] *Libere*, so also in Exet. Dom.
[4] Exet. Dom. *rectius*: 'Haltona.'
[5] Exet. Dom.: '*pariter*.'

[6] Exet. Dom. adds: 'All this land has been added to the lands of Bristrit to which it did not belong.'
[7] Exet. Dom.: '15.'
[8] Collinson suggested Warley in Bathford. 'Herleia' was purchased from 'Hugelin cum barba' by Bp. John de Villula in 1106 and given to the Abbey of Bath (*S.R.S.* vii. i. 53). Eyton's identification with Woolley cannot be correct, as the latter belonged to the Abbey of Wherwell.

ing between (*inter*) length and breadth. Formerly and now it is worth 50 shillings.

The same [Hugolin] holds ESTONE [Bath Easton]. Ingulf held (it) 'in parage (*pariter*)' T.R.E. and paid geld for 3 hides. There is land for 5 ploughs. There are 3 ploughs and 3 villeins and 6 bordars and 2 serfs and a mill paying 5 shillings. 'In demesne are 1½ hides and 1 plough and the villeins have 1½ hides and 2 ploughs.' Formerly (it was worth) 40 shillings. Now it is worth 60 shillings.

The same [Hugolin] holds CLAFTERTONE [Claverton]. Suain held (it) T.R.E. and paid geld for 5 hides. There is land for 6 ploughs, and so many are there and 4 villeins and 7 bordars and 4 serfs and a mill paying 7 shillings and 6 pence, and 20 acres of meadow and 12 furlongs of pasture (reckoning) in length and breadth. 'In demesne are 2½ hides and 2 ploughs and the villeins have 2½ hides and 4 ploughs. There are 1 riding-horse and 4 beasts and 29 swine and 120 sheep and 20 she-goats.' Formerly and now it is worth 7 pounds.

Drogo de Montagud holds CHENOLLE [Knowle in Shepton Montague]. Alnod held (it) T.R.E. and paid geld for 1½ hides. There is land for 3 ploughs, and as many are there and 6 villeins and 4 serfs with 1 cottar. 'In demesne are 3 virgates and 1 ferling and 2 ploughs and the villeins have 3 virgates less 1 ferling and 1 plough. There are 26 swine.' There (are) 15 acres of meadow. Wood(land) 4 furlongs in length and 3 furlongs in breadth. Formerly (it was worth) 40 shillings. Now it is worth 4 pounds.[1]

From this land has been taken away 1 hide of land which was there T.R.E. Turstin son of Rolf holds (it), 'and an Englishman of him.' It is worth 20 shillings.

Hugh 'de Vale torta' holds FODINDONE [Foddington in Babcary]. Alward held (it) T.R.E. and paid geld for 2 hides and 1 virgate of land. There is land for 3 ploughs and as many are there and 2 villeins and 1 cottar and 6 serfs and 14 acres of meadow. 'In demesne are 1¾ hides and 2 ploughs and the villeins have half a hide and 1 plough.

There are 2 riding-horses and 20 beasts and 15 swine and 28 sheep.' Formerly (it was worth) 30 shillings. Now it is worth 40 shillings.

Richard 'the interpreter' holds in RODE [Road] 1 hide which he (*ipse*) held [2] of Rainbold the priest (*presbytero* [3]) by leave of the king as he says. Reinbold indeed (*vero*) held (it) T.R.E. There is land for half a plough. There is 1 bordar. Formerly and now it is worth 10 shillings.

Schelin holds FODINDONE [Foddington in Babcary]. Bricstoward held (it) T.R.E. and paid geld for 1 hide and 1½ virgates of land. There is land for 2 ploughs which are there with 1 serf and 1 bordar. 'There is 1 riding-horse.' There (are) 6 acres of meadow. Formerly [4] and now it is worth 20 shillings.

Eldred holds BROCHELIE [Brockley]. He also (*idem ipse*) held (it) T.R.E. and paid geld for 4 hides. There is land for 4 ploughs, and as many are there and 6 villeins and 7 bordars and 16 acres of meadow. 'In demesne are 2 hides and the villeins have 2 hides and 4 ploughs. There are 2 beasts and 2 swine.' It is worth 30 shillings.

'fo. 465b'

ELDRED holds GRENEDONE [Crandon in Bawdrip]. He also (*idem ipse*) held (it) T.R.E. and paid geld for half a hide. There is land for half a plough. 'It is all in demesne and' there are 4 bordars with 1 serf, and a mill paying 30 pence 'and 1 pig' and 3 acres of meadow and 2 acres of underwood. It is worth 5 shillings.

'fo. 467'

Ansger de Montagud holds of the king PRESTETONE [Preston Plucknett]. Alward held (it) T.R.E. and paid geld for 2 hides. There is land for 1 plough which is there in demesne with 1 serf and 8 bordars. 'There are 1 riding-horse and 5 beasts and 80 sheep.' There (are) 10 acres of meadow. Formerly (it was worth) 15 shillings. Now it is worth 40 shillings.

---

[1] Exet. Dom. reverses the values.

[2] *Tenuit.* Exet. Dom. reads '*emit*,' which explains why the king's leave was mentioned.

[3] Exet. Dom. reads '*sacerdote*.'

[4] For '*olim*' Exet. Dom. reads : '*quando accepit ad firmam de rege*.'

GELD INQUEST

THESE ARE THE HUNDREDS OF SUMERSETA

[Exon. Domesday, fol. 75 seq.]

In the Hundred of Tantotone (Taunton) and in the Hundred of Pipeministre (Pitminster) are 120 hides and 3 virgates and 1 ferling. Thence the king has 30 pounds and 3 shillings for his geld from 100½ hides, and his barons have in demesne 20½ hides and 1 ferling. Of these (hides) bishop Walchelin has 11 hides and 1 virgate and 3 ferlings, and Wiliiam the sheriff 2½ hides, and Roger Arundel 3 hides and 3 ferlings, and John the usher (*hostiarius*) 1 hide and 1½ virgates, and the priests of Tantona 2 hides and 1 virgate. Besides the hides reckoned above bishop W(alchelin) has in Tontona 20 carrucates of land which never paid geld.

Analysis

	h.	v.	f.
Geld received for	100	2	0
Free of geld :	h.	v.	f.
Bishop Walchelin .	11	1	3
William the sheriff.	2	2	0
Roger Arundel . .	3	0	3
John the usher . .	1	1	2
Priests of Taunton .	2	1	0
	20	3	0
	121	1	0

In the Hundred of Milvertone (Milverton) are 24½ hides. Thence the king has 6 pounds and 7 shillings and 6 pence for his geld from 21 hides and 1 virgate. The king has no geld from 2½ hides which Britel holds. And Robert de Oburgivilla has 3 virgates which he holds of the king free (of geld).

	h.	v.	f.
Geld received for	21	1	0
Free of geld :	h.	v.	f.
Robert de Oburgivilla.	0	3	0
	0	3	0
Geld not received :			
Britel.	2	2	0
	2	2	0
	24	2	0

In the Hundred of Witestane (Whitstone) are 115 hides. Thence the king has 15 pounds for his geld from 50 hides, and the abbot (of Glastonbury) has in demesne 40 hides. The king has no geld from 1 hide and 3 virgates which Serlo de Burgei holds ; nor from 4 hides and 3½ virgates which Roger de Corcella holds ; nor from 5 hides and 1½ virgates which the villeins of the abbot hold. From these 3 pounds and 12 shillings are due to the king for his geld. Drogo did not pay geld in this Hundred for 7 hides which he held of the abbot of Glastingebery. Nigel the physician (*medicus*) did not pay geld in this Hundred for 5 hides. And Alvric and Evurard did not pay geld for 1 hide in this Hundred.

		h.	v.	f.
Geld received for		50	0	0
Free of geld :	h. v. f.			
Abbot of Glastonbury 40 0 0				
		40	0	0
Geld not received :				
Serlo de Burgei . .	1	3	0	
Roger de Corcella .	4	3	2	
Abbot's villeins. . .	5	1	2	
		12	0	0
Geld not paid here :				
Drogo	7	0	0	
Nigel	5	0	0	
Aluric and Evurard .	1	0	0	
		13	0	0
		115	0	0

In the Hundred of Cainesham (Keynsham) are 104 hides. Thence the king has 15 pounds for his geld from 50 hides. The king and his barons have in demesne 30½ hides. Of these (hides) the king has in demesne 15 hides, and the bishop of Coutances 3 hides and 3 virgates, and the abbot of Glastingebery 4½ hides, and the abbot of Bada 5 hides and 1 virgate, and the priest of Cainesham 1 hide, and Aluuric of Cainesham 1 hide. The king has no geld from 17½ hides which the king's villeins at Cainesham hold, nor from half a hide which William holds of the bishop of Coutances ; nor from 1¼ hides which Herald holds of Alvred; nor from 1 hide which Nicholas holds of Alvred; nor from 3 hides which Roger de Stanton holds. From this Hundred are due to the king for his geld 7 pounds and 12 pence.

	h.	v.	f.
Geld received for	50	0	0
Free of geld :	h.	v.	f.
King	15	0	0
Bishop of Coutances .	3	3	0
Abbot of Glastonbury .	4	2	0
Abbot of Bath . .	5	1	0
Priest of Keynsham .	1	0	0
Aluuric of Keynsham .	1	0	0
	30	2	0
Geld not received :			
King's villeins . . .	17	2	0
William	0	2	0
Herald	1	2	0
Nicholas	1	0	0
Roger de Stanton . .	3	0	0
	23	2	0
	104	0	0

In the Hundred of Porberie (Portbury) are 86½ hides. Thence the king has 19 pounds less 6 pence for 63 hides and 1 virgate. And his barons have in demesne 13 hides and 3 virgates less 1 ferling. Of these (hides) the bishop of Coutances has 8 hides and 3 virgates in demesne, and William de Ou 5 hides less 1 ferling. The king has no geld from 1 hide which Osbern holds of the bishop of Coutances; nor from 2 hides which Ori holds of the bishop of Coutances; nor from 1 hide and 1 virgate which Engeler holds of Arnulf of Hesdinc; nor from 5 hides and 1 virgate and 1 ferling for which the collectors (fegadri) acknowledge that they have received the money. From this Hundred 57 shillings and 4 pence and a halfpenny are still kept back which are due to the king for his geld.

	h.	v.	f.
Geld received for	63	1	0
Free of geld :	h.	v.	f.
Bishop of Coutances .	8	3	0
William de Ou . . .	4	3	3
	13	2	3
Geld not received :			
Osbern	1	0	0
Ori	2	0	0
Engeler	1	1	0
Not specified	5	1	1
	9	2	1
	86	2	0

In the Hundred of Bade (Bath) are 95 hides. Thence the king has 10 pounds and 18 shillings and 3 pence for his geld from 36 hides and 1½ virgates. The king and his barons have in demesne 43 hides and half a virgate. Of these (hides) the king has 1 in demesne, and the abbot of Bath 29 hides, and the abbess of St. Edward (Shaftesbury Nunnery) 3 hides, and Arnulf of Hesdinc 4 hides and half a virgate, and the bishop of St. Lo 3 hides, and William Hosat 1 hide and 1½ virgates, and Alvred of Wica 1 hide and half a virgate, and Ralf of Bercelai half a hide. The king has no geld from 1 hide and 1 virgate which Robert Greno holds; nor from 1 hide which the king's villeins hold in Estona; nor from 1 virgate which Sawyn the steward (prepositus) of Arnulf of Hesdinc holds; nor from 13 hides which Hugolin the officer (legatus) holds. Besides the 95 hides above written the king had no geld from the burgh of Bade (Bath) which used to pay geld for 20 hides in the time of King Edward. From this Hundred and from the burgh of Bade are still detained 10 pounds and 13 shillings of the geld which the king ought to have; he has not had his geld.

	h.	v.	f.
Geld received for	36	1	2
Free of geld :	h.	v.	f.
King	1	0	0
Abbot of Bath . . .	29	0	0
Abbess of St. Edward . .	3	0	0
Arnulf of Hesdinc . .	4	0	2
Bishop of St. Lo . .	3	0	0
William Hosat . . .	1	1	2
Alvred of Wica . . .	1	0	2
Ralf of Bercelai . .	0	2	0
	43	0	2
Geld not received :			
Robert Greno . . .	1	1	0
Villeins of Estona . .	1	0	0
Sawyn	0	1	0
Hugolin	13	0	0
	15	2	0
	95	0	0

In the Hundred of Cetdre (Cheddar) are 7 hides and 3 virgates. Thence the king has 30 shillings for his geld from 5 hides. Of these (hides) Godwyn has 1 virgate in demesne. The king has no geld from 1 hide and 1 virgate which Roger Wytent holds of the bishop of St. Lo; nor from 1 hide and 1 virgate which Robert son of Herbert holds of Roger de Corcella. From this Hundred there are still due to the king 15 shillings for his geld.

	h.	v.	f.
Geld received for	5	0	0
Free of geld : Godwyn	0	1	0
Geld not received :	h.	v.	f.
Roger Wytent . . .	1	1	0
Robert son of Herbert .	1	1	0
	2	2	0
	7	3	0

In the Hundred of Cŏdecoma (Cutcombe) and in the Hundred of Manehefve (Minehead) are 10 hides and 1 virgate. Thence the king has (32) shillings and 3 pence for his geld from 5 hides and 1½ virgates. William de Moione has in demesne 5 hides less half a virgate.

	h.	v.	f.
Geld received for	5	1	2
Free of geld	4	3	2
	10	1	0

In the Hundred of Hareclive (Hartcliffe) are 80 hides and 1 virgate. Thence the king has of his geld 18 pounds and 6 shillings for 61 hides, and his barons have 16 hides and 3 virgates in demesne. Of these (hides) the bishop of St. Lo has 5 hides and 3 virgates in demesne, and the abbot of Glastingbery 11 hides. And for 1½ hides which Fulcherar holds of the bishop of St. Lo the king has no geld. And for half a hide which Nigel de Gornay holds the king has no geld. And for half a hide which Godwyn the Englishman holds the king has no geld. From this Hundred there are still due 15 shillings to the king for his geld.

		h.	v.	f.
Geld received for		61	0	0
Free of geld :	h. v. f.			
Bishop of St. Lo . . .	5 3 0			
Abbot of Glastonbury	11 0 0			
		16	3	0
Geld not received :				
Fulcherar	1 2 0			
Nigel de Gornay . .	0 2 0			
Godwyn 'anglicus'. .	0 2 0			
		2	2	0
		80	1	0

In the Hundred of Betministre (Bedminster) are 6½ hides. Thence the king has 24 shillings for his geld from 4 hides. And Osbert Giffard has 1 hide in demesne. And Turstin 1 hide which he holds of the king exempt in almoin. And for half a hide of which the collectors (fegadri) had received the money the king has no geld, and they have given security for its payment (vadiaverunt foris) to the king's barons. From this Hundred there are due to the king of his geld 3 shillings.

		h.	v.	f.
Geld received for		4	0	0
Free of geld :	h. v. f.			
Osbert Giffard . . .	1 0 0			
Turstin	1 0 0			
		2	0	0
Geld not received		0	2	0
		6	2	0

In the Hundred of Carentone (Carhampton)
are 40 hides and 1 virgate and 3½ ferlings. Thence the king has 10 pounds and 11 shillings and 6 pence for his geld from 35 hides and 1 virgate, and his barons have in demesne 5 hides less 1 ferling. Of these (hides) Ralf de Limesy has 1½ hides. And Ralf de Pomeray half a hide. And William de Faleise 1 hide and 1½ virgates. And 2 nuns (2 virgates[1]) and a half. And William the sheriff 3 virgates and a ferling. . . . . Roger Corcelle half a virgate.

		h.	v.	f.
Geld received for		35	1	0
Free of geld :	h. v. f.			
Ralf de Limesy . .	1 2 0			
Ralf de Pomeray . .	0 2 0			
William de Faleise . .	1 1 2			
Two nuns	0 2 2			
William the sheriff . .	0 3 1			
Roger Corcelle . .	0 0 2			
		4	3	3
		40	0	3

In the Hundred of Winest . . . (Winterstoke) . . . 120 hides . . . virgates.[2] Thence the king has 13[3] pounds and 3 shillings and 60 pence and one halfpenny for his geld from 77 . . . (his) barons have in demesne 40 . . . bishop Walchelin has 10 hides in demesne. And bishop Giso 6 . . . (abbot of Glastonbury) 4 hides and 3 virgates. And count Eustace 3 hides and 1 ferling. And Serlo de Burci 5 hides and 1½ virgates. And Willaim de Faleise 7½ hides and 3 ferlings. And Walter de Dowai 3 hides and 1½ virgates. And for 4 hides which Ralf Tortemains holds of bishop Giso the king has no geld. From a manor called Harp(tree) which Robert son of Walter holds for 5 hides the king has no geld. . . . hide which Osbern holds of Gilbert son of Turold the king has no geld. And for half a hide which Alward holds of Anschetill parcar the king has no geld. And for half a hide which Aselin holds of the bishop of St. Lo the king has no geld. And for 1 virgate and 3 ferlings which William de Faleise holds the king has no geld. For 1 ferling of the land of Serlo de Burci the king has no geld. And for half a hide and 3 ferlings the king has received no geld, for which the collectors can give no account. From this Hundred there are still due to the king of his geld 70 shillings and 3 halfpennies which the king ought to have had, and security has been given to the king's satisfaction (vadiati sunt isti [the arrears] in misericordia Regis).

[1] Two nuns held 2½ virgates at Honecote.
[2] Eyton reckons 129 hides 3 virgates.
[3] rectius, '23.'

	h.	v.	f.
Geld received for	77	I	I
Free of geld :	h.	v.	f.
Bishop Walchelin . .	10	0	0
Bishop Giso	6	0	0
Abbot of Glastonbury .	4	3	0
Count Eustace . . .	3	0	I
Serlo de Burci . . .	5	I	2
William de Faleise . .	7	2	3
Walter de Dowai . .	3	I	2
		40	I	0
Geld not received :			
Ralf Tortemains . .	4	0	0
Robert son of Walter .	5	0	0
Osbern	?	0	2	0
Alward	0	2	0
Aselin	0	2	0
William de Faleise . .	0	I	3
Serlo de Burci . . .	0	0	I
Account lost	0	2	3
		11	2	3
		129	I	0[1]

In the Hundred of Brunetone (Brompton Ralph) are 5 hides. Thence the king has 24 shillings for his geld from 4 hides. From half a hide for which the collectors received the money the king had no geld. And from half a hide which Ogisus holds unaware (*ignorans*) that he ought to pay the geld the king has no geld. From this Hundred there are still due 6 shillings of the king's geld.

	h.	v.	f.
Geld received for	4	0	0
Geld not received :	h.	v.	f.
Ogisus	0	2	0
Collectors	0	2	0
		I	0	0
		5	0	0

In the Hundred of Bimastane (Bempstone) are 43 hides and 3 ferlings. Thence the king has 9 pounds and 13[2] shillings and 3 pence for his geld from 32 hides and 1½ virgates, and his barons have in demesne 10½ hides. Of these bishop Giso has 5 hides and 3 virgates in demesne, and Walter de Dowai 2 hides and 3 virgates, and Letaoldus 2 hides which he holds of the abbot of Glastingbery

which never paid geld. And the king has no geld from 1½ virgates which Roger de Corcelle holds. From this Hundred are still retained 18 pence which ought to be paid. Besides the 9 pounds 14 shillings and 3 pence written above, the men of Walter de Dowai have paid in this Hundred 27[3] shillings and 6 pence from 6 hides and I virgate, and besides these Walter has in demesne 1½ hides. And the king has no geld from half a hide of this land which Rainewalo holds of Walter. The thegns of Walter say that the land which they hold belongs to the Hundred of Bimestane.

	h.	v.	f.
Geld received for	32	I	2
Free of geld :	h.	v.	f.
Bishop Giso . . .	5	3	0
Walter de Dowai . .	2	3	0
Letaoldus	2	0	0
		10	2	0
Geld not received :			
Roger de Corcelle . .	0	I	2
		0	I	2
		43	I	0
Supplemental Inquest :			
Geld received ;	6	I	0
Free of geld ; Walter de Dowai .	I	2	0
Geld not received; Rainewalo .	0	2	0
		51	2	0

In the Hundred of Hunespille (Huntspil) which Walter de Dowai holds is exactly (*tantum*) I hide. From this the king has 6 shillings for his geld ; and with this Hundred 18 shillings have been received for 3 hides which belonged to the Hundred of Locheslege.

In the Hundred of Cumētone (Chewton) are 127½ hides. Thence the king has 21 pounds and 5 shillings and 3 pence for his geld from 70 hides and 3½ virgates. Of these (hides) the king and his barons have in demesne 33 hides and half a virgate. Of these (*inde*) the king has 18 hides in demesne, and bishop Giso 6 hides, and the bishop of St. Lo 4 hides and 3 virgates, and Aldret 1½ hides, and Serlo de Burci 3 hides less half a virgate. And the king has no geld from 11 hides which his men hold at Cumetona ; nor from 4 hides and 3 virgates which Serlo holds of the bishop of St. Lo ; nor from I virgate which Hugh Malus-transitus[4] holds ; nor from 4 hides and I virgate which Walter of Mans (*Cenomannensis*) holds of Gilbert son of Turold ; nor from 3 hides and I virgate[5] of

---

[1] The text of this Hundred has disappeared in part, and in several places is apparently corrupt. The sum received by the king, at 6 shillings to the hide, would give an area 33 hides short of the total required to complete the Hundred. I have therefore followed Eyton in reading 23 for 13 pounds. The total area of the different manors in this Hundred according to the identifications adopted in the translation amounts to 130 hides 3 virgates.

[2] *rectius*, 14, as below.

[3] *recte*, 37.   [4] i.e. Maltravers.

[5] Also a 'half' marked for cancellation.

the land of Manasseh. From this Hundred there are still due 7 pounds and 12 pence of the king's geld.

		h.	v.	f.
Geld received for		70	3	2
Free of geld :	h.	v.	f.	
King	18	0	0	
Bishop Giso . . .	6	0	0	
Bishop of St. Lo	4	3	0	
Aldret	1	2	0	
Serlo de Burci . .	2	3	2	
		33	0	2
Geld not received :				
King's men	11	0	0	
Serlo	4	3	0	
Hugh Malus-transitus .	0	1	0	
Walter of Mans . . .	4	1	0	
Land of Manasseh . .	3	1	0	
		23	2	0
		127	2	0

In the Hundred of Congresberie (Congresbury) are 19 hides. Thence the king has 13 shillings and 6 pence of his geld from 2 hides and 1 virgate. And the king and his barons have 5 hides and 1 virgate in demesne. Of these (hides) the king has $3\frac{1}{2}$ hides in demesne, and Ordric 3 virgates, and Ordulf half a hide, and Alward half a hide. The king has no geld from 11 hides which the king's villeins of Congresbury hold, nor for half a hide which the villeins of the church of Congresbury hold. From this Hundred 69 shillings remain to be paid.

		h.	v.	f.
Geld received for		2	1	0
Free of geld :	h.	v.	f.	
King	3	2	0	
Ordric	0	3	0	
Ordulf	0	2	0	
Alward	0	2	0	
		5	1	0
Geld not received :				
King's villeins . . .	11	0	0	
Church villeins . . .	0	2	0	
		11	2	0
		19	0	0

From a part of the land of bishop Giso which belongs to the Honour of his bishopric 218 hides are here (reckoned). Thence the king has 40 pounds and 4 shillings for his geld from 134 hides. Of these hides the bishop has in demesne 48 hides. And the king has no geld from 3 hides which Osmund the bishop's nephew holds; nor from 2 hides which Manases holds; nor from $1\frac{1}{2}$ hides which Alvered the man of Roger Arundell holds; nor from 2 hides which John the usher holds; nor from 1 hide which Teoderic and Egebert hold; nor from 1 hide which Richard of Sutuna holds; nor from 1 hide

which Worno and Macarius hold; nor from $4\frac{1}{2}$ hides which the bishop's tenants hold uncultivated (*vacuas*); nor from 7 hides which Isaac the provost (*prepositus*) of the canons of St. Andrew hold; nor from 6 hides which the canons of St. Andrew (hold); nor from $1\frac{1}{2}$ hides which Benselin the archdeacon (holds); nor from $5\frac{1}{2}$ hides which 6 parochial priests hold. And from 1 hide from which Ansger and his fellows who collected the geld acknowledge that they received the money the king has no geld.[1] From the said 218 hides 10 pounds and 16 shillings are still kept back which must be paid to the king's treasury.

		h.	v.	f.
Geld received for		134	0	0
Free of geld :	h.	v.	f.	
Bishop	48	0	0	
		48	0	0
Geld not received :				
Osmund	3	0	0	
Manases	2	0	0	
Alvered	1	2	0	
John the usher . . .	2	0	0	
Teoderic and Egebert	1	0	0	
Richard of Sutun .	1	0	0	
Worno and Macarius .	1	0	0	
Bishop's tenants . .	4	2	0	
Isaac the provost . .	7	0	0	
Canons of St. Andrew .	6	0	0	
Benselin, archdeacon .	1	2	0	
Parochial clergy .	5	2	0	
		36	0	0
		218	0	0

In the Hundred of Tierleberge (Thurlbear) are 3 hides. From these (hides) the king had 18 shillings for his geld. The men of the count (of Mortain) did not pay this (money) except in the last geld.

In the Hundred of Givele (Yeovil) are $157\frac{1}{2}$ hides. Thence the king has 30 pounds and 7 shillings and 6 pence for his geld from 101 hides and 1 virgate. And the king's barons have 31 hides in demesne. Of these (hides) the Count of Mortain has $18\frac{1}{2}$ hides, and Roger de Corcelle 4 hides and 1 virgate, and Brismar 5 hides, and Garmund 2 hides, and Ansger Brito 1 hide and 1 virgate. The king has no geld from 1 hide which Saward the fowler (*accipitrarius*) holds; nor from 5 hides which the monks of Egresten (Grestain) hold; nor from 6 hides which Britel holds and Drogo and Alvered and the count's villeins at Montacute; nor from 3 hides and 1 virgate which Britel holds; nor from 3 virgates which Ansger holds; nor from 2 hides which . . . *erna* (Alvred *pincerna*); nor from 2 hides at Achilei (Oakley); .

[1] The total is complete without this.

(one hide) which Roger de Corcelle holds; nor from 1 hide . . . ; nor from 1 virgate which Drogo holds; nor from 1 virgate which Roger *calvus* holds. In this Hundred Osbern holds 2 hides and 3 virgates of the bishop of St. Lo for which he paid geld in the Hundred of Liet. From this Hundred 6 pounds and 15 shillings of the king's geld are still unpaid (*restant*).

	h.	v.	f.
Geld received for	101	1	0
Free of geld :	h.	v.	f.
Count of Mortain . . 18	2	0	
Roger de Corcelle . . 4	1	0	
Brismar 5	0	0	
Garmund . . . 2	0	0	
Ansger Brito . . 1	1	0	
	31	0	0
Geld not received :			
Saward the hawker . 1	0	0	
Monks of Grestain . . 5	0	0	
Britel and others . . 6	0	0	
Britel 3	1	0	
Ansger 0	3	0	
(Alvred pincerna) . . 2	0	0	
At Oakley . . . 2	0	0	
Roger de Corcelle . . (1	0	0)	
Illegible 1	0	0	
Drogo 0	1	0	
Roger calvus . . . 0	1	0	
	22	2	0
Osbern 2	3	0	
	2	3	0
	157	2	0

In the Hundred of Cruche (Crewkerne) are 39 hides. Thence the king has 6 pounds and 10 shillings and 6 pence for his geld from 21 hides and 3 virgates, and the king's barons have 14 hides in demesne. Of these (hides) the (church of) St. Stephen of Caen has 7 hides, which never paid geld, and William de Ou 5 hides, and Harding 2 hides. The king has no geld from 2 hides and 1 virgate, which the villeins of William de Ou hold; nor from 1 hide which the villeins of Hardin of Meriet hold. From this Hundred there are due to the king 19 shillings and 6 pence of his geld.

	h.	v.	f.
Geld received for	21	3	0
Free of geld :	h.	v.	f.
St. Stephen of Caen . 7	0	0	
William de Ou . . . 5	0	0	
Harding 2	0	0	
	14	0	0
Geld not received :			
Villeins of W. de Ou . 2	1	0	
Villeins of Hardin . . 1	0	0	
	3	1	0
	39	0	0

In the Hundred of Willetone (Williton) are

92½ hides. Thence the king has 16 pounds and 11 shillings and 6 pence for his geld from 55 hides and 1 virgate. And the king and his barons have in demesne 24 hides less 1 ferling. Of these (hides) the king has 1 hide and 1 virgate in demesne, and the abbot of Muceleneia (Muchelney) 1 hide, and Dodo of Cori half a hide, and William the sheriff 12½ hides and 3 ferlings, and . . . . and Richer of Stoches 2 hides which he holds in almoin of the church, and Roger de Corcelle 4½ hides, and Alvred de Ispania 2 hides. The king has no geld from 6 hides and 1 virgate and 1 ferling which the villeins of Netelcoma (Nettlecombe) and of Winnesforda (Winsford) and of Dolvertona (Dulverton) hold; nor from 3 hides which Ansger the cook (*cocus*) holds of Count Robert (of Mortain); nor from 1 hide in Imela and Oda and Waiestow; nor from 1 virgate which Robert son of Rotscelin holds; nor from 1 virgate which Ranulph of Strangestona (Stringston) holds; nor from 1 virgate in Letfort; nor from 1 virgate in Pirtochesworda, which Dodeman holds and Richard; nor from 2 hides which Mauger de Kartrai holds, but he has paid in another Hundred. From this Hundred are still due 3 pounds and 7 shillings and 10 pence and 1 halfpenny of the king's geld.

	h.	v.	f.
Geld received for	55	1	0
Free of geld :	h.	v.	f.
King 1	1	0	
Abbot of Muchelney . 1	0	0	
Dodo of Cori . . . 0	2	0	
William the sheriff . 12	2	3	
Richer of Stoches . . 2	0	0	
Roger de Corcelle . . 4	2	0	
Alvred de Ispania . . 2	0	0	
	23	3	3
Geld not received :			
Villeins of Nettlecombe 6	1	1	
Ansger cocus 3	0	0	
Imela and elsewhere . 1	0	0	
Robert son of Rotscelin 0	1	0	
Ranulph of Stringston . 0	1	0	
In Letfort 0	1	0	
In Pirtochesworda . . 0	1	0	
Mauger de Kartrai . . 2	0	0	
	13	1	1
	92	2	0

In Winesfort (Winsford) Hundred are 2 hides and 1 ferling. Of this the king has half a hide in demesne, and he has no geld from 1½ hides and 1 ferling. From this Hundred are due to the king 9 shillings and 4 pence and 1 halfpenny.

In the Hundred of Cantetone (Cannington) are 45 hides and 1 virgate and 3 ferlings. Thence the king has 9 pounds and 18 shillings of his geld from 33 hides, and his barons have 10½ hides and 2 ferlings in demesne. Of this demesne William the sheriff has 4 hides and 1 virgate and 2 ferlings, and William de Faleise 2 hides, and Roger de Corcelle 1 hide and 3 virgates and 1 ferling, . . . 1½ virgates, and Anscetil *parcarius* 1 hide, and Levo 1 virgate, and Osmer 1 virgate, and the church of Cantelona (Cannington) half a hide, and a nun 1 ferling. The king has no geld from half a hide which Fulcer of Stochelande holds; nor from half a hide which Robert of Spachestone (Spaxton) holds; nor from half a virgate which William son of Robert holds; nor from half a hide which Bristri holds; nor from half a hide which Hugh de Ispania holds; nor from 1 ferling which Hugh de Tevera holds. From this Hundred there is still due of the king's geld 10 shillings and 10 pence and 1 halfpenny.

	h.	v.	f.
Geld received for	33	0	0
Free of geld :			
Will. the sheriff . . .	4	1	2
William de Faleise . .	2	0	0
Roger de Corcelle . .	1	3	1
. . . .	0	1	2
Anscetil parcar . . .	1	0	0
Levo	0	1	0
Osmer.	0	1	0
Cannington church .	0	2	0
A nun.	0	0	1
	10	2	2
Geld not received :			
Fulcer of Stochelande .	0	2	0
Robert of Spachestone .	0	2	0
William son of Robert .	0	0	2
Bristri	0	0	2
Hugh de Ispania . .	0	2	0
Hugh de Tevera . .	0	0	1
	1	3	1
	45	1	3

In the Hundred of Meleborne (Milborne Port) are 115 hides and 1 virgate. Thence the king has 18 pounds and 8 shillings and 4 pence and 1 halfpenny for his geld from 63 hides and 1 ferling, and his barons have 34½ hides and 3 ferlings in demesne. Of these William son of Guy has 8 hides and 1 virgate and 1 ferling, and Humphrey the chamberlain has 3 hides and 1 virgate and 3 ferlings, and the abbess of St. Edward (Shaftesbury) has 2½ hides, and the monks of St. Sever 3½ hides, and Robert son of Gerald 4 hides, and Ulward Wyta 7 hides and 1 virgate and 1 ferling, and the count of Mortain 2 hides and 3 virgates, and bishop Walcelin (of Winchester) 2 hides and 1½ virgates, and the church of Meleburne has 1 hide which never paid geld. The collectors

have retained for themselves 3 shillings (due) from half a hide. The king has no geld from 10 hides which his villeins hold at Hasteriga (Henstridge); nor from 5 hides and 3 virgates which Sanson holds of the bishop of Bayeux; nor from half a hide which William de Lestra holds; nor from 1 virgate which Ralph de Contevilla holds. From this Hundred there are still due of the king's geld 100 shillings less 23 pence.

				h.	v.	f.
Geld received for				63	0	1
Free of geld :	h.	v.	f.			
William son of Guy .	8	1	1			
Humphrey	3	1	3			
Abbess of St. Edward .	2	2	0			
Abbey of St. Sever . .	3	2	0			
Robert son of Gerald .	4	0	0			
Ulward Wyta . . .	7	1	1			
Count of Mortain . .	2	3	0			
Bishop Walcelin . . .	2	1	2			
Church of Milborne .	1	0	0			
				35	0	3
Geld not received :						
Collectors' fee on . .	0	2	0			
Villeins of Henstridge .	10	0	0			
Sanson.	5	3	0			
William de Lestra . .	0	2	0			
Ralph de Contevilla .	0	1	0			
				17	0	0
				115	1	0

In the Hundred of Nortpedret (North Petherton) are 38 hides and 3 virgates and half a ferling. Thence the king has 9 pounds and 10 shillings and 8 pence and 1 farthing for his geld from 31 hides and 3 virgates and half a ferling, and his barons have in demesne 5½ hides and half a virgate. Of these (hides) Walter de Dowai holds 2 hides, and John the usher 1½ virgates, and Ansger *focarius* 5 virgates, and Robert de Otburgivilla 1½ hides, and the church of the same manor (North Petherton) half a hide. The king has no geld from half a hide and half a virgate which John holds; nor from 1 virgate which Ansger holds of Walter; nor from 1 virgate which Robert son of William holds; nor from half a virgate which the men of Robert de Otburgivilla holds; nor from half a virgate which Walter de Ispania holds. From this Hundred there are still due to the king 8 shillings and 3 pence of his geld.

				h.	v.	f.
Geld received for				31	3	0½
Free of geld :	h.	v.	f.			
Walter de Dowai . .	2	0	0			
John the usher . . .	0	1	2			
Ansger focarius . . .	1	1	0			
Robert de Otburgivilla	1	2	0			
Church (of N. Petherton)	0	2	0			
				5	2	2

Geld not received :	h.	v.	f.	h.	v.	f.
John	0	2	2			
Ansger	0	1	0			
Robert son of William .	0	1	0			
Men of Robert de O. .	0	0	2			
Walter de Ispania . .	0	0	2			
				1	1	2
				38	3	0½

In the Hundred of Cui (Chew) are 35 hides. Thence the king has 6 pounds less 18 pence for his geld from 19 hides and 3 virgates, and his barons have 5 hides in demesne. Of these (hides) Odo of Flanders has 3 hides and 3 virgates, and Serlo de Burci 1 virgate, and Alduin 1 hide. The king has no geld from 4 hides which Ulveva holds, nor from 6 hides and 1 virgate which the king's villeins at Stocha (Chewstoke) hold. From this Hundred there are still due to the king for his geld 61 shillings and 6 pence.

	h.	v.	f.
Geld received for	19	3	0
Free of geld :			
Odo of Flanders . .	3	3	0
Serlo de Burci . .	0	1	0
Alduin	1	0	0
	5	0	0
Geld not received :			
Ulveva	4	0	0
Villeins of Stocha . .	6	1	0
	10	1	0
	35	0	0

In the Hundred of Andretesfelt (Andersfield) are 9 hides and 1 virgate. Thence the king has 42 shillings for his geld from 7 hides, and his barons have 2 hides and 1 virgate in demesne. Of the same William the sheriff has 1 hide and 1 virgate,[1] and Ansger *focarius* half a hide.

	h.	v.	f.
Geld received for	7	0	0
Free of geld :			
William the sheriff .	1	3	0
Ansger focarius . .	0	2	0
	2	1	0
	9	1	0

In the Hundred of Sutperetone (South Petherton) are 66½ hides. Thence the king has 12 pounds and 9 shillings for his geld from 41½ hides, and the king and his barons have 11 hides in demesne. Of these (hides) the king has 2 hides, and the clerk (priest) of the vill of South Petherton has 1 hide, and Siward 4 hides and 3 virgates, and John

the usher 1½ hides and 1 ferling, and Harding 1½ hides and 3 ferlings. The king has no geld from 6 hides which Leveva holds; nor from 1 hide which the villeins of the abbot of Adelingeia (Athelney) hold; nor from 2 hides which Turstan holds; nor from 1 hide which Stephen holds of William de Ou; nor from half a hide which William de Dalmereio holds; nor from 1 virgate which William de Monticut holds; nor from half a hide which Roger de Luxonio holds; nor from 1 hide and 1 virgate which Ralph Rufus holds; nor from half a hide which Odo de Fornelt holds; nor from 2 hides which Robert son of Gilbert holds of William de Moione. From this Hundred there are due to the king for his geld 4 pounds and 4 shillings.

				h.	v.	f.
Geld received for				41	2	0
Free of geld :	h.	v.	f.			
King	2	0	0			
Priest of South Pether-						
ton	1	0	0			
Siward	4	3	0			
John the usher . . .	1	2	1			
Harding	1	2	3			
				11	0	0
Geld not received :						
Leveva	6	0	0			
Villeins of A. of Athel-						
ney	1	0	0			
Turstan	2	0	0			
Stephen	1	0	0			
Will. de Dalmereio . .	0	2	0			
Will. de Monticut . .	0	1	0			
Roger de Luxonio . .	0	2	0			
Ralph Rufus . .	1	1	0			
Odo de Fornelt . .	0	2	0			
Robert son of Gilbert .	2	0	0			
				15[2]	0	0
				67	2	0

In the Hundred of Abbdiche (Abdick) are 138 hides.[3] Thence the king has 18 pounds and 5 shillings and 1 halfpenny and 1 farthing for his geld from 60 hides and 3 virgates and 1½ ferlings, and his barons have 32 hides and 3 virgates and 3 ferlings in demesne. Of these (hides) the Count of Mortain has 7 hides, and the abbot of Adelingeres (Athelney) 4 hides, and the abbot of Muceleneia 13½ hides and half a virgate, and Roger de Corcelle half a hide, and Sauard 2½ hides and half a virgate, and Roger Arundel 5 hides and 1 virgate and 3 ferlings. The king has no geld from 10 hides which Osmund bishop

[1] For 1 hide and 1 virgate read 1 hide and 3 virgates, which was William de Moione's demesne at Broomfield in this Hundred.

[2] This figure makes the sum total too large; it is corrected by the amount of the arrears, 84 shillings, which at 6 shillings for each hide gives 14 hides instead of 15.

[3] The items give a total of 137 hides only.

Giso's neph ew holds ; nor from 3 hides which William de Lestra holds ; nor from 3 hides which Malger[1] de Cartrai holds ; nor from half a hide which the villeins of the Count of Mortain hold ; nor from half a hide which Godewin de Cicemetona holds ; nor from half a hide which the villeins of Roger Arundel hold ; nor from 1½ hides and half a virgate which the priest and the villeins of Illeministre (Ilminster) hold.

Twenty hides belonging to this Hundred pay geld in the Hundred of Bishop Giso ; and the abbot of Muchelney (*Micelinensis*) pays geld on 3 hides and 3 virgates in another Hundred. The king has had no geld from 1½ ferlings for which the collectors were unable to give us any account. From this Hundred there still remains to be paid 115 shillings and 2 pence and 1 halfpenny and 1 farthing of the king's geld.

	h.	v.	f.
Geld received for	60	3	1½

Free of geld :	h.	v.	f.
Count of Mortain .	7	0	0
Abbot of Athelney .	4	0	0
Abbot of Muchelney .	13	2	2
Roger de Corcelle .	0	2	0
Sauard	2	2	2
Roger Arundel . .	5	1	3
	33	0	3

Geld not received :			
Osmund	10	0	0
William de Lestra . .	3	0	0
Malger de Cartrai . .	3	0	0
Villeins of Count of Mortain	0	2	0
Godwin de Cicemetona	0	2	0
Villeins of Roger Arundel . . .	0	2	0
In Ilminster . . .	1	2	2
Not accounted for .	0	0	1½
	19	0	3½
Paid in Bishop Giso's Hundred .	20	0	0
Paid by Abbot of Muchelney in another Hundred	3	3	0
	137	0	0

In the Hundred of Bruiwetone (Bruton) are 232 hides. Thence the king has 50 pounds and 2 shillings for his geld from 167 hides, and his barons have in demesne 37½ hides and half a virgate. Of these (hides) William the sheriff has 6 hides and 3 virgates, and Drogo half a virgate[2] and 3 ferlings, and Turstin son of Rolf 4 hides, and Serlo de Burci 3 hides, and Humphrey the chamberlain 1 hide, and Edmund 2 hides and 1½ virgates, and Escelin 1 hide and 1½ virgates, and Walter of Baden-

tona 7 hides and 3½ virgates, and Hugh de Valtort 1 hide and 3 virgates, Hardinc 1 virgate and 3 ferlings, the countess of Boulogne (*Bolonia*) 2 hides and 3 virgates, and Aluuric 5½ hides and half a virgate. Lambert of Watileia is quit of (the payment for) 1 hide, *tenementum fegadrorum*.[3] The king has no geld from 1 hide which Rannewalo holds ; nor from 2 hides which Turstin son of Rolf holds ; nor from 4 hides which Ralph Hastent (holds) ; nor from 4 hides which Britel holds ; nor from 1 hide which William de Radio holds ; nor from 1 hide which Gonsel . . . (Gozelin de Rivaria) holds ; nor from 1½ virgates which Drogo de Monte-accuto holds ; nor from half a hide which . . . etona ; nor from 1 hide and 3 virgates and 1 ferling which Isaac holds ; nor from 1 hide . . . (1 virgate and) a half which Hugh de Valtort holds ; nor from half a virgate which Erneis holds ; nor from 1½ hides which William de Durvile holds ; nor from 3 hides for which Alger of Halton has not paid geld in this Hundred ; nor from 5 hides for which Malger has not paid geld in this Hundred ; nor from 1 virgate and 3 ferlings for which the collectors are not able to give any account. From this Hundred there are due to the king for his geld 8 pounds and 2 shillings and 9 pence.

		h.	v.	f.
Geld received for		167	0	0

Free of geld :	h.	v.	f.
William the sheriff . .	6	3	0
Drogo	0	2	3
Turstin son of Rolf . .	4	0	0
Serlo de Burci . . .	3	0	0
Humphrey the chamberlain	1	0	0
Edmund	2	1	2
Escelin	1	1	2
Walter of Baden tone .	7	3	2
Hugh de Valtort . .	1	3	0
Hardinc	0	1	3
Countess of Boulogne .	2	3	0
Aluuric	5	2	2
	37	2	2
Lambert of 'Watileia'	1	0	0

Geld not received :	h.	v.	f.
Rannewalo	1	0	0
Turstin son of Rolf . .	2	0	0
Ralph Hastent . . .	4	0	0
Britel	4	0	0
William de Radio .	1	0	0
Gozelin	1	0	0
Drogo de Montacute .	0	1	2
. . . etona	0	2	0

---

[3] Lambert held 1 hide in Lovington, but there is nothing in Domesday as to its being the holding annexed to the office of collector of the geld. 'Tenementum' apparently means the fee which he set off against the payment due from his holding.

---

[1] Malger written over Roger.
[2] A clerical error for hide.

	h.	v.	f.	h.	v.	f.
Isaac	1	3	1			
Hugh de Valtort . .	1	1	2			
Erneis	0	0	2			
William de Durvile .	1	2	0			
Algar of Halton . .	3	0	0			
Mauger	5	0	0			
Not accounted for . .	0	1	3			
				27	0	2
				232	3	0

In the Hundred of Lochesleie [1] are 47 hides. Thence the king has 7 pounds and 16 shillings for his geld from 26 hides, and (the church of) St. Peter of Rome and the abbot of Glastingesberia have in demesne 11 hides. Of these (hides) St. Peter has 6 hides, and the abbot 5 hides. The king has no geld from 3 hides which Alvred de Hispania holds of the abbot of Glasting(bury) ; nor from 3 hides and 3 virgates which Roger Witenc holds of the honour of the said abbot ; nor from 1 virgate which Anschetil *parcarius* holds. From this Hundred there are due to the king 42 shillings.

	h.	v.	f.	h.	v.	f.
Geld received for				26	0	0
Free of geld :						
St. Peter of Rome	6	0	0			
Abbot of Glastonbury.	5	0	0			
				11	0	0
Geld not received :						
Alvred de Hispania .	3	0	0			
Roger Witenc . . .	3	3	0			
Anschetil	0	1	0			
				7	0	0
				44	0	0
Paid in Hundred of Huntspill				3	0	0
				47	0	0

In the Hundred of Ringoltdeswee [1] are 59 hides. Thence the king has 8 pounds and 8 shillings and 9 pence for his geld from 28 hides and half a virgate, and the abbot of Glastingesberia has in demesne 17 hides. The king has no geld from 7 hides and 1½ virgates which Roger de Corcelle holds of the abbot of Glasting(bery), nor from 2 hides which Humphrey the chamberlain holds ; nor from 4½ hides which the villeins of the abbot hold. From this Hundred are due to the king 4 pounds and 3 shillings and 3 pence.

	h.	v.	f.
Geld received for	28	0	2
Free of geld :			
Abbot of Glastonbury .	17	0	0
	17	0	0

[1] These two form the modern hundred of Whitley.

	h.	v.	f.	h.	v.	f.
Geld not received :						
Roger de Corcelle . .	7	1	2			
Humphrey	2	0	0			
Abbot's villeins . .	4	2	0			
				13	3	2
				59	0	0

In the manor of Hame (High Ham) are 17 hides. Thence the king has 42 shillings for his geld from 7 hides, and the abbot of Glastingesberia has in demesne 5½ hides and half a virgate. The king has no geld from 2 hides and half a virgate which Serlo de Burci holds of the abbot of Glasting(bury) ; nor from 5 virgates which Robert de Otborvilla holds of the said abbot ; nor from 1 hide which the villeins of the abbot hold. From this vill (*villa*) are due to the king 26 shillings and 3 pence.

	h.	v.	f.	h.	v.	f.
Geld received for				7	0	0
Free of geld :						
Abbot of Glastonbury	5	2	2			
Geld not received :						
Serlo de Burci . . .	2	0	2			
Robert de Otborvilla .	1	1	0			
Abbot's villeins . . .	1	0	0			
				4	1	2
				17	0	0

In the Hundred of Monachetone (West Monkton) are 15 hides. Thence the king has 55 shillings and 6 pence for his geld from 9 hides and 1 virgate. Godfrey the constable and Edret owe to the king 34 shillings and 6 pence for the geld from 5 hides and 3 virgates.

	h.	v.	f.
Geld received for . . .	9	1	0
Geld not received :			
Godfrey and Edret . .	5	3	0
	15	0	0

fol. 526.]

In the Hundred of Bolestane (Bulstone) are 18 hides and half a virgate. Thence the king has 4 pounds and 2 shillings and 6 pence for his geld from 13 hides and 3 virgates, and his barons have 2 hides and half a virgate in demesne. Of these (hides) Girard has 1 hide and Harding son of Alnod 1 hide and half a virgate. The king has no geld from 1 hide which Ansger Brito holds ; nor from half a hide which Britel de St. Clare holds ; nor from half a virgate which Ogissius holds ; nor from half a hide from which the collectors (*fegadri*) have received payment which they claim by prescription (*per consuetudinem*).

	h.	v.	f.
Geld received for	13	3	0

Free of geld :	h.	v.	f.
Girard	1	0	0
Harding son of Alnod .	1	0	2
	2	0	2

Geld not received :			
Ansger Brito . . .	1	0	0
Britel de St. Clare . .	0	2	0
Ogissius	0	0	2
Kept back by custom .	0	2	0
	2	0	2
	18	0	0[1]

In the manor of Torne (Thorne Falcon) are 7 hides. Thence the king has 30 shillings of his geld from 5 hides, and Robert has kept back the king's geld from 2 hides.

In the manor of Torleberge (Thurlbeare) are 6 hides. Thence the king has 18 shillings for his geld.

Malger de Carrai gives to the king for his geld 56 shillings and 3 pence from his land (which is) 9 hides and 1½ virgates.

In the Hundred of Frome are 300 hides less 2. The king has 50 pounds and 18 shillings and 6 pence for his geld from 169 hides and 3 virgates, and his barons have 115 hides less half a virgate in demesne. Of these (hides) the bishop of St. Lo has 13 hides and half a virgate, and Hardin de Uiltona 9 hides, and Roger Arundel 7 hides and 1½ virgates, and the abbot of Montebor (Montebourg) 2½ hides, and the abbot of Glastingbery 20½ hides, and Osbern Giffard 5 hides and 1 virgate, and Baldwin the sheriff 14½ hides, and Dū (Donno in Domesday) 9 hides, and Alvered 4 hides and 3 virgates, and Edmund 2 hides and 3 virgates, and Bristward the priest 5 hides, and Edward 10 hides and half a virgate, and the abbot of Bath 6 hides, and the king has 5 hides in demesne at Crenemere (Cranmore). The king has no geld from half a hide which Alvered the butler holds ; nor from 2½ hides which Humphrey the chamberlain holds ; nor from 1 hide which Richard holds ; nor from half a hide which Herbert holds ; nor from 1 virgate which Vital holds ; nor from half a virgate which Pancevold holds ;

1 Two ferlings are not accounted for.

nor from half a hide (held) in almoin at Cenemerresduna (Kilmersdon) ; nor from 3 virgates which Robert son of Herbert holds ; nor the geld from 1½ hides which the collectors have retained by prescription (*per consuetudinem*). And the king has not had 34 shillings and 6 pence of his geld from 5 hides and 3 virgates which the collectors (*fegadri*) have received.

	h.	v.	f.
Geld received for	169	3	0

Free of geld	h.	v.	f.
Bishop of St. Lo . .	13	0	2
Hardin de Uiltona .	9	0	0
Roger de Arundel . .	7	1	2
Abbot of Montebourg	2	2	0
Abbot of Glastingbery.	20	2	0
Osbern Giffard . . .	5	1	0
Baldwin the sheriff .	14	2	0
Dū	9	0	0
Alvered	4	3	0
Edmund	2	3	0
Bristuard the priest .	5	0	0
Edward	10	0	2
Abbot of Bath . . .	6	0	0
King in demesne . .	5	0	0
	114	3	2

Geld not received :			
Alvered the butler. .	0	2	0
Humphrey the chamberlain	2	2	0
Richard	1	0	0
Herbert	0	2	0
Vital	0	1	0
Pancevold	0	0	2
Almoin at Kilmersdon	0	2	0
Robert son of Herbert	0	3	0
Retained by custom .	1	2	0
Not accounted for . .	5	3	0
	13	1	2
	298	0	0

The king has 509 pounds of his geld from Somerset (paid) in his treasury at Winchester ; and the men who brought it to Winchester have had 40 shillings for their maintenance (*conregio*) ; and they paid 9 shillings and 8 pence to waggoners (*saginarii*) employed (*conducendos*), and to a scribe, and for coverings (*forellos*) bought, and wax. And the king has not (been paid) 51 shillings and 3 pence which the bearers of the geld have received, but for which they cannot give any account. They have given security that these monies will be paid to the king's officers (*legati*).